Fundamentals of
FINANCIAL ACCOUNTING

Seventh Edition

FRED PHILLIPS
University of Saskatchewan

SHANA CLOR-PROELL
Texas Christian University

ROBERT LIBBY
Cornell University

PATRICIA A. LIBBY
Ithaca College

McGraw Hill

FUNDAMENTALS OF FINANCIAL ACCOUNTING, SEVENTH EDITION

Published by McGraw Hill LLC, 1325 Avenue of the Americas, New York, NY 10121. Copyright © 2022 by McGraw Hill LLC. All rights reserved. Printed in the United States of America. Previous editions © 2021, 2019, and 2016. No part of this publication may be reproduced or distributed in any form or by any means, or stored in a database or retrieval system, without the prior written consent of McGraw Hill LLC, including, but not limited to, in any network or other electronic storage or transmission, or broadcast for distance learning.

Some ancillaries, including electronic and print components, may not be available to customers outside the United States.

This book is printed on acid-free paper.

1 2 3 4 5 6 7 8 9 LWI 24 23 22 21

ISBN 978-1-260-77138-1 (bound edition)
MHID 1-260-77138-5 (bound edition)
ISBN 978-1-264-23929-0 (loose-leaf edition)
MHID 1-264-23929-7 (loose-leaf edition)

Portfolio Manager: *Rebecca Olson*
Product Developers: *Danielle McLimore, Christina Sanders*
Marketing Manager: *Lauren Schur*
Content Project Managers: *Amy Gehl, Angela Norris*
Buyer: *Sandy Ludovissy*
Designer: *Matt Diamond*
Content Licensing Specialists: *Beth Cray*
Cover Image: *nadla/Getty Images*
Compositor: *SPi Global*

All credits appearing on page or at the end of the book are considered to be an extension of the copyright page.

Library of Congress Cataloging-in-Publication Data

Names: Phillips, Fred, author. | Clor-Proell, Shana, author. | Libby,
  Robert, author. | Libby, Patricia A., author.
Title: Fundamentals of financial accounting / Fred Phillips, University of
  Saskatchewan, Shana Clor-Proell, Texas Christian University, Robert
  Libby, Cornell University, Patricia A. Libby, Ithaca College.
Description: Seventh Edition. | New York : McGraw Hill LLC, 2021. | Revised
  edition of the authors' Fundamentals of financial accounting, [2019] |
  Audience: Ages 18+
Identifiers: LCCN 2020031349 (print) | LCCN 2020031350 (ebook) | ISBN
  9781260771381 (hardcover) | ISBN 9781264239313 (ebook)
Subjects: LCSH: Accounting.
Classification: LCC HF5636 .P545 2021 (print) | LCC HF5636 (ebook) | DDC
  657—dc23
LC record available at https://lccn.loc.gov/2020031349
LC ebook record available at https://lccn.loc.gov/2020031350

mheducation.com/highered

Dedicated to

Barb, Harrison, and Daniel, my Mom, and (memory of) my Dad.
FRED PHILLIPS

Chad, Abigail, and Emily.
SHANA CLOR-PROELL

Herman and Doris Hargenrater; Laura, Oscar, and Selma Libby;
Brian and Bennett Plummer.
PATRICIA AND ROBERT LIBBY

Meet the Authors

Fred Phillips

Dawn Stranden Photography

Fred Phillips is professor emeritus at the University of Saskatchewan. Most of his teaching has focused on introductory financial accounting at the University of Saskatchewan, the University of Texas at Austin, and the University of Manitoba. Fred has an undergraduate accounting degree and a PhD from the University of Texas at Austin. He is a nonpracticing CPA, CA (Canada), having previously worked as an audit manager at KPMG.

Fred has been recognized with numerous accounting education awards, as chosen by his students and peers. Most notably, Fred was awarded the title Master Teacher at the University of Saskatchewan and he was admitted to the 3M National Teaching Fellowship, the highest honor for undergraduate teaching in Canada. His peer-reviewed publications include education-focused research and instructional cases in *Issues in Accounting Education*, as well as professional judgment studies in *Journal of Accounting Research* and *Organizational Behavior and Human Decision Processes*, among others. His most recent publication, in *Issues in Accounting Education* in February 2020, examines effective use of SmartBook technology. In his spare time, Fred is a professional tennis line umpire, having worked ATP, ITF, WTA, and Grand Slam tournaments in Canada, Mexico, New Zealand, and the United States.

Shana Clor-Proell

Courtesy of Glen Ellman

Shana Clor-Proell is an associate professor at Texas Christian University, where she teaches introductory financial accounting and advanced accounting. She has also taught at Cornell University, the University of Wisconsin, the University of California–San Diego, and San Diego State University. Shana received her BS, MS, and PhD from Cornell University. She is a CPA (Wisconsin) and previously worked as an auditor for Arthur Andersen.

Shana's research examines judgment and decision making in financial accounting contexts. Her work has been published in *The Accounting Review*, *Journal of Accounting Research*, *Contemporary Accounting Research*, *Journal of Financial Reporting*, and *Journal of Business Ethics*. Shana is a member of the Teaching, Learning and Curriculum (TLC), Financial Accounting and Reporting (FAR), and Accounting, Behavior and Organizations (ABO) sections of the American Accounting Association. In her spare time, Shana enjoys long walks, meditation, and spending time with her husband and two daughters.

Robert Libby

Robert Libby is the David A. Thomas Professor of Accounting and Accounting Area Coordinator at Cornell University, where he teaches the introductory financial accounting course. He previously taught at the University of Illinois, Pennsylvania State University, the University of Texas at Austin, the University of Chicago, and the University of Michigan. He received his BS from Pennsylvania State University and his MAS and PhD from the University of Illinois; he also successfully completed the CPA exam (Illinois).

Courtesy of Robert Libby

Bob was selected as the AAA Outstanding Educator in 2000 and received the AAA Outstanding Service Award in 2006 and the AAA Notable Contributions to the Literature Award in 1985 and 1996. He has received the Core Faculty Teaching Award multiple times at Cornell. Bob is a widely published author and researcher specializing in behavioral accounting. He has published numerous articles in *The Accounting Review*; *Journal of Accounting Research; Accounting, Organizations, and Society*; and other accounting journals. He has held a variety of offices, including vice president, in the American Accounting Association, and he is a member of the American Institute of CPAs.

Patricia A. Libby

Patricia Libby is a retired associate professor of accounting at Ithaca College, where she taught the undergraduate and graduate financial accounting courses. She previously taught graduate and undergraduate financial accounting at Eastern Michigan University and the University of Texas. Before entering academia, she was an auditor with Price Waterhouse (now PricewaterhouseCoopers) and a financial administrator at the University of Chicago. She was also faculty advisor to Beta Alpha Psi (Mu Alpha chapter), the National Association of Black Accountants (Ithaca College chapter), and Ithaca College Accounting Association.

Courtesy of Patricia A. Libby

Patricia received her BS from Pennsylvania State University, her MBA from DePaul University, and her PhD from the University of Michigan; she also successfully completed the CPA exam (Illinois). She has published articles in *The Accounting Review*, *Issues in Accounting Education*, and *The Michigan CPA*.

Engaging Students with Real-World Context and Business

One of the most widely used introductory accounting textbooks, Phillips, *Fundamentals of Financial Accounting* focuses on four key attributes:

- **Engaging Writing and Illustrations**
- **Data-Driven Pedagogy**
- **Entrepreneurial Approach**
- **Video Asset Variety**

> *Phillips does an excellent job of writing at a level the average student will understand. [The authors] . . . know how to engage the students by using real companies; discussing relevant current events; using colorful, enticing-to-read graphs that are efficient at making a point; and most importantly, they know the frequent misconceptions and typical issues students have.*
>
> —Nancy Lynch, *West Virginia University*

Engaging Writing and Illustrations

Not all students learn financial accounting easily. In today's fast-paced world, it can be difficult to keep both majors and nonmajors focused on how accounting is relevant to them and their future careers. Through clear and engaging writing paired with vibrant illustrations, the financial decisions that companies make and the financial statements that they use come alive for students. The Phillips text helps students see the big picture of how accounting relates to the real world—their world.

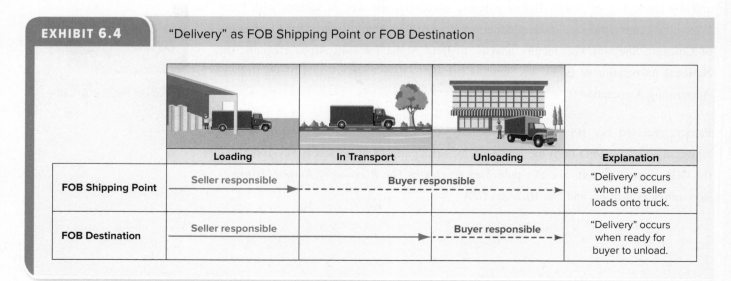

EXHIBIT 6.4   "Delivery" as FOB Shipping Point or FOB Destination

	Loading	In Transport	Unloading	Explanation
FOB Shipping Point	Seller responsible	Buyer responsible		"Delivery" occurs when the seller loads onto truck.
FOB Destination	Seller responsible		Buyer responsible	"Delivery" occurs when ready for buyer to unload.

Driving Learning with Clear, Effective, and Innovative Ideas

Data-Driven Pedagogy: A Proven Teaching and Learning Methodology

Faculty agree that for students studying financial accounting, the accounting cycle is the most critical topic to learn and master. The approach to this topic in the Phillips text is based on the belief that students struggle with the accounting cycle when transaction analysis is covered in one chapter. If students are exposed to the accounting equation, journal entries, and T-accounts for both balance sheet and income statement accounts in a single chapter, they can feel overwhelmed and are unable to grasp material in the next chapter, which typically covers adjustments and financial statement preparation.

The authors' peer-reviewed research on various approaches to teaching the accounting cycle informed the step-by-step model used in the text—a model proven to lead to better results in short-term assessment as well as in long-term understanding and application of the material. In a study published in *Issues in Accounting Education*, author Fred Phillips and his research partner Lindsay Heiser studied the effects of teaching the accounting cycle by initially restricting the scope of transactions to only those affecting balance sheet accounts, while waiting to introduce transactions involving both balance sheet and income statement accounts until later.

The results showed that students who learned the accounting cycle via the scaffolded approach were better able to prepare journal entries on similar types of transactions both immediately and one week later. Importantly, these same students later performed just as well on complex transactions affecting balance sheet *and* income statement accounts despite having had less practice with them. The scaffolded accounting cycle approach that proved so effective in this study is the same that is used in *Fundamentals of Financial Accounting*, helping students to "work smarter," and better preparing them for success in financial accounting and beyond.

The graphic below shows how, unlike other texts, Phillips spreads transaction analysis coverage over two chapters so that students have the time to master the material. In Chapter 2, students are exposed to the accounting equation and transaction analysis for transactions that affect only balance sheet accounts. This provides students with the opportunity to learn the basic structure and tools used in accounting in a simpler setting. In Chapter 3, students are exposed to more complex transactions that affect both balance sheet and income statement accounts. As a result of this progressive approach to transaction analysis, students learn more, as documented in peer-reviewed research.* This innovative organization also prepares students to better understand adjustments, financial statement preparation, and more advanced topics.

In addition, the accounting cycle approach used here tells a natural business story—one that would be familiar to any modern entrepreneur. From planning and establishing the business to opening and evaluating the business, the first few chapters clearly break out each key stage in starting a company. The accounting cycle coverage steadily unfolds as students move along this company's journey, allowing them to keep pace and absorb how accounting events unfold in the real world of business.

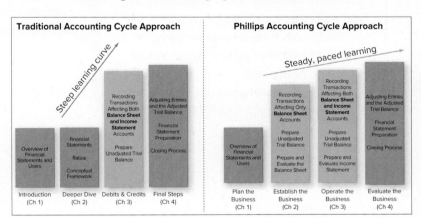

> [The topics covered in the first three chapters are] the toughest for students and require the most practice. Phillips understands this and expertly navigates through the two statements and demonstrates how the two interconnect and depend upon each other, setting the stage for an easier adjustment and closing process ahead.
>
> —Margaret Costello Lambert, *Oakland Community College*

*F. Phillips and L. Heiser, "A Field Experiment Examining the Effects of Accounting Equation Emphasis and Transaction Scope on Students Learning to Journalize," *Issues in Accounting Education* 26 (2011), pp. 681–699.

Modern Businesses Engage Students

Doug Lemke/Shutterstock

Entrepreneurial Approach: Inspiring Students

The authors of *Fundamentals of Financial Accounting* understand the challenges instructors face and the need for a financial accounting text that is relevant, easy to read, and current.

Fundamentals of Financial Accounting responds by using **carefully chosen focus companies that students recognize and engage with in their everyday lives.** From tech start-ups to some of the world's most familiar trademark brands, each chapter opens with an engaging scenario or story using a familiar company. The same focus company, such as Walmart, Cedar Fair, American Eagle, National Beverage, Under Armour, or General Mills, is used throughout the entire chapter so that students can see how the concepts and calculations apply to a real-world company they are already familiar with.

Today's students have grown up hearing about start-up culture, and many are entrepreneurially minded having seen the rise of Apple, Facebook, and the "gig economy." The authors showcase accounting's relevance by using Noodlecake Studios, a digital start-up, as the company profiled in Chapters 1–4. With this example, students see how a new small business uses accounting, from planning to evaluation of financial performance.

by Bringing Accounting Concepts to Life

Video Asset Variety: Present, Expand, and Reinforce Key Concepts

Modern businesses expect their employees to be lifelong learners. As a result, businesses and educators increasingly rely on videos as "just-in-time" resources to present, reinforce, and augment critical concepts. Whether the viewer is a student in a classroom or a newly hired CPA at a Big 4 accounting firm, learning on the go via a variety of multimedia-based assets is key in both the corporate world and academic settings. *Fundamentals of Financial Accounting* provides a range of video offerings and formats to facilitate understanding and help students learn wherever and whenever they need to.

Video Type/Purpose	Description
Tutorial Videos: Explaining the basics	
Concept Overview Videos	**Assignable in Connect**, these videos cover each chapter's learning objectives followed by auto-graded knowledge checks that confirm students' comprehension. A great tool for introducing students to new topics.
Guided Examples	Narrated, animated, step-by-step walkthroughs of an exercise similar to assignment exercises, that provide just-in-time help for students when they are working on assignments.
In Action Videos	**Assignable in Connect**, these tutorial videos illustrate the thought processes applicable to a sample of topics in *Fundamentals of Financial Accounting*, including how to analyze transactions, adjust accounts, account for inventory and receivables, and prepare a statement of cash flows.
Featured Videos: Engaging deeper	
Spotlight Videos	**Assignable in Connect**, selected Spotlight on Ethics, Financial Reporting, and Business Decisions feature boxes in the text are brought to life in 2- to 5-minute news magazine-style videos. Assign students the tasks of watching the video and answering comprehension-check questions.
Flash Topic Videos	**Assignable in Connect**, these videos extend ideas in the text for hot topics including revenue recognition, big data, sales returns, stock buybacks, and sustainability. Assign students the tasks of watching the video and answering comprehension-check questions.
	NEW! Several new videos illustrate the impact of the Covid-19 pandemic on selected business operations and financial results using companies familiar to students.

*"Clear, concise, and the **most reader-friendly text** I've come across. Most importantly, **it is based on sound learning theory, which greatly enhances the learning experience.**"*

—Professor Audrey Agnello, *Niagara County Community College*

From Concepts to Comprehension—Reinforcement Is Key

Whether you're presenting, discussing, or problem solving, you want materials that will motivate students and hold their interest. Motivating today's students requires materials that connect them with the workplace and encourage them to think about course topics before, during, and after class. *Fundamentals of Financial Accounting* offers students many tools to help reinforce the concepts discussed throughout the text.

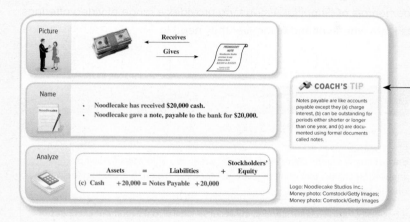

Logo: Noodlecake Studios Inc.;
Money photo: Comstock/Getty Images;
Money photo: Comstock/Getty Images

Coach's Tips

Every student needs encouragement and Coach's Tips are just one way *Fundamentals of Financial Accounting* fulfills that need. Coach's Tips appear throughout the text and in selected end-of-chapter problems to offer tips, advice, and suggestions.

How's it going? Self-Study Practice

Research shows that students learn best when they are actively engaged in the learning process. This active learning feature engages the student, provides interactivity, and promotes efficient learning. These quizzes ask students to pause at strategic points throughout each chapter to ensure they understand key points before moving ahead.

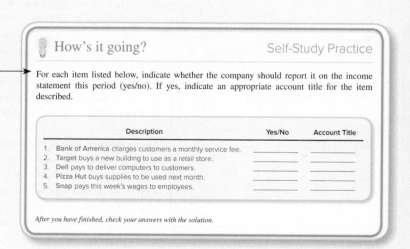

*Phillips does an **outstanding job of incorporating real-world data into the text**, which increases a student's engagement with the material and enhances their learning. I think that the writing style is very conversational, which makes reading the chapter a manageable task for the students.*

—Anne Clem, *Iowa State University*

Financial Reporting

Expected Impacts of COVID-19

A surge of 8-Ks were filed soon after the COVID-19 crisis reached the United States in early 2020. An example excerpted from Disney's 8-K follows:

> The impact of the novel coronavirus ("COVID-19") and measures to prevent its spread are affecting our businesses in a number of ways. We have closed our theme parks; suspended our cruises and theatrical shows; delayed theatrical distribution of films both domestically and internationally; and experienced supply chain disruption and ad sales impacts.

Source: The Walt Disney Company, Form 8-K filed March 18, 2020. Retrieved on March 19, 2020, from sec.gov.

Spotlight Features

Each chapter includes Spotlight features focusing on business decisions, ethics, internal controls, financial reporting, big data and analytics, and the world (IFRS). These features are designed to further engage students and provide instructors with material for in-class discussion.

- **Spotlight on Big Data and Analytics**—highlights topics relating to big data, data visualization, and data and business analytics.

- **Spotlight on the World**—highlights significant differences between U.S. GAAP and IFRS.

- **Spotlight on Financial Reporting**—connects chapter topics with real-world disclosures provided in the financial statements of our focus companies and other contrast companies.

- **Spotlight on Controls**—highlights applications of internal control principles in the workplace.

- **Spotlight on Ethics**—emphasizes ethical issues and the importance of acting responsibly.

- **Spotlight on Business Decisions**—helps students develop strong decision-making skills by illustrating the relevance of accounting in real-world decision making.

Practice and Review Materials
Build Confidence and Success

To effectively evaluate and guide student success with the appropriate feedback, instructors need homework and test materials that are easy to use and tied to the chapter discussions. Each chapter of *Fundamentals of Financial Accounting* is followed by an extensive variety of end-of-chapter material that applies and integrates topics presented in the chapter.

- **Demonstration Case:** End-of-chapter review material begins with a demonstration case that provides another self-study opportunity for students. The demonstration case is practice material that previews what students will see in the homework problems.

- **Homework Helper** immediately precedes each chapter's homework materials, highlighting subtleties discussed in the chapter and providing practical advice so students avoid common pitfalls when completing homework assignments.

- **Multiperspective Discussion Questions:** These questions ask students to explain and discuss terms and concepts presented in the chapter. Selected questions, denoted with an icon 🔄, help students begin developing critical thinking skills.

- **Mini Exercises, Exercises, Problems (Coached, Group A, and Group B):** Each chapter includes a wide variety of assignment material from questions that illustrate and apply a single learning objective to problem sets that help students develop decision-making skills.

  - **Level-up Questions:**

     In each chapter, particularly challenging questions, designated by the level-up icon, require students to combine multiple concepts to advance to the next level of accounting knowledge.

- **Comprehensive Problems:** Selected chapters include problems that cover topics from earlier chapters to refresh, reinforce, and build an integrative understanding of the course material. These are a great resource for helping students stay up-to-date throughout the course.

- **Questions** designated with the **general ledger** icon have been written to take advantage of Connect's general ledger simulation. A much-improved student experience when working with accounting cycle questions, students' work in the general journal is automatically posted to the ledger, navigation is much simpler, and students can easily link back to their original entries simply by clicking in the ledger if edits are needed. These questions include critical thinking components to maximize students' foundational knowledge of accounting concepts and principles.

- **Skills Development Cases:** Each chapter offers cases designed to help students develop analytical, critical thinking, and technology skills. These cases are ideal for individual assignments and group projects. They also encourage your students to find financial information in an actual annual report. The first two cases of every chapter present, in multiple-choice format, an opportunity to connect your students with real-world financial reporting. These are assignable in Connect.

- **Continuing Case:** In Chapter 1, students are introduced to Nicole's Getaway Spa (NGS). In the following chapters, this continuing case is extended to encompass each new topic.

- **Data Analytics Exercises:** These auto-graded exercises, assignable in Connect, introduce students to data visualization, interpretation, and analysis relevant to topics in selected chapters.

> *The end-of-chapter problems and exercises are ample, diverse (in terms of rigor), and congruent with the material covered in the chapter.*
>
> —Brian Nagle, *Duquesne University*

What's New in the Seventh Edition?

In response to feedback and guidance from numerous financial accounting faculty, the authors have made many important changes in the seventh edition of *Fundamentals of Financial Accounting,* including the following:

- Integrated **new companies,** including a new focus company (Dave & Buster's) and many other companies familiar to students (Alphabet, Apple, Domino's Pizza, Facebook, Garmin, Sonos, Zumiez, and so on).
- Reviewed, updated, and introduced new end-of-chapter material in each chapter to support new topics and learning objectives, including auto-graded **Data Analytics Exercises** in Connect involving data visualization, interpretation, and analysis.
- Incorporated throughout the text are discussions of the **effect of the COVID-19 pandemic** on businesses to drive relevancy and engagement.

CHAPTER 1: BUSINESS DECISIONS AND FINANCIAL ACCOUNTING

Focus Company: Noodlecake Studios

- **Updated** chapter opener describing the latest developments at this private company and its development of award-winning video games
- **Updated** Supplement 1B to describe the SEC's direct listing option, as pursued by Spotify
- **New** discussion of COVID-19 impact on 8-K reporting in Spotlight on Financial Reporting
- **Updated** demonstration case featuring WD-40 Company
- Reviewed and updated all end-of-chapter material, including financial data for Apple, Alphabet, Intel, Designer Brands, Cinemark, Garmin, and others

CHAPTER 2: THE BALANCE SHEET

Focus Company: Noodlecake Studios

- **Updated** analysis of current ratios in Exhibit 2.14 for video game companies Activision Blizzard, Electronic Arts, and Take-Two Interactive Software
- Reviewed and updated all end-of-chapter material, including financial data for Columbia Sportswear, Ethan Allen Interiors, Facebook, Shake Shack, and others

CHAPTER 3: THE INCOME STATEMENT

Focus Company: Noodlecake Studios

- **Updated** illustrations in Exhibits 3.6 and 3.7
- **Updated** net profit margin ratios at Electronic Arts and Nintendo in Spotlight on Financial Reporting
- **Updated** demonstration case featuring Carnival Corporation
- Reviewed and updated all end-of-chapter material, including financial data for Expedia, Booking.com, The Home Depot, and others

CHAPTER 4: ADJUSTMENTS, FINANCIAL STATEMENTS, AND FINANCIAL RESULTS

Focus Company: Noodlecake Studios

- **Updated** illustrations in Exhibit 4.14
- **New** analysis of stock price and earnings for Sears Holdings in Spotlight on Financial Reporting
- Reviewed and updated all end-of-chapter material, including financial data for FedEx Corporation, Regis Corporation, Lowe's, and others

CHAPTER 5: FRAUD, INTERNAL CONTROL, AND CASH

Focus Company: Koss Corporation

- **Updated** data relating to frequency and losses from employee fraud in Exhibit 5.1
- **Updated** illustration of restricted cash reporting at Domino's Pizza (Exhibit 5.10)
- Reviewed, updated, and introduced new end-of-chapter material, including financial data for Expedia, The Home Depot, and others

CHAPTER 6: MERCHANDISING OPERATIONS AND THE MULTISTEP INCOME STATEMENT

Focus Company: Walmart

- **Updated** focus company illustrations (Walmart) and contrasted with Planet Fitness (Exhibit 6.2)
- **Updated** data regarding inventory shrinkage costs in Spotlight on Controls
- **New** illustration of FOB Shipping Point and FOB Destination in Exhibit 6.4
- **New** discussion of using a contra-revenue account for sales returns and allowances
- **Updated** illustration of gross profit percentage analysis at Walmart and Nordstrom

CHAPTER 6: (continued)

- Reviewed, updated, and introduced new end-of-chapter material, including financial data for Dillard's, Luxottica, Fortune Brands, The Gap, Macy's, and others

CHAPTER 7: INVENTORY AND COST OF GOODS SOLD

Focus Company: American Eagle Outfitters

- **Updated** focus company illustrations
- **New** discussion of Burberry destroying its inventory in Spotlight on Business Decisions
- **Updated** inventory turnover analysis in Exhibit 7.7, involving Harley-Davidson, McDonald's, and American Eagle
- Reviewed and updated all end-of-chapter material, including financial data for Sonos, Amazon, Polaris Industries, GameStop, and others

CHAPTER 8: RECEIVABLES, BAD DEBT EXPENSE, AND INTEREST REVENUE

Focus Company: VF Corporation (VFC)

- **Updated** focus company illustrations for VF Corp.—the maker of North Face jackets, JanSport backpacks, Timberland boots, and Vans shoes
- **New** discussion of co-branded credit cards in Spotlight on Business Decisions
- **New** discussion of COVID-19 impact on collection of accounts receivable in Spotlight on Business Decisions
- **Updated** receivables turnover analysis in Exhibit 8.7, involving VF Corp., Post, and Apple
- Reviewed and updated all end-of-chapter material, including financial data for Adobe, Callaway Golf, Microsoft, FedEx, and others

CHAPTER 9: LONG-LIVED TANGIBLE AND INTANGIBLE ASSETS

Focus Company: Cedar Fair

- **Updated** focus company illustrations
- **New** discussion of COVID-19 impact on asset impairment losses
- **New** discussion of leased assets in Spotlight on Financial Reporting
- **Updated** fixed asset turnover analysis in Exhibit 9.5, involving Cedar Fair, Six Flags, and Facebook

- Reviewed and updated all end-of-chapter material, including financial data for Apple, Hasbro, and others

CHAPTER 10: LIABILITIES

Focus Company: General Mills

- **Updated** focus company illustrations
- **Updated** discussion of bond pricing
- **Updated** analysis of debt-to-assets and times interest earned ratios for Kellogg, Post, and Campbell Soup comparison companies
- **Simplified** presentation of installment notes in Supplement 10D
- Reviewed and updated all end-of-chapter material, including financial data for FedEx Corporation, Lowe's, and others

CHAPTER 11: STOCKHOLDERS' EQUITY

Focus Company: National Beverage Corp.

- **Updated** focus company illustrations, as well as stock prices of rivals Coca-Cola and PepsiCo
- **Updated** Spotlight on Business Decisions relating to the impact of stock repurchases on EPS at Boeing, and more recently at Delta and Southwest Airlines
- **Updated** Spotlight on Business Decisions relating to National Beverage's investor loyalty plan
- **Updated** ratio analyses in Exhibit 11.6, involving National Beverage and PepsiCo
- Reviewed and updated all end-of-chapter material, including financial data for General Mills, Stanley Black & Decker, Delta, Southwest Airlines, and others

CHAPTER 12: STATEMENT OF CASH FLOWS

Focus Company: Dave & Buster's

- **New** focus company
- **Updated** illustration of cash flow patterns in Exhibit 12.8
- **New** Spotlight on Financial Reporting relating to Dave & Buster's free cash flow
- Reviewed and updated all end-of-chapter material, including financial data for Colgate-Palmolive, Walt Disney Company, Zumiez, Cedar Fair, and others

CHAPTER 13: MEASURING AND EVALUATING FINANCIAL PERFORMANCE

Focus Company: Lowe's

- **Updated** focus company analyses
- **New** discussion of COVID-19 impact on going-concern status in Spotlight on Financial Reporting
- Reviewed and updated all end-of-chapter material, including financial data for Chevron, Cintas, Procter & Gamble, Dollar General, Kohl's, and others

APPENDIXES A & B: EXCERPTS FROM ANNUAL REPORTS OF THE HOME DEPOT AND LOWE'S

- Updated excerpts from the Fiscal 2019 10-K Annual Reports of The Home Depot and Lowe's

APPENDIX C: PRESENT AND FUTURE VALUE CONCEPTS

- Reviewed and updated all end-of-chapter material

APPENDIX D: INVESTMENTS IN OTHER CORPORATIONS

Focus Company: Alphabet Inc.

- **Updated** focus company illustrations
- Reviewed and updated all end-of-chapter material

Students: Get Learning That Fits You

Effective tools for efficient studying

Connect is designed to make you more productive with simple, flexible, intuitive tools that maximize your study time and meet your individual learning needs. Get learning that works for you with Connect.

Study anytime, anywhere

Download the free ReadAnywhere app and access your online eBook or SmartBook 2.0 assignments when it's convenient, even if you're offline. And since the app automatically syncs with your eBook and SmartBook 2.0 assignments in Connect, all of your work is available every time you open it. Find out more at **www.mheducation.com/readanywhere**

> *"I really liked this app—it made it easy to study when you don't have your text-book in front of you."*
>
> - Jordan Cunningham, Eastern Washington University

Everything you need in one place

Your Connect course has everything you need—whether reading on your digital eBook or completing assignments for class, Connect makes it easy to get your work done.

Calendar: owattaphotos/Getty Images

Learning for everyone

McGraw Hill works directly with Accessibility Services Departments and faculty to meet the learning needs of all students. Please contact your Accessibility Services Office and ask them to email accessibility@mheducation.com, or visit **www.mheducation.com/about/accessibility** for more information.

Top: Jenner Images/Getty Images, Left: Hero Images/Getty Images, Right: Hero Images/Getty Images

Remote Proctoring & Browser-Locking Capabilities

 New remote proctoring and browser-locking capabilities, hosted by Proctorio within Connect, provide control of the assessment environment by enabling security options and verifying the identity of the student. Seamlessly integrated within Connect, these services allow instructors to control students' assessment experience by restricting browser activity, recording students' activity, and verifying students are doing their own work. Instant and detailed reporting gives instructors an at-a-glance view of potential academic integrity concerns, thereby avoiding personal bias and supporting evidence-based claims.

Online Assignments

Connect helps students learn more efficiently by providing feedback and practice material when they need it, where they need it. Connect grades homework automatically and gives immediate feedback on any questions students may have missed. The extensive assignable, gradable end-of-chapter content includes a general journal application that looks and feels more like what you would find in a general ledger software package. Also, select questions have been redesigned to test students' knowledge more fully. They now include tables for students to work through rather than requiring that all calculations be done offline.

End-of-chapter questions in Connect include

- Mini-Exercises
- Exercises
- Problems (Coached, Group A, and Group B)
- Comprehensive Problems
- Skills Development Cases
- Continuing Cases

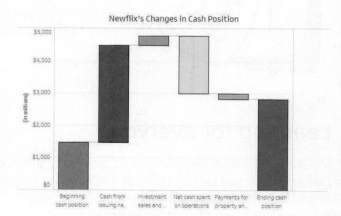

NEW! Writing Assignment

Available within McGraw Hill Connect,® the Writing Assignment tool delivers a learning experience to help students improve their written communication skills and conceptual understanding. As an instructor you can assign, monitor, grade, and provide feed-back on writing more efficiently and effectively.

NEW! Tableau Dashboard Activities

Tableau Dashboard Activities allow students to explore live Tableau dashboards directly integrated into Connect, and include auto-graded questions focused on both calculations and analysis. Students can check their understanding and apply what they are learning within the framework of analytics and critical thinking.

General Ledger Problems

General Ledger Problems provide a much-improved student experience when working with accounting cycle questions, offering improved navigation and less scrolling. Students can audit their mistakes by easily linking back to their original entries and

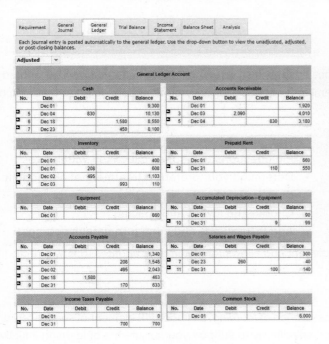

can see how the numbers flow through the various financial statements. Many General Ledger Problems include an analysis tab that allows students to demonstrate their critical thinking skills and a deeper understanding of accounting concepts.

Concept Overview Videos

The **Concept Overview Videos** provide engaging narratives of key topics in an assignable and interactive online format. They follow the structure of the text and are organized to match the chapter's learning objectives. The Concept Overview Videos provide additional explanation and enhancement of material from the text chapter, allowing students to learn, study, and practice with instant feedback, at their own pace.

Excel Simulations

Simulated Excel Questions, assignable within Connect, allow students to practice their Excel skills—such as basic formulas and formatting—within the context of financial accounting. These questions feature animated, narrated Help and Show Me tutorials (when enabled), as well as automatic feedback and grading for both students and professors.

Guided Examples/Hint Videos

The **Guided Examples** in Connect provide a narrated, animated, step-by-step walk-through of select exercises similar to those assigned. These short presentations can be turned on or off by instructors and provide reinforcement when students need it most.

Unadjusted Trial Balance

Debits = Credits

SONICGATEWAY, INC.
Unadjusted Trial Balance
At September 30

Account Name	Debits	Credits
Cash	$16,900	
Accounts Receivable	500	
Supplies	600	
Prepaid Rent	7,200	
Equipment	9,600	
Software	9,000	
Logo and trademarks	300	
Accounts Payable		$10,700
Unearned Revenue		300
Note Payable		20,000
Common Stock		10,000
Retained Earnings		0
Sales Revenue		12,000
Salaries and Wages Expense	7,800	
Utilities Expense	600	
Advertising Expense	500	
Totals	$53,000	$53,000

Knowledge Check 01
A trial balance can best be explained as a list of:

Test Builder in Connect

Available within Connect, **Test Builder** is a cloud-based tool that enables instructors to format tests that can be printed or administered within an LMS. Test Builder offers a modern, streamlined interface for easy content configuration that matches course needs, without requiring a download.

Test Builder allows you to:

- Access all test bank content from a particular title.
- Easily pinpoint the most relevant content through robust filtering options.
- Manipulate the order of questions or scramble questions and/or answers.

- Pin questions to a specific location within a test.
- Determine your preferred treatment of algorithmic questions.
- Choose the layout and spacing.
- Add instructions and configure default settings.

Test Builder provides a secure interface for better protection of content and allows for just-in-time updates to flow directly into assessments.

ASSURANCE OF LEARNING READY

Many educational institutions today are focused on the notion of *assurance of learning*, an important element of some accreditation standards. *Fundamentals of Financial Accounting* is designed specifically to support your assurance of learning initiatives with a simple, yet powerful solution.

Each test bank question for *Fundamentals of Financial Accounting* maps to a specific chapter learning objective listed in the text. You can use Connect to easily query for learning outcomes/objectives that directly relate to the learning objectives for your course. You can then use the reporting features of Connect to aggregate student results in a similar fashion, making the collection and presentation of assurance of learning data simple and easy.

AACSB STATEMENT

360b/Shutterstock

McGraw Hill Education is a proud corporate member of AACSB International. Understanding the importance and value of AACSB accreditation, *Fundamentals of Financial Accounting* recognizes the curricula guidelines detailed in the AACSB standards for business accreditation by connecting selected questions in the test bank to the six general knowledge and skill guidelines in the AACSB standards.

The statements contained in *Fundamentals of Financial Accounting* are provided only as a guide for the users of this textbook. The AACSB leaves content coverage and assessment within the purview of individual schools, the mission of the school, and the faculty. While *Fundamentals of Financial Accounting* and the teaching package make no claim of any specific AACSB qualification or evaluation, within the test bank to accompany *Fundamentals of Financial Accounting* we have labeled selected questions according to the six general knowledge and skill areas.

McGraw Hill Education Customer Experience Group Contact Information

At McGraw Hill Education, we understand that getting the most from new technology can be challenging. That's why our services don't stop after you purchase our products. You can contact our Product Specialists 24 hours a day to get product training online. Or you can search the knowledge bank of Frequently Asked Questions on our support website. For Customer Support, call **800-331-5094,** or visit www.mhhe.com/support. One of our Technical Support Analysts will be able to assist you in a timely fashion.

Acknowledgments

We are deeply indebted to the following individuals who helped develop, critique, and shape the extensive ancillary package:

Muriel Anderson, *SUNY–Buffalo*
Jean Bissell, *Bissell Consulting, LLC*
Jeannie Folk, *College of DuPage*
Debra L. Johnson, *Cerritos College*
Beth Kobylarz, *Accuracy Counts*
Nancy Lynch, *West Virginia University*
Brandy Mackintosh, *University of Saskatchewan*
Mark McCarthy, *Eastern Carolina Unviersity*
Barbara Muller, *Arizona State University*
Annieka Philo, *Clemson University*
Kevin Smith, *Utah Valley University*
Teri Zuccaro, *Clarke University*

We thank Linda Vaello and the University of Texas–San Antonio for letting us adapt their projects for our comprehensive problems. We also are grateful to Sharon Garvin at Wayne State College for contributing the financial calculator app instructional materials in Appendix C. We also received invaluable input and support from present and former colleagues and students, in particular Jocelyn Allard, Anders Bergstrom, Shari Boyd, Kara Chase, Nicole Dewan, Erin Ferguson, Aaron Ferrara, Genevieve Gallagher, Sarah Guina, Robin Harrington, Lee Harris, Blair Healy, Candice Heidt, Devon Hennig, Carrie Hordichuk, Lorraine Hurst, Jennifer Johnson, Nancy Kirzinger, Paul Knepper, Deborah Loran, Nicole Mackisey, Diana Mark, Roger Martin, Jason Matshes, Jennifer Millard, Kimberley Olfert, Ryan Olson, Daniel Phillips, David Pooler, Jessica Pothier, Abigail Proell, Chad Proell, Nick Purich, Emery Salahub, Bailey Schergevitch, Kendra Sigfusson, Marie Tait, and Kory Wickenhauser.

Last, we thank the extraordinary efforts of a talented group of individuals at McGraw Hill Education who made all of this come together. We would especially like to thank Tim Vertovec, vice president of the BEC portfolio; Rebecca Olson, portfolio director; Danielle McLimore and Christina Sanders, product developers; Kevin Moran, director of digital content; Xin Lin, lead product manager; Amy Gehl and Angela Norris, content and assessment project managers; Matt Diamond, designer; Sandy Ludovissy, buyer; and Beth Cray, content licensing specialist.

We also want to recognize the valuable input of all those who helped guide our developmental decisions for this edition.

Editorial Review Board

Kristine Baron, *Western Kentucky University*
Amy Bentley, *Tallahassee Community College*
Elizabeth Capener, *American University of Paris*
Anne Clem, *Iowa State University*
Debora Constable, *Georgia State University*
Nancy Coster, *Loyola Marymount University*
Dori Danko, *Grand Valley State University*
Annette Davis, *Glendale Community College*
Vicki Dominguez, *College of Southern Nevada*
Samantha Falgout, *Nicolls State University*
Robert Hogan, *College of Charleston*
Todd Jensen, *Sierra College*
Lara Kessler, *Grand Valley State University*
Patrick Lee, *University of Texas–San Antonio*
Jeffrey McMillan, *Clemson University*
Jennifer Miller, *Georgia State University*
Matthew Njoku, *Central Piedmont Community College*
Annieka Philo, *Clemson University*
Chris Proschko, *Texas State University*
Atul Rai, *Wichita State University*
Richard Sarkisian, *Camden County College*
Claire Yan, *Rutgers University*
Linda Vaello, *University of Texas–San Antonio*

We are equally grateful to the reviewers over the past six editions who have helped inform the development of this text, and whose ideas have aided thousands of students.

Brief Contents

Contents

Fundamentals of
FINANCIAL ACCOUNTING

1

Business Decisions and Financial Accounting

CHAPTER ONE

YOUR LEARNING OBJECTIVES

LO 1-1   Describe various organizational forms and business decision makers.

LO 1-2   Describe the purpose, structure, and content of the four basic financial statements.

LO 1-3   Explain how financial statements are used by decision makers.

LO 1-4   Describe factors that contribute to useful financial information.

LO 1-S1   Describe examples where accounting helps in pursuing other business careers.

LO 1-S2   Describe the decision to become a public company and explain the implications for accounting.

THAT WAS THEN

If you think accounting is far removed from your personal life, you might be in for a surprise. Your ordinary life experiences, especially as a student, actually prepare you well to learn accounting.

CHAMELEON RUN

Noodlecake Studios, Inc.

noodlecake
games

Welcome to the world of business and financial accounting. One of our goals for this book is to help you see the role accounting plays in helping people turn their good ideas into successful businesses. In the first four chapters of this book, you will learn how two video game developers started a business and learned to use accounting to run their business with great success.

For Jordan Schidlowsky and Ty Bader, the last few years have been incredible. Their *Super Stickman Golf* series and other game apps they've developed for mobile devices have won awards and recognitions on iTunes and Google Play. The crowning achievement (so far) was being awarded an Apple Design Award for their game *Chameleon Run*. Their chief operating officer, Ryan Holowaty, says it's like winning an Academy Award. They continue to grow their business, now developing and publishing games for not only the iPhone and Android, but also game consoles, PCs, and Apple Arcade. They have benefited greatly from the advice of Laurie Norris—a CPA (certified public accountant)—who has helped them establish their business and understand how to monitor its success. As you will read in this chapter, things got rolling when Laurie met with Jordan in June to answer his questions about how to get started. By following Laurie's business and accounting advice, Jordan and Ty successfully launched their company, named Noodlecake Studios, Inc. (noodlecake.com).

THIS IS NOW

This chapter focuses on the key financial reports that business people rely on when evaluating a company's performance.

Logo: Noodlecake Studios, Inc.

ORGANIZATION OF THE CHAPTER

Understand the business	Study the accounting methods	Evaluate the results	Supplement 1A	Supplement 1B	Review the chapter
• Organizational forms • Accounting for business decisions	• The basic accounting equation • Financial statements	• Using financial statements • Useful financial information	• Careers that depend on accounting knowledge	• Public companies	• Demonstration case • Chapter summary • Key terms • Homework helper • Practice material

Understand the Business

"Jordan, we should start by talking about how you want to organize your business."

 "Well, I'm starting a technology company to sell apps in Apple's App Store and on Google Play. What else do I need to know?"

ORGANIZATIONAL FORMS

> **Learning Objective 1-1**
> Describe various organizational forms and business decision makers.

Laurie outlined three primary ways businesses can be organized: sole proprietorship, partnership, and corporation.

Sole Proprietorship

This is a form of business owned (and usually operated) by one individual. It is the easiest form of business to start because it doesn't require any special legal maneuvers. Just get a business license and you're good to go. A sole proprietorship is considered a part of the owner's life, with all profits (or losses) becoming part of the taxable income of the owner, and the owner being personally liable for all debts of the business.

Partnership

A partnership is similar to a sole proprietorship, except that profits, taxes, and legal liability are the responsibility of two or more owners instead of just one. It is slightly more expensive to form than a sole proprietorship because a lawyer typically is needed to draw up a partnership agreement, which describes how profits are shared between partners and how that would

Photo: Eclipse Studios/McGraw-Hill;
Photo: Jill Braaten/McGraw-Hill Education

change if new partners are added or existing partners leave. The key advantage of a partnership over a sole proprietorship is that, by having more owners, a partnership typically has more resources available to it, which can help the business grow faster.

Corporation

Unlike sole proprietorships and partnerships, a corporation is a separate entity from both legal and accounting perspectives. This means the corporation, not its owners, is legally responsible for its own taxes and debts. Because legal liability is limited in this way, owners cannot lose more than their investment in the corporation, which is a major advantage to the owners. Two disadvantages of incorporation are the legal fees for creating a corporation can be expensive and income taxes must be paid by both the corporation and its owners.

Corporations can raise large amounts of money for growth because they divide ownership of the corporation into shares that can be sold to new owners. A share of the corporation's ownership is indicated on a legal document called a stock certificate. The owners of a company's stock (stockholders) can buy and sell stock privately or publicly on a stock exchange if the company has legally registered to do so. Most corporations start out as **private companies** and, as explained in Chapter Supplement 1B, will apply to become **public companies** ("go public") if they need a lot of financing, which they obtain from issuing new stock certificates to investors. Some big-name corporations, like Cargill and Chick-fil-A, haven't gone public because they get enough financing from private sources, but many that you are familiar with (and most examples in this book) are public companies.

Other

Other organizational forms exist, such as a limited liability company (LLC), which combines characteristics of a partnership and a corporation. We focus on corporations in this book.

> "I'm interested in limiting my legal liability and getting some financing by selling ownership shares to investors, so I will create a private corporation called Noodlecake Studios, Inc. What's next?"

ACCOUNTING FOR BUSINESS DECISIONS

Most companies exist to earn profits for their stockholders. They earn profits by selling goods or services to customers for more than they cost to produce. Noodlecake will be successful if it is able to sell enough apps to cover the costs of making them and running the company. To know just how successful the company is, Jordan and Ty will need to establish and maintain a good system of financial record-keeping—an accounting system. **Accounting** is an information system designed by an organization to capture (analyze, record, and summarize) the activities affecting its financial condition and performance and then report the results to decision makers, both inside and outside the organization. It's such a key part of business that businesspeople typically talk about their companies using accounting terms, which is why they often call it the "language of business."

Every organization needs accountants to assist in reporting financial information for decision making and to help its owners understand the financial effects of those business decisions. Jordan can get this help in one of two ways. He can hire an accountant to work as an employee of his business (a **private accountant**) or he can contract with someone like Laurie who provides advice to several businesses (a **public accountant**). Because Jordan's business is small, he doesn't yet need a full-time accountant. Instead, he agrees for Noodlecake to pay fees to Laurie for basic services. She'll help him to set up an accounting system and advise him on key business decisions.

> "How will an accounting system help me run my business?"

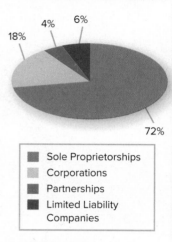

Percentage of Organizational Forms in the U.S.

4% 6%
18%
72%

- Sole Proprietorships
- Corporations
- Partnerships
- Limited Liability Companies

Source: IRS.gov.

YOU SHOULD KNOW

Accounting: A system of analyzing, recording, and summarizing the results of a business's operating, investing, and financing activities and then reporting them to decision makers.

Photo: Jill Braaten/McGraw-Hill Education

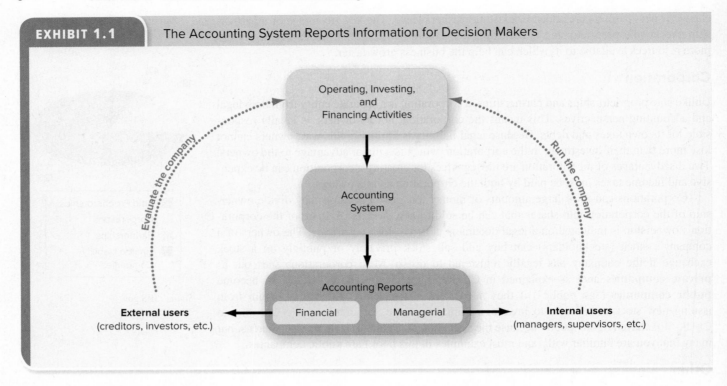

EXHIBIT 1.1   The Accounting System Reports Information for Decision Makers

The main goal of an accounting system is to capture information about the operating, investing, and financing activities of a company so that it can be reported to decision makers, both inside and outside the business. Exhibit 1.1 illustrates this role and shows that this information can be presented in two kinds of reports. **Managerial accounting reports** include detailed financial plans and continually updated reports about the operating performance of the company. These reports are made available only to the company's employees (internal users) for making business decisions related to production, marketing, human resources, and finance. For example, managerial accounting reports are needed when determining whether to build, buy, or rent a building; whether to continue or discontinue making particular products; how much to pay employees; and how much to borrow. As manager of Noodlecake, Jordan will regularly need managerial accounting reports to monitor the number of app downloads and evaluate the various costs associated with making and selling apps.

"Financial information about your business will be needed by others outside your company. For example, where will the money come from to start your business?"

"Ty and I will contribute $5,000 each from personal savings. But I'll still need to ask the bank for a $20,000 loan to buy computer equipment and software. What will the bank want to know?"

Photo: Eclipse Studios/McGraw-Hill;
Photo: Jill Braaten/McGraw-Hill
Education

YOU SHOULD KNOW

Financial Statements: Reports that summarize the financial results of business activities.

Laurie described **financial accounting reports,** called **financial statements**, which are prepared periodically to provide information to people not employed by the business. These external financial statement users aren't given access to detailed internal records of the company, so they rely extensively on the financial statements. The four main groups of external users are (1) creditors, (2) investors, (3) directors, and (4) government.

1. **Creditors** include suppliers, banks, and anyone to whom money is owed. *Suppliers* want to be sure they will be paid for the goods and services they deliver, so they will evaluate a company's financial statements and check its credit history before allowing it to buy on credit. *Banks* use financial statements to evaluate the risk they will not be repaid the money they've loaned to a company. Because banks take a risk when they loan money to a company, they want periodic financial reports to evaluate how well the company is doing so they can intervene if it looks like the company will have trouble repaying its loan.

2. **Investors** include existing and potential stockholders. *Stockholders* look to accounting information to assess the financial strength of a business and, ultimately, to estimate its value.

3. **Directors** is the short title for the members of a company's *board of directors.* The stockholders of public companies or large private companies elect directors to oversee the company's managers. Directors use financial statements to ensure the company's managers make decisions that are in the best financial interests of its stockholders.

4. **Government** agencies look closely at companies' financial statements. The *Securities and Exchange Commission (SEC),* for example, is responsible for the functioning of stock markets, so it keeps a close watch on the information public companies report in financial statements. Also, the *Internal Revenue Service (IRS)* and state and local governments use financial statement information to ensure taxes are computed using correct amounts.

Exhibit 1.2 shows that, along with managers inside the company, these external user groups are key users of financial statement information. In Noodlecake's case, the bank will be the

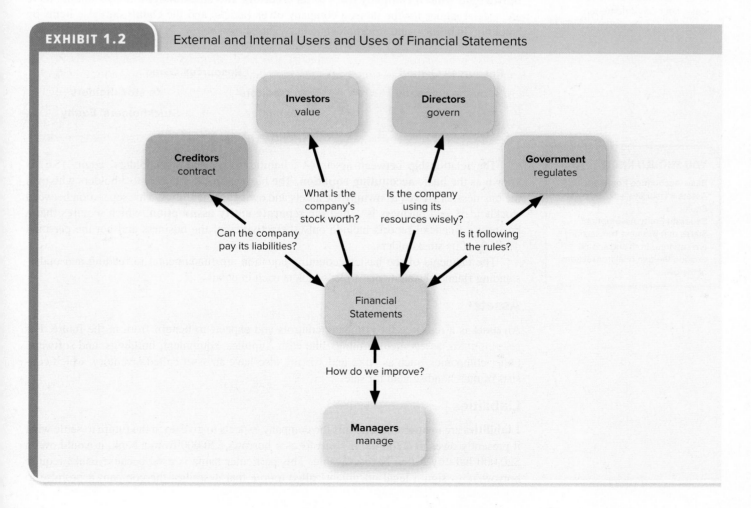

EXHIBIT 1.2 External and Internal Users and Uses of Financial Statements

main external user. Jordan will be expected to prepare financial statements to obtain a bank loan and then regularly provide updated financial reports until the loan is repaid.

While Jordan understood everything Laurie had told him up to this point, he had another major concern.

"I want to sound intelligent when I talk to my banker, but I don't know much about accounting."

"This is a common concern for new business owners, so let's start with the most basic thing you need to know about accounting."

Study the Accounting Methods

THE BASIC ACCOUNTING EQUATION

One of the central concepts to understanding financial reports is that **what a company owns must equal what a company owes to its creditors and stockholders.** In accounting, there are special names for the items a company owns (assets) and the claims on these items by creditors (liabilities) and stockholders (equity), as shown below.

Resources Owned . . .	=	Resources Owed . . .	
by the **company**		to **creditors**	to **stockholders**
Assets	**=**	**Liabilities**	**+** **Stockholders' Equity**

The relationship between assets (A), liabilities (L), and stockholders' equity (SE) is known as the **basic accounting equation**. The business itself, not the stockholders who own the business, is viewed as owning the assets and owing the liabilities. This separation between stockholders and business is called the **separate entity assumption**, which requires that a business's financial reports include only the activities of the business and not the personal dealings of its stockholders.

The elements of the basic accounting equation are fundamental to reading and understanding financial statements, so let's look at each in detail.

Assets

An **asset** is a resource the company controls and expects to benefit from in the future. For Noodlecake, assets include things like cash, supplies, equipment, buildings, and software. Other companies, such as Nike and Target, also have an asset called inventory, which consists of merchandise held for sale.

Liabilities

Liabilities are measurable amounts the company expects to give up in the future to settle what it presently owes to creditors. If Noodlecake borrows $20,000 from a bank, it would owe a $20,000 liability called Notes Payable. This particular name is used because banks require borrowers to sign a legal document called a *note* that describes the company's promise to repay the bank. If Noodlecake receives paper, pens, and toner bought on credit from suppliers, it would owe a liability called Accounts Payable. This particular name is used because purchases made using credit are said to be "on account." Noodlecake could also owe salaries and wages to employees (Salaries and Wages Payable) and taxes to governments (Taxes Payable).

Stockholders' Equity

Stockholders' equity represents the owners' claims on assets of the business after creditors' claims have been fulfilled. From a legal perspective, creditors have priority over stockholders. Thus, if a company goes out of business, liabilities must be paid before any amounts are paid to stockholders. Owners' claims arise from two sources.

1. **Paid-in capital.** The owners have a claim for amounts they contributed directly to the company in exchange for its stock (Common Stock).

2. **Earned capital.** The owners have a claim on profits the company has earned for them through its business operations (Retained Earnings).

The second item listed above is particularly important because a business can survive only if it is profitable. It will be profitable if the total amount earned from selling goods and services is greater than the costs incurred to generate those sales. Theoretically, these profits belong to the company's owners, so they increase stockholders' equity. Through these profits, owners can get more money back from the company than they paid in (a return on their investment).

Given the importance of a company's profits, accounting systems separately track the two components of profit: revenues and expenses.

Revenues   Revenues are earned by selling goods or services to customers. For Noodlecake, revenues are measured at the amount the company charges customers for its apps.

Expenses   Expenses are all costs of doing business that are necessary to earn revenues. Noodlecake incurs expenses for advertising, utilities, rent, salaries and wages, insurance, and supplies used up in the office. Notice that expenses are said to be "incurred" to generate revenues. The word *incurred* means the activities giving rise to a cost (e.g., running an ad, using electricity) have occurred in the period in which the related revenues have been generated.

Net Income   Although *profit* is used in casual conversation, the preferred term in accounting is *net income*. Net income is calculated as revenues minus expenses. For Noodlecake to be profitable, its revenues must be greater than its expenses. (If revenues are less than expenses, the company would have a net loss, but for now we'll assume Noodlecake is going to earn a profit.) **By generating net income, a company increases its stockholders' equity,** as illustrated below. This net income can be left in the company to accumulate (with earnings that have been retained from prior years), or it can be paid out to the company's stockholders for their own personal use (called *dividends*).

Stockholders' Equity

Common Stock
(equity paid in by stockholders)

Retained Earnings
(equity earned by the company)

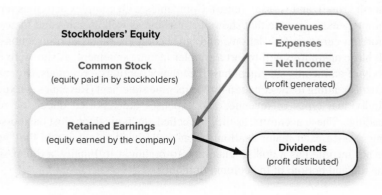

Dividends   A company's profits are accumulated in Retained Earnings until a decision is made to distribute them to stockholders in what is called a dividend. The simplest type of dividend, and the most common for a small business like Noodlecake, is a dividend paid in cash. Dividends are reported as a reduction in Retained Earnings. **Dividends are not an expense incurred to generate earnings.** Rather, dividends are an optional distribution of earnings to stockholders, approved by the company's board of directors. If Jordan and Ty wanted, they could choose to leave all the profits in Noodlecake by never declaring a dividend.

Photo: Jill Braaten/McGraw-Hill Education

> **"Okay, I think I get it, but can you tell me how all those items relate to each other and where they are reported in the financial statements?"**

FINANCIAL STATEMENTS

Assets, liabilities, stockholders' equity, revenues, expenses, and dividends appear in different reports that collectively are called financial statements. The term *financial statements* refers to four accounting reports, typically prepared in the following order:

1. **Income Statement**
2. **Statement of Retained Earnings**
3. **Balance Sheet**
4. **Statement of Cash Flows**

Financial statements can be prepared at any time during the year, although they are most commonly prepared monthly, every three months (quarterly reports), and at the end of the year (annual reports). Companies are allowed to choose a calendar or fiscal year-end. A calendar year is a 12-month period ending on December 31, and a fiscal year is a 12-month period ending on a day other than December 31. The toy maker Mattel uses a calendar year-end because this is the start of its slow business period. Green Bay Packers, Inc., has chosen a fiscal year-end of March 31, after the football season ends.

The Income Statement

The first financial statement prepared is the **income statement** (also called the statement of operations). Laurie gives Jordan Exhibit 1.3 to show what Noodlecake's income statement might look like for one month of operations ended September 30. The heading of the income statement identifies who, what, and when: the name of the business, the title of the report, and the time period covered by the financial statement. Larger businesses with thousands or millions of dollars in revenues and expenses add a fourth line under the date to indicate if the reported numbers are rounded to the nearest thousand or million. For international companies, this fourth line also reports the currency used in the report. An international company based in the United States, like Apple, will translate any foreign currency into U.S. dollars—basically assuming all its business was done in U.S. dollars. This is the **unit of measure assumption**. We see it in the reporting currency used by Nestlé (Swiss franc), LEGO (Danish krone), and Adidas (euro). Companies with complex activities report a statement of comprehensive income that shows net income as well as gains and losses relating to pensions, foreign currency translations, and other complex financial transactions. But companies with basic operations will report a simpler income statement, as shown in Exhibit 1.3.

The body of an income statement has three major captions—revenues, expenses, and net income—corresponding to the equation for the income statement (Revenues − Expenses = Net Income). Individual types of revenues and expenses are reported under the revenue and expense headings. These **accounts**, as they are called, are typical for most businesses, whether small or big. Notice each major caption has an underlined subtotal, and the "bottom line" amount for net income has a double underline to highlight it. Finally, a dollar sign appears (only) at the top and bottom of the column of numbers.

EXHIBIT 1.3 Income Statement

NOODLECAKE STUDIOS, INC. Income Statement (Projected) For the Month Ended September 30, 2021		Explanation **Who: Name of the business** **What: Title of the statement** **When: Accounting period**
Revenues		
Sales Revenue	$ 9,000	Price charged when selling apps to customers in September
Service Revenue	3,000	Price charged when providing consulting services to others
Total Revenues	12,000	**Total revenues generated during September**
Expenses		
Salaries and Wages Expense	5,000	Cost of salaries and wages for work done in September
Rent Expense	2,500	Cost of rent for the month of September
Utilities Expense	1,600	Cost of utilities used in September
Insurance Expense	300	Cost of insurance coverage for September
Advertising Expense	100	Cost of advertising done in September
Income Tax Expense	500	Cost of taxes on September's income
Total Expenses	10,000	**Total expenses incurred during September**
Net Income	$ 2,000	**Difference between total revenues and total expenses**

When listing the accounts on the income statement, revenues are on top, usually with the largest, most relevant revenue listed first. Then expenses are subtracted, again from largest to smallest, except that Income Tax Expense is the last expense listed. Net Income is the difference between total revenues and total expenses. This format, which groups revenues separately from expenses and reports a single measure of income, is called a **"single-step income statement."** Other income statement formats are possible, as explained in Chapter 6.

"So, does the $2,000 of Net Income mean I'll have that much more cash?"

 "No. Net income is a measure of how much better off your business is, not how much cash you made."

Laurie's point is one of the key ideas of the income statement. It's quite common for a business to provide goods or services to customers in one month but not collect cash from them until a later month. Similarly, expenses for the current month's activities may actually be paid in a different month. You'll have a chance to learn this in more detail later, but it's worth trying to understand from the beginning that the month's revenues don't necessarily equal cash coming in during the month and expenses don't always equal cash going out during the month.

Jordan seemed disappointed to see only $2,000 of projected net income for the first month. Laurie reassured him it's typical for new businesses like Noodlecake to initially struggle to generate a profit because the company has lots of expenses related to employee wages but relatively little revenues because it hasn't yet built a reputation that attracts customers. Noodlecake's net income will likely increase in the future as its apps gain in popularity. By selling more apps, revenues will increase without a major increase in expenses.

"I guess that's not so bad. It does make me want to watch my expenses and try to boost my sales quickly. What about the amount Noodlecake owes to the bank? Should we talk about the balance sheet?"

Photo: Eclipse Studios/McGraw-Hill;
Photo: Jill Braaten/McGraw-Hill
Education

Photo: Eclipse Studios/McGraw-Hill

 "**Before we look at that, I want to show you the next statement that connects the income statement to the balance sheet, so you'll understand the relationships between the reports.**"

The Statement of Retained Earnings

Noodlecake will report a **statement of retained earnings**, as shown in Exhibit 1.4. A more comprehensive statement of stockholders' equity that explains changes in all stockholders' equity accounts is provided by large corporations. But for Noodlecake, most changes in stockholders' equity relate to generating and distributing earnings, so a statement of retained earnings is just as good as a full-blown statement of stockholders' equity. The heading in Exhibit 1.4 identifies the name of the company, the title of the report, and the accounting period. The statement starts with the Retained Earnings balance at the beginning of the period. Remember that retained earnings are the profits that have accumulated in the company over time. Because this is a new business, there aren't any accumulated profits yet, so the beginning balance is $0. Next, the statement adds Net Income and subtracts any Dividends for the current period to arrive at Retained Earnings at the end of the period.[1] Again, a dollar sign is used at the top and bottom of the column of numbers and a double underline appears at the bottom.

EXHIBIT 1.4   Statement of Retained Earnings

		Explanation
NOODLECAKE STUDIOS, INC.		**Who: Name of the business**
Statement of Retained Earnings (Projected)		**What: Title of the statement**
For the Month Ended September 30, 2021		**When: Accounting period**
Retained Earnings, September 1, 2021	$ 0	Last period's ending Retained Earnings balance
Add: Net Income	2,000	Reported on the income statement (Exhibit 1.3)
Subtract: Dividends	(1,000)	Distributions to stockholders in the current period
Retained Earnings, September 30, 2021	$1,000	This period's ending Retained Earnings balance

The Balance Sheet

The next financial report is the **balance sheet**. It is also known as the statement of financial position. The balance sheet's purpose is to report the amount of a business's assets, liabilities, and stockholders' equity at a specific point in time. Exhibit 1.5 presents Noodlecake's projected balance sheet. Think of the balance sheet as a picture or screen capture of Noodlecake's resources and claims on those resources at the end of a particular day (in this case, September 30, 2021).

Notice again the heading specifically identifies the name of the company and title of the statement. Unlike the other financial reports, the balance sheet is presented for a point in time (at September 30, 2021, in this case). Assets are listed in order of how soon they are to be used or turned into cash. Likewise, liabilities are listed in order of how soon each is to be paid or settled.

The balance sheet first lists the assets of the business, which for Noodlecake total $36,000. The second section lists the business's liabilities and stockholders' equity balances, also totaling $36,000. The balance sheet "balances" because the resources equal the claims on

---

[1] For companies that have a net loss (expenses exceed revenues), the statement of retained earnings would subtract the net loss rather than add net income.

EXHIBIT 1.5 | Balance Sheet

		Explanation
NOODLECAKE STUDIOS, INC.		**Who:** Name of the business
Balance Sheet (Projected)		**What:** Title of the statement
At September 30, 2021		**When:** Point in time
Assets		**Resources controlled by the company**
Cash	$13,000	Amount of cash on hand and in the business's bank account
Accounts Receivable	2,500	Noodlecake's right to collect for sales/services provided on account
Supplies	500	Cost of paper and other supplies on hand
Equipment	14,000	Cost of computers, desks, etc.
Software	6,000	Cost of software and programming code purchased from others
Total Assets	**$36,000**	**Total amount of the company's resources**
Liabilities and Stockholders' Equity		**Claims on the company's resources**
Liabilities		*Creditors'* claims on the company's resources
Accounts Payable	$ 5,000	Amount owed to suppliers for prior credit purchases (on account)
Notes Payable	20,000	Amount of loan owed to the bank (for promissory note)
Total Liabilities	25,000	Total claims on the resources by creditors
Stockholders' Equity		*Stockholders'* claims on the company's resources
Common Stock	10,000	Amount stockholders contributed for the company's common stock
Retained Earnings	1,000	Total earnings retained in the business (Exhibit 1.4)
Total Stockholders' Equity	11,000	Total claims on the company's resources by stockholders
Total Liabilities and Stockholders' Equity	**$36,000**	**Total claims on the company's resources**

the resources. The basic accounting equation (also called the balance sheet equation) reflects the business's financial position at September 30:

Assets	=	Liabilities	+	Stockholders' Equity
$36,000	**=**	**$25,000**	**+**	**$11,000**

Cash is the first asset reported on the balance sheet. The $13,000 would represent the total amount of cash on hand and in Noodlecake's bank account. The $2,500 reported as Accounts Receivable would represent Noodlecake's right to collect from customers for sales and services provided on credit. Noodlecake intends to sell consulting services to other companies on account. The $500 reported for Supplies indicates the cost of office supplies on hand at the balance sheet date. Likewise, the $14,000 for Equipment and $6,000 for Software represent Noodlecake's cost of buying these assets. According to the **cost principle** of accounting, assets are initially reported on the balance sheet based on their original cost to the company.

Under liabilities, Laurie includes $5,000 of Accounts Payable as the amount Noodlecake owes suppliers for equipment, supplies, and other items purchased on account. Notes Payable is the written promise to repay the loan from the bank. As with all liabilities, these are financial obligations of the business arising from past business activities.

Finally, within stockholders' equity, Common Stock reflects the dollar amount of the company's stock given when Jordan and Ty contribute $10,000 to the company. Retained Earnings reports the earnings expected to be retained in the company as of September 30. It matches the ending amount of Retained Earnings on the statement of retained earnings (Exhibit 1.4).

 **COACH'S TIP**

Any account name containing "receivable" is an asset and any containing "payable" is a liability.

"**Besides monitoring my revenues and expenses, it looks like I need to make sure I have enough assets to pay my liabilities.**"

Photo: Jill Braaten/McGraw-Hill Education

Photo: Eclipse Studios/McGraw-Hill

"Sharp observation! Your creditors are most interested in your ability to pay cash to them in the future. However, not all assets can be easily turned into cash and not all revenues and expenses are received or paid in cash. So, there is one more important financial statement."

The Statement of Cash Flows

Noodlecake's projected income statement (back in Exhibit 1.3) shows a positive net income of $2,000. However, net income is not necessarily equal to cash because revenues and expenses are reported when generated or incurred regardless of when cash is received or paid. The fourth financial report of interest to external users, then, is the **statement of cash flows**. It includes only those activities that result in cash changing hands. Exhibit 1.6 shows Noodlecake's projected statement of cash flows for the month ended September 30.

The statement of cash flows is divided into three types of activities:

1. **Operating:** These cash flows arise directly from running the business to earn profit. They include cash received from selling apps and services, and cash paid for wages, advertising, rent, insurance, supplies, and so on.

2. **Investing:** These cash flows arise from buying and selling productive resources with long lives (such as buildings, land, equipment, and software), purchasing investments, and lending to others. As Exhibit 1.6 shows, Noodlecake expects to spend $20,000 cash to purchase equipment and software.

3. **Financing:** These cash flows include borrowing from banks, repaying bank loans, receiving cash from stockholders for company stock, or paying dividends to stockholders.

The bank will assess Noodlecake's ability to make cash payments on its loan by watching how the cash flows reported on this statement change in the future.

EXHIBIT 1.6   Statement of Cash Flows

NOODLECAKE STUDIOS, INC.
Statement of Cash Flows (Projected)
For the Month Ended September 30, 2021

Explanation

Who: Name of the entity
What: Title of the statement
When: Accounting period

		Explanation
Cash Flows from Operating Activities		**Activities directly related to earning income**
Cash received from customers	$ 9,500	Cash received from customers
Cash paid to employees and suppliers	(5,500)	Cash paid to employees and suppliers of goods/services
Cash Provided by Operating Activities	4,000	Cash inflows minus outflows ($9,500 − $5,500)
Cash Flows from (used in) Investing Activities		**Activities related to the sale/purchase of productive assets**
Cash used to buy equipment and software	(20,000)	Cash spent on equipment/software
Cash from (used in) Investing Activities	(20,000)	
Cash Flows from Financing Activities		**Activities involving investors and banks**
Cash received for stock issuance	10,000	Cash received from owners for company stock
Cash dividends paid to stockholders	(1,000)	Cash paid to distribute profit to owners
Cash borrowed from the bank	20,000	Cash received on loan from the bank
Cash Provided by Financing Activities	29,000	Cash inflows minus outflows ($10,000 − $1,000 + $20,000)
Change in Cash	13,000	Sum of the three cash flow categories ($4,000 − $20,000 + $29,000)
Beginning Cash, September 1, 2021	0	Cash balance at the beginning of the accounting period
Ending Cash, September 30, 2021	$13,000	Cash balance reported on the balance sheet (Exhibit 1.5)

COACH'S TIP

Parentheses are used on the statement of cash flows to indicate negative cash flows (outflows rather than inflows).

Notes to the Financial Statements

The four basic financial statements are not complete without notes to help financial statement users understand how the amounts were derived and what other information may affect their decisions. We'll talk about notes in more detail in later chapters.

Relationships among the Financial Statements

Exhibit 1.7 shows how the four basic financial statements connect to one another:

1 Net Income, from the income statement, is a component in determining ending Retained Earnings on the statement of retained earnings.

2 Ending Retained Earnings from the statement of retained earnings is then reported on the balance sheet.

3 Cash on the balance sheet is equal to the ending Cash on the statement of cash flows.

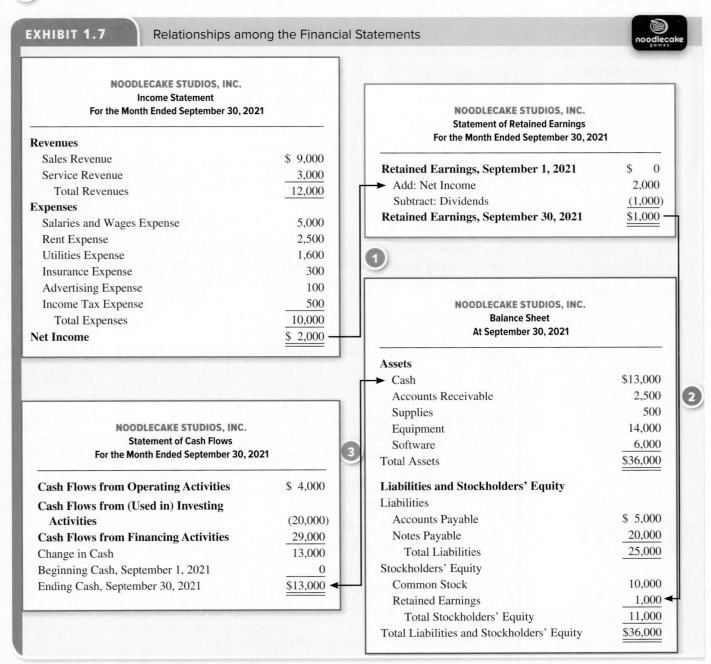

EXHIBIT 1.7 — Relationships among the Financial Statements

NOODLECAKE STUDIOS, INC.
Income Statement
For the Month Ended September 30, 2021

Revenues	
Sales Revenue	$ 9,000
Service Revenue	3,000
Total Revenues	12,000
Expenses	
Salaries and Wages Expense	5,000
Rent Expense	2,500
Utilities Expense	1,600
Insurance Expense	300
Advertising Expense	100
Income Tax Expense	500
Total Expenses	10,000
Net Income	$ 2,000

NOODLECAKE STUDIOS, INC.
Statement of Retained Earnings
For the Month Ended September 30, 2021

Retained Earnings, September 1, 2021	$ 0
Add: Net Income	2,000
Subtract: Dividends	(1,000)
Retained Earnings, September 30, 2021	$1,000

NOODLECAKE STUDIOS, INC.
Balance Sheet
At September 30, 2021

Assets	
Cash	$13,000
Accounts Receivable	2,500
Supplies	500
Equipment	14,000
Software	6,000
Total Assets	$36,000
Liabilities and Stockholders' Equity	
Liabilities	
Accounts Payable	$ 5,000
Notes Payable	20,000
Total Liabilities	25,000
Stockholders' Equity	
Common Stock	10,000
Retained Earnings	1,000
Total Stockholders' Equity	11,000
Total Liabilities and Stockholders' Equity	$36,000

NOODLECAKE STUDIOS, INC.
Statement of Cash Flows
For the Month Ended September 30, 2021

Cash Flows from Operating Activities	$ 4,000
Cash Flows from (Used in) Investing Activities	(20,000)
Cash Flows from Financing Activities	29,000
Change in Cash	13,000
Beginning Cash, September 1, 2021	0
Ending Cash, September 30, 2021	$13,000

A summary of the four basic financial statements is presented in Exhibit 1.8.

	EXHIBIT 1.8	Summary of the Four Basic Financial Statements

Financial Statement	Purpose: To report . . .	Structure	Examples of Content
Income Statement	The financial performance of the business *during the current accounting period.*	Revenues – Expenses = Net Income (Loss)	Sales revenue, wages expense, supplies expense, rent expense
Statement of Retained Earnings	Earnings retained in the business *during the current accounting period* added to those of prior periods.	Beginning Retained Earnings + Net Income (this period) – Dividends (this period) = Ending Retained Earnings	Net income is from the income statement. Dividends are amounts distributed this period.
Balance Sheet	The financial position of a business *at a point in time.*	Liabilities Assets = + Stockholders' Equity	Cash, receivables, supplies, equipment, accounts payable, notes payable, common stock, retained earnings
Statement of Cash Flows	Activities that caused increases and decreases in cash *during the current accounting period.*	+/– Operating Cash Flows +/– Investing Cash Flows +/– Financing Cash Flows = Change in Cash + Beginning Cash = Ending Cash	Cash collected from customers, cash paid to suppliers, cash paid for equipment, cash borrowed from banks, cash received from issuing stock

You have seen lots of new and important material in this section. Before moving on, take a moment to complete the self-study practice. This is the best way to make sure you've paid enough attention when reading about how business activities are reported in financial statements.

 How's it going?   Self-Study Practice

For each account, indicate (1) the type of account (A = asset, L = liability, SE = stockholders' equity, R = revenue, E = expense) and (2) whether it is reported on the income statement (I/S), statement of retained earnings (SRE), balance sheet (B/S), or statement of cash flows (SCF).

Account Title	Type	Statement
1. Land	_____	_____
2. Advertising Expense	_____	_____
3. Accounts Receivable	_____	_____
4. Service Revenue	_____	_____
5. Common Stock	_____	_____
6. Notes Payable	_____	_____

After you have finished, check your answers with the solution.

Solution to Self-Study Practice

	Type	Statement
1.	A	B/S
2.	E	I/S
3.	A	B/S
4.	R	I/S
5.	SE	B/S
6.	L	B/S

"So, you've just seen how your financial statements should look in one month and how they relate. Are you feeling okay with all this?"

"It actually makes me anxious to get started. What will my external users look for?"

Evaluate the Results

USING FINANCIAL STATEMENTS

Learning Objective 1-3
Explain how financial statements are used by decision makers.

The financial statements are a key source of information when external users, like creditors and investors, make decisions concerning a company. As you will see throughout this course, the amounts reported in the financial statements can be used to calculate percentages and ratios that reveal important insights about a company's performance. For now, however, let's consider how creditors and investors might gain valuable information simply by reading the dollar amounts reported in each financial statement.

- **Creditors are mainly interested in assessing:**
  1. **Is the company generating enough cash to pay what it owes?** The statement of cash flows helps answer this question. In particular, creditors would be interested in seeing whether operating activities are producing positive cash flows. Noodlecake's expected net inflow of $4,000 cash from operating activities is very good for a new business. Find it in Exhibit 1.6.
  2. **Does the company have enough assets to cover its liabilities?** Answers to this question come from comparing assets and liabilities reported on the balance sheet. Noodlecake is expected to own more than it owes at September 30 (total assets of $36,000 versus total liabilities of $25,000). With $13,000 in Cash, Noodlecake would be able to immediately pay all of its Accounts Payable and part of Notes Payable if needed.

- **Investors expect a return on their contributions to a company.** The return may be immediate (through dividends) or long term (through selling their stock certificates at a price higher than their original cost). Dividends and higher stock prices are more likely if a company is profitable. As a result, investors look closely at the income statement (and statement of retained earnings) for information about the company's ability to generate profits (and distribute dividends).

"I've heard a lot about fraud and 'cooking the books.' How do users know the information they're getting is useful and can be trusted?"

USEFUL FINANCIAL INFORMATION

Learning Objective 1-4
Describe factors that contribute to useful financial information.

Laurie indicated that useful financial information arises when businesses apply generally accepted accounting principles in an ethical business environment.

Generally Accepted Accounting Principles

The system of financial statement reporting used today has a long history—all the way back to a publication in 1494 by Italian monk and mathematician Luca Pacioli. Currently, the Financial Accounting Standards Board (FASB) has the primary responsibility for setting the underlying rules of accounting in the United States. As a group, these rules are called **generally accepted accounting principles, or GAAP** for short (pronounced like the name of the clothing store).

The accounting rules in the United States are similar, for the most part, to those used elsewhere in the world, but some important differences exist. The FASB has been working with the International Accounting Standards Board (IASB) to eliminate differences so that investors can more easily compare the financial statements of companies from different countries. Throughout this course, we'll use a pullout feature called Spotlight on the World to alert you to important differences.

SPOTLIGHT ON The World

The accounting rules developed by the IASB are called **International Financial Reporting Standards, or IFRS** for short. As the map indicates, many countries already require or permit the use of IFRS (purple), or have expressed an acceptance of IFRS in other ways (blue). For example, foreign companies whose stock is traded in the United States use IFRS.

The main goal of GAAP and IFRS is to ensure companies produce financial information that is useful to existing and potential investors, lenders, and other creditors in making decisions about providing resources to the companies. As shown in Exhibit 1.9, for financial information to be judged useful, it must possess two fundamental characteristics: **relevance** and **faithful representation**. Information is relevant if it makes a difference in

EXHIBIT 1.9 Key Concepts for External Financial Reporting

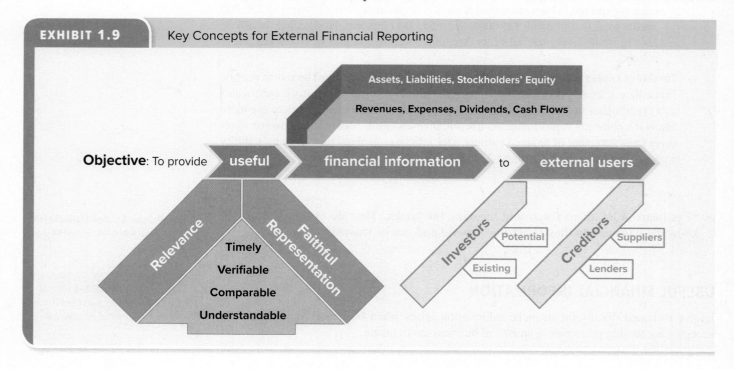

decision making, and it is a faithful representation if it fully depicts the economic substance of business activities. The usefulness of financial information is enhanced when it is (i) timely, (ii) verifiable, (iii) comparable, and (iv) understandable. Information is *timely* if it is available in time to influence decision makers. That's why large public companies in the United States must issue annual financial statements within 60 days of year-end. Information is *verifiable* if others, such as external auditors, reach similar values using similar methods. It is *comparable* if the same accounting principles are used over time and across companies. It is *understandable* if reasonably informed users can comprehend and interpret it. To achieve these objectives, the FASB and IASB have developed a framework that outlines the financial elements to be measured (shown in green in Exhibit 1.9) and the main external users for whom the financial information is intended (shown in beige in Exhibit 1.9).

"Who is responsible for ensuring that businesses follow GAAP?"

Laurie told Jordan that a company's managers have primary responsibility for following GAAP. To provide additional assurance, some private companies and all public companies hire independent auditors to scrutinize their financial records. Following rules approved by the Public Company Accounting Oversight Board (PCAOB) and other accounting bodies, these auditors report whether, beyond reasonable doubt, the financial statements represent what they claim to represent, whether they comply with GAAP, and what issues they struggled with when assessing whether the financial statements follow GAAP. In a sense, GAAP is to auditors and accountants what the criminal code is to lawyers and the public. The Securities and Exchange Commission (SEC) is the government agency that oversees stock exchanges and financial reporting by public companies in the United States. More information about public company reporting is presented in Chapter Supplement 1B.

 "Overall, users expect information that is truthful, and this assumes that the company is following strong ethical business and accounting practices."

Ethical Conduct

Ethics refers to the standards of conduct for judging right from wrong, honest from dishonest, and fair from unfair. Intentional misreporting is both unethical and illegal. As you will see throughout this course, some accounting and business issues have clear answers that are either right or wrong. However, many situations require accountants, auditors, and managers to weigh the pros and cons of alternatives before making final decisions. To help ensure these decisions are made in a professional and ethical manner, the American Institute of Certified Public Accountants (AICPA) requires that all its members adhere to a **Code of Professional Conduct.** Yet, despite this code of conduct, some individuals have been involved in accounting scandals and fraud.

In response to frauds, the government introduced laws through the **Sarbanes-Oxley Act (SOX).** SOX requires top managers of public companies to sign a report certifying their responsibilities for the financial statements, maintain an audited system of **internal controls** to ensure accuracy in the accounting reports, and maintain an independent committee to oversee top management and ensure they cooperate with auditors. SOX ensures corporate executives face severe consequences—20 years in prison and $5 million in fines—if found guilty of committing accounting fraud.

Ethical conduct is just as important for small private businesses as it is for large public companies. Laurie's advice to Jordan and to all managers is to create an ethical environment and establish a strong system of checks and controls inside the company. Do not tolerate blatant acts of fraud, such as employees making up false expenses for reimbursement, punching in a time card belonging to a fellow employee late for work, or copying someone's

Photo: Eclipse Studios/McGraw-Hill; Photo: Jill Braaten/McGraw-Hill Education

SPOTLIGHT ON | # Ethics

Accounting Scandals

Accounting scandals are often driven by greed and the fear of personal or business failure. Initially, some people may appear to benefit from fraudulent reporting. In the long run, however, fraud harms most individuals and organizations. When it is uncovered, the corporation's stock price drops dramatically. For example, Valeant Pharmaceuticals' stock price dropped 51 percent on a single day, leading its biggest investor to lose $1.3 billion in a matter of hours. Creditors are also harmed by fraud. WorldCom's creditors recovered only 42 percent of what they were owed. They lost $36 billion. Innocent employees also are harmed by fraud. At Enron, 5,600 employees lost their jobs and many lost all of their retirement savings. The auditing firm Arthur Andersen, which once employed 28,000, disbanded after becoming entangled in the WorldCom and Enron frauds.

ideas and claiming them as his or her own. Also be aware that not all ethical dilemmas are clear-cut. Some situations will require you to weigh one moral principle (e.g., honesty) against another (e.g., loyalty). When faced with an ethical dilemma, you should follow a three-step process:

1. **Identify who will be affected by the situation**—both those who will appear to benefit (often the manager or employee) and those who will be harmed (other employees, the company's reputation, owners, creditors, and the public in general).

2. **Identify and evaluate the alternative courses of action.**

3. **Choose the alternative that is the most ethical**—and that you would be proud to have reported in the news.

Often, there is no one right answer to ethical dilemmas and hard choices will need to be made. In the end, however, following strong ethical practices is a key factor in business success and in ensuring good financial reporting.

Epilogue and What's Coming Up

Jordan got going quickly and, in August, created a corporation called Noodlecake Studios, Inc. Things didn't turn out exactly as he had planned, but the business has been successful. Noodlecake started developing apps only for the iPhone but then created software to port these apps to Android devices for sale on Google Play. Noodlecake also provides software consulting services to other companies and is now looking to publish games for Sony and other gaming consoles.

The next three chapters will take you step by step through some of the financing, investing, and operating decisions during Noodlecake's first month of business. We will look at the way accountants collect data about business activities and process them to construct the financial statements. The key to success in this course is to regularly **practice** the skills presented in this textbook. It is very difficult to learn accounting without doing the assignments and keeping up with the reading.

SUPPLEMENT 1A CAREERS THAT DEPEND ON ACCOUNTING KNOWLEDGE

Learning Objective 1-S1
Describe examples where accounting helps in pursuing other business careers.

Accounting knowledge can make the difference in your ability to land a dream job, whether you hope to work in production and operations management, human resources, finance, or marketing. Exhibit 1A.1 displays nonaccounting jobs that could be available to you at the world's leading companies and explains how accounting knowledge can be vital to these positions. If, instead, you have your eyes set on an accounting career, see Supplement 2A in Chapter 2 for further information.

EXHIBIT 1A.1   Accounting Knowledge Can Benefit All Majors

Production and Operations Management

Production Manager, Nintendo: Figure out how to make a $300 Switch for $257.

Outsourcing Specialist, Apple: Coordinate more than 20 suppliers of parts for the next iPad, at the same total cost as legacy iPads.

Human Resources

Compensation Analyst, Google: Develop affordable, attractive global pay programs.

Labor Relations Manager, National Basketball Players Association union: Assist in salary renegotiations involving the $133 million salary cap.

Accounting

Finance

Investment Analyst, Goldman Sachs: Assess value of investing $50 million in Quirky Incorporated.

Financial Analyst, Amazon Web Services: Build financial models to forecast revenue and other key business measures.

Marketing

Brand Manager, Kraft Heinz Company: Set prices to achieve 5% annual sales growth.

Customer Business Developer, Procter & Gamble: Collaborate with accounting to enhance customer profits and cash flows.

Sources: https://venturebeat.com/2017/04/05/teardown-reveals-nintendo-switch-costs-257-to-build/, http://blogs.forbes.com/johnray/2011/03/11/isuppli-teardown-of-the-ipad-2-investor-edition/, http://www.isuppli.com/Teardowns/News/Pages/iPad-2-Carries-Bill-of-Materials-of-$326-60-IHS-iSuppli-Teardown-Analysis-Shows.aspx, https://www.nba.com/article/2019/06/29/nba-salary-cap-2019-20-season-set-10914-million.

Photo: Rubberball/Getty Images

SUPPLEMENT 1B   PUBLIC COMPANIES

When a company needs more financing than it can access privately, it may choose to issue its shares to investors through an **initial public offering (IPO)** on a public stock exchange. This process offers many positive outcomes. The company (1) keeps the money it raises when issuing shares, (2) can more easily raise money in the future by issuing additional shares, (3) can pay employees using company shares not just cash, (4) gives founders and other stockholders a way to sell their shares, and (5) can buy other companies by paying with shares rather than cash. A company also can *go public* through **"direct listing"** rules approved by the Securities and Exchange Commission in 2018 and 2019. In a direct listing, the company's existing stockholders (not the company itself) exchange their shares of the company for cash provided by new investors. Spotify used this new approach to go public in 2018 because the company didn't need more cash, but its stockholders did want to sell some of their shares.

> **Learning Objective 1-S2**
> Describe the decision to become a public company and explain the implications for accounting.

Public Company Financial Reporting

Whether a company goes public through an IPO or direct listing process, there are downsides to being a public company: (1) greater public reporting of significant events affecting the company, (2) increased accounting disclosures, and (3) greater risk of litigation for misstatements in and omissions from these reports. In addition, public companies are required to give frequent updates about their business through press releases, financial statement reports, and various filings with the SEC.

Press Releases   To keep external financial statement users informed, a public company will announce annual (and quarterly) results through a press release sent to news agencies. The press release typically includes highlights of key financial results for the period, management's discussion of these results, and attachments containing a condensed income statement and balance sheet. The press release is issued three to five weeks after the accounting period ends to give the company's accountants time to make final adjustments to the accounting records, to allow time for the company's management to prepare a written analysis of the results, and in the case of annual results, to enable external auditors to complete most of their work.

Many companies follow up the press release with a conference call broadcast on the Internet, which allows analysts to ask questions of the company's senior executives. By listening to these calls (or later reading their transcripts), you can learn a lot about the company's business strategy, its expectations for the future, and the key factors analysts consider when they evaluate the company. Archived conference calls are available at the company's website or conferencecalltranscripts.org.

Financial Statement Reports Several weeks after the preliminary press release, a public company will release its complete financial statements as part of an annual (or quarterly) report posted at its investor relations website. A typical annual report contains two parts. The first part usually begins with a letter to investors from the company's Chief Executive Officer (CEO), followed by glossy pictures and comments about the company's business. The second part presents the financial section. The typical elements of the financial section are listed and described in Exhibit 1B.1. The comparative financial statements (list item 5) are similar to the financial statements in the body of this chapter, except they cover multiple years by including a column of numbers for each year.

A company's quarterly report is a highly condensed version of its annual report. Following a short letter to stockholders and abbreviated discussion of the financial results, a quarterly report presents a condensed income statement for the quarter, a condensed balance sheet dated at the end of the quarter, and a condensed statement of cash flows. This condensed report typically shows less detail than the annual report, often omitting items 3, 4, 7, 8, and 9 in Exhibit 1B.1. Quarterly financial statements are not audited, so they are labeled as unaudited. Obviously, with all these limitations, the quarterly reports aren't as informative as the annual report, but at least they are released on a timelier basis (every three months rather than every year).

EXHIBIT 1B.1 Typical Elements of an Annual Report's Financial Section

Section Name	Information Presented
1. Summarized financial data	• key figures covering a 5- or 10-year period
2. Management's discussion and analysis (MD&A)	• detailed analysis of the company's financial condition and operating results; a must-read
3. Management's report on internal control	• statements that describe management's responsibility for ensuring effective control over the financial reporting
4. Auditor's report	• the auditor's conclusion about whether: (i) GAAP was followed, (ii) any matters were especially challenging, and (iii) the company's controls were effective
5. Comparative financial statements	• multiyear presentation of the four basic financial statements
6. Financial statement notes	• further information crucial for interpreting the financial statements
7. Recent stock price data	• brief summary of highs and lows during the year
8. Unaudited quarterly data	• condensed summary of results by quarter
9. Directors and officers	• list of those overseeing and running the company

---

Securities and Exchange Commission (SEC) Filings To ensure sufficient, relevant information is available to investors, the SEC requires each public company to file certain reports with the SEC, including an **annual report on Form 10-K, quarterly reports on Form 10-Q, and current event reports on Form 8-K.** (We wouldn't burden you with the details of the form numbers except that most people refer to them by number.) Form 10-K requires disclosure of information beyond that listed in Exhibit 1B.1 (e.g., description of properties owned, legal proceedings, executive pay), so often companies will use the 10-K in place of a glossy annual report. The 8-K is prepared any time a significant business event occurs between financial statement dates. The 8-K could report a change in the company's top management, its acquisition of another company, the filing of a press release, or the release of new financial data.

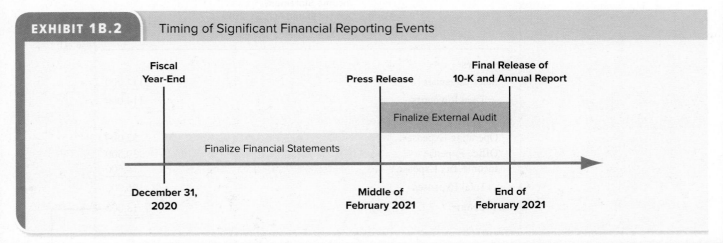

SPOTLIGHT ON Financial Reporting

Expected Impacts of COVID-19

A surge of 8-Ks were filed soon after the COVID-19 crisis reached the United States in early 2020. An example excerpted from Disney's 8-K follows:

> The impact of the novel coronavirus ("COVID-19") and measures to prevent its spread are affecting our businesses in a number of ways. We have closed our theme parks; suspended our cruises and theatrical shows; delayed theatrical distribution of films both domestically and internationally; and experienced supply chain disruption and ad sales impacts.

Source: The Walt Disney Company, Form 8-K filed March 18, 2020. Retrieved on March 19, 2020, from sec.gov.

To find a public company's SEC filings, click on "Company Filings Search" in the Filings tab at sec.gov. These filings are available soon after the SEC's Electronic Data Gathering, Analysis, and Retrieval (EDGAR) service receives them. The typical timing of these releases and filings for a company with a December 31 year-end is shown in Exhibit 1B.2.

Throughout the remaining chapters of this book, you will learn how to evaluate the results reported in financial statements, using ratios and other measures commonly considered by analysts.

EXHIBIT 1B.2	Timing of Significant Financial Reporting Events

Fiscal Year-End — Press Release — Final Release of 10-K and Annual Report

Finalize External Audit

Finalize Financial Statements

December 31, 2020 — Middle of February 2021 — End of February 2021

REVIEW THE CHAPTER

DEMONSTRATION CASE

The introductory case presented here reviews the items reported on the income statement, statement of retained earnings, and balance sheet, using the financial statements of the **WD-40 Company**, maker of the household lubricant and squeak stopper with the same name. Following is a list of items and amounts (in thousands of U.S. dollars) adapted from WD-40 Company's financial statements for the quarter ended May 31, 2019.

WD-40 Company

Accounts Payable	$ 50,000	Office Expense	$ 39,500
Accounts Receivable	76,000	Operating Expenses	52,000
Cash	36,000	Retained Earnings, March 1, 2019	19,000
Common Stock	121,000	Retained Earnings, May 31, 2019	29,000
Dividends	8,000	Sales Revenues	114,000
Equipment	155,000	Total Assets	310,000
Income Tax Expense	4,500	Total Expenses	96,000
Inventory	43,000	Total Liabilities	160,000
Net Income	18,000	Total Liabilities and Stockholders' Equity	310,000
Notes Payable	110,000	Total Revenues	114,000
		Total Stockholders' Equity	150,000

Required:

1. Prepare an income statement, a statement of retained earnings, and a balance sheet for the quarter, following the formats in Exhibits 1.3, 1.4, and 1.5.
2. Describe the content of these three statements.
3. Name the other statement WD-40 Company would include in its financial statements.
4. Did more of the financing for WD-40 Company's assets come from liabilities or stockholders' equity?
5. Explain why WD-40 Company would subject its statements to an independent audit.

Suggested Solution

1. The first step to reach a solution is to distinguish accounts as belonging to the income statement (revenues and expenses), statement of retained earnings (retained earnings and dividends), and balance sheet (assets, liabilities, and stockholders' equity). Organize the accounts in proper format and follow the flow from one to another (as shown by the following arrows).

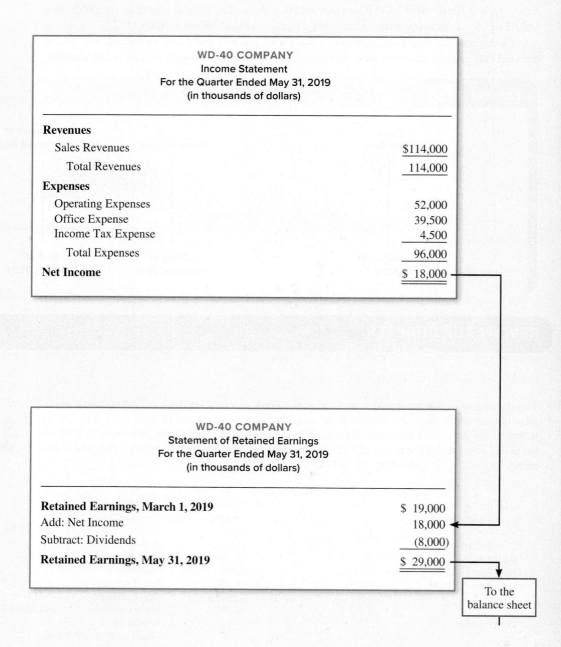

WD-40 COMPANY
Income Statement
For the Quarter Ended May 31, 2019
(in thousands of dollars)

Revenues

| Sales Revenues | $114,000 |
| Total Revenues | 114,000 |

Expenses

Operating Expenses	52,000
Office Expense	39,500
Income Tax Expense	4,500
Total Expenses	96,000
Net Income	**$ 18,000**

WD-40 COMPANY
Statement of Retained Earnings
For the Quarter Ended May 31, 2019
(in thousands of dollars)

Retained Earnings, March 1, 2019	$ 19,000
Add: Net Income	18,000
Subtract: Dividends	(8,000)
Retained Earnings, May 31, 2019	$ 29,000

To the balance sheet

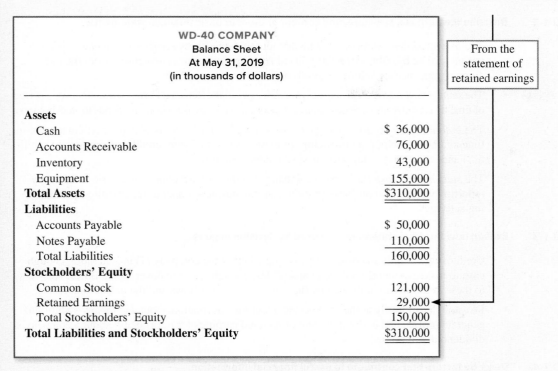

WD-40 COMPANY
Balance Sheet
At May 31, 2019
(in thousands of dollars)

From the
statement of
retained earnings

Assets	
Cash	$ 36,000
Accounts Receivable	76,000
Inventory	43,000
Equipment	155,000
Total Assets	**$310,000**
Liabilities	
Accounts Payable	$ 50,000
Notes Payable	110,000
Total Liabilities	160,000
Stockholders' Equity	
Common Stock	121,000
Retained Earnings	29,000
Total Stockholders' Equity	150,000
Total Liabilities and Stockholders' Equity	**$310,000**

2. The income statement reports the most common measure of financial performance for a business: net income (revenues minus expenses during the accounting period). The statement of retained earnings links the net income number from the income statement to the end-of-period retained earnings balance on the balance sheet. The balance sheet reports the amount of assets, liabilities, and stockholders' equity of a business at a point in time.

3. WD-40 Company would also present a statement of cash flows.

4. The balance sheet indicates slightly more financing for WD-40 Company's assets is provided from liabilities ($160,000) than stockholders' equity ($150,000).

5. Like all public companies, WD-40 Company will subject its financial statements to an audit because it is required by the SEC to have an independent audit. Also, an audit will give users greater confidence in the accuracy of financial statement information because the people who audited the statements are required to meet professional standards of ethics and competence.

CHAPTER SUMMARY

Describe various organizational forms and business decision makers.   LO 1-1

- Sole proprietorships are owned by one individual, are relatively inexpensive to form, and are not treated legally as separate from their owners. Thus, all profits or losses become part of the taxable income to the owner, who is also responsible personally for all debts of the business.

- Partnerships are businesses legally similar to proprietorships but with two or more owners.

- Corporations are separate legal entities (thus, corporations pay taxes) that issue shares of stock to investors (stockholders) and are more costly to establish. Stockholders cannot be held liable for more than their investment in the corporation. Private corporations issue stock to a few individuals while public corporations issue stock to many in the stock market.

- Business decision makers include creditors (banks, suppliers), investors (stockholders), customers, governments, and other external users.

LO 1-2 **Describe the purpose, structure, and content of the four basic financial statements.**

- The *income statement* reports the net amount that a business earned (net income) over a period of time by subtracting the costs of running the business (expenses) from the total amount generated by selling its goods and services (revenues).
- The *statement of retained earnings* explains changes in the Retained Earnings account over a period of time by considering increases (from net income) and decreases (from dividends to stockholders).
- The *balance sheet* reports what the business owns (reported as assets) at a particular point in time and how much of the financing for these assets came from creditors (reported as liabilities) and stockholders (reported as stockholders' equity).
- The *statement of cash flows* explains changes in the cash account over a period of time by reporting inflows and outflows of cash from the business's operating, investing, and financing activities.

LO 1-3 **Explain how financial statements are used by decision makers.**

- Creditors are mainly interested in assessing whether the company (1) is generating enough cash to make payments on its loan and (2) has enough assets to cover its liabilities. Answers to these questions are indicated by the statement of cash flows and the balance sheet.
- Investors look closely at the income statement for information about a company's ability to generate profits, and at the statement of retained earnings for information about a company's dividend distributions.

LO 1-4 **Describe factors that contribute to useful financial information.**

- Companies generate useful financial information by applying generally accepted accounting principles (GAAP) or International Financial Reporting Standards (IFRS) in an ethical business environment.
- To be useful, information must be relevant and a faithful representation of reality. Information is more useful when it is timely, verifiable, comparable, and understandable.

KEY TERMS

Accounting p. 5
Accounts p. 10
Balance Sheet p. 12
Basic Accounting Equation p. 8
Financial Statements p. 6

Generally Accepted Accounting Principles (GAAP) p. 18
Income Statement p. 10
International Financial Reporting Standards (IFRS) p. 18

Sarbanes-Oxley Act (SOX) p. 19
Separate Entity Assumption p. 8
Statement of Cash Flows p. 14
Statement of Retained Earnings p. 12
Unit of Measure Assumption p. 10

See complete definitions in the glossary in the back of this text.

HOMEWORK HELPER

Alternative terms

- The balance sheet also can be called the statement of financial position.
- The income statement also can be called the statement of operations.
- Net Income also can be called Net Earnings.

Helpful reminders

- The balance in each account is reported once and only once in either the balance sheet, income statement, or statement of retained earnings.

Frequent mistakes

- Dividends are not expenses. Dividends relate to distributing (not generating) earnings. Consequently, a company's dividends are reported on its statement of retained earnings (not its income statement).

PRACTICE MATERIAL

QUESTIONS (⊖ Symbol indicates questions that require analysis from more than one perspective.)

1. Define *accounting*.

2. Val is opening a hair salon, but she does not know what business form it should take. Tell her about the advantages and disadvantages of operating as a sole proprietorship versus a corporation. ⊖

3. Briefly distinguish financial accounting from managerial accounting.

4. The accounting process generates financial reports for both internal and external users. Describe some of the specific groups of internal and external users.

5. Explain what the separate entity assumption means when it says a business is treated as separate from its owners for accounting purposes.

6. List the three main types of business activities on the statement of cash flows and give an example of each.

7. What information should be included in the heading of each of the four primary financial statements?

8. What are the purposes of (*a*) the balance sheet, (*b*) the income statement, (*c*) the statement of retained earnings, and (*d*) the statement of cash flows?

9. Explain why the income statement, statement of retained earnings, and statement of cash flows would be dated "For the Year Ended December 31, 2021," whereas the balance sheet would be dated "At December 31, 2021."

10. Briefly explain the difference between *net income* and *net loss*.

11. Describe the basic accounting equation that provides the structure for the balance sheet. Define the three major components reported on the balance sheet.

12. Describe the equation that provides the structure for the income statement. Explain the three major items reported on the income statement.

13. Describe the equation that provides the structure for the statement of retained earnings. Explain the four major items reported on the statement of retained earnings.

14. Describe the equation that provides the structure for the statement of cash flows. Explain the three major types of activities reported on the statement.

15. Briefly describe the organization responsible for developing accounting measurement rules (generally accepted accounting principles) in the United States.

16. What is the main goal for accounting rules in the United States and around the world? What characteristics must financial information possess to reach that goal?

17. Briefly define what an ethical dilemma is and describe the steps to consider when evaluating ethical dilemmas.

18. In what ways might accounting frauds be similar to cases of academic dishonesty?

MULTIPLE CHOICE

1. Which of the following is *not* one of the four basic financial statements?

   a. The balance sheet
   b. The audit report
   c. The income statement
   d. The statement of cash flows

2. Which of the following is true regarding the income statement?

   a. The income statement is sometimes called the statement of operations.
   b. The income statement reports revenues, expenses, and liabilities.
   c. The income statement only reports revenue for which cash was received at the point of sale.
   d. The income statement reports the financial position of a business at a particular point in time.

3. Which of the following is false regarding the balance sheet?

   a. The accounts shown on a balance sheet represent the basic accounting equation for a particular business.
   b. The retained earnings balance shown on the balance sheet must agree with the ending retained earnings balance shown on the statement of retained earnings.

   c. The balance sheet summarizes the net changes in specific account balances over a period of time.
   d. The balance sheet reports the amount of assets, liabilities, and stockholders' equity of a business at a point in time.

4. Which of the following regarding retained earnings is false?

   a. Retained earnings is increased by net income.
   b. Retained earnings is a component of stockholders' equity on the balance sheet.
   c. Retained earnings is an asset on the balance sheet.
   d. Retained earnings represents earnings not yet distributed to stockholders in the form of dividends.

5. Which of the following is *not* one of the items required to be shown in the heading of a financial statement?

   a. The financial statement preparer's name
   b. The title of the financial statement
   c. The financial reporting date or period
   d. The name of the business entity

6. Which of the following statements regarding the statement of cash flows is false?

   a. The statement of cash flows separates cash inflows and outflows into three major categories: operating, investing, and financing.

b. The ending cash balance shown on the statement of cash flows must agree with the amount shown on the balance sheet at the end of the same period.

c. The total increase or decrease in cash shown on the statement of cash flows must agree with the "bottom line" (net income or net loss) reported on the income statement.

d. The statement of cash flows covers a period of time.

7. Which of the following regarding GAAP is true?

a. GAAP is an abbreviation for generally applied accounting principles.

b. Changes in GAAP always affect the amount of income reported by a company.

c. GAAP is the abbreviation for generally accepted accounting principles.

d. Changes to GAAP must be approved by the Senate Finance Committee.

8. Which of the following is true?

a. FASB creates SEC.

b. GAAP creates FASB.

c. SEC creates CPA.

d. FASB creates GAAP.

9. Which of the following would *not* be a goal of external users reading a company's financial statements?

a. Understanding the current financial state of the company

b. Assessing the company's contribution to social and environmental policies

c. Predicting the company's future financial performance

d. Evaluating the company's ability to generate cash from sales

10. Which of the following is *not* required by the Sarbanes-Oxley Act?

a. Top managers of public companies must sign a report certifying their responsibilities for the financial statements.

b. Public companies must maintain an audited system of internal control to ensure accuracy in accounting reports.

c. Public companies must maintain an independent committee to meet with the company's independent auditors.

d. Top managers of public companies must be members of the American Institute of Certified Public Accountants.

> For answers to the Multiple-Choice Questions **see page Q1** located in the last section of the book.

MINI-EXERCISES

LO 1-4 **M1-1 Identifying Definitions with Abbreviations**

The following is a list of important abbreviations used in the chapter. These abbreviations also are used widely in business. For each abbreviation, give the full designation. The first one is an example.

Abbreviation	Full Designation
1. CPA	Certified Public Accountant
2. GAAP	
3. FASB	
4. SEC	
5. IFRS	

LO 1-1, 1-2, 1-4 **M1-2 Matching Definitions with Terms or Abbreviations**

Match each definition with its related term or abbreviation by entering the appropriate letter in the space provided. Use each definition only once.

Term or Abbreviation	Definition
____ 1. SEC	A. A system that collects and processes financial information about an organization and reports that information to decision makers.
____ 2. Investing activities	
____ 3. Private company	B. Measurement of information about a business in the monetary unit (dollars or other national currency).
____ 4. Corporation	
____ 5. Accounting	C. An unincorporated business owned by two or more persons.
____ 6. Partnership	
____ 7. FASB	D. A company that sells shares of its stock privately and is not required to release its financial statements to the public.
____ 8. Financing activities	
____ 9. Unit of measure	

25

_____ 10. GAAP

_____ 11. Public company

_____ 12. Operating activities

E. An incorporated business that issues shares of stock as evidence of ownership.

F. Buying and selling productive resources with long lives.

G. Transactions with lenders (borrowing and repaying cash) and stockholders (selling company stock and paying dividends).

H. Activities directly related to running the business to earn profit.

I. Securities and Exchange Commission.

J. Financial Accounting Standards Board.

K. A company that has its stock bought and sold on stock exchanges and is required to publicly release its financial statements.

L. Generally accepted accounting principles.

M1-3 Matching Definitions with Terms

LO 1-2, 1-4

Match each definition with its related term by entering the appropriate letter in the space provided.

Term	Definition
_____ 1. Relevance	A. The financial reports of a business are assumed to include the results of only that business's activities.
_____ 2. Faithful representation	
_____ 3. Expenses	B. The resources owned by a business.
_____ 4. Separate entity	C. Financial information that depicts the economic substance of business activities.
_____ 5. Assets	D. The total amounts invested and reinvested in the business by its owners.
_____ 6. Liabilities	
_____ 7. Stockholders' equity	E. The costs of business necessary to earn revenues.
_____ 8. Revenues	F. A feature of financial information that allows it to influence a decision.
	G. Earned by selling goods or services to customers.
	H. The amounts owed by the business.

M1-4 Matching Financial Statement Items to Balance Sheet and Income Statement Categories

LO 1-2

Procter & Gamble

For each of the following items in Procter & Gamble's financial statements, indicate (1) whether it is reported in the income statement (I/S) or balance sheet (B/S) and (2) whether it is an asset (A), liability (L), stockholders' equity (SE), revenue (R), or expense (E) account. The first item is given as an example.

Item	(1) Statement	(2) Account Type
(Example) Cash	B/S	A
1. Accounts Payable		
2. Accounts Receivable		
3. Income Tax Expense		
4. Sales Revenue		
5. Notes Payable		
6. Retained Earnings		

LO 1-2

M1-5 Matching Financial Statement Items to Balance Sheet and Income Statement Categories

For each item, indicate (1) whether it is reported on the income statement (I/S) or balance sheet (B/S) and (2) the type of account (A = asset, L = liability, SE = stockholders' equity, R = revenue, E = expense).

Item	(1) Statement	(2) Account Type
1. Accounts Receivable		
2. Sales Revenue		
3. Equipment		
4. Supplies Expense		
5. Cash		
6. Advertising Expense		
7. Accounts Payable		
8. Retained Earnings		

LO 1-2

Tootsie Roll Industries

M1-6 Matching Financial Statement Items to Balance Sheet and Income Statement Categories

Tootsie Roll Industries manufactures and sells more than 64 million Tootsie Rolls each day. The following items were listed on Tootsie Roll's recent income statement and balance sheet. For each item, indicate (1) the type of account (A = asset, L = liability, SE = stockholders' equity, R = revenue, E = expense) and (2) whether it is reported on the income statement (I/S) or balance sheet (B/S).

1. Accounts Receivable
2. Office Expense
3. Cash
4. Equipment
5. Advertising Expense

6. Sales Revenue
7. Notes Payable
8. Retained Earnings
9. Accounts Payable

LO 1-2

General Mills

M1-7 Matching Financial Statement Items to Balance Sheet and Income Statement Categories

General Mills is a manufacturer of food products, such as Lucky Charms cereal, Pillsbury crescent rolls, and Green Giant vegetables. The following items were presented in the company's financial statements. For each item, indicate (1) the type of account (A = asset, L = liability, SE = stockholders' equity, R = revenue, E = expense) and (2) whether it is reported on the income statement (I/S) or balance sheet (B/S).

1. Accounts Payable
2. Common Stock
3. Equipment
4. Accounts Receivable
5. Notes Payable

6. Cash
7. Retained Earnings
8. Office Expense
9. Sales Revenue
10. Supplies

LO 1-2

Oakley, Inc.

M1-8 Matching Financial Statement Items to the Basic Financial Statements

Oakley, Inc., reported the following items in its financial statements. For each item, indicate (1) the type of account (A = asset, L = liability, SE = stockholders' equity, R = revenue, E = expense, D = dividend) and (2) whether it is reported on the income statement (I/S), statement of retained earnings (SRE), and/or balance sheet (B/S).

1. Dividends
2. Common Stock
3. Sales Revenue
4. Equipment

5. Cash
6. Notes Payable
7. Accounts Payable
8. Retained Earnings, Beginning of Year

LO 1-2

M1-9 Matching Financial Statement Items to the Four Basic Financial Statements

Match each element with its financial statement by entering the appropriate letter in the space provided.

Element	Financial Statement
_____ 1. Cash Flows from Financing Activities	A. Balance Sheet
_____ 2. Expenses	B. Income Statement
_____ 3. Cash Flows from Investing Activities	C. Statement of Retained Earnings
_____ 4. Assets	D. Statement of Cash Flows
_____ 5. Dividends	
_____ 6. Revenues	
_____ 7. Cash Flows from Operating Activities	
_____ 8. Liabilities	

M1-10 Reporting Amounts on the Statement of Cash Flows   LO 1-2

Learning which items belong in each cash flow statement category is an important first step in understanding their meaning. Use a letter to mark each item in the following list as a cash flow from Operating, Investing, or Financing activities. **Put parentheses around the letter if it is a cash *outflow* and use no parentheses if it's an *inflow*.**

_____ **1.** Cash paid for dividends   _____ **4.** Cash paid to employees
_____ **2.** Cash collected from customers   _____ **5.** Cash paid to purchase equipment
_____ **3.** Cash received when signing a note payable   _____ **6.** Cash received from issuing stock

M1-11 Reporting Amounts on the Statement of Cash Flows   LO 1-2

Learning which items belong in each category of the statement of cash flows is an important first step in understanding their meaning. Use a letter to mark each item in the following list as a cash flow from Operating, Investing, or Financing activities. **Put parentheses around the letter if it is a cash *outflow* and use no parentheses if it's an *inflow*.**

_____ **1.** Cash paid to purchase land   _____ **4.** Cash paid for dividends
_____ **2.** Cash collected from clients   _____ **5.** Cash paid to suppliers
_____ **3.** Cash received from selling equipment   _____ **6.** Cash received from issuing stock

M1-12 Preparing a Statement of Retained Earnings   LO 1-2

Stone Culture Corporation was organized on January 1, 2020. For its first two years of operations, it reported the following:

Net Income for 2020	$40,000	Dividends for 2021	$ 20,000
Net Income for 2021	45,000	Total assets at the end of 2020	125,000
Dividends for 2020	15,000	Total assets at the end of 2021	242,000

On the basis of the data given, prepare a statement of retained earnings for both 2020 (its first year of operations) and 2021.

M1-13 Relationships among Financial Statements   LO 1-2

Items from the income statement, statement of retained earnings, and balance sheet are listed below in alphabetical order. For the companies shown in each column, solve for the missing amounts.

Alphabet, Inc.
Apple, Inc.
Intel Corp.

TIP: Use Exhibit 1.7 to identify relations among the items, then solve for amounts.

	Alphabet, Inc.	Apple, Inc.	Intel Corp.
Common Stock	$43	$28	$26
Dividends	0	14	6
Net Income	(a)	(d)	(g)
Retained Earnings, Beginning of Year	104	15	24
Retained Earnings, End of Year	(b)	(e)	(h)
Total Assets	(c)	(f)	(i)
Total Expenses	106	195	50
Total Liabilities	56	269	63
Total Revenues	137	264	71

LO 1-2   **M1-14 Relationships among Financial Statements**

Items from the income statement, statement of retained earnings, and balance sheet are listed below in alphabetical order. For the companies shown in each column, solve for the missing amounts.

	Amazin' Corp.	Best Tech, Inc.	Colossal Corp.
Common Stock	$ 5	$15	$100
Dividends	10	5	50
Net Income	(a)	(d)	(g)
Retained Earnings, Beginning of Year	30	0	200
Retained Earnings, End of Year	(b)	(e)	(h)
Total Assets	(c)	(f)	(i)
Total Expenses	75	30	200
Total Liabilities	30	30	350
Total Revenues	100	50	300

LO 1-2

Activision Blizzard, Inc.

M1-15 Relationships among Financial Statements

Items from the 2018 income statement, statement of retained earnings, and balance sheet of Activision Blizzard, Inc., are listed below in alphabetical order. Solve for the missing amounts, and explain whether the company was profitable.

> **TIP:** Use Exhibit 1.7 to identify relations among the items, then work backward to solve for amounts.

	Activision Blizzard, Inc.
Common Stock	$ 4,799
Dividends	259
Net Income (Loss)	(a)
Retained Earnings, Beginning of Year	5,004
Retained Earnings, End of Year	(b)
Total Assets	17,835
Total Expenses	(c)
Total Liabilities	6,478
Total Revenues	7,500

LO 1-2, 1-3   **M1-16 Preparing an Income Statement, Statement of Retained Earnings, and Balance Sheet**

The following information was reported in the December 31 financial statements of National Airways, Inc. (listed alphabetically, amounts in millions).

Accounts Payable	$ 4,650	Interest Expense	$ 130
Accounts Receivable	580	Landing Fees Expense	3,100
Aircraft Fuel Expense	8,700	Notes Payable	6,950
Cash	2,970	Repairs and Maintenance Expense	1,200
Common Stock	1,220	Retained Earnings (as of December 31)	5,780
Dividends	20	Salaries and Wages Expense	3,280
Equipment	14,370	Supplies	680
Income Tax Expense	260	Ticket Revenues	17,100

1. Prepare an income statement for the year ended December 31.
2. Prepare a statement of retained earnings for the year ended December 31.
   TIP: Assume the balance in Retained Earnings was $5,370 (million) at January 1.
3. Prepare a balance sheet at December 31.
4. Using the balance sheet, indicate whether the total assets of National Airways at the end of the year were financed primarily by liabilities or stockholders' equity.

EXERCISES

E1-1 Reporting Amounts on the Four Basic Financial Statements

LO 1-2

Using the following table and the equations underlying each of the four basic financial statements, show (*a*) that the balance sheet is in balance, (*b*) that net income is properly calculated, (*c*) what caused changes in the retained earnings account, and (*d*) what caused changes in the cash account.

Assets	$18,200	Beginning Retained Earnings	$3,500
Liabilities	13,750	Ending Retained Earnings	4,300
Stockholders' Equity	4,450	Cash Flows from Operating Activities	1,600
Revenue	10,500	Cash Flows from Investing Activities	(1,000)
Expenses	9,200	Cash Flows from Financing Activities	(900)
Net Income	1,300	Beginning Cash	1,000
Dividends	500	Ending Cash	700

E1-2 Reporting Amounts on the Four Basic Financial Statements

LO 1-2

Using the following table and the equations underlying each of the four basic financial statements, show (*a*) that the balance sheet is in balance, (*b*) that net income is properly calculated, (*c*) what caused changes in the retained earnings account, and (*d*) what caused changes in the cash account.

Assets	$79,500	Beginning Retained Earnings	$20,500
Liabilities	18,500	Ending Retained Earnings	28,750
Stockholders' Equity	61,000	Cash Flows from Operating Activities	15,700
Revenue	32,100	Cash Flows from Investing Activities	(7,200)
Expenses	18,950	Cash Flows from Financing Activities	(5,300)
Net Income	13,150	Beginning Cash	3,200
Dividends	4,900	Ending Cash	6,400

E1-3 Preparing a Balance Sheet

LO 1-2, 1-3

Designer Brands, Inc., previously called DSW, sells luxurious and fashionable shoes. Its balance sheet, at August 3, 2019 (the first Saturday of the month), contained the following items and approximate amounts (in millions).

Designer Brands, Inc.

Amounts owed to suppliers	$650	Warehouses, stores, and offices	$1,700
Designer Brands' right to collect on account	85	Merchandise held for sale	700
Currency and bank account balances	75	Amounts owed for promissory notes	1,180
Common stock issued to stockholders	460	Accumulated profits of the company	270

Required:

1. Give the account name commonly used for each item listed.
2. Prepare the balance sheet as of August 3, 2019, providing appropriate totals and subtotals.
3. As of August 3, did most of the financing for assets come from creditors or stockholders?

LO 1-2, 1-3

E1-4 Completing a Balance Sheet and Inferring Net Income

Ken Young and Kim Sherwood organized Reader Direct as a corporation; each contributed $49,000 cash to start the business and received 4,000 shares of stock. The store completed its first year of operations on December 31, 2020. On that date, the following financial items for the year were determined: cash on hand and in the bank, $47,500; amounts due from customers from sales of books, $26,900; equipment, $48,000; amounts owed to publishers for books purchased, $8,000; one-year notes payable to a local bank for $2,850. No dividends were declared or paid to the stockholders during the year.

Required:

1. Complete the following balance sheet at December 31, 2020.

Assets		Liabilities and Stockholders' Equity	
Cash	$_____	**Liabilities**	
Accounts Receivable	_____	Accounts Payable	$_____
Equipment	_____	Notes Payable	_____
		Total Liabilities	_____
		Stockholders' Equity	
		Common Stock	_____
		Retained Earnings	13,550
		Total Stockholders' Equity	_____
Total Assets	$_____	Total Liabilities and Stockholders' Equity	$_____

2. Using the retained earnings equation and an opening balance of $0, work backwards to compute the amount of net income for the year ended December 31, 2020.
3. As of December 31, 2020, did most of the financing for assets come from creditors or stockholders?
4. Assuming that Reader Direct generates net income of $3,000 and pays dividends of $2,000 in 2021, what would be the ending Retained Earnings balance at December 31, 2021?

LO 1-2

K·Swiss Inc.

E1-5 Labeling and Classifying Business Transactions

The following items relate to business transactions involving K·Swiss Inc.
a. Coins and currency
b. Amounts K·Swiss owes to suppliers of shoes
c. Amounts K·Swiss can collect from customers
d. Amounts owed to bank for loan to buy building
e. Property on which buildings will be built
f. Amounts distributed from profits to stockholders
g. Amounts earned by K·Swiss by selling shoes
h. Unused paper in K·Swiss head office
i. Cost of paper used up during month
j. Amounts contributed by stockholders for K·Swiss stock

Required:

1. Identify an appropriate label (account name) for each item as it would be reported in the company's financial statements. Choose from the following: Accounts Payable, Accounts Receivable, Cash, Common Stock, Dividends, Land, Notes Payable, Sales Revenue, Supplies, and Supplies Expense.
2. Classify each item (*a* through *j*) as an asset (A), liability (L), stockholders' equity (SE), revenue (R), or expense (E).

E1-6 Preparing an Income Statement and Inferring Missing Values

LO 1-2, 1-3

Cinemark Holdings, Inc., operates movies and food concession counters throughout the United States. Its income statement for the quarter ended June 30, 2019, reported the following (accounts are listed alphabetically in thousands):

Cinemark Holdings, Inc.

Admissions Revenue	$521,000	Office Expense	$171,000
Concessions Expense	63,000	Rent Expense	89,000
Concessions Revenue	345,000	Salaries and Wages Expense	109,000
Film Rental Expense	295,000	Net Income	?
Income Tax Expense	38,000		

Required:

1. Solve for the missing amount by preparing an income statement for the quarter ended June 30, 2019.
2. What are Cinemark's main source of revenue and two biggest expenses?

E1-7 Preparing an Income Statement

LO 1-2

Home Realty, Incorporated, has been operating for three years and is owned by three investors. J. Doe owns 60 percent of the total outstanding stock of 9,000 shares and is the managing executive in charge. On December 31, the following financial items for the entire year were determined: sales revenue, $166,000; salaries and wages expense, $97,000; interest expense, $6,300; advertising expense, $9,025; and income tax expense, $18,500. Also during the year, the company declared and paid the owners dividends amounting to $12,000. Prepare the company's income statement.

E1-8 Inferring Values Using the Income Statement and Balance Sheet Equations

LO 1-2

Review the chapter explanations of the income statement and the balance sheet equations. Apply these equations in each of the following independent cases to compute the two missing amounts for each case. Assume that it is the end of the first full year of operations for the company.

TIP: First identify the numerical relations among the columns using the balance sheet and income statement equations. Then compute the missing amounts.

Independent Cases	Total Revenues	Total Expenses	Net Income (Loss)	Total Assets	Total Liabilities	Stockholders' Equity
A	$110,000	$82,000	$ ☐	$150,000	$70,000	$ ☐
B	☐	80,000	12,000	112,000	☐	70,000
C	80,000	86,000	☐	104,000	26,000	☐
D	50,000	☐	20,000	☐	22,000	77,000
E	☐	81,000	(6,000)	☐	73,000	28,000

LO 1-2, 1-3 **E1-9 Preparing an Income Statement and Balance Sheet**

Five individuals organized Miami Music Corporation on January 1. At the end of January 31, the following monthly financial data are available:

Total Revenues	$131,000
Operating Expenses	90,500
Cash	30,800
Accounts Receivable	25,300
Supplies	40,700
Accounts Payable	25,700
Common Stock	30,600

No dividends were declared or paid during January.

Required:

1. Complete the following income statement and balance sheet for the month of January.

MIAMI MUSIC CORPORATION
Income Statement
For the Month Ended January 31

Total Revenues	$_____
Operating Expenses	_____
Net Income	$_____

MIAMI MUSIC CORPORATION
Balance Sheet
At January 31

Assets	
Cash	$_____
Accounts Receivable	_____
Supplies	_____
Total Assets	$_____
Liabilities	
Accounts Payable	$_____
Total Liabilities	_____
Stockholders' Equity	
Common Stock	_____
Retained Earnings	_____
Total Stockholders' Equity	_____
Total Liabilities and Stockholders' Equity	$_____

2. Did Miami Music Corporation generate a profit? Which financial statement indicates this?
3. Does Miami Music Corporation have sufficient resources to pay its liabilities? Which financial statement indicates this?

E1-10 Analyzing and Interpreting an Income Statement   LO 1-2, 1-3

Three individuals organized Pest Away Corporation on January 1 to provide insect extermination services. The company paid dividends of $10,000 during the year. At the end of the first year of operations, the following income statement was prepared:

PEST AWAY CORPORATION	
Income Statement	
For the Year Ended December 31	
Revenues	
Service Revenue	$192,000
Sales Revenue	24,000
Total Revenues	216,000
Expenses	
Supplies Expense	76,000
Salaries and Wages Expense	33,000
Advertising Expense	22,000
Office Expense	46,000
Total Expenses	177,000
Net Income	$ 39,000

Required:

1. Did the company generate more revenue from selling goods or providing services to customers?
2. If salaries and wages were to double, how much net income would the company report?
3. If the company paid $20,000 of its advertising expense during the current year, what amount is owed for advertising at the end of the year? In what account would the amount still owing be reported?
4. Would the $10,000 of dividends be reported on the balance sheet or statement of retained earnings?

E1-11 Matching Cash Flow Statement Items to Business Activity Categories   LO 1-2

Tech Data Corporation is a leading distributor of computer peripherals and network solutions. The following items were taken from its recent cash flow statement. Mark each item in the following list with a letter to indicate whether it is a cash flow from Operating, Investing, or Financing activities. **Put parentheses around the letter if it is a cash *outflow* and use no parentheses if it's an *inflow*.**

Tech Data Corporation

_____ 1. Cash paid to suppliers and employees

_____ 2. Cash received from customers

_____ 3. Cash received from borrowing using a long-term note

_____ 4. Cash received from issuing stock

_____ 5. Cash paid to purchase equipment

E1-12 Matching Cash Flow Statement Items to Business Activity Categories   LO 1-2

The Coca-Cola Company is one of the world's leading manufacturers, marketers, and distributors of nonalcoholic beverage concentrates and syrups, producing more than 500 beverage brands. Mark each item in the following list with a letter to indicate whether it is a cash flow from Operating, Investing, or Financing activities. **Put parentheses around the letter if it is a cash *outflow* and use no parentheses if it's an *inflow*.**

Coca-Cola Company

_____ 1. Purchases of equipment

_____ 2. Cash received from customers

_____ **3.** Cash received from issuing stock

_____ **4.** Cash paid to suppliers and employees

_____ **5.** Cash paid on notes payable

_____ **6.** Cash received from selling equipment

COACHED PROBLEMS
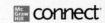

LO 1-2

CP1-1 Preparing an Income Statement, Statement of Retained Earnings, and Balance Sheet

Assume you are the president of Nuclear Company. At the end of the first year of operations (December 31), the following financial data for the company are available:

Accounts Payable	$30,000
Accounts Receivable	59,500
Cash	12,000
Common Stock	62,280
Dividends	200
Equipment	36,000
Notes Payable	1,470
Operating Expenses	57,200
Other Expenses	8,850
Sales Revenue	88,000
Supplies	8,000

Required:

1. Prepare an income statement for the year ended December 31.

    TIP: Begin by classifying each account as asset, liability, stockholders' equity, revenue, or expense. Each account is reported on only one financial statement.

2. Prepare a statement of retained earnings for the year ended December 31.

    TIP: Because this is the first year of operations, the beginning balance in Retained Earnings will be zero.

3. Prepare a balance sheet at December 31.

    TIP: The balance sheet includes the ending balance from the statement of retained earnings.

LO 1-3

CP1-2 Interpreting the Financial Statements

Refer to CP1-1. When answering the questions in requirements 1-4 that follow, refer to each financial statement only once in your answers.

Required:

1. Was the company profitable? Which financial statement provides the information to answer this question?

2. Did the company's dividends exceed its net income? Which financial statement provides the information to answer this question?

3. Is the company financed mainly by creditors or stockholders? Which financial statement provides the information to answer this question?

4. By how much did cash increase (decrease)? Which financial statement would report the business activities responsible for this change in cash?

LO 1-2

Garmin Ltd.

CP1-3 Reporting Amounts on the Four Basic Financial Statements

Garmin Ltd. reported the following information for the six-month period ended June 29, 2019. Items are listed alphabetically and are in thousands of dollars.

Accounts Payable	$1,027,700	Income Tax Expense	$ 78,000
Accounts Receivable	584,000	Inventory	648,000
Advertising Expense	69,000	Notes Payable	347,300
Cash (January 1, 2019)	1,383,000	Office Expense	656,000
Cash (June 29, 2019)	1,060,000	Operating Expenses	693,000
Common Stock	1,510,000	Retained Earnings (January 1, 2019)	2,725,000
Dividends	309,000	Sales Revenue	1,720,000
Equipment	3,065,000	Supplies	168,000

Other cash flow information:

Cash received from issuing common stock	$ 57,000
Cash paid to purchase equipment	529,000
Cash paid to suppliers and employees	1,431,000
Cash received from customers	1,706,000
Cash received from sale of long-term assets	183,000
Dividends paid to stockholders	309,000

Required:

Prepare the four basic financial statements for the six months ended June 29, 2019.

TIP: Prepare the four statements in the following order: (1) income statement, (2) statement of retained earnings, (3) balance sheet, (4) statement of cash flows.

CP1-4 Evaluating Financial Statements

Refer to CP1-3.

LO 1-3

Garmin Ltd.

Required:

1. Did Garmin rely more on creditors or stockholders for its financing at June 29, 2019? What is your information source?
2. Was the stockholders' equity at June 29, 2019, comprised more of contributions made by stockholders directly to the company or amounts earned and retained through profitable business operations? What is your information source?

GROUP A PROBLEMS

Mc Graw Hill **connect**

PA1-1 Preparing an Income Statement, Statement of Retained Earnings, and Balance Sheet

LO 1-2

Assume you are the president of High Power Corporation. At the end of the first year of operations (December 31), the following financial data for the company are available:

Accounts Payable	$32,100
Accounts Receivable	9,550
Cash	13,300
Common Stock	59,090
Dividends	1,950
Equipment	86,000
Notes Payable	1,160
Operating Expenses	58,700
Other Expenses	7,850
Sales Revenue	90,000
Supplies	5,000

Required:

1. Prepare an income statement for the year ended December 31.
2. Prepare a statement of retained earnings for the year ended December 31.
3. Prepare a balance sheet at December 31.

LO 1-3   **PA1-2 Interpreting the Financial Statements**

Refer to PA1-1. When answering the questions in requirements 1-4 that follow, refer to each financial statement only once in your answers.

Required:

1. Is the company financed mainly by creditors or stockholders? Which financial statement provides the information to answer this question?
2. By how much did cash increase (decrease)? Which financial statement would report the business activities responsible for this change in cash?
3. Was the company profitable? Which financial statement provides the information to answer this question?
4. Did the company's dividends exceed its net income? Which financial statement provides the information to answer this question?

LO 1-2   **PA1-3 Reporting Amounts on the Four Basic Financial Statements**

The following information for the year ended December 31, 2021, was reported by Nice Bite, Inc.

Accounts Payable	$ 45,000	Inventory	$ 17,200
Accounts Receivable	22,800	Notes Payable	23,600
Cash (balance on January 1, 2021)	103,500	Office Expense	14,300
Cash (balance on December 31, 2021)	102,800	Prepaid Rent	7,000
Common Stock	180,500	Retained Earnings (beginning)	6,300
Dividends	0	Salaries and Wages Expenses	35,700
Equipment	136,700	Service Revenue	137,800
Income Tax Expense	10,100	Utilities Expense	25,100
Interest Expense	29,500	Salaries and Wages Payable	8,000

Other cash flow information:	
Cash from issuing common stock	$ 21,000
Cash paid to reacquire common stock	23,500
Cash paid for income taxes	11,000
Cash paid to purchase long-term assets	41,000
Cash paid to suppliers and employees	83,200
Cash received from customers	137,000

Required:

Prepare the four basic financial statements for 2021.

LO 1-3   **PA1-4 Evaluating Financial Statements**

Refer to PA1-3.

Required:

1. Did Nice Bite rely more on creditors or stockholders for its financing at December 31, 2021? What is your information source?
2. Did the retained earnings at December 31, 2021, arise primarily from current year earnings or earnings retained from prior years? What is your information source?

GROUP B PROBLEMS

PB1-1 Preparing an Income Statement and Balance Sheet   LO 1-2

At the end of the first year of operations (December 31, 2021), the following financial data for APEC Aerospace Corporation are available:

Accounts Payable	$33,130
Accounts Receivable	9,500
Cash	13,900
Common Stock	10,000
Dividends	1,100
Equipment	86,000
Notes Payable	51,220
Operating Expenses	60,000
Other Expenses	8,850
Sales Revenue	94,000
Supplies	9,000

Required:

1. Prepare an income statement for the year ended December 31.
2. Prepare a statement of retained earnings for the year ended December 31.
3. Prepare a balance sheet at December 31.

PB1-2 Interpreting the Financial Statements   LO 1-3

Refer to PB1-1. When answering the questions in requirements 1-4 that follow, refer to each financial statement only once in your answers.

Required:

1. Is the company financed mainly by creditors or stockholders? Which financial statement provides the information to answer this question?
2. Was the company profitable? Which financial statement provides the information to answer this question?
3. By how much did cash increase (decrease)? Which financial statement would report the business activities responsible for this change in cash?
4. Did the company's dividends exceed its net income? Which financial statement provides the information to answer this question?

PB1-3 Reporting Amounts on the Four Basic Financial Statements   LO 1-2

Cheese Factory Incorporated reported the following information for the fiscal year ended August 31, 2021.

Accounts Payable	$145,000	Office Expense	$ 95,000
Accounts Receivable	15,000	Prepaid Rent	50,000
Cash (balance on September 1, 2020)	75,000	Retained Earnings (beginning)	410,000
Cash (balance on August 31, 2021)	80,000	Salaries and Wages Expense	955,000
Common Stock	100,000	Salaries and Wages Payable	170,000
Dividends	10,000	Sales Revenue	1,660,000
Equipment	755,000	Supplies	25,000
Notes Payable	30,000	Utilities Expense	530,000

Other cash flow information:	
Additional investments by stockholders	$ 34,000
Cash paid to purchase equipment	40,000
Cash paid to suppliers and employees	1,490,000
Repayments of borrowings	155,000
Cash received from customers	1,661,000
Cash received from borrowings	5,000
Dividends paid in cash	10,000

Required:

Prepare the four basic financial statements for the fiscal year ended August 31, 2021.

LO 1-3   **PB1-4 Evaluating Financial Statements**

Refer to PB1-3.

Required:

1. Did Cheese Factory's cash balance increase or decrease during the year ended August 31, 2021? Which financial statement shows the reasons for this change?
2. What would Cheese Factory's 2021 net income have been had it given a 5 percent pay increase to all employees on September 1, 2020? Which financial statement did you use to answer this?

SKILLS DEVELOPMENT CASES

LO 1-1, LO 1-2, LO 1-3   **S1-1 Finding Financial Information**

The Home Depot

Answer the following questions by referring to the financial statements of The Home Depot in Appendix A at the end of this book. (**Note: Fiscal 2019 for The Home Depot runs from February 4, 2019, to February 2, 2020.** As with many retail companies, **The Home Depot labels the period "Fiscal 2019" even though it ends in the 2020 calendar year.** The label "Fiscal 2019" is appropriate because Fiscal 2019 includes 11 months from the 2019 calendar year. The Home Depot explains its choice of fiscal period in Note 1 to its financial statements.)

1. What amount of net income was reported (in millions) for the year ended February 2, 2020?
   a. $110,225
   b. $15,843
   c. $11,242
   d. $11,121

2. What amount of sales revenue (in millions) was earned for the year ended February 2, 2020?
   a. $110,225
   b. $15,843
   c. $11,242
   d. $11,121

3. What was the cost (in millions) of the company's inventory on February 2, 2020?
   a. $2,133
   b. $14,531
   c. $13,925
   d. $7,787

4. How much cash (in millions) does The Home Depot have on February 2, 2020?
   a. $2,133
   b. $1,778
   c. $3,595
   d. $236

S1-2 Finding Financial Information

LO 1-1, LO 1-2, LO 1-3

Lowe's

Answer the following questions by referring to the financial statements of Lowe's Companies, Inc., in Appendix B at the end of this book. (**Note: Fiscal 2019 for Lowe's runs from February 2, 2019, to January 31, 2020.** As with many retail companies, **Lowe's labels the period "Fiscal 2019" even though it ends in the 2020 calendar year** because it includes 11 months of the 2019 calendar year.)

1. What amount of net income was reported (in millions) for the year ended January 31, 2020?
   - **a.** $4,281
   - **b.** $2,314
   - **c.** $3,447
   - **d.** $72,148
2. What amount of sales revenue (in millions) was earned for the year ended January 31, 2020?
   - **a.** $68,619
   - **b.** $4,281
   - **c.** $6,314
   - **d.** $72,148
3. What was the cost (in millions) of the company's inventory on January 31, 2020?
   - **a.** $12,561
   - **b.** $49,205
   - **c.** $13,179
   - **d.** $48,401
4. How much cash (in millions) does Lowe's have on January 31, 2020?
   - **a.** $511
   - **b.** $716
   - **c.** $160
   - **d.** $218

S1-3 Internet-Based Team Research: Examining an Annual Report

LO 1-1, LO 1-2, LO 1-3

Reuters

As a team, select an industry to analyze. Reuters provides lists of industries in the online stock screener at stockscreener.us.reuters.com/Stock/US. Another source is csimarket.com. Each group member should access the annual report (or Form 10-K filed with the SEC) for one publicly traded company in the industry, with each member selecting a different company. In addition to the company's own website, a great source is the SEC's Electronic Data Gathering, Analysis, and Retrieval (EDGAR) service. This free source is available by going to the "Filings" section of www.sec.gov and clicking on "Company Filings Search" and then entering the "Company name."

Required:

1. On an individual basis, each team member should write a short report that lists the following information:
   - **a.** What type of business organization is it?
   - **b.** What types of products or services does it sell?
   - **c.** On what day of the year does its fiscal year end?
   - **d.** For how many years does it present complete balance sheets? Income statements? Cash flow statements?
   - **e.** Are its financial statements audited by independent CPAs? If so, by whom?
   - **f.** Did its total assets increase or decrease over the last year?
   - **g.** Did its net income increase or decrease over the last year?
2. Then, as a team, write a short report comparing and contrasting your companies using these attributes. Discuss any patterns across the companies that you as a team observe. Provide potential explanations for any differences discovered.

S1-4 Ethical Decision Making: A Real-Life Example

LO 1-2, LO 1-3, LO 1-4

Adelphia Communications

Complete this case involving Adelphia Communications, which your instructor may access from and make available to you in the Connect eBook. By completing the requirements of this case, which ask you to explain how accounting concepts apply to Adelphia's business, you will learn the challenges and importance of distinguishing between personal and business activities when accounting for a family-owned business.

S1-5 Ethical Decision Making: A Mini-Case

LO 1-4

You are one of three stockholders who own and operate Mary's Maid Service. The company has been operating for seven years. One of the other stockholders has prepared the company's annual financial statements. Recently, you proposed the financial statements be audited each year because it would benefit the stockholders. The stockholder who prepares the statements proposed that his uncle, who has a lot of financial experience, can do the job at little cost. The third stockholder remained silent.

Required:

1. What position would you take on the proposal? Justify your response in writing.
2. What would you recommend? Give the basis for your recommendation.

LO 1-2, LO 1-3, LO 1-4   **S1-6   Critical Thinking: Developing a Balance Sheet and Income Statement**

On September 30, Ashley and Jason started arguing about who is better off. Jason said he was better off because he owned a video game console that he bought last year for $250. He figures that, if needed, he could sell it to a friend for $180. Ashley argued she was better off because she had $1,000 cash in her bank account and a piece of art she bought two years ago for $800 but could now probably sell for $1,400. Jason countered that Ashley still owed $250 on a loan and Jason's dad promised to buy him a Porsche if he does really well in accounting. Jason said he had $6,000 cash in his bank account right now because he just received a $4,800 student loan. Ashley knows that Jason also owes a tuition installment of $800 for this term.

Ashley and Jason met again in early November. They asked how each other was doing. Ashley claimed that she'd become much more successful than Jason. She had a part-time job, where she earned $1,500 per month. Jason mocked Ashley because he had won $1,950 on a lottery ticket he bought in October, and that was merely for the "work" of standing in line for a minute. It was just what he needed because his apartment costs $800 each month. Ashley, on the other hand, pays $470 for her share of the rent. Both Ashley and Jason have other normal living costs that total $950 each month.

Required:

1. Prepare a financial report that compares what Ashley and Jason each owns and owes on September 30. Make a list of any decisions you had to make when preparing your report.
2. In a written report, identify and justify which of the two characters is better off. If you were a creditor, to whom would you rather lend money?
3. Prepare a report that compares what Ashley and Jason each earned during October. Make a list of any decisions you had to make when preparing your report.
4. In a written report, identify and justify which of the two characters is more successful. If you were a creditor considering a three-year loan to one of these characters, to whom would you rather lend money?

LO 1-2   **S1-7   Preparing an Income Statement and Balance Sheet**

Electronic Arts

Complete this case involving Electronic Arts, which your instructor may access from and make available to you online in the Connect eBook. By completing this case, you will learn to use a spreadsheet to prepare a balance sheet and income statement. Detailed advice is included in the case to help you set up and complete the spreadsheet.

CONTINUING CASE

LO 1-2, 1-3   **CC1-1   Financial Statements for a Business Plan**

Nicole Mackisey is thinking of forming her own spa business, Nicole's Getaway Spa (NGS). Nicole expects that she and two family members will each contribute $10,000 to the business and receive 1,000 shares each. Nicole forecasts the following amounts for the first year of operations, ending December 31, 2021: cash on hand and in the bank, $2,150; amounts due from customers from spa treatments, $1,780; building and equipment, $70,000; amounts owed to beauty supply outlets for spa equipment, $4,660; notes payable to a local bank for $38,870. Cash dividends of $2,000 will be paid to the stockholders during the year. Nicole also forecasts that first-year sales revenues will be

$40,000; wages will be $24,000; the cost of supplies used up will be $7,000; office expenses will be $5,000; and income taxes will be $1,600.

Required:

1. Based on Nicole's estimates, prepare a (forecasted) income statement for Nicole's Getaway Spa for the year ended December 31, 2021.
2. Prepare a (forecasted) statement of retained earnings for Nicole's Getaway Spa for the year ended December 31, 2021.
3. Prepare a (forecasted) balance sheet for Nicole's Getaway Spa at December 31, 2021.
4. Are creditors or stockholders expected to supply most of the financing for NGS's assets at December 31, 2021?

DATA ANALYTICS EXERCISES

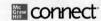

Data Analytics Exercises are auto-graded exercises offering detailed data visualization, interpretation, and analysis, and are available for assignment in Connect.

Design elements: Video camera: ©McGraw-Hill Education; Handshake, cash exchange: ©McGraw-Hill Education; Notepad with pen: ©McGraw-Hill Education; Calculator: ©McGraw-Hill Education; Light bulb: ©McGraw-Hill Education; Spotlight: ©McGraw-Hill Education; Whistle: ©Siede Preis/Getty Images; GL: ©McGraw-Hill Education; Level up: ©McGraw-Hill Education; Excel icon: ©McGraw-Hill Education; Magnifying glass: ©McGraw-Hill Education; Video icon: ©McGraw-Hill Education

2

The Balance Sheet

YOUR LEARNING OBJECTIVES

LO 2-1   Identify financial effects of common business activities that affect the balance sheet.

LO 2-2   Apply transaction analysis to accounting transactions.

LO 2-3   Use journal entries and T-accounts to show how transactions affect the balance sheet.

LO 2-4   Prepare a trial balance and a classified balance sheet.

LO 2-5   Interpret the balance sheet using the current ratio and an understanding of related concepts.

LO 2-S1   Describe examples of common career paths in accounting.

THAT WAS THEN

In the previous chapter, you were introduced to the four main financial statements: the balance sheet, income statement, statement of retained earnings, and statement of cash flows.

FOCUS COMPANY: NOODLECAKE STUDIOS, INC.

I n Chapter 1 you heard about Jordan's plans for starting an app development company. Building on initial success of the *Super Stickman Golf* game, Noodlecake has plans for releasing many more games including *Golf Blitz* (pictured above). Jordan's local CPA, Laurie, advised him all businesses, big and small, need systems for gathering and organizing financial information. Like most public accounting firms, Laurie offers professional services to help smaller companies like Noodlecake Studios track the financial results of their activities. With Laurie's help, Jordan will implement an accounting system to do this for Noodlecake. This system will provide the financial information he needs to manage the company and report its results to others interested in his business.[1]

The focus in this chapter is on activities that occurred during August, when Jordan was establishing Noodlecake. You will learn how these activities are captured in an accounting system, leading to the assets, liabilities, and stockholders' equity that are reported in a balance sheet. Later, in Chapter 3, you will learn about the operating activities that occur after a business is open to customers and begins generating the revenues and expenses that are reported in an income statement. Your introduction to the accounting system will conclude in Chapter 4, where you will learn about the steps needed to adjust the accounting records before finalizing and evaluating a company's financial results.

THIS IS NOW

This chapter focuses on just the balance sheet and the accounting system used to produce it.

---

[1]See Supplement 2A for a list of other services offered by public accounting firms, and for a summary of accounting careers available in private and public accounting.

Logo: Noodlecake Studios, Inc.

ORGANIZATION OF THE CHAPTER

Understand the business	The accounting cycle	Evaluate the results	Supplement 2A	Review the chapter
• Building a balance sheet from business activities • Transactions and other activities	• Step 1: Analyze transactions • Steps 2 and 3: Record and summarize • The debit/credit framework • Preparing a trial balance and balance sheet	• Assessing the ability to pay • Balance sheet concepts and values	• Accounting careers	• Demonstration case • Chapter summary • Key terms • Homework helper • Practice material

Understand the Business

BUILDING A BALANCE SHEET FROM BUSINESS ACTIVITIES

Learning Objective 2-1
Identify financial effects of common business activities that affect the balance sheet.

YOU SHOULD KNOW

Assets: Probable future economic benefits owned by the business as a result of past transactions.
Liabilities: Probable debts or obligations of the entity that result from past transactions, which will be fulfilled by providing assets or services.
Stockholders' Equity: The financing provided by the owners and the operations of the business.

After meeting with Laurie, Jordan understood that before he could start selling apps, he would first have to establish the business. This would involve acquiring **assets** that Noodlecake would use for many months or years to come. The assets would be owned by Noodlecake, but creditors would have a claim to those assets equal to the amount of **liabilities** the company owes. As owners of Noodlecake, Jordan and his friend Ty also would have a claim on the company's assets (**stockholders' equity**), but their claim would be secondary to creditors' claims. Jordan remembered that the balance sheet was structured like the basic accounting equation (A = L + SE), but it was only by accounting for Noodlecake's activities that he truly learned how a balance sheet was built.

A key activity for any start-up company is to obtain **financing.** Two sources of financing are available to businesses: equity and debt. Equity refers to financing a business through owners' contributions and reinvestments of profit. Debt refers to financing a business through loans and other amounts that must be repaid. A business is obligated to repay debt financing, but it is not obligated to repay its equity financing.

Like most small business owners, Jordan and Ty used their personal savings to make an initial cash contribution to the company. They decided to contribute $5,000 each ($10,000 in total). In exchange for their investment in the company, Jordan and Ty will receive common stock as evidence of their ownership.

Jordan had determined that Noodlecake would need additional money to become established, so, on behalf of the company, he applied for a loan from a bank. Soon after the loan was approved, Noodlecake received $20,000 cash in exchange for its promise to repay the loan in two years. The terms for repaying the loan were described in detail on a legal document called a promissory note. Noodlecake's initial financing activities are pictured in Exhibit 2.1.

After obtaining initial financing, a company will start **investing** in assets that will be used after the business opens. In the case of Noodlecake, Jordan felt an important first step was to develop a logo to visually represent his company's name. Using a company check, he paid

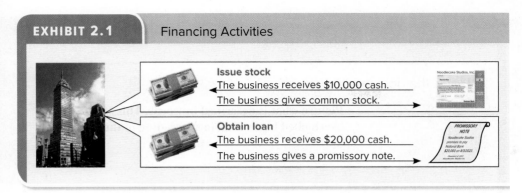

EXHIBIT 2.1 Financing Activities

a graphic designer $300 cash for the logo shown in Exhibit 2.2. The company also needed equipment, such as desks and computers. This equipment could be purchased with cash, but that would be inconvenient and inefficient. Instead, businesses typically buy goods or services from others on credit, by promising to pay within 30 or 60 days of the purchase. Noodlecake bought $9,600 of equipment on credit, as indicated by the supplier's bill (or "invoice"). These examples are pictured in Exhibit 2.2.

EXHIBIT 2.2 Investing Activities

By carefully reading Exhibits 2.1 and 2.2, you will see three features that will be important for understanding how accounting works.

1. The company always **documents** its activities. Promissory notes, electronic stock certificates, checks, invoices, and other documents indicate the nature of the underlying business activity.

2. The company always **receives** something and **gives** something. This is a basic feature of all business activities. A business enters into an exchange either to earn a profit immediately or to obtain resources that will allow it to earn a profit later. This is the fundamental idea of business: to create value through exchange. Any exchange that affects the company's assets, liabilities, or stockholders' equity must be captured in and reported by the accounting system. Because the accounting system captures both what is received and what is given, it is often referred to as a "double-entry" system.

3. Each exchange is analyzed to determine a dollar amount that represents the value of items given and received. This value is called the **cost** and is used to measure the financial effects of the exchange, as required by the **cost principle**.

As illustrated in Exhibit 2.3, these three features are key inputs into the process used when accounting for business activities. After each activity is documented, accountants assign names to the items exchanged and then analyze their financial effects on the accounting equation. The ultimate goal is to capture these financial effects so that they can be reported in the financial statements for use by decision makers inside and outside the company. Take a moment right now to read Exhibit 2.3.

EXHIBIT 2.3	Accounting for Business Activities

Picture the documented activity

Picture what is described in words. This step is easily overlooked but is vital to succeeding in the next step.

Name what's exchanged

Noodlecake

Building on the previous step, assign names to what your business has received and given.

Analyze the financial effects

A = L + SE

Building on the last step, show how the costs cause elements of the accounting equation to increase and/or decrease.

TRANSACTIONS AND OTHER ACTIVITIES

Business activities that affect the basic accounting equation (A = L + SE) are called **transactions**. Transactions are of special importance because they are the only activities that enter the financial accounting system. Transactions include two types of events:

1. **External exchanges:** These are exchanges involving assets, liabilities, and/or stockholders' equity between the company and someone else. When Starbucks sells you a Frappuccino®, it is exchanging an icy taste of heaven for your cash, so Starbucks would record this in its accounting system.

2. **Internal events:** These events do not involve exchanges with others outside the business, but rather occur within the company itself. For example, when the company Red Bull combines sugar, water, taurine, and caffeine, something magical happens: These ingredients turn into Red Bull Energy Drink. This internal event is a transaction because it has a direct financial effect whereby some assets (supplies of sugar, etc.) are used up to create a different asset (an inventory of Red Bull drinks).

Some important activities that occur will not be captured by the accounting system because they are not transactions. For example, during the first month of business, Jordan signed a contract on behalf of Noodlecake to rent office space the following month. This activity was not a transaction because no assets or services were exchanged at that time. The landlord exchanged a promise to rent the building for Noodlecake's promise to pay rent, but **an exchange of only promises is not an accounting transaction.** For this same reason, Noodlecake's accounting system did not capture other activities such as placing orders with suppliers or promising to hire employees. Documents were created to indicate these activities occurred, but they were appropriately excluded from the accounting records because these were not transactions. Later, when these promises result in actually receiving or giving an asset or service, they become transactions to be captured by the accounting system.

The Accounting Cycle

A systematic accounting process is used to capture and report the financial effects of a company's activities. This process, represented by the circular graphic below, is called the accounting cycle because it repeats itself over and over. For now, we will focus on the first three steps:

Learning Objective 2-2
Apply transaction analysis to accounting transactions.

STEP 1: ANALYZE TRANSACTIONS

The process shown earlier in Exhibit 2.3 is referred to as transaction analysis, which involves determining whether a transaction exists and, if it does, analyzing its impact on the accounting equation. Two simple ideas are used when analyzing transactions:

1. **Duality of effects.** It's a fancy name, but the idea is simple. Every transaction has at least two effects on the basic accounting equation. To remember this, just think of expressions like "give and receive" or "push and pull" or, if you're a closet scientist, Newton's third law of motion.

2. **A = L + SE.** You know this already, right? Well, just remember the dollar amount for assets must always equal the total of liabilities plus stockholders' equity for every accounting transaction. If it doesn't, you are missing something and you should go back to the first (duality of effects) idea.

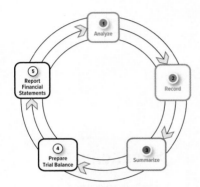

As part of transaction analysis, a name is given to each item exchanged. Accountants refer to these names as account titles. To ensure account titles are used consistently, every company establishes a **chart of accounts**—a list that designates a name and reference number the company will use when accounting for each item it exchanges. A partial chart of accounts for **Noodlecake** is shown in Exhibit 2.4. (The chart of accounts shown in Chapter 2

YOU SHOULD KNOW

Chart of Accounts: A summary of all account names and corresponding account numbers used to record financial results in the accounting system.

EXHIBIT 2.4	Noodlecake's (Partial) Chart of Accounts

Account Number	Account Name	Description
100	Cash	– Dollar amount of coins, paper money, funds in bank
140	Supplies	– Cost of paper, pens, business forms, etc.
173	Equipment	– Cost of computers, printers, desks, etc.
181	Logo and Trademarks	– Cost of purchased logo and trademarks
186	Software	– Cost of purchased software and technology
201	Accounts Payable	– Owed to suppliers for goods or services bought on credit
220	Notes Payable (long-term)	– Owed to lenders, as per terms of promissory note
301	Common Stock	– Stock issued for contributions made to the company
305	Retained Earnings	– Accumulated earnings (not yet distributed as dividends)

includes only balance sheet accounts. Chapter 3 will expand this to include additional assets and liabilities as well as revenue and expense accounts.) **A more comprehensive chart of accounts to use when completing homework assignments is presented in the Homework Helper at the end of this chapter, and a chart of accounts containing every account used in this book is shown at the end of this book and can be downloaded from the Additional Student Resources in Connect.**

The chart of accounts is tailored to each company's business, so although some account titles are common across all companies (Cash, Accounts Payable), others may be unique to a particular company (such as "Current Content Library" for Netflix's movies). Depending on the company, you may see a liability for a bank loan called Notes Payable or Loans Payable.[2]

The best way to learn how to analyze transactions is to work through examples. So skim the names and descriptions in Exhibit 2.4 one more time and then look closely at the following business activities.

(a) Issue Stock to Owners   **Jordan incorporates Noodlecake Studios, Inc., on August 1. The company issues common stock to Jordan and Ty as evidence of their total contribution of $10,000 cash, which is deposited in the company's bank account.**

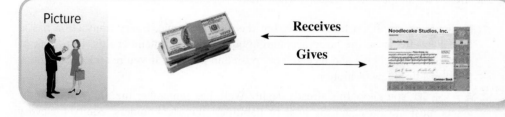

Picture   Receives   Gives

Name
- Noodlecake has received $10,000 cash.
- Noodlecake gave $10,000 of common stock.

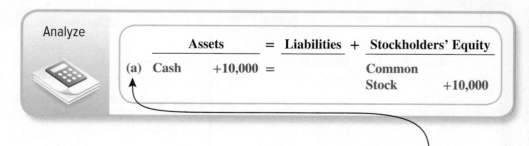

Analyze

		Assets	=	Liabilities +	Stockholders' Equity	
(a)	Cash	+10,000 =			Common Stock	+10,000

In the accounting equation analysis above, we included the reference "(a)" to relate it to the original transaction.

---

[2] The account names you see in the financial statements of most large businesses are actually aggregations of several specific accounts. For example, Apple keeps separate accounts for land, buildings, and equipment but combines them into one title on its balance sheet called Property, Plant, and Equipment.

(b) **Invest in Logo/Trademarks**   Noodlecake pays $300 cash to create the company's logo.

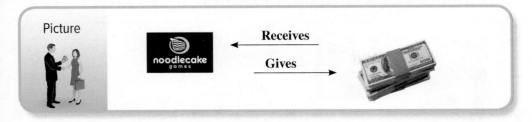

Name

- **Noodlecake has received a logo costing $300.**
- **Noodlecake gave $300 cash.**

Analyze

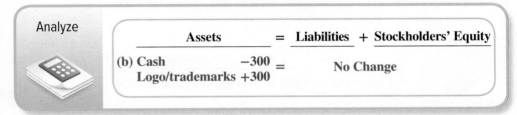

	Assets	=	Liabilities	+	Stockholders' Equity
(b) Cash	**−300**	=		**No Change**	
Logo/trademarks	**+300**				

Notice that even though transaction (b) did not affect liabilities or stockholders' equity, the accounting equation remained in balance because the decrease in one asset was offset by the increase in another asset. **The accounting equation must always "balance" (be equal) for each transaction.**

(c) **Obtain Loan from Bank**   Noodlecake borrows $20,000 from a bank, depositing those funds in its bank account and signing a formal agreement to repay the loan in **two years** (on August 3, 2023).

Name

- **Noodlecake has received $20,000 cash.**
- **Noodlecake gave a note, payable to the bank for $20,000.**

> **COACH'S TIP**
>
> Notes payable are like accounts payable except they (a) charge interest, (b) can be outstanding for periods either shorter or longer than one year, and (c) are documented using formal documents called notes.

Analyze

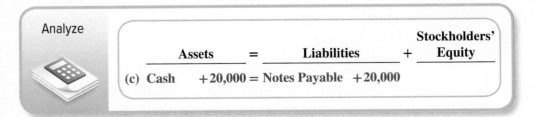

	Assets	=	Liabilities	+	Stockholders' Equity
(c) Cash	**+20,000**	=	**Notes Payable**	**+20,000**	

Logo: Noodlecake Studios Inc.;
Money photo: Comstock/Getty Images;
Money photo: Comstock/Getty Images

(d) Invest in Equipment   Noodlecake purchases and receives $9,600 in computers, printers, and desks, in exchange for its promise to pay $9,600 at the end of the month.

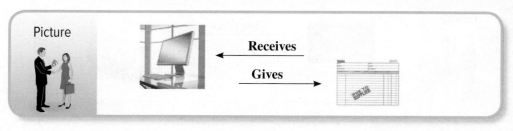

Picture

Name

- Noodlecake has received $9,600 of equipment.
- Noodlecake gave a promise to pay $9,600 on account.

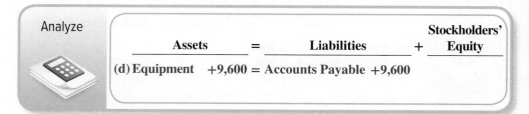

Analyze

	Assets	=	Liabilities	+	Stockholders' Equity
(d) Equipment	+9,600	=	Accounts Payable	+9,600	

Noodlecake would typically wait until the end of the month to pay the amount owed to the supplier in (d). But to show you how the payment is accounted for, we will present it here in (e).

(e) Pay Supplier   Noodlecake pays $5,000 to the equipment supplier in (d).

Picture

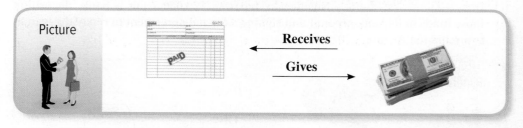

Name

- Noodlecake has received a release from $5,000 of its promise to pay on account.
- Noodlecake gave $5,000 cash.

Analyze

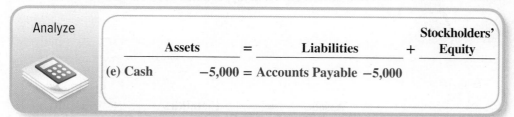

	Assets	=	Liabilities	+	Stockholders' Equity
(e) Cash	−5,000	=	Accounts Payable	−5,000	

Computer photo: Don Farrall/Getty Images; Invoice photo: Studio 101/Alamy Stock Photo; Invoice paid photo: Studio 101/Alamy Stock Photo; Money photo: Comstock/Getty Images

In (e), Noodlecake fulfills part of its liability owed to a supplier. Thus, the Accounts Payable is decreased because, in exchange for its payment to the supplier, Noodlecake receives a release from $5,000 of its promise to pay the supplier.

(f) Order Software for App Noodlecake signs a contract with an independent developer for program code for the Enchanted World game app for $9,000. No code has been received yet.

Picture

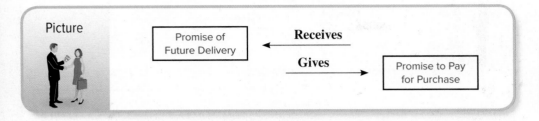

Promise of Future Delivery ← Receives

Gives → Promise to Pay for Purchase

Name

Noodle**cake**

- An exchange of only promises is not a transaction.
- This does not affect the accounting equation.

Analyze

Assets	=	Liabilities	+	Stockholders' Equity
(f) No Change	=		No Change	

Not all documented business activities are considered accounting transactions. As shown in (f), Noodlecake and the app programmer have documented the order, but it involves an exchange of only promises, so it is not an accounting transaction.

(g) Receive Software Noodlecake receives the $9,000 of app game code ordered in (f), pays $4,000 cash, and promises to pay the remaining $5,000 next month.

Picture

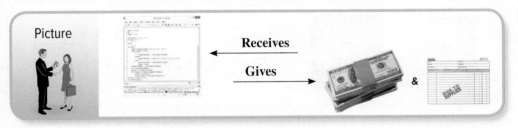

Receives ←

Gives → &

Name

Noodle**cake**

- Noodlecake has received software costing $9,000.
- Noodlecake gave $4,000 cash and a promise to pay $5,000 on account.

Analyze

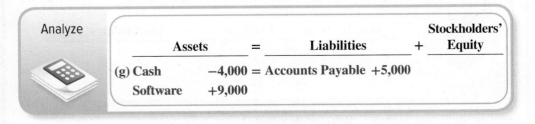

Assets		=	Liabilities	+	Stockholders' Equity
(g) Cash	−4,000	=	Accounts Payable +5,000		
Software	+9,000				

(h) Receive Supplies.   **Noodlecake receives supplies costing $600 on account.**

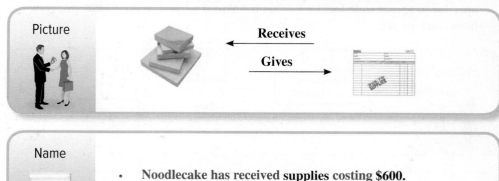

Picture

Receives

Gives

Name

Noodlecake

- **Noodlecake has received supplies costing $600.**
- **Noodlecake gave a promise to pay $600 on account.**

Analyze

	Assets	=	Liabilities	+	Stockholders' Equity
(h) Supplies	+600	=	Accounts Payable	+600	

As we said, the best way to learn accounting is to do examples, so try the following practice question.

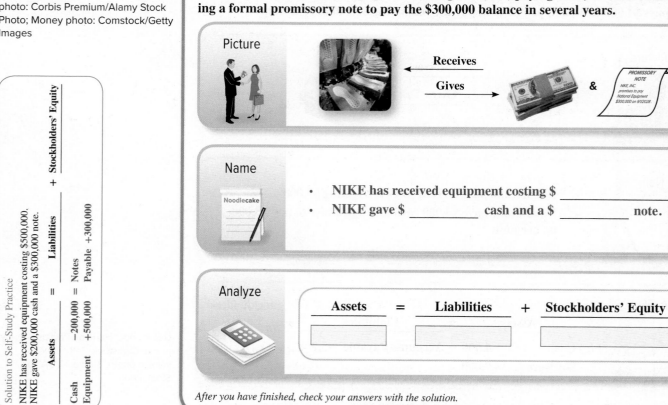

💡 How's it going?   Self-Study Practice

Complete the following transaction analysis steps by filling in the blanks and empty boxes.

NIKE, Inc., **purchased equipment costing $500,000, paying $200,000 cash and signing a formal promissory note to pay the $300,000 balance in several years.**

Picture

Receives

Gives   &

PROMISSORY NOTE
NIKE, INC.
promises to pay
National Equipment
$300,000 on 9/1/2028

Name

Noodlecake

- **NIKE has received equipment costing $ _____ .**
- **NIKE gave $ _____ cash and a $ _____ note.**

Analyze

Assets	=	Liabilities	+	Stockholders' Equity
☐	=	☐	+	☐

After you have finished, check your answers with the solution.

Notes photo: Comstock Images/Alamy Stock Photo; Invoice photo: Studio 101/Alamy Stock Photo; Shoe photo: Corbis Premium/Alamy Stock Photo; Money photo: Comstock/Getty Images

Solution to Self-Study Practice

NIKE has received equipment costing $500,000.
NIKE gave $200,000 cash and a $300,000 note.

Assets		=	Liabilities	+	Stockholders' Equity
Cash	−200,000	=	Notes		
Equipment	+500,000		Payable +300,000		

STEPS 2 AND 3: RECORD AND SUMMARIZE

In the previous section, you learned how to analyze transactions, which ended with an understanding of the financial effects of each transaction on a company's asset, liability, and stockholders' equity accounts. In our academic setting, we have encouraged you to write down these accounting equation effects. In the workplace, an accountant would not capture the effects in this way. Instead, after determining the financial effects of a transaction, an accountant would capture the effects through two additional steps: recording and summarizing.

One way to record and summarize the financial effects of transactions is to enter your understanding of their effects into a spreadsheet like the one shown in Exhibit 2.5. By summing each spreadsheet column, you could compute new balances at the end of each month and report them on a balance sheet.

EXHIBIT 2.5	Using a Spreadsheet to Record and Summarize Transactions

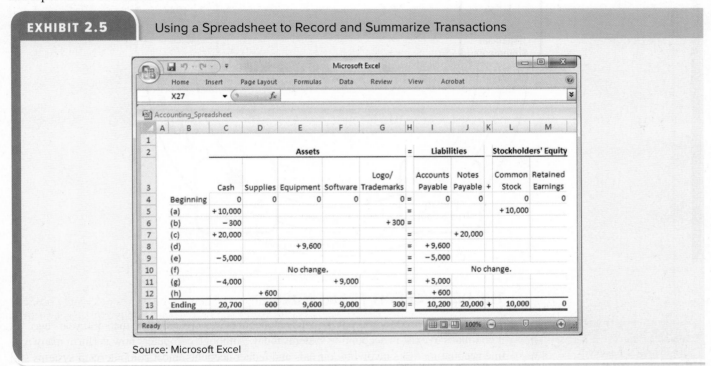

Source: Microsoft Excel

A spreadsheet makes it easy to see the individual impact of each transaction and how transactions combine with beginning balances to yield ending balances, but it is impractical for most large organizations. Instead, most companies record and summarize the financial effects of transactions with computerized accounting systems, which can handle a large number of transactions. These systems follow **the accounting cycle, which is repeated day after day, month after month, and year after year.** As shown in Exhibit 2.6, the three-step analyze-record-summarize process is applied to **daily transactions,** as well as adjustments at the end of each month, before preparing a trial balance and the financial statements. The same three steps also are part of the closing process that occurs at the end of each year. Our focus in Chapter 2 is on applying the three-step process during the period to activities that affect only balance sheet accounts. After you've become comfortable with this process, you will learn (in Chapter 3) to apply this process to operating activities that affect both balance sheet and income statement accounts. In Chapter 4, you will learn how the process is applied at the end of the accounting period, when the accounting records are adjusted and closed.

The three-step process of analyzing, recording, and summarizing is similar to what you do when attending class, taking notes, and preparing for exams. Day after day, you analyze what is said in class and you record important points in a notebook, which is kind of like an academic diary or "journal." Later, when preparing for exams, you transform your notes into summary sheets. The same ideas are used in the accounting cycle. Transactions are analyzed and their financial effects are entered into **journals** each day they occur. These journal entries are then summarized in **ledger** accounts to keep track of the financial effects on each account. To make this process efficient, journals and ledger accounts share the same underlying framework discussed in the following section.

EXHIBIT 2.6 | Elements of the Accounting Cycle

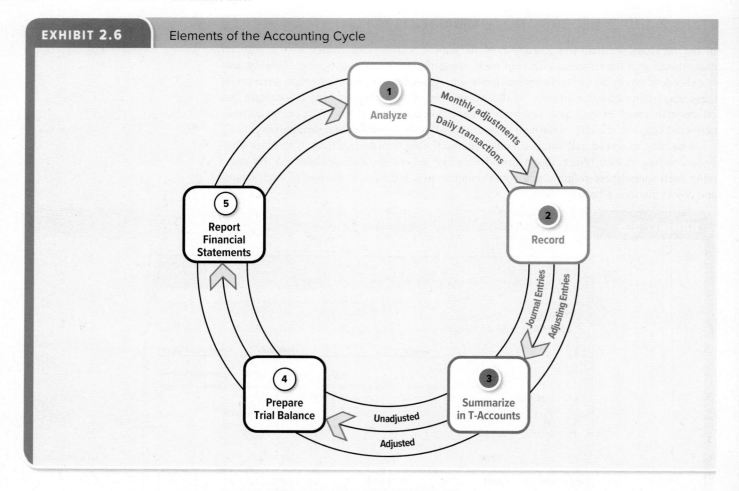

THE DEBIT/CREDIT FRAMEWORK

Learning Objective 2-3
Use journal entries and T-accounts to show how transactions affect the balance sheet.

The framework used for journals and ledger accounts was created more than 500 years ago, yet it continues to exist in accounting systems today. Although computers now perform many routine accounting tasks involving journals and ledger accounts, most computerized systems still require you to know how these accounting records work. To understand this framework, think of the accounting equation (A = L + SE) as an old-fashioned weight scale that tips at the equals sign. Assets—like Cash and Equipment—are put on the left side of the scale and liabilities and stockholders' equity accounts are put on the right. Each individual account has two sides, with one side used for increases and the other for decreases, similar to what is shown in Exhibit 2.7.

Take special note of three important rules illustrated in Exhibit 2.7:

1. **Accounts increase on the same side as they appear in A = L + SE.** Accounts on the left side of the accounting equation increase on the left side of the account and accounts on the right side of the equation increase on the right. So
   - **Assets increase on the left** side of the account.
   - **Liabilities increase on the right** side of the account.
   - **Stockholders' equity accounts increase on the right** side of the account.
   - Decreases are the opposite, as shown in Exhibit 2.7.

2. **Left is debit (dr); right is credit (cr).** The terms (and abbreviations) **debit** (*dr*) and **credit** (*cr*) come from Latin words that had meaning back in the day, but today they just mean *left* and *right*. When combined with how increases and decreases are entered into accounts, the following rules emerge:
   - **Use debits for increases in assets** (and for decreases in liabilities and stockholders' equity accounts).
   - **Use credits for increases in liabilities and stockholders' equity** accounts (and for decreases in assets).

YOU SHOULD KNOW

Debit: When used as a noun, debit is the left side of an account; when used as a verb, debit is the act of recording the debit portion of a journal entry to a particular account.
Credit: When used as a noun, credit is the right side of an account; when used as a verb, credit is the act of recording the credit portion of a journal entry to a particular account.

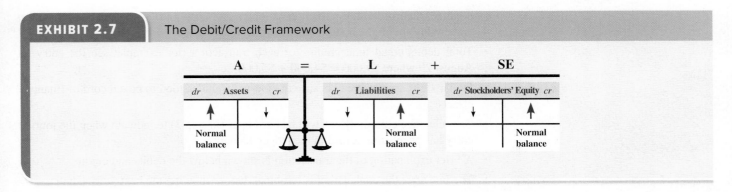

EXHIBIT 2.7   The Debit/Credit Framework

3. **The normal balance for an account is the side on which it increases.** Assets normally have debit balances, whereas liabilities and stockholders' equity accounts normally have credit balances.

Accountants didn't dream up this debit/credit framework to confuse you. The purpose of this double-entry system is to introduce another check on the accuracy of accounting numbers. In addition to requiring that A = L + SE, the double-entry system also requires that **debits = credits.** If either of these relationships is not equal, you know for sure you've made an error that needs to be corrected.

Step 1: Analyzing Transactions

The debit/credit framework does not change this first step of the accounting process. Continue to use the approach shown in Exhibit 2.3 to determine the financial effects of transactions, which you will learn to enter into the accounting system in step 2.

Step 2: Recording Journal Entries

The financial effects of transactions are entered into a journal using a debits-equal-credits format, as shown in Exhibit 2.8. When looking at these **journal entries**, as they are called, notice the following:

- A date is included for each transaction.
- Debits appear first (on top). Credits are shown below the debits and are indented to the right (both the words and the amounts). If more than one account is debited or

EXHIBIT 2.8   Formal Journal Page

General Journal				Page G1
Date	Account Titles and Explanation	Ref.	Debit	Credit
Aug. 1	Cash		10,000	
	Common Stock			10,000
	(Financing from stockholders.)			
Aug. 2	Logo and Trademarks		300	
	Cash			300
	(Bought logo using cash.)			
Aug. 29	**Software**		**9,000**	
	Cash			**4,000**
	Accounts Payable			**5,000**
	(Bought app using cash and credit.)			

credited, their order doesn't matter as long as for each journal entry debits are on top and credits are on the bottom and indented.

- Total debits equal total credits for each transaction (for example, see the entry on August 29 where $9,000 = $4,000 + $5,000).
- Dollar signs are not used because the journal is understood to be a record of financial effects.
- The reference column (Ref.) will be used later (in step 3) to indicate when the journal entry has been summarized in the ledger accounts.
- A brief explanation of the transaction is shown below the debits and credits.
- The line after the explanation is left blank before showing the next journal entry.

When writing journal entries in this course, we'll make a few minor changes to the formal entries, to make it easier for you to learn the most important aspects of recording journal entries. The way we show the journal entry for August 29 is:

		Debit	Credit
(g)	Software (+A)	9,000	
	Cash (−A)		4,000
	Accounts Payable (+L)		5,000

The main differences between our simplified format and a formal journal entry are

- When a date is not given, use some form of reference for each transaction, such as (g), to identify the event.
- Omit the reference column and transaction explanation to simplify the entry.
- Include the appropriate account type (A, L, or SE) along with the direction of the effect (+ or −) next to each account title to clarify the effects of the transaction on each account. This parenthetical note will reinforce the debit/credit framework and help you ensure the accounting equation remains in balance.

Step 3: Summarizing in Ledger Accounts

By themselves, journal entries show the effects of transactions, but they do not provide account balances. That's why ledger accounts are needed. After journal entries have been recorded (in step 2), their dollar amounts are copied ("posted") to each ledger account affected by the transaction, so that account balances can be computed. In most computerized accounting systems, this happens automatically. In homework assignments, you may have to do it yourself, so Exhibit 2.9 shows you how this is done using the journal entry for August 29. If account numbers are provided, keep track of the posting of journal entries to general ledger accounts by writing the account number in the Ref. column of the journal and the journal page number in the Ref. column of the ledger.

As we did earlier for journal entries, we will use a simplified format for ledger accounts to make it easier to focus on their main features. The simplified version of a ledger account is called a **T-account**. Each T-account represents the debit and credit columns of a ledger account. Exhibit 2.10 shows the T-accounts for **Noodlecake**'s Software, Cash, and Accounts Payable, based on transactions (a) through (g) presented earlier in this chapter. It also shows how an individual journal entry's effects would be summarized in these T-accounts. The debit to Software in the journal entry is copied into the debit (left) side of its T-account. The credits to Cash and Accounts Payable are copied into the credit (right) side of those T-accounts. (If you've forgotten why it is recorded this way, look back at Exhibit 2.7.)

YOU SHOULD KNOW

T-Account: A simplified version of a ledger account used for summarizing transaction effects and determining balances for each account.

EXHIBIT 2.9   Posting from the Journal to the Ledger

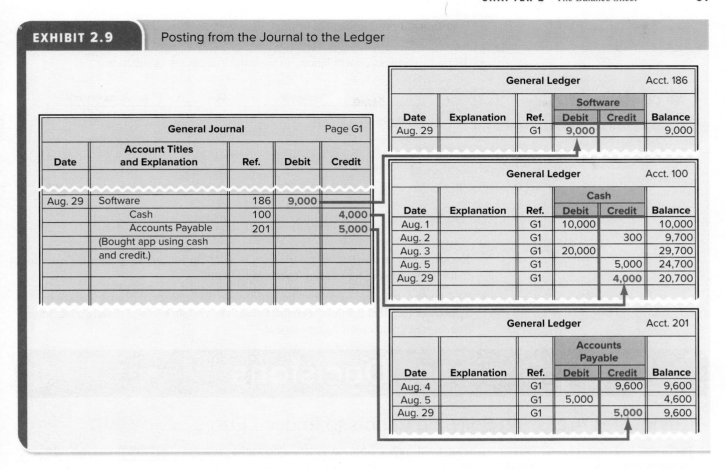

In Exhibit 2.10, notice the following:

- Every account starts with a beginning balance, normally on the side where increases are summarized. For balance sheet accounts, the ending balance from the prior period is the beginning balance for the current period. Because Noodlecake is in its first month of business, the beginning balance in each account is zero in this example.

- Dollar signs are not needed in journal entries and T-accounts.

EXHIBIT 2.10   Posting from a Simplified Journal Entry to T-Accounts

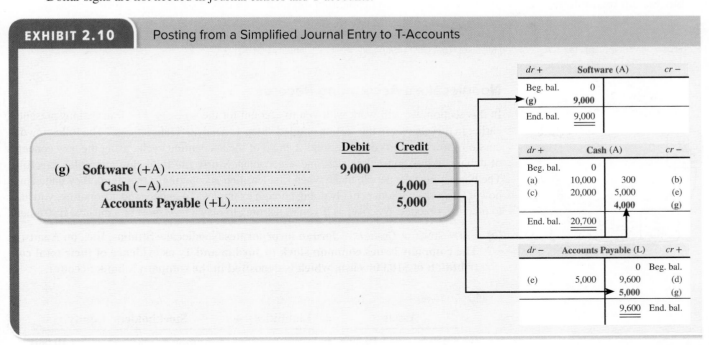

- Each amount is accompanied by a reference to the related journal entry, which makes it easy to trace back to the original transaction should errors occur.

- To find ending account balances, express the T-accounts as equations:

<table>
<thead>
<tr><th></th><th>Software</th><th>Cash</th><th>Accounts Payable</th></tr>
</thead>
<tbody>
<tr><td>Beginning balance</td><td>0</td><td>0</td><td>0</td></tr>
<tr><td>Add: "+" side</td><td>+9,000</td><td>+10,000</td><td>+9,600</td></tr>
<tr><td></td><td></td><td>+20,000</td><td>+5,000</td></tr>
<tr><td>Subtract: "−" side</td><td></td><td>−300</td><td>−5,000</td></tr>
<tr><td></td><td></td><td>−5,000</td><td></td></tr>
<tr><td></td><td></td><td>−4,000</td><td></td></tr>
<tr><td>Ending balance</td><td>9,000</td><td>20,700</td><td>9,600</td></tr>
</tbody>
</table>

COACH'S TIP

Assets normally end with a debit balance (because debits to assets normally exceed credits) and liabilities and stockholders' equity accounts normally end with credit balances (credits exceed debits).

Knowing how to use T-accounts in this way will help you answer homework questions that involve solving for missing values in accounts.

- The ending balance is double underlined to distinguish it from transactions and symbolize the final result of a computation. The ending balance is shown on the side that has the greater total dollar amount.

SPOTLIGHT ON

Business Decisions

Companies Are Using Software Robots to Reduce Errors

That's the headline of a CNBC report describing how mundane accounting tasks, such as entering data and paying suppliers, are increasingly being performed by computerized accounting systems.* By automating these repetitive activities, accountants now spend more time analyzing data to find ways to cut costs and increase sales. It also helps reduce human-caused accounting mistakes. A survey of accounting professionals reports more than a quarter of all accounting mistakes (28 percent) were caused by inputting incorrect data into computerized accounting systems. Excel spreadsheet errors (17 percent) and manual override of system data (13 percent) were the next most common causes.[†] Innovations, such as **blockchain technology,** promise to make data errors a problem of the past.

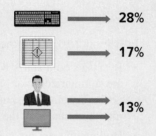

Sources: *A. Wong, "Companies Are Using Software Robots to Reduce Errors, CFO Says," CNBC, February 7, 2018, https://www.cnbc.com/2018/02/07/software-robots-are-helping-companies-reduce-errors-says-robotic-automation-process-company.html. [†]*Bloomberg* BNA, "Top Tax & Accounting Mistakes That Cost Companies Millions," January 2015.

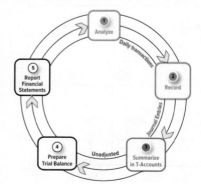

Noodlecake's Accounting Records

In this section, we will work with you to account for the Noodlecake transactions presented earlier in this chapter in the section entitled "Step 1: Analyze Transactions." The following discussion shows how to complete steps 2 and 3 of the accounting cycle, using the new concepts of debits, credits, journal entries, and T-accounts. **Study the following examples carefully.** The biggest mistake people make when first learning accounting is they think they understand how it all works without actually doing enough examples. To understand accounting, you have to practice, practice, practice, as if you're learning to play a new sport or a musical instrument.

(a) **Issue Stock to Owners** Jordan incorporates Noodlecake Studios, Inc., on August 1. **The company issues common stock to Jordan and Ty as evidence of their total contribution of $10,000 cash, which is deposited in the company's bank account.**

1 Analyze

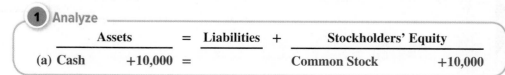

	Assets		=	Liabilities	+	Stockholders' Equity	
(a) Cash	+10,000		=			Common Stock	+10,000

2 Record

	Debit	Credit
(a) Cash (+A)..	10,000	
Common Stock (+SE)		10,000

3 Summarize

dr +	Cash (A)	cr –	dr –	Common Stock (SE)	cr +
Beg. bal.	0			0	Beg. bal.
(a)	10,000			10,000	(a)

(b) Invest in Logo and Trademarks Noodlecake pays $300 cash to create the company's logo.

1 Analyze

	Assets	= Liabilities + Stockholders' Equity
(b) Cash	–300	
Logo/trademarks	+300	

2 Record

	Debit	Credit
(b) Logo and Trademarks (+A)	300	
Cash (–A)...		300

3 Summarize

dr +	Cash (A)	cr –	dr +	Logo and Trademarks (A)	cr –
Beg. bal.	0		Beg. bal.	0	
(a)	10,000	300 (b)	(b)	300	

(c) Obtain Loan from Bank Noodlecake borrows $20,000 from a bank, depositing those funds in its bank account and signing a formal agreement to repay the loan in two years (on August 3, 2023).

1 Analyze

	Assets	=	Liabilities	+ Stockholders' Equity
			Notes Payable	
(c) Cash	+20,000	=	(long-term) +20,000	

2 Record

	Debit	Credit
(c) Cash (+A)...	20,000	
Notes Payable (long-term) (+L)		20,000

3 Summarize

dr +	Cash (A)		cr −	dr −	Notes Payable (long-term) (L)		cr +
Beg. bal.	0					0	Beg. bal.
(a)	10,000	300	(b)			20,000	(c)
(c)	**20,000**						

(d) Invest in Equipment Noodlecake purchases and receives $9,600 in computers, printers, and desks, in exchange for its promise to pay $9,600 at the end of the month.

1 Analyze

Assets	=	Liabilities	+	Stockholders' Equity
(d) Equipment +9,600	=	Accounts Payable +9,600		

2 Record

		Debit	Credit
(d)	Equipment (+A)	9,600	
	Accounts Payable (+L)..		9,600

3 Summarize

dr +	Equipment (A)		cr −	dr −	Accounts Payable (L)		cr +
Beg. bal.	0					0	Beg. bal.
(d)	**9,600**					9,600	(d)

(e) Pay Supplier Noodlecake pays $5,000 to the equipment supplier in (d).

1 Analyze

Assets	=	Liabilities	+	Stockholders' Equity
(e) Cash −5,000	=	Accounts Payable −5,000		

2 Record

		Debit	Credit
(e)	Accounts Payable (−L)	5,000	
	Cash (−A)...		5,000

3 Summarize

dr +	Cash (A)		cr −	dr −	Accounts Payable (L)		cr +
Beg. bal.	0					0	Beg. bal.
(a)	10,000	300	(b)	(e)	5,000	9,600	(d)
(c)	20,000	5,000	(e)				

(f) Order Software Noodlecake signs a contract for program code for a game app for $9,000. No code has been received yet. Because this event involves the exchange of only promises, it is not considered a transaction. No journal entry is needed.

(g) Receive Software Noodlecake receives the $9,000 of app game code ordered in (f), pays $4,000 cash, and promises to pay the remaining $5,000 next month.

1 Analyze

Assets	=	Liabilities	+	Stockholders' Equity
(g) Cash −4,000	=	Accounts Payable +5,000		
Software +9,000				

2 Record

	Debit	Credit
(g) Software (+A)	9,000	
Cash (−A)...		4,000
Accounts Payable (+L)...		5,000

3 Summarize

dr +	Cash (A)		cr −		dr −	Accounts Payable (L)		cr +
Beg. bal.	0						0	Beg. bal.
(a)	10,000	300	(b)	(e)	5,000		9,600	(d)
(c)	20,000	5,000	(e)				5,000	(g)
		4,000	(g)					

dr +	Software (A)	cr −
Beg. bal.	0	
(g)	9,000	

(h) Receive Supplies Noodlecake receives supplies costing $600 on account.

1 Analyze

Assets	=	Liabilities	+	Stockholders' Equity
(h) Supplies +600	=	Accounts Payable +600		

2 Record

	Debit	Credit
(h) Supplies (+A)..	600	
Accounts Payable (+L)...		600

3 Summarize

dr +	Supplies (A)	cr −		dr −	Accounts Payable (L)		cr +
Beg. bal.	0					0	Beg. bal.
(h)	600			(e)	5,000	9,600	(d)
						5,000	(g)
						600	(h)

Exhibit 2.11 summarizes the journal entries and T-accounts affected by events (a) through (h) for Noodlecake. It also reports the ending balances for each account.

EXHIBIT 2.11 Journal Entries and T-Accounts for Noodlecake Studios, Inc.

Journal Entries	Debit	Credit
(a) Cash (+A)	10,000	
Common Stock (+SE).........		10,000
(b) Logo and Trademarks (+A).....	300	
Cash (−A).........................		300
(c) Cash (+A)	20,000	
Notes Payable (+L)		20,000
(d) Equipment (+A)........................	9,600	
Accounts Payable (+L)		9,600
(e) Accounts Payable (−L)	5,000	
Cash (−A).........................		5,000
(f) Not a transaction so no journal entry.		
(g) Software (+A)	9,000	
Cash (−A).........................		4,000
Accounts Payable (+L)		5,000
(h) Supplies (+A)	600	
Accounts Payable (+L)		600

ASSETS = LIABILITIES

Cash (A)

Beg. bal.	0			
(a)	10,000	300	(b)	
(c)	20,000	5,000	(e)	
		4,000	(g)	
End. bal.	20,700			

Software (A)

Beg. bal.	0	
(g)	9,000	
End. bal.	9,000	

Accounts Payable (L)

		0	Beg. bal.	
(e)	5,000	9,600	(d)	
		5,000	(g)	
		600	(h)	
		10,200	End. bal.	

Supplies (A)

Beg. bal.	0	
(h)	600	
End. bal.	600	

Logo and Trademarks (A)

Beg. bal.	0	
(b)	300	
End. bal.	300	

Notes Payable (L)

		0	Beg. bal.
		20,000	(c)
		20,000	End. bal.

Equipment (A)

Beg. bal.	0	
(d)	9,600	
End. bal.	9,600	

+

STOCKHOLDERS' EQUITY

Common Stock (SE)

		0	Beg. bal.
		10,000	(a)
		10,000	End. bal.

PREPARING A TRIAL BALANCE AND BALANCE SHEET

The next step in the accounting cycle is to prepare an internal accounting report called a **trial balance**. It checks that the accounting records are in balance by determining whether debits = credits. The trial balance lists the ending balance in every T-account and then computes total debits and total credits, as shown in Exhibit 2.12. Because the column totals are equal, Noodlecake's balance sheet can be prepared. (If total debits don't equal total credits, the balance sheet will not balance.)

Exhibit 2.13 shows Noodlecake's balance sheet based on the transactions in this chapter. The balance sheet is prepared by taking the ending balances for each account and grouping them as assets, liabilities, and stockholders' equity in balance sheet format. We've used a balance sheet format in Exhibit 2.13 called the **classified balance sheet**. A classified balance

EXHIBIT 2.12 Trial Balance for Noodlecake Studios, Inc.

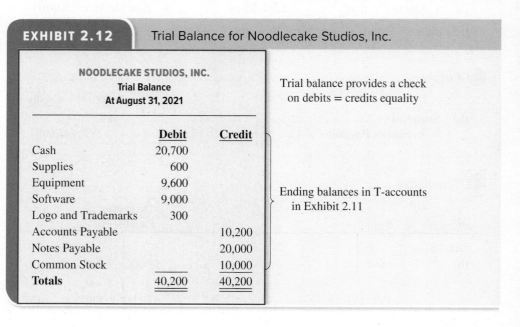

NOODLECAKE STUDIOS, INC.
Trial Balance
At August 31, 2021

	Debit	Credit
Cash	20,700	
Supplies	600	
Equipment	9,600	
Software	9,000	
Logo and Trademarks	300	
Accounts Payable		10,200
Notes Payable		20,000
Common Stock		10,000
Totals	**40,200**	**40,200**

Trial balance provides a check on debits = credits equality

Ending balances in T-accounts in Exhibit 2.11

EXHIBIT 2.13   Classified Balance Sheet

NOODLECAKE STUDIOS, INC. Balance Sheet At August 31, 2021		Explanation of Classification
Assets		
Current Assets		Current assets will be used up or turned into cash within 12 months.
Cash	$20,700	Cash in the company's bank account will be used up before August 31, 2022.
Supplies	600	Paper and other supplies will be used up or replaced before August 31, 2022.
Total Current Assets	21,300	
Equipment	9,600	Computers and desks will be used for a few years.
Software	9,000	Software for app is expected to be used for several years.
Logo and Trademarks	300	Logo will be used indefinitely, for as long as the company exists.
Total Assets	$40,200	
Liabilities and Stockholders' Equity		
Current Liabilities		Current liabilities will be paid or fulfilled within 12 months.
Accounts Payable	$10,200	Amounts owed to suppliers are usually paid within one or two months.
Total Current Liabilities	10,200	
Notes Payable	20,000	The promissory note is not required to be repaid until August 3, 2023.
Total Liabilities	30,200	
Stockholders' Equity		
Common Stock	10,000	Stockholders' equity accounts are not classified as current or noncurrent.
Retained Earnings	0	
Total Stockholders' Equity	10,000	
Total Liabilities and Stockholders' Equity	$40,200	

sheet contains subcategories for assets and liabilities labeled *current*. **Current assets** are assets the business will use up or turn into cash within 12 months of the balance sheet date. **Current liabilities** are debts and other obligations that will be paid or fulfilled within 12 months of the balance sheet date. In our example, Accounts Payable is the only current liability. The other liability—Notes Payable—is expected to be paid in two years, so it is considered **noncurrent**. **Companies list assets in order of liquidity (how soon they will be used up or turned into cash) and liabilities in order of maturity (how soon they will be paid in cash or fulfilled by providing a service).**

Like Noodlecake's Equipment and Notes Payable accounts, the stockholders' equity accounts are understood to be long-term in nature, although they are not labeled as such. Exhibit 2.13 includes the Retained Earnings account in stockholders' equity despite its zero balance because we don't want you to forget about this account. It will become a key link to the income statement, which we return to in Chapter 3 when we study operating activities.

Evaluate the Results

ASSESSING THE ABILITY TO PAY

The classified balance sheet format makes it easy to see whether current assets are sufficient to pay current liabilities. In Noodlecake's case, $21,300 of current assets is greater than the $10,200 of current liabilities, making it obvious the company's current assets are sufficient to cover its current liabilities.

The only problem with looking at total dollar amounts is the difficulty in comparing across companies. It's far easier to express the relationship as a ratio, by dividing current assets by current liabilities. This calculation is known as the current ratio. It is used to

Learning Objective 2-5
Interpret the balance sheet using the current ratio and an understanding of related concepts.

evaluate liquidity, which is the ability to pay liabilities as they come due in the short run. Generally speaking, a high current ratio suggests good liquidity. Noodlecake's current ratio ($21,300 ÷ $10,200 = 2.09$) is in line with many other video game companies, as shown in Exhibit 2.14. Current ratios typically vary from 1.0 to 2.0.

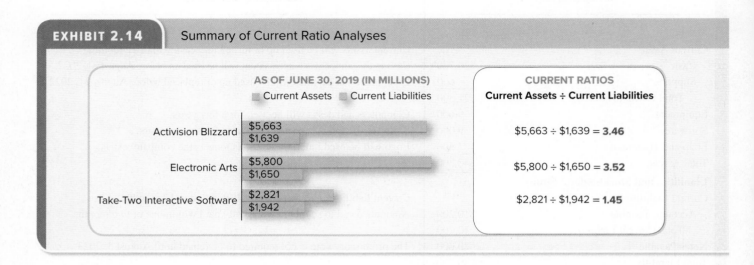

EXHIBIT 2.14	Summary of Current Ratio Analyses

	AS OF JUNE 30, 2019 (IN MILLIONS) ■ Current Assets ■ Current Liabilities	CURRENT RATIOS **Current Assets ÷ Current Liabilities**
Activision Blizzard	$5,663 $1,639	$5,663 ÷ $1,639 = **3.46**
Electronic Arts	$5,800 $1,650	$5,800 ÷ $1,650 = **3.52**
Take-Two Interactive Software	$2,821 $1,942	$2,821 ÷ $1,942 = **1.45**

Accounting Decision Tools		
Name of Measure	**Formula**	**What It Tells You**
Current ratio	$\dfrac{\text{Current Assets}}{\text{Current Liabilities}}$	• Whether current assets are sufficient to pay current liabilities • A higher ratio means better ability to pay

BALANCE SHEET CONCEPTS AND VALUES

The purpose of a balance sheet is to report what a company owns and owes, but not necessarily what the company is worth. Some people mistakenly believe the balance sheet reports a company's current value. To them, this isn't a crazy idea because the balance sheet lists a company's assets and liabilities, so the net difference between the two must be the company's worth. In fact, *net worth* is a term that many accountants and analysts use when referring to stockholders' equity. So why is it wrong to think the balance sheet reports a company's current value?

The answer comes from knowing accounting is based on recording and reporting transactions, which affects (1) what is (and is not) recorded and (2) the amounts assigned to recorded items.

1. **What is (and is not) recorded?**
   - Measurable exchanges, such as a purchase of equipment and software, are recorded. Items not acquired through exchange, such as Jordan's creativity and vision, are not listed on the balance sheet, but they can still affect the value of a company.

2. **What amounts are assigned to recorded items?**
   - Following the **cost principle,** assets and liabilities are first recorded at cost, which is their cash-equivalent value on the date of the transaction. Later, if an asset's value increases, the increase is generally not recorded under GAAP unless it is a

particular type of financial investment (as discussed in Appendix D). However, if an asset's value falls, it is generally reported at that lower value. Thus, the amount reported on the balance sheet may not be the asset's current value.

Summary of the Accounting Cycle

To show that the accounting process explained in this chapter can apply to any business, Exhibit 2.15 illustrates it for a fictitious construction company.

EXHIBIT 2.15	Summary of the Accounting Cycle

During the Accounting Period:

Transaction takes place	(e) Doe Construction purchases a loader, writing a check for $50,000.
Picture the documented activity.	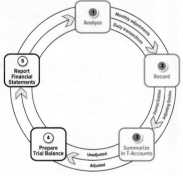 Receives ← Gives →
Name what's exchanged.	• Received a $50,000 loader. • Gave $50,000 cash.

Analyze the financial effects.

Assets	= Liabilities + Stockholders' Equity
(e) Cash −50,000 Equipment +50,000	

Record a journal entry.

		Debit	Credit
(e)	Equipment (+A)	50,000	
	Cash (−A)		50,000

Summarize in T-accounts.

dr+	Equipment (A)	cr−		dr+	Cash (A)	cr−
Beg. bal. 160,000				Beg. bal. 62,000		
(e) 50,000					50,000	(e)
End. bal. 210,000				End. bal. 12,000		

Prepare a trial balance.

	Debit	Credit
Cash	12,000	
Supplies	2,000	
Equipment	210,000	
Accounts Payable		10,000
Common Stock		214,000
Retained Earnings		0
Totals	224,000	224,000

Adjust the accounts.	Covered in Chapter 4

At the End of the Accounting Period:

Prepare financial statements from the trial balance and distribute to users.

(Because the company does not report any operations here, it prepares only the balance sheet.)

DOE CONSTRUCTION
Balance Sheet
At December 31, 2021

Assets	
Current Assets:	
Cash	$ 12,000
Supplies	2,000
Total Current Assets	14,000
Equipment	210,000
Total Assets	$224,000
Liabilities and Stockholders' Equity	
Current Liabilities:	
Accounts Payable	$ 10,000
Total Current Liabilities	10,000
Stockholders' Equity:	
Common Stock	214,000
Retained Earnings	0
Total Stockholders' Equity	214,000
Total Liabilities and Stockholders' Equity	$224,000

Close the books.	Covered in Chapter 4

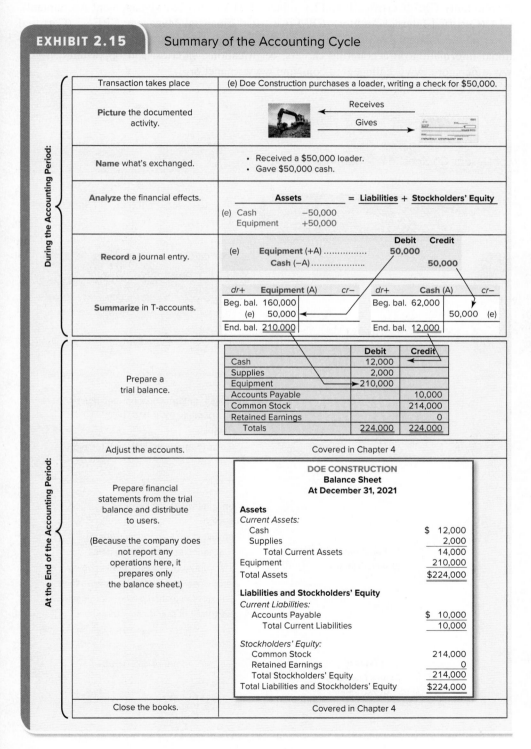

Construction photo: Steve Allen/ Brand X Pictures/Alamy Stock Photo; Check photo: GeorgeManga/Getty Images

SUPPLEMENT 2A ACCOUNTING CAREERS

Every business, government, and not-for-profit organization needs financial advice from an accountant. As shown in Exhibit 2A.1, accountants provide advice as an employee in a single organization (private accounting) or in a CPA firm (public accounting). Because accounting is in great demand, it continues to be a popular career choice for college graduates. According to the U.S. Department of Labor's projections, employment in accounting is expected to grow 6 percent over the next 10 years, resulting in about 9,000 new accounting jobs added each year.

Accountants may pursue a variety of certifications, including the CPA (Certified Public Accountant), CFE (Certified Fraud Examiner), CMA (Certified Management Accountant), CIA (Certified Internal Auditor), CFM (Certified Financial Manager), CRFAC (Certified Forensic Accountant), and CFA (Chartered Financial Analyst), among others. For additional information on accounting careers, certifications, salaries, and opportunities, visit www.aicpa.org, www.collegegrad.com, and www.imanet.org.

EXHIBIT 2A.1 Overview of Career Choices in Accounting

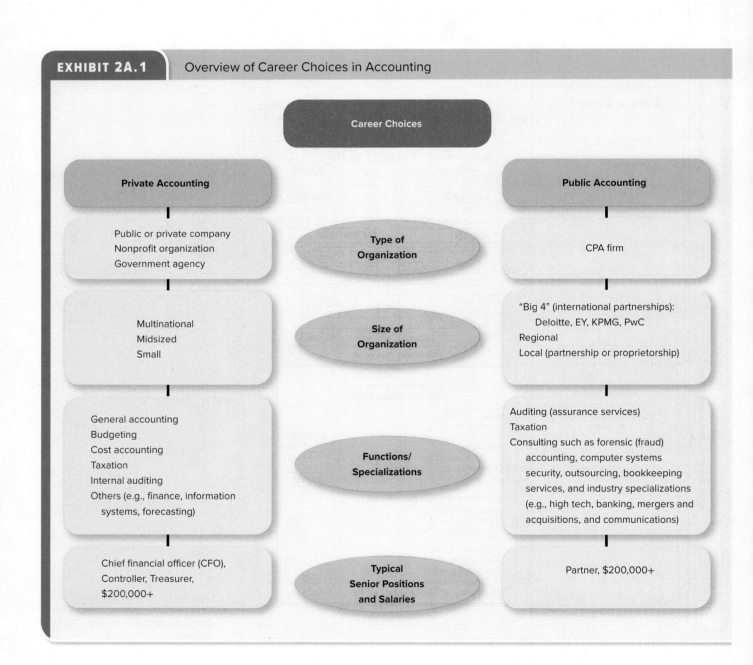

REVIEW THE CHAPTER

This section provides a chance to solidify your understanding of key points. It's worth your time to work through the following demonstration case, scan the chapter summary, test your understanding of key terms, and then practice, practice, practice.

DEMONSTRATION CASE

On April 1, 2021, three college students started Goodbye Grass Corporation (GGC). A summary of GGC's transactions completed through April 30 follows:

 **COACH'S TIP**

For account names, see the Homework Helper that precedes the practice material.

a. Issued shares of common stock to the investors in exchange for cash contributions totaling $9,000.
b. Acquired rakes and other hand tools (equipment) for $600, paying the hardware store $200 cash and agreeing informally to pay the balance in three months.
c. Ordered lawn mowers and edgers costing $4,000 from XYZ Lawn Supply, Inc.
d. Purchased four acres of land for the future site of a storage garage. Paid cash, $5,000.
e. Received the mowers and edgers that had been ordered and signed a promissory note to pay XYZ Lawn Supply in full in 60 days.
f. Sold for $1,250 one acre of land to the city for a park and accepted a note from the city indicating payment will be received by GGC in six months.
g. One of the owners borrowed $3,000 from a local bank for personal use.

Required:

1. Analyze each event to determine its effects on the accounting equation.
2. Prepare journal entries to record transactions listed above (omit explanations).
3. Set up T-accounts for Cash, Notes Receivable (from the city), Equipment (hand tools and mowing equipment), Land, Accounts Payable (to hardware store), Notes Payable (to equipment supply company), and Common Stock. Indicate the beginning balances of $0 in each T-account, and then summarize the effects of each journal entry in the appropriate T-accounts. Determine the ending balance in each account.
4. Use the amounts in the T-accounts, developed in requirement 3, to prepare a classified balance sheet for Goodbye Grass Corporation at April 30, 2021. Show the balances for all assets, liabilities, and stockholders' equity accounts.
5. As of April 30, 2021, has financing for GGC's assets come primarily from liabilities or stockholders' equity?

Suggested Solution

1. Analyze transactions:

	Assets				=	Liabilities		+	Stockholders' Equity
	Cash	Notes Receivable	Equipment	Land	=	Accounts Payable	Notes Payable		Common Stock
(a)	+9,000				=				+9,000
(b)	−200		+600		=	+400			
(c)		No change*			=		No change		
(d)	−5,000			+5,000	=		No change		
(e)			+4,000		=		+4,000		
(f)		+1,250		−1,250	=		No change		
(g)		No change*			=		No change		

*Event (c) is not considered a transaction because it involves only the exchange of promises. Event (g) is not considered a transaction of the company because the separate entity assumption (from Chapter 1) states that transactions of the owners are separate from transactions of the business.

2. Record journal entries:

		Debit	Credit
a.	Cash (+A)	9,000	
	Common Stock (+SE)		9,000
b.	Equipment (+A)	600	
	Cash (−A)		200
	Accounts Payable (+L)		400
c.	This is not an accounting transaction, so a journal entry is not needed.		
d.	Land (+A)	5,000	
	Cash (−A)		5,000
e.	Equipment (+A)	4,000	
	Notes Payable (+L)		4,000
f.	Notes Receivable (+A)	1,250	
	Land (−A)		1,250
g.	This is not a transaction of the business, so a journal entry is not needed.		

3. Summarize journal entries in T-accounts:

Assets = Liabilities + Stockholders' Equity

Cash (A)

Beg. bal.	0		
(a)	9,000	200	(b)
		5,000	(d)
End. bal.	3,800		

Equipment (A)

Beg. bal.	0		
(b)	600		
(e)	4,000		
End. bal.	4,600		

Accounts Payable (L)

		0	Beg. bal.
		400	(b)
		400	End. bal.

Common Stock (SE)

		0	Beg. bal.
		9,000	(a)
		9,000	End. bal.

Notes Receivable (A)

Beg. bal.	0		
(f)	1,250		
End. bal.	1,250		

Land (A)

Beg. bal.	0		
(d)	5,000	1,250	(f)
End. bal.	3,750		

Notes Payable (L)

		0	Beg. bal.
		4,000	(e)
		4,000	End. bal.

4. Prepare a trial balance and a classified balance sheet:

GOODBYE GRASS CORPORATION
Trial Balance
At April 30, 2021

	Debit	Credit
Cash	$ 3,800	
Notes Receivable	1,250	
Equipment	4,600	
Land	3,750	
Accounts Payable		$ 400
Notes Payable		4,000
Common Stock		9,000
Retained Earnings		0
Total	$13,400	$13,400

GOODBYE GRASS CORPORATION
Balance Sheet
At April 30, 2021

Assets		Liabilities	
Current Assets		Current Liabilities	
Cash	$ 3,800	Accounts Payable	$ 400
Notes Receivable	1,250	Notes Payable	4,000
Total Current Assets	5,050	Total Current Liabilities	4,400
Equipment	4,600		
Land	3,750	**Stockholders' Equity**	
		Common Stock	9,000
		Retained Earnings	0
		Total Stockholders' Equity	9,000
		Total Liabilities and	
Total Assets	$13,400	Stockholders' Equity	$13,400

5. The primary source of financing for GGC's assets (totaling $13,400) has come from stockholders' equity ($9,000) rather than liabilities ($4,400).

CHAPTER SUMMARY

Identify financial effects of common business activities that affect the balance sheet.

- Financing activities involve debt transactions with lenders (e.g., Notes Payable) or equity transactions with investors (e.g., Common Stock).
- Investing activities involve buying and selling long-term assets (e.g., Buildings, Equipment).
- Operating activities involve day-to-day transactions with suppliers, employees, and customers and typically affect current assets and current liabilities.

Apply transaction analysis to accounting transactions.

- Transactions include external exchanges and internal events.
- Transaction analysis is based on the duality of effects and the basic accounting equation. *Duality of effects* means that every transaction affects at least two accounts.
- Transaction analysis follows a systematic approach of picturing the documented business activity; naming the exchanged asset, liability, and stockholders' equity accounts; and analyzing the financial effects on the basic accounting equation.

Use journal entries and T-accounts to show how transactions affect the balance sheet.

- Debit means left and credit means right.
- Debits increase assets and decrease liabilities and stockholders' equity.
- Credits decrease assets and increase liabilities and stockholders' equity.
- Journal entries express, in debits-equal-credits form, the effects of a transaction on various asset, liability, and stockholders' equity accounts. Journal entries are used to record financial information in the accounting system, which is later summarized by accounts in the ledger (T-accounts).
- T-accounts are a simplified version of the ledger, which summarizes transaction effects for each account. T-accounts show increases on the left (debit) side for assets, which are on the left side of the accounting equation. T-accounts show increases on the right (credit) side for liabilities and stockholders' equity, which are on the right side of the accounting equation.

Prepare a trial balance and a classified balance sheet.

- A trial balance checks on the equality of debit and credit balances.
- A *classified balance sheet* separately classifies assets as current if they will be used up or turned into cash within one year. Liabilities are classified as current if they will be paid, settled, or fulfilled within one year.

Interpret the balance sheet using the current ratio and an understanding of related concepts.

- The current ratio divides current assets by current liabilities to determine the extent to which current assets are likely to be sufficient for paying current liabilities.
- Because accounting is transaction-based, the balance sheet does not necessarily represent the current value of a business. Some assets are not recorded because they do not arise from transactions.
- The amounts recorded for assets and liabilities may not represent current values because under the cost principle they generally are recorded at cost, using the exchange amounts established at the time of the initial transaction.

Accounting Decision Tools		
Name of Measure	**Formula**	**What It Tells You**
Current ratio	$\dfrac{\text{Current Assets}}{\text{Current Liabilities}}$	- Whether current assets are sufficient to pay current liabilities - A higher ratio means better ability to pay

KEY TERMS

Assets p. 48	**Current Liabilities** p. 67	**Noncurrent** p. 67
Chart of Accounts p. 51	**Debit** p. 58	**Stockholders' Equity** p. 48
Classified Balance Sheet p. 66	**Journal** p. 57	**T-Account** p. 60
Cost Principle p. 49	**Journal Entries** p. 59	**Transaction** p. 50
Credit p. 58	**Ledger** p. 57	**Trial Balance** p. 66
Current Assets p. 67	**Liabilities** p. 48	

See complete definitions in the glossary in the back of this text.

HOMEWORK HELPER

Account Name	Description
Assets	
Cash	Includes cash in the bank and in the cash register
Short-Term Investments	Investments in government securities and certificates of deposit
Accounts Receivable	The right to collect from customers for prior sales on credit
Interest Receivable	The right to collect interest from others
Inventory	Goods on hand that are being held for resale
Supplies	Items on hand that will be used to make goods or provide services
Prepaid Insurance	Amount paid to obtain insurance covering future periods
Prepaid Rent	Amount paid for rent relating to future periods
Notes Receivable	The right to collect from others under a formal agreement ("note")
Land	Cost of land to be used by the business
Buildings	Cost of buildings the business will use for operations
Equipment	Cost of equipment used to produce goods or provide services
Software	Cost of purchased computer programs and code
Intangible Assets	Brand names, goodwill, and other assets that lack a physical presence
Liabilities	
Accounts Payable	Amounts owed to suppliers for goods or services bought on credit
Salaries and Wages Payable	Amounts owed to employees for salaries, wages, and bonuses
Accrued Liabilities	Amounts owed to others for advertising, utilities, interest, etc.
Deferred Revenue	Amounts (customer deposits) received in advance of providing goods or services to customers
Notes Payable	Amounts borrowed from lenders; involves signing a promissory note
Interest Payable	Amount owed on loans as the cost of borrowing
Bonds Payable	Amounts borrowed from lenders; involves issuance of bonds
Other Liabilities	A variety of liabilities with smaller balances
Stockholders' Equity	
Common Stock	Amount of cash (or other property) contributed in exchange for the company's common stock
Retained Earnings	Amount of accumulated earnings not distributed as dividends

> **COACH'S TIP**
>
> Read this chart of accounts but don't memorize it. Also, don't try to force this chart of accounts on all problems. Account names vary from company to company.

Alternative terms

- Stockholders' equity also can be called shareholders' equity.
- The balance sheet also can be called the statement of financial position.

Helpful reminders

- It's easier to account for a transaction if you can accurately determine how it might affect Cash before determining its impact on the other account(s).
- The word *pay* and the expression *purchase with cash* both imply a reduction in Cash. The words *on account* mean to either buy something now by promising to pay cash later (accounts payable) or sell something now in exchange for a promise to receive cash later (accounts receivable).

Frequent mistakes

- When accounting for transactions, avoid thinking of yourself as the customer, investor, or creditor. Instead, put yourself in the position of the company you're accounting for.
- Stockholders' is plural; stockholder's is singular.

PRACTICE MATERIAL

QUESTIONS (⊖Symbol indicates questions that require analysis from more than one perspective.)

1. Define the following:

   a. Asset
   b. Current asset
   c. Liability
   d. Current liability
   e. Common stock
   f. Retained earnings

2. Define a transaction and give an example of each of the two types of events that are considered transactions.

3. For accounting purposes, what is an account? Explain why accounts are used in an accounting system.

4. What is the basic accounting equation?

5. Explain what *debit* and *credit* mean.

6. Briefly explain what is meant by *transaction analysis*. What are the two principles underlying transaction analysis?

7. What two different accounting equalities must be maintained in transaction analysis and recording?

8. What is a journal entry? What is the typical format of a journal entry?

9. What is a T-account? What is its purpose?

10. Explain the cost principle.

11. To obtain financing for her hair salon, Valeri asked you to prepare a balance sheet for her business. When she sees it, she is disappointed that the assets exclude a value for her list of loyal customers. What can you tell her to explain why this "asset" has been excluded? Knowing this, what should she tell her banker when they meet next week? ⊖

MULTIPLE CHOICE

1. Which of the following is not an asset account?

   a. Cash
   b. Land
   c. Equipment
   d. Common Stock

2. Which of the following statements describes transactions that would be recorded in the accounting system?

   a. An exchange of an asset for a promise to pay
   b. An exchange of a promise for another promise
   c. Both of the above
   d. None of the above

3. Total assets on a balance sheet prepared on any date must agree with which of the following?

   a. The sum of total liabilities and net income as shown on the income statement
   b. The sum of total liabilities and common stock
   c. The sum of total liabilities and retained earnings
   d. The sum of total liabilities and common stock and retained earnings

4. The *duality of effects* can best be described as follows:

   a. When a transaction is recorded in the accounting system, at least two effects on the basic accounting equation will result.
   b. When an exchange takes place between two parties, both parties must record the transaction.
   c. When a transaction is recorded, both the balance sheet and the income statement must be impacted.
   d. When a transaction is recorded, one account will always increase and one account will always decrease.

5. The T-account is used to summarize which of the following?

   a. Increases and decreases to a single account in the accounting system
   b. Debits and credits to a single account in the accounting system
   c. Changes in a specific account balance over time
   d. All of the above describe how T-accounts are used by accountants.

6. Which of the following describes how assets are listed on the balance sheet?

   a. In alphabetical order
   b. In order of magnitude, lowest value to highest value
   c. In the order they will be used up or turned into cash
   d. From least current to most current

7. A company was recently formed with $50,000 cash contributed to the company by stockholders for common stock. The company then borrowed $20,000 from a bank and bought $10,000 of supplies on account. The company also purchased $50,000 of equipment by paying $20,000 in cash and issuing a note for the remainder. What is the amount of total assets to be reported on the balance sheet?

   a. $110,000
   b. $100,000
   c. $90,000
   d. None of the above

8. Which of the following statements would be considered true regarding debits and credits?

   a. In any given transaction, the total dollar amount of the debits and the total dollar amount of the credits must be equal.

   b. Debits decrease certain accounts and credits decrease certain accounts.

   c. Liabilities and stockholders' equity accounts usually end in credit balances, while assets usually end in debit balances.

   d. All of the above are true.

9. Which of the following statements would be considered true regarding the balance sheet?

   a. One cannot determine the true current value of a company by reviewing just its balance sheet.

   b. The balance sheet reports assets only if they have been acquired through identifiable transactions.

   c. A balance sheet shows only the ending balances, in a summarized format, of balance sheet accounts in the accounting system as of a particular date.

   d. All of the above are true.

10. If a publicly traded company is trying to maximize its perceived value to decision makers external to the corporation, the company is most likely to report too small a value for which of the following on its balance sheet?

    a. Assets

    b. Liabilities

    c. Retained Earnings

    d. Common Stock

> For answers to the Multiple-Choice Questions **see page Q1** located in the last section of the book.

MINI-EXERCISES

LO 2-3 **M2-1 Identifying Increase and Decrease Effects on Balance Sheet Accounts**

Complete the following table by entering either the word *increases* or *decreases* in each column.

	Debit	Credit
Assets	_____	_____
Liabilities	_____	_____
Stockholders' Equity	_____	_____

LO 2-3 **M2-2 Identifying Debit and Credit Effects on Balance Sheet Accounts**

Complete the following table by entering either the word *debit* or *credit* in each column.

	Increase	Decrease
Assets	_____	_____
Liabilities	_____	_____
Stockholders' Equity	_____	_____

LO 2-2, LO 2-3 **M2-3 Matching Terms with Definitions**

Match each term with its related definition by entering the appropriate letter in the space provided. There should be only one definition per term. (That is, there are more definitions than terms.)

Term	Definition
_____ 1. Journal entry	A. An exchange or event that has a direct and measurable financial effect.
_____ 2. A = L + SE; Debits = Credits	B. Four periodic financial statements.
_____ 3. Transaction	C. The two equalities in accounting that aid in providing accuracy.
_____ 4. Liabilities	D. The results of transaction analysis in debits-equal-credits format.
_____ 5. Assets	E. The account that is debited when money is borrowed from a bank.
_____ 6. Income statement, balance sheet, statement of retained earnings, and statement of cash flows	F. A resource owned by a business, with measurable value and expected future benefits.
	G. Cumulative earnings of a company that are not distributed to the owners.
	H. Every transaction has at least two effects.
	I. Amounts presently owed by a business.
	J. Assigning dollar amounts to transactions.

M2-4 Classifying Accounts on a Balance Sheet

LO 2-1, LO 2-4

The following are a few of the accounts of Aim Delivery Corporation:

____	**1.** Salaries and Wages Payable	____	**7.** Land
____	**2.** Accounts Payable	____	**8.** Income Tax Payable
____	**3.** Accounts Receivable	____	**9.** Equipment
____	**4.** Buildings	____	**10.** Notes Payable (due in six months)
____	**5.** Cash	____	**11.** Retained Earnings
____	**6.** Common Stock	____	**12.** Supplies

In the space provided, classify each as it would be reported on a balance sheet. Use the following codes:

CA = Current Asset   CL = Current Liability   SE = Stockholders' Equity

NCA = Noncurrent Asset   NCL = Noncurrent Liability

M2-5 Identifying Accounts on a Classified Balance Sheet and Their Normal Debit or Credit Balances

LO 2-1, LO 2-3, LO 2-4

Hasbro, Inc., produces popular games such as Trivial Pursuit, Scrabble, and Monopoly. The following are several of the accounts from a recent balance sheet:

Hasbro, Inc.

1. Accounts Receivable
2. Notes Payable (short-term)
3. Common Stock
4. Notes Payable (long-term)
5. Income Tax Payable
6. Equipment
7. Retained Earnings
8. Accounts Payable
9. Cash

Required:

1. Indicate how each account normally should be categorized on a classified balance sheet. Use CA for current asset, NCA for noncurrent asset, CL for current liability, NCL for noncurrent liability, and SE for stockholders' equity.
2. Indicate whether the account normally has a debit or credit balance.

M2-6 Identifying Accounts on a Classified Balance Sheet and Their Normal Debit or Credit Balances

LO 2-1, LO 2-3, LO 2-4

Netflix, Inc., is the world's leading Internet subscription service for movies and TV shows. The following are several of the accounts included in a recent balance sheet:

Netflix, Inc.

1. Accrued Liabilities
2. Prepaid Rent
3. Cash
4. Common Stock
5. Notes Payable (long-term)
6. Equipment
7. Retained Earnings
8. Accounts Payable

Required:

1. Indicate how each account normally should be categorized on a classified balance sheet. Use CA for current asset, NCA for noncurrent asset, CL for current liability, NCL for noncurrent liability, and SE for stockholders' equity.
2. Indicate whether the account normally has a debit or credit balance.

M2-7 Identifying Events as Accounting Transactions

LO 2-2

Do the following events result in a recordable transaction for **The Toro Company**? Answer yes or no for each.

The Toro Company

____ **1.** Toro purchased robotic manufacturing equipment that it paid for by signing a note payable.

____ **2.** Toro's president purchased stock in another company for his own portfolio.

_____ **3.** The company lent $550 to an employee.

_____ **4.** Toro ordered supplies from Office Depot to be delivered next week.

_____ **5.** Six investors in Toro sold their stock to another investor.

_____ **6.** The company borrowed $2,500,000 from a local bank.

LO 2-2

M2-8 Identifying Events as Accounting Transactions

Half Price Books

Half Price Books is the country's largest family-owned new and used bookstore chain. Do the following events result in a recordable transaction for Half Price Books? Answer yes or no for each.

_____ **1.** Half Price Books bought an old laundromat in Dallas.

_____ **2.** The privately held company issued stock to new investors.

_____ **3.** The company signed an agreement to rent store space in Columbia Plaza near Cleveland.

_____ **4.** The company paid for renovations to prepare its Seattle store for operations.

_____ **5.** The vice president of the company spoke at a literacy luncheon in Indiana, which contributed to building the company's reputation as a responsible company.

LO 2-2

M2-9 Determining Financial Statement Effects of Several Transactions

For each of the following transactions of Spotlighter, Inc., for the month of January, indicate the accounts, amounts, and direction of the effects on the accounting equation. A sample is provided.

a. *(Sample)* Borrowed $3,940 from a local bank on a note due in six months.

b. Received $4,630 cash from investors and issued common stock to them.

c. Purchased $1,000 in equipment, paying $200 cash and promising the rest on a note due in one year.

d. Paid $300 cash for supplies.

e. Bought and received $700 of supplies on account.

	Assets		=	Liabilities		+ Stockholders' Equity
a. Sample	Cash	+3,940		Notes Payable (short-term)	+3,940	

LO 2-3

M2-10 Preparing Journal Entries

For each of the transactions in M2-9 (including the sample), write the journal entry using the format shown in this chapter (omit explanations).

LO 2-3

M2-11 Posting to T-Accounts

For each of the transactions in M2-9 (including the sample), post the effects to the appropriate T-accounts and determine ending account balances. Show a beginning balance of zero.

Cash (A)			Supplies (A)			Equipment (A)

Accounts Payable (L)			Notes Payable (L)			Common Stock (SE)

LO 2-4

M2-12 Reporting a Classified Balance Sheet

Given the transactions in M2-9 (including the sample), prepare a classified balance sheet for Spotlighter, Inc., as of January 31.

LO 2-3

M2-13 Identifying Transactions and Preparing Journal Entries

J.K. Builders was incorporated on July 1. Prepare journal entries for the following events from the first month of business. If the event is not a transaction, write "no transaction."

a. Received $70,000 cash invested by owners and issued common stock.

b. Bought an unused field from a local farmer by paying $60,000 cash. As a construction site for smaller projects, it is estimated to be worth $65,000 to J.K. Builders.

c. A lumber supplier delivered lumber supplies to J.K. Builders for future use. The lumber supplies would have normally sold for $10,000, but the supplier gave J.K. Builders a 10 percent discount. J.K. Builders has not yet received the $9,000 bill from the supplier.

d. Borrowed $25,000 from the bank with a plan to use the funds to build a small workshop in August. The loan must be repaid in two years.

e. One of the owners sold $10,000 worth of his common stock to another shareholder for $11,000.

M2-14 Determining Financial Statement Effects of Transactions

LO 2-3

Analyze the accounting equation effects of the transactions in M2-13 using the format shown in the chapter and compute total assets, total liabilities, and total stockholders' equity.

M2-15 Identifying Transactions and Preparing Journal Entries

LO 2-3

At the beginning of August, Joel Henry founded Bookmart.com, which sells new and used books online. He is passionate about books but does not have a lot of accounting experience. Help Joel by preparing journal entries for the following events. If the event is not a transaction, write "no transaction."

a. The company purchased equipment for $4,000 cash. The equipment is expected to be used for 10 or more years.

b. Joel's business bought $7,000 worth of inventory from a publisher. The company will pay the publisher within 45–60 days.

c. Joel's friend Sam lent $4,000 to the business. Sam had Joel write a note promising that Bookmart.com would repay the $4,000 in four months. Because they are good friends, Sam is not going to charge Joel interest.

d. The company paid $1,500 cash for books purchased on account earlier in the month.

e. Bookmart.com repaid the $4,000 loan established in (*c*).

M2-16 Determining Financial Statement Effects of Transactions

LO 2-3

Analyze the accounting equation effects of the transactions in M2-15 using the format shown in the chapter and compute total assets, total liabilities, and total stockholders' equity.

M2-17 Identifying Transactions and Preparing Journal Entries

LO 2-3

Sweet Shop Co. is a chain of candy stores that has been in operation for the past 10 years. Prepare journal entries for the following events, which occurred at the end of the most recent year. If the event is not a transaction, write "no transaction."

a. Ordered and received $12,000 worth of cotton candy machines from Candy Makers Inc., which Sweet Shop Co. will pay for in 45 days.

b. Sent a check for $6,000 to Candy Makers Inc. for the cotton candy machines from (*a*).

c. Received $400 from customers who bought candy on account in previous months.

d. To help raise funds for store upgrades estimated to cost $20,000, Sweet Shop Co. issued 1,000 common shares for $15 each to existing stockholders.

e. Sweet Shop Co. bought ice cream trucks for $60,000 total, paying $10,000 cash and signing a long-term note for $50,000.

M2-18 Determining Financial Statement Effects of Transactions

LO 2-3

Analyze the accounting equation effects of the transactions in M2-17 using the format shown in the chapter and compute total assets, total liabilities, and total stockholders' equity.

M2-19 Identifying Transactions and Preparing Journal Entries

LO 2-3

Katy Williams is the manager of Blue Light Arcade. The company provides entertainment for parties and special events. Prepare journal entries for the following events relating to the year ended December 31. If the event is not a transaction, write "no transaction."

a. Blue Light Arcade received $50 cash on account for a birthday party held two months ago.

b. Agreed to hire a new employee at a monthly salary of $3,000. The employee starts work next month.

c. Paid $2,000 for a tabletop hockey game purchased last month on account.

d. Repaid a $5,000 bank loan that had been outstanding for six months. (Ignore interest.)

e. The company purchased an air hockey table for $2,200, paying $1,000 cash and signing a short-term note for $1,200.

LO 2-3   **M2-20 Determining Financial Statement Effects of Transactions**

Analyze the accounting equation effects of the transactions in M2-19 using the format shown in the chapter and compute total assets, total liabilities, and total stockholders' equity.

LO 2-4   **M2-21 Ordering Current Assets and Current Liabilities within a Classified Balance Sheet**

Charlie's Crispy Chicken (CCC) operates a fast-food restaurant. When accounting for its first year of business, CCC created several accounts. Using the following descriptions, prepare a classified balance sheet at September 30. Are CCC's current assets sufficient to be converted into cash to cover its current liabilities? How can you tell?

Account Name	Balance	Description
Accounts Payable	$ 2,000	Payment is due in 30 days
Cash	1,800	Includes cash in register and in bank account
Common Stock	30,000	Stock issued in exchange for owners' contributions
Equipment	38,000	Includes deep fryers, microwaves, dishwasher, etc.
Land	18,900	Held for future site of new restaurant
Notes Payable (long-term)	25,000	Payment is due in six years
Retained Earnings	3,000	Total earnings through September 30
Salaries and Wages Payable	200	Payment is due in 7 days
Supplies	1,500	Includes serving trays, condiment dispensers, etc.

LO 2-4, LO 2-5   **M2-22 Preparing a Classified Balance Sheet**

Facebook Inc.

The following accounts are taken from the financial statements of Facebook Inc. at June 30, 2019. (Amounts are in millions.)

Accounts Payable	$13,000
Accounts Receivable	7,500
Cash	13,900
Common Stock	43,800
Equipment	37,270
Income Tax Expense	2,200
Interest Expense	200
Notes Payable (long-term)	15,200
Prepaid Rent	1,850
Retained Earnings	45,000
Service Revenue	16,900
Short-Term Investments	34,700
Software	21,780

Required:

1. Prepare a classified balance sheet at June 30, 2019.
   TIP: This exercise requires you to remember material from Chapter 1. (Some of the above accounts are not reported on the balance sheet.)

2. Using the balance sheet, indicate whether the total assets of Facebook Inc. at the end of June were financed primarily by liabilities or by stockholders' equity.

3. Were the current assets sufficient to cover the current liabilities at June 30, 2019? Show the ratio calculation (rounded to two decimal places) that indicates this.

M2-23 Calculating and Interpreting the Current Ratio

LO 2-5

The balance sheet of Mister Ribs Restaurant reports current assets of $30,000 and current liabilities of $15,000. Calculate and interpret the current ratio. Does it appear likely that Mister Ribs will be able to pay its current liabilities as they come due in the next year?

M2-24 Evaluating the Impact of Transactions on the Current Ratio

LO 2-5

Refer to M2-23. Evaluate whether the current ratio of Mister Ribs Restaurant will increase or decrease as a result of the following transactions. Consider each item, (a)–(d), independent of the others.

a. Paid $2,000 cash for a new oven.
b. Received a $2,000 cash contribution from an investor for the company's common stock.
c. Borrowed $5,000 cash from a bank, issuing a note that must be repaid in three years.
d. Purchased $500 of napkins, paper cups, and other disposable supplies on account.

M2-25 Analyzing the Impact of Transactions on the Current Ratio

LO 2-5

BSO, Inc., has current assets of $1,000,000 and current liabilities of $500,000, resulting in a current ratio of 2.0. For each of the following transactions, determine whether the current ratio will increase, decrease, or remain the same. Consider each item, (a)–(d), independent of the others.

a. Purchased $20,000 of supplies on credit.
b. Paid Accounts Payable in the amount of $50,000.
c. Recorded $100,000 of cash contributed by a stockholder for common stock.
d. Borrowed $250,000 from a local bank, to be repaid in 90 days.

EXERCISES

E2-1 Matching Terms with Definitions

LO 2-1, 2-2, 2-3

Match each term with its related definition by entering the appropriate letter in the space provided. There should be only one definition per term (that is, there are more definitions than terms).

Term	Definition
_____ 1. Transaction	A. Economic resources to be used or turned into cash within one year.
_____ 2. Separate Entity Assumption	
_____ 3. Balance Sheet	B. Reports assets, liabilities, and stockholders' equity.
_____ 4. Liabilities	C. Decrease assets; increase liabilities and stockholders' equity.
_____ 5. Assets = Liabilities + Stockholders' Equity	D. Increase assets; decrease liabilities and stockholders' equity.
_____ 6. Current Assets	
_____ 7. Notes Payable	E. An exchange or event that has a direct and measurable financial effect.
_____ 8. Duality of Effects	F. Accounts for a business separate from its owners.
_____ 9. Retained Earnings	G. The principle that assets should be recorded at their original cost to the company.
_____ 10. Debit	H. A standardized format used to accumulate data about each item reported on financial statements.
	I. The basic accounting equation.
	J. The idea that accounts can both increase and decrease.
	K. The account credited when money is borrowed from a bank using a promissory note.
	L. Cumulative earnings of a company that have not yet been distributed to the owners.
	M. Every transaction has at least two effects.
	N. Amounts presently owed by the business.

LO 2-1, 2-2, 2-5

E2-2 Identifying Account Titles

The following are independent situations.

a. A company orders and receives 10 personal computers for office use for which it signs a note promising to pay $25,000 within three months.

b. A company purchases for $21,000 cash a new delivery truck that has a list ("sticker") price of $24,000.

c. A women's clothing retailer orders 30 new display stands for $300 each for future delivery.

d. A new company is formed and issues 100 shares of stock for $12 per share to investors.

e. A company purchases a piece of land for $50,000 cash. An appraiser for the buyer valued the land at $52,500.

f. The owner of a local company uses a personal check to buy a $10,000 car for personal use. Answer from the company's point of view.

g. A company borrows $2,000 from a local bank and signs a six-month note for the loan.

h. A company pays $1,500 owed on its 10-year notes payable (ignore interest).

Required:

1. For each of the preceding events, indicate appropriate titles of the affected accounts, if any, listing first the item received (to be debited) followed by the item given (to be credited).

2. At what amount would you record the delivery truck in (b)? The piece of land in (e)? What measurement principle are you applying?

3. What reasoning did you apply in (c)? For (f), what accounting concept did you apply?

LO 2-1, 2-3, 2-4

E2-3 Classifying Accounts and Their Usual Balances

As described in a recent annual report, Digital Diversions, Inc. (DDI), designs, develops, and distributes video games for computers and advanced game systems. DDI has been operating for only one full year.

Required:

For each of the following accounts from DDI's recent balance sheet, complete the following table. Indicate whether the account is classified as a current asset (CA), noncurrent asset (NCA), current liability (CL), noncurrent liability (NCL), or stockholders' equity (SE), and whether the account usually has a debit (dr) or credit (cr) balance.

Account	Balance Sheet Classification	Debit or Credit Balance
1. Land	_____	_____
2. Retained Earnings	_____	_____
3. Notes Payable (due in three years)	_____	_____
4. Accounts Receivable	_____	_____
5. Supplies	_____	_____
6. Common Stock	_____	_____
7. Equipment	_____	_____
8. Accounts Payable	_____	_____
9. Cash	_____	_____
10. Income Taxes Payable	_____	_____

LO 2-1, 2-2

E2-4 Determining Financial Statement Effects of Several Transactions

The following events occurred for Favata Company:

a. Received $10,000 cash from owners and issued stock to them.

b. Borrowed $7,000 cash from a bank and signed a note due later this year.

c. Bought and received $800 of equipment on account.

d. Purchased land for $12,000; paid $1,000 in cash and signed a long-term note for $11,000.

e. Purchased $3,000 of equipment; paid $1,000 in cash and charged the rest on account.

Required:

For each of the events (*a*) through (*e*), perform transaction analysis and indicate the account, amount, and direction of the effect (+ for increase and − for decrease) on the accounting equation. Check that the accounting equation remains in balance after each transaction. Use the following headings:

Event	Assets	=	Liabilities	+	Stockholders' Equity

E2-5 Recording Journal Entries   LO 2-3

Refer to E2-4.

Required:

For each of the events in E2-4, prepare journal entries, checking that debits equal credits.

E2-6 Determining Financial Statement Effects of Several Transactions   LO 2-1, 2-2, 2-5

NIKE, Inc., with headquarters in Beaverton, Oregon, is one of the world's leading manufacturers   NIKE, Inc.
of athletic shoes and sports apparel. Assume the following activities occurred during a recent year.
The dollar amounts in (*a*) and (*b*) are presented "in millions," and the dollar amount in (*c*) is per
share. When reporting amounts "in millions," exclude the 000,000.

a. Purchased $216 in equipment; paid by signing a $5 long-term note and fulfilling the rest with cash.
b. Issued $21 in additional common stock for cash contributions made by stockholders.
c. Several NIKE investors sold their own stock to other investors on the stock exchange for $110
      per share of stock.

Required:

1. For each of these events, perform transaction analysis and indicate the account, amount (in
    millions), and direction of the effect on the accounting equation. Check that the accounting
    equation remains in balance after each transaction. Use the following headings:

Event	Assets	=	Liabilities	+	Stockholders' Equity

2. Explain your response to transaction (*c*).
3. Did these transactions change the extent to which NIKE relied on creditors versus stockhold-
    ers for financing? Explain.

E2-7 Recording Journal Entries   LO 2-3, 2-5

Refer to E2-6.

Required:

1. For each of the events in E2-6, prepare journal entries, checking that debits equal credits.
2. Explain your response to event (*c*).

E2-8 Analyzing the Effects of Transactions in T-Accounts   LO 2-2, 2-3, 2-5

Mulkeen Service Company, Inc., was incorporated by Conor Mulkeen and five other managers.
The following activities occurred during the year:

a. Received $60,000 cash from the managers; each was issued 1,000 shares of common stock.
b. Purchased equipment for use in the business at a cost of $12,000; one-fourth was paid in cash
      and the company signed a note for the balance (due in six months).
c. Signed an agreement with a cleaning service to pay it $120 per week for cleaning the corpo-
      rate offices, beginning next year.
d. Conor Mulkeen borrowed $10,000 for personal use from a local bank, signing a one-year note.

Required:

1. Create T-accounts for the following accounts: Cash, Equipment, Notes Payable, and Common
    Stock. Beginning balances are zero. For each of the above transactions, record its effects in the
    appropriate T-accounts. Include referencing and totals for each T-account.
2. Using the balances in the T-accounts, fill in the following amounts for the accounting equation:

    Assets $_____ = Liabilities $_____ + Stockholders' Equity $_____

3. Explain your response to events (*c*) and (*d*).

LO 2-1, 2-2, 2-4

E2-9 Inferring Investing and Financing Transactions and Preparing a Balance Sheet

Home Comfort Furniture Company completed four transactions, with the dollar effects indicated in the following schedule:

	Assets		=	Liabilities	+	Stockholders' Equity
	Cash	**Equipment**		**Notes Payable**		**Common Stock**
Beginning	$ 0	$ 0	=	$ 0		$ 0
(1)	+12,000		=			+12,000
(2)	+50,000		=	+50,000		
(3)	−4,000	+12,000	=	+8,000		
(4)	+4,000		=	+4,000		
Ending	$	$	=	$		$

Required:

1. Write a brief explanation of transactions (1) through (4). Explain any assumptions you made.
2. Compute the ending balance in each account.
3. Has most of the financing for Home Comfort's investments in assets come from liabilities or stockholders' equity?

LO 2-2, 2-3, 2-4

E2-10 Analyzing Accounting Equation Effects, Recording Journal Entries, and Summarizing Financial Statement Impact

Rawlco Communications operates 15 radio stations. The following events occurred during September.

a. Placed an order for office supplies costing $2,000. Supplier intends to deliver later in the month.
b. Purchased equipment that cost $30,000; paid $10,000 cash and signed a promissory note to pay $20,000 in one month.
c. Negotiated and signed a one-year bank loan, and then deposited $5,000 cash in the company's checking account.
d. Hired a new finance manager on the last day of the month.
e. Received an investment of $10,000 cash from the company's owners in exchange for issuing common shares.
f. Supplies [ordered in (*a*)] were received, along with a bill for $2,000.

Required:

1. Indicate the specific account, amount, and direction of effects for each transaction on the radio station's accounting equation. If an event is not considered a transaction, explain why.
2. Prepare journal entries to record each transaction.
3. Rawlco began the month with $220,000 in total assets. What total assets would be reported on the balance sheet after events (*a*)–(*f*)?

LO 2-1, 2-2, 2-4, 2-5

Despair, Inc.

E2-11 Recording Journal Entries and Preparing a Classified Balance Sheet

Assume Down, Inc., was organized on May 1 to compete with Despair, Inc.—a company that sells de-motivational posters and office products. Down, Inc., encountered the following events during its first month of operations.

a. Received $60,000 cash from the investors who organized Down, Inc.
b. Borrowed $20,000 cash and signed a note due in two years.
c. Ordered equipment costing $16,000.
d. Purchased $9,000 in equipment, paying $2,000 in cash and signing a six-month note for the balance.
e. Received the equipment ordered in (*c*), paid for half of it, and put the rest on account.

Required:

1. Summarize the financial effects of items (*a*)–(*e*) in a table or spreadsheet similar to Exhibit 2.5.
2. Prepare journal entries for each transaction. Be sure to use referencing and categorize each account as an asset (A), liability (L), or stockholders' equity (SE). If a transaction does not require a journal entry, explain the reason.
3. Prepare a classified balance sheet at May 31. Include Retained Earnings with a balance of zero.

E2-12 Analyzing the Effects of Transactions Using T-Accounts; Preparing and Interpreting a Balance Sheet

LO 2-2, 2-3, 2-4

Laser Delivery Services, Inc. (LDS), was incorporated January 1. The following transactions occurred during the year:

a. Received $40,000 cash from the company's founders in exchange for common stock.
b. Purchased land for $12,000, signing a two-year note (ignore interest).
c. Bought two used delivery trucks at the start of the year at a cost of $10,000 each; paid $2,000 cash and signed a note due in three years for $18,000 (ignore interest).
d. Paid $2,000 cash to a truck repair shop for a new motor, which increased the cost of one of the trucks.
e. Stockholder Jonah Lee paid $300,000 cash for a house for his personal use.

Required:

1. Analyze each item for its effects on the accounting equation of LDS for the year ended December 31.
   TIP: Transaction (*a*) is presented below as an example.

	Assets	**=**	**Liabilities**	**+**	**Stockholders' Equity**	
(*a*) Cash	+40,000	=			Common Stock	+40,000

   TIP: The new motor in transaction (*d*) is treated as an increase to the cost of the truck.
2. Record the effects of each item using a journal entry.
   TIP: Use the simplified journal entry format shown in this chapter's demonstration case.
3. Summarize the effects of the journal entries by account, using the T-account format shown in the chapter.
4. Prepare a classified balance sheet for LDS at December 31.
5. Using the balance sheet, indicate whether LDS's assets at the end of the year were financed primarily by liabilities or stockholders' equity.

E2-13 Explaining the Effects of Transactions on Balance Sheet Accounts Using T-Accounts

LO 2-1, 2-2, 2-3

Heavey and Lovas Furniture Repair Service, a company with two stockholders, began operations on June 1. The following T-accounts indicate the activities for the month of June.

Cash (A)		
(*a*) 17,000	10,000	(*b*)
	1,500	(*c*)

Supplies (A)	
(*c*) 1,500	

Buildings (A)	
(*b*) 50,000	

Notes Payable (L)	
	40,000 (*b*)

Common Stock (SE)	
	17,000 (*a*)

Required:

For each of the events (*a*)–(*c*), explain what transaction resulted in the indicated increases and/or decreases in the T-accounts.

E2-14 Calculating and Evaluating the Current Ratio

LO 2-1, 2-5

Columbia Sportswear Company

Columbia Sportswear Company reported the following in recent balance sheets (amounts in millions).

(in millions)	June 30, 2019	December 31, 2018
Assets		
Current Assets		
Cash	$ 524	$ 714
Accounts Receivable	281	449
Inventory	756	522
Prepaid Rent	101	80
Total Current Assets	1,662	1,765
Software	318	292
Equipment	682	312
Total Assets	$2,662	$2,369
Liabilities and Shareholders' Equity		
Liabilities		
Current Liabilities		
Accounts Payable	$ 511	$ 550
Notes Payable (short-term)	61	0
Income Tax Payable	6	23
Total Current Liabilities	578	573
Notes Payable (long-term)	429	105
Total Liabilities	1,007	678
Stockholders' Equity		
Common Stock	1	1
Retained Earnings	1,654	1,690
Total Shareholders' Equity	1,655	1,691
Total Liabilities and Shareholders' Equity	$2,662	$2,369

Required:

1. Calculate the current ratio (rounded to two decimal places) at June 30, 2019, and December 31, 2018.

2. Did the company's current ratio increase or decrease? What does this imply about the company's ability to pay its current liabilities as they come due?

3. What would Columbia's current ratio have been on June 30, 2019, if the company were to have paid down $10 (million) of its Accounts Payable? Does paying down Accounts Payable in this case increase or decrease the current ratio?

4. Are the company's total assets financed primarily by liabilities or stockholders' equity at June 30, 2019?

LO 2-1, 2-2, 2-3, 2-4, 2-5

E2-15 Analyzing and Recording Transactions, and Preparing and Evaluating a Balance Sheet

Business Sim Corp. (BSC) entered into the following four transactions: (a) Issued 1,000 common shares to Kelly in exchange for $12,000. (b) Borrowed $30,000 from the bank, promising to repay it in two years. (c) Bought computer equipment by signing check number 101 in the amount of $35,000 and signing a promissory note for $5,000 due in six months. This loan contains a clause ("covenant") that requires BSC to maintain a ratio of current assets to current liabilities of at least 1.3. (d) Received $900 of supplies and promised to pay for them in 30 days.

Required:

1. Analyze the accounting equation effects of each of these four transactions, using the format shown in the chapter.

2. Prepare journal entries for the transactions described above and post them to T-accounts.

3. Assuming BSC entered into no other activities during its first year ended September 30, prepare the company's classified balance sheet. Include a balance of zero in Retained Earnings.

4. Determine and explain whether BSC is complying with or violating its loan covenant.

COACHED PROBLEMS

CP2-1 Determining Financial Statement Effects of Various Transactions

LO 2-1, 2-2, 2-5

Ag Bio Tech (ABT) was organized on January 1 by four friends. Each organizer invested $10,000 in the company and, in turn, was issued 8,000 shares of common stock. To date, they are the only stockholders. During the first month (January), the company had the following five events:

a. Collected a total of $40,000 from the organizers and, in turn, issued common stock.
b. Purchased a building for $65,000, equipment for $16,000, and three acres of land for $18,000; paid $13,000 in cash and signed a note for the balance, which is due to be paid in 15 years.
c. One stockholder reported to the company that 500 shares of his ABT stock had been sold and transferred to another stockholder for $5,000 cash.
d. Purchased supplies for $3,000 cash.
e. Sold one acre of land for $6,000 cash to another company.

Required:

1. Was ABT organized as a partnership or corporation? Explain the basis for your answer.
2. During the first month, the records of the company were inadequate. You were asked to prepare a summary of the preceding transactions. To develop a quick assessment of their economic effects on ABT, you have decided to complete the spreadsheet that follows and to use plus (+) for increases and minus (−) for decreases for each account.

   TIP: Transaction (a) is presented below as an example.

Assets					=	Liabilities	+	Stockholders' Equity	
						Notes		**Common**	**Retained**
Cash	**Supplies**	**Land**	**Buildings**	**Equipment**	=	**Payable**		**Stock**	**Earnings**
(a) +40,000								+40,000	

3. Did you include the transaction between the two stockholders—event (c)—in the spreadsheet? Why?

   TIP: Think about whether this event caused ABT to receive or give up anything.

4. Based only on the completed spreadsheet, provide the following amounts (show computations):

   a. Total assets at the end of the month.
   b. Total liabilities at the end of the month.
   c. Total stockholders' equity at the end of the month.
   d. Cash balance at the end of the month.
   e. Total current assets at the end of the month.

5. As of January 31, has the financing for ABT's investment in assets primarily come from liabilities or stockholders' equity?

CP2-2 Recording Transactions (in a Journal and T-Accounts); Preparing a Trial Balance; Preparing and Interpreting the Balance Sheet

LO 2-1, 2-2, 2-3, 2-4, 2-5

Athletic Performance Company (APC) was incorporated as a private company. The company's accounts included the following at July 1:

Accounts Payable	$ 4,000	Land	$90,000
Buildings	200,000	Notes Payable (long-term)	17,000
Cash	16,000	Retained Earnings	0
Common Stock	308,000	Supplies	5,000
Equipment	18,000		

During the month of July, the company had the following activities:

a. Issued 2,000 shares of common stock for $200,000 cash.
b. Borrowed $30,000 cash from a local bank, payable in two years.
c. Bought a building for $141,000; paid $41,000 in cash and signed a three-year note for the balance.
d. Paid cash for equipment that cost $100,000.
e. Purchased supplies for $10,000 on account.

Required:

1. Analyze transactions (*a*)–(*e*) to determine their effects on the accounting equation. Use a spreadsheet format with a column for each account, enter the July 1 amounts in the first line under the account headings, and calculate ending balances as shown in Exhibit 2.5.

    TIP: You won't need new accounts to record the transactions described above, so have a quick look at the ones listed before you begin.

    TIP: In transaction (*c*), three different accounts are affected.

2. Record the transaction effects determined in requirement 1 using journal entries.

3. Summarize the journal entry effects from requirement 2 using T-accounts.

    TIP: Create a T-account for each account listed above. Enter the July 1 balances as the month's beginning balances.

4. Prepare a trial balance at July 31.

5. Prepare a classified balance sheet at July 31.

6. As of July 31, has the financing for APC's investment in assets primarily come from liabilities or stockholders' equity?

LO 2-1, 2-2, 2-3, 2-4, 2-5   **CP2-3   Recording Transactions (in a Journal and T-Accounts); Preparing and Interpreting the Balance Sheet**

Performance Plastics Company (PPC) has been operating for three years. The beginning account balances are:

Cash	$ 35,000	Buildings	$120,000
Accounts Receivable	5,000	Land	30,000
Inventory	40,000	Accounts Payable	37,000
Supplies	5,000	Notes Payable (due in three years)	80,000
Notes Receivable (due in three years)	2,000	Common Stock	150,000
Equipment	80,000	Retained Earnings	50,000

During the year, the company had the following summarized activities:

a. Purchased equipment that cost $21,000; paid $5,000 cash and signed a two-year note for the balance.

b. Issued an additional 2,000 shares of common stock for $20,000 cash.

c. Borrowed $50,000 cash from a local bank, payable June 30, in two years.

d. Purchased supplies for $4,000 cash.

e. Built an addition to the factory buildings for $41,000; paid $12,000 in cash and signed a three-year note for the balance.

f. Hired a new president to start January 1 of next year. The contract was for $95,000 for each full year worked.

Required:

1. Analyze transactions (*a*)–(*f*) to determine their effects on the accounting equation.

    TIP: You won't need new accounts to record the transactions described above, so have a quick look at the ones listed in the beginning of this question before you begin.

    TIP: In transaction (*e*), three different accounts are affected.

    TIP: In transaction (*f*), consider whether PPC owes anything to its new president for the current year ended December 31.

2. Record the transaction effects determined in requirement 1 using journal entries.

3. Summarize the journal entry effects from requirement 2. Use T-accounts if this requirement is being completed manually; if you are using the general ledger tool in Connect, the journal entries will have been posted automatically to general ledger accounts that are similar in appearance to Exhibit 2.9.

4. Explain your response to event (*f*).

5. Prepare a classified balance sheet at December 31.

6. As of December 31, has the financing for PPC's investment in assets primarily come from liabilities or stockholders' equity?

GROUP A PROBLEMS

 connect

PA2-1 Determining Financial Statement Effects of Various Transactions

LO 2-1, 2-2, 2-5

Mallard Incorporated (MI) is a small manufacturing company that makes model trains to sell to toy stores. It has a small service department that repairs customers' trains for a fee. The company has been in business for five years. At the end of the previous year, the accounting records reflected total assets of $500,000 and total liabilities of $200,000. During the current year, the following summarized events occurred:

a. Issued additional shares of common stock for $100,000 cash.
b. Borrowed $120,000 cash from the bank and signed a 10-year note.
c. Built an addition on the buildings for $200,000 and paid cash to the contractor.
d. Purchased equipment for the new addition for $30,000, paying $3,000 in cash and signing a note for the balance due in two years.
e. Returned a $3,000 piece of equipment, from (*d*), because it proved to be defective; received a reduction of the notes payable.
f. Purchased a delivery truck (equipment) for $10,000; paid $7,000 cash and signed a two-year note for the remainder.
g. A stockholder sold $5,000 of his stock in Mallard Incorporated to his neighbor.

Required:

1. Complete the spreadsheet that follows, using plus (+) for increases and minus (−) for decreases for each account. The first transaction is used as an example.

	Assets			=	Liabilities	+	Stockholders' Equity	
							Common Stock	Retained Earnings
	Cash	Equipment	Buildings	=	Notes Payable			
(*a*)	+100,000						+100,000	

2. Did you include event (*g*) in the spreadsheet? Why or why not?
3. Based on beginning balances plus the completed spreadsheet, provide the following amounts (show computations):
   a. Total assets at the end of the year.
   b. Total liabilities at the end of the year.
   c. Total stockholders' equity at the end of the year.
4. As of the current year-end, has the financing for MI's investment in assets primarily come from liabilities or stockholders' equity?

PA2-2 Recording Transactions (in a Journal and T-Accounts); Preparing a Trial Balance; Preparing and Interpreting the Balance Sheet

LO 2-1, 2-2, 2-3, 2-4, 2-5

Deliberate Speed Corporation (DSC) was incorporated as a private company. The company's accounts included the following at June 30:

Accounts Payable	$ 20,000	Land	$200,000
Buildings	100,000	Notes Payable (long-term)	2,000
Cash	36,000	Retained Earnings	259,000
Common Stock	180,000	Supplies	7,000
Equipment	118,000		

During the month of July, the company had the following activities:

a. Issued 4,000 shares of common stock for $400,000 cash.
b. Borrowed $100,000 cash from a local bank, payable in two years.
c. Bought a building for $182,000; paid $82,000 in cash and signed a three-year note for the balance.
d. Paid cash for equipment that cost $200,000.
e. Purchased supplies for $30,000 on account.

Required:

1. Analyze transactions (*a*)–(*e*) to determine their effects on the accounting equation, similar to Exhibit 2.5.
2. Record the transaction effects determined in requirement 1 using a journal entry format.
3. Summarize the journal entry effects from requirement 2 using T-accounts.
4. Prepare a trial balance at July 31.
5. Prepare a classified balance sheet at July 31.
6. As of July 31, has the financing for DSC's investment in assets primarily come from liabilities or stockholders' equity?

LO 2-1, 2-2, 2-3, 2-4, 2-5

PA2-3 Recording Transactions (in a Journal and T-Accounts); Preparing and Interpreting the Balance Sheet

Ethan Allen Interiors Inc.

Ethan Allen Interiors Inc. is a leading manufacturer and retailer of home furnishings in the United States and abroad. The following is adapted from Ethan Allen's June 30, 2019, trial balance. (The amounts shown represent millions of dollars.)

Accounts Payable	$ 93	Notes Payable (long-term)	$23
Accounts Receivable	14	Notes Payable (short-term)	9
Cash	21	Prepaid Rent	19
Common Stock	363	Retained Earnings	1
Equipment	245	Salaries and Wages Payable	21
Inventory	162	Software	49

Assume that the following events occurred in the following quarter.

a. Paid $10 cash for additional inventory.
b. Issued additional shares of common stock for $20 in cash.
c. Purchased equipment for $170; paid $15 in cash and signed a note to pay the remaining $155 in two years.
d. Signed a short-term note to borrow $10 cash.
e. Conducted negotiations to purchase a sawmill, which is expected to cost $36.

Required:

Noodlecake

1. Calculate Ethan Allen's current ratio at June 30, 2019, prior to the transactions listed above. Based on this calculation and the analysis of Noodlecake's current ratio in the chapter, indicate which company is in a better position to pay liabilities as they come due in the next year.
2. Analyze transactions (*a*)–(*e*) to determine their effects on the accounting equation. Use the format shown in the demonstration case.
3. Record the transaction effects determined in requirement 2 using journal entries.
4. Using the June 30, 2019, ending balances as the beginning balances for the July–September 2019 quarter, summarize the journal entry effects from requirement 3. Use T-accounts if this requirement is being completed manually; if you are using the general ledger tool in Connect, the journal entries will have been posted automatically to general ledger accounts that are similar in appearance to Exhibit 2.9.
5. Explain your response to event (*e*).
6. Prepare a classified balance sheet at September 30, 2019.
7. Use your response to requirement 6 to calculate Ethan Allen's current ratio after the transactions listed in (*a*)–(*e*). Based on this calculation and the calculation in requirement 1, indicate whether the above transactions increase or decrease the company's ability to pay current liabilities as they come due in the next year.

GROUP B PROBLEMS

PB2-1 Determining Financial Statement Effects of Various Transactions

LO 2-1, 2-2, 2-5

Swish Watch Corporation manufactures, sells, and services expensive watches. The company has been in business for three years. At the end of the previous year, the accounting records reported total assets of $2,255,000 and total liabilities of $1,780,000. During the current year, the following summarized events occurred:

a. Issued additional shares of common stock for $109,000 cash.
b. Borrowed $186,000 cash from the bank and signed a 10-year note.
c. A stockholder sold $5,000 of his stock in Swish Watch Corporation to another investor.
d. Built an addition on the factory buildings for $200,000 and paid cash to the contractor.
e. Purchased equipment for the new addition for $44,000, paying $12,000 in cash and signing a two-year note for the balance.
f. Returned a $4,000 piece of equipment, from (e), because it proved to be defective; received a cash refund.

Required:

1. Complete the spreadsheet that follows, using plus (+) for increases and minus (−) for decreases for each account. The first transaction is used as an example.

	Assets			=	Liabilities	+	Stockholders' Equity	
	Cash	Equipment	Buildings	=	Notes Payable		Common Stock	Retained Earnings
(a)	+109,000						+109,000	

2. Did you include event (c) in the spreadsheet? Why?
3. Based on beginning balances plus the completed spreadsheet, provide the following amounts (show computations):
    a. Total assets at the end of the year.
    b. Total liabilities at the end of the year.
    c. Total stockholders' equity at the end of the year.
4. At the end of the current year, has the financing for Swish Watch Corporation's investment in assets primarily come from liabilities or stockholders' equity?

PB2-2 Recording Transactions (in a Journal and T-Accounts); Preparing a Trial Balance; Preparing and Interpreting the Balance Sheet

LO 2-1, 2-2, 2-3, 2-4, 2-5

Bearings & Brakes Corporation (B&B) was incorporated as a private company. The company's accounts included the following at June 30:

Accounts Payable	$ 50,000	Land	$444,000
Buildings	500,000	Notes Payable (long-term)	5,000
Cash	90,000	Retained Earnings	966,000
Common Stock	170,000	Supplies	9,000
Equipment	148,000		

During the month of July, the company had the following activities:

a. Issued 6,000 shares of common stock for $600,000 cash.
b. Borrowed $60,000 cash from a local bank, payable in four years.
c. Bought a building for $166,000; paid $66,000 in cash and signed a three-year note for the balance.
d. Paid cash for equipment that cost $90,000.
e. Purchased supplies for $90,000 on account.

Required:

1. Analyze transactions (*a*)–(*e*) to determine their effects on the accounting equation. Use the format shown in the demonstration case.
2. Record the transaction effects determined in requirement 1 using a journal entry format.
3. Summarize the journal entry effects from requirement 2 using T-accounts.
4. Prepare a trial balance at July 31.
5. Prepare a classified balance sheet at July 31.
6. As of July 31, has the financing for B&B's investment in assets primarily come from liabilities or stockholders' equity?

LO 2-1, 2-2, 2-3, 2-4, 2-5

PB2-3 Recording Transactions (in a Journal and T-Accounts); Preparing and Interpreting the Balance Sheet

Shake Shack

Shake Shack Inc., which began as a hot dog stand in 2001, now has more than 200 locations worldwide. The following is adapted from Shake Shack's financial statements for the quarter ended June 26, 2019. Dollars are reported in millions.

Accounts Payable	$ 38	Inventory	$ 2
Accounts Receivable	14	Notes Payable (long-term)	519
Cash	29	Notes Payable (short-term)	40
Common Stock	255	Prepaid Rent	6
Equipment	544	Retained Earnings	46
Intangible Assets	267	Short-Term Investments	36

Assume that the following events occurred in the following quarter, which ended September 26, 2019. Dollars are in millions.

a. Paid $10 cash for additional intangible assets.
b. Issued additional shares of common stock for $50 in cash.
c. Purchased equipment; paid $30 in cash and signed additional long-term loans for $70.
d. Paid $9 cash for accounts payable owed at June 26.
e. Conducted negotiations to purchase a farm, which is expected to cost $15.

Required:

1. Calculate Shake Shack's current ratio at June 26, 2019, prior to the transactions listed above.
2. Analyze transactions (*a*)–(*e*) to determine their effects on the accounting equation. Use the format shown in the demonstration case.
3. Record the transaction effects determined in requirement 2 using journal entries.
4. Using the June 26, 2019, ending balances (reported above) as the beginning balances for the July–September 2019 quarter, summarize the journal entry effects from requirement 3. Use T-accounts if this requirement is being completed manually; if you are using the general ledger tool in Connect, the journal entries will have been posted automatically to general ledger accounts that are similar in appearance to Exhibit 2.9.
5. Explain your response to event (*e*).
6. Prepare a classified balance sheet at September 26, 2019.
7. Use your response to requirement 6 to calculate Shake Shack's current ratio after the transactions listed in (*a*)–(*e*). Based on this calculation and the calculation in requirement 1, indicate whether the above transactions increase or decrease the company's ability to pay liabilities as they come due in the next year.

SKILLS DEVELOPMENT CASES

LO 2-1, 2-4, 2-5

S2-1 Finding and Analyzing Financial Information

The Home Depot

Refer to the financial statements of **The Home Depot** in Appendix A at the end of this book. (Note: Fiscal 2019 for The Home Depot runs from February 4, 2019, to February 2, 2020. See S1-1 for further explanation of its fiscal periods.)

1.   What were the year-end dates for the "Fiscal 2019" and "Fiscal 2018" periods?

	Fiscal 2019	Fiscal 2018
a.	February 3, 2019	February 2, 2018
b.	February 4, 2019	January 28, 2018
c.	February 4, 2019	February 2, 2020
d.	February 2, 2020	February 3, 2019

2.   Which of the following are the amounts in the company's accounting equation (A = L + SE) for the 2019 fiscal year-end?

   a. $51,236 = $54,352 + $(3,116)
   b. $54,352 = $51,236 + $3,116
   c. $110,225 = $72,653 + $37,372
   d. $14,715 = $3,473 + $11,242

3.   What is the company's current ratio at February 2, 2020?

   a. 1.08
   b. 0.34
   c. 0.39
   d. 1.07

4.   What does the company's current ratio in requirement 3 indicate?

   a. The company has more than one dollar of current assets for every dollar of current liabilities due in the next year.
   b. The company has less than one dollar of current assets for every dollar of current liabilities due in the next year.
   c. Less than half of the company's assets are current.
   d. Less than half of the company's liabilities are current.

S2-2 Finding and Analyzing Financial Information

LO 2-1, 2-4, 2-5

Refer to the financial statements of Lowe's Companies, Inc., in Appendix B. (Note: Fiscal 2019 for Lowe's runs from February 2, 2019, to January 31, 2020. See S1-1 for further explanation.)

Lowe's

1.   What were the year-end dates for the "Fiscal 2019" and "Fiscal 2018" periods?

	Fiscal 2019	Fiscal 2018
a.	January 31, 2019	February 1, 2018
b.	January 31, 2020	February 1, 2019
c.	February 2, 2019	January 31, 2020
d.	January 31, 2020	February 2, 2019

2.   Which of the following are the amounts in the company's accounting equation (A = L + SE) for the 2019 fiscal year-end?

   a. $34,508 = $30,864 + $3,644
   b. $39,471 = $37,499 + $1,972
   c. $72,148 = $49,205 + $22,943
   d. $5,623 = $1,342 + $4,281

3.   What is the company's current ratio at February 2, 2020?

   a. 0.39
   b. 0.41
   c. 0.98
   d. 1.01

4.   What does the company's current ratio in requirement 3 indicate?

   a. The company has more than one dollar of current assets for every dollar of current liabilities due in the next year.
   b. The company has less than one dollar of current assets for every dollar of current liabilities due in the next year.
   c. Less than half of the company's assets are current.
   d. Less than half of the company's liabilities are current.

LO 2-1, 2-4, 2-5

S2-3 Team Research, Financial Analysis, Technology, and Communication: Examining the Balance Sheet

As a team, select an industry to analyze. Using your web browser, each team member should access the annual report or 10-K for one publicly traded company in the industry, with each member selecting a different company. (See S1-3 in Chapter 1 for a description of possible resources for these tasks.)

Required:

1. On an individual basis, each team member should write a short report that lists the following information.
   a. The date of the balance sheet.
   b. The major noncurrent asset accounts and any significant changes in them.
   c. The major noncurrent liability accounts and any significant changes in them.
   d. Any significant changes in total stockholders' equity.
   e. Whether financing for the investment in assets primarily comes from liabilities or stockholders' equity.

2. Then, as a team, write a short report comparing and contrasting your companies using the above dimensions. Discuss any similarities across the companies that you as a team observe and provide potential explanations for any differences discovered.

LO 2-1, 2-4, 2-5

S2-4 Ethical Reasoning, Critical Thinking, and Communication: A Real-Life Fraud

In the world of financial fraud, a "Ponzi scheme" is famous. Here is the story behind how the scam got its name. Charles Ponzi started the Security Exchange Company on December 26, 1919. He thought he had discovered a way to purchase American stamps in a foreign country at significantly lower amounts than they were worth in the United States. He claimed his idea was so successful that anyone who gave money to his company would be repaid their original loan plus 50 percent interest within 90 days. Friends and family quickly offered their money to Ponzi and they were handsomely rewarded, being repaid their original loan and the 50 percent interest within just 45 days. Thanks to an article in *The New York Times*, word spread quickly about Ponzi's business, attracting thousands of people seeking a similar payback. He might have had a successful business had his idea actually worked. The problem, however, was that it didn't. The 50 percent interest paid to early investors did not come from the profits of a successful underlying business idea (which didn't even exist) but instead was obtained fraudulently from funds contributed by later lenders. Eventually, the Ponzi scheme collapsed on August 10, 1920, after an auditor examined his accounting records.

Required:

1. Assume that on December 27, 1919, Ponzi's first three lenders provided his company with $5,000 each. Use the basic accounting equation to show the effects of these transactions on December 27, 1919.
2. If the first two lenders are repaid their original loan amounts plus the 50 percent interest promised to them, how much cash is left in Ponzi's business to repay the third lender? Given what you discovered, how was it possible for Ponzi's company to remain in "business" for over eight months?
3. Who was harmed by Ponzi's scheme?

Epilogue: After taking in nearly $15 million from 40,000 people, Ponzi's company failed with just $1.5 million in total assets. Ponzi spent four years in prison before jumping bail, to become involved in fraudulently selling swampland in Florida. We're not kidding. In December 2008, Bernard Madoff was arrested for using a modern-day Ponzi scheme to defraud investors of $65,000,000,000. On June 29, 2009, he was sentenced to 150 years in prison.

LO 2-1, 2-5

S2-5 Ethical Reasoning, Critical Thinking, and Communication: A Mini-Case

You work as an accountant for a small land development company that desperately needs additional financing to continue in business. The president of your company is meeting with the manager of a local bank at the end of the month to try to obtain this financing. The president has approached you with two ideas to improve the company's reported financial position. First, he claims that because a big part of the company's value comes from its knowledgeable and dedicated employees, you should report their "Intellectual Abilities" as an asset on the balance sheet. Second, he claims that by reporting the company's land on the balance sheet at its cost, rather than the much higher amount that real estate appraisers say it's really worth, the company is understating the true value of its assets.

Required:

1. Thinking back to Chapter 1, why do you think the president is so concerned with the amount of assets reported on the balance sheet?
2. What accounting concept introduced in Chapter 2 relates to the president's first suggestion to report "Intellectual Abilities" as an asset?
3. What accounting concept introduced in Chapter 2 relates to the president's second suggestion to report the land's current value?
4. Who might be hurt by the president's suggestions, if you were to do as he asks? What should you do?

S2-6 Financial Analysis and Critical Thinking: Evaluating the Reliability of a Balance Sheet

LO 2-1, 2-4, 2-5

Complete this case, available online in the Connect eBook, which involves identifying flaws in a company's balance sheet.

S2-7 Using Technology to Analyze Transactions and Prepare a Balance Sheet

LO 2-1, 2-2

Complete this case involving Elizabeth Arden, available online in the Connect eBook. By completing this case, you will learn to use a spreadsheet to capture the accounting equation effects of basic transactions.

Elizabeth Arden

CONTINUING CASE

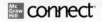

CC2-1 Accounting for the Establishment of a Business

LO 2-1, 2-2, 2-3, 2-4, 2-5

Nicole has decided that she is going to start her business, Nicole's Getaway Spa (NGS). A lot has to be done when starting a new business. Here are some transactions that have occurred prior to April 30.

a. Received $80,000 cash when issuing 8,000 new common shares.
b. Purchased land by paying $2,000 cash and signing a note payable for $7,000 due in three years.
c. Hired a new aesthetician for a salary of $1,000 a month, starting next month.
d. NGS purchased a company car for $18,000 cash (list price of $21,000) to assist in running errands for the business.
e. Bought and received $1,000 in supplies for the spa on credit.
f. Paid $350 of the amount owed in (e).
g. Nicole sold 100 of her own personal shares to Raea Gooding for $300.

Required:

1. For each of the events, prepare journal entries if a transaction exists, checking that debits equal credits. If a transaction does not exist, explain why there is no transaction.
2. Assuming that the beginning balances in each of the accounts are zero, complete T-accounts to summarize the transactions in (a)–(g).
3. Prepare a classified balance sheet at April 30 using the information given in the transactions.
4. Calculate the current ratio at April 30. What does this ratio indicate about the ability of NGS to pay its current liabilities?

DATA ANALYTICS EXERCISES

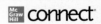

Data Analytics Exercises are auto-graded exercises offering detailed data visualization, interpretation, and analysis, and are available for assignment in Connect.

3

CHAPTER THREE

The Income Statement

YOUR LEARNING OBJECTIVES

LO 3-1 Describe common operating transactions and select appropriate income statement account titles.

LO 3-2 Explain and apply the revenue and expense recognition principles.

LO 3-3 Analyze, record, and summarize the effects of operating transactions using the accounting equation, journal entries, and T-accounts.

LO 3-4 Prepare an unadjusted trial balance.

LO 3-5 Evaluate net profit margin, but beware of income statement limitations.

THAT WAS THEN

In the previous chapter, you learned how to analyze, record, and summarize the effects of transactions on balance sheet accounts.

FOCUS COMPANY: NOODLECAKE STUDIOS, INC.

I n Chapter 2, Jordan and Ty established their game app company, Noodlecake Studios. Using money they had contributed to the company plus a loan from the bank, Noodlecake purchased computer equipment, software, and other assets needed to run the business. The company's first game was the *Super Stickman Golf* series, which they initially sold in the App Store. Later, they added award-winner *Chameleon Run* to their list of successful games. They also learned to "port" these games to Android-friendly versions for sale in Google Play, and soon started offering similar porting services to other app developers for a fee. Most recently, they have begun producing games for Apple Arcade, such as *The Enchanted World* (pictured above). Such day-to-day **operating activities determine whether the company makes a profit.**

The first goal of this chapter is to help you understand common operating activities and see how an income statement indicates whether a business generated a profit (or loss). Then, we'll show how the transaction analysis approach from Chapter 2 can be used to analyze and record transactions affecting the income statement. Finally, at the end of the chapter, we will highlight some uses and limitations of the income statement.

THIS IS NOW

This chapter focuses on analyzing, recording, and summarizing the effects of operating transactions on balance sheet and income statement accounts.

Logo: Noodlecake Studios, Inc.

97

Understand the business	Study the accounting methods	Evaluate the results	Review the chapter
• Operating activities • Income statement accounts	• Cash basis accounting • Accrual basis accounting • The expanded accounting equation • Unadjusted trial balance • Review of revenues and expenses	• Net profit margin • Income statement limitations	• Demonstration cases • Chapter summary • Key terms • Homework helper • Practice material

Understand the Business

Learning Objective 3-1
Describe common operating transactions and select appropriate income statement account titles.

OPERATING ACTIVITIES

Operating activities are the day-to-day functions involved in running a business. Unlike the investing and financing activities in Chapter 2 that occur infrequently and typically produce long-lasting effects, operating activities occur regularly and often have a shorter duration of effect. Operating activities include buying goods and services from suppliers and employees, selling goods and services to customers, and collecting cash from customers. The period from buying goods and services through to collecting cash from customers is known as the operating cycle. Exhibit 3.1 illustrates the operating cycle for Noodlecake.

EXHIBIT 3.1 Typical Operating Cycle Activities

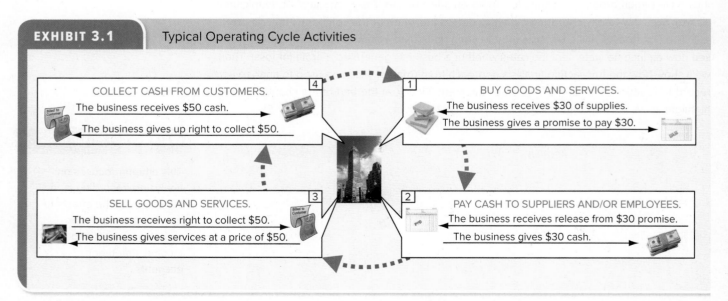

COLLECT CASH FROM CUSTOMERS. [4]
The business receives $50 cash.
The business gives up right to collect $50.

BUY GOODS AND SERVICES. [1]
The business receives $30 of supplies.
The business gives a promise to pay $30.

SELL GOODS AND SERVICES. [3]
The business receives right to collect $50.
The business gives services at a price of $50.

PAY CASH TO SUPPLIERS AND/OR EMPLOYEES. [2]
The business receives release from $30 promise.
The business gives $30 cash.

Building photo: Glow Images/Getty Images; Money photo: Comstock/Getty Images; Notes photo: Comstock Images/Alamy Stock Photo; Invoice photo: Studio 101/Alamy Stock Photo; Invoice paid photo: Studio 101/Alamy Stock Photo; App photo: Noodlecake Studios, Inc.

Although most businesses have the same steps in their operating cycles, the length of time for each step varies from company to company. For example, Noodlecake collects cash from some customers within moments of making a sale, whereas Microsoft might wait several weeks to collect on software it sells to Dell and other computer companies.

To be successful, Jordan must closely monitor Noodlecake's operating activities. **Operating activities are the primary source of revenues and expenses** and, thus, can determine whether a company earns a profit (or incurs a loss). Although Jordan may intuitively sense how his business is doing, a more reliable management approach is to evaluate the revenues and expenses reported on the income statement. Jordan takes a quick look at the income statement Laurie had prepared (Exhibit 3.2) based on the operating activities that were expected for Noodlecake (in Chapter 1). This projected income statement will provide a benchmark for him to evaluate actual results.

EXHIBIT 3.2	Income Statement		
			Explanation

NOODLECAKE STUDIOS, INC. Income Statement (Projected) For the Month Ended September 30, 2021		Who: Name of the business What: Title of the statement When: Accounting period
Revenues		
Sales Revenue	$9,000	Price charged for apps sold to customers in September
Service Revenue	3,000	Price charged for services provided in September
Total Revenues	12,000	**Total revenues generated during September**
Expenses		
Salaries and Wages Expense	5,000	Cost of employee wages for work done in September
Rent Expense	2,500	Cost of rent for the month of September
Utilities Expense	1,600	Cost of utilities used in September
Insurance Expense	300	Cost of insurance coverage for September
Advertising Expense	100	Cost of advertising done in September
Income Tax Expense	500	Cost of taxes on September's income
Total Expenses	10,000	**Total expenses in September to generate revenues**
Net Income	$2,000	**Difference between total revenues and total expenses**

INCOME STATEMENT ACCOUNTS

The income statement summarizes the financial impact of operating activities undertaken by the company during the accounting period. It includes three main sections: revenues, expenses, and net income.

Revenues

Revenues are the prices a business charges its customers when it provides goods or services. If Noodlecake sells 9,000 downloads of its apps in September and charges $1 per download, Sales Revenue would total $9,000. Revenue is reported when the company fulfills its promise to transfer control of a good or service to a customer, regardless of when the company is paid by the customer. Revenue generated during the period is reported in the first section of the income statement body.

Expenses

Expenses are costs of operating the business, incurred to generate revenues in the period covered by the income statement. Expenses are reported when the company uses something, like space in a building, supplies for providing services, or the efforts of employees. Basically,

> **YOU SHOULD KNOW**
>
> **Revenues:** Prices charged when providing goods or services, resulting in increases in assets or decreases in liabilities.
> **Expenses:** Costs incurred when providing goods or services during the current period, resulting in decreases in assets or increases in liabilities.

Logo: Noodlecake Studios, Inc.

whenever a business uses up its resources to generate revenues during the period, it reports an expense, regardless of when the company pays for the resources. Expenses follow revenues in the body of the income statement. Some of Noodlecake's typical expenses are listed in the income statement shown in Exhibit 3.2.

Net Income

Net income is calculated by subtracting expenses from revenues; it is a total, not an account like Sales Revenue or Rent Expense. Because it is a total, net income summarizes the overall impact of revenues and expenses in a single number. It is called a net loss if expenses are greater than revenues, and net income if revenues are greater than expenses. Net income indicates the amount by which stockholders' equity increases as a result of a company's profitable operations. For this reason, net income (or loss) is a closely watched measure of a company's success.

Exhibit 3.2 shows how revenues, expenses, and net income would be reported in Noodlecake's income statement. Each account title describes the specific type of revenue or expense arising from the business's particular operations. Noodlecake reports "Sales Revenue," whereas Netflix reports "Movie Subscription Revenue."

The income statement in Exhibit 3.2 is for the month ended September 30, 2021. As it turns out, September 30, 2021, is a Thursday. There is nothing particularly special about this date—it's just the last day of the month. By dividing the company's long life into shorter chunks of time, Jordan applies the **time period assumption**. It allows him to measure and evaluate Noodlecake's financial performance on a timely basis. If net income is low in the current month, Jordan will find out about it quickly and be able to take steps to become more profitable in the following month.

Notice that the income statement reports the financial effects of business activities from just the current period. This is a key distinction between the income statement and the balance sheet. **The revenues and expenses on an income statement report the financial impact of activities in just the current period, whereas items on a balance sheet will continue to have a financial impact beyond the end of the current period. Balance sheet accounts are considered permanent, whereas income statement accounts are considered temporary.** Another way people describe this difference is **the balance sheet takes stock of what exists at a point in time, whereas the income statement depicts a flow of what happened over a period of time.**

💡 How's it going? — Self-Study Practice

For each item listed below, indicate whether the company should report it on the income statement this period (yes/no). If yes, indicate an appropriate account title for the item described.

Description	Yes/No	Account Title
1. Bank of America charges customers a monthly service fee.	_____	_____
2. Target buys a new building to use as a retail store.	_____	_____
3. Dell pays to deliver computers to customers.	_____	_____
4. Pizza Hut buys supplies to be used next month.	_____	_____
5. Snap pays this week's wages to employees.	_____	_____

After you have finished, check your answers with the solution.

Solution to Self-Study Practice

	Yes/No	Account Title
1.	Yes	Service Revenue
2.	No	(a building is an asset, not an expense)
3.	Yes	Delivery Expense
4.	No	(supplies are assets until used up)
5.	Yes	Salaries and Wages Expense

SPOTLIGHT ON	Ethics

35 Days Hath September?

It's too bad the managers at CA, Inc., didn't learn the **time period assumption.** They were charged with financial statement fraud for improperly recording 35 days of sales in September—a month that has only 30 days. To make it look like managers had met their September sales targets, CA included sales from the first five days of October in its September income statement. This accounting fraud led managers to be paid bonuses they hadn't earned and tricked investors into thinking CA was a successful company. When the truth was revealed later, CA's stockholders quickly abandoned the company, causing its stock price to fall 43 percent in a single day. CA ultimately paid stockholders $225 million to make up for its bad accounting and agreed to ensure all inappropriate management bonuses were paid back to the company. In addition, marketing and accounting personnel were sent to jail. In November 2019, *The Wall Street Journal* reported the Securities and Exchange Commission was investigating Under Armour for similar issues. Proper revenue reporting is obviously a very serious matter.

Study the Accounting Methods

CASH BASIS ACCOUNTING

Many people gauge their financial performance by monitoring increases and decreases in their bank account balance. The change in bank balance can give a decent measure of financial performance if the cash flows (in and out) occur close in time to the activities that cause those cash flows. Reporting income on this basis, called **cash basis accounting**, may be fine for managing personal finances, but not for running a business.

Cash basis accounting doesn't measure financial performance very well when transactions are conducted using credit rather than cash. Credit often introduces a significant delay between the time an activity occurs and the time it impacts a bank account balance. If you are paid for work once a month, for example, the results of your hard work don't show up until the end of the month. Similarly, if you go crazy with your credit card at the mall, these transactions won't affect your bank balance until you pay the bill the following month.

Because most companies use credit for their transactions, cash basis accounting is not likely to correspond to the business activities that actually occur during a given period. Imagine Noodlecake paying its employees to provide services in one month but not receiving the customer's payment for these services until the following month. Under cash basis accounting, Noodlecake would report expenses in Month 1 but wouldn't report revenue until Month 2 when it received payment from its customer. This cash basis accounting leads to a distorted view of the company's financial performance, as shown in Exhibit 3.3.

> **YOU SHOULD KNOW**
>
> **Cash Basis Accounting:** Recording revenues when cash is received and expenses when cash is paid.

EXHIBIT 3.3	Cash Basis Can Distort Reported Profits

	MONTH 1		MONTH 2
	(No cash received, but **cash is paid**)		(No cash paid, but **cash is received**)
Revenues	$ 0	Revenues	$15,000
Expenses	10,000	Expenses	0
Net Income (Loss)	$ (10,000)	Net Income	$15,000

Under cash basis accounting, the company would report a net loss in Month 1 and a huge net income in Month 2, when the truth is the business activities generate revenue of $15,000, expenses of $10,000, and net income of $5,000, all of which relate to activities in Month 1 when the services were given. A better method of accounting is needed—one that reports the revenues and related expenses during the same period.

ACCRUAL BASIS ACCOUNTING

An alternative method of accounting is to report revenues and expenses when services are provided, regardless of when cash is received or paid. This approach, called **accrual basis accounting**, more accurately measures the profits arising from a company's activities. As shown in Exhibit 3.4, accrual basis accounting would require that Noodlecake report all its revenues, expenses, and net income in the period the service occurs (Month 1). In the following month, if Noodlecake doesn't provide additional services, it does not report revenues and expenses.

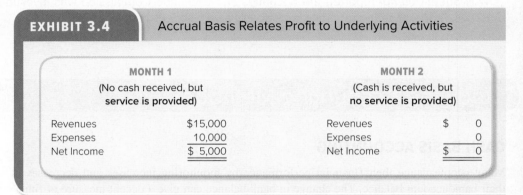

EXHIBIT 3.4	Accrual Basis Relates Profit to Underlying Activities		
MONTH 1 (No cash received, but service is provided)		**MONTH 2** (Cash is received, but no service is provided)	
Revenues	$15,000	Revenues	$ 0
Expenses	10,000	Expenses	0
Net Income	$ 5,000	Net Income	$ 0

According to GAAP and IFRS, the accrual basis is the only acceptable method for external reporting of income. The cash basis can be used internally by some small companies, but GAAP and IFRS do not allow it for external reporting. The "rule of accrual" is the financial effects of business activities are measured and reported when the activities actually occur, not when the cash related to them is received or paid. The two basic accounting principles that determine when revenues and expenses are recognized under accrual basis accounting are called the revenue recognition and expense recognition principles.

Revenue Recognition Principle

At its core, **the revenue recognition principle says a seller should report revenue when it provides goods or services to customers, in the amount the seller expects to be entitled to receive.** The core revenue recognition principle answers two questions:

Q1: When? Revenue is reported when the seller performs work promised to the customer,

Q2: How much? in the amount the seller expects to be entitled to receive from the customer.

The core revenue recognition principle is applied by following five steps, shown in Exhibit 3.5. We explain these five steps below.

Step 1.   **Identify the contract.** A contract is any agreement between a seller and customer that creates legal rights and obligations. It can be written, verbal, or merely implied. Starbucks establishes a contract when it agrees to sell you a Frappuccino, even though there's no legal paperwork.

Step 2.   **Identify the seller's performance obligation(s).** A performance obligation is the work the seller promises to do for the customer. Usually, performance obligations involve transferring control of goods or services to a customer. Some contracts involve only one performance obligation ("*a tall mocha Frappuccino, please*"). Others involve multiple obligations: Lifetime Fitness makes two promises when it sells a membership that includes a

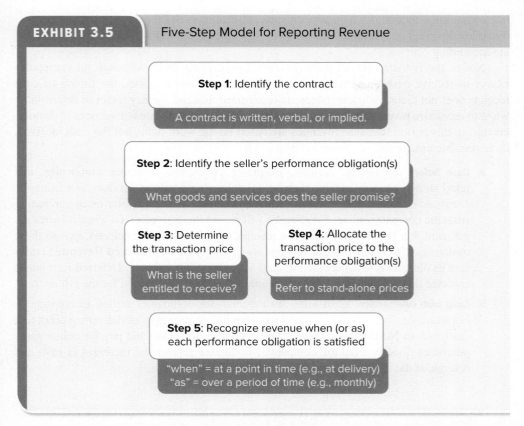

EXHIBIT 3.5 | Five-Step Model for Reporting Revenue

Step 1: Identify the contract

A contract is written, verbal, or implied.

Step 2: Identify the seller's performance obligation(s)

What goods and services does the seller promise?

Step 3: Determine the transaction price

What is the seller entitled to receive?

Step 4: Allocate the transaction price to the performance obligation(s)

Refer to stand-alone prices

Step 5: Recognize revenue when (or as) each performance obligation is satisfied

"when" = at a point in time (e.g., at delivery)
"as" = over a period of time (e.g., monthly)

session with a personal trainer, so it has two performance obligations: provide a year of member privileges plus offer a training session.

Step 3. **Determine the transaction price.** The transaction price is the amount the seller expects to be entitled to receive from the customer. This is the amount shown on Macy's clothing tags or in the menu at The Cheesecake Factory. The words "entitled to" imply any problems in later collecting those amounts are accounted for separately (as we show in Chapter 8).

Step 4. **Allocate the transaction price to the performance obligation(s).** This step determines how much revenue the seller reports when (or as) it does the work it promised the customer. If a contract involves only one performance obligation, the full price relates to that work. If more than one obligation exists, the total price is split by referring to the prices of each part sold separately. For example, the total price charged by Lifetime Fitness is split between membership dues and personal training fees based on their individual, stand-alone prices.

Step 5. **Recognize revenue when (or as) each performance obligation is satisfied.** Many performance obligations, such as delivering goods or providing one-time services (such as a personal training session), are satisfied at a point in time, so revenue for them is reported *when* the goods or services are delivered. In contrast, service contracts covering months or years are satisfied over time, so their revenue is reported *as* the seller provides those services. For example, Lifetime Fitness reports one-twelfth of its annual membership dues as revenue each month of the year.

For most contracts discussed in this course, this five-step model is easy to apply. For example, when Starbucks agrees to sell you a Frappuccino, (1) it creates a contract with you (2) involving just one performance obligation to deliver a delicious beverage (3) at the price displayed, whereby the price (4) relates entirely to providing the drink and (5) is reported as revenue when Starbucks satisfies its performance obligation by delivering the drink to you. We introduce you to slightly more complex uses of the five-step model in Chapter 6 when accounting for merchandising operations. Its application to even more complex and interesting sales contracts, where performance obligations exist for extended warranties, customer loyalty programs, coupons, and software upgrades, is saved for discussion in intermediate accounting courses.

Notice the five-step model does not refer to receiving cash. Although all companies expect to receive cash in exchange for providing goods and services, the timing of cash receipts does not dictate when revenues are recognized. Instead, the key factor in determining when to recognize revenue is whether the company has provided goods or services to customers during this period. Because revenues are based on the work done, not the cash received, three possible cases exist, as shown in Exhibit 3.6.

A. **Cash before sale/service.** Airlines, magazine publishers, insurance companies, and retail stores routinely receive cash before delivering goods or services. For example, Noodlecake receives cash for gift cards customers can redeem later when purchasing from the company online. Noodlecake will record the cash received when it issues the gift card, but it will defer reporting revenue until later when it delivers apps to these customers. Until then, Noodlecake reports a liability called **Deferred Revenue** to indicate its obligation to accept the gift card as payment in the future. Deferred Revenue is reported on the balance sheet equal in amount to the cash received for the gift card.

B. **Cash with sale/service.** Cash sales are common for companies selling to consumers. For example, Domino's Pizza collects cash within moments of delivering pizza to a customer. In Noodlecake's case, when customers download and pay for online game purchases directly from the company, Noodlecake reports the increases in cash and revenue at the same time, as shown in Case B in Exhibit 3.6.

EXHIBIT 3.6 | Timing of Reporting Revenue versus Cash Receipts

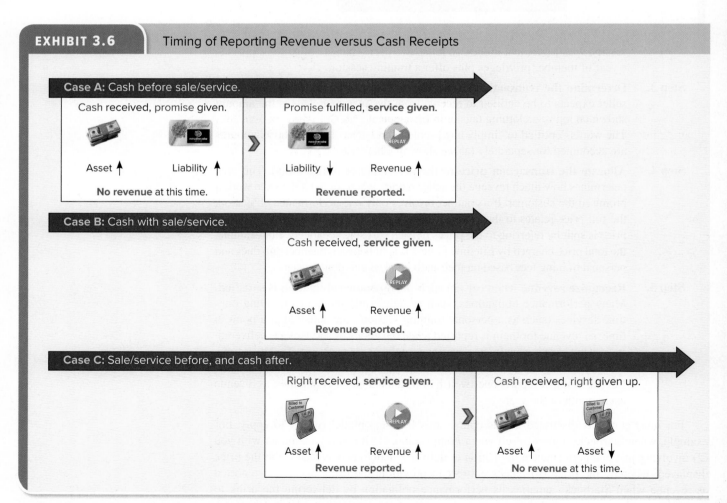

Money photo: Comstock/Getty Images; Gift card photo: duckycards/Getty Images; Logo: Noodlecake Studios, Inc.;
App photo: Noodlecake Studios, Inc.

C. Sale/service before, and cash after. This situation typically arises when a company sells on account. Selling on account means the company provides goods or services to a customer not for cash, but instead for the right to collect cash in the future. This right is an asset called Accounts Receivable. For example, Noodlecake sells consulting services on account to other companies. As the consulting services are provided, Noodlecake reports Service Revenue on the income statement and Accounts Receivable on the balance sheet. Later, when payment is received, Noodlecake increases its Cash account and decreases its Accounts Receivable account. No additional revenue is reported when the payment is received because the revenue was already recorded as the consulting services were provided.

SPOTLIGHT ON | **Financial Reporting**

Revenue Recognition Policy

Every company describes its revenue recognition policy in its notes to the financial statements. Noodlecake would explain its policy as follows.

> **Noodlecake Studios, Inc.**
>
> We recognize revenue when (or as) we fulfill the performance obligations we promise our customers. For sales of game apps, our performance obligation is fulfilled when customers successfully download our apps from a digital store. For sales of consulting services, our performance obligation is fulfilled each month, as we provide consulting services to clients.

It's worthwhile making sure you understand what sparks the recording of revenues because, in the next section, you'll see this also triggers the recording of expenses. To ensure you have a handle on this, spend a minute on the following Self-Study Practice.

 How's it going?   Self-Study Practice

The following transactions are typical operating activities for Florida Flippers (FF), a scuba diving and instruction company. Indicate the amount of revenue, if any, that should be recognized in May, June, and July for each activity, using the accrual basis of accounting.

Operating Activity	Amount of Revenue		
	May	June	July
1. In June, FF provided $32,000 in diving instruction to customers for cash.			
2. In May, customers booked and paid $8,000 cash for $5,000 of trips given in June and $3,000 in July.			
3. In June, customers paid $3,900 cash for instruction they received in May. In July, FF received $400 for FF gift cards used in August.			

After you have finished, check your answers with the solution.

Expense Recognition Principle ("Matching")

The business activities that generate revenues also create expenses. **Under accrual basis accounting, expenses are recognized in the same period as the revenues to which they relate,** not necessarily the period in which cash is paid for them. For example, for Noodlecake to create games for sale in September, it must rent space in a building and have its employees work that month. Under accrual basis accounting, Noodlecake would report rent expense and wages expense in September, even if the rent were paid in August and the wages were paid in October. This is what accountants call the **expense recognition principle (or "matching")**: Record expenses in the same period as the revenues with which they can be reasonably associated. If an expense cannot be directly associated with revenues, it is recorded in the period the underlying business activity occurs. For example, because it's not clear exactly when advertising yields revenue, advertising expense is simply reported in the period ads are run. Notice it is the timing of the underlying business activities, not the cash payments, that dictates when expenses are recognized. Three possible cases are shown in Exhibit 3.7.

> **YOU SHOULD KNOW**
>
> **Expense Recognition Principle:**
> Expenses are recorded when incurred in earning revenue; also called "matching."

A. **Cash before expense.**   It is common for businesses to pay for something that provides benefits only in future periods. For example, Noodlecake might buy office supplies now but not use them until next month. Under the expense recognition principle, the

---

EXHIBIT 3.7   Timing of Reporting Expenses versus Cash Payments

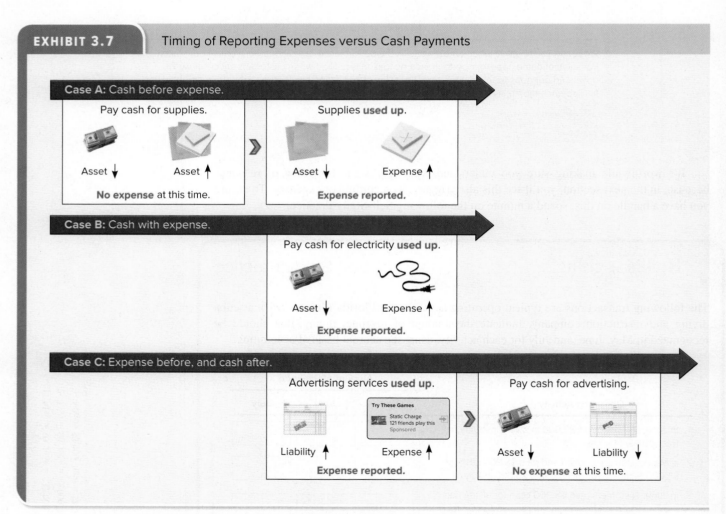

Money photo: Comstock/Getty Images; Notes photo: Ingram Publishing/SuperStock and Mark Dierker/McGraw-Hill Education; Purple notes photo: Mark Dierker/McGraw-Hill Education; Written notes photo: Ingram Publishing/SuperStock; Cord photo: Creatas/Jupiter Images/Alamy Stock Photo; Invoice photo: Studio 101/Alamy Stock Photo; Ad photo: Noodlecake Studios, Inc.; Invoice paid photo: Studio 101/Alamy Stock Photo

expense from using these supplies (Supplies Expense) is reported next month, when the supplies are used to generate revenue, not in the current month, when the supplies were purchased. This month, the supplies represent an asset (Supplies). Similar situations arise when a company prepays rent or insurance this month and uses up these assets in a later month.

B. **Cash with expense.** Noodlecake has arranged to make automatic monthly payments to its utility company for electricity at the end of each month. Because the electricity is used up in the current month, it is an expense of the current month.

C. **Expense before, and cash after.** Most businesses acquire goods or services on credit, so it is common for them to incur the expense of using up the benefits of goods or services in the current month, before paying for them in a later month. For example, Noodlecake places ads online but does not pay for this service until next month. Because the ads run in the current month, they are an expense that will be reported on this month's income statement. Because the cost has not yet been paid at the end of the month, the balance sheet reports a corresponding liability called Accounts Payable. Similar situations arise when employees work in the current period but are not paid their wages until the following period. This period's wages are reported as Salaries and Wages Expense on the income statement and any unpaid wages are reported as Salaries and Wages Payable on the balance sheet.

It's time for you to practice determining which costs should be reported as expenses on an income statement prepared using accrual basis accounting. As you work through the next Self-Study Practice, feel free to glance at Exhibit 3.7 for help.

COACH'S TIP

Promises exchanged for promises are not considered transactions, as you learned in Chapter 2. In Case C of Exhibit 3.7, a *service* has been received in exchange for a promise (of future payment), so it is considered a transaction.

 How's it going?　　　　　Self-Study Practice

The following transactions are typical operating activities for Florida Flippers (FF), a scuba diving and instruction company. Indicate the amount of expense, if any, that should be recognized in June and July for each activity, using the accrual basis of accounting.

	Amount of Expense	
Operating Activity	June	July
1. In June, FF paid $6,000 cash for six months of insurance covering July–December.		
2. On July 1, FF paid $4,000 in wages to employees for work done in June. July wages of $4,500 will be paid in August.		
3. FF used $2,400 of electricity in June and paid for it in July. FF used $2,500 of electricity in July and paid for it July 31.		

After you have finished, check your answers with the solution.

Solution to Self-Study Practice
1. June = $0, July = $1,000.
2. June = $4,000, July = $4,500.
3. June = $2,400, July = $2,500.

THE EXPANDED ACCOUNTING EQUATION

When we introduced the basic accounting equation in Chapter 2, we didn't mention how to account for the income statement effects of operating activities. You already had enough to learn, relating to the effects of business activities on assets, liabilities, and common stock.

Learning Objective 3-3
Analyze, record, and summarize the effects of operating transactions using the accounting equation, journal entries, and T-accounts.

The time has now come for you to learn how to analyze, record, and summarize the effects of activities affecting the income statement. To do this, you first need to know how the debit/credit framework works with revenues and expenses.

Let's start with the basic accounting equation from Chapter 2: Assets equal liabilities plus stockholders' equity, or A = L + SE. For now, focus on the stockholders' equity category. As you already know from Chapters 1 and 2, stockholders' equity includes (1) **Common Stock,** given to stockholders when they contribute capital to the company, and (2) **Retained Earnings,** generated by the company itself through profitable operations. Retained Earnings is the part that expands to include revenues and expenses, as shown in Exhibit 3.8.

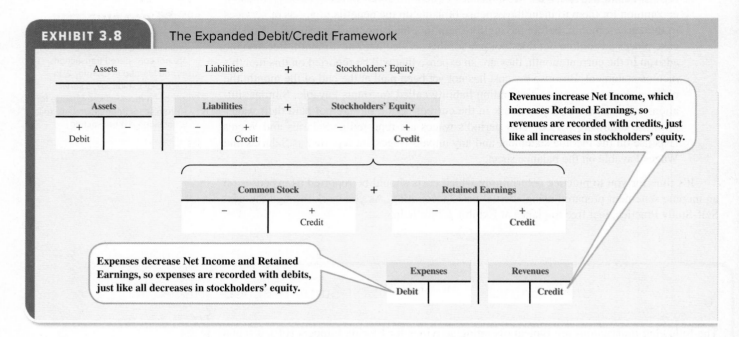

EXHIBIT 3.8   The Expanded Debit/Credit Framework

Take a moment to look at how Exhibit 3.8 encourages you to **think of revenues and expenses as subcategories within retained earnings.** They are shown this way because revenues and expenses eventually flow into Retained Earnings, but they aren't initially recorded there. Instead, each revenue and expense is accumulated in a separate account, making it easier to identify the amount to report for each item on the income statement. At the end of each accounting year, these separate revenue and expense accounts are transferred to (or "closed" into) Retained Earnings through a process we'll demonstrate in Chapter 4. For now, just focus on learning how revenues and expenses are recorded to indicate increases and decreases in the company's earnings, with corresponding effects recorded in the company's asset and/or liability accounts.

Because revenue and expense accounts are subcategories of Retained Earnings, they are affected by debits and credits in the same way as all stockholders' equity accounts. You already know increases in stockholders' equity are recorded on the right side. You also know revenues increase net income, which increases the stockholders' equity account Retained Earnings. So putting these ideas together should lead to the conclusion **revenues are recorded on the right (credit).** Here's the logic again: Increases in stockholders' equity are on the right; revenues increase stockholders' equity, so revenues are recorded on the right (credit). Decreases in stockholders' equity are recorded on the left side, so to show that expenses decrease net income and retained earnings, **expenses are recorded on the left (debit).** Exhibit 3.8 summarizes these effects.

Transaction Analysis, Recording, and Summarizing

To learn how to use your new knowledge of the revenue and expense recognition principles, the expanded accounting equation, and the debit/credit framework, you'll need lots of practice. Let's continue analyzing, recording, and summarizing as we did in Chapter 2, except now we'll focus on Noodlecake's operating activities in September.

(a) Sell Games for Cash **In September, Noodlecake sold $3,000 of apps online.** Customers paid online using a system similar to PayPal, where payments are deposited immediately into Noodlecake's accounts when the games are downloaded. This increase in Cash (an asset) must be recorded (with a debit) along with the revenue (which, as a subcategory of stockholders' equity, is recorded with a credit). To indicate game sales increase revenue (and net income), which ultimately increases stockholders' equity, we include a callout bubble in the transaction analysis and the notation (+R, +SE) in the journal entry. The increase in Cash is summarized in the Cash T-account, which carried a debit balance of $20,700 forward from the end of August (Chapter 2). The revenues are recorded in a new account called Sales Revenue, which has a beginning balance of zero because the company began operating only this month.

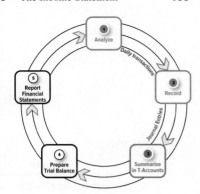

1 Analyze

	Assets	=	Liabilities	+	Stockholders' Equity	
(a) Cash	+3,000	=			Sales Revenue (+R)	+3,000

Revenues	↑3,000
− Expenses	−
Net Income	↑3,000

2 Record

	Debit	Credit
(a) Cash (+A)..	3,000	
Sales Revenue (+R, +SE)...		3,000

3 Summarize

dr +	Cash (A)	cr −	dr −	Sales Revenue (R, SE)	cr +
Beg. bal.	20,700			0	Beg. bal.
(a)	3,000			3,000	(a)

(b) Receive Cash for Future Services **Noodlecake issued three $100 gift cards at the beginning of September.** Noodlecake receives cash but gives only gift cards, which creates an obligation to accept the gift cards as payment for games in the future. This obligation is recorded as a liability called Deferred Revenue.

> 🔧 **COACH'S TIP**
>
> The word *deferred* in the Deferred Revenue account means the company defers or postpones reporting the revenue until it fulfills its promise represented by the gift card.

1 Analyze

	Assets	=	Liabilities		+ Stockholders' Equity
(b) Cash	+300	=	Deferred Revenue	+300	

2 Record

	Debit	Credit
(b) Cash (+A)	300	
Deferred Revenue (+L)		300

3 Summarize

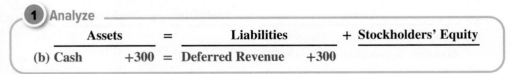

dr +	Cash (A)	cr −	dr −	Deferred Revenue (L)	cr +
Beg. bal.	20,700			0	Beg. bal.
(a)	3,000			300	(b)
(b)	300				

(c) Sell Apps on Credit   **Noodlecake sold $9,000 of apps in the App Store and on Google Play.** Apple and Google will release customer payments to Noodlecake later in the month. Because customers have downloaded the apps, Noodlecake has fulfilled its performance obligation, so it has earned revenue and now has the right to collect $9,000 from Apple and Google. The right to collect money in the future is an asset called Accounts Receivable. Use a debit to increase this asset and a credit to increase Sales Revenue.

1 Analyze

Assets	= Liabilities +	Stockholders' Equity	
(c) Accounts Receivable +9,000 =		Sales Revenue (+R) +9,000	

Revenues	↑9,000
− Expenses	−
Net Income	↑9,000

2 Record

		Debit	Credit
(c)	Accounts Receivable (+A)...	9,000	
	Sales Revenue (+R, +SE)..		9,000

3 Summarize

dr +	Accounts Receivable (A) cr −		dr −	Sales Revenue (R, SE) cr +	
Beg. bal.	0			0	Beg. bal.
(c)	9,000			3,000	(a)
				9,000	(c)

(d) Receive Payment on Account   **Noodlecake received checks totaling $8,500 from Apple and Google, on account.** This transaction does not involve additional app downloads, so no additional revenue is generated. Instead, the receipt of cash reduces the amount Noodlecake has the right to collect in the future, so it causes a decrease in Accounts Receivable.

1 Analyze

Assets		= Liabilities + Stockholders' Equity
(d) Cash	+8,500	
Accounts Receivable	−8,500	

2 Record

		Debit	Credit
(d)	Cash (+A)...	8,500	
	Accounts Receivable (−A)		8,500

3 Summarize

dr +	Cash (A)	cr −	dr +	Accounts Receivable (A) cr −		
Beg. bal.	20,700		Beg. bal.	0		
(a)	3,000		(c)	9,000	8,500	(d)
(b)	300					
(d)	8,500					

How's it going? — Self-Study Practice

Analyze and record the following June transaction: **Florida Flippers provided $3,000 of diving instruction in June to customers who will pay cash in July.** (The correct journal entry already has been summarized for you in the T-accounts in the "Summarize" step.)

1 Analyze

Assets	=	Liabilities	+	Stockholders' Equity

2 Record

		Debit	Credit
( ) ( )			
( ) ( )			

3 Summarize

dr +	Accounts Receivable	cr −	dr −	Service Revenue	cr +
	3,000			3,000	

After you have finished, check your answers with the solution.

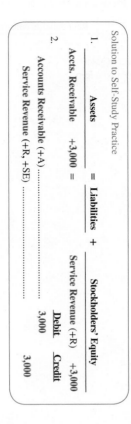

Solution to Self-Study Practice

1.

Assets	=	Liabilities	+	Stockholders' Equity
Accts. Receivable +3,000	=			Service Revenue (+R) +3,000

2.

	Debit	Credit
Accounts Receivable (+A)	3,000	
Service Revenue (+R, +SE)		3,000

(e) Pay Cash to Employees   **Noodlecake wrote checks to employees, totaling $7,800 for wages related to hours worked in September.** Because the efforts of employees are used this period to make and sell Noodlecake's games, their wages are an expense of this period. **We show (+E, −SE) because as expenses increase, net income decreases, which causes stockholders' equity to decrease.**

COACH'S TIP

To review why expenses are recorded using a debit, see Exhibit 3.8.

1 Analyze

Assets	=	Liabilities	+	Stockholders' Equity
(e) Cash −7,800	=			Wages Expense (+E) −7,800

Revenues		−
− Expenses		↑7,800
Net Income		↓7,800

2 Record

	Debit	Credit
(e) Salaries and Wages Expense (+E, −SE)	7,800	
Cash (−A)		7,800

3 Summarize

dr +	Cash (A)		cr −	dr +	Salaries and Wages Expense (E, SE)	cr −
Beg. bal.	20,700			Beg. bal.	0	
(a)	3,000	7,800	(e)	(e)	7,800	
(b)	300					
(d)	8,500					

Pay rent now

	Rent benefits consumed later
	Rent Expense recorded later

Record asset now
(Prepaid Rent)

(f) Pay Cash in Advance **On September 1, Noodlecake paid $7,200 in advance for September, October, and November rent.** This transaction involves paying for the right to use the rented building for three months following the payment. This payment provides an economic resource to Noodlecake (building space for three months), so it will be initially reported as an asset called Prepaid Rent, as shown in blue on the timeline. Each month, when the rented space has been used, Noodlecake will reduce Prepaid Rent and show the amount used up as Rent Expense. The adjustment needed to report September's share of the total rent expense (1/3 × $7,200 = $2,400) will be discussed later, in Chapter 4. For now, we will record just the $7,200 rent prepayment.

1 Analyze

	Assets	=	Liabilities	+ Stockholders' Equity
(f) Cash	−7,200			
Prepaid Rent	+7,200			

2 Record

	Debit	Credit
(f) Prepaid Rent (+A)	7,200	
Cash (−A)		7,200

3 Summarize

dr +	Cash (A)		cr −	dr +	Prepaid Rent (A)	cr −
Beg. bal.	20,700			Beg. bal.	0	
(a)	3,000	7,800	(e)	(f)	7,200	
(b)	300	**7,200**	(f)			
(d)	8,500					

Prepayments for insurance, advertising, and other time-based services would be analyzed and recorded in a similar manner.

(g) Incur Cost to Be Paid Later **Noodlecake displayed online ads in September and received a bill for $500, to be paid in October.** This cost was incurred for September advertising services, so according to the expense recognition principle it should be recorded as an expense in September. Rather than pay cash for this expense, Noodlecake gave a promise to pay, which increases the liability called Accounts Payable.

> **COACH'S TIP**
>
> The beginning balance in the Accounts Payable T-account is carried forward from the previous month's activities discussed in Chapter 2.

1 Analyze

Assets	=	Liabilities	+	Stockholders' Equity			
(g)		Accounts Payable +500		Advertising Expense (+E) −500			

Revenues		−
− Expenses		↑500
Net Income		↓500

2 Record

	Debit	Credit
(g) Advertising Expense (+E, −SE)	500	
Accounts Payable (+L)		500

3 Summarize

dr −	Accounts Payable (L)		cr +	dr +	Advertising Expense (E, SE)		cr −
		10,200	Beg. bal.	Beg. bal.	0		
		500	(g)	(g)	500		

(h) Pay Cash for Expenses Noodlecake was notified by its bank that an automatic monthly payment of $600 was transmitted to its utility company for electricity use in **September.** Just like transaction (e), the cash payment and expense occurred during the same period.

1 Analyze

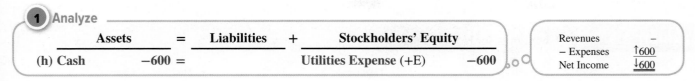

Assets	=	Liabilities	+	Stockholders' Equity		Revenues	–
(h) Cash −600 =				Utilities Expense (+E) −600		– Expenses	↑600
						Net Income	↓600

2 Record

	Debit	Credit
(h) Utilities Expense (+E, −SE)	600	
Cash (−A)		600

3 Summarize

dr +	Cash (A)		cr −
Beg. bal.	20,700		
(a)	3,000	7,800	(e)
(b)	300	7,200	(f)
(d)	8,500	600	(h)

dr +	Utilities Expense (E, SE)	cr −
Beg. bal.	0	
(h)	600	

💡 **How's it going?** Self-Study Practice

For a little break and some practice, let's return one last time to Florida Flippers. Analyze and record the effects of the following transaction for June: **Florida Flippers paid $4,000 cash in June for wages to employees who worked in June.** (Once again, the correct journal entry has already been summarized for you in the T-accounts.)

1 Analyze

Assets	=	Liabilities	+ Stockholders' Equity

2 Record

	Debit	Credit
[ ] ([ ])..	[ ]	
[ ] ([ ])		[ ]

3 Summarize

dr +	Cash (A)	cr −
		4,000

dr +	Wages Expense (E, SE)	cr −
	4,000	

After you have finished, check your answers with the solution.

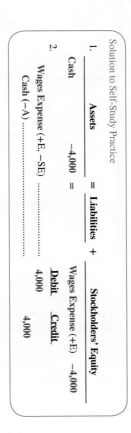

Solution to Self-Study Practice

1.

Assets	=	Liabilities	+	Stockholders' Equity
Cash −4,000	=			Wages Expense (+E) −4,000

2.

	Debit	Credit
Wages Expense (+E, −SE)	4,000	
Cash (−A)		4,000

Calculating Account Balances After entering ("posting") the effects of each journal entry into the T-accounts, we can calculate the ending balances. In Exhibit 3.9, we have included all the T-accounts for Noodlecake (from this chapter as well as Chapter 2). You've heard it before, but we'll just remind you the ending balance in each account is the amount by which the total of the increase (+) side exceeds the total of the decrease (−) side.

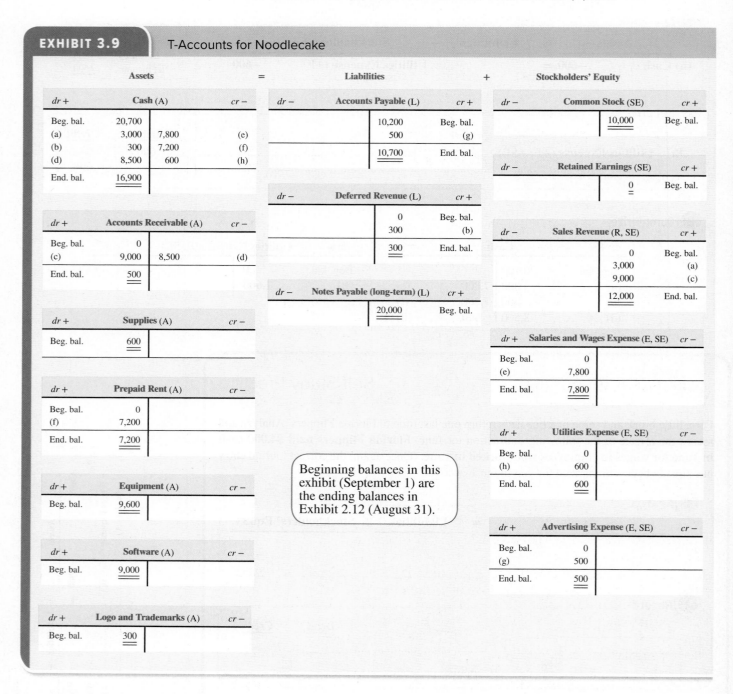

EXHIBIT 3.9 | T-Accounts for Noodlecake

Beginning balances in this exhibit (September 1) are the ending balances in Exhibit 2.12 (August 31).

UNADJUSTED TRIAL BALANCE

Learning Objective 3-4
Prepare an unadjusted trial balance.

After summarizing journal entries in the various accounts and then calculating ending balances for each account, you should prepare an unadjusted trial balance. The unadjusted trial balance shown in Exhibit 3.10 is similar to the one shown in Chapter 2. The only difference

EXHIBIT 3.10	Sample Unadjusted Trial Balance

NOODLECAKE STUDIOS, INC.
Unadjusted Trial Balance
At September 30, 2021

Account Name	Debits	Credits
Cash	$16,900	
Accounts Receivable	500	
Supplies	600	
Prepaid Rent	7,200	
Equipment	9,600	
Software	9,000	
Logo and Trademarks	300	
Accounts Payable		$ 10,700
Deferred Revenue		300
Notes Payable		20,000
Common Stock		10,000
Retained Earnings		0
Sales Revenue		12,000
Salaries and Wages Expense	7,800	
Utilities Expense	600	
Advertising Expense	500	
Totals	$53,000	$53,000

Balance sheet accounts

Income statement accounts

COACH'S TIP

A trial balance is prepared by simply listing and summing the T-account balances.

is we now have income statement accounts (revenues, expenses) to list after the balance sheet accounts. As before, use the debit column for accounts showing an ending debit balance and the credit column for accounts showing an ending credit balance. Lastly, add the two columns (and hope they balance).

If your trial balance indicates total debits don't equal total credits, you will experience a sickening feeling in your stomach because this means you've made an error somewhere in preparing or posting the journal entries to the T-accounts. Don't panic or start randomly changing numbers. When you find yourself in a hole, stop digging. Calmly look at the difference between total debits and credits and consult the Homework Helper section at the end of this chapter for tips on how to find the error causing that difference.

Be aware that even if total debits equal total credits, it's still possible you've made an error. For example, if you accidentally debit an asset rather than an expense or credit Accounts Payable instead of Deferred Revenue, total debits would still equal total credits. So if the trial balance doesn't balance, you know you've made an error for sure. If the trial balance does balance, it's still possible you've made a mistake.

If you haven't already scanned the trial balance in Exhibit 3.10, take a moment to do it now. Notice the title says **unadjusted trial balance**. It is called this because several

YOU SHOULD KNOW

Unadjusted Trial Balance: An internal report, prepared before end-of-period adjustments, listing the unadjusted balances of each account to check the equality of total debits and credits.

adjustments will have to be made at the end of the accounting period to update the accounts. For example, some of the benefits of Prepaid Rent were used up in September, but this wasn't recorded yet. If you're really sharp, you'll also have noticed income taxes haven't been calculated and recorded yet. Although it's possible to prepare preliminary financial statements using the numbers on the unadjusted trial balance, most companies don't. They wait until after the final adjustments are made. These adjustments will ensure the revenues and expenses are up to date and complete, so that the (adjusted) net income number will provide a good indication about whether the company was profitable during the period. Don't worry about how to make the end-of-period adjustments yet. We'll spend most of Chapter 4 on that. For now, just realize the accounts still have to be adjusted before we can prepare financial statements that follow GAAP or IFRS.

REVIEW OF REVENUES AND EXPENSES

Up to this point of the chapter, you've analyzed some transactions—eight actually—that involve operating activities. While this is a good introduction, it doesn't prepare you entirely for the variety of operating activities that most companies engage in. What you need is a general summary of everything you've learned about revenues, expenses, and journal entries, and then lots of practice applying it to a broad range of activities. Let's start with revenues.

Remember that revenues are recorded when the business fulfills its promise to provide goods or services to customers, which is not necessarily the same time that cash is received. Because of this, we look at three cases, where cash is received (A) before the revenue is generated by delivering goods or services, (B) in the same period in which the revenue is generated, and (C) after the period in which the revenue is generated. The journal entries for these situations are shown in the following panels.

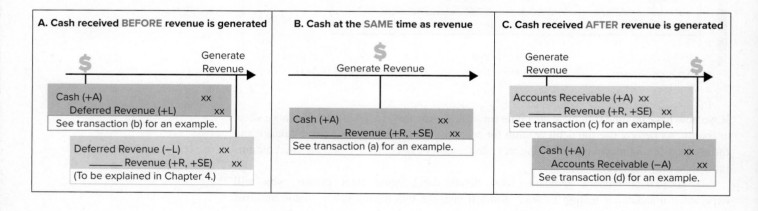

These three panels correspond to the revenue transactions for Noodlecake analyzed earlier in this chapter, but they can be applied to any business. We use a generic label "_____ Revenue" with the expectation that you will fill in the blank with whatever type of revenue you are recording. That is, when accounting for revenue from selling games, you should use an account name like Sales Revenue. A more complete list of account names is provided in the Homework Helper at the end of this chapter.

Let's look at a similar summary for expenses now. Under accrual accounting, expenses are recorded when incurred (by using up the economic benefits of the company's resources). Expenses are not necessarily incurred at the same time that cash is paid. Because of this, we look at three cases, where cash is paid (A) before the expense is incurred, (B) in the same period in which the expense is incurred, and (C) after the expense is incurred. The corresponding journal entries are summarized in the following panels.

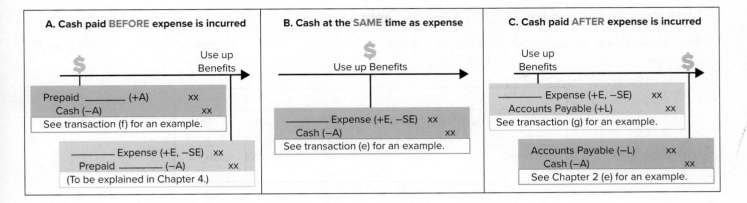

Again, we use generic labels like "Prepaid _____" and "_____ Expense." Just fill in the blank with whatever type of item you are recording (e.g., Prepaid Rent, Rent Expense, Prepaid Insurance, Insurance Expense).

Evaluate the Results

NET PROFIT MARGIN

The income statement provides the main measure of a company's operating performance. The key thing to look for is whether net income is positive (revenues exceed expenses). Beyond that, it's useful to consider whether revenues are growing faster than expenses. If so, the company's net income will be increasing.

Currently, Noodlecake's accounting records report revenues of $12,000 and expenses of $8,900 (= $7,800 + $600 + $500), suggesting a net income of $3,100 (= $12,000 − $8,900). This $3,100 of net income is 25.8 percent of the $12,000 of revenues ($3,100 ÷ $12,000 = 0.258). This **net profit margin**, as it is called, implies Noodlecake earned 25.8 cents of net income from each dollar of sales revenue. But Laurie cautions Jordan that these measures are preliminary and will change when the accounting records are adjusted at the end of September. The adjustment process is the main topic of Chapter 4.

Accounting Decision Tools		
Name of Measure	**Formula**	**What It Tells You**
Net profit margin	$\dfrac{\text{Net Income}}{\text{Revenues}}$	• How much profit from each dollar of revenue • A higher ratio means better performance

As Jordan realized, a good accountant like Laurie monitors how well other companies are doing. Based on the analysis that follows, she was able to advise Jordan that Noodlecake's preliminary net profit margin of 25.8 percent was slightly higher than that of two big competitors (Electronic Arts and Nintendo).

Net Profit Margin for Video Game Companies

The following table shows the net profit margin calculations for two of Noodlecake's competitors: Electronic Arts and Nintendo.

(in millions of U.S. dollars)	Electronic Arts		Nintendo	
	2018	2019	2018	2019
Net Income	$1,043	$1,019	$1,259	$ 1,749
Revenues	$5,150	$4,950	$9,524	$10,825
Net profit margin (%)	20.3	20.6	13.2	16.2

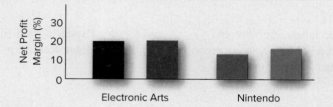

Electronic Arts is a picture of consistency, just like its two most popular games (*FIFA* soccer and *Madden* football), which dependably come out every year. With revenues around $5 billion and net incomes just over $1 billion, its net profit margins were just above 20 percent in both 2018 and 2019. In contrast, Nintendo had a more exciting year in 2019, with its new *Switch* hardware system more popular than ever. Download-only software sales also increased, causing Nintendo's net profit margin to jump from 13.2 percent to 16.2 percent. Nintendo's higher net profit margin was still less than that of Electronic Arts, though, mostly because of differences in income tax expense. (If Nintendo were to enjoy the same low tax rate as Electronic Arts, its 2019 net profit margin would have been 21.4 percent.)

INCOME STATEMENT LIMITATIONS

Although an income statement is useful for assessing a company's performance, it does have some limitations and resulting misconceptions. One of the most common is that some people think net income equals the amount of cash generated by the business during the period. While this is the way many of us think about our own income, it's not the way companies recognize revenues and expenses on the income statement when using accrual basis accounting. Net income is not cash.

A second, related misconception is that a company's net income represents the change in the company's value during the period. While a company's net income is one source of value to the company, many other determinants of its value are not included in the income statement. A good example is the increase in the value of Noodlecake's name as it grows its reputation for making great apps and games.

A third common misconception is that the measurement of income involves only counting. Proper counting is critical to income measurement, but estimation also plays a role. For example, Noodlecake's equipment will not last forever. Instead, its benefits will be "used up" over time to generate the company's revenue. These benefits should therefore be expensed over the period in which they are used up. Doing so requires estimating the number of total years over which its equipment will be used. We will discuss this particular example in Chapter 4; many other estimates affecting income measurement will arise in later chapters.

REVIEW THE CHAPTER

DEMONSTRATION CASE A

1. From the following list of balance sheet and income statement account balances for Carnival Corporation, prepare an income statement for the quarter ended May 31, 2019. (Amounts are reported in millions of U.S. dollars.)

2. Explain what the results suggest about the cruise ship company's operating performance. For the same period last year, net income was $561 (in millions of U.S. dollars) and net profit margin was 12.9 percent.

Carnival Corporation

Transportation Expenses	$ 613	Wage Expenses	$566	Selling Expenses	$ 621
Passenger Ticket Revenue	3,257	Fuel Expenses	423	Prepaid Expenses	727
Onboard Revenue	1,581	Accounts Payable	792	Ship Expenses	1,887
Food Expenses	269	Income Tax Expense	8	Deferred Revenue	5,815

Suggested Solution

1. Income Statement

CARNIVAL CORPORATION
Income Statement
For the Quarter Ended May 31, 2019
(amounts in millions of U.S. dollars)

Revenues	
Passenger Ticket Revenue	$3,257
Onboard Revenue	1,581
Total Revenues	4,838
Expenses	
Ship Expenses	1,887
Selling Expenses	621
Transportation Expenses	613
Wage Expenses	566
Fuel Expenses	423
Food Expenses	269
Income Tax Expense	8
Total Expenses	4,387
Net Income	$ 451

 **COACH'S TIP**

Prepaid Expenses of $727 includes Prepaid Rent and Prepaid Insurance, so it is an asset on the balance sheet and therefore is excluded from the income statement. Accounts Payable of $792 and Deferred Revenue of $5,815 are excluded from the income statement because they are liabilities on the balance sheet.

2. The net income of $451 (million) indicates Carnival Corporation was profitable, meaning the revenues it earned were greater than the expenses it incurred. Its net profit margin was 9.3 percent of total revenues ($451 ÷ $4,838 = 0.093). These 2019 results are worse than the same period last year, when Carnival reported (higher) net income of $561 (million) and 12.9 percent net profit margin.

DEMONSTRATION CASE B

This case is a continuation of the Goodbye Grass Corporation case introduced in Chapter 2. The company was established and property and equipment were purchased. The balance sheet at April 30, 2021, based on only the investing and financing activities (from Chapter 2) is as follows:

GOODBYE GRASS CORPORATION Balance Sheet At April 30, 2021			
Assets		**Liabilities**	
Current Assets		Current Liabilities	
Cash	$ 3,800	Accounts Payable	$ 400
Notes Receivable	1,250	Notes Payable	4,000
Total Current Assets	5,050	Total Current Liabilities	4,400
Equipment	4,600	**Stockholders' Equity**	
Land	3,750	Common Stock	9,000
		Retained Earnings	0
		Total Stockholders' Equity	9,000
Total Assets	$13,400	Total Liabilities and Stockholders' Equity	$13,400

The following activities also occurred during April:

a. Purchased and used gasoline for mowers and edgers, paying $90 in cash at a local gas station.

b. In early April, received $1,600 cash from the city in advance for lawn maintenance service for April through July ($400 each month). The entire amount is to be recorded as Deferred Revenue.

c. In early April, purchased $300 of insurance covering six months, April through September. The entire payment is to be recorded as Prepaid Insurance.

d. Mowed lawns for residential customers who are billed every two weeks. A total of $5,200 of service was billed and is to be recorded in April.

e. Residential customers paid $3,500 on their accounts.

f. Paid wages every two weeks. Total cash paid in April was $3,900.

g. Received a bill for $320 from the local gas station for additional gasoline purchased on account and used in April.

h. Paid $100 on accounts payable.

Required:

1. Analyze activities (*a*)–(*h*) with the goal of indicating their effects on the basic accounting equation (Assets = Liabilities + Stockholders' Equity), using the format shown in the chapter.

2. Prepare journal entries to record the transactions identified among activities (*a*)–(*h*).
   TIP: Treat insurance (in *c*) in the same manner as Noodlecake's rent in transaction (*f*).

3. Summarize the effects of each transaction in the appropriate T-accounts. Before entering these effects, set up T-accounts for Cash, Accounts Receivable, Notes Receivable, Prepaid Insurance, Equipment, Land, Accounts Payable, Deferred Revenue, Notes Payable, Common Stock, Retained Earnings, Service Revenue, Salaries and Wages Expense, and Fuel Expense. The beginning balance in each T-account should be the amount shown on the balance sheet above or $0 if the account does not appear on the above balance sheet. After posting the journal entries to the T-accounts, compute ending balances for each of the T-accounts.

4. Use the amounts in the T-accounts to prepare an unadjusted trial balance for Goodbye Grass Corporation at April 30, 2021.

5. Alongside the trial balance, indicate which accounts would be reported on the balance sheet and which would be reported on the income statement.

After completing the above requirements, check your answers with the following solution.

Suggested Solution

1. Transaction analysis:

	Assets		=	Liabilities		+	Stockholders' Equity	
a.	Cash	−90	=				Fuel Expense (+E)	−90
b.	Cash	+1,600	=	Deferred Revenue	+1,600			
c.	Cash	−300	=		No change			
	Prepaid Insurance	+300						
d.	Accounts Receivable	+5,200	=				Service Revenue (+R)	+5,200
e.	Cash	+3,500	=		No change			
	Accounts Receivable	−3,500						
f.	Cash	−3,900	=				Salaries and Wages Expense (+E)	−3,900
g.	No change		=	Accounts Payable	+320		Fuel Expense (+E)	−320
h.	Cash	−100	=	Accounts Payable	−100			

2. Journal entries:

		Debit	Credit
a.	Fuel Expense (+E, −SE).............................	90	
	Cash (−A)...		90
b.	Cash (+A)...	1,600	
	Deferred Revenue (+L).......................		1,600
c.	Prepaid Insurance (+A)...........................	300	
	Cash (−A)...		300
d.	Accounts Receivable (+A)	5,200	
	Service Revenue (+R, +SE)		5,200
e.	Cash (+A)...	3,500	
	Accounts Receivable (−A)		3,500
f.	Salaries and Wages Expense (+E, −SE)...............	3,900	
	Cash (−A)...		3,900
g.	Fuel Expense (+E, −SE).............................	320	
	Accounts Payable (+L)...........................		320
h.	Accounts Payable (−L).............................	100	
	Cash (−A)...		100

3. T-Accounts:

Assets	=	Liabilities	+	Stockholders' Equity

dr +   Cash (A)   **cr −**

Beg. bal.	3,800		
(b)	1,600	90	(a)
(e)	3,500	300	(c)
		3,900	(f)
		100	(h)
End. bal.	4,510		

dr + Accounts Receivable (A) **cr −**

Beg. bal.	0		
(d)	5,200	3,500	(e)
End. bal.	1,700		

dr + Notes Receivable (A) **cr −**

Beg. bal.	1,250
End. bal.	1,250

dr + Prepaid Insurance (A) **cr −**

Beg. bal.	0
(c)	300
End. Bal.	300

dr +   Equipment (A)   **cr −**

Beg. bal.	4,600
End. bal.	4,600

dr +   Land (A)   **cr −**

Beg. bal.	3,750
End. bal.	3,750

dr − Accounts Payable (L) **cr +**

		400	Beg. bal.
(h)	100	320	(g)
		620	End. bal.

dr − Deferred Revenue (L) **cr +**

0	Beg. bal.
1,600 (b)	
1,600	End. bal.

dr −   Notes Payable (L)   **cr +**

4,000	Beg. bal.
4,000	End. bal.

dr + Salaries and Wages Expense (E)   **cr −**

Beg. bal.	0
(f)	3,900
End. bal.	3,900

dr +   Fuel Expense (E)   **cr −**

Beg. bal.	0
(a)	90
(g)	320
End. bal.	410

dr −   Common Stock (SE)   **cr +**

9,000	Beg. bal.
9,000	End. bal.

dr − Retained Earnings (SE) **cr +**

0	Beg. bal.
0	End. bal.

dr − Service Revenue (R) **cr +**

0	Beg. bal.
5,200	(d)
5,200	End. bal.

4. Unadjusted trial balance:

5. Reported on the ...

GOODBYE GRASS CORPORATION
Unadjusted Trial Balance
At April 30, 2021

Account Name	Debits	Credits	
Cash	$ 4,510		
Accounts Receivable	1,700		
Notes Receivable	1,250		
Prepaid Insurance	300		
Equipment	4,600		
Land	3,750		Balance sheet
Accounts Payable		$ 620	
Deferred Revenue		1,600	
Notes Payable		4,000	
Common Stock		9,000	
Retained Earnings		0	
Service Revenue		5,200	
Salaries and Wages Expense	3,900		Income statement
Fuel Expense	410		
Totals	$20,420	$20,420	

CHAPTER SUMMARY

Describe common operating transactions and select appropriate income statement account titles.   LO 3-1

- The income statement reports the results of transactions that affect net income, including

    Revenues—amounts charged to customers for sales of goods or services provided.

    Expenses—costs of business activities undertaken to generate revenues.

- See Exhibit 3.2 for basic income statement format.

Explain and apply the revenue and expense recognition principles.   LO 3-2

- The two key concepts underlying accrual basis accounting and the income statement are

    Revenue recognition principle—recognize revenues when the seller fulfills its performance obligation to customers by delivering goods or services, regardless of when cash is received.

    Expense recognition principle ("matching")—recognize expenses when they are incurred in generating revenue, regardless of when cash is paid.

- A five-step model guides revenue reporting: (1) Identify the contract, (2) Identify the seller's performance obligation(s), (3) Determine the transaction price, (4) Allocate the transaction price to the performance obligations, and (5) Recognize revenue when (or as) each performance obligation is satisfied.

Analyze, record, and summarize the effects of operating transactions using the accounting equation, journal entries, and T-accounts.   LO 3-3

- The expanded transaction analysis model includes revenues and expenses as subcategories of Retained Earnings. Increases, decreases, and normal account balances (*dr* or *cr*) follow:

Assets	=	Liabilities	+	Stockholders' Equity
+ *dr* / −		− / + *cr*		

Common Stock: − / + *cr*

Retained Earnings: − / + *cr*

Expenses: + *dr* / −

Revenues: − / + *cr*

Prepare an unadjusted trial balance.   LO 3-4

- The unadjusted trial balance is a list of all accounts and their unadjusted balances and is used to check on the equality of recorded debits and credits.

Evaluate net profit margin, but beware of income statement limitations.   LO 3-5

- Net profit margin expresses net income as a percentage of revenues.

- The income statement indicates whether the company is profitable, but this might not explain whether cash increased or decreased. Also, the income statement does not directly measure the change in company value during the period, and estimation affects income measurement.

Accounting Decision Tools		
Name of Measure	**Formula**	**What It Tells You**
Net profit margin	$\dfrac{\text{Net Income}}{\text{Revenues}}$	• How much profit from each dollar of revenue • A higher ratio means better performance

KEY TERMS

See complete definitions in the glossary in the back of this text.

HOMEWORK HELPER

Account Name	Description
Revenues	
Sales Revenue	Arise from delivering products in the ordinary course of business
Service Revenue	Arise from providing services in the ordinary course of business
Rent Revenue	Amounts earned by renting out company property
Interest Revenue	Amounts earned on savings and loans to others
Dividend Revenue	Dividends earned from investing in other companies

Account Name	Description
Expenses	
Cost of Goods Sold	Cost of products sold in the ordinary course of business
Repairs & Maintenance Expense	Cost of routine maintenance and upkeep of buildings/equipment
Advertising Expense	Cost of advertising services obtained during the period
Depreciation Expense	Cost of buildings and equipment used up during the period
Insurance Expense	Cost of insurance coverage for the current period
Salaries and Wages Expense	Cost of employees' salaries and wages for the period
Rent Expense	Cost of rent for the period
Supplies Expense	Cost of supplies used up during the period
Delivery Expense	Cost of transportation to deliver goods to customers
Utilities Expense	Cost of power, light, heat, Internet, and telephone for the period
Amortization Expense	Cost of intangible assets used up or expired during the period
Interest Expense	Cost of interest charged on outstanding debts owed during the period
Income Tax Expense	Taxes charged on net income reported for the period

Alternative terms

- Net income also can be called net earnings or net profit.
- Prepaid Rent and Prepaid Insurance can be called Prepaid Expenses, which is reported as a current asset on the balance sheet.
- The income statement may also be called the statement of comprehensive income, statement of earnings, or statement of operations.

Helpful reminders

- To properly understand why Prepaid Expenses is an asset and Deferred Revenue is a liability, emphasize the first word (prepaid and deferred).
- If the trial balance doesn't balance, look at the difference between total debits and total credits. If it is . . .
  - **The same as** one of your T-account balances, you probably forgot to include the account in your trial balance.

- **Twice the amount of an account balance,** you may have included it in the wrong column of the trial balance.
- **Twice the amount of a transaction,** you may have posted a debit as a credit or a credit as a debit in your T-accounts.
- **Evenly divisible by 9,** you may have reversed the order of two digits in a number (a transposition error) or left a zero off the end of a number.
- **Evenly divisible by 3,** you may have hit the key above or below the one you intended to hit (like a 9 instead of a 6) on your numeric keypad.

Frequent mistakes

- Accrual is <u>not</u> spelled accural.

PRACTICE MATERIAL

QUESTIONS (⊖ Symbol indicates questions that require analysis from more than one perspective.)

1. Show the income statement equation and define each element.

2. When accounting was developed in the 14th and 15th centuries, some businesses had very short lives. For instance, a business might have been created for a ship to sail from Europe to North America and return with furs and other goods. After the goods were delivered and profits were distributed among those who financed the shipment, the business ceased to exist. In more recent centuries, businesses began to experience longer lives. Identify the accounting concept that is needed when accounting for businesses with long lives. Explain what this concept means and why it is necessary for modern-day accounting. ⊖

3. Define *accrual basis accounting* and contrast it with *cash basis accounting*.

4. Why is it appropriate to use cash basis accounting in your personal life but not in the business world? ⊖

5. What two questions are answered by the core revenue recognition principle?

6. What five steps are to be followed when applying the core revenue recognition principle?

7. What is a performance obligation?

8. How do you report revenue from a contract that contains more than one performance obligation but specifies only one (total) transaction price?

9. Explain the expense recognition principle ("matching").

10. Explain why stockholders' equity is increased by revenues and decreased by expenses.

11. Explain why revenues are recorded as credits and expenses as debits.

12. Complete the following table by entering either *debit* or *credit* in each cell:

Item	Increase	Decrease
Revenues		
Expenses		

13. Complete the following table by entering either *increase* or *decrease* in each cell:

Item	Debit	Credit
Revenues		
Expenses		

14. What basic characteristic distinguishes items reported on the income statement from items reported on the balance sheet?

15. Which of the four basic accounting reports indicates that it is appropriate to consider revenues and expenses as subcategories of retained earnings? Explain.

16. What is the difference between Accounts Receivable and Revenue?

17. What is the difference between Accounts Payable for advertising and Advertising Expense?

18. For each of the following situations, indicate whether it represents an accounting error and explain why it is or is not an error. Also state whether a trial balance would indicate that an error exists for each situation. ⊖

   a. Cash received from a customer on account was debited to Accounts Receivable and credited to Cash.
   b. Revenue was recognized when a customer purchased a gift card for future use.
   c. An expense was recorded as an asset.
   d. The debit side of a journal entry was recorded in the accounts, but the credit side was not.
   e. A company shareholder purchased a new car, but this was not recorded by the company.

19. What are three limitations of the income statement that often lead to misconceptions?

MULTIPLE CHOICE

1. Which of the following items is not a specific account in a company's accounting records?

   a. Accounts Receivable
   b. Net Income
   c. Sales Revenue
   d. Deferred Revenue

2. Which of the following accounts normally has a debit balance?

   a. Deferred Revenue
   b. Rent Expense
   c. Retained Earnings
   d. Sales Revenue

3. The expense recognition principle ("matching") controls

   a. Where on the income statement expenses should be presented.
   b. When revenues are recognized on the income statement.
   c. The ordering of current assets and current liabilities on the balance sheet.
   d. When costs are recognized as expenses on the income statement.

4. Which of the following would the core revenue recognition principle consider a contract?

   a. A concert ticket issued by a Ticketmaster customer service representative
   b. An order automatically generated by Target's computer system to restock its shelves
   c. A rental agreement signed by Gables Residential for an apartment rented by a tenant
   d. All of the above

5. If a company incorrectly records a payment as an asset, rather than as an expense, how will this error affect net income in the current period?

   a. Net income will be too high.
   b. Net income will be too low.
   c. Net income will not be affected by this error.
   d. It's a mystery; nobody really knows.

6. When should a company report the cost of an insurance policy as an expense?

   a. When the company first signs the policy
   b. When the company pays for the policy
   c. When the company receives the benefits from the policy over its period of coverage
   d. When the company receives payments from the insurance company for its insurance claims

7. When expenses exceed revenues in a given period,

   a. Stockholders' equity will not be impacted.
   b. Stockholders' equity will be increased.
   c. Stockholders' equity will be decreased.
   d. One cannot determine the impact on stockholders' equity without information about the specific revenues and expenses.

8. Which account is *least* likely to be debited when revenue is recorded?

   a. Accounts Payable
   b. Accounts Receivable
   c. Cash
   d. Deferred Revenue

9. Webby Corporation reported the following amounts on its income statement: service revenues, $32,500; utilities expense, $300; net income, $1,600; and income tax expense, $900. If the only other amount reported on the income statement was for selling expenses, what amount would it be?

   a. $2,200   c. $30,000
   b. $29,700   d. $30,900

10. Which of the following is the entry to be recorded by a law firm when it receives a payment from a new client that will be earned when services are provided in the future?

   a. *Debit* Accounts Receivable; *credit* Service Revenue.
   b. *Debit* Deferred Revenue; *credit* Service Revenue.
   c. *Debit* Cash; *credit* Deferred Revenue.
   d. *Debit* Deferred Revenue; *credit* Cash.

> For answers to the Multiple-Choice Questions **see page Q1** located in the last section of the book.

MINI-EXERCISES

LO 3-2   **M3-1 Identifying Performance Obligations**

Lakeside Indoor Tennis Club (LITC) sells a tennis membership for $2,400 per year, which entitles members to 50 "free" court bookings. The price for nonmembers is $40 per court booking. LITC's membership also allows members to participate in a competitive league without charge, whereas nonmembers pay a league fee of $500. How many different types of performance obligations exist for LITC when it sells a tennis membership?

M3-2 Reporting Cash Basis versus Accrual Basis Income

Mostert Music Company had the following transactions in March:

a. Sold music lessons to customers for $10,000; received $6,000 in cash and the rest on account.
b. Paid $600 in wages for the month.
c. Received a $200 bill for utilities that will be paid in April.
d. Received $1,000 from customers as deposits on music lessons to be given in April.

Complete the following statements for March:

Cash Basis Income Statement		Accrual Basis Income Statement	
Revenues		Revenues	
Cash Sales	$	Sales	$
Customer Deposits			
Expenses		Expenses	
Wages Paid		Salaries and Wages Expense	
		Utilities Expense	
Cash Income	$	Net Income	$

M3-3 Identifying Accrual Basis Revenues

The following transactions are July activities of Bill's Extreme Bowling, Inc., which operates several bowling centers. If revenue is to be recognized in July, indicate the amount. If revenue is not to be recognized in July, explain why.

Activity	Amount or Explanation
a. Bill's collected $12,000 from customers for services related to games played in July.	
b. Bill's billed a customer for $250 for a party held at the center on the last day of July. The bill is to be paid in August.	
c. The men's and women's bowling leagues gave Bill's advance payments totaling $1,500 for the fall season that starts in September.	
d. Bill's received $1,000 from credit sales made to customers last month (in June).	

M3-4 Identifying Accrual Basis Expenses

The following transactions are July activities of Bill's Extreme Bowling, Inc., which operates several bowling centers. If an expense is to be recognized in July, indicate the amount. If an expense is not to be recognized in July, explain why.

Activity	Amount or Explanation
a. Bill's paid $1,500 to plumbers for repairing a broken pipe in the restrooms.	
b. Bill's paid $2,000 for the June electricity bill and received the July bill for $2,500, which will be paid in August.	
c. Bill's paid $5,475 to employees for work in July.	

M3-5 Recording Accrual Basis Revenues

For each of the transactions in M3-3, write the journal entry using the format shown in the chapter.

M3-6 Recording Accrual Basis Expenses

For each of the transactions in M3-4, write the journal entry using the format shown in the chapter.

M3-7 Determining the Accounting Equation Effects of Operating Activities Involving Revenues

The following transactions are July activities of Bill's Extreme Bowling, Inc., which operates several bowling centers. For each of the following transactions, complete the spreadsheet, indicating the amount and effect (+ for increase and − for decrease) of each transaction under the accrual basis. Write NE if there is no effect on the category. Indicate +/− if the effects offset within a category. Include revenues as a subcategory of stockholders' equity, as shown for the first transaction, which is provided as an example.

Transaction	Assets	Liabilities	Stockholders' Equity
a. Bill's collected $12,000 from customers for services related to games played in July.	+12,000	NE	Service Revenue (+R) +12,000
b. Bill's billed a customer for $250 for a party held at the center on the last day of July. The bill is to be paid in August.			
c. The men's and women's bowling leagues gave Bill's advance payments totaling $1,500 for the fall season that starts in September.			
d. Bill's received $1,000 from credit sales made to customers last month (in June).			

LO 3-2, 3-3   **M3-8 Determining the Accounting Equation Effects of Operating Activities Involving Expenses**

The following transactions are July activities of Bill's Extreme Bowling, Inc., which operates several bowling centers. For each of the following transactions, complete the spreadsheet, indicating the amount and effect (+ for increase and − for decrease) of each transaction under the accrual basis. Write NE if there is no effect on the category. Indicate +/− if the effects offset within a category. Include expenses as a subcategory of stockholders' equity, as shown for the first transaction, which is provided as an example.

Transaction	Assets	Liabilities	Stockholders' Equity
a. Bill's paid $1,500 to plumbers for repairing a broken pipe in the restrooms.	−1,500	NE	Repairs Expense (+E) −1,500
b. Bill's paid $2,000 for the June electricity bill and received the July bill for $2,500, which will be paid in August.			
c. Bill's paid $5,475 to employees for work in July.			

LO 3-1, 3-5   **M3-9 Preparing an Income Statement and Calculating Net Profit Margin**

Given the transactions in M3-7 and M3-8 (including the examples), prepare an income statement for Bill's Extreme Bowling, Inc., for the month ended July 31. (This income statement would be considered "preliminary" because it uses unadjusted balances.) What is the company's net profit margin, expressed as a percent (to one decimal place)?

LO 3-2   **M3-10 Identifying Accrual Basis Revenues**

The following transactions are February activities of Swing Hard Incorporated, which offers indoor golfing lessons in the northeastern United States. If revenue is to be recognized in February, indicate the amount. If revenue is not to be recognized in February, explain why.

Activity	Amount or Explanation
a. Swing Hard collected $15,000 from customers for lesson services given in February.	
b. Swing Hard sold a gift card for golf lessons for $150 cash in February.	
c. Swing Hard received $4,000 from services provided on account to customers in January.	
d. Swing Hard collected $2,250 in advance payments for services to start in June.	
e. Swing Hard billed a customer $125 for services provided between February 25 and February 28. The bill is to be paid in March.	

M3-11 Identifying Accrual Basis Expenses

The following transactions are February activities of Swing Hard Incorporated, which offers indoor golfing lessons in the northeastern United States. If an expense is to be recognized in February, indicate the amount. If an expense is not to be recognized in February, explain why.

Activity	Amount or Explanation
a. Swing Hard paid $4,750 to its golf instructors for the month of February.	
b. Swing Hard paid $1,750 for electricity used in the month of January.	
c. Swing Hard received an electricity bill for $800 for the month of February, to be paid in March.	

M3-12 Recording Accrual Basis Revenues

For each of the transactions in M3-10, write the journal entry using the format shown in the chapter.

M3-13 Recording Accrual Basis Expenses

For each of the transactions in M3-11, write the journal entry using the format shown in the chapter.

M3-14 Preparing Accrual Basis Journal Entries for Business Activities

Quick Cleaners, Inc. (QCI), has been in business for several years. It specializes in cleaning houses but has some small business clients as well. Prepare journal entries for the following transactions, which occurred during a recent month, and determine QCI's preliminary net income.

a. Issued $25,000 of QCI stock for cash.
b. Incurred $600 of utilities costs this month and will pay them next month.
c. Incurred and paid wages for the current month, totaling $2,000.
d. Performed cleaning services on account worth $2,800.
e. Some of Quick Cleaners's equipment was repaired at a total cost of $150. The company paid the full amount at the time the repair work was done.

M3-15 Preparing Accrual Basis Journal Entries for Business Activities

Junktrader is an online company that specializes in matching buyers and sellers of used items. Buyers and sellers can purchase a membership with Junktrader, which provides them advance notice of potentially attractive offers. Prepare journal entries for the following transactions, which occurred during a recent month, and determine Junktrader's preliminary net income.

a. Junktrader provided online advertising services for another company for $200 on account.
b. On the last day of the month, Junktrader paid $50 cash to run an ad promoting the company's services. The ad ran that day in the local newspaper.
c. Received $200 cash in membership fees for the month from new members.
d. Received an electricity bill for $85 for usage this month. The bill will be paid next month.
e. Billed a customer $180 for helping sell some junk. Junktrader expects to receive the customer's payment by the end of next month.

M3-16 Preparing Accrual Basis Journal Entries for Business Activities

An international charity collects donations, which are used to pay its operating expenses and buy equipment for others. The charity records donations of cash and other items as Donations Revenue when received. Prepare journal entries for the following transactions, which occurred during a recent month, and determine the charity's preliminary net income.

a. Received $4,000 in cash and checks from a door-to-door campaign.
b. Incurred and paid $2,000 cash for employee wages this month.
c. Paid $1,000 cash on a short-term loan from the bank (ignore interest).
d. Bought $3,000 of equipment from a manufacturer, paying $1,000 cash and signing a short-term note for $2,000.
e. The manufacturer generously donated to the charity an additional $2,500 of equipment.

LO 3-3

M3-17 Preparing Accrual Basis Journal Entries and Reporting Financial Statements

Andy's Autobody Shop has the following balances at the beginning of September: Cash, $10,000; Accounts Receivable, $1,450; Equipment, $40,000; Accounts Payable, $2,000; Common Stock, $20,000; and Retained Earnings, $29,450. Prepare journal entries for the following transactions, which occurred during September; update the account balances for the journal entries; and then prepare an income statement, statement of retained earnings, and classified balance sheet as of and for the month ended September 30. (These financial statements would be considered "preliminary" because they use unadjusted balances.)

a. Signed a long-term note and received a $150,000 loan from a local bank.
b. Billed a customer $2,000 for repair services just completed. Payment is expected in 45 days.
c. Wrote a check for $600 of rent for the current month.
d. Received $450 cash on account from a customer for work done last month.
e. The company incurred $400 in advertising costs for the current month and is planning to pay these costs next month.

LO 3-2, 3-3

M3-18 Determining the Accounting Equation Effects of Operating Activities Involving Revenues

The following transactions are February activities of Swing Hard Incorporated, which offers golfing lessons in the northeastern United States. For each of the following transactions, complete the spreadsheet, indicating the amount and effect (+ for increase and − for decrease) of each transaction under the accrual basis. Write NE if there is no effect on the category. Indicate +/− if the effects offset within a category. Include revenues as a subcategory of stockholders' equity, as shown for the first transaction, which is provided as an example.

Transaction	Assets	Liabilities	Stockholders' Equity
a. Swing Hard collected $15,000 from customers for lesson services provided in February.	+15,000	NE	Service Revenue (+R) +15,000
b. Swing Hard sold a gift card for golf lessons for $150 cash in February.			
c. Swing Hard received $4,000 from credit sales made to customers in January.			
d. Swing Hard collected $2,250 in advance payments for golf lessons to start in June.			
e. Swing Hard billed a customer $125 for services provided between February 25 and February 28. The bill is to be paid in March.			

LO 3-2, 3-3

M3-19 Determining the Accounting Equation Effects of Operating Activities Involving Expenses

The following transactions are February activities of Swing Hard Incorporated, which offers golfing lessons in the northeastern United States. For each of the following transactions, complete the spreadsheet, indicating the amount and effect (+ for increase and − for decrease) of each transaction under the accrual basis. Write NE if there is no effect on the category. Indicate +/− if the effects offset within a category. Include expenses as a subcategory of stockholders' equity, as shown for the first transaction, which is provided as an example.

Transaction	Assets	Liabilities	Stockholders' Equity
a. Swing Hard paid $4,750 for wages to its golf instructors for the month of February.	−4,750	NE	Salaries and Wages Expense (+E) −4,750
b. Swing Hard paid $1,750 for electricity used in the month of January.			
c. Swing Hard received an electricity bill for $800 for the month of February, to be paid in March.			

LO 3-1, 3-5

M3-20 Preparing an Income Statement and Calculating Net Profit Margin

Given the transactions in M3-18 and M3-19 (including the examples), prepare an income statement for Swing Hard Incorporated for the month ended February 28. (This income statement would be considered "preliminary" because it uses unadjusted balances.) What is the company's net profit margin, expressed as a percent (to one decimal place)?

M3-21 Preparing Financial Statements from a Trial Balance   LO 3-1, 3-4

The following accounts are taken from Equilibrium Riding, Inc., a company that specializes in occupational therapy and horseback riding lessons, as of December 31.

EQUILIBRIUM RIDING, INC.
Unadjusted Trial Balance
At December 31

Account Name	Debits	Credits
Cash	$ 59,750	
Accounts Receivable	3,300	
Prepaid Insurance	4,700	
Equipment	64,600	
Land	23,000	
Accounts Payable		$ 29,230
Deferred Revenue		1,500
Notes Payable (long-term)		74,000
Common Stock		5,000
Retained Earnings		14,500
Dividends	0	
Service Revenue		35,700
Salaries and Wages Expense	3,900	
Repairs and Maintenance Expense	410	
Office Expense	270	
Totals	$159,930	$159,930

Required:

Using the unadjusted trial balance provided, create a classified Balance Sheet, Statement of Retained Earnings, and Income Statement for Equilibrium Riding, Inc., for the year ended December 31. (These financial statements would be considered "preliminary" because they use unadjusted balances.)

> **TIP:** Create the Income Statement first, followed by the Statement of Retained Earnings, and finally the classified Balance Sheet. Follow the formats presented in Exhibits 1.3, 1.4, and 2.13.

M3-22 Preparing an Income Statement and Calculating Net Profit Margin   LO 3-1, 3-5

For each of the following items in Old Time Cable, Inc.'s financial statements, indicate (1) whether it is reported in the income statement (I/S) or balance sheet (B/S) and (2) whether it is an asset (A), liability (L), stockholders' equity (SE), revenue (R), or expense (E) account. The first item is given as an example.

Item		(1) Statement	(2) Account Type
Example. Cash	$ 880	B/S	A
1. Service Revenue	5,500		
2. Accounts Receivable	900		
3. Interest Expense	380		
4. Deferred Revenue	200		
5. Income Tax Expense	250		
6. Retained Earnings	120		

Old Time Cable also reported $4,340 in operating expenses. Based on the available information, determine the company's net profit margin expressed as a percent (to one decimal place).

LO 3-5

Expedia
Booking.com

M3-23 Calculating and Interpreting Net Profit Margin

Expedia and Booking.com compete as online travel agencies. The following amounts were reported by the two companies in the three months ended June 30, 2019. Calculate each company's net profit margin expressed as a percent (to one decimal place). Which company has generated a greater return of profit from each revenue dollar?

(in millions)	Net Income	Total Assets	Total Liabilities	Total Revenues
Expedia	$183	$22,201	$16,294	$3,153
Booking.com	979	21,494	16,187	3,850

LO 3-5

M3-24 Calculating and Interpreting Net Profit Margin

Kijijo Auctions runs an online auction company. Its end-of-year financial statements indicate the following results. Calculate the company's net profit margin expressed as a percent (to one decimal place) and indicate whether it represents an improvement or deterioration relative to the 15.0 percent net profit margin earned in the previous year.

Total assets = $100,000   Total liabilities = $60,000   Common stock = $10,000
Dividends = $5,000   Expenses = $80,000   Retained earnings (beginning of year)
                                                          = $15,000

EXERCISES

LO 3-1

E3-1 Matching Definitions with Terms

Match each definition with its related term by entering the appropriate letter in the space provided.

Term	Definition
____ 1. Expenses	A. A liability account used to record the obligation to provide future services or return cash that has been received before services have been provided.
____ 2. Deferred Revenue	
____ 3. Prepaid Expenses	B. Costs that result when a company sacrifices resources to generate revenues in the current period.
____ 4. Revenue	C. A type of asset account used to record the benefits obtained, when cash is paid before expenses are incurred.
	D. The amount charged to customers for providing goods or services.

LO 3-1

E3-2 Matching Definitions with Terms

Match each definition with its related term by entering the appropriate letter in the space provided.

Term	Definition
____ 1. Accrual basis accounting	A. Record expenses when incurred in earning revenue.
____ 2. Expense recognition principle	
____ 3. Revenue recognition principle	B. Record revenues when or as work is done, not necessarily when cash is received.
____ 4. Cash basis accounting	C. Record revenues when received and expenses when paid.
	D. Record revenues when or as work is done, and expenses when incurred.

E3-3 Identifying Performance Obligations and Timing Revenue Recognition

LO 3-1, 3-2

Sirius XM Holdings Inc.

Sirius XM Holdings Inc. sells a dash-top satellite radio receiver and one-year subscription for a total price of $80. By purchasing this deal, the subscriber is entitled to receive hardware (i.e., the radio), a software update that is automatically downloaded every second month to the radio, and continuous music service for one year from the date the hardware is delivered.

Required:

Identify the performance obligation(s) in this contract, and indicate whether the revenue should be recognized at a point in time ("when") or over time ("as") for each identified performance obligation.

E3-4 Identifying Accrual Basis Revenues

LO 3-1, 3-2

Apple
The Home Depot
AT&T
American Airlines

According to the revenue recognition principle, revenues should be recognized when or as the company performs acts promised to the customer. For many businesses, this condition is met at the point of delivery of goods or services. The following transactions occurred in September:

a. A customer paid for and downloaded song files from Apple's iTunes store for $10 cash. Answer from Apple's standpoint.

b. The Home Depot provided a carpet installation for $2,000 cash. A comparable installation from other companies costs $3,000.

c. AT&T is scheduled to install digital cable at 1,000 Austin area homes next week. The installation charge is $100 per home. The terms require payment within 30 days of installation. Answer from AT&T's standpoint.

d. AT&T completed the installations described in (*c*). Answer from AT&T's standpoint.

e. AT&T received payment from customers for the installations described in (*c*). Answer from AT&T's standpoint.

f. A customer purchased a ticket from American Airlines in September for $500 cash to travel in December. Answer from American Airlines's standpoint.

Required:

For each of the transactions, if revenue is to be recognized in September, indicate the amount. If revenue is not to be recognized in September, explain why.

E3-5 Identifying Accrual Basis Revenues

LO 3-1, 3-2

T-Mobile

According to the revenue recognition principle, revenues should be recognized when or as the company performs acts promised to the customer. For many businesses, this condition is met at the point of delivery of goods or services. The following transactions occurred in September:

a. Gillespie Enterprises Inc. issued $26 million in new common stock.

b. Cal State University received $20,000,000 cash for 80,000 five-game-season football tickets. None of the games have been played.

c. Cal State played the first football game referred to in (*b*).

d. Hall Construction Company signed a contract with a customer for the construction of a new $500,000 warehouse. At the signing, Hall received a check for $50,000 as a deposit to be applied against amounts earned during the first phase of construction. Answer from Hall's standpoint.

e. A popular snowboarding magazine company received a total of $1,800 today from subscribers. The subscriptions begin in the next fiscal year. Answer from the magazine company's standpoint.

f. T-Mobile sold a $100 cell phone plan for service in September to a customer who charged the sale on his credit card. Answer from the standpoint of T-Mobile.

Required:

For each of the transactions, if revenue is to be recognized in September, indicate the amount. If revenue is not to be recognized in September, explain why.

E3-6 Identifying Accrual Basis Expenses

LO 3-1, 3-2

Dell
McGraw-Hill Education

Under accrual basis accounting, expenses are recognized when incurred, which means the activity giving rise to the expense has occurred. Assume the following transactions occurred in January:

a. Dell paid its computer service technicians $90,000 in salary for work done in January. Answer from Dell's standpoint.

b. At the beginning of January, Turner Construction Company paid $3,000 in rent for February–April.

c. McGraw-Hill Education—publisher of this textbook—used $3,000 worth of electricity and natural gas in January, which it has not paid or recorded.

d. Pooler Company received and paid in January a $1,500 invoice from a consulting firm for services received in January.

e. The campus bookstore received consulting services at a cost of $5,000. The terms indicate that payment is due within 30 days of the consultation.

f. Schergevitch Incorporated had its delivery van repaired in January for $280 and charged the amount on account.

Required:

For each of the transactions, if an expense is to be recognized in January, indicate the amount. If an expense is not to be recognized in January, indicate why.

LO 3-1, 3-2

American Express
Waste Management, Inc.

E3-7 Identifying Accrual Basis Expenses

Under accrual basis accounting, expenses are recognized when incurred. The following transactions occurred in January:

a. American Express paid its salespersons $3,500 in commissions related to December sales of financial advisory services. Answer from American Express's standpoint.

b. On January 31, American Express determined that it will pay its salespersons $4,200 in commissions related to January sales. The payment will be made in early February. Answer from American Express's standpoint.

c. The city of Omaha hired Waste Management, Inc., to provide trash collection services beginning January 1. The city paid $12 million for the entire year. Answer from the city's standpoint.

d. The University of Florida paid $10,000 in advance for refundable airline tickets to fly the baseball team to a tournament in California. The first game will be played in March. Answer from the university's standpoint.

e. A Houston Community College employee worked eight hours, at $15 per hour, on January 31; payday is not until February 3. Answer from the college's point of view.

f. Wang Company paid $3,600 for a fire insurance policy on January 1. The policy covers 12 months beginning on January 1. Answer from Wang's point of view.

g. Ziegler Company, a farm equipment company, received a phone bill for $230 of January calls. The bill has not been paid to date.

Required:

For each of the transactions, if an expense is to be recognized in January, indicate the amount. If an expense is not to be recognized in January, indicate why.

LO 3-2, 3-3

E3-8 Determining Accounting Equation Effects and Net Income

The following transactions occurred during a recent year:

a. Paid wages of $1,000 for the current period (example).
b. Borrowed $5,000 cash from local bank using a short-term note.
c. Purchased $2,000 of equipment on credit.
d. Earned $400 of sales revenue; collected cash.
e. Received $800 of utilities services, on credit.
f. Earned $1,700 of service revenue, on credit.
g. Paid $300 cash on account to a supplier.
h. Incurred $70 of travel expenses; paid cash.
i. Earned $400 of service revenue; collected half in cash, with balance on credit.
j. Collected $100 cash from customers on account.
k. Incurred $300 of advertising costs; paid half in cash, with balance on credit.

Required:

For each of the transactions, complete the following table, indicating the account, amount, and direction of the effect (+ for increase and − for decrease) of each transaction under the accrual basis. Write NE if there is no effect. Include revenues and expenses as subcategories of stockholders' equity, as shown for the first transaction, which is provided as an example. Also, determine the company's preliminary net income.

Transaction	Assets	=	Liabilities	+	Stockholders' Equity	
(a) (example)	Cash −1,000		NE		Wages Expense (+E)	−1,000

E3-9 Determining Accounting Equation Effects and Net Income

LO 3-2, 3-3

Wolverine World Wide, Inc.

Wolverine World Wide, Inc., manufactures military, work, sport, and casual footwear and leather accessories under a variety of brand names, such as Caterpillar, Hush Puppies, Wolverine, and Steve Madden. The following transactions occurred during a recent month.

a. Made cash sales of $49,000 (example).
b. Purchased $3,000 of additional supplies on account.
c. Borrowed $58,000 on long-term notes.
d. Purchased $18,600 in additional equipment, paying in cash.
e. Incurred $27,000 in selling expenses, paying two-thirds in cash and owing the rest on account.
f. Paid $4,700 in rent for this month, and also paid $4,700 for next month.

Required:

For each of the transactions, complete the table below, indicating the account, amount, and direction of the effect (+ for increase and − for decrease) of each transaction under the accrual basis. Write NE if there is no effect. Include revenues and expenses as subcategories of stockholders' equity, as shown for the first transaction, which is provided as an example. Also, determine the company's preliminary net income.

Transaction	Assets	=	Liabilities	+	Stockholders' Equity	
(a) (example)	Cash +49,000		NE		Sales Revenue (+R)	+49,000

E3-10 Recording Journal Entries and Determining Net Income

LO 3-2, 3-3

Sysco

Sysco, formed in 1969, is America's largest marketer and distributor of food service products, serving nearly 250,000 restaurants, hotels, schools, hospitals, and other institutions. The following transactions are typical of those that occurred in a recent year, but the amounts are simplified.

a. Borrowed $80,000 from a bank, signing a short-term note payable.
b. Provided $100,000 in service to customers, with $95,000 on account and the rest received in cash.
c. Purchased equipment for $130,000 in cash.
d. Incurred and paid employee wages of $1,000.
e. Received $410 on account from a customer.
f. Incurred and paid $4,000 cash for travel costs during the year.
g. Paid $8,200 cash on accounts payable.
h. Incurred $20,000 in utility expenses during the year, of which $15,000 was paid in cash and the rest owed on account.

Required:

For each of the transactions, prepare accrual basis journal entries and determine whether the accounting equation remains in balance and debits equal credits after each entry. Also, calculate the company's preliminary net income.

E3-11 Recording Journal Entries and Determining Net Income

LO 3-2, 3-3

Greek Peak

Greek Peak is a ski resort in upstate New York. The company sells lift tickets, ski lessons, and ski equipment. It operates several restaurants and rents townhouses to vacationing skiers. The following hypothetical December transactions are typical of those that occur at the resort.

a. Borrowed $500,000 from the bank on December 1, signing a note payable, due in six months.
b. Purchased a new snowplow for $20,000 cash on December 31.
c. Purchased ski supplies for $10,000 on account.
d. Incurred $22,000 in routine maintenance expenses for the chairlifts; paid cash.

    e. Received $72,000 for season passes (beginning in the new year).
    f. Daily lift passes were sold this month for a total of $76,000 cash.
    g. Received a $320 deposit on a townhouse to be rented for five days in January.
    h. Paid half the charges incurred on account in (*c*).
    i. Incurred and paid $18,000 in wages to employees for the month of December.

Required:

Prepare accrual basis journal entries for each transaction. Be sure to categorize each account as an Asset (A), Liability (L), Stockholders' Equity (SE), Revenue (R), or Expense (E) and check that debits equal credits for each journal entry. Also, calculate the company's preliminary net income.

LO 3-2, 3-3, 3-5
E3-12 Recording Journal Entries and Determining Net Income and Net Profit Margin

Rowland & Sons Air Transport Service, Inc., has been in operation for three years. The following transactions occurred in February:

Feb. 1	Paid $200 for rent of hangar space in February.
Feb. 4	Received customer payment of $800 to ship several items to Philadelphia next month.
Feb. 7	Flew cargo from Denver to Dallas; the customer paid in full ($900 cash).
Feb. 10	Incurred and paid $1,200 in pilot wages for flying in February.
Feb. 14	Paid $100 for an advertisement run in the local paper on February 14.
Feb. 18	Flew cargo for two customers from Dallas to Albuquerque for $1,700; one customer paid $500 cash and the other asked to be billed $1,200.
Feb. 25	Purchased on account $1,350 in supplies for future use on the planes.

Required:

Prepare accrual basis journal entries for each transaction. Be sure to categorize each account as an Asset (A), Liability (L), Stockholders' Equity (SE), Revenue (R), or Expense (E). Also, calculate the company's preliminary net income and net profit margin expressed as a percent (to one decimal place).

LO 3-2, 3-3, 3-4
E3-13 Recording and Posting Accrual Basis Journal Entries, and Preparing an Unadjusted Trial Balance and Preliminary Financial Statements

Ricky's Piano Rebuilding Company has been operating for one year. On January 1, at the start of its second year, its income statement accounts had zero balances and its balance sheet account balances were as follows:

Cash	$ 6,000	Accounts Payable	$ 8,000
Accounts Receivable	25,000	Deferred Revenue (deposits)	3,200
Supplies	1,200	Notes Payable (long-term)	40,000
Equipment	8,000	Common Stock	8,000
Land	6,000	Retained Earnings	9,000
Buildings	22,000		

Required:

1. Create T-accounts for the balance sheet accounts and for these additional accounts: Service Revenue, Rent Revenue, Salaries and Wages Expense, and Utilities Expense. Enter the beginning balances. (If you are using the general ledger tool in Connect, this requirement will be completed for you.)

2. Prepare journal entries for the following January transactions, using the letter of each transaction as a reference:

    a. Received a $500 deposit from a customer who wanted her piano rebuilt in February.
    b. Rented a part of the building to a bicycle repair shop; $300 rent received for January.
    c. Delivered five rebuilt pianos to customers who paid $14,500 in cash.
    d. Delivered two rebuilt pianos to customers for $7,000 charged on account.
    e. Received $6,000 from customers as payment on their accounts.
    f. Received an electric and gas utility bill for $350 for January services to be paid in February.
    g. Ordered $800 in supplies.
    h. Paid $1,700 on account in January.
    i. Paid $10,000 in wages to employees in January for work done this month.
    j. Received and paid cash for the supplies in (*g*).

3. Post the journal entries to the T-accounts. Show the unadjusted ending balances in the T-accounts. (If you are using the general ledger tool, this requirement will be completed for you.)

4. Use the balances in the completed T-accounts to prepare an unadjusted trial balance at January 31. (If you are using the general ledger tool, this requirement will be completed for you.)

5. Using the unadjusted balances, prepare a preliminary income statement for the month ended January 31 and a classified balance sheet at January 31.

E3-14 Analyzing Transactions from the Perspectives of Different Companies

LO 3-2, 3-3

Over-the-Top Technologies (OTT) operates a computer repair and web consulting business. News Now (NN) publishes a local newspaper. The two companies entered into the following transactions.

a. NN billed OTT for $500 of advertising services provided this month on account.
b. OTT repaired some of NN's equipment this month, for $135 on account.
c. NN collected $500 cash from OTT for the advertising services provided in (a).
d. NN paid $60 cash to OTT for OTT advertising NN's online newspaper this month on OTT's website.
e. OTT and NN signed a promissory note, documenting OTT's $1,000 cash loan to NN this month with repayment to occur in six months.

Required:

Show the journal entries that OTT and NN would record for items (a)–(e). Use a two-part table, with the left side showing OTT's journal entries and the right side showing NN's journal entries.

E3-15 Inferring Transactions and Computing Effects Using T-Accounts

LO 3-1, 3-2, 3-3

A company's accounting records included the following accounts.

Accounts Receivable (A)			Prepaid Rent (A)			Deferred Revenue (L)		
1/1	313		1/1	25			240	1/1
	2,573	a		43	b	c	328	
12/31	295		12/31	26			253	12/31

Required:

1. For each T-account, describe the typical transactions that cause it to increase and decrease.

2. Express each T-account in equation format (Beginning + Increase Side − Decrease Side = Ending) and then solve for the missing amounts. For example, the Accounts Receivable T-account can be expressed as: $313 + 2{,}573 - a = 295$. By rearranging the equation, you can solve for $313 + 2{,}573 - 295 = a$.

E3-16 Determining Accounting Equation Effects of Several Transactions

LO 3-2, 3-3

In January, Tongo, Inc., a branding consultant, had the following transactions. Indicate the accounts, amounts, and direction of the effects on the accounting equation under the accrual basis. A sample is provided.

a. (Sample) Received $9,500 cash for consulting services rendered in January.
b. Issued common stock to investors for $10,000 cash.
c. Purchased $12,000 of equipment, paying 25 percent in cash and owing the rest on a note due in two years.
d. Received $7,500 cash for consulting services to be performed in February.
e. Bought and received $1,000 of supplies on account.
f. Received utility bill for January for $1,250, due February 15.
g. Consulted for customers in January for fees totaling $15,900, due in February.
h. Received $12,000 cash for consulting services rendered in December.
i. Paid $500 toward supplies purchased in (e).

	Assets		=	Liabilities	+	Stockholders' Equity	
a.	Cash	+9,500	=			Service Revenue (+R)	+9,500

LO 3-3 **E3-17 Preparing Journal Entries**

For each of the transactions in E3-16 (including the sample), write the journal entry using the format shown in this chapter.

LO 3-3 **E3-18 Posting to T-Accounts**

For each of the transactions in E3-16 (including the sample), post the effects to the appropriate T-accounts and determine ending account balances. Beginning account balances have been given. The sample transaction has been posted as an example.

Cash (A)		Accounts Payable (L)		Common Stock (SE)	
Jan 1 10,000			5,000 Jan 1		12,000 Jan 1
a. 9,500					

Accounts Receivable (A)		Deferred Revenue (L)		Retained Earnings (SE)	
Jan 1 12,500			2,500 Jan 1		8,800 Jan 1

Supplies (A)		Notes Payable (L)		Service Revenue (R)	
Jan 1 800			0 Jan 1		0 Jan 1
					9,500 a.

Equipment (A)				Utilities Expense (E)	
Jan 1 5,000				Jan 1 0	

LO 3-4 **E3-19 Creating an Unadjusted Trial Balance**

Based on the transactions posted to T-accounts in E3-18, create an unadjusted trial balance for Tongo, Inc., for the month ended January 31. Distinguish the balance sheet and income statement accounts as shown in Exhibit 3.10.

LO 3-3, 3-4, 3-5 **E3-20 Analyzing, Recording, and Evaluating the Effects of Income Statement Transactions**

MyBnB started a home rental company on January 1. As of November 30, MyBnB reported the following balances. The company does not yet have a balance in Retained Earnings because this is its first year of operations so no net income has been reported in prior years.

Accounts Payable	$ 300	Equipment	$2,400
Cash	1,000	Repairs Expense	200
Cleaning Expense	900	Service Revenue	2,000
Common Stock	3,000	Wages Expense	800

Required:

1. Prepare an unadjusted trial balance, a preliminary income statement, statement of retained earnings, and classified balance sheet as of and for the 11-month period ended November 30.
2. The owner of MyBnB was hoping the company would generate a net profit margin of at least 10 percent. Based on the financial statements prepared in requirement 1, determine whether the owner met her goal as of November 30.
3. Prepare journal entries for the following December transactions.

   a. Provided rental services at a price of $300 and collected the full amount in cash.
   b. Paid $70 cash to a cleaning company for December work.
   c. Paid $60 cash to MyBnB's part-time employee for December wages.
   d. Paid $100 cash on account for amounts owed from a prior equipment purchase.
   e. Obtained repair services in December at a cost of $40, to be paid in January.

4. Prepare T-accounts that show the November 30 balances as December 1 beginning balances and then post the journal entries from your answer to requirement 3 to calculate updated December 31 balances. Retained Earnings has a beginning balance of $0.

5. Prepare an unadjusted trial balance, a preliminary income statement, statement of retained earnings, and classified balance sheet as of and for the year ended December 31.

6. Based on the financial statements prepared in requirement 5, determine whether the owner met her 10 percent net profit margin goal as of December 31.

E3-21 Determining the Effects of Various Transactions

LO 3-3, 3-5

EZ Reader was founded in January to provide text reading and recording services. Selected transactions for EZ Reader's first month of business are as follows:

a. Issued common stock to investors for $50,000 cash.
b. Billed customers $10,500 for services performed in January.
c. Purchased equipment for $24,500 for use in the business. Paid in cash.
d. Purchased and received $2,400 of supplies on account.
e. Received $7,500 cash from customers billed in transaction (b).
f. Used $1,500 in utilities, which will be paid in February.
g. Paid employees $3,500 cash for work done in January.
h. Paid $1,200 cash toward supplies purchased in transaction (d).

Required:

For each transaction, give (1) the name of the account being debited or credited, (2) the basic account type (A, L, SE, R, E), (3) whether the account is increased (+) or decreased (−) due to the transaction, and (4) whether the account normally holds a debit or credit balance. Transaction (a) has been given as an example. Also, calculate the company's preliminary net income and net profit margin (expressed as a percent to one decimal place).

Debit Side of Journal Entry			
Account Name	Account Type	Direction of Change	Normal Balance
(a) Cash	A	+	Debit

Credit Side of Journal Entry			
Account Name	Account Type	Direction of Change	Normal Balance
(a) Common Stock	SE	+	Credit

COACHED PROBLEMS

Mc Graw Hill **connect**

CP3-1 Recording Nonquantitative Journal Entries

LO 3-1, 3-2, 3-3

The following list includes a series of accounts for B-ball Corporation, which has been operating for three years. These accounts are listed alphabetically and numbered for identification. Following the accounts is a series of transactions. For each transaction, indicate the account(s) that should be debited and credited by entering the appropriate account number(s) to the right of each transaction. If no journal entry is needed, write *none* after the transaction. The first transaction is used as an example.

> **TIP:** In transaction (h), remember what the expense recognition principle says.
> **TIP:** Think of transaction (i) as two transactions: (1) incur expenses and liability and (2) pay part of the liability.

Account No.	Account Title	Account No.	Account Title
1	Accounts Payable	8	Notes Payable
2	Accounts Receivable	9	Prepaid Insurance
3	Cash	10	Rent Expense
4	Common Stock	11	Service Revenue
5	Equipment	12	Supplies
6	Income Tax Expense		
7	Income Tax Payable		

Transactions	Debit	Credit
a. Example: Purchased equipment for use in the business; paid one-third cash and signed a note payable for the balance.	5	3, 8
b. Issued common stock to new investors.	——	——
c. Collected cash for services performed this period.	——	——
d. Paid cash for rent this period.	——	——
e. Performed services this period on credit.	——	——
f. Collected cash on accounts receivable for services performed last period.	——	——
g. Paid cash on accounts payable for expenses incurred last period.	——	——
h. Purchased supplies to be used later; paid cash.	——	——
i. Paid three-fourths of the income tax expense for the year; the balance will be paid next year.	——	——
j. On the last day of the current period, paid cash for an insurance policy covering the next two years.	——	——

LO 3-2, 3-3   **CP3-2 Recording Journal Entries**

Ryan Olson organized a new company, MeToo, Inc. The company provides networking management services on social network sites. You have been hired to record the following transactions.

a. May   1: Issued 1,000 shares of common stock to investors for $30 per share.
b. May 15: Borrowed $50,000 from the bank to provide additional funding to begin operations; the note is due in two years.
c. May 31: Paid $2,400 for a one-year fire insurance policy with coverage starting June 1.
   TIP: For convenience, simply record the full amount of the payment as an asset (Prepaid Insurance). At the end of June, this account will be adjusted to its proper balance. We will study this adjustment process in Chapter 4, so just leave it as Prepaid Insurance for now.
d. June   3: Purchased furniture for the store for $15,000 on account. The amount is due within 30 days.
e. June   5: Placed advertisements in local college newspapers today for a total of $250 cash.
f. June   9: Provided services for $400 cash.
g. June 14: Made full payment for the furniture purchased on account on June 3.

Required:

For each of the transactions, prepare journal entries. Be sure to categorize each account as an asset (A), liability (L), stockholders' equity (SE), revenue (R), or expense (E).

LO 3-1, 3-2, 3-3, 3-4, 3-5   **CP3-3 Analyzing the Effects of Transactions Using T-Accounts, Preparing an Unadjusted Trial Balance, and Determining Net Income and Net Profit Margin**

Barbara Jones opened Barb's Book Business on February 1. You have been hired to maintain the company's financial records. The following transactions occurred in February, the first month of operations.

a. Received shareholders' cash contributions on February 1 totaling $16,000 to form the corporation; issued 1,000 shares of common stock.
b. Paid $2,400 cash on February 2 for three months' rent for office space.
   TIP: For convenience, simply record the full amount of the payment as an asset (Prepaid Rent). At the end of the month, this account will be adjusted to its proper balance. We will study this adjustment process in Chapter 4, so just leave it as Prepaid Rent for now.
c. Purchased and received supplies on February 3 for $300 cash.
d. Signed a promissory note on February 4, payable in two years; deposited $10,000 in the company's bank account.
e. On February 5, paid cash to buy equipment for $2,500 and land for $7,500.
f. Placed an advertisement in the local paper on February 6 for $425 cash.
g. Recorded sales on February 7 totaling $1,800; $1,525 was in cash and the rest on accounts receivable.
h. Collected accounts receivable of $50 from customers on February 8.
i. On February 9, repaired one of the computers for $120 cash.
   TIP: Most repairs involve costs that do not provide additional future economic benefits.
j. Incurred and paid employee wages on February 28 of $420.

Required:

1. Record the effects of transactions (*a*) through (*j*) using journal entries.

2. If this requirement is being completed manually, set up appropriate T-accounts for Cash, Accounts Receivable, Supplies, Prepaid Rent, Land, Equipment, Notes Payable, Common Stock, Sales Revenue, Advertising Expense, Salaries and Wages Expense, and Repairs and Maintenance Expense. All accounts begin with zero balances because this is the first month of operations. Summarize the journal entries from requirement 1, referencing each transaction in the accounts with the transaction letter. Show the unadjusted ending balances in the T-accounts. If you are using the general ledger tool in Connect, your answers to requirement 1 will have been posted automatically to general ledger accounts that are similar in appearance to Exhibit 2.9.

3. Prepare an unadjusted trial balance at the end of February. If you are using the general ledger tool in Connect, this requirement is completed automatically using your previous answers.

4. Refer to the revenues and expenses shown on the unadjusted trial balance. Based on this information, calculate preliminary net income and net profit margin (expressed as a percent to one decimal place), and determine whether the net profit margin is better or worse than the 10.0 percent earned by a close competitor.

CP3-4 Analyzing, Journalizing, and Interpreting Business Activities

LO 3-3, 3-5

Lakewood Tennis Club (LTC) operates an indoor tennis facility. The company charges a $150 annual membership fee plus a member rental rate of $20 per court per hour. LTC's fiscal year-end is August 31. LTC's revenue recognition policy is described in its financial statement notes as follows:

> *Revenue Recognition*—LTC generates revenue from two sources. Annual membership fees arise from providing 12 months of services to members, so they are reported as membership revenue each month as these services are provided. Court rental fees are generated by renting courts each day, so they are reported as service revenue when courts are used by members.

The following events occurred.

a. On August 31, 10 new members joined and paid the annual membership fee in cash. The memberships do not begin until September 1.

b. For the week ended September 11, LTC provided 190 court-hours of rental services for members and collected its fees in cash.

c. On September 13, LTC purchased and received tennis balls and other supplies. The regular retail price was $220, but LTC negotiated a lower amount ($200) that is to be paid in October.

d. On September 15, LTC paid $1,500 to employees for the hours they worked from September 1–15.

e. For the two weeks ended September 25, LTC provided 360 court-hours for members and collected its fees in cash.

f. On September 26, LTC's courts were used for a member's birthday party. LTC expects the member to pay the special event booking fee of $210 on Saturday, October 2.

g. On September 27, LTC wrote a $300 check to an advertising company to prepare advertising flyers that will be inserted in local newspapers on October 1.

h. On September 29, LTC received $210 on account for the member's birthday party that was held on September 26.

i. On September 30, LTC submitted its electricity and natural gas meter readings online. According to the suppliers' websites, the total charges for the month will be $300. This amount will be paid on October 17 through a preauthorized online payment.

Required:

1. Indicate the accounting equation effects of the August and September events, using a table similar to the one shown for Demonstration Case B. Reference each transaction by date.

2. Prepare journal entries to record the August and September events described in items (*a*)–(*i*).

3. Using your answer to requirement 1 or 2, calculate LTC's preliminary net income for September. Is LTC profitable, based on its preliminary net income?

4. Identify at least two adjustments that LTC will be required to make before it can prepare a final income statement for September.

   TIP: Scan the accounts used to answer requirements 1 and 2, looking for amounts that are no longer accurate at September 30.

GROUP A PROBLEMS

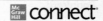

LO 3-1, 3-2, 3-3   **PA3-1 Recording Nonquantitative Journal Entries**

The following is a series of accounts for Dewan & Allard, Incorporated, which has been operating for two years. The accounts are listed alphabetically and numbered for identification. Following the accounts is a series of transactions. For each transaction, indicate the account(s) that should be debited and credited by entering the appropriate account number(s) to the right of each transaction. If no journal entry is needed, write *none* after the transaction. The first transaction is given as an example.

Account No.	Account Title	Account No.	Account Title
1	Accounts Payable	9	Land
2	Accounts Receivable	10	Notes Payable
3	Advertising Expense	11	Prepaid Insurance
4	Buildings	12	Salaries and Wages Expense
5	Cash	13	Service Revenue
6	Common Stock	14	Supplies
7	Income Tax Expense	15	Supplies Expense
8	Income Tax Payable		

Transactions	Debit	Credit
a. *Example:* Issued common stock to new investors.	5	6
b. Performed services for customers this period on credit.		
c. Purchased on credit but did not use supplies this period.		
d. Prepaid a fire insurance policy this period to cover the next 12 months.		
e. Purchased a building this period by making a 20 percent cash down payment and signing a note payable for the balance.		
f. Collected cash for services that had been provided and recorded in the prior year.		
g. Paid cash for wages incurred this period.		
h. Paid cash for supplies that had been purchased on accounts payable in the prior period.		
i. Paid cash for advertising expense incurred in the current period.		
j. Incurred advertising expenses this period to be paid next period.		
k. Received cash for services rendered this period.		
l. Recorded income taxes for this period to be paid at the beginning of the next period.		
m. This period a shareholder sold some shares of her stock to another person for an amount above the original issuance price.		

LO 3-2, 3-3   **PA3-2 Recording Journal Entries**

Diana Mark is the president of ServicePro, Inc., a company that provides temporary employees for not-for-profit companies. ServicePro has been operating for five years; its revenues are increasing with each passing year. You have been hired to help Diana in analyzing the following transactions for the first two weeks of April:

April 2	Purchased and received office supplies for $500 on account.
April 5	Billed the local United Way office $3,000 for temporary services provided.
April 8	Paid $250 for supplies purchased and recorded on account last period.
April 8	Placed an advertisement in the local paper for $400 cash.
April 9	Purchased new equipment for the office costing $2,300 cash.
April 10	Paid employee wages of $1,200 incurred in April.
April 11	Received $1,000 on account from the local United Way office billed on April 5.
April 12	Purchased land as the site of a future office for $10,000. The land value was appraised as $11,000. Paid $2,000 down and signed a long-term note payable for the balance.

April 13	Issued 2,000 additional shares of common stock for $40 per share in anticipation of building a new office.
April 14	Billed Family & Children's Services $2,000 for services rendered this month.
April 15	Received the April utilities bill for $300 to be paid next month.

Required:

For each of the transactions, prepare journal entries. Be sure to categorize each account as an asset (A), liability (L), stockholders' equity (SE), revenue (R), or expense (E).

PA3-3 Analyzing the Effects of Transactions Using T-Accounts, Preparing an Unadjusted Trial Balance, and Determining Net Income and Net Profit Margin

LO 3-1, 3-2, 3-3, 3-4, 3-5

Spicewood Stables, Inc., was established in Dripping Springs, Texas, on April 1. The company provides stables, care for animals, and grounds for riding and showing horses. You have been hired as the new assistant controller. The following transactions for April are provided for your review.

a. Received contributions from investors and issued $200,000 of common stock on April 1.
b. Acquired a barn for $142,000. On April 2, the company paid half the amount in cash and signed a three-year note payable for the balance.
c. Provided $16,000 in animal care services for customers on April 3, all on credit.
d. Rented stables to customers who cared for their own animals; received cash of $13,000 on April 4 for rent earned this month.
e. On April 5, received $1,500 cash from a customer to board her horse in May, June, and July (record as Deferred Revenue).
f. Purchased and received hay and feed supplies on account on April 6 for $3,000.
g. Paid $1,700 on accounts payable on April 7 for previous purchases.
h. Received $1,000 from customers on April 8 on accounts receivable.
i. On April 9, prepaid a two-year insurance policy for $3,600 for coverage starting in May.
j. On April 28, paid $800 in cash for water and utilities used this month.
k. Paid $14,000 in wages on April 29 for work done this month.
l. Received an electric utility bill on April 30 for $1,200 for usage in April; the bill will be paid next month.

Required:

1. Record the effects of transactions (a) through (l) using journal entries.
2. If you are completing this requirement manually, set up appropriate T-accounts. All accounts begin with zero balances. Summarize the journal entries from requirement 1 in the T-accounts, referencing each transaction in the accounts with the transaction number. Show the unadjusted ending balances in the T-accounts. If you are using the general ledger tool in Connect, your answers to requirement 1 will have been posted automatically to general ledger accounts that are similar in appearance to Exhibit 2.9.
3. Prepare an unadjusted trial balance as of April 30. If you are using the general ledger tool in Connect, this requirement is completed automatically using your previous answers.
4. Refer to the revenues and expenses shown on the unadjusted trial balance. Based on this information, calculate preliminary net income and determine whether the net profit margin is better or worse than the 30.0 percent earned by a close competitor.

PA3-4 Analyzing, Journalizing, and Interpreting Business Activities

LO 3-3, 3-5

The following events occurred soon after Pat Hopkins established Ona Cloud Corporation (OCC) as a provider of cloud computing services.

a. On September 1, Pat contributed $10,000 for 1,000 shares of OCC.
b. On September 8, OCC borrowed $30,000 from a bank, promising to repay the bank in two years.
c. On September 10, OCC wrote a check for $20,000 to acquire computer equipment.
d. On September 15, OCC received $1,000 of supplies purchased on account.
e. On September 16, OCC paid $1,500 for September rent.
f. Through September 22, OCC provided its customers $8,000 of services, of which OCC collected $6,000 in cash.
g. On September 28, OCC paid $200 for Internet and phone service this month.
h. On September 29, OCC paid wages of $4,000 for the month.
i. On September 30, OCC submitted its electricity meter reading online and determined that the total charges for the month will be $300. This amount will be paid on October 14 through a preauthorized online payment.

Required:

1. Indicate the accounting equation effects of the September events, using a table similar to the one shown for Demonstration Case B. Reference each transaction by date.

2. Prepare journal entries to record the September events described above.

3. Using your answer to requirement 1 or 2, calculate OCC's preliminary net income for September. Is OCC profitable, based on its preliminary net income?

4. Identify at least two adjustments that OCC will be required to make before it can prepare a final income statement for September.

GROUP B PROBLEMS

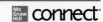

LO 3-1, 3-2, 3-3

Abercrombie & Fitch Co.

PB3-1   Recording Nonquantitative Journal Entries

Abercrombie & Fitch Co. (ANF) is a specialty retailer of casual apparel. The following is a series of accounts for ANF. The accounts are listed alphabetically and numbered for identification. Following the accounts is a series of transactions. For each transaction, indicate the account(s) that should be debited and credited by entering the appropriate account number(s) to the right of each transaction. If no journal entry is needed, write *none* after the transaction. The first transaction is given as an example.

Account No.	Account Title	Account No.	Account Title
1	Accounts Payable	6	Equipment
2	Accounts Receivable	7	Interest Revenue
3	Cash	8	Prepaid Rent
4	Common Stock	9	Rent Expense
5	Deferred Revenue	10	Salaries and Wages Expense

Transactions	Debit	Credit
a. *Example:* Incurred wages expense; paid cash.	10	3
b. Collected cash on account.		
c. Customers purchased ANF gift cards; none redeemed this period.		
d. Purchased equipment, paying part in cash and charging the balance on account.		
e. Paid cash to suppliers on account.		
f. Issued additional common stock for cash.		
g. Paid rent to landlords for next month's use of mall space.		
h. Earned and received cash for interest on investments.		

LO 3-2, 3-3

PB3-2   Recording Journal Entries

Robin Harrington established Time Definite Delivery on January 1. The following transactions occurred during the company's most recent quarter.

a. Issued common stock for $80,000.
b. Provided delivery service to customers, receiving $16,000 in cash and $72,000 on account.
c. Purchased and received equipment costing $82,000 and signed a long-term note for the full amount.
d. Incurred repair costs of $3,000 on account.
e. Collected $65,000 from customers on account.
f. Borrowed and deposited $90,000 cash upon signing a long-term note.
g. Prepaid $74,400 cash to rent equipment next quarter.
h. Paid employees $38,000 for work done this period.
i. Incurred $49,000 of delivery costs this quarter, all paid in cash.
j. Paid $2,000 on accounts payable.
k. Ordered, but haven't yet received, $700 in supplies.

Required:

For each of the transactions, prepare journal entries. Be sure to categorize each account as an asset (A), liability (L), stockholders' equity (SE), revenue (R), or expense (E).

PB3-3 Analyzing the Effects of Transactions Using T-Accounts, Preparing an Unadjusted Trial Balance, and Determining Net Income and Net Profit Margin

LO 3-1, 3-2, 3-3, 3-4, 3-5

Jessica Pothier opened FunFlatables on June 1. The company rents out moon walks and inflatable slides for parties and corporate events. The company also has obtained the use of an abandoned ice rink located in a local shopping mall, where its rental products are displayed and available for casual hourly rental by mall patrons. The following transactions occurred during the first month of operations.

a. Jessica contributed $50,000 cash to the company on June 1 in exchange for its common stock.
b. Purchased inflatable rides and inflation equipment on June 2, paying $20,000 cash.
c. Received $5,000 cash from casual hourly rentals at the mall on June 3.
d. Rented rides and equipment to customers for $10,000. Received cash of $2,000 on June 4 and the rest is due from customers.
e. Received $2,500 from a large corporate customer on June 5 as a deposit on a party booking for July 4.
f. Began to prepare for the July 4 party by purchasing and receiving various party supplies on June 6 on account for $600.
g. On June 7, paid $6,000 in cash for renting the mall space this month.
h. On June 8, prepaid next month's mall space rental charge of $6,000.
i. Received $1,000 on June 9 from customers on accounts receivable.
j. Paid $1,000 for running a television ad on June 10.
k. Paid $4,000 in wages to employees on June 30 for work done during the month.

Required:

1. Record the effects of transactions (*a*) through (*k*) using journal entries.
2. If you are completing this requirement manually, set up appropriate T-accounts. All accounts begin with zero balances. Summarize the journal entries from requirement 1 in the T-accounts, referencing each transaction in the accounts with the transaction number. Show the unadjusted ending balances in the T-accounts. If you are using the GL tool in Connect, your answers to requirement 1 will have been posted automatically to general ledger accounts that are similar in appearance to Exhibit 2.9.
3. Prepare an unadjusted trial balance for the end of June. If you are using the GL tool in Connect, this requirement is completed automatically using your previous answers.
4. Refer to the revenues and expenses shown on the unadjusted trial balance to calculate preliminary net income and determine whether the net profit margin is better or worse than the 30.0 percent earned by a close competitor.

PB3-4 Analyzing, Journalizing, and Interpreting Business Activities

LO 3-3, 3-5

The following items present a sample of business activities involving Dry Cleaner Corporation (DCC) for the year ended December 31. DCC provides cleaning services for individual customers and for employees of several large companies in the city.

Dec 1:   DCC's owner paid $10,000 cash to acquire 200 of DCC's common shares.

Dec 7:   DCC ordered cleaning supplies at a total cost of $2,000. The supplies are expected to be received in early January.

Dec 17:   Customers paid $200 cash to DCC to obtain DCC gift cards that they could use to obtain future cleaning services at no additional cost.

Dec 21:   DCC ran advertising in the local newspaper today at a total cost of $500. DCC is not required to pay for the advertising until January 21.

Dec 22:   DCC paid $1,000 to the landlord for January rent.

Dec 23:   DCC's owner sold 20 of his own DSS common shares to a private investor, at a selling price of $1,200.

Dec 28:   DCC paid in full for the advertising run in the local newspaper on December 21.

Dec 29:   The cleaning supplies ordered on December 7 were received today. DCC does not have to pay for these supplies until January 29.

Dec 31:   Today, DCC completed cleaning services for several large companies at a total price of $2,000. The companies are expected to pay for the services by January 31.

Required:

1. Indicate the accounting equation effects of each item, using a table similar to the one shown for Demonstration Case B. Reference each item by date.

2. Prepare journal entries to record each item. Reference each item by date. If a journal entry is not required, explain.

3. Identify at least two adjustments that DCC will be required to make before it can prepare a final income statement for December.

COMPREHENSIVE PROBLEM

LO 3-2, 3-3, 3-4, 3-5

C3-1 Analyzing, Recording, and Posting, and Preparing and Evaluating Financial Statements (Chapters 1–3)

Vanishing Games Corporation (VGC) operates a massively multiplayer online game, charging players a monthly subscription of $15. At the start of January 2021, VGC's income statement accounts had zero balances and its balance sheet account balances were as follows:

Cash	$1,500,000	Accounts Payable	$ 108,000
Accounts Receivable	150,000	Deferred Revenue	73,500
Supplies	14,700	Notes Payable (due 2025)	60,000
Equipment	874,500	Common Stock	2,500,000
Buildings	422,000	Retained Earnings	1,419,700
Land	1,200,000		

In addition to the above accounts, VGC's chart of accounts includes the following: Service Revenue, Salaries and Wages Expense, Advertising Expense, and Utilities Expense.

Required:

1. Analyze the effect of the January transactions (shown below) on the accounting equation, using the format shown in this chapter's Demonstration Case B.

    a. Received $50,000 cash from customers on 1/1 for subscriptions that had already been earned in 2020.

    b. Purchased 10 new computer servers for $33,500 on 1/2; paid $10,000 cash and signed a three-year note for the remainder owed.

    c. Paid $10,000 for an Internet advertisement run on 1/3.

    d. On January 4, purchased and received $3,000 of supplies on account.

    e. Received $170,000 cash on 1/5 from customers for service revenue earned in January.

    f. Paid $3,000 cash to a supplier on January 6.

    g. On January 7, sold 15,000 subscriptions at $15 each for services provided during January. Half was collected in cash and half was sold on account.

    h. Paid $378,000 in wages to employees on 1/30 for work done in January.

    i. On January 31, received an electric and gas utility bill for $5,350 for January utility services. The bill will be paid in February.

2. Prepare journal entries for the January transactions listed in requirement 1, using the letter of each transaction as a reference.

3. If you are completing this requirement manually, create T-accounts, enter the beginning balances shown above, post the journal entries to the T-accounts, and show the unadjusted ending balances in the T-accounts. If you are completing this problem using the general ledger tool in Connect, this requirement will be automatically completed using your answers to earlier requirements.

4. Prepare an unadjusted trial balance as of January 31, 2021. If you are completing this problem using the general ledger tool in Connect, this requirement will be automatically completed using your answers to earlier requirements.

5. Prepare an Income Statement for the month ended January 31, 2021, using unadjusted balances from requirement 4.

6. Prepare a Statement of Retained Earnings for the month ended January 31, 2021, using the beginning balance given above and the net income from requirement 5. Assume VGC has no dividends.

7. Prepare a classified Balance Sheet at January 31, 2021, using your response to requirement 6.

8. Calculate net profit margin, expressed as a percent (to one decimal place).

SKILLS DEVELOPMENT CASES

S3-1 Finding Financial Information

LO 3-1

Refer to the financial statements of The Home Depot in Appendix A at the end of this book. (Note: Fiscal 2019 for The Home Depot runs from February 4, 2019, to February 2, 2020. See S1-1 for further explanation.)

The Home Depot

1. How much did The Home Depot's sales revenue increase or decrease in the year ended February 2, 2020?
   a. Decreased $2,022 (million)
   c. Increased $2,022 (million)
   b. Decreased $121 (million)
   d. Increased $121 (million)

2. What is the largest expense on the income statement for the year ended February 2, 2020, and how much did it change from the previous year?
   a. Cost of Sales, which increased $1,610 (million)
   b. Cost of Sales, which decreased $1,610 (million)
   c. Selling, General and Administrative Expenses, which decreased $331 (million)
   d. Selling, General and Administrative Expenses, which increased $227 (million)

3. Which of the following was The Home Depot's net profit margin in the year ended February 2, 2020?
   a. $37,572
   c. 34.1 percent
   b. $10.29
   d. 10.2 percent

S3-2 Finding Financial Information

LO 3-1

Refer to the financial statements of Lowe's Companies, Inc., in Appendix B. (Note: Fiscal 2019 for Lowe's runs from February 2, 2019, to January 31, 2020. See S1-1 for further explanation.)

Lowe's

1. How much did Lowe's sales revenue increase or decrease in the year ended January 31, 2020?
   a. Decreased $839 (million)
   b. Increased $839 (million)
   c. Increased $1,967 (million)
   d. Decreased $1,967 (million)

2. What is the largest expense on the income statement for the year ended January 31, 2020, and how much did it change from the previous year?
   a. Cost of Sales, which decreased $804 (million)
   b. Cost of Sales, which increased $804 (million)
   c. Selling, General and Administrative Expenses, which decreased $2,046 (million)
   d. Selling, General and Administrative Expenses, which increased $2,046 (million)

3. Which of the following was Lowe's net profit margin in the year ended January 31, 2020?
   a. 5.9 percent
   c. 31.8 percent
   b. $5.49
   d. 5.02 percent

S3-3 Internet-Based Team Research: Examining the Income Statement

LO 3-1, 3-5

As a team, select an industry to analyze. Using your web browser, each team member should access the annual report or 10-K for one publicly traded company in the industry, with each member selecting a different company. (See S1-3 in Chapter 1 for a description of possible resources for these tasks.)

Required:

1. On an individual basis, each team member should write a short report that lists the following information:
   a. The major revenue and expense accounts on the most recent income statement.
   b. Description of how the company has followed the conditions of the revenue recognition principle.
   c. The percentage of revenues that go to covering expenses and that are in excess of expenses (in other words, net profit margin expressed as a percentage).

2. Then, as a team, write a short report comparing and contrasting your companies using these attributes. Discuss any patterns across the companies that you as a team observe. Provide potential explanations for any differences discovered.

LO 3-1, 3-2, 3-3, 3-5

S3-4 Ethical Decision Making: A Real-Life Example

WorldCom

Read the following excerpt from a complaint filed by the Securities and Exchange Commission against WorldCom (posted online at www.sec.gov/litigation/complaints/comp17829.htm).

> WorldCom officers and employees fraudulently made and caused the making of false and fictitious entries in WorldCom's general ledger which effectively "transferred" a significant portion of its line cost expenses to a variety of capital asset accounts, thereby effectively recharacterizing, without any supporting documentation, and in a manner inconsistent with GAAP, the operating expenses it had incurred for access to third party networks as "assets."

1. When a company incurs a cost, its accountants have to decide whether to record the cost as an asset or expense. When costs are recorded as an asset, they are said to be *capitalized*. This builds on ideas first presented in Chapter 2, where you learned that it was appropriate to record costs as assets, provided that they possess certain characteristics. What are those characteristics?

2. Some authors claim that even with clear rules like those referenced in question 1 above, accounting still allows managers to use "tricks" like *capitalizing* expenses. What do you suppose is meant by the expression "*capitalizing* expenses"?

3. Suppose that, in the current year, a company inappropriately records a cost as an asset when it should be recorded as an expense. What is the effect of this accounting decision on the current year's net income? What is the effect of this accounting decision on the following year's net income?

4. Do you think it is always easy and straightforward to determine whether costs should be capitalized or expensed? Do you think it is always easy and straightforward to determine whether a manager is acting ethically or unethically? Give examples to illustrate your views.

LO 3-1, 3-2, 3-5

S3-5 Ethical Decision Making: A Mini-Case

Mike Lynch is the manager of an upstate New York regional office for an insurance company. As the regional manager, his pay package includes a base salary, commissions, and a bonus, when the region sells new policies in excess of its quota. Mike has been under enormous pressure lately, stemming largely from two factors. First, he is experiencing mounting personal debt due to a family member's illness. Second, compounding his worries, the region's sales of new insurance policies have dipped below the normal quota for the first time in years.

You have been working for Mike for two years, and like everyone else in the office, you consider yourself lucky to work for such a supportive boss. You also feel great sympathy for his personal problems over the last few months. In your position as accountant for the regional office, you are only too aware of the drop in new policy sales and the impact this will have on the manager's bonus. While you are working on the year-end financial statements, Mike stops by your office.

Mike asks you to change the manner in which you have accounted for a new property insurance policy for a large local business. A check for the premium, substantial in amount, came in the mail on December 31, the last day of the reporting year. The premium covers a period beginning on January 5. You deposited the check and correctly debited Cash and credited Deferred Revenue. Mike says, "Hey, we have the money this year, so why not count the revenue this year? I never did understand why you accountants are so picky about these things anyway. I'd like you to change the way you've recorded the transaction. I want you to credit a revenue account. And anyway, I've done favors for you in the past, and I am asking for such a small thing in return." With that, he leaves your office.

Required:

How should you handle this situation? What are the ethical implications of Mike's request? Who are the parties who would be helped or harmed if you went along with the request? If you fail to comply with his request, how will you explain your position to him? Justify your answers in writing.

LO 3-1, 3-2, 3-4

S3-6 Critical Thinking: Analyzing Changes in Accounts and Preparing an Unadjusted Trial Balance

Complete this case, available online in the Connect eBook. By completing this case, you will learn to identify changes in spreadsheet values and infer the underlying transactions responsible for those changes.

S3-7 Analyzing Transactions and Preparing an Unadjusted Trial Balance   LO 3-2, 3-3, 3-4

Complete this case, available online in the Connect eBook. By completing this case, you will learn to use a spreadsheet to capture transactions and use cell linking to prepare an end-of-period trial balance.

CONTINUING CASE

CC3-1 Accounting for Business Operations   LO 3-2, 3-3, 3-5

Starting in May, Nicole has decided that she has everything she needs to open her doors to customers. To keep up with competition, Nicole has added gift certificates and has started to advertise her company more to keep her business going in the long term. Here is a sample of some transactions that occurred in the month of May at Nicole's Getaway Spa (NGS).

May 1	Paid $3,000 cash for an insurance policy that covers the period from June 1 until May 31 next year.
May 4	Ordered five new massage tables from Spa Supplies Unlimited for $250 each for future delivery.
May 7	Provided $860 of spa services to customers on account.
May 10	Received spa supplies purchased for $800 on account to use at Nicole's Getaway Spa.
May 13	Received a bill for $60 for running an advertisement in the newspaper in May. The bill was paid in cash.
May 16	Paid one-quarter of the amount owed from May 10.
May 19	Customers paid $1,900 cash for NGS gift cards. No gift cards have been used.
May 20	Obtained financing from the bank by signing a $5,000 two-year note payable. The $5,000 cash was deposited in NGS's bank account.
May 22	Received two of the massage tables ordered on May 4 and paid for the two tables in cash.
May 25	Paid $500 cash for utility bills for services received and billed in May.

Required:

1. For each of the transactions, prepare journal entries, using the date of the transaction as the reference.
2. Identify the transactions affecting revenues and/or expenses, and then calculate NGS's preliminary net income and net profit margin for the month.
3. Which of the following best describes the adjustment(s) that will have to be made before the income statement is finalized?

   a. Record supplies used up in May.
   b. Record income taxes on May's net income.
   c. All of the above.
   d. None of the above.

DATA ANALYTICS EXERCISES

Data Analytics Exercises are auto-graded exercises offering detailed data visualization, interpretation, and analysis, and are available for assignment in Connect.

4

Adjustments, Financial Statements, and Financial Results

CHAPTER FOUR

YOUR LEARNING OBJECTIVES

LO 4-1 Explain why adjustments are needed.

LO 4-2 Prepare adjustments needed at the end of the period.

LO 4-3 Prepare an adjusted trial balance.

LO 4-4 Prepare financial statements.

LO 4-5 Explain the closing process.

LO 4-6 Explain how adjustments affect financial results.

THAT WAS THEN

In the previous chapter, you learned how to analyze, record, and summarize the effects of operating transactions on balance sheet and income statement accounts.

10'000 Hours/
Getty Images

noodlecake
games

I n Chapter 3, you saw that Noodlecake sold a lot of games during its first month of operations—more than Jordan (the company's co-founder) had expected. Jordan was curious to know how the business performed, so he computed net income based on the company's unadjusted balances. When he saw that $12,000 of revenue had led to net income of $3,100 (a net profit margin of 25.8 percent), Jordan was excited.

Jordan's CPA, Laurie, cautioned him that, because he had been using unadjusted amounts in his computations, the results should be considered preliminary. She emphasized that under accrual accounting, adjustments need to be made at the end of an accounting period to (1) update amounts already recorded in the accounting records and (2) include events that had occurred but had not yet been recorded. These adjustments ensure that the recognition of revenues and expenses occurs in the proper period and assets and liabilities are reported at appropriate amounts.

In the first section of this chapter, we'll help you to understand why adjustments are a necessary part of accrual basis accounting. In the second part of the chapter, we'll show you how to determine what adjustments are needed and how they are recorded and summarized in the accounting system. This second section concludes with the final steps involved in the accounting cycle. In the third part of this chapter, you will learn the importance of adjustments for financial statement users and, as always, the final section provides lots of opportunities for you to review and work with the material presented in this chapter.

THIS IS NOW

This chapter concludes the accounting cycle by focusing on adjustments, financial statement preparation, and the closing process.

Logo: Noodlecake Studios, Inc.

ORGANIZATION OF THE CHAPTER

Understand the business	Study the accounting methods	Evaluate the results	Review the chapter
• Why adjustments are needed	• Making required adjustments • Preparing an adjusted trial balance and the financial statements • Closing temporary accounts	• Adjusted financial results	• Demonstration case • Chapter summary • Key terms • Homework helper • Practice material

Understand the Business

WHY ADJUSTMENTS ARE NEEDED

Accounting systems record most recurring daily transactions, particularly any involving cash. As cash is received or paid, it is recorded in the accounting system. This focus on cash works well, especially when cash receipts and payments occur in the same period as the activities that lead to revenues and expenses. However, as you learned in Chapter 3, cash is not always received in the period the company fulfills its promises to customers and thereby generates revenue; likewise, cash is not always paid in the period the company incurs the related expense. In these situations, **adjustments** are made to the accounting records at the end of the period to ensure assets and liabilities are reported at appropriate amounts. These adjustments also ensure the related revenues and expenses are reported in the proper period, as required by the revenue and expense recognition principles.

Adjustments involve both income statement and balance sheet accounts. They are needed to ensure

- **Revenues** are recorded when (or as) the seller fulfills its performance obligation to the customer (the revenue recognition principle).

- **Expenses** are recorded in the same period as the revenues to which they relate (the expense recognition or "matching" principle).

- **Assets** are reported at amounts representing economic benefits that remain at the end of the current period.

- **Liabilities** are reported at amounts owed at the end of the current period that will require a future sacrifice of resources.

Companies wait until the **end of the accounting period** to adjust their accounts because daily adjustments would be time-consuming and costly. In practice, almost every financial statement account could require adjustment. Rather than memorize endless examples, instead focus on learning the nature of adjustments and the process for determining them. In general, adjustments can be grouped into two categories: (1) deferrals and (2) accruals.

1. Deferral Adjustments

The word *defer* means to postpone until later. In accounting, we say an expense or revenue has been deferred if we have postponed reporting it on the income statement until a later period. As you saw in Chapter 3, when Noodlecake pays its rent in advance, the expense is initially deferred as an asset on the balance sheet (in an account called Prepaid Rent). The adjustment part comes later, at the end of the month, when one month of the prepaid rent benefits has been used up. The deferral adjustment involves reducing Prepaid Rent on the balance sheet and increasing Rent Expense on the income statement.

Deferral adjustments also can involve revenues. For example, when GQ receives cash for subscription service before it has delivered magazines to subscribers, this revenue is initially deferred as a liability on the balance sheet (in an account called Deferred Revenue). The liability indicates the company's obligation to deliver magazines in the future. Later, when the company delivers the magazines, thereby fulfilling its obligation and earning the revenue, a deferral adjustment is made to reduce Deferred Revenue on the balance sheet and increase Service Revenue on the income statement.

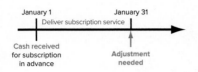

You should note two key ideas here.

1. **Deferral adjustments are used to decrease balance sheet accounts and increase corresponding income statement accounts.** Previously deferred amounts exist on the balance sheet because the company paid cash before incurring the expense or received cash before earning revenue. When revenues are generated (as defined by the revenue recognition principle) or expenses incurred (as defined by the expense recognition principle), the previously deferred amounts are adjusted and amounts are transferred to the income statement using a deferral adjustment.

2. **Each deferral adjustment involves one asset and one expense account, or one liability and one revenue account.** The left side of Exhibit 4.1 shows a partial list of accounts that commonly require deferral adjustments.

EXHIBIT 4.1	Examples of Accounts Affected by Adjustments

	Deferral Adjustments				**Accrual Adjustments**		
	Balance Sheet	Income Statement			Balance Sheet	Income Statement	
Assets	Supplies ———————— Supplies Expense		**Expenses**	**Assets**	Interest Receivable ———————— Interest Revenue		**Revenues**
	Prepaid Rent ———————— Rent Expense				Rent Receivable ———————— Rent Revenue		
	Prepaid Insurance ———————— Insurance Expense						
Liabilities	Deferred Revenue ———————— Sales Revenue or Service Revenue		**Revenues**	**Liabilities**	Income Tax Payable ———————— Income Tax Expense		**Expenses**
					Wages Payable ———————— Wages Expense		
					Interest Payable ———————— Interest Expense		

---

2. Accrual Adjustments

Accrual adjustments are needed when a company has generated revenue or incurred an expense in the current period but has not yet recorded it because the related cash will not be received or paid until a later period. The first timeline shows an accrual adjustment for an expense. Noodlecake will eventually pay taxes on the income it earns this period, so an accrual adjustment is needed at the end of the month to record increases in its Income Tax Expense and Income Tax Payable accounts. This adjustment matches Income Tax Expense to the period in which the company generated the income that caused the income taxes,

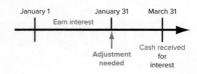

and it adjusts Income Tax Payable to show the amount owed. The next timeline shows an accrual adjustment for revenue. If interest revenue is earned on investments this month but not received in cash until a later month, an accrual adjustment is needed at the end of the current month to record increases in the company's Interest Revenue and Interest Receivable accounts.

You should note two key ideas here.

1. **Accrual adjustments are used to record revenue or expenses when they occur prior to receiving or paying cash and to adjust corresponding balance sheet accounts.**

2. **Each accrual adjustment involves one asset and one revenue account, or one liability and one expense account.** Notice that this differs from deferral adjustments, which pair assets with expenses and liabilities with revenues. The right side of Exhibit 4.1 shows a partial list of accounts that require accrual adjustments.

💡 How's it going?   Self-Study Practice

Match each situation below to two applicable reasons that require an adjustment to be made.

_____ 1. **Brand Affinity Technologies** received a $500 bill for this month's celebrity advertising services, which it will pay next month.

_____ 2. Concerts, for which **Live Nation Entertainment** had sold $10,000 of tickets last month, were performed this month.

_____ 3. **Chiquita Brands International** used up $5,000 of the benefits of its banana harvesting and transportation equipment.

_____ 4. **International Flavors and Fragrances** completed a project to develop a new scent for Hilton Hotels, for which it will be paid $1,000 next month.

A. Revenue has been generated.
B. Expense has been incurred.
C. Liability has been incurred.
D. Liability has been fulfilled.
E. Asset has been acquired.
F. Asset has been used up.

After you have finished, check your answers with the solution.

Study the Accounting Methods

MAKING REQUIRED ADJUSTMENTS

The process of making adjustments is similar to the process you learned in Chapters 2 and 3 when accounting for daily transactions. As shown in Exhibit 4.2, the main difference is adjustments are made at the end of each accounting period immediately prior to preparing an adjusted trial balance and financial statements. Adjustments are not made daily because it's more efficient to do them all at once at the end of each period. After analyzing the necessary adjustments (in Step 1), they are recorded using **adjusting journal entries** (in Step 2) and then summarized in the accounts (in Step 3). An adjusted trial balance is prepared to ensure total debits still equal total credits after posting the adjusting journal entries to the accounts. If the trial balance is in balance, the financial statements can be prepared.

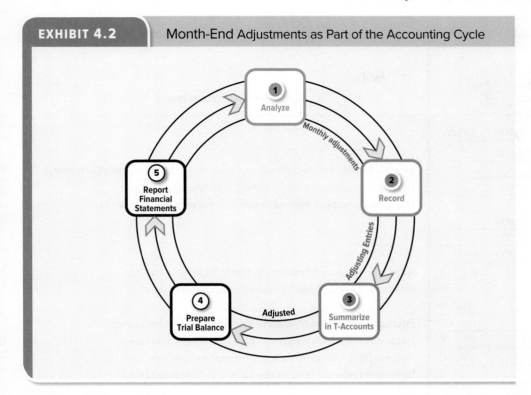

EXHIBIT 4.2 Month-End Adjustments as Part of the Accounting Cycle

Adjustment Analysis, Recording, and Summarizing

The first step, Analyze, involves determining the necessary adjustments to make to the accounting records. To complete this step, you need to know the balance currently reported in each account, then determine what should be reported as the balance, and finally figure out the adjustment that will take you from the current (unadjusted) balance to the desired (adjusted) balance. Exhibit 4.3 illustrates this thinking process.

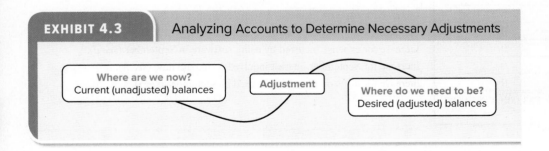

EXHIBIT 4.3 Analyzing Accounts to Determine Necessary Adjustments

The unadjusted trial balance is a key starting point for the adjustment process because it presents the unadjusted balances for every account, which will help you identify accounts that require adjustment. Exhibit 4.4 shows Noodlecake's unadjusted trial balance at the end of September. This trial balance is identical to Exhibit 3.10, except we've included balances for all accounts in Noodlecake's chart of accounts, including those that currently have zero balances. Alongside the unadjusted trial balance, we've identified accounts requiring adjustment at the end of September.

In the remainder of this section, we show how to analyze, record, and summarize the required adjustments. Read this section carefully. It contains the topics people typically find the most challenging in this chapter.

EXHIBIT 4.4   Unadjusted Trial Balance

NOODLECAKE STUDIOS, INC.
Unadjusted Trial Balance
At September 30, 2021

Account Name	Debit	Credit	Explanation of Adjustments Needed
Cash	$16,900		
Accounts Receivable	500		Increase for right to collect for services given on account to app developers (*see f*).
Supplies	600		Decrease for supplies used up during September (*see a*).
Prepaid Rent	7,200		Decrease for prepaid September rent benefits now used up (*see b*).
Equipment	9,600		
Software	9,000		
Logo and Trademarks	300		
Accumulated Depreciation		$ 0	Adjust for equipment benefits used up in September (*see c*).
Accumulated Amortization		0	Adjust for software benefits used up in September (*see d*).
Accounts Payable		10,700	
Deferred Revenue		300	Decrease for gift card obligations fulfilled in September (*see e*).
Salaries and Wages Payable		0	Increase for September wages incurred but not yet paid (*see g*).
Income Tax Payable		0	Increase for tax owed on income generated in September (*see i*).
Interest Payable		0	Increase for interest owed on unpaid note in September (*see h*).
Notes Payable (long-term)		20,000	
Common Stock		10,000	
Retained Earnings		0	
Dividends	0		
Sales Revenue		12,000	Increase for revenues generated by accepting gift cards for sales (*see e*).
Service Revenue		0	Increase for revenues generated by providing services to app developers (*see f*).
Salaries and Wages Expense	7,800		Increase for employees' September wages not yet recorded (*see g*).
Rent Expense	0		Increase for expense incurred for September rent (*see b*).
Utilities Expense	600		
Advertising Expense	500		
Depreciation Expense	0		Increase for expense incurred by using equipment in September (*see c*).
Supplies Expense	0		Increase for supplies used up in September (*see a*).
Amortization Expense	0		Increase for expense incurred by using software in September (*see d*).
Interest Expense	0		Increase for September interest incurred on unpaid note (*see h*).
Income Tax Expense	0		Increase for taxes on income generated in September (*see i*).
Totals	**$53,000**	**$53,000**	

Deferral Adjustments   Let's begin by looking at deferral adjustments, which are used to update amounts previously deferred on the balance sheet.

(a) Supplies Used during the Period   **Noodlecake counts its supplies on hand at September 30. Of the supplies previously purchased for $600, only $250 are now on hand.**

The supplies were initially recorded as an asset at the end of August (in Chapter 2), but some of them have now been used up as of September 30. The **expense recognition principle** requires an adjustment be made to report the cost of supplies used up this month as an expense (to match against revenues). To determine the cost of supplies used up, just do a little calculating. If you had $600 of supplies available for use and only $250 are left at the end of the month, then the $350 difference must be the cost of supplies used this month. In accounting terms, you should reduce the asset (Supplies) by $350 and show this amount as an expense (Supplies Expense).

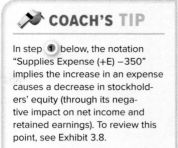

COACH'S TIP

In step ❶ below, the notation "Supplies Expense (+E) −350" implies the increase in an expense causes a decrease in stockholders' equity (through its negative impact on net income and retained earnings). To review this point, see Exhibit 3.8.

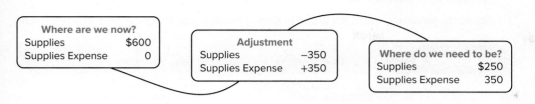

Where are we now?	
Supplies	$600
Supplies Expense	0

Adjustment	
Supplies	−350
Supplies Expense	+350

Where do we need to be?	
Supplies	$250
Supplies Expense	350

The effects of this adjustment on the accounting equation are shown below, along with the required adjusting journal entry (AJE) and the accounts affected by it.

1 Analyze

Assets		=	Liabilities	+	Stockholders' Equity	
(a) Supplies	−350	=			Supplies Expense (+E)	−350

Revenues	−
− Expenses	↑ 350
Net Income	↓ 350

2 Record

		Debit	Credit
(a)	Supplies Expense (+E, −SE)..	350	
	Supplies (−A)...		350

3 Summarize

dr +	Supplies (A)		cr −
Unadj. bal.	600		
		350	AJE (a)
Adj. bal.	250		

dr +	Supplies Expense (E, SE)		cr −
Unadj. bal.	0		
AJE (a)	350		
Adj. bal.	350		

The financial statement effects of this adjustment are pictured in Exhibit 4.5.

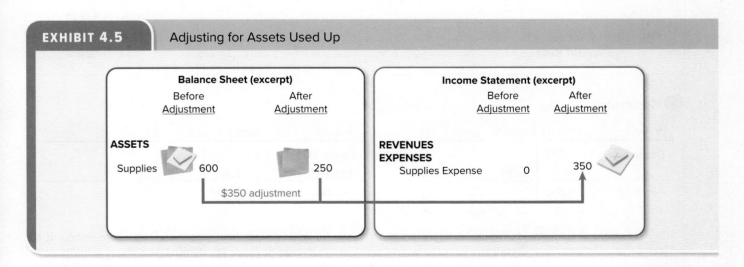

EXHIBIT 4.5 | Adjusting for Assets Used Up

Balance Sheet (excerpt)

	Before Adjustment	After Adjustment
ASSETS		
Supplies	600	250

$350 adjustment

Income Statement (excerpt)

	Before Adjustment	After Adjustment
REVENUES		
EXPENSES		
Supplies Expense	0	350

(b) Rent Benefits Expired during the Period   **Three months of rent were prepaid on September 1 for $7,200, but one month has now expired, leaving only two months prepaid at September 30.**

To picture the passage of time, it's useful to draw a timeline like the one shown in Exhibit 4.6.

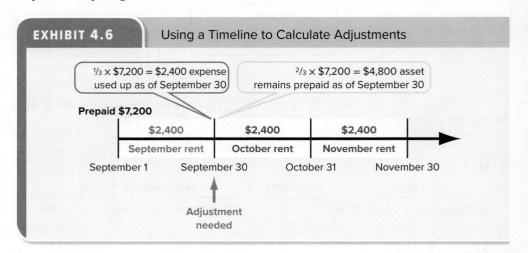

EXHIBIT 4.6	Using a Timeline to Calculate Adjustments

⅓ × $7,200 = $2,400 expense used up as of September 30

⅔ × $7,200 = $4,800 asset remains prepaid as of September 30

Prepaid $7,200

$2,400	$2,400	$2,400
September rent	October rent	November rent

September 1   September 30   October 31   November 30

↑
Adjustment
needed

The timeline in Exhibit 4.6 shows the September prepayment of $7,200 represented as three equal pieces of $2,400. The benefits of the first piece (pictured in red) have now expired, so they should be reported as an expense on the September income statement. Only two of the three months (2/3) remain prepaid on September 30. Thus, the $7,200 that was prepaid on September 1 has to be adjusted on September 30 to $4,800 (2/3 × $7,200), which is the cost of the two remaining months of Prepaid Rent.

The preceding analysis has determined an adjustment is needed to reduce Prepaid Rent by $2,400, from $7,200 to $4,800. Likewise, the adjustment needs to increase Rent Expense by $2,400. These effects are accounted for as follows:

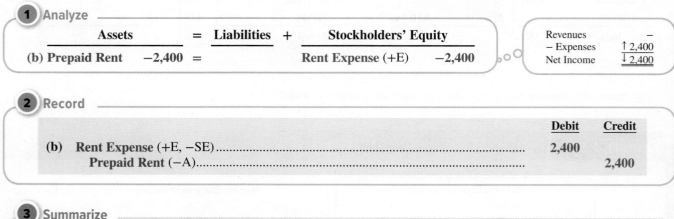

1 Analyze

	Assets	=	Liabilities	+	Stockholders' Equity	
(b) Prepaid Rent	−2,400	=			Rent Expense (+E)	−2,400

Revenues	−
− Expenses	↑ 2,400
Net Income	↓ 2,400

2 Record

		Debit	Credit
(b)	**Rent Expense (+E, −SE)**	2,400	
	Prepaid Rent (−A)		2,400

3 Summarize

dr +	Prepaid Rent (A)		cr −
Unadj. bal.	7,200		
		2,400	AJE (b)
Adj. bal.	4,800		

dr +	Rent Expense (E, SE)		cr −
Unadj. bal.	0		
AJE (b)	2,400		
Adj. bal.	2,400		

Similar adjustments are made for other prepayments, such as Prepaid Insurance. If the company pays the cost of services in advance of receiving them, the company initially defers that cost as an asset on the balance sheet. At the end of each accounting period in which the services are used up, a deferral adjustment is made to decrease the asset and increase the related expense on the income statement. Practice doing this one more time in the following Self-Study Practice.

How's it going?   Self-Study Practice

On September 30, Apple, Inc., paid $24,000 for insurance for October, November, and December. On October 31, **unadjusted** balances for Prepaid Insurance and Insurance Expense were $24,000 and $0, respectively. Based on this information, determine the **adjusted** amounts that should be reported on October 31 for (1) Prepaid Insurance and (2) Insurance Expense. Finally, (3) what adjusting journal entry is needed to change these accounts from their unadjusted balances to their desired adjusted balances?

After you have finished, check your answers with the solution.

Solution to Self-Study Practice

1. $16,000 ($24,000 × 2/3)
2. $8,000 ($24,000 × 1/3)
3.

	Debit	Credit
Insurance Expense (+E, −SE)	8,000	
Prepaid Insurance (−A)		8,000

Notice that for events in (*a*), (*b*), and the Self-Study Practice, the deferral adjustments have two effects: (1) They reduce the **carrying value** of assets on the balance sheet and (2) they transfer the amount of the reductions to related expense accounts on the income statement. This happens whether we're adjusting supplies, prepaid rent, or even long-term assets like buildings, equipment, and software. When accounting for the use of long-term assets like buildings, equipment, and software, there is one slight difference in how the carrying value is reduced, as we'll explain next.

(c) Depreciation Is Recorded for Use of Equipment   **The computer equipment, which was estimated to last two years, has now been used for one month, representing an estimated expense of $400.**

The **expense recognition principle ("matching")** indicates that when equipment is used to generate revenues in the current period, part of its cost should be transferred to an expense account in that period. This process is referred to as **depreciation**, so an income statement account named Depreciation Expense reports the cost of equipment use in the current period. On the balance sheet, we reduce the amount reported for equipment, but we don't take the depreciation directly out of the Equipment account. Rather, a **contra-account** is created to track all the depreciation recorded against the equipment. This contra-account, named Accumulated Depreciation, is like a negative asset account that is subtracted from the Equipment account in the assets section of the balance sheet, as shown in Exhibit 4.7.

> **YOU SHOULD KNOW**
>
> **Carrying Value:** The amount at which an asset or liability is reported after deducting any contra-accounts. Also called *Book Value, Net Book Value.*
>
> **Depreciation:** Process of allocating the cost of buildings and equipment over their productive lives using a systematic and rational method of allocation.
>
> **Contra-Account:** An account that is an offset to, or reduction of, another account.

EXHIBIT 4.7	Reporting Accumulated Depreciation on the Balance Sheet

NOODLECAKE STUDIOS, INC.
Balance Sheet (excerpt)
At September 30, 2021

Assets		
Equipment	$9,600	← Original cost of equipment
Accumulated Depreciation	(400)	← Running total of depreciation
Equipment, Net of Accumulated Depreciation	9,200	← Carrying value (or book value)

> 🔨 **COACH'S TIP**
>
> Recording depreciation for the use of long-lived assets is a lot like recording the use of supplies. The only difference is a contra-account is used so that a record of the original cost is maintained for long-lived assets throughout their long lives.

In the following analyses, we use a small "x" to indicate a contra-account, so the notation for a contra-account for an asset is "xA." An increase in a contra-asset account (+xA) decreases total assets on the balance sheet (−A).

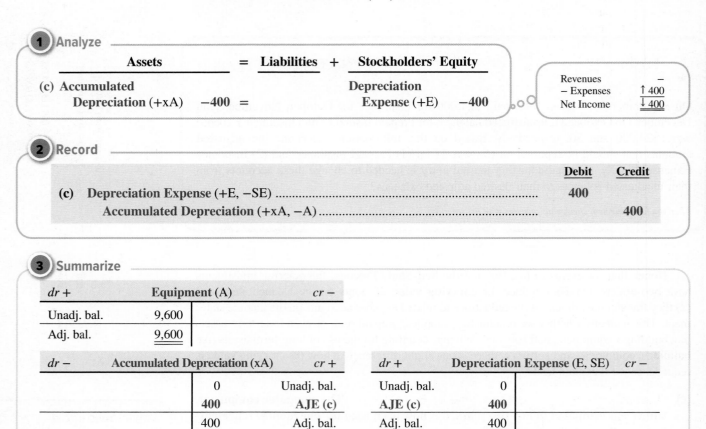

1 Analyze

	Assets	=	Liabilities	+	Stockholders' Equity
(c) Accumulated Depreciation (+xA)	−400	=			Depreciation Expense (+E) −400

Revenues   −
− Expenses   ↑ 400
Net Income   ↓ 400

2 Record

		Debit	Credit
(c)	Depreciation Expense (+E, −SE)	400	
	Accumulated Depreciation (+xA, −A)		400

3 Summarize

dr +	Equipment (A)	cr −
Unadj. bal.	9,600	
Adj. bal.	9,600	

dr −	Accumulated Depreciation (xA)	cr +
	0	Unadj. bal.
	400	AJE (c)
	400	Adj. bal.

dr +	Depreciation Expense (E, SE)	cr −
Unadj. bal.	0	
AJE (c)	400	
Adj. bal.	400	

There are four aspects of this example you should note:

1. **Accumulated Depreciation is a balance sheet account and Depreciation Expense is an income statement account.** As a balance sheet account, Accumulated Depreciation will increase each year as it accumulates the depreciation of each period. In contrast, the income statement account, Depreciation Expense, will include the depreciation of only the current accounting year.

2. **By recording depreciation in Accumulated Depreciation, distinct from the Equipment account, you can report both the original cost of equipment and a running total of the amount that has been depreciated.** This gives financial statement users a rough idea of how much of the asset's original cost (representing its original usefulness) has been used up as of the balance sheet date. In our example, approximately 1/24 ($400/$9,600) of the equipment's total usefulness has been used up as of September 30.

3. **The normal balance in a contra-account is always the opposite of the account it offsets.** Accumulated Depreciation is recorded with a credit because the account that it offsets, Equipment, is recorded with a debit.

4. **The amount of depreciation depends on the method used for determining it.** Depreciation methods (and their formulas) will be discussed in Chapter 9.

(d) Amortization Is Recorded for Use of Software   **The app software developed for Noodlecake, estimated to have three years of usefulness, has now been used for one month at an estimated expense of $250.**

Similar to depreciation, *amortization* is the concept that applies to using up long-term assets that lack physical substance and have a limited period of usefulness. Because Noodlecake's app will eventually decline in popularity, its software has a limited period of usefulness. To show that some of this usefulness is used up this period, part of the cost of the app software needs to be transferred to an expense this period. To show this, Noodlecake will record the following deferral adjustment at the end of every month to report amortization as an expense on the income statement (Amortization Expense) and accumulate it in a contra-asset account on the balance sheet (Accumulated Amortization).

COACH'S TIP

Amortization is not reported for long-term assets that have an unlimited period of usefulness. For example, Noodlecake's logo will be useful indefinitely, so it is not amortized.

1 Analyze

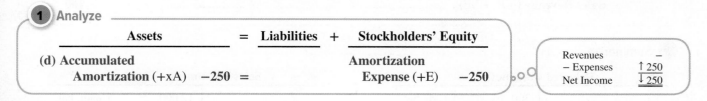

Assets	=	Liabilities	+	Stockholders' Equity
(d) Accumulated Amortization (+xA) −250	=			Amortization Expense (+E) −250

Revenues	−
− Expenses	↑ 250
Net Income	↓ 250

2 Record

		Debit	Credit
(d)	Amortization Expense (+E, −SE)	250	
	Accumulated Amortization (+xA, −A)		250

3 Summarize

dr +	Software (A)		cr −
Unadj. bal.	9,000		
Adj. bal.	9,000		

dr −	Accumulated Amortization (xA)	cr +
	0	Unadj. bal.
	250	AJE (d)
	250	Adj. bal.

dr +	Amortization Expense (E, SE)		cr −
Unadj. bal.	0		
AJE (d)	250		
Adj. bal.	250		

Just as deferral adjustments are used to record expenses incurred when assets are used up, they also are used to record the revenues generated when (or as) a company fulfills its obligation to provide goods or services to customers. For example, when American Airlines, USA Today, and T-Mobile receive cash in advance of providing flights, newspapers, and cell phone service, they initially increase (debit) Cash and increase (credit) a liability account called Deferred Revenue. Later, when they meet their obligations, a deferral adjustment is recorded, reducing the liability (with a debit) and reporting the revenue generated from these services (with a credit). Let's see how this idea applies to Noodlecake.

(e) Gift Cards Redeemed **Noodlecake accepted $100 of gift cards from customers as payment for game downloads.**

The unadjusted trial balance reports $300 of Deferred Revenue, which represents Noodlecake's obligation to honor gift cards previously issued to customers. By now accepting $100 of gift cards in exchange for game downloads this month, Noodlecake has fulfilled a portion of its obligation and has generated additional sales. Thus, a deferral adjustment is needed to reduce Deferred Revenue and increase Sales Revenue.

COACH'S TIP

The word "deferred" in the Deferred Revenue account means a company defers or postpones reporting revenue until it completes the work it was paid to do. When (or as) it completes its work, it reduces the liability Deferred Revenue and reports the revenue it has generated.

1 Analyze

Assets	=	Liabilities	+	Stockholders' Equity			Revenues	↑ 100
(e)		Deferred Revenue −100		Sales Revenue (+R) +100			− Expenses	−
							Net Income	↑ 100

2 Record

	Debit	Credit
(e) Deferred Revenue (−L)	100	
Sales Revenue (+R, +SE)...		100

3 Summarize

dr −	Deferred Revenue (L)		cr +
		300	Unadj. bal.
AJE (e)	100		
		200	Adj. bal.

dr −	Sales Revenue (R, SE)		cr +
		12,000	Unadj. bal.
		100	AJE (e)
		12,100	Adj. bal.

Accrual Adjustments   Let's now look at common examples of accrual adjustments, which are adjustments to make the accounting records complete by including transactions that occurred but have not yet been recorded.

(f) Services Given but Revenue Not Yet Recorded   **Noodlecake provided $3,250 of consulting services to other app developers in September, with payment to be received in October.**

Companies that provide accounting, consulting, or other services that span more than one month are unlikely to receive cash or bill customers until the services have been provided in full. In Noodlecake's case, some of its services have been provided in September but have not yet been recorded. Because these revenues and the right to collect them (Accounts Receivable) arise from work occurring in September, the **revenue recognition principle** indicates they should be recorded in September. Thus, an accrual adjustment is needed on September 30 to increase Accounts Receivable on the balance sheet and increase Service Revenue on the income statement.

1 Analyze

Assets	=	Liabilities	+	Stockholders' Equity			Revenues	↑ 3,250
(f) Accounts Receivable +3,250	=			Service Revenue (+R) +3,250			− Expenses	−
							Net Income	↑ 3,250

2 Record

	Debit	Credit
(f) Accounts Receivable (+A)	3,250	
Service Revenue (+R, +SE)..		3,250

3 Summarize

dr +	Accounts Receivable (A)		cr −
Unadj. bal.	500		
AJE (f)	3,250		
Adj. bal.	3,750		

dr −	Service Revenue (R, SE)		cr +
		0	Unadj. bal.
		3,250	AJE (f)
		3,250	Adj. bal.

Other situations require accrual adjustments for revenue that has been generated but not yet recorded. For example, interest on investments is earned daily but typically is received in cash on a yearly basis, so each month an accrual adjustment is made to increase Interest Receivable and Interest Revenue for amounts earned but not yet recorded.

(g) Wage Expense Incurred but Not Yet Recorded   **Noodlecake owes $1,950 of wages to employees for work done in the last six days of September.**

Back in Chapter 3, Noodlecake paid employees $7,800 for work done through September 24 ($325 per day). As of September 30, six additional days of work have been completed at a cost of $1,950 (= $325 × 6). Although this amount will not be paid until October, the expense relates to work done (and revenues generated) in September, so the **expense recognition principle** (**"matching"**) requires an adjustment be made to accrue the $1,950 of wages incurred and owed by Noodlecake, as follows.

September 2021

SU	MO	TU	WE	TH	FR	SA
Paid	1	2	3	4
5	6	7	8	9	10	11
12	13	14	15	16	17	18
19	20	21	22	23	24	25
26	27	28	29	30 Owed

① Analyze

Assets	=	Liabilities	+	Stockholders' Equity
(g)		Salaries and Wages Payable +1,950		Salaries and Wages Expense (+E) −1,950

Revenues	−
− Expenses	↑ 1,950
Net Income	↓ 1,950

② Record

	Debit	Credit
(g) Salaries and Wages Expense (+E, −SE)	1,950	
Salaries and Wages Payable (+L)..		1,950

③ Summarize

dr −	Salaries and Wages Payable (L)	cr +
	0	Unadj. bal.
	1,950	AJE (g)
	1,950	Adj. bal.

dr +	Salaries and Wages Expense (E, SE)	cr −
Unadj. bal.	7,800	
AJE (g)	1,950	
Adj. bal.	9,750	

When these $1,950 of wages are paid in cash the following month, Noodlecake will decrease Salaries and Wages Payable (with a debit) and decrease Cash (with a credit).

Accrual adjustments also may be required for other expenses, like property taxes and interest, if incurred and owed (but not yet recorded) during the current period. The adjusting journal entry required for each of these items would be similar to the one shown in (g), with an expense recorded (with a debit) and a liability increased (with a credit). For purposes of our Noodlecake example, we'll assume the only remaining expenses to record are accruals for interest (in h) and income taxes (in i), both of which are incurred this month but won't be paid until a later period.

(h) Interest Expense Incurred but Not Yet Recorded   **Noodlecake has not paid or recorded the $100 interest that it owes for this month on its note payable.**

Noodlecake incurs interest each month on its unpaid note payable to the bank. An adjustment is needed to record the Interest Expense relating to September and, because this interest has not yet been paid, the adjustment also must record a liability called Interest Payable.

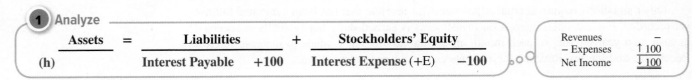

1 Analyze

Assets	=	Liabilities	+	Stockholders' Equity
(h)		Interest Payable +100		Interest Expense (+E) −100

Revenues	−
− Expenses	↑ 100
Net Income	↓ 100

2 Record

		Debit	Credit
(h)	Interest Expense (+E, −SE)..	100	
	Interest Payable (+L)		100

3 Summarize

dr −	Interest Payable (L)	cr +		dr +	Interest Expense (E, SE)	cr −
	0	Unadj. bal.		Unadj. bal.	0	
100		AJE (h)		AJE (h)	100	
	100	Adj. bal.		Adj. bal.	100	

(i) Income Taxes Incurred but Not Yet Recorded   Noodlecake pays income tax at an average rate equal to 20 percent of the company's income before taxes.

Just like you, a corporation is responsible for income tax on the income it generates. Income tax is calculated by multiplying (1) the company's adjusted income (before income tax expense) by (2) the company's tax rate. To calculate adjusted income (before income tax), the following table starts with the unadjusted revenue and expense numbers from the unadjusted trial balance (Exhibit 4.4) and then includes the effects of adjustments to revenues and expenses. Multiply the adjusted income before income tax ($1,000) by the tax rate (20%) to get the amount of income tax for September ($200).

COACH'S TIP

Always calculate income tax expense after taking into account all other adjustments.

	Revenues	Expenses	
Unadjusted totals	**$12,000**	**$ 8,900**	← Calculated from Exhibit 4.4 ($8,900 = $7,800 + $600 + $500)
Adjustments:			
(a) Supplies Used		+ 350	
(b) Rent Expired		+ 2,400	
(c) Depreciation		+ 400	
(d) Amortization		+ 250	
(e) Gift Cards	+ 100		
(f) Services Given	+ 3,250		
(g) Wages Incurred		+ 1,950	
(h) Interest Incurred		+ 100	
Adjusted totals	**$ 15,350** −	**$14,350**	= $1,000 Adjusted income before income tax expense
			× 20% Tax rate
			$ 200 **Income tax**

The unadjusted trial balance indicates no income tax has been recorded (both Income Tax Payable and Income Tax Expense are $0). Because income was reported in September, the **expense recognition principle** requires that we record the $200 tax expense in September. The tax hasn't been paid yet, so a liability also is recorded.

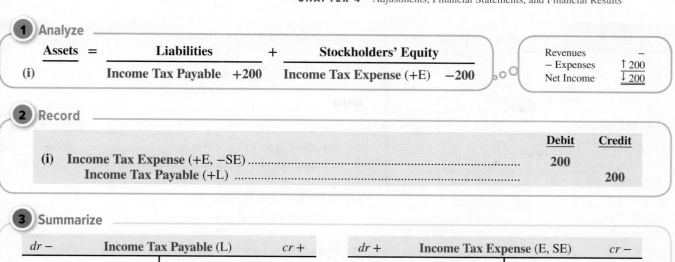

1 Analyze

	Assets	=	Liabilities	+	Stockholders' Equity		Revenues	–
(i)			Income Tax Payable +200		Income Tax Expense (+E) −200		– Expenses	↑ 200
							Net Income	↓ 200

2 Record

		Debit	Credit
(i)	Income Tax Expense (+E, −SE)	200	
	Income Tax Payable (+L)		200

3 Summarize

dr −	Income Tax Payable (L)	cr +		dr +	Income Tax Expense (E, SE)	cr −
	0	Unadj. bal.		Unadj. bal.	0	
	200	AJE (i)		AJE (i)	200	
	200	Adj. bal.		Adj. bal.	200	

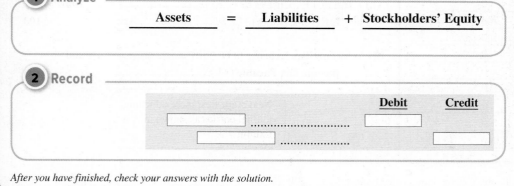

💡 **How's it going?**   **Self-Study Practice**

Prior to accruing marketing expenses of $5 million, **Pixar**'s adjusted income before income taxes was $245 million. Assuming the company's average tax rate was 40%, (1) analyze the effect of the required income tax adjustment on the accounting equation and (2) prepare the adjusting journal entry, assuming no amounts have been recorded yet for income taxes.

1 Analyze

	Assets	=	Liabilities	+	Stockholders' Equity

2 Record

		Debit	Credit
	....		
	....		

After you have finished, check your answers with the solution.

Solution to Self-Study Practice

1. Adjusted income before taxes = $245 − $5 = $240 (million).
   Income tax = $240 × 40% = $96 (million).

Assets	=	Liabilities	+	Stockholders' Equity
		Income Tax Payable +96		Income Tax Expense (+E) −96

2.

		Debit	Credit
Income Tax Expense (+E, −SE)		96	
Income Tax Payable (+L)			96

Additional Comments

There are two final points to notice before finishing this section. First, none of the adjusting journal entries affected the Cash account. **Cash is never part of an accrual or deferral adjusting journal entry.** Second, each adjusting entry affects one balance sheet and one income statement account.

Exhibit 4.8 summarizes the work we've done to this point. Starting with the unadjusted trial balance prepared at the end of Chapter 3 (see the left side of Exhibit 4.8), we determined the adjusting journal entries to be recorded at the end of this month (see the right side of Exhibit 4.8).

Next, we post journal entries (a)–(i) to the T-accounts, as summarized in Exhibit 4.9. Then, we need to check that the accounting records are still in balance by using the adjusted T-account balances to prepare an adjusted trial balance, as shown in the following section. Assuming the trial balance shows debits equal credits, we will finally be able to prepare the financial statements.

EXHIBIT 4.8	Summary of Unadjusted Balances and Adjusting Journal Entries

NOODLECAKE STUDIOS, INC.
Unadjusted Trial Balance
At September 30, 2021

Account Name	Debit	Credit
Cash	$16,900	
Accounts Receivable	500	
Supplies	600	
Prepaid Rent	7,200	
Equipment	9,600	
Accumulated Depreciation		$ 0
Software	9,000	
Accumulated Amortization		0
Logo and Trademarks	300	
Accounts Payable		10,700
Deferred Revenue		300
Salaries and Wages Payable		0
Income Tax Payable		0
Interest Payable		0
Notes Payable (long-term)		20,000
Common Stock		10,000
Retained Earnings		0
Dividends	0	
Sales Revenue		12,000
Service Revenue		0
Salaries and Wages Expense	7,800	
Rent Expense	0	
Utilities Expense	600	
Advertising Expense	500	
Depreciation Expense	0	
Supplies Expense	0	
Amortization Expense	0	
Interest Expense	0	
Income Tax Expense	0	
Totals	**$53,000**	**$53,000**

NOODLECAKE STUDIOS, INC.
General Journal

		Debit	Credit
(a)	Supplies Expense (+E, −SE)	350	
	Supplies (−A)		350
(b)	Rent Expense (+E, −SE)	2,400	
	Prepaid Rent (−A)		2,400
(c)	Depreciation Expense (+E, −SE)	400	
	Accumulated Depreciation (+xA, −A)		400
(d)	Amortization Expense (+E, −SE)	250	
	Accumulated Amortization (+xA, −A)		250
(e)	Deferred Revenue (−L)	100	
	Sales Revenue (+R, +SE)		100
(f)	Accounts Receivable (+A)	3,250	
	Service Revenue (+R, +SE)		3,250
(g)	Salaries and Wages Expense (+E, −SE)	1,950	
	Salaries and Wages Payable (+L)		1,950
(h)	Interest Expense (+E, −SE)	100	
	Interest Payable (+L)		100
(i)	Income Tax Expense (+E, −SE)	200	
	Income Tax Payable (+L)		200

Next step: Post these adjusting journal entries as shown in Exhibit 4.9.

PREPARING AN ADJUSTED TRIAL BALANCE AND THE FINANCIAL STATEMENTS

Adjusted Trial Balance

An **adjusted trial balance** is prepared to check that the accounting records are still in balance, after having posted all adjusting entries to the T-accounts. To prepare an adjusted trial balance, just copy the adjusted T-account balances (Exhibit 4.9) into the debit or credit columns of the adjusted trial balance (left side of Exhibit 4.10).

The trial balance lists accounts in the order they will appear in the balance sheet, statement of retained earnings, and income statement. As you can see in Exhibit 4.10, the trial balance proves Noodlecake's accounting records are in balance (total debits = $59,150 = total credits), so the financial statements can be prepared. The balance for each account in the trial balance is reported only once on either the income statement, statement of retained earnings, or balance sheet. Typically, the income statement is prepared first because its final number,

EXHIBIT 4.9 Noodlecake's Adjusted Accounts

dr +	Cash (A)	cr −
Adj. bal.	**16,900**	

dr +	Accounts Receivable (A)	cr −
Unadj. bal.	500	
AJE (f)	3,250	
Adj. bal.	**3,750**	

dr +	Supplies (A)	cr −
Unadj. bal.	600	
		350	AJE (a)
Adj. bal.	**250**	

dr +	Prepaid Rent (A)	cr −
Unadj. bal.	7,200	
		2,400	AJE (b)
Adj. bal.	**4,800**	

dr +	Equipment (A)	cr −
Adj. bal.	**9,600**	

dr −	Accumulated Depreciation (xA)	cr +
	0	Unadj. bal.
	400	AJE (c)
	400	Adj. bal.

dr +	Software (A)	cr −
Adj. bal.	**9,000**	

dr −	Accumulated Amortization (xA)	cr +
	0	Unadj. bal.
	250	AJE (d)
	250	Adj. bal.

dr +	Logo and Trademarks (A)	cr −
Adj. bal.	**300**	

dr −	Accounts Payable (L)	cr +
	10,700	Adj. bal.

dr −	Deferred Revenue (L)	cr +
	300	Unadj. bal.
AJE (e)	100	
	200	Adj. bal.

dr −	Salaries and Wages Payable (L)	cr +
	0	Unadj. bal.
	1,950	AJE (g)
	1,950	Adj. bal.

dr −	Income Tax Payable (L)	cr +
	0	Unadj. bal.
	200	AJE (i)
	200	Adj. bal.

dr −	Interest Payable (L)	cr +
	0	Unadj. bal.
	100	AJE (h)
	100	Adj. bal.

dr −	Notes Payable (long-term) (L)	cr +
	20,000	Adj. bal.

dr −	Common Stock (SE)	cr +
	10,000	Adj. bal.

dr −	Retained Earnings (SE)	cr +
	0	Adj. bal.

dr +	Dividends (D, SE)	cr −
Adj. bal.	**0**	

dr −	Sales Revenue (R, SE)	cr +
	12,000	Unadj. bal.
	100	AJE (e)
	12,100	Adj. bal.

dr −	Service Revenue (R, SE)	cr +
	0	Unadj. bal.
	3,250	AJE (f)
	3,250	Adj. bal.

dr +	Salaries and Wages Expense (E, SE)	cr −
Unadj. bal.	7,800	
AJE (g)	1,950	
Adj. bal.	**9,750**	

dr +	Rent Expense (E, SE)	cr −
Unadj. bal.	0	
AJE (b)	2,400	
Adj. bal.	**2,400**	

dr +	Utilities Expense (E, SE)	cr −
Adj. bal.	**600**	

dr +	Advertising Expense (E, SE)	cr −
Adj. bal.	**500**	

dr +	Depreciation Expense (E, SE)	cr −
Unadj. bal.	0	
AJE (c)	400	
Adj. bal.	**400**	

dr +	Supplies Expense (E, SE)	cr −
Unadj. bal.	0	
AJE (a)	350	
Adj. bal.	**350**	

dr +	Amortization Expense (E, SE)	cr −
Unadj. bal.	0	
AJE (d)	250	
Adj. bal.	**250**	

dr +	Interest Expense (E, SE)	cr −
Unadj. bal.	0	
AJE (h)	100	
Adj. bal.	**100**	

dr +	Income Tax Expense (E, SE)	cr −
Unadj. bal.	0	
AJE (i)	200	
Adj. bal.	**200**	

> **Next step:** Summarize these adjusted balances in an adjusted trial balance as shown in Exhibit 4.10.

net income, flows into the statement of retained earnings, from which the ending balance then flows into the balance sheet. As you will see in later chapters of this book, the statement of cash flows and notes to the financial statements are prepared last because they include information obtained from the income statement, statement of retained earnings, and balance sheet (plus other sources).

Income Statement and Statement of Retained Earnings

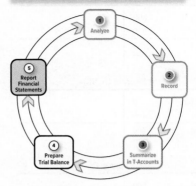

Prepare the income statement by creating the usual heading (who, what, when) and listing the names and amounts for each revenue and expense account from the adjusted trial balance, as shown in the right side of Exhibit 4.10. Notice that each major category of items on the income statement is subtotaled prior to computing net income for the period.

Account balances from the adjusted trial balance are also used in the statement of retained earnings, as shown in Exhibit 4.10. Notice **the amount coming from the adjusted trial balance is the beginning-of-year balance for Retained Earnings.** This account balance doesn't yet include revenues, expenses, and dividends for the current period because they've been recorded in their own separate accounts. Eventually we will transfer ("close") those accounts into Retained Earnings, but that's done only at the end of the year. For now, the Retained Earnings account on the adjusted trial balance provides the opening amount

EXHIBIT 4.10   Preparing the Income Statement and Statement of Retained Earnings

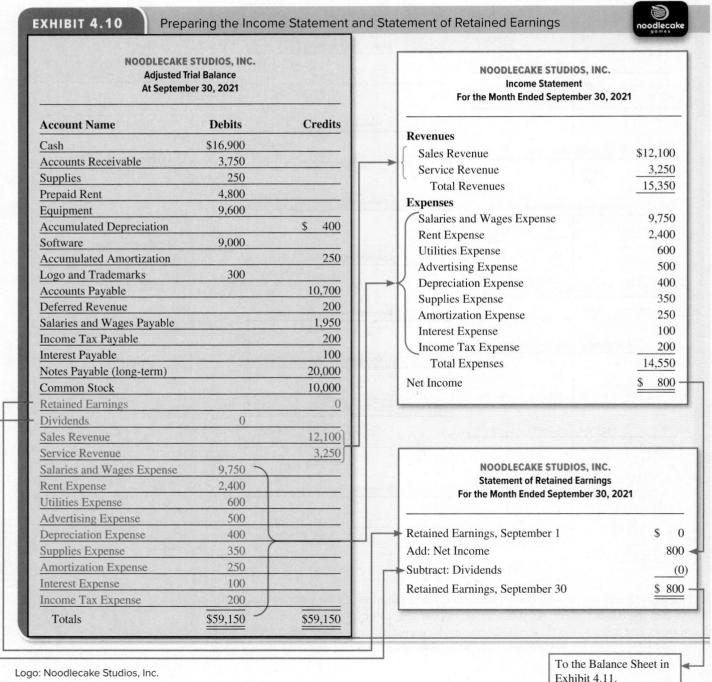

NOODLECAKE STUDIOS, INC.
Adjusted Trial Balance
At September 30, 2021

Account Name	Debits	Credits
Cash	$16,900	
Accounts Receivable	3,750	
Supplies	250	
Prepaid Rent	4,800	
Equipment	9,600	
Accumulated Depreciation		$ 400
Software	9,000	
Accumulated Amortization		250
Logo and Trademarks	300	
Accounts Payable		10,700
Deferred Revenue		200
Salaries and Wages Payable		1,950
Income Tax Payable		200
Interest Payable		100
Notes Payable (long-term)		20,000
Common Stock		10,000
Retained Earnings		0
Dividends	0	
Sales Revenue		12,100
Service Revenue		3,250
Salaries and Wages Expense	9,750	
Rent Expense	2,400	
Utilities Expense	600	
Advertising Expense	500	
Depreciation Expense	400	
Supplies Expense	350	
Amortization Expense	250	
Interest Expense	100	
Income Tax Expense	200	
Totals	$59,150	$59,150

NOODLECAKE STUDIOS, INC.
Income Statement
For the Month Ended September 30, 2021

Revenues	
Sales Revenue	$12,100
Service Revenue	3,250
Total Revenues	15,350
Expenses	
Salaries and Wages Expense	9,750
Rent Expense	2,400
Utilities Expense	600
Advertising Expense	500
Depreciation Expense	400
Supplies Expense	350
Amortization Expense	250
Interest Expense	100
Income Tax Expense	200
Total Expenses	14,550
Net Income	$ 800

NOODLECAKE STUDIOS, INC.
Statement of Retained Earnings
For the Month Ended September 30, 2021

Retained Earnings, September 1	$ 0
Add: Net Income	800
Subtract: Dividends	(0)
Retained Earnings, September 30	$ 800

To the Balance Sheet in Exhibit 4.11.

Logo: Noodlecake Studios, Inc.

on the statement of retained earnings. The amount for Net Income on the next line of the statement of retained earnings comes from the income statement, and the Dividends number comes from the adjusted trial balance.

Balance Sheet

Like the other statements, the balance sheet is prepared from the adjusted trial balance, as shown in Exhibit 4.11. When preparing the balance sheet, watch out for three things. First, remember to classify assets as current if they will be turned into cash or used up within 12 months. Liabilities should be classified as current if they will be fulfilled (paid) within 12 months. Second, note that Accumulated Depreciation and Accumulated Amortization are reported in the assets section (and are subtracted from the accounts to which

COACH'S TIP

The account Dividends is reported only on the statement of retained earnings.

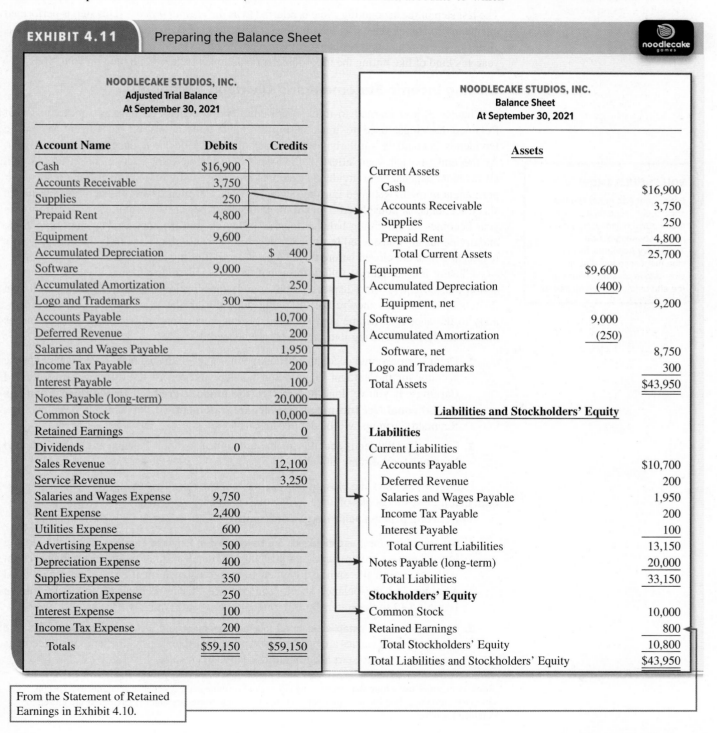

EXHIBIT 4.11 Preparing the Balance Sheet

NOODLECAKE STUDIOS, INC.
Adjusted Trial Balance
At September 30, 2021

Account Name	Debits	Credits
Cash	$16,900	
Accounts Receivable	3,750	
Supplies	250	
Prepaid Rent	4,800	
Equipment	9,600	
Accumulated Depreciation		$ 400
Software	9,000	
Accumulated Amortization		250
Logo and Trademarks	300	
Accounts Payable		10,700
Deferred Revenue		200
Salaries and Wages Payable		1,950
Income Tax Payable		200
Interest Payable		100
Notes Payable (long-term)		20,000
Common Stock		10,000
Retained Earnings		0
Dividends	0	
Sales Revenue		12,100
Service Revenue		3,250
Salaries and Wages Expense	9,750	
Rent Expense	2,400	
Utilities Expense	600	
Advertising Expense	500	
Depreciation Expense	400	
Supplies Expense	350	
Amortization Expense	250	
Interest Expense	100	
Income Tax Expense	200	
Totals	$59,150	$59,150

NOODLECAKE STUDIOS, INC.
Balance Sheet
At September 30, 2021

Assets

Current Assets		
Cash		$16,900
Accounts Receivable		3,750
Supplies		250
Prepaid Rent		4,800
Total Current Assets		25,700
Equipment	$9,600	
Accumulated Depreciation	(400)	
Equipment, net		9,200
Software	9,000	
Accumulated Amortization	(250)	
Software, net		8,750
Logo and Trademarks		300
Total Assets		$43,950

Liabilities and Stockholders' Equity

Liabilities	
Current Liabilities	
Accounts Payable	$10,700
Deferred Revenue	200
Salaries and Wages Payable	1,950
Income Tax Payable	200
Interest Payable	100
Total Current Liabilities	13,150
Notes Payable (long-term)	20,000
Total Liabilities	33,150
Stockholders' Equity	
Common Stock	10,000
Retained Earnings	800
Total Stockholders' Equity	10,800
Total Liabilities and Stockholders' Equity	$43,950

From the Statement of Retained Earnings in Exhibit 4.10.

Logo: Noodlecake Studios, Inc.

they are contra-accounts). Third, get the Retained Earnings balance from the statement of retained earnings, not from the adjusted trial balance. (The adjusted trial balance still reports the period's opening Retained Earnings balance.)

Statement of Cash Flows and Notes

We don't want you to forget the statement of cash flows (SCF) and notes to the financial statements also must be prepared as part of the financial statements. But you look a little tired, so we'll leave the SCF for Chapter 12 and we'll slide information about financial statement notes into each of the remaining chapters.

CLOSING TEMPORARY ACCOUNTS

Learning Objective 4-5
Explain the closing process.

The last step of the accounting cycle is referred to as the *closing process*. This step is performed only at the end of the year, after the financial statements have been prepared. The closing process cleans up the accounting records to get them ready to begin tracking the results in the following year. It's kind of like hitting the trip odometer on your car or the reset button on your Xbox.

Closing Income Statement and Dividend Accounts

In Chapter 3, you learned to think of revenue and expense accounts as subcategories of Retained Earnings, used to track earnings-related transactions of the current year. The Dividends account is similarly used to track dividends declared during the current year. At the end of each year, after all the year's transactions and adjustments are recorded, all revenue, expense, and dividends accounts are "closed" by moving their balances to their permanent home in Retained Earnings. The Retained Earnings account, like all other balance sheet accounts, is considered a **permanent account** because its ending balance from one year becomes its beginning balance for the following year. In contrast, revenues, expenses, and dividends are considered **temporary accounts** because they track only the current year's results and then are closed before the next year's activities are recorded.

> **YOU SHOULD KNOW**
>
> **Permanent Accounts:** The balance sheet accounts that carry their ending balances into the next accounting period.
> **Temporary Accounts:** Income statement accounts that are closed to *Retained Earnings* at the end of the accounting period.

Closing journal entries follow the usual debits-equal-credits format used for the transaction journal entries (in Chapters 2 and 3) and adjusting journal entries (shown earlier in this chapter). Because they're the last thing done during the year, they're posted immediately to the accounts. (Some computerized systems record and post closing journal entries automatically.) Two closing journal entries are needed:[1]

1. Debit each revenue account for the amount of its credit balance, credit each expense account for the amount of its debit balance, and record the difference in Retained Earnings. If you've done it correctly, **the amount credited to Retained Earnings should equal Net Income on the income statement.** (If the company has a net loss, Retained Earnings will be debited.)

2. Credit the Dividends account for the amount of its debit balance and debit Retained Earnings for the same amount.

Exhibit 4.12 shows the closing process for Noodlecake (assuming, for sake of illustration, that it closes its books on the last day of September).

The closing process achieves two outcomes:

1. **Net income (or loss) and dividends are transferred to Retained Earnings.** After the closing journal entries are prepared and posted, the balance in the Retained Earnings account will agree with the ending Retained Earnings balance on the statement of retained earnings and the balance sheet. You can see this by comparing the T-account in Exhibit 4.12 to the statement of retained earnings in Exhibit 4.10.

2. **Zero balances are established in all income statement and dividend accounts.** After the closing journal entries are prepared and posted, the balances in the temporary accounts are reset to zero to start accumulating next year's results.

---

[1]Some companies use a four-step process, by closing (1) revenue and (2) expense accounts to a special summary account, called Income Summary. Then, (3) Income Summary and (4) Dividends are closed to Retained Earnings.

EXHIBIT 4.12   Analyzing, Preparing, and Summarizing the Closing Journal Entries

① Analyze

The analysis step for closing the temporary accounts only requires that you identify, from the adjusted trial balance, the temporary accounts with debit balances (to be credited below) and the temporary accounts with credit balances (to be debited below).

② Record

CJE 1. Close revenue and expense accounts:	**Debit**	**Credit**
Sales Revenue (−R)	12,100	
Service Revenue (−R)	3,250	
Salaries and Wages Expense (−E)		9,750
Rent Expense (−E)		2,400
Utilities Expense (−E)		600
Advertising Expense (−E)		500
Depreciation Expense (−E)		400
Supplies Expense (−E)		350
Amortization Expense (−E)		250
Interest Expense (−E)		100
Income Tax Expense (−E)		200
Retained Earnings (+SE)		800

CJE 2. Close the dividends account:

Like most tech companies, Noodlecake decided to not declare or pay dividends. If it had, the following closing journal entry would be required for the existing balance in the Dividends account.

Retained Earnings (−SE)	xx	
Dividends (−D)		xx

③ Summarize

dr −	**Sales Revenue (R, SE)**	cr +
	12,100	Adj. bal.
CJE (1)	12,100	
	0	Closed bal.

dr +	**Depreciation Expense (E, SE)**	cr −
Adj. bal.	400	
		400	CJE (1)
Closed bal.	0	

dr −	**Service Revenue (R, SE)**	cr +
	3,250	Adj. bal.
CJE (1)	3,250	
	0	Closed bal.

dr +	**Supplies Expense (E, SE)**	cr −
Adj. bal.	350	
		350	CJE (1)
Closed bal.	0	

dr +	**Salaries and Wages Expense (E, SE)**	cr −
Adj. bal.	9,750	
		9,750	CJE (1)
Closed bal.	0	

dr +	**Amortization Expense (E, SE)**	cr −
Adj. bal.	250	
		250	CJE (1)
Closed bal.	0	

dr +	**Rent Expense (E, SE)**	cr −
Adj. bal.	2,400	
		2,400	CJE (1)
Closed bal.	0	

dr +	**Interest Expense (E, SE)**	cr −
Adj. bal.	100	
		100	CJE (1)
Closed bal.	0	

dr +	**Utilities Expense (E, SE)**	cr −
Adj. bal.	600	
		600	CJE (1)
Closed bal.	0	

dr +	**Income Tax Expense (E, SE)**	cr −
Adj. bal.	200	
		200	CJE (1)
Closed bal.	0	

dr +	**Advertising Expense (E, SE)**	cr −
Adj. bal.	500	
		500	CJE (1)
Closed bal.	0	

dr −	**Retained Earnings (SE)**	cr +
	0	Adj. bal.
	800	CJE (1)
	800	Closed bal.

Post-Closing Trial Balance

After the closing journal entries are posted, all temporary accounts should have zero balances. These accounts will be ready for summarizing transactions recorded next year. The ending balance in Retained Earnings is now up to date (it matches the year-end amount on the statement of retained earnings and the balance sheet) and is carried forward as the beginning Retained Earnings balance for the next year. To ensure no errors occurred during the closing process, you could prepare a **post-closing trial balance** (as shown in Exhibit 4.13). In this context, *post* means "after," so a post-closing trial balance is an "after-closing" trial balance prepared as a final check that total debits still equal total credits and that all temporary accounts have been closed.

EXHIBIT 4.13	Noodlecake's Post-Closing Trial Balance

NOODLECAKE STUDIOS, INC.
Post-Closing Trial Balance
At September 30, 2021

Account Name	Debits	Credits
Cash	$16,900	
Accounts Receivable	3,750	
Supplies	250	
Prepaid Rent	4,800	
Equipment	9,600	
Accumulated Depreciation		$ 400
Software	9,000	
Accumulated Amortization		250
Logo and Trademarks	300	
Accounts Payable		10,700
Deferred Revenue		200
Salaries and Wages Payable		1,950
Income Tax Payable		200
Interest Payable		100
Notes Payable (long-term)		20,000
Common Stock		10,000
Retained Earnings		800
Dividends	0	
Sales Revenue		0
Service Revenue		0
Salaries and Wages Expense	0	
Rent Expense	0	
Utilities Expense	0	
Advertising Expense	0	
Depreciation Expense	0	
Supplies Expense	0	
Amortization Expense	0	
Interest Expense	0	
Income Tax Expense	0	
Totals	$44,600	$44,600

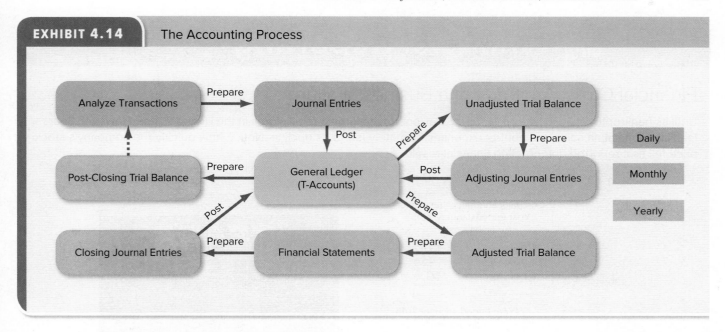

EXHIBIT 4.14 | The Accounting Process

Now that we've completed the accounting cycle, it seems appropriate to summarize it one more time. Exhibit 4.2 showed one way to think about the accounting cycle. Exhibit 4.14 presents a slightly different format.[2] Follow the path along the arrows clockwise from the top left through each boxed item in the exhibit, noticing the central role of the general ledger (T-accounts). The steps involving the coral, blue, and gold boxes are done daily, monthly, and yearly, respectively.

Evaluate the Results

ADJUSTED FINANCIAL RESULTS

Learning Objective 4-6
Explain how adjustments affect financial results.

Throughout this chapter, you have learned various adjustments that must be made to the accounting records when finalizing and preparing the financial statements. These adjustments help to ensure all revenues and expenses are reported in the period in which they are generated and incurred. As a result of these adjustments, the financial statements present the best picture of whether the company's business activities were profitable that period and what economic resources the company owns and owes at the end of that period. Without these adjustments, the financial statements present an incomplete and misleading picture of the company's financial performance.

Noodlecake provides a good example of the extent to which unadjusted balances may change during the adjustment process. Chapter 3 ended with Jordan believing Noodlecake had earned a sizable profit (net income of $3,100 from revenue of $12,000, resulting in a net profit margin of 25.8%). After making the required adjustments in this chapter, the company's adjusted results indicated a much different picture (net income of $800 from revenue of $15,350, yielding a net profit margin of 5.2%). Consequently, Jordan learned he had much to improve upon in the upcoming months. He set a goal of attempting to increase the company's revenue by expanding his customer base, while at the same time trying to control expenses. He was well aware that even large companies go out of business if they fail to maintain revenues and control their expenses.

---

[2]Thanks to Robert Hogan for this illustration.

SPOTLIGHT ON Financial Reporting

Financial Crisis: Anatomy of a Business Failure

Until its bankruptcy filing in late 2018, Sears was one of the largest retail stores in the United States. However, Sears's inability to maintain sales and control expenses ultimately led to its decline. Notice how quickly the company's stock price fell as it reported deteriorating financial results.

Company announces results for
Year Ended January 2015
(in billions)

Revenues	$31.2
Expenses	32.9
Net Income	$(1.7)

Year Ended January 2016
(in billions)

Revenues	$25.1
Expenses	26.3
Net Income	$(1.2)

Year Ended January 2017
(in billions)

Revenues	$22.1
Expenses	24.4
Net Income	$(2.3)

Year Ended January 2018
(in billions)

Revenues	$16.7
Expenses	17.1
Net Income	$(0.4)

Quarter Ended
May 5, 2018
(in billions)

Revenues	$2.9
Expenses	3.3
Net Income	$(0.4)

Quarter Ended
August 4, 2018
(in billions)

Revenues	$3.2
Expenses	3.7
Net Income	$(0.5)

Company files for bankruptcy protection.

Stock prices: $36.05, $17.52, $8.01, $2.42, $2.81, $1.21, $0.31

Dates: February 26, 2015; February 25, 2016; March 9, 2017; March 14, 2018; May 31, 2018; September 13, 2018; October 15, 2018

ShotStalker/Shutterstock

REVIEW THE CHAPTER

DEMONSTRATION CASE

We take our final look at accounting for Goodbye Grass Corporation by illustrating the end of the accounting cycle: the adjustment process, financial statement preparation, and the closing process. No adjustments have been made to the accounts yet. Your starting point will be the following unadjusted trial balance dated April 30, 2021:

GOODBYE GRASS CORPORATION
Unadjusted Trial Balance
At April 30, 2021

Account Name	Debits	Credits
Cash	$ 4,510	
Accounts Receivable	1,700	
Notes Receivable	1,250	
Interest Receivable	0	
Prepaid Insurance	300	
Equipment	4,600	
Accumulated Depreciation		$ 0
Land	3,750	
Accounts Payable		620
Deferred Revenue		1,600
Salaries and Wages Payable		0
Interest Payable		0
Income Tax Payable		0
Notes Payable (short-term)		4,000
Common Stock		9,000
Retained Earnings		0
Service Revenue		5,200
Interest Revenue		0
Salaries and Wages Expense	3,900	
Fuel Expense	410	
Insurance Expense	0	
Depreciation Expense	0	
Interest Expense	0	
Income Tax Expense	0	
Totals	$20,420	$20,420

By reviewing the unadjusted trial balance, you identify three deferral accounts (Prepaid Insurance, Equipment, and Deferred Revenue) that may need to be adjusted in addition to accruals that may be necessary relating to wages, income taxes, and interest on the Notes Receivable and Notes Payable. The following information is determined at the end of the accounting cycle:

Deferral Adjustments

a. The $1,600 in Deferred Revenue represents four months of service (April through July). Service for one month (April) has now been provided.
b. Insurance purchased at the beginning of April for $300 provides coverage for six months (April through September). The insurance coverage for April has now been used.
   TIP: Account for the expiry of prepaid insurance just like the expiry of prepaid rent.
c. Mowers, edgers, rakes, and hand tools (equipment) have been used in April to generate revenues. The company estimates $300 in depreciation each year.

Accrual Adjustments

d. Salaries and wages have been paid through April 28. Employees worked the last two days of April and will be paid in May. Salaries and wages amount to $200 per day.
e. Interest incurred and payable on the Notes payable is $45 for the month of April.
f. Interest earned and receivable on the Notes receivable is $10 for the month of April.
g. The estimated income tax rate for Goodbye Grass Corporation is 35 percent.

Required:

1. Analyze items (*a*)–(*g*) with the goal of identifying the effects of required adjustments on the basic accounting equation (Assets = Liabilities + Stockholders' Equity), using the format shown in the chapter.

2. Record the adjusting journal entries required at the end of April.

3. Summarize the effects of each adjusting journal entry in T-accounts for each account affected. Obtain beginning balances from the unadjusted trial balance, then post the adjusting journal entries from requirement 2, and calculate adjusted April 30 balances.

4. Prepare an adjusted trial balance to ensure debit and credit balances are equal, remembering to include all accounts in the trial balance (and not just the ones affected by the adjusting journal entries).

5. Prepare an income statement, statement of retained earnings, and classified balance sheet from the amounts in the adjusted trial balance.

6. Prepare the closing journal entries that would be required if Goodbye Grass Corporation's fiscal year ended April 30, 2021.

After completing requirements 1–6, check your answers with the following solution.

Suggested Solution

1. Adjustment analysis:

   a. The unadjusted balances are $1,600 for Deferred Revenue and $5,200 for Service Revenue. Service for one-fourth of the $1,600 has now been provided in April ($400 = ¼ × $1,600), bringing total service revenues for the month to $5,600 ($5,200 + $400). Three-fourths of the $1,600 remains deferred at the end of April ($1,200 = ¾ × $1,600). To reach these desired balances, we need an adjustment that decreases Deferred Revenue by $400 and increases Service Revenue by $400.

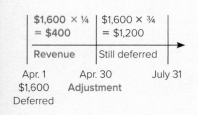

Assets	=	Liabilities	+	Stockholders' Equity
		Deferred Revenue −400		Service Revenue (+R) +400

   b. The unadjusted balances are $300 for Prepaid Insurance and $0 for Insurance Expense. One-sixth of the $300 has expired in April, resulting in an insurance expense for the month of $50 (= ⅙ × $300). Five of the six months of insurance coverage remain unused at the end of April ($250 = ⅚ × $300). To reach these desired balances, we need an adjustment that decreases Prepaid Insurance by $50 and increases Insurance Expense by $50.

Assets	=	Liabilities	+	Stockholders' Equity
Prepaid Insurance −50				Insurance Expense (+E) −50

   c. The unadjusted balances are $0 for Accumulated Depreciation and $0 for Depreciation Expense. Yearly depreciation of $300 equals $25 for just one month ($300 × 1/12). To go from the unadjusted balances of $0 to the desired adjusted balances of $25, we increase the expense and contra-account balances by $25.

Assets	=	Liabilities	+	Stockholders' Equity
Accumulated Depreciation (+xA) −25				Depreciation Expense (+E) −25

   d. The unadjusted balances are $0 for Salaries and Wages Payable and $3,900 for Salaries and Wages Expense. Because the final two days of work done in April are unpaid, we need to record a liability for $400 (2 × $200). Total wages expense for the month should include the $3,900 paid for work from April 1–28 plus the $400 not yet paid for work on April 29 and 30. To reach these desired balances, we need an adjustment increasing Wages Payable by $400 and increasing Wages Expense by $400.

Assets	=	Liabilities	+	Stockholders' Equity
		Salaries and Wages Payable +400		Salaries and Wages Expense (+E) −400

   e. The unadjusted balances are $0 for Interest Payable and $0 for Interest Expense. Interest of $45 was incurred in April, so the adjustment needs to increase both accounts by $45.

Assets	=	Liabilities	+	Stockholders' Equity
		Interest Payable +45		Interest Expense (+E) −45

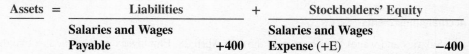

f. The unadjusted balances are $0 for Interest Receivable and $0 for Interest Revenue. Interest of $10 was earned and became receivable in April, so the adjustment needs to increase both accounts by $10.

Assets	=	Liabilities	+	Stockholders' Equity	
Interest Receivable +10				**Interest Revenue (+R)**	**+10**

g. The unadjusted balances are $0 for Income Tax Payable and $0 for Income Tax Expense. The amount of calculated income taxes will increase both of these accounts. Income taxes are calculated as 35 percent of adjusted income before tax for the month, as follows:

	Revenues	Expenses	
Unadjusted totals	$5,200	$4,310	← Calculated from unadjusted trial balance
Adjustments:			($4,310 = $3,900 + $410)
(a) Service Given	+ 400		
(b) Insurance Expired		+ 50	
(c) Depreciation		+ 25	
(d) Wages Incurred		+ 400	
(e) Interest Incurred		+ 45	
(f) Interest Earned	+ 10		
Adjusted totals	$5,610	– $4,830	= $780 Adjusted income before income tax
			× 35% Tax rate
			$273 **Income tax**

Assets	=	Liabilities	+	Stockholders' Equity	
		Income Tax Payable +273		**Income Tax Expense (+E)**	**−273**

2. Adjusting journal entries:

		Debit	Credit
a.	**Deferred Revenue (−L)**	**400**	
	Service Revenue (+R, +SE)		**400**
b.	**Insurance Expense (+E, −SE)**	**50**	
	Prepaid Insurance (−A)		**50**
c.	**Depreciation Expense (+E, −SE)**	**25**	
	Accumulated Depreciation (+xA, −A)		**25**
d.	**Salaries and Wages Expense (+E, −SE)**	**400**	
	Salaries and Wages Payable (+L)		**400**
e.	**Interest Expense (+E, −SE)**	**45**	
	Interest Payable (+L)		**45**
f.	**Interest Receivable (+A)**	**10**	
	Interest Revenue (+R, +SE)		**10**
g.	**Income Tax Expense (+E, −SE)**	**273**	
	Income Tax Payable (+L)		**273**

3. T-accounts affected by adjusting journal entries:*

dr +	Interest Receivable (A)	cr −
Beg. bal.	0	
(f)	10	
End. bal.	10	

dr −	Interest Payable (L)	cr +
	0	Beg. bal.
	45	(e)
	45	End. bal.

dr +	Insurance Expense (E)	cr −
Beg. bal.	0	
(b)	50	
End. bal.	50	

dr +	Prepaid Insurance (A)	cr −
Beg. bal.	300	
	50	(b)
End. bal.	250	

dr −	Income Tax Payable (L)	cr +
	0	Beg. bal.
	273	(g)
	273	End. bal.

dr +	Depreciation Expense (E)	cr −
Beg. bal.	0	
(c)	25	
End. bal.	25	

*See Chapter 3's Demonstration Case B for balances of T-accounts not affected by adjusting journal entries.

dr − Accumulated Depreciation (xA) cr +		
	0	Beg. bal.
	25	(c)
	25	End. bal.

dr − Service Revenue (R, SE) cr +		
	5,200	Beg. bal.
	400	(a)
	5,600	End. bal.

dr + Interest Expense (E, SE) cr −		
Beg. bal.	0	
(e)	45	
End. bal.	45	

dr − Deferred Revenue (L) cr +		
	1,600	Beg. bal.
(a) 400		
	1,200	End. bal.

dr − Interest Revenue (R, SE) cr +		
	0	Beg. bal.
	10	(f)
	10	End. bal.

dr + Income Tax Expense (E, SE) cr −		
Beg. bal.	0	
(g)	273	
End. bal.	273	

dr − Salaries and Wages Payable (L) cr +		
	0	Beg. bal.
	400	(d)
	400	End. bal.

dr + Salaries and Wages Expense (E, SE) cr −		
Beg. bal.	3,900	
(d)	400	
End. bal.	4,300	

4. Adjusted trial balance:

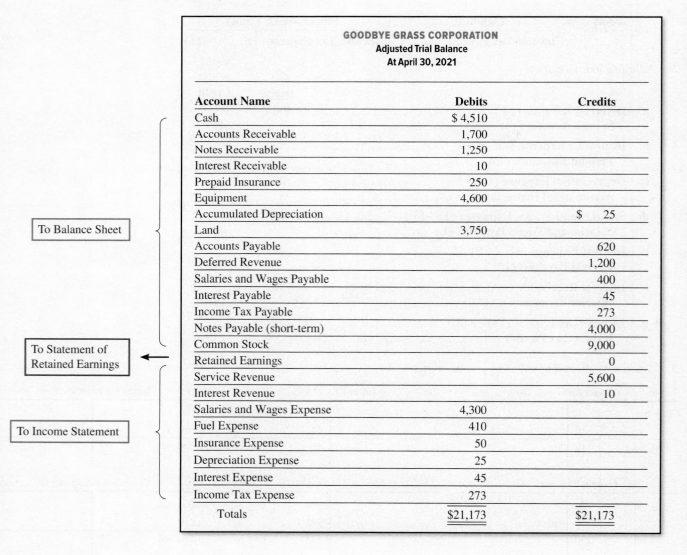

GOODBYE GRASS CORPORATION
Adjusted Trial Balance
At April 30, 2021

Account Name	Debits	Credits
Cash	$ 4,510	
Accounts Receivable	1,700	
Notes Receivable	1,250	
Interest Receivable	10	
Prepaid Insurance	250	
Equipment	4,600	
Accumulated Depreciation		$ 25
Land	3,750	
Accounts Payable		620
Deferred Revenue		1,200
Salaries and Wages Payable		400
Interest Payable		45
Income Tax Payable		273
Notes Payable (short-term)		4,000
Common Stock		9,000
Retained Earnings		0
Service Revenue		5,600
Interest Revenue		10
Salaries and Wages Expense	4,300	
Fuel Expense	410	
Insurance Expense	50	
Depreciation Expense	25	
Interest Expense	45	
Income Tax Expense	273	
Totals	$21,173	$21,173

To Balance Sheet

To Statement of Retained Earnings

To Income Statement

5. Income statement, statement of retained earnings, and balance sheet:

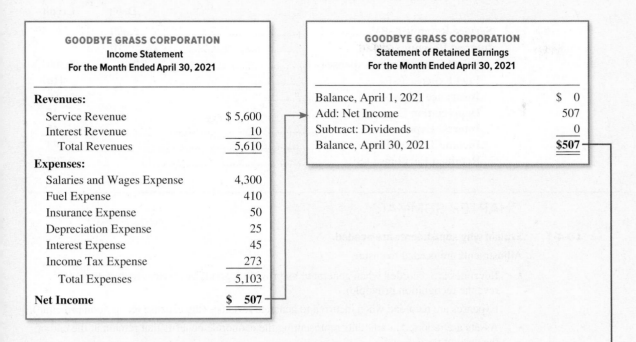

GOODBYE GRASS CORPORATION
Income Statement
For the Month Ended April 30, 2021

Revenues:

Service Revenue	$ 5,600
Interest Revenue	10
Total Revenues	5,610

Expenses:

Salaries and Wages Expense	4,300
Fuel Expense	410
Insurance Expense	50
Depreciation Expense	25
Interest Expense	45
Income Tax Expense	273
Total Expenses	5,103
Net Income	**$ 507**

GOODBYE GRASS CORPORATION
Statement of Retained Earnings
For the Month Ended April 30, 2021

Balance, April 1, 2021	$ 0
Add: Net Income	507
Subtract: Dividends	0
Balance, April 30, 2021	**$507**

GOODBYE GRASS CORPORATION
Balance Sheet
At April 30, 2021

Assets			**Liabilities and Stockholders' Equity**	
Current Assets:			Liabilities	
Cash		$ 4,510	Current Liabilities:	
Accounts Receivable		1,700	Accounts Payable	$ 620
Notes Receivable		1,250	Deferred Revenue	1,200
Interest Receivable		10	Salaries and Wages Payable	400
Prepaid Insurance		250	Interest Payable	45
Total Current Assets		7,720	Income Tax Payable	273
Equipment	$ 4,600		Notes Payable (short-term)	4,000
Accumulated Depreciation	(25)		Total Current Liabilities	6,538
Equipment, Net		4,575	Stockholders' Equity	
			Common Stock	9,000
Land		3,750	Retained Earnings	507
Total Assets		$16,045	Total Liabilities and Stockholders' Equity	$16,045

6. Closing journal entry:

If Goodbye Grass Corporation had adopted an April 30 year-end, the company would require a journal entry to close its revenue and expense accounts into Retained Earnings. Because the company has not declared a dividend, a Dividends account does not exist to be closed into Retained Earnings. The closing journal entry needed to close revenues and expenses into Retained Earnings is

	Debit	Credit
Service Revenue (−R)	5,600	
Interest Revenue (−R)	10	
Salaries and Wages Expense (−E)		4,300
Fuel Expense (−E)		410
Insurance Expense (−E)		50
Depreciation Expense (−E)		25
Interest Expense (−E)		45
Income Tax Expense (−E)...		273
Retained Earnings (+SE)		507

CHAPTER SUMMARY

LO 4-1   **Explain why adjustments are needed.**

Adjustments are needed to ensure

- Revenues are recorded when generated by providing goods or services to customers (the revenue recognition principle),
- Expenses are recorded when incurred to generate revenues (the expense recognition principle),
- Assets are reported at amounts representing the economic benefits that remain at the end of the current period, and
- Liabilities are reported at amounts owed at the end of the current period that will require a future sacrifice of resources.

LO 4-2   **Prepare adjustments needed at the end of the period.**

- The process for preparing adjustments includes
    1. Analyzing the unadjusted balances in balance sheet and income statement accounts and calculating the amount of the adjustment needed, using a timeline where appropriate.
    2. Preparing an adjusting journal entry to make the adjustment.
    3. Summarizing the adjusting journal entry in the applicable ledger (T-accounts).
- Each adjusting journal entry affects one balance sheet and one income statement account.

LO 4-3   **Prepare an adjusted trial balance.**

An adjusted trial balance is a list of all accounts with their adjusted debit or credit balances indicated in the appropriate column to provide a check on the equality of total debits and credits.

LO 4-4   **Prepare financial statements.**

Adjusted account balances are used in preparing the following financial statements:

- Income Statement: Revenues − Expenses = Net Income.
- Statement of Retained Earnings: Beginning Retained Earnings + Net Income − Dividends = Ending Retained Earnings.
- Balance Sheet: Assets = Liabilities + Stockholders' Equity.
- The statement of cash flows and notes to the financial statements are important components of adjusted financial statements, but they will be studied in later chapters.

LO 4-5   **Explain the closing process.**

- Closing journal entries are required to (*a*) transfer net income (or loss) and dividends into Retained Earnings and (*b*) prepare all temporary accounts (revenues, expenses, dividends) for the following year by establishing zero balances in these accounts.
- Two closing journal entries are needed:
    1. Debit each revenue account for the amount of its balance, credit each expense account for the amount of its balance, and record the difference (equal to net income) in Retained Earnings.
    2. Credit the Dividends account for the amount of its balance and debit Retained Earnings for the same amount.

Explain how adjustments affect financial results.   **LO 4-6**

Adjustments help ensure all revenues and expenses are reported in the period in which they are earned and incurred, as a result of a company's activities. Without these adjustments, the financial statements present an incomplete and potentially misleading picture of the company's financial performance.

KEY TERMS

Adjusted Trial Balance p. 166

Adjusting Journal
    Entries p. 154

Adjustments p. 152

Carrying Value (Net Book Value,
    Book Value) p. 159

Contra-Account p. 159

Depreciation p. 159

Permanent Accounts p. 170

Post-Closing Trial
    Balance p. 172

Temporary Accounts p. 170

See complete definitions in the glossary in the back of this text.

HOMEWORK HELPER

Alternative terms

- Accrued Liabilities is a generic account name that can include liabilities recorded using accrual adjustments for salaries, interest, income taxes, and many other items.

Helpful reminders

- When determining each adjustment, draw timelines to picture where we are now, where we need to be, and the adjustment to get us there.
- Cash is never part of an accrual or deferral adjustment.
- The income statement is the temporary home for revenue and expense accounts, and their permanent home is Retained Earnings in the stockholders' equity section of the balance sheet.

Frequent mistakes

- Accumulated Depreciation and Depreciation Expense are not the same accounts. Accumulated Depreciation is a permanent balance sheet account that accumulates each period of depreciation. Depreciation Expense is a temporary income statement account that reports the depreciation of only the current year.
- Dividends are not expenses, but rather are distributions to stockholders of the company's prior profits that have accumulated in Retained Earnings.
- The amount in Retained Earnings on an adjusted trial balance is not reported on the balance sheet; it is the beginning balance on the statement of retained earnings. The ending balance from the statement of retained earnings is reported on the balance sheet. Also, the Retained Earnings account is a permanent account, so it is never closed.

PRACTICE MATERIAL

QUESTIONS (⊖ Symbol indicates questions that require analysis from more than one perspective.)

1. Briefly explain the purposes of adjustments.

2. Explain the relationships between adjustments and the following Chapter 3 concepts: (*a*) the time period assumption, (*b*) the revenue recognition principle, and (*c*) the expense recognition principle.

3. List the two types of adjustments and give an example of an adjustment affecting revenues and expenses for each type.

4. Explain the effect of adjusting journal entries on cash.

5. What is a contra-asset? Give an example of one.

6. Explain the differences between depreciation expense and accumulated depreciation.

7. What is an adjusted trial balance? What is its purpose?

8. On December 31, a company makes a $9,000 payment for renting a warehouse in January, February, and March of the following year. Show the accounting equation effects of the transaction on December 31, as well as the adjustments required on January 31, February 28, and March 31.

9. Using the information in question 8, determine the amounts and accounts that will be reported on the January 31

balance sheet and the income statement for the month ended January 31.

10. Using the information in question 8, prepare the journal entry and adjusting journal entries to be made on December 31, January 31, February 28, and March 31.

11. What is the equation for each of the following statements: (*a*) income statement, (*b*) balance sheet, and (*c*) statement of retained earnings?

12. Explain how the financial statements in question 11 relate to each other.

13. What is the purpose of closing journal entries?

14. How do permanent accounts differ from temporary accounts?

15. Why are the income statement accounts closed but the balance sheet accounts are not?

16. What is a post-closing trial balance? Is it a useful part of the accounting cycle? Explain.

17. The owner of a local business complains that the adjustments process consumes a lot of time and delays reporting month-end financial results. How would you convince her of the importance of this process? ⊜

MULTIPLE CHOICE

1. Which of the following accounts would not appear in a closing journal entry?

    a. Interest Revenue
    b. Accumulated Depreciation
    c. Retained Earnings
    d. Salaries and Wages Expense

2. Which account is least likely to appear in an adjusting journal entry?

    a. Cash
    b. Interest Receivable
    c. Income Tax Expense
    d. Salaries and Wages Expense

3. When a concert promotions company collects cash for ticket sales two months in advance of the show date, which of the following accounts is affected?

    a. Accounts Payable
    b. Accounts Receivable
    c. Prepaid Expense
    d. Deferred Revenue

4. On December 31, an adjustment is made to reduce Deferred Revenue and report Service Revenue generated. How many accounts will be included in this adjusting journal entry?

    a. None
    b. One
    c. Two
    d. Three

5. An adjusting journal entry to recognize accrued salaries payable would cause which of the following?

    a. A decrease in assets and stockholders' equity
    b. A decrease in assets and liabilities
    c. An increase in expenses, liabilities, and stockholders' equity
    d. An increase in expenses and liabilities and a decrease in stockholders' equity

6. An adjusted trial balance

    a. Shows the ending balances in a debit and credit format before posting the adjusting journal entries.
    b. Is prepared after closing entries have been posted.

    c. Is a tool used by financial analysts to review the performance of publicly traded companies.
    d. Shows the ending balances resulting from the adjusting journal entries in a debit-and-credit format.

7. Company A has owned a building for several years. Which of the following statements regarding depreciation is false from an accounting perspective?

    a. Depreciation Expense for the year will equal Accumulated Depreciation.
    b. Depreciation is an estimated expense to be recorded each period during the building's life.
    c. As depreciation is recorded, stockholders' equity is reduced.
    d. As depreciation is recorded, total assets are reduced.

8. Which of the following trial balances is used as a source for preparing the income statement?

    a. Unadjusted trial balance
    b. Pre-adjusted trial balance
    c. Adjusted trial balance
    d. Post-closing trial balance

9. Assume the balance in Prepaid Insurance is $2,500, but it should be $1,500. The adjusting journal entry should include which of the following?

    a. Debit to Prepaid Insurance for $1,000
    b. Credit to Insurance Expense for $1,000
    c. Debit to Insurance Expense for $1,000
    d. Debit to Insurance Expense for $1,500

10. Assume a company receives a bill for $10,000 for advertising done during the current year. If this bill is not yet recorded at the end of the year, what will the adjusting journal entry include?

    a. Debit to Advertising Expense of $10,000
    b. Credit to Advertising Expense of $10,000
    c. Debit to Accrued Liabilities of $10,000
    d. Need more information to determine

For answers to the Multiple-Choice Questions **see page Q1** located in the last section of the book.

MINI-EXERCISES

Mc Graw Hill **connect**

M4-1 Understanding Concepts Related to Adjustments

LO 4-1

Match each situation below to two applicable reasons that require an adjustment to be made.

_____ 1. Delta Airlines provided flights this month for customers who paid cash last month for tickets.

_____ 2. GSD&M completed work on an advertising campaign that will be collected next month.

_____ 3. Snap received a telephone bill for services this month, which must be paid next month.

_____ 4. The Tiger Woods Foundation used up some of the benefits of its 35,000-square-foot building.

A. Revenue has been generated.

B. Expense has been incurred.

C. Liability has been incurred.

D. Liability has been fulfilled.

E. Asset has been acquired.

F. Asset has been used up.

Delta Airlines
GSD&M
Snap
Tiger Woods Foundation

M4-2 Understanding Concepts Related to Adjustments

LO 4-1

Match each situation below to two applicable reasons that require an adjustment to be made.

_____ 1. IBM completed a consulting project for the CDC to simulate the spread of contagious viruses and will be paid next month.

_____ 2. This month Apple, Inc., redeemed iTunes gift cards that had been issued last month.

_____ 3. Schutt Sports used up some of the benefits of its football helmet manufacturing equipment.

_____ 4. Procter & Gamble received a bill for this month's advertising services, which it will pay next month.

A. Revenue has been generated.

B. Expense has been incurred.

C. Liability has been incurred.

D. Liability has been fulfilled.

E. Asset has been acquired.

F. Asset has been used up.

IBM
Apple, Inc.
Schutt Sports
Procter & Gamble

M4-3 Matching Transactions with Type of Adjustment

LO 4-1, 4-2

Match each transaction with the type of adjustment that will be required, by entering the appropriate letter in the space provided.

Transaction	Type of Adjustment
_____ 1. Supplies for office use were purchased during the year for $500, of which $100 remained on hand (unused) at year-end.	A. Accrual adjustment
	B. Deferral adjustment
_____ 2. Interest of $250 on a note receivable was earned at year-end, although collection of the interest is not due until the following year.	
_____ 3. At year-end, salaries and wages payable of $3,600 had not been recorded or paid.	
_____ 4. At year-end, one-half of a $2,000 advertising project had been completed for a client, but nothing had been billed or collected.	
_____ 5. Redeemed a gift card for $600 of services.	

M4-4 Recording Adjusting Journal Entries

LO 4-2

Using the information in M4-3, prepare the adjusting journal entries required.

M4-5 Determine Accounting Equation Effects of Deferral Adjustments

LO 4-2

For each of the following transactions for the Sky Blue Corporation, give the accounting equation effects of the adjustments required at the end of the month on October 31:

a. Collected $2,400 rent for the period October 1 to December 31, which was credited to Deferred Revenue on October 1.

    b. Paid $1,200 for a two-year insurance premium on October 1 and debited Prepaid Insurance for that amount.

    c. Used a machine purchased on October 1 for $48,000. The company estimates *annual* depreciation of $4,800.

LO 4-2   **M4-6** **Recording Adjusting Journal Entries**

Using the information in M4-5, prepare the adjusting journal entries required on October 31.

LO 4-2   **M4-7** **Determining Accounting Equation Effects of Accrual Adjustments**

For each of the following transactions for New Idea Corporation, give the accounting equation effects of the adjustments required at the end of the month on July 31:

    a. Received a $600 utility bill for electricity usage in July to be paid in August.

    b. Owed wages to 10 employees who worked three days at $100 each per day at the end of July. The company will pay employees at the end of the first week of August.

    c. On July 1, loaned money to an employee who agreed to repay the loan in one year along with $1,200 for one full year of interest. No interest has been recorded yet.

LO 4-2   **M4-8** **Recording Adjusting Journal Entries**

Using the information in M4-7, prepare the adjusting journal entries required on July 31.

LO 4-2   **M4-9** **Preparing Journal Entries for Deferral Transactions and Adjustments**

For each of the following independent situations, prepare journal entries to record the initial transaction on September 30 and the adjustment required on October 31.

    a. Hockey Helpers paid $4,000 cash on September 30 to rent an arena for the months of October and November.

    b. Super Stage Shows received $16,000 on September 30 for season tickets that admit patrons to a theatre event that will be held twice (on October 31 and November 30).

    c. Risky Ventures paid $3,000 on September 30 for insurance coverage for the months of October, November, and December.

LO 4-2   **M4-10** **Preparing Journal Entries for Deferral Transactions and Adjustments**

For each of the following independent situations, prepare journal entries to record the initial transaction on December 31 and the adjustment required on January 31.

    a. Magnificent Magazines received $12,000 on December 31, 2021, for subscription services related to magazines that will be published and distributed in January through December 2022.

    b. Walker Window Washing paid $1,200 cash for supplies on December 31, 2021. As of January 31, 2022, $200 of these supplies had been used up.

    c. Indoor Raceway received $3,000 on December 31, 2021, from race participants for providing services for three races. One race is held January 31, 2022, and the other two will be held in March 2022.

LO 4-2   **M4-11** **Preparing Journal Entries for Deferral and Accrual Adjustments**

Service Pro Corp. (SPC) is preparing adjustments for its September 30 year-end. For the following transactions and events, show the September 30 adjusting entries SPC would make.

    a. Prepaid Insurance shows a balance of zero at September 30, but Insurance Expense shows a debit balance of $2,340, representing the cost of a three-year fire insurance policy purchased on September 1 of the current year.

    b. On August 31 of this year, Cash was debited and Service Revenue was credited for $1,500. The $1,500 related to fees for a three-month period beginning September 1 of the current year.

    c. The company's income tax rate is 20%. After making the above adjustments, SPC's net income before tax is $10,000. No income tax has been paid or recorded.

LO 4-3, 4-4   **M4-12** **Reporting Adjusted Account Balances**

Indicate whether each of the following accounts would be reported on the balance sheet (B/S) or income statement (I/S) of Home Repair Company. Further, if the account is reported on the balance sheet, indicate whether it would be classified with current assets (CA), noncurrent assets (NCA), current liabilities (CL), noncurrent liabilities (NCL), or stockholders' equity (SE). If the account is reported on the income statement, indicate whether it would be classified as revenue (R) or expense (E). Finally, for each account, indicate whether the company's accounting records would normally show a debit (*dr*) or credit (*cr*) balance.

Account	Financial Statement?	Classification?	Normal *dr* or *cr* Balance?
Interest Expense			
Prepaid Rent			
Amortization Expense			
Deferred Revenue			
Retained Earnings			
Accumulated Depreciation			

M4-13 Preparing an Adjusted Trial Balance

LO 4-3

Macro Company has the following adjusted accounts and balances at (June 30):

Accounts Payable	$ 300	Depreciation Expense	$ 40	Rent Expense	$ 400
Accounts Receivable	550	Equipment	1,400	Retained Earnings	120
Accumulated Amortization	150	Income Tax Expense	110	Salaries and	
Accumulated		Income Tax Payable	30	Wages Expense	660
Depreciation	250	Interest Expense	180	Sales Revenue	3,600
Amortization Expense	20	Notes Payable		Software	200
Cash	1,020	(long-term)	1,300	Supplies	710
Common Stock	300	Office Expense	820		
Deferred Revenue	100	Prepaid Rent	40		

Required:

Prepare an adjusted trial balance for Macro Company at June 30.

M4-14 Reporting an Income Statement

LO 4-4

The Sky Blue Corporation has the following adjusted trial balance at December 31.

	Debit	Credit
Cash	$ 1,230	
Accounts Receivable	2,000	
Prepaid Insurance	2,300	
Notes Receivable (long-term)	3,000	
Equipment	12,000	
Accumulated Depreciation		$ 2,600
Accounts Payable		5,420
Salaries and Wages Payable		1,000
Income Taxes Payable		2,900
Deferred Revenue		600
Common Stock		2,400
Retained Earnings		1,000
Dividends	300	
Sales Revenue		42,030
Rent Revenue		300
Salaries and Wages Expense	21,600	
Depreciation Expense	1,300	
Utilities Expense	4,220	
Insurance Expense	1,400	
Rent Expense	6,000	
Income Tax Expense	2,900	
Total	$58,250	$58,250

Prepare an income statement for the year ended December 31. How much net income did the Sky Blue Corporation generate during the year?

LO 4-4   **M4-15   Reporting a Statement of Retained Earnings**

Refer to M4-14. Prepare a statement of retained earnings for the year.

LO 4-4   **M4-16   Reporting a Balance Sheet**

Refer to M4-14. Prepare a classified balance sheet at December 31. Are the Sky Blue Corporation's assets financed primarily by debt or equity?

LO 4-5   **M4-17   Recording Closing Journal Entries**

Refer to the adjusted trial balance in M4-14. Prepare closing journal entries on December 31.

LO 4-2   **M4-18   Preparing and Posting Adjusting Journal Entries**

At December 31, the unadjusted trial balance of H&R Tacks reports Supplies of $9,000 and Supplies Expense of $0. On December 31, supplies costing $7,700 are on hand. Prepare the adjusting journal entry on December 31. In separate T-accounts for each account, enter the unadjusted balances, post the adjusting journal entry, and report the adjusted balance.

LO 4-2   **M4-19   Preparing and Posting Adjusting Journal Entries**

At December 31, the unadjusted trial balance of H&R Tacks reports Equipment of $30,000 and zero balances in Accumulated Depreciation and Depreciation Expense. Depreciation for the period is estimated to be $6,000. Prepare the adjusting journal entry on December 31. In separate T-accounts for each account, enter the unadjusted balances, post the adjusting journal entry, and report the adjusted balance.

LO 4-2   **M4-20   Preparing and Posting Adjusting Journal Entries**

At December 31, the unadjusted trial balance of H&R Tacks reports Prepaid Insurance of $7,200 and Insurance Expense of $0. The insurance was purchased on July 1 and provides coverage for 24 months. Prepare the adjusting journal entry on December 31. In separate T-accounts for each account, enter the unadjusted balances, post the adjusting journal entry, and report the adjusted balance.

LO 4-2   **M4-21   Preparing and Posting Adjusting Journal Entries**

At December 31, the unadjusted trial balance of H&R Tacks reports Deferred Revenue of $5,000 and Service Revenues of $33,800. Obligations for one-half of the deferred revenue have been fulfilled as of December 31. Prepare the adjusting journal entry on December 31. In separate T-accounts for each account, enter the unadjusted balances, post the adjusting journal entry, and report the adjusted balance.

LO 4-2   **M4-22   Preparing and Posting Adjusting Journal Entries**

At December 31, the unadjusted trial balance of H&R Tacks reports Salaries and Wages Payable of $0 and Salaries and Wages Expense of $20,000. Employees have been paid for work done up to December 27, but the $1,200 they have earned for December 28–31 has not yet been paid or recorded. Prepare the adjusting journal entry on December 31. In separate T-accounts for each account, enter the unadjusted balances, post the adjusting journal entry, and report the adjusted balance.

LO 4-2   **M4-23   Preparing and Posting Adjusting Journal Entries**

At December 31, the unadjusted trial balance of H&R Tacks reports Interest Payable of $0 and Interest Expense of $0. Interest incurred and owed in December totals $500. Prepare the adjusting journal entry on December 31. In separate T-accounts for each account, enter the unadjusted balances, post the adjusting journal entry, and report the adjusted balance.

LO 4-2   **M4-24   Preparing and Posting Journal Entries for Amortization**

At December 31, the unadjusted trial balance of H&R Tacks reports Software of $25,000 and zero balances in Accumulated Amortization and Amortization Expense. Amortization for the period is estimated to be $5,000. Prepare the adjusting journal entry on December 31. In separate T-accounts for each account, enter the unadjusted balances, post the adjusting journal entry, and report the adjusted balance.

M4-25 Preparing an Adjusted Trial Balance   LO 4-3

The adjusted trial balance for PI Detectives reported the following account balances: Accounts Receivable $500; Supplies $9,000; Prepaid Insurance $7,200; Equipment $28,000; Accumulated Depreciation $4,000; Accounts Payable $200; Deferred Revenue $5,000; Notes Payable $3,000; Common Stock $22,000; Retained Earnings $5,700; Dividends $3,000; Service Revenue $33,800; Salaries and Wages Expense $20,000; and Depreciation Expense $1,000. Prepare an adjusted trial balance as of December 31, and solve for its missing Cash balance.

M4-26 Progression of Prepaid Expenses over Several Periods   LO 4-2, 4-4, 4-5

Midwest Manufacturing purchased a three-year insurance policy for $30,000 on January 2, 2021. Prepare any journal entries, adjusting journal entries, and closing journal entries required on January 2, 2021, December 31, 2021, and December 31, 2022. Summarize these entries in T-accounts for Prepaid Insurance, Insurance Expense, Cash, and Retained Earnings. Assume the January 2, 2021, balances in these accounts were $0, $0, $90,000, and $80,000, respectively. Given only the entries for insurance, indicate what amounts would be reported for each of these accounts on the balance sheet and income statement prepared on December 31, 2021, and December 31, 2022.

EXERCISES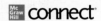

E4-1 Explaining Why Adjustments Are Needed and Preparing Adjustments   LO 4-1, 4-2

A list of various reasons for adjusting account balances is presented below, along with an unadjusted trial balance presented for the year ended December 31.

a. As of December 31, the equipment has been used for two full years. Approximately $1,200 of the equipment's usefulness is consumed each year.

b. On December 31, the company performed $400 of services for a customer but has not yet recorded or billed the customer.

c. On December 31, the company received an e-mail from its utility company indicating the company used $250 of services during December. The company has not recorded this item because the $250 will not be paid until January 15.

d. Salaries and wages totaling $333 for the second half of December have not yet been paid or recorded.

e. No adjustment is needed for this account.

	Account Name	Debit	Credit
1.	Cash	$ 6,000	
2.	Accounts Receivable	500	
3.	Equipment	12,000	
4.	Accumulated Depreciation		$ 2,300
5.	Accounts Payable		700
6.	Salaries and Wages Payable		0
7.	Common Stock		10,000
8.	Retained Earnings		5,017
9.	Service Revenue		12,000
10.	Salaries and Wages Expense	7,667	
11.	Depreciation Expense	1,100	
12.	Utilities Expense	2,750	
	Totals	$30,017	$30,017

Required:

1. For each account balance numbered 1-12, choose an appropriate reason from (*a*)–(*d*) that explains why that particular account balance needs to be adjusted or choose "*e.* No adjustment is needed."

2. Prepare the adjusting journal entries required as of December 31.

LO 4-1, 4-4   **E4-2   Identifying Adjustments and Preparing Financial Statements from a Trial Balance**

FedEx Corporation

FedEx Corporation reported its balance sheet at May 31, 2019. Assume the following alphabetically listed accounts were included in its trial balance immediately prior to preparing the financial statements. (Amounts represent millions of dollars.)

	Debit	Credit
Accounts Payable		$ 2,960
Accounts Receivable	$ 9,200	
Accumulated Depreciation		29,100
Cash	2,300	
Common Stock		3,200
Depreciation Expense	3,300	
Dividends	710	
Equipment	59,500	
Goodwill	10,900	
Income Tax Expense	120	
Income Tax Payable		3,300
Interest Expense	590	
Interest Receivable	200	
Interest Revenue		60
Notes Payable (long-term)		27,600
Notes Payable (short-term)		1,000
Office Expenses	13,760	
Prepaid Rent	900	
Rent Expense	3,300	
Repairs and Maintenance Expense	2,800	
Retained Earnings		14,770
Salaries and Wages Expense	24,800	
Salaries and Wages Payable		1,740
Service Revenue		69,700
Supplies	500	
Transportation Expense	20,550	
	$153,430	$153,430

Required:

1. Based on the trial balance, provide the name of the account that would accompany (*a*) Prepaid Rent and (*b*) Depreciation Expense in deferral adjustments at May 31.

2. Based on the trial balance, provide the name of the account that would accompany (*a*) Interest Revenue and (*b*) Salaries and Wages Expense in accrual adjustments at May 31.

3. Prepare an income statement, statement of retained earnings, and classified balance sheet for the year ended May 31, 2019.

LO 4-1, 4-2   **E4-3   Recording Initial Transactions and Subsequent Adjustments**

During the month of September, the Texas Go-Kart Company had the following business activities:

a. On September 1, paid rent on the track facility for six months at a total cost of $12,000.
b. On September 1, received $60,000 for season tickets for 12-month admission to the race track.
c. On September 1, booked the race track for a private organization that will use the track one day per month for $2,000 each time, to be paid in the following month. The organization uses the track on September 30.
d. On September 1, hired a new manager at a monthly salary of $3,000, to be paid the first Monday following the end of the month.

Required:

First prepare the journal entry, if any, required to record each of the initial business activities on September 1. Then, prepare the adjusting journal entries, if any, required on September 30.

E4-4 Determining Adjustments and Accounting Equation Effects

LO 4-1, 4-2

Mobo, a wireless phone carrier, completed its first year of operations on October 31. All of the year's entries have been recorded, except for the following:

a. At year-end, employees earned wages of $6,000, which will be paid on the next payroll date, November 6.
b. At year-end, the company had earned interest revenue of $3,000. It will be collected December 1.

Required:

1. What is the annual reporting period for this company?
2. Identify whether each required adjustment is a deferral or an accrual.
3. Show the accounting equation effects of each required adjustment, using the format shown in the demonstration case.
4. Why are these adjustments needed?

E4-5 Recording Adjusting Journal Entries

LO 4-1, 4-2

Refer to E4-4.

Required:

Record the required adjusting journal entry for transactions (*a*) and (*b*).

E4-6 Determining Adjustments and Accounting Equation Effects

LO 4-1, 4-2

Fes Company is making adjusting journal entries for the year ended December 31, 2021. In developing information for the adjusting journal entries, you learned the following:

a. A two-year insurance premium of $7,200 was paid on January 1, 2021, for coverage beginning on that date. As of December 31, 2021, the unadjusted balances were $7,200 for Prepaid Insurance and $0 for Insurance Expense.
b. At December 31, 2021, you obtained the following data relating to supplies.

Unadjusted balance in Supplies on December 31	$15,000
Unadjusted balance in Supplies Expense on December 31	72,000
Supplies on hand, counted on December 31	10,000

Required:

1. Of the $7,200 paid for insurance, what amount should be reported on the 2021 income statement as Insurance Expense? What amount should be reported on the December 31, 2021, balance sheet as Prepaid Insurance?
2. What amount should be reported on the 2021 income statement as Supplies Expense? What amount should be reported on the December 31, 2021, balance sheet as Supplies?
3. Using the format shown in the demonstration case, indicate the accounting equation effects of the adjustment required for (*a*) insurance and (*b*) supplies.

E4-7 Recording Adjusting Journal Entries

LO 4-1, 4-2

Refer to E4-6.

Required:

Prepare adjusting journal entries at December 31, 2021, for (*a*) insurance and (*b*) supplies.

E4-8 Recording Typical Adjusting Journal Entries

LO 4-1, 4-2, 4-6

Jaworski's Ski Store is completing the accounting process for its first year ended December 31, 2021. The transactions during 2021 have been journalized and posted. The following data are available to determine adjusting journal entries:

a. The unadjusted balance in Supplies was $850 at December 31, 2021. The unadjusted balance in Supplies Expense was $0 at December 31, 2021. A year-end count showed $100 of supplies on hand.

b. Wages earned by employees during December 2021, unpaid and unrecorded at December 31, 2021, amounted to $3,700. The last paychecks were issued December 28; the next payments will be made on January 6, 2022. The unadjusted balance in Salaries and Wages Expense was $40,000 at December 31, 2021.

c. A portion of the store's basement is now being rented for $1,100 per month to K. Frey. On November 1, 2021, the store collected six months' rent in advance from Frey in the amount of $6,600. It was credited in full to Deferred Revenue when collected. The unadjusted balance in Rent Revenue was $0 at December 31, 2021.

d. The store purchased delivery equipment at the beginning of the year. The estimated depreciation for 2021 is $2,000, although none has been recorded yet.

e. On December 31, 2021, the unadjusted balance in Prepaid Insurance was $3,000. This was the amount paid in the middle of the year for a two-year insurance policy with coverage beginning on July 1, 2021. The unadjusted balance in Insurance Expense was $600, which was the cost of insurance from January 1 to June 30, 2021.

f. Jaworski's store did some ski repair work for Frey. At the end of December 31, 2021, Frey had not paid for work completed amounting to $750. This amount has not yet been recorded as Service Revenue. Collection is expected during January 2022.

Required:

For each situation, prepare the adjusting journal entry that Jaworski's should record at December 31, 2021.

LO 4-2, 4-6 **E4-9 Determining Accounting Equation Effects of Typical Adjusting Journal Entries**

Refer to E4-8.

Required:

For each of the transactions in E4-8, indicate the amount and direction of effects of the adjusting journal entry on the elements of the accounting equation. Using the following format, indicate + for increase, − for decrease, and NE for no effect. Include account names using the format shown for the following sample.

Transaction	Assets	Liabilities	Stockholders' Equity
a	Supplies −750	NE	Supplies Expense (+E) −750
etc.			

LO 4-1, 4-2 **E4-10 Determining Adjusted Income Statement Account Balances**

Partial comparative income statements are presented below for Commonplace Corporation.

COMMONPLACE CORPORATION
(Partial) Income Statements
For the Years Ended December 31

	2021	2020
Service Revenue	$705,000	$730,000
Utilities Expense	20,000	24,000
Salaries and Wages Expense	405,000	460,000
Rent, Insurance, and Supplies Expense	163,000	142,000
Depreciation and Amortization Expense	17,000	4,000
Income before Income Tax Expense	100,000	100,000

The company's manager provides the following additional information:

a. The company received a bill for $2,400 of electricity and other utility services used in December 2021, but recorded it only when paid in January 2022.

b. A customer's $15,000 payment was received and included as service revenue on January 2, 2021, even though it was for services performed in December 2020.

c. The company ordered $5,000 of supplies in December 2021, but only recorded them when they were received, used, and paid for in January 2022.

d. The company did not record December 2019 salaries of $30,000 until the employees were paid on January 2, 2020. Salaries for December 2020 and December 2021 were recorded in the proper years.

Required:

Using the above information, revise the comparative income statement to report the proper amounts for each year. (Assume all other transactions and events, such as income taxes, have been properly recorded but are just not displayed on the partial income statements.)

E4-11 Reporting Depreciation

LO 4-4

The adjusted trial balance for Rowdy Profits Corporation reports that its equipment cost $250,000. For the current year, the company has recorded $30,000 of depreciation, which brings the total depreciation to date to $150,000.

Balance Sheet	Income Statement
Assets	Revenues
Liabilities	Expenses
Stockholders' Equity	

Required:

Using the headings shown above, indicate the location and amounts that would be used to report the three items on the company's balance sheet and income statement.

E4-12 Recording Transactions Including Adjusting and Closing Journal Entries

LO 4-2, 4-5

The following accounts are used by Mouse Potato, Inc., a computer game maker.

Codes	Accounts	Codes	Accounts
A	Accounts Receivable	I	Interest Revenue
B	Accumulated Depreciation	J	Notes Payable (long-term)
C	Cash	K	Retained Earnings
D	Deferred Revenue	L	Salaries and Wages Expense
E	Depreciation Expense	M	Salaries and Wages Payable
F	Equipment	N	Service Revenue
G	Interest Expense	O	Supplies
H	Interest Payable	P	Supplies Expense

Required:

For each of the following independent situations, give the journal entry by entering the appropriate code(s) and amount(s). We've done the first one for you as an example.

		Debit		Credit	
	Independent Situations	**Code**	**Amount**	**Code**	**Amount**
a.	Accrued wages, unrecorded and unpaid at year-end, $400 (example).	L	400	M	400
b.	Service revenue collected in advance, $600.				
c.	At year-end, interest on notes payable not yet recorded or paid, $220.				
d.	Depreciation expense for year, $1,000.				
e.	Service revenue earned but not yet collected at year-end, $1,000.				
f.	Balance in Supplies account, $400; supplies on hand at year-end, $150.				
g.	Adjusted balance at year-end in Service Revenue account, $75,000. Give the journal entry to close this one account at year-end.				

LO 4-2, 4-6   **E4-13 Analyzing the Effects of Adjusting Journal Entries on the Income Statement and Balance Sheet**

On December 31, 2021, Alan and Company prepared an income statement and balance sheet but failed to take into account four adjusting journal entries. The income statement, prepared on this incorrect basis, reported income before income tax of $30,000. The balance sheet (before the effect of income taxes) reflected total assets, $90,000; total liabilities, $40,000; and stockholders' equity, $50,000. The data for the four adjusting journal entries follow:

a.   Amortization of $8,000 for the year on software was not recorded.
b.   Salaries and wages amounting to $17,000 for the last three days of December 2021 were not paid and not recorded (the next payroll will be on January 10, 2022).
c.   Rent revenue of $4,800 was collected on December 1, 2021, for office space for the three-month period December 1, 2021, to February 28, 2022. The $4,800 was credited in full to Deferred Revenue when collected.
d.   Income taxes were not recorded and not paid. The income tax rate for the company is 30 percent.

Required:

Complete the following table to show the effects of the four adjusting journal entries (indicate deductions with parentheses):

Items	Net Income	Total Assets	Total Liabilities	Stockholders' Equity
Amounts reported	$30,000	$90,000	$40,000	$50,000
Effect of amortization				
Effect of salaries and wages				
Effect of rent revenue				
Adjusted balances	6,600	82,000	55,400	26,600
Effect of income tax				
Correct amounts				

LO 4-2, 4-4, 4-6   **E4-14 Reporting an Adjusted Income Statement**

Dyer, Inc., completed its first year of operations on December 31, 2021. Because this is the end of the annual accounting period, the company bookkeeper prepared the following preliminary income statement:

Income Statement, 2021

Rent Revenue		$114,000
Expenses:		
Salaries and Wages Expense	$28,500	
Repairs and Maintenance Expense	13,000	
Rent Expense	9,000	
Utilities Expense	4,000	
Travel Expense	3,000	
Total Expenses		57,500
Income		$ 56,500

You are an independent CPA hired by the company to audit the firm's accounting systems and financial statements. In your audit, you developed additional data as follows:

a.   Wages for the last three days of December amounting to $310 were not recorded or paid.
b.   The $400 telephone bill for December 2021 has not been recorded or paid.
c.   Depreciation of equipment amounting to $23,000 for 2021 was not recorded.
d.   Interest of $500 was not recorded on the notes payable by Dyer, Inc.
e.   The Rental Revenue account includes $4,000 of revenue to be earned in January 2022.
f.   Supplies costing $600 were used during 2021, but this has not yet been recorded.
g.   The income tax expense for 2021 is $7,000, but it won't actually be paid until 2022.

Required:

1. What adjusting journal entry for each item (*a*) through (*g*) should be recorded at December 31, 2021? If none is required, explain why.
2. Prepare, in proper form, an adjusted income statement for 2021.
3. Did the adjustments have a significant overall effect on the company's net income? By what dollar amount did net income change as a result of the adjustments?

E4-15 Recording Adjusting Entries and Preparing an Adjusted Trial Balance   LO 4-2, 4-3

North Star prepared the following unadjusted trial balance at the end of its second year of operations ending December 31.

Account Titles	Debit	Credit
Cash	$12,000	
Accounts Receivable	6,000	
Prepaid Rent	2,400	
Equipment	21,000	
Accumulated Depreciation		$ 1,000
Accounts Payable		1,000
Income Tax Payable		0
Common Stock		24,800
Retained Earnings		2,100
Sales Revenue		50,000
Salaries and Wages Expense	25,000	
Utilities Expense	12,500	
Rent Expense	0	
Depreciation Expense	0	
Income Tax Expense	0	
Totals	$78,900	$78,900

Other data not yet recorded at December 31:

a. Rent expired during the year, $1,200.
b. Depreciation expense for the year, $1,000.
c. Utilities used and unpaid, $9,000.
d. Income tax expense, $390.

Required:

1. Using the format shown in the demonstration case, indicate the accounting equation effects of each required adjustment.
2. Prepare the adjusting journal entries required at December 31.
3. Summarize the adjusting journal entries in T-accounts. After entering the beginning balances and computing the adjusted ending balances, prepare an adjusted trial balance as of December 31.
4. Compute the amount of net income using (*a*) the preliminary (unadjusted) numbers and (*b*) the final (adjusted) numbers. Had the adjusting entries not been recorded, would net income have been overstated or understated, and by what amount?

E4-16 Recording Four Adjusting Journal Entries and Preparing an Adjusted Trial Balance   LO 4-2, 4-3

Mint Cleaning Inc. prepared the following unadjusted trial balance at the end of its second year of operations ending December 31. (Assume amounts are reported in thousands of dollars.)

Account Titles	Debit	Credit
Cash	$ 38	
Accounts Receivable	9	
Prepaid Insurance	6	
Equipment	80	
Accumulated Depreciation		$ 0
Accounts Payable		9
Salaries and Wages Payable		0
Income Tax Payable		0
Common Stock		76
Retained Earnings		4
Sales Revenue		80
Insurance Expense	0	
Salaries and Wages Expense	10	
Supplies Expense	26	
Income Tax Expense	0	
Totals	$169	$169

Other data not yet recorded at December 31:

a. Insurance expired during the year, $5.
b. Depreciation expense for the year, $4.
c. Salaries and wages payable, $7.
d. Income tax expense, $9.

Required:

1. Prepare the adjusting journal entries for the year ended December 31.
2. Using T-accounts, determine the adjusted balances in each account and prepare an adjusted trial balance as of December 31.
3. By what amount would net income have been understated or overstated had the adjusting journal entries not been recorded?

LO 4-4   **E4-17 Reporting an Income Statement, Statement of Retained Earnings, and Balance Sheet**

Refer to E4-16.

Required:

Using the adjusted balances in E4-16, prepare an income statement, statement of retained earnings, and classified balance sheet for the year ended December 31.

LO 4-5   **E4-18 Recording Closing Entries**

Refer to E4-16.

Required:

Using the adjusted balances in E4-16, give the closing journal entry for the year ended December 31.

LO 4-1, 4-2, 4-3, 4-4   **E4-19 Preparing Adjusting Entries, an Adjusted Trial Balance, and Financial Statements**

Daily Driver, Inc. (DDI), operates a driving service through a popular ride-sharing app. DDI has prepared a list of unadjusted account balances at its December 31 year-end. You have reviewed the balances and made notes shown in the right column.

DAILY DRIVER, INC.
Unadjusted Trial Balance
At December 31

Account Name	Debit	Credit	Notes
Cash	$ 1,000		This equals the bank balance.
Supplies	50		Only windshield washer fluid that cost $30 remains at December 31.
Prepaid Insurance	1,200		This amount was paid January 2 for car insurance from January 1 through December 31 of this year.
Equipment	40,000		This is the car's purchase price.
Accumulated Depreciation		$ 2,400	The car will be two years old at the end of December.
Salaries and Wages Payable		0	DDI has not yet paid or recorded $800 of salary for December.
Income Tax Payable		0	DDI paid all its taxes from last year.
Common Stock		25,000	DDI issued 5,000 shares at $5 each.
Retained Earnings		5,430	This is the total accumulated earnings to January 1 of this year.
Service Revenue		19,570	All revenue is received in cash when the service is given.
Salaries and Wages Expense	8,800		DDI's only employee receives a monthly salary of $800 to December 31.
Supplies Expense	100		This is the cost of windshield washer fluid used to November 30.
Depreciation Expense	0		The car's benefits are being used up about $2,400 per year.
Insurance Expense	0		No car insurance has been paid for next year.
Fuel Expense	1,250		All fuel is paid for in cash.
Income Tax Expense	0		DDI's tax rate is 20 percent of income before tax.
Totals	$ 52,400	$ 52,400	

Required:

1. Use the notes to determine and record adjusting entries needed on December 31 for (*a*) supplies used up, (*b*) insurance costs, (*c*) using up the car's benefits, (*d*) salaries not yet accounted for, and (*e*) income taxes for the year.

2. Post the adjusting entries from requirement 1 to T-accounts to determine new adjusted balances, and prepare an adjusted trial balance. (If you are completing this exercise using the general ledger tool in Connect, this requirement will be completed automatically for you.)

3. Using the adjusted balances from requirement 2, prepare an income statement, statement of retained earnings, and classified balance sheet.

E4-20 Preparing Adjusting Entries, an Adjusted Trial Balance, and Financial Statements

LO 4-1, 4-2, 4-3, 4-4

Bill's Boards (BB) is an outdoor advertising company founded by William Longfall. William knows very little accounting so he hired a friend to "keep the books." Unfortunately, William did not review his friend's work and now it seems his friend has made a mess of the accounting records. William has provided you the following list of unadjusted account balances at BB's September 30 fiscal year-end. You have reviewed the balances with William and made notes shown in the right column.

BILL'S BOARDS
Unadjusted Trial Balance
At September 30

Account Name	Debits	Credits	Notes
Cash	$13,000		This balance equals the balance reported by the bank.
Accounts Receivable	1,000		A customer ordered $1,000 of advertising services to be provided in October. The accountant recorded this service by debiting Accounts Receivable and crediting Service Revenue.
Prepaid Rent	800		Starting January 1, BB agreed to pay $1,200 cash to rent the land on which its billboards are located, for the January–December period. The accountant adjusted this account on April 30 but has not adjusted it since.
Supplies	0		BB still has supplies costing $200 on hand on September 30.
Equipment	6,000		BB bought scaffolding and billboards in October last year.
Accumulated Depreciation		$ 0	Because the equipment was bought at the beginning of the fiscal year, no depreciation is carried forward from prior years.
Accounts Payable		2,000	BB purchased and received $2,000 of supplies used for creating advertising displays. The supplier is to be paid in October.
Deferred Revenue		1,500	This balance relates to $1,500 cash paid by a customer in August for advertising from September 1–November 30.
Salaries and Wages Payable		0	BB's employees are still waiting to be paid for the last half of September.
Income Tax Payable		250	BB hasn't paid the $250 tax owed from the last fiscal year.
Common Stock		1,000	BB has issued 2,000 shares for $1,000 cash.
Retained Earnings		3,750	BB started business a few years ago, so this is the total accumulated earnings up to October 1 of last year.
Service Revenue		60,700	BB has provided $2,000 of services for which it hasn't yet billed customers or recorded in its accounting records.
Salaries and Wages Expense	46,000		BB's employees earn $4,000 per month. The employees were paid in full on August 31, and were paid again on September 15.
Depreciation Expense	0		About $1,500 of the usefulness of the equipment's $6,000 cost has been used up during the current fiscal year.
Rent Expense	400		BB incurs a small cost to rent the land on which its billboards are located. Rent for the current year has been paid in full.
Supplies Expense	2,000		BB's accountant expensed $2,000 of supplies purchased during the year because he assumed the supplies would be completely used by year-end. As noted above, he was wrong.
Income Tax Expense	0		BB's tax rate is 20 percent of income before tax.
Totals	$69,200	$69,200	

Required:

1. Use the notes to determine and record the adjusting journal entries needed on September 30 to (*a*) fix the premature recording of advertising revenue, (*b*) update the rent accounts, (*c*) account for the use of equipment, (*d*) update deferred revenue, (*e*) accrue revenue not yet billed, (*f*) accrue unpaid wages, (*g*) correct the supplies accounts, and (*h*) accrue income taxes for the year.

2. Post the adjusting journal entries from requirement 1 to T-accounts to determine new adjusted balances, and prepare an adjusted trial balance. (If you are completing this exercise using the general ledger tool in Connect, this requirement will be completed automatically for you.)

3. Using the adjusted account balances from requirement 2, prepare an income statement, statement of retained earnings, and classified balance sheet.

COACHED PROBLEMS

CP4-1 Preparing an Adjusted Trial Balance, Closing Journal Entry, and Post-Closing Trial Balance   LO 4-3, 4-5

The following is a list of accounts and amounts reported for Rollcom, Inc., for the fiscal year ended September 30, 2021. The accounts have normal debit or credit balances.

Accounts Payable	$39,100	Notes Payable (long-term)	$ 1,500
Accounts Receivable	66,500	Office Expense	6,300
Accumulated Depreciation	21,500	Rent Expense	164,200
Cash	80,300	Retained Earnings	99,900
Common Stock	94,800	Salaries and Wages Expense	128,700
Equipment	90,700	Sales Revenue	325,600
Income Tax Expense	10,500	Supplies	35,200

Required:

1. Prepare an adjusted trial balance at September 30, 2021. Is the Retained Earnings balance of $99,900 the amount that would be reported on the balance sheet as of September 30, 2021?
    TIP: The company did not declare a dividend during 2021, but it did earn net income.
2. Prepare the closing entry required at September 30, 2021.
3. Prepare a post-closing trial balance at September 30, 2021.

CP4-2 Analyzing and Recording Adjusting Journal Entries   LO 4-1, 4-2, 4-6

Jordan Company's annual accounting year ends on December 31. It is now December 31, 2021, and all of the 2021 entries have been made except for the following:

a. The company owes interest of $700 on a bank loan. The interest will be paid when the loan is repaid on September 30, 2022. No interest has been recorded.
b. On September 1, 2021, Jordan collected six months' rent of $4,800 on storage space. At that date, Jordan debited Cash and credited Deferred Revenue for $4,800.
c. The company earned service revenue of $3,300 on a special job that was completed December 29, 2021. Collection will be made during January 2022. No entry has been recorded.
d. On November 1, 2021, Jordan paid a one-year premium for property insurance of $4,200, for coverage starting on that date. Cash was credited and Prepaid Insurance was debited for this amount.
e. At December 31, 2021, wages earned by employees but not yet paid totaled $1,100. The employees will be paid on the next payroll date, January 15, 2022.
f. Depreciation of $1,000 must be recognized on a service truck purchased this year.
g. The income after all adjustments other than income taxes was $30,000. The company's income tax rate is 30 percent. Compute and record income tax expense.

Required:

1. Give the adjusting journal entry required for each transaction at December 31, 2021.
    TIP: In transaction (b), Jordan Company has met its obligation for four of the six months, thereby earning 4/6 of the rent collected.
    TIP: In transaction (d), two months of insurance coverage have now expired.
2. If adjustments were not made each period, the financial results could be materially misstated. Determine the amount by which Jordan Company's net income would have been understated, or overstated, had the adjustments in requirement 1 not been made.

LO 4-2, 4-6

CP4-3 Determining Accounting Equation Effects of Adjusting Journal Entries

Refer to CP4-2.

Required:

Indicate the effects (account, amount, and direction) of each adjusting journal entry. Use + for increase, − for decrease, and NE for no effect. Provide an appropriate account name for any revenue and expense effects.

TIP: The first transaction is done for you as an example.

Transaction	Assets	Liabilities	Stockholders' Equity
a	NE	Interest Payable +700	Interest Expense (+E) −700
b			
etc.			

LO 4-1, 4-2, 4-3, 4-6

CP4-4 Identifying and Preparing Adjusting Journal Entries

Golf Academy, Inc., provides private golf lessons. Its unadjusted trial balance at December 31, 2021, follows, along with information about selected accounts.

Account Names	Debit	Credit	Further Information
Cash	$31,900		As reported on December 31 bank statement.
Supplies	600		Based on count, only $200 of supplies still exist.
Deferred Revenue		$ 3,500	Of this amount, $3,000 was received for December lessons and $500 for January lessons.
Salaries and Wages Payable		0	Employees were paid $1,000 for 10 days of work through December 28. They have not yet been paid for work on December 29 and 30.
Income Tax Payable		0	The company has paid last year's income tax but not this year's tax.
Interest Payable		0	The company has not paid the $100 of interest owed on its notes payable for the current period.
Notes Payable (long-term)		12,000	This one-year note was taken out this year on December 1.
Common Stock		1,000	This amount was contributed for common stock in prior years.
Retained Earnings		3,000	This is the balance reported at the end of last year.
Service Revenue		51,500	Most customers pay cash for lessons each time they are provided, but some customers pay in advance.
Salaries and Wages Expense	36,100		Employees worked through December 30 but did not work on December 31.
Supplies Expense	2,400		This is the cost of supplies used through November 30.
Interest Expense	0		The company has not paid the $100 of interest owed on its notes payable for the current period.
Income Tax Expense	0		The company has an average tax rate of 30 percent.
Totals	$71,000	$71,000	

Required:

1. Calculate the (preliminary) unadjusted net income for the year ended December 31, 2021.
2. Name the five pairs of balance sheet and income statement accounts that require adjustment and indicate the amount of adjustment for each pair.
3. Prepare the adjusting journal entries that are required at December 31, 2021.
4. Calculate the adjusted net income that the company should report for the year ended December 31, 2021. By what dollar amount did the adjustments in requirement 3 cause net income to increase or decrease?

GROUP A PROBLEMS

Mc Graw Hill **connect**

PA4-1 Preparing a Trial Balance, Closing Journal Entry, and Post-Closing Trial Balance

LO 4-3, 4-5

Starbooks Corporation provides an online bookstore for electronic books. The following is a simplified list of accounts and amounts reported in its accounting records. The accounts have normal debit or credit balances. Assume the year ended on September 30, 2021.

Accounts Payable	$ 600	Notes Payable (long-term)	$ 200
Accounts Receivable	300	Notes Payable (short-term)	500
Accumulated Depreciation	900	Prepaid Rent	100
Cash	300	Rent Expense	400
Common Stock	200	Retained Earnings	1,500
Deferred Revenue	200	Salaries and Wages Expense	2,200
Depreciation Expense	300	Service Revenue	6,200
Equipment	3,200	Supplies	500
Income Tax Expense	300	Supplies Expense	200
Interest Revenue	100	Travel Expense	2,600

Required:

1. Prepare an adjusted trial balance at September 30, 2021. Is the Retained Earnings balance of $1,500 the amount that would be reported on the balance sheet as of September 30, 2021?
2. Prepare the closing entry required at September 30, 2021.
3. Prepare a post-closing trial balance at September 30, 2021.

PA4-2 Analyzing and Recording Adjusting Journal Entries

LO 4-1, 4-2, 4-6

Brokeback Towing Company is at the end of its accounting year, December 31, 2021. The following data that must be considered were developed from the company's records and related documents:

a. On July 1, 2021, a two-year insurance premium on equipment in the amount of $600 was paid and debited in full to Prepaid Insurance on that date. Coverage began on July 1.
b. At the end of 2021, the unadjusted balance in the Supplies account was $1,000. A physical count of supplies on December 31, 2021, indicated supplies costing $300 were still on hand.
c. On December 31, 2021, YY's Garage completed repairs on one of Brokeback's trucks at a cost of $800. The amount is not yet recorded. It will be paid during January 2022.
d. On December 31, 2021, the company completed a contract for an out-of-state company for $7,950 payable by the customer within 30 days. No cash has been collected and no journal entry has been made for this transaction.
e. On July 1, 2021, the company purchased a new hauling van. Depreciation for July–December 2021, estimated to total $2,750, has not been recorded.
f. As of December 31, the company owes interest of $500 on a bank loan taken out on October 1, 2021. The interest will be paid when the loan is repaid on September 30, 2022. No interest has been recorded yet.
g. Assume the income after the preceding adjustments but before income taxes was $30,000. The company's federal income tax rate is 30%. Compute and record income tax expense.

Required:

1. Give the adjusting journal entry required for each item at December 31, 2021.
2. If adjustments were not made each period, the financial results could be materially misstated. Determine the amount by which Brokeback's net income would have been understated, or overstated, had the adjustments in requirement 1 not been made.

LO 4-2, 4-6   **PA4-3 Determining Accounting Equation Effects of Adjusting Journal Entries**

Refer to PA4-2.

Required:

Indicate the accounting equation effects (amount and direction) of each adjusting journal entry. Use + for increase, − for decrease, and NE for no effect. Provide an appropriate account name for any revenue and expense effects.

Transaction	Assets	Liabilities	Stockholders' Equity
a			
b			
etc.			

LO 4-1, 4-2, 4-3, 4-6   **PA4-4 Identifying and Preparing Adjusting Journal Entries**

Val's Hair Emporium operates a hair salon. Its unadjusted trial balance as of December 31, 2021, follows, along with information about selected accounts.

Account Names	Debit	Credit	Further Information
Cash	$ 3,800		As reported on December 31 bank statement.
Supplies	4,300		Based on count, only $1,300 of supplies still exist.
Prepaid Rent	6,000		This amount was paid November 1 for rent through the end of January.
Accounts Payable		$ 1,500	This represents the total amount of bills received for supplies and utilities through December 15. Val estimates that the company has received $450 of utility services through December 31 for which it has not yet been billed.
Salaries and Wages Payable		0	Stylists have not yet been paid $150 for their work on December 31.
Income Tax Payable		0	The company has paid last year's income taxes but not this year's taxes.
Common Stock		2,000	This amount was contributed for common stock in prior years.
Retained Earnings		900	This is the balance reported at the end of last year.
Service Revenue		75,800	Customers pay cash when they receive services.
Salaries and Wages Expense	29,100		This is the cost of stylist wages through December 30.
Utilities Expense	12,200		This is the cost of utilities through December 15.
Rent Expense	20,000		This year's rent was $2,000 per month.
Supplies Expense	4,800		This is the cost of supplies used through November 30.
Income Tax Expense	0		The company has an average tax rate of 30 percent.
Totals	**$80,200**	**$80,200**	

Required:

1. Calculate the (preliminary) unadjusted net income for the year ended December 31, 2021.
2. Name the five pairs of balance sheet and income statement accounts that require adjustment and indicate the amount of adjustment for each pair.
3. Prepare the adjusting journal entries that are required at December 31, 2021.
4. Calculate the adjusted net income that the company should report for the year ended December 31, 2021. By what dollar amount did the adjustments in requirement 3 cause net income to increase or decrease?

GROUP B PROBLEMS

Mc Graw Hill **connect**

PB4-1 Preparing a Trial Balance, Closing Journal Entry, and Post-Closing Trial Balance

LO 4-3, 4-5

Regis Corporation operates hair salons under various brand names including Supercuts, Magicuts, and Style America. The following is a simplified list of accounts and amounts (in millions) reported in the company's accounts for the year ended June 30, 2019.

Regis Corporation

Accounts Payable	$ 48	Notes Payable (long-term)	$ 230
Accounts Receivable	30	Office Expense	188
Accumulated Amortization	20	Prepaid Rent	33
Accumulated Depreciation	310	Rent Expense	272
Amortization Expense	3	Retained Earnings	280
Cash	70	Salaries and Wages Expense	453
Common Stock	58	Salaries and Wages Payable	81
Depreciation Expense	35	Service Revenue	1,070
Equipment	458	Software	345
Income Tax Expense	2	Supplies	77
Interest Expense	1	Supplies Expense	130

Required:

1. Prepare an adjusted trial balance at June 30, 2019. Is the Retained Earnings balance of $280 the amount that would be reported on the balance sheet as of June 30, 2019?
2. Prepare the closing entry required at June 30, 2019.
   TIP: The company reported a net loss of $14 in 2019, so the closing entry will need to debit (not credit) Retained Earnings for that amount.
3. Prepare a post-closing trial balance at June 30, 2019.

PB4-2 Recording Adjusting Journal Entries

LO 4-1, 4-2, 4-6

Cactus Company's annual accounting year ends on June 30. Assume it is now June 30 and all of the entries except the following adjusting journal entries have been made:

a. The company earned service revenue of $2,000 on a special job that was completed June 29. Collection will be made during July; no entry has been recorded.
b. On March 31, Cactus paid a six-month premium for property insurance in the amount of $3,200 for coverage starting on that date. Cash was credited and Prepaid Insurance was debited for this amount.
c. At June 30, wages of $900 were earned by employees but not yet paid. The employees will be paid on the next payroll date, which is July 15.
d. On June 1, Cactus collected two months' revenue of $450. At that date, Cactus debited Cash and credited Deferred Revenue for $450. One-half of it has now been earned but not yet recorded.
e. Depreciation of $1,500 must be recognized on equipment purchased on July 1 of the previous year.
f. Cash of $4,200 was collected on May 1 for services to be rendered evenly over the next year beginning on May 1. Deferred Revenue was credited when the cash was received. Two months of this performance obligation have now been fulfilled but not yet recorded.
g. The company owes interest of $600 on a bank loan taken out on February 1. The interest will be paid when the loan is repaid next year on January 31.
h. The income after all adjustments except income taxes was $20,000. The company's federal income tax rate is 30 percent. Compute and record income tax expense.

Required:

1. Give the adjusting journal entry required for each transaction at June 30.
2. If adjustments were not made each period, the financial results could be materially misstated. Determine the amount by which Cactus Company's net income would have been understated, or overstated, had the adjustments in requirement 1 not been made.

LO 4-2, 4-6   **PB4-3 Determining Accounting Equation Effects of Adjusting Journal Entries**

Refer to PB4-2.

Required:

Indicate the accounting equation effects (amount and direction) of each adjusting journal entry. Use + for increase, − for decrease, and NE for no effect. Provide an appropriate account name for any revenue and expense effects.

Transaction	Assets	Liabilities	Stockholders' Equity
a			
b			
c			
etc.			

LO 4-1, 4-2, 4-3, 4-6   **PB4-4 Identifying and Preparing Adjusting Journal Entries**

Learn to Play, Inc., is a one-person company that provides private piano lessons. Its unadjusted trial balance at December 31, 2021, follows, along with information about selected accounts.

Account Names	Debit	Credit	Further Information
Cash	$ 23,800		As reported on December 31 bank statement.
Supplies	300		Based on count, only $200 of supplies still exist.
Deferred Revenue		$ 1,500	Of this amount, $500 was received for December lessons and $1,000 for January lessons.
Salaries and Wages Payable		0	The employee was paid $500 for 10 days of work through December 29. She has not yet been paid for work on December 30 and 31.
Income Tax Payable		0	The company has paid last year's income tax but not this year's taxes.
Interest Payable		0	The company has not paid the $100 of interest owed on its notes payable for the current period.
Notes Payable		12,000	This one-year note was taken out this year on December 1.
Common Stock		1,000	This amount was contributed for common stock in prior years.
Retained Earnings		3,000	This is the balance reported at the end of last year.
Service Revenue		25,500	Most customers pay cash for lessons each time they are provided, but some customers pay in advance.
Salaries and Wages Expense	18,100		The company's employee worked through December 31.
Supplies Expense	800		This is the cost of supplies used through November 30.
Interest Expense	0		The company has not paid the $100 of interest owed on its notes payable for the current period.
Income Tax Expense	0		The company has an average tax rate of 30 percent.
Totals	**$43,000**	**$43,000**	

Required:

1. Calculate the (preliminary) unadjusted net income for the year ended December 31, 2021.
2. Name the five pairs of balance sheet and income statement accounts that require adjustment and indicate the amount of adjustment for each pair.
3. Prepare the adjusting journal entries that are required at December 31, 2021.
4. Calculate the adjusted net income that the company should report for the year ended December 31, 2021. By what dollar amount did the adjustments in requirement 3 cause net income to increase or decrease?

COMPREHENSIVE PROBLEMS

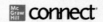

LO 2-3, 3-3, 4-2, 4-3, 4-4

C4-1 From Recording Transactions to Preparing Accrual and Deferral Adjustments and Reporting Results on the Balance Sheet and Income Statement (Chapters 2, 3, and 4)

RunHeavy Corporation (RHC) is a corporation that manages a local band. It had the following activities during its first month.

a. RHC was formed with an investment of $10,000 cash, paid in by the leader of the band on January 3 in exchange for common stock.

b. On January 4, RHC purchased music equipment by paying $2,000 cash and signing an $8,000 promissory note payable in three years.

c. On January 5, RHC booked the band for six concert events, at a price of $2,500 each, but no cash was collected yet.

d. Of the six events, four were completed between January 10 and 20.

e. On January 22, cash was collected for three of the four events.

f. The other two bookings were for February concerts, but on January 24, RHC collected half of the $2,500 fee for one of them.

g. On January 27, RHC paid $3,140 cash for the band's travel-related costs.

h. On January 28, RHC paid its band members a total of $2,400 cash for salaries and wages for the first three events.

i. As of January 31, the band members hadn't yet been paid wages for the fourth event completed in January, but they would be paid in February at the same rate as for the first three events.

j. As of January 31, RHC has not yet recorded the $100 of monthly depreciation on the equipment.

k. Also, RHC has not yet paid or recorded the $60 interest owed on the promissory note at January 31.

l. RHC is subject to a 15 percent tax rate on the company's income before tax.

Required:

1. Prepare journal entries to record the transactions and appropriate adjustments.

2. Post the entries from requirement 1 to T-accounts, calculate ending balances, and prepare an adjusted trial balance.

3. Prepare a classified balance sheet and income statement for January 31.

C4-2 From Recording Transactions (Including Adjusting Journal Entries) to Preparing Financial Statements and Closing Journal Entries (Chapters 2, 3, and 4)

LO 2-3, 3-3, 4-1, 4-2, 4-3, 4-4, 4-5, 4-6

Brothers Harry and Herman Hausyerday began operations of their machine shop (H & H Tool, Inc.) on January 1, 2020. The annual reporting period ends December 31. The trial balance on January 1, 2021, follows (the amounts are rounded to thousands of dollars to simplify):

Account Titles	Debit	Credit
Cash	$ 3	
Accounts Receivable	5	
Supplies	12	
Land	0	
Equipment	60	
Accumulated Depreciation		$ 6
Software	15	
Accumulated Amortization		5
Accounts Payable		5
Notes Payable (short-term)		0
Salaries and Wages Payable		0
Interest Payable		0
Income Tax Payable		0
Common Stock		71
Retained Earnings		8
Service Revenue	0	
Salaries and Wages Expense	0	
Depreciation Expense	0	
Amortization Expense	0	
Income Tax Expense	0	
Interest Expense	0	
Supplies Expense	0	
Totals	$95	$95

Transactions and events during 2021 (summarized in thousands of dollars) follow:

a.   Borrowed $12 cash on March 1 using a short-term note.
b.   Purchased land on March 2 for future building site; paid cash, $9.
c.   Issued additional shares of common stock on April 3 for $23.
d.   Purchased software on July 4, $10 cash.
e.   Purchased supplies on account on October 5 for future use, $18.
f.   Paid accounts payable on November 6, $13.
g.   Signed a $25 service contract on November 7 to start February 1, 2022.
h.   Recorded revenues of $160 on December 8, including $40 on credit and $120 collected in cash.
i.   Recognized salaries and wages expense on December 9, $85 paid in cash.
j.   Collected accounts receivable on December 10, $24.

Data for adjusting journal entries as of December 31:

k.   Unrecorded amortization for the year on software, $5.
l.   Supplies counted on December 31, 2021, $10.
m.   Depreciation for the year on the equipment, $6.
n.   Interest of $1 to accrue on notes payable.
o.   Salaries and wages earned but not yet paid or recorded, $12.
p.   Income tax for the year was $8. It will be paid in 2022.

Required:

1.   Set up T-accounts for the accounts on the trial balance and enter beginning balances. If you are completing this problem in Connect using the general ledger tool, this requirement will be completed for you.

2.   Record journal entries for transactions (a) through (j).

3.   Post the journal entries from requirement 2 to T-accounts and prepare an unadjusted trial balance. If you are completing this problem in Connect using the general ledger tool, this requirement will be completed for you using your answers to requirement 2.

4.   Record the adjusting journal entries (k) through (p).

5.   Post the adjusting entries from requirement 4 and prepare an adjusted trial balance. If you are completing this problem in Connect using the general ledger tool, this requirement will be completed for you using your previous answers.

6.   Prepare an income statement, statement of retained earnings, and balance sheet.

7.   Prepare the closing journal entry.

8.   Post the closing entry from requirement 7 and prepare a post-closing trial balance. If you are completing this problem in Connect using the general ledger tool, this requirement will be completed for you using your previous answers.

9.   How much net income did H & H Tool, Inc., generate during 2021? What was its net profit margin? Is the company financed primarily by liabilities or stockholders' equity? What is its current ratio (rounded to two decimal places)?

LO 2-3, 3-3, 4-1, 4-2, 4-3, 4-4,
4-5, 4-6

C4-3   Recording Transactions (Including Adjusting Journal Entries), Preparing Financial Statements and Closing Journal Entries, and Computing Net Profit Margin and Current Ratio (Chapters 2, 3, and 4)

Drs. Glenn Feltham and David Ambrose began operations of their physical therapy clinic, called Northland Physical Therapy, on January 1, 2020. The annual reporting period ends December 31. The trial balance on January 1, 2021, was as follows (the amounts are rounded to thousands of dollars to simplify):

Account Titles	Debit	Credit
Cash	$ 7	
Accounts Receivable	3	
Supplies	3	
Equipment	8	
Accumulated Depreciation		$ 1
Software	5	
Accumulated Amortization		1
Accounts Payable		5
Notes Payable (short-term)		0
Salaries and Wages Payable		0
Interest Payable		0
Income Taxes Payable		0
Deferred Revenue		0
Common Stock		15
Retained Earnings		4
Service Revenue		0
Depreciation Expense	0	
Amortization Expense	0	
Salaries and Wages Expense	0	
Supplies Expense	0	
Interest Expense	0	
Income Tax Expense	0	
Totals	$26	$26

Transactions during 2021 (summarized in thousands of dollars) follow:

a. Borrowed $22 cash on July 1, 2021, signing a six-month note payable.
b. Purchased equipment for $25 cash on July 2, 2021.
c. Issued additional shares of common stock for $5 on July 3.
d. Purchased software on July 4, $3 cash.
e. Purchased supplies on July 5 on account for future use, $7.
f. Recorded revenues on December 6 of $55, including $8 on credit and $47 received in cash.
g. Recognized salaries and wages expense on December 7 of $30; paid in cash.
h. Collected accounts receivable on December 8, $9.
i. Paid accounts payable on December 9, $10.
j. Received a $3 cash deposit on December 10 from a hospital for a contract to start January 5, 2022.

Data for adjusting journal entries on December 31:

k. Amortization for 2021, $1.
l. Supplies of $3 were counted on December 31, 2021.
m. Depreciation for 2021, $4.
n. Accrued interest of $1 on notes payable.
o. Salaries and wages incurred but not yet paid or recorded, $3.
p. Income tax expense for 2021 was $4 and will be paid in 2022.

Required:

1. Set up T-accounts for the accounts on the trial balance and enter beginning balances. If you are completing this problem in Connect using the general ledger tool, this requirement will be completed for you.
2. Record journal entries for transactions (a) through (j).

3. Post the journal entries from requirement 2 to T-accounts and prepare an unadjusted trial balance. If you are completing this problem in Connect using the general ledger tool, this requirement will be completed for you using your answers to requirement 2.

4. Record the adjusting journal entries (*k*) through (*p*).

5. Post the adjusting entries from requirement 4 and prepare an adjusted trial balance. If you are completing this problem in Connect using the general ledger tool, this requirement will be completed for you using your previous answers.

6. Prepare an income statement, statement of retained earnings, and balance sheet.

7. Prepare the closing journal entry.

8. Post the closing entry from requirement 7 and prepare a post-closing trial balance. If you are completing this problem in Connect using the general ledger tool, this requirement will be completed for you using your previous answers.

9. How much net income did the physical therapy clinic generate during 2021? What was its net profit margin? Is the business financed primarily by liabilities or stockholders' equity? What is its current ratio?

LO 2-3, 3-3, 4-1, 4-2, 4-3, 4-4, 4-5, 4-6

C4-4 From Recording Transactions (Including Adjusting Journal Entries) to Preparing Financial Statements and Closing Journal Entries (Chapters 2, 3, and 4)

Alison and Chuck Renny began operations of their furniture repair shop (Lazy Sofa Furniture, Inc.) on January 1, 2020. The annual reporting period ends December 31. The trial balance on January 1, 2021, follows (amounts are rounded to thousands of dollars to simplify).

Account Titles	Debit	Credit
Cash	$ 5	
Accounts Receivable	4	
Supplies	2	
Equipment	6	
Accumulated Depreciation		$ 0
Software	12	
Accumulated Amortization		3
Accounts Payable		7
Notes Payable (short-term)		0
Salaries and Wages Payable		0
Interest Payable		0
Income Tax Payable		0
Deferred Revenue		0
Common Stock		15
Retained Earnings		4
Service Revenue		0
Supplies Expense	0	
Depreciation Expense	0	
Salaries and Wages Expense	0	
Amortization Expense	0	
Interest Expense	0	
Income Tax Expense	0	
Totals	$29	$29

Transactions during 2021 (summarized in thousands of dollars) follow:

a. Borrowed $21 cash on July 1, 2021, signing a six-month note payable.
b. Purchased equipment for $18 cash on July 2.
c. Issued additional shares of common stock on July 3 for $5.

d. Purchased additional equipment on August 4, $3 cash.
e. Purchased, on account, supplies on September 5 for future use, $10.
f. On December 6, recorded revenues in the amount of $65, including $9 on credit and $56 received in cash.
g. Paid salaries and wages expenses on December 7, $35.
h. Collected accounts receivable on December 8, $8.
i. Paid accounts payable on December 9, $11.
j. Received a $3 deposit on December 10 for work to start January 15, 2022.

Data for adjusting journal entries on December 31:

k. Amortization for 2021, $3.
l. Supplies of $4 were counted on December 31, 2021.
m. Depreciation for 2021, $2.
n. Accrued interest on notes payable of $1.
o. Salaries and wages earned but not yet paid, $3.
p. Income tax for 2021 was $4 and will be paid in 2022.

Required:

1. Set up T-accounts for the accounts on the trial balance and enter beginning balances. If you are completing this problem in Connect using the general ledger tool, this requirement will be completed for you.
2. Record journal entries for transactions (a) through (j).
3. Post the journal entries from requirement 2 to T-accounts and prepare an unadjusted trial balance. If you are completing this problem in Connect using the general ledger tool, this requirement will be completed for you using your answers to requirement 2.
4. Record adjusting journal entries (k) through (p).
5. Post the adjusting entries from requirement 4 and prepare an adjusted trial balance. If you are completing this problem in Connect using the general ledger tool, this requirement will be completed for you using your previous answers.
6. Prepare an income statement, statement of retained earnings, and balance sheet.
7. Prepare the closing journal entry.
8. Post the closing entry from requirement 7 and prepare a post-closing trial balance. If you are completing this problem in Connect using the general ledger tool, this requirement will be completed for you using your previous answers.
9. How much net income did Lazy Sofa Furniture, Inc., generate during 2021? Is the company financed primarily by liabilities or stockholders' equity?

C4-5 From Recording Transactions to Preparing Accrual and Deferral Adjustments and Reporting Results on the Balance Sheet and Income Statement (Chapters 2, 3, and 4)

LO 2-2, 2-3, 3-3, 4-2, 4-4

House of Tutors, Inc. (HTI), is a company that runs a tutoring service for high school and university students. The company reported the following amounts in its post-closing trial balance, prepared at the end of its first fiscal year, at August 31.

Accounts Payable	$ 60	Equipment	$12,000
Accounts Receivable	220	Interest Payable	40
Accumulated Depreciation	1,200	Notes Payable (long-term)	8,000
Cash	700	Retained Earnings	820
Common Stock	2,900	Supplies	100

The company encountered the following events during September:

a. HTI provided 100 hours of regular hourly tutoring at the rate of $20 per hour, all of which was collected in cash.
b. HTI paid tutors at the hourly rate of $10 per hour. On September 28, HTI paid for 90 hours of tutor time and promised to pay the remaining hours worked.
   TIP: The total hours of expense in (b). should match the total hours of revenue in (a).

c. HTI hosted an all-night review session on September 29 for people cramming for midterm exams, at a special price of $10 per attendee. Rather than collect cash at the time of the review session, HTI will send bills in October to the 75 people who attended the review session.

d. At the beginning of the night-long review session, HTI paid $200 cash to its tutors for wages. No additional salaries and wages will be paid for the review session.

e. HTI collected $200 cash on account from students who received tutoring during the summer.

f. HTI also collected $250 cash from a high school for a tutoring session to be held in October.

g. HTI determined that depreciation for September should be $100.

h. Although HTI adjusted its accounts on August 31, it has not yet paid the $40 monthly interest owed on the promissory note, for either August or September. The note is due in three years.

i. HTI has only $40 of supplies left at September 30.

j. HTI's income taxes are approximately 30 percent of income before tax.

Required:

1. Prepare HTI's journal entries and adjusting journal entries.

2. Prepare HTI's income statement and statement of retained earnings for the month ended September 30.

3. Prepare HTI's classified balance sheet at September 30.

LO 2-3, 3-3, 4-2, 4-4

C4-6 Recording/Posting Transactions and Adjustments, and Preparing Trial Balances and Financial Statements—Requires Calculating Depreciation and Interest (Chapters 2, 3, and 4)

Fast Deliveries, Inc. (FDI), was organized in December last year and had limited activity last year. The resulting balance sheet at the beginning of the current year is provided below:

FAST DELIVERIES, INC.			
Balance Sheet at January 1			
Assets:		**Liabilities:**	
Cash	$10,900	Accounts Payable	$ 500
Accounts Receivable	800	**Stockholders' Equity:**	
Supplies	400	Common Stock	11,000
		Retained Earnings	600
		Total Liabilities and Stockholders'	
Total Assets	$12,100	**Equity**	$12,100

Two employees have been hired, at a monthly salary of $2,200 each. The following transactions occurred during January of the current year. For your reference, the chapter to which each event relates is indicated in the first column.

Ch.	January	
2	1	$5,700 is paid for 12 months' insurance starting January 1. (Record as an asset.)
2	2	$4,200 is paid for 12 months of rent beginning January 1. (Record as an asset.)
2	3	FDI borrows $30,000 cash from First State Bank at 6 percent annual interest; this note is payable in two years.
2	4	A delivery van is purchased using cash. Including tax, the total cost was $24,000.
2	5	Stockholders contribute $6,000 of additional cash to FDI for its common stock.
2	6	Additional supplies costing $1,000 are purchased on account and received.
2	7	$600 of accounts receivable arising from last year's December sales are collected.
2	8	$400 of accounts payable from December of last year are paid.
3	9	Performed services for customers on account. Sent invoices totaling $10,400.
3	10	$7,600 of services are performed for customers who paid immediately in cash.
3	16	$2,200 of salaries are paid for the first half of the month.
3	20	FDI receives $3,500 cash from a customer for an advance order for services to be provided later in January and in February.
3	25	$4,500 is collected from customers on account (see January 9 transaction).

Ch.	January	Additional information for adjusting entries:
4	31a.	A $1,200 bill arrives for January utility services. Payment is due February 15.
4	31b.	Supplies on hand on January 31 are counted and determined to have cost $250.
4	31c.	As of January 31, FDI had completed 60 percent of the deliveries for the customer who paid in advance on January 20.
4	31d.	Accrue one month of interest on the bank loan. Yearly interest is determined by multiplying the amount borrowed by the annual interest rate (expressed as 0.06). For convenience, calculate January interest as one-twelfth of the annual interest.
4	31e.	Assume the van will be used for four years, after which it will have no value. Thus, each year, one-fourth of the van's benefits will be used up, which implies annual depreciation equal to one-fourth of the van's total cost. Record depreciation for the month of January, equal to one-twelfth of the annual depreciation expense.
4	31f.	Salaries earned by employees for the period from January 16–31 are $1,100 per employee and will be paid on February 3.
4	31g.	Adjust the prepaid asset accounts (for rent and insurance) as needed.

Required:

1. Record journal entries for the transactions that occurred from January 1–25.

2. If you are completing this problem manually, set up T-accounts using the beginning balances shown in the January 1 balance sheet, post the transactions from requirement 1, and prepare an unadjusted trial balance at January 31. If you are completing this problem in Connect using the general ledger tool, this requirement will be completed for you.

3. Using the given information, record all adjusting journal entries needed at January 31. Ignore income taxes.

4. If you are completing this problem manually, post the adjusting journal entries from requirement 3 into T-accounts and prepare an adjusted trial balance. If you are completing this problem in Connect using the general ledger tool, this requirement will be completed for you.

5. Prepare an income statement and statement of retained earnings for the month ended January 31, and prepare a classified balance sheet at January 31.

SKILLS DEVELOPMENT CASES

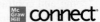

S4-1 Finding Financial Information

Refer to the financial statements of The Home Depot in Appendix A at the end of this book. (Note: Fiscal 2019 for The Home Depot runs from February 4, 2019, to February 2, 2020. See S1-1 for further explanation.)

LO 4-1, 4-6

The Home Depot

1. How much did The Home Depot owe for salaries and related expenses at February 2, 2020? Was this an increase or decrease from the previous year?

   a. $1,494 million (Decrease)
   b. $1,494 million (Increase)
   c. $1,506 million (Decrease)
   d. $1,506 million (Increase)

2. Refer to the Revenues note in the Summary of Significant Accounting Policies that follows The Home Depot's statements of cash flows. How does the company account for customer payments received in advance of providing merchandise or services?

   a. Record the prepayment as revenue.
   b. The funds are deposited in the bank account and no entry is recorded.
   c. The funds are not deposited in the bank account and no entry is recorded.
   d. The revenue is deferred until the goods or services are provided to the customer.

3. What adjusting journal entry must The Home Depot make when it provides services paid by gift card?

   a. *debit* Cash, *credit* Deferred Revenue
   b. *debit* Deferred Revenue, *credit* Net Sales Revenue
   c. *debit* Net Sales Revenue, *credit* Deferred Revenue
   d. *debit* Deferred Revenue, *credit* Cash

LO 4-1, 4-6

Lowe's

S4-2 Finding Financial Information

Refer to the financial statements of Lowe's Companies, Inc., in Appendix B. (Note: Fiscal 2019 for Lowe's runs from February 2, 2019, to January 31, 2020. See S1-1 for further explanation.)

1. How much did Lowe's owe for compensation and employee benefits at January 31, 2020? Was this an increase or decrease from the previous year?
   a. $684 million (Decrease)   c. $662 million (Decrease)
   b. $684 million (Increase)   d. $662 million (Increase)

2. What journal entry must Lowe's make when a customer purchases and pays for, but does not yet use, a gift card?
   a. *debit* Cash, *credit* Deferred Revenue
   b. *debit* Deferred Revenue, *credit* Net Sales Revenue
   c. *debit* Net Sales Revenue, *credit* Deferred Revenue
   d. *debit* Deferred Revenue, *credit* Cash

LO 4-1, 4-4

S4-3 Internet-Based Team Research: Examining Deferrals and Accruals

As a team, select an industry to analyze. Using your web browser, each team member should access the annual report or 10-K for one publicly traded company in the industry, with each member selecting a different company. (See S1-3 in Chapter 1 for a description of possible resources for these tasks.)

Required:

1. On an individual basis, each team member should write a short report listing the following:
   a. The company's total assets and total liabilities at the end of each year.
   b. The company's prepaid expenses and accrued liabilities at the end of each year.
   c. The percentage of prepaid expenses to total assets and the percentage of accrued liabilities to total liabilities.
   d. Describe and explain the types of accrued liabilities reported in the notes to the financial statements.

2. Discuss any patterns that you as a team observe. Then, as a team, write a short report comparing and contrasting your companies according to the preceding attributes. Provide potential explanations for any differences discovered.

LO 4-1, 4-2, 4-6

Safety-Kleen Corp.

S4-4 Ethical Decision Making: A Real-Life Example

On December 12, 2002, the SEC filed a lawsuit against four executives of Safety-Kleen Corp., one of the country's leading providers of industrial waste collection and disposal services. The primary issue was that the executives had directed others in the company to record improper adjustments, which had the effect of overstating net income during those periods. Complete this case by downloading, from the Connect eBook, excerpts from the SEC's court documents and questions about adjustments related to Safety-Kleen's operating expenses and management bonuses.

LO 4-1, 4-2, 4-6

Outerwall

S4-5 Ethical Decision Making: A Mini-Case

Assume you work as an assistant accountant in the head office of a DVD movie kiosk business, similar to Outerwall's Redbox machines. With the popularity of online movie rental operations, your company has struggled to meet its earnings targets for the year. It is important for the company to meet its earnings targets this year because the company is renegotiating a bank loan next month, and the terms of that loan are likely to depend on the company's reported financial success. Also, the company plans to issue more stock to the public in the upcoming year, to obtain funds for establishing its own presence in the online movie rental business. The chief financial officer (CFO) has approached you with a solution to the earnings dilemma. She proposes that the depreciation period for the stock of reusable DVDs be extended from 3 months to 15 months. She explains that by lengthening the depreciation period, a smaller amount of depreciation expense will be recorded in the current year, resulting in a higher net income. She claims that generally accepted accounting principles require estimates like this, so it wouldn't involve doing anything wrong.

Required:

Discuss the CFO's proposed solution. In your discussion, consider the following questions: Will the change in depreciation affect net income in the current year in the way that the CFO described?

How will it affect net income in the following year? Is the CFO correct when she claims that the change in estimated depreciation is allowed by GAAP? Who relies on the video company's financial statements when making decisions? Why might their decisions be affected by the CFO's proposed solution? Is it possible that their decisions would not be affected? What should you do?

S4-6 Critical Thinking: Adjusting an Income Statement and Balance Sheet for Deferrals and Accruals   LO 4-1, 4-2, 4-4, 4-6

Complete this case, available online at the Connect eBook. By completing this case, you will learn to identify misstatements and make adjustments to correct the financial statements.

S4-7 Aggregating Accounts on an Adjusted Trial Balance to Prepare an Income Statement,   LO 4-3, 4-4, 4-6
Statement of Retained Earnings, and Balance Sheet

Complete this case involving Escalade, Inc., available online at the Connect eBook. By completing this case, you will learn to use a spreadsheet to link account balances on an adjusted trial balance to produce aggregated amounts reported in an income statement, statement of retained earnings, and balance sheet.

Escalade, Inc.

CONTINUING CASE

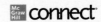

CC4-1 Adjusting the Accounting Records   LO 4-1, 4-2

Assume it is now December 31, 2021, and Nicole has just completed her first year of operations at Nicole's Getaway Spa. After looking through her trial balance, she noticed that there are some items that have either not been recorded or are no longer up-to-date.

a. Nicole's Getaway Spa is renting its space at a cost of $600 per month. On September 1, 2021, Nicole paid eight months' rent in advance using cash. This prepayment was recorded in the account Prepaid Rent back in September.

b. The building, purchased at the beginning of the year for $47,000 cash, has estimated depreciation of $2,000 for 2021, but none has been recorded yet.

c. Salaries and wages to the support staff at Nicole's Getaway Spa have been paid up to December 26, 2021. The support staff worked both December 27 and 28 and will be paid on January 5, 2022. Salaries and wages amount to $1,000 per day. The spa was closed December 29–31.

d. The insurance policy, purchased on June 1 for $3,000 cash, provides coverage for 12 months. The part of the insurance coverage for June–December has now been used up.

e. The unadjusted amount in the Spa Supplies account was $2,000 at December 31, 2021, for supplies purchased on account. A year-end count showed $700 of supplies remain on hand.

f. On the last day of December, a customer obtained spa services by using a $90 gift certificate that was purchased earlier in the month. Use of the gift certificate to pay for these services had not yet been recorded.

Required:

1. For each of the items listed above, identify whether an accrual adjustment, a deferral adjustment, or no adjustment is required.

2. For each of the deferral adjustments, prepare the initial journal entry that would have been recorded.

3. Prepare the adjusting journal entries that should be recorded for Nicole's Getaway Spa at December 31, 2021, assuming that the items have not been adjusted prior to December 31, 2021.

DATA ANALYTICS EXERCISES

Data Analytics Exercises are auto-graded exercises offering detailed data visualization, interpretation, and analysis, and are available for assignment in Connect.

5

Fraud, Internal Control, and Cash

CHAPTER FIVE

YOUR LEARNING OBJECTIVES

LO 5-1   Define fraud and internal control.

LO 5-2   Explain common principles and limitations of internal control.

LO 5-3   Apply internal control principles to cash receipts and payments.

LO 5-4   Perform the key control of reconciling cash to bank statements.

LO 5-5   Explain the reporting of cash.

LO 5-S1 Describe the operations of petty cash systems.

THAT WAS THEN

In the previous chapters you learned about the accounting system that produces the basic financial statements.

FOCUS COMPANY: KOSS CORPORATION

C hapters 1 through 4 explained the key roles that accounting systems and financial statements play when establishing and operating a small business like Noodlecake. Chapter 5 introduces another key part of an accounting system: internal controls, which are the behind-the-scenes practices that help businesses achieve their objectives. When operating effectively, internal controls can improve operations, enhance the reporting of financial and nonfinancial information, and enable compliance with laws and regulations. But when internal controls fail, the results can be disastrous. Just ask the people at Koss Corporation—the Milwaukee-based maker of headphones and earbuds. The company's former vice president of finance admitted she exploited weaknesses in the company's internal controls and stole $31.5 million to pay for extravagant purchases she made with personal credit cards. This chapter will help you understand why frauds occur and how internal controls can help prevent them. The chapter also will help you learn an internal control practice to use in your personal life every month to protect your own cash. Had it been used properly at Koss, the company could have avoided much of its losses.[1]

---

[1]Information regarding the Koss fraud has been obtained from the following sources: Koss Corporation 2011 Form 10-K, 2009 Form 10-K, and 2009 Schedule 14A; http://www.milwaukeemag.com/article/3162011-thediva; *Puskala v. Koss* class action complaint (http://securities.stanford.edu/1044/KOSS00_01/2010115_ f01c_1000041.pdf); *SEC v. Koss* civil action complaint (http://www.sec.gov/litigation/complaints/2011/ comp22138.pdf); and *SEC v. Sachdeva/Mulvaney* civil action complaint (http://www.sec.gov/litigation/ complaints/2010/comp21640.pdf).

THIS IS NOW

This chapter explains how internal control works behind the scenes to improve operations and prevent fraud, particularly for one key asset: cash.

Fraud and internal control	Internal control for cash	Cash reporting	Supplement 5A	Review the chapter
• Fraud • The Sarbanes-Oxley Act (SOX) • Internal control	• Controls for cash receipts • Controls for cash payments • Controls from bank procedures	• Bank statement • Bank reconciliation • Reporting cash • Restricted cash	• Petty cash systems	• Demonstration case • Chapter summary • Key terms • Homework helper • Practice material

Fraud and Internal Control

FRAUD

A **fraud** is generally defined as an attempt to deceive others for personal gain. Employee fraud is often grouped into three categories:

- *Corruption.* Corruption involves misusing one's position for inappropriate personal gain. A former mayor of Detroit was sentenced to 28 years in federal prison for corruption after he accepted payments from people seeking to do business with the city (bribery) and awarded contracts to a friend who redirected money to him (kickbacks).

- *Asset misappropriation.* Asset misappropriation is, quite simply, theft (embezzlement). Cash is usually the target, but other assets can be misappropriated. A vice president of product development at Tiffany & Co. admitted to stealing and reselling $1.3 million of jewelry that belonged to her employer. The company discovered the pieces missing when counting its inventory.

- *Financial statement fraud.* This type of fraud involves misreporting amounts in the financial statements, usually to portray more favorable financial results than what actually exist. The most famous cases occurred at Enron (now bankrupt) and WorldCom (now part of Verizon). WorldCom violated GAAP by recording $11 billion of expenses as assets, the result of which was larger total assets on the balance sheet and more net income on the income statement.

As Exhibit 5.1 shows, financial statement fraud occurs infrequently but causes the greatest losses. In contrast, asset misappropriation is more frequent but tends to involve smaller amounts.

Why would an employee commit fraud? Research has found three factors exist when fraud occurs. These factors work together, as suggested by the *fraud triangle*.

1. **Incentive.** The employee has a reason for committing fraud. For example, personal financial pressure may lead to asset misappropriation. The VP at Koss stole because

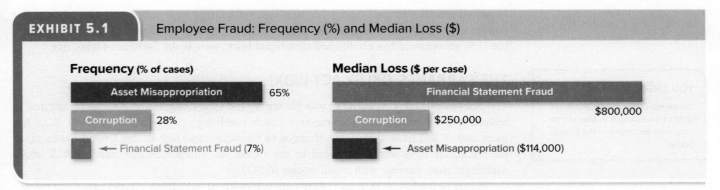

| EXHIBIT 5.1 | Employee Fraud: Frequency (%) and Median Loss ($) |

Frequency (% of cases)

Asset Misappropriation	65%
Corruption	28%
← Financial Statement Fraud (7%)	

Median Loss ($ per case)

Financial Statement Fraud	$800,000
Corruption	$250,000
← Asset Misappropriation ($114,000)	

Source: Association of Certified Fraud Examiners 2018 Report to the Nations on Occupational Fraud and Abuse.

her $145,000 salary was not enough to pay for the monthly credit card bills that reached as high as $1 million. In financial statement fraud cases, the incentive can be to make the business appear successful so as to attract investors, bring in new business partners, or meet loan requirements. The **loan covenants** in lending agreements may require the company to achieve financial targets, such as maintaining specific levels of assets or stockholders' equity. If loan covenants are not met, the lender can require the company to pay a higher interest rate, repay its loan balance on demand, or put up extra collateral to secure the loan. To avoid this, dishonest managers may misreport the company's financial statements.

2. **Opportunity.** The employee has a means of committing fraud. Opportunities to commit fraud usually stem from weak internal controls. That was certainly the case at Koss, where the VP transferred $16 million out of the company without approval or review by the chief financial officer. She also took advantage of deficiencies in the company's petty cash authorizations to pay $390,000 of her personal purchases. Finally, she was able to cover up these thefts because she did not require proper authorization for journal entries she recorded.

3. **Rationalization.** The employee perceives the misdeed as unavoidable or justified. In the Koss case, the defense attorney argued the VP suffered from addiction and mental illness, which led to uncontrollable compulsive behavior. In many other cases, fraudsters rationalize their actions through a feeling of personal entitlement, which outweighs moral principles, such as honesty and concern for others. These employees often feel they are underpaid, so fraud is their way to get even and be paid what they think they deserve.

> **YOU SHOULD KNOW**
>
> **Loan Covenants:** Terms of a loan agreement that, if broken, entitle the lender to renegotiate loan terms or force repayment.

The Fraud Triangle

SPOTLIGHT ON | Ethics

You Can't Count That!

Most of the big accounting frauds involve uncertain judgments or complex accounting decisions that later are found to be inappropriate. However, some frauds have involved blatantly unethical acts. In one famous case, managers at Bausch & Lomb shipped as much as two years' worth of contact lenses to opticians who hadn't even ordered them. These shipments were counted as sales revenue, which led to overstated financial results and unwarranted bonuses. An investigation later found (1) an environment of extreme pressure created incentives, (2) weak internal controls provided opportunities, and (3) unscrupulous managers rationalized the fraud.

Fraud affects all sizes and types of companies, but its impact on public companies is a major concern. When investors lose, the economy suffers. To reduce fraud among public companies, the U.S. government has established significant laws, such as the Sarbanes-Oxley Act.

THE SARBANES-OXLEY ACT (SOX)

The **Sarbanes-Oxley Act (SOX)** was passed by the U.S. Congress in 2002 in an attempt to restore investor confidence after massive frauds involving Enron and WorldCom. SOX has been one of the most significant changes to financial reporting in the United States since the Securities Acts were introduced in the 1930s. All companies that trade on U.S. stock exchanges must comply with requirements of SOX.

Some of the key SOX requirements are summarized in Exhibit 5.2 and explained below.

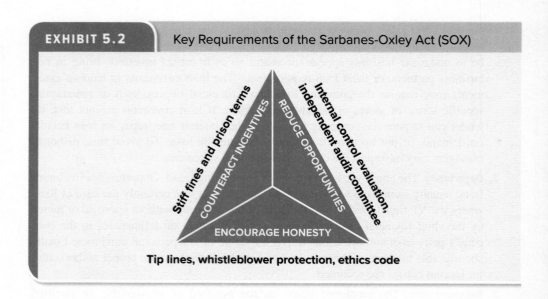

EXHIBIT 5.2 — Key Requirements of the Sarbanes-Oxley Act (SOX)

Internal control evaluation, independent audit committee

Stiff fines and prison terms

COUNTERACT INCENTIVES

REDUCE OPPORTUNITIES

ENCOURAGE HONESTY

Tip lines, whistleblower protection, ethics code

1. **Counteract incentives.** Those who willfully misrepresent financial results face stiff penalties, including fines of up to $5 million plus repayment of any fraud proceeds. Also, maximum jail sentences have been increased to 20 years, which can quickly add up because federal sentencing guidelines allow judges to declare consecutive jail terms for each violation. The VP at Koss was charged with six counts of fraud, so she was facing a maximum prison term of 120 years.

2. **Reduce opportunities.** This is the part of the fraud triangle most affected by SOX. To reduce fraud opportunities and improve companies' internal control over financial reporting, SOX requires all public companies to

   - *Establish an audit committee of independent directors.* This committee strives to ensure the company's accounting, internal control, and audit functions are effective.

   - *Evaluate and report on the effectiveness of internal control over financial reporting.* This evaluation must be completed by management and, for large public companies, by external auditors as well. An external audit of control effectiveness can be expensive, so it is optional for small public companies. Sadly, Koss executives felt the company's resources "would be better spent on strategic planning" than auditing, so they did not ask external auditors to test and report on their company's internal control. Had they done so, the massive fraud might have been detected earlier. You will learn more about internal control in the following section.

3. **Encourage honesty.** Admittedly, it's difficult for any law to achieve this, but some parts of SOX help honest employees confront those inclined to rationalize and conceal fraud. For example, public companies must have tip lines that allow employees to secretly submit concerns about questionable accounting or auditing practices. These whistleblower tips are the most common means for detecting fraud, according to the 2018 report referenced in Exhibit 5.1. SOX grants legal protection to whistleblowers so they aren't retaliated against by those charged with fraud. If you tattle on your boss for submitting a fraudulent expense claim, you can't be fired for it. Finally, companies are required to adopt a code of ethics for their senior financial officers. Google ends its code by simply saying, "don't be evil."

 How's it going?   Self-Study Practice

Identify whether each of the following increases (+) or decreases (−) the risk of fraud, arising from incentives (I), opportunities (O), or rationalizing/concealing (R).

	+/−	I/O/R
1. Enron was notorious for its "rank and yank" practice that involved ranking the financial performance of each business unit and then firing managers in the lowest 20 percent.		
2. Nintendo of America conducts preemployment screening before hiring anyone.		
3. The Walt Disney Company has a strong board of directors, according to *Corporate Responsibility Magazine.*		

After you have finished, check your answers with the solution.

INTERNAL CONTROL

Objectives

Internal control consists of the actions taken by people at every level of an organization to achieve its objectives relating to

- *Operations.* Operational objectives focus on completing work efficiently and effectively and protecting assets by reducing the risk of fraud.
- *Reporting.* Reporting objectives include producing reliable and timely accounting information for use by people internal and external to the organization.
- *Compliance.* Compliance objectives focus on adhering to laws and regulations.

In your personal life, these actions include basic steps such as locking your door (operations), checking the accuracy of your banking records (reporting), and staying within the speed limit when driving (compliance).

Components

Most organizations use the following control components as a framework when analyzing their internal control systems.

1. **Control environment.** The control environment refers to the attitude people in the organization hold regarding internal control. Do they appreciate its importance, or do they view internal control as just bureaucratic hurdles? The control environment is influenced by the policies a company's board of directors and senior managers set, their demonstrated commitment to integrity and ethical values, the character of the people they hire, and how they evaluate others. A strong control environment helps employees understand the value of internal controls to their organization's success.

YOU SHOULD KNOW

Internal Control: Actions taken to promote efficient and effective operations, protect assets, enhance accounting information, and adhere to laws and regulations.

2. **Risk assessment.** Managers should continuously assess the potential for fraud and other risks that could prevent the company from achieving its objectives.

3. **Control activities.** Control activities include various work responsibilities and duties completed by employees to reduce risks to an acceptable level. We discuss these activities in detail in the next section of this chapter.

4. **Information and communication.** An effective internal control system generates and communicates information about activities affecting the organization to support sound decision making.

5. **Monitoring activities.** The internal control system is evaluated often to determine whether it is working as intended. Deficiencies should be communicated to those responsible for taking corrective action, including senior management and/or the board of directors.

As shown in Exhibit 5.3, the control objectives and components apply to all levels of an organization. Although a chief financial officer and a cashier are assigned different responsibilities, their work combines to achieve the same control objectives through the components of control shown below.

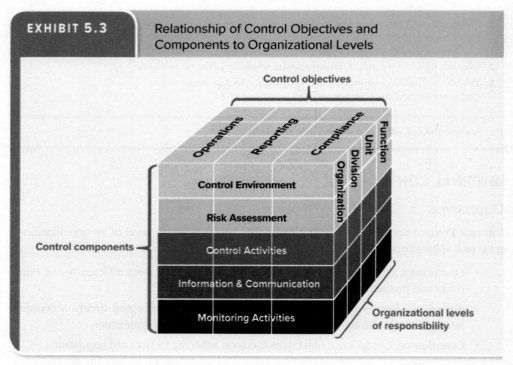

EXHIBIT 5.3   Relationship of Control Objectives and Components to Organizational Levels

Source: AICPA on behalf of Committee of Sponsoring Organizations of the Treadway Commission (COSO). *Internal Control—Integrated Framework.* New York, NY: COSO, 2013.

Principles of Control Activities

Learning Objective 5-2
Explain common principles and limitations of internal control.

The control objectives and components outlined in the previous sections are supported by fundamental principles of control. We focus this section on how five key principles, shown in Exhibit 5.4, are used in control activities you are likely to see early in your career. We want you to understand these control examples so that when you encounter them or other controls on the job, you will appreciate them and ensure others respect them. The principles apply to all areas of business, including human resource management, finance, marketing, and general business operations, but our focus here is on accounting.

EXHIBIT 5.4	Five Common Principles of Internal Control

Principle	Explanation	Examples
1 **Establish responsibility**	Assign each task to only one employee.	Give a separate cash register drawer to each cashier at the beginning of a shift.
2 **Segregate duties**	Do not make one employee responsible for all parts of a process.	Inventory buyers do not also approve payments to suppliers.
3 **Restrict access**	Do not provide access to assets or information unless it is needed to fulfill assigned responsibilities.	Secure valuable assets such as cash and restrict access to computer systems (via passwords, firewalls).
4 **Document procedures**	Prepare documents to show activities that have occurred.	Pay suppliers using prenumbered checks and digitally documented electronic fund transfers.
5 **Independently verify**	Check others' work.	Compare the cash balance in the company's accounting records to the cash balance reported by the bank and account for any differences.

1 **Establish responsibility.** Whenever possible, assign each task to only one employee. Doing so will allow you to determine who caused any errors or thefts that occur. That's why retail companies assign a separate cash register drawer to each employee at the beginning of a shift. If two cashiers were to use the same drawer, it would be impossible to know which cashier caused the drawer to be short on cash. With only one person responsible for adding and removing money from the drawer, there's no doubt about who is responsible for a cash shortage.

2 **Segregate duties.** **Segregation of duties** involves assigning responsibilities so that one employee can't make a mistake or commit a dishonest act without someone else discovering it. That's why inventory buyers do not approve payments to suppliers. Without this control, buyers could create their own fictitious supply company and approve unwarranted payments to the supply company. Segregation of duties is most effective when a company assigns responsibilities for related activities to two or more people and assigns responsibilities for record-keeping to people who do not have access to the assets for which they are accounting. One employee should not initiate, approve, record, and have access to the items involved in the same transaction. A lack of segregation of duties at Koss created the opportunity for fraud because the VP had access to both the company's cash and record-keeping that allowed her to conceal her theft through fraudulent journal entries.

3 **Restrict access.** Some controls involve rather obvious steps such as physically locking up valuable assets and electronically securing access to other assets and information. Companies

YOU SHOULD KNOW

Segregation of Duties: An internal control designed into the accounting system to prevent an employee from making a mistake or committing a dishonest act as part of one assigned duty and then also covering it up through another assigned duty.

Pointing hand: Tatiana Popova/ Shutterstock; Cubicles: Andersen Ross/Getty Images; Padlock: Ragnar Schmuck/Getty Images; Check photo: Tetra Images/Getty Images; Magnifying glass: Ingram Publishing/ Alamy Stock Photo

restrict access to check-signing equipment, require a passcode to open cash registers, and protect computer systems with firewalls. If employees do not need assets or information to fulfill their assigned responsibilities, they are denied access.

4 Document procedures. Digital and paper documents are such common features of business that you may not realize they represent an internal control. By documenting each business activity, a company creates a record of whether goods were shipped, customers were billed, cash was received, and so on. Without these documents, a company wouldn't know what transactions have been or need to be entered into the accounting system. To enhance this control, most companies assign sequential numbers to their documents and check they are used in numerical sequence. This check occurs frequently, sometimes daily, to ensure every transaction is recorded and each document number corresponds to one and only one accounting entry.

5 Independently verify. A business can perform independent verification in various ways. The most obvious is to hire someone (an auditor) to ensure the work done by others within the company is appropriate and supported by documentation. Independent verification also can be made part of a person's job. For example, before a check is issued to pay the bill for a truckload of merchandise, a clerk first verifies the bill relates to goods actually received and is calculated correctly. A third form of independent verification involves comparing the company's accounting information to information kept by an independent third party. For example, the company may compare internal cash records to a statement of account issued by the bank. The next section of this chapter demonstrates this procedure, called a bank reconciliation.

Control Limitations

Internal controls can never completely prevent and detect errors and fraud for two reasons. First, an organization will implement internal controls only to the extent their benefits exceed their costs. Companies could nearly eliminate shoplifting by body searching every customer who leaves the store, but such an irritating policy would soon drive customers away. The cost of the lost sales would far exceed the benefits of reduced shoplifting. For smaller companies, the cost of hiring additional employees to fully segregate duties exceeds the benefits. In these cases, other controls such as independent verification by top management must compensate for the lack of segregation of duties. A second limitation is internal controls can fail as a result of human error or fraud. People do make simple mistakes when performing control procedures, especially if they are tired, careless, or confused. Criminally minded employees also have been known to **override** (disarm) internal controls or **collude** (work together) to get around them. The fraud at Koss involved collusion between the VP and her assistant.

SPOTLIGHT ON Controls

Is That a Control, Too?

The five principles covered in this section do not represent all possible forms of internal control. Many other policies and procedures exist, some of which contribute in subtle ways to enhancing internal control. For example, most businesses establish a **mandatory vacation** policy for employees who handle cash because it is difficult for them to cover prior thefts while they are away from the business. Another simple control is an **anonymous hotline** that allows anyone to tip off independent auditors about suspected fraud. The Association of Certified Fraud Examiners reports about 40 percent of workplace fraud cases are identified in this way. American Express alerted Koss to more than $1.7 million in transfers from a Koss bank account to its VP's personal credit card. A final example of a control that can limit losses from theft is **bonding** employees, which involves obtaining an insurance policy that partially reimburses the organization for losses caused by employee fraud.

Internal Control for Cash

Internal control for cash is important for two main reasons. First, because the volume of cash transactions is enormous, the risk of cash-handling errors is significant. Second, because cash is valuable, portable, and "owned" by the person who possesses it, it poses a high risk of theft. To reduce these risks, internal controls are vital.

Learning Objective 5-3
Apply internal control principles to cash receipts and payments.

CONTROLS FOR CASH RECEIPTS

Businesses can receive cash in two different ways. They can receive it in person at the time of a sale or from a remote source as payment on an account. Most businesses receive cash either physically, in the form of dollars, coins, and checks payable to the business, or through electronic transactions involving credit cards, debit cards, and electronic funds transfers. Regardless of the way or form in which a business receives cash, **the primary internal control goal for cash receipts is to ensure the business receives the appropriate amount of cash and safely deposits it in the bank.**

Cash Received in Person

To properly segregate duties involving cash receipts, specific responsibilities are assigned to employees, as shown in Exhibit 5.5. Cashiers collect cash and issue a receipt at the point of sale. Supervisors take custody of the cash at the end of each cashier's shift and deposit it in the bank. Accounting staff then ensure the receipts from cash sales are properly recorded in the accounting system. Segregating these duties ensures those who handle the cash (cashiers and supervisors) do not have access to those who record it (the accounting staff). If this segregation of duties did not exist, employees could steal the cash and cover up the theft by changing the accounting records.

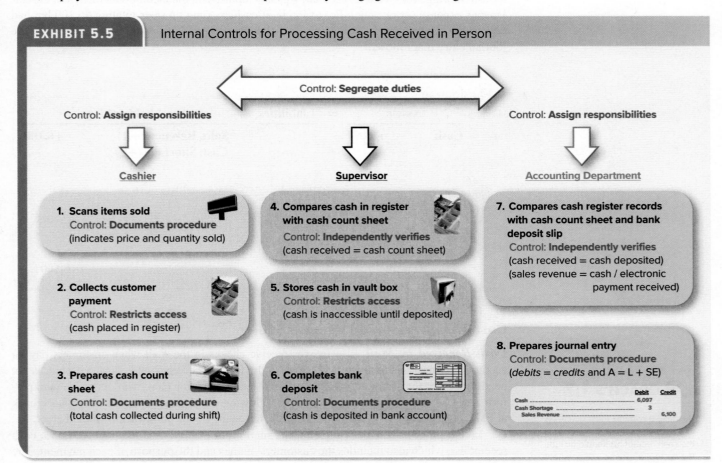

EXHIBIT 5.5 Internal Controls for Processing Cash Received in Person

Control: **Segregate duties**

Control: **Assign responsibilities**

Control: **Assign responsibilities**

Cashier

1. **Scans items sold**
   Control: **Documents procedure**
   (indicates price and quantity sold)

2. **Collects customer payment**
   Control: **Restricts access**
   (cash placed in register)

3. **Prepares cash count sheet**
   Control: **Documents procedure**
   (total cash collected during shift)

Supervisor

4. **Compares cash in register with cash count sheet**
   Control: **Independently verifies**
   (cash received = cash count sheet)

5. **Stores cash in vault box**
   Control: **Restricts access**
   (cash is inaccessible until deposited)

6. **Completes bank deposit**
   Control: **Documents procedure**
   (cash is deposited in bank account)

Accounting Department

7. **Compares cash register records with cash count sheet and bank deposit slip**
   Control: **Independently verifies**
   (cash received = cash deposited)
   (sales revenue = cash / electronic payment received)

8. **Prepares journal entry**
   Control: **Documents procedure**
   (*debits = credits* and A = L + SE)

	Debit	Credit
Cash	6,097	
Cash Shortage	3	
Sales Revenue		6,100

Display photo: Tom Hahn/Getty Images; Cash drawer photo: Tetra Images/Getty Images; Safe photo: PhotoDisc/Getty Images; Cash count photo: Radius/SuperStock

Exhibit 5.5 shows, in boxes 1–3, the cashier uses the cash register and its accompanying point-of-sale accounting system to perform three important functions: (1) document the amount charged for each item sold, (2) restrict access to cash, and (3) document the total cash sales. In documenting each item sold (both on screen and on a paper or e-mailed receipt), the cash register reduces errors by allowing customers to dispute overcharges. By restricting access, the cash register reduces the risk of cash being lost or stolen. By documenting the total cash sales, the cash register provides an independent record of the amount of cash the cashier should have collected and passed on for deposit at the bank. The cashier uses this information when completing a cash count sheet at the end of each shift. The cash count sheet documents the amount of cash the cashier received and determines any cash short or over that occurred during the shift.

Exhibit 5.5 also shows, in boxes 4–6, that the supervisor performs important controls such as independently verifying each cashier's count sheet, a copy of which is sent to the accounting department. The supervisor is also responsible for placing the cash in a locked vault until it is taken to the bank for deposit. At that time, a deposit slip listing the amounts included in the deposit is prepared and presented to the bank. After verifying and receiving the funds, the bank employee issues a verified deposit slip, which is then forwarded to the company's accounting department.

The accounting department performs two key tasks, shown in boxes 7 and 8 of Exhibit 5.5. It compares the record of cash sales maintained by the cash register with the count sheet prepared by the cashier and the bank deposit slip returned by the bank. This comparison provides independent verification that the amount of cash rung up at the time of sale was deposited into the bank account. Based on this information, a journal entry is prepared to record Sales Revenue at the amount rung up by the cash register and increase the Cash account for the amount deposited in the bank. Any difference between the two amounts is recorded in a Cash Shortage (or Overage) account, which is reported on the income statement as a miscellaneous expense (or revenue). For example, if cashiers rung up sales totaling $6,100 but had only $6,097 to deposit, the following financial statement effects would be recorded with the journal entry that follows.

1 Analyze

Assets		=	Liabilities	+	Stockholders' Equity	
Cash	+6,097				Sales Revenue (+R)	+6,100
					Cash Shortage (+E)	−3

2 Record

	Debit	Credit
Cash	6,097	
Cash Shortage	3	
Sales Revenue		6,100

Cash Received from a Remote Source

Cash Received by Mail   Businesses receive checks in the mail when customers pay on account. Because this cash is not received in the form of currency and coins, a cashier is not needed to enter these amounts into a cash register. Instead, the clerk who opens the mail performs this function. In fact, to visualize the following description, you need only glance back at Exhibit 5.5 and replace boxes 1–3 with the following duties performed by a mail clerk.

Like a point-of-sale cash register, the mail clerk lists all amounts received on a cash receipt list, which also includes the customers' names and the purpose of each payment. The customer usually includes with the payment a note (called a **remittance advice**) explaining what is being paid. Ideally, someone supervises the clerk who opens the mail to ensure

COACH'S TIP

Because payments must be credited to each customer's account, the cash receipt list should include the customer's name and payment purpose.

he or she takes no cash that may have been remitted by a customer. As evidence of this supervision, both the mail clerk and the supervisor sign the completed cash receipts list. To ensure no one diverts the checks for personal use, the clerk stamps each check "For Deposit Only," which instructs the bank to deposit the check in the company's account rather than exchange it for cash.

After these steps have been completed, the cash received is separated from the *record* of cash received. Checks and money orders are given to the person who prepares the bank deposit, whereas the cash receipts list and remittance advices are sent to the accounting department. As in step 7 of Exhibit 5.5, the accounting department then compares the total on the cash receipts list with the deposit slip received from the bank. This comparison serves to independently verify that all cash received by mail was deposited in the bank. The accounting department then uses the cash receipts list to record the journal entries that debit Cash and credit Accounts Receivable from each customer.

Cash Received Electronically Businesses also receive payments from customers via **electronic funds transfer (EFT).** An EFT occurs when a customer electronically transfers funds from his or her bank account to the company's bank account. Most businesses encourage customers to use EFTs because they speed up collections. A company may not receive mailed payments for five to seven days, but it receives EFTs almost immediately. And because these payments are deposited directly into the company's bank account, EFTs eliminate the need for some internal controls. To process an EFT, the accounting department merely records journal entries to debit Cash and credit Accounts Receivable from each customer.

How's it going? — Self-Study Practice

The five internal control principles are represented in the following diagram. (One principle appears twice.) Identify the principle associated with each numbered box.

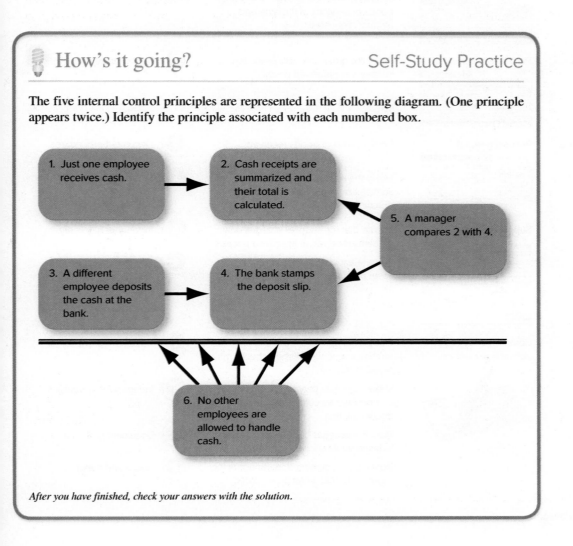

After you have finished, check your answers with the solution.

Solution to Self-Study Practice
1. Establish responsibility
2. Document procedures
3. Segregate duties
4. Document procedures
5. Independently verify
6. Restrict access

CONTROLS FOR CASH PAYMENTS

Most cash payments involve (1) writing a check or completing an electronic funds transfer (EFT) to a supplier or (2) paying employees via EFT. In the rare case where a company pays for purchases with dollar bills and coins, it uses (3) a petty cash system. **The primary goal of internal controls for all cash payments is to ensure the business pays only for properly authorized transactions.**

Cash Paid by Check for Purchases on Account

Businesses usually purchase goods and services on account and pay for them later by check or EFT. Most companies rely on a voucher system to control these transactions. A **voucher system** is a process for approving and documenting all purchases and payments made on account. A voucher is simply a collection of documents prepared at each step in the system. Exhibit 5.6 lists typical steps involved in obtaining goods or services from a supplier, documents prepared at each step, and examples of the related cash controls and applicable control principles.

EXHIBIT 5.6   Steps, Documentation, and Controls in a Voucher System

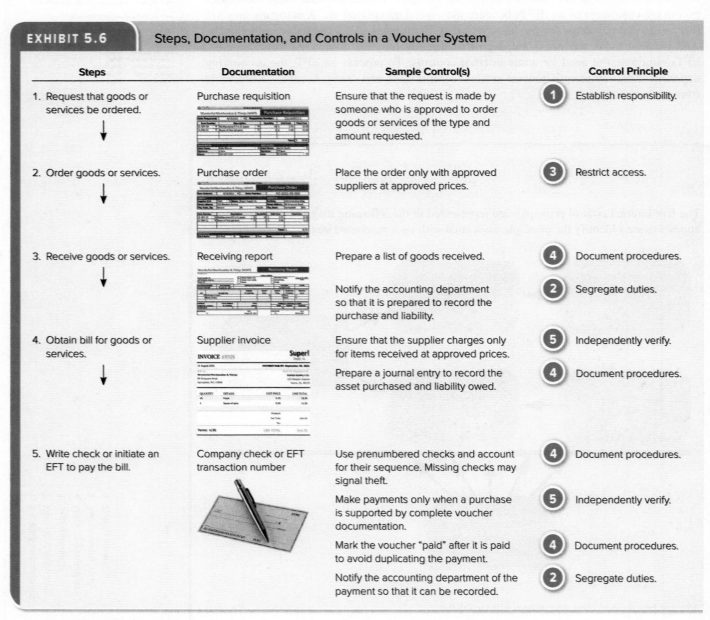

Steps	Documentation	Sample Control(s)	Control Principle
1. Request that goods or services be ordered.	Purchase requisition	Ensure that the request is made by someone who is approved to order goods or services of the type and amount requested.	**1** Establish responsibility.
2. Order goods or services.	Purchase order	Place the order only with approved suppliers at approved prices.	**3** Restrict access.
3. Receive goods or services.	Receiving report	Prepare a list of goods received.	**4** Document procedures.
		Notify the accounting department so that it is prepared to record the purchase and liability.	**2** Segregate duties.
4. Obtain bill for goods or services.	Supplier invoice	Ensure that the supplier charges only for items received at approved prices.	**5** Independently verify.
		Prepare a journal entry to record the asset purchased and liability owed.	**4** Document procedures.
5. Write check or initiate an EFT to pay the bill.	Company check or EFT transaction number	Use prenumbered checks and account for their sequence. Missing checks may signal theft.	**4** Document procedures.
		Make payments only when a purchase is supported by complete voucher documentation.	**5** Independently verify.
		Mark the voucher "paid" after it is paid to avoid duplicating the payment.	**4** Document procedures.
		Notify the accounting department of the payment so that it can be recorded.	**2** Segregate duties.

Check photo: Tetra Images/Getty Images

Below we illustrate how Exhibit 5.6 is applied in practice by Wonderful Merchandise & Things (WMT).

1. As Exhibit 5.6 indicates, the purchasing system begins with an authorized employee completing a manual or electronic purchase requisition form. In the purchase requisition example shown, Kelly Watson has requested office supplies. These items are requested regularly, so they are selected from a drop-down list of items that Kelly is authorized to request. The purchase requisition is sequentially numbered so that missing requisitions can be easily identified. The purchase requisition must be approved by a supervisor before an order is placed with a supplier. No journal entry is made at this stage because the company has not entered into an exchange, so a transaction has not yet occurred.

2. After the purchase requisition is approved, the company's purchasing agent completes a prenumbered purchase order. Unlike the purchase requisition, the purchase order identifies the company that will supply the goods. In the example shown here, this company is chosen from a drop-down list of approved suppliers. In this case, the supplier is Super Supply Co. The purchase order also indicates the specific location to which the goods are to be delivered, as well as the approved cost for the items. The purchase order is then sent to the company supplying the goods. A copy of the purchase order is also transmitted to the company's own accounting department to forewarn them of the pending purchase. However, at this point, the company has only promised to pay for the items on order, but it has not received them, so a journal entry is not recorded yet.

3. When the goods are received, a receiving report is prepared. As shown in this example, the receiving report indicates the date, quantity, and condition of items received. A copy of the receiving report is sent to WMT's accounting department to notify them that the goods have been received and are in good order, so that the purchase can be recorded (in step 4).

4. The next piece of documentation in the voucher system will be an invoice sent to WMT from Super Supply Co. The employees at WMT's accounting department will verify that information on the invoice matches information on both the receiving report and purchase order (often called a three-way match). Specifically, they will check that the quantity of items billed on the invoice matches the quantity WMT received, as indicated on its receiving report, and that the cost per item on the invoice matches the approved cost indicated previously on the purchase order. **Assuming the supplier invoice is accurate, the accounting department will prepare a journal entry to record the purchase of office supplies on account.** Then, the supplier invoice will be included with the other documents in a voucher that will be submitted for payment. An example of the voucher package of documents is shown here, with the supplier invoice on top.

5. The final step in the voucher system, shown in Exhibit 5.6, is for WMT to process a check or electronic funds transfer to pay for the items purchased and received. When the check or funds transfer is prepared, WMT's accounting department reduces both the Cash account and the Accounts Payable to the supplier (created in step 4). The voucher also is marked "paid" so that it cannot be accidentally or intentionally resubmitted for duplicate payment.

Notice in the preceding discussion and in Exhibit 5.6 how employee responsibilities are limited to specific tasks that occur only after obtaining and documenting proper authorization in the prior step. The purchasing, receiving, and bill payment duties are segregated to ensure

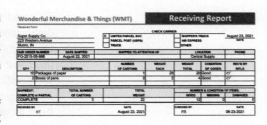

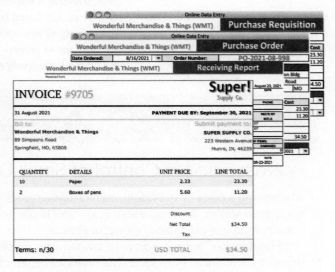

the company obtains and pays only for the goods or services that have been properly authorized and received. Increasingly, these responsibilities are completed using **robotic process automation (RPA)**, which combines automation and artificial intelligence to perform many of these activities without human involvement. As a result, accountants spend more of their time resolving exceptions in this process, rather than executing the basic steps of a voucher system.

Cash Paid to Employees via Electronic Funds Transfer

Most companies pay salaries and wages to employees through EFTs, which are known by employees as **direct deposits.** The company initiates the EFT when it instructs its bank to transfer the pay due each employee directly from the company's bank account to each employee's checking account. This system is convenient and efficient for the employer because it eliminates the tasks of physically writing and distributing the checks and for the employee, who has access to the funds without having to deposit a check. One risk, however, is the bank might accidentally overpay or underpay an employee by transferring the wrong amount of money out of the company's bank account.

To reduce this risk, many companies use an imprest system for paying employees. An **imprest system** restricts the total amount paid to others by limiting the amount of money available to be transferred. Using an imprest payroll system, the company instructs the bank to transfer the total net pay of all employees for the pay period out of the company's general bank account and into a special payroll account established for that purpose. Then the bank transfers the individual amounts from the payroll account to the employees' checking accounts. If the transfers occur without error, the special payroll account equals zero after all employees have been paid. If the account is overdrawn or a balance remains, the company knows an error has occurred.

Cash Paid to Reimburse Employees (Petty Cash)

To avoid the time and cost of writing checks for business expenses that are small in amount, organizations may use a petty cash fund. A **petty cash fund** is a system to reimburse employees for expenditures they have made on behalf of the organization. Like the imprest payroll account described above, a petty cash fund acts as a control by establishing a limited amount of cash to use for specific types of expenses. The main difference between the two is that rather than transfer funds from a general bank account to another special account at the bank, the company removes cash from its general bank account to hold at its premises in a locked cash box. The company's petty cash custodian is responsible for operating the petty cash fund. Because this employee has access to cash, he or she should be supervised and the petty cash fund should be subject to surprise audits. At Koss, the fund was operated by the VP's assistant with review only by the VP, who colluded with her assistant to process $390,000 of personal purchases. The fund was not audited. Step-by-step procedures for properly establishing and operating a petty cash fund are explained in Supplement 5A.

SPOTLIGHT ON | **Controls**

Pcards: Efficient Control of Small-Dollar Transactions

When using a petty cash system, administrative costs of processing small-dollar purchases can exceed the cost of the items themselves. To avoid these costs and implement tighter controls over small-dollar purchases, many organizations instead use purchasing cards, or Pcards.

Pcards work like a credit card by allowing employees to purchase business-related items using a plastic card issued by a financial institution. The financial institution keeps track of the purchases and sends a monthly bill to the company for all purchases the company's employees made. With all small transactions combined into one monthly bill, the company avoids having to reimburse each employee for each individual transaction. The company can also tighten controls *before* the purchases occur by setting limits on the amounts and types of allowable purchases. Pcards are estimated to cut processing costs for each typical transaction from $50–$75 to under $5.[*]

---

[*]"Do You Know How Much It Costs to Process a P-card Transaction?," *Managing Accounts Payable* 14, no. 3 (March 2014), p. 13.

CONTROLS FROM BANK PROCEDURES

Banks provide important services to individuals and businesses. They accept deposits, process payments to others, and provide statements that account for these and other transactions. Their services help businesses control cash in several ways:

1. **Restricting access.** Because banks provide a secure place to deposit cash, businesses need to keep only a limited amount of cash on hand, which reduces the risk it will be stolen or misplaced.

2. **Documenting procedures.** By processing payments made by check or EFT, banks facilitate and document business transactions.

3. **Independently verifying.** Company accountants can use the bank's statement of account to double-check the accuracy of the company's cash records. By comparing these two sets of records and investigating any differences, they can verify the company's records are accurate or identify necessary adjustments.

Cash Reporting

The balance in a company's cash records usually differs from the balance in the bank's records for a variety of valid reasons described in this part of the chapter. To determine the appropriate amount to report on the balance sheet and statement of cash flows, an internal accounting report is prepared to compare the company's cash records with the bank's. The process of comparing two sets of records is called *reconciling*, so the report is called a **bank reconciliation**. A bank reconciliation is a key internal control because it provides independent verification of all cash transactions the bank has processed for the company. This procedure is done monthly, ideally by a company employee whose duties are segregated from recording and handling cash. This segregation of duties did not exist at Koss, which allowed the VP's embezzlement to remain undetected through six years. You should prepare a monthly bank reconciliation in your own life. To prepare a bank reconciliation, you must first understand the items on a bank statement.

> **YOU SHOULD KNOW**
>
> **Bank Reconciliation:** Process of using both the bank statement and the cash accounts of a business to determine the appropriate amount of cash in a bank account, after taking into consideration delays or errors in processing cash transactions.

BANK STATEMENT

For each account a business opens, the bank generates a statement that it makes available online. The format varies from bank to bank, but the statement in Exhibit 5.7 is typical. This statement, prepared by Texas Commerce Bank for one of the accounts opened by WMT, provides an overall summary of the account (labeled ① in Exhibit 5.7). The summary is followed by a list of specific transactions posted to the account (labeled ② through ④) and a running balance in the account (labeled ⑤). In the following section, we explain the transactions that caused changes in the account's balance.

> **Learning Objective 5-4**
> Perform the key control of reconciling cash to bank statements.

Checks Cleared

After a check is written, the payee (to whom the check is written) either gives the check or sends a digital image of it to a financial institution for deposit. That financial institution contacts the check writer's bank, which in turn withdraws the amount of the check from the check writer's account and reports it as a deduction on the bank statement. The check is then said to have **cleared the bank.**

Checks are listed on the bank statement in the order they clear the bank. Look closely at column ② in Exhibit 5.7 and you will see four checks cleared the bank in June. Because WMT's checks are used in their prenumbered order, the bank statement provides a hint that check 103 did not clear the bank this month. (This fact will be important later when we prepare the bank reconciliation.)

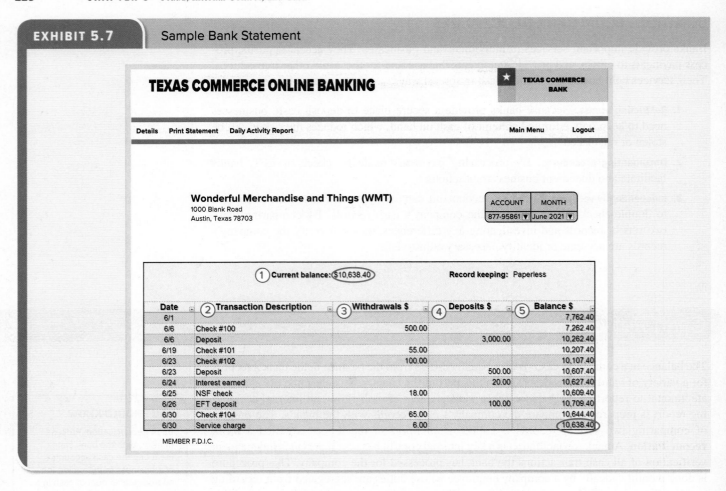

EXHIBIT 5.7 Sample Bank Statement

Deposits Made

Deposits are listed on the bank statement in the order in which the bank processes them. If you make a deposit after the bank closes (using an ATM, night deposit chute, or digital image deposit), it will not appear on the bank statement until the bank processes it the following business day. Knowing this detail will help you to prepare the bank reconciliation.

Other Transactions

The balance in a bank account can change for a variety of reasons other than checks and deposits. For example, the account balance increases when the account earns interest and when funds are transferred into the account electronically. The account balance decreases when the bank charges a service fee or transfers funds out of the account electronically.

To understand how these items are reported on a bank statement, it is important to realize **the bank statement is presented from the bank's point of view.** The bank views amounts in a company's bank account as liabilities because they will eventually be used by or returned to the account holder. As with all liabilities, increases are reported as credits on the bank statement. Amounts that are removed from a bank account reduce the bank's liability, so they are reported as debits on the bank statement. Banks typically explain the reasons for these increases (credits) and decreases (debits) with symbols or in a short memo, appropriately called a credit memo or debit memo.

BANK RECONCILIATION

A bank reconciliation involves comparing the company's records to the bank's statement of account to determine whether they agree. The company's records can differ from the bank's records for two basic reasons: (1) the company has recorded items the bank doesn't know about at the time it prepares the statement of account or (2) the bank has recorded items the company doesn't know about until the bank statement is examined. Exhibit 5.8 lists examples of these differences, which we discuss below.

EXHIBIT 5.8 — Reconciling Differences

Your Bank May Not Know About	You May Not Know About

1. Errors made by the bank
2. Time lags
   a. Deposits you made recently
   b. Checks you wrote recently
	3. Interest the bank has put into your account
	4. Electronic funds transfers (EFTs)
	5. Service charges taken out of your account
	6. Customer checks you deposited for which the customer had non-sufficient funds (NSF)
	7. Errors made by you

> **COACH'S TIP**
>
> You'll need to change your cash records only for items that appear on the right-hand side of Exhibit 5.8.

1. **Bank errors.** Bank errors happen in real life, just as they do in Monopoly. If you discover a bank error, you should ask the bank to correct its records, but you should not change yours.

2. **Time lags.** Time lags are common. A time lag occurs, for example, when you make a deposit after the bank's normal business hours. *You* know you made the deposit, but your bank does not know until it processes the deposit the next day. Time lags involving deposits are called **deposits in transit.** Another common time lag is an **outstanding check.** This lag occurs when you write a check to a company, but your bank doesn't find out about it until that company deposits the check in its own bank, which then notifies your bank. As you will see later, although deposits in transit and outstanding checks may be a significant part of a bank reconciliation, they do not require any further action on your part because you have already recorded them.

3. **Interest deposited.** You may know your bank pays interest, but you probably do not know exactly how much interest you'll get because it varies depending on the average balance in your account. When you read your bank statement, you'll learn how much interest you need to add to your records.

4. **Electronic funds transfer (EFT).** It doesn't happen every day, but occasionally funds may be transferred into or out of your account without your knowing about it. If you discover these electronic transfers on your bank statement, you will need to adjust your records.

5. **Service charges.** These are amounts the bank charges for processing your transactions. Rather than send you a bill and wait for you to pay it, the bank just takes the amount directly out of your account. You will need to reduce the Cash balance in your accounting records for these charges and record them as Bank Charges Expense.

6. **NSF checks.** Your customers' checks that you deposited in the bank but were later rejected ("bounced") because of insufficient funds in your customers' own bank accounts are referred to as **NSF (non-sufficient funds) checks**. Because the bank increased your account when the check was deposited, the bank decreases your account when it discovers the deposit was not valid. You will need to reduce your Cash balance by the amount of these bounced checks (and any additional bank charges), and you will have to try to collect these amounts from the check writer.

7. **Your errors.** You may have made mistakes or forgotten to record some amounts in your records. If so, you will need to adjust your records for these items.

> **YOU SHOULD KNOW**
>
> **NSF (Non-Sufficient Funds) Checks:** Checks written for an amount greater than the funds available to cover them.

Bank Reconciliation Illustrated

The ending cash balance shown on the bank statement does not usually agree with the ending cash balance shown by the related Cash account on the books of the company. For example, the Cash account of WMT at the end of June might contain the information shown in the following T-account.

Cash (A)			
June 1 balance	7,762.40		
June 6 deposit	3,000.00	500.00	Check #100 written June 4
June 23 deposit	500.00	55.00	Check #101 written June 17
June 30 deposit	1,800.00	100.00	Check #102 written June 20
		145.00	Check #103 written June 24
		56.00	Check #104 written June 30
		815.00	Check #105 written June 30
Ending balance	11,391.40		

WMT's ending cash balance of $11,391.40 differs from the $10,638.40 ending cash balance shown on the bank statement in Exhibit 5.7. The appropriate cash balance is determined by reconciling these balances.

Exhibit 5.9 shows the bank reconciliation prepared by WMT for the month of June. The completed reconciliation finds that the up-to-date cash balance is $11,478.40, an amount that differs from both the bank's statement and WMT's accounting records. This balance is the amount WMT will report as Cash on its balance sheet after adjusting its records with the journal entries that we present later.

EXHIBIT 5.9	Sample Bank Reconciliation

WMT BANK RECONCILIATION
At June 30

UPDATES TO BANK STATEMENT			UPDATES TO COMPANY'S BOOKS	
Ending cash balance per bank statement		$10,638.40	Ending cash balance per books	$11,391.40
Additions			Additions	
(1) Deposit in transit (June 30)		1,800.00	(3a) Interest received from the bank	20.00
		12,438.40	(3b) EFT received from customer	100.00
				11,511.40
Deductions			Deductions	
(2) Outstanding checks:			(3c) NSF check of R. Smith	18.00
#103 (June 24)	145.00		(3d) Bank service charges	6.00
#105 (June 30)	815.00	960.00	(3e) Error in recording check #104	9.00
Up-to-date ending cash balance		$11,478.40	Up-to-date ending cash balance	$11,478.40

To prepare the bank reconciliation in Exhibit 5.9, WMT compared the entries in its Cash account to the bank statement (Exhibit 5.7) with the following goals:

1. **Identify the deposits in transit.** A comparison of WMT's recorded deposits with those on the bank statement revealed WMT made a deposit of $1,800 on June 30 that was not listed on the bank statement. More than likely, the bank will process this deposit the next business day (July 1). WMT doesn't have to change its records for this item because it already was recorded in WMT's books on June 30. It is simply a timing difference, so WMT entered the amount on the bank reconciliation as an addition to update the bank's records.

2. **Identify the outstanding checks.** A comparison of the checks listed on the bank statement with the company's record of written checks showed checks numbered 103 and 105 were still

outstanding at the end of June (that is, they had not cleared the bank). They were entered on the reconciliation (in Exhibit 5.9) as a deduction from the bank balance because the bank will eventually reduce the account balance when these checks clear the bank. (WMT had already deducted checks #103 and #105, so WMT does not change its cash records.)

3. **Record other transactions on the bank statement and correct your errors.**

   a. **Interest received** from the bank, $20—entered on the bank reconciliation in Exhibit 5.9 as an addition to the company's books because it's included in the bank balance but not yet in the company's books.

   b. **Electronic funds transfer** received from customer, $100—entered on the bank reconciliation as an addition to the book balance because it's included in the bank balance but not yet in the company's books.

   c. **NSF check** rejected, $18—entered on the bank reconciliation as a deduction from the company's books because it was deducted from the bank statement balance but has not yet been deducted from the company's cash records.

   d. **Service charges,** $6—entered on the bank reconciliation as a deduction from the company's books because it has been deducted from the bank balance but not yet removed from the Cash account in the company's books.

   e. **Your company errors,** $9—after accounting for the items listed above, WMT found the reconciliation was out of balance by $9. Upon checking the journal entries made during the month, WMT discovered check #104 was recorded in the company's accounts as $56 when, in fact, the check had been filled out for $65 (in payment of Accounts Payable). As Exhibit 5.7 shows, the bank correctly processed the check (on June 30) as $65. To correct its own error, WMT must deduct $9 ($65 − $56) from the company's books side of the bank reconciliation and record a corresponding journal entry (below).

COACH'S TIP

This example involves the company's error in recording the amount of the check. In other cases, the bank errs if it processes the check at the wrong amount. In all instances, the amount written on the check is the correct amount at which the transaction should be recorded.

Now that we know the up-to-date cash balance is $11,478.40, we need to prepare and record journal entries that will bring the Cash account to that balance. The entries on the Bank Statement side of the bank reconciliation do not need to be recorded by WMT because they will automatically work out when the bank processes them next month. **Only the items on the Company's books side of the bank reconciliation need to be recorded in the company's records,** using the following journal entries:

	Debit	Credit
Interest Received:		
(a) Cash	20	
Interest Revenue		20
To record interest received from the bank.		
EFT Received from Customer:		
(b) Cash	100	
Accounts Receivable		100
To record electronic funds transfer received from customer.		
Customer's Check Rejected as NSF:		
(c) Accounts Receivable	18	
Cash		18
To record amount rejected by bank and still owed by customer.		
Service Charges:		
(d) Bank Charges Expense	6	
Cash		6
To record service charge deducted by bank.		
Company Error (Understated Payment to Supplier):		
(e) Accounts Payable	9	
Cash		9
To correct error made in recording a check paid to a creditor.		

After the reconciling entries are posted, the Cash balance matches the bank reconciliation ($11,478.40).

Cash (A)			
Before reconciliation	11,391.40		
(a)	20.00	18.00	(c)
(b)	100.00	6.00	(d)
		9.00	(e)
Up-to-date balance	11,478.40		

 How's it going?   Self-Study Practice

Indicate whether (yes or no) each of the following items discovered when preparing a bank reconciliation will need to be recorded in the Cash account in the company's books.

1. Outstanding checks.
2. Deposits in transit.
3. Bank service charges.
4. NSF checks that were deposited.

After you have finished, check your answers with the solution.

Solution to Self-Study Practice

1. No (this item already was recorded when the check was written).
2. No (this item already was recorded when the cash was deposited).
3. Yes (this item will be recorded as a decrease in Cash and increase in Bank Charges Expense).
4. Yes (this item will be recorded as a decrease in Cash and increase in Accounts Receivable).

SPOTLIGHT ON   **Controls**

Granny Does Time

Grandmothers seem so trustworthy. But in one well-known case, a granny stole nearly half a million dollars from the small company where she worked as a bookkeeper. How did she do it? It was easy because the owner knew little accounting, so he gave her responsibility for all of the company's accounting work but never independently verified her work. Granny realized this lack of internal control gave her unlimited opportunity, so she wrote checks to herself and recorded them as inventory purchases. Then, when she did the bank reconciliation, she destroyed the checks to cover her tracks. Granny kept this fraud going for eight years, but then confessed after becoming overwhelmed with guilt. If you're wondering why no one ever became suspicious about the recorded inventory purchases that didn't actually occur, the next chapter will tell you why.

Learning Objective 5-5
Explain the reporting of cash.

YOU SHOULD KNOW

Cash: Money or any instrument that banks will accept for deposit and immediately credit to the company's account, such as a check, money order, or bank draft.
Cash Equivalents: Short-term, highly liquid investments purchased within three months of maturity.

REPORTING CASH

Cash, as reported on the balance sheet, includes **cash** deposited with banks, petty cash on hand, and cash equivalents. **Cash equivalents** are short-term, highly liquid investments purchased within three months of maturity. They are considered equivalent to cash because they are both readily convertible to known amounts of cash and so near to maturity that there is little risk their value will change. In your personal life, cash equivalents could include certificates of deposit (CDs) you've purchased within three months of maturity. For companies, cash equivalents include money market funds, government Treasury bills, and other highly liquid investments. Exhibit 5.10 shows how Domino's Pizza reported its $108 million in cash and cash equivalents on its year-end balance sheet. Its financial statement notes explained the $108 million included $15 million of cash and $93 million of cash equivalents.

EXHIBIT 5.10 Example of Cash Reporting

DOMINO'S PIZZA, INC.
Balance Sheet (excerpts)
At June 16, 2019

(in millions)

Assets

Current assets

Cash and Cash Equivalents	$108
Restricted Cash	153
Accounts Receivable	183
Inventory	44
Prepaids and Other Assets	37
Advertising fund assets, restricted	118
Total Current Assets	643

RESTRICTED CASH

Companies are sometimes legally or contractually required to set aside cash for a specific purpose and are not allowed to use it for day-to-day operations. This **restricted cash** must be reported separately on the balance sheet, in the manner shown in Exhibit 5.10. The notes to the financial statements of Domino's Pizza explained that the company was restricted from using its cash for day-to-day operations for two reasons. First, its financing agreements required the company to set aside $153 million in cash for future debt payments. Second, its franchise agreements required the company to set aside $118 million to be used only for promoting the Domino's Pizza brand. By reporting restricted amounts separately from the $108 million in cash and cash equivalents, Domino's more clearly conveys to financial statement users the actual amount of cash available to pay liabilities. The restricted cash in Exhibit 5.10 was classified as a current asset because it was expected to be used up within a year. Restricted cash that is not expected to be used up within a year is classified as a noncurrent asset.

> **YOU SHOULD KNOW**
>
> **Restricted Cash:** Not available for general use but rather restricted for a specific purpose.

SUPPLEMENT 5A   PETTY CASH SYSTEMS

A petty cash system involves three steps: (1) putting money into petty cash to establish a fund, (2) paying money out to reimburse others, and (3) putting money back into petty cash to replenish the fund.

> **Learning Objective 5-S1**
> Describe the operations of petty cash systems.

1. **Put money into the fund.** The company establishes the fund by writing a check to the petty cash custodian. The amount of the check equals the total estimated payments to be made from the fund over a fairly short period, such as a month or quarter. The custodian cashes the check and places the funds in the locked cash box. At this time, the petty cash still belongs to the company, so it represents an asset that must be recorded in the accounting system. Establishing a $100 petty cash fund involves the following accounting equation effects and journal entry.

>  **COACH'S TIP**
>
> Journal entries affect the Petty Cash account only when a petty cash fund is established or when its approved total increases or decreases.

1 **Analyze**

Assets		=	Liabilities	+	Stockholders' Equity
Cash	−100				
Petty Cash	+100				

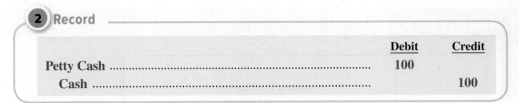

2. **Pay money out of the fund.** The custodian determines when to make payments out of the cash box following policies established by the company's managers. Usually, these policies limit the size and nature of payments to items such as postage, taxi fares, and low-cost supplies. Petty cash policies require that payments be documented using a petty cash receipt signed by both the custodian and the payee. The custodian attaches any related documents, such as a bill of sale or an invoice, to the petty cash receipt and places it in the cash box. Documents such as these act as controls to ensure petty cash payments are made only for approved purchases. Because these receipts involve small amounts, **payments out of petty cash are not recorded in the accounting system until the fund is replenished.** To ensure the fund is operating appropriately, however, most companies require that an internal auditor or manager conduct surprise audits of the fund. At any point, the sum of the petty cash receipts and the funds in the cash box should equal the fund's total when it was established.

3. **Replenish the fund.** When the amount of cash in the cash box runs low, the petty cash custodian asks that the fund be replenished. To support this request, the petty cash custodian presents a summary of payments and all supporting petty cash receipts to the accounting department. After reviewing these items, the accounting department marks the receipts "paid" and issues a check to the custodian for the total amount spent. The amount of the check is recorded as a reduction in Cash (with a credit), and the various items that were paid are recorded in their corresponding accounts (with debits). For example, the following accounting equation effects and journal entry would be recorded if the custodian requested a check for $67 to replenish the fund after payments were made for supplies ($40), travel ($21), and a dozen Krispy Kreme donuts awarded to the employee of the month ($6).

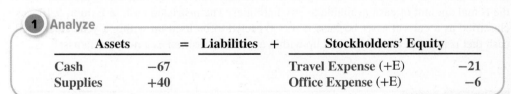

Assets		=	Liabilities	+	Stockholders' Equity	
Cash	−67				Travel Expense (+E)	−21
Supplies	+40				Office Expense (+E)	−6

2 **Record**

	Debit	Credit
Supplies	40	
Travel Expense	21	
Office Expense	6	
Cash		67

Because petty cash transactions are recorded only when the fund is replenished, some companies have a policy of replenishing all petty cash funds at the end of each accounting period so that the expenses are recorded in the appropriate period. Other companies do not observe this policy on the grounds that unrecorded petty cash transactions are "immaterial" (too small to affect the decisions of financial statement users).

No. 22   **Petty Cash Receipt**

Paid:	$21.00	**Date:**	September 9
To:	Yellow Checker Cab (receipt attached)		
For:	Taxi Fare to Airport	**Account:**	Travel Expense

Payment Approved by: Payment Received by:

Chris Cattan   *John Giovanni*
Custodian

🔨 **COACH'S TIP**

If the total of cash and receipts in the cash box is less (or more) than the fund total, the fund is referred to as being **short** (or **over**). Shortages (overages) are recorded in an account called **Cash Shortage (Overage)** and reported on the income statement as a miscellaneous expense (or revenue).

---

2 **Record**

	Debit	Credit
Petty Cash	100	
Cash		100

REVIEW THE CHAPTER

DEMONSTRATION CASE

Bardash Corporation has just viewed its checking account statement for the month ended September 30. The bank's statement of account showed the following:

Bank balance, September 1	$1,150
Deposits during September	650
Checks cleared during September	900
Bank service charge	25
Interest earned	5
EFT received from Bardash customer	20
NSF check written by Bardash customer	15
Bank balance, September 30	885

The bank had not yet reported a deposit of $50 made on September 29 and a Bardash check for $200 had not cleared its account. Bardash's September 30 Cash balance was $759. The company's accountant discovered that one of Bardash's checks for $19 paid on account to a supplier had been recorded as $10.

Required:

1. Complete the September bank reconciliation. What changes, if any, does Bardash need to make to its cash records?
2. Why is it important for individuals and businesses to prepare a bank reconciliation each month?

Suggested Solution

1. Bardash's bank reconciliation:

Updates to Bank Statement		Updates to Company's Books	
September 30 cash balance	$ 885	September 30 cash balance	$759
Additions		Additions	
Deposit in transit	50	(a) Interest earned	5
Deductions		(b) EFT from customer	20
Outstanding check	(200)	Deductions	
Up-to-date cash balance	$ 735	(c) Bank service charge	(25)
		(d) NSF check	(15)
		(e) Recording error	(9)
		Up-to-date cash balance	$735

Bardash needs to record the following reconciling entries:

		Debit	Credit
(a)	**Cash**	5	
	Interest Revenue		5
(b)	**Cash**	20	
	Accounts Receivable		20
(c)	**Bank Charges Expense**	25	
	Cash		25
(d)	**Accounts Receivable**	15	
	Cash		15
(e)	**Accounts Payable**	9	
	Cash		9

2. Bank statements, whether personal or business, should be reconciled each month to help ensure that a correct balance is reflected in the depositor's books. Failure to reconcile a bank statement increases the chance an error will not be discovered and may result in NSF checks being written. Businesses prepare a bank reconciliation for an additional reason: The up-to-date balance calculated during the reconciliation is included in Cash on the balance sheet.

CHAPTER SUMMARY

LO 5-1   **Define fraud and internal control.**

- Fraud is an attempt to deceive others for personal gain. Employee fraud includes collusion, asset misappropriation, and financial statement fraud.

- Internal control consists of the actions taken by people at every level of an organization to achieve its objectives relating to operations, reporting, and compliance. The components of internal control include the control environment, risk assessment, control activities, information and communication, and monitoring activities.

LO 5-2   **Explain common principles and limitations of internal control.**

- Most employees working within a company will encounter five basic principles: (1) establish responsibility for each task; (2) segregate duties so that one employee cannot initiate, record, approve, and handle a single transaction; (3) restrict access to those employees who have been assigned responsibility; (4) document procedures performed; and (5) independently verify work done by others inside and outside the business.

- Internal controls may be limited by cost, human error, and fraud.

LO 5-3   **Apply internal control principles to cash receipts and payments.**

- When applied to cash receipts, internal control principles require that (1) cashiers be held individually responsible for the cash they receive; (2) different individuals be assigned to receive, maintain custody of, and record cash; (3) cash be stored in a locked safe until it has been securely deposited in a bank; (4) cash register receipts, cash count sheets, daily cash summary reports, and bank deposit slips be prepared to document the cash received and deposited; and (5) cash register receipts be matched to cash counts and deposit slips to independently verify that all cash was received and deposited.

- When applied to cash payments, internal control principles require that (1) only certain individuals or departments initiate purchase requests; (2) different individuals be assigned to order, receive, and pay for purchases; (3) access to checks and valuable property be restricted; (4) purchase requisitions, purchase orders, receiving reports, and prenumbered checks be used to document the work done; and (5) each step in the payment process occurs only after the preceding step has been independently verified using the documents listed in (4).

LO 5-4   **Perform the key control of reconciling cash to bank statements.**

- The bank reconciliation requires determining two categories of items: (1) those that have been recorded in the company's books but not in the bank's statement of account and (2) those that have been reported in the bank's statement of account but not in the company's books. The second category of items provides the data needed to change the Cash account to the balance that will be reported on the balance sheet.

LO 5-5   **Explain the reporting of cash.**

- Cash is combined with cash equivalents in current assets. Cash equivalents are highly liquid investments purchased within three months of maturity.

- Restricted cash is reported separately, as a current asset if expected to be used up within one year or, if not, as a noncurrent asset.

KEY TERMS

Bank Reconciliation p. 227
Cash p. 232
Cash Equivalents p. 232
Fraud p. 214
Imprest System p. 226

Internal Control p. 217
Loan Covenants p. 215
NSF (Non-Sufficient Funds)
   Checks p. 229
Restricted Cash p. 233

Robotic Process Automation (RPA) p. 226
Sarbanes-Oxley Act (SOX) p. 216
Segregation of Duties p. 219
Voucher System p. 224

See complete definitions in the glossary in the back of this text.

HOMEWORK HELPER

Alternative terms

- The up-to-date ending cash balance is also called the true cash balance or correct cash balance.

Helpful reminders

- When preparing a bank reconciliation, your goals are to determine which transactions the bank has not yet processed and which transactions your company has not yet processed. You will record transactions correctly processed by the bank but not yet processed by your company.
- If you are having trouble reconciling cash balances, you may be overlooking an outstanding check or deposit. Try counting the number of checks or deposits processed by the bank and by your company to ensure you have identified them all. Or use the out-of-balance tips in the Chapter 3 Homework Helper.

Frequent mistakes

- Do not change your cash records for reconciling items related to updating the bank statement.

PRACTICE MATERIAL

QUESTIONS (⊖ Symbol indicates questions that require analysis from more than one perspective.)

1. What are three categories of employee fraud? Which is most common? Which is associated with the largest losses?

2. What are the three points of the fraud triangle? Is fraud more or less likely to occur if one of these elements is missing?

3. Why would managers misrepresent the financial results of their companies?

4. What aspect(s) of the Sarbanes-Oxley Act might counteract the incentive to commit fraud?

5. What aspect(s) of the Sarbanes-Oxley Act might reduce opportunities for fraud?

6. What aspect(s) of the Sarbanes-Oxley Act might allow honest employees to prevail?

7. What three types of objectives are the focus of internal control?

8. What are the five components of an internal control system?

9. What are five common internal control principles?

10. Why is it a good idea to assign each task to only one employee?

11. Why should responsibilities for certain duties, like cash handling and cash recording, be separated? What types of responsibilities should be separated?

12. What are some of the methods for restricting access?

13. In what ways does documentation act as a control?

14. In what ways can independent verification occur?

15. In what way does a mandatory vacation policy act as a control?

16. What are two limitations of internal control?

17. What is the primary internal control goal for cash receipts?

18. What internal control functions are performed by a cash register and point-of-sale system? How are these functions performed when cash is received by mail? ⊖

19. How is cash received in person independently verified?

20. What is the primary internal control goal for cash payments?

21. What are the purposes of a bank reconciliation? What balances are reconciled?

22. Define cash and cash equivalents and indicate the types of items that should be reported as cash and cash equivalents.

23. Define restricted cash and indicate how it should be reported on the balance sheet.

24. (Supplement 5A) What are the arguments for and against replenishing all petty cash funds at the end of each accounting period? ⊖

MULTIPLE CHOICE

1. Which of the following is **not** an element of the fraud triangle?
   a. Opportunity
   b. Control environment
   c. Incentive
   d. Rationalization

2. Which of the following is **not** a Sarbanes-Oxley Act requirement intended to reduce fraud opportunities?
   a. Increase fines and jail sentences for fraud perpetrators.
   b. All public companies establish an audit committee of independent directors.
   c. Management of all public companies evaluates and reports on the effectiveness of internal control over financial reporting.
   d. External auditors of large public companies evaluate and report on the effectiveness of internal control over financial reporting.

3. Which of the following is **not** a component of internal control?
   a. Environmental assessment
   b. Control activities
   c. Information and communication
   d. Monitoring activities

4. Which of the following does not enhance internal control?
   a. Assigning different duties to different employees
   b. Ensuring adequate documentation is maintained
   c. Allowing access only when required to complete assigned duties
   d. None of the above—all enhance internal control.

5. Which of the following internal control principles underlies the requirement that all customers be given a sales receipt?
   a. Segregate duties
   b. Establish responsibility
   c. Restrict access
   d. Document procedures

6. A company indicates the condition of goods obtained on which of the following documents?
   a. Purchase requisition
   b. Purchase order
   c. Receiving report
   d. Supplier invoice

7. What document signals that a company should record the purchase of goods on account?
   a. Purchase requisition
   b. Purchase order
   c. Receiving report
   d. Supplier invoice

8. Upon review of your company's bank statement, you discover that you recently deposited a check from a customer that was rejected by your bank as NSF. Which of the following describes the actions to be taken when preparing your company's bank reconciliation?

	Balance per Bank	Balance per Book
a.	Decrease	No change
b.	Increase	Decrease
c.	No change	Decrease
d.	Decrease	Increase

9. Upon review of the most recent bank statement, you discover that a check was made out to your supplier for $76 but was recorded in your Cash and Accounts Payable accounts as $67. Which of the following describes the actions to be taken when preparing your bank reconciliation?

	Balance per Bank	Balance per Book
a.	Decrease	No change
b.	Increase	Decrease
c.	No change	Decrease
d.	Decrease	Increase

10. Which of the following correctly describes how to report cash?
    a. Restricted cash is always reported as a current asset.
    b. Cash can be combined with cash equivalents.
    c. Cash can be combined with restricted cash.
    d. Cash equivalents can be combined with restricted cash.

> For answers to the Multiple-Choice Questions **see page Q1** located in the last section of the book.

MINI-EXERCISES

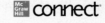

LO 5-1   M5-1 Matching Circumstances to the Fraud Triangle

Match each of the following circumstances to the corresponding element of the fraud triangle by entering the appropriate letter in the space provided.

_____ 1. Employee has significant personal debt.

_____ 2. One employee receives and deposits customer checks.

_____ 3. CFO feels she is underpaid relative to other financial officers.

_____ 4. Manager approval is not required for expense reports.

A. Incentive

B. Opportunity

C. Rationalization

M5-2 Identifying Internal Controls over Financial Reporting   LO 5-2, 5-3

Fox Erasing has a system of internal control with the following procedures. Match the procedure to the corresponding internal control principle.

Procedure	Internal Control Principle
____ 1. The treasurer signs checks.	A. Establish responsibility
____ 2. The treasurer is not allowed to make bank deposits.	B. Segregate duties
	C. Restrict access
____ 3. The company's checks are prenumbered.	D. Document procedures
____ 4. Unused checks are stored in the vault.	E. Independently verify
____ 5. A bank reconciliation is prepared each month.	

M5-3 Identifying Internal Control Principles Applied by a Merchandiser   LO 5-2, 5-3

Identify the internal control principle represented by each point in the following diagram.

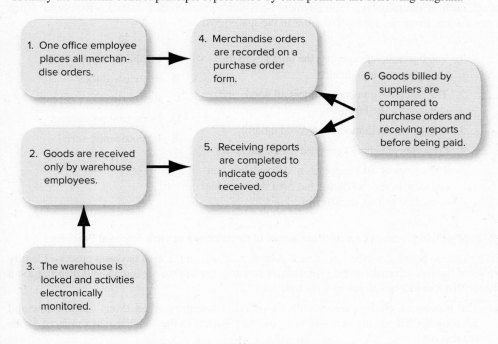

1. One office employee places all merchandise orders.

4. Merchandise orders are recorded on a purchase order form.

6. Goods billed by suppliers are compared to purchase orders and receiving reports before being paid.

2. Goods are received only by warehouse employees.

5. Receiving reports are completed to indicate goods received.

3. The warehouse is locked and activities electronically monitored.

M5-4 Matching Cash Receipt Processes to Internal Control Principles   LO 5-2, 5-3

Match each of the following cash receipt activities to the internal control principle to which it best relates. Enter the appropriate letter in the space provided.

____ 1. A list of checks received in the mail is prepared.	A. Establish responsibility
____ 2. Total cash receipts are compared to the amount on the bank deposit slip.	B. Segregate duties
	C. Restrict access
____ 3. A password is required to open the cash register.	D. Document procedures
____ 4. Price changes at the checkout require a manager's approval.	E. Independently verify
____ 5. Cashiers are required to count the cash in their register at the beginning and end of each shift.	

M5-5 Identifying Internal Control Weaknesses in Descriptions of Cash Receipts Process   LO 5-3

Each situation below describes an internal control weakness in the cash receipts process. Identify which of the five internal control principles is violated, explain the weakness, and then suggest a change that would improve internal control.

a. Cashiers prepare a cash count summary, attach tapes from the cash register showing total receipts, and then prepare a bank deposit slip, which they take to the bank for deposit. After the deposit is made, all documents are forwarded to the accounting department for review and recording.

b.   The receptionist opens the mail each morning, sorts it into piles, and then gives checks received from customers to the mail clerk for delivery to the accounting department, where a cash receipts list is prepared.

c.   The accounting department receives cash register totals each day and promptly files them by cash register number. The accounting department also receives cash count sheets from cashiers each day and files them by employee number. The accounting department receives stamped bank deposit slips the morning after the bank deposit is made, prepares the journal entry, and files the deposit slips by date.

d.   To avoid boredom, the employee who works the cash register at the movie theater trades off with either the employee who collects the tickets or an employee who works at the concessions stand.

e.   To enhance efficiency, cashiers are assigned the responsibility of authorizing price changes at the cash register.

LO 5-3   **M5-6**   **Matching Cash Payment Processes to Internal Control Principles**

Match each of the following cash payment activities to the internal control principle to which it best relates. Enter the appropriate letter in the space provided.

____ 1. The business manager has the only key to the check-signing equipment.	A.	Establish responsibility
____ 2. The purchasing manager orders all goods and services for the business.	B.	Segregate duties
	C.	Restrict access
____ 3. A bank reconciliation is prepared monthly.	D.	Document procedures
____ 4. Prenumbered checks are used for all payments.	E.	Independently verify
____ 5. The company asks suppliers to deliver their merchandise to the warehouse but mail their invoices to the accounting department.		

LO 5-3   **M5-7**   **Identifying Internal Control Weaknesses in Descriptions of Cash Payment Processes**

Each situation below describes an internal control weakness in the cash payment process. Identify which of the five internal control principles is violated, explain the weakness, and then suggest a change that would improve internal control.

a.   The warehouse clerk is responsible for ordering inventory when levels become low and advising the accounting department to issue a payment to the supplier when ordered goods are received.

b.   At the end of each week, the accountant gives the owner a stack of checks to sign. Rather than examine the supporting documentation, the owner simply asks the accountant what each check is for and then merrily signs it.

c.   The check-signing machine is stored with a supply of blank checks in the lunch room closet.

d.   Purchase orders can be approved by the purchasing manager, accountant, or warehouse supervisor, depending on who is least busy.

LO 5-4   **M5-8**   **Organizing Items on the Bank Reconciliation**

Indicate whether the following items would be added (+) or subtracted (−) from the company's books or the bank statement side of a bank reconciliation.

Reconciling Item	Bank Statement	Company's Books
a. Outstanding checks of $12,000		
b. Bank service charge of $15		
c. Deposit in transit of $2,300		
d. Interest earned of $5		

LO 5-4   **M5-9**   **Preparing Journal Entries after a Bank Reconciliation**

Using the information in M5-8, prepare any journal entries needed to adjust the company's books.

M5-10 Identifying Outstanding Checks   LO 5-4

Use the following bank statement and T-account to identify outstanding checks that should be included in the May 31 bank reconciliation.

BANK STATEMENT				
Date	Checks	Deposits	Other	Balance
May 1				$200
4	#2 $ 10	$ 50		240
12	#4 100		NSF Check $50	90
28	#5 20			70
30	#6 15	200		255
May 31	#8 55		Service charge 5	195

Cash (A)			
May 1	200		
May 3	50	10	May 3 #2
		70	May 4 #3
		100	May 8 #4
		20	May 11 #5
		15	May 21 #6
May 29	200	25	May 29 #7
May 30	150	55	May 30 #8
May 31	305		

M5-11 Identifying Outstanding Deposits   LO 5-4

Use the information in M5-10 to identify outstanding deposits that should be included in the May 31 bank reconciliation.

M5-12 Preparing a Bank Reconciliation   LO 5-4

Use the information in M5-10 to prepare the May 31 bank reconciliation.

M5-13 Accounting for Unrecorded Items on Bank Reconciliation   LO 5-4

Use your answer to M5-12 to prepare any journal entries needed as a result of the May 31 bank reconciliation.

M5-14 Reporting Cash and Cash Equivalents   LO 5-5

Indicate (Yes or No) whether each of the following is properly included in Cash and Cash Equivalents.

_____ 1. $10,000 of government Treasury bills purchased 10 days prior to their maturity.

_____ 2. $50,000 of government Treasury bills purchased to satisfy a legal requirement to set aside funds for a landfill cleanup.

_____ 3. $10,000 of cash owed by customers on sales made within 20 days of year-end.

_____ 4. $1,000 of cash in the petty cash custodian's locked cash box.

M5-15 (Supplement 5A) Accounting for Petty Cash Transactions   LO 5-S1

The petty cash custodian reported the following transactions during the month. Prepare the journal entry to record the replenishment of the fund.

A $10 cash payment is made to Starbucks to purchase coffee for a business client, a $40 cash payment is made for supplies purchased from Office Depot, and a $30 cash payment is made to UPS to deliver goods to a customer.

Starbucks
Office Depot
UPS

M5-16 (Supplement 5A) Accounting for Petty Cash Transactions   LO 5-S1

On September 30, Hector's petty cash fund of $100 is replenished. At the time, the cash box contained $18 cash and receipts for taxi fares ($40), delivery charges ($12), and office supplies ($30). Prepare the journal entry to record the replenishment of the fund.

EXERCISES

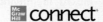

LO 5-1, 5-2 **E5-1 Identifying Internal Control Principle and Financial Reporting Control Objective**

At most movie theaters, one employee sells tickets and another employee collects them. One night, when you're at the movies, your friend comments that this is a waste of the theater's money.

Required:

1. Identify the name of the control principle to which this situation relates.
2. Explain to your friend what kind of fraud could occur if the same person did both jobs.

LO 5-1, 5-2 **E5-2 Identifying Financial Reporting Control Objectives**

Your student club recently volunteered to go door-to-door collecting cash donations on behalf of a local charity. The charity's accountant went berserk when you said you wrote receipts only for donors who asked for one.

Required:

Identify the control principle that you violated and explain how that violation could allow fraud to occur. What controls might be appropriate to use in the future?

LO 5-3 **E5-3 Identifying Internal Control Principles in Cash Receipt Processes**

Locker Rentals Corp. (LRC) operates locker rental services at several locations throughout the city including the airport, bus depot, shopping malls, and athletics facilities. Unlike some of the old mechanical lockers that charge a fixed amount per use, LRC's lockers operate electronically and are able to charge based on hours of use. The locker system transmits a daily message to LRC's office indicating the number of hours that lockers have been used, which the office manager uses to determine when cash should be picked up at each location. LRC's cash receipts system is described below.

   a. Two employees ("cash collection clerks") are responsible for collecting cash from the lockers. Based on instructions from the office manager, one clerk collects cash from specific locations on the west side of the city and the other collects from specific locations on the east side.

   b. When each cash collection clerk returns with the cash, a supervisor counts the cash and prepares a cash count sheet.

   c. The supervisor summarizes the cash count sheets in a prenumbered daily cash summary and files the prenumbered cash count sheets by date.

   d. The supervisor places the cash in a locked cashbox until it is taken to the bank for deposit.

   e. The supervisor, not the cash collection clerks, takes the cash to the bank for deposit.

   f. The supervisor prepares a duplicate deposit slip, which the bank stamps after the deposit is made to indicate the date and amount of the deposit.

   g. The supervisor sends the stamped bank deposit slip and daily cash summary to the accountant, who compares them before preparing a journal entry debiting Cash and crediting Locker Rental Revenue.

Required:

1. For each statement (*a*)–(*g*), identify the internal control principle being applied.
2. After several months, LRC's supervisor is arrested for stealing nearly $10,000 from the company. Identify the internal control weakness that allowed this theft to occur.

LO 5-3 **E5-4 Identifying Internal Control Principles in Cash Payment Processes**

Home Repair Corp. (HRC) operates a building maintenance and repair business. The business has three office employees—a sales manager, a materials/crew manager, and an accountant. HRC's cash payments system is described below.

   a. After a contract is signed with a customer, the sales manager prepares a prenumbered purchase requisition form that indicates the materials needed for the work at the repair site.

b. Based on the purchase requisition form, the materials/crew manager prepares and sends a prenumbered purchase order to suppliers of materials, advising them of the specific materials needed and the repair site to which they should be delivered.

c. The materials/crew manager is the only employee authorized to order goods.

d. Upon receiving a supplier's invoice, the accountant compares it to terms indicated on the purchase order, noting in particular the prices charged and quantities ordered.

e. If these documents are in agreement, the accountant prepares a prenumbered check, stamps the invoice "paid," and prepares a journal entry to record the payment. The journal entry explanation references the sequential number on the purchase order.

f. HRC's owner prepares a monthly bank reconciliation and reviews checks returned with the bank statement to ensure they have been issued to valid suppliers.

Required:

1. For each statement (a)–(f), identify the internal control principle being applied.

2. Using the above description, prepare a list of steps and documentation similar to the first two columns of Exhibit 5.6. Also include a third column that lists the individuals performing each step. Which document in Exhibit 5.6 is excluded from the above description?

3. After several months, HRC's materials/crew manager is arrested for having $20,000 of materials delivered to his home but charged to the company. Identify the internal control weakness that allowed this theft to occur.

E5-5 Preparing a Bank Reconciliation and Journal Entries and Reporting Cash　　　　**LO 5-4**

Hills Company's June 30 bank statement and the June ledger account for cash are summarized here:

BANK STATEMENT				
	Checks	**Deposits**	**Other**	**Balance**
Balance, June 1				$ 7,200
Deposits during June		$18,000		25,200
Checks cleared during June	$19,100			6,100
Bank service charges			$30	6,070
Balance, June 30				6,070

Cash (A)					
June 1	Balance	6,800			
June	Deposits	19,000	19,400	Checks written	June
June 30	Balance	6,400			

Required:

1. Prepare a bank reconciliation. A comparison of the checks written with the checks that have cleared the bank shows outstanding checks of $700. Some of the checks that cleared in June were written prior to June. No deposits in transit were noted in May, but a deposit is in transit at the end of June.

2. Give any journal entries that should be made as a result of the bank reconciliation.

3. What is the balance in the Cash account after the reconciliation entries?

4. In addition to the balance in its bank account, Hills Company also has $300 of petty cash on hand. This amount is recorded in a separate account called Petty Cash on Hand. What is the total amount of cash that should be reported on the balance sheet at June 30?

LO 5-4

E5-6 Preparing a Bank Reconciliation and Journal Entries and Reporting Cash

The September 30 bank statement for Cadieux Company and the September ledger account for cash are summarized here:

BANK STATEMENT				
	Checks	**Deposits**	**Other**	**Balance**
Balance, September 1				$2,000
September 7			NSF check $100	1,900
September 11		$3,000		4,900
September 12	#101 $ 800			4,100
September 17	#102 1,700			2,400
September 26	#103 2,300			100
September 29			EFT deposit 150	250
September 30			Service charge 20	230

Cash (A)					
Sept 1	Balance	2,000			
Sept 10		3,000	800	Sept 10	#101
Sept 30		2,500	1,700	Sept 15	#102
			2,300	Sept 22	#103
			50	Sept 28	#104
Sept 30	Balance	2,650			

No outstanding checks and no deposits in transit were noted in August. However, there are deposits in transit and checks outstanding at the end of September. The NSF check and EFT involved transactions with Cadieux Company's customers.

Required:

1. Prepare a bank reconciliation.
2. Give any journal entries that should be made as the result of the bank reconciliation.
3. What should the balance in the Cash account be after recording the journal entries in requirement 2?
4. If the company also has $400 of petty cash on hand (recorded in a separate account), what total amount of cash should the company report on the September 30 balance sheet?

LO 5-5

E5-7 Reporting Cash, Cash Equivalents, and Restricted Cash

Expedia, Inc.

Expedia, Inc., reported total cash of $4,877 million at June 30, 2019. Of this amount, $619 million was set aside and could be used only for specific purposes, as defined in legal contracts and regulations; $1,439 million was invested in money market funds and time deposits with original maturities of less than 90 days; and the remaining $2,819 million was held in bank accounts. Expedia also reported $631 million in short-term investments (maturing in 90–360 days), $522 million of deferred revenue, $3,021 million of accounts receivable, and $295 million of prepaid insurance.

TIP: Not all accounts listed are current assets.

Required:

Show the current assets section of Expedia's balance sheet.

LO 5-5

E5-8 Preparing a Balance Sheet

Gatti Corporation reported the following balances at June 30.

Accounts Payable	$110	Deferred Revenue	$ 40	Petty Cash	$ 5
Accounts Receivable	70	Depreciation Expense	15	Restricted Cash (short-term)	20
Accumulated Depreciation—Equipment	40	Dividends	5	Retained Earnings	40
Cash	10	Equipment	300	Salaries and Wages Expense	400
Cash Equivalents	15	Notes Payable (long-term)	60	Service Revenue	480
Common Stock	100	Notes Payable (short-term)	30	Utilities Expense	60

Required:

1. What amount should be reported as "Cash and Cash Equivalents"?
2. Prepare a classified balance sheet. Do not show the components that add up to your answer in requirement 1, but rather show only the line "Cash and Cash Equivalents."

E5-9 (Supplement 5A) Recording Petty Cash Transactions

LO 5-S1

Sunshine Health established a $100 petty cash fund on January 1. From January 2 through 10, payments were made from the fund, as listed below. On January 12, the fund had only $10 remaining; a check was written to replenish the fund.

a. January 2—Paid cash for deliveries to customers—$23.
b. January 7—Paid cash for taxi fare incurred by office manager—$50.
c. January 10—Paid cash for pens and other office supplies—$17.

Required:

1. Prepare the journal entry, if any, required on January 1.
2. Prepare the journal entries, if any, required on January 2 through 10.
3. Prepare the journal entries, if any, required on January 12.

E5-10 (Supplement 5A) Recording Petty Cash Transactions

LO 5-S1

Mountain Air Company established a $200 petty cash fund on January 1. From January 3 through 15, payments were made from the fund, as listed below. On January 17, the fund was replenished with a check for $158.

a. January 3—Paid cash for deliveries to customers—$43.
b. January 8—Paid cash to restaurant for catering office lunch—$83.
c. January 15—Paid cash for supplies—$32.

Required:

1. Prepare the journal entry, if any, required on January 1.
2. Prepare the journal entries, if any, required on January 3 through 15.
3. Prepare the journal entries, if any, required on January 17.

COACHED PROBLEMS

LO 5-3

CP5-1 Identifying Internal Control Principles in Cash Receipts and Disbursements

The following procedures are used by Richardson Light Works.

a. When customers pay cash for lighting products, a receipt is issued to the customer.
b. When customers pay cash for lighting products, the cash is placed in a cash register.
c. At the end of each day, a cash count sheet is prepared.
d. The manager checks the accuracy of the cash count sheet before taking the cash to the bank for deposit.
e. Receiving reports are prepared to indicate the quantity and condition of goods received from suppliers.
f. Warehouse personnel are not allowed to fill in for absent accounting department staff, and accounting department staff are not allowed to fill in for absent warehouse personnel.

Required:

1. For each statement (a)–(f), identify the internal control principle being applied.
2. If the company's accountant pays supplier invoices by check without comparing to purchase orders and receiving reports, what internal control principle is violated?

LO 5-4, 5-5   **CP5-2 Preparing a Bank Reconciliation and Journal Entries and Reporting Cash**

The April 30 bank statement for KMaxx Company and the April ledger account for cash are summarized here:

BANK STATEMENT					
	Checks		**Deposits**	**Other**	**Balance**
Balance, April 1					$6,000
April 5	#101	$ 700			5,300
April 9			$2,500		7,800
April 12	#102	200			7,600
April 19	#103	500			7,100
April 22	#104	1,000			6,100
April 27				EFT payment $200	5,900
April 29				NSF check 100	5,800
April 30				Service charge 25	5,775

Cash (A)					
April 1 Balance	6,000				
April 8	2,500	700	April 2	#101	
April 28	500	200	April 10	#102	
		500	April 15	#103	
		1,100	April 20	#104	
		300	April 29	#105	
April 30 Balance	6,200				

No outstanding checks and no deposits in transit were noted in March. However, there are deposits in transit and checks outstanding at the end of April. The EFT involved an automatic monthly payment to one of KMaxx's creditors. Check #104 was written for $1,100. The NSF check had been received from a customer.

Required:

1. Prepare a bank reconciliation for April.
    TIP: Put a check mark beside each item that appears on both the bank statement and what's already been recorded in the accounting records (shown in the T-account). Items left unchecked will be used in the bank reconciliation.
2. Give any journal entries that should be made as a result of the bank reconciliation.
    TIP: Remember to make entries only for items that affect the company's books, not the bank.
3. What should the balance in the Cash account be after recording the journal entries in requirement 2?
4. If the company also has $1,000 of petty cash on hand (recorded in a separate account), what total amount should the company report as Cash and Cash Equivalents on the April 30 balance sheet?

LO 5-4, 5-5   **CP5-3 Identifying Outstanding Checks and Deposits in Transit and Preparing a Bank Reconciliation and Journal Entries**

The August bank statement and cash T-account for Martha Company follow:

BANK STATEMENT				
Date	**Checks**	**Deposits**	**Other**	**Balance**
Aug. 1				$17,470
2	$ 300			17,170
3		$12,000		29,170
4	400			28,770
5	250			28,520
9	890			27,630
10	310			27,320
15		4,000		31,320
21	400			30,920
24	21,000			9,920
25		7,000		16,920
30	800			16,120
30			Interest earned $20	16,140
31			Service charge 10	16,130

Cash (A)				
Aug. 1 Balance	17,470			
Deposits		Checks written		
Aug. 2	12,000	300	Aug. 1	
12	4,000	400	2	
24	7,000	250	3	
31	5,000	310	4	
		890	5	
		290	15	
		550	17	
		800	18	
		400	19	
		21,000	23	
Aug. 31 Balance	20,280			

No deposits were in transit and no checks were outstanding at the end of July.

Required:

1. Identify and list the deposits in transit at the end of August.
   TIP: Put a check mark beside each item that appears on both the bank statement and what's already been recorded in the accounting records (shown in the T-account).
2. Identify and list the outstanding checks at the end of August.
3. Prepare a bank reconciliation for August.
   TIP: Any item in the accounting records without check marks should appear on the bank statement side of the bank reconciliation. Any items in the bank statement without check marks should appear on the company's books side of the bank reconciliation.
4. Give any journal entries that the company should make as a result of the bank reconciliation.
5. After the reconciliation journal entries are posted, what balance will be reflected in the Cash account in the ledger?
6. If the company also has $100 of petty cash on hand, which is recorded in a different account called Petty Cash on Hand, what total amount of Cash and Cash Equivalents should be reported on the August 31 balance sheet?

LO 5-5, 5-S1   **CP5-4 (Supplement 5A) Reporting Petty Cash Transactions**

Superior Cabinets maintains a petty cash fund for minor business expenditures. The petty cash custodian, Mo Smith, describes the events that occurred during the last two months:

a.   I established the fund by cashing a Superior Cabinets check for $300 made payable to me.
b.   Liz Clay provided a receipt for $50 for various supplies. I paid $50 cash to her.
c.   James Flyer provided a $70 taxi receipt, so I paid $70 cash to him.
d.   Ricky Ricota claimed to do photocopying for Superior Cabinets at The UPS Store for $97 but had misplaced the receipt. He gave me a signed memo explaining what happened and I paid $97 cash to him.
e.   On the last day of the month, I prepared a summary of expenditures and requested the fund be replenished. I received and cashed a Superior Cabinets check for $217, placing the cash into the locked cash box.
f.   James Flyer provided receipts for taxi costs ($75), so I paid $75 cash to him.
g.   Woo Riun provided a $147 receipt from a local delivery company for an expedited delivery to a customer. I paid her $147 cash.
h.   Ricky Ricota claimed to have purchased $35 of envelopes, but again he had misplaced the receipt. He showed me a big stack of envelopes and signed another memo explaining what happened, so I paid him $35 cash.
i.   After requesting that the fund be replenished, I received and cashed a Superior Cabinets check for $257, placing the cash into the locked cash box.
j.   After suggesting that the petty cash fund be increased, I received and cashed a Superior Cabinets check for $100 cash, which I placed in the locked cash box.

Required:

1. Prepare journal entries where required.
    TIP: Remember that petty cash journal entries are recorded only when the fund is established and reimbursed, not when each payment is made.
2. If Superior Cabinets has $1,000 cash in the bank, $500 of government Treasury bills purchased last month with a six-week maturity, and $750 of cash set aside for legal reasons, how much will the company report on the balance sheet as "Cash and Cash Equivalents"?
    TIP: Don't forget to include the amount in the Petty Cash fund.

GROUP A PROBLEMS

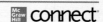

LO 5-3   **PA5-1 Identifying Internal Control Principles in Cash Receipts and Disbursements**

The following procedures are used by The Taco Truck (TTT).

a.   TTT has two employees given the following tasks: the counter staff person's job is to handle all customer interactions, whereas it is up to the manager to do all food preparation and business management.
b.   Customers pay for all food orders in cash, which is placed in a cash register.
c.   At the end of each day, the counter staff person counts the cash and prepares a cash count sheet.
d.   At the end of the day, the manager counts the cash and signs the cash count sheet if he agrees with the amount reported by the counter staff person, and takes it for deposit.
e.   Orders for drink cups, straws, condiments, and other supplies are written on prenumbered purchase order forms.

Required:

1. For each statement (a)–(e), identify the internal control principle being applied.
2. If the counter staff person were to count the cash *and* take it for deposit, what internal control principle would be violated?

LO 5-4, 5-5   **PA5-2 Preparing a Bank Reconciliation and Journal Entries and Reporting Cash**

The bookkeeper at Martin Company has asked you to prepare a bank reconciliation as of May 31. The May 31 bank statement and the May T-account for cash (summarized) are below.
    Martin Company's bank reconciliation at the end of April showed a cash balance of $18,800. No deposits were in transit at the end of April, but a deposit was in transit at the end of May.

BANK STATEMENT

	Checks		Deposits	Other		Balance
Balance, May 1						$18,800
May 2			$ 8,000			26,800
May 5	#301	$11,000				15,800
May 7	#302	6,000				9,800
May 8			10,000			19,800
May 14	#303	500				19,300
May 17				Interest	$120	19,420
May 22				NSF check	280	19,140
May 27	#304	4,600				14,540
May 31				Service charge	60	14,480
Balance, May 31						14,480

Cash (A)

May 1	Balance	18,800			
May 1		8,000	11,000	#301	May 2
May 7		10,000	6,000	#302	May 4
May 29		6,000	500	#303	May 11
			4,600	#304	May 23
			1,300	#305	May 29
May 31	Balance	19,400			

Required:

1. Prepare a bank reconciliation for May.
2. Prepare any journal entries required as a result of the bank reconciliation. Why are they necessary?
3. After the reconciliation journal entries are posted, what balance will be reflected in the Cash account in the ledger?
4. If the company also has $50 of petty cash on hand, which is recorded in a different account called Petty Cash on Hand, what total amount of Cash and Cash Equivalents should be reported on the balance sheet at the end of May?

PA5-3 Identifying Outstanding Checks and Deposits in Transit and Preparing a Bank Reconciliation and Journal Entries

LO 5-4, 5-5

The December bank statement and cash T-account for Stewart Company follow:

BANK STATEMENT

Date	Checks	Deposits	Other		Balance
Dec. 1					$48,000
6	$ 7,620				40,380
11	550	$28,000			67,830
17	13,900				53,930
23		36,000			89,930
26	960				88,970
30	19,200	19,000	NSF*	$300	88,470
31			Interest earned	50	88,520
31			Service charge	150	88,370

*NSF check from J. Left, a customer.

Cash (A)			
Dec. 1 Balance	48,000		
Deposits		Checks written during December:	
Dec. 11	28,000		7,620
23	36,000		550
30	19,000		13,900
31	13,000		960
			150
			19,200
			4,500
Dec. 31 Balance	97,120		

There were no deposits in transit or outstanding checks at November 30.

Required:

1. Identify and list the deposits in transit at the end of December.
2. Identify and list the outstanding checks at the end of December.
3. Prepare a bank reconciliation for December.
4. Give any journal entries that the company should make as a result of the bank reconciliation.
5. After the reconciliation journal entries are posted, what balance will be reflected in the Cash account in the ledger?
6. If the company also has $300 of petty cash on hand, which is recorded in a different account called Petty Cash on Hand, what total amount of Cash and Cash Equivalents should be reported on the December 31 balance sheet?

LO 5-5, 5-S1   **PA5-4 (Supplement 5A) Reporting Petty Cash Transactions**

Harristown Hockey Club (HHC) maintains a petty cash fund for minor club expenditures. The petty cash custodian, Wayne Crosby, describes the events that occurred during the last two months:

a.   I established the fund by cashing a check from HHC for $250 made payable to me.
b.   Tom Canuck provided a $70 receipt for repairs to the club's computer, so I paid $70 cash to him.
c.   Kim Harra provided a receipt for $50 for various supplies she planned to use to decorate the arena later this year. I paid $50 cash to her.
d.   Trainer Jim bought some equipment that the club intends to use for the next few years. He gave me the receipt and I paid him $80.
e.   On the last day of the month, I prepared a summary of expenditures and requested the fund be replenished. I received and cashed a check from HHC for $200, placing the cash into a locked cash box.
f.   Wendy Wignes provided receipts for supplies purchased for the club's office for use next month. I paid $125 cash to her.
g.   Destiny Hook provided a phone bill showing she had paid $30 for telephone calls made to contact referees for the annual tournament. I paid her $30 cash.
h.   Gutty McTavish submitted a receipt for $35 for a haircut he received. I did not pay him.
i.   On the last day of the month, I received and cashed a check from HHC for $155, placing the cash into the locked cash box.

Required:

1. Prepare journal entries where required.
2. If HHC has $1,000 cash, $500 of government Treasury bills purchased four months ago, and $750 of cash set aside for its workers' compensation insurance, how much will the company report on the balance sheet as "Cash and Cash Equivalents"?

GROUP B PROBLEMS

PB5-1 Identifying Internal Control Principles in Cash Receipts and Disbursements   LO 5-3

The following procedures are used by Complete Wholesale Incorporated (CWI).

a. All sales are made on account, with each sale being indicated on a sequentially numbered sales invoice.
b. A cashier deposits all customer checks received in the mail, but entries in the customer records are made only by the accounting department.
c. The office receptionist is given the job of handling all customer complaints.
d. When a customer has a legitimate complaint about goods sold to the customer on account, the receptionist will send a credit memo to the accounting department to request that the customer's account be reduced.
e. The company's inventory is stored in a locked warehouse that is monitored by surveillance cameras.
f. Payments to the company's suppliers are made only after the invoice from the supplier is compared to the receiving report prepared by CWI's warehouse personnel.

Required:

1. For each statement (*a*)–(*f*), identify the internal control principle being applied.
2. CWI suspects customer account balances are being reduced for fraudulent reasons, so it will ask one of its employees to review all customer account reductions to ensure they were appropriate. For this review to be considered independent verification, should this responsibility be given to (*a*) the accounting department, (*b*) the receptionist, or (*c*) the cashier?

PB5-2 Preparing a Bank Reconciliation and Journal Entries and Reporting Cash   LO 5-4, 5-5

The bookkeeper at Tony Company has asked you to prepare a bank reconciliation as of February 29. The February bank statement and the February T-account for cash showed the following (summarized):

BANK STATEMENT						
		Checks	**Deposits**	**Other**		**Balance**
Balance, February 1						$49,400
February 2	#101	$15,000				34,400
February 4			$ 7,000			41,400
February 5				NSF	$320	41,080
February 9	#102	11,000				30,080
February 12	#103	7,500				22,580
February 14			9,500			32,080
February 19	#104	9,000				23,080
February 23			14,150			37,230
February 26	#105	6,700				30,530
February 27				Interest earned	150	30,680
February 28				Service charge	40	30,640

Cash (A)				
Feb. 1	Balance	49,400		
Feb. 2		7,000	15,000	Feb. 1 #101
Feb. 13		9,500	11,000	Feb. 7 #102
Feb. 21		14,150	7,500	Feb. 11 #103
Feb. 28		7,800	9,000	Feb. 17 #104
			6,700	Feb. 25 #105
			1,200	Feb. 29 #106
Feb. 29	Balance	37,450		

Tony Company's bank reconciliation at the end of January showed no outstanding checks. No deposits were in transit at the end of January, but a deposit was in transit at the end of February.

Required:

1. Prepare a bank reconciliation for February.
2. Prepare any journal entries required as a result of the bank reconciliation. Why are they necessary?
3. After the reconciliation journal entries are posted, what balance will be reflected in the Cash account in the ledger?
4. If the company also has $50 of petty cash on hand, which is recorded in a different account called Petty Cash on Hand, what total amount of Cash and Cash Equivalents should be reported on the balance sheet at the end of February?

LO 5-4, 5-5   **PB5-3 Identifying Outstanding Checks and Deposits in Transit and Preparing a Bank Reconciliation and Journal Entries**

The September bank statement and cash T-account for Terrick Company follow:

BANK STATEMENT				
Date	**Checks**	**Deposits**	**Other**	**Balance**
Sept. 1				$ 75,900
6	$ 4,120			71,780
13	950	$14,000		84,830
23	10,090	27,000		101,740
28	8,700			93,040
29	1,130	17,000	NSF* $500	108,410
30			Interest earned 60	108,470
30			Service charge 40	108,430
*NSF check from B. Frank, a customer.				

Cash (A)			
Sept. 1 Balance	75,900	Checks written during September:	
Deposits			4,120
Sept. 11	14,000		950
23	27,000		10,090
29	17,000		8,700
30	21,000		500
			1,130
			6,000
Sept. 30 Balance	123,410		

There were no deposits in transit or outstanding checks at August 31.

Required:

1. Identify and list the deposits in transit at the end of September.
2. Identify and list the outstanding checks at the end of September.
3. Prepare a bank reconciliation for September.
4. Give any journal entries that the company should make as a result of the bank reconciliation.
5. After the reconciliation journal entries are posted, what balance will be reflected in the Cash account in the ledger?
6. If the company also has $200 of petty cash on hand, which is recorded in a different account called Petty Cash on Hand, what total amount of Cash and Cash Equivalents should be reported on the September 30 balance sheet?

PB5-4 (Supplement 5A) Reporting Petty Cash Transactions   LO 5-5, 5-S1

Service World maintains a petty cash fund. The fund custodian encountered the following events.

a. The fund was established when a check for $300 was cashed and deposited into a locked cash box.

b. An employee submitted a receipt for a customer delivery costing $20 and was reimbursed in full from petty cash.

c. Another employee submitted a receipt for $60 for locksmith repairs to the office door and was reimbursed in full from petty cash.

d. An employee submitted a receipt for newspaper advertising that cost the company $50. She was given $50 from the petty cash box.

e. The petty cash custodian received and cashed a check that fully replenished the petty cash fund.

f. An employee submitted a receipt for $35 for supplies and was reimbursed in full from petty cash.

g. An employee submitted a receipt for $65 for filling up his personal vehicle. He was not reimbursed because it would violate company policy.

h. At the end of the month, a check was given to the petty cash custodian to not only replenish the petty cash fund but also increase the total fund to $400.

Required:

1. Prepare any required journal entries.
2. If Service World has $1,000 cash, $500 of government Treasury bills purchased last month with a six-week maturity, and $750 of cash set aside for legal reasons, how much will the company report on the balance sheet as "Cash and Cash Equivalents"?

COMPREHENSIVE PROBLEM

C5-1 Recording Transactions and Adjustments, Reconciling Items, and Preparing Financial Statements   LO 2-2, 2-4, 2-5, 3-3, 3-5, 4-2, 4-3, 4-4, 5-4, 5-5

On January 1, Pulse Recording Studio (PRS) had the following account balances.

Accounts Payable	$ 8,500	Deferred Revenue	$ 4,000
Accounts Receivable	7,000	Equipment	30,000
Accumulated Depreciation—Equipment	6,000	Notes Payable (long-term)	12,000
Cash	3,800	Prepaid Rent	3,000
Cash Equivalents	1,500	Retained Earnings	5,300
Common Stock	10,000	Supplies	500

The following transactions occurred during January.

a. Received $2,500 cash on 1/1 from customers on account for recording services completed in December.

b. Wrote checks on 1/2 totaling $4,000 for amounts owed on account at the end of December.

c. Purchased and received supplies on account on 1/3, at a total cost of $200.

d. Completed $4,000 of recording sessions on 1/4 that customers had paid for in advance in December.

e. Received $5,000 cash on 1/5 from customers for recording sessions started and completed in January.

f. Wrote a check on 1/6 for $4,000 for an amount owed on account.

g. Converted $1,000 of cash equivalents into cash on 1/7.

h. On 1/15, completed EFTs for $1,500 for employees' salaries and wages for the first half of January.

i. Received $3,000 cash on 1/31 from customers for recording sessions to start in February.

Required:

1. Prepare journal entries for the January transactions.
2. Enter the January 1 balances into T-accounts, post the journal entries from requirement 1, and calculate January 31 balances. (If you are completing this requirement in Connect, this requirement will be completed for you.)

3. Use the January 31 balance in Cash from requirement 2 and the following information to prepare a bank reconciliation. PRS's bank reported a January 31 balance of $6,300.

    j. The bank deducted $500 for an NSF check from a customer deposited on January 5.
    k. The check written January 6 has not cleared the bank, but the January 2 payment has cleared.
    l. The cash received and deposited on January 31 was not processed by the bank until February 1.
    m. The bank added $5 cash to the account for interest earned in January.
    n. The bank deducted $5 for service charges.

4. Prepare journal entries for items (j)–(n) from the bank reconciliation, if applicable, and post them to the T-accounts. If a journal entry is not required for one or more of the reconciling items, indicate "no journal entry required." (If you are using Connect, journal entries will be automatically posted after you enter them.)

5. Prepare adjusting journal entries on 1/31, using the following information.

    o. Depreciation for the month is $200.
    p. Salaries and wages totaling $1,500 have not yet been recorded for January 16–31.
    q. Prepaid Rent will be fully used up by March 31.
    r. Supplies on hand at January 31 were $500.
    s. Received $600 invoice for January electricity charged on account to be paid in February but is not yet recorded.
    t. Interest on the promissory note of $60 for January has not yet been recorded or paid.
    u. Income tax of $1,000 on January income has not yet been recorded or paid.

6. Post the adjusting journal entries from requirement 5 to the T-accounts and prepare an adjusted trial balance. (If you are completing this requirement in Connect, it will be completed for you using your previous answers.)

7. Prepare an income statement for January and a classified balance sheet at January 31. Report PRS's cash and cash equivalents as a single line on the balance sheet.

8. Calculate the current ratio at January 31 and indicate whether PRS has met its loan covenant that requires a minimum current ratio of 1.2.

9. Calculate the net profit margin and indicate whether PRS has achieved its objective of 10 percent.

SKILLS DEVELOPMENT CASES

LO 5-2, 5-5

S5-1 Finding Financial Information

The Home Depot

Refer to the financial statements of The Home Depot in Appendix A at the end of this book. (Note: Fiscal 2019 for The Home Depot runs from February 4, 2019, to February 2, 2020. See S1-1 for further explanation.)

1. How much does The Home Depot report for Cash and Cash Equivalents and Restricted Cash (in millions) at February 2, 2020?
    a. $2,133 and $2,106
    b. $2,133 and $53
    c. $8 and $53
    d. $2,133 and $0

2. Accompanying the financial statements are reports issued by management and an independent registered public accounting firm regarding the company's internal control. According to these reports, did the company maintain effective internal control over financial reporting?
    a. Management concluded: yes; independent registered public accounting firm concluded: yes.
    b. Management concluded: yes; independent registered public accounting firm concluded: no.
    c. Management concluded: no; independent registered public accounting firm concluded: yes.
    d. Management concluded: no; independent registered public accounting firm concluded: no.

LO 5-2, 5-5

S5-2 Finding Financial Information

Lowe's

Refer to the financial statements of Lowe's Companies, Inc., in Appendix B. (Note: Fiscal 2019 for Lowe's runs from February 2, 2019, to January 31, 2020. See S1-1 for further explanation.)

1. How much does Lowe's report for Cash and Cash Equivalents (in millions) at January 31, 2020?
   a. $511
   c. $205
   b. $716
   d. $588

2. Lowe's does not report Restricted Cash at January 31, 2020, but Note 1 to its financial statements indicates it does include Restricted Balances in its investment accounts for its extended protection plan program. How much of its short-term and long-term investments (in millions) were restricted at January 31, 2020?
   a. $160 and $218
   c. $160 and $372
   b. $372 and $256
   d. $218 and $256

S5-3 Internet-Based Team Research: Examining an Annual Report

LO 5-2, 5-5

As a team, select an industry to analyze. Using your web browser, each team member should access the annual report or 10-K for one publicly traded company in the industry, with each member selecting a different company. (See S1-3 in Chapter 1 for a description of possible resources for these tasks.)

Required:

1. On an individual basis, each team member should write a short report that incorporates the following:
   a. Read management's report on internal control effectiveness. Did any material weaknesses or deficiencies exist during the year? Did the external auditors agree with management's assessment?
   b. How much did the company report in total Cash and Cash Equivalents? Does the company present sufficient information to determine the proportion of Cash versus Cash Equivalents? Does the company report Restricted Cash?

2. Then, as a team, write a short report comparing and contrasting your companies using these attributes. Discuss any patterns across the companies that you as a team observe. Provide potential explanations for any differences discovered.

S5-4 Ethical Decision Making: A Real-Life Example

LO 5-1, 5-2

Famous Footwear
Caleres

When some people think about inventory theft, they imagine a shoplifter running out of a store with goods stuffed inside a jacket or bag. But that's not what the managers thought at the Famous Footwear store on Chicago's Madison Street. No, this company owned by Caleres suspected its own employees were the main cause of their unusually high inventory theft. One scam involved dishonest cashiers who would let their friends take a pair of Skechers without paying for them. To make it look like the shoes had been bought, cashiers would ring up a sale, but instead of charging $50 for shoes, they would charge only $2 for a bottle of shoe polish. That's when the company's managers decided to put its register-monitoring system to work. In just two years, the company cut its Madison Street inventory losses in half. Here's how a newspaper described the store's improvements:

Retailers Crack Down on Employee Theft
SouthCoast Today
By Calmetta Coleman, *Wall Street Journal* Staff Writer

CHICAGO . . . Famous Footwear installed a chainwide register-monitoring system to sniff out suspicious transactions, such as unusually large numbers of refunds or voids, or repeated sales of cheap goods.

. . . [B]efore an employee can issue a cash refund, a second worker must be present to see the customer and inspect the merchandise.

. . . [T]he chain has set up a toll-free hotline for employees to use to report suspicions about co-workers.

Source: www.southcoasttoday.com/article/20000910/news/309109951.

Required:

1. To which of the three types of employee fraud does this article relate?
2. Explain how the register-monitoring system would allow Famous Footwear to cut down on employee theft.
3. What is the name of the control principle that is addressed by Famous Footwear's new cash refund procedure?
4. Think of and describe at least four different parties that are harmed by the type of inventory theft described in this case.

LO 5-1, 5-5

S5-5 Ethical Decision Making: A Mini-Case

You are an assistant in the accounting department of Hasher Electronics, a small electronics retailer. Hasher has a loan that requires the company to maintain a minimum cash balance of $125,000, as reported on its year-end balance sheet. Although Hasher has struggled in recent years, as of yesterday it looked as though Hasher would be able to meet this requirement. The cash balance in Hasher's general ledger was $130,000 and the company's credit manager was expecting to receive a $30,000 electronic funds transfer that day on account from your biggest customer. Your department supervisor had been worried about meeting the loan requirement, so she had delayed making payments to Hasher's suppliers for several days. But in anticipation of receiving the EFT, she decided yesterday to issue checks to suppliers totaling $15,000.

It is now the last day of the fiscal year and your supervisor approaches you with a problem. Your big customer has backed out at the last minute, indicating it has "some financial issues to sort out" before it can transfer money to Hasher. The supervisor says the only way Hasher can meet its loan requirement is to put the $15,000 back into the Cash account and pretend as if the supplier checks were not issued until after year-end. You question whether this would be ethical. Her reply is, "Well, we don't really have a choice. Either we do this, or we violate the terms of the loan agreement and possibly be forced to repay the loan immediately. That could put us out of business. Think of all the people who would lose their jobs! Just make a journal entry today to increase Cash and Accounts Payable. Then tomorrow we can reduce Cash and Accounts Payable—probably before many of our suppliers even get the checks we have written to them."

Required:

1. Who might suffer in the short term if you go along with your supervisor's request? What might happen in the future if you go along with her request this time? If you do not go along, who might suffer in the short term and what could be the long-term consequences?

2. You want to be loyal to your supervisor but honest to others who rely on your work. As an accounting assistant, which of these concerns should be most important? Why?

3. What alternative courses of action can you take? Which of these is "best" given the circumstances?

LO 5-1, 5-2

S5-6 Critical Thinking: Analyzing Internal Control Weaknesses

This case is available online in the Connect eBook. By completing this case, you will learn to quantify cash embezzlement, identify missing cash controls, and recommend control improvements.

CONTINUING CASE

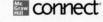

LO 5-3, 5-4, 5-5

CC5-1 Accounting for Cash Receipts, Purchases, and Cash Payments and Reconciling Items

Nicole's Getaway Spa (NGS) continues to grow and develop. Nicole is now evaluating a computerized accounting system and needs your help in understanding how source documents inform accounting processes. She also needs some help reconciling NGS's bank account.

Required:

1. For each source document shown below, prepare the appropriate journal entry or indicate that no journal entry is required.

    a. Purchase order dated October 13 for massage chairs costing $765 and oil supplies costing $240.

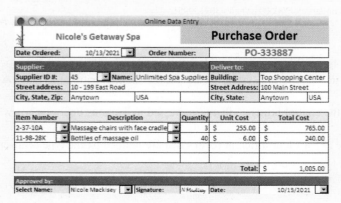

Bamboo photo: Nella/Shutterstock

b. Remittance advice from customer for $93, received October 17.

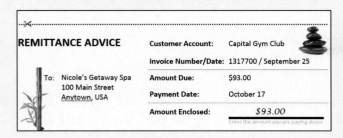

c. Receiving report indicating October 22 receipt of October 13 order. Also received supplier invoice totaling $1,005.

d. NGS check for payment in full of October 13 order.

2. Nicole has asked you to prepare a bank reconciliation for NGS. According to her records, NGS's cash balance is $6,000 at December 31, but the bank reports a balance of $5,500.

   a. The bank deducted $250 for an NSF check from a customer deposited on December 22.
   b. NGS has written checks totaling $3,500 that have not yet cleared the bank.
   c. The bank added $10 cash to the account for interest earned in December.
   d. NGS made a $3,480 deposit on December 31, which will be recorded by the bank in January.
   e. The bank deducted $10 for service charges.
   f. NGS wrote a check to a supplier on account for $300 but mistakenly recorded it as $30.

3. Prepare journal entries for items (a)–(f) from the bank reconciliation, if applicable. If a journal entry is not required for one or more of the reconciling items, indicate "no journal entry required."

4. If NGS also has $120 of petty cash and $1,000 invested in government Treasury bills purchased in August, what is the amount of Cash and Cash Equivalents on NGS's December 31 balance sheet?

Bamboo photo: Nella/Shutterstock; Stones photo: Ingram Publishing/ SuperStock

---

DATA ANALYTICS EXERCISES

Data Analytics Exercises are auto-graded exercises offering detailed data visualization, interpretation, and analysis, and are available for assignment in *Connect*.

6

Merchandising Operations and the Multistep Income Statement

CHAPTER SIX

YOUR LEARNING OBJECTIVES

LO 6-1   Distinguish between service and merchandising operations.

LO 6-2   Explain the differences between periodic and perpetual inventory systems.

LO 6-3   Analyze purchase transactions under a perpetual inventory system.

LO 6-4   Analyze sales transactions under a perpetual inventory system.

LO 6-5   Analyze sales of bundled items under a perpetual inventory system.

LO 6-6   Prepare and analyze a merchandiser's multistep income statement.

LO 6-S1 Record purchase and sales discounts under a perpetual inventory system.

LO 6-S2 Record inventory transactions in a periodic system.

THAT WAS THEN

Earlier chapters have focused on companies whose operating activities relate to providing services to customers, rather than selling goods.

Dutourdumonde
Photography/Shutterstock

FOCUS COMPANY: WALMART

Seventeen years after the company was founded, Walmart rang up yearly sales of $1 billion. Fourteen years later, it sold that much in a week. Thanks to you and the 275 million other customers who shop at Walmart, its sales now average nearly $1.4 billion a day. And that's not all. Walmart has been able to earn sizable profits, even during difficult economic times. One secret to its success is the state-of-the-art accounting system that controls Walmart's merchandise purchase and sales transactions. In this chapter, you will learn about this kind of system and the other aspects of merchandising companies that make them unique and interesting. You'll also learn how to analyze a merchandiser's financial statements to figure out the amount of markup that it includes in the prices you pay. You might be surprised by how much you're contributing to Walmart's profits.

THIS IS NOW

This chapter focuses on companies that sell merchandise to customers and the way they control and report their operating results.

Understand the business	Study the accounting methods	Evaluate the results	Supplement 6A	Supplement 6B	Review the chapter
• Operating cycles • Inventory systems	• Recording inventory purchases • Recording inventory sales	• Multistep income statement • Gross profit analysis	• Recording early payment ("cash") discounts on purchases and sales	• Recording inventory transactions in a periodic system	• Demonstration cases • Chapter summary • Key terms • Homework helper • Practice material

Understand the Business

OPERATING CYCLES

For any company to be successful, it must complete its operating cycle efficiently. **The operating cycle is a series of activities that a company undertakes to generate revenues, which ultimately lead to collecting cash.** Exhibit 6.1 contrasts the operating cycles of service and merchandising companies.

Service companies such as Planet Fitness follow a simple operating cycle: sell services to customers, collect cash from them, and use that money to pay for operating expenses. **Merchandising companies** differ in that their cycle begins with buying products. These products, called **Inventory**, are sold to customers, which leads to collecting cash that can be used to pay operating expenses and buy more inventory. Merchandising companies such as Walmart and Costco are called **retailers** when they sell directly to individual consumers and **wholesalers** when they sell their inventory to retail businesses for resale to consumers. This chapter applies equally to both retail and wholesale merchandisers. This chapter does not include manufacturing companies such as Mattel and Goodyear because they make rather than buy the products they sell, which introduces complexities that are beyond this introductory course. Accounting for manufacturing companies is explained in managerial and cost accounting courses.

EXHIBIT 6.1	Operating Cycles for Service and Merchandising Companies

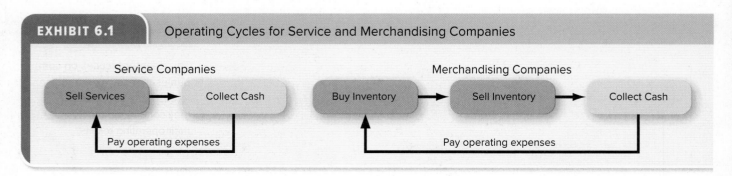

The operating cycle differences in Exhibit 6.1 lead to important differences in how service and merchandising companies report their financial results. Exhibit 6.2 shows **three key differences** in the balance sheet and income statement of a service company (Planet Fitness) and a merchandising company (Walmart). The balance sheet excerpts show that **(1)** merchandisers report Inventory as a current asset, whereas service companies are more likely to report Supplies. Supplies differ from Inventory because *supplies are goods acquired for internal use whereas inventory includes goods acquired for resale to customers.* The income statement excerpts show that **(2)** service companies earn revenue from services whereas merchandisers earn revenue from sales. Finally, **(3)** merchandisers report an expense called Cost of Goods Sold, which represents the total cost of all goods sold to customers during the period. Service companies do not incur this expense because they do not sell goods.

Of course, some companies operate as both service and merchandising companies. Supercuts, for example, buys shampoo for both internal use (Supplies) and resale to customers (Inventory). The financial statements of such companies separately report all the items shown in Exhibit 6.2.

EXHIBIT 6.2　Financial Reporting Differences for Service and Merchandising Companies

Service Company Example

PLANET FITNESS, INC.
Balance Sheet (*excerpt*)
At June 30, 2019
(*in thousands*)

Assets
Current Assets

Cash and Cash Equivalents	$330,550
Accounts Receivable	26,600
Supplies	5,800
Prepaid Insurance	10,100
etc.	

Income Statement (*excerpt*)
(*in thousands*)

Service Revenue	$181,700
Depreciation Expense	10,600
etc.	

Merchandising Company Example

WALMART STORES, INC.
Balance Sheet (*excerpt*)
At July 31, 2019
(*in millions*)

Assets
Current Assets

Cash and Cash Equivalents	$ 9,300
Accounts Receivable	5,400
Inventory	44,100
Prepaid Insurance	2,600
etc.	

Income Statement (*excerpt*)
(*in millions*)

Sales Revenue	$129,400
Cost of Goods Sold	97,900
Gross Profit	31,500
Depreciation Expense	5,400
etc.	

Sources: Walmart Stores, Inc., and Planet Fitness, Inc. Amounts simplified for presentation.

INVENTORY SYSTEMS

Three accounts are particularly important to a merchandiser: Inventory, Sales Revenue, and Cost of Goods Sold. **Inventory** reports the merchandiser's total **cost** of acquiring goods that it has not yet sold, whereas **Sales Revenue** and **Cost of Goods Sold** indicate the total **selling price** and **cost** of all goods that the merchandiser did sell to customers during the period. By subtracting Cost of Goods Sold from Sales Revenue, a merchandiser determines its *gross profit*, which represents the profit earned before taking into account other expenses such as salaries, wages, depreciation, and so on.

Learning Objective 6-2
Explain the differences between periodic and perpetual inventory systems.

Before we discuss the systems for tracking changes in Inventory, Sales Revenue, and Cost of Goods Sold, you should understand a key relationship between Inventory and Cost of Goods Sold. A merchandiser starts each accounting period with a stock of inventory that we will call **beginning inventory (BI).** During the accounting period, the cost of new inventory **purchases (P)** is added to the cost of beginning inventory. As in Exhibit 6.3, the sum of these two amounts (BI + P) represents the cost of **goods available for sale**.

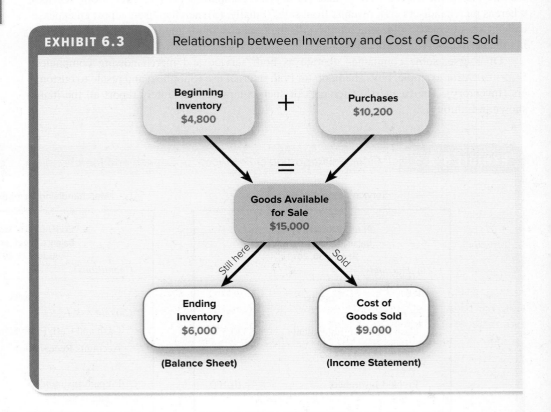

EXHIBIT 6.3   Relationship between Inventory and Cost of Goods Sold

Goods available for sale either will be sold during the period (reported as **Cost of Goods Sold (CGS)** on the income statement) or will remain on hand (reported as **ending inventory (EI)** on the balance sheet). Ending inventory for one accounting period becomes beginning inventory for the next period. A **cost of goods sold equation** can express the relationship among these items in two ways, as given below using the numbers from Exhibit 6.3:

BI + P − EI = CGS	or	**BI + P − CGS = EI**
$4,800 + 10,200 − 6,000 = $9,000		$4,800 + 10,200 − 9,000 = $6,000

Companies track these costs using either a periodic or perpetual inventory system. As explained below, the equation above on the left is used for a periodic inventory system and the equation above on the right depicts a perpetual inventory system.

If one of the values in the cost of goods sold equation is unknown, you can use either version of the cost of goods sold equation or the inventory T-account to solve for the missing value. See for yourself in the following Self-Study Practice.

How's it going? Self-Study Practice

Cases 1 and 2 below contain the same information but use the cost of goods sold equation in different ways to calculate inventory costs. Solve for the missing information for cases 1 and 2. Then enter the information for either case 1 or case 2 into the T-account on the right.

		Case 1	Case 2
Beginning Inventory	5 units × $10	$ 50	$ 50
+ Purchases	20 units × $10	200	200
Goods Available for Sale		☐	250
− Ending Inventory		100	☐
Cost of Goods Sold		☐	$150

Inventory

Beginning	50		
Purchases	200		
Goods Available	☐		
		☐	Goods Sold
Ending Inventory	☐		

After you have finished, check your answers with the solution.

Solution to Self-Study Practice
Case 1: Goods available = $250, CGS = $150
Case 2: Ending inventory = $100

Inventory

Beginning	50		
Purchases	200		
Goods Available	250		
		150	Goods Sold
Ending Inventory	100		

Periodic Inventory System

A **periodic inventory system** updates the inventory records for merchandise purchases, sales, and returns only at the end of the accounting period. Although simple to maintain, a major drawback of a periodic system is that accurate records of the inventory on hand and the inventory that has been sold are unavailable during the accounting period. To determine these amounts, employees must physically count the inventory, which they do at the end of the period, when the store is "closed for inventory." Based on the inventory count, the cost of ending inventory (EI) is determined and subtracted to calculate the cost of goods sold (CGS) (BI + P − EI = CGS). These amounts are then used to adjust the balances in the Inventory and Cost of Goods Sold accounts.

Perpetual Inventory System

A **perpetual inventory system** updates inventory records every time an item is bought, sold, or returned. You may not realize it, but the bar-code scanners at Walmart's checkouts serve two purposes: (1) they calculate and record the sales revenue for each product you're buying and (2) they remove the product and its cost from Walmart's inventory records. Similar scanners are used back in the "employees only" part of the store, where products are unloaded from the trucks or returned to suppliers. As a result of this continuous, or "perpetual," updating, the balances in Walmart's Inventory and Cost of Goods Sold accounts are always up to date.

Inventory Control A perpetual inventory system provides the best inventory control because its continuous tracking of transactions allows companies to instantly determine the quantity of products on the shelves and to evaluate the amount of time they have spent there. Using this information, companies can better manage their inventory and save a great deal of money in financing and storage charges. Another benefit of a perpetual inventory system is that it allows managers to estimate **shrinkage**, the term for loss of inventory from theft, fraud, and error. You might wonder how companies can estimate how much of their inventory is missing because isn't it, by definition, *missing*? They use the information in the perpetual inventory system and the following version of the cost of goods sold equation: BI + P − CGS = EI.

To illustrate, assume Walmart reports the following for one of its lines of cell phones.

Equation	Information in the company's perpetual records					Physical inventory count
	Quantity		Cost per Unit		Total Cost	
Beginning Inventory	3	×	$100	=	$300	
+ Purchases	3	×	$100	=	300	
− Goods Sold	(2)	×	$100	=	(200)	vs.
= Ending Inventory	4	×	$100	=	$400	

Because a perpetual inventory system records all goods purchased and sold, the ending inventory in the company's perpetual records indicates how many units should be on hand. In our example, four units should be on hand at a unit cost of $100, for a total cost of $400. By physically counting the inventory actually on hand, the company can determine whether items have been physically removed without being recorded as an approved transaction. Calculate shrinkage by subtracting the cost of inventory counted from that recorded in the perpetual inventory system. In our example, just three units were on hand, so the shrinkage was one unit, with a cost of $100. This shrinkage of one unit will be accounted for by recording a "book-to-physical" adjustment that reduces the Inventory account (with a credit of $100) and increases Cost of Goods Sold (with a debit of $100). In a perpetual inventory system, Inventory and Cost of Goods Sold are not complete until this book-to-physical adjustment is made.

You can't do this kind of analysis with a periodic inventory system because it doesn't provide an up-to-date record of the inventory that should be on hand when you count it. Notice, however, that even if you're using a perpetual inventory system, you still need to count the inventory occasionally (at least yearly) to ensure the accounting records are accurate and any shrinkage is detected. If you don't do this physical count, you could end up like the company in the Spotlight on Controls in Chapter 5. The grandmother was able to falsely record payments to herself as if they were inventory purchases because no one checked to see whether the recorded inventory actually existed.

SPOTLIGHT ON | Controls

Sources of Inventory Shrinkage

Independent verification of inventory quantities is important. A recent study suggests that more than $50.6 billion of inventory goes missing from U.S. retailers each year.* Although shoplifting is a major cause of shrinkage, a nearly equal proportion results from employee theft. To avoid hiring dishonest employees, companies screen job applicants using employment and criminal background checks. To deter and detect employee theft, they use security tags, surveillance cameras, and data analytics to detect suspicious inventory transactions.

*Richard Hollinger, "2019 National Retail Security Survey," University of Florida, June 2019.

Study the Accounting Methods

RECORDING INVENTORY PURCHASES

Learning Objective 6-3
Analyze purchase transactions under a perpetual inventory system.

In this section, we demonstrate the accounting for inventory purchases, as well as transportation, purchase returns and allowances, and purchase discounts. For purposes of this demonstration, we record all inventory-related transactions in the Inventory account. This approach is generally associated with a **perpetual inventory system** because it maintains an up-to-date balance in the Inventory account at all times. An alternative approach, which maintains separate accounts for purchases, transportation, and so on, is generally used in a **periodic inventory system** and is demonstrated in Supplement 6B at the end of this chapter. Notice for each of the following transactions, the Inventory T-account tracks the **cost** of inventory, not the number of units of inventory.

Inventory Purchases

Most large retailers use perpetual inventory systems that not only monitor inventory quantities, but also automatically issue purchase orders to replenish inventory on hand. The purchase order instructs the supplier to send specified quantities of particular products on certain dates. At the time the purchase order is transmitted, Walmart and the supplier have exchanged only promises, so no journal entry is recorded. A transaction arises when Walmart receives the inventory and is invoiced for it. For example, if Walmart receives $10,500 of bikes purchased on account, the transaction would affect the accounting equation and would be recorded at cost as follows.

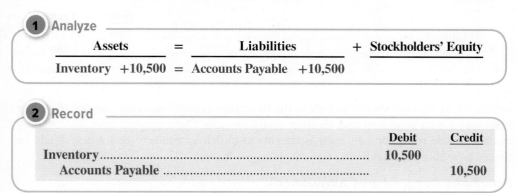

1 Analyze

Assets	=	Liabilities	+ Stockholders' Equity
Inventory +10,500	=	Accounts Payable +10,500	

2 Record

	Debit	Credit
Inventory..	10,500	
Accounts Payable		10,500

The $10,500 owed to the supplier remains in Accounts Payable until it is paid, at which time Accounts Payable is decreased (with a debit) and Cash is decreased (with a credit). The Inventory account remains at $10,500, unless the inventory is sold or any of the following transactions occur.

Transportation Cost

The inventory that Walmart purchases must be shipped from the supplier to Walmart. Depending on the terms of sale, the transportation cost may be paid by either Walmart or the supplier. If the terms of sale are **FOB shipping point**, ownership of the goods transfers to Walmart at the supplier's shipping point, so Walmart would pay the transportation cost. This transportation cost (sometimes called freight-in) is recorded as an addition to Walmart's Inventory account because it is a cost Walmart incurs to obtain the inventory. If the terms are **FOB destination**, ownership transfers at the destination, so the supplier incurs the transportation cost. Exhibit 6.4 summarizes these differences.

> **YOU SHOULD KNOW**
>
> **FOB Shipping Point:** Term of sale indicating that goods are owned by the buyer the moment they leave the seller's premises.
> **FOB Destination:** Term of sale indicating that goods are owned by the seller until delivered to the buyer.

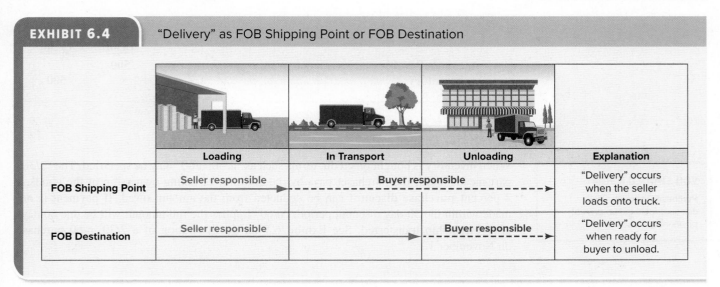

EXHIBIT 6.4 "Delivery" as FOB Shipping Point or FOB Destination

	Loading	In Transport	Unloading	Explanation
FOB Shipping Point	Seller responsible	Buyer responsible		"Delivery" occurs when the seller loads onto truck.
FOB Destination	Seller responsible		Buyer responsible	"Delivery" occurs when ready for buyer to unload.

To show how to account for transportation cost, let's assume the $10,500 of bikes were sold to Walmart with terms FOB shipping point. These terms imply the buyer (Walmart) must pay the transportation cost, which in this example is $200 cash paid to a trucker. Walmart would account for this transportation cost as follows:

1 Analyze

Assets		=	Liabilities	+ Stockholders' Equity
Cash	−200			
Inventory	+200			

2 Record

	Debit	Credit
Inventory	200	
Cash		200

In general, a purchaser should **include in the Inventory account any costs needed to get the inventory into a condition and location ready for sale.** Costs incurred after the inventory has been made ready for sale, such as freight-out to deliver goods to customers, should be treated as selling expenses.

Purchase Returns and Allowances

When goods purchased from a supplier arrive in damaged condition or fail to meet specifications, the buyer can (1) return them for a full refund or (2) keep them and ask for a cost reduction, called an allowance. Either way, these **purchase returns and allowances** are accounted for by reducing the cost of the inventory and either recording a cash refund or reducing the liability owed to the supplier.

Assume, for example, Walmart returned some of the bikes to the supplier and received a $500 reduction in the balance owed. This purchase return would be analyzed and recorded by Walmart as follows:

1 Analyze

Assets		=	Liabilities		+ Stockholders' Equity
Inventory	−500	=	Accounts Payable	−500	

2 Record

	Debit	Credit
Accounts Payable	500	
Inventory		500

Purchase Discounts

When inventory is bought on credit, terms such as "2/30, n/60" may be specified. The "2/30" part means that if the purchaser pays by the 30th day of taking ownership of the goods, a 2 percent **purchase discount** can be deducted from the amount owed. If payment is not made within the 30-day discount period, "n/60" implies the full amount will be due 60 days after ownership transferred. See Exhibit 6.5 for an illustration of a 2/30, n/60 purchase on November 1.

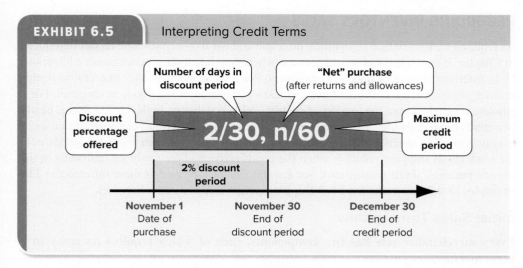

EXHIBIT 6.5 | Interpreting Credit Terms

Number of days in discount period

"Net" purchase (after returns and allowances)

Discount percentage offered

2/30, n/60

Maximum credit period

2% discount period

November 1
Date of purchase

November 30
End of discount period

December 30
End of credit period

A company accounts for purchase discounts either when the goods are first purchased and received (the "net method") or later when the payment is made (the "gross method"). The net method is convenient when a company is routinely offered and takes advantage of purchase discounts. The gross method may be appropriate when a company does not regularly take purchase discounts. Either way, **inventory ultimately is recorded at its cost after subtracting any purchase discounts taken.** The journal entries for discounts taken, using the gross and net methods, are presented in Supplement 6A.

SPOTLIGHT ON Business Decisions

"The Terms, They Are a-Changin'"

It's not quite the lyrics of Nobel Prize winner Bob Dylan, but the heading does describe the evolution of credit terms. In the 1990s, discounts and credit periods such as 2/10, n/30 were common. However, two academic studies reveal that such discounts are much less common since the mid-2000s. One study that analyzed more than 29,000 contracts found the average credit period is 60 days and only 13 percent of contracts had early payment discounts, offered mostly to retailers of electronics, appliances, and other hard goods.[*] Another study reports less than 60 percent of the discounts *offered* are actually taken.[†] These new studies suggest you are less likely to encounter early payment discounts than your bosses who grew up listening to Dylan.

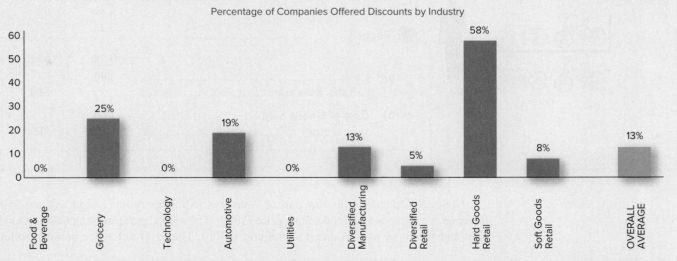

Percentage of Companies Offered Discounts by Industry

Industry	Percentage
Food & Beverage	0%
Grocery	25%
Technology	0%
Automotive	19%
Utilities	0%
Diversified Manufacturing	13%
Diversified Retail	5%
Hard Goods Retail	58%
Soft Goods Retail	8%
OVERALL AVERAGE	13%

Sources: [*]Leora Klapper, Luc Laeven, and Raghuram Rajan, "Trade Credit Contracts," *Review of Financial Studies* 25, no. 3 (2012), pp. 838–867.
[†]Mariassunta Giannetti, Mike Burkart, and Tore Ellingsen, "What You Sell Is What You Lend? Explaining Trade Credit Contracts," *Review of Financial Studies* 24, no. 4 (2011), pp. 1261–1298.

Learning Objective 6-4
Analyze sales transactions under a perpetual inventory system.

RECORDING INVENTORY SALES

As required by the revenue recognition principle and the five-step revenue model introduced in Chapter 3, merchandisers record revenue when they fulfill their performance obligations by transferring control of goods to customers. For a retail merchandiser like Walmart, this transfer occurs when a customer buys and takes possession of the goods at checkout. For a wholesale merchandiser, the transfer of control occurs at delivery. In the United States, nearly two-thirds of all deliveries are made by truck.[1] Because trucking times can span several days, it is important to specify whether "delivery" occurs when the seller loads the goods onto the truck (FOB shipping point) or when the goods arrive and are ready for unloading at the buyer's premises (FOB destination). See Exhibit 6.4 for a picture of these differences. **The examples in this book assume FOB shipping point** (unless stated otherwise).

Initial Sales Transactions

Every merchandise sale has two components, each of which requires an entry in a perpetual inventory system:

a. **Selling price.** Walmart's *sales price* is recorded as an increase in Sales Revenue and a corresponding increase in either Cash (for a cash sale) or Accounts Receivable (for a sale on account).

b. **Cost.** The *cost* that Walmart incurred to initially buy the merchandise is removed from its Inventory account and reported as an expense called Cost of Goods Sold (CGS).

For example, assume Walmart sells four mountain bikes at a selling price of $200 per bike, for a total of $800 cash. The bikes had previously been recorded in Walmart's Inventory at a cost of $175 per bike, for a total cost of $700. This transaction is illustrated, analyzed, and recorded in Exhibit 6.6.

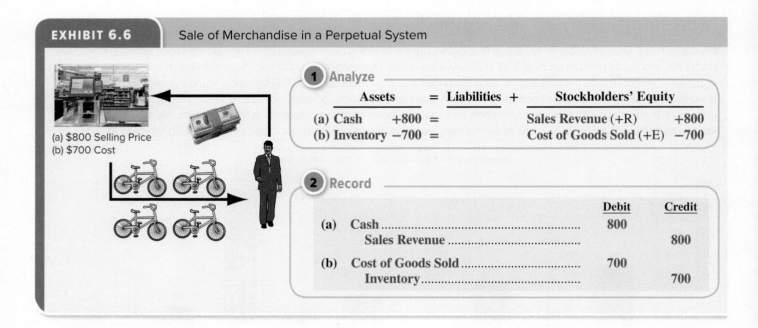

EXHIBIT 6.6   Sale of Merchandise in a Perpetual System

(a) $800 Selling Price
(b) $700 Cost

1 Analyze

	Assets	= Liabilities +	Stockholders' Equity	
(a) Cash	+800 =		Sales Revenue (+R)	+800
(b) Inventory	−700 =		Cost of Goods Sold (+E)	−700

2 Record

		Debit	Credit
(a)	Cash	800	
	Sales Revenue		800
(b)	Cost of Goods Sold	700	
	Inventory		700

Notice in Exhibit 6.6 the first part of Walmart's journal entry involving Cash and Sales Revenue is recorded at the total selling price ($800). The second part involving Cost of Goods Sold and Inventory uses Walmart's total cost ($700). The $100 difference between selling

[1]United States Department of Transportation, Bureau of Transportation Statistics, *Freight Facts and Figures 2017.* Downloaded October 4, 2019, from https://roasp.ntl.bts.gov/view/dot/34923.

price and cost ($800 − $700) is called the *gross profit*. **Gross profit is not directly recorded in an account by itself** but instead is a subtotal on the income statement produced by subtracting Cost of Goods Sold from Sales Revenue.

To simplify our examples, we will use only one Sales Revenue account and one Cost of Goods Sold account. In the workplace, however, merchandising companies use different Sales and Cost of Goods Sold accounts for different product lines. This allows managers at Walmart to separately evaluate sales of different products. When reporting to external financial statement users, Walmart combines these individual accounts into a single number for Sales Revenue and a single number for Cost of Goods Sold, which avoids cluttering its income statement with numerous accounts and also prevents its competitors from discovering details about its sales of specific products.

Sales Returns and Allowances

When goods sold to a customer arrive in damaged condition or are otherwise unsatisfactory, the customer can (1) return them for a full refund or (2) keep them and ask for a reduction in the selling price, called an *allowance*. These **sales returns and allowances** reduce the amount the seller expects to receive from the customer. The five-step revenue model introduced in Chapter 3 requires the seller to report sales revenue at the amount the seller expects to be entitled to receive from customers, so technically sales returns and allowances should be subtracted from sales revenue when a sale is initially reported. However, it is impractical to account for sales returns and allowances when the initial sale is recorded because returns and allowances arise *after* the initial sale. Companies resolve this dilemma by recording *actual* sales returns and allowances as they occur, and then adjusting the accounts at month-end for further returns and allowances *expected* to occur in the following months.

Actual Returns   To illustrate how to account for sales returns and allowances as they occur, assume one mountain bike is returned to Walmart in good condition.[2] The customer is given $200 cash, which was the original selling price paid by the customer. (The bike had originally cost Walmart $175.) To account for this transaction, Walmart would basically reverse the original sale of the bike. We say "basically" because there is a catch: Walmart does not directly reduce its Sales Revenue account. Instead, Walmart tracks sales returns using a contra-account as follows.

1 Analyze

Assets	= Liabilities +	Stockholders' Equity	
Cash −200 =		Sales Returns and Allowances (+xR, −R)	−200
Inventory +175 =		Cost of Goods Sold (−E)	+175

2 Record

	Debit	Credit
Sales Returns and Allowances	200	
Cash		200
Inventory	175	
Cost of Goods Sold		175

Sales Returns and Allowances is a contra-account that is deducted from Sales Revenue on the income statement, as shown in Exhibit 6.7. By tracking amounts originally sold (Sales Revenue) separate from the reversal of sales (Sales Returns and Allowances), Walmart can estimate the proportion of sales that are reversed, providing clues about whether customers are happy with the quality and price of Walmart's products.

---

[2]Chapter 7 describes how to account for damaged inventory.

EXHIBIT 6.7 | Reporting Effects of Sales-Related Transactions

Sales Revenue	$800	**Selling price** of 4 bikes (4 × $200 = $800)
Sales Returns and Allowances	(200)	**Selling price** of returned bike ($200)
Net Sales	600	**Subtotal** ($800 − $200 = $600)
Cost of Goods Sold	525	**Cost** of 4 bikes ($700) − returned bike ($175)
Gross Profit	75	**Subtotal** ($600 − $525 = $75)

Reported Externally / Reported Internally

The previous example showed how to account for a sales return that results in a cash refund. A sales return that results instead in issuing a store gift card is accounted for the same way, except the reduction in Cash (recorded with a credit) is replaced with an increase in the liability Deferred Revenue (recorded with a credit) for the store gift card that is issued, as follows:

1 Analyze

Assets	=	Liabilities	+	Stockholders' Equity	
		Deferred Revenue +200		Sales Returns and Allowances (+xR, −R)	−200
Inventory +175	=			Cost of Goods Sold (−E)	+175

2 Record

	Debit	Credit
Sales Returns and Allowances	200	
Deferred Revenue		200
Inventory	175	
Cost of Goods Sold		175

A sales *allowance* (i.e., a reduction in sales without the return of goods) is accounted for just like the sales return, except the increase in Inventory and decrease in Cost of Goods Sold are not recorded (because no goods are returned to the seller).

Expected Returns The month-end adjustment for expected additional returns is similar to that shown for actual returns, with two differences. The first difference is the refund or store gift card has not yet been given; it is only expected to be given. To report this, replace Cash or Deferred Revenue in the journal entry with an increase in a liability called Refund Liability (recorded with a credit). The second difference is the inventory has not been returned; it is only expected to be returned. To designate this, an account called Inventory—Estimated Returns is used rather than Inventory. The methods for estimating and further adjusting the balances in Refund Liability and Inventory—Estimated Returns at the end of each period will be discussed in an intermediate accounting course.

Sales Discounts

Earlier in this chapter, you saw that merchandisers sometimes are offered purchase discounts from their suppliers to encourage prompt payment on account. In the same way, merchandisers can entice their own customers to pay promptly for sales on account by offering a **sales discount**, such as "2/30, n/60." Sales discounts offered to and taken by customers within the discount period are accounted for using a contra-revenue account, similar to sales returns and allowances shown earlier in this chapter. The journal entries for recording sales discounts are presented in Supplement 6A.

YOU SHOULD KNOW

Sales Discount: Cash discount offered to customers to encourage prompt payment of an account receivable.

Reporting Sales-Related Transactions

The amount of sales returns, allowances, and discounts provides important but sensitive information about a merchandiser's operations. For example, a large dollar amount of sales returns and allowances, relative to initial sales revenue, could suggest problems with product quality. Companies track this information internally to inform management decisions, but to avoid revealing it to competitors, most externally reported income statements begin with **Net Sales.** For an example, see Walmart's income statement in Exhibit 6.9 later in this chapter.

Sales of Bundled Items

A common practice for many businesses is to package several items into a "bundle" and sell the bundle at a single price. (See the Spotlight on Business Decisions for examples.) When the bundle includes only products, this situation is easy to account for because the seller fulfills its performance obligations at the same time: delivery of the product bundle. In other cases, when a bundle includes both a product and a service, accounting for a sale is slightly more complex because the performance obligations are likely to be fulfilled over different periods.

> **Learning Objective 6-5**
> Analyze sales of bundled items under a perpetual inventory system.

SPOTLIGHT ON | # Business Decisions

Customers Who Bought This Item Also Bought . . .

Amazon isn't the only company encouraging customers to combine two or more items into a single sale. Bundling exists in nearly every industry, as shown below. The challenge for accounting occurs when two or more bundled items offer different patterns of benefits but are sold together for a single price.

Automotive **BMW** offers maintenance "free" with new car purchases

Finance **Citibank** offers travel insurance "free" with its credit card

Technology **Microsoft's** Office suite bundles many software applications

Broadcasting **Comcast** sells cable TV equipment with TV programming

Health Care **Johnson & Johnson** provides training and repair service with hospital equipment sales

Tele-communications **Verizon** sells cell phones at a discount when bundled with cellular service

Education **McGraw Hill** sells print books and multimonth Connect access

Hospitality **Marriott** provides hotel rooms with "free" breakfast and Wi-Fi

Transportation **United Airlines** gives "free" baggage service on select fares

Entertainment **Nintendo** sells console/game bundles

Quick Service Restaurants **McDonald's** bundles burgers, fries, and a drink in its Extra Value meal

Utilities **GridPoint, Inc.** offers home automation and energy services

It's important to understand how revenue from bundled items is reported. When Apple first started accounting for its iPhone software upgrades as a separate performance obligation, its financial results differed from analyst expectations by billions of dollars. The NASDAQ stock market even halted trading of Apple's shares temporarily to allow time for investors to grasp the impact of the accounting method on its financial results.

Let's consider a simple example where Sirius XM sells a vehicle equipment kit and 12-month radio service package for a combined price of $200. Separately, the equipment and radio service sell for $100 and $150, respectively. The performance obligation for the equipment

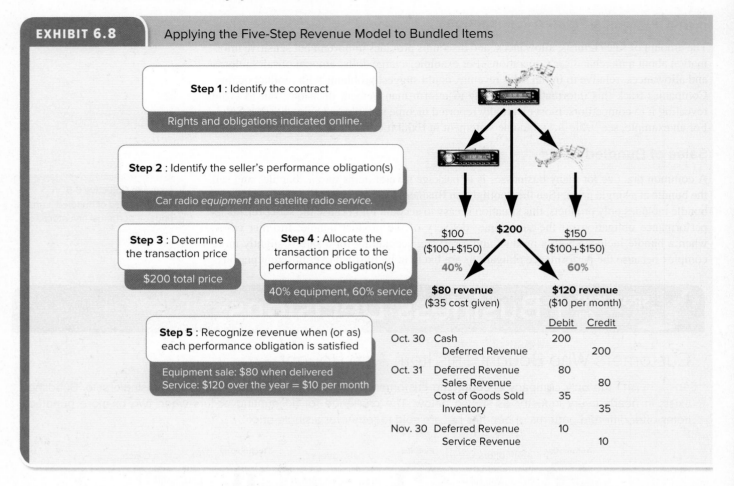

EXHIBIT 6.8   Applying the Five-Step Revenue Model to Bundled Items

sale is fulfilled at the point of delivery, whereas the performance obligation for the radio service is fulfilled over the 12 months of the service subscription. Assume the customer pays the $200 price on October 30, the equipment is shipped and received on October 31, and the subscription begins November 1. Sirius XM held the equipment in its inventory at its $35 cost. To ensure proper reporting of the revenue generated by fulfilling each performance obligation, Sirius XM follows the five-step revenue model, as illustrated in Exhibit 6.8 and explained below.

Step 1.   **Identify the contract.** A contract is agreed to online, establishing responsibilities relating to shipping, radio signal access, payment, pricing, and more.

Step 2.   **Identify the seller's performance obligation(s).** Sirius XM promises to deliver radio equipment and provide one year of radio service, so it has two performance obligations.

Step 3.   **Determine the transaction price.** The total price for the transaction is stated as $200.

Step 4.   **Allocate the transaction price to the performance obligation(s).** This allocation is made based on the stand-alone selling prices of the equipment and service. When sold separately, the price of the equipment is $100 and the 12-month service is $150, equaling a total of $250. Relative to this total, the $100 equipment price is 40% (calculated as $100 divided by $250) and the $150 radio service is 60% (calculated as $150 divided by $250). Thus, the $200 total price for the bundle is allocated 40% to equipment and 60% to the radio service. In dollars, sales revenue for delivering the equipment is $80 (40% of $200) and service revenue from providing the radio service is $120 (60% of $200).

Step 5.   **Recognize revenue when (or as) each performance obligation is satisfied.** When the $200 cash is received October 30, Sirius XM has not yet satisfied either of its performance obligations, so it accounts for a $200 liability (Deferred Revenue), as follows on October 30.

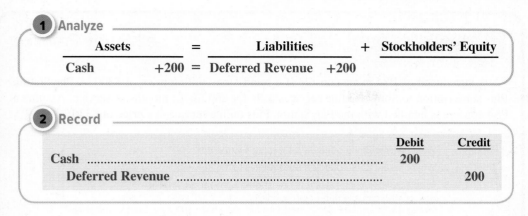

1 Analyze

Assets		=	Liabilities		+	Stockholders' Equity
Cash	+200	=	Deferred Revenue	+200		

2 Record

	Debit	Credit
Cash	200	
Deferred Revenue		200

On October 31, when Sirius XM delivers the radio kit, it fulfills the performance obligation to deliver equipment, so at that point it reduces its liability and records Sales Revenue of $80 (calculated in Step 4). If Sirius XM uses a perpetual inventory system, it also records an expense for its cost of goods sold of $35 and reduces Inventory by the same amount. No service revenue for the radio signal is recorded on October 31 because the performance obligation to provide radio service is fulfilled after October 31, as each month of service is provided.

1 Analyze

Assets		=	Liabilities		+	Stockholders' Equity	
			Deferred Revenue	−80		Sales Revenue (+R)	+80
Inventory	−35	=				Cost of Goods Sold (+E)	−35

2 Record

	Debit	Credit
Deferred Revenue	80	
Sales Revenue		80
Cost of Goods Sold	35	
Inventory		35

On November 30, Sirius XM will adjust its accounts to indicate it has fulfilled 1/12 of its promised radio services, resulting in $10 of service revenue for the month (1/12 × $120 total service revenue), as shown below.

1 Analyze

Assets	=	Liabilities		+	Stockholders' Equity	
	=	Deferred Revenue	−10		Service Revenue (+R)	+10

2 Record

	Debit	Credit
Deferred Revenue	10	
Service Revenue		10

A similar adjustment to decrease Deferred Revenue and report $10 of Service Revenue is made each month-end as the promised services are provided.

How's it going?   Self-Study Practice

Sony introduced its PS4 game console at a stand-alone selling price of $300. A PlayStation Plus subscription to Sony's online services sells for $60 for 12 months of service. Assume a PS4 console is bundled with the PlayStation Plus online service at a price of $330.

1. What percent of the bundled price relates to the console?   ☐
2. What percent of the bundled price relates to the service?   ☐
3. In dollars, how much sales revenue should Sony report when it   ☐
   delivers the console part of the bundle?

After you have finished, check your answers with the solution.

Evaluate the Results

Learning Objective 6-6
Prepare and analyze a merchandiser's multistep income statement.

MULTISTEP INCOME STATEMENT

YOU SHOULD KNOW

Multistep Income Statement:
Reports alternative measures of income by calculating subtotals for core and peripheral business activities.
Gross Profit (Gross Margin, Margin): Net sales less cost of goods sold.

To survive, a merchandiser must sell goods for more than their cost. That's the only way companies like **Walmart** can cover their operating expenses. To show how much profit is earned from product sales, without being clouded by other operating expenses, merchandise companies often present their income statement using a multistep format.

A **multistep income statement** is similar to what you saw in the first few chapters, with expenses being subtracted from revenues to arrive at net income. The difference is that a multistep format separates the revenues and expenses that relate to core operations from all the other (peripheral) items that affect net income. For merchandisers, a key measure is the amount of profit earned over the cost of goods sold, so their multistep income statements separate Cost of Goods Sold from other expenses. As shown in Exhibit 6.9, this extra step produces a subtotal called **gross profit**, which is the profit the company earned from selling goods, over and above the cost of the goods. If you buy inventory for $70 and sell it for $100, you'll have a gross profit of $30.

EXHIBIT 6.9   Sample Multistep Income Statement

WALMART STORES, INC.
Income Statements
For the Years Ended January 31
(amounts in millions)

	2019	2018	2017
Net Sales	$510,329	$495,761	$481,317
Cost of Goods Sold	385,301	373,396	361,256
Gross Profit	125,028	122,365	120,061
Selling, General, and Administrative Expenses	103,071	101,928	97,297
Income from Operations	21,957	20,437	22,764
Other Expenses, net	11,006	5,975	2,917
Income before Income Tax Expense	10,951	14,462	19,847
Income Tax Expense	4,281	4,600	6,204
Net Income	$ 6,670	$ 9,862	$ 13,643

Source: Walmart Stores, Inc. Some items have been combined and simplified.

Notice in Exhibit 6.9, after the gross profit line, the multistep income statement presents other items in a format similar to what you saw for a service company in Chapter 3 (Exhibit 3.2). The category called *Selling, General, and Administrative Expenses* includes a variety of operating expenses such as salaries and wages, utilities, advertising, rent, and the costs of delivering merchandise to customers. These expenses are subtracted from gross profit to yield Income from Operations, which is a subtotal measuring the company's income from regular operating activities. The category called *Other Expenses, net* includes miscellaneous expenses and revenues that do not involve the company's main business operations (e.g., interest expense or interest revenue).

GROSS PROFIT ANALYSIS

Exhibit 6.9 presents Walmart's income statement in **comparative format** by showing results for more than one year. This format reveals the dollar amount of Walmart's gross profit increased throughout the three years. The difficulty in interpreting the increasing dollars of gross profit is Walmart also increased its net sales over the same period, so we don't know whether the increase in gross profit dollars arises solely because Walmart increased its sales volume or whether it also is generating more profit per sale. To determine the amount of gross profit included in each dollar of sales, analysts typically evaluate the gross profit percentage.

Accounting Decision Tools		
Name of Measure	**Formula**	**What It Tells You**
Gross profit percentage	$\dfrac{\text{Net Sales} - \text{CGS}}{\text{Net Sales}}$	• The percentage of profit earned on each dollar of sales, after considering the cost of products sold • A higher ratio means that greater profit is available to cover operating and other expenses

The **gross profit percentage** measures the percentage of profit earned on each dollar of sales. A higher gross profit percentage means the company is selling products for a greater markup over its cost. This ratio can be used to (1) analyze changes in the company's operations over time, (2) compare one company to another, and (3) determine whether a company is earning enough from sales to cover its operating expenses.

Calculations show that Walmart's gross profit percentage decreased from 24.9 percent to 24.7 and then 24.5 percent over the years ended January 31, 2017 through 2019. Thus, the increase in total dollars of gross profit over these years could only be caused by an increase in sales volume (because Walmart was earning less gross profit on each dollar of sales).

You might wonder whether it's worth talking about a mere 0.4 percent decrease in the gross profit percentage, but a small change in this ratio can lead to a big change in net income. In Walmart's case, because the company has such a huge sales volume (over $500 billion), even just one-tenth of a percentage point change in gross profit translates into about half a billion dollars of profit ($500 billion × 0.001 = $0.5 billion). Yes, that's billion with a b.

> **YOU SHOULD KNOW**
>
> **Gross Profit Percentage:** Indicates how much above cost a company sells its products; calculated as Gross Profit divided by Net Sales.

> **WALMART'S GROSS PROFIT PERCENTAGE**
>
> | Year-ended January 31, | 2019 | 2018 | 2017 |
> |---|---|---|---|
> | $\dfrac{\text{Gross Profit}}{\text{Net Sales}} =$ | $\dfrac{\$125,028}{\$510,329}$ | $\dfrac{\$122,365}{\$495,761}$ | $\dfrac{\$120,061}{\$481,317}$ |
> | = | 0.245 | 0.247 | 0.249 |
> | or | 24.5% | 24.7% | 24.9% |

Comparing Gross Profit Percentages

Be aware that gross profit percentages can vary greatly between industries (as shown in the margin) and between companies in the same industry. Walmart's gross profit percentage of 24.5 percent is characteristic of its slogan and mission statement: "Saving people money so they can live better." Walmart's strategy is to earn a relatively small amount of profit on each dollar of sales, but to compensate by generating a huge volume of sales. In contrast, high-end department stores carry brand-name fashions with high-end prices, resulting in fewer sales but more profit on each sale. For example, Nordstrom reported a 34.4 percent gross profit percentage in fiscal 2019.

As the following spotlight indicates, gross profit percentages can reveal problems in a merchandiser's operations.

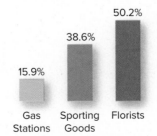

Gross Profit Percentage by Industry
Source: eStatement Studies, 2018–19.

SPOTLIGHT ON Controls

"Shoppers Are Buying More. They're Also Stealing More."

That's how a *Wall Street Journal* story described the results at JCPenney (JCP) Co. a few years ago, when explaining a drop in JCP's gross profit percentage.* What attracted thieves to JCP? For one, customers were given cash refunds even when they didn't have a sales receipt, so that gave them an *incentive* to steal. Second, they had an *opportunity* to steal because JCP had removed antitheft sensor tags from its products to avoid interfering with radio frequency identification (RFID) tags, which had just been introduced to better track inventory. This blunder led to a loss of inventory totaling $28 million, which was expensed in the company's Cost of Goods Sold.

_____
*S. Kapner, "Jump in Shoplifting Hurt Penney," *The Wall Street Journal* (Online), November 21, 2013.

Learning Objective 6-S1
Record purchase and sales discounts under a perpetual inventory system.

SUPPLEMENT 6A RECORDING EARLY PAYMENT ("CASH") DISCOUNTS ON PURCHASES AND SALES

Purchase and sales discounts can be recorded either at the time of the initial purchase/sale (the "net method") or later when cash is paid/received (the "gross method"). Essentially, the net method records discounts when they are first offered, in anticipation they will be taken later, whereas the gross method records discounts only when they are actually taken. Companies use the net method when discounts are common and they use the gross method when discounts are less frequent. For example, if a company regularly is offered and takes purchase discounts from suppliers but rarely offers sales discounts to its own customers, it will use the net method for recording purchase discounts and the gross method for recording sales discounts. Ultimately, the net and gross methods enter the same amounts into the accounting system, so either method could be acceptable depending on the circumstances; they just differ in timing and journal entries used. The middle column in Exhibit 6A.1 shows journal entries for the gross method, and the final column illustrates journal entries for the net method.

Gross Method   The middle column of Exhibit 6A.1 shows the purchase is recorded initially at the full ("gross") cost ($1,000), without considering the purchase discount. If Walmart pays $980 cash within the discount period, it will fulfill its $1,000 Accounts Payable balance and the $20 discount will be recorded as a reduction in the Inventory account. Walmart records the discount as a reduction in Inventory because the inventory ultimately cost $20 less as a result of the discount. If Walmart does not pay within the discount period, it will pay the full $1,000 Accounts Payable balance and Inventory will remain at $1,000.

When the goods are sold, the gross method records Sales Revenue at the full ("gross") selling price ($1,500), without considering the sales discount. If the customer takes advantage of the discount by paying the Accounts Receivable balance within the discount period, the discount ($30) reduces the selling price of the merchandise, so it is recorded in a contra-account for revenue called Sales Discounts.[3]

Net Method   The right column of Exhibit 6A.1 shows how the net method records the initial inventory purchase at the "net" cost ($980), in anticipation the purchase discount ($20) will be taken later. If payment is made within the discount period, Walmart pays only the net amount ($980) to satisfy the Accounts Payable balance. If payment is not made within the discount period, Walmart must pay $1,000, which covers both the $980 accounts payable and an extra $20 for the forgone discount. The extra $20 is considered a fee Walmart is charged for late payment, so Walmart would report it as an Other Operating Expense (recorded with a debit).

When the goods are sold, the net method records Sales Revenue at the net selling price ($1,470), as if the sales discount ($30) is taken. If the customer pays within the discount

_____
[3]Similar to Sales Returns and Allowances (shown earlier in this chapter), this contra-revenue account is recorded with a debit and is subtracted from Sales Revenue in the income statement.

EXHIBIT 6A.1   Journal Entries for Purchase and Sale Discounts Using the Gross and Net Methods

Assume **Walmart** purchases merchandise at a cost of $1,000, with terms 2/30, n/60, offered by its supplier. Walmart's warehouse store (Sam's Club) then sells the merchandise to a local business at a price of $1,500, with terms 2/30, n/60, offered to the customer. Walmart pays its supplier within the discount period and the customer pays Walmart within the discount period.

Transactions:	Gross Method			Net Method		
Purchase		**Debit**	**Credit**		**Debit**	**Credit**
When goods are received	Inventory..........................	1,000		Inventory..........................	980	
	Accounts Payable........		1,000	Accounts Payable........		980
				($980 = $1,000 × 98%)		
		Debit	**Credit**		**Debit**	**Credit**
When payment is made in the discount period	Accounts Payable............	1,000		Accounts Payable............	980	
	Cash.............................		980	Cash.............................		980
	Inventory.....................		20			
	($20 = $1,000 × 2%)					
Sale		**Debit**	**Credit**		**Debit**	**Credit**
When goods are delivered	Accounts Receivable.......	1,500		Accounts Receivable.......	1,470	
	Sales Revenue		1,500	Sales Revenue		1,470
				($1,470 = $1,500 × 98%)		
	Cost of Goods Sold	980		Cost of Goods Sold	980	
	Inventory.....................		980	Inventory.....................		980
		Debit	**Credit**		**Debit**	**Credit**
When payment is received in discount period	Cash..............................	1,470		Cash..............................	1,470	
	Sales Discounts	30		Accounts Receivable...		1,470
	Accounts Receivable...		1,500			
	($30 = $1,500 × 2%)					

period, Walmart will receive $1,470 cash, which will satisfy the Accounts Receivable balance. If the customer does not pay within the discount period, Walmart will be entitled to receive $1,500, which includes both the $1,470 account receivable and an extra $30 for the forfeited discount. The extra $30 represents a fee Walmart charges for late payment, so Walmart would report it as Other Revenue (recorded with a credit).

SUPPLEMENT 6B   RECORDING INVENTORY TRANSACTIONS IN A PERIODIC SYSTEM

> **Learning Objective 6-S2**
> Record inventory transactions in a periodic system.

Businesses that use a periodic inventory system update their inventory records only at the end of the accounting period. Unlike a perpetual inventory system, a periodic system does not track the cost of goods sold during the accounting period.

This supplement illustrates typical journal entries made when using a periodic inventory system, and contrasts them with the journal entries that would be recorded using a perpetual inventory system. A summary of the effects of the journal entries on the accounting equation, shown in the following table, reveals that the total effects and the financial statements produced under periodic and perpetual inventory systems are identical. Only the timing and nature of the entries differ.

Assume for the purposes of this illustration that an electronics retailer stocks and sells just one item and that only the following events occurred:

Jan. 1	Beginning inventory: 80 units at a unit cost of $60.
Apr. 14	Purchased 170 additional units on account at a unit cost of $60.
Nov. 30	Sold 150 units on account at a unit sales price of $80.
Dec. 31	Counted 100 units at a unit cost of $60.

PERIODIC RECORDS	PERPETUAL RECORDS

A. Record purchases:

April 14:

	Debit	Credit
Purchases (170 units at $60)	10,200	
Accounts Payable		10,200

B. Record sales (but not cost of goods sold):

November 30:

Accounts Receivable	12,000	
Sales Revenue (150 units at $80)		12,000

No cost of goods sold entry

C. Record end-of-period adjustments:

    a. Count the number of units on hand.
    b. Compute the dollar valuation of the ending inventory.
    c. Compute and record the cost of goods sold.

Beginning Inventory (last period's ending) (80 units at $60)	$ 4,800
Add: Net Purchases	10,200
Cost of Goods Available for Sale	15,000
Deduct: Ending Inventory (physical count—100 units at $60)	6,000
Cost of Goods Sold	$ 9,000

December 31:

Record cost of goods sold (as computed above), **record ending inventory, remove beginning inventory, and remove the balance in net purchases**

Cost of Goods Sold	9,000	
Inventory (ending)	6,000	
Inventory (beginning)		4,800
Purchases		10,200

A. Record purchases:

April 14:

	Debit	Credit
Inventory (170 units at $60)	10,200	
Accounts Payable		10,200

B. Record sales and cost of goods sold:

November 30:

Accounts Receivable	12,000	
Sales Revenue (150 units at $80)		12,000

Cost of Goods Sold	9,000	
Inventory (150 units at $60)		9,000

C. Record end-of-period adjustments:

At the end of the accounting period, the balance in the Cost of Goods Sold account is reported on the income statement. Computing the cost of goods sold is not necessary because the **Cost of Goods Sold** account is up to date. Also, the **Inventory** account shows the ending inventory amount reported on the balance sheet. A physical inventory count is still necessary to assess the accuracy of the perpetual records and identify theft and other forms of shrinkage. Any shrinkage would be recorded by reducing the **Inventory** account and increasing an expense account (**Cost of Goods Sold**). This illustration assumes that no shrinkage has been detected.

No entries

PERIODIC	PERPETUAL

Assets	=	Liabilities	+	Stockholders' Equity
Purchases +10,200		Accounts Payable +10,200		
Accts. Rec. +12,000				Sales Revenue (+R) +12,000
Inventory −4,800				Cost of Goods Sold (+E) −9,000
Purchases −10,200				
Inventory +6,000				
Totals +13,200 =		+10,200		+3,000

Assets	=	Liabilities	+	Stockholders' Equity
Inventory +10,200		Accounts Payable +10,200		
Accts. Rec. +12,000				Sales Revenue (+R) +12,000
Inventory −9,000				Cost of Goods Sold (+E) −9,000
Totals +13,200 =		+10,200		+3,000

REVIEW THE CHAPTER

DEMONSTRATION CASE A: PURCHASES AND SALES OF MERCHANDISE

Assume Oakley, Inc.—the maker of sunglasses, goggles, and other products—made merchandise costing $137,200 and sold it on credit to Sunglass Hut for $405,000, with terms n/60, FOB shipping point. Oakley shipped the goods on October 1, and Sunglass Hut received them on October 2. On October 5, Oakley agreed to give Sunglass Hut an allowance of $5,000. On October 25, Sunglass Hut paid in full the balance owed to Oakley.

Oakley, Inc.
Sunglass Hut
Luxottica Group

Required:

1. Assume Sunglass Hut (the purchaser) uses a perpetual inventory system. Analyze the accounting equation effects and record the journal entries Sunglass Hut would use for the following transactions. Include dates.

 a. Sunglass Hut purchases goods shipped by Oakley on October 1.
 b. Allowance granted by Oakley on October 5.
 c. Payment made by Sunglass Hut to Oakley on October 25.

2. Assume Oakley (the seller) uses a perpetual inventory system. Analyze the accounting equation effects and record the journal entries Oakley would use for the following transactions. Include dates.

 a. Oakley sells and ships goods to Sunglass Hut on October 1.
 b. Allowance granted by Oakley on October 5.
 c. Payment made by Sunglass Hut to Oakley on October 25.

3. Assume the same facts as requirement 2, except Oakley's terms were 2/30, n/60. Compute Oakley's net sales, after sales returns/allowances and sales discounts.

4. Using your answer from requirement 3, compute Oakley's gross profit and gross profit percentage on the sale. Compare this ratio to the 64.0 percent gross profit percentage reported in 2018 by the Luxottica Group—the Italian company that makes Persol® and Ray-Ban® sunglasses. What does it imply about the two companies?

> **COACH'S TIP**
>
> Transaction b depicts an allowance but no return of goods. Because no goods are returned, Oakley does not increase its Inventory and decrease its Cost of Goods Sold, but it does account for the allowance's effect on the selling price.

Suggested Solution

1. **a.** Purchase from Oakley, recorded October 1 when ownership transfers.

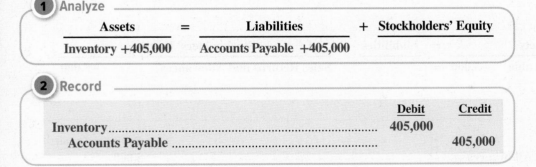

1 Analyze

Assets	=	Liabilities	+ Stockholders' Equity
Inventory +405,000		Accounts Payable +405,000	

2 Record

	Debit	Credit
Inventory	405,000	
Accounts Payable		405,000

b. Allowance granted by Oakley, recorded October 5.

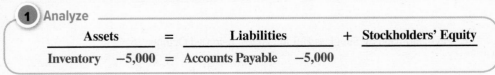

1 Analyze

Assets	=	Liabilities	+ Stockholders' Equity
Inventory −5,000	=	Accounts Payable −5,000	

2 Record

	Debit	Credit
Accounts Payable	5,000	
Inventory		5,000

c. Payment made by Sunglass Hut to Oakley, recorded October 25.

1 Analyze

Assets		=	Liabilities	+	Stockholders' Equity
Cash	−400,000	=	Accounts Payable −400,000		

2 Record

	Debit	Credit
Accounts Payable	400,000	
Cash		400,000

2. a. Sale from Oakley to Sunglass Hut, recorded October 1 when ownership transfers.

1 Analyze

Assets		=	Liabilities	+	Stockholders' Equity	
Accounts Receivable	+405,000	=			Sales Revenue (+R)	+405,000
Inventory	−137,200	=			Cost of Goods Sold (+E)	−137,200

2 Record

	Debit	Credit
Accounts Receivable	405,000	
Sales Revenue		405,000
Cost of Goods Sold	137,200	
Inventory		137,200

b. Allowance granted by Oakley (no goods returned), recorded October 5.

1 Analyze

Assets		=	Liabilities	+	Stockholders' Equity	
Accounts Receivable	−5,000	=			Sales Returns and Allowances	−5,000

2 Record

	Debit	Credit
Sales Returns and Allowances	5,000	
Accounts Receivable		5,000

c. Payment made by Sunglass Hut to Oakley, recorded October 25.

1 Analyze

Assets		=	Liabilities	+	Stockholders' Equity
Cash	+400,000				
Accounts Receivable	−400,000				

2 Record

	Debit	Credit
Cash	400,000	
Accounts Receivable		400,000

3. Sales returns/allowances and sales discounts should be subtracted from sales revenue to compute net sales:

Sales Revenue, gross	$405,000
Sales Returns/Allowances	(5,000)
Sales Discounts	(8,000)*
Net Sales	$392,000

*$8,000 = 2% × ($405,000 − $5,000)

4. Gross profit and gross profit percentage are calculated as follows:

	In Dollars	Percent of Net Sales
Net Sales (calculated in 3.)	$392,000	100.0%
Cost of Goods Sold	137,200	35.0
Gross Profit	$254,800	65.0%

The 65 percent gross profit percentage indicates that Oakley generates 65 cents of gross profit on each dollar of sales. This is one cent more gross profit on each dollar of sales than Luxottica (1.0 = 65.0 − 64.0). This difference implies Oakley is including a slightly higher markup in its selling prices than Luxottica.

DEMONSTRATION CASE B: SALES OF BUNDLED ITEMS

Scholastic Incorporated sells loose-leaf textbooks and 12 months of online learning system access as a bundle for a price of $160. When sold separately, the textbook sells for $50 and the online learning system service sells for $150. A customer paid $160 for the bundle on October 28, the textbook was sent FOB shipping point on October 30, and 12 months of system service started November 1. Scholastic Incorporated has many loose-leaf textbooks in its inventory, each at a cost of $15.

Required:

1. Compute the dollar amount of revenue that should be allocated to Sales Revenue (for textbooks) and Service Revenue (for learning system access).
2. When should the revenue be recognized for (a) textbook sales and (b) learning system service?
3. Record the journal entries required on October 28, October 30, November 1, and November 30.

Suggested Solution

1. The stand-alone prices of a textbook ($50) and learning system service ($150) sum to $200. Of this total, the textbook is 25% ($50/$200 = 25%) and the learning system service is 75% ($150/$200 = 75%). Thus, the textbook should be allocated 25% of the bundled price of $160, or $40 (0.25 × $160). The learning system service should be allocated 75% of the bundled price of $160, or $120 (0.75 × $160).

2. The performance obligation for the textbook sale is satisfied (and the related $40 of revenue should be recognized) at the point of delivery, which under the terms FOB shipping point is fulfilled at the time of shipment (October 30). The performance obligation for the learning system service is satisfied over the 12 months of service, so its revenue of $120 should be recognized each month as the service is provided ($10 per month).

3. Journal entries:

		Debit	Credit
Oct. 28	Cash	160	
	Deferred Revenue......................................		160
Oct. 30	Deferred Revenue	40	
	Sales Revenue..		40
	Cost of Goods Sold..	15	
	Inventory..		15
Nov. 1	No journal entry required because no service has been given yet.		
Nov. 30	Deferred Revenue	10	
	Service Revenue		10

CHAPTER SUMMARY

LO 6-1 **Distinguish between service and merchandising operations.**

- Service companies sell services rather than physical goods; consequently, their income statements show operating expenses from providing services but no cost of goods sold.

- Merchandise companies sell goods that have been obtained from a supplier. Retail merchandise companies sell directly to consumers whereas wholesale merchandise companies sell to retail companies.

LO 6-2 **Explain the differences between periodic and perpetual inventory systems.**

- Periodic inventory records are updated only when inventory is counted, usually at the end of each accounting period.

- Perpetual inventory systems promote efficient and effective operations because they provide an up-to-date record of inventory that should be on hand at any given time. They protect against undetected theft because this up-to-date record can be compared to a count of the physical quantity that actually is on hand.

LO 6-3 **Analyze purchase transactions under a perpetual inventory system.**

- The Inventory account should include costs incurred to get inventory into a condition and location ready for sale.

- The cost of inventory includes its purchase price and transportation (freight-in) minus cost reductions for purchase returns and allowances, purchase discounts, and goods sold. Costs to deliver inventory to customers (freight-out) are a selling expense and are not included in inventory.

LO 6-4 **Analyze sales transactions under a perpetual inventory system.**

- In a perpetual inventory system, journal entries are needed for each sale to record two amounts: (i) selling price (debit Cash or Accounts Receivable and credit Sales Revenue) and (ii) cost (debit Cost of Goods Sold and credit Inventory).

- Sales discounts and sales returns and allowances are subtracted from (gross) Sales Revenue to yield Net Sales.

Analyze sales of bundled items under a perpetual inventory system.

- When goods and services are sold together for a single "bundled" price, the price is allocated to the goods and services based on their stand-alone selling prices. Revenue is then recognized when (as) each performance obligation is satisfied by delivering goods (providing services).

Prepare and analyze a merchandiser's multistep income statement.

- One of the key items in a merchandiser's multistep income statement is gross profit, which is a subtotal calculated by subtracting cost of goods sold from net sales. The gross profit percentage is calculated and interpreted as follows.

Accounting Decision Tools		
Name of Measure	**Formula**	**What It Tells You**
Gross profit percentage	$\dfrac{\text{Net Sales} - \text{CGS}}{\text{Net Sales}}$	• The percentage of profit earned on each dollar of sales, after considering the cost of products sold • A higher ratio means that greater profit is available to cover operating and other expenses

KEY TERMS

Cost of Goods Sold Equation p. 262
FOB Destination p. 265
FOB Shipping Point p. 265
Goods Available for Sale p. 262
Gross Profit (Gross Margin, Margin) p. 274
Gross Profit Percentage p. 275

Inventory p. 260
Merchandising Company p. 260
Multistep Income Statement p. 274
Periodic Inventory System p. 263
Perpetual Inventory System p. 263
Purchase Discount p. 266

Purchase Returns and Allowances p. 266
Sales Discount p. 270
Sales Returns and Allowances p. 269
Service Company p. 260
Shrinkage p. 263

See complete definitions in the glossary in the back of this text.

HOMEWORK HELPER

Multistep Income Statement Format (heading omitted)

Sales Revenue	$100,000
Sales Returns and Allowances	(2,500)
Sales Discounts	(1,500)
Net Sales	96,000
Cost of Goods Sold	55,000
Gross Profit	41,000
Selling, General, and Administrative Expenses	21,000
Income from Operations	20,000
Other Revenue (Expenses)	5,000
Income before Income Tax Expense	25,000
Income Tax Expense	10,000
Net Income	$ 15,000

Reported Externally

Reported Internally

Alternative terms

- Gross profit is also called gross margin or margin.
- Purchase and sales discounts are also called early payment and cash discounts.

Helpful reminders

- As sales returns occur, record two components: (1) adjust the initial selling price (by recording a contra-revenue and either decreasing Cash or Accounts Receivable or increasing Deferred Revenue, depending on whether cash, a reduction in the right to collect cash, or a gift card is given to the customer) and (2) record the return of goods previously recorded as sold (increase Inventory and decrease Cost of Goods Sold). Sales allowances involve only the first component because no goods are returned to the seller.
- Purchase and sales discounts are calculated after taking into account any returns and allowances. A partial payment within the discount period (such as one-half the total amount owed) usually qualifies for a partial discount (one-half of the discount on the total).

Frequent mistakes

- Discounts (or "markdowns") in the selling price of merchandise prior to making a sale are not recorded. Sales Discounts, given to customers after making a sale, are recorded by the seller in a contra-revenue account, to offset the Sales Revenue recorded on the initial sales transaction.
- Gross profit percentage is calculated as a percentage of Net Sales, not as a percentage of Total Revenue or Cost of Goods Sold.

PRACTICE MATERIAL

QUESTIONS (● Symbol indicates questions that require analysis from more than one perspective.)

1. What is the distinction between service and merchandising companies? What is the distinction between merchandising and manufacturing companies? What is the distinction between retail and wholesale merchandising companies?

2. If a Chicago-based company ships goods on September 30 to a customer in Hawaii with sales terms FOB destination, does the Chicago-based company include the inventory or the sale in its September financial statements?

3. Define *goods available for sale*. How does it differ from cost of goods sold?

4. Define *beginning inventory* and *ending inventory*.

5. Describe how transportation costs to obtain inventory (freight-in) are accounted for by a merchandising company using a perpetual inventory system. Explain the reasoning behind this accounting treatment.

6. What is the main distinction between perpetual and periodic inventory systems? Which type of system provides better internal control over inventory? Explain why.

7. Why is a physical count of inventory necessary in a periodic inventory system? Why is it still necessary in a perpetual inventory system?

8. What is the difference between FOB shipping point and FOB destination? How do these terms relate to the revenue principle?

9. Describe in words the journal entries that are made in a perpetual inventory system when inventory is sold on credit.

10. What is the distinction between *Sales Returns* and *Sales Allowances*?

11. What is a sales discount? Use 2/30, n/45 in your explanation.

12. In response to the weak economy, your company's sales force is urging you, the sales manager, to change sales terms from 1/10, n/30 to 2/30, n/60. Explain what these terms mean and how this switch could increase or decrease your company's profits. ●

13. Explain the difference between Sales Revenue (gross) and Net Sales.

14. Why is revenue from selling a product/service bundle allocated between the product and service?

15. What is gross profit? How is the gross profit percentage computed? Illustrate its calculation and interpretation assuming Net Sales is $100,000 and Cost of Goods Sold is $60,000.

MULTIPLE CHOICE

1. Mountain Gear, Inc., buys bikes, tents, and climbing supplies from Rugged Rock Corporation for sale to consumers. What type of company is Mountain Gear, Inc.?

    a. Service
    b. Retail merchandiser
    c. Wholesale merchandiser
    d. Manufacturer

2. Each period, the Cost of Goods Available for Sale is allocated between

    a. Assets and Liabilities.
    b. Assets and Expenses.
    c. Assets and Revenues.
    d. Expenses and Liabilities.

3. A company that purchases inventory costing $10,000 on terms 2/30, n/60, but first returns one-half of those goods, will receive a discount of what amount if it pays on the last day of the discount period?

a. $0 b. $100
c. $200 d. $5,000

4. If beginning inventory is $200 and purchases are $800, which of the following could be true?

a. Ending inventory is $400 and Cost of Goods Sold is $600.
b. Ending inventory is $800 and Cost of Goods Sold is $800.
c. Ending inventory is $200 and Cost of Goods Sold is $200.
d. Ending inventory is $200 and Cost of Goods Sold is $600.

5. Which of the following is false regarding a perpetual inventory system?

a. Physical counts are never needed because records are maintained on a transaction-by-transaction basis.
b. The Inventory records are updated with each inventory purchase, sale, or return transaction.
c. Cost of Goods Sold is increased as sales are recorded.
d. A perpetual inventory system can be used to detect shrinkage.

6. Sales discounts with terms 2/10, n/30 mean

a. 10 percent discount for payment received within 30 days of the date of sale.
b. 2 percent discount for payment received within 10 days or the full amount (less returns) is due within 30 days.
c. Two-tenths of a percent discount for payment received within 30 days.
d. None of the above.

7. Which of the following does not affect Net Sales?

a. Sales Returns and Allowances
b. Sales Discounts
c. Cost of Goods Sold
d. Sales Revenue

8. A $1,000 sale is made on May 1 with terms 2/30, n/60. Items with a $100 selling price are returned on May 3. What amount, if received on May 9, will be considered payment in full?

a. $700 b. $800
c. $882 d. $900

9. A company bundles a product and service that separately sell for $40 and $60, respectively. If the bundled price is $80, how much revenue is recognized for delivering the product?

a. $32 b. $40
c. $60 d. $80

10. This year your company has purchased less expensive merchandise inventory but has not changed its selling prices. What effect will this change have on the company's gross profit percentage this year, in comparison to last year?

a. The ratio will not change.
b. The ratio will increase.
c. The ratio will decrease.
d. Cannot determine.

> For answers to the Multiple-Choice Questions **see page Q1** located in the last section of the book.

MINI-EXERCISES

Mc Graw Hill **connect**

M6-1 Distinguishing among Operating Cycles

LO 6-1

Identify the type of business as service (S), retail merchandiser (RM), or wholesale merchandiser (WM) for each of the following.

____ **1.** The company reports no inventory on its balance sheet.

____ **2.** The company is a true "middleman," buying from a manufacturer and selling to other companies.

____ **3.** The company sells goods to consumers.

M6-2 Calculating Shrinkage in a Perpetual Inventory System

LO 6-2

Corey's Campus Store has $4,000 of inventory on hand at the beginning of the month. During the month, the company buys $41,000 of merchandise and sells merchandise that had cost $30,000. At the end of the month, $13,000 of inventory is on hand. How much shrinkage occurred during the month?

M6-3 Accounting for Inventory Transportation Costs

LO 6-3

XO Group sells merchandise to companies (and individuals) for significant milestones in life, such as getting married, moving in together, and having a baby. Indicate (yes/no) whether the following costs should be recorded in the Inventory account in XO Group's perpetual inventory system.

XO Group

a. Transportation costs incurred by XO Group when it buys goods from suppliers under terms FOB shipping point.

b. Transportation costs incurred by XO Group when it delivers goods to customers under terms FOB destination.

c. Transportation costs incurred by XO Group's customers when XO Group sells goods under terms FOB shipping point.

LO 6-3

Dillard's, Inc.

M6-4 Inferring Purchases Using the Cost of Goods Sold Equation

Dillard's, Inc., operates department stores located primarily in the Southwest, Southeast, and Midwest. In its 2019 second-quarter report, the company reported Cost of Goods Sold of $1,030 million, ending inventory for the second quarter of $1,600 million, and ending inventory for the previous quarter of $1,830 million. Determine the amount of merchandise purchases for the second quarter.

LO 6-3

M6-5 Evaluating Inventory Cost Components

Assume Anderson's General Store bought, on credit, a truckload of merchandise from American Wholesaling costing $23,000. If Anderson's paid National Trucking $650 cash for transportation, immediately returned goods to American Wholesaling costing $1,200, and then paid American Wholesaling within the 2/30, n/60 purchase discount period, how much did this inventory cost Anderson's? Assume Anderson's uses a perpetual inventory system.

LO 6-3, 6-4, 6-6

M6-6 Preparing Journal Entries for Inventory Purchases and Sales in a Perpetual System

Inventory at the beginning of the year cost $13,400. During the year, the company purchased (on account) inventory costing $84,000. Inventory that had cost $80,000 was sold on account for $95,000. At the end of the year, inventory was counted and its cost was determined to be $17,400. (*a*) Show the cost of goods sold equation using these numbers. (*b*) What was the dollar amount of gross profit? (*c*) Prepare journal entries to record these transactions, assuming a perpetual inventory system is used.

LO 6-3, 6-4

M6-7 Recording Journal Entries for Purchases, Purchase Returns, Sales, and Sales Returns Using a Perpetual Inventory System

During its first year of operations, Tron Auto Dealership (TAD) bought vehicles from a manufacturer on account at a cost of $608,000. TAD returned $152,000 of these vehicles to the manufacturer for credit on its account. TAD then sold $380,000 of the remaining vehicles for cash at a selling price of $685,000. TAD's customers rarely return vehicles, so TAD records sales returns only as they occur. One customer did return a vehicle to TAD for cash, which had been sold to the customer for $137,000. The vehicle was in perfect condition, so it was put back into TAD's inventory at TAD's cost of $76,000. Prepare journal entries to record these transactions, assuming TAD uses a perpetual inventory system.

LO 6-3, 6-4

M6-8 Recording Journal Entries for Purchases, Purchase Returns, Sales, and Actual and Estimated Sales Returns Using a Perpetual Inventory System

During its first year of operations, Drone Zone Corporation (DZC) bought goods from a manufacturer on account at a cost of $50,000. DZC returned $8,000 of this merchandise to the manufacturer for credit on its account. DZC then sold $38,000 of the remaining goods for cash at a selling price of $64,600. DZC records sales returns as they occur and then records estimated additional returns at year-end. During the year, customers returned goods and were issued gift cards equal in amount to the initial selling price of $6,800. These goods were in perfect condition, so they were put back into DZC's inventory at their cost of $4,000. At year-end, DZC estimated $9,010 of current-year merchandise sales would be returned to DZC in the following year; DZC estimates $5,300 as its cost of this merchandise. Prepare journal entries to record DZC's transactions and estimates, assuming DZC uses a perpetual inventory system.

LO 6-4

M6-9 Reporting Net Sales and Gross Profit with Sales Discounts

Merchandise costing $2,000 is sold for $3,000 on terms 2/30, n/60. If the customer pays within the discount period, what amount will be reported on the income statement as net sales and as gross profit?

LO 6-4

American Eagle Outfitters

M6-10 Choosing between FOB Shipping Point and FOB Destination

In its annual report, American Eagle Outfitters states that its "e-commerce operation records revenue upon the estimated customer receipt date of the merchandise." Is this FOB shipping point or FOB destination? If American Eagle were to change to the other terms of shipment, would it report its Sales Revenues earlier or later?

LO 6-2, 6-6

M6-11 Calculating Shrinkage and Gross Profit in a Perpetual System

Nord Store's perpetual accounting system indicated ending inventory of $20,000, cost of goods sold of $100,000, and net sales of $150,000. A year-end inventory count determined goods costing

$15,000 were actually on hand. Calculate (*a*) the cost of shrinkage, (*b*) an adjusted cost of goods sold (assuming shrinkage is charged to cost of goods sold), (*c*) gross profit percentage before shrinkage, and (*d*) gross profit percentage after shrinkage. Round gross profit percentages to one decimal place.

M6-12 Allocating Transaction Price to Performance Obligations

A company that usually sells satellite TV equipment for $50 and two years of satellite TV service for $450 has a special, time-limited offer in which it sells the equipment for $300 and gives the two years of satellite service for "free." If the company sells one of these packages on July 1, how much revenue should the company recognize on July 1 when it delivers the equipment and receives the full price in cash?

LO 6-5

M6-13 Preparing a Multistep Income Statement

Sellall Department Stores reported the following amounts as of its December 31 year-end: Administrative Expenses, $2,400; Cost of Goods Sold, $22,728; Income Tax Expense, $3,000; Interest Expense, $1,600; Interest Revenue, $200; General Expenses, $2,600; Net Sales, $37,880; and Delivery (freight-out) Expense, $300. Prepare a multistep income statement for distribution to external financial statement users, using a format similar to Exhibit 6.9.

LO 6-6

M6-14 Computing and Interpreting the Gross Profit Percentage

Using the information in M6-13, calculate the gross profit percentage (rounded to one decimal place). How has Sellall performed, relative to the 24.5 percent gross profit percentage reported for Walmart in 2019?

LO 6-6

Walmart

M6-15 Computing and Interpreting the Gross Profit Percentage

Ziehart Pharmaceuticals reported Net Sales of $178,000 and Cost of Goods Sold of $58,000. Candy Electronics Corp. reported Net Sales of $36,000 and Cost of Goods Sold of $26,200. Calculate the gross profit percentage for both companies (rounded to one decimal place). Which company has a greater proportion of its sales available to cover expenses other than cost of goods sold?

LO 6-6

M6-16 Interpreting Changes in Gross Profit Percentage

Luxottica Group, the Italian company that sells Ray Ban and Oakley sunglasses, reported net sales of €8.9 billion in 2018 and €9.2 billion in 2017. Gross profit decreased from €5.9 billion in 2017 to €5.7 billion in 2018. Was the change in gross profit caused by (*a*) a decrease in gross profit per sale, (*b*) a decrease in sales volume, or (*c*) a combination of (*a*) and (*b*)?

LO 6-6

Luxottica Group

M6-17 Determining the Cause of Increasing Gross Profit

Fortune Brands Home & Security, Inc., sells Master Lock padlocks. It reported an increase in net sales from $5.3 billion in 2017 to $5.5 billion in 2018, and an increase in gross profit from $1.2 billion in 2017 to $1.3 billion in 2018. Based on these numbers, determine whether the change in gross profit represents (*a*) an increase in gross profit per sale, (*b*) an increase in sales volume, or a combination of (*a*) and (*b*).

LO 6-6

Fortune Brands Home & Security, Inc.

M6-18 Understanding Relationships among Gross Profit and Inventory

If net sales are $300,000, cost of goods available for sale is $280,000, and gross profit percentage is 35 percent, what is the amount of ending inventory?

LO 6-2, 6-6

LEVEL UP

M6-19 Recording Journal Entries for Purchase Discounts (Gross Method)

On October 5, your company buys and receives inventory costing $5,000, on terms 2/30, n/60. On October 20, your company pays the amount owed relating to the October 5 purchase. Prepare the journal entries needed on October 5 and 20, assuming the company uses a perpetual system and records purchase discounts using the gross method.

LO 6-S1

M6-20 Recording Journal Entries for Purchase Discounts (Net Method)

Using the information in M6-19, prepare the journal entries needed on October 5 and 20, assuming the company uses a perpetual system and records purchase discounts using the net method.

LO 6-S1

M6-21 Recording Journal Entries for Sales and Sales Discounts (Gross Method)

Using the information in M6-9, prepare the journal entries needed at (*a*) time of sale and (*b*) collection of payment from the customer, assuming the company uses a perpetual inventory system with the gross method of recording sales discounts.

LO 6-S1

LO 6-S1   **M6-22 Recording Journal Entries for Sales and Sales Discounts (Net Method)**

Using the information in M6-9, prepare the journal entries needed at (*a*) time of sale and (*b*) collection of payment from the customer, assuming the company uses a perpetual inventory system with the net method of recording sales discounts.

LO 6-S1   **M6-23 Journal Entries to Record Sales Discounts (Gross Method)**

Inventory that cost $500 is sold for $700, with terms of 2/30, n/60. Give the journal entries to record (*a*) the sale of merchandise and (*b*) collection of the accounts receivable. Assume the sales discount is taken and accounted for using the gross method, and a perpetual inventory system is used.

LO 6-S1   **M6-24 Journal Entries to Record Sales Discounts (Net Method)**

Inventory that cost $500 is sold for $700, with terms of 2/30, n/60. Give the journal entries to record (*a*) the sale of merchandise and (*b*) collection of the accounts receivable. Assume the sales discount is taken and accounted for using the net method, and a perpetual inventory system is used.

EXERCISES

LO 6-1   **E6-1 Relating Financial Statement Reporting to Type of Company**

For each of the following, indicate whether the item would be reported on the balance sheet (B/S), reported on the income statement (I/S), or not shown in the financial statements (Not). Also indicate whether it relates to a service company (SC) or merchandising company (MC).

	Financial Statement	Type of Company
Inventory		
Sales Revenue		
Number of Units Available for Sale		
Service Revenue		

LO 6-2   **E6-2 Inferring Merchandise Purchases**

The Gap, Inc.

The Gap, Inc., is a specialty retailer that operates stores selling clothes under the trade names Gap, Banana Republic, Athleta, and Old Navy. Assume that you are employed as a stock analyst and your boss has just completed a review of The Gap, Inc., for the first quarter of 2019. She provided you with her notes, but they are missing some information that you need. Her notes show the inventory for Gap was $2,240 million at the end of the quarter and $2,130 million at the beginning of the quarter. Net Sales for the quarter were $3,700 million. Gross Profit was $1,340 million and Net Income was $227 million.

Required:

Determine the Cost of Goods Sold and cost of purchases for the first quarter.

LO6-2   **E6-3 Identifying Shrinkage and Other Missing Inventory Information**

Calculate the missing information for each of the following independent cases:

Cases	Beginning Inventory	Purchases	Cost of Goods Sold	Ending Inventory (perpetual system)	Ending Inventory (as counted)	Shrinkage
A	$100	$700	$300	?	$420	$?
B	200	800	?	150	150	?
C	150	500	200	450	?	10
D	260	?	650	210	200	?

LO 6-2   **E6-4 Inferring Shrinkage Using a Perpetual Inventory System**

Macy's

In the year ended February 2, 2019, Macy's reported cost of goods sold (before shrinkage) of $15.2 billion; February 2, 2019, inventory of $5.3 billion; and ending inventory for the previous year (February 3, 2018) of $5.2 billion.

Required:

If the cost of inventory purchases was $15.5 billion, what was the cost of shrinkage during the year ended February 2, 2019?

E6-5 Inferring Missing Amounts Based on Income Statement Relationships   **LO 6-2, 6-6**

Supply the missing dollar amounts for each of the following independent cases:

Cases	Sales Revenue	Beginning Inventory	Purchases	Cost of Goods Available for Sale	Cost of Goods Sold	Cost of Ending Inventory	Gross Profit
A	$ 700	$100	$800	?	$300	$?	$?
B	900	200	800	?	?	150	?
C	?	100	?	?	200	300	400
D	800	?	600	?	650	250	?
E	1,000	50	900	?	?	?	500

E6-6 Inferring Missing Amounts Based on Income Statement Relationships   **LO 6-2, 6-6**

Supply the missing dollar amounts for each of the following independent cases:

Cases	Sales Revenue	Beginning Inventory	Purchases	Total Available	Ending Inventory	Cost of Goods Sold	Gross Profit	Selling and General Expenses	Income from Operations
A	$800	$100	$700	$?	$500	$?	$?	$200	$?
B	900	200	700	?	?	?	?	150	0
C	?	100	?	?	200	200	400	150	?
D	800	?	600	?	300	?	?	250	100

E6-7 Reporting Purchases and Purchase Discounts Using a Perpetual Inventory System   **LO 6-3**

During the months of January and February, Axe Corporation purchased goods from three suppliers. The sequence of events was as follows:

Jan. 6	Purchased goods for $1,200 from Green with terms 2/10, n/30.
6	Purchased goods from Munoz for $900 with terms 2/10, n/30.
14	Paid Green in full.
Feb. 2	Paid Munoz in full.
28	Purchased goods for $350 from Reynolds with terms n/45.

Required:

Assume that Axe uses a perpetual inventory system, the company had no inventory on hand at the beginning of January, and no sales were made during January and February. Calculate the cost of inventory as of February 28.

E6-8 Reporting Purchases, Purchase Discounts, and Purchase Returns Using a Perpetual Inventory System   **LO 6-3**

During the month of June, Ace Incorporated purchased goods from two suppliers. The sequence of events was as follows:

June 3	Purchased goods for $4,100 from Diamond Inc. with terms 2/10, n/30.
5	Returned goods costing $1,100 to Diamond Inc. for credit on account.
6	Purchased goods from Club Corp. for $1,000 with terms 2/10, n/30.
11	Paid the balance owed to Diamond Inc.
22	Paid Club Corp. in full.

Required:

Assume that Ace uses a perpetual inventory system and that the company had no inventory on hand at the beginning of the month. Calculate the cost of inventory as of June 30.

LO 6-3, 6-4   **E6-9   Items Included in Inventory**

PCM, Inc.   PCM, Inc., is a direct marketer of computer hardware, software, peripherals, and electronics. In its 2018 annual report, the company reported, "we changed the terms of sale in the fourth quarter of 2017 such that all of our businesses have terms where title and risk of loss transfer upon delivery to the customer."

Required:

1. Indicate whether PCM's sales terms are FOB shipping point or FOB destination.
2. Assume PCM sold inventory on account to eCOST.com on December 28 that was to be delivered January 3. The inventory cost PCM $25,000 and the selling price was $30,000. What amounts, if any, related to this transaction would be reported on PCM's balance sheet and income statement in December? In January?
3. Assume PCM purchased electronics on December 29 that were shipped that day and received on January 2. For these goods to be included in PCM's inventory on December 31, would the terms have been FOB destination or FOB shipping point?

LO 6-4   **E6-10   Reporting Net Sales after Sales Discounts**

During the months of January and February, Solitare Corporation sold goods to two customers. The sequence of events was as follows:

Jan. 6	Sold goods for $100 to Wizard Inc. with terms 2/30, n/60. The goods cost Solitare $70.
6	Sold goods to Spyder Corp. for $80 with terms 5/10, n/60. The goods cost Solitare $60.
14	Collected cash for the amount due from Wizard Inc.
Feb. 28	Collected cash for the amount due from Spyder Corp.

Required:

Compute the Net Sales Solitare would report over the two months.

LO 6-4   **E6-11   Reporting Net Sales after Sales Discounts**

The following transactions were selected from the records of Evergreen Company:

July 12	Sold merchandise to Wally Butler, who paid the $1,000 purchase with cash. The goods cost Evergreen Company $600.
15	Sold merchandise to Claudio's Chair Company at a selling price of $5,000 on terms 3/10, n/30. The goods cost Evergreen Company $3,500.
16	Sold merchandise to Otto's Ottomans at a selling price of $3,000 on terms 3/10, n/30. The goods cost Evergreen Company $1,900.
23	Received cash from Claudio's Chair Company for the amount due from July 15.
31	Received cash from Otto's Ottomans for the amount due from July 16.

Required:

Compute the amount of Net Sales to be reported for the month ended July 31.

LO 6-4   **E6-12   Reporting Net Sales after Sales Discounts and Sales Returns**

The following transactions were selected from among those completed by Bear's Retail Store:

Nov. 20	Sold two items of merchandise to Cheryl Jahn, who paid the $400 sales price in cash. The goods cost Bear's $300.
25	Sold 20 items of merchandise to Vasko Athletics at a selling price of $4,000 (total); terms 3/10, n/30. The goods cost Bear's $2,500.
28	Sold 10 identical items of merchandise to Nancy's Gym at a selling price of $6,000 (total); terms 3/10, n/30. The goods cost Bear's $4,000.

29	Nancy's Gym returned one of the items purchased on the 28th. The item was in perfect condition and credit was given to the customer on account. No further returns are expected.
Dec. 6	Nancy's Gym paid the account balance in full.
30	Vasko Athletics paid in full for the invoice of November 25.

Required:

Compute the Net Sales to be reported over the two months.

E6-13 Determining the Effects of Credit Sales, Sales Discounts, and Sales Returns and Allowances on the Income Statement

LO 6-4, 6-6

Complete the following table, indicating the amount and direction of effect (+ for increase, − for decrease, and NE for no effect) of each transaction on each item in Rockland Shoe Company's income statement. Be sure to compute the total effects in the final column. Rockland allows returns within only two weeks of the initial sale.

July 12	Rockland sold merchandise to Kristina Zee at its factory store. Kristina paid for the $300 purchase in cash. The goods cost Rockland $160.
15	Sold merchandise to Shoe Express at a selling price of $5,000, with terms n/30. Rockland's cost was $3,000.
23	Shoe Express returned $1,000 of the shoes purchased July 15. The returned shoes were in perfect condition and had cost Rockland $600.
31	Shoe Express paid the balance owing after the events on July 15 and 23.

	July 12	July 15	July 23	July 31	Totals
Sales Revenues					
Sales Returns and Allowances					
Net Sales					
Cost of Goods Sold					
Gross Profit					

E6-14 Analyzing and Recording Sales and Gross Profit with Sales Returns

LO 6-4, 6-6

Cycle Wholesaling sold merchandise on account, with terms n/60, to Sarah's Cycles on February 1 for $800 (cost of goods sold of $500). On February 9, Sarah's Cycles returned to Cycle Wholesaling one-quarter of the merchandise from February 1 (cost of goods returned was $125). Cycle Wholesaling uses a perpetual inventory system, and it allows returns only within 15 days of initial sale.

Required:

1. Prepare the journal entry Cycle Wholesaling makes to record the sale to Sarah's Cycles.
2. Prepare the journal entry Cycle Wholesaling makes to record the goods returned on February 9.
3. Prepare the journal entry Cycle Wholesaling makes when the remaining balance owed by Sarah's Cycles is collected in full on March 2.
4. Calculate the gross profit percentage for the sale to Sarah's Cycles (rounded to one decimal place).

E6-15 Allocating Transaction Price to Performance Obligations

LO 6-5

A company separately sells home security equipment and 12 months of system monitoring service for $120 and $240, respectively. The company sells an equipment/monitoring bundle on January 1 for a total price of $270. The monitoring service begins immediately after the equipment is delivered and installed on January 1.

Required:

1. Determine the dollars of revenue that should be allocated to the equipment for each bundled sale.
2. Determine the dollars of revenue that should be allocated to the service for each bundled sale.
3. Determine the dollars of Sales Revenue and Service Revenue from the January 1 bundled sale that should be reported in the income statement for the period January 1–31.

LO 6-6   **E6-16 Inferring Missing Amounts Based on Income Statement Relationships**

Supply the missing dollar amounts for the income statement of Williamson Company for each of the following independent cases:

	Case A	Case B	Case C
Sales Revenues, gross	$8,000	$6,000	$?
Sales Returns and Allowances	150	?	275
Net Sales	?	?	5,920
Cost of Goods Sold	5,750	4,050	5,400
Gross Profit	?	1,450	?

LO 6-6   **E6-17 Analyzing Gross Profit Percentage on the Basis of a Multistep Income Statement**

The following data were provided by Mystery Incorporated for the year ended December 31:

Cost of Goods Sold	$165,000
Income Tax Expense	17,600
Merchandise Sales (gross revenue) for Cash	240,000
Merchandise Sales (gross revenue) on Credit	42,000
Office Expense	19,000
Sales Returns and Allowances	7,000
Salaries and Wages Expense	40,200

Required:

1. Based on these data, prepare a multistep income statement for external reporting purposes (showing appropriate subtotals and totals).
2. What was the dollar amount of gross profit? What was the gross profit percentage (calculated using the formula shown in this chapter and rounded to one decimal place)? Explain what these two amounts mean.
3. Did the gross profit percentage in the current year improve, or decline, relative to the 38.0 percent gross profit percentage in the prior year?

LO 6-6   **E6-18 Analyzing Gross Profit Percentage on the Basis of an Income Statement**

Wolverine World Wide, Inc.

Wolverine World Wide, Inc., prides itself as being the "world's leading marketer of U.S. branded non-athletic footwear." The following data (in millions) were reported for the second quarter of 2019:

Net Sales	$570
Income Tax Expense	10
Dividends	9
Salaries and Wages Expense	170
Cost of Goods Sold	345
Interest Expense	5

Required:

1. Based on these data, prepare a multistep income statement.
2. How much was the gross profit in dollars? What was the gross profit percentage? (Round to one decimal place.) Explain what these two amounts mean.
3. Did the gross profit percentage in the current quarter improve, or decline, relative to the 42.1 percent gross profit percentage in the prior quarter?

LO 6-S1   **E6-19 (Supplement 6A) Recording Journal Entries for Purchases and Purchase Discounts (Gross Method) Using a Perpetual Inventory System**

Using the information in E6-7, prepare journal entries to record the transactions, assuming Axe records discounts using the gross method in a perpetual inventory system.

E6-20 (Supplement 6A) Recording Journal Entries for Purchases and Purchase Discounts   **LO 6-S1**
(Net Method) Using a Perpetual Inventory System

Using the information in E6-7, prepare journal entries to record the transactions, assuming Axe records discounts using the net method in a perpetual inventory system. Forfeited discounts are charged to Other Operating Expenses.

E6-21 (Supplement 6A) Recording Journal Entries for Purchases, Purchase Discounts (Gross   **LO 6-S1**
Method), and Purchase Returns Using a Perpetual Inventory System

Using the information in E6-8, prepare journal entries to record the transactions, assuming Ace records discounts using the gross method in a perpetual inventory system.

E6-22 (Supplement 6A) Recording Journal Entries for Purchases, Purchase Discounts (Net   **LO 6-S1**
Method), and Purchase Returns Using a Perpetual Inventory System

Using the information in E6-8, prepare journal entries to record the transactions, assuming Ace records discounts using the net method in a perpetual inventory system. Forfeited discounts are charged to Other Operating Expenses.

E6-23 (Supplement 6A) Recording Journal Entries for Net Sales with Credit Sales and Sales   **LO 6-S1**
Discounts (Gross Method)

Using the information in E6-10, prepare journal entries to record the transactions, assuming Solitare records discounts using the gross method in a perpetual inventory system.

E6-24 (Supplement 6A) Recording Journal Entries for Net Sales with Credit Sales and Sales   **LO 6-S1**
Discounts (Net Method)

Using the information in E6-10, prepare journal entries to record the transactions, assuming Solitare records discounts using the net method in a perpetual inventory system. Forfeited discounts are recorded as Other Revenue.

E6-25 (Supplement 6A) Recording Journal Entries for Net Sales with Credit Sales and Sales   **LO 6-S1**
Discounts (Gross Method)

Using the information in E6-11, prepare journal entries to record the transactions, assuming Evergreen Company records discounts using the gross method in a perpetual inventory system.

E6-26 (Supplement 6A) Recording Journal Entries for Net Sales with Credit Sales and Sales   **LO 6-S1**
Discounts (Net Method)

Using the information in E6-11, prepare journal entries to record the transactions, assuming Evergreen Company records discounts using the net method in a perpetual inventory system. Forfeited discounts are recorded as Other Revenue.

E6-27 (Supplement 6A) Recording Journal Entries for Net Sales with Credit Sales, Sales Discounts   **LO 6-S1**
(Gross Method), and Sales Returns

Using the information in E6-12, prepare journal entries to record the transactions, assuming Bear's Retail Store records discounts using the gross method in a perpetual inventory system.

E6-28 (Supplement 6A) Recording Journal Entries for Net Sales with Credit Sales, Sales Discounts   **LO 6-S1**
(Net Method), and Sales Returns

Using the information in E6-12, prepare journal entries to record the transactions, assuming Bear's Retail Store records discounts using the net method in a perpetual inventory system. Forfeited discounts are recorded as Other Revenue.

E6-29 (Supplement 6B) Recording Purchases and Sales Using Perpetual and Periodic Inventory   **LO 6-S2**
Systems

Kangaroo Jim Company reported beginning inventory of 100 units at a per unit cost of $25. It had the following purchase and sales transactions during the year:

Jan. 14	Sold 25 units at unit sales price of $45 on account.
Apr. 9	Purchased 15 additional units at a per unit cost of $25 on account.
Sept. 2	Sold 50 units at a sales price of $50 on account.
Dec. 31	Counted inventory and determined 40 units were still on hand.

Required:

Record each transaction, assuming that Kangaroo Jim Company uses (*a*) a perpetual inventory system and (*b*) a periodic inventory system.

COACHED PROBLEMS

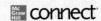

LO 6-3   **CP6-1 Purchase Transactions between Wholesale and Retail Merchandisers, Using Perpetual Inventory Systems**

The transactions listed below are typical of those involving Amalgamated Textiles and American Fashions. Amalgamated is a wholesale merchandiser and American Fashions is a retail merchandiser. Assume all sales of merchandise from Amalgamated to American Fashions are made with terms n/60, and the two companies use perpetual inventory systems. Assume the following transactions between the two companies occurred in the order listed during the year ended December 31.

a.   Amalgamated sold merchandise to American Fashions at a selling price of $230,000. The merchandise had cost Amalgamated $175,000.

b.   Two days later, American Fashions returned goods that had been sold to the company at a price of $20,000 and complained to Amalgamated that some of the remaining merchandise differed from what American Fashions had ordered. Amalgamated agreed to give an allowance of $5,000 to American Fashions. The goods returned by American Fashions had cost Amalgamated $15,270. No further returns are expected.

c.   Just three days later, American Fashions paid Amalgamated, which settled all amounts owed.

Required:

1.   Indicate the effect (direction and amount) of each transaction on the Inventory balance of American Fashions.

2.   Prepare the journal entries American Fashions would record and show any computations.
     TIP: The selling price charged by the seller is the purchaser's cost.

LO 6-4, 6-6   **CP6-2 Reporting Sales Transactions between Wholesale and Retail Merchandisers Using Perpetual Inventory Systems**

Use the information in CP6-1 to complete the following requirements.

Required:

1.   For each of the events (a) through (c), indicate the amount and direction of the effect (+ for increase, − for decrease, and NE for no effect) on Amalgamated Textiles in terms of the following items.

Sales Revenues	Sales Returns	Sales Allowances	Net Sales	Cost of Goods Sold	Gross Profit

2.   Prepare the journal entries that Amalgamated Textiles would record, and show any computations.
     TIP: When using a perpetual inventory system, the seller always makes two journal entries when goods are sold.

LO 6-4, 6-6   **CP6-3 Recording Cash Sales, Credit Sales, Estimated and Actual Sales Returns, and Sales Allowances, and Analyzing Gross Profit Percentage**

Campus Stop, Inc., is a student co-op. Campus Stop uses a perpetual inventory system. The following transactions (summarized) have been selected for analysis:

a.	Sold merchandise for cash (cost of merchandise $152,070).	$275,000
b.	Received merchandise returned by customers as unsatisfactory (but in perfect condition) for cash refund (original cost of merchandise $600).	1,600
c.	Sold merchandise (costing $9,000) to a customer on account with terms n/30.	20,000
d.	Collected half of the balance owed by the customer in (c).	10,000
e.	Granted a partial allowance relating to credit sales the customer in (c) had not yet paid.	1,100
f.	Anticipate further returns of merchandise (costing $200) after month-end from sales made during the month.	700

Required:

1.   Compute Net Sales and Gross Profit for Campus Stop. No additional sales returns/allowances are expected.

2. Compute the gross profit percentage (using the formula shown in this chapter and rounding to one decimal place).

3. Prepare journal entries to record transactions (a)–(f).

4. Campus Stop is considering a contract to sell merchandise to a campus organization for $15,000. This merchandise will cost Campus Stop $12,000. Would this contract increase (or decrease) Campus Stop's dollars of gross profit and its gross profit percentage (round to one decimal place)?

   TIP: The impact on gross profit dollars may differ from the impact on gross profit percentage.

CP6-4 Recording Journal Entry after Allocating Transaction Price to Performance Obligations

LO 6-5

Great American Oilchange (GAO) sells a combined oil change service and parts package for $30. A customer who supplies the parts (oil and filter) is charged $20 for only the service, whereas a customer who buys only the oil and filter (for do-it-yourself use) is charged $20 for the parts. The parts cost GAO $14.

Required:

1. Determine the dollar amount of revenue from the oil change service versus the sale of parts for each combined oil change package.

   TIP: To calculate the percentage of the combined package that relates to the service, divide the stand-alone selling price of the service by the combined *stand-alone* selling prices of both the service and parts.

2. Show the journal entry GAO would record if GAO provides a combined oil change service and parts package to a customer on October 7. Assume GAO distinguishes Service Revenue from Sales Revenue arising from the sale of parts, it uses a perpetual inventory system for recording the cost of goods sold, and it collects cash the day the oil change is performed.

CP6-5 Preparing a Multistep Income Statement and Computing the Gross Profit Percentage

LO 6-6

Psymon Company, Inc., sells construction equipment. The annual fiscal period ends on December 31. The following adjusted trial balance was created from the general ledger accounts on December 31:

Account Titles	Debits	Credits
Cash	$ 42,000	
Accounts Receivable	18,000	
Inventory	65,000	
Property and Equipment	50,000	
Accumulated Depreciation		$ 21,000
Accounts Payable		30,000
Common Stock		90,000
Retained Earnings, January 1		11,600
Sales Revenue		167,000
Cost of Goods Sold	98,000	
Salaries and Wages Expense	17,000	
Office Expense	18,000	
Interest Expense	2,000	
Income Tax Expense	9,600	
Totals	$319,600	$319,600

Required:

1. Prepare a multistep income statement that would be used for external reporting purposes.

   TIP: Some of the accounts listed will appear on the balance sheet rather than the income statement.

2. Compute and interpret the gross profit percentage (using the formula shown in this chapter and rounding to one decimal place).

LO 6-S2   **CP6-6** **(Supplement 6B) Recording Inventory Transactions Using Periodic and Perpetual Inventory Systems**

Frigid Supplies reported beginning inventory of 200 units, for a total cost of $2,000. The company had the following transactions during the month:

Jan. 3	Sold 20 units on account at a selling price of $15 per unit.
6	Bought 30 units on account at a cost of $10 per unit.
16	Sold 30 units on account at a selling price of $15 per unit.
19	Sold 20 units on account at a selling price of $20 per unit.
26	Bought 10 units on account at a cost of $10 per unit.
31	Counted inventory and determined that 160 units were on hand.

Required:

1. Prepare the journal entries that would be recorded using a periodic inventory system.
2. Prepare the journal entries that would be recorded using a perpetual inventory system, including any "book-to-physical" adjustment that might be needed.
   TIP: Adjust for shrinkage by decreasing Inventory and increasing Cost of Goods Sold.
3. What is the dollar amount of shrinkage that you were able to determine in (*a*) requirement 1 and (*b*) requirement 2? Enter CD (cannot determine) if you were unable to determine the dollar amount of shrinkage.

GROUP A PROBLEMS

LO 6-3   **PA6-1** **Reporting Purchase Transactions between Wholesale and Retail Merchandisers Using Perpetual Inventory Systems**

The transactions listed below are typical of those involving New Books Inc. and Readers' Corner. New Books is a wholesale merchandiser and Readers' Corner is a retail merchandiser. Assume all sales of merchandise from New Books to Readers' Corner are made with terms n/30, and the two companies use perpetual inventory systems. Assume the following transactions between the two companies occurred in the order listed during the year ended August 31.

a. New Books sold merchandise to Readers' Corner at a selling price of $550,000. The merchandise had cost New Books $415,000.
b. Two days later, Readers' Corner complained to New Books that some of the merchandise differed from what Readers' Corner had ordered. New Books agreed to give an allowance of $10,000 to Readers' Corner. Readers' Corner also returned some books, which had cost New Books $2,000 and had been sold to Readers' Corner for $3,500. No further returns are expected.
c. Just three days later, Readers' Corner paid New Books, which settled all amounts owed.

Required:

1. Indicate the effect (direction and amount) of each transaction on the Inventory balance of Readers' Corner.
2. Prepare the journal entries that Readers' Corner would record and show any computations.

LO 6-4, 6-6   **PA6-2** **Reporting Sales Transactions between Wholesale and Retail Merchandisers Using Perpetual Inventory Systems**

Use the information in PA6-1 to complete the following requirements.

Required:

1. For each of the events (*a*) through (*c*), indicate the amount and direction of the effect (+ for increase, − for decrease, and NE for no effect) on New Books in terms of the following items.

Sales Revenues	Sales Returns	Sales Allowances	Net Sales	Cost of Goods Sold	Gross Profit

2. Prepare the journal entries New Books would record, and show any computations.

PA6-3 Recording Sales with Discounts and Estimated and Actual Returns, and Analyzing Gross Profit Percentage   **LO 6-4, 6-5**

Hair World Inc. is a wholesaler of hair supplies. Hair World uses a perpetual inventory system. The following transactions (summarized) have been selected for analysis:

a.	Sold merchandise for cash (cost of merchandise $28,797).	$51,200
b.	Received merchandise returned by customers as unsatisfactory (but in perfect condition) for cash refund (original cost of merchandise $220).	250
c.	Sold merchandise (costing $4,750) to a customer on account with terms n/60.	10,000
d.	Collected half of the balance owed by the customer in (*c*).	5,000
e.	Granted a partial allowance relating to credit sales the customer in (*c*) had not yet paid.	160
f.	Anticipate further returns of merchandise (costing $140) after year-end from sales made during the year.	350

Required:

1. Compute Net Sales and Gross Profit for Hair World. No additional sales returns/allowances are expected.
2. Compute the gross profit percentage (using the formula shown in this chapter and rounding to one decimal place).
3. Prepare journal entries to record transactions (*a*)–(*f*).
4. Hair World is considering a contract to sell merchandise to a hair salon chain for $15,000. This merchandise will cost Hair World $10,000. Would this contract increase (or decrease) Hair World's dollars of gross profit and its gross profit percentage?

PA6-4 Recording Journal Entry after Allocating Transaction Price to Performance Obligations   **LO 6-5**

Hospital Equipment Company (HEC) acquired several fMRI machines for its inventory at a cost of $2,300 per machine. HEC usually sells these machines to hospitals at a price of $5,800. HEC also separately sells 12 months of training and repair services for fMRI machines for $1,450. HEC is paid $5,800 cash on November 30 for the sale of an fMRI machine delivered on December 1. HEC sold the machine at its regular price but included one year of free training and repair service.

Required:

1. For the machine sold at its regular price, but with one year of "free" training and repair service, determine the dollar amount of revenue earned from the equipment sale versus the revenue earned from the training and repair service.
2. What journal entries would HEC record on November 30 and December 1? (Assume HEC uses a perpetual inventory system for recording the cost of goods sold.)

PA6-5 Preparing a Multistep Income Statement and Computing the Gross Profit Percentage   **LO 6-6**

Big Tommy Corporation is a local grocery store organized seven years ago as a corporation. The bookkeeper prepared the following statement at year-end (assume that all amounts are correct, but note the incorrect format):

BIG TOMMY CORPORATION **Profit and Loss** **December 31**		
	Debit	**Credit**
Net Sales		$404,000
Cost of Goods Sold	$279,000	
Salaries and Wages Expense	58,000	
Office Expense	16,000	
Travel Expenses	1,000	
Income Tax Expense	15,000	
Net Profit	35,000	
Totals	$404,000	$404,000

Required:

1. Prepare a properly formatted multistep income statement that would be used for external reporting purposes.
2. Compute and interpret the gross profit percentage (using the formula shown in this chapter and rounding to one decimal place).

LO 6-S2   **PA6-6 (Supplement 6B) Recording Inventory Transactions Using Periodic and Perpetual Inventory Systems**

Home Hardware reported beginning inventory of 20 shovels, for a total cost of $100. The company had the following transactions during the month:

Jan. 2	Sold 4 shovels on account at a selling price of $10 per unit.
16	Sold 10 shovels on account at a selling price of $10 per unit.
18	Bought 5 shovels on account at a cost of $5 per unit.
19	Sold 10 shovels on account at a selling price of $10 per unit.
24	Bought 10 shovels on account at a cost of $5 per unit.
31	Counted inventory and determined that 10 units were on hand.

Required:

1. Prepare the journal entries that would be recorded using a periodic inventory system.
2. Prepare the journal entries that would be recorded using a perpetual inventory system, including any "book-to-physical" adjustment that might be needed.
3. What is the dollar amount of shrinkage that you were able to determine in (a) requirement 1 and (b) requirement 2? Enter CD (cannot determine) if you were unable to determine the dollar amount of shrinkage.

GROUP B PROBLEMS

LO 6-3   **PB6-1 Reporting Purchase Transactions between Wholesale and Retail Merchandisers Using Perpetual Inventory Systems**

The transactions listed below are typical of those involving Southern Sporting Goods (SSG) and Sports R Us (SRU). SSG is a wholesale merchandiser and SRU is a retail merchandiser. Assume all sales of merchandise from SSG to SRU are made with terms n/30, and the two companies use perpetual inventory systems. Assume the following transactions between the two companies occurred in the order listed during the year ended December 31.

a. SSG sold merchandise to SRU at a selling price of $125,000. The merchandise had cost SSG $94,000.
b. Two days later, SRU complained to SSG that some of the merchandise differed from what SRU had ordered. SSG agreed to give an allowance of $3,000 to SRU. SRU also returned some sporting goods, which had cost SSG $12,000 and had been sold to SRU for $16,500. No further returns are expected.
c. Just three days later SRU paid SSG, which settled all amounts owed.

Required:

1. Indicate the effect (direction and amount) of each transaction on the Inventory balance of SRU.
2. Prepare the journal entries that SRU would record and show any computations.

LO 6-4, 6-6   **PB6-2 Reporting Sales Transactions between Wholesale and Retail Merchandisers Using Perpetual Inventory Systems**

Use the information in PB6-1 to complete the following requirements.

Required:

1. For each of the events (a) through (c), indicate the amount and direction of the effect (+ for increase, − for decrease, and NE for no effect) on SSG in terms of the following items.

| Sales Revenues | Sales Returns | Sales Allowances | Net Sales | Cost of Goods Sold | Gross Profit |

2. Prepare the journal entries SSG would record and show any computations.

PB6-3 Recording Sales and Estimated and Actual Returns, and Analyzing Gross Profit Percentage

Larry's Building Supplies (LBS) is a local hardware store. LBS uses a perpetual inventory system. The following transactions (summarized) have been selected for analysis:

a.	Sold merchandise for cash (cost of merchandise $224,350).	$500,000
b.	Received merchandise returned by customers as unsatisfactory (but in perfect condition) for cash refund (original cost of merchandise $1,000).	1,600
c.	Sold merchandise (costing $3,000) to a customer on account with terms n/30.	5,000
d.	Collected half of the balance owed by the customer in (*c*).	2,500
e.	Granted a partial allowance relating to credit sales the customer in (*c*) had not yet paid.	950
f.	Anticipate further returns of merchandise (costing $900) after year-end from sales made during the year.	1,400

Required:

1. Compute Net Sales and Gross Profit for LBS. No additional sales returns/allowances are expected.

2. Compute the gross profit percentage (using the formula shown in this chapter and rounding to one decimal place).

3. Prepare journal entries to record transactions (*a*)–(*f*).

4. LBS is considering a contract to sell building supplies to a local home builder for $20,000. These materials will cost LBS $16,000. Would this contract increase (or decrease) LBS's dollars of gross profit and its gross profit percentage?

PB6-4 Recording Journal Entry after Allocating Transaction Price to Performance Obligations

Sky Communcations (SKY) usually sells a cell phone for $320 plus 12 months of cellular service for $480. SKY has a special, time-limited offer in which it gives the phone for free and sells the 12 months of cellular service for $420. Each phone costs SKY $120, which it accounts for in its perpetual inventory system. On July 1, SKY sells one of the special packages, delivers the phone, collects the $420 cash, and starts the cellular service.

Required:

1. For the special offer, how much of the $420 relates to the sale of the cell phone versus the sale of the cellular service?

2. What journal entries would SKY record on July 1 and July 31?

PB6-5 Preparing a Multistep Income Statement and Computing the Gross Profit Percentage

Emily's Greenhouse Corporation is a local greenhouse organized 10 years ago as a corporation. The bookkeeper prepared the following statement at year-end (assume that all amounts are correct, but note the incorrect format):

EMILY'S GREENHOUSE CORPORATION
Profit and Loss
December 31

	Debit	Credit
Net Sales		$485,000
Cost of Goods Sold	$311,000	
Salaries and Wages Expense	61,000	
Office Expense	13,000	
Travel Expenses	3,000	
Income Tax Expense	18,000	
Net Profit	79,000	
Totals	$485,000	$485,000

Required:

1. Prepare a properly formatted multistep income statement that would be used for external reporting purposes.
2. Compute and interpret the gross profit percentage (using the formula shown in this chapter and rounding to one decimal place).

LO 6-S2 | **PB6-6** **(Supplement 6B) Recording Inventory Transactions Using Periodic and Perpetual Inventory Systems**

Sigfusson Supplies reported beginning inventory of 100 units, for a total cost of $2,000. The company had the following transactions during the month:

Jan. 6	Sold 20 units on account at a selling price of $30 per unit.
9	Bought 10 units on account at a cost of $20 per unit.
11	Sold 10 units on account at a selling price of $35 per unit.
19	Sold 20 units on account at a selling price of $40 per unit.
27	Bought 10 units on account at a cost of $20 per unit.
31	Counted inventory and determined that 60 units were on hand.

Required:

1. Prepare the journal entries that would be recorded using a periodic inventory system.
2. Prepare the journal entries that would be recorded using a perpetual inventory system, including any "book-to-physical" adjustment that might be needed.
3. What is the dollar amount of shrinkage that you were able to determine in (*a*) requirement 1 and (*b*) requirement 2? Enter CD (cannot determine) if you were unable to determine the dollar amount of shrinkage.

COMPREHENSIVE PROBLEMS

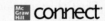

LO 5-4, 6-3, 6-4, 6-6 | **C6-1** **Reporting Cash, Inventory Orders, Purchases, Sales, Returns, and (Gross Method) Discounts (Chapters 5 and 6)**

(*a*) On October 1, the Business Students' Society (BSS) placed an order for 100 golf shirts at a unit cost of $20, under terms 2/10, n/30. (*b*) The order was received on October 10, but some golf shirts differed from what had been ordered. Uncertain whether the shirts would be returned or kept, BSS decided to record any purchase discount only when taken (using the gross method). (*c*) On October 11, 20 golf shirts were returned to the supplier. (*d*) On October 12, BSS complained the remaining golf shirts were slightly defective so the supplier granted a $100 allowance. (*e*) BSS paid for the golf shirts on October 13. (*f*) During the first week of October, BSS received student and faculty orders for 80 golf shirts, at a unit price of $60, on terms 2/10, n/30. (*g*) The golf shirts were delivered to these customers on October 18. Unfortunately, customers were unhappy with the golf shirts, so BSS permitted them to be returned or given an allowance (see *h* and *i*). Uncertain whether customers would keep or return the shirts, BSS decided to record any sales discount only when taken (using the gross method). (*h*) On October 19, one-half of the golf shirts were returned by customers to BSS. (*i*) On October 20, an allowance was given on account equal to $12.50 per shirt for the remaining 40 shirts. (*j*) The customers paid their remaining balances on the last day of the month, October 31. No further returns are expected.

Required:

1. Create a five-column table, in which the first column lists events (*a*) through (*j*), and the second through fifth columns show the impact of the events on Inventory, Net Sales, Cost of Goods Sold, and Gross Profit.
2. Determine the percentage of net sales that is available to cover operating expenses other than cost of goods sold. By what name is this percentage commonly known?
3. As of October 31, the check dated October 13 had not cleared the bank. How should BSS report this on its October 31 bank reconciliation? Give the journal entry, if any, needed as a result of including this item in the bank reconciliation.

C6-2 **Preparing Journal Entries for Inventory Purchases, Sales, Returns, and (Gross Method) Discounts, and Adjusting Income Tax (Chapters 4 and 6)**

LO 6-3, 6-4, 6-6, 6-S1

Use the information in C6-1 to complete the following requirements.

Required:

1. Prepare journal entries for the transactions described in events (*a*) through (*j*), using the date of each transaction as its reference. Assume BSS uses perpetual inventory accounts. If you complete this problem in Connect, these journal entries will be summarized for you in T-accounts and an unadjusted trial balance.

2. Prepare adjusting journal entries to accrue office expenses of $500 incurred on account and to accrue income taxes of $133. If you complete this problem in Connect, these adjusting entries will be summarized for you in T-accounts and an adjusted trial balance.

3. Report the financial effects of the above transactions in a multistep income statement for the month ended October 31 prepared for external use.

SKILLS DEVELOPMENT CASES

S6-1 **Finding Financial Information**

LO 6-2, 6-6

Refer to the financial statements of **The Home Depot** in Appendix A at the end of this book. (Note: Fiscal 2019 for The Home Depot runs from February 4, 2019, to February 2, 2020. See S1-1 for further explanation.)

The Home Depot

1. What amount of Net Sales does the company report during the year ended February 2, 2020?
   a. $110,225
   b. $72,653
   c. $37,572
   d. $11,242

2. Assuming that Cost of Sales is the company's term for Cost of Goods Sold, compute the company's gross profit percentage for fiscal 2019 and the year immediately prior to that.
   a. 65.9% and 65.7%
   b. 34.1% and 34.3%
   c. 67.1% and 70.4%
   d. 32.9% and 29.6%

3. Assume that The Home Depot experienced no shrinkage in the most current year. Using the balance sheet and income statement, estimate the amount of purchases in the year ended February 2, 2020.
   a. $110,831
   b. $73,259
   c. $72,653
   d. $72,047

S6-2 **Comparing Financial Information**

LO 6-2, 6-6

Refer to the financial statements of **Lowe's Companies, Inc.**, in Appendix B. (Note: Fiscal 2019 for Lowe's runs from February 2, 2019, to January 31, 2020. See S1-1 for further explanation.)

Lowe's

1. What amount of Net Sales does the company report during the year ended January 31, 2020?
   a. $72,148
   b. $49,205
   c. $71,309
   d. $68,619

2. Which of the following is consistent with and could explain the changes in Lowe's dollars of gross profit and gross profit percentage in fiscal 2019 (compared to fiscal 2018)?
   a. Sales volume increased in fiscal 2019, but unit costs decreased.
   b. Sales volume decreased in fiscal 2019, and per unit selling prices decreased.
   c. Sales volume increased in fiscal 2019, and unit costs increased.
   d. Sales volume and unit costs did not change, but per unit selling prices increased.

3. Assume that Lowe's experienced no shrinkage in the most current year. Using the balance sheet and income statement, estimate the amount of purchases in the year ended January 31, 2020.
   a. $72,766
   b. $49,823
   c. $49,205
   d. $48,587

LO 6-1, 6-6   **S6-3 Internet-Based Team Research: Examining an Annual Report**

As a team, select an industry to analyze. Using your web browser, each team member should access the annual report or 10-K for one publicly traded company in the industry, with each member selecting a different company. (See S1-3 in Chapter 1 for a description of possible resources for these tasks.)

Required:

1. On an individual basis, each team member should write a short report that incorporates the following:
   a. Describe the company's business in sufficient detail to be able to classify it as a service or merchandising company. What products or services does the company provide?
   b. Calculate the gross profit percentage at the end of the current and prior years, and explain any change between the two years.

2. Then, as a team, write a short report comparing and contrasting your companies using these attributes. Discuss any patterns across the companies that you as a team observe. Provide potential explanations for any differences discovered.

LO 6-6   **S6-4 Ethical Decision Making: A Mini-Case**

Assume you work as an accountant in the merchandising division of a large public company that makes and sells athletic clothing. To encourage the merchandising division to earn as much profit on each individual sale as possible, the division manager's pay is based, in part, on the division's gross profit percentage. To encourage control over the division's operating expenses, the manager's pay also is based on the division's net income.

You are currently preparing the division's financial statements. The division had a good year, with initial (gross) sales revenue of $100,000, cost of goods sold of $50,000, sales returns and allowances of $6,000, sales discounts of $4,000, and salaries and wages expenses of $30,000. (Assume the division does not report income taxes.) The division manager stresses that "*it would be in your personal interest*" to classify sales returns and allowances and sales discounts as selling expenses rather than subtract them from sales revenue as contra-accounts on the division's income statement. He justifies this "friendly advice" by saying that he's not asking you to fake the numbers—he just believes that those items are more accurately reported as expenses. Plus, he claims, being a division of a larger company, you don't have to follow GAAP.

Required:

1. Prepare an income statement for the division using the format shown in this chapter for external reporting purposes. Using this income statement, calculate the division's gross profit percentage.

2. Prepare an income statement for the division using the classifications advised by the manager. Using this income statement, calculate the division's gross profit percentage.

3. What reason (other than reporting "more accurately") might be motivating the manager's advice to you?

4. Do you agree with the manager's statement that "he's not asking you to fake the numbers"?

5. Do you agree with the manager's statement about not having to follow GAAP?

6. How should you respond to the division manager's "friendly advice"?

S6-5 Evaluating the Results of Merchandising Operations

LO 6-6

Merchandise Mavens Corporation sells goods throughout North America. One of its product lines has recently reported the following information to you at the head office. Based on this information, you have become concerned that the company is experiencing difficulties selling the product.

	2020	2019	2018
Cost of Goods Sold	$375,000	$358,000	$334,000
Gross Sales Revenue	400,000	400,000	400,000
Inventory	56,410	34,000	29,425
Sales Returns and Allowances	10,000	2,000	3,000

Required:

1. Prepare a multistep income statement for external reporting purposes, stopping at the gross profit subtotal. Use a separate column to report each year's results, similar to Exhibit 6.9.
2. Compute gross profit percentage for each year.
3. Analyze the information to identify two observations that led to your concern.

S6-6 Preparing Multistep Income Statements and Calculating Gross Profit Percentage

LO 6-6

Assume that you have been hired by Big Sky Corporation as a summer intern. The company is in the process of preparing its annual financial statements. To help in the process, you are asked to prepare an income statement for internal reporting purposes and an income statement for external reporting purposes. Your boss also has requested that you determine the company's gross profit percentage based on the statements that you are to prepare. The following adjusted trial balance was created from the general ledger accounts on December 31.

Account Titles	Debits	Credits
Cash	$ 57,000	
Accounts Receivable	67,000	
Inventory	103,000	
Property and Equipment	252,000	
Accumulated Depreciation		$103,000
Accounts Payable		75,000
Common Stock		120,000
Retained Earnings		145,900
Sales Revenue		369,000
Sales Returns and Allowances	9,500	
Sales Discounts	14,000	
Cost of Goods Sold	248,000	
Salaries and Wages Expense	19,000	
Office Expense	23,000	
Travel Expenses	5,000	
Income Tax Expense	15,400	
Totals	$812,900	$812,900

As the trial balance shows, Big Sky tracks sales returns and allowances and sales discounts in separate contra-accounts that are subtracted from the (gross) Sales Revenue to determine Net Sales. Your boss wants you to create the spreadsheet in a way that automatically recalculates net sales and any other related amounts whenever changes are made to the contra-revenue accounts. To do this, you know that you'll have to use formulas throughout the worksheets and even import or link cells from one worksheet to another. Your friend Owen, an accountant, is willing to help.

From: Owentheaccountant@yahoo.com
To: Helpme@hotmail.com
Cc:
Subject: Excel Help

Sounds like you are going to get some great experience this summer. Okay, to import a number from another spreadsheet, you first click on the cell where you want the number to appear. For example, if you want to enter the Net Sales balance in the external income statement, click on the cell in the external income statement where the Net Sales number is supposed to appear. Enter the equals sign (=) and then click on the tab that takes you to the worksheet containing the internal income statement. In that worksheet, click on the cell that contains the amount you want to import into the external income statement and then press enter. This will create a link from the internal income statement cell to the external income statement cell. Here's a screen shot showing the formula that will appear after you import the number.

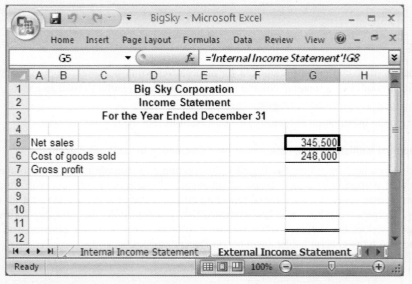

Source: Microsoft Excel.

Don't forget to save the file using a name that indicates who you are.

Required:

Enter the trial balance information into a spreadsheet and complete the following:

1. Prepare a multistep income statement that would be used for internal reporting purposes, by classifying sales returns and allowances and sales discounts as contra-revenue accounts, and subtracting them from Sales Revenue to show Net Sales.

2. Prepare a multistep income statement that would be used for external reporting purposes, beginning with the amount for Net Sales.

3. Compute the gross profit percentage (round to one decimal place).

CONTINUING CASE   Mc Graw Hill **connect**

LO 6-4, 6-5, 6-6   **CC6-1 Accounting for Merchandising Operations**

Nicole's Getaway Spa (NGS) has been so successful that Nicole has decided to expand her spa by selling merchandise. She sells things such as nail polish, at-home spa kits, cosmetics, and aromatherapy items. Nicole uses a perpetual inventory system and is starting to realize all of the work that is created when inventory is involved in a business. The following transactions were selected from among those completed by NGS in August.

Aug. 2	Sold a bundle of spa services with a merchandise basket. When sold separately, the spa service part of the bundle sells for $400 and the merchandise basket normally sells for $100. Together, the bundle was sold to Val Amy for cash at a selling price of $450 (total). Val booked a spa treatment for August 10, and she took the basket of goods with her. The goods had cost NGS $80.
Aug. 3	Sold five identical items of merchandise to Cosmetics R Us on account at a selling price of $500 (total); terms n/30. The goods cost NGS $400.
Aug. 6	Cosmetics R Us returned one of the five items purchased on August 3. The item could still be sold by NGS in the future and credit was given to the customer.
Aug. 10	Val Amy used one of the three spa treatments she had purchased as part of the bundle sold to her on August 2.
Aug. 20	Sold two at-home spa kits to Meghan Witzel for $300 cash. The goods cost NGS $96.
Aug. 22	Cosmetics R Us paid its remaining account balance in full.

Required:

1. Prepare journal entries for each transaction. No additional sales returns are expected.
2. Calculate the Sales Revenue and Cost of Goods Sold for the transactions listed above (but exclude Service Revenue for spa services). What is Nicole's Getaway Spa's gross profit percentage (excluding Service Revenue)? Explain to Nicole what gross profit percentage means.

DATA ANALYTICS EXERCISES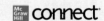

Data Analytics Exercises are auto-graded exercises offering detailed data visualization, interpretation, and analysis, and are available for assignment in Connect.

7

Inventory and Cost of Goods Sold

CHAPTER SEVEN

THAT WAS THEN

In the previous chapter, we focused on selling goods that were purchased at the same cost per unit.

James Leynse/The Image Bank/
Getty Images

Like you, companies encounter changing costs when they purchase or produce goods. For some products, unit costs increase over time and, for others, technological innovation drives unit costs down. Either way, inventory is likely to include some items that were acquired at a lower unit cost and others that were acquired at a higher unit cost.

Suppose clothing retailer American Eagle Outfitters buys three batches of its AE Fleece Jackets at a cost of $20 per jacket for the first batch, $30 per jacket for the second batch, and $40 per jacket for the third. When American Eagle sells a jacket, what cost should it use to compute the Cost of Goods Sold? And what happens at the end of the season when the value of its jackets falls below cost? As you will learn in this chapter, accounting rules allow different methods to be used when accounting for inventory, each of which leads to reporting different dollar amounts for Cost of Goods Sold (and the items remaining in inventory). This flexibility allows managers to choose the method that best fits their business environment. But it also means that you must know which method managers are using and how it works. That's what we'll look at in this chapter.

THIS IS NOW

This chapter demonstrates how to account for goods purchased at different unit costs.

Understand the business	Study the accounting methods	Evaluate inventory management	Supplement 7A	Supplement 7B	Review the chapter
• Types of inventory • Inventory management decisions	• Balance sheet and income statement reporting • Inventory costing methods • Lower of cost or market/net realizable value	• Inventory turnover analysis	• FIFO, LIFO, and weighted average in a perpetual inventory system	• The effects of errors in ending inventory	• Demonstration case • Chapter summary • Key terms • Homework helper • Practice material

Understand the Business

Learning Objective 7-1
Describe the issues in managing different types of inventory.

TYPES OF INVENTORY

The generic term *inventory* means goods that are held for sale in the normal course of business or are used to produce other goods for sale. Merchandisers hold **merchandise inventory,** which consists of products acquired in a finished condition, ready for sale without further processing. Manufacturers often hold three types of inventory, with each representing a different stage in the manufacturing process. They start with **raw materials inventory** such as plastic, steel, or fabrics. When these raw materials enter the production process, they become part of **work in process inventory,** which includes goods that are in the process of being manufactured. When completed, work in process inventory becomes **finished goods inventory,** which is ready for sale just like merchandise inventory. For purposes of this chapter, we'll focus on merchandise inventory, but the concepts we cover apply equally to manufacturers' inventory.

Two other accounting terms may be used to describe inventory. **Consignment inventory** refers to goods a company is holding on behalf of the goods' owner. Typically, this arises when a company is willing to sell the goods for the owner (for a fee) but does not want to take ownership of the goods in the event the goods are difficult to sell. Consignment inventory is reported on the balance sheet of the owner, not the company holding the inventory. **Goods in transit** are inventory items being transported. This type of inventory is reported on the balance sheet of the owner, not the company transporting it. As you may remember from Exhibit 6.4 in Chapter 6, ownership of inventory is determined by the terms of the inventory sales agreement. If a sale is made FOB destination, goods in transit belong to the seller until they reach their destination (the customer). If a sale is made FOB shipping point, goods in transit belong to the customer at the point of shipping (from the seller's premises).

INVENTORY MANAGEMENT DECISIONS

The primary goals of inventory managers are to

1. Maintain a sufficient **quantity** of inventory to meet customers' needs.
2. Ensure inventory **quality** meets customers' expectations and company standards.

3. Minimize the **cost** of acquiring and carrying inventory (including costs related to purchasing, production, storage, spoilage, theft, obsolescence, and financing).

These factors are tricky to manage because as one of them changes (e.g., quality), so, too, do the others (e.g., cost). Ultimately, inventory management often comes down to purchasing goods that can be sold soon after they are acquired.

Study the Accounting Methods

BALANCE SHEET AND INCOME STATEMENT REPORTING

Because inventory will be used or converted into cash within one year, it is reported on the balance sheet as a current asset. Goods are initially recorded in inventory at cost, which is the amount paid to acquire the asset and prepare it for sale. See Exhibit 7.1 for the way American Eagle reports inventory.

> **Learning Objective 7-2**
> Explain how to report inventory and cost of goods sold.

EXHIBIT 7.1   Reporting Inventory on the Balance Sheet (Partial)

AMERICAN EAGLE OUTFITTERS, INC.
Balance Sheets (Partial)

(in millions)	February 2, 2019	February 3, 2018
Assets		
Current Assets		
Cash and Cash Equivalents	$425	$415
Inventory	420	400
Accounts Receivable	95	80
Prepaid Expenses and Other	105	80

When a company sells goods, it removes their cost from the Inventory account and reports the cost on the income statement as the expense Cost of Goods Sold. As Exhibit 7.2 shows, Cost of Goods Sold (CGS) is subtracted from Net Sales to yield the income statement subtotal called Gross Profit.

EXHIBIT 7.2   Reporting Cost of Goods Sold on the Income Statement (Partial)

AMERICAN EAGLE OUTFITTERS, INC.
Income Statements (Partial)
For the Years Ended

(in millions)	February 2, 2019	February 3, 2018	January 28, 2017
Net Sales	$4,035	$3,795	$3,610
Cost of Goods Sold	2,550	2,425	2,245
Gross Profit	1,485	1,370	1,365

Cost of Goods Sold Equation

Chapter 6 explained that the balance sheet account Inventory is related to the income statement account Cost of Goods Sold through the cost of goods sold equation. The cost of goods sold equation can take one of two forms, depending on whether the inventory costs are updated periodically at year-end (or month-end) when inventory is counted, or perpetually each time inventory is bought or sold:

Periodic Updating:

Beginning Inventory + Purchases − Ending Inventory = Cost of Goods Sold

Perpetual Updating:

Beginning Inventory + Purchases − Cost of Goods Sold = Ending Inventory

Exhibit 7.3 illustrates how to use these equations with a simple case where a company has beginning inventory of 5 units that each costs $10, then purchases 20 units with a cost of $10 each, sells 15 units, and is left with 10 units in ending inventory. Exhibit 7.3 shows that, in a periodic inventory system, you must calculate the cost of Ending Inventory and then use the cost of goods sold equation to "force out" the Cost of Goods Sold (left table). In a perpetual inventory system, the Cost of Goods Sold is updated with each inventory transaction, which "forces out" the cost of Ending Inventory (right table). With a perpetual inventory system, you can "prove" the cost of Ending Inventory by calculating it directly using the number of units on hand. Be sure you understand all of the calculations in Exhibit 7.3 before moving on because we use it as a basis for more calculations later in this chapter.

EXHIBIT 7.3	Calculations Involving Constant Inventory Costs

PERIODIC INVENTORY

Description	# of Units		Unit Cost	Total Cost
Beginning	5	×	$10	$ 50
+ Purchases	20	×	$10	200
Available	25	×	$10	250
− Ending Inventory	(10)	×	$10	(100)
= Cost of Goods Sold				$150

PERPETUAL INVENTORY

Description	# of Units		Unit Cost	Total Cost
Beginning	5	×	$10	$ 50
+ Purchases	20	×	$10	200
Available	25	×	$10	250
− Goods Sold	(15)	×	$10	(150)
= Ending Inventory				$100

INVENTORY COSTING METHODS

Learning Objective 7-3
Compute costs using four inventory costing methods.

In the example presented in the previous section, the cost of all units of the item was the same—$10. If inventory costs normally remained constant, we'd be done right now. But just as you notice every time you fill up your car with gas, the cost of goods does not always stay the same. In recent years, the costs of many items have risen moderately. In other cases, such as electronic products, costs have dropped dramatically.

When the costs of inventory change over time, it is not obvious how to determine the cost of goods sold (and the cost of ending inventory). To see why, think about the following simple example:

May 3	Purchased 1 unit for **$70**.
May 5	Purchased 1 more unit for **$75**.
May 6	Purchased 1 more unit for **$95**.
May 8	Sold 2 units for $125 each.

The sale on May 8 of two units, at a selling price of $125 each, would generate sales revenue of $250 ($125 × 2), but what amount would be considered the cost of goods sold? The answer depends on which goods are reported as sold.

Four generally accepted inventory costing methods are available for determining the cost of goods sold and the cost of goods remaining in ending inventory, regardless of whether a company uses a perpetual or periodic inventory system. The method chosen does not have to correspond to the physical flow of goods, so any one of these four methods is acceptable under GAAP in the United States.

The **specific identification method** individually identifies and records the cost of each item sold as Cost of Goods Sold. This method requires accountants to keep track of the purchase cost of each item. In the example just given, if the items sold were identified as the ones received on May 3 and May 6, which cost $70 and $95, the total cost of those items ($70 + $95 = $165) would be reported as Cost of Goods Sold. The cost of the remaining item ($75) would be reported as Inventory on the balance sheet at the end of the period. Companies tend to use the specific identification method when accounting for individually expensive and unique items. CarMax, a national auto dealership, uses specific identification.

The units within each American Eagle product line are identical, so the company does not use the specific identification method. Like most companies, American Eagle uses one of the three other cost flow methods to account for inventory items. These three other inventory costing methods are **not based on the physical flow** of goods on and off the shelves. Instead, these methods are based on **assumptions** accountants make about the flow of inventory costs. These three cost flow assumptions are applied to our simple three-unit example in Exhibit 7.4.

1. **First-in, first-out (FIFO)** assumes the inventory costs flow out in the order the goods are received. As in Exhibit 7.4, the earliest items received, the $70 and $75 units received on May 3 and 5, become the $145 Cost of Goods Sold on the income statement, and the remaining $95 unit received on May 6 becomes ending Inventory on the balance sheet.

2. **Last-in, first-out (LIFO)** assumes the inventory costs flow out in the opposite of the order the goods are received. As in Exhibit 7.4, the latest items received, the $95 and $75 units received on May 6 and 5, become the $170 Cost of Goods Sold on the

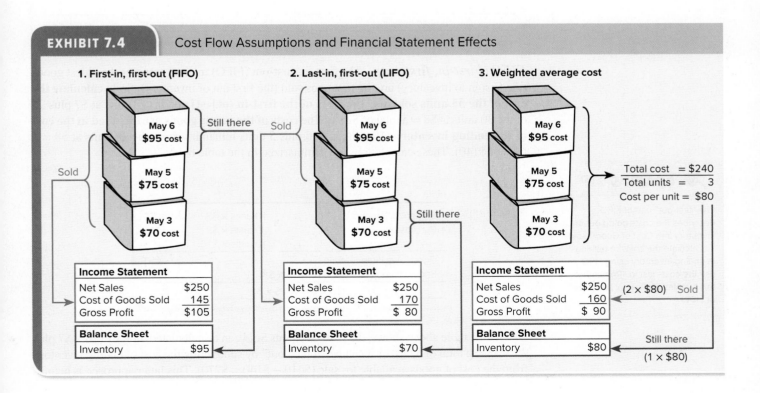

EXHIBIT 7.4 Cost Flow Assumptions and Financial Statement Effects

income statement, and the remaining $70 unit received on May 3 becomes ending
Inventory on the balance sheet.

3. **Weighted average cost** uses the weighted average of the costs of goods available for
sale for both the cost of each item sold and those remaining in inventory. As in
Exhibit 7.4, the average of the costs [($70 + $75 + $95) ÷ 3 = $80] is assigned to the
two items sold, resulting in $160 as Cost of Goods Sold on the income statement.
The same $80 average cost is assigned to the one item in ending Inventory reported
on the balance sheet.

As Exhibit 7.4 illustrates, the choice of cost flow assumption can have a major effect on Gross
Profit on the income statement and Inventory on the balance sheet. Walgreens, for example,
would report $3.2 billion more in inventory cost if it used FIFO rather than LIFO. But doing
so would also increase the company's income taxes, so it stays with LIFO.

Notice that **although they're called "inventory" costing methods, their names
actually describe how to calculate the cost of goods sold.** That is, the "first-out" part of
FIFO and LIFO refers to the goods that are sold (i.e., first out), not the goods that are still
in ending inventory. Also notice that the cost flows assumed for LIFO are the opposite of
FIFO, and weighted average is a middle-of-the-road method.

Inventory Cost Flow Computations

Now that you've seen how these cost flow assumptions work and that they actually make a
difference in a company's balance sheet and income statement, you're ready for a more realistic example. So, let's assume that during the first week of October American Eagle entered
into the following transactions for its Henley T-shirt product line. All sales were made at a
selling price of $15 per unit. These sales occurred after American Eagle made two batches of
T-shirt purchases, which were added to inventory purchased the previous month.

Date	Description	# of Units	Cost per Unit	Total Cost
Oct. 1	Beginning Inventory	10	$ 7	$ 70
Oct. 3	Purchase	30	8	240
Oct. 5	Purchase	10	10	100
	Goods Available for Sale	50		410
Oct. 6	Goods Sold	(35)	To calculate	To calculate
	Ending Inventory	15	To calculate	To calculate

FIFO (First-in, first-out)   The first-in, first-out (FIFO) method assumes the oldest goods
(the first in to inventory) are the first ones sold (the first out of inventory). So **to calculate the
cost of the 35 units sold, use the costs of the first-in (oldest) goods** (10 units at $7 plus 25
of the 30 units at $8 = a total of $270). The **costs of the newer goods are included in the cost
of the ending inventory** (10 units at $10 plus 5 units remaining from the 30 units at $8 = a
total of $140). These calculations are summarized in the table below.

FIFO		
Beginning Inventory	10 units × $7	$ 70
+ Purchases	30 units × $8	240
	10 units × $10	100
Goods Available for Sale		410
− Ending Inventory (10 × $10) + (5 × $8)		**140**
Cost of Goods Sold (10 × $7) + (25 × $8)		$270

As the table above shows, the Cost of Goods Sold can be calculated directly (10 × $7 plus
25 × $8 = a total of $270) or it can be "forced out" by subtracting the cost of ending inventory
from the cost of goods available for sale ($410 − $140 = $270). This latter approach is helpful

if the number of units sold is not known, which is always the case when a company uses a periodic inventory system.[1]

LIFO (Last-in, first-out)   The last-in, first-out (LIFO) method assumes the newest goods (the last in to inventory) are the first ones sold (the first out of inventory). So **to calculate the cost of the 35 units sold, use the costs of the last-in (newest) goods** (10 units at $10 plus 25 of the 30 units at $8 = total of $300). The **costs of the older goods, including those in beginning inventory, are included in the cost of the ending inventory** (10 units at $7 plus 5 units remaining from the 30 units at $8 = a total of $110). These calculations are summarized in the table below.

LIFO		
Beginning Inventory	10 units × $7	$ 70
+ Purchases	30 units × $8	240
	10 units × $10	100
Goods Available for Sale		410
− Ending Inventory (10 × $7) + (5 × $8)		**110**
Cost of Goods Sold (10 × $10) + (25 × $8)		$300

As in the table, Cost of Goods Sold can be calculated directly (10 × $10 plus 25 × $8 = a total of $300) or it can be "forced out" by subtracting the cost of ending inventory from the cost of goods available for sale ($410 − $110 = $300). We recommend you do both, as a way to double-check your calculations.

Weighted Average Cost   The weighted average cost method is applied in two steps. The first step is to calculate the total cost of the goods available for sale. You multiply the number of units at each cost by the cost per unit and then sum these amounts to get the total cost:

Beginning Inventory	10 units × $7	$ 70
+ Purchases	30 units × $8	240
	10 units × $10	100
Goods Available for Sale	**50 units**	**$410**

Then you calculate the weighted average cost per unit using the following formula:

$$\frac{\text{Weighted}}{\text{Average Cost}} = \frac{\text{Cost of Goods Available for Sale}}{\text{Number of Units Available for Sale}} = \frac{\$410}{50 \text{ units}} = \frac{\$8.20}{\text{per unit}}$$

Cost of goods sold and ending inventory are both calculated using the same weighted average cost per unit, as in the following table.

Weighted Average		
Beginning Inventory	10 units × $7	$ 70
+ Purchases	30 units × $8	240
	10 units × $10	100
Goods Available for Sale	**50 units**	410
− Ending Inventory (15 × $8.20)		**123**
Cost of Goods Sold (35 × $8.20)		$287

COACH'S TIP

The "first-out" part of LIFO describes the costs going out of inventory into Cost of Goods Sold. To calculate the costs remaining in ending inventory using LIFO, use the costs first in. (Remember this by thinking "first in, still there," or FIST.)

COACH'S TIP

To calculate weighted average cost, be sure to **weight** the costs by the number of units at each unit cost. Don't simply average the unit costs [($7 + $8 + $10) ÷ 3 = $8.33]. That is a simple average— not a weighted average.

---

[1]By showing all purchases taking place before any Sales and Cost of Goods Sold are computed, we are demonstrating a periodic inventory system. You might think it's odd we use a periodic system when we said in Chapter 6 that most modern companies use perpetual inventory systems. We actually have several good reasons for doing this, which we explain in Supplement 7A at the end of this chapter. To learn how cost flow assumptions are applied in more complex situations involving perpetual inventory systems, see Supplement 7A. For purposes of examples shown in the chapter and for problem materials at the end of this chapter, we assume no shrinkage (a topic discussed in Chapter 6).

Financial Statement Effects Exhibit 7.5 summarizes the financial statement effects of the FIFO, LIFO, and weighted average cost methods. Remember these methods differ only in the way they split the cost of goods available for sale between ending Inventory and Cost of Goods Sold. If a cost goes into Inventory, it doesn't go into Cost of Goods Sold. Thus, the method that assigns the highest cost to ending Inventory will assign the lowest cost to Cost of Goods Sold (and vice versa). As you can see in Exhibit 7.5, the effect on Cost of Goods Sold affects many other items on the income statement including Gross Profit, Income from Operations, Income before Income Tax Expense, Income Tax Expense, and Net Income.

EXHIBIT 7.5	Financial Statement Effects of Inventory Costing Methods		

Effects on the Income Statement	FIFO	LIFO	Weighted Average
Sales	$525	$525	$525
Cost of Goods Sold	270	300	287
Gross Profit	**255**	**225**	**238**
Operating Expenses	125	125	125
Income from Operations	**130**	**100**	**113**
Other Revenue (Expenses)	20	20	20
Income before Income Tax Expense	**150**	**120**	**133**
Income Tax Expense (assume 30%)	**45**	**36**	**40**
Net Income	**$105**	**$ 84**	**$ 93**

Effects on the Balance Sheet	FIFO	LIFO	Weighted Average
Inventory	**$140**	**$110**	**$123**

Depending on whether costs are rising or falling, different methods have different effects on the financial statements. **When costs are rising,** as they were in our example, FIFO produces a larger inventory value (making the balance sheet **appear** to be stronger) and a smaller cost of goods sold (resulting in a larger gross profit, which makes the company **look** more profitable). **When costs are falling,** these effects are reversed; FIFO produces a smaller ending inventory value and a larger cost of goods sold—a double whammy. These are not "real" economic effects, however, because the inventory cost flow assumption does not affect the number of units sold or held in ending inventory. The following graphic summarizes the relative amounts reported:

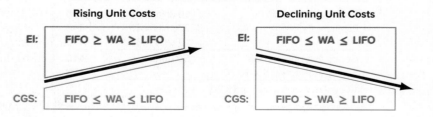

Tax Implications and Cash Flow Effects Given the financial statement effects, you might wonder why a company would ever use a method that produces a smaller inventory amount and a larger cost of goods sold. The answer is suggested in Exhibit 7.5, in the line called Income Tax Expense. **When faced with increasing costs per unit,** as in our example, **a company that uses FIFO will have a larger income tax expense.** This income tax effect is a real cost, in the sense that the company will actually have to pay more income taxes in the current year, thereby reducing the company's cash.

Consistency in Reporting A common question is whether managers are free to choose LIFO one period, FIFO the next, and then go back to LIFO, depending on whether unit costs are rising or declining during the period. Because this switching would make it difficult to compare financial results across periods, accounting rules discourage it. A change in method is allowed only if it improves the accuracy of the company's financial results. A company can, however, use different methods for different types of inventory that differ in nature or use, provided the methods are used consistently over time. Tax rules also limit the methods that can be used. **In the United States, the LIFO Conformity Rule requires that if LIFO is used on the income tax return, it also must be used in financial statement reporting.**

 How's it going?   Self-Study Practice

Ultimo Euromoda, Inc., purchases one designer suit at a cost of $200 and then purchases three more identical suits for $400 each. Three of the suits are then sold at a price of $1,000 each. Compute the Sales Revenue, Cost of Goods Sold, Gross Profit, and the cost of ending Inventory using (*a*) FIFO, (*b*) weighted average, and (*c*) LIFO.

After you have finished, check your answers with the solution.

SPOTLIGHT ON | The World

IFRS Does Not Allow LIFO

U.S. GAAP allows companies to use any of the four inventory costing methods presented in this chapter, but **LIFO is not allowed under International Financial Reporting Standards (IFRS).** This difference can create difficulties when comparing companies across international borders. For example, home appliance maker **Whirlpool Corporation** uses LIFO for its U.S. inventory, but companies in Germany (e.g., **Bosch**), Korea (e.g., **LG**), Sweden (e.g., **Electrolux**), and Switzerland (e.g., **Miele**) do not. If Whirlpool were to switch from LIFO to FIFO, its total inventory cost would increase by approximately $160 million.

LOWER OF COST OR MARKET/NET REALIZABLE VALUE

The value of inventory can fall below its recorded cost for two reasons: (1) it's easily replaced by identical goods at a lower cost or (2) it's become outdated or damaged. The first case is common for high-tech electronics. As companies become more efficient at making these cutting-edge products, they become cheaper to make. The second case commonly occurs with fad items or seasonal goods such as **American Eagle**'s winter coats, which tend to drop in value at the end of the season.

When inventory value falls below its cost, GAAP requires the inventory to be written down to its lower value. This rule is known as reporting inventory at the **lower of cost or market/ net realizable value (LCM/NRV)**. "Market value" focuses on how much the inventory would cost to replace in current *market* conditions (replacement cost). "Net realizable value" focuses on the inventory value likely to be *realized* when sold (selling price minus selling costs such as delivery). Technically, accounting rules require companies using FIFO and weighted average cost to compare inventory cost to net realizable value, and companies using LIFO to compare cost to market value. Either way, the main point of the LCM/NRV rule is to ensure inventory is reported at no more than it is worth. Also, by recording the write-down in the period in which a loss in value occurs, companies better match their revenues and expenses of that period.

> **Learning Objective 7-4**
> Report inventory at the lower of cost or market/net realizable value.

> **YOU SHOULD KNOW**
> **Lower of Cost or Market/Net Realizable Value (LCM/NRV):** Valuation method departing from the cost principle; recognizes a loss when inventory value drops below cost.

Let's look at how an inventory write-down is determined and recorded. Included in American Eagle's ending inventory are two items whose values have recently changed: vintage jeans and leather coats.[2] The vintage jeans are recorded in Inventory at their average cost of $20 per item. These jeans are expected to sell for $25 each, so they do not need to be written down because they already are reported at the **lower** amount (i.e., their **$20** cost). However, the leather coats are estimated to have a lower value (**$150**) than their recorded cost ($165 each). Thus, the inventory of leather coats needs to be written down by $15 per leather coat or, in total, $15,000 ($15 × 1,000 units).

Item	Cost per Item	Value per Item	Write-down per Item	Quantity	Total Write-down
Vintage jeans	$ 20	$ 25	—		
Leather coats	165	**150**	$15	1,000	**$15,000**

The effect of a $15,000 write-down on the accounting equation and the journal entry to record it are

1 Analyze

Assets	=	Liabilities	+	Stockholders' Equity
Inventory −15,000	=			Cost of Goods Sold (+E) −15,000

2 Record

	Debit	Credit
Cost of Goods Sold	15,000	
Inventory		15,000

Fashion Is on Fire

But not in a good way. Apparently, British fashion company Burberry has been incinerating its unsold products in blast furnaces, to limit supply and prop up prices. Burberry felt the burn on social media—tagged #burnberry—soon after its annual report disclosed the "cost of finished goods physically destroyed in the year was £28.6m" (nearly $40 million U.S. dollars).* Cartier watchmaker Richemont had a similar program to reduce the supply of its watches: buying them back from retailers and destroying them or dismantling them for parts. The company's annual report said Richemont recovered €481 million of watches over a two-year period. But broken down into parts, the watches were worth only 20 percent of what Richemont paid to recover them, leading to inventory write-downs totaling €388 million (about $460 million U.S. dollars).† Fortunately, some companies are starting to rethink how to design products to keep them in use as long as possible. Even Burberry is helping to extend the life of its products by promoting their reuse through The RealReal marketplace for authenticated, consignment luxury goods.‡

*Burberry Annual Report, FY2018, p. 165.
†Richemont Annual Report and Accounts 2018 (p. 27) and 2017 (p. 29).
‡"Burberry and The RealReal Join Forces to Make Fashion Circular," *Dow Jones Institutional News*, October 7, 2019.

---

[2]Common practice is to apply lower of cost or market/net realizable value to each item of inventory. However, in some circumstances, GAAP also allows it to be applied to entire inventory totals.

Most companies report the expense of an inventory write-down as Cost of Goods Sold, even though the written-down goods may not have been sold. This reporting is appropriate because writing down goods that haven't yet sold is a necessary cost of carrying the goods that did sell. By recording the write-down in the period in which a loss in value occurs, companies better match their revenues and expenses of that period.

Because investors and analysts view an inventory write-down as a sign of inventory management problems, some managers are reluctant to fairly apply the LCM/NRV rules. The failure to follow inventory LCM/NRV rules is one of the most common types of financial statement misstatements. To learn more about how this misstatement and other inventory errors can affect the financial statements, see Supplement 7B at the end of this chapter.

Evaluate Inventory Management

INVENTORY TURNOVER ANALYSIS

Learning Objective 7-5
Evaluate inventory management by computing and interpreting the inventory turnover ratio.

How can you tell whether an increase in a company's inventory balance is good news or bad news? If the increase occurs because management is building up stock in anticipation of higher sales, it could be good news. But if it results from an accumulation of old inventory items that nobody wants, it is probably bad news. Those who work inside the company can determine whether the change is good or bad news by talking with the sales managers. But if you are looking at the company's financial statements from the outside, how can you tell?

The method most analysts use to evaluate such changes is called inventory turnover analysis. Exhibit 7.6 illustrates the idea behind inventory turnover analysis. As a company buys goods, its inventory balance goes up; as it sells goods, its inventory balance goes down. This process of buying and selling, which is called **inventory turnover**, is repeated over and over during each accounting period for each line of products.

YOU SHOULD KNOW

Inventory Turnover: The process of buying and selling inventory.
Days to Sell: Measure of the average number of days from the time inventory is bought to the time it is sold.

EXHIBIT 7.6 Inventory Turnover Analysis

Analysts can assess how many times, on average, inventory has been bought and sold during the period by calculating the inventory turnover ratio. A higher ratio indicates that inventory moves more quickly from purchase to sale, reducing storage and obsolescence costs. Because less money is tied up in inventory, the excess can be invested to earn interest or reduce borrowing, which reduces interest expense. More efficient purchasing and production techniques as well as high product demand will boost this ratio. A sudden decline in the inventory turnover ratio may signal an unexpected drop in demand for the company's products or sloppy inventory management.

Rather than evaluate the **number of times** inventory turns over during the year, some analysts prefer to think in terms of the **length of time** (in days) required to sell inventory. Converting the inventory turnover ratio to the number of days needed to sell the inventory is easy. You simply divide 365 days by the year's inventory turnover ratio to get the **days to sell**. This measure provides the same basic information, but it is a little easier to interpret than the inventory turnover ratio. In terms of Exhibit 7.6, the inventory turnover ratio indicates the number of loops in a given period; days to sell indicates the average number of days between loops.

Accounting Decision Tools		
Name of Measure	**Formula**	**What It Tells You**
Inventory turnover ratio	$\dfrac{\text{Cost of Goods Sold}}{\text{Average Inventory}}$	• The number of times inventory turns over during the period • A higher ratio means faster turnover
Days to sell	$\dfrac{365}{\text{Inventory Turnover Ratio}}$	• Average number of days from purchase to sale • A higher number means a longer time to sell

Comparison to Benchmarks

Inventory turnover ratios and the number of days to sell can be helpful in comparing different companies' inventory management practices. But use them cautiously because these measures can vary significantly between industries. For merchandisers, inventory turnover refers to buying and selling goods, whereas for manufacturers, it refers to producing inventory and delivering it to customers. Industry differences are reflected in Exhibit 7.7, which shows that McDonald's has a turnover ratio of 57.4, which means it takes almost a week (6.4 days to be precise) to sell its entire food inventory (including the stuff in its freezers). The motorcycles at Harley-Davidson hog more time, as indicated by its inventory turnover ratio of 6.1, which equates to nearly two months (59.8 days) to produce and sell. American Eagle's inventory turned over only 6.2 times during the year, which is just once every 58.9 days.

EXHIBIT 7.7 Summary of Inventory Turnover Ratio Analyses

Company	Relevant Information (in millions)				Fiscal 2018 Inventory Turnover Calculation	Fiscal 2018 Days to Sell Calculation
			Fiscal 2018	**Fiscal 2017**		
Harley-Davidson Motorcycles		CGS	$3,350	$3,270	$\dfrac{\$3,350}{(\$560+\$540)/2}=6.1$ times	$\dfrac{365 \text{ days}}{6.1 \text{ times}}=59.8$ days
		Inventory	560	540		
			Fiscal 2018	**Fiscal 2017**		
McDonald's		CGS	$3,155	$4,035	$\dfrac{\$3,155}{(\$50+\$60)/2}=57.4$ times	$\dfrac{365 \text{ days}}{57.4 \text{ times}}=6.4$ days
		Inventory	50	60		
			Fiscal 2018	**Fiscal 2017**		
American Eagle		CGS	$2,550	$2,425	$\dfrac{\$2,550}{(\$420+\$400)/2}=6.2$ times	$\dfrac{365 \text{ days}}{6.2 \text{ times}}=58.9$ days
		Inventory	420	400		

Inventory turnover also can vary significantly between companies within the same industry, particularly if they take different approaches to pricing their inventory. In Chapter 6, we saw that Walmart follows a low-cost pricing policy, which means setting its sales prices only slightly above cost. This policy led Walmart to earn about 24.5 cents of gross profit on each dollar of sales, whereas Nordstrom earned 34.4 cents of gross profit. But when you consider the inventory turnover measures, you can see the full implications of this pricing policy. Walmart turns its inventory over about 8.8 times a year (41.5 days), whereas Nordstrom turns its inventory over 5.1 times a year (71.6 days). **Often, the company with a lower gross profit percentage has a faster inventory turnover.**

With inventory turnover ratios varying between industries and companies, it's most useful to compare a company's turnover with its own results from prior periods. For practice at computing and comparing to prior periods, try the following Self-Study Practice.

How's it going?

Self-Study Practice

American Eagle's balance sheet and income statement information for prior years are presented in Exhibits 7.1 and 7.2.

(a) Calculate American Eagle's inventory turnover and days to sell for the year ended February 3, 2018 (Fiscal 2017). The inventory balance on January 28, 2017, was $360 (million).

Fiscal 2017 Inventory Turnover:	Fiscal 2017 Days to Sell:
$$\frac{\boxed{}}{(\boxed{} + \boxed{})/2} = \boxed{} \text{ times}$$	$$\frac{365 \text{ days}}{\boxed{} \text{ times}} = \boxed{} \text{ days}$$

(b) Did American Eagle's inventory turnover improve, deteriorate, or remain unchanged between Fiscal 2017 (calculated in *a*) and Fiscal 2018 (shown in Exhibit 7.7)?

After you have finished, check your answers with the solution.

Solution to Self-Study Practice

a. $\dfrac{\$2,425}{(\$400 + \$360)/2} = 6.4$ times

$365 \div 6.4 = 57.0$ days

b. American Eagle's inventory turnover (and days to sell) deteriorated in Fiscal 2018 (58.9 − 57.0 = 1.9 days longer).

SPOTLIGHT ON | Big Data and Analytics

Applying Inventory Turnover and Gross Profit to LCM/NRV Judgments

Accountants and managers often use **data visualization** techniques to identify key relationships between financial measures. For example, to identify particular inventory items at risk of requiring an LCM/NRV write-down, accounting analysts plot the *days to sell* and *gross profit percentage* by product line on a graph such as the following:

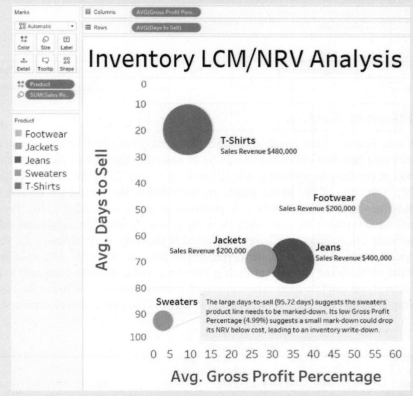

YOU SHOULD KNOW

Data Visualization: Presenting large quantities of data in maps, charts, and graphs, to reveal important relationships and trends within the data.

The inventory items in the bottom left section of this graph are most likely to require a write-down because they *(a)* take more days to sell than other products and *(b)* have the smallest gross profit percentage (i.e., the margin of difference between cost and selling price). Thus, even a small reduction in selling price could drop the company's anticipated net realizable value below its cost. **Accountants watch for worsening inventory turnover and low gross profit percentages as signs a write-down may be needed to report inventory at LCM/NRV.**

Learning Objective 7-S1
Compute inventory costs in perpetual systems.

SUPPLEMENT 7A FIFO, LIFO, AND WEIGHTED AVERAGE IN A PERPETUAL INVENTORY SYSTEM

Most modern companies use a perpetual inventory system to monitor the number of *units* in inventory, but revert to a periodic inventory system at year-end when assigning costs to those units. This occurs because companies typically adjust their records to match a physical count of the inventory on hand at year-end. There are three more reasons for showing, in the previous sections of this chapter, how cost flow assumptions are applied in a periodic inventory system. First, only the LIFO and weighted average calculations differ between periodic and perpetual inventory systems. As we show in the following example, FIFO calculations don't differ between periodic and perpetual systems. Nearly half of all U.S. companies use FIFO, so even if they calculate costs under a perpetual system, it is identical to calculating costs under a periodic system. Second, most LIFO companies actually use FIFO or a standard costing system during the period and then adjust to LIFO at the end of the period. By waiting to the end of the period to calculate this LIFO adjustment, it's *as if* all purchases during the period were recorded before the Cost of Goods Sold is calculated and recorded. In other words, it's as if these companies use a periodic inventory system to determine their LIFO inventory numbers, even though they actually track the number of units bought and sold on a perpetual basis. Third, the periodic inventory system is easier to visualize, so it's easier for you to learn.

Despite these reasons, it can be useful to know how to apply cost flow assumptions in a perpetual inventory system. In this supplement, we show how to calculate the Cost of Goods Sold and cost of ending Inventory on a perpetual basis using the same cost flow information used in the body of the chapter. The only difference in the following table is we have assumed the sales occurred on October 4, prior to the final inventory purchase.

Date	Description	# of Units	Cost per Unit	Total Cost
Oct. 1	Beginning Inventory	10	$ 7	$ 70
Oct. 3	Purchase	30	$ 8	240
Oct. 4	Sales	(35)	To calculate	To calculate
Oct. 5	Purchase	10	$10	100
	Ending Inventory	**15**	**To calculate**	**To calculate**

FIFO (First-in, First-out)

The first-in, first-out (FIFO) method assumes the oldest goods (the first in to inventory) are the first ones sold (the first out of inventory). So **to calculate the cost of the 35 units sold, use the costs of the first-in (oldest) goods** (10 units at $7 plus 25 of the 30 units at $8 = a total of $270). The **costs of the newer goods are included in the cost of the ending inventory** (5 units remaining from the 30 units at $8 plus 10 units at $10 = a total of $140). These calculations are summarized in the left-hand side of the following table (the right-hand side summarizes periodic calculations, which were explained in the body of the chapter). As you can see, FIFO yields identical amounts under perpetual and periodic. The only difference is perpetual allows you to "force out" the cost of Ending Inventory so that it can be compared to the cost of goods actually on hand (to determine shrinkage). Periodic requires you to use the cost of goods in Ending Inventory to force out the Cost of Goods Sold (so you cannot determine shrinkage).

FIFO—Perpetual		
Beginning Inventory	10 units × $7	$ 70
+ Purchases	30 units × $8	240
	10 units × $10	100
Goods Available for Sale		410
− **Cost of Goods Sold** (10 × $7) + (25 × $8)		270
Ending Inventory (10 × $10) + (5 × $8)		**$140**

FIFO—Periodic		
Beginning Inventory	10 units × $7	$ 70
+ Purchases	30 units × $8	240
	10 units × $10	100
Goods Available for Sale		410
− **Ending Inventory** (10 × $10) + (5 × $8)		**140**
Cost of Goods Sold (10 × $7) + (25 × $8)		**$270**

LIFO (Last-in, First-out)

The last-in, first-out (LIFO) method assumes the newest goods (the last in to inventory) as of the date of the sale are the first ones sold (the first out of inventory). So **to calculate the cost of the 35 units sold, use the costs of the last-in (newest) goods as of the date of the sale** (30 units at $8 plus 5 of the 10 units at $7 = a total of $275). **The costs of the older goods** (5 units remaining from the 10 units at $7 = $35) **plus any later purchases** (10 units at $10 = $100) **are included in the cost of the ending inventory** ($35 + $100 = $135). These calculations appear in the following table on the left.

LIFO—Perpetual		
Beginning Inventory	10 units × $7	$ 70
+ Purchase	30 units × $8	240
Goods Available for Sale		310
− Cost of Goods Sold (30 × $8) + (5 × $7)		275
Goods Available for Sale	5 units × $7	35
+ Purchase	10 units × $10	100
Ending Inventory (5 × $7) + (10 × $10)		**$135**

LIFO—Periodic		
Beginning Inventory	10 units × $7	$ 70
+ Purchases	30 units × $8	240
	10 units × $10	100
Goods Available for Sale		410
− **Ending Inventory** (10 × $7) + (5 × $8)		**110**
Cost of Goods Sold (10 × $10) + (25 × $8)		**$300**

Notice that LIFO–Perpetual calculates Cost of Goods Sold using the cost of goods last in at the time of the sale, whereas LIFO–Periodic uses the cost of goods last in at the end of the period.

Weighted Average Cost

In a perpetual inventory system, the weighted average cost must be calculated each time a sale is recorded. Using the same two steps shown in the body of the chapter: (1) calculate the total cost of the goods available for sale and (2) divide by the number of units available for sale. For example, in the following table on the left, the weighted average cost at the time of sale is calculated by dividing $310 by the 40 units available for sale ($310 ÷ 40 = $7.75 per unit). This cost is then multiplied by the number of units sold to calculate Cost of Goods Sold (35 × $7.75 = $271.25). The remaining 5 units are also valued at the same weighted average cost (5 × $7.75 = $38.75). Additional inventory purchases ($100) are added to these inventory costs to calculate the cost of ending inventory ($38.75 + $100 = $138.75).[3]

Weighted Average—Perpetual		
Beginning Inventory	10 units × $7	$ 70.00
+ Purchase	30 units × $8	240.00
Goods Available for Sale	40 units	310.00
− Cost of Goods Sold (35 × $7.75)		271.25
Goods Available for Sale	5 units	38.75
+ Purchase	10 units × $10	100.00
Ending Inventory	15 units	**$138.75**

Weighted Average—Periodic		
Beginning Inventory	10 units × $7	$ 70
+ Purchases	30 units × $8	240
	10 units × $10	100
Goods Available for Sale	50 units	410
− **Ending Inventory** (15 × $8.20)		**123**
Cost of Goods Sold (35 × $8.20)		**$287**

Financial Statement Effects

Exhibit 7A.1 summarizes the financial statement effects of using a perpetual inventory system with FIFO, LIFO, or weighted average cost methods. These methods differ only in the way they split the cost of goods available for sale between ending inventory and cost of goods sold.

---

[3]If inventory is sold immediately after the $100 purchase, the weighted average cost will need to be calculated again ($138.75 ÷ 15 = $9.25 per unit). Notice the change in weighted average cost from $7.75 to $9.25 per unit. Because the weighted average unit cost changes, weighted average perpetual is also called the moving average method.

If a cost goes into Cost of Goods Sold, it must be taken out of Inventory. Thus, the method that assigns the highest cost to cost of goods sold assigns the lowest cost to ending inventory (and vice versa).

EXHIBIT 7A.1	Financial Statement Effects of Inventory Costing Methods (Perpetual)		
Effects on the Income Statement	**FIFO**	**LIFO**	**Weighted Average**
Sales	$525	$525	$ 525.00
Cost of Goods Sold	270	275	271.25
Gross Profit	255	250	253.75
Effects on the Balance Sheet			
Inventory	**$140**	**$135**	**$138.75**

SUPPLEMENT 7B THE EFFECTS OF ERRORS IN ENDING INVENTORY

Learning Objective 7-S2
Determine the effects of inventory errors.

As mentioned earlier in the chapter, the failure to correctly apply the LCM/NRV rule to ending inventory is considered an error. Other errors can occur by using inappropriate quantities or unit costs in inventory costing calculations. These errors can arise in either periodic or perpetual inventory systems. Regardless of the reason, errors in inventory can significantly affect both the balance sheet and the income statement. As the cost of goods sold equation indicates, a direct relationship exists between ending inventory and cost of goods sold because items not in the ending inventory are assumed to have been sold. Thus, any errors in ending inventory will affect the balance sheet (current assets) and the income statement (Cost of Goods Sold, Gross Profit, and Net Income). The effects of inventory errors are felt in more than one year because the ending inventory for one year becomes the beginning inventory for the next year.

To determine the effects of inventory errors in the current and following year, use the cost of goods sold equation. For example, assume inventory was overstated at the end of Year 1 by $10,000 due to an error that was not discovered until Year 2. This would have the following Year 1 effects:

Year 1	
Beginning Inventory	**Accurate**
+ Purchases	**Accurate**
− Ending Inventory	**Overstated $10,000**
= Cost of Goods Sold	**Understated $10,000**

Because Cost of Goods Sold was understated, Gross Profit and Income before Income Tax Expense would be overstated by $10,000 in Year 1, as shown in Exhibit 7B.1. (Net Income would be overstated as well, although the effects would be offset somewhat by overstated Income Tax Expense.)

The Year 1 ending inventory becomes the Year 2 beginning inventory, so even if Year 2 ending inventory is calculated correctly, the error in Year 1 creates an error in Year 2, as shown in the following table:

Year 2	
Beginning Inventory	**Overstated $10,000**
+ Purchases	**Accurate**
− Ending Inventory	**Accurate**
= Cost of Goods Sold	**Overstated $10,000**

EXHIBIT 7B.1	Two-Year Income Effects of Inventory Error

| | Year 1 | | Year 2 | |
	With an Error	Without an Error	With an Error	Without an Error
Sales	$120,000	$120,000	$110,000	$110,000
Beginning Inventory	$ 50,000	$ 50,000	**$45,000**	**$35,000**
+ Purchases	75,000	75,000	70,000	70,000
Cost of Goods Available for Sale	125,000	125,000	115,000	105,000
− Ending Inventory	**45,000**	**35,000**	20,000	20,000
Cost of Goods Sold	80,000	90,000	95,000	85,000
Gross Profit	40,000	30,000	15,000	25,000
Operating Expenses	10,000	10,000	10,000	10,000
Net Income (before income tax)	$ 30,000	$ 20,000	$ 5,000	$ 15,000

Net Income overstated by $10,000 → Cancels out ← Net Income understated by $10,000

Because Cost of Goods Sold is overstated in Year 2, that year's Gross Profit and Income before Income Tax Expense would be understated by the same amount in Year 2. (Net Income would be understated as well, although the effects would be offset somewhat by understated Income Tax Expense.)

Ignoring income taxes, the effects of these errors on Net Income in each of the two years is shown in Exhibit 7B.1. Notice that the Cost of Goods Sold is understated in the first year and overstated in the second year. Over the two years, these errors offset one another. Inventory errors will "self-correct" like this only if ending inventory is accurately calculated at the end of the following year and adjusted to that correct balance. (That these errors are self-correcting does not make them "OK." They are errors.)

REVIEW THE CHAPTER

DEMONSTRATION CASE

Ebert Electronics sells one line of consumer electronics. Assume the following summarized transactions were completed during the month ended January 31, in the order given.

	Units	Unit Cost
Beginning inventory (January 1)	11	$200
New inventory purchases (January 3)	5	209
New inventory purchases (January 4)	9	220
Sale (January 5 at a price of $420 per item)	(12)	
Ending inventory (January 31)	13	

Required:

1. Using the formats shown in the chapter, compute the Cost of Goods Available for Sale, Ending Inventory, and Cost of Goods Sold under (*a*) FIFO, (*b*) LIFO, (*c*) weighted average and (*d*) specific identification. Assume the 12 units sold on January 5 included all of the beginning inventory and one unit from the purchase on January 4.

2. Which method would minimize income taxes? Explain your answer.

3. Assuming that operating expenses were $500 and the income tax rate is 25 percent, prepare the income statement for the month using the method selected in requirement 2.

4. If the inventory value at the end of January fell to $205 per unit, compute the adjustment to the Inventory account assuming the company uses (*a*) FIFO, (*b*) LIFO, (*c*) weighted average and (*d*) specific identification.

5. Describe the impact of an adjustment in requirement 4 on the inventory turnover ratio. Computations are not required.

Suggested Solution

1.

(a) FIFO

Beginning Inventory	11 units × $200	$ 2,200
+ Purchases	5 units × $209	1,045
	9 units × $220	1,980
Goods Available for Sale		5,225
− **Ending Inventory** (9 × $220) + (4 × $209)		**2,816**
Cost of Goods Sold (11 × $200) + (1 × $209)		**$2,409**

(b) LIFO

Beginning Inventory	11 units × $200	$ 2,200
+ Purchases	5 units × $209	1,045
	9 units × $220	1,980
Goods Available for Sale		5,225
− **Ending Inventory** (11 × $200) + (2 × $209)		**2,618**
Cost of Goods Sold (9 × $220) + (3 × $209)		**$2,607**

(c) Weighted Average

Beginning Inventory	11 units × $200	$ 2,200
+ Purchases	5 units × $209	1,045
	9 units × $220	1,980
Goods Available for Sale	25 units	5,225

$$\text{Weighted Average Cost} = \frac{\text{Cost of Goods Available for Sale}}{\text{Number of Units Available for Sale}} = \frac{\$5,225}{25 \text{ units}} = \frac{\$209}{\text{per unit}}$$

(c) Weighted Average

Beginning Inventory	11 units × $200	$ 2,200
+ Purchases	5 units × $209	1,045
	9 units × $220	1,980
Goods Available for Sale		5,225
− **Ending Inventory** (13 × $209)		**2,717**
Cost of Goods Sold (12 × $209)		**$2,508**

(d) Specific Identification

	Ending Inventory	Cost of Goods Sold
January 1 inventory (11 × $200)	$ 0	$2,200
January 3 purchase (5 × $209)	1,045	
January 4 purchase ($220 each)	1,760*	220
Total	$ 2,805	2,420

*$220 per unit × 8 units = $1,760

2. LIFO would minimize income taxes. Because costs are rising, LIFO produces higher Cost of Goods Sold, lower Income before Income Tax Expense, and lower Income Tax Expense.

3.

EBERT ELECTRONICS	
Income Statement	
For the Month Ended January 31	
Sales (12 × $420)	$5,040
Cost of Goods Sold	2,607
Gross Profit	2,433
Operating Expenses	500
Income before Income Tax Expense	1,933
Income Tax Expense (25%)	483
Net Income	$1,450

4. The total value of the 13 units in ending inventory, with a per unit market/net realizable value of $205, is $2,665 (13 × $205 = $2,665). The LCM/NRV analysis follows:

	Cost	Market/NRV	LCM/NRV	Adjustment Needed
(a) FIFO	$2,816	$2,665	$2,665	$(151) = $2,816 − $2,665
(b) LIFO	$2,618	$2,665	$2,618	0
(c) Weighted Average	$2,717	$2,665	$2,665	(52) = $2,717 − $2,665
(d) Specific Identification	$2,805	$2,665	$2,665	(140) = $2,805 − $2,665

5. An adjustment for LCM/NRV decreases the Inventory balance and increases the Cost of Goods Sold. Both of these changes (individually or together) increase the inventory turnover ratio.

CHAPTER SUMMARY

Describe the issues in managing different types of inventory.   **LO 7-1**

- Make or buy a sufficient *quantity* of *quality* products, at the lowest possible *cost*, so they can be sold as quickly as possible to earn the desired gross profit.

- *Merchandise inventory* is bought by merchandisers in a ready-to-sell format. When *raw materials* enter a manufacturer's production process, they become *work in process* inventory, which is further transformed into *finished goods* that are ultimately sold to customers.

Explain how to report inventory and cost of goods sold.   **LO 7-2**

- The costs of goods purchased are added to Inventory (on the balance sheet).

- The costs of goods sold are removed from Inventory and reported as an expense called Cost of Goods Sold (on the income statement).

- The costs remaining in Inventory at the end of a period become the cost of Inventory at the beginning of the next period.

- The relationships among beginning inventory (BI), purchases (P), ending inventory (EI), and cost of goods sold (CGS) are BI + P − EI = CGS or BI + P − CGS = EI.

Compute costs using four inventory costing methods.   **LO 7-3**

- Under GAAP, any of four generally accepted methods can be used to allocate the cost of inventory available for sale between goods that are sold and goods that remain on hand at the end of the accounting period.

- Specific identification assigns costs to ending inventory and cost of goods sold by tracking and identifying each specific item of inventory.

- Under FIFO, the costs first in are assigned to cost of goods sold and the costs last in (most recent) are assigned to the inventory that is still on hand in ending inventory.

- Under LIFO, the costs last in are assigned to cost of goods sold and the costs first in (oldest) are assigned to the inventory that is still on hand in ending inventory.

- Under weighted average cost, the weighted average cost per unit of inventory is assigned equally to goods sold and those still on hand in ending inventory.

LO 7-4 **Report inventory at the lower of cost or market/net realizable value.**

- The LCM/NRV rule ensures inventory assets are not reported at more than they are worth.

LO 7-5 **Evaluate inventory management by computing and interpreting the inventory turnover ratio.**

- The inventory turnover ratio measures the efficiency of inventory management. It reflects how many times average inventory was acquired and sold during the period. The inventory turnover ratio is calculated by dividing Cost of Goods Sold by Average Inventory.

Accounting Decision Tools		
Name of Measure	**Formula**	**What It Tells You**
Inventory turnover ratio	$\dfrac{\text{Cost of Goods Sold}}{\text{Average Inventory}}$	• The number of times inventory turns over during the period • A higher ratio means faster turnover
Days to sell	$\dfrac{365}{\text{Inventory Turnover Ratio}}$	• Average number of days from purchase to sale • A higher number means a longer time to sell

KEY TERMS

See complete definitions in the glossary in the back of this text.

HOMEWORK HELPER

Alternative terms
- Cost of Goods Sold is also called Cost of Sales.
- Days to Sell is also called "days in inventory" and "days' sales in inventory."

Helpful reminders
- The "first-out" part of FIFO and LIFO describes the costs going out of inventory into Cost of Goods Sold. To calculate ending inventory cost using LIFO, think FIST (first in, still there). For FIFO inventory, think LIST (last in, still there).

Frequent mistakes
- When calculating weighted average cost, do not simply average the costs per unit. Instead, divide the total cost of goods available for sale by the number of goods available for sale.
- Do not use Sales Revenue when calculating inventory turnover (use Cost of Goods Sold). Also, use the average inventory, not the ending Inventory balance.

PRACTICE MATERIAL

QUESTIONS (⊖ Symbol indicates questions that require analysis from more than one perspective.)

1. What are three goals of inventory management?

2. Describe the specific types of inventory reported by merchandisers and manufacturers.

3. The chapter discussed four inventory costing methods. List the four methods and briefly explain each.

4. Which inventory cost flow method is most similar to the flow of products involving (*a*) a gumball machine, (*b*) bricks off a stack, and (*c*) gasoline out of a tank?

5. "Where possible, the inventory costing method should mimic actual product flows." Do you agree? Explain.

6. Contrast the effects of LIFO versus FIFO on ending inventory when (*a*) costs are rising and (*b*) costs are falling.

7. Contrast the income statement effect of LIFO versus FIFO (on Cost of Goods Sold and Gross Profit) when (*a*) costs are rising and (*b*) costs are falling.

8. Several managers in your company are experiencing personal financial problems and have asked that your company switch from LIFO to FIFO so that they can receive bigger bonuses, which are tied to the company's net income. How would you respond to this request if you were the company's chief financial officer (CFO)? Would such a switch help the managers? Who could it hurt? ⊖

9. Explain briefly the application of the LCM/NRV rule to ending inventory. Describe its effect on the balance sheet and income statement when inventory value is lower than cost.

10. As a sales representative for a publicly traded pharmaceutical company, you become aware of new evidence that one of your company's main drugs has significant life-threatening side effects that were not previously reported. Your company has a significant inventory of this drug. What income statement accounts other than Net Sales will be affected by the news? A friend asks you whether he should invest in your company. What should you say? ⊖

11. You work for a made-to-order clothing company, whose reputation is based on its fast turnaround from order to delivery. The owner of your company is considering outsourcing much of the clothing production because she thinks this will improve inventory turnover and customer satisfaction. In what way is she correct? In what way might she be wrong? ⊖

12. (Supplement 7A) Distinguish perpetual inventory systems from periodic inventory systems by describing when and how cost of goods sold is calculated when using LIFO.

13. (Supplement 7B) Explain why an error in ending inventory in one period affects the following period.

MULTIPLE CHOICE

1. Which of the following statements are true regarding Cost of Goods Sold?

   i. Cost of Goods Sold represents the costs that a company incurred to purchase or produce inventory in the current period.
   ii. Cost of Goods Sold is an expense on the income statement.
   iii. Cost of Goods Sold is affected by the inventory method selected by a company (FIFO, LIFO, etc.).

   a. (i) only
   b. (ii) and (iii)
   c. (ii) only
   d. All of the above.

2. The inventory costing method selected by a company can affect

   a. The balance sheet.
   b. The income statement.
   c. The statement of retained earnings.
   d. All of the above.

3. Which of the following is not a name for a specific type of inventory?

   a. Finished goods.
   b. Merchandise inventory.
   c. Raw materials.
   d. Goods available for sale.

4. Which of the following correctly expresses the cost of goods sold equation, as used in a periodic system?

   a. $BI + CGS - P = EI$
   b. $BI + P - EI = CGS$
   c. $BI + P - Sales = EI$
   d. $BI + EI - P = CGS$

5. A New York bridal dress designer that makes high-end custom wedding dresses and needs to know the exact cost of each dress most likely uses which inventory costing method?

   a. FIFO
   b. LIFO
   c. Weighted Average
   d. Specific Identification

6. If costs are rising, which of the following will be true?

   a. The cost of goods sold will be greater if LIFO is used rather than weighted average.
   b. The cost of ending inventory will be greater if FIFO is used rather than LIFO.
   c. The gross profit will be greater if FIFO is used rather than LIFO.
   d. All of the above are true.

7. Which inventory method provides a better matching of current costs with sales revenue on the income statement but also results in older values being reported for inventory on the balance sheet?

a. FIFO

c. LIFO

b. Weighted Average

d. Specific Identification

8. Which of the following regarding the *lower of cost or market/net realizable value* rule for inventory are true?

   i. When the value of inventory increases above the cost of inventory shown in the financial records, the inventory should be increased to that higher value.

   ii. When the value of inventory drops below the cost of inventory shown in the financial records, net income is reduced.

   iii. When the value of inventory drops below the cost of inventory shown in the financial records, total assets are reduced.

   a. (i) only

   b. (ii) only

   c. (ii) and (iii)

   d. All of the above.

9. An increasing inventory turnover ratio

   a. Indicates a longer time span between the ordering and receiving of inventory.

   b. Indicates a shorter time span between the ordering and receiving of inventory.

   c. Indicates a shorter time span between the purchase and sale of inventory.

   d. Indicates a longer time span between the purchase and sale of inventory.

10. In which of the following situations is an LCM/NRV write-down most likely required?

    a. Increasing inventory turnover ratio, decreasing gross profit percentage.

    b. Decreasing inventory turnover ratio, decreasing gross profit percentage.

    c. Increasing inventory turnover ratio, increasing gross profit percentage.

    d. Decreasing inventory turnover ratio, increasing gross profit percentage.

> For answers to the Multiple-Choice Questions **see page Q1** located in the last section of the book.

MINI-EXERCISES

LO 7-1　**M7-1 Matching Inventory Items to Type of Business**

Match the type of inventory with the type of business by placing checkmarks in the applicable columns:

Type of Inventory	Type of Business	
	Merchandising	Manufacturing
Merchandise		
Finished goods		
Work in process		
Raw materials		

LO 7-1

Abercrombie & Fitch Co.

M7-2 Reporting Goods in Transit

Abercrombie & Fitch Co. reported the following in its financial statement notes.

> Ending inventory balances . . . include inventory in transit. Inventory in transit is considered to be all merchandise owned by Abercrombie & Fitch that has not yet been received at an Abercrombie & Fitch distribution center.

Has the inventory in transit been sold to Abercrombie & Fitch as FOB shipping point or FOB destination?

LO 7-1

XO Group

M7-3 Items Included in Inventory

Indicate whether the following items should be included in the inventory of XO Group, a company that arranges and supplies wedding services for couples and other wedding consultants.

a. Goods being held by XO Group on consignment from Emerald Bridal.

b. Goods in transit to Winston Wedding Consultants, sold FOB shipping point by XO Group.

c. Goods in transit to XO Group, purchased FOB shipping point by XO Group.

LO 7-2　**M7-4 Reporting Inventory-Related Accounts in the Financial Statements**

For each of the following, indicate whether it would be reported on the balance sheet (B/S), reported on the income statement (I/S), or not shown in the company's financial statements (Not).

_____ *a.* Sales Revenue

_____ *b.* Inventory (held on consignment)

_____ *c.* Cost of Goods Sold

_____ *d.* Inventory (out on consignment)

M7-5 Matching Financial Statement Effects to Inventory Costing Methods LO 7-3

Complete the following table by indicating which inventory costing method (FIFO or LIFO) would lead to the effects noted in the rows, for each of the circumstances described in the columns.

	1. Declining Costs	2. Rising Costs
a. Lowest net income		
b. Lowest ending inventory		

M7-6 Matching Inventory Costing Method Choices to Company Circumstances LO 7-3

Indicate whether a company interested in minimizing its income taxes should choose the FIFO or LIFO inventory costing method under each of the following circumstances.

_____ *a.* Declining costs
_____ *b.* Rising costs

M7-7 Calculating Cost of Goods Available for Sale, Ending Inventory, Sales, Cost of Goods Sold, and Gross Profit under Periodic FIFO LO 7-3

Given the following information, calculate cost of goods available for sale and ending inventory, then sales, cost of goods sold, and gross profit, under FIFO. Assume a periodic inventory system is used.

		Units	Unit Cost	Unit Selling Price
July 1	Beginning Inventory	50	$10	
July 13	Purchase	250	13	
July 25	Sold	(100)		15
July 31	Ending Inventory	200		

M7-8 Calculating Cost of Goods Available for Sale, Ending Inventory, Sales, Cost of Goods Sold, and Gross Profit under Periodic LIFO LO 7-3

Complete the requirements for M7-7 assuming a periodic LIFO inventory system is used.

M7-9 Calculating Cost of Goods Available for Sale, Ending Inventory, Sales, Cost of Goods Sold, and Gross Profit under Periodic Weighted Average Cost LO 7-3

Complete the requirements for M7-7 assuming weighted average cost is used in a periodic inventory system.

M7-10 Calculating Cost of Goods Available for Sale, Cost of Goods Sold, and Ending Inventory under FIFO, LIFO, and Weighted Average Cost (Periodic Inventory) LO 7-3

Aircard Corporation tracks the number of units purchased and sold throughout each accounting period but applies its inventory costing method at the end of each period as if it uses a periodic inventory system. Given the following information, calculate the cost of goods available for sale, ending inventory, and cost of goods sold if Aircard uses (*a*) FIFO, (*b*) LIFO, or (*c*) weighted average cost.

		Units	Unit Cost
July 1	Beginning Inventory	2,000	$40
July 5	Sold	1,000	
July 13	Purchased	6,000	44
July 17	Sold	3,000	
July 25	Purchased	8,000	50
July 27	Sold	5,000	

LO 7-3

M7-11 Calculating Cost of Goods Available for Sale, Cost of Goods Sold, and Ending Inventory under Periodic FIFO

In its first month of operations, Literacy for the Illiterate opened a new bookstore and bought merchandise in the following order: (1) 300 units at $7 on January 1, (2) 450 units at $8 on January 8, and (3) 750 units at $9 on January 29. Assuming 900 units are on hand at the end of the month, calculate the cost of goods available for sale, ending inventory, and cost of goods sold under FIFO. Assume a periodic inventory system is used.

LO 7-3

M7-12 Calculating Cost of Goods Available for Sale, Cost of Goods Sold, and Ending Inventory under Periodic LIFO

Complete the requirements for M7-11 assuming LIFO is used in a periodic inventory system.

LO 7-3

M7-13 Calculating Cost of Goods Available for Sale, Cost of Goods Sold, and Ending Inventory under Periodic Weighted Average Cost

Complete the requirements for M7-11 assuming weighted average cost is used in a periodic inventory system.

LO 7-4

M7-14 Reporting Inventory under Lower of Cost or Market/Net Realizable Value

The Jewel Fool had the following inventory items on hand at the end of the year.

	Quantity	Cost per Item	Value per Item
Necklaces	10	$75	$70
Bracelets	50	40	60

Determine the lower of cost or market/net realizable value per unit and the total amount that should be reported on the balance sheet for each item of inventory.

LO 7-4

BlackBerry Limited

M7-15 Preparing the Journal Entry to Record Lower of Cost or Market/Net Realizable Value (LCM/NRV) Adjustment

During fiscal 2014, BlackBerry Limited wrote down its BB10 smartphone inventory by approximately $1,700,000,000 because its cost exceeded its net realizable value. Show the effects of this adjustment on the accounting equation and show the journal entry the company would have made to record it.

LO 7-5

M7-16 Determining the Effects of Inventory Management Changes on the Inventory Turnover Ratio

Indicate the most likely effect of the following changes in inventory management on the inventory turnover ratio (+ for increase, − for decrease, and NE for no effect).

_____ *a.* Inventory delivered by suppliers daily (small amounts) instead of weekly (larger amounts).
_____ *b.* Shorten production process from 10 days to 8 days.
_____ *c.* Extend payments for inventory purchases from 15 days to 30 days.

LO 7-5

Zumiez Inc.

M7-17 Interpreting LCM/NRV Financial Statement Note Disclosure

Zumiez Inc. is a leading action sports retailer, selling its skateboarding, snowboarding, surfing, and BMX merchandise under the Blue Tomato brand. The company's financial statement notes reported, "Merchandise inventories may include items that have been written down to our best estimate of their net realizable value. Our decisions to write down our merchandise inventories are based on their current rate of sale, the age of the inventory, the profitability of the inventory and other factors." What ratios and financial measure(s) discussed in this chapter is the company likely using to monitor . . .

a. ". . . the current rate of sale"?
b. ". . . the age of the inventory"?
c. ". . . the profitability of the inventory"?

LO 7-5

M7-18 Calculating the Inventory Turnover Ratio and Days to Sell

Solve for the missing information designated by "?" in the following table. Round the Inventory Turnover Ratio and Days to Sell to one decimal.

Case	BI	Purchases	CGS	EI	Inventory Turnover Ratio	Days to Sell
a.	$100	$700	$ 600	?	?	?
b.	200	?	1,200	?	6.0	?
c.	?	?	1,000	150	?	36.5

M7-19 (Supplement 7A) Calculating Cost of Goods Sold and Ending Inventory under FIFO and LIFO (Perpetual Inventory)   LO 7-S1

Refer to M7-10. Calculate the cost of ending inventory and cost of goods sold assuming a perpetual inventory system is used in combination with (a) FIFO and (b) LIFO.

M7-20 (Supplement 7A) Calculating Cost of Goods Sold and Ending Inventory under Perpetual FIFO   LO 7-S1

Repeat M7-11, except assume Literacy for the Illiterate uses a perpetual inventory system and it sold 600 units between January 9 and January 28.

M7-21 (Supplement 7A) Calculating Cost of Goods Sold and Ending Inventory under Perpetual LIFO   LO 7-S1

Repeat M7-12, except assume Literacy for the Illiterate uses a perpetual inventory system and it sold 600 units between January 9 and January 28.

M7-22 (Supplement 7A) Calculating Cost of Goods Sold and Ending Inventory under Perpetual Weighted Average Cost   LO 7-S1

Repeat M7-13, except assume Literacy for the Illiterate uses a perpetual inventory system and it sold 600 units between January 9 and January 28.

M7-23 (Supplement 7B) Determining the Financial Statement Effects of Inventory Errors   LO 7-S2

Assume the 2021 ending inventory of Shea's Shrimp Shack was understated by $10,000. Explain how this error would affect the amounts reported for cost of goods sold and gross profit for 2021 and 2022.

M7-24 (Supplement 7B) Determining the Financial Statement Effects of Inventory Errors   LO 7-S2

Repeat M7-23, except assume the 2021 ending inventory was *over*stated by $10,000.

EXERCISES   Mc Graw Hill connect

E7-1 Reporting Goods in Transit and Consignment Inventory   LO 7-1

The RealReal, Inc., is a public company that sells authenticated luxury goods, similar to Second Chance Clothing (SCC). SCC acquires its goods on consignment and through purchase. The following events occurred close to SCC's October 31 year-end.   The RealReal, Inc.

_____ a. On November 2, SCC received goods on consignment from Apparel Corp.
_____ b. On October 31, SCC received goods on consignment from Apparel Corp.
_____ c. Goods in transit to SCC were shipped by Shoe, Inc., on October 31, FOB shipping point.
_____ d. Goods in transit to SCC were shipped by Shoe, Inc., on October 31, FOB destination.

Required:

Indicate (Yes or No) whether SCC should include each item in its inventory balance at October 31.

E7-2 Determining the Correct Inventory Balance   LO 7-1, 7-2, 7-4

Seemore Lens Company (SLC) sells contact lenses FOB destination. For the year ended December 31, the company reported Inventory of $70,000 and Cost of Goods Sold of $420,000.

a. Included in Inventory (and Accounts Payable) are $10,000 of lenses SLC is holding on consignment.
b. Included in SLC's Inventory balance are $5,000 of office supplies held in SLC's warehouse.

c. Excluded from SLC's Inventory balance are $8,000 of lenses in the warehouse, ready to send to customers on January 2. SLC reported these lenses as sold on December 31, at a price of $15,000.

d. Included in SLC's Inventory balance are $3,000 of lenses that were damaged in December and will be scrapped in January, with zero realizable value.

Required:

Create a table showing the balances presently reported for Inventory and Cost of Goods Sold, and then displaying the adjustment(s) needed to correctly account for each of items (a)–(d), and finally determining the appropriate Inventory and Cost of Goods Sold balances.

LO 7-1, 7-2, 7-4   **E7-3   Recording Journal Entries to Correct Inventory Misreporting**

Refer to the information in E7-2.

Required:

For each item (a)–(d), prepare the journal entry to correct the balances presently reported. If a journal entry is not required, indicate so.

LO 7-3   **E7-4   FIFO Inventory Calculations**

Just One Product (JOP) began operating on June 26 with no inventory on hand. It then made the purchases listed below. JOP sold and delivered 46 units on June 30.

Date	Description	Units	Unit Cost	Total Cost
June 27	Purchase	12	$ 8	$ 96
28	Purchase	38	9	342
29	Purchase	20	11	220

Required:

1. Calculate the number and cost of goods available for sale.
2. Calculate the number of units in ending inventory at June 30.
3. Calculate the cost of ending inventory and the cost of goods sold under FIFO.

LO 7-3   **E7-5   LIFO Inventory Calculations**

Refer to the information in E7-4. Complete requirements 1–3 using LIFO (not FIFO).

LO 7-3   **E7-6   Weighted Average Cost Inventory Calculations**

Refer to the information in E7-4. Complete requirements 1–3 using Weighted Average Cost (not FIFO).

LO 7-3   **E7-7   Calculating Cost of Ending Inventory and Cost of Goods Sold under Periodic FIFO, LIFO, and Weighted Average Cost**

Oahu Kiki tracks the number of units purchased and sold throughout each accounting period but applies its inventory costing method at the end of each month, as if it uses a periodic inventory system. Assume Oahu Kiki's records show the following for the month of January. Sales totaled 240 units.

	Date	Units	Unit Cost	Total Cost
Beginning Inventory	January 1	120	$ 80	$ 9,600
Purchase	January 15	380	90	34,200
Purchase	January 24	200	110	22,000

Required:

1. Calculate the number and cost of goods available for sale.
2. Calculate the number of units in ending inventory.
3. Calculate the cost of ending inventory and cost of goods sold using the (a) FIFO, (b) LIFO, and (c) weighted average cost methods.

E7-8 Analyzing and Interpreting the Financial Statement Effects of Periodic FIFO, LIFO, and Weighted Average Cost

Orion Iron Corp. tracks the number of units purchased and sold throughout each year but applies its inventory costing method at the end of the year, as if it uses a periodic inventory system. Assume its accounting records provided the following information at the end of the annual accounting period, December 31.

Transactions	Units	Unit Cost
a. Inventory, Beginning	300	$12
For the year:		
b. Purchase, April 11	900	10
c. Purchase, June 1	800	13
d. Sale, May 1 (sold for $40 per unit)	300	
e. Sale, July 3 (sold for $40 per unit)	600	
f. Operating expenses (excluding income tax expense), $19,500		

Required:

1. Calculate the number and cost of goods available for sale.
2. Calculate the number of units in ending inventory.
3. Compute the cost of ending inventory and cost of goods sold under (*a*) FIFO, (*b*) LIFO, and (*c*) weighted average cost.
4. Prepare an income statement that shows the FIFO method in one column, the LIFO method in another column, and the weighted average method in a final column. Include the following line items in the income statement: Sales, Cost of Goods Sold, Gross Profit, Operating Expenses, and Income from Operations.
5. Compare the Income from Operations and the ending inventory amounts that would be reported under the three methods. Explain the similarities and differences.
6. Which inventory costing method minimizes income taxes?

E7-9 Analyzing and Interpreting the Financial Statement Effects of FIFO, LIFO, and Weighted Average Cost

Scoresby Inc. tracks the number of units purchased and sold throughout each year but applies its inventory costing method at the end of the year, as if it uses a periodic inventory system. Assume its accounting records provided the following information at the end of the annual accounting period, December 31.

Transactions	Units	Unit Cost
a. Inventory, Beginning	3,000	$ 8
For the year:		
b. Purchase, March 5	9,500	9
c. Purchase, September 19	5,000	11
d. Sale, April 15 (sold for $29 per unit)	4,000	
e. Sale, October 31 (sold for $31 per unit)	8,000	
f. Operating expenses (excluding income tax expense), $250,000		

Required:

1. Calculate the number and cost of goods available for sale.
2. Calculate the number of units in ending inventory.
3. Compute the cost of ending inventory and cost of goods sold under (*a*) FIFO, (*b*) LIFO, and (*c*) weighted average cost.

4. Prepare an income statement that shows the FIFO method in one column, the LIFO method in another column, and the weighted average method in a final column. Include the following line items in the income statement: Sales, Cost of Goods Sold, Gross Profit, Operating Expenses, and Income from Operations.

5. Compare the Income from Operations and the ending inventory amounts that would be reported under the three methods. Explain the similarities and differences.

6. Which inventory costing method minimizes income taxes?

LO 7-3   **E7-10 Evaluating the Effects of Inventory Methods on Income from Operations, Income Taxes, and Net Income (Periodic)**

Courtney Company uses a periodic inventory system. The following data were available: beginning inventory, 1,000 units at $35; purchases, 4,000 units at $38; operating expenses (excluding income taxes), $91,500; ending inventory per physical count at December 31, 900 units; sales price per unit, $75; and average income tax rate, 30%.

Required:

1. Complete the body of the following income statements and the cost of goods sold calculation under the FIFO, LIFO, and weighted average costing methods.

		Inventory Costing Method		
Income Statement	Units	FIFO	LIFO	Weighted Average
Sales Revenue	____	$ ____	$ ____	$ ____
Cost of Goods Sold*	____	____	____	____
Gross Profit		____	____	____
Operating Expenses		____	____	____
Income from Operations		____	____	____
Income Tax Expense		____	____	____
Net Income		____	____	____

Cost of goods sold equation:

Beginning Inventory	____	$ ____	$ ____	$ ____
Purchases	____	____	____	____
Goods Available for Sale	____	____	____	____
Ending Inventory	____	____	____	____
Cost of Goods Sold	____	____	____	____

2. Between FIFO and LIFO, which method is preferable in terms of (*a*) maximizing income from operations or (*b*) minimizing income taxes? Explain.

3. What would be your answer to requirement 2 if costs were falling? Explain.

LO 7-3   **E7-11 Choosing LIFO versus FIFO When Costs Are Rising and Falling**

Use the following information to complete this exercise: sales, 550 units for $12,500; beginning inventory, 300 units; purchases, 400 units; ending inventory, 150 units; and operating expenses, $4,000. Begin by setting up the following table and then complete the requirements that follow.

		Costs Rising			Costs Falling	
		Situation A	Situation B	Situation C	Situation D
		FIFO	LIFO	FIFO	LIFO
Sales Revenue		$12,500	$12,500	$12,500	$12,500
Beginning Inventory	$3,600				
Purchases	5,200	____	____	____	
Goods Available for Sale	8,800				
Ending Inventory	1,950	____	____	____	
Cost of Goods Sold		6,850	____	____	____
Gross Profit		5,650			
Operating Expenses		4,000	4,000	4,000	4,000
Income from Operations		1,650			
Income Tax Expense (30%)		495	____	____	____
Net Income		$ 1,155			

Required:

1. Complete the table for each situation. In Situations A and B (costs rising), assume the following: beginning inventory, 300 units at $12 = $3,600; purchases, 400 units at $13 = $5,200. In Situations C and D (costs falling), assume the opposite; that is, beginning inventory, 300 units at $13 = $3,900; purchases, 400 units at $12 = $4,800. Use periodic inventory procedures.

2. Describe the relative effects on Income from Operations as demonstrated by requirement 1 when costs are rising and when costs are falling.

3. Describe the relative effects on Income Tax Expense for each situation.

E7-12 Using FIFO for Multiproduct Inventory Transactions (Chapters 6 and 7)

LO 6-3, 6-4, 7-3

TrackR, Inc., (TI) has developed a coin-sized tracking tag that attaches to key rings, wallets, and other items and can be prompted to emit a signal using a smartphone app. TI sells these tags, as well as water-resistant cases for the tags, with terms FOB shipping point. Assume TI has no inventory at the beginning of the month, and it has outsourced the production of its tags and cases. TI uses FIFO and has entered into the following transactions:

TrackR, Inc.

Jan. 2:	TI purchased and received 300 tags from Xioasi Manufacturing (XM) at a cost of $9 per tag, n/15.
Jan. 4:	TI purchased and received 100 cases from Bachittar Products (BP) at a cost of $2 per case, n/20.
Jan. 6:	TI paid cash for the tags purchased from XM on Jan. 2.
Jan. 8:	TI mailed 200 tags via the U.S. Postal Service (USPS) to customers at a price of $30 per tag, on account.
Jan. 11:	TI purchased and received 400 tags from XM at a cost of $12 per tag, n/15.
Jan. 14:	TI purchased and received 200 cases from BP at a cost of $3 per case, n/20.
Jan. 16:	TI paid cash for the cases purchased from BP on Jan. 4.
Jan. 19:	TI mailed 160 cases via the USPS to customers at a price of $10 per case, on account.
Jan. 21:	TI mailed 300 tags to customers at a price of $30 per tag.

Required:

1. Prepare journal entries for each of the above dates, assuming TI uses a perpetual inventory system.

2. Calculate the dollars of gross profit and the gross profit percentage from selling (*a*) tags and (*b*) cases.

3. Which product line yields more dollars of gross profit?

4. Which product line yields more gross profit per dollar of sales?

LO 7-4

E7-13 Reporting Inventory at Lower of Cost or Market/Net Realizable Value

Peterson Furniture Designs is preparing the annual financial statements dated December 31. Ending inventory information about the five major items stocked for regular sale follows:

Item	Unit Cost (FIFO)	NRV per Item	Write-Down per Item	Quantity on Hand	Total Write-Down
Alligator Armoires	$30	$24		50	
Bear Bureaus	40	40		75	
Cougar Credenzas	50	52		10	
Dingo Cribs	30	30		30	
Elephant Dressers	15	12		400	

Required:

1. Complete the table column "Write-Down per Item" and then sum the final column to compute the amount of the total write-down when the LCM/NRV rule is applied to each item.
2. Prepare the journal entry Peterson Furniture Designs would record on December 31 to write down its inventory to LCM/NRV.

LO 7-4

E7-14 Reporting Inventory at Lower of Cost or Market/Net Realizable Value

Sandals Company is preparing the annual financial statements dated December 31. Ending inventory is presently recorded at its total cost of $5,465. Information about its inventory items follows:

Product Line	Quantity on Hand	Unit Cost When Acquired (FIFO)	Value at Year-End
Air Flow	20	$12	$14
Blister Buster	75	40	38
Coolonite	35	55	50
Dudesly	10	30	35

Required:

1. Compute the LCM/NRV write-down per unit and in total for each item in the table. Also compute the total overall write-down for all items.
2. How will the write-down of inventory to lower of cost or market/net realizable value affect the company's expenses reported for the year ended December 31?
3. Compute the amount that should be reported for the inventory on December 31, after the LCM/NRV rule has been applied to each item.

LO 7-5

Polaris Industries Inc.
Arctic Cat
Textron, Inc.

E7-15 Analyzing and Interpreting the Inventory Turnover Ratio

Polaris Industries Inc. is the biggest snowmobile manufacturer in the world. It reported the following amounts in its financial statements (in millions):

	2017	2018
Net Sales Revenue	$5,430	$6,080
Cost of Goods Sold	4,100	4,580
Average Inventory	765	880

Required:

1. Calculate to one decimal place the inventory turnover ratio and average days to sell inventory for 2018 and 2017.
2. Did inventory turnover at Polaris improve or decline in 2018?
3. Calculate the 2018 gross profit percentage.
4. The main competitor for Polaris is Arctic Cat. Prior to being acquired by Textron, Inc., Arctic Cat reported its inventory turnover was 2.9 and its gross profit percentage was 3.5 percent.

Why was Arctic Cat more likely than Polaris to require a write-down for LCM/NRV? (Select all that apply.)

    a. Arctic Cat had a higher number of days to sell than Polaris.
    b. Arctic Cat had a lower gross profit percentage than Polaris.
    c. Arctic Cat had a greater number of inventory turns than Polaris.

E7-16 Analyzing and Interpreting the Effects of the LIFO/FIFO Choice on Inventory Turnover Ratio   LO 7-2, 7-3, 7-5

Simple Plan Enterprises uses a periodic inventory system. Its records showed the following:

> Inventory, December 31, using FIFO → 38 units @ $14 = $532
>
> Inventory, December 31, using LIFO → 38 units @ $10 = $380

Transactions in the Following Year	Units	Unit Cost	Total Cost
Purchase, January 9	50	15	$ 750
Purchase, January 20	100	16	1,600
Sale, January 11 (at $38 per unit)	80		
Sale, January 27 (at $39 per unit)	56		

Required:

1. Compute the number and cost of goods available for sale, the cost of ending inventory, and the cost of goods sold under FIFO and LIFO.

2. Compute the inventory turnover ratio under the FIFO and LIFO inventory costing methods (show computations and round to one decimal place).

3. Based on your answer to requirement 2, explain whether analysts should consider the inventory costing method when comparing companies' inventory turnover ratios.

E7-17 (Supplement 7A) Calculating Cost of Ending Inventory and Cost of Goods Sold under Perpetual FIFO and LIFO   LO 7-S1

Refer to the information in E7-7. Assume Oahu Kiki applies its inventory costing method perpetually at the time of each sale. The company sold 240 units between January 16 and 23. Calculate the cost of ending inventory and the cost of goods sold using the FIFO and LIFO methods.

E7-18 (Supplement 7A) Calculating Cost of Ending Inventory and Cost of Goods Sold under Perpetual FIFO and LIFO   LO 7-S1

Refer to the information in E7-8. Assume Orion Iron applies its inventory costing method perpetually at the time of each sale. Calculate the cost of ending inventory and the cost of goods sold using the FIFO and LIFO methods.

E7-19 (Supplement 7B) Analyzing and Interpreting the Impact of an Inventory Error   LO 7-S2

Dallas Corporation prepared the following two income statements:

	First Quarter		Second Quarter	
Sales Revenue		$15,000		$18,000
Cost of Goods Sold				
Beginning Inventory	$ 3,000		$ 4,000	
Purchases	7,000		12,000	
Goods Available for Sale	10,000		16,000	
Ending Inventory	4,000		9,000	
Cost of Goods Sold		6,000		7,000
Gross Profit		9,000		11,000
Operating Expenses		5,000		6,000
Income from Operations		$ 4,000		$ 5,000

During the third quarter, the company's internal auditors discovered that the ending inventory for the first quarter should have been $4,400. The ending inventory for the second quarter was correct.

Required:

1. What effect would the error have on total Income from Operations for the two quarters combined? Explain.
2. What effect would the error have on Income from Operations for each of the two quarters? Explain.
3. Prepare corrected income statements for each quarter. Ignore income taxes.

COACHED PROBLEMS

LO 7-3   **CP7-1 Analyzing the Effects of Four Alternative Inventory Costing Methods**

Scrappers Supplies tracks the number of units purchased and sold throughout each accounting period but applies its inventory costing method at the end of each period, as if it uses a periodic inventory system. Assume its accounting records provided the following information at the end of the annual accounting period, December 31.

Transactions	Units	Unit Cost
Beginning inventory, January 1	200	$30
Transactions during the year:		
a. Purchase on account, March 2	300	32
b. Cash sale, April 1 ($46 each)	(350)	
c. Purchase on account, June 30	250	36
d. Cash sale, August 1 ($46 each)	(50)	

> **TIP:** Although the purchases and sales are listed in chronological order, Scrappers determines the cost of goods sold *after* all of the purchases have occurred.

Required:

1. Compute the cost of goods available for sale, cost of ending inventory, and cost of goods sold at December 31 under each of the following inventory costing methods:
   a. Last-in, first-out.
   b. Weighted average cost.
   c. First-in, first-out.
   d. Specific identification, assuming that the April 1 sale was selected one-fifth from the beginning inventory and four-fifths from the purchase of March 2. Assume that the sale of August 1 was selected from the purchase of June 30.
2. Of the four methods, which will result in the highest gross profit? Which will result in the lowest income taxes?

LO 7-4   **CP7-2 Evaluating the Income Statement and Income Tax Effects of Lower of Cost or Market/Net Realizable Value**

Smart Company prepared its annual financial statements dated December 31. The company reported its inventory using the FIFO inventory costing method and failed to evaluate its net realizable value at December 31. The preliminary income statement follows:

Sales Revenue		$280,000
Cost of Goods Sold		
Beginning Inventory	$ 30,000	
Purchases	182,000	
Goods Available for Sale	212,000	
Ending Inventory	44,000	
Cost of Goods Sold		168,000
Gross Profit		112,000
Operating Expenses		61,000
Income from Operations		51,000
Income Tax Expense (30%)		15,300
Net Income		$ 35,700

Assume you have been asked to restate the financial statements to incorporate LCM/NRV. You have developed the following data relating to the ending inventory:

Item	Quantity	Purchase Cost Per Unit	Total	Net Realizable Value per Unit
A	3,000	$3	$ 9,000	$4
B	1,500	4	6,000	2
C	7,000	2	14,000	4
D	3,000	5	15,000	2
			$44,000	

TIP: Inventory write-downs do not affect the cost of goods available for sale. Instead, the effect of the write-down is to reduce ending inventory, which increases Cost of Goods Sold and then affects other amounts in the income statement.

Required:

1. Restate the income statement to reflect LCM/NRV valuation of the ending inventory. Apply LCM/NRV on an item-by-item basis and show computations.
2. Compare and explain the LCM/NRV effect on each amount in the income statement that was changed in requirement 1.

CP7-3 Calculating and Interpreting the Inventory Turnover Ratio and Days to Sell

LO 7-5

GameStop Corp. is a multichannel video game and consumer electronics retailer. The company reported the following amounts (in millions) in its annual financial statements at the end of January.

GameStop Corp.
Best Buy

	2018	2017
Net Sales Revenue	$8,290	$8,550
Cost of Goods Sold	5,980	6,060
Beginning Inventory	1,250	1,120
Ending Inventory	1,250	1,250

Required:

1. Determine the inventory turnover ratio and average days to sell inventory for 2018 and 2017. Round your answers to one decimal place.
   TIP: In both the numerator (CGS) and denominator (average inventory), use costs (not selling prices).
2. Comment on any changes in these measures, and compare the effectiveness of inventory managers at GameStop with those at Best Buy, where inventory turned over 6.2 times during 2018 (58.9 days to sell).

CP7-4 (Supplement 7A) Analyzing the Effects of the LIFO Inventory Method in a Perpetual Inventory System

LO 7-S1

Using the information in CP7-1, calculate the Cost of Goods Sold and Ending Inventory for Scrappers Supplies assuming it applies the LIFO cost method perpetually at the time of each sale. Compare these amounts to the periodic LIFO calculations in requirement 1a of CP7-1. Does the use of a perpetual inventory system result in a higher or lower Cost of Goods Sold when costs are rising?
   TIP: In CP7-4, the sale of 350 units on April 1 is assumed, under LIFO, to consist of the 300 units purchased March 2 and 50 units from beginning inventory.

CP7-5 (Supplement 7B) Analyzing and Interpreting the Effects of Inventory Errors

LO 7-S2

Partial income statements for Murphy & Murphy (M & M) reported the following summarized amounts:

	Quarter 1	Quarter 2	Quarter 3	Quarter 4
Net Sales	$50,000	$49,000	$71,000	$58,000
Cost of Goods Sold	32,500	35,000	43,000	37,000
Gross Profit	17,500	14,000	28,000	21,000

After these amounts were reported, M & M's accountant determined the inventory at the end of Quarter 2 was understated by $3,000. The inventory balance at the end of the other three quarters was accurately stated.

Required:

1. Restate the partial income statements to reflect the correct amounts, after fixing the inventory error.

2. Compute the gross profit percentage for all four quarters both (*a*) before the correction and (*b*) after the correction. Does the pattern of gross profit percentages lend confidence to your corrected amounts? Explain. Round your answer to the nearest percentage.

   TIP: Gross profit percentage is calculated as (Gross Profit ÷ Net Sales) × 100.

GROUP A PROBLEMS

LO 7-3

PA7-1 Analyzing the Effects of Four Alternative Inventory Methods in a Periodic Inventory System

Gladstone Company tracks the number of units purchased and sold throughout each accounting period but applies its inventory costing method at the end of each period, as if it uses a periodic inventory system. Assume its accounting records provided the following information at the end of the annual accounting period, December 31.

Transactions	Units	Unit Cost
Beginning inventory, January 1	1,800	$50
Transactions during the year:		
a. Purchase, January 30	2,500	62
b. Sale, March 14 ($100 each)	(1,450)	
c. Purchase, May 1	1,200	80
d. Sale, August 31 ($100 each)	(1,900)	

Required:

1. Compute the amount of goods available for sale, ending inventory, and cost of goods sold at December 31 under each of the following inventory costing methods:

   a. Last-in, first-out.
   b. Weighted average cost.
   c. First-in, first-out.
   d. Specific identification, assuming that the March 14 sale was selected two-fifths from the beginning inventory and three-fifths from the purchase of January 30. Assume that the sale of August 31 was selected from the remainder of the beginning inventory, with the balance from the purchase of May 1.

2. Of the four methods, which will result in the highest gross profit? Which will result in the lowest income taxes?

LO 7-4

PA7-2 Evaluating the Income Statement and Income Tax Effects of Lower of Cost or Market/Net Realizable Value

Springer Anderson Gymnastics prepared its annual financial statements dated December 31. The company reported its inventory using the LIFO inventory costing method but did not compare the cost of its ending inventory to its market value (replacement cost). The preliminary income statement follows:

Sales Revenue		$140,000
Cost of Goods Sold		
Beginning Inventory	$ 15,000	
Purchases	91,000	
Goods Available for Sale	106,000	
Ending Inventory	22,000	
Cost of Goods Sold		84,000
Gross Profit		56,000
Operating Expenses		31,000
Income from Operations		25,000
Income Tax Expense (30%)		7,500
Net Income		$ 17,500

Assume that you have been asked to restate the financial statements to incorporate the LCM/NRV rule. You have developed the following data relating to the ending inventory:

Item	Quantity	Purchase Cost Per Unit	Purchase Cost Total	Replacement Cost per Unit
A	1,500	$3	$ 4,500	$4
B	750	4	3,000	2
C	3,500	2	7,000	1
D	1,500	5	7,500	3
			$22,000	

Required:

1. Restate the income statement to reflect LCM/NRV valuation of the ending inventory. Apply LCM/NRV on an item-by-item basis and show computations.
2. Compare and explain the LCM/NRV effect on each amount that was changed in the preliminary income statement in requirement 1.

PA7-3 Calculating and Interpreting the Inventory Turnover Ratio and Days to Sell

LO 7-5

Sonos, Inc.
Koss Corporation

Sonos, Inc., was founded with the mission of filling every home with music. The company reported the following amounts in its financial statements (in millions):

	2018	2017
Net Sales	$1,140	$990
Cost of Goods Sold	650	540
Beginning Inventory	115	55
Ending Inventory	195	115

Required:

1. Determine the inventory turnover ratio and average days to sell inventory for 2018 and 2017. Round to one decimal place.
2. Comment on any changes in these measures and compare the effectiveness of inventory managers at Sonos to inventory managers at Koss Corporation, where inventory turns over 2.3 times per year (158.7 days to sell).

PA7-4 (Supplement 7A) Analyzing the Effects of the LIFO Inventory Method in a Perpetual Inventory System

LO 7-S1

Using the information in PA7-1, calculate the cost of goods sold and ending inventory for Gladstone Company assuming it applies the LIFO cost method perpetually at the time of each sale. Compare these amounts to the periodic LIFO calculations in requirement 1a of PA7-1. Does the use of a perpetual inventory system result in a higher or lower cost of goods sold when costs are rising?

PA7-5 (Supplement 7B) Analyzing and Interpreting the Effects of Inventory Errors

LO 7-S2

Partial income statements for Sherwood Company summarized for a four-year period show the following:

	2018	2019	2020	2021
Net Sales	$2,000,000	$2,400,000	$2,500,000	$3,000,000
Cost of Goods Sold	1,400,000	1,660,000	1,770,000	2,100,000
Gross Profit	600,000	740,000	730,000	900,000

An audit revealed that in determining these amounts, the ending inventory for 2019 was overstated by $20,000. The inventory balance on December 31, 2020, was accurately stated. The company uses a periodic inventory system.

Required:

1. Restate the partial income statements to reflect the correct amounts, after fixing the inventory error.

2. Compute the gross profit percentage for each year (*a*) before the correction and (*b*) after the correction, rounding to the nearest percentage. Do the results lend confidence to your corrected amounts? Explain.

GROUP B PROBLEMS

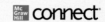

LO 7-3   **PB7-1 Analyzing the Effects of Four Alternative Inventory Methods in a Periodic Inventory System**

Mojo Industries tracks the number of units purchased and sold throughout each accounting period but applies its inventory costing method at the end of each period, as if it uses a periodic inventory system. Assume its accounting records provided the following information at the end of the accounting period, January 31. The inventory's selling price is $9 per unit.

Transactions	Unit Cost	Units	Total Cost
Inventory, January 1	$2.50	250	$625
Sale, January 10		(200)	
Purchase, January 12	3.00	300	900
Sale, January 17		(150)	
Purchase, January 26	4.00	80	320

Required:

1. Compute the amount of goods available for sale, ending inventory, and cost of goods sold at January 31 under each of the following inventory costing methods:

   a. Weighted average cost. (Round the weighted-average unit cost to two decimal places.)
   b. First-in, first-out.
   c. Last-in, first-out.
   d. Specific identification, assuming that the January 10 sale was from the beginning inventory and the January 17 sale was from the January 12 purchase.

2. Of the four methods, which will result in the highest gross profit? Which will result in the lowest income taxes?

LO 7-4   **PB7-2 Evaluating the Income Statement and Income Tax Effects of Lower of Cost or Market/Net Realizable Value**

Mondetta Clothing prepared its annual financial statements dated December 31. The company used the FIFO inventory costing method, but it failed to evaluate the net realizable value of its ending inventory. The preliminary income statement follows:

Net Sales		$420,000
Cost of Goods Sold		
Beginning Inventory	$ 45,000	
Purchases	273,000	
Goods Available for Sale	318,000	
Ending Inventory	66,000	
Cost of Goods Sold		252,000
Gross Profit		168,000
Operating Expenses		93,000
Income from Operations		75,000
Income Tax Expense (30%)		22,500
Net Income		$ 52,500

Assume that you have been asked to restate the financial statements to incorporate LCM/NRV. You have developed the following data relating to the ending inventory:

Item	Quantity	Acquisition Cost Per Unit	Acquisition Cost Total	Net Realizable Value per Unit
A	3,000	$4.50	$13,500	$6.00
B	1,500	6.00	9,000	3.00
C	7,000	3.00	21,000	6.00
D	3,000	7.50	22,500	4.50
			$66,000	

Required:

1. Restate the income statement to reflect LCM/NRV valuation of the ending inventory. Apply LCM/NRV on an item-by-item basis and show computations.
2. Compare and explain the LCM/NRV effect on each amount that was changed in the preliminary income statement in requirement 1.

PB7-3 Calculating and Interpreting the Inventory Turnover Ratio and Days to Sell

Amazon.com reported the following amounts in its financial statements (in millions):

LO 7-5
Amazon.com
Costco Wholesale Corporation

	2018	2017
Net Sales	$232,900	$177,900
Cost of Goods Sold	139,200	111,900
Beginning Inventory	16,000	11,500
Ending Inventory	17,200	16,000

Required:

1. Determine the inventory turnover ratio and average days to sell inventory for 2018 and 2017. Round to one decimal place.
2. Comment on any changes in these measures and compare the inventory turnover at Amazon .com to inventory turnover at Costco Wholesale Corporation, where inventory turned over 11.9 times during 2019 (30.7 days to sell).

PB7-4 (Supplement 7A) Analyzing the Effects of the LIFO Inventory Method in a Perpetual Inventory System

LO 7-S1

Using the information in PB7-1, calculate the cost of goods sold and ending inventory for Mojo Industries assuming it applies the LIFO cost method perpetually at the time of each sale. Compare these amounts to the periodic LIFO calculations in requirement 1c of PB7-1. Does the use of a perpetual inventory system result in a higher or lower cost of goods sold when costs are rising?

PB7-5 (Supplement 7B) Analyzing and Interpreting the Effects of Inventory Errors

LO 7-S2

Spears & Cantrell announced inventory had been overstated by $30 at the end of its second quarter. The error wasn't discovered and corrected in the company's periodic inventory system until after the end of the third quarter. The following table shows the amounts that were originally reported by the company.

	Q1	Q2	Q3
Net Sales	$3,000	$3,600	$3,750
Cost of Goods Sold	2,100	2,490	2,655
Gross Profit	900	1,110	1,095

Required:

1. Restate the income statements to reflect the correct amounts, after fixing the inventory error.
2. Compute the gross profit percentage for each quarter (*a*) before the correction and (*b*) after the correction, rounding to the nearest percentage. Do the results lend confidence to your corrected amounts? Explain.

COMPREHENSIVE PROBLEMS

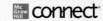

LO 2-5, 7-3

C7-1 Computing and Evaluating Financial Statement Effects of Alternative Inventory Costing Methods (Chapters 2 and 7)

You have been given responsibility for overseeing a bank's small business loans division. The bank has included loan covenants requiring a minimum current ratio of 1.80 in all small business loans. When you ask which inventory costing method the covenant assumes, the previous loans manager gives you a blank look. To explain to him that a company's inventory costing method is important, you present the following balance sheet information.

Current assets other than inventory	$ 10
Inventory	(*a*)
Other (noncurrent) assets	107
Total assets	$ (*b*)
Current liabilities	$ 36
Other (noncurrent) liabilities	44
Stockholders' equity	(*d*)
Total liabilities and stockholders' equity	$ (*c*)

You ask the former loans manager to find amounts for (*a*), (*b*), (*c*), and (*d*) assuming the company began the year with five units of inventory at a unit cost of $11, then purchased eight units at a cost of $12 each, and finally purchased six units at a cost of $16 each. A year-end inventory count determined that four units are on hand.

Required:

1. Determine the amount for (*a*) using FIFO, and then calculate (*b*) through (*d*).
2. Determine the amount for (*a*) using Weighted Average, and then calculate (*b*) through (*d*).
3. Determine the amount for (*a*) using LIFO, and then calculate (*b*) through (*d*).
4. Determine the current ratios, rounded to two decimal places, using (*i*) FIFO, (*ii*) Weighted Average, and (*iii*) LIFO and explain why these ratios differ.
5. Determine whether the company would be in violation or compliance with the loan covenant if the company were to use (*i*) FIFO, (*ii*) Weighted Average, and (*iii*) LIFO.

LO 4-2, 6-3, 6-4, 7-3, 7-5

C7-2 (Supplement 7A) Recording Inventory Transactions, Making Accrual and Deferral Adjustments, and Preparing and Evaluating Financial Statements (Chapters 4, 6, and 7)

College Coasters is a San Diego–based merchandiser specializing in logo-adorned drink coasters. The company reported the following balances in its unadjusted trial balance at December 1.

Cash	$10,005	Accounts Payable	$ 1,500	Cost of Goods Sold	$8,900
Accounts Receivable	2,000	Salaries and Wages Payable	300	Rent Expense	1,100
Inventory	500	Income Taxes Payable	0	Salaries and Wages Expense	2,000
Prepaid Rent	600	Common Stock	6,500	Depreciation Expense	110
Equipment	810	Retained Earnings	3,030	Income Tax Expense	0
Accumulated Depreciation—Equipment	110	Sales Revenue	15,985	Office Expense	1,400

The company buys coasters from one supplier. All amounts in Accounts Payable on December 1 are owed to that supplier. The inventory on December 1 consisted of 1,000 coasters, all of which were purchased in a batch on July 10 at a unit cost of $0.50. College Coasters records its inventory using perpetual inventory accounts and the FIFO cost flow method.

During December, the company entered into the following transactions. Some of these transactions are explained in greater detail below.

a.   Purchased 500 coasters on account from the regular supplier on 12/1 at a unit cost of $0.52, with terms of n/60.

b.   Purchased 1,000 coasters on account from the regular supplier on 12/2 at a unit cost of $0.55, with terms of n/60.

c.   Sold 2,000 coasters on account on 12/3 at a unit price of $0.90.

d.   Collected $1,000 from customers on account on 12/4.

e.   Paid the supplier $1,600 cash on account on 12/18.

f.   Paid employees $500 on 12/23, of which $300 related to work done in November and $200 was for wages up to December 22.

g.   Loaded 100 coasters on a cargo ship on 12/31 to be delivered the following week to a customer in Kona, Hawaii. The sale was made FOB destination with terms of n/60.

Other relevant information includes the following at 12/31:

h.   College Coasters has not yet recorded $200 of office expenses incurred in December on account.

i.   The company estimates that the equipment depreciates at a rate of $10 per month. One month of depreciation needs to be recorded.

j.   Wages for the period from December 23–31 are $100 and will be paid on January 15.

k.   The $600 of Prepaid Rent relates to a six-month period ending on May 31 of next year.

l.   The company incurred $789 of income tax but has made no tax payments this year.

m.   No shrinkage or damage was discovered when the inventory was counted on December 31.

n.   The company did not declare dividends and there were no transactions involving common stock.

Required:

1.   Analyze the accounting equation effects of items *a–n.*

2.   Prepare journal entries required for items *a–n.*

3.   Summarize the journal entries in T-accounts. Be sure to include the balances on December 1 as beginning account balances. Calculate ending balances and prepare a trial balance. (If you are completing this requirement in Connect, your journal entries will have been posted to T-accounts and a trial balance will have been prepared automatically.)

4.   Prepare the year-end Income Statement and classified Balance Sheet, using the formats presented in Exhibits 6.9 and 4.11.

5.   Calculate to one decimal place the inventory turnover ratio and days to sell, assuming that inventory was $500 on January 1 of this year. Evaluate these measures in comparison to an inventory turnover ratio of 21.0 during the previous year.

C7-3 (Supplement 7A) Recording Inventory Purchases, Allowances, Sales, and Shrinkage Using Perpetual FIFO (Chapters 6 and 7)

LO 6-2, 6-3, 6-4, 7-S1

Tracer Advance Corporation (TAC) sells a tracking implant that veterinarians surgically insert into pets. TAC began January with an inventory of 400 tags purchased from its supplier in November last year at a cost of $24 per tag, plus 200 tags purchased in December last year at a cost of $30 per tag. TAC uses a perpetual inventory system to account for the following transactions.

Jan. 3   TAC gave 500 tags to a courier company (UPS) to deliver to veterinarian customers. The sales price was $60 per tag, and the sales terms were n/30, FOB shipping point.

Jan. 4   UPS confirmed that all 500 tags were delivered today to customers.

Jan. 9   TAC ordered 700 tags from its supplier. The supplier was out of stock but promised to send them to TAC as soon as possible. TAC agreed to a cost of $43 per tag, n/30.

Jan. 19   The 700 tags ordered on January 9 were shipped to and received by TAC today. TAC complained about the delay between order and shipment date, so the supplier reduced the amount TAC owed by granting an allowance of $1 per tag ($700 total).

Jan. 23	TAC gave 750 tags to UPS, which were delivered "same day" to veterinarian customers at a price of $60 per tag, n/30, FOB shipping point.
Jan. 28	TAC received cash payment from customers for 400 of the tags delivered January 4.
Jan. 31	TAC counted its inventory and determined 40 tags were on hand. TAC made a "book-to-physical adjustment" to account for the missing 10 tags.

TIP: The book-to-physical adjustment is described in Chapter 6.

Required:

Assume TAC uses FIFO in its perpetual inventory system. For each date, prepare the journal entry or provide an appropriate reason for not recording a journal entry.

LO 6-2, 6-3, 6-4, 7-S1

C7-4 (Supplement 7A) Recording Inventory Purchases, Allowances, Sales, and Shrinkage Using Perpetual Weighted Average (Chapters 6 and 7)

Complete C7-3 but assume Tracer Advance Corporation (TAC) uses weighted average cost in its perpetual inventory system.

LO 6-2, 6-3, 6-4, 7-S1

C7-5 (Supplement 7A) Recording Inventory Purchases, Allowances, Sales, and Shrinkage Using Perpetual LIFO (Chapters 6 and 7)

Complete C7-3 but assume Tracer Advance Corporation (TAC) uses LIFO in its perpetual inventory system.

LO 6-2, 6-3, 6-4, 7-S1

C7-6 (Supplement 7A) Recording Inventory Purchases, Sales, and Shrinkage Using Perpetual FIFO (Chapters 6 and 7)

Chipolo
FedEx

Chipolo sells a coin-sized tracking tag that attaches to keys, wallets, and other personal items. Chipolo began January with an inventory of 200 tags purchased from its supplier in November last year at a cost of $12 per tag, plus 100 tags purchased in December last year at a cost of $15 per tag. Chipolo sells the tags at a price of $30 per tag, on account with terms n/30, FOB destination. Chipolo uses a perpetual inventory system to account for the following transactions.

Jan. 8	Chipolo gave 250 tags to a courier company (FedEx) to deliver to customers.
Jan. 9	FedEx confirmed that all 250 tags were delivered today to customers.
Jan. 11	Chipolo ordered 350 tags from its supplier. The supplier was out of stock but promised to send them to Chipolo as soon as possible. Chipolo agreed to a cost of $21 per tag, n/30.
Jan. 17	Chipolo received cash payment from customers for 125 of the tags delivered eight days earlier.
Jan. 21	The 350 tags ordered on January 11 were shipped to and received by Chipolo today.
Jan. 23	Chipolo gave 375 tags to FedEx, which were delivered "same day" to customers.
Jan. 31	Chipolo counted its inventory and determined 20 tags were on hand. Chipolo made a "book-to-physical adjustment" to account for the missing 5 tags.

Required:

Assume Chipolo uses FIFO in its perpetual inventory system. For each date, prepare the journal entry or provide an appropriate reason for not recording a journal entry.

LO 6-2, 6-3, 6-4, 7-S1

C7-7 (Supplement 7A) Recording Inventory Purchases, Sales, and Shrinkage Using Perpetual Weighted Average (Chapters 6 and 7)

Chipolo

Complete C7-6 but assume Chipolo uses weighted average cost in its perpetual inventory system.

LO 6-2, 6-3, 6-4, 7-S1

C7-8 (Supplement 7A) Recording Inventory Purchases, Sales, and Shrinkage Using Perpetual LIFO (Chapters 6 and 7)

Chipolo

Complete C7-6 but assume Chipolo uses LIFO in its perpetual inventory system.

LO 6-3, 6-4, 7-S1

C7-9 (Supplement 7A) Recording Inventory Purchases and Sales Using Perpetual FIFO (Chapters 6 and 7)

Stolte Trimble Corporation (STC) uses a perpetual inventory system. At the beginning of May, STC had 30 units of inventory, of which 10 units were purchased in March for $60 per unit and

20 units were purchased in April for $66 per unit. STC uses its perpetual inventory system to account for the following transactions.

May 2	STC shipped 25 units of inventory to customers for $150 per unit, on credit terms n/60, FOB shipping point.
May 4	STC purchased and received 20 units of inventory for $70 per unit, on credit terms n/45.
May 8	STC shipped 20 units of inventory to customers for $150 per unit, on credit terms n/60, FOB shipping point.

Required:

Assume STC uses FIFO in its perpetual inventory system. For each date, prepare the journal entry or provide an appropriate reason for not recording a journal entry.

C7-10 (Supplement 7A) Recording Inventory Purchases and Sales Using Perpetual Weighted Average (Chapters 6 and 7)   LO 6-3, 6-4, 7-S1

Complete C7-9 but assume Stolte Trimble Corporation (STC) uses weighted average cost in its perpetual inventory system.

C7-11 (Supplement 7A) Recording Inventory Purchases and Sales Using Perpetual LIFO (Chapters 6 and 7)   LO 6-3, 6-4, 7-S1

Complete C7-9 but assume Stolte Trimble Corporation (STC) uses LIFO in its perpetual inventory system.

C7-12 Evaluating Lower of Cost or Market/Net Realizable Value (LCM/NRV) (Chapters 6 and 7)   LO 6-6, 7-5

Refer to the financial information in S6-5 (in Chapter 6).

Required:

Analyze the financial information to identify *three* observations that lead to concerns that the inventory will need to be written down to comply with the LCM/NRV rule.

SKILLS DEVELOPMENT CASES

Mc Graw Hill connect

S7-1 Finding Financial Information   LO 7-2, 7-4, 7-5

Refer to the financial statements of The Home Depot in Appendix A at the end of this book. (Note: Fiscal 2019 for The Home Depot runs from February 4, 2019, to February 2, 2020. See S1-1 for further explanation.)   **The Home Depot**

1. How much inventory does the company hold on February 2, 2020? Does this represent an increase or decrease in comparison to the prior year?
    a. $13,925 (in millions), which is a decrease
    b. $13,925 (in millions), which is an increase
    c. $14,531 (in millions), which is a decrease
    d. $14,531 (in millions), which is an increase

2. What method(s) does the company use to determine the cost of its inventory? Where is this information reported?
    a. LIFO; Note 1
    b. FIFO; Note 1
    c. Weighted Average Cost; the Balance Sheet
    d. Specific Identification; Management's Discussion and Analysis

3. Compute to one decimal place the company's inventory turnover ratio and days to sell for the year ended February 2, 2020.
    a. 5.1 and 71.6   **c.** 7.6 and 48.0
    b. 5.0 and 73.0   **d.** 7.7 and 47.4

S7-2 Finding Financial Information   LO 7-2, 7-4, 7-5

Refer to the financial statements of Lowe's Companies, Inc., in Appendix B. (Note: Fiscal 2019 for Lowe's runs from February 2, 2019, to January 31, 2020. See S1-1 for further explanation.)   **Lowe's**

1. How much inventory does the company hold on January 31, 2020? Does this represent an increase or decrease in comparison to the prior year?

    a. $12,561 (in millions), which is a decrease   **c.** $13,179 (in millions), which is a decrease

    b. $12,561 (in millions), which is an increase   **d.** $13,179 (in millions), which is an increase

2. What method(s) does the company use to determine the cost of its inventory? Where is this information reported?

    a. LIFO; Note 1

    b. FIFO; Note 1

    c. Weighted Average Cost; the Balance Sheet

    d. Specific Identification; Management's Discussion and Analysis

3. Compute to one decimal place the company's inventory turnover ratio and days to sell for the year ended January 31, 2020.

    a. 5.6 and 65.2   **c.** 3.8 and 96.1

    b. 5.5 and 66.4   **d.** 3.7 and 98.6

LO 7-1, 7-2, 7-3, 7-4, 7-5

S7-3 Internet-Based Team Research: Examining an Annual Report

As a team, select an industry to analyze. Using your web browser, each team member should access the annual report or 10-K for one publicly traded company in the industry, with each member selecting a different company. (See S1-3 in Chapter 1 for a description of possible resources for these tasks.)

Required:

1. On an individual basis, each team member should write a short report that incorporates the following:

    a. Describe the types of inventory held by the company. Does the company indicate its inventory management goals anywhere in its annual report?

    b. Describe the inventory costing method that is used. Why do you think the company chose this method rather than the other acceptable methods? Do you think its inventory costs are rising or falling?

    c. Calculate the inventory turnover ratio for the current and prior years, and explain any change between the two years. (To obtain the beginning inventory number for the prior year, you will need the prior year's annual report.)

    d. Search the 10-K for information about the company's approach for applying the LCM/NRV rule to inventory. Did the company report the amount of inventory written down during the year?

2. Then, as a team, write a short report comparing and contrasting your companies using these attributes. Discuss any patterns across the companies that you as a team observe. Provide potential explanations for any differences discovered.

LO 7-2, 7-4

S7-4 Ethical Decision Making: A Real-Life Example

Phar-Mor

This case is based on an inventory fraud at Phar-Mor and is available online in the Connect eBook. By completing this case, you will learn to identify clues of inventory misreporting.

LO 7-3

S7-5 Ethical Decision Making: A Mini-Case

This case is available online in the Connect eBook. By completing this case, you will learn how the choice of inventory method can influence a manager's ability to meet profit expectations.

LO 7-3

S7-6 Critical Thinking: Income Manipulation under the LIFO Inventory Method

Mandalay Industries is a private company that sells electronic test equipment. During the year, the inventory records reflected the following:

	Units	Unit Cost	Total Cost
Beginning Inventory	15	$12,000	$180,000
Purchases	40	10,000	400,000
Sales (45 units at $25,000 each)			

To minimize income taxes, inventory is valued at cost using the LIFO inventory method. On December 28, Mandalay's supplier increased the unit cost of new test equipment to $15,000.

Required:

1. Determine the company's Income from Operations and the cost of ending inventory. The company's operating expenses (excluding Cost of Goods Sold) were $300,000 and the company applies LIFO with a periodic inventory system.

2. Mandalay's management is considering buying 20 additional units on December 31 at $15,000 each. Redo the income statement and ending inventory calculations, assuming that this purchase is made on December 31.

3. How much did Income from Operations change because of the decision to purchase additional units on December 31? Is there any evidence of deliberate income manipulation? Is this tax fraud? Explain.

S7-7 Calculating and Recording the Effects of Lower of Cost or Market/Net Realizable Value (LCM/NRV) on Ending Inventory

LO 7-4

This case is available online in the Connect eBook. By completing this case, you will learn to use a spreadsheet to compute the amount of write-down to record after applying LCM/NRV to inventory.

CONTINUING CASE

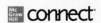

CC7-1 Accounting for Changing Inventory Costs

LO 7-3, 7-5

In October, Nicole eliminated all existing inventory of cosmetic items. The trouble of ordering and tracking each product line had exceeded the profits earned. In December, a supplier asked her to sell a prepackaged spa kit. Feeling she could manage a single product line, Nicole agreed. Nicole's Getaway Spa (NGS) would make monthly purchases from the supplier at a cost that included production costs and a transportation charge. NGS would keep track of its new inventory using a perpetual inventory system.

On December 31, NGS purchased 10 units at a total cost of $6 per unit. Nicole purchased 25 more units at $8 in February. In March, Nicole purchased 15 units at $10 per unit. In May, 50 units were purchased at $9.80 per unit. In June, NGS sold 50 units at a selling price of $12 per unit and 35 units at $10 per unit.

Required:

1. Explain whether the transportation cost included in each purchase should be recorded as a cost of the inventory or immediately expensed.

2. Compute the Cost of Goods Available for Sale, Cost of Goods Sold, and Cost of Ending Inventory using the first-in, first-out (FIFO) method.

3. Calculate the inventory turnover ratio (round to one decimal place), using the inventory purchased on December 31 as the beginning inventory. The supplier reported that the typical inventory turnover ratio was 6.0. How does NGS's ratio compare?

4. Would a different inventory cost flow assumption allow Nicole's Getaway Spa to better minimize its income tax?

DATA ANALYTICS EXERCISES

Data Analytics Exercises are auto-graded exercises offering detailed data visualization, interpretation, and analysis, and are available for assignment in *Connect*.

Design elements: Video camera: ©McGraw-Hill Education; Handshake, cash exchange: ©McGraw-Hill Education; Notepad with pen: ©McGraw-Hill Education; Calculator: ©McGraw-Hill Education; Light bulb: ©McGraw-Hill Education; Spotlight: ©McGraw-Hill Education; Whistle: ©Siede Preis/Getty Images; GL: ©McGraw-Hill Education; Level up: ©McGraw-Hill Education; Excel icon: ©McGraw-Hill Education; Magnifying glass: ©McGraw-Hill Education; Video icon: ©McGraw-Hill Education

8

CHAPTER EIGHT

Receivables, Bad Debt Expense, and Interest Revenue

YOUR LEARNING OBJECTIVES

LO 8-1   Describe the trade-offs of extending credit.

LO 8-2   Estimate and report the effects of uncollectible accounts.

LO 8-3   Compute and report interest on notes receivable.

LO 8-4   Compute and interpret the receivables turnover ratio.

LO 8-S1   Record bad debts using the direct write-off method.

THAT WAS THEN

In previous chapters, we quietly assumed that all sales on account ultimately are collected as cash.

FOCUS COMPANY: VF CORPORATION (VFC)

One company is responsible for making North Face jackets, JanSport backpacks, Timberland boots, and Vans shoes. That company, VF Corporation, or simply "VFC," sells its products on account to major customers including Walmart, Macy's, and Target, as well as to many smaller retailers that you likely haven't heard of, including Adventure 16, Paragon Sporting Goods, and Tactics. After making a sale to its customers, VFC faces the challenge of trying to collect the amount owed. Inevitably, some of VFC's customers will not pay the full amount owed, either because they dispute the price or quality of VFC's products or the customers have run into financial difficulties. This risk of failing to collect the full amount of its Accounts Receivable is a major concern for VFC's managers and investors, and it presents interesting challenges for the company's accountants, as you will read in this chapter.

THIS IS NOW

In this chapter, you'll learn how companies handle the situation where customers don't pay all that they owe.

Understand the business	Accounting for accounts receivable	Accounting for notes receivable	Evaluate receivables management	Supplement 8A	Review the chapter
• Pros and cons of extending credit	• Accounts receivable and bad debts • Methods for estimating bad debts	• Notes receivable and interest revenue • Recording notes receivable and interest revenue	• Receivables turnover analysis	• Direct write-off method	• Demonstration cases • Chapter summary • Key terms • Homework helper • Practice material

Understand the Business

What factors do managers consider when extending credit on account (accounts receivable) or lending to others under contract (notes receivable)?

PROS AND CONS OF EXTENDING CREDIT

Learning Objective 8-1
Describe the trade-offs of extending credit.

VFC allows business customers (like Walmart and Macy's) to open an account and buy items on credit, yet its outlet stores do not extend this option to you—the individual consumer. The reason VFC is willing to create accounts receivable from business customers but not individual consumers is that doing so involves different advantages and disadvantages. The advantage of extending credit is that it helps business customers buy products and services, thereby increasing the seller's revenues. The disadvantages of extending credit are the following additional costs introduced:

1. **Increased wage costs.** If credit is extended, VFC will have to hire people to (*a*) evaluate whether each customer is creditworthy, (*b*) track how much each customer owes, and (*c*) follow up to collect the receivable from each customer.

2. **Bad debt costs.** Inevitably, some customers dispute what they owe, or they run into financial difficulties and pay only a fraction of their account balances. These "bad debts," as they are called, can be a significant additional cost of extending credit. At September 30, 2019, VFC estimated that more than $20 million of its receivables would not be collected.

3. **Delayed receipt of cash.** Even if VFC were to collect in full from customers, it would likely have to wait 30–60 days before receiving the cash. During this period, VFC may have to take out a short-term bank loan to pay for other business activities. The interest on such a loan would be another cost of extending credit to customers.

Most managers find the additional revenue (or, more accurately, the gross profit) from selling on account to business customers is greater than the additional costs mentioned above.

SPOTLIGHT ON | Business Decisions

Co-branded Credit Comes to a Store Near You

Many companies, including VCF, do not grant credit to individual consumers because the expected costs outweigh the benefits. Instead, companies allow customers to pay for goods using PayPal or national credit cards like Visa, MasterCard, American Express, and Discover Card. Companies can also team up with banks to offer co-branded credit cards, such as the Starbucks Rewards Visa Card, which debuted in 2018.* By joining forces, both Starbucks and Chase benefit from the co-branded card. Starbucks saves itself the hassle of extending credit to individuals and builds brand loyalty with card members who can earn Starbucks Rewards stars on non-Starbucks purchases. Chase is responsible for collecting customer balances, but can also profit by charging annual fees, late payment fees, and interest on overdue balances.

* https://investor.starbucks.com/press-releases/financial-releases/press-release-details/2018/Starbucks-and-Chase-Launch-Starbucks-Rewards-Visa-Card/default.aspx.

Similar advantages and disadvantages are considered when deciding whether to create notes receivable. **Notes receivable** are created when formal written contracts ("notes") are established outlining the terms by which a company will receive amounts it is owed. Notes receivable differ from accounts receivable in that notes generally charge interest from the day they are signed to the day they are collected. Notes receivable are viewed as a stronger legal claim than accounts receivable, but new notes need to be created for every transaction, so they are used less frequently—typically when a company sells large dollar-value items (e.g., cars), offers extended payment periods, or lends money to individuals or businesses.[1]

Accounting for Accounts Receivable

ACCOUNTS RECEIVABLE AND BAD DEBTS

You already know from earlier chapters that **accounts receivable** arise from the sale of goods or services on credit. What you may not know is some accounts receivable are never collected. Like that "friend" of yours who *says* he'll pay you later but for one reason or another never gets around to it, some customers just do not pay their bills.

Learning Objective 8-2
Estimate and report the effects of uncollectible accounts.

Two objectives when accounting for accounts receivable and bad debts are to (1) report Accounts Receivable at the amount the company expects to collect ("Net Accounts Receivable") and (2) match the cost of bad debts to the accounting period in which the related credit sales are made. These two objectives point to the same solution: Reduce both Accounts Receivable and Net Income by the amount of credit sales that are unlikely to be collected.

The only problem with this solution is time will pass before VFC discovers which particular credit sales and customer balances aren't going to be collected. These bad debts will likely be discovered in an accounting period following the sale, rather than in the same period as the sale. As Exhibit 8.1 shows, if you record sales in one period when they occur and bad debts in a different period when they are discovered, you will violate the **expense recognition ("matching") principle.** This failure to match Bad Debt Expense with Sales Revenue in the same period will lead to distorted views of Net Income in the period of the sale as well as in the period the bad debt is discovered.

[1] Accounting for other notes, such as structured note securities, is discussed in Appendix D.

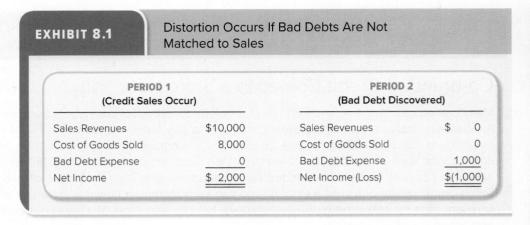

EXHIBIT 8.1	Distortion Occurs If Bad Debts Are Not Matched to Sales		
PERIOD 1 (Credit Sales Occur)		**PERIOD 2** (Bad Debt Discovered)	
Sales Revenues	$10,000	Sales Revenues	$ 0
Cost of Goods Sold	8,000	Cost of Goods Sold	0
Bad Debt Expense	0	Bad Debt Expense	1,000
Net Income	$ 2,000	Net Income (Loss)	$(1,000)

Clearly, we need to **record bad debts in the same period as the sale.** The only way to do this is to record an estimate of the amount of bad debts that are likely to arise. Later, the accounting records can be adjusted when uncollectible amounts become known with near certainty. This approach is called the **allowance method** and it follows a two-step process, which we'll walk you through below:

1. **Record the estimated bad debts in the period credit sales occur,** using an end-of-period adjustment, and

2. **Remove ("write off") specific customer balances when they are known to be uncollectible.**

1. Adjust for Estimated Bad Debts

Credit sales, when first recorded, affect both the balance sheet (an increase in Accounts Receivable) and the income statement (an increase in Sales Revenue). Thus, to account for any bad credit sales that have been included in Sales Revenue and Accounts Receivable, we record offsetting amounts in both the balance sheet and income statement. This adjustment, which is made at the end of each accounting period, reduces Accounts Receivable (using a contra-asset account called Allowance for Doubtful Accounts) and reduces Net Income (using an expense account called **Bad Debt Expense**). If **VFC** were to estimate $900 of bad debts this period, the effects on the accounting equation and adjusting journal entry to record them would be as follows:

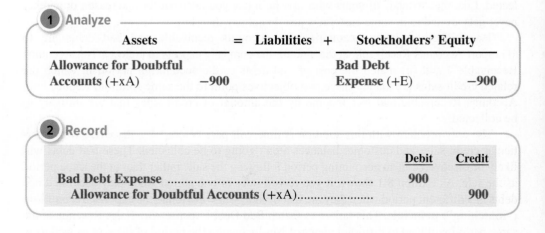

1 Analyze

Assets		= Liabilities +	Stockholders' Equity	
Allowance for Doubtful Accounts (+xA)	−900		Bad Debt Expense (+E)	−900

2 Record

	Debit	Credit
Bad Debt Expense	900	
Allowance for Doubtful Accounts (+xA)		900

Exhibit 8.2 uses blue and red text to show how the accounts in the end-of-period adjusting journal entry partially offset the original sales on account. The exhibit also shows where the accounts appear in the balance sheet and income statement.

EXHIBIT 8.2	Recording and Reporting Estimated Bad Debts

Jan. 1   Jan. 31
| Record sales on account | | | | Record estimate of bad sales/receivables |

	Debit	**Credit**		**Debit**	**Credit**
Accounts Receivable	120,000		Bad Debt Expense	900	
Sales Revenue		120,000	Allowance for Doubtful Accounts (+xA)		900

Balance Sheet (*excerpt*) At January 31		
Cash		$115,000
Accounts Receivable	$200,000	
Allowance for Doubtful Accounts	(15,000)	
Accounts Receivable, Net of Allowance		185,000
Inventory		260,000
Other Current Assets		40,000
Total Current Assets		600,000

Income Statement (*excerpt*) For the month ended January 31	
Sales Revenue	$120,000
Cost of Goods Sold	70,000
Gross Profit	50,000
Salaries and Wages Expense	44,000
Bad Debt Expense	900
Other Expenses	600
Income from Operations	4,500

Like all contra-asset accounts, such as Accumulated Depreciation, the Allowance for Doubtful Accounts is a permanent account, so its balance carries forward from one account-ing period to the next. Bad Debt Expense, which is a temporary account, will have its balance closed (zeroed out) at the end of each year. Consequently, the balance in the Allowance for Doubtful Accounts will differ from the balance in Bad Debt Expense, except during the first year the Allowance for Doubtful Accounts is used. This explains why the $15,000 Allowance for Doubtful Accounts in the balance sheet in Exhibit 8.2 does not equal the $900 Bad Debt Expense in the January income statement. The Bad Debt Expense relates only to January sales, whereas the Allowance for Doubtful Accounts relates to all credit sales still in Accounts Receivable, which haven't yet been collected.

For billing and collection purposes, VFC internally keeps a separate accounts receiv-able account (called a **subsidiary account**) for each customer. The total of these accounts is reported as Accounts Receivable on the balance sheet. Given this, you might wonder why the estimated uncollectible accounts aren't taken directly out of these individual accounts. The reason is, at the time the Allowance for Doubtful Accounts is estimated, no one knows which particular customers' accounts receivable are uncollectible. If VFC were to remove the specific customer accounts believed to be uncollectible, it would lose track of which custom-ers still owed money. If this were to happen, VFC would no longer know which customers it should continue pursuing for payment.

 **COACH'S TIP**

Accounts Receivable, Net of Allowance (shown in Exhibit 8.2) is not a separate account. It is a subtotal that is computed by sub-tracting the contra-asset account *Allowance for Doubtful Accounts* from the asset account *Accounts Receivable*.

2. Remove (Write Off) Specific Customer Balances

Throughout the year, when it becomes clear a particular customer will never pay, VFC removes the customer's account from the accounts receivable records. By removing the receivable, VFC no longer needs to make an allowance for it, so the company removes the corresponding amount from the Allowance for Doubtful Accounts. Removing the uncollectible account and a corresponding amount from the allowance is called a **receivable write-off**. The purpose of writing off some or all of a customer's account balance is to remove amounts that have virtu-ally no chance of collection.

YOU SHOULD KNOW

Receivable Write-Off: The act of removing an uncollectible account receivable and its cor-responding allowance from the accounting records.

To illustrate, assume VFC decides to write off an $800 receivable from Fast Fashions. VFC would record an $800 decrease in Accounts Receivable, which would be offset by an $800 decrease in the contra-account Allowance for Doubtful Accounts. These accounting equation effects and the journal entry to record them follow.

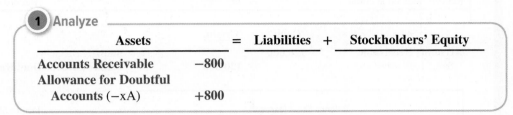

1 Analyze

Assets		= Liabilities +	Stockholders' Equity
Accounts Receivable	−800		
Allowance for Doubtful Accounts (−xA)	+800		

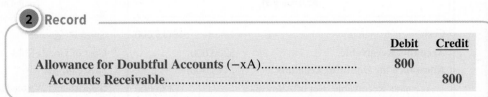

2 Record

	Debit	Credit
Allowance for Doubtful Accounts (−xA)............................	800	
Accounts Receivable...		800

Notice **a receivable write-off does not affect income statement accounts.** The estimated Bad Debt Expense relating to these uncollectible accounts was already recorded with an adjusting entry in the period the sale was recorded. Therefore, no additional expense is incurred when the account is finally written off.

The effects of these two steps on VFC's accounting records can be summarized in terms of the following changes in the related T-accounts:

Accounts Receivable (A)				Allow. for Doubtful Accts. (xA)			Bad Debt Expense (E, SE)		
1/1 Bal.	200,000				14,100	1/1 Bal.	1/1 Bal.	0	
					900	(1) Estimate	(1) Estimate	900	
1/31 Bal.	200,000				15,000	1/31 Bal.	1/31 Bal.	900	
		800 (2) Write-off		(2) Write-off	800				
End. Bal.	199,200				14,200	End. Bal.			

Notice the write-off decreased both the total Accounts Receivable and Allowance for Doubtful Accounts by the same amount ($800). Consequently, the **net** receivable balance after the write-off ($185,000 = $199,200 − $14,200) is unchanged from the net receivable balance before the write-off ($185,000 = $200,000 − $15,000). Write-offs merely remove receivable balances that were previously accounted for as uncollectible.

🔆 **How's it going?**   *Self-Study Practice*

Indicate the effect (+ / − / No Effect) of the following on net income and total assets.

	Net Income	Total Assets
1. **Polaris Industries** recorded an increase in estimated bad debts on December 31.		
2. **Kellogg** wrote off 12 customer account balances during the year.		

After you have finished, check your answers with the solution.

Solution to Self-Study Practice

	Net Income	Total Assets
1.	−	−
2.	NE	NE*

*The decrease in Accounts Receivable is offset by the decrease in Allowance for Doubtful Accounts.

METHODS FOR ESTIMATING BAD DEBTS

In the examples given so far, we simply stated the estimated amount of uncollectibles to record. In the workplace, these bad debts must be estimated based on historical loss information, current conditions, and economic forecasts. Such estimates may be based on either (1) a **percentage of credit sales** for the period or (2) an **aging of accounts receivable**. Both methods are acceptable under GAAP and IFRS. The percentage of credit sales method is simpler to apply, but the aging method uses more detailed data and therefore is generally more accurate.

Percentage of Credit Sales Method

The percentage of credit sales method estimates bad debt expense by multiplying the estimated percentage of bad debt losses by the current period's credit sales. For example, assume VFC anticipates bad debt losses of ¾ of 1 percent of credit sales. If credit sales this January total $120,000, VFC could estimate this month's bad debt expense as

Credit sales this month	$120,000
× Bad debt loss rate (0.75%)	× 0.0075
Bad debt expense this month	$ 900

This estimate would be recorded using the journal entry shown in the previous section.

Aging of Accounts Receivable Method

Whereas the percentage of credit sales method focuses on estimating this period's Bad Debt Expense, the aging of accounts receivable method focuses on estimating the Allowance for Doubtful Accounts ending balance. The aging method gets its name because it is based on the "age" of each amount in Accounts Receivable. The older and more overdue accounts receivable become, the less likely they are to be collectible. Based on this idea, credit managers and accountants use their experience and economic forecasts to estimate what portion of receivables of a specific age will not be paid.

   To illustrate the aging of accounts receivable method, we assume VFC applies this method to its accounts receivable balances on February 28, after taking into account February sales and cash collections. The aging method includes three steps, as shown in Exhibit 8.3:

 Prepare an aged listing of accounts receivable with totals for each age category. Most accounting software packages produce this report automatically by counting back the number of days to when each receivable was first recorded.

EXHIBIT 8.3   Estimating Uncollectible Amounts with an Aging of Accounts Receivable

Customer	Total	Number of Days Unpaid					
		0–30	31–60	61–90	Over 90		
Adam's Sports	$ 700	$ 400	$ 200	$ 100			
Momentum Clothes	2,300				$ 2,300		
Others (not shown to save space)	199,000	115,600	42,800	36,900	3,700	← Step ① – Age
Zoom Athletics	6,000	4,000	2,000				
Total Accounts Receivable	**$208,000**	**$120,000**	**$45,000**	**$37,000**	**$6,000**		
Estimated Uncollectible (%)		× 1%	× 10%	× 20%	× 40%	← Step ② – Estimate
Estimated Uncollectible ($)	**$ 15,500**	**$ 1,200**	**$ 4,500**	**$ 7,400**	**$2,400**	← Step ③ – Compute

② **Estimate bad debt loss percentages for each category.** The percentage each company uses varies according to its past experience, current conditions, and future forecasts. Generally, higher percentages are applied to increasingly older receivables.

③ **Compute the total estimate by multiplying the totals in Step 1 by the percentages in Step 2 and then summing across all categories.** The total across all aging categories ($1,200 + $4,500 + $7,400 + $2,400 = **$15,500**) equals the balance to which the Allowance for Doubtful Accounts will need to be adjusted at the end of the period.

The amount computed in Step 3 is the desired balance in the Allowance for Doubtful Accounts, not the amount of the adjustment. To compute the amount of the adjustment, you must determine how much to increase (credit) the Allowance for Doubtful Accounts to reach the desired adjusted balance computed in Step 3. For example, assume VFC had an unadjusted credit balance in the Allowance for Doubtful Accounts of $14,200 and computed a desired credit balance of $15,500, as shown in Exhibit 8.3. An adjustment of **$1,300** ($15,500 − $14,200) needs to be recorded as a credit to the account. A corresponding amount is debited to Bad Debt Expense, as follows.

Allowance for Doubtful Accounts (xA)	
	14,200 Unadj. bal.
	? AJE
	15,500 Desired bal.

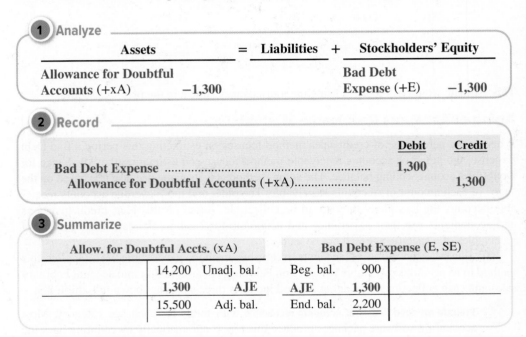

① Analyze

Assets	=	Liabilities	+	Stockholders' Equity
Allowance for Doubtful Accounts (+xA) −1,300				Bad Debt Expense (+E) −1,300

② Record

	Debit	Credit
Bad Debt Expense	1,300	
Allowance for Doubtful Accounts (+xA)		1,300

③ Summarize

Allow. for Doubtful Accts. (xA)		Bad Debt Expense (E, SE)	
	14,200 Unadj. bal.	Beg. bal. 900	
	1,300 AJE	AJE 1,300	
	15,500 Adj. bal.	End. bal. 2,200	

Although the Allowance for Doubtful Accounts normally has a credit balance, it may have a **debit balance** before it is adjusted. This happens when a company has recorded write-offs that exceed previous estimates of uncollectible accounts. If this happens, you can still calculate the amount of the adjustment needed to reach the desired balance under the aging of accounts receivable method. The only difference is that to reach the desired balance, you need to record an amount equal to the desired balance **plus** the existing debit balance. After the adjustment is recorded, the Allowance for Doubtful Accounts will once again return to a credit balance.

 **SPOTLIGHT ON** **Business Decisions**

Focus Collection Efforts with the Aged Listing of Accounts Receivable

The aged listing of accounts receivable, shown in Exhibit 8.3, is useful when estimating uncollectible accounts. It also is useful when credit managers identify customers at risk of failing to pay their accounts. Accounts receivable collections were especially difficult after the **COVID-19 pandemic** in 2020, resulting in older account balances, such as the $2,300 shown in Exhibit 8.3 from Momentum Clothes. If a follow-up phone call does not prompt the customer to pay, VFC could turn the account over to a collection agency.

How's it going? Self-Study Practice

For the years ended March 31, 2021 and 2020, Kat Inc. reported credit balances in the Allowance for Doubtful Accounts (AfDA) of $6,300 and $4,800, respectively. Assume it also reported write-offs during the year ended March 31, 2021, amounting to $7,500. Assuming no other changes in the account, what amount did Kat record as Bad Debt Expense for the period? Convert the following T-account to an equation and then solve for the missing value.

Allow. for Doubtful Accts. (xA)		
	4,800	March 31, 2020
Write-offs	7,500	☐ Bad Debt Estimate
	6,300	March 31, 2021

After you have finished, check your answers with the solution.

Solution to Self-Study Practice

Allow. for Doubtful Accts.		
	4,800	March 31, 2020
Write-offs 7,500	X	Estimate
	6,300	March 31, 2021

Beginning AfDA + Bad debt estimate − Write-offs = Ending AfDA
4,800 + X − 7,500 = 6,300; which implies **X = 9,000**

Other Issues

Revising Estimates Bad debt estimates always differ somewhat from the actual bad debt amounts, which are later written off. To ensure bad debts and the allowance for doubtful accounts do not become materially misstated over time, companies lower estimates in the current period to correct overestimates of prior periods, or they raise estimates in the current period to correct underestimates of prior periods.

Account Recoveries In the same way that someone you've written off as a friend might do something to win you back, a customer might pay an account balance that was previously written off. Collection of a previously written-off account is called a **recovery** and is accounted for in two parts. First, put the receivable back on the books by recording the opposite of the write-off. Second, record the collection of the account. To illustrate, let's assume **VFC** collects the $800 from Fast Fashions that was previously written off. This recovery would be recorded with the following journal entries:

> ***COACH'S TIP***
>
> Like the initial write-off, an account recovery does not affect Net Income.

		Debit	Credit
(1)	Accounts Receivable	800	
	Allowance for Doubtful Accounts (+xA)		800
(2)	Cash	800	
	Accounts Receivable		800

} Reverse the write-off

} Record the collection

Look closely at the journal entries for recording a recovery and you'll see Accounts Receivable is debited and then credited for $800. It's tempting to cancel these two out, but don't do it because it would create an inaccurate credit history for the customer. After all, the customer's balance was removed because it was actually collected, not written off, so the accounting records should reflect that.

Alternative Methods You should be aware some small companies don't use the allowance method. Instead, they use an alternative approach called the **direct write-off method,** which we demonstrate in Supplement 8A at the end of this chapter. This alternative method records Bad Debt Expense only when a company writes off specific accounts. Although this alternative method is easier to use, it overstates the value of Accounts Receivable and it violates the expense recognition principle, as explained in Supplement 8A. Thus, it is not considered a generally accepted accounting method. However, the Internal Revenue Service (IRS), which discourages use of accounting estimates, requires this method for tax purposes.

Accounting for Notes Receivable

NOTES RECEIVABLE AND INTEREST REVENUE

A company reports Notes Receivable if it uses a promissory note to document its right to collect money from another party and intends to retain that right until a specified future date (called the **maturity date**). This usually happens in the following three situations: (1) the company loans money to employees or businesses, (2) the company sells expensive items for which customers require an extended payment period, or (3) the company converts existing accounts receivable to notes receivable to allow an extended payment period.

The accounting issues for notes receivable are similar to those for accounts receivable, with one exception. Unlike accounts receivable, which are interest-free until they become overdue, notes receivable charge interest from the day they are created to their maturity date. Although interest on notes receivable is earned each day, interest payments typically are received only once or twice a year. This means that a company with notes receivable needs to accrue Interest Revenue and Interest Receivable. Let's look at how to calculate interest.

Calculating Interest

YOU SHOULD KNOW

Interest Formula: $I = P \times R \times T$, where I = interest calculated, P = principal, R = annual interest rate, and T = time period covered in the interest calculation (number of months out of 12).

To calculate interest, you need to consider three variables: (1) the **principal,** which is the amount of the notes receivable; (2) the annual **interest rate** charged on the notes; and (3) the **time** period covered in the interest calculation. **Interest rates are always stated as an annual percentage** (even if the notes are for more or less than a year), so the time period factor is the portion of a year for which interest is calculated. It is a fraction expressed as the number of months out of 12, or days out of 365, the interest period covers. Use the following **interest formula** to calculate the interest:

$$\text{Interest (I)} = \text{Principal (P)} \times \text{Interest Rate (R)} \times \text{Time (T)}$$

 **COACH'S TIP**

The "time" variable refers to the portion of a year for which interest is calculated, not the portion of the notes' entire life. A 2-month interest calculation on 3-year notes has a time variable of 2/12 not 2/36.

Financial institutions often use the number of days out of 365 to compute interest. But, for homework assignments, assume time is measured simply as the number of months out of 12. See Exhibit 8.4 for the computation of interest for three notes with different terms and different lengths of interest periods. Notice how the time variable in the calculation depends on the interest period, not the due date for the notes.

EXHIBIT 8.4 | Sample Interest Computations

GIVEN INFORMATION		INTEREST CALCULATION				
Terms of notes	Interest period	Principal	Rate	Time		Interest
$100,000, 6%, matures in 2 years	January 1–December 31	$100,000 ×	6% ×	12/12	=	$6,000
$100,000, 6%, matures in 10 months	January 1–October 31	100,000 ×	6% ×	10/12	=	5,000
$100,000, 6%, matures in 2 months	November 1–December 31	100,000 ×	6% ×	2/12	=	1,000

RECORDING NOTES RECEIVABLE AND INTEREST REVENUE

The four key events that occur with any notes receivable are (1) establishing the notes, (2) accruing interest earned but not received, (3) recording interest payments received, and (4) recording principal payments received. Assume on November 1, 2021, **VFC** lent $100,000 to a company by creating a note that required the company to pay VFC 6 percent interest and the $100,000 principal on October 31, 2022. VFC prepared year-end financial statements as of December 31, 2021, but made no other adjustments for interest during the year.

Establishing Notes Receivable

The $100,000 loan that created the note receivable has the following accounting equation effects, which **VFC** would record using the following journal entry:

1 Analyze

Assets		=	Liabilities	+	Stockholders' Equity
Notes Receivable	+100,000				
Cash	−100,000				

2 Record

	Debit	Credit
Notes Receivable	100,000	
Cash		100,000

Accruing Interest Earned

Under accrual basis accounting, interest revenue is earned over time. Rather than record the interest earned as each day passes, **VFC** waits until it either receives an interest payment or reaches the end of its accounting period.

The timeline in Exhibit 8.5 shows how VFC should account for interest on the note over its one-year term. Between the date of the note's creation (November 1, 2021) and the year-end (December 31, 2021), VFC earned two months of interest revenue (the red portion of the timeline). As you learned in Chapter 4, when a company has earned interest in the current period but has not yet recorded the interest, the company must make an adjusting entry at the end of the current period to accrue the interest earned. The amount of interest for **two** months is computed as

$$\text{Interest (I)} = \text{Principal (P)} \times \text{Interest Rate (R)} \times \text{Time (T)}$$
$$\$1,000 = \$100,000 \times 6\% \times 2/12$$

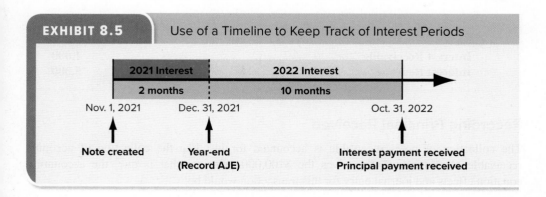

EXHIBIT 8.5	Use of a Timeline to Keep Track of Interest Periods

2021 Interest	2022 Interest
2 months	10 months

Nov. 1, 2021   Dec. 31, 2021   Oct. 31, 2022

Note created   Year-end (Record AJE)   Interest payment received / Principal payment received

The effect of this $1,000 adjustment, along with the adjusting journal entry to record the interest revenue that is receivable on December 31, 2021, follows:

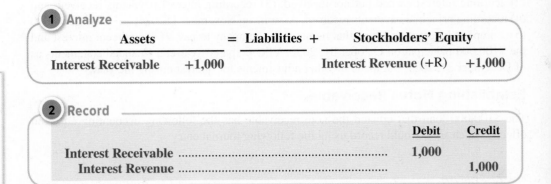

① Analyze

Assets		= Liabilities +	Stockholders' Equity	
Interest Receivable	+1,000		Interest Revenue (+R)	+1,000

② Record

	Debit	Credit
Interest Receivable	1,000	
Interest Revenue		1,000

Recording Interest Received

On October 31, 2022, VFC receives a cash interest payment of $6,000 (= $100,000 × 6% × 12/12). As shown on the following timeline, this $6,000 of interest includes the $1,000 that was accrued as Interest Receivable at December 31, 2021, plus $5,000 of interest revenue earned during the 10-month period from January 1 to October 31, 2022, which had yet to be recorded.

When VFC receives the interest payment, it will record the $6,000 Cash, and it will reduce the $1,000 Interest Receivable that was previously recorded and record the remaining $5,000 as Interest Revenue in 2022. These effects and the journal entry to record them follow:

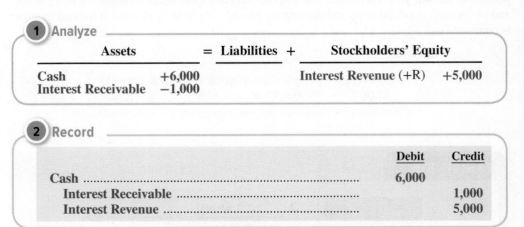

① Analyze

Assets		= Liabilities +	Stockholders' Equity	
Cash	+6,000		Interest Revenue (+R)	+5,000
Interest Receivable	−1,000			

② Record

	Debit	Credit
Cash	6,000	
Interest Receivable		1,000
Interest Revenue		5,000

Recording Principal Received

The collection of notes receivable is accounted for just like the collection of accounts receivable. Assuming VFC receives the $100,000 principal that is due, the accounting equation effects and journal entry for this transaction would be:

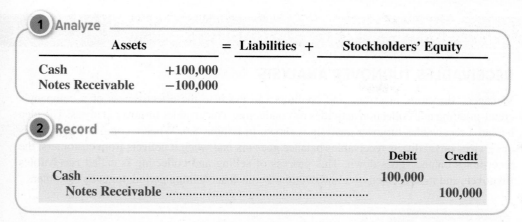

(1) Analyze

Assets	= Liabilities +	Stockholders' Equity
Cash	+100,000	
Notes Receivable	−100,000	

(2) Record

	Debit	Credit
Cash	100,000	
Notes Receivable		100,000

Accounting for Uncollectible Notes

Just as companies may not collect their accounts receivable in full, they also might not collect the full principal (and interest) that they are owed on notes receivable. When the collection of notes receivable is in doubt, a company should record an Allowance for Doubtful Accounts against the Notes Receivable, just as it records an Allowance for Doubtful Accounts against Accounts Receivable.

 How's it going?   Self-Study Practice

Assume Kat Inc. loaned $12,000 to an employee on October 1, 2021, by creating a note that required the employee to pay the principal and 8 percent interest on September 30, 2022. Assume the company makes adjusting entries only at year-end on December 31.

1. Calculate the amount of Interest Receivable and Interest Revenue to be recorded on December 31, 2021.
2. Calculate the amount of Interest Revenue to be recorded on September 30, 2022.

After you have finished, check your answers with the solution.

SPOTLIGHT ON # Ethics

Resetting the Clock

Earlier in this chapter, you saw that as customer balances get older, the Allowance for Doubtful Accounts should be increased. Because increases in the Allowance for Doubtful Accounts are accompanied by increases in Bad Debt Expense, the result of older customer accounts should be a decrease in net income.

    MCI (a company now owned by Verizon) employed a credit manager who knew about these accounting effects. To avoid reducing net income, he "reset the clock" on amounts owed by customers. He did so by making loans to customers, who then used the money to pay off their account balances. By replacing old accounts receivable with new notes receivable, he avoided recording approximately $70 million in bad debts. His scheme didn't last long, though. After the fraud was revealed, the credit manager spent several years in prison, and he has been working to pay off over $10 million in fines. To learn more about this fraud, see S8-4 at the end of this chapter.

Evaluate Receivables Management

RECEIVABLES TURNOVER ANALYSIS

Managers, directors, investors, and creditors can evaluate the effectiveness of a company's credit-granting and collection activities by conducting a receivables turnover analysis. The idea behind a receivables turnover analysis is shown in Exhibit 8.6. When a company sells goods or services on credit, its receivables balance goes up, and when it collects from customers, the receivables balance goes down. This process of selling and collecting is called **receivables turnover**, and it is repeated over and over during each accounting period, for each customer.

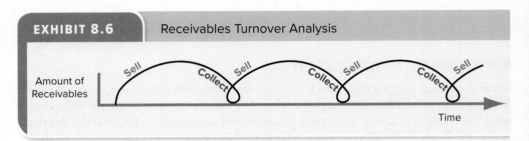

EXHIBIT 8.6 Receivables Turnover Analysis

The receivables turnover ratio indicates how many times, on average, this process of selling and collecting is repeated during the period. The higher the ratio, the faster the collection of receivables. And the faster the collection of receivables, the shorter your company's operating cycle, which means more cash available for running the business. A low turnover ratio can be a warning sign, suggesting the company is allowing too much time for customers to pay. As you learned earlier in this chapter (in the Spotlight), the longer an account goes uncollected, the bigger the risk it will never be collected. Analysts watch for changes in the receivables turnover ratio because a sudden decline may mean a company is recording sales of merchandise that customers are likely to return later. It also may mean the company is selling to less financially secure customers or is allowing customers more time to pay their accounts to entice them to buy more than they need—a practice known as **channel stuffing.**

Rather than evaluate the **number of times** accounts receivable turn over during a year, some people find it easier to think in terms of the **length of time** (in days) it takes to collect accounts receivable (called **days to collect**). Converting the year's receivables turnover ratio into the average days to collect is easy. Simply divide 365 by the year's receivables turnover ratio. This alternative measure provides the same basic information about the company's ability to collect receivables, but it's a little easier to interpret. In terms of Exhibit 8.6, the receivables turnover ratio counts the number of loops in a given period of time, whereas days to collect tells you the average number of days between loops.

Accounting Decision Tools		
Name of Measure	**Formula**	**What It Tells You**
Receivables turnover ratio	$\dfrac{\text{Net Sales Revenue}}{\text{Average Net Receivables}}$	• The number of times receivables turn over during the period • A higher ratio means faster (better) turnover
Days to collect	$\dfrac{365}{\text{Receivables Turnover Ratio}}$	• Average number of days from sale on account to collection • A higher number means a longer (worse) time to collect

Comparison to Benchmarks

Credit Terms By calculating days to collect, you can compare a company's collection performance to its stated collections policy. You might remember from Chapter 6 that when companies sell on account, they specify the length of credit period (as well as any discounts for prompt payment). The annual report of IBM explains its policy is to be paid within 30 days after it bills its customers. By comparing the number of days to collect to the length of credit period, you can gain a sense of whether customers are complying with the stated policy. In 2018, IBM turned over its receivables once every 37.5 days, slightly longer than its policy. Managers inside a company watch this closely, and so do investors and creditors on the outside. Why? If customers appear to be disregarding the stated credit period, that may be a sign they are dissatisfied with the product or service they bought.

Other Companies Receivables turnover ratios and the number of days to collect often are used to compare companies, but be aware they can vary across industries. To illustrate, we have calculated these measures in Exhibit 8.7 for VFC, Post (the cereal maker), and Apple. As Exhibit 8.7 shows, VFC turned over its receivables 8.9 times, which is once every 41 days. Post had a turnover ratio of 12.6 times, which means a collection period of less than a month (29 days). Apple had a collection period just over one month (32.3 days), as determined using its receivables turnover ratio of 11.3. Because these measures typically vary between industries, you should focus on comparing a company's turnover with those of other companies in the same industry or with its figures from prior periods. Post's collections, for example, did not change much from the prior period to the current period. If you detect a significant decline in receivables turnover and lengthening in days to collect, you should question whether the company has estimated a sufficient allowance for doubtful accounts.

SPOTLIGHT ON | Big Data and Analytics

Collection Analysis by Customer Region

Data visualization techniques allow managers to create geographic maps that combine customer location information with measures of liquidity (such as days to collect) and profitability (such as average gross profit percentage). The following map represents average rates of customer profitability by the size of dots, with larger dots representing more profitable customers, and the days to collect shaded in different colors, with green representing fewer days to collect and red representing longer collection times. As the map indicates, customers along the west and east coasts are more profitable and faster to pay, whereas those in the central part of the country are producing lower profits and taking longer to collect.

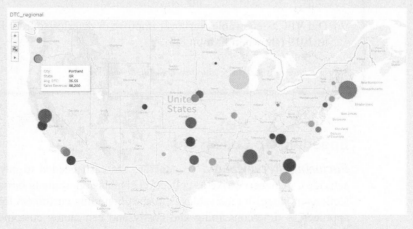

| EXHIBIT 8.7 | Summary of Receivables Turnover Ratio Analyses |

Company	Relevant Information (in millions)		Fiscal 2019 Receivables Turnover Calculation	Fiscal 2019 Days to Collect Calculation
VFC		**Fiscal 2019**	**Fiscal 2018**	$\dfrac{\$13,850}{(\$1,700 + \$1,400)/2} = 8.9$ times	$\dfrac{365 \text{ days}}{8.9 \text{ times}} = 41.0$ days
	Net Sales	$ 13,850	$ 12,350		
	Net Accounts Receivable	1,700	1,400		
Post		**Fiscal 2019**	**Fiscal 2018**	$\dfrac{\$5,680}{(\$445 + \$460)/2} = 12.6$ times	$\dfrac{365 \text{ days}}{12.6 \text{ times}} = 29.0$ days
	Net Sales	$ 5,680	$ 6,260		
	Net Accounts Receivable	445	460		
Apple		**Fiscal 2019**	**Fiscal 2018**	$\dfrac{\$260,170}{(\$22,925 + \$23,190)/2} = 11.3$ times	$\dfrac{365 \text{ days}}{11.3 \text{ times}} = 32.3$ days
	Net Sales	$260,170	$265,595		
	Net Accounts Receivable	22,925	23,190		

For practice at computing and comparing these measures to prior periods, try the Self-Study Practice that follows.

⚡ How's it going?   Self-Study Practice

VFC reported net accounts receivable of $1,430 (million) at the end of Fiscal 2017.

(a) Use this information, along with that in Exhibit 8.7, to calculate VFC's receivables turnover and days to collect in Fiscal 2018.

Fiscal 2018 Receivables Turnover:	**Fiscal 2018 Days to Collect:**

$$\frac{\boxed{}}{(\boxed{}+\boxed{})/2} = \boxed{} \text{ times} \qquad \frac{365 \text{ days}}{\boxed{} \text{ times}} = \boxed{} \text{ days}$$

(b) Did VFC's receivables turnover improve or deteriorate from Fiscal 2018 (calculated in *a*) to 2019 (shown in Exhibit 8.7)?

After you have finished, check your answers with the solution.

Solution to Self-Study Practice

a. $\dfrac{\$12,350}{(\$1,400 + 1,430)/2} = 8.7$ times

$365 \div 8.7 = 42.0$ days

b. VFC's receivables turnover improved in 2019 (1 day faster).

Speeding Up Collections

Factoring Receivables   To generate the cash needed to pay for a company's business activities, managers strive to collect receivables on a timely basis. One way to speed up collections of sluggish receivables is to start hounding customers for payment. But this forceful approach is time-consuming and costly and can annoy customers and cause them to take their business elsewhere. An alternative approach is to sell outstanding accounts receivable to another company (called a **factor**). Through a **factoring** arrangement, your company receives cash for the receivables it sells to the factor (minus a factoring fee) and the factor then takes over collecting the outstanding amounts owed by your customers. Factoring is a fast and easy way for your company to get cash for its receivables, but with costs. First, factoring could send a potentially negative message because it might be seen as a last resort for collecting accounts. Second, the factoring fee can be as much as 3 percent of the receivables sold. In a recent annual report, VFC reported that it sold $1,110 million of receivables to a factor and was charged a fee of $5.8 million, which VFC reported as a Miscellaneous Expense. Other companies that regularly sell receivables report the cost of factoring on the income statement as a selling expense.

Credit Card Sales   As you learned earlier in this chapter (in the Spotlight), companies can allow customers to pay for goods using PayPal or national credit cards. This is another way to avoid lengthy collection periods because national credit card companies and PayPal pay the seller within one to three days of the sale. Most banks process authorized credit card transactions as if they are overnight deposits of cash into the company's bank account. This not only speeds up the seller's cash collection, but also reduces losses from customers writing bad checks. But, just like factoring, these benefits come at a cost. PayPal and credit card companies charge a fee for their services, often around 3 percent of the total sales price. If sales amounted to $100,000, a fee of $3,000 would be deducted, leaving the equivalent of $97,000 cash. These transaction fees are included with selling expenses on the income statement.

SPOTLIGHT ON | Controls

Segregating Collections and Write-Offs

One way to control accounts receivable is to ensure the same person does not both receive collections from customers and write off account balances. This segregation of duties helps to prevent errors and fraud. Without adequate segregation between these duties, a single dishonest employee could divert customer payments to his or her own bank account and then cover up the theft by writing off the customer's balance.

SUPPLEMENT 8A   DIRECT WRITE-OFF METHOD

As described earlier in this chapter, an alternative method exists to account for uncollectible accounts. This alternative approach, called the **direct write-off method**, does not estimate bad debts and does not use an Allowance for Doubtful Accounts. Instead, it reports Sales when they occur and Bad Debt Expense when it is discovered. This is required for tax purposes, but it is not acceptable under generally accepted accounting principles or IFRS. Consequently, it isn't used very often for external financial reporting.

The direct write-off method is not allowed by GAAP because it reports Accounts Receivable at the total amount owed by customers (an overly optimistic point of view) rather than what is estimated to be collectible (a more realistic viewpoint). The direct write-off method also breaks the expense recognition ("matching") principle by recording Bad Debt Expense in the period customer accounts are determined to be bad rather than the period when the credit sales are made. As illustrated earlier in Exhibit 8.1, the failure to match Bad Debt Expense to Sales has a distorting effect on Net Income in the period of the sale as well as in later periods when bad debts are discovered. The only advantage of the direct write-off method is it doesn't require estimating uncollectible amounts.

Learning Objective 8-S1
Record bad debts using the direct write-off method.

Under the direct write-off method, no journal entries are made until a bad debt is discovered. The journal entry used by the direct write-off method to record $1,000 of Bad Debt Expense when a customer account is determined to be uncollectible is:

	Debit	Credit
Bad Debt Expense	1,000	
Accounts Receivable		1,000

REVIEW THE CHAPTER

DEMONSTRATION CASE A: BAD DEBTS

Shooby Dooby Shoe (SDS) reported credit sales of $95,000 during January 2021. Later in the year, SDS determined that it would not be able to collect a $500 account balance that was owed by a deceased customer (Captain Cutler). SDS used the percentage of credit sales method for estimating monthly Bad Debt Expense but then switched to the aging of accounts receivable method at its December 31 year-end.

Required:

1. If SDS estimates that 1 percent of credit sales will result in bad debts, what will be the effects on the accounting equation of recording the January 2021 estimate? Prepare the journal entry to record these effects.

2. Show how the write-off of the account receivable from Captain Cutler would affect the accounting equation, and prepare the journal entry to record these effects.

3. Assume SDS estimates that $11,000 of its year-end Accounts Receivable is uncollectible, as shown below. As of December 31, 2021, the Allowance for Doubtful Accounts had an unadjusted credit balance of $3,000. Show the accounting equation effects of recording the bad debt estimate and prepare a journal entry to record these effects.

		Number of Days Unpaid			
	Total	0–30	31–60	61–90	>90
Total Accounts Receivable	$171,000	$50,000	$80,000	$40,000	$1,000
Estimated uncollectible (%)		× 1%	× 5%	× 15%	× 50%
Estimated uncollectible ($)	$ 11,000	$ 500	$ 4,000	$ 6,000	$ 500

4. Assume SDS reported Net Sales of $950,000 in 2021 and Net Accounts Receivable of $160,000 at December 31, 2021, and $167,586 at December 31, 2020. Calculate the receivables turnover ratio for 2021.

5. If the receivables turnover ratio was 6.4 in 2020, what was the number of days to collect that year? Given your calculations in requirement 4, conclude whether SDS collections are faster in 2021 or 2020.

Suggested Solution

1. The percentage of credit sales method multiplies estimated bad debt losses (1%) by this period's credit sales ($95,000) to directly estimate the amount of Bad Debt Expense to record ($950 = 1% × $95,000).

Assets		= Liabilities +	Stockholders' Equity	
Allowance for Doubtful			Bad Debt Expense (+E)	−950
Accounts (+xA)	−950			

	Debit	Credit
Bad Debt Expense (0.01 × $95,000)	950	
Allowance for Doubtful Accounts (+xA).............................		950

2.

Assets		= Liabilities + Stockholders' Equity
Accounts Receivable	−500	
Allowance for Doubtful Accounts (−xA)	+500	

	Debit	Credit
Allowance for Doubtful Accounts (−xA)	500	
Accounts Receivable		500

3. Under the aging of accounts receivable method, we determine the estimated balance for the Allowance for Doubtful Accounts ($11,000) and then subtract its unadjusted balance ($3,000) to determine the amount of the adjustment ($8,000 = $11,000 − $3,000).

Assets		= Liabilities +	Stockholders' Equity	
Allowance for Doubtful			Bad Debt Expense (+E)	−8,000
Accounts (+xA)	−8,000			

	Debit	Credit
Bad Debt Expense	8,000	
Allowance for Doubtful Accounts (+xA)		8,000

4. Receivables turnover ratio is calculated as Net Sales ÷ Average Net Accounts Receivable. The average net accounts receivable in 2021 was $163,793 (= ($160,000 + $167,586)/2), so the receivables turnover ratio for 2021 was 5.8 (= $950,000 ÷ $163,793).

5. Days to collect is calculated as 365 ÷ receivables turnover ratio. The 6.4 turnover in 2020 equates to 57 days (and the 5.8 turnover in 2021 equates to 63 days). Collections were faster in 2020 than 2021.

DEMONSTRATION CASE B: NOTES RECEIVABLE

On March 1, 2021, Colorado Credit Company (CCC) loaned $600,000 to another company. The promissory note stated an annual interest rate of 8 percent, with interest payments due semiannually, on July 31 and January 31. CCC prepares financial statements for external reporting every quarter, ending on May 31, August 31, November 30, and February 28.

Required:

1. Using the interest formula, calculate the amount of interest CCC earns each month on the note receivable.

2. Using the interest formula, calculate the amount of interest payment CCC received on July 31, 2021, and on January 31, 2022.

3. Prepare a timeline showing the amount of interest earned each quarter and received on each payment date.

4. Prepare journal entries to record the note's issuance, interest earned, and interest payments received for each quarter and on each payment date.

Suggested Solution

1. Interest earned = Principal × Interest Rate × Time

= $600,000 × 8% × 1/12 = $4,000 per month.

2. The period from March 1 to July 31 is five months, whereas the period from August 1 to January 31 is six months.

Interest payment = Principal × Interest Rate × Time

$$= \$600{,}000 \times 8\% \times 5/12 = \$20{,}000 \text{ on July 31.}$$

Interest payment = Principal × Interest Rate × Time

$$= \$600{,}000 \times 8\% \times 6/12 = \$24{,}000 \text{ on January 31.}$$

3. Timeline

March 1	May 31	July 31	Aug. 31	Nov. 30	Jan. 31	Feb. 28
$12,000	$8,000	$4,000	$12,000	$8,000	$4,000	
$20,000			$24,000			

4. Journal Entries

	Debit	Credit
March 1, 2021 (Note Issued)		
Notes Receivable	600,000	
Cash		600,000
May 31 (Interest Accrued)		
Interest Receivable	12,000	
Interest Revenue		12,000
July 31 (Interest Payment Received)		
Cash	20,000	
Interest Receivable		12,000
Interest Revenue		8,000
August 31 (Interest Accrued)		
Interest Receivable	4,000	
Interest Revenue		4,000
November 30 (Interest Accrued)		
Interest Receivable	12,000	
Interest Revenue		12,000
January 31, 2022 (Interest Payment Received)		
Cash	24,000	
Interest Receivable		16,000
Interest Revenue		8,000
February 28 (Interest Accrued)		
Interest Receivable	4,000	
Interest Revenue		4,000

CHAPTER SUMMARY

LO 8-1 **Describe the trade-offs of extending credit.**

- By extending credit to customers, a company is likely to attract a greater number of customers willing to buy from it.

- The additional costs of extending credit include increased wage costs, bad debt costs, and delayed receipt of cash.

LO 8-2 **Estimate and report the effects of uncollectible accounts.**

- Under generally accepted accounting principles, companies must use the allowance method to account for uncollectibles. This method involves the following steps:
  1. Estimate and record uncollectibles with an end-of-period adjusting journal entry that increases Bad Debt Expense (debit) and increases the Allowance for Doubtful Accounts (credit).
  2. Identify and write off specific customer balances in the period that they are determined to be uncollectible.

- The adjusting entry (in 1) reduces Net Income as well as Net Accounts Receivable. The write-off (in 2) has offsetting effects on Accounts Receivable and the Allowance for Doubtful Accounts, ultimately yielding no net effect on Net Accounts Receivable or on Net Income.

Compute and report interest on notes receivable.   **LO 8-3**

- Interest is calculated by multiplying the principal, interest rate, and time period (number of months out of 12). As time passes and interest is earned on the notes, accountants must record an adjusting journal entry that accrues the interest revenue that is receivable on the notes.

Compute and interpret the receivables turnover ratio.   **LO 8-4**

- The receivables turnover ratio measures the effectiveness of credit-granting and collection activities. It reflects how many times average trade receivables were recorded and collected during the period.

- Analysts and creditors watch this ratio because a sudden decline may mean that a company is extending payment deadlines in an attempt to prop up lagging sales. Or it may mean that a company is recording sales of merchandise that customers are likely to return later.

Accounting Decision Tools		
Name of Measure	**Formula**	**What It Tells You**
Receivables turnover ratio	$\dfrac{\text{Net Sales Revenue}}{\text{Average Net Receivables}}$	• The number of times receivables turn over during the period • A higher ratio means faster (better) turnover
Days to collect	$\dfrac{365}{\text{Receivables Turnover Ratio}}$	• Average number of days from sale on account to collection • A higher number means a longer (worse) time to collect

KEY TERMS

Accounts Receivable p. 353
Aging of Accounts Receivable Method p. 357
Allowance Method p. 354
Bad Debt Expense p. 354

Days to Collect p. 364
Direct Write-Off Method p. 367
Factoring p. 367
Interest Formula p. 360
Notes Receivable p. 353

Percentage of Credit Sales Method p. 357
Receivable Write-Off p. 355
Receivables Turnover p. 364

See complete definitions in the glossary in the back of this text.

HOMEWORK HELPER

Alternative terms

- Days to Collect is also called "days' sales outstanding."

Helpful reminders

- The percentage of credit sales method calculates the amount to record as Bad Debt Expense. The aging of accounts receivable method calculates the desired balance in the Allowance for Doubtful

Accounts. This desired balance is compared to the existing balance to determine the amount to adjust the Allowance for Doubtful Accounts and the amount to record as Bad Debt Expense.

- Interest rates always are for a full year. To calculate interest for a shorter period, multiply the interest rate by the fraction of the year for which you are calculating interest.

Frequent mistakes

- Some students mistakenly think an account receivable write-off is an expense. It isn't. It is merely a way to clean up the accounts receivable records. Under the allowance method, no Bad Debt Expense is recorded when removing (writing off) specific customer accounts.

PRACTICE MATERIAL

QUESTIONS (⊖ Symbol indicates questions that require analysis from more than one perspective.)

1. What are the advantages and disadvantages of extending credit to customers?

2. In March 2021, Zengale Inc. decided to discontinue its credit card operations. What factors would this company have considered prior to making this decision? ⊖

3. Which basic accounting principles does the allowance method of accounting for bad debts satisfy?

4. Using the allowance method, is Bad Debt Expense recognized in the period in which (a) sales related to the uncollectible account were made or (b) the seller learns that the customer is unable to pay?

5. What is the effect of the write-off of uncollectible accounts (using the allowance method) on (a) net income and (b) net accounts receivable?

6. How does the use of calculated estimates differ between the aging of accounts receivable method and the percentage of credit sales method?

7. A local phone company had a customer who rang up $300 in charges during September 2021 but did not pay. Despite reminding the customer of this balance, the company was unable to collect in October, November, or December. In March 2022, the company finally gave up and wrote off the account balance. What amount of Sales, Bad Debt Expense, and Net Income would the phone company report from these events in 2021 and 2022 if it used the allowance method of accounting for uncollectible accounts? Assume the company estimates 5 percent of credit sales will go bad.

8. What is the primary difference between accounts receivable and notes receivable?

9. What are the three components of the interest formula? Explain how this formula adjusts for interest periods that are less than a full year.

10. As of December 30, 2018, The Wendy's Company had $2,857,000 of Notes Receivable due within one year, $111,887,000 of Accounts Receivable, and $4,939,000 in its Allowance for Doubtful Accounts (assume all related to accounts receivable). How should these accounts be reported on a balance sheet prepared using GAAP?

11. Does an increase in the receivables turnover ratio generally indicate faster or slower collection of receivables? Explain.

12. What two approaches discussed in this chapter can managers take to speed up sluggish collections of receivables? List one advantage and disadvantage for each approach.

13. When customers experience economic difficulties, companies consider extending longer credit periods. What are the possible consequences of longer credit periods on Sales, Accounts Receivable, Allowance for Doubtful Accounts, Net Income, and the receivables turnover ratio? ⊖

14. (Supplement 8A) Describe how (and when) the direct write-off method accounts for uncollectible accounts. What are the disadvantages of this method?

15. (Supplement 8A) Refer to question 7. What amounts would be reported if the direct write-off method were used? Which method (allowance or direct write-off) more accurately reports the financial results?

MULTIPLE CHOICE

1. When a company using the allowance method writes off a specific customer's account receivable from the accounting system, how many of the following are true?

   - Total stockholders' equity remains the same.
   - Total assets remain the same.
   - Total expenses remain the same.

   a. None   c. Two
   b. One   d. Three

2. When using the allowance method, as Bad Debt Expense is recorded,

   a. Total assets remain the same and stockholders' equity remains the same.
   b. Total assets decrease and stockholders' equity decreases.
   c. Total assets increase and stockholders' equity decreases.
   d. Total liabilities increase and stockholders' equity decreases.

3. For many years, Carefree Company has estimated Bad Debt Expense using the aging of accounts receivable method. Assuming Carefree has no write-offs or recoveries, its estimate of uncollectible receivables resulting from the aging analysis equals

  a. Bad Debt Expense for the current period.
  b. The ending balance in the Allowance for Doubtful Accounts for the period.
  c. The change in the Allowance for Doubtful Accounts for the period.
  d. Both (*a*) and (*c*).

4. Which of the following best describes the proper presentation of accounts receivable in the financial statements?

  a. Accounts Receivable plus the Allowance for Doubtful Accounts in the asset section of the balance sheet.
  b. Accounts Receivable in the asset section of the balance sheet and the Allowance for Doubtful Accounts in the expense section of the income statement.
  c. Accounts Receivable less Bad Debt Expense in the asset section of the balance sheet.
  d. Accounts Receivable less the Allowance for Doubtful Accounts in the asset section of the balance sheet.

5. If the Allowance for Doubtful Accounts opened with a $10,000 credit balance, had write-offs of $5,000 (with no recoveries) during the period, and had a desired ending balance of $20,000 based on an aging analysis, what was the amount of Bad Debt Expense?

  a. $5,000   **c.** $15,000
  b. $10,000   **d.** $20,000

6. When an account receivable is "recovered"

  a. Total assets increase.
  b. Total assets decrease.

  c. Stockholders' equity increases.
  d. None of the above.

7. If 5 percent notes receivable for $100,000 are created on January 1, 2021, and have a maturity date of December 31, 2024,

  a. No interest revenue will be recorded in 2021.
  b. The notes receivable will be classified as a current asset.
  c. Interest Revenue of $5,000 will be recorded in 2021.
  d. None of the above.

8. If the receivables turnover ratio decreased during the year,

  a. The days to collect also decreased.
  b. Receivables collections slowed down.
  c. Sales Revenues increased at a faster rate than Accounts Receivable increased.
  d. None of the above.

9. In 2018, Coca-Cola Bottling had a receivables turnover ratio of 9.0. Which of the following actions could Coca-Cola take to cause the ratio to increase?

  a. Pursue collections more aggressively.
  b. Increase the percentages used to estimate bad debts.
  c. Factor its receivables.
  d. All of the above.

10. All else equal, if VFC incurs a 3 percent fee to factor $10,000 of its Accounts Receivable, its Net Income will

  a. Increase by $10,000.
  b. Increase by $9,700.
  c. Increase by $300.
  d. Decrease by $300.

For answers to the Multiple-Choice Questions **see page Q1** located in the last section of the book.

MINI-EXERCISES

M8-1 Evaluating the Decision to Extend Credit

LO 8-1

Nutty Productions Inc. generated service revenue of $30,000 and income from operations of $10,000. The company estimates that, had it extended credit, it would have instead generated $60,000 of service revenue, but it would have incurred $25,000 of additional expenses for wages and bad debts. Using these estimates, calculate the amount by which Income from Operations would increase (decrease). Should the company extend credit?

M8-2 Evaluating the Decision to Extend Credit

LO 8-1

Last year, Pastis Productions reported $100,000 in sales and $40,000 in cost of goods sold. The company estimates it would have doubled its sales and cost of goods sold had it allowed customers to buy on credit, but it also would have incurred $50,000 in additional expenses relating to wages, bad debts, and interest. Should Pastis Productions extend credit?

M8-3 Reporting Accounts Receivable and Recording Write-Offs Using the Allowance Method

LO 8-2

On December 31, 2020, Extreme Fitness has adjusted balances of $800,000 in Accounts Receivable and $55,000 in Allowance for Doubtful Accounts. On January 2, 2021, the company learns that certain customer accounts are not collectible, so management authorizes a write-off of these accounts totaling $10,000.

a. Show how the company would have reported its receivable accounts on December 31, 2020. As of that date, what amount did Extreme Fitness expect to collect?

b. Prepare the journal entry to write off the accounts on January 2, 2021.

c. Assuming no other transactions occurred between December 31, 2020, and January 3, 2021, show how Extreme Fitness would have reported its receivable accounts on January 3, 2021. As of that date, what amount did Extreme Fitness expect to collect? Has this changed from December 31, 2020? Explain why or why not.

LO 8-2 **M8-4 Recording Recoveries Using the Allowance Method**

Let's go a bit further with the example from M8-3. Assume that on February 2, 2021, Extreme Fitness received a payment of $500 from one of the customers whose balance had been written off. Prepare the journal entries to record this transaction.

LO 8-2 **M8-5 Recording Write-Offs and Bad Debt Expense Using the Allowance Method**

Prepare journal entries for each transaction listed.

a. At the end of June, bad debt expense is estimated to be $14,000.

b. In July, customer balances are written off in the amount of $7,000.

LO 8-2 **M8-6 Determining Financial Statement Effects of Write-Offs and Bad Debt Expense Using the Allowance Method**

Using the following categories, indicate the effects of the following transactions. Use + for increase and − for decrease and indicate the accounts affected and the amounts.

Assets	=	Liabilities	+	Stockholders' Equity

a. During the period, customer balances are written off in the amount of $10,000.

b. At the end of the period, bad debt expense is estimated to be $8,000.

LO 8-2 **M8-7 Estimating Bad Debts Using the Percentage of Credit Sales Method**

Assume Simple Co. had credit sales of $250,000 and cost of goods sold of $150,000 for the period. Simple uses the percentage of credit sales method and estimates that 1 percent of credit sales would result in uncollectible accounts. Before the end-of-period adjustment is made, the Allowance for Doubtful Accounts has a credit balance of $250. What amount of Bad Debt Expense would the company record as an end-of-period adjustment?

LO 8-2 **M8-8 Estimating Bad Debts Using the Aging Method**

Assume that Simple Co. had credit sales of $250,000 and cost of goods sold of $150,000 for the period. Simple uses the aging method and estimates that the appropriate ending balance in the Allowance for Doubtful Accounts is $3,000. Before the end-of-period adjustment is made, the Allowance for Doubtful Accounts has a credit balance of $250. What amount of Bad Debt Expense would the company record as an end-of-period adjustment?

LO 8-2 **M8-9 Recording Bad Debt Estimates Using the Two Estimation Methods**

Using the information in M8-7 and M8-8, prepare the journal entry to record the end-of-period adjustment for bad debts under the (*a*) percentage of credit sales method and (*b*) aging of accounts receivable method. Which of these methods is required by GAAP?

LO 8-3 **M8-10 Using the Interest Formula to Compute Interest**

Complete the following table by computing the missing amounts (?) for the following independent cases.

Principal Amount on Notes Receivable	Annual Interest Rate	Time Period	Interest Earned
a. $100,000	10%	6 months	?
b. $50,000	?	9 months	$3,000
c. ?	10%	12 months	$4,000

LO 8-3 **M8-11 Recording Notes Receivable Transactions**

Nova Corporation hired a new product manager and agreed to provide her a $20,000 relocation loan on a six-month, 7 percent note. Prepare journal entries to record the following transactions for Nova Corporation. Rather than use letters to reference each transaction, use the date of the transaction.

a. The company loans the money on January 1.
b. The new employee pays Nova the interest owed on the maturity date.
c. The new employee pays Nova the full principal owed on the maturity date.

M8-12 Recording Notes Receivable Transactions

LO 8-3

RecRoom Equipment Company received an $8,000, six-month, 6 percent note to settle an $8,000 unpaid balance owed by a customer. Prepare journal entries to record the following transactions for RecRoom. Rather than use letters to reference each transaction, use the date of the transaction.

a. The note is accepted by RecRoom on November 1, causing the company to increase its Notes Receivable and decrease its Accounts Receivable.
b. RecRoom adjusts its records for interest earned to its December 31 year-end.
c. RecRoom receives the interest on the note's maturity date.
d. RecRoom receives the principal on the note's maturity date.

M8-13 Reporting Accounts and Notes Receivable in a Classified Balance Sheet

LO 8-2, 8-3

Adobe Inc.

Adobe Inc. reported the following accounts and amounts (in millions) in its financial statements for the year ended November 30, 2018. Prepare a classified balance sheet. The Allowance for Doubtful Accounts relates entirely to Accounts Receivable. (One of the accounts does not belong on the balance sheet.)

Accounts Payable	$ 1,350	Income Taxes Payable	$ 35
Accounts Receivable	1.330	Notes Payable (long-term)	5,105
Accumulated Amortization	650	Notes Receivable (long-term)	185
Accumulated Depreciation	1,400	Prepaid Rent	310
Allowance for Doubtful Accounts	15	Retained Earnings	8,915
Cash and Cash Equivalents	1,640	Service Revenue	485
Common Stock	450	Short-Term Investments	1,590
Deferred Revenue	2,915	Software	2,720
Equipment	13,060		

M8-14 Determining the Effects of Credit Policy Changes on Receivables Turnover Ratio and Days to Collect

LO 8-4

Indicate the most likely effect of the following changes in credit policy on the receivables turnover ratio and days to collect (+ for increase, − for decrease, and NE for no effect).

a. Granted credit with shorter payment deadlines.
b. Granted credit to less-creditworthy customers.
c. Increased effectiveness of collection methods.

M8-15 Evaluating the Effect of Factoring on the Receivables Turnover Ratio and Computing the Cost of Factoring

LO 8-4

After noting that its receivables turnover ratio had declined, Imperative Company decided for the first time in the company's history to sell $500,000 of receivables to a factoring company. The factor charges a factoring fee of 3 percent of the receivables sold. How much cash does Imperative receive on the sale? Calculate the factoring fee and describe how it is reported by Imperative Company. All else equal, how will this affect Imperative's receivables turnover ratio in the future?

M8-16 (Supplement 8A) Recording Write-Offs and Reporting Accounts Receivable Using the Direct Write-Off Method

LO 8-S1

Complete all the requirements of M8-3, except assume Extreme Fitness uses the direct write-off method. Note this means Extreme does not have an Allowance for Doubtful Accounts balance.

EXERCISES

LO 8-2   **E8-1   Recording Bad Debt Expense Estimates and Write-Offs Using the Aging of Receivables Method**

Blackhorse Productions, Inc., used the aging of accounts receivable method to estimate that its Allowance for Doubtful Accounts should be $19,750. The account had an unadjusted credit balance of $10,000 at that time.

Required:

Prepare journal entries for each of the following.

a.   The appropriate bad debt adjustment was recorded.
b.   Later, an account receivable for $1,000 was determined to be uncollectible and was written off.

LO 8-2   **E8-2   Determining Financial Statement Effects of Bad Debt Expense Estimates and Write-Offs**

For each transaction listed in E8-1, indicate the amount and direction (+ or −) of effects on the financial statement accounts and on the overall accounting equation.

Assets	=	Liabilities	+	Stockholders' Equity

LO 8-2   **E8-3   Recording, Reporting, and Evaluating a Bad Debt Estimate Using the Percentage of Credit Sales Method**

During the year ended December 31, 2021, Kelly's Camera Shop had sales revenue of $170,000, of which $85,000 was on credit. At the start of 2021, Accounts Receivable showed a $10,000 debit balance and the Allowance for Doubtful Accounts showed a $600 credit balance. Collections of accounts receivable during 2021 amounted to $68,000.
      Data during 2021 follow:

a.   On December 10, a customer balance of $1,500 from a prior year was determined to be uncollectible, so it was written off.
b.   On December 31, a decision was made to continue the accounting policy of basing estimated bad debt losses on 2 percent of credit sales for the year.

Required:

1.   Give the required journal entries for the two events in December.
2.   Show how the amounts related to Accounts Receivable and Bad Debt Expense would be reported on the balance sheet and income statement for 2021.
3.   On the basis of the data available, does the 2 percent rate appear to be reasonable? Explain.

LO 8-2   **E8-4   Recording Write-Offs and Recoveries**

Prior to recording the following, Elite Electronics, Inc., had a credit balance of $2,000 in its Allowance for Doubtful Accounts.

Required:

Prepare journal entries for each transaction.

a.   On August 31, a customer balance for $300 from a prior year was determined to be uncollectible and was written off.
b.   On December 15, the customer balance for $300 written off on August 31 was collected in full.

LO 8-2   **E8-5   Determining Financial Statement Effects of Write-Offs and Recoveries**

For each transaction listed in E8-4, indicate the amount and direction (+ or −) of effects on the financial statement accounts and on the overall accounting equation.

Assets	=	Liabilities	+	Stockholders' Equity

LO 8-2   **E8-6   Computing Bad Debt Expense Using Aging of Accounts Receivable Method**

Young and Old Corporation (YOC) uses two aging categories to estimate uncollectible accounts. Accounts less than 60 days are considered young and have a 5 percent uncollectible rate. Accounts more than 60 days are considered old and have a 40 percent uncollectible rate.

Required:

1. If YOC has $100,000 of young accounts and $400,000 of old accounts, how much should be reported in the Allowance for Doubtful Accounts?
2. If YOC's Allowance for Doubtful Accounts currently has an unadjusted credit balance of $40,000, how much should be credited to the account?
3. If YOC's Allowance for Doubtful Accounts has an unadjusted debit balance of $5,000, how much should be credited to the account?
4. Explain how YOC's Allowance for Doubtful Accounts could have a debit balance.

E8-7 Computing Bad Debt Expense Using Aging of Accounts Receivable Method

LO 8-2

Brown Cow Dairy uses the aging approach to estimate Bad Debt Expense. The balance of each account receivable is aged on the basis of three time periods as follows: (1) 1–30 days old, $12,000; (2) 31–90 days old, $5,000; and (3) more than 90 days old, $3,000. For each age group, the average loss rate on the amount of the receivable due to uncollectibility is estimated to be (1) 5 percent, (2) 10 percent, and (3) 20 percent, respectively. At December 31 (end of the current year), the Allowance for Doubtful Accounts balance was $800 (credit) before the end-of-period adjusting entry is made.

Required:

1. Prepare a schedule to estimate an appropriate year-end balance for the Allowance for Doubtful Accounts.
2. What amount of Bad Debt Expense should be recorded on December 31?
3. If the unadjusted balance in the Allowance for Doubtful Accounts was a $600 debit balance, what amount of Bad Debt Expense should be recorded on December 31?

E8-8 Recording and Reporting Allowance for Doubtful Accounts Using the Percentage of Credit Sales and Aging of Accounts Receivable Methods

LO 8-2

Innovative Tech Inc. (ITI) has been using the percentage of credit sales method to estimate bad debts. During November, ITI sold services on account for $100,000 and estimated that ½ of 1 percent of those sales would be uncollectible.

Required:

1. Prepare the November adjusting entry for bad debts.
2. Starting in December, ITI switched to using the aging method. At its December 31 year-end, total Accounts Receivable is $89,000, aged as follows: (1) 1–30 days old, $75,000; (2) 31–90 days old, $10,000; and (3) more than 90 days old, $4,000. The average rate of uncollectibility for each age group is estimated to be (1) 10 percent, (2) 20 percent, and (3) 40 percent, respectively. Prepare a schedule to estimate an appropriate year-end balance for the Allowance for Doubtful Accounts.
3. Before the end-of-year adjusting entry is made, the Allowance for Doubtful Accounts has a $1,600 credit balance at December 31. Prepare the December 31 adjusting entry.
4. Show how the various accounts related to accounts receivable should be shown on the December 31 balance sheet.

E8-9 Recording and Determining the Effects of Write-Offs, Recoveries, and Bad Debt Expense Estimates on the Balance Sheet and Income Statement

LO 8-2

Fraud Investigators Inc. operates a fraud detection service.

Required:

1. Prepare journal entries for each transaction below.
   a. On March 31, 10 customers were billed for detection services totaling $25,000.
   b. On October 31, a customer balance of $1,500 from a prior year was determined to be uncollectible and was written off.
   c. On December 15, a customer paid an old balance of $900, which had been written off in a prior year.
   d. On December 31, $500 of bad debts were estimated and recorded for the year.

2. Complete the following table, indicating the amount and effect (+ for increase, − for decrease, and NE for no effect) of each transaction.

Transaction	Net Receivables	Net Sales	Income from Operations
a.			
b.			
c.			
d.			

LO 8-3   **E8-10 Recording Notes Receivable Transactions, Including Accrual Adjustment for Interest**

The following transactions took place for Smart Solutions Inc.

<u>2020</u>

a. July 1   Loaned $70,000 to employees of the company and received back one-year, 10 percent notes.

b. Dec. 31   Accrued interest on the notes.

<u>2021</u>

c. July 1   Received interest on the notes. (No interest has been recorded since December 31.)

d. July 1   Received principal on the notes.

Required:

Prepare the journal entries that Smart Solutions Inc. would record for the above transactions.

LO 8-3   **E8-11 Recording Notes Receivable Transactions, Including Accrual Adjustment for Interest**

The following transactions took place for Parker's Grocery.

a. Jan. 1   Loaned $50,000 to cashiers of the company and received back one-year, 8 percent notes.

b. June 30   Accrued interest on the notes.

c. Dec. 31   Received interest on the notes. (No interest has been recorded since June 30.)

d. Dec. 31   Received principal on the notes.

Required:

Prepare the journal entries Parker's Grocery would record for the above transactions.

LO 8-3   **E8-12 Recording Notes Receivable Transactions, Including Accrual Adjustment for Interest**

To attract retailers to its shopping center, the Marketplace Mall will lend money to tenants under formal contracts, provided that they use it to renovate their store space. On November 1, 2020, the company loaned $100,000 to new tenants on one-year notes with stated annual interest rates of 9 percent. Interest is to be received by Marketplace Mall on April 30, 2021, and at maturity on October 31, 2021.

Required:

Prepare journal entries that Marketplace Mall would record related to these notes on the following dates: (*a*) November 1, 2020; (*b*) December 31, 2020 (Marketplace Mall's fiscal year-end); (*c*) April 30, 2021; and (*d*) October 31, 2021.

LO 8-2, 8-4   **E8-13 Using Financial Statement Disclosures to Infer Write-Offs and Bad Debt Expense and to Calculate the Receivables Turnover Ratio**

Microsoft Corporation

Microsoft Corporation develops, produces, and markets a wide range of computer software including the Windows operating system. Microsoft reported the following information about Net Sales Revenue and Accounts Receivable (all amounts in millions).

	June 30, 2019	June 30, 2018
Accounts Receivable, Net of Allowance for Doubtful Accounts of $410 and $375	$29,520	$26,480
Net Revenues	$125,840	$110,360

According to its Form 10-K, Microsoft recorded Bad Debt Expense of $150 and did not recover any previously written-off accounts during the year ended June 30, 2019.

Required:

1. What amount of accounts receivable was written off during the year ended June 30, 2019?
2. What was Microsoft's receivables turnover ratio (to one decimal place) in the current year?
3. Does your answer in requirement 2 suggest the collectibility of Accounts Receivable improved (or deteriorated) in 2019, relative to 2018 when the turnover was 5.0?

E8-14 Using Financial Statement Disclosures to Infer Bad Debt Expense   LO 8-2

The annual report for Fabeck Finishing Corporation contained the following information:

(in millions)	2021	2020
Accounts Receivable	$455	$455
Allowance for Doubtful Accounts	35	25
Accounts Receivable, Net	420	430

Assume that accounts receivable write-offs amounted to $1 during 2021 and $9 during 2020 and that Fabeck Finishing did not record any recoveries.

Required:

Determine the Bad Debt Expense for 2021 based on the above facts.

E8-15 Determining the Effects of Uncollectible Accounts on the Receivables Turnover Ratio   LO 8-2, 8-4

Refer to the information about Fabeck Finishing given in E8-14.

Required:

Complete the following table indicating the direction of the effect (+ for increase, − for decrease, and NE for no effect) of each transaction during 2021:

Transaction	Net Credit Sales	Average Net Accounts Receivable	Receivables Turnover Ratio
a. Writing off uncollectible accounts.			
b. Recording bad debt expense.			

E8-16 Analyzing and Interpreting Receivables Turnover Ratio and Days to Collect   LO 8-4

FedEx Corporation reported the following rounded amounts (in millions):   FedEx Corporation

	2019	2018
Accounts Receivable	$ 9,415	$ 8,880
Allowance for Doubtful Accounts	(300)	(400)
Accounts Receivable, Net of Allowance	$ 9,115	$ 8,480
Net Sales (assume all on credit)	$69,690	$65,450

Required:

1. Determine the receivables turnover ratio and days to collect for 2019. Round your answers to one decimal place.
2. Do the measures calculated in requirement 1 represent an improvement (or deterioration) in receivables turnover, compared to 2018, when the turnover was 8.1?

LO 8-S1

E8-17 (Supplement 8A) Recording Write-Offs and Reporting Accounts Receivable Using the Direct Write-Off Method

Trevorson Electronics is a small company privately owned by Jon Trevorson, an electrician who installs wiring in new homes. Because the company's financial statements are prepared only for tax purposes, Jon uses the direct write-off method. During 2021, its first year of operations, Trevorson Electronics sold $30,000 of services on account. The company collected $26,000 of these receivables during the year, and Jon believed that the remaining $4,000 was fully collectible. In 2022, Jon discovered that none of the $4,000 would be collected, so he wrote off the entire amount. To make matters worse, Jon sold only $5,000 of services during the year.

Required:

1. Prepare journal entries to record the transactions in 2021 and 2022.
2. Using only the information provided (ignore other operating expenses), prepare comparative income statements for 2021 and 2022. Was 2021 really as profitable as indicated by its income statement? Was 2022 quite as bad as indicated by its income statement? What should Jon do if he wants better information for assessing his company's ability to generate profit?

COACHED PROBLEMS

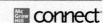

LO 8-2

Red Hat, Inc.

CP8-1 Recording Accounts Receivable Transactions Using Two Estimation Methods

Red Hat, Inc., is a software development company that recently reported the following amounts (in thousands) in its unadjusted trial balance as of February 28, 2019.

	Debits	Credits
Accounts Receivable	$984,750	
Allowance for Doubtful Accounts		$ 4,500
Sales and Service Revenue		3,300,000

Required:

1. Assume Red Hat uses ¼ of 1 percent of revenue to estimate its bad debt expense for the year. Prepare the adjusting journal entry required at February 28 for recording Bad Debt Expense.
2. Assume instead that Red Hat uses the aging of accounts receivable method and estimates that $5,000 (thousand) of Accounts Receivable will be uncollectible. Prepare the adjusting journal entry required at February 28 for recording bad debt expense.

   TIP: The aging of accounts receivable method focuses on calculating what the adjusted Allowance for Doubtful Accounts balance should be. You need to consider the existing balance when determining the adjustment.
3. Repeat requirement 2, except this time assume the unadjusted balance in Red Hat's Allowance for Doubtful Accounts at February 28 was a debit balance of $1,000 (thousand).
4. If one of Red Hat's customers declared bankruptcy, what journal entry would be used to write off its $500 (thousand) balance?

LO 8-2

Callaway Golf Company

CP8-2 Interpreting Disclosure of Allowance for Doubtful Accounts

Callaway Golf Company sells on account to golf pro shops and general sporting goods retailers. In its financial statements for the year ended December 31, 2018, Callaway reported the following balances and changes in the Allowance for Doubtful Accounts (in thousands):

Balance at Beginning of Period	Charged to Bad Debt Expense	Amounts Written Off	Balance at End of Period
$4,450	$2,260	$1,100	$5,610

Required:

1. Create a T-account for the Allowance for Doubtful Accounts and enter into it the amounts from the above schedule. Then write the T-account in equation format to prove that the above items account for the changes in the account.

   TIP: The allowance increases when estimates are charged to Bad Debt Expense and when recoveries are reported. The allowance decreases when accounts are written off.

2. Record summary journal entries related to (*a*) estimating bad debt expense and (*b*) write-offs of specific balances during the year.

3. If Callaway had written off an additional $100 (thousand) of accounts receivable during the period, by how much would Net Receivables have decreased? How much would Net Income have decreased?

CP8-3 Recording Notes Receivable Transactions

LO 8-3

Jung & Newbicalm Advertising (JNA) recently hired a new creative director, Howard Rachell, for its Madison Avenue office in New York. To persuade Howard to move from San Francisco, JNA agreed to advance him $100,000 on April 30, 2021, on a one-year, 10 percent note, with interest payments required on October 31, 2021, and April 30, 2022. JNA issues quarterly financial statements on March 31, June 30, September 30, and December 31.

Required:

1. Prepare the journal entry that JNA will make to record the promissory note created on April 30, 2021.

   TIP: See Demonstration Case B for a similar problem.

2. Prepare the journal entries that JNA will make to record the interest accruals at each quarter-end and interest payments at each payment date.

   TIP: Interest receivable will be accrued at the end of each quarter, and then will be reduced when the interest payment is received.

3. Prepare the journal entry that JNA will make to record the principal payment at the maturity date.

CP8-4 Accounting for Accounts and Notes Receivable Transactions

LO 8-2, 8-3

Execusmart Consultants has provided business consulting services for several years. The company has been using the percentage of credit sales method to estimate bad debts but switched at the end of the first quarter this year to the aging of accounts receivable method. The company entered into the following partial list of transactions.

a. During January, the company provided services for $200,000 on credit.
b. On January 31, the company estimated bad debts using 1 percent of credit sales.
c. On February 4, the company collected $100,000 of accounts receivable.
d. On February 15, the company wrote off $500 of accounts receivable.
e. During February, the company provided services for $150,000 on credit.
f. On February 28, the company estimated bad debts using 1 percent of credit sales.
g. On March 1, the company loaned $12,000 to an employee, who signed a 10 percent note due in three months.
h. On March 15, the company collected $500 on the account written off one month earlier.
i. On March 31, the company accrued interest earned on the note.
j. On March 31, the company adjusted for uncollectible accounts, based on the following aging analysis, which includes the preceding transactions (as well as others not listed). Prior to the adjustment, Allowance for Doubtful Accounts had an unadjusted credit balance of $6,000.

		Number of Days Unpaid			
Customer	Total	0–30	31–60	61–90	Over 90
Arrow Ergonomics	$ 1,000	$ 500	$ 400	$ 100	
Asymmetry Architecture	2,000				$ 2,000
Others (not shown to save space)	85,000	34,000	42,000	5,000	4,000
Weight Whittlers	2,000	2,000			
Total Accounts Receivable	**$ 90,000**	**$ 36,500**	**$ 42,400**	**$ 5,100**	**$ 6,000**
Estimated Uncollectible (%)		**2%**	**10%**	**20%**	**40%**

Required:

1. For items (a)–(j), analyze the amount and direction (+ or −) of effects on specific financial statement accounts and the overall accounting equation.
    TIP: In item (j), you must first calculate the desired ending balance before adjusting the Allowance for Doubtful Accounts.

2. Prepare journal entries for items (a)–(j).

3. Show how Accounts Receivable, Notes Receivable, and their related accounts would be reported in the current assets section of a classified balance sheet at the end of the quarter on March 31.

4. Sales Revenue and Service Revenue are two income statement accounts that relate to Accounts Receivable. Name two other accounts related to Accounts Receivable and Notes Receivable that would be reported on the income statement and indicate whether each would appear before, or after, Income from Operations for Execusmart Consultants.

LO 8-4

Mattel, Inc.

Hasbro

CP8-5 Analyzing Allowance for Doubtful Accounts, Receivables Turnover Ratio, and Days to Collect

Mattel, Inc., and Hasbro are two of the largest and most successful toymakers in the world, in terms of the products they sell and their receivables management practices. To evaluate their ability to collect on credit sales, consider the following information reported in their annual reports (amounts in millions).

	Mattel			Hasbro		
Fiscal Year Ended:	2018	2017	2016	2018	2017	2016
Net Sales	$4,510	$4,880	$5,460	$4,580	$5,210	$5,020
Accounts Receivable	990	1,155	1,135	1,200	1,435	1,337
Allowance for Doubtful Accounts	20	25	20	10	30	17
Accounts Receivable, Net of Allowance	970	1,130	1,115	1,190	1,405	1,320

Required:

1. Calculate the receivables turnover ratios and days to collect for Mattel and Hasbro for 2018 and 2017. (Round your final answers to one decimal place.)
    TIP: In your calculations, use **average** Accounts Receivable, Net of Allowance.

2. Which of the companies was quicker to convert its receivables into cash in 2018? in 2017?

GROUP A PROBLEMS

LO 8-2

The Kraft Heinz Company

PA8-1 Recording Accounts Receivable Transactions Using the Aging Method

The Kraft Heinz Company was formed in 2015 with the merger of Kraft Foods and H. J. Heinz Corporation. The company reported the following rounded amounts for the year ended December 29, 2018 (all amounts in millions):

	Debits	Credits
Accounts Receivable	$2,130	
Allowance for Doubtful Accounts		$ 24
Sales (assume all on credit)		26,300

Required:

1. Assume Kraft Heinz uses ½ of 1 percent of sales to estimate its Bad Debt Expense for the year. Prepare the adjusting journal entry required for the year (rounded to the nearest million), assuming no Bad Debt Expense has been recorded yet.

2. Assume instead Kraft Heinz uses the aging of accounts receivable method and estimates that $80 of its Accounts Receivable will be uncollectible. Prepare the adjusting journal entry required at December 29, 2018, for recording Bad Debt Expense.

3. Repeat requirement 2, except this time assume the unadjusted balance in Kraft Heinz's Allowance for Doubtful Accounts at December 29, 2018, was a debit balance of $20.

4. If one of Kraft Heinz's customers declared bankruptcy, what journal entry would be used to write off its $15 balance?

PA8-2 Interpreting Disclosure of Allowance for Doubtful Accounts

LO 8-2

Expedia, Inc., disclosed the following rounded amounts (in millions) concerning the Allowance for Doubtful Accounts on its Form 10-K annual report.

Expedia, Inc.

		Allowance for Doubtful Accounts (dollars in millions)		
Year	Beginning Balance	Increases for Bad Debt Expense	Decreases for Write-Offs	Ending Balance
2018	$31	$19	$?	$34
2017	25	20	14	31
2016	27	9	11	25

Required:

1. Create a T-account for the Allowance for Doubtful Accounts and enter into it the 2016 amounts from the above schedule. Then write the T-account in equation format to prove the above items account for the changes in the account.

2. Record summary journal entries for 2017 related to (a) estimating Bad Debt Expense and (b) writing off specific customer account balances.

3. Supply the missing dollar amount noted by "?" for 2018.

4. If Expedia had written off an additional $20 of Accounts Receivable during 2018, by how much would Net Receivables have decreased? How much would Net Income have decreased?

PA8-3 Recording Notes Receivable Transactions

LO 8-3

C&S Marketing (CSM) recently hired a new marketing director, Jeff Otos, for its downtown Minneapolis office. As part of the arrangement, CSM agreed on February 28, 2021, to advance Jeff $50,000 on a one-year, 8 percent note, with interest to be paid at maturity on February 28, 2022. CSM prepares financial statements on June 30 and December 31.

Required:

1. Prepare the journal entry CSM will make when the note is established.

2. Prepare the journal entries CSM will make to accrue interest on June 30 and December 31.

3. Prepare the journal entry CSM will make to record the interest and principal payments on February 28, 2022.

PA8-4 Accounting for Accounts and Notes Receivable Transactions

LO 8-2, 8-3

Web Wizard, Inc., has provided information technology services for several years. For the first two months of the current year, the company has used the percentage of credit sales method to estimate bad debts. At the end of the first quarter, the company switched to the aging of accounts receivable method. The company entered into the following *partial* list of transactions during the first quarter.

a. During January, the company provided services for $40,000 on credit.

b. On January 31, the company estimated bad debts using 1 percent of credit sales.

c. On February 4, the company collected $20,000 of accounts receivable.
d. On February 15, the company wrote off $100 of accounts receivable.
e. During February, the company provided services for $30,000 on credit.
f. On February 28, the company estimated bad debts using 1 percent of credit sales.
g. On March 1, the company loaned $2,400 to an employee, who signed a 6 percent note, due in six months.
h. On March 15, the company collected $100 on the account written off one month earlier.
i. On March 31, the company accrued interest earned on the note.
j. On March 31, the company adjusted for uncollectible accounts, based on the following aging analysis, which includes the preceding transactions (as well as others not listed). Prior to the adjustment, Allowance for Doubtful Accounts had an unadjusted credit balance of $1,200.

		Number of Days Unpaid			
Customer	Total	0–30	31–60	61–90	Over 90
Alabama Tourism	$ 200	$ 100	$ 80	$ 20	
Bayside Bungalows	400				$ 400
Others (not shown to save space)	17,000	6,800	8,400	1,000	800
Xciting Xcursions	400	400			
Total Accounts Receivable	**$18,000**	**$7,300**	**$8,480**	**$1,020**	**$1,200**
Estimated Uncollectible (%)		**2%**	**10%**	**20%**	**40%**

Required:

1. For items (a)–(j), analyze the amount and direction (+ or −) of effects on specific financial statement accounts and the overall accounting equation.
2. Prepare journal entries for items (a)–(j).
3. Show how Accounts Receivable, Notes Receivable, and their related accounts would be reported in the current assets section of a classified balance sheet at the end of the first quarter.
4. Sales Revenue and Service Revenue are two income statement accounts that relate to Accounts Receivable. Name two other accounts related to Accounts Receivable and Notes Receivable that would be reported on the income statement and indicate whether each would appear before, or after, Income from Operations.

LO 8-4
Coca-Cola
PepsiCo

PA8-5 Analyzing Allowance for Doubtful Accounts, Receivables Turnover Ratio, and Days to Collect

Coca-Cola and PepsiCo are two of the largest and most successful beverage companies in the world in terms of the products that they sell and their receivables management practices. To evaluate their ability to collect on credit sales, consider the following rounded amounts reported in their annual reports (amounts in millions).

	Coca-Cola			PepsiCo		
Fiscal Year Ended:	2018	2017	2016	2018	2017	2016
Net Sales	$31,860	$35,410	$41,860	$64,660	$63,525	$62,800
Accounts Receivable	3,890	4,150	4,330	7,240	7,155	6,835
Allowance for Doubtful Accounts	490	480	470	100	130	135
Accounts Receivable, Net of Allowance	3,400	3,670	3,860	7,140	7,025	6,700

Required:

1. Calculate the receivables turnover ratios and days to collect for Coca-Cola and PepsiCo for 2018 and 2017. (Round to one decimal place.)
2. Which of the companies is quicker to convert its receivables into cash in 2018? in 2017?

GROUP B PROBLEMS

LO 8-2

PB8-1 Recording Accounts Receivable Transactions Using the Allowance Method

Chipman Software recently reported the following amounts in its unadjusted trial balance at its year-end:

	Debits	Credits
Accounts Receivable	$3,000	
Allowance for Doubtful Accounts		$ 20
Sales (assume all on credit)		44,000

Required:

1. Chipman uses ¼ of 1 percent of sales to estimate its Bad Debt Expense for the year. Prepare the adjusting journal entry required for the year, assuming no Bad Debt Expense has been recorded yet.

2. Assume instead that Chipman uses the aging of accounts receivable method and estimates that $80 of its Accounts Receivable will be uncollectible. Prepare the year-end adjusting journal entry for recording Bad Debt Expense.

3. Repeat requirement 2, except this time assume Chipman's year-end unadjusted balance in Allowance for Doubtful Accounts was a debit balance of $20.

4. If one of Chipman's main customers declared bankruptcy after year-end, what journal entry would be used to write off its $15 balance?

PB8-2   Interpreting Disclosure of Allowance for Doubtful Accounts

Xerox Corporation is the company that made the photocopier popular, but since then has grown a new business related to business process outsourcing. It recently disclosed the following information concerning the Allowance for Doubtful Accounts on its Form 10-K annual report.

		Allowance for Doubtful Accounts (dollars in millions)		
Year	Beginning Balance	Increases for Bad Debt Expense	Decreases for Write-Offs	Ending Balance
2018	$ 59	$ 14	$ 17	$ 56
2017	64	16	*a*	59
2016	74	*b*	25	64

Required:

1. Create a T-account for the Allowance for Doubtful Accounts and enter into it the 2018 amounts from the above schedule. Then, write the T-account in equation format to prove that the above items account for the changes in the account.

2. Record summary journal entries for 2018 related to (*i*) estimating bad debt expense and (*ii*) writing off specific balances.

3. Supply the missing dollar amounts for *a* and *b*.

4. If Xerox had written off an additional $20 of accounts receivable during 2016, by how much would its Net Accounts Receivable have decreased? How much would the write-off have decreased Income from Operations?

PB8-3   Recording Notes Receivable Transactions

Stinson Company recently agreed to loan an employee $100,000 for the purchase of a new house. The loan was executed on May 31, 2021, and is a one-year, 6 percent note, with interest payments required on November 30, 2021, and May 31, 2022. Stinson issues quarterly financial statements on March 31, June 30, September 30, and December 31.

Required:

1. Prepare the journal entry Stinson will make when the note is established.

2. Prepare the journal entries Stinson will make to record the interest accruals at each quarter-end and interest payments at each payment date.

3. Prepare the journal entry Stinson will make to record the principal payment at the maturity date.

LO 8-2, 8-3

PB8-4 Accounting for Accounts and Notes Receivable Transactions

Elite Events Corporation has provided event planning services for several years. The company has been using the percentage of credit sales method to estimate bad debts but switched at the end of the first quarter to the aging of accounts receivable method. The company entered into the following partial list of transactions during the first quarter.

a. During January, the company provided services for $300,000 on credit.
b. On January 31, the company estimated bad debts using 1 percent of credit sales.
c. On February 4, the company collected $250,000 of accounts receivable.
d. On February 15, the company wrote off $3,000 of accounts receivable.
e. During February, the company provided services for $250,000 on credit.
f. On February 28, the company estimated bad debts using 1 percent of credit sales.
g. On March 1, the company loaned $15,000 to an employee who signed a 4 percent note, due in nine months.
h. On March 15, the company collected $3,000 on the account written off one month earlier.
i. On March 31, the company accrued interest earned on the note.
j. On March 31, the company adjusted for uncollectible accounts, based on the following aging analysis, which includes the preceding transactions (as well as others not listed). Prior to the adjustment, Allowance for Doubtful Accounts had an unadjusted credit balance of $9,000.

| Customer | Total | Number of Days Unpaid | | | |
		0–30	31–60	61–90	Over 90
Aerosmith	$ 2,000	$ 1,000	$ 1,000		
Biggie Small	2,000			$ 1,000	$ 1,000
Others (not shown to save space)	99,000	39,000	42,000	9,000	9,000
ZZ Top	7,000	7,000			
Total Accounts Receivable	**$110,000**	**$47,000**	**$43,000**	**$10,000**	**$10,000**
Estimated Uncollectible (%)		**5%**	**10%**	**20%**	**40%**

Required:

1. For items (a)–(j), analyze the amount and direction (+ or −) of effects on specific financial statement accounts and the overall accounting equation.
2. Prepare journal entries for items (a)–(j).
3. Show how Accounts Receivable, Notes Receivable, and their related accounts would be reported in the current assets section of a classified balance sheet at the end of the first quarter.
4. Sales Revenue and Service Revenue are two income statement accounts that relate to Accounts Receivable. Name two other accounts related to Accounts Receivable and Notes Receivable that would be reported on the income statement and indicate whether each would appear before, or after, Income from Operations.

LO 8-4

J. M. Smucker
Seneca Foods Corporation

PB8-5 Analyzing Allowance for Doubtful Accounts, Receivables Turnover Ratio, and Days to Collect

J. M. Smucker is well known for its fruit jams and Seneca Foods Corporation is the company behind Green Giant canned vegetables. To evaluate their ability to collect on credit sales, consider the following rounded information in their annual reports (amounts in millions).

| | J.M. Smucker | | | Seneca Foods | | |
Fiscal Year Ended April 30:	2019	2018	2017	2019	2018	2017
Net Sales	$7,840	$7,360	$7,390	$1,200	$1,160	$1,260
Accounts Receivable	507	386	440	85	67	73
Allowance for Doubtful Accounts	2	1	2	1	1	1
Accounts Receivable, Net of Allowance	505	385	440	84	66	72

Required:

1. Calculate the receivables turnover ratios and days to collect for Smucker and Seneca for the fiscal years ended in 2019 and 2018. (Round to one decimal place.)
2. Which of the companies is quicker to convert its receivables into cash?

COMPREHENSIVE PROBLEMS

C8-1 Recording and Reporting Credit Sales and Bad Debts Using the Aging of Accounts Receivable Method (Chapters 6 and 8)

LO 6-4, 8-2

Walgreens

Okay Optical, Inc. (OOI), began operations in January, selling inexpensive sunglasses to large retailers like Walgreens and other smaller stores. Assume the following transactions occurred during its first six months of operations.

January 1 Sold merchandise to Walgreens for $20,000; the cost of these goods to OOI was $12,000.

February 12 Received payment in full from Walgreens.

March 1 Sold merchandise to Bravis Pharmaco on account for $3,000; the cost of these goods to OOI was $1,400.

April 1 Sold merchandise to Tony's Pharmacy on account for $8,000. The cost to OOI was $4,400.

May 1 Sold merchandise to Anjuli Stores on account for $2,000; the cost to OOI was $1,200.

June 17 Received $6,500 on account from Tony's Pharmacy.

Required:

1. Complete the following aged listing of customer accounts at June 30.

		Unpaid Since			
Customer	Total Balance	June (one month)	May (two months)	April (three months)	March (greater than three months)
Anjuli Stores	$2,000		$2,000		
Bravis Pharmaco	3,000				$3,000
Tony's Pharmacy					
Walgreens					

2. Estimate the Allowance for Doubtful Accounts required at June 30 assuming the following uncollectible rates: one month, 1 percent; two months, 5 percent; three months, 20 percent; more than three months, 40 percent.

3. Show how OOI would report its accounts receivable on its June 30 balance sheet. What amounts would be reported on an income statement prepared for the six-month period ended June 30?

4. Bonus Question: In July, OOI collected the balance due from Bravis Pharmaco but discovered that the balance due from Tony's Pharmacy needed to be written off. Using this information, determine how accurate OOI was in estimating the Allowance for Doubtful Accounts needed for each of these two customers and in total.

C8-2 Evaluating Accounts Receivable Management (Chapters 6 and 8)

LO 6-4, 8-4

WorldBiz operates divisions around the world. Its European division—EuroBiz (EB)—has recently reported the following information to you at WorldBiz's head office. You are trying to decide whether to direct your internal audit staff to investigate more closely.

From the Financial Statement Notes	Year 5	Year 4	Year 3
Accounts Receivable (gross)	$100,000	$ 60,000	$ 40,000
Allowance for Doubtful Accounts	(5,000)	(6,000)	(4,000)
Accounts Receivable, Net	95,000	54,000	36,000
Other Information Gathered			
Net Sales Revenue	$590,000	$540,000	$490,000
Accounts Receivable Write-offs	6,900	6,100	6,100
Bad Debt Expense	5,900	8,100	7,350
Sales Discounts (2/10, n/30)	3,000	9,000	5,000

Required:

1. For each of the years, calculate the proportion of gross accounts receivable estimated to be uncollectible as allowed for in the Allowance for Doubtful Accounts. Round to one decimal place. Which year does not align with the other two?

2. For each of the years, calculate the proportion of Net Sales Revenue that Bad Debt Expense represents. Round to one decimal place. Which year does not align with the other two?

3. Did customers take greater (or lesser) advantage of sales discounts in Year 5 than in Year 4 and Year 3? Does this indicate customers were more (or less) likely to promptly pay their balances in Year 5 as compared to prior years?

4. Calculate the average days to collect in Year 5 and Year 4. Round to one decimal place. Does this measure indicate customers paid their balances faster (or slower) in Year 5 as compared to Year 4?

5. Given your answers to requirements 1 through 4, indicate (yes or no) whether you should direct your internal audit staff to investigate EB's receivables management practices more closely.

LO 3-3, 4-2, 4-3, 4-4, 6-3, 6-4, 6-6, 7-3, 8-2, 8-3

C8-3 Recording Daily and Adjusting Entries Using FIFO in a Perpetual Inventory System (Chapters 3, 4, 6, 7, and 8)

One Trick Pony (OTP) incorporated and began operations near the end of the year, resulting in the following post-closing balances at December 31:

Cash	$18,620	Deferred Revenue (30 units)	$ 4,350
Accounts Receivable	9,650	Accounts Payable	1,300
Allowance for Doubtful Accounts	900*	Notes Payable (long-term)	15,000
Inventory	2,800	Common Stock	5,000
		Retained Earnings	4,520

* Credit balance.

The following information is relevant to the first month of operations in the following year:

- OTP will sell inventory at $145 per unit. OTP's January 1 inventory balance consists of 35 units at a total cost of $2,800. OTP's policy is to use the FIFO method, recorded using a perpetual inventory system.
- In December, OTP received a $4,350 payment for 30 units OTP is to deliver in January; this obligation was recorded in Deferred Revenue. Rent of $1,300 was unpaid and recorded in Accounts Payable at December 31.
- OTP's notes payable mature in three years, and accrue interest at a 10% annual rate.

January Transactions

a. Included in OTP's January 1 Accounts Receivable balance is a $1,500 balance due from Jeff Letrotski. Jeff is having cash flow problems and cannot pay the $1,500 balance at this time. On 01/01, OTP arranges with Jeff to convert the $1,500 balance to a six-month note, at 12 percent annual interest. Jeff signs the promissory note, which indicates the principal and all interest will be due and payable to OTP on July 1 of this year.

b. OTP paid a $500 insurance premium on 01/02, covering the month of January; the payment is recorded directly as an expense.

c. OTP purchased an additional 150 units of inventory from a supplier on account on 01/05 at a total cost of $9,000, with terms n/30.

d. OTP paid a courier $300 cash on 01/05 for same-day delivery of the 150 units of inventory.

e. The 30 units that OTP's customer paid for in advance in December are delivered to the customer on 01/06.

f. On 01/07, OTP received a purchase allowance of $1,350 on account, and then paid the amount necessary to settle the balance owed to the supplier for the 1/05 purchase of inventory (in c).

g. Sales of 40 units of inventory occurring during the period of 01/07–01/10 are recorded on 01/10. The sales terms are n/30.

h. Collected payments on 01/14 from sales to customers recorded on 01/10.

i. OTP paid the first two weeks' wages to the employees on 01/16. The total paid is $2,200.

j. Wrote off a $1,000 customer's account balance on 01/18. OTP uses the allowance method, not the direct write-off method.

k. Paid $2,600 on 01/19 for December and January rent. See the earlier bullets regarding the December portion. The January portion will expire soon, so it is charged directly to expense.

l. OTP recovered $400 cash on 01/26 from the customer whose account had previously been written off on 01/18.

m. An unrecorded $400 utility bill for January arrived on 01/27. It is due on 02/15 and will be paid then.

n. Sales of 65 units of inventory during the period of 01/10–01/28, with terms n/30, are recorded on 01/28.

o. Of the sales recorded on 01/28, 15 units are returned to OTP on 01/30. The inventory is not damaged and can be resold. OTP charges sales returns to a contra-revenue account.

p. On 01/31, OTP records the $2,200 employee salary that is owed but will be paid February 1.

q. OTP uses the aging method to estimate and adjust for uncollectible accounts on 01/31. All of OTP's accounts receivable fall into a single aging category, for which 8 percent is estimated to be uncollectible. (Update the balances of both relevant accounts prior to determining the appropriate adjustment, and round your calculation to the nearest dollar.)

r. Accrue interest for January on the notes payable on 01/31.

s. Accrue interest for January on Jeff Letrotski's note on 01/31 (see *a*).

Required:

1. Prepare all January journal entries and adjusting entries for items (*a*)–(*s*).

2. If you are completing this problem manually, set up T-accounts using the December 31 balances as the beginning balances, post the journal entries from requirement 1, and prepare an adjusted trial balance at January 31. If you are completing this problem in Connect using the general ledger tool, this requirement will be completed automatically using your previous answers.

3. Prepare an income statement, statement of retained earnings, and classified balance sheet at the end of January.

4. For the month ended January 31, indicate the (*i*) gross profit percentage (rounded to one decimal place), (*ii*) number of units in ending inventory, and (*iii*) cost per unit of ending inventory (include dollars *and* cents).

5. If OTP had used the percentage of sales method (using 2 percent of Net Sales) rather than the aging method, what amounts would OTC's January financial statements have reported for (*i*) Bad Debt Expense and (*ii*) Accounts Receivable, net?

6. If OTP had used LIFO rather than FIFO, what amount would OTC have reported for Cost of Goods Sold on 01/10?

SKILLS DEVELOPMENT CASES

S8-1 Finding Financial Information

LO 8-2, 8-4

The Home Depot

Refer to the financial statements of The Home Depot in Appendix A at the end of this book. (Note: Fiscal 2019 for The Home Depot runs from February 4, 2019, to February 2, 2020. See S1-1 for further explanation.)

1. Where does the company disclose the amount of its Allowance for Doubtful Accounts? (*Hint:* The company refers to its Allowance for Doubtful Accounts as a "Valuation Allowance.")

   a. On the income statement.
   b. On the statement of cash flows.
   c. On both the income statement and balance sheet.
   d. In the notes to the financial statements.

2. Compute the company's receivables turnover ratio and days to collect for the year ended February 2, 2020.

   a. 52.3 times and 7.0 days
   b. 54.5 times and 6.7 days
   c. 6.6 times and 55.3 days
   d. 10.2 times and 35.8 days

LO 8-2, 8-4

Lowe's

S8-2 Finding Financial Information

Refer to the financial statements of Lowe's in Appendix B at the end of this book. (Note: Fiscal 2019 for Lowe's runs from February 2, 2019, to January 31, 2020. See S1-1 for further explanation.)

1. Where does the company report information about its Accounts Receivable?
   a. On the income statement.
   b. On the statement of cash flows.
   c. On both the income statement and balance sheet.
   d. In the notes to the financial statements.

2. For companies that are involved in home improvement retail sales, the receivables turnover ratio and days to collect analyses are useful
   a. Regardless of whether the companies sell their receivables to a factor.
   b. Only if the companies do not have significant credit sales.
   c. Only if the companies do not sell their receivables to a factor.
   d. Regardless of whether the companies have significant credit sales.

LO 8-2, 8-4

S8-3 Internet-Based Team Research: Examining an Annual Report

As a team, select an industry to analyze. Using your web browser, each team member should access the annual report or 10-K for one publicly traded company in the industry, with each member selecting a different company. (See S1-3 in Chapter 1 for a description of possible resources for these tasks.)

Required:

1. On an individual basis, each team member should write a short report that incorporates the following:
   a. Calculate the receivables turnover ratio for the current and prior year, and explain any change between the two years. (To obtain the beginning accounts receivable number for the prior year, you will need the prior year's annual report.)
   b. Look in the 10-K for the Schedule II analysis of "Valuation and Qualifying Accounts," which provides additional disclosures concerning the Allowance for Doubtful Accounts. From this schedule, determine the level of Bad Debt Expense, as a percentage of sales, for the current and prior years.

2. Then, as a team, write a short report comparing and contrasting your companies using these attributes. Discuss any patterns across the companies that you as a team observe. Provide potential explanations for any differences discovered.

LO 8-2, 8-3

MCI
WorldCom

S8-4 Ethical Decision Making: A Real-Life Example

You work for a company named MCI and you have been assigned the job of adjusting the company's Allowance for Doubtful Accounts balance. You obtained the following aged listing of customer account balances for December.

Accounts Receivable Aged Listing—December 31						
Customer	Total	0–30 days	31–60 days	61–90 days	91–120 days	>120 days
AfriTel	40,000	20,000	10,000	5,000	5,000	0
CT&T	0	0	0	0	0	0
GlobeCom	28,000	0	18,000	8,000	1,000	1,000
Hi-Rim	35,000	0	0	0	0	35,000
Level 8	162,000	63,000	44,000	29,000	13,000	13,000
NewTel	0	0	0	0	0	0
Telemedia	0	0	0	0	0	0
Others	485,000	257,000	188,000	28,000	11,000	1,000
TOTAL	**750,000**	**340,000**	**260,000**	**70,000**	**30,000**	**50,000**

Bad debt loss rates for each aging category are estimated to be 1 percent (0–30 days), 5 percent (31–60 days), 8 percent (61–90 days), 10 percent (91–120 days), and 50 percent (> 120 days). Using these rates, you calculate a desired balance for the allowance. No entries have been made to the account since the end of November, when the account had a credit balance of $46,820.

To check the reasonableness of the calculated balance, you obtain the aged listings for prior months (shown below). As you scan the listings, you notice an interesting pattern. Several account balances, which had grown quite large by the end of November, had disappeared in the final month of the year. You ask the accounts receivable manager, Walter Pavlo, what happened. He said the customers "obtained some financing . . . I guess out of nowhere" and they must have used it to pay off their account balances.

	Total Accounts Receivable as of . . .					
	Q1	Q2	Q3	Q4		
Customer	(March 31)	(June 30)	(September 30)	(October 31)	(November 30)	(December 31)
AfriTel	19,000	19,000	21,000	16,000	20,000	40,000
CT&T	0	30,000	100,000	100,000	100,000	0
GlobeCom	29,000	28,000	31,000	27,000	28,000	28,000
Hi-Rim	0	0	25,000	35,000	35,000	35,000
Level 8	229,000	229,000	198,000	174,000	190,000	162,000
NewTel	0	0	25,000	25,000	25,000	0
Telemedia	0	0	2,000	2,000	2,000	0
Others	524,000	489,000	375,000	503,000	463,000	485,000
TOTAL	**801,000**	**795,000**	**777,000**	**882,000**	**863,000**	**750,000**

Required:

1. Calculate the balance that should be reported in Allowance for Doubtful Accounts as of December 31.
2. Prepare the adjusting journal entry that is required on December 31.
3. Show how Accounts Receivable would be reported on the balance sheet at December 31.
4. If the balances for CT&T, NewTel, and Telemedia at the end of November continued to exist at the end of December (in the over-120-days category), what balance would you have estimated for the Allowance for Doubtful Accounts on December 31? Would this have changed MCI's net income in the current year? Explain.
5. A few days later, you overhear Mr. Pavlo talking about the accounts receivable from Hi-Rim. Apparently, MCI will soon loan Hi-Rim some money, creating notes receivable. Hi-Rim will use the money to pay off the Accounts Receivable balance it owes to MCI. You are aware that Mr. Pavlo receives a bonus based on MCI's net income. Should you investigate this matter further? Explain why or why not.

Epilogue: The events described above are based on an article in the June 10, 2002, issue of *Forbes* magazine that describes how Walter Pavlo was pressured to commit accounting fraud at MCI. Ironically, MCI was later taken over by WorldCom—the company that went on to commit the world's largest accounting fraud at the time.

S8-5 Ethical Decision Making: A Mini-Case

LO 8-2

This case is available online in the Connect eBook. By completing this case, you will learn what "earnings management" and "smoothing earnings" mean, and you will see how it occurs when estimates of uncollectible accounts are unethically biased.

S8-6 Critical Thinking: Analyzing the Impact of Credit Policies

LO 8-1, 8-4

Problem Solved Company has been operating for five years as a software consulting firm. During this period, it has experienced rapid growth in Sales Revenue and in Accounts Receivable. To solve its growing receivables problem, the company hired you as its first corporate controller. You have put into place more stringent credit-granting and collection procedures that you expect will reduce receivables by approximately one-third by year-end. You have gathered the following data related to the changes (in thousands):

	(in thousands)	
	Beginning of Year	End of Year (projected)
Accounts Receivable	$1,000,608	$660,495
Allowance for Doubtful Accounts	36,800	10,225
Accounts Receivable, Net	$ 963,808	$650,270
	Prior Year	Current Year (projected)
Net Sales (assume all on credit)	$7,515,444	$7,015,069

Required:

1. Compute, to one decimal place, the accounts receivable turnover ratio based on three different assumptions:

   a. The stringent credit policies reduce Accounts Receivable, Net, and decrease Net Sales as projected in the table.

   b. The stringent credit policies reduce Accounts Receivable, Net, as projected in the table but do not decrease Net Sales from the prior year.

   c. The stringent credit policies are not implemented, resulting in no change from the beginning-of-the-year Accounts Receivable balance and no change in Net Sales from the prior year.

2. On the basis of your findings in requirement 1, write a brief memo to the chief financial officer explaining the potential benefits and drawbacks of more stringent credit policies and how they are likely to affect the accounts receivable turnover ratio.

LO 8-2

Caffe D'Amore

S8-7 Using an Aging Schedule to Estimate Bad Debts and Improve Collections from Customers

Assume you were recently hired by Caffe D'Amore, the company that formulated the world's first flavored instant cappuccino and now manufactures several lines of flavored cappuccino mixes. Given the company's tremendous sales growth, Caffe D'Amore's receivables also have grown. Your job is to evaluate and improve collections of the company's receivables.

To determine this year's uncollectible receivables, you jotted down the estimated loss rates on the last page of a recent aged listing of outstanding customer balances (see below).

		Number of Days Unpaid				
Customer	Total	1–30	31–60	61–90	91–120	Over 120
Subtotal from previous page	$280,000	$150,000	$60,000	$40,000	$20,000	$10,000
Jumpy Jim's Coffee	1,000					1,000
Pasadena Coffee Company	24,500	14,500	8,000	2,000		
Phillips Blender House	17,000	12,000	4,000		1,000	
Pugsly's Trading Post	26,600	19,600	7,000			
Q-Coffee	12,400	8,400	3,000	1,000		
Special Sips	10,000	6,000	4,000			
Uneasy Isaac's	3,500	500				3,000
Total accounts receivable	**375,000**	**211,000**	**86,000**	**43,000**	**21,000**	**14,000**
Bad debt loss rates		1%	5%	10%	15%	30%

Required:

1. Enter the above totals in a spreadsheet and then insert formulas to calculate the total estimated uncollectible balance.

2. Prepare the year-end adjusting journal entry to adjust the Allowance for Doubtful Accounts to the balance you calculated above. Assume the allowance account has an unadjusted credit balance of $8,000.

3. Of the customer account balances shown above on the last page of the aged listing, which should be your highest priority for contacting and pursuing collection?

4. Assume Jumpy Jim's Coffee account is determined to be uncollectible. Prepare the journal entry to write off the entire account balance.

CONTINUING CASE

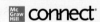

CC8-1 Accounting for Receivables and Uncollectible Accounts

LO 8-2, 8-4

The following transactions occurred over the months of September to December at Nicole's Getaway Spa (NGS).

September	Sold spa merchandise to Ashley Welch Beauty for $1,800 on account; the cost of these goods to NGS was $900.
October	Sold merchandise to Kelly Fast Nail Gallery for $450 on account; the cost of these goods to NGS was $200.
November	Sold merchandise to Raea Gooding Wellness for $300 on account; the cost of these goods to NGS was $190.
December	Received $1,200 from Ashley Welch Beauty for payment on its account.

Required:

1. Prepare journal entries for each of the transactions. Assume a perpetual inventory system.
2. Estimate the Allowance for Doubtful Accounts required at December 31, assuming the only receivables outstanding at December 31 arise from the transactions listed above. NGS uses the aging of accounts receivable method with the following uncollectible rates: one month, 2 percent; two months, 5 percent; three months, 20 percent; more than three months, 35 percent.
3. The Allowance for Doubtful Accounts balance was $47 (credit) before the end-of-period adjusting entry is made. Prepare the journal entry to account for the Bad Debt Expense.
4. Assume the end of the previous year showed net accounts receivable of $800, and net sales for the current year are $9,000. Calculate the accounts receivable turnover ratio (round to one decimal place).
5. Audrey's Mineral Spa has an accounts receivable turnover ratio of 12.0 times. How does NGS compare to this competitor?

DATA ANALYTICS EXERCISES

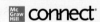

Data Analytics Exercises are auto-graded exercises offering detailed data visualization, interpretation, and analysis, and are available for assignment in *Connect*.

9

Long-Lived Tangible and Intangible Assets

CHAPTER NINE

THAT WAS THEN

In the past few chapters, you learned about the sale of goods and services to customers.

Doug Lemke/Shutterstock

FOCUS COMPANY: CEDAR FAIR

Most people agonize over how much money to spend on a house or which car to buy. After all, they will own these expensive items for many years to come. The same concerns exist when companies acquire long-lived assets. A major challenge business managers face is determining the right amount to invest in long-lived assets.

The task is especially challenging for companies such as Disney, Six Flags, and Cedar Fair, which operate amusement parks. Unlike merchandising companies, an amusement park cannot build up an inventory of unused roller-coaster seats to be sold sometime in the future. If managers build more rides than needed to satisfy park-goers, some rides will run with empty seats. Although the company will still incur all the costs of running the rides, it will generate only a fraction of the potential revenue. On the other hand, amusement parks also can run into trouble if they have too few rides to satisfy patrons. Fortunately for managers, accounting reports provide information to evaluate a company's investment in long-lived assets.

In this chapter, you will study specific long-lived asset decisions at Cedar Fair, which is headquartered in Sandusky, Ohio, and owns and operates 11 amusement parks, three water parks, and four hotels throughout North America. You will see the significant effect that long-lived assets can have on a company's financial statements. Although manufacturing companies, retailers, and even airlines must deal with the same issues as Cedar Fair, the impact on this amusement park company is particularly significant because it relies almost exclusively on long-lived assets. As of December 31, 2018, in fact, Cedar Fair's rides, hotels, and other long-lived assets accounted for about 90 percent of its total assets.

THIS IS NOW

This chapter focuses on the assets that enable companies to produce and sell goods and services.

ORGANIZATION OF THE CHAPTER

Understand the business	Study the accounting methods	Evaluate the results	Supplement 9A	Supplement 9B	Review the chapter
• Definition and classification	• Tangible assets • Intangible assets	• Turnover analysis • Impact of depreciation differences	• Natural resources	• Changes in depreciation	• Demonstration case • Chapter summary • Key terms • Homework helper • Practice material

Understand the Business

DEFINITION AND CLASSIFICATION

Long-lived assets are business assets acquired for use over one or more years. These assets are not intended for resale. Instead, they are considered "productive" assets in the sense they produce the goods or services the business then sells to customers. Examples include the computers Noodlecake Studios uses to make its game apps, the stores where Walmart sells merchandise, and the legal rights that restrict use of the American Eagle Outfitters logo. So when you hear the term "long-lived assets," think more broadly than just rusty old equipment. This class of assets includes two major types: tangible and intangible.

1. **Tangible assets.** These are long-lived assets that have physical substance, which simply means you can see, touch, or kick them. The most prominent examples of tangible assets are land, buildings, machinery, vehicles, office equipment, and furniture and fixtures. These assets are typically grouped into a single line item on the balance sheet called Property, Plant, and Equipment. They are also known as **fixed assets** because they are often fixed in place. Cedar Fair's tangible assets include roller coasters, hotels, and land in the western, midwestern, and northeastern United States.

2. **Intangible assets.** These long-lived assets have special rights but no physical substance. The existence of most intangible assets is indicated only by legal documents that describe their rights. Compared to the tangible assets you see in daily life, intangible assets are probably less familiar to you. For this reason, we'll describe the various types of intangibles in detail later in this chapter. For now you can think of this category as including brand names, trademarks, and licensing rights such as the ones that allow Cedar Fair's exclusive use of PEANUTS® characters throughout its amusement parks until 2025.

A third category of long-lived assets that are depleted over time, like an oil well or gold mine, is common in natural resource industries. Chapter Supplement 9A describes how to account for these natural resource assets.

EXHIBIT 9.1	Cedar Fair's Assets		

		AT DECEMBER 31	
(in millions)		**2018**	**2017**
Assets			
Current Assets (details omitted to save space)		$ 200	$ 250
Property and Equipment			
Land		270	270
Land Improvements		435	420
Buildings		735	695
Equipment		1,810	1,740
Construction in Progress		80	75
Property and Equipment, at cost		3,330	3,200
Accumulated Depreciation		(1,730)	(1,615)
Property and Equipment, net		1,600	1,585
Goodwill and Other Intangible Assets, net		215	220
Other Assets		10	10
Total Assets		$2,025	$2,065

>  **COACH'S TIP**
>
> Accumulated Depreciation is reported here as a total for the entire tangible assets category. Alternatively, it can be reported separately for each type of tangible asset.

Exhibit 9.1 shows how Cedar Fair reported long-lived assets on its balance sheet. From this exhibit, you can see how important tangible and intangible assets are to Cedar Fair. Of the $2.0 billion in total assets at December 31, 2018, Cedar Fair owned long-lived assets totaling more than $1.8 billion ($1,600 + $215 = $1,815, in millions).

Study the Accounting Methods

In this section, you will study the accounting decisions that relate to long-lived assets. We'll start with tangible long-lived assets and consider key accounting decisions related to their (1) acquisition, (2) use, and (3) disposal. Accounting for intangible assets will be the focus of the last part of this section.

TANGIBLE ASSETS

Most companies own a variety of tangible assets. Earlier chapters introduced you to the most common examples: land, buildings, equipment, and automobiles. Other, less common examples include land improvements and construction in progress—both of which Cedar Fair reported on its balance sheet in Exhibit 9.1. **Land improvements** include the sidewalks, pavement, landscaping, fencing, lighting, and sprinkler systems that are added to improve the usefulness of land. Land improvements differ from land in that they deteriorate over time, whereas land is assumed to last forever. **Construction in progress** includes the costs of constructing new buildings and equipment. When construction is finished, these costs are moved from this account into the building or equipment account to which they relate.

> **Learning Objective 9-2**
> Apply the cost principle to the acquisition of long-lived assets.

Acquisition of Tangible Assets

The general rule for tangible assets under the cost principle is that **all reasonable and necessary costs to acquire and prepare an asset for use should be recorded as a cost of the asset.** Accountants say costs have been **capitalized** when they are recorded as assets (rather than as expenses).

> **YOU SHOULD KNOW**
> **Capitalize:** To record a cost as an asset, rather than an expense.

Deciding whether a cost is a reasonable and necessary cost to acquire or prepare tangible assets for use can involve a great deal of judgment. Because capitalizing costs has a significant impact on both the balance sheet (it increases assets) and the income statement (it decreases expenses), some dishonest accountants and managers have exploited the judgment involved in this decision by capitalizing costs that should have been expensed. A well-known example of this tactic is described in the following Spotlight on Ethics feature. As you read this Spotlight and the discussion that follows, focus on distinguishing between what costs should be capitalized and what costs should be expensed.

SPOTLIGHT ON | Ethics

Simple Violations, Serious Consequences

In the early 2000s, executives at WorldCom (now part of Verizon) committed an $11 billion fraud by capitalizing costs that should have been expensed. In 2017, the SEC charged Obsidian Energy for the same type of fraud. These decisions led the companies to report huge increases in assets (rather than expenses) when the costs were incurred. As a result, their balance sheets appeared stronger (more total assets) and income statements appeared more profitable (lower expenses) than would have been the case had the costs been properly expensed. Learn more about the WorldCom fraud in Case S9-4 at the end of this chapter.

The illustration that follows shows the types of costs that should be capitalized when a tangible asset is acquired. All are necessary for acquiring and preparing tangible assets for use. Notice they are not limited to the amounts paid to purchase or construct the assets. For example, the Land account at Cedar Fair would include legal fees for title searches, fees for land surveys, and commissions paid to brokers when purchasing the land on Ohio's Sandusky Bay shown in the photograph on the left. Take a moment right now to read the lists of costs that should be capitalized when buildings (middle) and equipment (right) are acquired.

Land

Purchase cost
Legal fees
Survey fees
Title search fees

Buildings

Purchase/construction cost
Legal fees
Appraisal fees
Architect fees

Equipment

Purchase/construction cost
Sales taxes
Transportation costs
Installation costs

If a company buys land, a building, or a piece of used equipment and incurs demolition, renovation, or repair costs before it can be used, these additional costs are capitalized as a cost of the land, building, or equipment. These costs are capitalized because they are needed to prepare the asset for use.

Aerial photo: Courtesy of Cedar Point; Hotel photo: Courtesy of Cedar Point; Coaster photo: Courtesy of Cedar Point

In some cases, land, buildings, and equipment are purchased together, such as when Cedar Fair bought five amusement parks from Paramount Parks. When this type of "basket purchase" occurs, the total cost is split among the assets in proportion to the market value of the assets as a whole. For example, if Cedar Fair were to pay $10 million for a hotel and the land surrounding it, based on an appraisal that estimates the land contributes 40 percent of the property's value and the building contributes 60 percent, Cedar Fair would record 40 percent of the total cost as land ($4 million) and the other 60 percent as buildings ($6 million). Splitting the total purchase price among individual assets is necessary because they may be used over different periods. For example, the hotel may be used over 50 years. However, **land is never used up,** so any costs assigned to Land will remain undepreciated in that account until Cedar Fair sells the land.

Total Cost
$10 million

40%   Percent of total value   60%

$4 million
Land

$6 million
Buildings

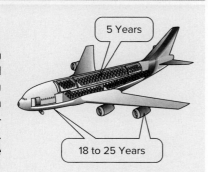

SPOTLIGHT ON | The World

Component Allocation

IFRS takes the idea of a basket purchase one step further. The cost of an individual asset's components is allocated among each significant component and then depreciated separately over that component's useful life. For example, British Airways (now merged into International Airlines Group) separates the cost of an aircraft between its body and engines versus interior cabin space, and then depreciates the body and engines over 18 to 25 years, and the cabin interior over 5 years. Likewise, TWC Enterprises distinguishes the cost and useful life of its golf course bunkers (20 years) from its fairways (unlimited life).

5 Years

18 to 25 Years

To illustrate how the costs of tangible assets are recorded, let's consider the Top Thrill Dragster that Cedar Fair purchased from Intamin, a Swiss roller-coaster manufacturer. When it was purchased, the Top Thrill Dragster was the biggest, fastest roller coaster in the world. Some of its specs are shown in the following graphic.

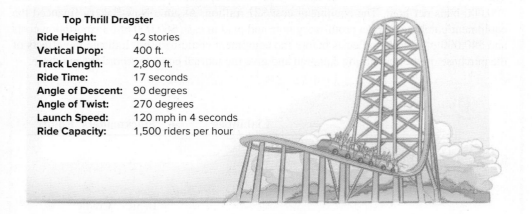

Top Thrill Dragster

Ride Height:	42 stories
Vertical Drop:	400 ft.
Track Length:	2,800 ft.
Ride Time:	17 seconds
Angle of Descent:	90 degrees
Angle of Twist:	270 degrees
Launch Speed:	120 mph in 4 seconds
Ride Capacity:	1,500 riders per hour

Assume the list price for the roller coaster (including sales tax) was $26 million, but Cedar Fair received a $1 million discount. In other words, the roller coaster's net purchase price to Cedar Fair was $25 million. Assume too that Cedar Fair paid $125,000 to have the roller coaster delivered and another $625,000 to have it assembled and prepared for use.

Because these expenditures are necessary to acquire and prepare the asset for use, Cedar Fair would capitalize the expenditures as part of the cost of the asset as follows:

List price	$26,000,000
Less: Discount	1,000,000
Net invoice price	25,000,000
Add: Transportation costs paid by Cedar Fair	125,000
Installation costs paid by Cedar Fair	625,000
Total cost of the roller coaster	$25,750,000

The total $25,750,000 cost would be the amount Cedar Fair recorded in the Equipment account regardless of how the company paid for or financed the roller coaster. If we assume Cedar Fair signed a note payable for the new roller coaster and paid cash for the transportation and installation costs, the accounting equation effects and journal entry would be:

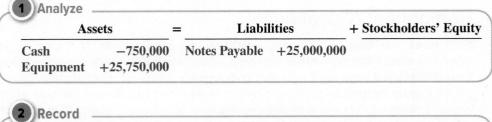

1 Analyze

Assets	=	Liabilities	+ Stockholders' Equity
Cash −750,000		Notes Payable +25,000,000	
Equipment +25,750,000			

2 Record

	Debit	Credit
Equipment	25,750,000	
Cash		750,000
Notes Payable		25,000,000

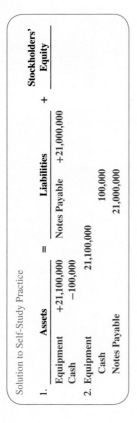

Solution to Self-Study Practice

	Assets	=	Liabilities	+	Stockholders' Equity
1. Equipment	+21,100,000		Notes Payable +21,000,000		
Cash	−100,000				
2. Equipment	21,100,000				
Cash			100,000		
Notes Payable			21,000,000		

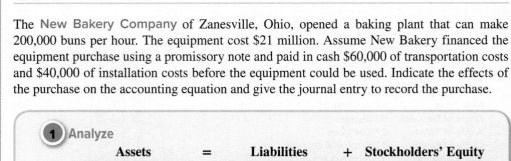

💡 **How's it going?**   Self-Study Practice

The **New Bakery Company** of Zanesville, Ohio, opened a baking plant that can make 200,000 buns per hour. The equipment cost $21 million. Assume New Bakery financed the equipment purchase using a promissory note and paid in cash $60,000 of transportation costs and $40,000 of installation costs before the equipment could be used. Indicate the effects of the purchase on the accounting equation and give the journal entry to record the purchase.

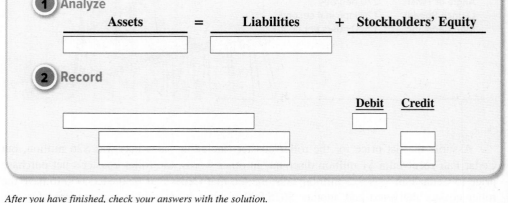

1 Analyze

Assets	=	Liabilities	+	Stockholders' Equity

2 Record

	Debit	Credit

After you have finished, check your answers with the solution.

Before we leave this section, we should mention that not all fixed asset costs are capitalized. The cost of some fixed assets, like staplers or hole punches, is such a small dollar amount that it's not worth the trouble of recording them as fixed assets. Such policies are acceptable because immaterial amounts (small in relation to the company) will not affect users' analysis of financial statements. **Other costs that are expensed as incurred include insurance for fixed assets in use, interest on loans to purchase fixed assets, and ordinary repairs and maintenance,** as discussed in the next section.

Use of Tangible Assets

Maintenance Costs Incurred during Use   Most tangible assets require substantial expenditures over the course of their lives to maintain or enhance their operation. Maintenance is a big deal in the roller-coaster industry, where safety is vital. Companies in this industry spend a lot of money on two types of maintenance: (1) ordinary repairs and maintenance and (2) extraordinary repairs and maintenance.

1. **Ordinary repairs and maintenance. Ordinary repairs and maintenance** are expenditures for the routine maintenance and upkeep of long-lived assets. Just like an oil change for your car, these are recurring, relatively small expenditures that do not directly increase an asset's usefulness. Because these costs occur frequently to maintain the asset's productive capacity for a short time, they are recorded as expenses in the current period. Because these expenses are matched to revenues, ordinary repairs and maintenance are sometimes called **revenue expenditures.**

   In the case of Cedar Fair, ordinary repairs and maintenance includes applying orange paint to the tracks of The Bat roller coaster at Kings Island outside Cincinnati, replacing the lights on the eight-story Giant Gondola wheel at Michigan's Adventure, and fixing the harnesses on the Rougarou roller coaster at Cedar Point in Ohio.

2. **Extraordinary repairs, replacements, and additions.** In contrast to ordinary repairs and maintenance, **extraordinary repairs occur infrequently, involve large expenditures, and increase an asset's usefulness through enhanced efficiency, capacity, or lifespan.** Examples include additions, major overhauls, complete reconditioning, and major replacements and improvements, such as the replacement of the passenger train on a roller coaster. Because these costs increase the usefulness of tangible assets beyond their original condition, they are added to the appropriate long-lived asset accounts. Because doing so means capitalizing costs, these extraordinary repairs, replacements, and additions are called **capital expenditures.**

Alan Schein/The Image Bank/Getty

> **YOU SHOULD KNOW**
>
> **Ordinary Repairs and Maintenance:** Expenditures for the normal operating upkeep of long-lived assets, recorded as expenses. **Extraordinary Repairs:** Infrequent expenditures that increase an asset's economic usefulness in the future and that are capitalized.

 How's it going?   Self-Study Practice

As you know from living in a house, apartment, or residence hall, buildings often require maintenance and repair. For each of the following expenditures, indicate whether it should be expensed in the current period or capitalized.

Expense or Capitalize?

1. Replacing electrical wiring throughout the building.
2. Repairing the hinge on the front door of the building.
3. Yearly cleaning of the building's air-conditioning filters.
4. Replacing load-bearing walls with a laminated beam.

After you have finished, check your answers with the solution.

Solution to Self-Study Practice
1. Capitalize—extends life.
2. Expense—does not increase usefulness.
3. Expense—does not increase usefulness.
4. Capitalize—extends life and usefulness.

Depreciation Expense In addition to repairs and maintenance expense, a company reports depreciation expense every period buildings and equipment are used to generate revenue. Depreciation doesn't involve new payments for using the asset. Rather, **depreciation** is the allocation of existing costs that were already recorded as a long-lived asset. Think of the cost of a long-lived asset as a big prepayment for future benefits. As that asset is used, those prepaid benefits are used up, so the asset needs to be decreased each period. This decrease in the asset creates an expense, which is reported on the income statement and matched against the revenue generated by the asset, as required by accrual accounting.

As you learned in Chapter 4, depreciation affects one income statement account and one balance sheet account. The income statement account, Depreciation Expense, reports the depreciation of the current period. The balance sheet account, Accumulated Depreciation, contains the current period's depreciation as well as that of prior periods. It is an **accumulation** over several periods. The effects of $125 of depreciation on the accounting equation and the journal entry to record these effects follow:

1 Analyze

Assets	= Liabilities +	Stockholders' Equity	
Accumulated Depreciation (+xA)	−125	Depreciation Expense (+E)	−125

2 Record

	Debit	Credit
Depreciation Expense	125	
Accumulated Depreciation (+xA)		125

Exhibit 9.2 shows how Cedar Fair reported its depreciation in 2018. The income statement on the right shows the $155 million of Depreciation Expense in 2018. The balance sheet on the left shows that this depreciation, when combined with depreciation of prior years, brought the total Accumulated Depreciation to $1,730 million at December 31, 2018. The $1,600 difference between the Property and Equipment's $3,330 cost and $1,730 of Accumulated Depreciation is called the **book (or carrying) value**. Most companies report a breakdown of these totals by class of asset (e.g., buildings, equipment) in their financial statement notes.

EXHIBIT 9.2 Reporting Depreciation on the Balance Sheet and Income Statement

Balance Sheet (in millions)	Dec. 31, 2018
Assets	
Property and Equipment, at cost	$3,330
Accumulated Depreciation	(1,730)
Property and Equipment, net	1,600

(in millions) Income Statement	2018
Net Revenues	$1,350
Operating Expenses:	
Food and Operating Expenses	701
Selling, General, and Other	195
Depreciation Expense	155
Impairment Loss	10
Loss (Gain) on Disposals	(1)
Total Operating Expenses	1,060
Income from Operations	290

One way to interpret the information on the left side of Exhibit 9.2 is the Property and Equipment's $3,330 million cost represents the assets' total economic benefits. Thus, $155 million of Depreciation Expense means Cedar Fair used up about 4.7 percent

($155/$3,330 = 0.047) of the assets' benefits in 2018. As of December 31, 2018, 52 percent ($1,730/$3,330 = 0.520) of their total benefits had been used up.

To fully understand the depreciation numbers in Exhibit 9.2, you need to know how they are calculated. Depreciation calculations are based on the following three items:

1. **Asset cost.** This includes all the asset's capitalized costs, including the purchase cost, sales tax, legal fees, and other costs needed to acquire and prepare the asset for use.

2. **Useful life. Useful life** is an estimate of the asset's useful economic life to the company (not its economic life to all potential users). It may be expressed in terms of years or units of capacity, such as the number of units it can produce or the number of miles it will travel. **Land is the only tangible asset that's assumed to have an unlimited (indefinite) useful life. Because of this, land is not depreciated.**

3. **Residual value. Residual (or salvage) value** is an estimate of the amount the company will receive when it disposes of the asset. Cedar Fair will recover some of the initial cost of its roller coasters when it disposes of them either by selling them "as is" to local amusement companies or by dismantling them and selling their parts to other roller-coaster or scrap metal companies.

The basic idea of depreciation is to match the economic benefit that will be used up (asset cost minus residual value) to the periods the asset is used to generate revenue (useful life). Residual value is considered when calculating depreciation because we want to leave a little of the asset's cost in the accounts after we have finished depreciating it. We do this because, when we dispose of the asset, we're likely to get back some of the money we initially paid for the asset. So the amount to be depreciated over the asset's life is the difference between its cost and residual value, an amount called the **depreciable cost**. A company should record depreciation each year of an asset's useful life until its total accumulated depreciation equals its depreciable cost. After that, the company should report no additional depreciation expense, even if the company continues to use the asset.

If every company used the same techniques for calculating depreciation, we'd stop right here. But they don't. Companies own different assets and use them differently, so they are allowed to choose from several alternative depreciation methods. These alternative depreciation methods produce different patterns of depreciation, as represented by the depreciation amounts recorded each year.

Depreciation Methods   **The depreciation method chosen for each type of property, plant, and equipment should reflect the pattern in which those assets' economic benefits are used up.** We discuss the three most common depreciation methods:

1. **Straight-line**—when usage is the same each period.

2. **Units-of-production**—when usage varies each period.

3. **Declining-balance**—when the asset is more efficient (generates more revenues) in early years but less so over time; also used for tax.

To show how each method works, let's assume Cedar Fair acquired a new go-kart ride on January 1. The relevant information is shown in Exhibit 9.3.

EXHIBIT 9.3	Information for Depreciation Computations

CEDAR FAIR—Acquisition of a New Go-Kart Ride

Cost, purchased on January 1	$62,500
Estimated residual value	$2,500
Estimated useful life	3 years; 100,000 miles

Straight-Line Method Managers choose the **straight-line depreciation method** when an asset is expected to be used up in equal amounts each period of the asset's estimated useful life. The straight-line formula for estimating annual depreciation expense is

Straight-Line Formula

$$(\text{Cost} - \text{Residual Value}) \times \frac{1}{\text{Useful Life}} = \text{Depreciation Expense}$$

Depreciable cost   Depreciation rate

In the straight-line formula, Cost − Residual Value is the total amount to be depreciated (the depreciable cost). The depreciation rate is 1/Useful Life. Using the information in Exhibit 9.3, the depreciation expense for Cedar Fair's new ride is $20,000 per year, calculated in the following depreciation schedule:

Straight-line (Cost − Residual Value) × (1/Useful Life)			INCOME STATEMENT		BALANCE SHEET		
Year	Yearly Computation		Depreciation Expense	Cost −	Accumulated Depreciation =	Book Value	
At acquisition				$62,500	$ 0	$ 62,500	
Year 1	($62,500 − $2,500) × (1/3)	amounts for	$20,000	62,500	20,000	42,500	
Year 2	($62,500 − $2,500) × (1/3)	adjusting entry	20,000	62,500	40,000	22,500	
Year 3	($62,500 − $2,500) × (1/3)	each year	20,000	62,500	60,000	2,500	
	Total		$60,000		↑ used cost to-date	↑ unused cost to-date	

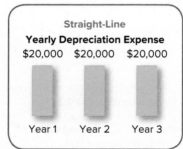

Straight-Line
Yearly Depreciation Expense
$20,000 $20,000 $20,000
Year 1   Year 2   Year 3

Take a moment to study the straight-line depreciation schedule. Notice that as the name *straight-line* suggests,

1. **Depreciation Expense** is a constant amount each year.
2. **Accumulated Depreciation** increases by an equal amount each year.
3. **Book Value** decreases by the same equal amount each year.

Notice too that at the end of the asset's life, accumulated depreciation ($60,000) equals the asset's depreciable cost ($62,500 − $2,500), and book value ($2,500) equals residual value.

As you will see with other depreciation methods, the amount of depreciation depends on estimates of an asset's useful life and residual value at the end of that life. A question people often ask is: **How do accountants estimate useful lives and residual values?** While some of this information can be obtained from the asset's supplier or from other sources such as reseller databases or insurance companies, the simple answer is that professional judgment is required. Because useful lives and residual values are difficult to estimate with precision, accountants are encouraged to update their calculations regularly (see Supplement 9B at the end of this chapter).

Units-of-Production Method Choose the **units-of-production depreciation method** if the amount of asset production varies significantly from period to period. An asset's production can be defined in terms of miles, products, or machine-hours. The units-of-production formula for estimating depreciation expense is

Units-of-Production
Yearly Depreciation Expense
$30,000
$18,000
$12,000
Year 1   Year 2   Year 3

Units-of-Production Formula

$$(\text{Cost} - \text{Residual Value}) \times \frac{\text{Actual Production This Period}}{\text{Estimated Total Production}} = \text{Depreciation Expense}$$

Depreciable cost   Depreciation rate

If the go-kart ride in Exhibit 9.3 was driven 30,000 miles in Year 1, 50,000 miles in Year 2, and 20,000 miles in Year 3, the units-of-production method would calculate depreciation in each year of the asset's life as follows:

Units-of-production
(Cost − Residual Value) × (Actual/Estimated Total Production)

| | | INCOME STATEMENT | BALANCE SHEET | | |
| | | Depreciation | | Accumulated | Book |
Year	Yearly Computation	Expense	Cost −	Depreciation =	Value
At acquisition			$62,500	$ 0	$62,500
Year 1	($62,500 − $2,500) × (30,000/100,000 miles)	$18,000	62,500	18,000	44,500
Year 2	($62,500 − $2,500) × (50,000/100,000 miles)	30,000	62,500	48,000	14,500
Year 3	($62,500 − $2,500) × (20,000/100,000 miles)	12,000	62,500	60,000	2,500
	Total	$60,000			

An alternative, but equivalent, approach to calculating units-of-production depreciation is to determine the depreciation per unit and then multiply that by the current period's actual production. For our example, depreciation per unit is $0.60 per mile [($62,500 − $2,500)/100,000], so the year 2 depreciation is $0.60 × 50,000 miles = $30,000. Regardless of the approach you use, **under the units-of-production method, the depreciation expense, accumulated depreciation, and book value vary from period to period, depending on the number of units produced.**

Declining-Balance Method   The **declining-balance depreciation method** is used to report more depreciation expense in the early years of an asset's life when the asset is more efficient and less in later years as the asset becomes less efficient. Because this method speeds up depreciation reporting, it is sometimes called an accelerated method. Although accelerated methods are used infrequently for financial reporting purposes in the United States, they are used commonly in financial reporting in other countries, such as Japan and Canada, as well as in tax reporting in the United States (a point we discuss in greater detail later).

Notice the declining-balance formula below uses book value (Cost − Accumulated Depreciation) rather than depreciable cost (Cost − Residual Value). This slight difference in the formula produces declining amounts of depreciation as the asset ages. In the first year of an asset's life, the beginning balance in Accumulated Depreciation is zero. However, with each passing year as additional depreciation is recorded, the Accumulated Depreciation balance increases, which causes (Cost − Accumulated Depreciation) to decrease, which then causes the amount of double-declining depreciation expense to decline each year.

> **YOU SHOULD KNOW**
>
> Declining-Balance Depreciation Method: Allocates the cost of an asset over its useful life based on a multiple of (often two times) the straight-line rate.

Double-Declining-Balance Formula

$$(\text{Cost} - \text{Accumulated Depreciation}) \times \frac{2}{\text{Useful Life}} = \text{Depreciation Expense}$$

Book value at beginning of period   Depreciation rate

The depreciation rate for the declining balance method also differs from that used in the straight-line method. In the formula above, we show a rate of 2/Useful Life, which is the most common declining depreciation rate. Because the 2/Useful Life rate used in the formula is double the straight-line rate, this particular version of the declining-balance method is called the **double-declining-balance depreciation method.**

Because **residual value is not included in the formula for the declining-balance method of computing depreciation expense,** you must take extra care to ensure an asset's book value is not depreciated beyond its residual value. If the calculated amount of depreciation for the year would reduce the book value below the asset's residual value, you must record a smaller amount of depreciation so the book value will equal the residual value. No depreciation is recorded after the book value reaches the residual value, even if the asset continues to be used. The following depreciation schedule illustrates this point.

Double-declining-balance
(Cost − Accumulated Depreciation) × (2/Useful Life)

		INCOME STATEMENT	BALANCE SHEET			
Year	Yearly Computation	Depreciation Expense	Cost	− Accumulated Depreciation	=	Book Value
At acquisition			$62,500	$ 0		$62,500
Year 1	($62,500 − $0) × (2/3)	$41,667	62,500	41,667		20,833
Year 2	($62,500 − $41,667) × (2/3)	13,889	62,500	55,556		6,944
Year 3	($62,500 − $55,556) × (2/3)	~~4,629~~	62,500	~~60,185~~		~~2,315~~
		4,444	62,500	60,000		**2,500**
	Total	$60,000				

Double-Declining
Yearly Depreciation Expense

Notice the calculated depreciation expense for Year 3 ($4,629) would not be recorded because it would cause the asset's book value to fall below its $2,500 residual value. Instead, in the final year of the asset's life, just enough depreciation ($4,444) is recorded to make the book value of the asset equal its residual value of **$2,500.**

Summary of Depreciation Methods   See Exhibit 9.4 for a summary of the depreciation expense that would be reported in each year of our example under the three alternative depreciation methods. Notice **the amount of depreciation expense recorded in each year of an asset's life depends on the method used. That means the amount of reported net income can vary depending on the depreciation method used.** At the end of an asset's life, after it has been fully depreciated, total depreciation will equal the asset's depreciable cost regardless of the depreciation method used.

EXHIBIT 9.4 | Differences in Depreciation Expense by Method

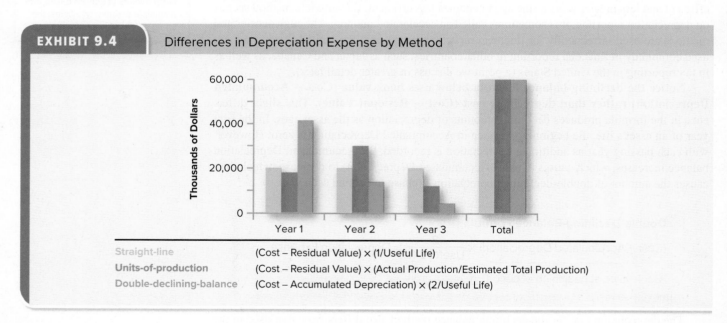

Straight-line   (Cost − Residual Value) × (1/Useful Life)
Units-of-production   (Cost − Residual Value) × (Actual Production/Estimated Total Production)
Double-declining-balance   (Cost − Accumulated Depreciation) × (2/Useful Life)

Different depreciation methods can be used for different classes of assets provided the methods are used consistently over time so that financial statement users can compare results across periods. Tesla, for example, uses straight-line for buildings and units-of-production for tooling. The straight-line method is the most commonly used method because it is easy to use and understand, and it does a good job of matching depreciation expense to revenues, especially when assets are used evenly over their useful lives. The units-of-production method is the typical choice when asset use fluctuates significantly from period to period, as is often the case in extractive resource industries. Declining-balance methods apply best to assets that are most productive when they are new but quickly lose their usefulness as they get older.

How's it going?   Self-Study Practice

Assume **Cedar Fair** has acquired new equipment at a cost of $24,000. The equipment has an estimated life of six years, an estimated operating life to the company of 5,000 hours, and an estimated residual value of $3,000. Determine depreciation expense for the **second year** under each of the following methods:

1. Straight-line method.

   $(24,000 − ☐) × ☐/6 = $☐

2. Double-declining-balance method.

   Year 1: $(24,000 − ☐) × ☐/☐ = $☐
   Year 2: $(24,000 − ☐) × ☐/☐ = $☐

3. Units-of-production method (assume the equipment ran for 800 hours in Year 2).

   $(☐ − ☐) × ☐/5,000 = $☐

After you have finished, check your answers with the solution.

Partial-Year Depreciation Calculations   Purchases of long-lived assets seldom occur on the first day of the accounting period. Consequently, the need arises to calculate depreciation for periods shorter than a year. **Under the straight-line and declining-balance methods, the annual depreciation is multiplied by the fraction of the year for which depreciation is being calculated.**

For purposes of these calculations, accountants typically assume assets were purchased at the beginning of the month nearest to the actual purchase date. For example, if Cedar Fair purchased a ride on October 7, it would have owned the asset for about three months during the year ended December 31. Thus, straight-line depreciation for the ride that year would be calculated by multiplying the annual straight-line depreciation of $20,000 by 3 ÷ 12, representing the 3 months of 12 that Cedar Fair owned it. Similarly, if an asset is disposed of during the year, the annual depreciation is multiplied by the fraction of the year during which the asset was owned. **These partial-year modifications are not required in the units-of-production method because that method is based on actual production for the period.** If the accounting period is shorter than a year, the level of actual production already reflects that shorter period.

Tax Depreciation   Before we leave the topic of depreciation methods, we should note that most companies use one method of depreciation for reporting to stockholders and a different method for determining income taxes. These differences affect the amount of depreciation reported on the company's income statement and tax return. Keeping two sets of accounting records like this is both ethical and legal because the primary objective of financial reporting differs from that of income tax reporting.

Financial Reporting	**Income Tax Reporting**
Objective: Provide economic information about a business that is useful in projecting its future cash flows.	Objective: Raise sufficient tax revenues to pay for the expenditures of the federal government and to encourage certain social and economic behaviors.

One of the behaviors the government wants to encourage is economic renewal and growth. Thus, the IRS allows companies to deduct larger amounts of tax depreciation in the early years of an asset's life than what GAAP allows.[1] The larger tax deduction reduces the company's income taxes significantly in the years immediately following the purchase of a long-lived asset.

Although the IRS allows super-sized deductions in the early years of an asset's life, it doesn't allow a company to depreciate more than an asset's depreciable cost over its life. So the tax savings enjoyed in the early years of an asset's life will eventually be returned to the government in later years of that asset's life. The tax payment that is temporarily put off (deferred) as a result of taking large tax deductions for depreciation is reported as a long-term liability called Deferred Income Tax. The following companies report they deferred significant tax obligations in recent years by choosing different depreciation methods for tax and financial reporting purposes.

Company	Deferred Income Tax Liabilities	Percentage Due to Applying Different Depreciation Methods
AT&T Inc.	$57,860 million	74%
Exxon Mobil Corp.	42,300 million	85
Cedar Fair	110 million	100

The preceding table shows that, like most individuals, companies follow an economic rule called the **least and latest rule.** Taxpayers want to pay the least tax that is legally permitted, and at the latest possible date. If you had the choice of paying taxes of $1,000 at the end of this year or at the end of next year, you would rationally choose the end of next year. Doing so would allow you to invest the money for an extra year and earn a return on your investment.

Asset Impairment Losses

Learning Objective 9-4
Explain the effect of asset impairment on the financial statements.

As a result of recording depreciation, a depreciable asset's book value declines as the asset ages. However, because **depreciation is not intended to report an asset at its current value,** it does not capture a sudden drop in asset value that arises if the asset becomes impaired. **Impairment** occurs when events or changed circumstances interfere with a company's ability to recover the value of the asset through future operations. Impairment can be company-wide, as when Cedar Fair closed its theme parks when the COVID-19 crisis occurred in 2020, or it can be specific to a particular asset. For example, many years ago, one of the steel towers on Cedar Fair's VertiGo slingshot ride mysteriously snapped during the winter (a bizarre phenomenon known as vortex shedding), so the company recorded a $3 million impairment loss when it wrote down the book value of the ride. More recently, in 2018, the company recorded $10 million of impairment losses (see Exhibit 9.2), which included an impairment loss for its Firehawk roller coaster at Kings Island.

YOU SHOULD KNOW

Impairment: Occurs when the cash to be generated by an asset is estimated to be less than the carrying value of that asset and requires that the carrying value of the asset be written down.

An asset impairment is accounted for in two steps: (1) eliminate the asset's Accumulated Depreciation against the asset account and (2) write down the asset to its fair value (what it is worth). For example, assume the Firehawk roller coaster originally cost $10.6 million and had $2.0 million in Accumulated Depreciation when its impairment was recorded. The first step is to net the $2.0 million against the Equipment account, as follows:

1 Analyze

Assets		= Liabilities + Stockholders' Equity
Equipment	−2,000,000	
Accumulated Depreciation (−xA)	+2,000,000	

2 Record

	Debit	Credit
Accumulated Depreciation (−xA)	2,000,000	
Equipment		2,000,000

---

[1]Most corporations use the IRS-approved Modified Accelerated Cost Recovery System (MACRS) to calculate depreciation expense for their tax returns. MACRS is similar to the declining-balance method and is applied over relatively short asset lives set by the IRS to yield high tax deductions for depreciation expense in the early years.

After the first step, the asset account showed a balance of $8.6 million ($10.6 million cost − $2.0 million). The second step is to write down this balance to the asset's fair value, which in this case is presumed to be $0. The accounting equation effects and journal entry for this second step follow:

1 Analyze

Assets	=	Liabilities	+	Stockholders' Equity
Equipment −8,600,000				Impairment Loss (+E) −8,600,000

2 Record

	Debit	Credit
Impairment Loss (+E)	8,600,000	
Equipment		8,600,000

Impairment Loss is classified as an operating expense on the income statement and reported above the Income from Operations subtotal, as shown in Exhibit 9.2.[2]

Disposal of Tangible Assets

A business may voluntarily dispose of an asset before the end of its life. For example, your local gym might replace its treadmills with elliptical trainers. Or, if a company discontinues a product, it may sell the equipment that was used to make the product. To get rid of used assets, companies do just what you do. They trade them in on a new asset, sell them on eBay, or "retire" them to a junkyard.

The disposal of a depreciable asset usually requires two accounting adjustments:

1. **Update the Depreciation Expense and Accumulated Depreciation accounts.** If a long-lived asset is disposed of during the year, it should be depreciated to the date of disposal using the partial-year calculations explained earlier.

2. **Record the disposal.** All disposals of long-lived assets require that you account for (1) the book value of the items given up, (2) the value of the items received on disposal, and (3) any difference between these two amounts, which reflects a gain or loss on the disposal to be reported on the income statement.

Earlier in this chapter, you saw how to compute and record depreciation expense on a long-lived asset (step 1 above), so let's look instead at an example where we only have to record the disposal (step 2). Assume that, at the end of year 6, Cedar Fair sold one of its junior roller coasters for $50,000 cash. The original $100,000 cost of this equipment was depreciated using the straight-line method over 10 years with no residual value ($10,000 depreciation expense per year), resulting in $60,000 of accumulated depreciation at the time of disposal. **A gain (or loss) on disposal represents the difference between the proceeds from selling the asset and the asset's book value (BV),** computed as follows:

Received

Proceeds on disposal		$50,000
− **Book value** of asset sold:		
Cost	$100,000	
Accumulated depreciation	(60,000)	40,000
= **Gain** (loss) on disposal		$10,000

Given up

---

[2]Financial Accounting Standards Board, *Accounting Standards Codification,* sec. 360-10-45-4, Property, Plant, and Equipment.

Money photo: Comstock/Getty Images; Coaster photo: Image State/Alamy Stock Photo

This roller coaster disposal would be analyzed and recorded as follows.

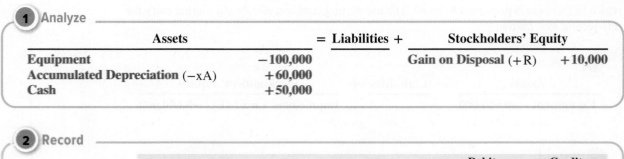

1 Analyze

Assets		= Liabilities +	Stockholders' Equity	
Equipment	−100,000		Gain on Disposal (+R)	+10,000
Accumulated Depreciation (−xA)	+60,000			
Cash	+50,000			

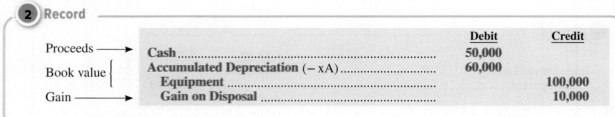

2 Record

		Debit	Credit
Proceeds →	Cash	50,000	
Book value {	Accumulated Depreciation (− xA)	60,000	
	Equipment		100,000
Gain →	Gain on Disposal		10,000

Gains on disposal are included in the income statement, as shown in Exhibit 9.2. A loss on disposal is recorded just like any expense (with a debit), as shown in the following Self-Study Practice.

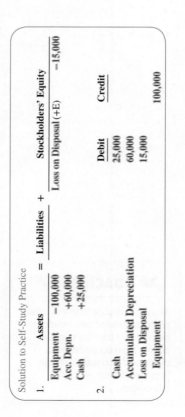

Solution to Self-Study Practice

1.

	Assets	= Liabilities +	Stockholders' Equity	
			Loss on Disposal (+E)	−15,000
Equipment	−100,000			
Acc. Depn.	+60,000			
Cash	+25,000			

2.

	Debit	Credit
Cash	25,000	
Accumulated Depreciation	60,000	
Loss on Disposal	15,000	
Equipment		100,000

💡 How's it going?   Self-Study Practice

Assume **Cedar Fair** sold the roller coaster from our example at the end of year 6 for $25,000 cash. Also assume depreciation had been updated to that point in time, resulting in Accumulated Depreciation of $60,000 on the asset that originally cost $100,000. Complete the accounting equation effects and the journal entry for this disposal below.

1 Analyze

Assets		= Liabilities + Stockholders' Equity	
Equipment	−100,000	[ ]	
Accumulated Depreciation (−xA)	[ ]		
Cash	+25,000		

2 Record

	Debit	Credit
[ ]	[ ]	
[ ]	[ ]	
[ ]	[ ]	
[ ]		[ ]

After you have finished, check your answers with the solution.

SPOTLIGHT ON | **Financial Reporting**

Tragic Events Can Lead to Reporting Gains on Disposal

Avoid the temptation to think of gains as "good" management performance and losses as "bad." Often, they are greatly influenced by the amount of depreciation recorded prior to disposal. To clearly see how gains sometimes arise from "bad" events, consider the following tragic disposals.

Disposal Event	Insurance Proceeds	Book Value	Gain
Loss of Malaysia Airlines MH370	$230 million	$100 million	$130 million
Capsizing of *Costa Concordia*	€395 million	€381 million	€14 million
Collapse of World Trade Center	$1.37 billion	$1.1 billion	$270 million

Sources: P. Greenberg and N. Rapp, "The Big Money Surprise About Malaysia Airlines Flight 370," *Fortune,* May 1, 2014; Carnival Cruises 2012 Annual Report on Form 10-K; Port Authority of New York and New Jersey, 2002, 2003, and 2004 Annual Financial Statements.

INTANGIBLE ASSETS

Intangible assets are long-lived assets that lack physical substance. Their existence is indicated by legal documents of the types described below.

- **Trademarks.** A **trademark** is a special name, image, or slogan identified with a product or company, like the name Kleenex or the image of McDonald's golden arches. The symbol ® signifies a trademark registered with the U.S. Patent and Trademark Office and ™ indicates unregistered trademarks. Both are intangible assets.
- **Copyrights.** A **copyright** gives the owner the exclusive right to publish, use, and sell a literary, musical, artistic, or dramatic work for a period not exceeding 70 years after the author's death.
- **Patents.** A **patent** is an exclusive right granted by the federal government to the patent owner that prevents others from using, manufacturing, or selling the patented item for 20 years.
- **Technology. Technology assets** include software and web development work. IBM reported $1.8 billion of these assets at the end of 2018. Most companies use up intangible technology assets over a relatively short time (three to seven years).
- **Licensing rights. Licensing rights** are limited permissions to use something according to specific terms and conditions. Your university or college likely has obtained the licensing right to make computer programs available for use on your campus network. A licensing right also allows Cedar Fair to showcase Snoopy at its parks.
- **Franchises.** A **franchise** is a contractual right to sell certain products or services, use certain trademarks, or perform activities in a geographical region. For example, a business can buy franchise rights that allow it to use the Krispy Kreme name, store format, recipes, and ingredients by paying an up-front fee ranging from $12,500 to $25,000 per store plus ongoing fees of 4.5 percent of store sales.[3]
- **Goodwill. Goodwill** tops the charts as the most frequently reported intangible asset. It encompasses lots of good stuff like a favorable location, an established customer base, a great reputation, and successful business operations. Although many companies have probably built up their own goodwill, GAAP does not allow it to be reported as an intangible asset on the balance sheet unless it has been purchased from another company. To understand the reasons behind this, keep reading. We explain them in the next section.

Learning Objective 9-6
Analyze the acquisition, use, and disposal of long-lived intangible assets.

YOU SHOULD KNOW

Trademark: An exclusive legal right to use a special name, image, or slogan.
Copyright: A form of protection provided to the original authors of literary, musical, artistic, dramatic, and other works of authorship.
Patent: A right to exclude others from making, using, selling, or importing an invention.
Technology Assets: Capitalized computer software and web development costs; an intangible asset.
Licensing Right: The limited permission to use property according to specific terms and conditions set out in a contract.
Franchise: A contractual right to sell certain products or services, use certain trademarks, or perform activities in a certain geographical region.
Goodwill (Cost in Excess of Net Assets Acquired): For accounting purposes, the excess of the purchase price of a business over the market value of the business's assets and liabilities.

---

[3]Krispy Kreme, Form 10-K annual report for the year ended January 31, 2016.

Acquisition, Use, and Disposal

Acquisition   **The costs of intangible assets are recorded as assets ("capitalized") if they have been purchased.** If an intangible asset is being self-constructed or internally developed, its costs *generally* are reported as **research and development expenses**. The cost of self-developed intangibles is reported as an expense rather than an asset because it's easy for people to claim they've developed a valuable (but invisible) intangible asset. But to believe what they are saying, you really need to see evidence that it's actually worth what they say it's worth. And that usually only happens when hard-earned cash is used to buy it. At that time, the purchaser records the intangible asset at its acquisition cost. This general rule to expense costs to self-develop intangible assets applies to trademarks, copyrights, patents, licensing rights, franchises, and goodwill. However, technology assets are an exception: Costs incurred to develop internal-use computer software during application development are capitalized.

Goodwill is a peculiar intangible asset because it represents the value paid for the unidentifiable assets of another business. You might wonder how you can value something you can't identify, but it is possible. When one company buys another business, the purchase price often is greater than the appraised value of all of the **net assets** of the business. Why would a company pay more for a business as a whole than if it bought the assets individually? The answer is to obtain its goodwill, which encompasses intangible benefits such as its good location or strong management team.

SPOTLIGHT ON | # Financial Reporting

Reporting Goodwill after a Business Acquisition

When Cedar Fair bought five theme parks from Paramount Parks, it paid $1.2 billion, which exceeded the fair value of Paramount's net assets ($890 million). As shown below, Cedar Fair paid the extra $310 million to acquire the goodwill associated with the theme parks' businesses.

Cedar Fair Purchases Paramount Parks		
(in millions)		
Purchase price		$ 1,200
Assets purchased and liabilities assumed		
Current assets	$ 70	
Property and equipment	1,000	
Intangible assets	80	
Debt and other liabilities	(260)	
Net assets, at fair value		890
Goodwill		$ 310

For most companies, goodwill is not amortized but instead is tested annually for impairment and written down if its value is found to be impaired. Private companies can forgo annual impairment testing and instead amortize goodwill using the straight-line method over 10 years or less.

Use   The accounting rules that apply to the use of intangible assets, after they have been purchased, depend on whether the intangible asset has an unlimited or limited life.

- **Unlimited life.** Intangibles with unlimited or indefinite lives (trademarks and most goodwill) are not amortized.

- **Limited life.** The cost of intangible assets with a limited life (copyrights, patents, licensing rights, franchises, and technology assets) initially is capitalized and, later, is expensed on a **straight-line** basis over each period of useful life in a process called **amortization**, similar to depreciation. Most companies do not estimate a residual value for intangible assets because, unlike tangible assets that can be sold as scrap, intangibles usually have no value at the end of their useful lives. Amortization is reported as an expense each period on the income statement and accumulated on the balance sheet in the contra-asset account Accumulated Amortization.

> **YOU SHOULD KNOW**
>
> **Amortization:** For intangible assets, this is the systematic and rational allocation of the cost of an intangible asset over its useful life.

To illustrate, assume Cedar Fair purchased a patent for a water-coaster for $800,000 and intends to use it for 20 years. Each year, the company would record $40,000 in Amortization Expense ($800,000 ÷ 20 years). The effect of this amortization and the journal entry to record it follow:

1 Analyze

Assets	= Liabilities +	Stockholders' Equity
Accumulated Amortization (+xA) −40,000		Amortization Expense (+E) −40,000

2 Record

	Debit	Credit
Amortization Expense	40,000	
Accumulated Amortization (+xA)		40,000

Beyond amortization, which reports the gradual consumption of the benefits of intangible assets over time, companies also may need to report impairment losses for sudden declines in the usefulness of intangible assets. For example, Cedar Fair's closure of all its amusement parks for COVID-19 in the first quarter of 2020 led to write-downs of goodwill and trade names it had acquired, resulting in a total impairment loss of $88 million.

Disposal Just like long-lived tangible assets, disposals of intangible assets result in gains (or losses) if the amounts received on disposal are greater than (less than) their book values.

The accounting rules for long-lived tangible and intangible assets are summarized and compared in the Homework Helper in this chapter.

 SPOTLIGHT ON # Financial Reporting

New Rules for Leases to Add $2 Trillion in Assets and Liabilities

During 2019, new accounting rules came into effect for leases. A **lease** is a contract in which one party (the **lessee**) pays for the right to use an asset owned by another party (the **lessor**). Cedar Fair, for example, was the lessee in its agreement to pay $5 million every year to use land owned by the City of Santa Clara. Previously, Cedar Fair accounted for this payment simply as rent expense each year. The new accounting rules, however, now require lessees to account for long-term leases by recording both a "right-of-use" asset and a lease liability, as if the asset is bought and a loan is taken out to cover all lease payments until the end of the lease. In Cedar Fair's case, this new accounting rule amounts to an extra $75 million in assets and lease liabilities.* Summed across all public companies worldwide, total assets and liabilities are estimated to increase by $2.2 trillion.† As a result, starting in 2019, analysts expect huge changes in many financial statement ratios, including the one discussed in the following section.

---

*Cedar Fair 2018 Form 10-K.
†International Accounting Standards Board. *Effects Analysis: Leases,* January 2016.

Evaluate the Results

TURNOVER ANALYSIS

Learning Objective 9-7
Interpret the fixed asset
turnover ratio.

A primary goal of financial analysts is to evaluate how well management uses long-lived tangible assets to generate revenues. The fixed asset turnover ratio provides a good measure of this aspect of managerial performance. It is calculated as shown in the table that follows. The denominator uses the value of **average** net fixed assets (property and equipment) over the same period as the revenue in the numerator. You can calculate the average net fixed assets by summing the beginning and ending balances in fixed assets (net of accumulated depreciation) and dividing by 2.

Accounting Decision Tools		
Name of Measure	**Formula**	**What It Tells You**
Fixed asset turnover ratio	$\dfrac{\text{Net Revenue}}{\text{Average Net Fixed Assets}}$	• Indicates dollars of revenue generated for each dollar invested in fixed assets (long-lived tangible assets) • A higher ratio implies greater efficiency

The fixed asset turnover ratio measures the dollars of revenue generated by each dollar invested in (tangible) fixed assets. Just as the number of miles per gallon provides a measure of a car's fuel efficiency, the fixed asset turnover ratio provides a measure of fixed asset operating efficiency. Generally speaking, a high or increasing turnover ratio relative to others in the industry suggests better-than-average use of fixed assets in the sense that each dollar of fixed assets is generating higher-than-average revenue.

Be aware that fixed asset turnover ratios can vary across industries because capital intensity—the need for tangible assets—varies widely. Compared to Cedar Fair and Six Flags, a company such as Facebook needs fewer fixed assets to generate revenue, so it has a higher turnover ratio. Exhibit 9.5 shows the fixed asset turnover ratios for the three companies in 2018. Cedar Fair generated about 85 cents of revenue for every dollar invested in net fixed assets, whereas Six Flags generated about $1.18. Look closely at the ratios and you can see the main reason for the difference. Cedar Fair has invested more in long-lived tangible assets than Six Flags.

EXHIBIT 9.5   Summary of Fixed Asset Turnover Ratio Analyses

Company	(in millions)	2018	2017	Calculation of 2018 Fixed Asset Turnover
Cedar Fair	Net revenue	$ 1,350	$ 1,320	$\dfrac{\$1,350}{(\$1,600 + \$1,590)/2} = 0.85$
	Net fixed assets	1,600	1,590	
Six Flags	Net revenue	$ 1,465	$ 1,360	$\dfrac{\$1,465}{(\$1,250 + \$1,240)/2} = 1.18$
	Net fixed assets	1,250	1,240	
Facebook	Net revenue	$55,800	$40,650	$\dfrac{\$55,800}{(\$24,700 + \$13,700)/2} = 2.91$
	Net fixed assets	24,700	13,700	

Check that you can compute the fixed asset turnover ratio by trying the Self-Study Practice that follows.

 How's it going?   Self-Study Practice

Cedar Fair reported net fixed assets of $1,540 (million) at December 31, 2016.

a. Use this information, along with that in Exhibit 9.5, to calculate Cedar Fair's fixed asset turnover ratio in 2017.

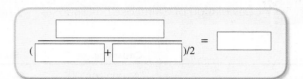

$$ \left(\boxed{} + \boxed{} \right)/2 = \boxed{} $$

b. Did Cedar Fair's fixed asset turnover improve or decline from 2017 (calculated in *a*) to 2018 (shown in Exhibit 9.5)?

After you have finished, check your answers with the solution.

Solution to Self-Study Practice

a. $\dfrac{\$1,320}{(\$1,590 + \$1,540)/2} = 0.84$

b. Cedar Fair's fixed asset turnover improved in 2018.

IMPACT OF DEPRECIATION DIFFERENCES

Learning Objective 9-8
Describe factors to consider when comparing companies' long-lived assets.

Just as differences in the nature of business operations affect financial analyses and the conclusions you draw from them, so too do differences in depreciation. Depreciation varies from one company to the next as a result of differences in depreciation methods, estimated useful lives, and estimated residual values. In this section, we present a simple example to show how different depreciation methods can affect financial analysis throughout the life of a long-lived asset. Do not be fooled by the simplicity of the example. Differences in depreciation can have a significant impact in the real world.

Assume Cedar Fair and Six Flags each acquired a new roller coaster at the beginning of the year for $15.5 million. The two companies estimate the roller coasters will have residual values of $1.5 million at the end of their seven-year useful lives. Assume too that everything about the roller coasters is identical. However, Cedar Fair uses the straight-line depreciation method and Six Flags uses the double-declining-balance method. Exhibit 9.6 shows the yearly depreciation reported by the two companies (rounded to the nearest thousand dollars). Exhibit 9.6 shows that early in the asset's life, before year 4, the straight-line depreciation expense reported by Cedar Fair is less than the declining-balance depreciation expense

✏️ **COACH'S TIP**

For tips and practice involving the calculations in Exhibit 9.6, try S9-7 at the end of this chapter.

EXHIBIT 9.6   Straight-Line versus Double-Declining-Balance Depreciation Schedules

CEDAR FAIR (STRAIGHT-LINE)				SIX FLAGS (DOUBLE-DECLINING-BALANCE)		
Depreciation Expense	Accumulated Depreciation	Book Value	Year	Depreciation Expense	Accumulated Depreciation	Book Value
$2,000,000	$ 2,000,000	$13,500,000	1	$4,429,000	$ 4,429,000	$11,071,000
2,000,000	4,000,000	11,500,000	2	3,163,000	7,592,000	7,908,000
2,000,000	6,000,000	9,500,000	3	2,259,000	9,851,000	5,649,000
2,000,000	8,000,000	7,500,000	4	1,614,000	11,465,000	4,035,000
2,000,000	10,000,000	5,500,000	5	1,153,000	12,618,000	2,882,000
2,000,000	12,000,000	3,500,000	6	823,000	13,441,000	2,059,000
2,000,000	14,000,000	1,500,000	7	559,000	14,000,000	1,500,000

reported by Six Flags. Thus, even if the two companies attract exactly the same number of customers and earn exactly the same total revenues, their reported net incomes will differ each year simply because they use two different (but equally acceptable) methods of depreciation. This example shows why a user of financial statements needs to understand the accounting methods companies use.

These differences in depreciation affect more than just depreciation expense, however. Taking this example one step further, assume the two companies sell the roller coasters on the last day of year 4 for $6,000,000. Exhibit 9.7 shows the calculation of the gain or loss on disposal for the two companies.

EXHIBIT 9.7	Calculation of Gain/Loss on Disposal	
	Cedar Fair	**Six Flags**
Selling price	$6,000,000	$6,000,000
Book value (see Exhibit 9.6)	(7,500,000)	(4,035,000)
Gain (loss) on disposal	$(1,500,000)	$1,965,000

Based on the information in Exhibit 9.7, which company appears better managed? Someone who does not understand accounting is likely to say Six Flags is better managed because it reported a gain on disposal whereas Cedar Fair reported a loss. You know that cannot be right, however, because both companies experienced exactly the same events. They bought the same asset at the same cost ($15.5 million) and sold it for the same amount of money ($6 million). The only difference between them is Cedar Fair reported less depreciation over the years leading up to the disposal, so its roller coaster had a larger book value at the time of disposal. Six Flags reported more depreciation, so its roller coaster had a smaller book value at the time of disposal. As a financial statement user, it is useful to know that **any gain or loss on disposal on the income statement tells you as much about the method used to depreciate assets as about management's apparent ability to successfully negotiate the sale of long-lived assets.**

Although the previous example concerned different depreciation methods, the same effects can occur for two companies that use the same depreciation method but different estimated useful lives or residual values. Useful lives can vary for several reasons, including differences in (1) the type of equipment used, (2) the frequency of repairs, (3) the frequency and duration of use, and (4) the accuracy of management's estimates. How large can these differences be? Even within the same industry, sizable differences can occur. The notes to the financial statements of various companies in the airline industry, for example, reveal the following differences in the estimated useful lives of airplanes and other flight equipment:

Company	Estimated Life (in years)
Alaska Air Group	15–25
American Airlines Group	20–30
Delta Air Lines, Inc.	20–34
Southwest Airlines	25

YOU SHOULD KNOW

EBITDA: Abbreviation for "earnings before interest, taxes, depreciation, and amortization," which is a measure of operating performance that some managers and analysts use in place of net income.

Some analysts try to sidestep such differences in depreciation calculations by focusing on financial measures that exclude depreciation. One popular measure is called **EBITDA** (pronounced something like *'e bit, duh*), which stands for "earnings before interest, taxes, depreciation, and amortization." Analysts calculate EBITDA by starting with net income and then adding back depreciation and amortization expense (as well as nonoperating expenses such as interest and taxes). The idea is this measure allows analysts to conduct financial analyses without having to deal with possible differences in depreciation and amortization. Unfortunately, it doesn't handle other differences, such as those between GAAP and IFRS discussed next.

SPOTLIGHT ON **The World**

Differences between GAAP and IFRS

IFRS differs from GAAP somewhat in accounting for tangible and intangible assets. Two of the most significant differences are summarized below. GAAP requires tangible and intangible assets to be recorded at cost and not revalued for later increases in asset values. In contrast, IFRS allows companies the option of reporting these assets at fair values (e.g., appraisals), provided they use the fair value method consistently each year. IFRS also requires companies to capitalize costs of developing intangible assets, such as prototypes for making new products or tools. GAAP *generally* expenses such development costs because of the uncertainty of their value.

GAAP	IFRS
Cost versus Fair Value	**Cost versus Fair Value**
• Must record at cost	• Choose between either cost **or fair value**
• Do not record increases in value	• **If using fair value, record increases in value**
Research and Development	**Research and Development**
• Expense all costs of researching and developing intangible assets (except some technology costs)	• Expense research costs but **capitalize measurable costs of developing intangible assets**

SUPPLEMENT 9A NATURAL RESOURCES

Industries such as oil and gas, mining, and timber harvesting rely significantly on a third category of long-lived assets called *natural resources.* These natural resources, whether in the form of oil wells, mineral deposits, or timber tracts, provide the raw materials for products that are sold by companies like ExxonMobil and International Paper. When a company first acquires or develops a natural resource, the cost of the natural resource is recorded in conformity with the **cost principle.** As the natural resource is used up, its acquisition cost must be split among the periods in which revenues are generated, in conformity with the **expense recognition ("matching") principle.** The term **depletion** describes the process of allocating a natural resource's cost over the period of its extraction or harvesting. The units-of-production method is often used to compute depletion.

Depletion is similar to the concepts of depreciation and amortization discussed earlier in the chapter for tangible and intangible assets, with one important exception. When a natural resource such as timberland is depleted, the company obtains inventory (logs). Because depletion of the natural resource is necessary to obtain the inventory, the depletion computed during a period is added to the cost of the inventory, not expensed in the period. For example, if a timber tract costing $530,000 is depleted over its estimated cutting period based on a "cutting" rate of approximately 20 percent per year, it would be depleted by $106,000 each year. Recording this depletion would have the following effects on the company's accounting equation, which would be recorded with the journal entry shown below.

Learning Objective 9-S1
Analyze and report depletion of natural resources.

YOU SHOULD KNOW

Depletion: Process of allocating a natural resource's cost over the period of its extraction or harvesting.

1 Analyze

Assets		= Liabilities +	Stockholders' Equity
Timber Inventory	+106,000		
Accumulated Depletion (+xA)	−106,000		

2 Record

	Debit	Credit
Timber Inventory...	106,000	
Accumulated Depletion (+xA)		106,000

Just as Accumulated Depreciation is subtracted from Equipment, Accumulated Depletion is subtracted from the long-lived asset Timber Tract on the balance sheet. Timber Inventory is reported as a current asset on the balance sheet until it is sold, at which time its cost is removed from the balance sheet and reported on the income statement as an expense called Cost of Goods Sold.

Learning Objective 9-S2
Calculate changes in deprecia-tion arising from changes in estimates or capitalized cost.

SUPPLEMENT 9B   CHANGES IN DEPRECIATION

The amount of depreciation and amortization depends on three items: an asset's recorded cost, its estimated useful life, and its estimated residual value. When any one of these items changes, the amount of depreciation and amortization needs to change. For example, Cedar Fair changed its amortization calculations when it shortened the estimated useful life of cer-tain intangible assets after deciding to discontinue its licensing agreement with Nickelodeon. In other instances, when the company made extraordinary repairs that increased a roller coaster's recorded cost, it revised depreciation for the remaining years of that asset's life.

To compute the new depreciation expense due to the changes described above, substitute the book value for the original acquisition cost, the new residual value for the original resid-ual value, and the estimated remaining life for the original useful life. As an illustration, the formula using the straight-line method follows:

$$\textbf{(Cost} \; - \; \textbf{Residual Value)} \; \times \; \frac{1}{\textbf{Useful Life}} \; = \textbf{Depreciation Expense}$$

$$\textbf{(Book Value} - \textbf{New Residual Value)} \times \frac{1}{\textbf{Remaining Life}} = \textbf{Depreciation Expense}$$

Assume Cedar Fair purchased a roller coaster for $60,000,000 with an estimated useful life of 20 years and estimated residual value of $3,000,000. Shortly after the start of year 5, Cedar Fair changed the initial estimated life to 25 years and lowered the estimated residual value to $2,400,000. At the end of year 5, the computation of the new amount for depreciation expense is as follows:

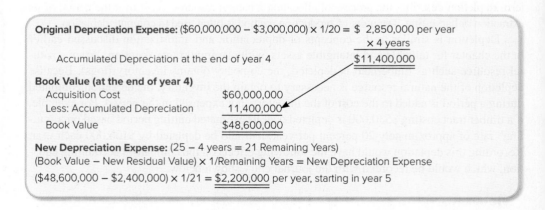

Original Depreciation Expense: ($60,000,000 − $3,000,000) × 1/20 = $ 2,850,000 per year
                                                                              × 4 years
   Accumulated Depreciation at the end of year 4 $11,400,000

Book Value (at the end of year 4)
   Acquisition Cost $60,000,000
   Less: Accumulated Depreciation   11,400,000
   Book Value $48,600,000

New Depreciation Expense: (25 − 4 years = 21 Remaining Years)
(Book Value − New Residual Value) × 1/Remaining Years = New Depreciation Expense
($48,600,000 − $2,400,000) × 1/21 = $2,200,000 per year, starting in year 5

Companies also may change depreciation *methods* (for example, from declining-balance to straight-line), although such a change requires more disclosure, as described in intermedi-ate accounting textbooks. Under GAAP, changes in accounting estimates and depreciation methods should be made only when a new estimate or accounting method "better measures" the periodic income of the business.

REVIEW THE CHAPTER

DEMONSTRATION CASE

Diversified Industries (DI) started as a house construction company. In recent years, it has expanded into heavy construction, ready-mix concrete, sand and gravel, construction supplies, and earth-moving services. The company completed the following transactions during the year. Amounts have been simplified.

Jan. 1   The management decided to buy a 10-year-old building for $175,000 and the land on which it was situated for $130,000. DI paid $100,000 in cash and signed a 5-year note payable for the rest.

Jan. 3   DI paid $38,000 in cash for renovations to the building prior to its use.

July 10   DI paid $1,200 cash for ordinary repairs on the building.

Dec. 31   DI considered the following information to determine year-end adjustments:

    a. The building will be depreciated on a straight-line basis over an estimated useful life of 30 years. The estimated residual value is $33,000.

    b. DI purchased another company two years ago at $100,000 more than the fair values of the net assets acquired. The goodwill has an unlimited life.

    c. At the beginning of the year, DI owned equipment with a cost of $650,000 and accumulated depreciation of $150,000. The equipment is being depreciated using the double-declining-balance method, with a useful life of 20 years and no residual value.

    d. At year-end, DI tested its long-lived assets for possible impairment of their value. Goodwill was found to be not impaired. Included in its equipment was a piece of excavation equipment with a cost of $156,000 and accumulated depreciation of $36,000 after making the adjustment for (*c*). The old equipment has limited use, so its future cash flows and fair value are expected to be $35,000.

The end of the annual accounting period is December 31.

Required:

1. Indicate the accounts affected and the amount and direction (+ for increase and − for decrease) of the effect of each of the preceding events and required adjustments on the financial statement categories at the end of the year. Use the following headings:

Date	Assets	=	Liabilities	+	Stockholders' Equity

2. Prepare the journal entries to record each event that occurred during the year and the adjusting journal entries required at December 31.
3. Which accounts would be reported on the income statement? Where?
4. Show how the December 31 balance sheet would report these long-lived tangible and intangible assets.
5. Assuming that the company had Net Revenue of $1,000,000 for the year and a book value of $500,000 for fixed assets at the beginning of the year, compute the fixed asset turnover ratio. Explain its meaning and evaluate it relative to the prior year's ratio of 1.5.

Suggested Solution

1. Effects of events (with computations in notes below the table):

Date	Assets		=	Liabilities	+	Stockholders' Equity	
Jan. 1	Cash Land Building	−100,000 +130,000 +175,000		Notes Payable +205,000 (long-term)			
Jan. 3 (Note 1)	Cash Building	−38,000 +38,000					
July 10 (Note 2)	Cash	−1,200				Repairs and Maintenance Expense (+E)	−1,200
Dec. 31 (a) (Note 3)	Accumulated Depreciation (+xA)	−6,000				Depreciation Expense (+E)	−6,000
Dec. 31 (b) (Note 4)	No entry						
Dec. 31 (c) (Note 5)	Accumulated Depreciation (+xA)	−50,000				Depreciation Expense (+E)	−50,000
Dec. 31 (d) (Note 6)	Equipment Accumulated Depreciation (−xA)	−36,000 +36,000					
	Equipment	−85,000				Impairment Loss (+E)	−85,000

Notes

(1) Capitalize the $38,000 expenditure because it is necessary to prepare the asset for use.

(2) This is an ordinary repair and should be expensed.

(3)

Cost of building		**Straight-line depreciation (building)**
Initial payment	$175,000	($213,000 cost − $33,000 residual value) ×
Renovations prior to use	38,000	1/30 years = $6,000 annual depreciation
Acquisition cost	$213,000	

(4) Goodwill has an indefinite life and is therefore not amortized. Goodwill is tested for impairment but, as described later in the case, was found to be not impaired.

(5) **Double-declining-balance depreciation (equipment)**

($650,000 cost − $150,000 accumulated depreciation) × 2/20 years = $50,000 depreciation for the year.

(6) **Asset impairment test**

The book value of the old equipment ($120,000 = $156,000 − $36,000) exceeds expected future cash flows ($35,000). The asset has become impaired, so it needs to be written down to its fair value.

Impairment loss:	
Book Value	$120,000
Fair Value	(35,000)
Impairment Loss	$ 85,000

2. Journal entries for events during the year:

			Debit	Credit
Jan. 1	Land		130,000	
	Building..		175,000	
	Cash..			100,000
	Notes Payable (long-term)...			205,000
Jan. 3	Building..		38,000	
	Cash..			38,000
July 10	**Repairs and Maintenance Expense**		1,200	
	Cash..			1,200

Adjusting journal entries at December 31:	Debit	Credit
a. **Depreciation Expense**	**6,000**	
Accumulated Depreciation—Building (+xA)		**6,000**
b. No adjusting journal entry required because goodwill is assumed to have an unlimited (or indefinite) life.		
c. **Depreciation Expense**	**50,000**	
Accumulated Depreciation—Equipment (+xA)		**50,000**
d. **Accumulated Depreciation—Equipment (−xA)**	**36,000**	
Equipment		**36,000**
Impairment Loss	**85,000**	
Equipment		**85,000**

3. The income statement would report Depreciation Expense, Repairs and Maintenance Expense, and Impairment Loss as operating expenses included in the computation of Income from Operations.

4. Partial balance sheet, December 31:

Assets	
Property, Plant, and Equipment	
Land	$130,000
Building	213,000
Equipment	529,000*
Property, Plant, and Equipment, at cost	872,000
Accumulated Depreciation	(170,000)†
Property, Plant, and Equipment, net	702,000
Goodwill	100,000

* $529,000 = $650,000 − $36,000 − $85,000
† $170,000 = $150,000 + $6,000 + $50,000 − $36,000

5. Fixed asset turnover ratio:

$$\frac{\text{Net Revenue}}{(\text{Beginning Net Fixed Asset Balance} + \text{Ending Net Fixed Asset Balance})/2} = \frac{\$1,000,000}{(\$500,000 + \$702,000)/2} = 1.66$$

The fixed asset turnover ratio measures the company's efficiency at using its investment in property, plant, and equipment to generate revenue. Approximately $1.66 of revenue was generated for each dollar of fixed assets, which is an improvement over last year's 1.5.

CHAPTER SUMMARY

Define, classify, and explain the nature of long-lived assets.   LO 9-1

- Long-lived assets are those that a business retains for long periods of time for use in the course of normal operations rather than for sale. They may be divided into tangible assets (land, buildings, equipment) and intangible assets (including goodwill, patents, and franchises).

Apply the cost principle to the acquisition of long-lived assets.   LO 9-2

- The acquisition cost of property, plant, and equipment is the cash-equivalent purchase price plus all reasonable and necessary expenditures made to acquire and prepare the asset for its intended use. Expenditures made after the asset is in use are either expensed or capitalized as a cost of the asset:
  a. Expenditures are expensed if they recur frequently, involve relatively small amounts, and do not directly lengthen the asset's useful life. These are considered ordinary repairs and maintenance expense.

    b. Expenditures are capitalized as a cost of the asset if they provide benefits for one or more accounting periods beyond the current period. This category includes extraordinary repairs, replacements, and additions.

LO 9-3   **Apply various depreciation methods as economic benefits are used up over time.**

- In conformity with the matching principle, the cost of long-lived tangible assets (less any estimated residual value) is allocated to depreciation expense over each period benefited by the assets.
- Because of depreciation, the book value of an asset declines over time and net income is reduced by the amount of the expense.
- Common depreciation methods include straight-line (a constant amount over time), units-of-production (a variable amount over time), and double-declining-balance (a decreasing amount over time).

LO 9-4   **Explain the effect of asset impairment on the financial statements.**

- When events or changes in circumstances reduce the estimated future cash flows of a long-lived asset below its book value, the accumulated depreciation should be eliminated against the asset's cost and then the book value of the asset should be written down, with the amount of the write-down reported as an impairment loss.

LO 9-5   **Analyze the disposal of long-lived tangible assets.**

When assets are disposed of through sale or abandonment,

- Record additional depreciation arising since the last adjustment was made.
- Remove the cost of the old asset and its related accumulated depreciation.
- Recognize the cash proceeds (if any).
- Recognize any gains or losses when the asset's book value is not equal to the cash received.

LO 9-6   **Analyze the acquisition, use, and disposal of long-lived intangible assets.**

- Intangible assets are recorded at cost, but only when purchased. The costs of most internally developed intangible assets are expensed as research and development when incurred.
- Intangibles are reported at book value on the balance sheet.
- Amortization is calculated for intangibles with limited useful lives, using the straight-line method.
- Intangibles with unlimited useful lives, including most goodwill, are not amortized but are reviewed for impairment.

LO 9-7   **Interpret the fixed asset turnover ratio.**

- The fixed asset turnover ratio measures the company's efficiency at using its investment in property, plant, and equipment to generate sales. Higher turnover ratios imply greater efficiency.

LO 9-8   **Describe factors to consider when comparing companies' long-lived assets.**

- Companies in different industries require different levels of investment in long-lived assets. Beyond that, you should consider whether differences exist in depreciation methods, estimated useful lives, and estimated residual values, which can affect the book value of long-lived assets as well as ratios calculated using these book values and any gains or losses reported at the time of asset disposal.

Accounting Decision Tools		
Name of Measure	**Formula**	**What It Tells You**
Fixed asset turnover ratio	$\dfrac{\text{Net Revenue}}{\text{Average Net Fixed Assets}}$	• Dollars of revenue generated for each dollar invested in (tangible) fixed assets • A higher ratio implies greater efficiency

KEY TERMS

Amortization p. 413

Book (or Carrying) Value p. 402

Capitalize p. 397

Copyright p. 411

Declining-Balance Depreciation
Method p. 405

Depletion p. 417

Depreciable Cost p. 403

Depreciation p. 402

EBITDA p. 416

Extraordinary Repairs p. 401

Franchise p. 411

Goodwill p. 411

Impairment p. 408

Licensing Right p. 411

Long-Lived Assets p. 396

Net Assets p. 412

Ordinary Repairs and
Maintenance p. 401

Patent p. 411

Research and Development
Expenses p. 412

Residual (or Salvage) Value p. 403

Straight-Line Depreciation
Method p. 404

Technology Assets p. 411

Trademark p. 411

Units-of-Production Depreciation
Method p. 404

Useful Life p. 403

See complete definitions in the glossary in the back of this text.

HOMEWORK HELPER

Stage	Subject	Tangible Assets	Intangible Assets
Acquire	**Purchased asset**	Capitalize all related costs	Capitalize all related costs
Use	***Repairs and maintenance***		
	Ordinary	Expense related costs	Not applicable
	Extraordinary	Capitalize related costs	Not applicable
	Depreciation/amortization		
	Limited life	One of several methods: • Straight-line • Units-of-production • Declining-balance	Straight-line method
	Unlimited life	Do not depreciate (e.g., land)	Do not amortize (e.g., goodwill)
	Impairment test	Write down if necessary	Write down if necessary
Dispose	***Report gain (loss) when . . .***	Receive more (less) on disposal than book value	Receive more (less) on disposal than book value

Alternative terms

• Declining-balance depreciation methods are also called accelerated methods.

• Tangible assets are also called fixed assets or plant assets.

Helpful reminders

• Declining-balance depreciation methods subtract Accumulated Depreciation, not residual value, from the asset's cost. For this reason, take extra care to ensure that you stop depreciating the asset when its book value equals its residual value.

• The following T-accounts illustrate changes in long-lived asset accounts:

Equipment (A)		Accumulated Depreciation (xA)	
Beg. bal.			Beg. bal.
Purchases (at cost)	**Impairment** (loss in value) **Disposals** (at cost)	**Impairment** (amount accumulated) **Disposals** (amount accumulated)	**Depreciation** (this year)
End. bal.			End. bal.

Frequent mistakes

- Depreciation does not represent a decline in the current value of an asset; declines in asset values are recorded as impairment losses, not depreciation. The purpose of depreciation is to allocate the cost of a long-lived asset as an expense in each period in which the asset is used to generate revenue.

- To record an asset disposal, remove its cost and accumulated depreciation separately, rather than removing just its book value from the asset's account.

PRACTICE MATERIAL

QUESTIONS (● Symbol indicates questions that require analysis from more than one perspective.)

1. Define *long-lived assets.* What are the two common categories of long-lived assets? Describe each.

2. Under the cost principle, what amounts should be recorded as a cost of a long-lived asset?

3. What is the term for recording costs as assets rather than as expenses? Describe how the decision to record costs as assets, rather than expenses, affects the balance sheet and income statement.

4. Waste Management, Inc., regularly incurs costs (e.g., salaries, legal fees, travel) to find new locations for landfill sites. What reasons support capitalizing these costs? What reasons support expensing these costs? ●

5. Distinguish between ordinary repairs and extraordinary repairs. How is each accounted for?

6. Describe the relationship between the expense recognition ("matching") principle and accounting for long-lived assets.

7. Why are different depreciation methods allowed?

8. In computing depreciation, three values must be known or estimated. Identify and describe each.

9. What type of depreciation expense pattern is used under each of the following methods and when is its use appropriate?

   a. The straight-line method.
   b. The units-of-production method.
   c. The double-declining-balance method.

10. After merging with Northwest Airlines, Delta Airlines increased the estimated useful life and increased the estimated residual value of its flight equipment. All else equal, how will each of these changes affect Delta's Depreciation Expense and Net Income? ●

11. A local politician claimed, "to reduce the government's deficit, it's time we require companies to start paying their deferred income tax liabilities." Explain to the politician what deferred income taxes represent and why they should not be viewed as accounts payable to the government. ●

12. What is an asset impairment? How is it accounted for?

13. What is book value? When equipment is sold for more than book value, how is the transaction recorded? How is it recorded when the selling price is less than book value?

14. Distinguish between depreciation and amortization.

15. Define *goodwill.* When is it appropriate to record goodwill as an intangible asset? When is its value decreased?

16. FedEx Corporation reports the cost of its aircraft in a single category called Flight Equipment. What impact would adopting IFRS have on this aspect of FedEx's accounting? ●

17. How is the fixed asset turnover ratio computed? Explain its meaning.

18. Johnson & Johnson, the maker of Tylenol, uses GAAP. Bayer, the maker of aspirin, uses IFRS. Explain what complications might arise when comparing the long-lived assets of these two companies. ●

19. (Supplement 9A) How does depletion affect the balance sheet and income statement? Why is depletion accounted for in a manner that differs from depreciation and amortization?

20. (Supplement 9B) Over what period should an addition to an existing long-lived asset be depreciated? Explain.

MULTIPLE CHOICE

1. Which of the following should be capitalized when a piece of production equipment is acquired for a factory?

   a. Sales tax
   b. Transportation costs
   c. Installation costs
   d. All of the above

2. When recording depreciation, which of the following statements is true?

   a. Total assets increase and stockholders' equity increases.
   b. Total assets decrease and total liabilities increase.
   c. Total assets decrease and stockholders' equity increases.
   d. None of the above are true.

3. Under what depreciation method(s) is an asset's book value used to calculate depreciation each year?

a. Straight-line method
b. Units-of-production method
c. Declining-balance method
d. Weighted-average-cost method

4. A company wishes to report the highest earnings possible according to GAAP. Therefore, when calculating depreciation for financial reporting purposes,

a. It will follow the MACRS depreciation rates prescribed by the IRS.
b. It will estimate the shortest lives possible for its assets.
c. It will estimate the longest lives possible for its assets.
d. It will estimate lower residual values for its assets.

5. Barber, Inc., depreciates its building on a straight-line basis. A building was purchased on January 1 that had an estimated useful life of 20 years and a residual value of $20,000. The company's Depreciation Expense for that year was $20,000 on the building. What was the original cost of the building?

a. $360,000
b. $380,000
c. $400,000
d. $420,000

6. Thornton Industries purchased a machine part-way through the year on July 1 for $45,000 and is depreciating it with the straight-line method over a life of 10 years, using a residual value of $3,000. Depreciation Expense for the machine for that year ended December 31 is

a. $2,100
b. $2,250
c. $4,200
d. $4,500

7. ACME, Inc., uses straight-line depreciation for all of its depreciable assets. ACME sold a used piece of machinery on December 31 that it had purchased two years earlier on January 1 for $10,000. When the asset was first acquired, its estimated life was five years and the estimated residual value was zero. At the time of disposal, Accumulated Depreciation was $4,000. If the sales price of the used

machine was $7,500, the resulting gain or loss on disposal was which of the following amounts?

a. Loss of $2,500
b. Gain of $3,500
c. Loss of $1,500
d. Gain of $1,500

8. What assets should be amortized using the straight-line method?

a. Land
b. Intangible assets with limited lives
c. Intangible assets with unlimited lives
d. All of the above

9. How many of the following statements regarding goodwill are true?

• Goodwill is not reported unless purchased in an exchange.
• Private companies can elect to amortize goodwill over 10 years or less.
• Impairment of goodwill results in a decrease in net income.

a. None
b. One
c. Two
d. Three

10. The Simon Company and the Allen Company each bought a new delivery truck on January 1. Both companies paid exactly the same cost, $30,000, for their respective vehicles. Two years later, on December 31, the book value of Simon's truck was less than the Allen Company's book value for the same vehicle. Which of the following are acceptable explanations for the difference in book value?

a. Both companies elected straight-line depreciation, but the Simon Company used a longer estimated life.
b. The Simon Company estimated a lower residual value, but both estimated the same useful life and both elected straight-line depreciation.
c. Because GAAP specifies rigid guidelines regarding the calculation of depreciation, this situation is not possible.
d. None of the above explain the difference in book value.

> For answers to the Multiple-Choice Questions **see page Q1** located in the last section of the book.

MINI-EXERCISES

Mc Graw Hill connect

M9-1 Classifying Long-Lived Assets and Related Cost Allocation Concepts

LO 9-1, 9-3, 9-6

For each of the following long-lived assets, indicate its nature and related cost allocation concept. Use the abbreviations shown on the right:

Asset	Nature	Cost Allocation		Nature
1. Property	_____	_____	B	Building
2. Delivery vans	_____	_____	E	Equipment
3. Warehouse	_____	_____	I	Intangible
4. Trademark	_____	_____	L	Land
5. New engine	_____	_____		
6. Franchise	_____	_____		**Cost Allocation**
7. Software license	_____	_____	A	Amortization
8. Computers	_____	_____	D	Depreciation
9. Production plant	_____	_____	NO	No cost allocation

LO 9-2, 9-6

American Golf Corporation

M9-2 Deciding Whether to Capitalize or Expense

American Golf Corporation operates golf courses throughout the country. For each of the following items, enter the correct letter to show whether the cost should be capitalized (C) or expensed (E).

Transactions

_____ 1. Purchased a golf course in Orange County, California.

_____ 2. Paid a landscaping company to clear 100 acres of land on which to build a new course.

_____ 3. Paid a landscaping company to apply fertilizer to the fairways on its Coyote Hills Golf Course.

_____ 4. Hired a building maintenance company to build a 2,000-square-foot addition on a clubhouse.

_____ 5. Hired a building maintenance company to replace the locks on a clubhouse and equipment shed.

_____ 6. Paid an advertising company to create a campaign to build goodwill.

LO 9-2, 9-6

M9-3 Deciding Whether to Capitalize an Expense

For each of the following items, enter the correct letter to show whether the expenditure should be capitalized (C) or expensed (E).

Transactions

_____ 1. Purchased a machine, $70,000; gave long-term note.

_____ 2. Paid $600 for ordinary repairs.

_____ 3. Purchased a patent, $45,300 cash.

_____ 4. Paid cash, $200,000, for addition to old building.

_____ 5. Paid $20,000 for monthly salaries.

_____ 6. Paid $250 for routine maintenance.

_____ 7. Paid $16,000 for extraordinary repairs.

LO 9-3

M9-4 Computing Book Value (Straight-Line Depreciation)

A machine that cost $400,000 has an estimated residual value of $40,000 and an estimated useful life of four years. The company uses straight-line depreciation. Calculate its book value at the end of year 3.

LO 9-3

M9-5 Computing Book Value (Units-of-Production Depreciation)

A machine that cost $400,000 has an estimated residual value of $40,000 and an estimated useful life of 20,000 machine hours. The company uses units-of-production depreciation and ran the machine 3,000 hours in year 1, 8,000 hours in year 2, and 6,000 hours in year 3. Calculate its book value at the end of year 3.

LO 9-3

M9-6 Computing Book Value (Double-Declining-Balance Depreciation)

A machine that cost $400,000 has an estimated residual value of $40,000 and an estimated useful life of four years. The company uses double-declining-balance depreciation. Calculate its book value at the end of year 3. Round to the nearest dollar.

LO 9-3

M9-7 Calculating Partial-Year Depreciation

Calculate the amount of depreciation to report during the year ended December 31 for equipment that was purchased at a cost of $43,000 on October 1. The equipment has an estimated residual value of $3,000 and an estimated useful life of five years or 20,000 hours. Assume the equipment was used for 1,000 hours from October 1 to December 31 and the company uses (*a*) straight-line, (*b*) double-declining-balance, or (*c*) units-of-production depreciation.

LO 9-4, 9-5

M9-8 Recording Asset Impairment Losses

After recording depreciation for the current year, Media Mania Incorporated decided to discontinue using its printing equipment. The equipment had cost $750,000, accumulated depreciation was $550,000, and its fair value (based on estimated future cash flows from selling the equipment) was $50,000. Determine whether the equipment is impaired and, if it is impaired, show any necessary journal entries.

M9-9 Recording the Disposal of a Long-Lived Asset

LO 9-5

Prepare journal entries to record these transactions: (*a*) Morrell Corporation disposed of two computers at the end of their useful lives. The computers had cost $4,800 and their Accumulated Depreciation was $4,800. No residual value was received. (*b*) Assume the same information as (*a*), except that Accumulated Depreciation, updated to the date of disposal, was $3,600.

M9-10 Reporting and Recording the Disposal of a Long-Lived Asset (Straight-Line Depreciation)

LO 9-5

As part of a major renovation at the beginning of the year, Atiase Pharmaceuticals, Inc., sold shelving units (recorded as Equipment) that were 10 years old for $800 cash. The shelves originally cost $6,400 and had been depreciated on a straight-line basis over an estimated useful life of 10 years with an estimated residual value of $400. Assuming that depreciation has been recorded to the date of sale, show the effect of the disposal on the accounting equation. Prepare the journal entry to record the sale of the shelving units.

M9-11 Capitalizing versus Expensing Intangible Asset Costs

LO 9-6

Most highly visible companies spend significant amounts of money to protect their intellectual property, ensuring that no one uses this property without direct permission. Discuss whether companies should capitalize or expense the money paid to employees who evaluate requests for use of their logos and who search for instances where the companies' intellectual property has been used without permission. Draw an analogy to similar costs incurred for employees responsible for the use and upkeep of tangible assets.

M9-12 Computing Goodwill and Patents

LO 9-6

Taste-T Company has been in business for 30 years and has developed a large group of loyal restaurant customers. Down Home Foods made an offer to buy Taste-T Company for $6,000,000. The market value of Taste-T's tangible assets, net of liabilities, on the date of the offer is $5,600,000. Taste-T also holds a patent for a fluting machine that the company invented (the patent with a market value of $200,000 was never recorded by Taste-T because it was developed internally). How much has Down Home Foods included for intangibles in its offer of $6,000,000? Assuming Taste-T accepts this offer, which company will report Goodwill on its balance sheet and at what amount?

M9-13 Computing and Evaluating the Fixed Asset Turnover Ratio

LO 9-7

Cedar Fair

The following information was reported by Amuse Yourself Parks (AYP):

Net fixed assets (beginning of year)	$8,450,000
Net fixed assets (end of year)	8,250,000
Net sales for the year	4,175,000
Net income for the year	1,700,000

Compute the company's fixed asset turnover ratio for the year. What can you say about AYP's fixed asset turnover ratio when compared to Cedar Fair's ratio of 0.85 in Exhibit 9.5?

M9-14 (Supplement 9A) Recording Depletion for a Natural Resource

LO 9-S1

Saskatchewan Forestry Company purchased a timber tract for $600,000 and estimates that it will be depleted evenly over its 10-year useful life with no residual value. Show the journal entry that would be recorded if 10 percent of the total timber is cut and placed into inventory during the current year.

M9-15 (Supplement 9B) Computing Revised Depreciation after Change in Cost and Estimated Life

LO 9-S2

Plummer Industries purchased a machine for $43,800 and is depreciating it with the straight-line method over a life of 8 years, using a residual value of $3,000. At the beginning of the sixth year, an extraordinary repair was made costing $7,500, the estimated useful life was extended to 15 years, and no change was made to the estimated residual value. Calculate depreciation expense for year 6, rounded to the nearest dollar.

EXERCISES

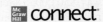

LO 9-1, 9-7

Hasbro, Inc.

E9-1 Preparing a Classified Balance Sheet

The following is a list of account titles and amounts (in millions) reported at December 30, 2018, by Hasbro, Inc., a leading manufacturer of games, toys, and interactive entertainment software for children and families:

Accounts Receivable	$1,200	Equipment	$ 530
Accumulated Amortization	720	Goodwill	485
Accumulated Depreciation	465	Inventory	445
Allowance for Doubtful Accounts	10	Land	5
Buildings	190	Licensing Rights	2,160
Cash and Cash Equivalents	1,180	Prepaid Rent	270

Required:

1. Prepare the asset section of a classified balance sheet for Hasbro, Inc.
2. Using Hasbro's 2018 Net Sales Revenue of $4,580 (million) and its average Net Fixed Assets of $260 (million), calculate the fixed asset turnover ratio for 2018. Has the company generated more or less revenue from each dollar of fixed assets than in 2017, when the ratio was 19.77?

LO 9-2, 9-3

E9-2 Computing and Recording a Basket Purchase and Straight-Line Depreciation

Bridge City Consulting bought a building and the land on which it is located for $182,000 cash. The land is estimated to represent 70 percent of the purchase price. The company paid $22,000 for building renovations before it was ready for use.

Required:

1. Explain how the renovation costs should be accounted for.
2. Give the journal entry to record all expenditures. Assume that all transactions were for cash and they occurred at the start of the year.
3. Compute straight-line depreciation on the building at the end of one year, assuming an estimated 12-year useful life and a $4,600 estimated residual value.
4. What should be the book value of (*a*) the land and (*b*) the building at the end of year 2?

LO 9-2, 9-3

E9-3 Determining Financial Statement Effects of an Asset Acquisition and Straight-Line Depreciation

O'Connor Company ordered a machine on January 1 at a purchase price of $40,000. On the date of delivery, January 2, the company paid $10,000 on the machine and signed a long-term note payable for the balance. On January 3, it paid $350 for freight on the machine. On January 5, O'Connor paid cash for installation costs relating to the machine amounting to $2,400. On December 31 (the end of the accounting period), O'Connor recorded depreciation on the machine using the straight-line method with an estimated useful life of 10 years and an estimated residual value of $4,750.

Required:

1. Indicate the effects (accounts, amounts, and + or −) of each transaction (on January 1, 2, 3, and 5) on the accounting equation. Use the following schedule:

Date	Assets	=	Liabilities	+	Stockholders' Equity

2. Compute the acquisition cost of the machine.
3. Compute the depreciation expense to be reported for the first year.
4. What should be the book value of the machine at the end of the second year?

E9-4 Recording Straight-Line Depreciation and Repairs

Wiater Company operates a small manufacturing facility. On January 1, 2021, an asset account for the company showed the following balances:

Equipment	$160,000
Accumulated Depreciation (beginning of year)	100,000

During the first week of January 2021, the following expenditures were incurred for repairs and maintenance:

Routine maintenance and repairs on the equipment	$ 1,850
Major overhaul of the equipment that improved efficiency	24,000

The equipment is being depreciated on a straight-line basis over an estimated life of 15 years with a $10,000 estimated residual value. The annual accounting period ends on December 31.

Required:

Indicate the effects (accounts, amounts, and + or −) of the following two items on the accounting equation, using the headings shown below.

1. The adjustment for depreciation made last year at the end of 2020.
2. The two expenditures for repairs and maintenance during January 2021.

Item	Assets	=	Liabilities	+	Stockholders' Equity

E9-5 Determining Financial Statement Effects of Straight-Line Depreciation and Repairs

Refer to the information in E9-4.

Required:

1. Give the adjusting journal entry that would have been made at the end of 2020 for depreciation on the manufacturing equipment.
2. Starting at the beginning of 2021, what is the remaining estimated life?
3. Give the journal entries to record the two expenditures for repairs and maintenance during 2021.

E9-6 Computing and Recording Straight-Line Depreciation

Solar Innovations Corporation bought a machine at the beginning of the year at a cost of $22,000. The estimated useful life was five years and the residual value was $2,000.

Required:

1. Complete a depreciation schedule with the following headings. Assume the straight-line method is used and round answers to the nearest dollar.

		Income Statement		Balance Sheet		
Year	Computation	Depreciation Expense	Cost	Accumulated Depreciation	Book Value
At acquisition					
1					

2. Prepare the journal entry to record Year 2 depreciation.

LO 9-3

E9-7 Computing and Recording Units-of-Production Depreciation

Refer to the information in E9-6. Further assume the estimated productive life of the machine is 10,000 units. Expected annual production was year 1, 2,000 units; year 2, 3,000 units; year 3, 2,000 units; year 4, 2,000 units; and year 5, 1,000 units. Complete requirements 1 and 2 assuming the units-of-production method is used.

LO 9-3

E9-8 Computing and Recording Double-Declining-Balance Depreciation

Refer to the information in E9-6. Complete requirements 1 and 2 assuming the double-declining-balance method is used.

LO 9-3

E9-9 Computing Depreciation under Alternative Methods

Sonic Corporation

Sonic Corporation purchased and installed electronic payment equipment at its drive-in restaurants in San Marcos, TX, at a cost of $27,000. The equipment has an estimated residual value of $1,500. The equipment is expected to process 255,000 payments over its three-year useful life. Per year, expected payment transactions are 61,200, year 1; 140,250, year 2; and 53,550, year 3.

Required:

Complete a depreciation schedule for each of the alternative methods.

1. Straight-line.
2. Units-of-production.
3. Double-declining-balance.

		Income Statement	Balance Sheet		
Year	Computation	Depreciation Expense	Cost	Accumulated Depreciation	Book Value
At acquisition					
1					

LO 9-3

E9-10 Inferring Asset Age from Straight-Line Depreciation

On January 1, the records of Tasty Treats Corporation (TTC) showed the following regarding production equipment:

Equipment (estimated residual value, $4,000)	$16,000
Accumulated Depreciation (straight-line, one year)	2,000

Required:

Based on the data given, compute the estimated useful life of the equipment.

LO 9-5

E9-11 Demonstrating the Effect of Book Value on Reporting an Asset Disposal

FedEx Corporation

FedEx Corporation is the world's leading express-distribution company. In addition to its 643 aircraft, the company has more than 91,000 ground vehicles that pick up and deliver packages. Assume that FedEx sold a delivery truck for $16,000. FedEx had originally purchased the truck for $28,000 and had recorded depreciation for three years.

Required:

1. Calculate the amount of gain or loss on disposal, assuming that Accumulated Depreciation was (a) $12,000, (b) $10,000, and (c) $15,000.
2. Using the following structure, indicate the effects (accounts, amounts, and + or −) of the disposal of the truck, assuming Accumulated Depreciation was (a) $12,000, (b) $10,000, and (c) $15,000.

Assets	=	Liabilities	+	Stockholders' Equity

3. Based on the three preceding situations, explain how the amount of depreciation recorded up to the time of disposal affects the amount of gain or loss on disposal.
4. Prepare the journal entry to record the disposal of the truck, assuming Accumulated Depreciation was (*a*) $12,000, (*b*) $10,000, and (*c*) $15,000.

E9-12 Evaluating the Impact of Estimated Useful Lives of Intangible Assets

LO 9-6

Onlineshop Inc., Ubiquitous Inc., and Travelmore Corp. rely on various intangible assets to operate their businesses. These companies amortize the cost of these assets using the straight-line method over the following average estimated useful lives (in years), as reported in their annual reports.

Type of Intangible Asset	Onlineshop, Inc.	Ubiquitous, Inc.	Travelmore Corp.
Developed Technology	3.9	4.1	2.0
Trade Names	4.4	8.6	10.0
Customer Relationships	3.6	4.0	6.0

Required:

Based on these estimates, identify the company that uses the longest periods for amortizing most of its classes of intangible assets. Will these estimates increase or decrease that company's net income relative to its competitors? Explain.

E9-13 Calculating the Impact of Estimated Useful Lives of Intangible Assets

LO 9-6

Refer to the data in E9-12. Assume each company spent $319,800 at the beginning of the current year for additional Developed Technology. Because of its proprietary nature, the technology is estimated to have no residual value at the end of its estimated life.

Required:

Calculate the impact (direction and amount) that the amortization of such expenditures would have on each company's Income from Operations in the current year.

E9-14 Computing and Reporting the Acquisition and Amortization of Three Different Intangible Assets

LO 9-6

Bluestone Company had three intangible assets at the end of the current year:

a. A patent purchased this year from Miller Co. on January 1 for a cash cost of $9,300. When purchased, the patent had an estimated life of 15 years.
b. A trademark was registered with the federal government for $10,000. Management estimated that the trademark could be worth as much as $200,000 because it has an indefinite life.
c. Computer licensing rights were purchased this year on January 1 for $60,000. The rights are expected to have a five-year useful life to the company.

Required:

1. Compute the acquisition cost of each intangible asset.
2. Compute the amortization of each intangible for the current year ended December 31.
3. Show how these assets and any related expenses should be reported on the balance sheet and income statement for the current year.

E9-15 Computing and Interpreting the Fixed Asset Turnover Ratio from a Financial Analyst's Perspective

LO 9-7

Apple Inc.
Microsoft Corp.

The following data were included in a recent Apple Inc. annual report (in millions):

	2015	2016	2017	2018
Net revenue	$233,715	$215,640	$229,230	$265,600
Net property, plant, and equipment	22,471	27,010	33,780	41,300

Required:

1. Compute Apple's fixed asset turnover ratio for 2016, 2017, and 2018. Round your answer to one decimal place.
2. During 2018, Microsoft reported a fixed asset turnover ratio of 3.8. Was Apple's turnover better or worse than Microsoft's in that year?

LO 9-3, 9-7   **E9-16   Computing Depreciation and Book Value for Two Years Using Alternative Depreciation Methods and Interpreting the Impact on the Fixed Asset Turnover Ratio**

Torge Company bought a machine for $65,000 cash. The estimated useful life was five years and the estimated residual value was $5,000. Assume that the estimated useful life in productive units is 150,000. Units actually produced were 40,000 in year 1 and 45,000 in year 2.

Required:

1. Determine the appropriate amounts to complete the following schedule. Show computations.

	Depreciation Expense for		Book Value at the End of	
Method of Depreciation	Year 1	Year 2	Year 1	Year 2
Straight-line				
Units-of-production				
Double-declining-balance				

2. Which method would result in the lowest net income for year 1? For year 2?
3. Which method would result in the lowest fixed asset turnover ratio for year 1? Why?

LO 9-S1   **E9-17   (Supplement 9A) Calculating and Reporting Depletion**

Texas Oil Company (TOC) paid $3,000,000 for an oil reserve estimated to hold 50,000 barrels of oil. Oil production is expected to be 10,000 barrels in year 1, 30,000 barrels in year 2, and 10,000 barrels in year 3. TOC expects to begin selling barrels from its oil inventory in year 4.

Required:

Assuming these estimates prove to be accurate, show the balances in the oil reserve, accumulated depletion, and oil inventory accounts in each of the three years. What effect does this yearly depletion have on the income statement?

LO 9-S2   **E9-18   (Supplement 9B) Determining Financial Statement Effects of a Change in Estimate**

Refer to E9-4.

Required:

1. Indicate the effects (accounts, amounts, and + or −) of the 2021 adjustment for depreciation of the manufacturing equipment, assuming no change in the estimated life or residual value. Show computations.

Date	Assets	=	Liabilities	+	Stockholders' Equity

2. Give the adjusting entry that should be made at the end of 2021 for depreciation.

COACHED PROBLEMS

   Mc Graw Hill **connect**

LO 9-2, 9-3   **CP9-1   Computing Acquisition Cost and Recording Depreciation under Three Alternative Methods**

At the beginning of the year, Young Company bought machinery, shelving, and a forklift.

The machinery initially cost $25,600 but had to be overhauled (at a cost of $1,200) before it could be installed (at a cost of $600) and finally put into use. The machinery's total life was estimated as 40,000 hours, with an estimated residual value of $1,000. The machinery was actually used 5,000 hours in year 1 and 7,000 hours in year 2. Repair costs were $350 in each year.

The shelving cost $9,300 and was expected to last five years, with a residual value of $600.

The forklift cost $10,800 and was expected to last six years, with a residual value of $2,000.

Required:

1. Compute the amount to be capitalized for the machinery.
2. Compute year 2 units-of-production depreciation expense for the machinery.
3. Give the journal entry to record year 2 depreciation expense for the machinery.
4. Compute year 2 straight-line depreciation expense for the shelving and give the journal entry to record it.
5. Compute double-declining-balance depreciation expense for years 1 and 2 for the forklift.
   TIP: Remember that the formula for double-declining-balance uses cost minus accumulated depreciation (not residual value).
6. Give the journal entry to record double-declining balance depreciation expense for the forklift for year 2.

CP9-2 Recording and Interpreting the Disposal of Long-Lived Assets

LO 9-5

During the current year, Martinez Company disposed of two different assets. On January 1, prior to their disposal, the accounts reflected the following:

Asset	Original Cost	Residual Value	Estimated Life	Accumulated Depreciation (straight-line)
Machine A	$76,200	$4,200	15 years	$62,400 (13 years)
Machine B	20,000	2,000	8 years	13,500 (6 years)

The machines were disposed of in the following ways:

a. Machine A: Sold on January 2 for $20,000 cash.
b. Machine B: On January 2, this machine was scrapped with zero proceeds (and zero cost of removal).

Required:

1. Give the journal entry related to the disposal of Machine A on January 2 of the current year.
2. Give the journal entry related to the disposal of Machine B on January 2 of the current year.
   TIP: When no cash is received on disposal, the loss on disposal will equal the book value of the asset at the time of disposal.

CP9-3 Analyzing and Recording Long-Lived Asset Transactions with Partial-Year Depreciation

LO 9-2, 9-3, 9-6

Palmer Cook Music Productions manages and operates two bands. The company entered into the following transactions during a recent year.

January 2	Purchased a tour bus for $80,000 by paying $20,000 cash and signing a $60,000 note due in two years. In its accounting system, the company records the vehicle distinct from other types of equipment.
January 8	After the bus was used for nearly one week, it was painted with the logos of the two bands at a cost of $350, on account. The logos did not increase the lifespan, operating capacity, or operating efficiency of the bus, but they were thought to be useful in promoting the bands.
January 30	Wrote a check for the amount owed on account for the work completed on January 8.
February 1	Purchased new speakers and amplifiers and wrote a check for the full $12,000 cost.
February 8	Paid $250 cash for minor repairs to the tour bus.
March 1	Paid $20,000 cash and signed a $190,000 five-year note to purchase a small office building and land. An appraisal indicated that the building and land contributed equally to the total price.
March 31	Paid $90,000 cash to acquire the goodwill and certain tangible assets of Kris' Myth, Inc. The fair values of the tangible assets acquired were $20,000 for band equipment and $60,000 for recording equipment.

Required:

1. Analyze the accounting equation effects and record journal entries for each of the transactions.

   TIP: Goodwill is recorded as the excess of the purchase price over the fair value of individual assets.

2. For the tangible and intangible assets acquired in the preceding transactions, determine the amount of depreciation and amortization that Palmer Cook Music Productions should report for the quarter ended March 31. For convenience, the equipment and vehicle are depreciated the same way, using the straight-line method with a useful life of five years and no residual value. The building is depreciated using the double-declining-balance method, with a 10-year useful life and residual value of $20,000.

   TIP: Calculate depreciation from the acquisition date to the end of the quarter.

3. Prepare a journal entry to record the depreciation calculated in requirement 2.

GROUP A PROBLEMS

LO 9-2, 9-3

PA9-1 Computing Acquisition Cost and Recording Depreciation under Three Alternative Methods

At the beginning of the year, Grillo Industries bought three used machines. The machines immediately were overhauled, were installed, and started operating. Because the machines were different, each was recorded separately in the accounts. Details for Machine A are provided below.

Cost of the asset	$9,000
Installation costs	800
Renovation costs prior to use	600
Repairs after production began	500

Required:

1. Compute the amount to be capitalized for Machine A. Explain the rationale for capitalizing or expensing the various costs.
2. Compute year 2 straight-line depreciation expense for Machine A, assuming an estimated life of four years and $1,000 residual value.
3. Give the journal entry to record year 2 depreciation expense for Machine A.
4. Compute year 2 units-of-production depreciation expense for Machine B, assuming a capitalized cost of $42,000, an estimated life of 30,000 hours, $4,500 residual value, and actual year 2 use of 8,000 hours.
5. Give the journal entry to record year 2 units-of-production depreciation expense for Machine B.
6. Compute years 1 and 2 double-declining-balance depreciation expense for Machine C, which has a cost of $25,400, an estimated life of 10 years, and $1,400 residual value.
7. Give the journal entry to record year 2 double-declining-balance depreciation expense for Machine C.

LO 9-5 ### PA9-2 Recording and Interpreting the Disposal of Long-Lived Assets

Ly Company disposed of two different assets. On January 1, prior to their disposal, the accounts reflected the following:

Asset	Original Cost	Residual Value	Estimated Life	Accumulated Depreciation (straight-line)
Machine A	$30,000	$3,000	5 years	$21,600 (4 years)
Machine B	59,200	3,200	14 years	$44,000 (11 years)

The machines were disposed of in the following ways:

a. Machine A: Sold on January 1 for $9,000 cash.
b. Machine B: On January 1, this machine was scrapped with zero proceeds (and zero cost of removal).

Required:

1. Give the journal entry related to the disposal of Machine A at the beginning of the current year.
2. Give the journal entry related to the disposal of Machine B at the beginning of the current year.

PA9-3 Analyzing and Recording Long-Lived Asset Transactions with Partial-Year Depreciation

LO 9-2, 9-3, 9-6

Precision Construction entered into the following transactions during a recent year.

January 2	Purchased a bulldozer for $250,000 by paying $20,000 cash and signing a $230,000 note due in five years.
January 3	Replaced the steel tracks on the bulldozer at a cost of $20,000, purchased on account. The new steel tracks increase the bulldozer's operating efficiency.
January 30	Wrote a check for the amount owed on account for the work completed on January 3.
February 1	Repaired the leather seat on the bulldozer and wrote a check for the full $800 cost.
March 1	Paid $3,600 cash for the rights to use computer software for a two-year period.

Required:

1. Analyze the accounting equation effects and record journal entries for each of the transactions.
2. For the tangible and intangible assets acquired in the preceding transactions, determine the amount of depreciation and amortization that Precision Construction should report for the quarter ended March 31. The equipment is depreciated using the double-declining-balance method with a useful life of five years and $40,000 residual value.
3. Prepare a journal entry to record the depreciation calculated in requirement 2.

PA9-4 Recording Transactions and Adjustments for Tangible and Intangible Assets

LO 9-1, 9-2, 9-3, 9-4, 9-5, 9-6

The following transactions and adjusting entries were completed by a paper-packaging company called Gravure Graphics International. The company uses straight-line depreciation for trucks and other vehicles, double-declining-balance depreciation for buildings, and straight-line amortization for patents.

2020	
January 2	Paid $95,000 cash to purchase storage shed components.
January 3	Paid $5,000 cash to have the storage shed erected. The storage shed has an estimated life of 10 years and a residual value of $10,000.
April 1	Paid $38,000 cash to purchase a pickup truck for use in the business. The truck has an estimated useful life of five years and a residual value of $8,000.
May 13	Paid $250 cash for minor repairs to the pickup truck's upholstery.
July 1	Paid $20,000 cash to purchase patent rights on a new paper bag manufacturing process. The patent is estimated to have a remaining useful life of five years.
December 31	Recorded depreciation and amortization on the pickup truck, storage shed, and patent.
2021	
June 30	Sold the pickup truck for $33,000 cash. (Record the depreciation on the truck prior to recording its disposal.)
December 31	Recorded depreciation on the storage shed. Recorded the patent amortization. After recording the patent amortization, determined that the patent was impaired and wrote off its remaining book value (i.e., wrote down the book value to zero).

Required:

Give the journal entries required on each of the above dates.

GROUP B PROBLEMS

LO 9-2, 9-3   **PB9-1 Computing Acquisition Cost and Recording Depreciation under Three Alternative Methods**

At the beginning of the year, Oakmont Company bought a shed, a machine, and a trailer.

The shed initially cost $19,600 but had to be renovated at a cost of $400. The shed was expected to last seven years, with a residual value of $1,100. Repairs costing $220 were incurred at the end of the first year of use.

The machine cost $10,900, and is estimated to have a total life of 40,000 hours and residual value of $900. The machine was actually used 2,000 hours in year 1 and 4,000 hours in year 2.

The trailer cost $10,600 and was expected to last four years, with a residual value of $2,000.

Required:

1. Compute the amount to be capitalized for the shed.
2. Compute year 2 straight-line depreciation expense for the shed and give the journal entry to record it.
3. Compute year 2 units-of-production depreciation expense for the machine.
4. Give the journal entry to record year 2 units-of-production depreciation expense for the machine.
5. Compute years 1 and 2 double-declining-balance depreciation expense for the trailer.
6. Give the journal entry to record year 2 double-declining-balance depreciation expense for the trailer.

LO 9-5   **PB9-2 Recording and Interpreting the Disposal of Long-Lived Assets**

During the current year, Rayon Corporation disposed of two different assets. On January 1, prior to their disposal, the accounts reflected the following:

Asset	Original Cost	Residual Value	Estimated Life	Accumulated Depreciation (straight-line)
Machine A	$60,000	$11,000	7 years	$28,000 (4 years)
Machine B	14,200	1,925	5 years	7,365 (3 years)

The machines were disposed of in the following ways:

a. Machine A: Sold on January 2 for $33,500 cash.
b. Machine B: On January 2, this machine was scrapped with zero proceeds (and zero cost of removal).

Required:

1. Give the journal entry related to the disposal of Machine A on January 2 of the current year.
2. Give the journal entry related to the disposal of Machine B on January 2 of the current year.

LO 9-2, 9-3, 9-6   **PB9-3 Analyzing and Recording Long-Lived Asset Transactions with Partial-Year Depreciation**

Rudy's Restaurant Company (RRC) entered into the following transactions during a recent year.

April 1	Purchased equipment (a new walk-in cooler) for $5,000 by paying $1,000 cash and signing a $4,000 note due in six months.
April 2	Enhanced the equipment (by replacing the air-conditioning system in the walk-in cooler) at a cost of $3,000, purchased on account.
April 30	Wrote a check for the amount owed on account for the work completed on April 2.
May 1	A local carpentry company repaired the restaurant's front door, for which RRC wrote a check for the full $120 cost.
June 1	Paid $9,120 cash for the rights to use the name and store concept created by a different restaurant that has been successful in the region.

Required:

1. Analyze the accounting equation effects and record journal entries for each of the transactions.
2. For the tangible and intangible assets acquired in the preceding transactions, determine the amount of depreciation and amortization that Rudy's Restaurant Company should report for the quarter ended June 30. Equipment is depreciated using the straight-line method with a useful life of five years and no residual value. The RRC franchise right is amortized using the straight-line method with a useful life of four years and no residual value.
3. Prepare a journal entry to record the depreciation calculated in requirement 2.

PB9-4   Recording Transactions and Adjustments for Tangible and Intangible Assets

LO 9-1, 9-2, 9-3, 9-4, 9-5, 9-6

The following transactions and adjusting entries were completed by a local delivery company called Fast Delivery. The company uses straight-line depreciation for delivery vehicles, double-declining-balance depreciation for buildings, and straight-line amortization for franchise rights.

<u>2020</u>

January 2	Paid $175,000 cash to purchase a small warehouse building near the airport. The building has an estimated life of 20 years and a residual value of $15,000.
July 1	Paid $40,000 cash to purchase a delivery van. The van has an estimated useful life of five years and a residual value of $8,000.
October 2	Paid $500 cash to paint a small office in the warehouse building.
October 13	Paid $150 cash to get the oil changed in the delivery van.
December 1	Paid $90,000 cash to UPS to begin operating Fast Delivery business as a franchise using the name The UPS Store. This franchise right expires in five years.
December 31	Recorded depreciation and amortization on the delivery van, warehouse building, and franchise right.

<u>2021</u>

June 30	Sold the warehouse building for $140,000 cash. (Record the depreciation on the building prior to recording its disposal.)
December 31	Recorded depreciation on the delivery van and amortization on the franchise right. Determined that the franchise right was not impaired in value.

Required:

Give the journal entries required on each of the above dates.

COMPREHENSIVE PROBLEM

C9-1   Accounting for Operating Activities (Including Depreciation) and Preparing Financial Statements (Chapters 3, 4, 8, and 9)

LO 3-3, 4-2, 8-2, 9-2, 9-3

Grid Iron Prep Inc. (GIPI) is a service business incorporated in January of the current year to provide personal training for athletes aspiring to play college football. The following transactions occurred during the month ended January 31.

a. GIPI issued stock in exchange for $100,000 cash on 1/01.
b. GIPI purchased a gymnasium building and gym equipment on 1/02 for $50,000, 80 percent of which related to the gymnasium and 20 percent to the equipment.
c. GIPI paid $260 cash on 1/03 to have the gym equipment refurbished before it could be used.
d. GIPI provided $4,000 in training on 1/04 and expected collection in February.
e. GIPI collected $36,000 cash in training fees on 1/10, of which $34,000 related to January and $2,000 related to February.
f. GIPI paid $23,000 of wages and $7,000 in utilities on 1/30.
g. GIPI will depreciate the gymnasium building using the straight-line method over 20 years with a residual value of $2,000. Gym equipment will be depreciated using the double-declining-balance method, with an estimated residual value of $2,250 at the end of its four-year useful life. Record depreciation on 1/31 equal to one-twelfth the yearly amount.

h. GIPI received a bill on 1/31 for $350 for advertising done on 1/31. The bill has not been paid or recorded.

i. GIPI uses the aging method for estimating doubtful accounts and, on 1/31, will record an estimated 3 percent of its under-30-day-old accounts as not collectible.

j. GIPI's income tax rate is 30 percent. Assume depreciation for tax is the same amount as depreciation for financial reporting purposes.

Required:

1. Prepare journal entries to record the transactions and adjustments listed in (*a*)–(*j*).

2. If you are completing this problem manually, post the entries from requirement 1 to T-accounts and then prepare an adjusted trial balance at December 31. Show a zero balance for Retained Earnings in the adjusted trial balance. (If you are completing this problem in Connect, this requirement will be completed automatically for you using your responses to requirement 1.)

3. Prepare GIPI's annual income statement, statement of retained earnings, and classified balance sheet.

SKILLS DEVELOPMENT CASES

LO 9-2, 9-3, 9-6, 9-7

The Home Depot

S9-1 Finding Financial Information

Refer to the financial statements of The Home Depot in Appendix A at the end of this book. (Note: Fiscal 2019 for The Home Depot runs from February 4, 2019, to February 2, 2020. See S1-1 for further explanation.)

1. The total cost of Property and Equipment is $44,860 (million) at February 2, 2020. Use this information, along with other data reported on the balance sheet, to determine the amount of "Accumulated Depreciation and Amortization" at February 2, 2020. What percentage is this of the total cost of property and equipment?
   a. $67,630 (million); 150.8%
   b. $22,090 (million); 49.2%
   c. $22,375 (million); 49.9%
   d. $1,989 (million); 4.4%

2. What amount of Depreciation and Amortization Expense was reported for the year ended February 2, 2020? What percentage of net sales is it?
   a. $1,989 (million); 1.8%
   b. $1,989 (million); 17.7%
   c. $22,770 (million); 20.7%
   d. $1,989 (million); 4.4%

3. What is the fixed asset turnover ratio for the year ended February 2, 2020?
   a. 2.03
   b. 3.11
   c. 4.84
   d. 4.88

LO 9-2, 9-3, 9-6, 9-7, 9-8

Lowe's

S9-2 Comparing Financial Information

Refer to the financial statements of Lowe's Companies, Inc. in Appendix B. (Note: Fiscal 2019 for Lowe's runs from February 2, 2019, to January 31, 2020.)

1. The total cost of Property is $35,945 (million) at January 31, 2020. Use this information, along with other data reported on the balance sheet, to determine the amount of Accumulated Depreciation at January 31, 2020. What percentage is this of the total cost of property?
   a. $17,276 (million); 48.1%
   b. $54,614 (million); 151.9%
   c. $18,432 (million); 51.3%
   d. $1,262 (million); 3.5%

2. What amount of Depreciation and Amortization Expense was reported for the year ended January 31, 2020? What percentage of net sales is it?
   a. $1,404 (million); 2.1%
   b. $1,262 (million); 29.5%
   c. $1,262 (million); 1.7%
   d. $1,477 (million); 2.1%

3. What is the fixed asset turnover ratio for the year ended January 31, 2020?
   a. 1.94
   b. 3.89
   c. 4.29
   d. 57.17

S9-3 Internet-Based Team Research: Examining an Annual Report

LO 9-1, 9-3, 9-6, 9-7

As a team, select an industry to analyze. Using your web browser, each team member should access the annual report or 10-K for one publicly traded company in the industry, with each member selecting a different company. (See S1-3 in Chapter 1 for a description of possible resources for these tasks.)

Required:

1. On an individual basis, each team member should write a short report that incorporates the following:
   a. Describe the depreciation methods used.
   b. Compute the percentage of fixed asset cost that has been depreciated. What does this imply about the length of time the assets have been depreciated?
   c. Compute the fixed asset turnover ratios for the current and prior years. What does this tell you about the efficiency of the company's asset use?
   d. Describe the kinds of intangible assets, if any, that the company reports on the balance sheet.

2. Then, as a team, write a short report comparing and contrasting your companies using these attributes. Discuss any patterns across the companies that you as a team observe. Provide potential explanations for any differences discovered.

S9-4 Ethical Decision Making: A Real-Life Example

LO 9-2, 9-7

WorldCom

This case is based on a cost capitalization fraud at WorldCom. The case is available online in the Connect eBook. To complete this case, you will identify information that suggests certain costs are not appropriately capitalized and you will calculate the effects of capitalizing those costs on the financial statements.

S9-5 Ethical Decision Making: A Mini-Case

LO 9-3

Assume you are one of three members of the accounting staff working for a small, private company. At the beginning of this year, the company expanded into a new industry by acquiring equipment that will be used to make several new lines of products. The owner and general manager of the company has indicated that, as one of the conditions for providing financing for the new equipment, the company's bank will receive a copy of the company's annual financial statements. Another condition of the loan is that the company's total assets cannot fall below $250,000. Violation of this condition gives the bank the option to demand immediate repayment of the loan. Before making the adjustment for this year's depreciation, the company's total assets are reported at $255,000. The owner has asked you to take a look at the facts regarding the new equipment and "work with the numbers to make sure everything stays onside with the bank."

A depreciation method has not yet been adopted for the new equipment. Equipment used in other parts of the company is depreciated using the double-declining-balance method. The cost of the new equipment was $35,000 and the manager estimates it will be worth "at least $7,000" at the end of its four-year useful life. Because the products made with the new equipment are only beginning to catch on with consumers, the company used the equipment to produce just 4,000 units this year. It is expected that, over all four years of its useful life, the new equipment will make a total of 28,000 units.

Required:

1. Calculate the depreciation that would be reported this year under each of the three methods shown in this chapter. Which of the methods would meet the owner's objective?

2. Evaluate whether it is ethical to recommend that the company use the method identified in requirement 1. What two parties are most directly affected by this recommendation? How would each party benefit from or be harmed by the recommendation? Does the recommendation violate any laws or applicable rules? Are there any other factors that you would consider before making a recommendation?

S9-6 Critical Thinking: Analyzing the Effects of Depreciation Policies on Income

LO 9-3, 9-5, 9-8

As an aspiring financial analyst, you have applied to a major Wall Street firm for a summer job. To screen potential applicants, the firm provides you a short case study and asks you to evaluate the financial success of two hypothetical companies that started operations last year on January 1. Both companies operate in the same industry, use very similar assets, and have very similar customer bases. Among the additional information provided about the companies are the following comparative income statements.

	Fast Corporation		Slow Corporation	
	Last Year	Current Year	Last Year	Current Year
Net Sales	$60,000	$60,000	$60,000	$60,000
Cost of Goods Sold	20,000	20,000	20,000	20,000
Gross Profit	40,000	40,000	40,000	40,000
Selling, General, and Administrative Expenses	19,000	19,000	19,000	19,000
Depreciation Expense	10,667	3,555	5,000	5,000
Loss (Gain) on Disposal	—	(2,222)	—	2,000
Income from Operations	$10,333	$ 19,667	$ 16,000	$ 14,000

Required:

Prepare an analysis of the two companies with the goal of determining which company is better managed. If you could request two additional pieces of information from these companies' financial statements, describe specifically what they would be and explain how they would help you to make a decision.

LO 9-3

Cedar Fair
Six Flags

S9-7 Preparing Depreciation Schedules for Straight-Line and Double-Declining-Balance

To make some extra money, you've started preparing templates of business forms and schedules for others to download from the Internet (for a small fee). After relevant information is entered into each template, it automatically performs calculations using formulas you have entered into the template. For the depreciation template, you decide to produce two worksheets: one that calculates depreciation and book value under the straight-line method and another that calculates these amounts using the double-declining-balance method. The templates perform straightforward calculations of depreciation and book value when given the cost of an asset, its estimated useful life, and its estimated residual value. These particular templates won't handle disposals or changes in estimates—you plan to create a deluxe version for those functions. To illustrate that your templates actually work, you enter the information used to produce the depreciation schedules shown in Exhibit 9.6, with Cedar Fair and Six Flags as examples (but replace the millions of dollars with thousands, as shown in the following spreadsheet).

Although you're confident you can use appropriate formulas in the spreadsheet to create a template for the straight-line method, you're a little uncertain about how to make the double-declining-balance method work. As usual, you e-mail your friend Owen for advice. Here's what he said:

From:	Owentheaccountant@yahoo.com
To:	Helpme@hotmail.com
Cc:	
Subject:	Excel Help

I wish I'd thought of charging money for showing how to do ordinary accounting activities. You'd have made me rich by now. Here's how to set up your worksheets. Begin by creating an "input values" section. This section will allow someone to enter the asset cost, residual value, and estimated life in an area removed from the actual depreciation schedule. You don't want someone accidentally entering amounts over formulas that you've entered into the schedule.

The cells from the input values section will be referenced by other cells in the depreciation schedule. You will want to enter formulas in the cells for the first year row, and then copy and paste them to rows for the other years. When doing this, you will need to use what is called an "absolute reference," which means the cell reference does not change when one row is copied and pasted to a different row. Unlike an ordinary cell reference that has a format of A1, an absolute reference has the format of A1, which prevents the spreadsheet from changing either the column (A) or row (1) when copying the cell to other cells. You may find this useful when preparing both the straight-line and double-declining-balance schedules.

To create the depreciation schedules, use five columns labeled (1) year, (2) beginning-of-year accumulated depreciation, (3) depreciation, (4) end-of-year accumulated depreciation, and (5) end-of-year book value.

The double-declining-balance template will be the trickiest to create because you need to be concerned that the book value is not depreciated below the residual value in the last year of the asset's life. To force the template to automatically watch for this, you will need to use the IF function.

I have included a screenshot of a template I created, using the IF function to properly calculate depreciation for all years of the asset's life. Notice the formula shown in the formula bar at the top

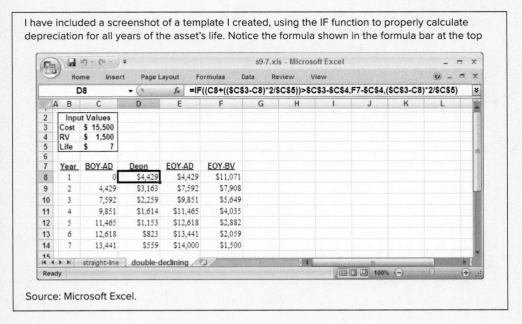

Source: Microsoft Excel.

Required:

Create the spreadsheet templates to calculate depreciation and book value using the straight-line and double-declining-balance methods. Demonstrate that the template works by reproducing the schedules in Exhibit 9.6 using thousands rather than millions of dollars.

> **TIP:** To switch between displaying cell formulas and their values, press CTRL and ~ (tilde) at the same time. Also, use Excel's help feature to obtain further information about the IF function.

CONTINUING CASE

CC9-1 Accounting for the Use and Disposal of Long-Lived Assets

LO 9-3, 9-5

Nicole's Getaway Spa (NGS) purchased a hydrotherapy tub system to add to the wellness programs at NGS. The machine was purchased at the beginning of the year at a cost of $7,000. The estimated useful life was five years and the residual value was $500. Assume that the estimated productive life of the machine is 13,000 hours. Expected annual production was year 1, 3,100 hours; year 2, 2,500 hours; year 3, 3,400 hours; year 4, 2,200 hours; and year 5, 1,800 hours.

Required:

1. Complete a depreciation schedule for each of the alternative methods.
   a. Straight-line.   c. Double-declining-balance.
   b. Units-of-production.

2. Assume NGS sold the hydrotherapy tub system for $2,100 at the end of year 3. Prepare the journal entry to account for the disposal of this asset under the three different methods.

3. The following amounts were forecast for year 3: Sales Revenues $42,000; Cost of Goods Sold $33,000; Other Operating Expenses $4,000; and Interest Expense $800. Create an income statement for year 3 for each of the different depreciation methods, ending at Income before Income Tax Expense. (Don't forget to include a loss or gain on disposal for each method.)

DATA ANALYTICS EXERCISES

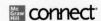

Data Analytics Exercises are auto-graded exercises offering detailed data visualization, interpretation, and analysis, and are available for assignment in *Connect*.

10

Liabilities

CHAPTER TEN

YOUR LEARNING OBJECTIVES

LO 10-1 Explain the role of liabilities in financing a business.

LO 10-2 Explain how to account for common types of current liabilities.

LO 10-3 Analyze and record bond liability transactions.

LO 10-4 Describe how to account for contingent liabilities.

LO 10-5 Calculate and interpret the debt-to-assets ratio and the times interest earned ratio.

LO 10-S1 Use straight-line bond amortization.

LO 10-S2 Use effective-interest bond amortization.

LO 10-S3 Use simplified effective-interest bond amortization.

LO 10-S4 Account for installment notes payable.

THAT WAS THEN

Previous chapters focused on items related to the assets section of the balance sheet.

FOCUS COMPANY: GENERAL MILLS

They've turned in the reports and they're just waiting to hear their letter grade. They're expecting an A and would be devastated if it's a B. Sounds like some high-achieving students, right? It could be. But it's actually Bernie the Bunny, Lucky the Leprechaun, the Pillsbury Doughboy, and their corporate bosses at General Mills. That's right. This magically delicious company and all its characters receive a letter grade just like you and your friends. Their grading process differs a bit from yours because their grade is assigned by credit rating agencies like Standard & Poor's, Fitch, and Moody's, indicating the company's ability to pay its liabilities on a timely basis. Another difference is their grades can range from AAA to D. The AAA rating is given to companies in rock-solid financial condition and the D goes to those likely to pay less than half of what they owe. In general, anything above BB is considered a good to high-quality credit rating, which is what General Mills typically earns. Anything below BB is called "junk."

In this chapter, you will learn about the accounting procedures and financial ratios used to report and interpret liabilities, and how they influence credit ratings. Although we focus on corporate reporting and analyses, this chapter also can help you to understand the kind of information others use to evaluate your own personal credit rating.

THIS IS NOW

This chapter focuses on items related to the liabilities section of the balance sheet.

ORGANIZATION OF THE CHAPTER

Understand the business	Study the accounting methods	Evaluate the results	Supplements 10A, 10B, 10C	Supplement 10D	Review the chapter
• The role of liabilities	• Measuring liabilities • Current liabilities • Long-term liabilities • Contingent liabilities	• Debt-to-assets ratio • Times interest earned ratio	• Straight-line method of amortization • Effective-interest method of amortization • Simplified effective-interest amortization	• Installment notes payable	• Demonstration cases • Chapter summary • Key terms • Homework helper • Practice material

Understand the Business

Learning Objective 10-1
Explain the role of liabilities in financing a business.

THE ROLE OF LIABILITIES

The balance sheet excerpt in Exhibit 10.1 shows that, at the end of its 2019 fiscal year, General Mills had financed its $30.1 billion of total assets using a combination of liabilities ($22.2 billion) and equity ($7.9 billion). For General Mills, and many other companies, liabilities play a significant role in financing business activities. Liabilities are created when a company buys goods and services on credit, obtains short-term loans to cover gaps in cash flows, and issues long-term debt to obtain money for expanding into new regions and markets.

To help financial statement users know when liabilities must be repaid, companies prepare a classified balance sheet, as shown in Exhibit 10.1. In Chapter 2, you learned that a classified balance sheet reports current liabilities separate from other liabilities. Technically, **current liabilities** are defined as short-term obligations that will be paid or fulfilled within the company's current operating cycle or within one year of the balance sheet date, whichever is longer. Practically, this definition can be simplified as liabilities that are due within one year (because most companies have operating cycles shorter than a year). This means that, as shown in Exhibit 10.1, General Mills will have to pay over $7 billion in the upcoming year. An additional $11.6 billion in long-term debt and $3.5 billion in other liabilities will need to be paid in the longer term. Although these long-term obligations rarely get a separate subheading of their own, people often refer to them as noncurrent or long-term liabilities.

YOU SHOULD KNOW

Current Liabilities: Short-term obligations that will be paid in cash (or fulfilled with other current assets) within 12 months or the next operating cycle, whichever is longer.

EXHIBIT 10.1	Excerpt from General Mills's Balance Sheet

Balance Sheet Excerpt

(in millions)

Assets		Liabilities and Stockholders' Equity	
Current Assets		Current Liabilities	
Cash and Cash Equivalents	$ 450	Accounts Payable	$ 2,850
Accounts Receivable, Net	1,680	Accrued Liabilities (see Exhibit 10.2)	1,370
Inventory	1,560	Notes Payable	1,470
Prepaid Rent and Other	500	Current Portion of Long-Term Debt	1,400
Total Current Assets	4,190	Total Current Liabilities	7,090
Land, Buildings, and Equipment	3,790	Long-Term Debt	11,600
Goodwill	13,990	Other Liabilities	3,510
Other Intangible Assets	7,160	Total Liabilities	22,200
Other Assets	980	Stockholders' Equity (summarized)	7,910
Total Assets	$30,110	Total Liabilities and Equity	$30,110

Study the Accounting Methods

MEASURING LIABILITIES

As Exhibit 10.1 illustrates, General Mills owed various types of liabilities. In this section, we will describe each of these liabilities and the methods used to account for them. In general, the amount reported for each liability is the result of three factors:

1. **The initial amount of the liability.** Initially, the company records each liability at the amount of cash a creditor would accept to settle the liability immediately after a transaction or event creates the liability.

2. **Additional amounts owed to the creditor.** The company increases liabilities whenever additional obligations arise, by purchasing goods and services, receiving customer deposits, or incurring interest charges over time.

3. **Payments or services provided to the creditor.** The company decreases liabilities whenever the company makes a payment or provides services to the creditor.

Notice that a liability is first recorded at the amount initially owed, which excludes interest charges. **Interest arises only when time passes, so no interest is recorded on the day the company purchases an item on account or the day the company receives a loan.**

> **Learning Objective 10-2**
> Explain how to account for common types of current liabilities.

CURRENT LIABILITIES

Let's look more closely at each current liability listed in Exhibit 10.1.

Accounts Payable

You've used this account in previous chapters, so we'll keep this discussion short. Accounts Payable is increased (credited) when a company receives goods or services on credit and it is decreased (debited) when the company pays on its account. Accounts Payable is generally interest free, but 50–70 percent of suppliers do charge a 1 percent penalty on overdue accounts.[1]

Accrued Liabilities

Chapter 4 showed how to use an adjusting journal entry at the end of the accounting period to record increases in both Salaries and Wages Expense (debit) and Salaries and Wages Payable (credit) when a company had incurred but not yet paid that period's salaries and

---

[1]Mariassunta Giannetti, Mike Burkart, and Tore Ellingsen, "What You Sell Is What You Lend? Explaining Trade Credit Contracts," *Review of Financial Studies* 24, no. 4 (2011), pp. 1261–1298.

EXHIBIT 10.2 | Accrued Liabilities Note (Excerpt)

(in millions)	2019
Accrued Advertising	$ 480
Accrued Payroll	350
Accrued Taxes	40
Accrued Interest	90
Other	410
Total Accrued Liabilities	$1,370

wages. Similar adjustments were made for interest incurred but not paid and income taxes incurred but not paid. Because these adjustments are called *accruals,* the liabilities (Salaries and Wages Payable, Interest Payable, etc.) are generally referred to as *accrued liabilities.* **Accrued liabilities** can include other unpaid expenses, including advertising, corporate income tax, interest, payroll tax, and warranties. General Mills itemizes its $1.4 billion of Accrued Liabilities in a note to its financial statements, similar to Exhibit 10.2.

Accrued Payroll   In addition to Salaries and Wages Payable, companies record liabilities for other aspects of payroll. Two significant payroll liabilities relate to payroll deductions and employer payroll taxes.

Payroll Deductions   Payroll deductions are amounts subtracted from employees' gross earnings to determine their net pay. **Gross earnings** are computed by multiplying the time worked by the pay rate promised by the employer (40 hours × $15 per hour = $600 gross earnings). From these gross earnings, certain **payroll deductions** are subtracted, for items such as income tax, FICA tax, and charitable donations. The tear-away portion of the paycheck shown in Exhibit 10.3 illustrates payroll deductions totaling $116.80. **Net pay** equals gross earnings less payroll deductions ($483.20 = $600.00 − $116.80).

You might think your employer keeps the deductions from your gross earnings, but that's not true. Your employer is obligated to remit those deductions to another organization or government agency on your behalf. As Exhibit 10.3 shows, **payroll deductions create current liabilities for your employer.**

Payroll deductions are either required by law or voluntarily requested by employees. The law requires that employers deduct federal income tax (and possibly state, county, and city income tax) from each employee's gross earnings. The law also requires, through the Federal Insurance Contributions Act, that each employee support Medicare and Social Security through employee payroll deductions called **FICA taxes.** In 2019, employers were

EXHIBIT 10.3 | Accounting for Gross Earnings, Payroll Deductions, and Net Pay

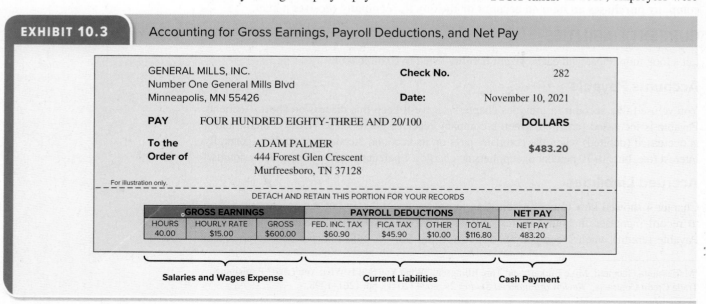

GROSS EARNINGS			PAYROLL DEDUCTIONS				NET PAY
HOURS	HOURLY RATE	GROSS	FED. INC. TAX	FICA TAX	OTHER	TOTAL	NET PAY
40.00	$15.00	$600.00	$60.90	$45.90	$10.00	$116.80	483.20

Salaries and Wages Expense   Current Liabilities   Cash Payment

required to deduct 1.45 percent from each employee's earnings for Medicare and 6.2 percent (on earnings up to $132,900) for Social Security. Voluntarily requested payroll deductions (for charitable donations, parking, union dues, retirement savings, etc.) also are accounted for as liabilities until they are paid on behalf of the employees to the various organizations for which they are intended. The employer classifies payroll deductions as *current* liabilities because they must be paid no more than one month after the payroll date.

To illustrate how to record these items, let's assume (for simplicity) that General Mills has 1,000 workers who earn the same amount as the employee in Exhibit 10.3. The accounting equation effects and journal entry for these 1,000 workers would be as follows:

1 Analyze

Assets	=	Liabilities		+	Stockholders' Equity	
Cash −483,200		Withheld Income Tax Payable	+60,900		Salaries and Wages Expense (+E)	−600,000
		FICA Payable	+45,900			
		Charitable Contributions Payable	+10,000			

2 Record

	Debit	Credit
Salaries and Wages Expense	600,000	
Withheld Income Tax Payable		60,900
FICA Payable		45,900
Charitable Contributions Payable		10,000
Cash		483,200

Employer Payroll Taxes   Beyond paying employees and remitting payroll deductions, employers have other responsibilities that lead to substantial additional labor costs. According to the U.S. Department of Labor, **in 2019, slightly more than 31 percent of labor costs were for costs other than salaries and wages.** In the remainder of this section, we consider two employer payroll taxes: FICA and unemployment taxes.

Like their employees, all employers are required to pay FICA taxes. The required contribution is 100 percent of total employee contributions (called a "matching" contribution). In addition, employers are required by the Federal Unemployment Tax Act (FUTA) and State Unemployment Tax Act (SUTA) to pay unemployment taxes. The rates for these taxes vary by industry, state, and employer history but can be substantial, as shown in the pie chart.

To illustrate how these payroll expenses affect the accounting records, let's assume General Mills was required to match $45,900 for FICA and contribute $4,750 for federal and state unemployment tax—a total of $50,650. These payroll taxes are extra costs the employer incurs beyond the costs of salaries and wages, so they are reported as an additional operating expense on the income statement. Until they have been paid, the liabilities for these taxes are recorded in current liability accounts, as follows:

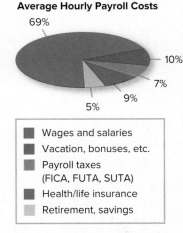

Average Hourly Payroll Costs

69%
10%
7%
9%
5%

- ■ Wages and salaries
- ■ Vacation, bonuses, etc.
- ■ Payroll taxes (FICA, FUTA, SUTA)
- ■ Health/life insurance
- ▢ Retirement, savings

Source: Bureau of Labor Statistics.

1 Analyze

Assets =	Liabilities		+	Stockholders' Equity	
	FICA Payable	+45,900		Payroll Tax	
	Unemployment Tax Payable	+4,750		Expense (+E) −50,650	

2 Record

	Debit	Credit
Payroll Tax Expense	50,650	
FICA Payable		45,900
Unemployment Tax Payable		4,750

When the employer pays these taxes (along with the payroll deductions shown earlier), it decreases the liability accounts (with debits) and decreases its Cash account (with a credit).

Accrued Income Taxes Corporations pay taxes not only on payroll but also on income they earn, just like you. The corporate tax return, which the IRS calls a Form 1120, is similar to the company's income statement, except that it calculates *taxable* income by subtracting tax-allowed expenses from revenues. This taxable income is then multiplied by a federal tax rate, which is 21 percent for corporations. Corporate income taxes are due three and a half months after year-end, although most corporations are required to pay advance installments during the year.

COACH'S TIP

The adjusting journal entry to accrue income taxes was presented in Chapter 4.

Notes Payable

The next liability reported by General Mills in Exhibit 10.1 is Notes Payable. This liability represents the amount the company owes to others as a result of issuing promissory notes. It is the flipside of the notes receivable transactions that were explained in Chapter 8.

Four key events occur with notes payable: (1) establishing the note, (2) accruing interest incurred but not paid, (3) recording interest paid, and (4) recording principal paid. Financial effects are recorded for each of these four events. As an example, assume that on November 1, 2021, General Mills borrowed $100,000 cash on a one-year note that required General Mills to pay 6 percent interest and the $100,000 principal, both on October 31, 2022.

1. **Establish the notes payable.** The $100,000 note has the following accounting equation effects, which General Mills would record using the following journal entry:

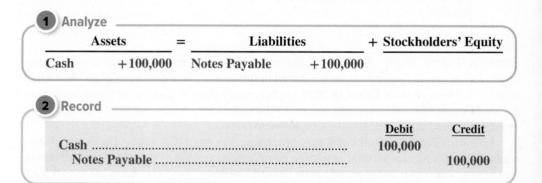

2. **Accrue interest incurred but not paid.** Interest occurs as time passes. It is not owed the day the note is established, but rather it accumulates as each day passes. Under accrual accounting, interest must be recorded as it is incurred over time. The timeline in Exhibit 10.4 shows how General Mills should account for the interest incurred on the note over its one-year term. In reality, General Mills would record an adjustment each month, but for simplicity, we have assumed it occurs only once, at the end of the year. From the date the note was established (November 1, 2021) to the end of the year (December 31, 2021), General Mills incurred two months of interest expense.

COACH'S TIP

This example shows how to account for the note from the borrower's perspective. The same example is presented in Chapter 8 from the lender's perspective.

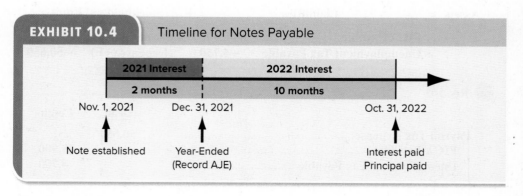

EXHIBIT 10.4 Timeline for Notes Payable

The amount of interest to record for **two** months is computed using the interest formula, as follows:

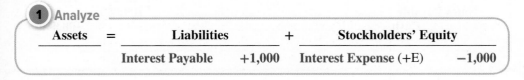

Interest (I) = Principal (P) × Interest Rate (R) × Time (T)
$1,000 = $100,000 × 6% × 2/12

The effect of this adjustment on December 31, 2021, along with the adjusting journal entry to record the $1,000 of interest expense that is payable, is as follows:

1 Analyze

Assets	=	Liabilities	+	Stockholders' Equity	
		Interest Payable +1,000		Interest Expense (+E)	−1,000

2 Record

	Debit	Credit
Interest Expense	1,000	
Interest Payable		1,000

3. **Record interest paid.** The timeline in Exhibit 10.4 shows that on October 31, 2022, General Mills pays both the principal and the interest. Although the company is likely to pay both amounts with a single check, it is instructive to consider these payments separately. In this step, we analyze and record the interest payment. The interest payment is calculated to be $6,000 (= $100,000 × 6% × 12/12). This $6,000 interest payment (shown below in green) includes the $1,000 that was accrued as Interest Payable (in red) at December 31, 2021, plus $5,000 interest expense incurred during the 10 months between January 1 and October 31, 2022 (in blue).

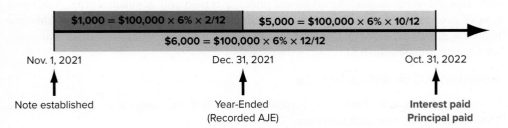

$1,000 = $100,000 × 6% × 2/12	$5,000 = $100,000 × 6% × 10/12
$6,000 = $100,000 × 6% × 12/12	

Nov. 1, 2021   Dec. 31, 2021   Oct. 31, 2022

↑   ↑   ↑

Note established   Year-Ended   Interest paid
              (Recorded AJE)   Principal paid

The $6,000 interest payment is analyzed and recorded as follows:

1 Analyze

Assets		=	Liabilities		+	Stockholders' Equity	
Cash	−6,000		Interest			Interest	
			Payable	−1,000		Expense (+E)	−5,000

2 Record

	Debit	Credit
Interest Payable	1,000	
Interest Expense	5,000	
Cash		6,000

4. **Record principal paid.** The accounting equation effects and journal entry to record the $100,000 principal payment on October 31, 2022, are as follows:

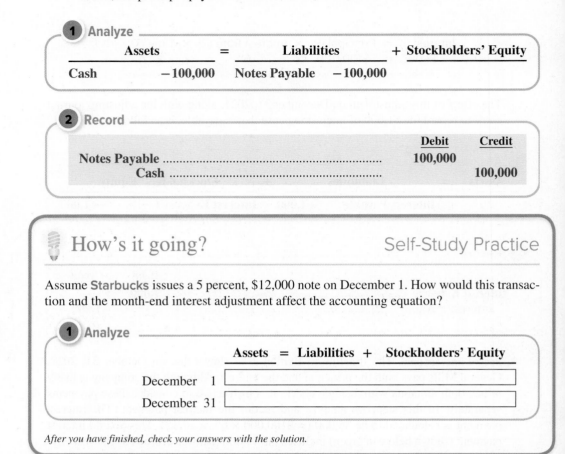

1 Analyze

Assets		=	Liabilities		+ Stockholders' Equity
Cash	−100,000		Notes Payable	−100,000	

2 Record

	Debit	Credit
Notes Payable	100,000	
Cash		100,000

💡 How's it going?   Self-Study Practice

Assume **Starbucks** issues a 5 percent, $12,000 note on December 1. How would this transaction and the month-end interest adjustment affect the accounting equation?

1 Analyze

	Assets	=	Liabilities	+	Stockholders' Equity
December 1					
December 31					

After you have finished, check your answers with the solution.

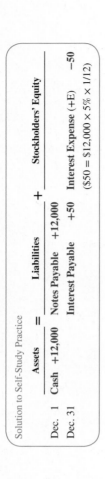

Solution to Self-Study Practice

	Assets	=	Liabilities	+	Stockholders' Equity
Dec. 1	Cash +12,000		Notes Payable +12,000		
Dec. 31			Interest Payable +50		Interest Expense (+E) −50

($50 = $12,000 × 5% × 1/12)

The previous example and Self-Study Practice illustrated promissory notes where interest is charged on the amount borrowed and principal is paid only at note maturity. A different type of note exists, where the loan is repaid through a series of installment payments that include a mix of principal and interest. For explanation of accounting for installment notes, see Chapter Supplement 10D.

Additional Current Liabilities

General Mills does not have some current liabilities that are common to other companies. This section covers two such liabilities.

Sales Tax Payable Retail companies are required to charge a sales tax in most states (excluding Alaska, Delaware, Montana, New Hampshire, and Oregon). Retailers collect sales tax from consumers at the time of sale and forward it to the state government. Just like payroll taxes, the tax collected by the company is reported as a current liability until it is forwarded to the government. Sales tax is not an expense to the retailer because it is simply collected and passed on to the government. So if Best Buy sold a television for $1,000 cash plus 5 percent sales tax, Best Buy would collect $1,050 cash, report $1,000 in sales revenue, and recognize a $50 liability (= 5% × $1,000) for the sales tax collected. The financial effects of this sale are analyzed below and would be recorded with the journal entry that follows:

**COACH'S TIP**

In a perpetual inventory system, the sales transaction would be accompanied by an increase in Cost of Goods Sold (recorded with a debit) and a decrease in Inventory (recorded with a credit).

1 Analyze

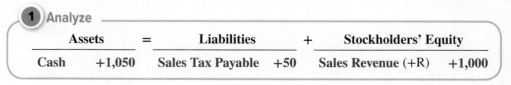

Assets		=	Liabilities		+	Stockholders' Equity	
Cash	+1,050		Sales Tax Payable	+50		Sales Revenue (+R)	+1,000

2 Record

	Debit	Credit
Cash	1,050	
Sales Tax Payable ($1,000 × 5%)		50
Sales Revenue		1,000

When Best Buy pays the sales tax to the state government, its accountants will reduce Sales Tax Payable (with a debit) and reduce Cash (with a credit).

Deferred Revenue   In Chapter 4, you learned that some companies receive cash before they provide goods or services to customers. Airlines are paid in advance of providing flights, retailers receive cash for gift cards that can be used for future purchases of goods and services, crowdfunded projects receive cash from people who are later repaid with goods or services, and other companies receive money for subscriptions and events before they begin. Live Nation Entertainment (LYV), the owner of Ticketmaster, provides a great example of this type of liability. Consider what happens when LYV receives $800,000 cash in January for two concerts, to be held May 12 and 15. Because LYV receives cash before providing concert services, accountants initially record a liability in the account Deferred Revenue to represent the company's obligation to provide future services. As the concert services are provided, LYV reduces this liability and reports the concert fees as revenue.

That is, LYV records the following financial effects and related journal entries when it receives $800,000 total for advance ticket sales in January and then provides the first of two concerts in May:

1. Receive cash and create a liability (on January 2):

1 Analyze

Assets	=	Liabilities	+ Stockholders' Equity
Cash +800,000		Deferred Revenue +800,000	

2 Record

	Debit	Credit
Cash	800,000	
Deferred Revenue		800,000

2. Fulfill part of the liability and report revenue (on May 12):

1 Analyze

Assets	=	Liabilities	+	Stockholders' Equity
		Deferred Revenue −400,000		Service Revenue (+R) +400,000

2 Record

	Debit	Credit
Deferred Revenue	400,000	
Service Revenue		400,000

When the May 15 concert is held, LYV makes another adjustment like the one in step 2 to show that it fulfilled its remaining performance obligation and generated $400,000 more in service revenue.

> ## SPOTLIGHT ON
> # Business Decisions

Jumpstarting a Business with Crowdfunding

Crowdfunding has become a popular way for small business ventures to raise funds from large numbers of individuals over the Internet. People have made movies, developed mobile apps, and published books using crowdfunding. These arrangements can take different forms, including presales, loans, and equity investments.

Presales

Made popular by Kickstarter, most presale arrangements use an all-or-nothing funding model where you ask people to pledge money to your venture and later you collect that money from them if your project reaches its funding goals. In exchange for their payments, you give these backers an "award" such as an exclusive service from your business. **How do you account for this arrangement?** The same way Live Nation accounts for its presales of concert tickets, shown in the previous section. At first, record nothing because your proposal and the backers' pledges represent only an exchange of promises. But when you reach your funding goal and receive the money, record increases in both Cash and Deferred Revenue for the service promised to backers. Later, when you fulfill that performance obligation, reduce Deferred Revenue and report the provided service as revenue, and also expense the cost of awards given out.

Loans

A different crowdfunding arrangement known as peer-to-peer lending, or P2P for short, makes it possible for people with money to lend to others without involving banks. The process at Prosper begins with borrowers requesting a loan amount and providing a reason for the loan. Lenders evaluate all the loan requests and then select the loans they want to fund. This form of crowdfunding is accounted for as notes payable with interest accrued and paid monthly.

Equity

We discuss equity in Chapter 11.

Current Portion of Long-Term Debt

Remember when you were in 9th grade and it seemed as if it would be forever before you'd graduate from high school? At that time, graduation was something that would happen in the long term. Later, when you became a senior, graduation became a current event—one that was less than a year away. A similar progression occurs with long-term debt.

If a company borrows money with the promise to repay it in two years, the loan is classified as long-term debt. The company reports only the accrued interest on the loan as a current liability in the balance sheet. After a year has passed, however, the loan becomes a current liability (just as your graduation became a current event when you reached your senior year). When that happens, the borrower must reclassify the loan into the Current Liabilities section of the balance sheet, just as General Mills has done in Exhibit 10.1. Rather than create different accounts for this, accountants often record the total loan in just one account and then, when preparing the balance sheet, reclassify the amount of principal to be repaid in the upcoming year as a current liability (Current Portion of Long-Term Debt) and leave the rest as Long-Term Debt.

Group photo: Chris Ryan/AGE Fotostock; Loan photo: Medioimages/Photodisc/Getty Images

The final line item in the Current Liabilities section of the General Mills balance sheet provides an example (see Exhibit 10.1). In 2019, General Mills reported a current liability for $1,400 (million) of long-term debt that it expected to pay in 2020. This reclassification of long-term debt into current liabilities is needed so that the balance sheet accurately reports the dollar amount of existing liabilities that will be paid in the upcoming year.

How's it going?   Self-Study Practice

Assume that on December 31, 2020, DIRECTV borrowed $10,000, a portion of which is to be repaid each year on November 30. Specifically, DIRECTV will make the following principal payments: $1,000 in 2021, $2,000 in 2022, $3,000 in 2023, and $4,000 in 2024. Show how this loan will be reported on the balance sheets on December 31, 2021 and 2020, assuming principal payments will be made when required.

| | At December 31 | |
	2021	2020
Current Liabilities		
Current Portion of Long-Term Debt	$	$
Long-Term Debt		
Total Liabilities	$9,000	$10,000

After you have finished, check your answers with the solution.

Solution to Self-Study Practice

| | At December 31 | |
	2021	2020
Current Liabilities		
Current Portion of Long-Term Debt	$ 2,000	$ 1,000
Long-Term Debt	7,000	9,000
Total Liabilities	$9,000	$10,000

LONG-TERM LIABILITIES

Like most companies, General Mills reports several long-term liabilities on its balance sheet (see Exhibit 10.1). Common long-term liabilities include long-term notes payable, deferred income taxes, and bonds payable. Long-term notes payable are accounted for in the same way as the short-term notes payable discussed in the previous section (except, of course, long-term notes are on the books for more than one year). Liabilities for deferred income taxes were explained in Chapter 9; they represent the amount of tax put off (deferred) by taking tax deductions on the corporation's income tax return that are greater than the expenses subtracted on the income statement. This section focuses on accounting for bonds that a company issues to obtain a significant amount of financing. Later, in Chapter 11, after you become more familiar with bonds as a form of long-term debt financing, we will compare it to alternative forms of long-term (equity) financing.

> **Learning Objective 10-3**
> Analyze and record bond liability transactions.

Bonds

Occasionally, governments and very large companies such as General Mills need to borrow more money than any single lender can provide. In January 2020, for example, General Mills needed to borrow $750 million. Because issuing a promissory note for such a large amount of money was impractical, the company instead issued bonds to thousands of different investors. A sample bond certificate is shown here. You can think of this as a formal version of an IOU.

Bonds are financial instruments that outline the future payments a company promises to make in exchange for receiving a sum of money now. From the company's perspective, the bond is a long-term liability. From the bondholder's perspective, the bond is an investment. For an investor, bonds can be attractive because they return higher interest rates than bank savings accounts, and after a company issues the bonds, they can be traded on established exchanges such as the New York Bond Exchange. This makes it easy for an investor to buy and sell bonds with other investors.

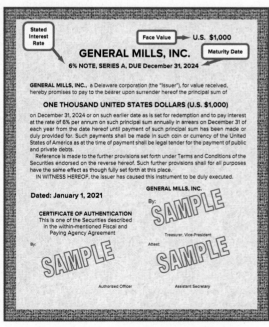

As you can see from the sample bond certificate, three key elements of a bond are (1) the **maturity date**, (2) the amount payable on the maturity date (often called the **face value**), and (3) the **stated interest rate**. In most cases, the face value of each bond is $1,000. This means that at the maturity date, the company will repay $1,000 for each bond. In the years prior to repayment, the company will make periodic interest payments. Interest payments are based on the stated rate, which is always expressed as an annual rate. However, many bonds require interest payments every six months (that is, semiannually). Each interest payment is computed by multiplying the face value times the stated interest rate (times the fraction of the year if payments are made semiannually). As you will see in a moment, for good economic reasons, bonds may be priced at amounts above or below their face value. A bond's price does not affect the amount of each interest payment, however. For example, a 6 percent bond with a face value of $1,000 always pays interest of $60 cash each year (= $1,000 × 6% × 12/12).

Bond Pricing

The company does not determine the price at which its bonds issue. Instead, investors in the market establish the issue price. The bond **issue price** represents the amount that investors are willing to pay on the issue date in exchange for the cash payments the company promises to make over the life of the bond. As we saw at the beginning of the chapter, companies receive ratings based on their ability to keep their promise. Not surprisingly, investors are willing to pay more for bonds issued by companies with higher ratings.

SPOTLIGHT ON | Financial Reporting

Bond Prices in the Financial Press

The financial press (and the NYSE Bond Directory) reports bond prices each day based on transactions that occurred on the bond exchange. The following is typical of the information you will find:

Company Name	Maturity	INTEREST RATE Stated	INTEREST RATE Market	Bond Price
Walt Disney Co.	2026	1.85	2.70	93.14
General Mills, Inc.	2024	6.00	4.00	107.26
McDonald's Corporation	2045	4.88	4.10	112.89

This listing reports that the General Mills bond will mature in the year 2024. It has a stated interest rate of 6.00 percent. At the present time, 4.00 is the typical interest rate earned by investors in the market when buying similar bonds. Because the 6.00 percent stated interest rate is better than the 4.00 percent market interest rate, investors are attracted to the General Mills bond. Consequently, they are willing to pay a higher bond price. **The bond price is quoted as a percentage of face value.** In this case, investors were willing to pay 107.26 percent of face value, or $1,072.60 for each $1,000 bond (107.26% × $1,000).

When companies issue bonds, they try to offer competitive interest rates. But they only get one opportunity to print the bond certificate, and there may be a time lag between the printing date and the issue date. During this time lag, changing economic events can cause the bond's stated interest rate to differ from the market's current interest rate, which affects the bond's attractiveness and its price. To see how, you need consider only the relationship between the stated interest rate on the bond (what the bond pays in cash) and the **market interest rate** (the return that bondholders require). Exhibit 10.5 illustrates this relationship.

If the stated interest rate is the same as the market rate, then investors will be willing to pay the face value to acquire the bond. If a bond offers something attractive, such as a stated rate that is higher than the market interest rate, bondholders may be willing to pay more than the face value to acquire it. A bond issued for more than its face value is said to have been issued at a **premium**. This is just like how you might pay a premium to acquire tickets to a great concert or a big game. Finally, if a bond promises to pay interest at a stated rate that is lower than the market interest rate, no one will be willing to acquire the bond unless the company issues the bond for less than its face value. A bond issued for less than its face value is said to have been issued at a **discount**.

EXHIBIT 10.5   Relationships between Interest Rates and Bond Pricing

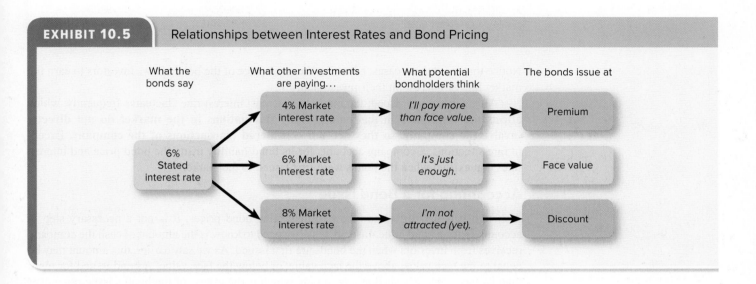

Before you continue, try the following Self-Study Practice.

 How's it going?   Self-Study Practice

For each of the following independent situations, indicate whether the bonds were issued at a premium, at a discount, or at face value.

1. Stated interest rate = 7% and market interest rate = 7%.
2. Stated interest rate = 5% and market interest rate = 6%.
3. Bond issue price = $10,100 and bond face value = $10,000.

After you have finished, check your answers with the solution.

You may wonder how we determine the amount of premium or discount in the examples above. Theoretically, this amount is based on a mathematical calculation called a **present value**, which is described in detail in Appendix C at the end of this book. (Case C in Appendix C shows the calculations for the four-year $1,000, 6 percent General Mills bond used in our example above.) The general idea behind this calculation is that we adjust the issue price of the bond so that investors earn the current market rate of interest on their investment. To see how this works, imagine a $1,000 bond that pays a stated interest rate of 6 percent and matures in one year. After one year, the bond pays the stated interest of $60 ($1,000 × 6% × 12/12) plus the face value of $1,000. The amount that you pay for this bond today will determine the return on your investment as follows:

When the market interest rate is:	What bondholders pay today:	What bondholders receive in one year:	Annual rate of return:
4% (Less than stated rate)	$1,019 (A Premium)	$1,060 ($60 + $1,000)	4% ($1,060 ÷ $1,019) = 1.04
6% (Equal to stated rate)	$1,000 (Face value)	$1,060 ($60 + $1,000)	6% ($1,060 ÷ $1,000) = 1.06
8% (More than stated rate)	$981 (A Discount)	$1,060 ($60 + $1,000)	8% ($1,060 ÷ $981) = 1.08

Notice that in all three cases, adjusting the issue price of the bond allows investors to earn the market rate of interest on their investment.

After a bond has issued, the market's (current) interest rate fluctuates frequently, which affects the bond price in the market. **Daily fluctuations in the market do not directly involve the company, so they are not considered transactions of the company.** Except in rare situations, a company accounts for its bond liability using the bond price and interest rates that existed when the bonds were first issued to the market.

Accounting for a Bond Issue

Although it is useful to know how to determine bond prices, it is not a necessary step in accounting for a bond issue. Instead, what we need to know is the amount of cash the company receives from investors when the bonds are first issued. As we saw earlier, this amount may be equal to the face value, above the face value, or below the face value. A bond issued for more than its face value is issued at a premium, which is the excess of the bond's issue price over its face value. A bond issued for less than its face value is issued at a discount, which is the amount by which the issue price falls short of the bond's face value. The following sections show how to account for bonds issued at face value, at a premium, and at a discount.

Bonds Issued at Face Value If General Mills receives $100,000 cash in exchange for issuing 100 bonds at their $1,000 face value, the transaction will be analyzed and recorded as follows:

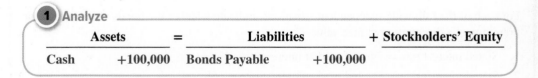

1 Analyze				
Assets	**=**	**Liabilities**		**+ Stockholders' Equity**
Cash	+100,000	Bonds Payable	+100,000	

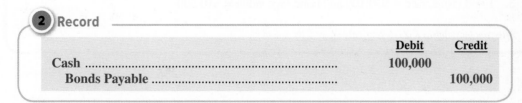

2 Record		
	Debit	**Credit**
Cash	100,000	
Bonds Payable		100,000

Bonds Issued at a Premium If General Mills issues 100 of its $1,000 bonds at a price of 107.26, the company will receive $107,260 (= 100 × $1,000 × 1.0726). Thus, the cash-equivalent amount is $107,260, which represents the total liability on the issue date. The company's accountants will distinguish the $100,000 total face value from the $7,260 premium by recording them in separate liability accounts as follows:

1 Analyze

	Assets	=	Liabilities	+ Stockholders' Equity
Cash	+107,260		Bonds Payable +100,000	
			Premium on	
			Bonds Payable +7,260	

2 Record

	Debit	Credit
Cash	107,260	
Bonds Payable		100,000
Premium on Bonds Payable		7,260

As we saw earlier, the premium increases the initial bond price for investors without changing the stated interest payments or the face value paid at maturity. In effect, a premium decreases the return that bondholders earn on their initial investment. You might think that it is strange to record the premium and the face value separately, but we will learn later why accountants do it this way.

Bonds Issued at a Discount   If General Mills receives $93,376 for bonds with a total face value of $100,000, the cash-equivalent amount of $93,376 represents the liability on the issue date. As shown in the analyze step below, the discount of $6,624 (= $100,000 − $93,376) offsets the face value, so accountants will record it in a contra-liability account, which we identify using "xL." To offset the liability, a contra-liability account is recorded as a debit, as in the journal entry that follows:

1 Analyze

	Assets	=	Liabilities	+ Stockholders' Equity
Cash	+93,376		Bonds Payable +100,000	
			Discount on Bonds	
			Payable (+xL) −6,624	

2 Record

	Debit	Credit
Cash	93,376	
Discount on Bonds Payable (+xL)	6,624	
Bonds Payable		100,000

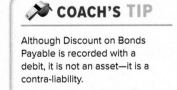

COACH'S TIP

Although Discount on Bonds Payable is recorded with a debit, it is not an asset—it is a contra-liability.

Again, the discount reduces the initial bond price for investors without changing the stated interest payments and the face value paid to them at maturity. In effect, a discount increases the return bondholders earn on their initial investment.

Reporting Bond Liabilities   The total face value of a bond plus any related premium or minus any related discount is reported in the liabilities section of the balance sheet, as in Exhibit 10.6 for our three examples. The amount of the bond liability, after taking into account any premium or discount, is referred to as the bond's **carrying value.**

EXHIBIT 10.6 | Balance Sheet Reporting of Bond Liabilities

Bonds issued at a premium

Bonds Payable	$100,000
Premium on Bonds Payable	7,260
Carrying Value	107,260

Bonds issued at face value

Bonds Payable	$100,000

Bonds issued at a discount

Bonds Payable	$100,000
Discount on Bonds Payable	(6,624)
Carrying Value	93,376

Interest Expense

As time passes, a bond liability creates interest expense, which is matched to each period in which the liability is owed. Because interest expense arises from a financing decision (not an operating decision), it is reported below the Income from Operations subtotal on the income statement.

Interest on Bonds Issued at Face Value   For bonds issued at face value, the process of calculating and recording interest is similar to that for Notes Payable. Assume, for example, General Mills issues bonds on January 1, 2021, at their total face value of $100,000. The bonds carry an annual stated interest rate of 6 percent payable in cash on December 31 of each year. Because interest arises as time passes, General Mills will need to accrue an expense and liability for interest at the end of each accounting period. For the first month ended January 31, 2021, assuming no previous accrual of interest, General Mills would record interest of $500 (= $100,000 × 6% × 1/12) as follows:

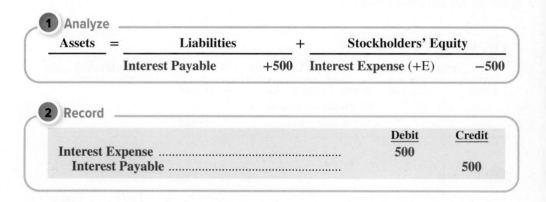

1 Analyze

Assets	=	Liabilities	+	Stockholders' Equity	
		Interest Payable	+500	Interest Expense (+E)	−500

2 Record

	Debit	Credit
Interest Expense	500	
Interest Payable		500

General Mills would continue to calculate and record interest this way each month until the interest is paid. When interest is paid, Interest Payable will be decreased (with a debit) and Cash will be decreased (with a credit) for the amount paid.

Interest on Bonds Issued at a Premium   When bonds issue at a premium, the bond issuer receives more cash on the issue date than it repays on the maturity date. For example, in our earlier illustration of bonds issued at a premium, General Mills received $107,260 but repays only $100,000 at maturity. The $7,260 difference isn't exactly "free money" for General Mills but rather is a reduction in the company's cost of borrowing. For accounting purposes, we match the reduced borrowing cost to the periods in which interest expense is recorded. This process, called **bond amortization,** makes the Interest Expense smaller than the actual interest payment and, at the same time, causes the balance in Premium on Bonds Payable to decline each period, as shown in Exhibit 10.7.

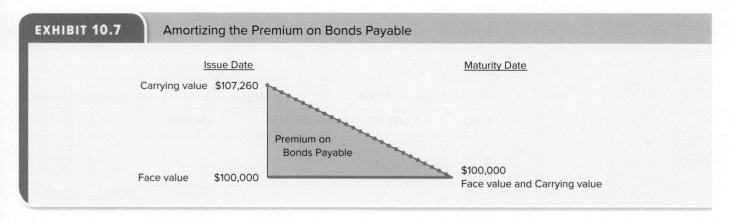

EXHIBIT 10.7 Amortizing the Premium on Bonds Payable

Issue Date

Carrying value $107,260

Premium on
Bonds Payable

Face value $100,000

Maturity Date

$100,000
Face value and Carrying value

Hopefully, Exhibit 10.7 makes it easier to see why accountants record the premium and face value in separate accounts. Although the premium decreases each period, the face value does not change. As the Premium on Bonds Payable decreases, the carrying value of the liability decreases until it reaches $100,000 on the maturity date. Procedures for amortizing bond premiums are explained in Chapter Supplements 10A, 10B, and 10C. If you have been assigned any of these supplements, don't jump to them yet. We'll tell you later when it's best to read them.

Interest on Bonds Issued at a Discount   When bonds issue at a discount, the bond issuer receives less cash on the issue date than it repays on the maturity date. For example, in our earlier illustration of bonds issued at a discount, General Mills receives $93,376 on the issue date but repays $100,000 at maturity. For General Mills, the $6,624 discount represents an extra cost of borrowing, over and above each interest payment. For accounting purposes, we match the extra borrowing cost to the periods in which interest is recorded. This amortization causes the Interest Expense to be more than the interest payment and, at the same time, causes Discount on Bonds Payable to decrease each period. As the Discount on Bonds Payable decreases, the carrying value of the liability increases until it reaches $100,000 on the maturity date, as illustrated in Exhibit 10.8.

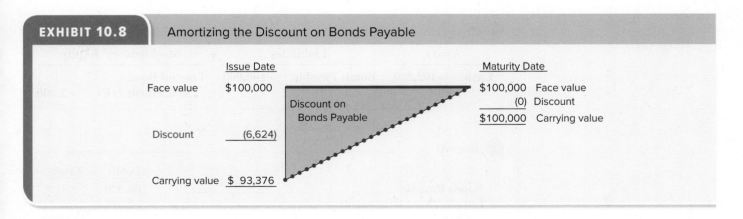

EXHIBIT 10.8 Amortizing the Discount on Bonds Payable

Issue Date

Face value $100,000

Discount on
Bonds Payable

Discount (6,624)

Carrying value $ 93,376

Maturity Date

$100,000 Face value
(0) Discount
$100,000 Carrying value

At this point, you should skip ahead in the textbook to Chapter Supplement 10A, 10B, or 10C —whichever you have been assigned to read—then come back here and continue with the remainder of this section.

Bond Retirements

Retirement at Maturity   Most bonds are retired (paid off) at maturity. If interest has been fully paid at the time of maturity, the only remaining account to settle will be Bonds Payable.

Assuming the General Mills bonds in our example were retired with a payment equal to their $100,000 face value, the transaction would be analyzed and recorded as follows:

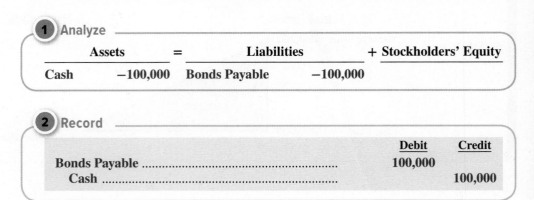

1 Analyze

	Assets	=	Liabilities	+ Stockholders' Equity
Cash	−100,000	Bonds Payable	−100,000	

2 Record

	Debit	Credit
Bonds Payable	100,000	
Cash		100,000

Early Retirement Rather than wait until the maturity date to retire bonds, a company may retire them early. Companies with a lot of cash often retire their bonds early to avoid the related interest expense. Even companies that do not have extra cash may decide to retire their bonds early if interest rates have fallen since issuing the original bonds. In this case, the companies would issue new bonds at the lower interest rate and use the money they receive from the new bonds to retire the old ones before maturity. Again, this decision reduces interest expense, which increases future earnings.

The early retirement of bonds has three financial effects. The company (1) pays cash, (2) eliminates the bond liability, and (3) reports either a gain or a loss. A gain arises if the cash paid to retire the bonds is less than the carrying value of the bond liability. A loss is incurred if the company pays more than the carrying value at the time of retirement.

To illustrate these effects, assume that 10 years ago General Mills issued $100,000 of bonds at face value. If the company retired the bonds now at a bond price of 102, General Mills would have to pay $102,000 (= $100,000 × 1.02) to retire the bonds. Even though the company is paying an extra $2,000 to retire the bonds, it may be worth it to avoid interest expense in the future. This transaction would be analyzed and recorded as follows:

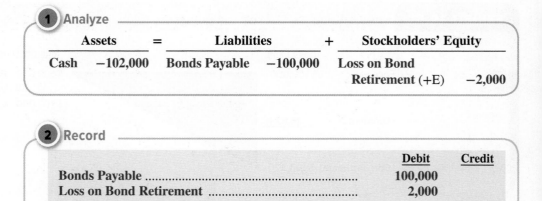

1 Analyze

	Assets	=	Liabilities	+	Stockholders' Equity	
Cash	−102,000	Bonds Payable	−100,000		Loss on Bond Retirement (+E)	−2,000

2 Record

	Debit	Credit
Bonds Payable	100,000	
Loss on Bond Retirement	2,000	
Cash		102,000

Notice two features of this example. First, because the bond retirement is a financing decision, the loss would be reported after the Income from Operations subtotal on the income statement. Second, this retirement example does not involve the removal of a bond discount or bond premium account because the bonds were issued at face value. If the bonds had been issued below or above face value, any premium or discount balance that existed at the time of retirement would need to be removed as well.

Types of Bonds

When you first start learning about bonds, it may seem the number of new terms that describe the bonds are limitless. These terms can generally be grouped into two categories: (1) those that describe the type of organization that issued the bonds and (2) those that describe specific features of the bond. In the first category are bonds issued by the U.S. Treasury Department ("treasuries"); municipal organizations such as states, cities, counties, and towns ("munis"); and corporations ("corporates"). In the second category are bonds that are backed by collateral ("secured") or not ("debentures"), that the issuing corporation can call in and exchange for cash ("callable") or convert into shares of its stock ("convertible"), and that mature in a series of installments ("serial bonds") rather than all at once ("term bonds") or include no periodic interest payments ("strips" and "zero-coupon bonds"). The basic procedures shown in the previous sections for recording bond liabilities and interest expense apply similarly to these various types of bonds.

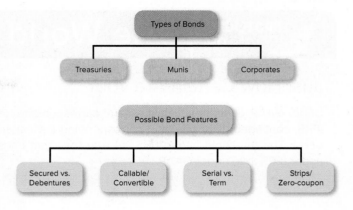

CONTINGENT LIABILITIES

Contingent liabilities are potential liabilities that arise as a result of past transactions or events, but their ultimate resolution depends (is contingent) on a future event. Contingent liabilities differ from other liabilities discussed in this chapter because their dependence on a future event introduces a great deal of uncertainty. For example, consider the quality-assurance warranty on computers. This warranty obligates the seller to repair defective products for a limited time, but the ultimate cost of those repairs depends on future events including the number of warranty claims, labor rates, and supply costs. Imagine trying to estimate the cost of the eight-year, unlimited-mile warranty on Tesla's battery pack. Even more uncertainty is introduced when accounting for lawsuits against a company. Some suits may be defended successfully, but others may result in huge penalties, such as the $20 billion BP was ordered to pay, five years after the *Deepwater Horizon* oil spill in the Gulf of Mexico. Given the uncertainties of contingent events, accounting rules require the company to evaluate whether it will probably be found liable and, if so, whether the amount of the liability is reasonably estimable (yes, that's a word). If the liability is both probable and estimable, an expense and liability are accrued, as shown in Exhibit 10.9. If a contingent liability is reasonably possible but not probable or its amount cannot be reasonably estimated, a liability is not recorded in the accounting records. Instead, any potential liability and related loss are described in a note to the financial statements, as shown in a General Mills excerpt in Exhibit 10.9.

> **Learning Objective 10-4**
> Describe how to account for contingent liabilities.

> **YOU SHOULD KNOW**
>
> **Contingent Liabilities:** Potential liabilities that have arisen as a result of a past transaction or event; their ultimate outcome will not be known until a future event occurs or fails to occur.

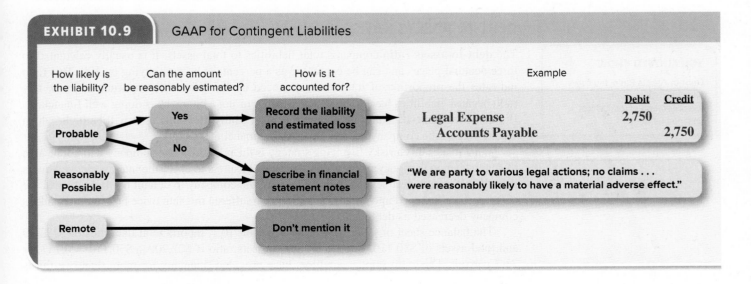

EXHIBIT 10.9   GAAP for Contingent Liabilities

The World

Just How Certain Are You?

Under GAAP, contingent liabilities (and corresponding losses) are recorded if the estimated loss is "probable." Under IFRS, contingent liabilities (and corresponding losses) are recorded if the estimated loss is "more likely than not" to occur. The threshold under IFRS is lower than that under GAAP, causing more contingent liabilities to be reported under IFRS than under GAAP.

Now that you have seen how liabilities are accounted for inside a company, let's consider them again from the outside. How do users evaluate liabilities?

Evaluate the Results

Learning Objective 10-5
Calculate and interpret the debt-to-assets ratio and the times interest earned ratio.

It's tempting to think of liabilities as bad, but debt can be good if it is managed well. What does it mean to manage it well? First, don't take on too much debt. Second, pay what is owed when it is owed. Two ratios commonly used in business to evaluate these two aspects of debt management are (1) the debt-to-assets ratio and (2) the times interest earned ratio.

Accounting Decision Tools		
Name of Measure	**Formula**	**What It Tells You**
Debt-to-assets ratio	$\dfrac{\text{Total Liabilities}}{\text{Total Assets}}$	• The percentage of assets financed by creditors • A higher ratio means greater financing risk
Times interest earned ratio	$\dfrac{(\text{Net Income} + \text{Interest Expense} + \text{Income Tax Expense})}{\text{Interest Expense}}$	• Whether sufficient resources are generated from operations to cover interest costs • The higher the number, the better the coverage

DEBT-TO-ASSETS RATIO

YOU SHOULD KNOW

Debt-to-Assets Ratio: Indicates financing risk by computing the proportion of total assets financed by debt.

The **debt-to-assets ratio** compares total liabilities to total assets. It is usually calculated to three decimal places and can be expressed as a percentage by multiplying by 100. This ratio indicates the proportion of total assets financed by liabilities. It's important to know this ratio because liabilities have to be repaid whether or not a company is doing well financially. If assets are financed mainly by debt, rather than equity, then this ratio will be high, which would suggest the company has adopted a risky financing strategy.

What makes this a risky financing strategy is the possibility the company will not be able to generate enough money from its debt-financed business to cover the interest charged on its debt. If this occurs over several periods, causing the company to default on its payments, the company can be forced into bankruptcy. Hostess suffered this fate twice before the Twinkies company decreased its debt load.

The balance sheet of General Mills, in Exhibit 10.1, reports total liabilities of $22,200 and total assets of $30,110. Thus, the debt-to-assets ratio is $22,200 ÷ $30,110 = 0.737, or 73.7 percent. This ratio implies creditors have provided financing for more than two-thirds of the assets of General Mills. Is this ratio too high? Not according to industry data reported by CSImarket.com, which indicates General Mills relies on debt financing to about the same extent as its competitors in the food processing industry. In late 2019, Kellogg had a ratio of 82.2 percent, Post's ratio was 75.4 percent, and Campbell Soup had a ratio of 91.5 percent. These comparisons suggest General Mills has adopted a financing strategy no riskier than its industry competitors. However, to be sure, analysts will also study the relationship between the company's interest expense and earnings, as discussed below.

TIMES INTEREST EARNED RATIO

One way to judge whether a company is generating enough income to cover its interest expense is to compute the **times interest earned ratio** (also called a fixed charge coverage ratio).

The accounting decision tools box shows the formula for the times interest earned ratio. Notice that in this ratio, interest and income tax expenses are added back into net income. The reason for this is simple: Analysts want to know whether a company covers its interest expense from earnings **before the costs of financing and taxes.** In general, a high times interest earned ratio is viewed more favorably than a low one. A high ratio indicates an extra margin of protection should the company's profitability decline in the future.

General Mills's 2019 income statement (online at sec.gov) reports Net Income of $1,760 after having subtracted Interest Expense of $520 and Income Tax Expense of $370 (all numbers in millions). We compute its times interest earned ratio as follows:

> **YOU SHOULD KNOW**
>
> **Times Interest Earned Ratio:**
> Divides net income before interest and taxes by interest expense to determine the extent to which earnings before taxes and financing costs are sufficient to cover interest incurred on debt.

$$\frac{\text{Net Income} + \text{Interest Expense} + \text{Income Tax Expense}}{\text{Interest Expense}} = \frac{\$1{,}760 + \$520 + \$370}{\$520} = 5.10$$

This ratio means that General Mills generates $5.10 of income (before the costs of financing and taxes) for each dollar of interest expense. Reaching this level of interest coverage was important to General Mills because its financial statement note for long-term debt indicated that the bank required the company to have a minimum ratio of 2.5.

You may see a times interest earned ratio less than 1.0 or even negative. **When the times interest earned ratio is less than 1.0, a company is not generating enough operating income to cover its interest expense.** Companies with recurring negative times interest earned ratios run the risk of defaulting on their interest payments and, in severe cases, face bankruptcy.

SPOTLIGHT ON | The World

Violated Loan Covenants

Most lending agreements allow the lender to revise loan terms (e.g., interest rates, due dates) if a borrower's financial condition deteriorates significantly. These escape hatches for the lender, called **loan covenants,** are often based on financial statement ratios such as debt-to-assets and times interest earned. Under GAAP, if a company violates loan covenants on long-term debt at the financial statement date, but the lender waives this covenant violation prior to the company releasing its financial statements, the debt stays classified as long-term. Under IFRS, the long-term debt would be reclassified as a current liability.

SUPPLEMENT 10A STRAIGHT-LINE METHOD OF AMORTIZATION

> **Learning Objective 10-S1**
> Use straight-line bond amortization.

Exhibits 10.7 and 10.8 illustrated how a bond premium or discount decreases each year, until it is completely eliminated on the bond's maturity date. This process is called amortizing the bond premium or discount. The **straight-line method of amortization** reduces the premium or discount by an equal amount each period. Because this method results in an equal amount each period, it is easy to apply. However, it distorts the financial results somewhat because it produces an equal amount of Interest Expense each period, even though the carrying value of the bond liability changes each period. Ideally, interest expense would be based on the amount owed (the carrying value) at any given time. For this reason, the straight-line method may be used only when it does not materially differ from the effective-interest method of amortization (presented in Supplement 10B).

Bond Premiums

In our earlier example of bonds issued at a premium, General Mills received $107,260 on the issue date (January 1, 2021) but repays only $100,000 at maturity (December 31, 2024). The $7,260 difference is considered a reduction in the company's borrowing cost over the four-year period the bond is owed. Under the straight-line method, this $7,260 is spread evenly as a reduction in interest expense over the four years ($7,260 ÷ 4 = $1,815 per year). So when General Mills makes its yearly $6,000 cash payment for interest, it will report Interest Expense of only $4,185 ($6,000 − $1,815). The remainder of the $6,000 cash payment is reported as a reduction in the carrying value of the bond liability, as follows:

1 Analyze

Assets	=	Liabilities	+	Stockholders' Equity
Cash −6,000		Premium on Bonds Payable −1,815		Interest Expense (+E) −4,185

2 Record

	Debit	Credit
Interest Expense	4,185	
Premium on Bonds Payable	1,815	
Cash		6,000

In effect, the $6,000 payment includes both an interest component ($4,185) and a partial reduction of the bond premium ($1,815). The accounting equation effects and journal entry shown above will be recorded each year on December 31 until the bonds mature. The following bond amortization schedule summarizes the amounts that must be recorded each period (on the left), producing the end-of-year balance sheet account balances (on the right):

Bond Premium Amortization Schedule: Straight-Line Method

	Journal Entry Components			Balance Sheet Accounts		
	(A)	(B) Amortized Premium	(C) (= A − B) Interest Expense	(D) Bonds Payable	(E) Premium on Bonds Payable	(F) (= D + E) Carrying Value
Period Ended	Cash Paid					
01/01/2021				$100,000	$7,260	$107,260
12/31/2021	$6,000	$1,815	$4,185	100,000	5,445	105,445
12/31/2022	6,000	1,815	4,185	100,000	3,630	103,630
12/31/2023	6,000	1,815	4,185	100,000	1,815	101,815
12/31/2024	6,000	1,815	4,185	100,000	0	100,000

Bond Discounts

A discount arises when the bond issuer receives less cash than the issuer repays at maturity. In effect, a discount increases the company's cost of borrowing, so amortization of the discount causes interest expense to be higher than the interest payment each period. To report this effect, accountants record a decrease in Discount on Bonds Payable and an increase in Interest Expense.

In our earlier example, General Mills received $93,376 for four-year bonds with a total face value of $100,000, implying a discount of $6,624. Using the straight-line method, amortization of the discount in each of the four years that the bonds remain unpaid would be $1,656 (= $6,624 ÷ 4). This amount would be added to the interest to be paid ($6,000) to calculate the amount of Interest Expense ($7,656). The effects would be recorded as follows:

1 Analyze

Assets	=	Liabilities	+	Stockholders' Equity
Cash −6,000		Discount on Bonds Payable (−xL) +1,656		Interest Expense (+E) −7,656

2 Record

	Debit	Credit
Interest Expense	7,656	
Discount on Bonds Payable (−xL)		1,656
Cash		6,000

The accounting equation effects and journal entry shown above would be recorded each year on December 31 until the bonds mature. The following bond amortization schedule summarizes the amounts that must be recorded each period (on the left), producing the end-of-year balance sheet account balances (on the right):

Bond Discount Amortization Schedule: Straight-Line Method

	Journal Entry Components				Balance Sheet Accounts		
Period Ended	(A) Cash Paid	(B) Amortized Discount	(C) (= A + B) Interest Expense		(D) Bonds Payable	(E) Discount on Bonds Payable	(F) (= D − E) Carrying Value
01/01/2021					$100,000	$6,624	$ 93,376
12/31/2021	$6,000	$1,656	$7,656		100,000	4,968	95,032
12/31/2022	6,000	1,656	7,656		100,000	3,312	96,688
12/31/2023	6,000	1,656	7,656		100,000	1,656	98,344
12/31/2024	6,000	1,656	7,656		100,000	0	100,000

SUPPLEMENT 10B EFFECTIVE-INTEREST METHOD OF AMORTIZATION

> **Learning Objective 10-S2**
> Use effective-interest bond amortization.

The **effective-interest method of amortization** is conceptually superior to the straight-line method of accounting for bonds (presented in Supplement 10A) because it correctly calculates interest expense by multiplying the true cost of borrowing times the amount of money actually owed to investors. The true cost of borrowing is the market interest rate that investors used to determine the bond issue price. The actual amount owed to investors is the carrying value of the bond, which equals the cash received when the bond was issued plus any interest that has been incurred but not yet paid. This means that as the carrying value of the bond changes, so too does the interest expense.

To clearly understand the effective-interest method, it helps to see how a bond's issue price depends on the market interest rate. As we mentioned in the chapter, investors in the market decide how much to pay for a bond by using a mathematical calculation called a **present value.** You can read instructions about how to calculate present values in Appendix C at the end of this book, but for now just focus on understanding what a present value is. Present value is the idea that something is worth more if you get it today than if you get it sometime in the future. For example, if someone offered to pay you $100,000 today or $100,000 five years from now, you'd be better off taking it today. You could invest the money and earn interest for five years, making

> **YOU SHOULD KNOW**
>
> **Effective-Interest Method of Amortization:** Allocates the amount of bond premium or discount over each period of a bond's life in amounts corresponding to the bond's carrying value and market interest rate.

it worth more than $100,000. The same idea explains why you could be equally happy with receiving $100,000 in five years or some smaller amount today. To figure out how much this smaller amount is, you just calculate the present value of $100,000. The only pieces of information you need for this calculation are (1) the amounts to be received in the future, (2) the number of months between now and then, and (3) the interest rate you expect to earn during that time.

In the bond context, investors calculate the present value of the amounts received periodically (at the stated interest rate) and at maturity (the face value), using the market interest rate. We have summarized this calculation in Exhibit 10B.1 for General Mills's 6 percent, four-year bond.

Exhibit 10B.1 shows three different scenarios, with each one involving different market interest rates but the same 6 percent stated interest rate. The first column calculates the amount of money that investors would be willing to give up if they needed to earn 4 percent on the amount they pay for the bond. The second column calculates the amount investors would pay if they wanted to earn an interest rate of 6 percent. The third column calculates the amount that investors would be willing to pay if they wanted to earn 8 percent on the amount they pay for the bond. (For detailed calculations underlying the amounts in Exhibit 10B.1, see Appendix C at the end of the book.)

EXHIBIT 10B.1	Computing the Present Value of Bond Payments		
	MARKET INTEREST RATES		
	4%	**6%**	**8%**
Present value of $100,000 face value (principal) paid four years from now	$ 85,480	$ 79,210	$73,503
Present value of $6,000 (6% stated interest rate) paid once a year for four years	21,780	20,790	19,873
Bond price	**$107,260**	**$100,000**	**$93,376**

As we saw earlier in the chapter, when the bond pays interest at a rate that exactly matches the rate required by investors in the market (6 percent), they are willing to pay face value ($100,000) for it. If the 6 percent interest rate stated on the bond is more than investors require (4 percent), they will be willing to pay a premium for the bond, as shown in the first column. If the 6 percent interest promised is less than the market interest rate (8 percent), investors pay less than face value for the bond, resulting in a discounted bond price, as indicated in the third column.

Bond Premiums

In our earlier example of a bond premium, General Mills promised to make cash interest payments each year at a stated rate of 6 percent. Investors found this stated interest rate attractive, so the bond issued at a $7,260 premium. When General Mills adds this $7,260 premium to the $100,000 face value, it reports a carrying value of $107,260 (= $100,000 + $7,260) on January 1, 2021. Exhibit 10B.1 indicates that the $107,260 total implies the market interest rate was 4 percent. General Mills uses this market interest rate to calculate its **Interest Expense** on the bond, using a variation of the interest formula. For example, General Mills calculates Interest Expense in the first year ended December 31, 2021, as follows:

2021:	**Interest (I)**	=	**Principal (P)**	×	**Interest Rate (R)**	×	**Time (T)**
	Interest Expense	=	Carrying Value	×	Market Interest Rate	×	n/12
	$4,290	=	$107,260	×	4%	×	12/12

Use the information *stated* on the *face* of the bond to calculate the **cash** interest payment:

	Interest (I)	=	**Principal (P)**	×	**Interest Rate (R)**	×	**Time (T)**
	Cash Payment	=	Face Value	×	Stated Interest Rate	×	n/12
	$6,000	=	$100,000	×	6%	×	12/12

Because the $6,000 cash interest payment exceeds the $4,290 Interest Expense by $1,710 ($6,000 − $4,290 = $1,710), General Mills records a $1,710 reduction in its bond liability. In effect, the $6,000 cash payment includes both an interest component ($4,290) and a partial reduction in the carrying value of the bond liability ($1,710), as analyzed and recorded below:

① Analyze

Assets	=	Liabilities	+	Stockholders' Equity	
Cash −6,000		Premium on Bonds Payable −1,710		Interest Expense (+E) −4,290	

② Record

	Debit	Credit
Interest Expense	4,290	
Premium on Bonds Payable	1,710	
Cash		6,000

Similar calculations and accounting effects occur each period until the bonds mature. The only thing to watch out for is **the carrying value of the bond liability decreases each year because the cash payment includes a partial reduction of the bond premium.** For example, after the above entry is recorded on December 31, 2021, the Premium on Bonds Payable decreases by $1,710, from $7,260 to $5,550.

Thus, the Interest Expense for the second year of the bond (for the year ended December 31, 2022) is:

Premium on Bonds Payable (L)	
	7,260 1/1/2021
12/31/2021 1,710	
	5,550 12/31/2021

2022:   **Interest (I) = Principal (P)   × Interest Rate (R)   × Time (T)**
Interest Expense = Carrying Value × Market Interest Rate × n/12
$4,222 = $105,550   × 4%   × 12/12

The following bond amortization schedule summarizes the amounts that must be recorded each period (on the left), producing the end-of-year balance sheet account balances (on the right):

Bond Premium Amortization Schedule: Effective-Interest Method

	Journal Entry Components			Balance Sheet Accounts		
	(A)	(B) Interest	(C) (= A − B) Amortized	(D) Bonds	(E) Premium on	(F) (= D + E) Carrying
Period Ended	Cash Paid	Expense	Premium	Payable	Bonds Payable	Value
01/01/2021				$100,000	$7,260	$107,260
12/31/2021	$6,000	$4,290	$1,710	100,000	5,550	105,550
12/31/2022	6,000	4,222	1,778	100,000	3,772	103,772
12/31/2023	6,000	4,151	1,849	100,000	1,923	101,923
12/31/2024	6,000	4,077	1,923	100,000	0	100,000

Bond Discounts

In our earlier example of a bond discount, General Mills promised to make cash interest payments each year at a stated rate of 6 percent. Investors did not find this stated interest rate attractive, so the bond issued at a $6,624 discount. When General Mills subtracts this $6,624 discount from the $100,000 face value, it reports a carrying value of $93,376 (= $100,000 − $6,624) on January 1, 2021. Exhibit 10B.1 indicates the $93,376 implies the market interest rate was 8 percent. General Mills uses this market interest rate to calculate its

Interest Expense on the bond, as we did in the case of a bond premium. The Interest Expense for the first year ended December 31, 2021, is calculated as

2021:	**Interest (I)**	**=**	**Principal (P)**	**× Interest Rate (R)**	**× Time (T)**
	Interest Expense	=	Carrying Value	× Market Interest Rate	× n/12
	$7,470	=	$93,376	× 8%	× 12/12

Use the information *stated* on the *face* of the bond to calculate the **cash** interest payment:

	Interest (I)	**=**	**Principal (P)**	**× Interest Rate (R)**	**× Time (T)**
	Cash Payment	=	Face Value	× Stated Interest Rate	× n/12
	$6,000	=	$100,000	× 6%	× 12/12

Because the $7,470 Interest Expense is more than the $6,000 cash paid, General Mills records the $1,470 difference ($7,470 − $6,000 = $1,470) as an increase in the carrying value of the bond liability. As illustrated in Exhibit 10.8, the increase in the carrying value of the bond liability is achieved by decreasing the contra-liability Discount on Bonds Payable. These effects are analyzed and recorded as follows:

1 Analyze

Assets	=	Liabilities	+	Stockholders' Equity
Cash −6,000		Discount on		Interest
		Bonds Payable (−xL) +1,470		Expense (+E) −7,470

2 Record

	Debit	Credit
Interest Expense	7,470	
Discount on Bonds Payable (−xL)		1,470
Cash		6,000

Discount on Bonds Payable decreases when the above journal entry is posted to its T-account. A reduction of this contra-liability account increases the carrying value of the long-term liability, as you can see by moving from left to right in Exhibit 10B.2.

Discount on Bonds Payable (xL)	
1/1/2021 6,624	
	1,470 12/31/2021
12/31/2021 5,154	

EXHIBIT 10B.2 Sample Balance Sheet Reporting of Bond Discount

GENERAL MILLS, INC.
Balance Sheet (excerpt)

	January 1, 2021	December 31, 2021
Long-Term Liabilities		
Bonds Payable	$100,000	$100,000
Discount on Bonds Payable	(6,624)	(5,154)
Carrying Value	93,376	94,846

Let's now consider the interest expense for 2022. As in 2021, the 2022 interest expense is calculated using the market interest rate. However, the carrying value of bonds owed at the end of 2021 increased to $94,846, as shown in Exhibit 10B.2. Thus, interest expense also will increase in 2022, calculated as follows:

2022:   Interest (I) = Principal (P) × Interest Rate (R) × Time (T)
Interest Expense = Carrying Value × Market Interest Rate × n/12
$7,588 = $94,846   × 8%   × 12/12

Because the Interest Expense ($7,588) is greater than the cash payment ($6,000), the carrying value of the bond liability is increased (by reducing the contra-liability). This is reflected in the accounting equation and recorded with the journal entry on December 31, 2022, as follows:

1 Analyze

Assets	=	Liabilities	+	Stockholders' Equity
Cash −6,000		Discount on Bonds Payable (−xL) +1,588		Interest Expense (+E) −7,588

2 Record

	Debit	Credit
Interest Expense	7,588	
Discount on Bonds Payable (−xL)		1,588
Cash		6,000

The following bond amortization schedule summarizes the amounts that must be recorded each period (on the left), producing the end-of-year balance sheet account balances (on the right):

Bond Discount Amortization Schedule: Effective-Interest Method

	Journal Entry Components			Balance Sheet Accounts		
Period Ended	(A) Cash Paid	(B) Interest Expense	(C) (= B − A) Amortized Premium	(D) Bonds Payable	(E) Premium on Bonds Payable	(F) (= D − E) Carrying Value
01/01/2021				$100,000	$6,624	$ 93,376
12/31/2021	$6,000	$7,470	$1,470	100,000	5,154	94,846
12/31/2022	6,000	7,588	1,588	100,000	3,566	96,434
12/31/2023	6,000	7,715	1,715	100,000	1,851	98,149
12/31/2024	6,000	7,851	1,851	100,000	0	100,000

SUPPLEMENT 10C SIMPLIFIED EFFECTIVE-INTEREST AMORTIZATION

Learning Objective 10-S3
Use simplified effective-interest bond amortization.

The approach shown in this supplement presents a simplified explanation of how to account for bond liabilities and interest expense. You should be aware this approach involves taking a shortcut. While the shortcut will help you to focus on the line items that ultimately are reported on the financial statements, it requires that we ignore a few accounts that are typically used behind the scenes in real-world accounting systems. Be sure to check your course syllabus to see whether you are expected to read this supplement.

If you're like most people, you probably have to concentrate really hard when you are told the carrying value of a bond is increased by decreasing a contra-liability account. You may even whisper this thought quietly to yourself a few times before it starts making sense. In this section, we present a shortcut when accounting for bonds that will allow you to avoid thinking in "double-negatives" like this. Hopefully it also will help you to stop whispering to yourself when you read.

Accounting for the Bond Issue

The shortcut involves simplifying only one aspect of what you studied earlier in this chapter. Rather than record a discount or premium in a separate account, we combine the discount or premium with the bond's face value in a single account that we will call Bonds Payable, Net. This name is used to remind you that we are focusing on what is ultimately reported in the financial statements rather than what is actually used behind the scenes. The following journal entries demonstrate how the shortcut is applied to the three earlier bond examples (issued at a premium, at face value, and at a discount).

	Premium		Face Value		Discount	
	Debit	Credit	Debit	Credit	Debit	Credit
Cash	107,260		100,000		93,376	
Bonds Payable, Net		107,260		100,000		93,376

Interest Expense

As time passes, the company incurs Interest Expense on its bond liability. Because the bond liability was recorded in a single account, the interest calculation is the same whether the bond has been issued at a premium or discount. The following version of the interest formula is used to compute Interest Expense.

Interest (I)	=	Principal (P)	×	Interest Rate (R)	×	Time (T)
Interest Expense	=	Bonds Payable, Net	×	Market Interest Rate	×	n/12

The market interest rate is determined by using present value techniques (discussed in Appendix C) that relate the bond's issue price to the payments promised over the life of the bond. The market interest rate also can be determined using the XIRR and RATE functions in Excel, or the online bond calculator app at fncalculator.com.

Bond Premiums   Our bond premium example indicated that General Mills received $107,260 on the issue date, which we would record in Bonds Payable, Net using the journal entry shown above. The $107,260 issue price implies a 4 percent market interest rate. The bonds promise to pay the 6 percent stated interest rate on their total face value of $100,000. This information is used to compute Interest Expense and the annual cash payment as follows:

2021:	Interest (I)	=	Principal (P)	×	Interest Rate (R)	×	Time (T)
	Interest Expense	=	Bonds Payable, Net	×	Market Interest Rate	×	n/12
	$4,290	=	$107,260	×	4%	×	12/12

	Interest (I)	=	Principal (P)	×	Interest Rate (R)	×	Time (T)
	Cash Payment	=	Face Value	×	Stated Interest Rate	×	n/12
	$6,000	=	$100,000	×	6%	×	12/12

Because the $6,000 cash interest payment exceeds the $4,290 Interest Expense by $1,710 ($6,000 − $4,290 = $1,710), General Mills records a $1,710 reduction in Bonds Payable, Net. In effect, the $6,000 cash payment includes both an interest component ($4,290) and a partial reduction in the carrying value of the bond liability ($1,710), as analyzed and recorded below:

1 Analyze

Assets	=	Liabilities	+	Stockholders' Equity	
Cash −6,000		Bonds Payable, Net −1,710		Interest Expense (+E)	−4,290

2 Record

	Debit	Credit
Interest Expense	4,290	
Bonds Payable, Net	1,710	
Cash		6,000

Similar calculations and accounting effects occur each period until the bonds mature. The only thing to watch out for is that Bonds Payable, Net decreases each year because the cash payment includes a partial reduction of the bond premium. For example, after the above entry is recorded on December 31, 2021, Bonds Payable, Net decreases by $1,710, from $107,260 to $105,550.

This new balance is used to compute Interest Expense for the second year of the bond (for the year ended December 31, 2022):

	Bonds Payable, Net (L)	
	107,260	1/1/2021
12/31/2021 1,710		
	105,550	12/31/2021

2022:   Interest (I) = Principal (P)   × Interest Rate (R)   × Time (T)
Interest Expense = Bonds Payable, Net × Market Interest Rate × n/12
    $4,222 = $105,550   × 4%   × 12/12

Because the $6,000 annual cash payment exceeds the $4,222 Interest Expense by $1,778 ($6,000 − $4,222 = $1,778), General Mills records a $1,778 reduction in Bonds Payable, Net in 2022. In effect, the $6,000 cash payment includes both an interest component ($4,222) and a partial reduction in the carrying value of the bond liability ($1,778). As the following amortization schedule shows, the bond liability continues to decrease until, at maturity, it reaches the bonds' face value ($100,000).

	Bond Premium Amortization Schedule: Simplified Method				
	Beginning of Year		Changes During the Year		End of Year
Period	(A) Bonds Payable, Net	(B) Interest Expense	(C) Cash Paid	(D) = (C − B) Reduction in Bonds Payable, Net	(E) = (A − D) Bonds Payable, Net
1/1/21–12/31/21	$107,260	$4,290	$6,000	$1,710	$105,550
1/1/22–12/31/22	105,550	4,222	6,000	1,778	103,772
1/1/23–12/31/23	103,772	4,151	6,000	1,849	101,923
1/1/24–12/31/24	101,923	4,077	6,000	1,923	100,000

Bond Discounts   Our bond discount example indicated that General Mills received $93,376 on the issue date, which we would record in Bonds Payable, Net using the journal entry shown at the beginning of this chapter supplement. This issue price implies an 8 percent market interest rate. The bonds promise to pay the 6 percent stated interest rate on their total face value of $100,000. This information is used to compute Interest Expense and the annual cash payment as follows:

2021:	**Interest (I)**	**=**	**Principal (P)**	**× Interest Rate (R)**	**× Time (T)**
	Interest Expense	=	Bonds Payable, Net	× Market Interest Rate	× n/12
	$7,470	=	$93,376	× 8%	× 12/12

	Interest (I)	**=**	**Principal (P)**	**× Interest Rate (R)**	**× Time (T)**
	Cash Payment	=	Face Value	× Stated Interest Rate	× n/12
	$6,000	=	$100,000	× 6%	× 12/12

Because the $7,470 Interest Expense is more than the $6,000 cash paid, General Mills records the $1,470 difference ($7,470 − $6,000 = $1,470) as an increase in its liability Bonds Payable, Net, as follows:

1 Analyze

Assets	=	Liabilities	+	Stockholders' Equity
Cash −6,000		Bonds Payable, Net +1,470		Interest Expense (+E) −7,470

2 Record

	Debit	Credit
Interest Expense	7,470	
Bonds Payable, Net		1,470
Cash		6,000

Recording the $1,470 as the liability Bonds Payable, Net is appropriate because General Mills will eventually pay this amount at maturity, as part of the face value of the bond.

Similar calculations and accounting effects occur each period until the bonds mature. The only thing to watch out for is that Bonds Payable, Net increases each year because the cash payment is less than the interest expense. For example, after the above entry is recorded on December 31, 2021, Bonds Payable, Net increases by $1,470, from $93,376 to $94,846.

This new balance is used to compute Interest Expense for the second year of the bond (for the year ended December 31, 2022):

Bonds Payable, Net (L)	
	93,376 1/1/2021
	1,470 12/31/2021
	94,846 12/31/2021

2022:	**Interest (I)**	**=**	**Principal (P)**	**× Interest Rate (R)**	**× Time (T)**
	Interest Expense	=	Bonds Payable, Net	× Market Interest Rate	× n/12
	$7,588	=	$94,846	× 8%	× 12/12

Because the $7,588 Interest Expense exceeds the $6,000 annual cash payment by $1,588 ($7,588 − $6,000 = $1,588), General Mills records a $1,588 increase in Bonds Payable, Net in 2022. In effect, the $1,588 in unpaid interest will be paid at maturity. As the following amortization schedule shows, the carrying value of the bond liability continues to increase until, at maturity, it reaches the bonds' face value ($100,000).

Bond Discount Amortization Schedule: Simplified Method					
	Beginning of Year		Changes During the Year		End of Year
Period	(A) Bonds Payable, Net	(B) Interest Expense	(C) Cash Paid	(D) = (B – C) Reduction in Bonds Payable, Net	(E) = (A + D) Bonds Payable, Net
1/1/21–12/31/21	$93,376	$7,470	$6,000	$1,470	$ 94,846
1/1/22–12/31/22	94,846	7,588	6,000	1,588	96,434
1/1/23–12/31/23	96,434	7,715	6,000	1,715	98,149
1/1/24–12/31/24	98,149	7,851	6,000	1,851	100,000

SUPPLEMENT 10D INSTALLMENT NOTES PAYABLE

Learning Objective 10-S4
Account for installment notes payable.

Earlier in this chapter, we described promissory notes where the amount borrowed (principal) is not repaid until the notes reach their maturity date. Because the borrower pays only interest between the date of initial borrowing and its later maturity, that type of note is known as an interest-only loan. In this chapter supplement, we describe a different type of promissory note—an installment note—that is commonly used for student loans, credit card loans, and home mortgages, as well as business loans.

Installment Notes

Like an interest-only note, an installment note requires the borrower to pay interest and principal to the lender over the note's life to maturity. Unlike an interest-only note, however, an installment note does not include a single "balloon" payment of principal at maturity because principal is blended with interest within the payment made each period. In effect, the borrower makes an interest *and* principal payment each period, resulting in no liability for interest or principal after the final periodic repayment. The figure below illustrates a $60,000 loan with 8% interest fully repaid in six equal annual installments.

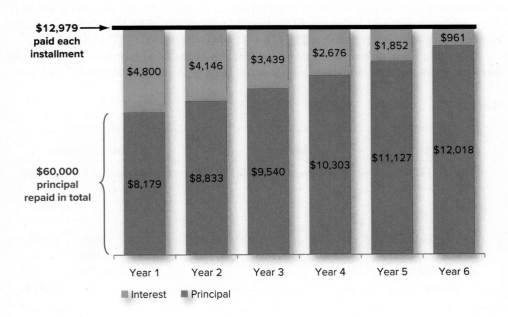

Notice that each year's installment payment is the same ($12,979), but the proportion of interest (shown in orange) decreases over the period while the proportion of principal (shown in blue) increases. This pattern occurs because the borrower repays some of the principal as part of each installment payment, so multiplying the fixed interest rate by the remaining principal balance results in a smaller dollar amount of interest expense in each following year.

You should be wondering how we determined the split between interest and principal amounts, as well as the amount of the equal annual payments of $12,979. All amounts shown in the previous figure were determined using basic spreadsheet calculations, which are commonly depicted in a loan **amortization schedule**, as follows.[2]

Year	(A) Beginning Notes Payable	(B) Interest Expense (8%)	(C) Repaid Principal on Notes Payable	(D) = (A − C) Ending Notes Payable
1	60,000	4,800	8,179	51,821
2	51,821	4,146	8,833	42,988
3	42,988	3,439	9,540	33,448
4	33,448	2,676	10,303	23,145
5	23,145	1,852	11,127	12,018
6	12,018	961	12,018	—
Total		17,874	60,000	

Reading from left to right, our amortization schedule shows the year of the loan, the amount owed at the beginning of the year, the interest expense for a full year (calculated as 8 percent times the amount owed), the principal included in the installment (calculated as the annual payment minus the interest portion), and the ending loan balance (calculated as the beginning balance minus the repaid principal).

Journal Entries: Installment Payment Occurs on Fiscal Year-End Of course, your knowledge of installment loans should not stop at merely generating a loan amortization schedule. You also should understand the implications for a company's financial reporting. The amortization schedule indicates that, of the $12,979 annual payment, the interest expense for the first year of the loan is $4,800 and the principal component is $8,179. By repaying $8,179 of principal in the first year, the Notes Payable balance decreases by that amount (to $51,821). Thus, in the second year, interest will be less ($51,821 × 8% = $4,146) and the principal component will be larger ($8,833 = $12,979 − $4,146).

Assuming the loan was taken out on the first day of the fiscal year and the installment payment is made at year-end, the following entries could be recorded at the end of years 1 and 2:

Year 1:

1 Analyze

Assets	=	Liabilities	+	Stockholders' Equity
Cash −12,979		Notes Payable −8,179		Interest Expense (+E) −4,800

2 Record

	Debit	Credit
Interest Expense	4,800	
Notes Payable	8,179	
Cash		12,979

(to record first annual installment payment)

---

[2]You can use a free online loan calculator to create your own amortization schedule. For our example, try the "loan calculator with annual payments" at mycalculators.com. Enter the original principal amount ($60,000), number of years (6), interest rate (8.0), and compounding frequency (annual). Click on the payment button to reveal an annual (rounded) payment of $12,979 that fully repays the interest and principal by the end of year 6. Click on "view amortization schedule" to produce a table similar to that shown in the text.

Year 2:

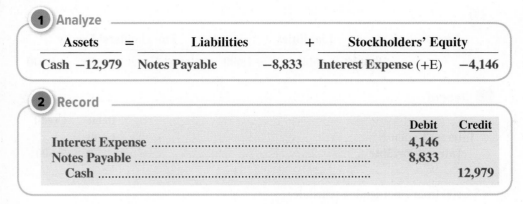

① Analyze

Assets	=	Liabilities	+	Stockholders' Equity
Cash −12,979		Notes Payable −8,833		Interest Expense (+E) −4,146

② Record

	Debit	Credit
Interest Expense	4,146	
Notes Payable	8,833	
Cash		12,979

(to record second annual installment payment)

Journal Entries: Installment Payment Date Differs from Fiscal Year-End In reality, it's unlikely your company establishes an installment loan only on the first day of the year. Instead, installment loans could start midyear. In this more realistic situation, the accounting is a little more complex. To illustrate, we will continue to use the information from the previous amortization schedule, but we **assume the loan was obtained September 1, 2021, and the company records interest on December 31 as it prepares its annual financial statements.** The first installment payment does not occur until August 31, 2022—one year after the loan is taken out—so the company will need to adjust its records to show the interest expense that results from having had the loan outstanding during 2021. The following timeline illustrates how the $4,800 of interest from the amortization schedule for the first year of the loan would be allocated to the fiscal years to which it relates.

The timeline shows that, because the loan was taken out on September 1, 2021, it is outstanding for only four months before the end of the year. Consequently, only part of the $4,800 will need to be recorded on December 31 ($1,600 = 4/12 × $4,800). The rest of the $4,800 interest ($3,200 = 8/12 × $4,800) will be recorded when the first installment is paid August 31, 2022.

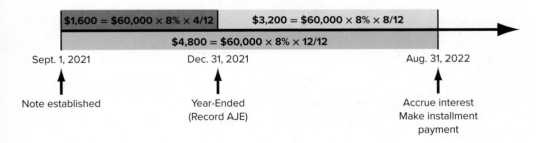

Sept. 1, 2021	Dec. 31, 2021	Aug. 31, 2022
Note established	Year-Ended (Record AJE)	Accrue interest Make installment payment

$1,600 = $60,000 × 8% × 4/12 $3,200 = $60,000 × 8% × 8/12

$4,800 = $60,000 × 8% × 12/12

The journal entries to be recorded on each of the dates shown on the timeline follow.

September 1, 2021—Receive the loan proceeds and establish the liability

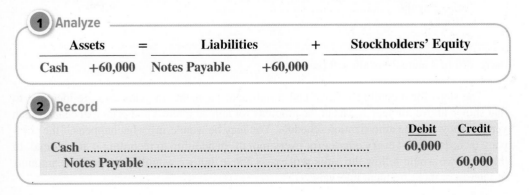

① Analyze

Assets	=	Liabilities	+	Stockholders' Equity
Cash +60,000		Notes Payable +60,000		

② Record

	Debit	Credit
Cash	60,000	
Notes Payable		60,000

December 31, 2021—Accrue interest for a four-month period

1 Analyze

Assets	=	Liabilities	+	Stockholders' Equity
		Interest Payable +1,600		Interest Expense (+E) −1,600

2 Record

	Debit	Credit
Interest Expense	1,600	
Interest Payable		1,600

($\frac{4}{12}$ × \$4,800 from amortization schedule)

The next date for recording interest would occur when the first installment is paid on August 31, 2022. One approach for recording the interest and the installment payment on August 31, 2022, is to accrue the interest owed from January 1 to August 31 (as follows in the first journal entry below) and then record the \$12,979 installment payment in a separate journal entry (in the second journal entry below):

August 31, 2022—Accrue interest and record the first installment payment

1 Analyze

Assets	=	Liabilities	+	Stockholders' Equity
		Interest Payable +3,200		Interest Expense (+E) −3,200

2 Record

	Debit	Credit
Interest Expense	3,200	
Interest Payable		3,200

($\frac{8}{12}$ × \$4,800 from amortization schedule)

1 Analyze

Assets		=	Liabilities		+	Stockholders' Equity
Cash	−12,979		Interest Payable	−4,800		
			Interest Payable	−8,179		

2 Record

	Debit	Credit
Interest Payable	4,800	
Notes Payable	8,179	
Cash		12,979

(to record first annual installment payment)

The steps for recording interest and installment payments in years 2–6 are identical to that shown above for year 1, except the amounts for annual interest and principal change each year, as shown in the amortization schedule. You may be wondering what happens if the company records interest every quarter (or every month) in addition to recording it at year-end. In this case, we would follow the same process as above, but we would record smaller amounts of interest at more frequent intervals.

REVIEW THE CHAPTER

DEMONSTRATION CASE A: ACCRUED LIABILITIES AND DEFERRED REVENUE

Online Games, Inc., reported the following information in its accounting records on December 31.

Annual subscription payments received in December for the following year	$12,000
Gross salaries earned by employees (December 26–31)	3,600
Income taxes withheld from employees (December 26–31)	550
FICA taxes withheld from employees (December 26–31)	210
Net payment to employees (made on December 31)	2,840

The subscription payments are for services to be provided equally throughout each month of the following year. The employees were paid $2,840 on December 31, but the withholdings have not yet been remitted nor have the matching employer FICA contributions.

Required:

1. Describe how the subscription payments should be reported in the balance sheet and income statement on (*a*) December 31 and (*b*) January 31.
2. Show the accounting equation effects and give the journal entries for (*a*) the receipt of annual subscription payments in December and (*b*) any required adjustments for the subscription payments on January 31 of the following year.
3. Compute the total payroll costs relating to the period December 26–31. (Assume $280 in total unemployment taxes.)
4. Show the accounting equation effects and give the journal entries (*a*) to record salaries and wages paid on December 31 and (*b*) to adjust for payroll taxes relating to December 26–31.

Suggested Solution

1. **a.** On December 31, the $12,000 of advance subscription payments would be reported on the balance sheet as a current liability called Deferred Revenue. No amounts relating to the following year's subscription services would be reported in the December income statement.

   b. On January 31, one month of subscription services would be earned, so Deferred Revenue on the balance sheet would be reduced by $1,000 (= $12,000 × 1/12) and Service Revenue on the income statement would be increased by $1,000.

2. **a.** December (receipt of the following year's subscription payments):

Assets	=	Liabilities		+	Stockholders' Equity
Cash +12,000		Deferred Revenue	+12,000		

	Debit	Credit
Cash	12,000	
Deferred Revenue		12,000

   b. January 31 (earned one month of subscriptions):

Assets	=	Liabilities		+	Stockholders' Equity	
		Deferred Revenue	−1,000		Service Revenue (+R)	+1,000

	Debit	Credit
Deferred Revenue	1,000	
Service Revenue		1,000

3. Computation of total payroll costs:

Salaries and wages:	Net pay to employees	$2,840
	Income taxes withheld from employees	550
	FICA taxes withheld from employees	210
	Total cost of salaries and wages	3,600
Employer payroll taxes:	FICA taxes (matching contribution)	210
	Unemployment taxes	280
Total payroll costs:		$4,090

4a. Salaries and wages costs:

Assets	=	Liabilities	+	Stockholders' Equity	
Cash −2,840		**Withheld Income**		**Salaries and Wages Expense (+E)** −3,600	
		Taxes Payable +550			
		FICA Payable +210			

	Debit	Credit
Salaries and Wages Expense	3,600	
Withheld Income Taxes Payable		550
FICA Payable		210
Cash		2,840

4b. Employer-related payroll costs:

Assets	=	Liabilities	+	Stockholders' Equity	
		FICA Payable +210		**Payroll Tax Expense (+E)** −490	
		Unemployment			
		Tax Payable +280			

	Debit	Credit
Payroll Tax Expense	490	
FICA Payable		210
Unemployment Tax Payable		280

DEMONSTRATION CASE B: NOTES PAYABLE AND ACCRUED INTEREST

Assume that on December 1, Caterpillar, Inc., received $350 million when it issued promissory notes that will mature in several years. The notes pay interest at the annual rate of 6.00 percent, comparable to other interest rates available in the market. Caterpillar's fiscal year ends on December 31.

Required:

1. Describe which sections of Caterpillar's classified balance sheet are affected by its issuance of promissory notes.
2. Give the journal entry on December 1 to record the issuance of the notes.
3. Give the journal entry on December 31 to record one month of interest expense, assuming none had been accrued prior to that date.

Suggested Solution

1. The issuance of notes increases Caterpillar's Cash (a current asset) and its Notes Payable (a long-term liability) by $350 million.

2. December 1 (issuance date):

	Debit	Credit
Cash	350,000,000	
Notes Payable		350,000,000

3. December 31 (accrual of interest expense for one month):

	Debit	Credit
Interest Expense..	1,750,000	
Interest Payable		1,750,000

($1,750,000 = $350,000,000 × 6% × 1/12)

DEMONSTRATION CASE C: BONDS PAYABLE ISSUED AT A PREMIUM

To raise funds to build a new plant, Reed Company issued bonds with the following terms:

> Face value of the bonds: $100,000.
> Dates: Issued January 1, 2021; due in 5 years on January 1, 2026.
> Interest rate: 6 percent per year, payable on December 31 each year.

The bonds were issued on January 1, 2021, at 104.3, implying a 5 percent market rate of interest. The annual accounting period for Reed Company ends on December 31.

Required:

1. How much cash did Reed Company receive from the issuance of the bonds? Show computations.
2. What was the amount of premium on the bonds payable? Over how many months should it be amortized?
3. Show the accounting equation effects and give the journal entry on January 1, 2021, for recording the issuance of the bonds.
4. (Supplement 10A) Show the accounting equation effects and give the journal entry required on December 31, 2021, relating to interest on the bond. Use the straight-line amortization method.
5. (Supplement 10B) Show the accounting equation effects and give the journal entry required on December 31, 2021, relating to interest on the bond. Use the effective-interest amortization method.
6. (Supplement 10C) Show the accounting equation effects and give the journal entries required on January 1, 2021, relating to the bond issuance and on December 31, 2021, relating to interest on the bond. Use the simplified effective-interest amortization method.

Suggested Solution

1. Issue price of the bonds: $100,000 × 104.3% = $104,300.
2. Premium on the bonds payable: $104,300 − $100,000 = $4,300.

   Months amortized: From date of issue, January 1, 2021, to maturity date, January 1, 2026 = 5 years × 12 months per year = 60 months.
3. January 1 (issuance date):

Assets		=	Liabilities		+	Stockholders' Equity
Cash	+104,300		Bonds Payable	+100,000		
			Premium on Bonds Payable	+4,300		

	Debit	Credit
Cash	104,300	
Premium on Bonds Payable		4,300
Bonds Payable		100,000

4. December 31, 2021 (straight-line amortization):

Assets	=	Liabilities	+	Stockholders' Equity	
Cash −6,000		Premium on Bonds Payable −860		Interest Expense (+E)	−5,140

	Debit	Credit
Premium on Bonds Payable ($4,300 × 12/60 months)	860	
Interest Expense ($6,000 − $860)	5,140	
Cash ($100,000 × 6% × 12/12)		6,000

5. December 31, 2021 (effective-interest amortization):

Assets	=	Liabilities	+	Stockholders' Equity	
Cash −6,000		Premium on Bonds Payable −785		Interest Expense (+E)	−5,215

	Debit	Credit
Interest Expense ($104,300 × 5% × 12/12)	5,215	
Premium on Bonds Payable ($6,000 − $5,215)	785	
Cash ($100,000 × 6% × 12/12)		6,000

6. January 1 (issuance date):

Assets	=	Liabilities	+	Stockholders' Equity
Cash +104,300		Bonds Payable, Net +104,300		

	Debit	Credit
Cash	104,300	
Bonds Payable, Net		104,300

December 31, 2021 (simplified effective-interest amortization):

Assets	=	Liabilities	+	Stockholders' Equity	
Cash −6,000		Bonds Payable, Net −785		Interest Expense (+E)	−5,215

	Debit	Credit
Interest Expense ($104,300 × 5% × 12/12)	5,215	
Bonds Payable, Net ($6,000 − $5,215)	785	
Cash ($100,000 × 6% × 12/12)		6,000

DEMONSTRATION CASE D: BONDS PAYABLE ISSUED AT A DISCOUNT

To raise funds to build a new plant, Morales Company issued bonds with the following terms:

> Face value of the bonds: $100,000
> Dates: Issued January 1, 2021; due in 5 years on January 1, 2026
> Interest rate: 6 percent per year, payable on December 31 each year

The bonds were issued on January 1, 2021, at 95.9, implying a 7 percent market rate of interest. The annual accounting period for Morales Company ends on December 31.

Required:

1. How much cash did Morales Company receive from the issuance of the bonds? Show computations.
2. What was the amount of discount on the bonds payable? Over how many months should it be amortized?
3. Show the accounting equation effects and give the journal entry on January 1, 2021, for recording the issuance of the bonds.
4. (Supplement 10A) Show the accounting equation effects and give the journal entry required on December 31, 2021, relating to interest on the bond. Use the straight-line amortization method.
5. (Supplement 10B) Show the accounting equation effects and give the journal entry required on December 31, 2021, relating to interest on the bond. Use the effective-interest amortization method.
6. (Supplement 10C) Show the accounting equation effects and give the journal entries required on January 1, 2021, relating to the bond issuance and on December 31, 2021, relating to interest on the bond. Use the simplified effective-interest amortization method.

Suggested Solution

1. Issue price of the bonds: $100,000 × 95.9% = $95,900.
2. Discount on the bonds payable: $100,000 × $95,900 = $4,100.

   Months amortized: From date of issue, January 1, 2021, to maturity date, January 1, 2026 = 5 years × 12 months per year = 60 months.
3. January 1 (issuance date):

Assets		=	Liabilities		+	Stockholders' Equity
Cash	+95,900		Bonds Payable	+100,000		
			Discount on			
			Bonds Payable (+xL)	−4,100		

	Debit	Credit
Cash	95,900	
Discount on Bonds Payable (+xL)	4,100	
Bonds Payable		100,000

4. December 31, 2021 (straight-line amortization):

Assets		=	Liabilities		+	Stockholders' Equity	
Cash	−6,000		Discount on			Interest	
			Bonds Payable (+xL)	+820		Expense (+E)	−6,820

	Debit	Credit
Interest Expense ($6,000 + $820)	6,820	
Discount on Bonds Payable (−xL) ($4,100 × 12/60)		820
Cash ($100,000 × 6% × 12/12)		6,000

5. December 31, 2021 (effective-interest amortization):

Assets		=	Liabilities		+	Stockholders' Equity	
Cash	−6,000		Discount on			Interest	
			Bonds Payable (+xL)	+713		Expense (+E)	−6,713

	Debit	Credit
Interest Expense ($95,900 × 7% × 12/12)	6,713	
Discount on Bonds Payable (−xL) ($6,713 − $6000)		713
Cash ($100,000 × 6% × 12/12)		6,000

6. January 1 (issuance date):

Assets		=	Liabilities		+	Stockholders' Equity
Cash	+95,900		Bonds Payable, Net	+95,900		

	Debit	Credit
Cash	95,900	
Bonds Payable, Net		95,900

December 31, 2021 (simplified effective-interest amortization):

Assets		=	Liabilities		+	Stockholders' Equity	
Cash	−6,000		Bonds Payable, Net	+713		Interest Expense (+E)	−6,713

	Debit	Credit
Interest Expense ($95,900 × 7% × 12/12)	6,713	
Bonds Payable, Net ($6,713 − $6,000)		713
Cash ($100,000 × 6% × 12/12)		6,000

CHAPTER SUMMARY

LO 10-1 Explain the role of liabilities in financing a business.

- Liabilities play a vital role in allowing a business to buy goods and services on credit, cover gaps in cash flows, and expand into new regions and markets.

- Liabilities are classified as current if due to be paid with current assets within the current operating cycle of the business or within one year of the balance sheet date (whichever is longer). All other liabilities are considered long term.

LO 10-2 Explain how to account for common types of current liabilities.

- Liabilities are initially reported at their cash equivalent value, which is the amount of cash that a creditor would accept to settle the liability immediately after the transaction or event occurred.

- Liabilities are increased whenever additional obligations arise (including interest) and are reduced whenever the company makes payments or provides services to the creditor.

LO 10-3 Analyze and record bond liability transactions.

- For most public issuances of debt (bonds), the amount borrowed by the company does not equal the amount repaid at maturity. The effect of a bond discount is to provide the borrower less money than the value stated on the face of the bond, which increases the cost of borrowing above the interest rate stated on the bond. The effect of a bond premium is to provide the borrower more money than the face value repaid at maturity, which decreases the cost of borrowing below the stated interest rate.

- Interest Expense reports the cost of borrowing, which equals the periodic interest payments plus (or minus) the amount of the bond discount (or premium) amortized in that interest period.

LO 10-4 Describe how to account for contingent liabilities.

- A contingent liability is a potential liability (and loss) that has arisen as a result of a past transaction or event. Its ultimate outcome will not be known until a future event occurs or fails to occur. Under GAAP, it is recorded when probable and reasonably estimable.

LO 10-5 Calculate and interpret the debt-to-assets ratio and the times interest earned ratio.

- The debt-to-assets ratio is calculated by dividing total liabilities by total assets. It indicates the percentage of assets financed by creditors, with a higher ratio indicating a riskier financing strategy.

- The times interest earned ratio measures a company's ability to meet its interest obligations with resources generated from its profit-making activities.

Accounting Decision Tools		
Name of Measure	**Formula**	**What It Tells You**
Debt-to-assets ratio	$\dfrac{\text{Total Liabilities}}{\text{Total Assets}}$	• The percentage of assets financed by creditors • A higher ratio means greater financing risk
Times interest earned ratio	$\dfrac{(\text{Net Income} + \text{Interest Expense} + \text{Income Tax Expense})}{\text{Interest Expense}}$	• Whether sufficient resources are generated from operations to cover interest costs • The higher the number, the better the coverage

KEY TERMS

Accrued Liabilities p. 446
Amortization Schedule p. 474
Contingent Liability p. 461
Current Liabilities p. 444
Debt-to-Assets Ratio p. 462
Discount p. 455

Effective-Interest Method of Amortization p. 465
Face Value p. 454
Issue Price p. 454
Market Interest Rate p. 454
Maturity Date p. 454

Premium p. 455
Present Value p. 455
Stated Interest Rate p. 454
Straight-Line Method of Amortization p. 464
Times Interest Earned Ratio p. 463

See complete definitions in the glossary in the back of this text.

HOMEWORK HELPER

Alternative terms

• The stated interest rate on a bond is also called the coupon rate or contract rate. The market interest rate is also called the effective interest rate or yield rate.
• The word *amortize* comes from the root word "mort," which means to kill or eliminate; as bond discounts and premiums are amortized, they are gradually eliminated.

Helpful reminders

• From the employer's perspective, payroll deductions create liabilities, not expenses. They are not expenses because they do not increase the employer's wages and salaries cost; they simply redirect part of the wages and salaries payments to a government agency or other organization, rather than to employees.
• Bonds issue above face value (at a premium) if their stated interest rate is attractive (more than the market interest rate). If bonds have issued at a premium, their periodic cash payments will be greater than the interest expense, causing a reduction in the bond liability's carrying value.
• Bonds issue below face value (at a discount) if their stated interest rate is unattractive (less than the market interest rate). If bonds have issued at a discount, their periodic cash payments will be less than the interest expense, causing an increase in the bond liability's carrying value.

Frequent mistakes

• Use the stated interest rate, not the market interest rate, to calculate the cash paid periodically on a bond. (The market interest rate is used to calculate Interest Expense when using the effective-interest method.)

PRACTICE MATERIAL

QUESTIONS (⊖ Symbol indicates questions that require analysis from more than one perspective.)

1. Describe three ways in which liabilities are used to finance business activities.

2. Define *liability*. What's the difference between a current liability and a long-term liability?

3. What three factors influence the dollar amount reported for liabilities?

4. Define *accrued liability*. Give an example of a typical accrued liability.

5. Why is Deferred Revenue considered a liability?

6. Why are payroll taxes and sales taxes considered liabilities?

7. Your company plans to hire an employee at a yearly salary of $70,000. Someone in your company says the actual cost will be lower because of payroll deductions. Someone else says it will be higher. Who is right? What is likely to be the total cost to the company? Explain. ⊖

8. If a company has a long-term loan that has only two years remaining until it matures, how is it reported on the balance sheet (*a*) this year and (*b*) next year?

9. What are the reasons that some bonds are issued at a discount and others are issued at a premium?

10. What is the difference between the stated interest rate and the market interest rate on a bond?

11. Will the stated interest rate be higher than the market interest rate or will the market interest rate be higher than the stated interest rate when a bond is issued at (*a*) face value, (*b*) a discount, and (*c*) a premium?

12. What is the carrying value of a bond payable?

13. What is the difference between a secured bond and a debenture? Which type carries more risk for the lender?

14. What is a contingent liability? How is a contingent liability reported under GAAP? How does this differ under IFRS?

15. (Supplement 10A) How is interest expense calculated using the straight-line method of amortization for a bond issued at (*a*) a discount and (*b*) a premium?

16. (Supplement 10B) How is interest expense calculated using the effective-interest method of amortization for a bond issued at (*a*) a discount and (*b*) a premium?

17. (Supplement 10C) How is interest expense calculated using the simplified approach to the effective-interest method for a bond issued at (*a*) a discount and (*b*) a premium?

18. (Supplement D) Over the period to maturity, why does yearly interest expense decrease on an installment note?

MULTIPLE CHOICE

1. Which of the following best describes Accrued Liabilities?
   a. Long-term liabilities.
   b. Current amounts owed to suppliers of inventory.
   c. Expenses incurred but not paid at the end of the accounting period.
   d. Revenues that have been collected but not earned.

2. As of December 31, 2018, Shutterfly, Inc. had 7,000 full-time and 12,500 part-time employees. Assume in the last pay period of the year, the company paid $8,000,000 to employees after deducting $2,000,000 for employee income taxes, $612,000 for FICA taxes, and $700,000 for other purposes. No payments have been made to the government relating to these taxes. Which of the following statements is true regarding this pay period?
   a. FICA Taxes Payable should be $612,000.
   b. FICA Taxes Payable should be $1,224,000.
   c. Salaries and Wages Expense should be $8,000,000.
   d. None of the above is true.

3. Assume PVH, the makers of Calvin Klein underwear, borrowed $100,000 from the bank to be repaid over the next five years, with principal payments beginning next month. Which of the following best describes the presentation of this debt in the balance sheet as of today (the date of borrowing)?
   a. $100,000 in the long-term liability section.
   b. $100,000 *plus* the interest to be paid over the five-year period in the long-term liability section.

   c. A portion of the $100,000 in the current liability section and the remainder of the principal in the long-term liability section.
   d. A portion of the $100,000 plus interest in the current liability section and the remainder of the principal plus interest in the long-term liability section.

4. Assume Speedo International received $400,000 for long-term promissory notes that were issued on November 1. The notes pay interest on April 30 and October 31 at the annual rate of 6 percent, which was comparable to other interest rates in the market at that time. Which of the following journal entries would be required at December 31?

	Debit	Credit
a. Interest Expense	4,000	
Interest Payable		4,000
b. Interest Expense	4,000	
Cash		4,000
c. Interest Expense	4,000	
Interest Payable	8,000	
Cash		12,000
d. Interest Expense	8,000	
Interest Payable	4,000	
Cash		12,000

5. Which of the following does not impact the calculation of the cash interest payments to be made to bondholders?

   a. Face value of the bond.
   b. Stated interest rate.
   c. Market interest rate.
   d. The length of time between payments.

6. Which of the following is false when a bond is issued at a premium?

   a. The bond will issue for an amount above its face value.
   b. Interest expense will exceed the cash interest payments.
   c. The market interest rate is lower than the stated interest rate.
   d. The issue price will be quoted at a number greater than 100.

7. To determine if a bond will be issued at a premium, discount, or face value, one must know which of the following pairs of information?

   a. The face value and the stated interest rate on the date the bonds were issued.
   b. The face value and the market interest rate on the date the bonds were issued.
   c. The stated interest rate and the market interest rate on the date the bonds were issued.
   d. You can't tell without having more information.

8. A bond is issued at a price of 103 and retired early at a price of 97. Which of the following is true?

   a. A gain will be reported on the income statement when the bond is issued.

   b. A loss will be reported on the income statement when the bond is issued.
   c. A gain will be reported on the income statement when the bond is retired.
   d. A loss will be reported on the income statement when the bond is retired.

9. Land O' Lakes, Inc., reported (in millions) Income from Operations of $206, Net Income of $160, Interest Expense of $63, and Income Tax Expense of $15. What was this dairy company's times interest earned ratio (rounded) for the year?

   a. 1.49
   b. 2.53
   c. 3.27
   d. 3.78

10. Big Hitter Corp. is facing a class-action lawsuit in the upcoming year. It is possible, but not probable, that the company will have to pay a settlement of approximately $2,000,000 in the upcoming year. How would this fact be reported, if at all, in the financial statements prepared at the end of the current month using GAAP?

   a. Report $2,000,000 as a current liability.
   b. Report $2,000,000 as a long-term liability.
   c. Describe the potential liability in the notes to the financial statements.
   d. Reporting is not required in this case.

> For answers to the Multiple-Choice Questions **see page Q1** located in the last section of the book.

MINI-EXERCISES

McGraw Hill connect

M10-1 Recording Deferred Revenues

LO 10-2

A local theater company sells 1,500 season ticket packages at a price of $250 per package. The first show in the 10-show season starts this week. Show the accounting equation effects and prepare the journal entries related to (a) the sale of the season tickets before the first show and (b) the revenue from fulfilling the performance obligation by putting on the first show.

M10-2 Recording Sales and State Tax

LO 10-2

Grandpa Clocks, Inc. (GCI), is a retailer of wall, mantle, and grandfather clocks. Assume GCI sells a grandfather clock for $10,000 cash plus 4 percent sales tax. The clock had originally cost GCI $6,000. Show the accounting equation effects and prepare the journal entries related to this transaction. Assume GCI uses a perpetual inventory system, as explained in Chapter 6.

M10-3 Calculating Net Pay and Total Payroll Costs

LO 10-2

Lightning Electronics is a midsize manufacturer of lithium batteries. The company's payroll records for the November 1–14 pay period show that employees earned wages totaling $50,000 but that employee income taxes totaling $7,000 and FICA taxes totaling $2,625 were withheld from this amount. The net pay was directly deposited into the employees' bank accounts. What was the amount of net pay? Assuming Lightning Electronics also must pay $250 of unemployment taxes for this pay period, what amount would be reported as the total payroll costs?

M10-4 Reporting Payroll Tax Liabilities

LO 10-2

Refer to M10-3. Prepare the journal entry or entries that Lightning would use to record the payroll. Include both employee and employer taxes.

LO 10-2

M10-5 Reporting Current and Noncurrent Portions of Long-Term Debt

On December 1, 2021, your company borrowed $15,000, a portion of which is to be repaid each year on November 30. Specifically, your company will make the following principal payments: 2022, $2,000; 2023, $3,000; 2024, $4,000; and 2025, $6,000. Show how this loan will be reported in the December 31, 2022 and 2021, balance sheets, assuming principal payments will be made when required.

LO 10-2

M10-6 Recording Notes Payable

Greener Pastures Corporation borrowed $1,000,000 on November 1, 2021. The note carried a 9 percent interest rate with the principal and interest payable on June 1, 2022. Show the accounting equation effects and prepare the journal entries for (a) the note issued on November 1 and (b) the interest accrual on December 31.

LO 10-2

M10-7 Reporting Interest and Long-Term Debt, Including Current Portion

Barton Chocolates used a promissory note to borrow $1,000,000 on July 1, 2021, at an annual interest rate of 6 percent. The note is to be repaid in yearly installments of $200,000, plus accrued interest, on June 30 of every year until the note is paid in full (on June 30, 2026). Show how the results of this transaction would be reported in a classified balance sheet prepared as of December 31, 2021.

LO 10-3

M10-8 Determining Bond Discount or Premium from Quoted Price

On February 6, 2021, there was a quoted bond price of 130.03 for Tough Motor Company's 7.45 percent bonds maturing on July 16, 2031. Were the bonds listed at a discount or premium? Does this mean the market interest rate for comparable bonds was higher or lower than 7.45 percent?

LO 10-3

M10-9 Computing and Reporting a Bond Liability at an Issuance Price of 97

E-Tech Initiatives Limited plans to issue $500,000, 10-year, 4 percent bonds. Interest is payable annually on December 31. All of the bonds will be issued on January 1, 2022. Show how the bonds would be reported on the January 2, 2022, balance sheet if they are issued at 97.

LO 10-3

M10-10 Computing and Reporting a Bond Liability at an Issuance Price of 102

Repeat M10-9 assuming the bonds are issued at 102.

LO 10-3

M10-11 Recording Bonds Issued at Face Value

Schlitterbahn Waterslide Company issued 25,000, 10-year, 5 percent, $100 bonds on January 1 at face value. Interest is payable each December 31. Show the accounting equation effects and prepare journal entries for (a) the issuance of these bonds on January 1 and (b) the first interest payment on December 31.

LO 10-4

McDonald's

M10-12 Reporting a Contingent Liability

Buzz Coffee Shops is famous for its large servings of hot coffee. After a famous case involving McDonald's, the lawyer for Buzz warned management (during 2017) that it could be sued if someone were to spill hot coffee and be burned. "With the temperature of your coffee, I can guarantee it's just a matter of time before you're sued for $1,000,000." Buzz felt the likelihood was remote. Unfortunately, in 2019, the lawyer's prediction came true when a customer filed suit. After consulting with his attorney, Buzz felt the loss was possible but not likely or probable. The case went to trial in 2020, and the jury awarded the customer $400,000 in damages, which the company immediately appealed. Buzz felt a loss was probable but believed a lower amount could be negotiated. During 2021, the customer and the company settled their dispute for $150,000. What is the proper reporting of this liability each year from 2019 through 2021 under GAAP? Would the reporting differ under IFRS?

LO 10-5

M10-13 Computing the Debt-to-Assets Ratio and the Times Interest Earned Ratio

The balance sheet for Shaver Corporation reported the following: cash, $5,000; short-term investments, $10,000; net accounts receivable, $35,000; inventory, $40,000; prepaids, $10,000; equipment, $100,000; current liabilities, $40,000; notes payable (long-term), $70,000; total stockholders' equity, $90,000; net income, $3,320; interest expense, $4,400; income before income taxes, $5,280. Compute Shaver's debt-to-assets ratio and times interest earned ratio. Based on these ratios, does it appear Shaver relies mainly on debt or equity to finance its assets? Is it probable that Shaver will be able to meet its future interest obligations?

M10-14 Analyzing the Impact of Transactions on the Debt-to-Assets Ratio   LO 10-5

BSO, Inc., has assets of $600,000 and liabilities of $450,000, resulting in a debt-to-assets ratio of 0.75. For each of the following transactions, determine whether the debt-to-assets ratio will increase, decrease, or remain the same. Each item is independent.

a. Purchased $20,000 of new inventory on credit.
b. Paid accounts payable in the amount of $50,000.
c. Recorded accrued salaries in the amount of $100,000.
d. Borrowed $250,000 from a local bank, to be repaid in 90 days.

**M10-15 (Supplement 10A) Recording Bond Issuance and Interest Payment (Straight-Line   LO 10-S1
Amortization)**

Simko Company issued $600,000, 10-year, 5 percent bonds on January 1, 2021. The bonds were issued for $580,000. Interest is payable annually on December 31. Using straight-line amortization, prepare journal entries to record (a) the bond issuance on January 1, 2021, and (b) the payment of interest on December 31, 2021.

**M10-16 (Supplement 10B) Recording Bond Issuance and Interest Payment (Effective-Interest   LO 10-S2
Amortization)**

Clem Company issued $800,000, 10-year, 5 percent bonds on January 1, 2021. The bonds sold for $741,000. Interest is payable annually on December 31. Using effective-interest amortization, prepare journal entries to record (a) the bond issuance on January 1, 2021, and (b) the payment of interest on December 31, 2021. The market interest rate on the bonds is 6 percent.

**M10-17 (Supplement 10C) Recording Interest Accrual and Interest Payment (Simplified   LO 10-S3
Approach to Effective-Interest Amortization)**

On January 1, 2021, Buchheit Enterprises reported $95,000 in a liability called "Bonds Payable, Net." This liability related to a $100,000 bond with a stated interest rate of 5 percent that was issued when the market interest rate was 6 percent. Assuming that interest is paid December 31 each year, prepare the journal entry to record interest paid on December 31, 2021, using the simplified effective-interest method shown in Chapter Supplement 10C.

M10-18 (Supplement 10D) Interpreting an Amortization Schedule   LO 10-S4

The following amortization schedule indicates the interest and principal that Chip's Cookie Corporation (CCC) must repay on an installment note established January 1, 2021. CCC has a December 31 year-end and makes the required annual payments on December 31. Use the amortization schedule to determine (a) the amount of the (rounded) annual payment; (b) the amount of interest expense to report in the year ended December 31, 2021 (Year 1); (c) the notes payable balance at January 1, 2024; and (d) the total interest and total principal paid over the note's entire life.

Year	Beginning Notes Payable	Interest Expense	Repaid Principal on Notes Payable	Ending Notes Payable
1	30,000	1,500	6,960	23,040
2	23,040	1,152	7,308	15,732
3	15,732	787	7,673	8,059
4	8,059	401	8,059	0
Total		3,840	30,000	

**M10-19 (Supplement 10D) Preparing Journal Entries from an Installment Note Amortization   LO 10-S4
Schedule**

Refer to M10-18. Prepare CCC's required journal entries on (a) January 1, 2021; (b) December 31, 2021; (c) December 31, 2022; (d) December 31, 2023; and (e) December 31, 2024.

**M10-20 (Supplement 10D) Using an Online Calculator to Produce and Interpret an Amortization   LO 10-S4
Schedule**

Access an online loan calculator with annual payments, such as the one at mycalculators.com, to produce an amortization schedule for Welton Corp.'s installment note that has original principal of $25,000, interest of 6 percent compounded annually, and a term of three years. (a) What is the annual payment (rounded to the nearest dollar)? (b) Of this amount, how much represents interest in year 1 (rounded to the nearest dollar)? (*c*) How much principal is included in the year 1 payment (rounded to the nearest dollar)? (*d*) How much interest is included in the year 2 payment (rounded to the nearest dollar)? (*e*) Over time, has the interest become a smaller or larger component of the annual payment?

LO 10-S4   **M10-21 (Supplement 10D) Preparing Journal Entries from an Installment Note Amortization Schedule**

Refer to M10-20. Welton Corp. established the note on the first day of its fiscal year and will fully repay the note by the end of year 3 on its December 31 fiscal year-end. Prepare Welton Corp.'s journal entries on (*a*) January 1, Year 1; (*b*) December 31, Year 1; (*c*) December 31, Year 2; and (*d*) December 31, Year 3. Round amounts in Years 1 and 2 to the nearest dollar. In Year 3, ensure the rounded amounts eliminate the Notes Payable balance and maintain the same annual cash repayment.

EXERCISES

LO 10-2   **E10-1   Determining Financial Statement Effects of Transactions Involving Notes Payable**

Mattel

Many businesses borrow money during periods of increased business activity to finance inventory and accounts receivable. For example, Mattel builds up its inventory to meet the needs of retailers selling to Christmas shoppers. A large portion of Mattel's sales are on credit. As a result, Mattel often collects cash from its sales several months after Christmas. Assume on November 1, 2021, Mattel borrowed $6 million cash from Metropolitan Bank and signed a promissory note that matures in six months. The interest rate was 8 percent payable at maturity. The accounting period ends December 31.

Required:

1.   Indicate the accounts, amounts, and effects (+ for increase, − for decrease, and NE for no effect) of the (*a*) issuance of the note on November 1; (*b*) impact of the adjusting entry on December 31, 2021; and (*c*) the payment of the note and interest on April 30, 2022, on the accounting equation. Use the following structure for your answer:

Date	Assets	=	Liabilities	+	Stockholders' Equity

2.   If Mattel needs extra cash prior to every Christmas season, should management borrow money on a long-term basis to avoid negotiating a new short-term loan each year? Explain your answer.

LO 10-2   **E10-2   Recording Notes Payable through the Time to Maturity**

Use the information in E10-1 to complete the following requirements.

Required:

1.   Give the journal entry to record the note on November 1, 2021.
2.   Give any adjusting entry required on December 31, 2021.
3.   Give the journal entry to record payment of the note and interest on the maturity date, April 30, 2022, assuming that interest has not been recorded since December 31, 2021.

LO 10-2   **E10-3   Recording Payroll Costs**

McLoyd Company completed the salaries and wages payroll for March. The payroll provided the following details:

Salaries and wages earned	$400,000
Employee income taxes withheld	37,000
FICA taxes withheld	28,600
Unemployment taxes	2,780

Required:

1.   Considering both employee and employer payroll taxes, use the preceding information to calculate the total labor cost for the company for March.
2.   Prepare the journal entry to record the payroll for March, including employee deductions (but excluding employer payroll taxes). Employees were paid in March but amounts withheld were not yet remitted.
3.   Prepare the journal entry to record the employer's FICA taxes and unemployment taxes.

E10-4 Recording Payroll Costs with and without Withholdings

Assume an employee of Rocco Rock Company earns $1,000 of gross wages during the current pay period and is required to remit to the government $100 for income tax and $50 for FICA. Consider the following two procedures for paying the employee:

Procedure 1 (Withholdings)	Procedure 2 (No Withholdings)
Rocco Rock Company pays the employee net wages of $850 and will remit income taxes and FICA on behalf of the employee.	Rocco Rock Company pays the employee gross wages of $1,000 and the employee is responsible for remitting income taxes and FICA himself.

Required:

1. Ignoring employer payroll taxes, under each procedure calculate (*a*) the total amount to be paid by the company and (*b*) the amount of cash the employee will have after satisfying all responsibilities to the government. Do your answers for procedures 1 and 2 differ for (*a*)? For (*b*)?
2. Explain why procedure 1 (withholdings) is the approach required by the government.
3. Considering that employers are responsible for matching employees' FICA contributions, explain why employers also might prefer procedure 1 over procedure 2.
4. Prepare the journal entries required by the employer under procedure 1, assuming the employee is paid in cash, but the withholdings and matching employer FICA contribution have not yet been paid. (Do not ignore employer payroll taxes, but assume no unemployment taxes.)

E10-5 Determining the Impact of Current Liability Transactions, Including Analysis of the Debt-to-Assets Ratio

Bryant Company sells a wide range of inventories, which are initially purchased on account. Occasionally, short-term notes payable are used to obtain cash for current use. The following transactions were selected from those occurring during the year:

a. On January 10, purchased merchandise on credit for $18,000. The company uses a perpetual inventory system.
b. On March 1, borrowed $40,000 cash from City Bank and signed a promissory note with a face amount of $40,000, due at the end of six months, accruing interest at an annual rate of 8 percent, payable at maturity.

Required:

1. For each of the transactions, indicate the accounts, amounts, and effects (+ for increase, − for decrease, and NE for no effect) on the accounting equation. Use the following structure:

Date	Assets	=	Liabilities	+	Stockholders' Equity

2. What amount of cash is paid on the maturity date of the note?
3. Indicate the impact of each transaction (+ for increase, − for decrease, and NE for no effect) on the debt-to-assets ratio. Assume Bryant Company had $300,000 in total liabilities and $500,000 in total assets, yielding a debt-to-assets ratio of 0.60, prior to each transaction.

E10-6 Determining and Recording the Financial Statement Effects of Deferred Revenue

The Tennis Times (TTT) is a publisher of magazines. Its accounting policy for subscriptions follows:

Revenues
Revenues from our magazine subscription services are deferred initially and later recognized as revenue as subscription services are provided.

Assume TTT (*a*) collected $420 million in 2021 for magazines that will be distributed later in 2021 and 2022, (*b*) provided $204 million of services on these subscriptions in 2021, and (*c*) provided $216 million of services on these subscriptions in 2022 .

Required:

1. Using the information given, indicate the accounts, amounts, and accounting equation effects (+ for increase, − for decrease, and NE for no effect) of transactions (*a*), (*b*), and (*c*).

2. Using the information given, prepare the journal entries that would be recorded for (*a*), (*b*), and (*c*).

LO 10-3   **E10-7 Preparing Journal Entries to Record Issuance of Bonds and Payment of Interest**

On January 1, Applied Technologies Corporation (ATC) issued $500,000 in bonds that mature in 10 years. The bonds have a stated interest rate of 10 percent. When the bonds were issued, the market interest rate was 10 percent. The bonds pay interest once per year on December 31.

Required:

1. Determine the price at which the bonds were issued and the amount that ATC received at issuance.
2. Prepare the journal entry to record the bond issuance.
3. Prepare the journal entry to record the first interest payment on December 31 assuming no interest has been accrued earlier in the year.

LO 10-3   **E10-8 Preparing Journal Entries to Record Issuance of Bonds at Face Value, Payment of Interest, and Early Retirement**

On January 1, Innovative Solutions, Inc., issued $200,000 in bonds at face value. The bonds have a stated interest rate of 6 percent. The bonds mature in 10 years and pay interest once per year on December 31.

Required:

1. Prepare the journal entry to record the bond issuance.
2. Prepare the journal entry to record the first interest payment on December 31. Assume no interest has been accrued earlier in the year.
3. Assume the bonds were retired immediately after the first interest payment at a quoted price of 101. Prepare the journal entry to record the early retirement of the bonds.

LO 10-3   **E10-9 Indicating the Effects of a Premium Bond Issue and Interest Payment on the Financial Statements**

Grocery Corporation received $300,328 for 11 percent bonds issued on January 1, 2021, at a market interest rate of 8 percent. The bonds had a total face value of $250,000, stated that interest would be paid each December 31, and stated that they mature in 10 years.

Required:

Complete the following table for each account by indicating (*a*) whether it is reported on the Balance Sheet (B/S) or Income Statement (I/S); (*b*) the dollar amount by which the account increases (+), decreases (−), or does not change (0) when Grocery Corporation issues the bonds; and (*c*) the direction of change in the account [increase (+), decrease (−), or no change (NC)] when Grocery Corporation records the interest payment on December 31.

Account	(a) Financial Statement	(b) Issuance	(c) Interest Paid
Bonds Payable			
Discount on Bonds Payable			
Interest Expense			
Premium on Bonds Payable			

LO 10-5   **E10-10 Calculating and Interpreting the Debt-to-Assets Ratio and Times Interest Earned Ratio**

FedEx Corporation   At May 31, 2019, FedEx Corporation reported the following amounts (in millions) in its financial statements:

	2019	2018
Total Assets	$54,400	$52,330
Total Liabilities	36,600	32,900
Interest Expense	590	560
Income Tax Expense	115	220
Net Income	540	4,570

Required:

1. Compute the debt-to-assets ratio and times interest earned ratio (to two decimal places) for 2019 and 2018.
2. Use your answers to requirement 1 to determine whether, in 2019, (*a*) creditors were providing a greater (or lesser) proportion of financing for FedEx's assets and (*b*) FedEx was more (or less) successful at covering its interest costs, as compared to 2018.

E10-11 (Supplement 10A) Recording the Effects of a Premium Bond Issue and First Interest Period (Straight-Line Amortization)   LO 10-S1

Refer to the information in E10-9 and assume Grocery Corporation uses the straight-line method to amortize the bond premium.

Required:

1. Prepare the journal entry to record the bond issuance.
2. Prepare the journal entry to record the first interest payment on December 31.

E10-12 (Supplement 10B) Recording the Effects of a Premium Bond Issue and First Interest Period (Effective-Interest Amortization)   LO 10-S2

Refer to the information in E10-9 and assume Grocery Corporation uses the effective-interest method to amortize the bond premium.

Required:

1. Prepare the journal entry to record the bond issuance.
2. Prepare the journal entry to record the first interest payment on December 31.

E10-13 (Supplement 10C) Recording the Effects of a Premium Bond Issue and First Interest Period (Simplified Effective-Interest Amortization)   LO 10-S3

Refer to the information in E10-9 and assume Grocery Corporation accounts for the bond using the shortcut approach shown in Chapter Supplement 10C.

Required:

1. Prepare the journal entry to record the bond issuance.
2. Prepare the journal entry to record the first interest payment on December 31.

E10-14 (Supplement 10A) Recording the Effects of a Discount Bond Issue and First Interest Payment and Preparing a Discount Amortization Schedule (Straight-Line Amortization)   LO 10-S1

On January 1, when the market interest rate was 9 percent, Seton Corporation completed a $200,000, 8 percent bond issue for $187,163. The bonds pay interest each December 31 and mature in 10 years. Seton amortizes the bond discount using the straight-line method.

Required:

1. Prepare the journal entry to record the bond issuance.
2. Prepare the journal entry to record the first interest payment on December 31.
3. Prepare a bond discount amortization schedule for these bonds. Round calculations to the nearest dollar.

E10-15 (Supplement 10B) Recording the Effects of a Discount Bond Issue and First Interest Payment and Preparing a Discount Amortization Schedule (Effective-Interest Amortization)   LO 10-S2

Refer to the information in E10-14 and assume Seton Corporation uses the effective-interest method to amortize the bond discount.

Required:

1. Prepare the journal entry to record the bond issuance.
2. Prepare the journal entry to record the first interest payment on December 31.
3. Prepare a bond discount amortization schedule for these bonds. Round calculations to the nearest dollar.

LO 10-S3   **E10-16 (Supplement 10C) Recording the Effects of a Discount Bond Issue and First Interest Payment and Preparing a Discount Amortization Schedule (Simplified Effective-Interest Amortization)**

Refer to the information in E10-14 and assume Seton Corporation accounts for the bond using the simplified effective-interest method shown in Chapter Supplement 10C.

Required:

1. Prepare the journal entry to record the bond issuance.
2. Prepare the journal entry to record the first interest payment on December 31.
3. Prepare a bond discount amortization schedule for these bonds. Round calculations to the nearest dollar.

LO 10-S4   **E10-17 (Supplement 10D) Interpreting an Amortization Schedule and Preparing Journal Entries**

The following amortization schedule indicates the interest and principal to be repaid on an installment note established January 1, 2021, for a company with a March 31 fiscal year-end.

Period	Beginning Notes Payable	Interest Expense	Repaid Principal on Notes Payable	Ending Notes Payable
1/1–12/31, Year 1	$10,000	$ 400	$ 2,355	$7,645
1/1–12/31, Year 2	7,645	306	2,449	5,196
1/1–12/31, Year 3	5,196	208	2,547	2,649
1/1–12/31, Year 4	2,649	106	2,649	0
Total		1,020	10,000	

Required:

1. Assuming the company makes the required annual payments on December 31, use the amortization schedule to determine (*a*) the amount of the (rounded) annual payment; (*b*) the amount of Interest Expense to report in the year ended March 31, 2021; (*c*) the amount of Interest Expense to report in the year ended March 31, 2022; (*d*) the Notes Payable balance at January 1, 2024; and (*e*) the total interest and total principal paid over the note's entire life.
2. Assuming the company makes adjustments at the end of each fiscal year, prepare the journal entries required on (*a*) January 1, 2021, and (*b*) March 31, 2021.

COACHED PROBLEMS

LO 10-2, 10-5   **CP10-1 Determining Financial Effects of Transactions Affecting Current Liabilities with Evaluation of Effects on the Debt-to-Assets Ratio**

EZ Curb Company completed the following transactions. The annual accounting period ends December 31.

Jan. 8	Purchased merchandise on account at a cost of $14,000. (Assume a perpetual inventory system.)
Jan. 17	Paid for the January 8 purchase.
Apr. 1	Received $40,000 from National Bank after signing a 12-month, 6 percent, promissory note.
June 3	Purchased merchandise on account at a cost of $18,000.
July 5	Paid for the June 3 purchase.
July 31	Rented out a small office in a building owned by EZ Curb Company and collected six months' rent in advance, amounting to $6,000. (Use an account called Deferred Revenue.)
Dec. 20	Collected $100 cash on account from a customer.
Dec. 31	Determined that wages of $6,500 were earned but not yet paid on December 31 (ignore payroll taxes).
Dec. 31	Adjusted the accounts at year-end, relating to interest.
Dec. 31	Adjusted the accounts at year-end, relating to rent.

Required:

1. For each listed transaction and related adjusting entry, indicate the accounts, amounts, and effects (+ for increase, − for decrease, and NE for no effect) on the accounting equation, using the following format:

Date	Assets	=	Liabilities	+	Stockholders' Equity

2. For each transaction and related adjusting entry, state whether the debt-to-assets ratio is increased or decreased or there is no change. (Assume EZ Curb Company's debt-to-assets ratio has always been less than 1.0.)

CP10-2 Recording and Reporting Current Liabilities with Evaluation of Effects on the Debt-to-Assets Ratio

LO 10-2, 10-5

Using data from CP10-1, complete the following requirements.

Required:

1. Prepare journal entries for each of the transactions through December 20.
2. Prepare any adjusting entries required on December 31.
3. Show how all of the liabilities arising from these items are reported on the balance sheet at December 31.
4. Complete requirement 2 of CP10-1, if you have not already done so.

CP10-3 Recording and Reporting Current Liabilities

LO 10-2

Riverside Company completed the following two transactions. The annual accounting period ends December 31.

a. On December 31, calculated the payroll, which indicates gross earnings for wages ($130,000), payroll deductions for income tax ($13,000), payroll deductions for FICA ($10,000), payroll deductions for United Way ($2,000), employer contributions for FICA (matching), and state and federal unemployment taxes ($1,300). Employees were paid in cash, but these payments and the corresponding payroll deductions and employer taxes have not yet been recorded.

b. Collected rent revenue of $3,600 on December 10 for office space that Riverside rented to another business. The rent collected was for 30 days from December 11 to January 10 and was credited in full to Deferred Revenue.

Required:

1. Give the journal entries to record payroll on December 31.
2. Give (*a*) the journal entry for the collection of rent on December 10 and (*b*) the adjusting journal entry on December 31.

    TIP: For (*b*), notice that the entry recorded on December 10 includes 10 days of rental space (out of 30) that isn't provided until after December 31.

3. Show how any liabilities related to these items should be reported on the company's balance sheet at December 31.

CP10-4 Comparing Bonds Issued at Par, Discount, and Premium

LO 10-3

Sikes Corporation, whose annual accounting period ends on December 31, issued the following bonds:

> Date of bonds: January 1, 2021
>
> Maturity amount and date: $200,000 due in 10 years (December 31, 2030)
>
> Interest: 10 percent per year payable each December 31
>
> Date issued: January 1, 2021

Required:

1. For each of the three independent cases that follow, provide the amounts to be reported on the January 1, 2021, financial statements immediately after the bonds are issued:

	Case A (issued at 100)	Case B (at 96)	Case C (at 102)
a. Bonds payable	$	$	$
b. Unamortized premium (or discount)			
c. Carrying value			

TIP: See Exhibit 10.6 for an illustration distinguishing Bonds Payable from their carrying value.

2. Someone posted the following comment on an investment discussion forum: "Why would I buy a bond at a premium when I can find one at a discount? Isn't that stupid? It's like paying list price for a car instead of negotiating a discount." Write a brief message in response to the posting.

LO 10-4

Brunswick Corporation

CP10-5 Determining Financial Statement Reporting of Contingent Liabilities

Brunswick Corporation is a multinational company that manufactures and sells marine and recreational products. A prior annual report contained the following information:

Litigation

A jury awarded $44.4 million in damages in a suit brought by Independent Boat Builders, Inc., a buying group of boat manufacturers and its 22 members. Under the antitrust laws, the damage award has been tripled and the plaintiffs will be entitled to their attorney's fees and interest. The Company has filed an appeal contending the verdict was erroneous as a matter of law, as to both liability and damages.

Required:

If Brunswick recorded a liability for $133.2 million (3 × $44.4 million), which of the following best describes the likelihood of having to pay this amount: (*a*) probable, (*b*) reasonably possible, or (*c*) remote?

TIP: Refer to Exhibit 10.9.

LO 10-S1

CP10-6 (Supplement 10A) Recording Bond Issuance and Interest Payments (Straight-Line Amortization)

Southwest Corporation issued bonds with the following details:

Face value: $600,000
Interest: 9 percent per year payable each December 31
Terms: Bonds dated January 1, 2021, due five years from that date

---

The annual accounting period ends December 31. The bonds were issued at 104 on January 1, 2021, when the market interest rate was 8 percent. Assume the company uses straight-line amortization and adjusts for any rounding errors when recording interest expense in the final year.

Required:

1. Compute the cash received from the bond issuance in dollars (show computations).
    TIP: The issue price typically is quoted at a percentage of face value.
2. Give the journal entry to record the issuance of the bonds.
3. Give the journal entries to record the payment of interest on December 31, 2021 and 2022.
4. How much interest expense would be reported on the income statements for 2021 and 2022? Show how the liability related to the bonds should be reported on the balance sheets at December 31, 2021 and 2022.

LO 10-S2

CP10-7 (Supplement 10B) Recording Bond Issuance and Interest Payments (Effective-Interest Amortization)

Complete the requirements of CP10-6, assuming Southwest Corporation uses effective-interest amortization.

LO 10-S3

CP10-8 (Supplement 10C) Recording Bond Issuance and Interest Payments (Simplified Approach to Effective-Interest Amortization)

Complete the requirements of CP10-6, assuming Southwest Corporation uses simplified effective-interest amortization shown in Chapter Supplement 10C.

CP10-9 (Supplement 10A) Completing an Amortization Schedule (Straight-Line Amortization)   LO 10-S1

The Peg Corporation (TPC) issued bonds and received cash in full for the issue price. The bonds were dated and issued on January 1, 2021. The stated interest rate was payable at the end of each year. The bonds mature at the end of four years. The following schedule has been prepared (amounts in thousands):

Date	Cash	Interest	Amortization	Balance
January 1, 2021				$6,101
End of year 2021	$450	$425	$25	?
End of year 2022	450	?	25	6,051
End of year 2023	450	?	25	6,026
End of year 2024	450	424	26	6,000

Required:

1. Complete the amortization schedule.
   TIP: The switch in amortization from $25 to $26 in the final year is caused by rounding.
2. What was the maturity amount (face value) of the bonds?
3. How much cash was received at date of issuance of the bonds?
4. Was there a premium or a discount? If so, which and how much was it?
5. How much cash is paid for interest each period and will be paid in total for the full life of the bond issue?
6. What is the stated interest rate?
7. What is the market interest rate?
8. What amount of interest expense should be reported on the income statement each year?
9. Show how the bonds should be reported on the balance sheet at the end of 2022 and 2023.

CP10-10 (Supplement 10B or 10C) Completing an Amortization Schedule (Effective-Interest Amortization or Simplified Effective-Interest)   LO 10-S2, 10-S3

Hondor Corporation issued bonds and received cash in full for the issue price. The bonds were dated and issued on January 1, 2021. The stated interest rate was payable at the end of each year. The bonds mature at the end of four years. The following schedule has been completed (amounts in thousands):

Date	Cash	Interest	Amortization	Balance
January 1, 2021				$6,101
End of year 2021	$450	$427	$23	6,078
End of year 2022	450	426	24	6,054
End of year 2023	450	?	?	?
End of year 2024	450	?	28	6,000

Required:

1. Complete the amortization schedule.
2. What was the maturity amount (face value) of the bonds?
3. How much cash was received at date of issuance (sale) of the bonds?
4. Was there a premium or a discount? If so, which and how much was it?
5. How much cash is paid for interest each period and will be paid in total for the full life of the bond issue?
6. What is the stated interest rate?
   TIP: The stated interest rate can be calculated by comparing the cash payment to the face value of the bond.
7. What is the market interest rate?
8. What amount of interest expense should be reported on the income statement each year?
9. Show how the bonds should be reported on the balance sheet at the end of 2022 and 2023.

GROUP A PROBLEMS

LO 10-2, 10-5

PA10-1 Determining Financial Effects of Transactions Affecting Current Liabilities with Evaluation of Effects on the Debt-to-Assets Ratio

Jack Hammer Company completed the following transactions. The annual accounting period ends December 31.

Apr. 30	Received $600,000 from Commerce Bank after signing a 12-month, 6 percent, promissory note.
June 6	Purchased merchandise on account at a cost of $75,000. (Assume a perpetual inventory system.)
July 15	Paid for the June 6 purchase.
Aug. 31	Signed a contract to provide security service to a small apartment complex starting in September, and collected six months' fees in advance, amounting to $24,000.
Dec. 31	Determined salary and wages of $40,000 were earned but not yet paid as of December 31 (ignore payroll taxes).
Dec. 31	Adjusted the accounts at year-end, relating to interest.
Dec. 31	Adjusted the accounts at year-end, relating to security service.

Required:

1. For each listed transaction and related adjusting entry, indicate the accounts, amounts, and effects (+ for increase, − for decrease, and NE for no effect) on the accounting equation, using the following format:

Date	Assets	=	Liabilities	+	Stockholders' Equity

2. For each item, state whether the debt-to-assets ratio is increased or decreased or there is no change. (Assume Jack Hammer's debt-to-assets ratio is less than 1.0.)

LO 10-2, 10-5

PA10-2 Recording and Reporting Current Liabilities with Evaluation of Effects on the Debt-to-Assets Ratio

Using data from PA10-1, complete the following requirements.

Required:

1. Prepare journal entries for each of the transactions through August 31.
2. Prepare all adjusting entries required on December 31.
3. Show how all of the liabilities arising from these items are reported on the balance sheet at December 31.
4. Complete requirement 2 of PA10-1, if you have not already done so.

LO 10-2

PA10-3 Recording and Reporting Current Liabilities

Lakeview Company completed the following two transactions. The annual accounting period ends December 31.

a. On December 31, calculated the payroll, which indicates gross earnings for wages ($80,000), payroll deductions for income tax ($8,000), payroll deductions for FICA ($6,000), payroll deductions for American Cancer Society ($3,000), employer contributions for FICA (matching), and state and federal unemployment taxes ($600). Employees were paid in cash, but payments for the corresponding payroll deductions have not yet been made and employer taxes have not yet been recorded.

b. Collected rent revenue of $6,000 on December 10 for office space that Lakeview rented to another business. The rent collected was for 30 days from December 11 to January 10 and was credited in full to Deferred Revenue.

Required:

1. Give the journal entries to record payroll on December 31.
2. Give (*a*) the journal entry for the collection of rent on December 10 and (*b*) the adjusting journal entry on December 31.
3. Show how any liabilities related to these items should be reported on the company's balance sheet at December 31.

PA10-4 Comparing Bonds Issued at Par, Discount, and Premium

LO 10-3

Net Work Corporation, whose annual accounting period ends on December 31, issued the following bonds:

> Date of bonds: January 1, 2021
>
> Maturity amount and date: $200,000 due in 10 years (December 31, 2030)
>
> Interest: 10 percent per year payable each December 31
>
> Date issued: January 1, 2021

Required:

For each of the three independent cases that follow, provide the amounts to be reported on the January 1, 2021, financial statements immediately after the bonds were issued:

	Case A (issued at 100)	Case B (at 98)	Case C (at 102)
a. Bonds payable	$	$	$
b. Unamortized premium (or discount)			
c. Carrying value			

PA10-5 Determining Financial Statement Reporting of Contingent Liabilities

LO 10-4

Macromedia, Inc.

Macromedia, Inc., is the original maker of shockwave and flash technologies. One of its annual reports indicated a lawsuit had been filed against the company and five of its former officers for securities fraud in connection with allegedly making false or misleading statements about its financial results. The lawsuit was settled out of court, as described in the following note:

Legal
The settlement amount was $48.0 million, of which approximately $19.5 million was paid by insurance. As a result, the Company recorded a $28.5 million charge as a component of other income (expense) in its consolidated statements of operations.

Required:

Macromedia did not record a liability or include a note to the financial statements prior to settling the lawsuit. Which of the following best describes the estimated likelihood of loss prior to settling the lawsuit: (*a*) probable, (*b*) reasonably possible, or (*c*) remote?

PA10-6 (Supplement 10A) Recording Bond Issue, Interest Payments (Straight-Line Amortization), and Early Bond Retirement

LO 10-S1

On January 1, 2021, Loop Raceway issued 600 bonds, each with a face value of $1,000, a stated interest rate of 5 percent paid annually on December 31, and a maturity date of December 31, 2023. On the issue date, the market interest rate was 6 percent, so the total proceeds from the bond issue were $583,950. Loop uses the straight-line bond amortization method and adjusts for any rounding errors when recording interest in the final year.

Required:

1. Prepare a bond amortization schedule.
2. Give the journal entry to record the bond issue.
3. Give the journal entries to record the interest payments on December 31, 2021 and 2022.

4. Give the journal entry to record the interest and face value payment on December 31, 2023.

5. Assume the bonds are retired on January 1, 2023, at a price of 98. Give the journal entries to record the bond retirement.

LO 10-S2   **PA10-7 (Supplement 10B) Recording Bond Issue, Interest Payments (Effective-Interest Amortization), and Early Bond Retirement**

On January 1, 2021, Surreal Manufacturing issued 600 bonds, each with a face value of $1,000, a stated interest rate of 3 percent paid annually on December 31, and a maturity date of December 31, 2023. On the issue date, the market interest rate was 4 percent, so the total proceeds from the bond issue were $583,352. Surreal uses the effective-interest bond amortization method and adjusts for any rounding errors when recording interest in the final year.

Required:

1. Prepare a bond amortization schedule.
2. Give the journal entry to record the bond issue.
3. Give the journal entries to record the interest payments on December 31, 2021 and 2022.
4. Give the journal entry to record the interest and face value payment on December 31, 2023.
5. Assume the bonds are retired on January 1, 2023, at a price of 101. Give the journal entry to record the bond retirement.

LO 10-S3   **PA10-8 (Supplement 10C) Recording Bond Issue, Interest Payments (Simplified Effective-Interest Amortization), and Early Bond Retirement**

Assume the same facts as PA10-7, except that Surreal uses the simplified effective-interest bond amortization method, as shown in Chapter Supplement 10C.

Required:

1. Prepare a bond amortization schedule.
2. Give the journal entry to record the bond issue.
3. Give the journal entries to record the interest payments on December 31, 2021 and 2022.
4. Give the journal entry to record the interest and face value payment on December 31, 2023.
5. Assume the bonds are retired on January 1, 2023, at a price of 101. Give the journal entry to record the bond retirement.

LO 10-S4   **PA10-9 (Supplement 10D) Generating an Amortization Schedule and Preparing Journal Entries**

Cucina Corp. signed a new installment note on January 1, 2021, and deposited the proceeds of $50,000 in its bank account. The note has a three-year term, compounds 5 percent interest annually, and requires an annual installment payment on December 31. Cucina Corp. has a December 31 year-end and adjusts its accounts only at year-end. Round calculations to the nearest dollar.

Required:

1. Use an online application, such as the loan calculator with annual payments at mycalculators.com, to generate an amortization schedule. Enter that information into an amortization schedule with the following headings: Year, Beginning Notes Payable, Interest Expense, Repaid Principal on Notes Payable, and Ending Notes Payable.
2. Prepare the journal entries on (*a*) January 1, 2021, and December 31 of (*b*) 2021, (*c*) 2022, and (*d*) 2023.
3. If Cucina Corp.'s year-end were March 31, rather than December 31, what adjusting journal entry would it make for this note on March 31, 2021?

GROUP B PROBLEMS

LO 10-2, 10-5   **PB10-1 Determining Financial Effects of Transactions Affecting Current Liabilities with Evaluation of Effects on the Debt-to-Assets Ratio**

Tiger Company completed the following transactions. The annual accounting period ends December 31.

Jan. 3	Purchased merchandise on account at a cost of $24,000. (Assume a perpetual inventory system.)	
Jan. 27	Paid for the January 3 purchase.	
Apr. 1	Received $80,000 from Atlantic Bank after signing a 12-month, 5 percent promissory note.	
June 13	Purchased merchandise on account at a cost of $8,000.	
July 25	Paid for the June 13 purchase.	
July 31	Rented out a small office in a building owned by Tiger Company and collected eight months' rent in advance amounting to $8,000.	
Dec. 31	Determined wages of $12,000 were earned but not yet paid on December 31 (ignore payroll taxes).	
Dec. 31	Adjusted the accounts at year-end, relating to interest.	
Dec. 31	Adjusted the accounts at year-end, relating to rent.	

Required:

1. For each listed transaction and related adjusting entry, indicate the accounts, amounts, and effects (+ for increase, – for decrease, and NE for no effect) on the accounting equation, using the following format:

Date	Assets	=	Liabilities	+	Stockholders' Equity

2. For each item, state whether the debt-to-assets ratio is increased or decreased or there is no change. (Assume Tiger Company's debt-to-assets ratio is less than 1.0.)

PB10-2 Recording and Reporting Current Liabilities with Evaluation of Effects on the Debt-to-Assets Ratio   LO 10-2, 10-5

Using data from PB10-1, complete the following requirements.

Required:

1. Prepare journal entries for each of the transactions through August 1.
2. Prepare any adjusting entries required on December 31.
3. Show how all of the liabilities arising from these items are reported on the balance sheet at December 31.
4. Complete requirement 2 of PB10-1, if you have not already done so.

PB10-3 Recording and Reporting Current Liabilities   LO 10-2

Sandler Company completed the following two transactions. The annual accounting period ends December 31.

a. On December 31, calculated the payroll, which indicates gross earnings for wages ($260,000), payroll deductions for income tax ($28,000), payroll deductions for FICA ($20,000), payroll deductions for United Way ($4,000), employer contributions for FICA (matching), and state and federal unemployment taxes ($2,000). Employees were paid in cash, but payments for the corresponding payroll deductions have not been made and employer taxes have not yet been recorded.

b. Collected rent revenue of $1,500 on December 10 for office space that Sandler rented to another business. The rent collected was for 30 days from December 11 to January 10 and was credited in full to Deferred Revenue.

Required:

1. Give the entries required on December 31 to record payroll.
2. Give (a) the journal entry for the collection of rent on December 10 and (b) the adjusting journal entry on December 31.
3. Show how any liabilities related to these items should be reported on the company's balance sheet at December 31.

LO 10-3   **PB10-4**   **Comparing Bonds Issued at Par, Discount, and Premium**

Marshalls Corporation completed a $500,000, 7 percent bond issue on January 1, 2021. The bonds pay interest each December 31 and mature 10 years from January 1, 2021.

Required:

For each of the three independent cases that follow, provide the amounts to be reported on the January 1, 2021, financial statements immediately after the bonds were issued:

	Case A (issued at 100)	Case B (at 98)	Case C (at 102)
a. Bonds payable	$	$	$
b. Unamortized premium (or discount)			
c. Carrying value			

LO 10-3   **PB10-5**   **Recording and Explaining the Early Retirement of Debt**

AMC Entertainment, Inc.

AMC Entertainment, Inc., owns and operates movie theaters worldwide. Assume the company issued 4 percent bonds at their $53,000,000 face value and then used all of these cash proceeds to retire bonds with a stated interest rate of 6 percent. At that time, the 6 percent bonds had a carrying value of $50,000,000.

Required:

1. Prepare the journal entries to record the issuance of the 4 percent bonds and the early retirement of the 6 percent bonds. Assume both sets of bonds were issued at face value.
2. Where should AMC report any gain or loss on this transaction?
3. What dollar amount of interest expense is AMC saving each year by replacing the 6 percent bonds with the 4 percent bonds?

LO 10-S1   **PB10-6**   **(Supplement 10A) Recording Bond Issue, Interest Payments (Straight-Line Amortization), and Early Bond Retirement**

On January 1, 2021, Methodical Manufacturing issued 100 bonds, each with a face value of $1,000, a stated interest rate of 5 percent paid annually on December 31, and a maturity date of December 31, 2023. On the issue date, the market interest rate was 4.25 percent, so the total proceeds from the bond issue were $102,070. Methodical uses the straight-line bond amortization method and adjusts for any rounding errors when recording interest in the final year.

Required:

1. Prepare a bond amortization schedule.
2. Give the journal entry to record the bond issue.
3. Give the journal entries to record the interest payments on December 31, 2021 and 2022.
4. Give the journal entry to record the interest and face value payment on December 31, 2023.
5. Assume the bonds are retired on January 1, 2023, at a price of 102. Give the journal entries to record the bond retirement.

LO 10-S2   **PB10-7**   **(Supplement 10B) Recording Bond Issue, Interest Payments (Effective-Interest Amortization), and Early Bond Retirement**

Refer to PB10-6. Assume Methodical uses the effective-interest bond amortization method.

Required:

1. Prepare a bond amortization schedule.
2. Give the journal entry to record the bond issue.
3. Give the journal entries to record the interest payments on December 31, 2021 and 2022.
4. Give the journal entry to record the interest and face value payment on December 31, 2023.
5. Assume the bonds are retired on January 1, 2023, at a price of 101. Give the journal entry to record the bond retirement.

PB10-8 (Supplement 10C) Recording Bond Issue, Interest Payments (Simplified Effective-Interest Amortization), and Early Bond Retirement   LO 10-S3

Assume the same facts as PB10-6, but now assume that Methodical uses the simplified effective-interest bond amortization method, as shown in Chapter Supplement 10C.

Required:

1. Prepare a bond amortization schedule.
2. Give the journal entry to record the bond issue.
3. Give the journal entries to record the interest payments on December 31, 2021 and 2022.
4. Give the journal entry to record the interest and face value payment on December 31, 2023.
5. Assume the bonds are retired on January 1, 2023, at a price of 101. Give the journal entry to record the bond retirement.

PB10-9 (Supplement 10D) Generating an Amortization Schedule and Preparing Journal Entries   LO 10-S4

Zarina Corp. signed a new installment note on January 1, 2021, and deposited the proceeds of $15,000 in its bank account. The note has a two-year term, compounds 4 percent interest annually, and requires an annual installment payment on December 31. Zarina Corp. has a March 31 year-end. Round calculations to the nearest dollar.

Required:

1. Use an online application, such as the loan calculator with annual payments at mycalculators.com, to generate an amortization schedule. Enter that information into an amortization schedule with the following headings: Year, Beginning Notes Payable, Interest Expense, Repaid Principal on Notes Payable, and Ending Notes Payable.
2. Prepare the journal entry on January 1, 2021.
3. Prepare the adjusting journal entry to accrue interest on March 31, 2021.
4. Prepare the journal entry to record the first annual installment payment on December 31, 2021.
5. Calculate the amount of interest expense that should be accrued for the year ended March 31, 2022.

COMPREHENSIVE PROBLEM   

C10-1 Recording Journal Entries and Adjusting Journal Entries Affecting Inventories and Current Liabilities (Chapters 6, 7, and 10)   LO 6-3, 6-4, 7-3, 10-2

Fit for Life (FFL) operates a fitness center and snack lounge. The following is a partial list of FFL transactions during its year ended December 31. FFL adjusts its records only at year-end.

Jan. 6	Purchased and received 50 nutritional bars for $95, n/45.
Jan. 8	FFL sold 60 nutritional bars to Big Jim for $264 cash, which includes $24 of sales tax.
Apr. 30	FFL received $55,000 from Commerce Bank after signing a 24-month, 6 percent, promissory note.
Aug. 31	FFL signed a six-month contract to sublease a portion of its building. FFL also received a $12,000 check for six months' rent.
Dec. 30	FFL paid employees' net pay through December 31, using direct deposits totaling $2,880, for 250 total hours at a $14 hourly wage. The company had withheld FICA of $260, United Way contributions of $20, and income tax of $340.
Dec. 31	FFL adjusted the accounts at year-end, relating to (a) employer payroll taxes, including FICA and $30 of unemployment taxes, (b) interest, and (c) rent.

Required:

1. Calculate the cost of goods sold on January 8, assuming FFL began the year with an inventory of 50 nutritional bars at a unit cost of $1.80 ($90 total cost), had no other inventory transactions prior to January 6 and 8, and reports its inventory costs using FIFO.

2. For each of the above dates, prepare the required journal entries (using a perpetual inventory system) and the adjusting journal entries.

SKILLS DEVELOPMENT CASES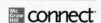

LO 10-5

The Home Depot

S10-1 Finding Financial Information

Refer to the financial statements of The Home Depot in Appendix A at the end of this book. (Note: Fiscal 2019 for The Home Depot runs from February 4, 2019, to February 2, 2020. See S1-1 for further explanation.)

1. Calculate and express as a percentage the company's debt-to-assets ratio using amounts reported in its financial statements for the years ended February 2, 2020, and February 3, 2019, respectively.
   a. 106.1 and 104.3 percent
   b. 92.8 and 90.2 percent
   c. 38.7 and 42.1 percent
   d. 33.8 and 36.4 percent

2. Using the company's interest expense, calculate the times interest earned ratio to two decimal places for the year ended February 2, 2020.
   a. 1.42
   b. 3.24
   c. 13.25
   d. 9.36

LO 10-5

Lowe's

S10-2 Finding Financial Information

Refer to the financial statements of Lowe's in Appendix B at the end of this book. (Note: Fiscal 2019 for Lowe's runs from February 2, 2019, to January 31, 2020. See S1-1 for further explanation.)

1. Calculate and express as a percentage the company's debt-to-assets ratio using amounts reported in its financial statements for the years ended January 31, 2020, and February 1, 2019, respectively.
   a. 99.1 and 101.9 percent
   b. 95.0 and 89.4 percent
   c. 40.5 and 47.0 percent
   d. 38.8 and 41.2 percent

2. Using the company's interest expense, calculate the times interest earned ratio to two decimal places for the year ended January 31, 2020.
   a. 1.47
   b. 3.19
   c. 6.20
   d. 9.14

LO 10-1, 10-2, 10-3, 10-4, 10-5

S10-3 Internet-Based Team Research: Examining an Annual Report

As a team, select an industry to analyze. Using your web browser, each team member should access the annual report or 10-K for one publicly traded company in the industry, with each member selecting a different company. (See S1-3 in Chapter 1 for a description of possible resources for these tasks.)

Required:

1. On an individual basis, each team member should write a short report that incorporates the following:

   a. What are the most significant types of current liabilities owed by the company?

   b. Read the company's financial statement note regarding long-term debt and commitments and contingencies. Does the company have any significant amounts coming due in the next five years?

   c. Compute and analyze the debt-to-assets ratio and times interest earned ratio.

2. Then, as a team, write a short report comparing and contrasting your companies using these attributes. Discuss any patterns across the companies that you as a team observe. Provide potential explanations for any differences discovered.

S10-4 Ethical Decision Making: A Real-Life Example

LO 10-3

Many retired people invest a significant portion of their money in bonds of corporations because of their relatively low level of risk. During the 1980s, significant inflation caused some interest rates to rise to as high as 15 percent. Retired people who bought bonds that paid only 6 percent continued to earn at the lower rate. During the 1990s, inflation subsided and interest rates declined. Many corporations took advantage of the callability feature of these bonds and retired the bonds early. Many of these early retirements of high-interest-rate bonds were replaced with low-interest-rate bonds.

Required:

In your judgment, is it ethical for corporations to continue paying low interest rates when rates increase but to retire bonds when rates decrease? Why or why not?

S10-5 Ethical Decision Making: A Mini-Case

LO 10-3

Assume you are a portfolio manager for a large insurance company. The majority of the money you manage is from retired school teachers who depend on the income you earn on their investments. You have invested a significant amount of money in the bonds of a large corporation and have just received news released by the company's president explaining that it is unable to meet its current interest obligations because of deteriorating business operations related to increased international competition. The president has a recovery plan that will take at least two years. During that time, the company will not be able to pay interest on the bonds and, she admits, if the plan does not work, bondholders will probably lose more than half of their money. As a creditor, you can force the company into immediate bankruptcy and probably get back at least 90 percent of the bondholders' money. You also know that your decision will cause at least 10,000 people to lose their jobs if the company ceases operations.

Required:

Given only these two options, what should you do? Consider who would be helped or harmed by the two options.

S10-6 Critical Thinking: Evaluating Effects on the Debt-to-Assets Ratio

LO 10-5

Assume you work as an assistant to the chief financial officer (CFO) of Fashions First, Inc. The CFO reminds you that the fiscal year-end is only two weeks away and that she is looking to you to ensure the company stays in compliance with its loan covenant to maintain a debt-to-assets ratio of no more than 75 percent. A review of the general ledger indicates that assets total $690,000 and liabilities are $570,000. Your company has an excess of Cash ($300,000) and an equally large balance in Accounts Payable ($270,000), although none of its Accounts Payable are due until next month.

Required:

1. Determine whether the company is currently in compliance with its loan covenant.

2. Assuming the level of assets and liabilities remains unchanged until the last day of the fiscal year, evaluate whether Fashions First should pay down $210,000 of its Accounts Payable on the last day of the year, before the Accounts Payable become due.

LO 10-S1

S10-7 (Supplement 10A) Preparing a Bond Amortization Schedule (Straight-Line Amortization)

Assume the authors of a popular introductory accounting text have hired you to create spreadsheets that will calculate bond discount amortization schedules like those shown in this chapter. As usual, you e-mail your friend Owen for some guidance. Much to your disappointment, you receive an auto-reply message from Owen indicating that he's gone skiing in New Zealand. After a bit of panicking, you realize you can refer to Owen's previous e-mail messages for spreadsheet advice that will help you complete this task. From his advice for Chapter 9, you decide to create a data input section for the stated interest rate, market interest rate, face value, issue price, and years to maturity. The spreadsheet file also will have a separate amortization schedule worksheet that contains only formulas, references to the cells in the data input section, and references to other cells in the amortization schedule. All amounts will be rounded to the nearest dollar (using the Round function in Excel), which means the discount amortization in the final year might be off a few dollars (unless you use the IF function in Excel to eliminate any remaining discount in the final year of the bond's life, in the same way that Owen showed in Chapter 9 for declining-balance depreciation).

Required:

Prepare a worksheet that uses formulas to reproduce the straight-line bond discount amortization schedule shown in Chapter Supplement 10A. Display both the completed spreadsheet and a "formulas revealed" (Ctrl ~) version of it.

LO 10-S2

S10-8 (Supplement 10B) Preparing a Bond Amortization Schedule (Effective-Interest Amortization)

Refer to the information in S10-7 and prepare a worksheet that uses formulas to reproduce the effective-interest bond discount amortization schedule shown in Chapter Supplement 10B. Display both the completed spreadsheet and a "formulas revealed" (Ctrl ~) version of it.

LO 10-S3

S10-9 (Supplement 10C) Preparing a Bond Amortization Schedule (Simplified Effective-Interest Amortization)

Refer to the information in S10-7 and prepare a worksheet that uses formulas to reproduce the bond discount amortization schedule shown for simplified effective-interest amortization in Chapter Supplement 10C. Display both the completed spreadsheet and a "formulas revealed" (Ctrl ~) version of it.

CONTINUING CASE

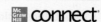

LO 10-2

CC10-1 Accounting for Debt Financing

Nicole thinks that her business, Nicole's Getaway Spa (NGS), is doing really well and she is planning a large expansion. With such a large expansion, Nicole will need to finance some of it using debt. She signed a one-year note payable with the bank for $50,000 with a 6 percent interest rate. The note was issued October 1, 2020; interest is payable annually; and the end of Nicole's accounting period is December 31.

Required:

Prepare the journal entries required from the issuance of the note until its maturity on September 30, 2021, assuming that no entries are made other than at the end of the accounting period and when the note reaches its maturity.

DATA ANALYTICS EXERCISES

Data Analytics Exercises are auto-graded exercises offering detailed data visualization, interpretation, and analysis, and are available for assignment in *Connect*.

11

Stockholders' Equity

YOUR LEARNING OBJECTIVES

LO 11-1 Explain the role of stock in financing a corporation.

LO 11-2 Explain and analyze common stock transactions.

LO 11-3 Explain and analyze cash dividends, stock dividends, and stock split transactions.

LO 11-4 Describe the characteristics of preferred stock and analyze transactions affecting preferred stock.

LO 11-5 Analyze the earnings per share (EPS), return on equity (ROE), and price/earnings (P/E) ratios.

LO 11-S1 Account for owners' equity in other forms of business.

LO 11-S2 Record journal entries for large and small stock dividends.

THAT WAS THEN

The last chapter focused on debt financing, as reported in the liabilities section of the balance sheet.

Darryl Brooks/
Shutterstock

FOCUS COMPANY: NATIONAL BEVERAGE CORP.

News about shares of stock is everywhere. You've probably read it in *The Wall Street Journal*, listened to it on CNBC, or searched for it online. Behind this fascination with stock is a dream many people share: taking a small amount of money and turning it into a fortune. That's what National Beverage Corp. has managed to do.

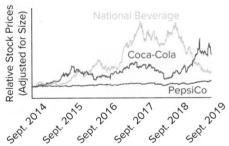

National Beverage started as a small regional drink maker but has expanded into a successful niche soft-drink company. This success has arisen through National Beverage's acquisition and development of brands such as Shasta and LaCroix. To obtain financing for growing these brands, National Beverage issued its shares to investors through the NASDAQ stock exchange, under the stock ticker symbol "FIZZ." Since it first became a public company in September 1991, National Beverage's stock price has soared. It was strongest in 2017 and 2018 when National Beverage dominated the sparkling water market. Since then rivals Coca-Cola and PepsiCo have countered with their own natural water products, knocking some of the fizz out of National Beverage's stock price.

In this chapter, you will see how companies like National Beverage account for a variety of stock transactions, including issuances, splits, and dividends. By the end of the chapter, you should understand how each individual National Beverage share that existed in September 1991 has multiplied into 16 shares.

THIS IS NOW

This chapter focuses on equity financing, as reported in the stockholders' equity section of the balance sheet.

Understand the business	Study the accounting methods	Evaluate the results	Supplement 11A	Supplement 11B	Review the chapter
• Corporate ownership • Equity versus debt financing	• Common stock transactions • Stock dividends and stock splits • Preferred stock • Retained earnings • Statement of stockholders' equity	• Earnings per share (EPS) • Return on equity (ROE) • Price/earnings (P/E) ratio	• Owners' equity for other forms of business	• Recording stock dividends	• Demonstration case • Chapter summary • Key terms • Homework helper • Practice material

Understand the Business

Learning Objective 11-1
Explain the role of stock in financing a corporation.

CORPORATE OWNERSHIP

According to the U.S. Census Bureau, corporations account for about 90 percent of the total sales reported by U.S. businesses.[1] Many Americans own shares in corporations, either directly or indirectly through a mutual fund or pension program.

You probably recall from Chapter 1 the act of creating a corporation is costly, so why is the corporate form so popular? One reason is it limits the legal liability of its owners. Another reason is corporations can raise large amounts of money because investors can easily participate in a corporation's ownership. This ease of participation is related to several factors.

- **Shares of stock can be purchased in small amounts.** You could become one of National Beverage's owners by buying a share of the company's stock.

- **Ownership interests are transferable.** The shares of public companies are regularly bought and sold on established markets such as the New York Stock Exchange. National Beverage's shares are traded on the NASDAQ under the ticker symbol FIZZ.

- **Stockholders are not liable for the corporation's debts.** Creditors have no legal claim on the personal assets of stockholders like they do on the personal assets belonging to owners of sole proprietorships and partnerships. So if you own stock in a company that goes bankrupt and is liquidated, you would lose what you paid to buy the stock but, unless you personally guaranteed the company's debt, you wouldn't have to pay the company's liabilities.

---

[1]Chapter Supplement 11A discusses accounting for owners' equity in proprietorships, partnerships, and other business forms.

The law recognizes a corporation as a separate legal entity. It may own assets, incur liabilities, expand and contract in size, sue others, be sued, and enter into contracts independently of its owners. A corporation exists separate and apart from its owners, which means it doesn't die when its owners die. Thomas Edison died in 1931, but the company he founded continues to exist today, operating under the name General Electric Company.

To protect everyone's rights, creation and oversight of corporations are tightly regulated by law. Corporations are created by submitting an application to a state government (not the federal government). Because laws vary from state to state, you might decide to create a corporation in a state other than the one in which it operates. Although National Beverage has its headquarters in Fort Lauderdale, it was actually incorporated in Delaware. More than half of the largest corporations in America are incorporated in Delaware because it has some of the most favorable laws for establishing corporations. If the application to create a corporation is approved, the state issues a charter, also called the articles of incorporation, which spells out information about the corporation such as its name, address, nature of business, and ownership structure.

The ownership structure of a corporation can vary from one company to the next. In the most basic form, a corporation must have one type of stock, fittingly called **common stock**. Owners of common stock usually enjoy a number of benefits:

> **YOU SHOULD KNOW**
>
> **Common Stock:** The basic voting stock issued by a corporation to stockholders.

1. **Voting rights.** For each share you own, you get a set number of votes on major issues. Some classes of common stock can carry more votes than others, so watch for this if you care about voting on which accounting firm will be appointed as external auditors and who will serve on the board of directors.

2. **Dividends.** Stockholders receive a share of the corporation's profits when distributed as dividends.

3. **Residual claim.** If the company ceases operations, stockholders share in any assets remaining after creditors have been paid.

4. **Preemptive rights.** To retain their ownership percentages, existing stockholders may be given the first chance to buy newly issued stock before it is offered to others.

EQUITY VERSUS DEBT FINANCING

Whenever a company needs a large amount of long-term financing, its executives will decide whether to obtain it by issuing new stock to investors (called **equity financing**) or borrowing money from lenders (**debt financing**). Each form of financing has certain advantages over the other, as listed in Exhibit 11.1. These factors play a big role in determining whether equity or debt financing is most appropriate for each particular corporation. One company, for example, might be primarily concerned about the impact of financing on income taxes and decide to rely on debt financing because its interest payments are tax deductible. A different company might be so concerned about being able to pay its existing liabilities that it can't afford to take on additional debt. By using equity financing, which doesn't have to be repaid, the company could obtain the financing it needs. Ultimately, the decision to pursue additional equity or debt financing depends on the circumstances.

EXHIBIT 11.1	Advantages of Equity and Debt Financing
Advantages of Equity Financing	**Advantages of Debt Financing**
1. Equity does not have to be repaid. Debt must be repaid or refinanced.	1. Interest on debt is tax deductible. Dividends on stock are not tax deductible.
2. Dividends are optional. Interest must be paid on debt.	2. Debt does not change stockholder control. In contrast, a stock issue gives new stockholders the right to vote and share in the earnings, diluting existing stockholders' control.

SPOTLIGHT ON | # Business Decisions

Equity Financing through Crowdfunding

Until recently, equity financing for start-up companies has typically been limited to the personal savings of company founders, or their friends and relatives. But now the Securities and Exchange Commission (SEC) allows companies to raise up to $1 million annually via crowdfunding portals, such as Wefunder.com. Companies have to fulfill certain requirements such as filing their financial statements with the SEC each year and limiting their shareholders to investing less than 10 percent of their annual income. Time will tell whether equity crowdfunding replaces your rich, surly uncle as a source of equity.

Monty Rakusen/Getty Images

Study the Accounting Methods

The first point to note is **all transactions between a company and its stockholders affect the company's balance sheet accounts only.** They do not affect the company's income statement.

COMMON STOCK TRANSACTIONS

Learning Objective 11-2
Explain and analyze common stock transactions.

Exhibit 11.2 shows the balance sheet accounts National Beverage reported in the stockholders' equity section of its balance sheet at the end of its 2019 fiscal year. It includes four main elements:

1. **Contributed Capital** reports the amount of capital the company received from investors' contributions. That is, contributed capital represents *paid-in* capital. As Exhibit 11.2 suggests, contributed capital can include several components, relating to common stock and preferred stock, as we'll explain later in this section.

2. **Retained Earnings** reports the cumulative amount of net income earned by the company less the cumulative amount of dividends since the corporation was first organized. Retained Earnings represents *earned* capital.

3. **Treasury Stock** reports shares that were previously issued to and owned by stockholders but have been reacquired and are now held by the corporation. To fully understand treasury stock, it's helpful to follow stock transactions through from authorization to issuance and repurchase, as we do in the following section.

4. **Accumulated Other Comprehensive Income (Loss)** reports unrealized gains and losses, which are temporary changes in the value of certain assets and liabilities the company holds. They can relate to pensions, foreign currencies, and financial investments, such as National Beverage's contracts to stabilize the cost of its aluminum cans. Accounting rules relating to Accumulated Other Comprehensive Income (Loss) are explained in advanced financial accounting courses.

EXHIBIT 11.2   Explanation of National Beverage's Stockholders' Equity

NATIONAL BEVERAGE CORP.
Partial Balance Sheets

(in thousands, except per share amounts)	2019	2018	Explanation
STOCKHOLDERS' EQUITY			
Contributed Capital			
Preferred Stock, 2.5%, $1 par value	$ 150	$ 150	Stock with special rights
Common Stock, $0.01 par value	507	506	Basic voting stock
Authorized: 200 million shares			Maximum number of shares
Issued: 50.7 million shares			Number of shares distributed
Additional Paid-In Capital	37,065	36,358	Amount in excess of par value
Total Contributed Capital	37,722	37,014	Total equity paid in by investors
Retained Earnings	313,430	307,824	Total equity earned by the company
Treasury Stock (4.0 million shares, at cost)	(18,000)	(18,000)	Stock reacquired by the company
Accumulated Other Comprehensive Income (Loss)	(1,543)	4,601	Unrealized gains and losses, net
Total Stockholders' Equity	331,609	331,439	

Authorization, Issuance, and Repurchase of Stock

A corporation's charter indicates the maximum number of shares of stock the corporation is allowed to issue. Look closely at the Contributed Capital section of Exhibit 11.2 and you will see National Beverage is **authorized** to issue 200 million common shares. The next line in Exhibit 11.2 tells us how many shares have actually been issued. At the end of 2019, 50.7 million common shares have been issued. **Issued shares** will be owned forever by one stockholder or another, unless the company repurchases them. Shares that have been repurchased by the corporation are called **treasury stock**. National Beverage's treasury stock is shown in Exhibit 11.2 as a negative amount because it represents shares that are no longer outstanding with investors. During the time treasury stock is held by the corporation, the shares do not carry voting, cash dividend, or other stockholder rights. Shares owned by stockholders (not the corporation itself) are called **outstanding shares**.

The relationships among authorized, issued, outstanding, and treasury stock are shown in Exhibit 11.3. Be aware that the number of outstanding shares (46.7 million) is not reported on the face of the balance sheet but instead has to be computed as the difference between issued shares (50.7 million) and treasury stock (4.0 million). Knowing this will help you compute earnings per share, which is a key financial ratio discussed later in this chapter and expressed in terms of the number of outstanding shares.

EXHIBIT 11.3   Authorized, Issued, Outstanding, and Treasury Stock

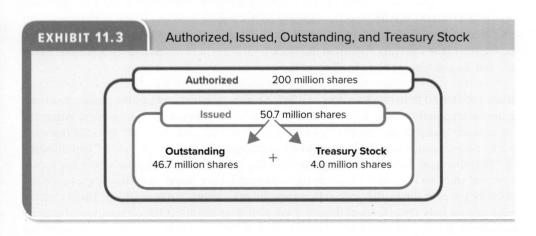

Stock Authorization Before stock can be issued, its specific rights and characteristics must be authorized and defined in the corporate charter. This authorization does not affect the accounting records, but it does establish certain characteristics that, later, will affect how stock transactions are recorded. One prominent characteristic is the stock's **par value**. Oddly enough, par value has little meaning today. It is an old concept from long ago, originally introduced to prevent stockholders from removing contributed capital of businesses that were about to go bankrupt. Stronger laws and regulations exist today to prevent this from happening, so par value no longer has this use. However, some states charge corporate fees based on total par value. Thus, par value is typically set at a token amount, such as $0.01 per share, as is the case with National Beverage's common stock in Exhibit 11.2. Other states allow the issuance of no-par value stock. **No-par value stock** is similar to stock with par value, except it does not have a specified legal value per share. In any event, par value is a legal concept and is not related in any way to the market value of the company's stock.

Stock Issuance A stock issuance occurs when a corporation distributes its shares to existing or new stockholders, usually in exchange for cash. The very first issuance of a company's stock to the public is called an **initial public offering,** or IPO. This is what most people are referring to when they say a private company is going public. If a company has issued stock previously, additional issuances of new stock by the company are called **seasoned new issues.** Whether stock is issued as part of an IPO or as a seasoned new issue, a company accounts for it in the same way.

Most stock issuances are cash transactions. To illustrate the accounting for a stock issuance, assume that during the next fiscal year, National Beverage issues 100,000 shares of its $0.01 par value stock at the market price existing at the time of issuance of $20 per share. The accounting equation effects of this stock issuance and the journal entry to record them would be:

① Analyze

	Assets	= Liabilities +	Stockholders' Equity	
Cash	+2,000,000		Common Stock	+1,000
			Additional Paid-In Capital	+1,999,000

② Record

	Debit	Credit
Cash (100,000 × $20)..	2,000,000	
Common Stock (100,000 × $0.01)....................................		1,000
Additional Paid-In Capital ($2,000,000 − $1,000)		1,999,000

Notice the increase in Common Stock is the number of shares issued times the par value per share (100,000 × 0.01) and the increase in Additional Paid-In Capital is the amount of cash received in excess of this amount. If the corporate charter does not specify a par value for the stock, the total proceeds from the stock issuance will be entered in the Common Stock account, as you learned to do in Chapter 2.

Stock Exchanged between Investors When a company issues stock to the public, the transaction is recorded because it is between the issuing corporation and an investor. After this initial stock issuance, an investor can exchange shares for cash provided by other investors without directly affecting the corporation. For example, if investor Dr. Anne Clem disposed of 1,000 shares of National Beverage stock to Darla Karnes, the company would not record a journal entry on its books. Dr. Clem received cash for the shares and Mrs. Karnes received stock for the cash she paid. National Beverage did not receive or pay anything. These transactions involve only the owners of the company so it does not affect the corporation's financial statements. It's like an auto dealership that records the initial sale of a car to a customer but doesn't later record another sale when the customer sells the car to someone else.

Stock Used to Compensate Employees To encourage employees to work hard for a corporation, employee pay packages often include a combination of base pay, cash bonuses, and stock options. Stock options give employees the option of acquiring the company's stock at a predetermined price, often equal to the then-current market price. If employees work hard and meet the corporation's goals, the company's stock price will increase. Employees can then exercise their option to acquire the company's stock at the lower predetermined price and sell it at the higher price for a profit. If the stock price declines, employees haven't lost anything. Accounting rules require that, at the time the company grants stock options, an expense must be reported for the estimated cost associated with stock options, even if the option price equals the current stock price. The specific accounting procedures for this will be discussed in an intermediate accounting course.

Repurchase of Stock A corporation may want to repurchase its stock from existing stockholders to (1) send a signal to investors that the company itself believes its own stock is worth acquiring, (2) obtain shares that can be reissued as payment for purchases of other companies, (3) obtain shares to reissue to employees as part of employee stock purchase plans, and (4) reduce the number of outstanding shares to increase per-share measures of earnings and stock value. Companies must maintain a specified minimum per-share stock price, for example, to be allowed to list on the NASDAQ and New York Stock Exchange.

SPOTLIGHT ON | # Business Decisions

Repurchasing Stock into Treasury Sends EPS Flying High

Airplane maker Boeing reported declines in net income in both 2015 and 2016. Yet, by repurchasing and holding its stock in treasury, its **earnings per share** (EPS) continued to climb skyward over the same period. Delta and Southwest Airlines reported the same outcomes in Q1 and Q2 of 2018, sending EPS up at the same time net income was descending. The lesson for you is to be careful when interpreting EPS. It's affected not only by profitability. And watch out if executive pay is linked to per-share financial measures, as it was at Humana* and Safeway,† where stock repurchases boosted bonuses by millions of dollars.

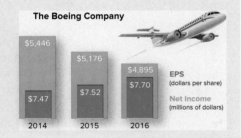

The Boeing Company

$5,446 | $5,176 | $4,895

$7.47 | $7.52 | $7.70

EPS (dollars per share)

Net Income (millions of dollars)

2014 | 2015 | 2016

---

*"Stock Buybacks Enrich the Bosses Even When Business Sags," *Reuters Special Report*, December 10, 2015.
†"As Companies Step Up Buybacks, Executives Benefit, Too," *The Wall Street Journal*, May 5, 2013.

Most companies record shares repurchased and held as treasury stock using the cost incurred to acquire the shares. This approach is called the cost method. Assume that during the next fiscal year, National Beverage repurchased 50,000 shares of its stock for $25 per share (50,000 shares × $25 = $1,250,000) and held these stock in treasury. Using the cost method, the effects of this repurchase on the accounting equation and the journal entry for it would be

1 Analyze

Assets	= Liabilities +	Stockholders' Equity	
Cash	−1,250,000	Treasury Stock (+xSE)	−1,250,000

2 Record

	Debit	Credit
Treasury Stock (+xSE)	1,250,000	
Cash		1,250,000

We use the notation +xSE in the journal entry to remind you that **Treasury Stock is not an asset.** It is a permanent account that is reported as contra-equity, subtracted from total stockholders' equity. Look at the third line from the bottom of Exhibit 11.2 to see how National Beverage reported its treasury stock.

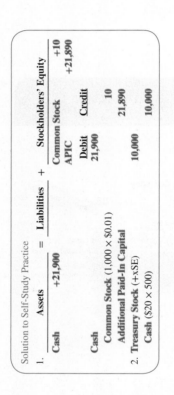

Solution to Self-Study Practice

1.

Assets	= Liabilities +	Stockholders' Equity	
Cash +21,900		Common Stock	+10
		APIC	+21,890

	Debit	Credit
Cash	21,900	
Common Stock (1,000 × $0.01)		10
Additional Paid-In Capital		21,890

2.

	Debit	Credit
Treasury Stock (+xSE)	10,000	
Cash ($20 × 500)		10,000

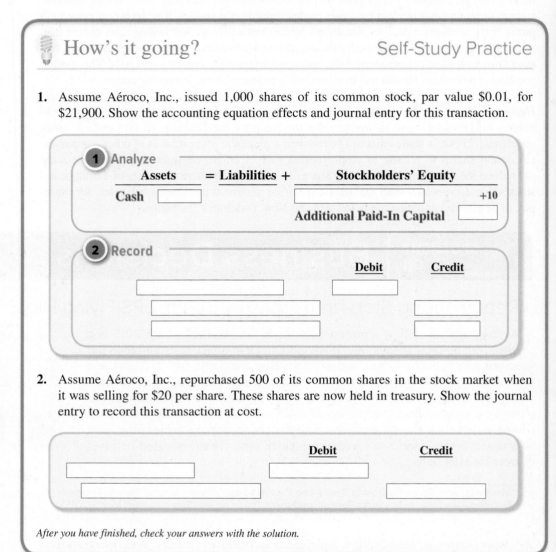

How's it going? — Self-Study Practice

1. Assume Aéroco, Inc., issued 1,000 shares of its common stock, par value $0.01, for $21,900. Show the accounting equation effects and journal entry for this transaction.

1 Analyze

	Assets	= Liabilities +	Stockholders' Equity	
Cash	[ ]		[ ]	+10
			Additional Paid-In Capital	[ ]

2 Record

	Debit	Credit
[ ]	[ ]	
[ ]		[ ]
[ ]		[ ]

2. Assume Aéroco, Inc., repurchased 500 of its common shares in the stock market when it was selling for $20 per share. These shares are now held in treasury. Show the journal entry to record this transaction at cost.

	Debit	Credit
[ ]	[ ]	
[ ]		[ ]

After you have finished, check your answers with the solution.

Reissuance of Treasury Stock When a company reissues shares previously reported as treasury stock, it does not report a gain or loss, even if it issues the shares for more or less than they cost the company to reacquire them. GAAP does not permit a corporation to report income or losses from investments in its own stock because transactions with the owners are not considered profit-making activities. Instead, this type of transaction affects only the balance sheet, just like other stock issuances. To illustrate, let's extend our previous example where National Beverage had repurchased its stock at a cost of $25 per share. If National Beverage reissues 5,000 shares of this treasury stock for $28 per share (5,000 × $28 = $140,000), the accounting equation effects and journal entry would be:

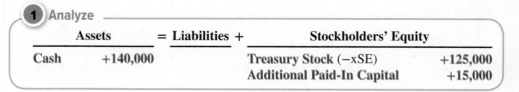

1 Analyze

	Assets	= Liabilities +	Stockholders' Equity	
Cash	+140,000		Treasury Stock (−xSE)	+125,000
			Additional Paid-In Capital	+15,000

2 Record

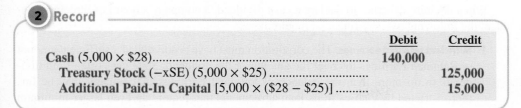

	Debit	Credit
Cash (5,000 × $28)...	140,000	
Treasury Stock (−xSE) (5,000 × $25)		125,000
Additional Paid-In Capital [5,000 × ($28 − $25)]		15,000

> **COACH'S TIP**
>
> The contra-account Treasury Stock is reduced only for the cost of each treasury share. Any amount received for treasury stock in excess of its cost is recorded as an increase in Additional Paid-In Capital.

Continuing with this example, assume that 5,000 shares of treasury stock were reissued later at a price below its repurchase price. The difference between the repurchase price ($25 per share × 5,000 = $125,000) and the reissue price (say, $23 per share × 5,000 = $115,000) is recorded as a reduction in Additional Paid-In Capital.[2] The accounting equation effects and journal entry for this case, reissuing at less than cost, are:

1 Analyze

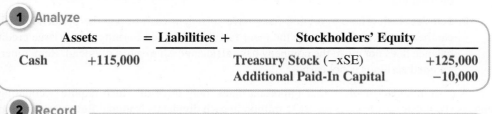

Assets	= Liabilities +	Stockholders' Equity	
Cash +115,000		Treasury Stock (−xSE)	+125,000
		Additional Paid-In Capital	−10,000

2 Record

	Debit	Credit
Cash (5,000 × $23)...	115,000	
Additional Paid-In Capital [5,000 × ($25 − $23)]	10,000	
Treasury Stock (−xSE) (5,000 × $25)		125,000

Cash Dividends on Common Stock

Investors acquire common stock because they expect a return on their investment. This return can come in two forms: dividends and increases in stock price. Some investors prefer to buy stocks that pay little or no dividends (called a **growth investment**). Alphabet (Google), Amazon, Facebook, Monster, and Netflix are just a few companies that had never paid a dividend at the time of writing this chapter. These companies instead reinvested their earnings to grow both the business and their stock price. Other investors, such as retirees who require a steady income, prefer to receive their return through dividends. Some stocks are known to consistently pay dividends (called an **income investment**). Coca-Cola, for example, has paid cash dividends each year since 1920.

> **Learning Objective 11-3**
> Explain and analyze cash dividends, stock dividends, and stock split transactions.

> **SPOTLIGHT ON** # Business Decisions
>
> ## A Dividend to Reward Stockholder Loyalty?
>
> In 2016, National Beverage announced its intention to pay a dividend based on the length of time each investor has owned National Beverage stock.* The hope was that a stockholder loyalty dividend would lead investors to hold the company's stock for the long term and discourage short-term trading. It's a clever idea, but is it allowed? Corporate laws require that dividends be distributed "pro-rata," which means an equal amount per share for a given class of stock, without considering length of ownership. The company hasn't yet been able to pay a loyalty dividend, but its 2018 annual report said it was still planning to find a way to make it happen.
>
> *"National Beverage Corp. announces special dividend for FIZZ shareholders," *Company Press Release*, November 18, 2016.

---

[2] If a company has Additional Paid-In Capital from both an initial issuance of common stock and the reissuance of treasury stock, the latter may be recorded in a separate account called Additional Paid-In Capital, Treasury Stock.

When deciding whether to declare a cash dividend, a company's board of directors considers the following two key financial requirements:

1. **Sufficient retained earnings.** The corporation must have accumulated a sufficient amount of Retained Earnings to cover the amount of the dividend. State laws often limit dividends to no more than the balance in Retained Earnings. A company may be further restricted by clauses in its loan agreements that require an even larger minimum balance in Retained Earnings. If the company were to violate such a loan covenant, a lender could require renegotiation of the loan and possibly demand its immediate repayment. **Because restrictions on Retained Earnings can severely limit dividends, accounting rules require that companies disclose any restrictions in their financial statement notes.** In a prior year, National Beverage reported in its financial statement notes that "$1,320,000 of retained earnings were restricted from distribution."

2. **Sufficient cash.** The corporation must have sufficient cash to pay the dividend. Cash can be used in many ways, so the mere fact that Retained Earnings has a large credit balance does not mean the company has sufficient cash to pay a dividend. Remember, retained earnings is not cash.

A cash dividend involves four important dates, only three of which require accounting entries. To illustrate, consider the $135 million in cash dividends National Beverage declared and paid during its 2019 fiscal year.

1. **Declaration Date.** On the **declaration date**, the company's board of directors formally approves the dividend, thereby creating a legal liability for the corporation. The dividend declaration is accounted for by increasing Dividends Payable and increasing a temporary account called Dividends. Because dividends are a distribution of the company's *prior* earnings, this Dividends account is deducted from Retained Earnings when it is closed at year-end. Until then, the temporary account is accounted for as a decrease in Stockholders' Equity, as shown below. Although they reduce Retained Earnings, **dividends are not an expense.** Rather, they are a distribution of prior profits.

1 Analyze

Assets	=	Liabilities	+	Stockholders' Equity
		Dividends Payable +135,000,000		Dividends −135,000,000

2 Record

	Debit	Credit
Dividends	135,000,000	
Dividends Payable		135,000,000

2. **Date of Record.** The shares of public companies are bought and sold all the time; it takes time to determine who should receive the dividend payment after the dividend has been declared. The **record date** is the cut-off date for determining the specific stockholders to be paid the dividend. No journal entry is recorded on this date.

3. **Date of Payment.** The **payment date** is the date on which cash is disbursed to pay the dividend liability owed to each stockholder. The distribution of cash and reduction in liability are recorded on this date, as follows:

1 Analyze

Assets	=	Liabilities	+	Stockholders' Equity
Cash −135,000,000		Dividends Payable −135,000,000		

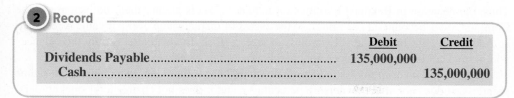

> **2 Record**
>
> | | Debit | Credit |
> |---|---|---|
> | Dividends Payable.. | 135,000,000 | |
> | Cash.. | | 135,000,000 |

4. Year-End. All temporary accounts, including Dividends, are closed into Retained Earnings at each accounting year-end. This closing journal entry zeroes out the temporary account Dividends by transferring its (debit) balance to its permanent home in Retained Earnings. The closing entry has no effect on total stockholders' equity.

> **1 Analyze**
>
> | Assets | = | Liabilities | + | Stockholders' Equity | |
> |---|---|---|---|---|---|
> | | | | | Dividends | +135,000,000 |
> | | | | | Retained Earnings | −135,000,000 |

> **2 Record**
>
> | | Debit | Credit |
> |---|---|---|
> | Retained Earnings.. | 135,000,000 | |
> | Dividends .... | | 135,000,000 |

💡 How's it going? — Self-Study Practice

Answer the following questions concerning dividends:

1. On which dividend date is a liability created?
2. A cash outflow occurs on which dividend date?
3. What are the two fundamental requirements for the payment of a dividend?

After you have finished, check your answers with the solution.

STOCK DIVIDENDS AND STOCK SPLITS

Stock Dividends

The term *dividend,* when used alone with no adjectives, implies a cash dividend. However, some dividends are not paid in cash but in additional shares of stock. These dividends, called **stock dividends**, are distributed to a corporation's stockholders on a pro rata basis at no cost to the stockholder. The phrase *pro rata basis* means that each stockholder receives additional shares equal to the percentage of shares held. A stockholder who owns 10 percent of the company's shares would receive 10 percent of any additional shares issued as a stock dividend.

How are stock dividends accounted for? Stock dividends are recorded by transferring an amount from Retained Earnings to contributed capital accounts. The value used to record a stock dividend varies depending on the size of the stock dividend. A large stock dividend (more than 25 percent of the company's outstanding stock) is recorded at par value; thus, the decrease in Retained Earnings equals the increase in the Common Stock account. A small stock dividend (less than 25 percent of the company's outstanding stock) is recorded at market value.

> **YOU SHOULD KNOW**
>
> **Stock Dividend:** A dividend that distributes additional shares of a corporation's own stock.

Thus, the decrease in Retained Earnings (at market value) is greater than the increase in the Common Stock account (at par value), so the excess of market value over par value is recorded as Additional Paid-In Capital.[3] Regardless of size, a stock dividend affects only the balances within stockholders' equity; it does not change a company's total stockholders' equity.

Why would a company issue a stock dividend? On the surface, a stock dividend seems pointless: It does not affect ownership percentages and it does not change total stockholders' equity. Company executives give three possible explanations for stock dividends:

1. **To lower the market price per share of stock.** If you increase the number of shares without changing the company in any other way, the stock price per share will fall proportionately: 20 shares at **$100** per share become 40 shares at **$50** per share after a 100 percent stock dividend. National Beverage has declared stock dividends four times since becoming a public company, each time to make the company's stock more affordable to small investors.

2. **To demonstrate commitment to stockholders while conserving cash during difficult times.** This reason was given by the hotel company Marriott during the financial crisis of 2009 when it replaced its regular cash dividend with a stock dividend. Unlike a cash dividend, a stock dividend does not involve cash payments or any distribution of assets. But the stock dividend did allow Marriott to continue boasting that it had declared a dividend "in every year since going public in 1953."

3. **To signal an expectation of significant future earnings.** Companies can declare future cash dividends only when they maintain an adequate balance in Retained Earnings through profitable operations. Because stock dividends cause a reduction in Retained Earnings, companies will declare stock dividends only if they expect sufficient future earnings to replenish the balance in Retained Earnings after a stock dividend. Nike used this reasoning to explain its 100 percent stock dividend in a recent year; the company's CEO said it was a sign of "the ongoing confidence we have in our strategy to generate long-term profitable growth."

Stock Splits

Stock splits are not dividends. While they are similar to a stock dividend, they are quite different in terms of how they occur and how they affect the stockholders' equity accounts. In a **stock split**, the total number of authorized shares is increased by a specified amount, such as 2-for-1. In this instance, each issued share is called in and two new shares are issued in its place. Cash is not affected when the company splits its stock, so the total resources of the company do not change. It's just like taking a four-piece pizza and cutting each piece into two smaller pieces.

Typically, a stock split involves revising the corporate charter to reduce the per-share par value of all authorized shares, so that the total par value across all shares is unchanged. For instance, if a company with 1 million shares executes a 2-for-1 stock split, it reduces the per-share par value of its stock from $0.01 to $0.005 and doubles the number of shares. The decrease in par value per share offsets the increase in the number of shares, so the financial position of the company is not affected and no journal entry is needed. By reading the following illustration from left to right, you can see these offsetting effects on the number of shares and par value per share.

Stockholders' Equity	Before a 2-for-1 Stock Split		After a 2-for-1 Stock Split	
Number of shares	1,000,000		2,000,000	
Par value per share	$ 0.01		$ 0.005	
Total par value	$ 10,000		$ 10,000	
Retained earnings	650,000		650,000	
Total stockholders' equity	$ 660,000		$ 660,000	

---

[3]The details of these journal entries are demonstrated in Chapter Supplement 11B.

SPOTLIGHT ON | # Business Decisions

Choosing between Stock Dividends and Stock Splits

Both stock dividends and stock splits increase the number of shares outstanding (as well as any in treasury) and decrease the per-share market price. A key difference between them is a stock dividend causes a reduction in Retained Earnings, whereas a "true" stock split doesn't. By itself, this accounting difference might not mean much. Remember, though, that to declare a cash dividend, a company must maintain an adequate balance in Retained Earnings. If you're managing a company that you expect will struggle financially in the future, you'll prefer a stock split because it doesn't reduce Retained Earnings, so it doesn't reduce your ability to declare cash dividends in the future. On the other hand, if you expect your company will be financially successful in the near future, you won't care that a stock dividend reduces Retained Earnings because future earnings will replenish that account to allow cash dividends to be declared. In fact, you'll *want* to declare a stock dividend to show how confident you are of your company's financial outlook. This reasoning suggests **a company's board of directors may declare a stock dividend rather than a stock split to signal to financial statement users that the company expects significant future earnings** (which will replenish the reduction in Retained Earnings caused by the stock dividend).

Exhibit 11.4 shows the typical components of the stockholders' equity section of the balance sheet and highlights amounts (in blue) that are changed by a 2-for-1 stock split, a 100 percent stock dividend, and an equivalent ($10,000) cash dividend. Notice that the cash dividend is the only distribution that affects total stockholders' equity because it is the only one that distributes the company's resources to stockholders.

EXHIBIT 11.4 | Comparison of Distributions to Stockholders

		AFTER		
Stockholders' Equity	BEFORE	2-for-1 Stock Split	100% Stock Dividend	$10,000 Cash Dividend
Contributed Capital				
Number of common shares	1,000,000	2,000,000	2,000,000	1,000,000
Par value per common share	$ 0.01	$ 0.005	$ 0.01	$ 0.01
Common stock, at par	$ 10,000	$ 10,000	$ 20,000	$ 10,000
Additional paid-in capital	30,000	30,000	30,000	30,000
Retained Earnings	650,000	650,000	640,000	640,000
Total stockholders' equity	$ 690,000	$ 690,000	$ 690,000	$ 680,000

💡 How's it going?   Self-Study Practice

Vandalay Industries wanted to reduce the market price of its stock, so it issued 100,000 new shares of common stock (par value $10) in a 100 percent stock dividend when the market value was $30 per share.

1. Is this a large or small stock dividend? What effect does it have on total stockholders' equity?

2. What journal entry would be required if the transaction instead involved a 2-for-1 stock split? Theoretically, what would be the new stock price after the split?

After you have finished, check your answers with the solution.

PREFERRED STOCK

In addition to common stock, some corporations issue **preferred stock** to a select group of investors. This special form of stock differs from common stock, typically in the following ways:

1. **Preferred stock allows different voting rights.** Preferred stock can carry anywhere from no voting rights to super-voting rights. This flexibility allows a corporation to separate stock ownership from voting control. No voting rights are useful if you want to raise financing from a key stockholder who already owns a lot of common stock and you don't want that stockholder to take control. Super-voting rights can let founding stockholders retain control and yet still issue shares to the public. Facebook and Snap have adopted stock structures that give super-voting rights to some stockholders and no voting rights to others.

2. **Dividends on preferred stock, if any, may be paid at a fixed rate,** specified as either a dollar amount or a percentage per share. For example, if dividends are declared on National Beverage's "2.5%, $1 par value" preferred stock, the dividend will equal 2.5 cents per share ($0.025 = 2.5% × $1.00). A fixed dividend can be attractive to certain investors, such as company founders or retirees, who seek stable investment income.

3. **Preferred stock carries priority over common stock.** Preferred stockholders have higher priority than common stockholders if a corporation distributes assets to its owners through dividends or at liquidation. That is, any dividends the corporation declares must be paid to preferred stockholders before they can be paid to common stockholders. Also, if the corporation goes out of business, its assets will be sold and used to pay creditors and then preferred stockholders. Common stockholders are paid last from whatever assets remain after paying preferred stockholders.

SPOTLIGHT ON | The World

Under IFRS, preferred stock is typically classified as stockholders' equity. However, if the issuing company is contractually obligated to pay dividends or redeem the stock at a future date, then preferred stock is classified as a liability. This classification can dramatically affect financial ratios that use total stockholders' equity (e.g., return on equity, discussed later in this chapter) or total liabilities (e.g., debt-to-assets ratio in Chapter 10).

Preferred Stock Issuance

Just like a common stock issuance, a preferred stock issuance increases a company's cash and its stockholders' equity. Several years ago, National Beverage issued 400,000 shares of its $1 par value preferred stock for $19,704,000. As shown below, the Preferred Stock account increased by its par value for each share issued ($1 × 400,000 = $400,000) and the amount of cash received in excess of par value was recorded as Additional Paid-In Capital—Preferred:

1 Analyze

Assets	= Liabilities +	Stockholders' Equity	
Cash +19,704,000		Preferred Stock	+400,000
		Additional Paid-In Capital—	
		Preferred	+19,304,000

2 Record

	Debit	Credit
Cash...	19,704,000	
Preferred Stock..		400,000
Additional Paid-In Capital—Preferred		19,304,000

Preferred Stock Redemption

In the same way a company can repurchase its common stock, it also can reacquire its previously issued preferred stock. The reacquisition of preferred stock typically is referred to as a redemption because, rather than being held in treasury, the preferred stock is formally retired as if it were never issued. To account for the redemption of preferred stock, a company reverses the original issuance. For example, in 2016, National Beverage redeemed 120,000 shares of its $1 par value preferred stock for $6 million. It accounted for this redemption by decreasing Cash (with a credit) for $6,000,000, decreasing Preferred Stock (with a debit) for the $120,000 par value, and decreasing Additional Paid-In Capital–Preferred (with a debit) for the $5,880,000 in excess of par.

Preferred Stock Dividends

Preferred stock offers dividend preferences. The two most common dividend preferences are called current and cumulative.

Current Dividend Preference A **current dividend preference** requires that preferred dividends be paid before paying any dividends to holders of common stock. This preference is a feature of all preferred stock. After the current dividend preference has been met, and if no other preference exists, dividends may be paid to the common stockholders. National Beverage has not recently declared dividends on its preferred stock, but for purposes of the following example, let's assume it does.

For this first illustration, assume the 150,000 shares of 2.5%, $1 preferred stock carry only a current dividend preference. Further assume the company declares dividends totaling $12,800 in 2021 and $15,800 in 2022. In each year, a fixed amount of the total dividends would first go to the preferred stockholders, and only the excess would go to the common stockholders, as shown and calculated below.

Year	Total Dividends Declared	Dividends on 2.5% Preferred Stock*	Dividends on Common Stock†
2021	$12,800	$3,750	$ 9,050
2022	15,800	3,750	12,050

* Dividends on preferred stock = 150,000 shares × $1 par value × 2.5% dividend = $3,750
† Dividends on common stock = Total dividends declared − Dividends on preferred stock

Had National Beverage declared dividends in 2022 but not 2021, preferred stockholders would have had preference to $3,750 of dividends in 2022 but not 2021. The current dividend preference does not carry over to later years unless the preferred stock is designated as cumulative, as discussed next.

Cumulative Dividend Preference A **cumulative dividend preference** states that if all or a part of the current dividend is not paid in full, the cumulative unpaid amount, known as **dividends in arrears**, must be paid before any future common dividends can be paid. Of course, if the preferred stock is noncumulative, dividends can never be in arrears; any preferred dividends that are not declared are permanently lost. Because preferred stockholders are unwilling to accept this unfavorable feature, preferred stock is usually cumulative, as it is with National Beverage.

To illustrate the cumulative preference, assume the same amount of stock outstanding as in the last example. In this case, however, assume dividends are in arrears for 2019 and 2020. The following table shows that, in 2021, dividends in arrears are satisfied first, followed by the current dividend preference, and the excess goes to common stockholders. In 2022, preferred dividends include only the current preference of that year because dividends in arrears from 2019 and 2020 were fulfilled in 2021.

		DIVIDENDS ON 2.5% PREFERRED STOCK		
Year	Total Dividends Declared	In Arrears*	Current†	Dividends on Common Stock‡
2021	$12,800	$7,500	$3,750	$ 1,550
2022	15,800	—	3,750	12,050

* Dividends in arrears preference = 150,000 shares × $1 par value × 2.5% dividend × 2 years = $7,500
† Current dividend preference = 150,000 shares × $1 par value × 2.5% dividend = $3,750
‡ Dividends on common stock = Total dividends declared − Total dividends on preferred stock

Because dividends are not a liability until the board of directors declares them, dividends in arrears (i.e., dividends not declared on cumulative preferred stock) are not reported on the balance sheet. Instead, they are disclosed in the notes to the financial statements as National Beverage did in a previous year: "Unpaid dividends at April 27, 2013 were $141,000."

RETAINED EARNINGS

As its name suggests, Retained Earnings represents the company's total earnings that have been retained in the business (rather than being distributed to stockholders). The balance in this account increases when the company reports net income and it decreases when the company reports a net loss (expenses greater than revenues) or declares cash or stock dividends to stockholders. **Think of retained earnings as the amount of equity the company itself has generated for stockholders (through profitable operations) but not yet distributed to them.**

Should a company ever accumulate more net losses than net income over its life, it will report a negative (debit) balance in the Retained Earnings account. This amount is (*a*) shown in parentheses in the stockholders' equity section of the balance sheet, (*b*) deducted when computing total stockholders' equity, and (*c*) typically called an **Accumulated Deficit** rather than Retained Earnings.

STATEMENT OF STOCKHOLDERS' EQUITY

Previous chapters indicated that companies report a statement of retained earnings to show how net income increased and dividends decreased the retained earnings balance during the period. While this information is useful, it doesn't tell the full story for public companies because Retained Earnings is only one of their stockholders' equity accounts. To show the causes of changes in all stockholders' equity accounts, public companies report a more comprehensive version of the statement of retained earnings called the statement of stockholders' equity. The statement of stockholders' equity has either separate sections or columns for each stockholder's equity account, in which to show the increases and decreases in each account balance during the period.

Exhibit 11.5 shows a modified version of National Beverage's statement for its fiscal year ended April 27, 2019. Notice how the beginning and ending balances for each

EXHIBIT 11.5	Statement of Stockholders' Equity

NATIONAL BEVERAGE CORP.
Statement of Stockholders' Equity

(in thousands)	Preferred Stock	Common Stock	Additional Paid-In Capital	Retained Earnings	Treasury Stock	Accumulated Other Comprehensive Income (Loss)
April 28, 2018	$150	$506	$36,358	$307,824	$(18,000)	$4,601
Net Income				140,853		
Dividends				(135,247)		
Stock Issuance		1	707			
Aluminum Contracts						(6,144)
April 27, 2019	$150	$507	$37,065	$313,430	$(18,000)	$(1,543)

account correspond to the comparative balance sheet (in Exhibit 11.2). From Exhibit 11.5, we can quickly see the most significant stock transactions for National Beverage during its 2019 fiscal year: its net income and dividends (both of which affected Retained Earnings) and the issuance of common stock (which affected both Common Stock and Additional Paid-In Capital).

Evaluate the Results

In this section, you will learn to use three ratios to evaluate how well a company appears to be using its capital to generate returns for the company and, ultimately, for its stockholders.

Learning Objective 11-5
Analyze the earnings per share (EPS), return on equity (ROE), and price/earnings (P/E) ratios.

EARNINGS PER SHARE (EPS)

The most famous of all ratios, earnings per share (EPS), reports how much profit is earned for each share of common stock outstanding. The calculation of EPS can involve many details and intricacies, but in its basic form, it is computed by dividing net income by the average number of common shares outstanding. Because preferred stock has priority over common stock, any dividends on preferred stock are subtracted from net income when computing EPS. Most companies report EPS on the income statement immediately below Net Income or in the notes to the financial statements.

Why is *earnings* per share so popular when dividends and stock prices ultimately determine the return to stockholders? The reason is that current earnings can predict future dividends and stock prices. If a company generates increased earnings in the current year, it will be able to pay higher dividends in future years. In other words, current EPS influences expectations about future dividends, which investors factor into the current stock price.

Another reason EPS is so popular is that it allows you to easily compare results over time. For example, for its 2019 fiscal year, National Beverage reported net income of $140.9 million and 46.7 million outstanding common stock shares, compared to $149.8 million of net income and 46.6 million outstanding common stock shares in the previous year. By considering earnings on a per-share basis, we adjust for the effect of additional stock issued, resulting in a clearer picture of what these changes mean for each investor. The decrease in net income between 2018 and 2019, combined with the issuance of additional stock, caused EPS to drop from $3.21 to $3.02.

Exhibit 11.6 shows how to calculate EPS for National Beverage and its rival PepsiCo. We should caution you against comparing EPS across companies. The number of shares

 **COACH'S TIP**

Outstanding shares are issued shares minus treasury shares.

	Accounting Decision Tools	
Name of Measure	**Formula**	**What It Tells You**
Earnings per share (EPS)	$\dfrac{\text{Net Income} - \text{Preferred Dividends}}{\text{Average Number of Common Shares Outstanding}}$	• The amount of income generated for each share of common stock owned by stockholders • A higher ratio means greater profitability
Return on equity (ROE)	$\dfrac{\text{Net Income} - \text{Preferred Dividends}}{\text{Average Common Stockholders' Equity}}$	• The amount of income earned for each dollar of common stockholders' equity • A higher ratio means stockholders are likely to enjoy greater returns
Price/Earnings (P/E) ratio	$\dfrac{\text{Stock Price (per share)}}{\text{Earnings per Share (annual)}}$	• How many times more than the current year's earnings investors are willing to pay for a company's common stock • A higher number means investors anticipate an improvement in the company's future results

EXHIBIT 11.6	Summary of EPS, ROE, and P/E Ratio Analyses

National Beverage

(in millions, except price)	2019	2018	2017
Net Income	$140.9	$ 149.8	$ 107.0
Preferred Dividends	0.0	0.0	0.0
Average # Shares Outstanding	46.7	46.6	46.6
Common Stockholders' Equity*	$336.6	$ 336.4	$ 250.6
Stock Price	$42.22	$106.90	$103.66

$$\text{EPS} = \frac{\text{Net Income} - \text{Preferred Dividends}}{\text{Avg. \# Shares}}$$

	2019	2018
	$\frac{\$140.9 - 0.0}{46.7}$	$\frac{\$149.8 - 0.0}{46.6}$
	= $3.02	= $3.21

$$\text{ROE} = \frac{\text{NI} - \text{Pref. div}}{\text{Avg. Common Stockholders' Equity}}$$

	2019	2018
	$\frac{\$140.9 - 0.0}{(\$333.6 + \$336.4)/2}$	$\frac{\$149.8 - 0.0}{(\$336.4 + \$250.6)/2}$
	= 0.419, or 41.9%	= 0.510, or 51.0%

$$\text{P/E} = \frac{\text{Stock Price (per share)}}{\text{Earnings per Share (annual)}}$$

	2019	2018
	$\frac{\$42.22}{\$3.02}$	$\frac{\$106.90}{\$3.21}$
	= 14.0	= 33.3

PepsiCo[+]

(in millions, except price)	2018	2017	2016
Net Income	$12,515	$ 4,857	$ 6,329
Preferred Dividends	0	0	1
Average # Shares Outstanding	1,415	1,425	1,439
Common Stockholders' Equity	$14,602	$11,137	$11,199
Stock Price	$115.85	$112.00	$105.35

$$\text{EPS} = \frac{\text{Net Income} - \text{Preferred Dividends}}{\text{Avg. \# Shares}}$$

	2018	2017
	$\frac{\$12,515 - 0}{1.415}$	$\frac{\$4,857 - 0}{1,425}$
	= $8.84	= $3.41

$$\text{ROE} = \frac{\text{NI} - \text{Pref. div}}{\text{Avg. Common Stockholders' Equity}}$$

	2018	2017
	$\frac{\$12,515 - 0}{(\$14,602 + \$11.137)/2}$	$\frac{\$4,857 - 0}{(\$11,137 + \$11,199)/2}$
	= 0.972, or 97.2%	= 0.435, or 43.5%

$$\text{P/E} = \frac{\text{Stock Price}}{\text{EPS}}$$

	2018	2017
	$\frac{\$115.85}{\$8.84}$	$\frac{\$112.00}{\$3.41}$
	= 13.1	= 32.8

*Common stockholders' equity equals total stockholders' equity minus preferred stock and additional paid-in capital on preferred stock.
[+]Rather than show PepsiCo's 2019 results, we show PepsiCo's 2018 fiscal year (ended December 31, 2018) because it has the greatest number of months in common with National Beverage's 2019 fiscal year (ended April 27, 2019).

outstanding for one company can differ dramatically from the number outstanding for a different company, simply because one chooses to issue more shares of stock than the other. Also, as you have seen in earlier chapters, net income can be affected by differences in how two companies cost inventory (Chapter 7), estimate bad debts (Chapter 8), depreciate long-lived tangible assets (Chapter 9), and estimate losses from contingent liabilities (Chapter 10). So, **while EPS is an effective and widely used measure for comparing a company with itself over time, it is not appropriate for comparing across companies.**

RETURN ON EQUITY (ROE)

Like EPS, return on equity (ROE) reports a company's return to common stockholders. However, rather than relate net income to the average *number* of shares outstanding, the return on equity (ROE) ratio relates net income to the average *dollars* of common stockholder investment in the company.[4] Because ROE uses dollars contributed to and reinvested in the company, this ratio can be appropriately compared across companies.

As Exhibit 11.6 reports, National Beverage's ROE was 41.9 percent for the year ended April 27, 2019, and 51.0 percent the year before that. The decrease in ROE resulted from a decrease in net income that was blamed on negative press claiming the company's sparkling water contained unnatural ingredients. Despite the decline, National Beverage's ROE still exceeded the industry average of 27.3 percent, as reported by csimarket.com. PepsiCo's ROE

[4]When a company has preferred stock outstanding, the ROE ratio deducts any preferred dividends from net income and excludes any preferred stock accounts from the calculation of average common stockholders' equity. The preferred stock, additional paid-in capital on preferred stock, and preferred stock held in treasury have been excluded from the common stockholders' equity for National Beverage in Exhibit 11.6.

also beat the industry average, but for two different reasons. First, PepsiCo sells more than just beverages. Sales of its Doritos and other Frito-Lay products increased significantly during its year ended December 31, 2018. Second, and perhaps more importantly, Pepsico is able to increase its return by using a strategy called **financial leverage.** Rather than rely solely on equity for financing, PepsiCo also relies heavily on debt. PepsiCo has been able to use borrowed money to expand its business and generate more profit than it incurs in interest expense on that debt. As a result, PepsiCo was able to generate a superior return on equity for stockholders. Financial leverage isn't always the best strategy, though, as Dr Pepper discovered during the global financial crisis when its Interest Expense on debt financing was greater than its Income from Operations.

PRICE/EARNINGS (P/E) RATIO

While EPS and ROE are useful for evaluating a company's return to stockholders, they don't help you evaluate the company's stock price. Sophisticated techniques to value a company are taught in advanced courses in finance, but for this course, let's focus on a simple tool. The price/earnings ratio is the most basic way to determine the value investors place on a company's common stock. The P/E ratio, as most people call it, measures how many times more than current year's earnings investors are willing to pay for a company's stock. It is calculated as shown in Exhibit 11.6 by dividing a company's EPS for the year into the stock price at the time its EPS is reported.

Generally, a relatively high P/E ratio means investors expect the company to improve in the future and increase its profits, so they have factored in the future earnings when determining the current stock price. A relatively low P/E ratio typically means they don't expect strong future performance. P/E ratios can vary significantly across industries, so you'll find them most meaningful when comparing a company over time with itself or with competitors in the same industry. Both National Beverage and PepsiCo saw big declines in their P/E ratios in the most recent fiscal years reported in Exhibit 11.6. These declines were consistent with investors growing concerned that the companies' stocks had been priced too high, as consumers were expected to move away from bottled beverages in the future.

🔆 How's it going?   Self-Study Practice

National Beverage reported common stockholders' equity of $206.0 (million) at its 2016 fiscal year-end.

(a) Use this information, along with that in Exhibit 11.6, to calculate National Beverage's earnings per share (EPS), return on equity (ROE), and price/earnings (P/E) ratios for 2017.

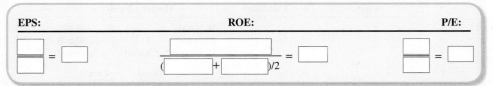

(b) Did National Beverage's EPS and ROE improve or decline from 2017 (calculated in [*a*]) to 2018 (shown in Exhibit 11.6)?

After you have finished, check your answers with the solution.

SUPPLEMENT 11A OWNERS' EQUITY FOR OTHER FORMS OF BUSINESS

Owner's Equity for a Sole Proprietorship

A sole proprietorship is an unincorporated business owned by one person. Only two owner's equity accounts are needed: (1) a capital account for the proprietor (H. Simpson, Capital) and (2) a drawing (or withdrawal) account for the proprietor (H. Simpson, Drawings).

The capital account of a sole proprietorship serves two purposes: to record capital contributions by the owner and to accumulate periodic income or loss. The drawing account is used to record the owner's withdrawals of cash or other assets from the business, similar to recording dividends declared by corporations. The drawing account is closed to the capital account at the end of each accounting period. Thus, after the drawing account is closed, the capital account reflects the cumulative total of all capital contributions by the owner and all earnings of the business less all withdrawals from the entity by the owner.

In most respects, the accounting for a sole proprietorship is the same as for a corporation. Exhibit 11A.1 presents the recording of selected transactions of Homer's Dough Store and a statement of owner's equity, which replaces the statement of retained earnings or statement of stockholders' equity.

EXHIBIT 11A.1   Accounting for Owner's Equity for a Sole Proprietorship

January 1
H. Simpson started a sole proprietorship by placing $150,000 cash in a bank account opened for the business. The accounting equation effects and journal entry follow:

Assets		=	Liabilities	+	Owner's Equity	
Cash	+150,000				H. Simpson, Capital	+150,000

	Debit	Credit
Cash	150,000	
H. Simpson, Capital		150,000

During the year
Each month during the year, Simpson withdrew $1,000 cash from the business for personal living costs. Accordingly, each month the financial effects and required journal entry are

Assets		=	Liabilities	+	Owner's Equity	
Cash	−1,000				H. Simpson, Drawings	−1,000

	Debit	Credit
H. Simpson, Drawings	1,000	
Cash		1,000

Note: At December 31, after the last withdrawal, the drawings account reflected a debit balance of $12,000.

December 31
The usual journal entries for the year, including adjusting and closing entries for the revenue and expense accounts, resulted in total revenue of $48,000 and total expenses of $30,000. The net income of $18,000 was closed to the capital account as follows:

Assets	=	Liabilities	+	Owner's Equity	
				Revenues	−48,000
				Expenses	+30,000
				H. Simpson, Capital	+18,000

	Debit	Credit
Individual Revenue Accounts	48,000	
Individual Expense Accounts		30,000
H. Simpson, Capital		18,000

December 31
The drawings account was closed as follows:

Assets	=	Liabilities	+	Owner's Equity	
				H. Simpson, Capital	−12,000
				H. Simpson, Drawings	+12,000

	Debit	Credit
H. Simpson, Capital	12,000	
H. Simpson, Drawings		12,000

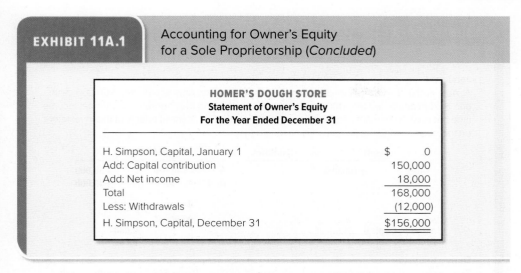

EXHIBIT 11A.1 Accounting for Owner's Equity for a Sole Proprietorship (*Concluded*)

HOMER'S DOUGH STORE
Statement of Owner's Equity
For the Year Ended December 31

H. Simpson, Capital, January 1	$ 0
Add: Capital contribution	150,000
Add: Net income	18,000
Total	168,000
Less: Withdrawals	(12,000)
H. Simpson, Capital, December 31	$156,000

Because a sole proprietorship does not pay income taxes, its financial statements do not report Income Tax Expense or Income Tax Payable. Instead, the net income of a sole proprietorship is taxed when it is included on the owner's personal income tax return. Likewise, the owner's salary is not recognized as an expense in a sole proprietorship because an employer/employee contractual relationship cannot exist with only one party involved. The owner's salary therefore is accounted for as a distribution of profits—a withdrawal—instead of salary expense, as it would be in a corporation.

Owner's Equity for a Partnership

The Uniform Partnership Act, which most states have adopted, defines a partnership as "an association of two or more persons to carry on as co-owners of a business for profit." Small businesses and professionals such as accountants, doctors, and lawyers often use the partnership form of business.

A partnership is formed by two or more persons reaching mutual agreement about the terms of the relationship. The law does not require an application for a charter as in the case of a corporation. Instead, the agreement between the partners constitutes a partnership contract. This agreement should specify matters such as division of income, management responsibilities, transfer or sale of partnership interests, disposition of assets upon liquidation, and procedures to be followed in case of the death of a partner. If the partnership agreement does not specify these matters, the laws of the resident state are binding.

In comparison to a corporation, the primary advantages of a partnership are (1) ease of formation, (2) complete control by the partners, and (3) lack of income taxes on the business itself. The primary disadvantage is the unlimited liability of each partner for the partnership's debts. If the partnership does not have sufficient assets to satisfy outstanding debt, creditors of the partnership can seize each partner's personal assets. In some cases, this can even result in one partner being held responsible for another partner's share of the partnership's debt.

As with a sole proprietorship, accounting for a partnership follows the same underlying principles as any other form of business organization, except for those entries that directly affect owners' equity. Accounting for partners' equity follows the same pattern as for a sole proprietorship, except that separate capital and drawings accounts must be established for each partner. Contributions by each partner are credited to that partner's Capital account and withdrawals are debited to the respective Drawings account. The net income of a partnership is divided among the partners in accordance with the partnership agreement and credited to each account. The respective Drawings accounts are closed to the partner Capital accounts. After the closing process, each partner's Capital account reflects the cumulative total of all that partner's contributions plus that partner's share of the partnership earnings less all that partner's withdrawals.

Exhibit 11A.2 presents selected journal entries and partial financial statements for AB Partnership to illustrate the accounting for the distribution of income and partners' equity.

EXHIBIT 11A.2 | Accounting for Partners' Equity

January 1

A. Able and B. Baker organized AB Partnership on this date. Able contributed $60,000 cash and Baker contributed $40,000 cash to the partnership and they agreed to divide net income (and net loss) 60 percent and 40 percent, respectively. The financial effects of this investment on the business and the journal entry to record them are

Assets		=	Liabilities	+	Partners' Equity	
Cash	+100,000				A. Able, Capital	+60,000
					B. Baker, Capital	+40,000

	Debit	Credit
Cash..	100,000	
A. Able, Capital..		60,000
B. Baker, Capital...		40,000

During the year

The partners agreed that Able would withdraw $1,000 and Baker $650 per month in cash. Accordingly, each month the following financial effects were recorded with the journal entry that appears below:

Assets		=	Liabilities	+	Partners' Equity	
Cash	−1,650				A. Able, Drawings (+D)	−1,000
					B. Baker, Drawings (+D)	−650

	Debit	Credit
A. Able, Drawings..	1,000	
B. Baker, Drawings	650	
Cash..		1,650

Note: At December 31, after the last withdrawals, the Drawings account for Able had a debit balance of $12,000 and the Drawings account for Baker had a debit balance of $7,800.

December 31

Assume that the normal closing entries for the revenue and expense accounts resulted in revenue of $78,000, expenses of $48,000, and net income of $30,000. The partnership agreement specified Able would receive 60 percent of net income ($18,000 = 60% × $30,000) and Baker would get 40 percent ($12,000 = 40% × $30,000). The financial effects and related closing entry follow:

Assets	=	Liabilities	+	Partners' Equity	
				Revenues	−78,000
				Expenses	+48,000
				A. Able, Capital	+18,000
				B. Baker, Capital	+12,000

	Debit	Credit
Individual Revenue Accounts..	78,000	
Individual Expense Accounts....................................		48,000
A. Able, Capital (60% × $30,000)		18,000
B. Baker, Capital (40% × $30,000)		12,000

December 31

The financial effects of closing the drawings accounts and the related closing journal entry are:

Assets	=	Liabilities	+	Partners' Equity	
				A. Able, Capital	−12,000
				B. Baker, Capital	−7,800
				A. Able, Drawings (−D)	+12,000
				B. Baker, Drawings (−D)	+7,800

	Debit	Credit
A. Able, Capital...	12,000	
B. Baker, Capital...	7,800	
A. Able, Drawings		12,000
B. Baker, Drawings		7,800

A separate statement of partners' capital, similar to a corporation's statement of stockholders' equity, is customarily prepared to supplement the balance sheet, as shown next:

EXHIBIT 11A.2	Accounting for Partners' Equity (*Concluded*)

AB PARTNERSHIP
Statement of Partners' Equity
For the Year Ended December 31

	A. Able	B. Baker	Total
Partners' equity, January 1	$ 0	$ 0	$ 0
Add: Additional contributions during the year	60,000	40,000	100,000
Add: Net income for the year	18,000	12,000	30,000
Totals	78,000	52,000	130,000
Less: Drawings during the year	(12,000)	(7,800)	(19,800)
Partners' equity, December 31	$66,000	$44,200	$110,200

Other Business Forms

In addition to sole proprietorships, partnerships, and corporations, other forms of business exist. These forms blend features of the "pure" organizational forms described earlier in this chapter to create hybrid business forms such as S corporations, limited liability partnerships (LLPs), and limited liability companies (LLCs). The LLC in particular is an increasingly common form of business that combines legal characteristics of corporations (such as a separate legal identity and limited liability) with the tax treatment of partnerships (where tax is paid by the individual owners rather than by the business entity itself). Accounting for these hybrid entities generally follows the methods shown earlier in this chapter.

The financial statements of an LLC follow the same format as those for a partnership, which differs from a corporation in the following ways: (1) the financial statements include an additional section entitled Distribution of Net Income; (2) the owners' equity section of the balance sheet is detailed for each owner; (3) the income statement does not report income tax expense because these forms of business do not pay income tax (owners must report their share of the entity's profits on their individual tax returns); and (4) unless other contractual arrangements exist, amounts paid to the owners are not recorded as expenses but instead are accounted for as withdrawals of capital.

SUPPLEMENT 11B	RECORDING STOCK DIVIDENDS

Learning Objective 11-S2
Record journal entries for large and small stock dividends.

Stock dividends are recorded by transferring an amount from Retained Earnings to Common Stock (and possibly other contributed capital accounts). This transfer is called *capitalizing retained earnings*. The amount transferred is either the stock's par value (for large dividends) or its market value (for small dividends). Initially, the distinction between large and small stock dividends was loosely defined in original accounting standards as 20–25 percent of outstanding shares. The dividing line between large and small was later refined to be 25 percent for public companies, which then became common practice for private companies as well.

Large Stock Dividends

A stock dividend is large when the issue is more than 25 percent of the outstanding shares. A large stock dividend is recorded at the stock's par value. National Beverage declared a large stock dividend several years ago, resulting in the issuance of 7.6 million common shares with a par value of $0.01 per share. The total par value (7.6 million × $0.01 = $76,000) was accounted for as

1 Analyze

Assets	=	Liabilities	+	Stockholders' Equity	
				Retained Earnings	−76,000
				Common Stock	+76,000

2 Record

	Debit	Credit
Retained Earnings..	76,000	
Common Stock		76,000

Small Stock Dividends

A stock dividend is small when less than 25 percent of the company's outstanding shares are issued. A small stock dividend is accounted for at the market value of the company's stock. Because market value exceeds par value, the company must record the excess as Additional Paid-In Capital.

To illustrate, assume National Beverage issues a small stock dividend of 10,000 common shares when its stock is trading at $20 per share. The total market value of the dividend is $200,000 ($20 × 10,000), whereas the total par value is $100 ($0.01 × 10,000), so the excess of market value over par value is $199,900 ($200,000 − $100). The effects of this small dividend would be accounted for as

1 Analyze

Assets	= Liabilities +	Stockholders' Equity	
		Common Stock	+100
		Additional Paid-In Capital	+199,900
		Retained Earnings	−200,000

2 Record

	Debit	Credit
Retained Earnings..	200,000	
Common Stock		100
Additional Paid-In Capital...		199,900

REVIEW THE CHAPTER

DEMONSTRATION CASE

This case focuses on selected transactions from the first year of operations of Zoogle Corporation, which was incorporated on January 1 for the purpose of operating a lost-pet search business. The charter authorized the following stock:

> Common stock, $0.10 par value, 20,000 shares
> Preferred stock, 5 percent noncumulative, $100 par value, 5,000 shares

The following summarized transactions were completed on the dates indicated:

a. Jan. 1   Issued a total of 8,000 shares of $0.10 par value common stock for cash at $50 per share.

b. Feb. 1   Issued 2,000 shares of preferred stock at $102 per share; cash collected in full.

c. July 1   Purchased 400 shares of common stock that had been issued earlier. Zoogle Corporation paid the stockholder $54 per share for the stock, which is currently held in treasury.

d. Aug. 1   Issued 30 shares of the common treasury stock at $54 per share.

e. Dec. 1   The board declared a cash dividend on the preferred stock, payable on December 22 to stockholders of record as of December 15.

f. Dec. 22   The cash dividends declared on December 1 were paid.

Required:

1. Give the appropriate journal entries, and show calculations for each transaction.
2. Prepare the stockholders' equity section of the balance sheet for Zoogle Corporation at December 31. Assume that the balance in Retained Earnings after closing entries is $31,000.

Suggested Solution

1. Journal entries:

			Debit	Credit
a.	Jan. 1	**Cash** ($50 × 8,000 shares)...	400,000	
		Common Stock ($0.10 × 8,000 shares)		800
		Additional Paid-In Capital: Common...........................		399,200
b.	Feb. 1	**Cash** ($102 × 2,000 shares)..	204,000	
		Preferred Stock ($100 par × 2,000 shares)		200,000
		Additional Paid-In Capital:		
		Preferred [($102 − $100) × 2,000 shares]		4,000
c.	July 1	**Treasury Stock** (+xSE)	21,600	
		Cash ($54 × 400 shares)..		21,600
d.	Aug. 1	**Cash** ($54 × 30 shares)...	1,620	
		Treasury Stock (−xSE) ($54 × 30 shares)		1,620
e.	Dec.1	**Dividends**	10,000	
		Dividends Payable...		10,000
		(2,000 preferred shares × $100 par × 5% dividend rate)		
f.	Dec. 22	**Dividends Payable**...	10,000	
		Cash..		10,000

2. Stockholders' equity section of the balance sheet:

ZOOGLE CORPORATION
Partial Balance Sheet
At December 31

Stockholders' Equity

Contributed Capital

Preferred Stock, 5% (par value $100; 5,000 authorized shares, 2,000 issued and outstanding shares)	$200,000
Additional Paid-In Capital, Preferred Stock	4,000
Common Stock ($.10 par value; authorized 20,000 shares, issued 8,000 shares of which 370 shares are held as treasury stock)	800
Additional Paid-In Capital, Common Stock	399,200
Total Contributed Capital	604,000
Retained Earnings	31,000
Treasury Stock, at cost, 370 common shares	(19,980)
Total Stockholders' Equity	615,020

CHAPTER SUMMARY

LO 11-1   **Explain the role of stock in financing a corporation.**

- The law recognizes corporations as separate legal entities. Owners invest in a corporation and receive capital stock that can be bought from and sold to other investors. Stock provides a number of rights, including the rights to vote, receive dividends, and share in residual assets at liquidation.

LO 11-2   **Explain and analyze common stock transactions.**

- A number of key transactions involve common stock: (1) initial issuance of stock, (2) repurchase of stock into treasury, and (3) reissuance of treasury stock. Each is illustrated in this chapter. Note that these transactions have only balance sheet effects; corporations do not report income arising from gains or losses on transactions involving their own stock.

LO 11-3   **Explain and analyze cash dividends, stock dividends, and stock split transactions.**

- Cash dividends reduce stockholders' equity (Retained Earnings) and create a liability (Dividends Payable) when they are declared by the board of directors (on the date of declaration). The liability is reduced when the dividends are paid (on the date of payment).
- Stock dividends are pro rata distributions of a company's stock to existing owners. The transaction typically is accounted for by transferring an amount out of Retained Earnings and into contributed capital accounts.
- A stock split also involves the distribution of additional shares to owners, but no additional amount is transferred into the contributed capital accounts. Instead, the per-share par value of stock is reduced.

LO 11-4   **Describe the characteristics of preferred stock and analyze transactions affecting preferred stock.**

- Preferred stock provides investors certain advantages including current dividend preferences and a preference on asset distributions in the event the corporation is liquidated.
- If preferred stock carries cumulative dividend rights, any part of a current dividend that is not paid (called *dividends in arrears*) must be paid in full before any additional dividends can be paid.

LO 11-5   **Analyze the earnings per share (EPS), return on equity (ROE), and price/earnings (P/E) ratios.**

- The earnings per share (EPS) ratio is calculated by dividing net income (less preferred dividends) by the average number of shares of common stock outstanding during the year. This ratio makes it easy to compare a company's earnings over time, but it does not allow reliable comparisons across companies because it does not adjust for likely differences in the number of shares that each company has outstanding.
- The return on equity (ROE) ratio relates earnings to each dollar contributed to and retained by the company on behalf of common stockholders. Because it is calculated using dollar amounts contributed to and retained by a company, it allows comparisons to be made across companies.
- The price/earnings (P/E) ratio relates the company's current stock price to its most recent annual earnings per share, indicating the value investors place on the company's stock.

Accounting Decision Tools		
Name of Measure	**Formula**	**What It Tells You**
Earnings per share (EPS)	$\dfrac{\text{Net Income} - \text{Preferred Dividends}}{\text{Average Number of Common Shares Outstanding}}$	• The amount of income generated for each share of common stock owned by stockholders • A higher ratio means greater profitability
Return on equity (ROE)	$\dfrac{\text{Net Income} - \text{Preferred Dividends}}{\text{Average Common Stockholders' Equity}}$	• The amount earned for each dollar invested by common stockholders • A higher ratio means stockholders are likely to enjoy greater returns
Price/Earnings (P/E) ratio	$\dfrac{\text{Current Stock Price (per share)}}{\text{Earnings per Share (annual)}}$	• How many times more than the current year's earnings investors are willing to pay for a company's common stock • A higher number means investors anticipate an improvement in the company's future results

KEY TERMS

Authorized Shares p. 511

Common Stock p. 509

Cumulative Dividend Preference p. 521

Current Dividend Preference p. 521

Declaration Date p. 516

Dividends in Arrears p. 521

Issued Shares p. 511

No-Par Value Stock p. 512

Outstanding Shares p. 511

Par Value p. 512

Payment Date p. 516

Preferred Stock p. 520

Record Date p. 516

Stock Dividend p. 517

Stock Split p. 518

Treasury Stock p. 511

See complete definitions in the glossary in the back of this text.

HOMEWORK HELPER

Alternative terms

- Stockholders are also called shareholders.
- Additional Paid-In Capital is also called Capital in Excess of Par.

Helpful reminders

- Large stock dividends are recorded at par value; small stock dividends are recorded at the stock market price, with the excess of market over par accounted for as Additional Paid-In Capital.

Frequent mistakes

- Do not record a liability for dividends in arrears at the end of each year. They are recorded as a liability only when dividends are declared on the cumulative preferred stock.

PRACTICE MATERIAL

QUESTIONS (● Symbol indicates questions that require analysis from more than one perspective.)

1. Identify the primary advantages of the corporate form of business.

2. What are the relative advantages of equity versus debt financing?

3. Just prior to filing for bankruptcy protection in 2009, General Motors asked its bondholders to exchange their investment in GM's bonds for GM stock. The bondholders rejected this proposal. Why might GM have proposed this exchange? Why might the bondholders have rejected it? ●

4. Explain each of the following terms: (*a*) authorized common stock, (*b*) issued common stock, and (*c*) outstanding common stock.

5. What are the differences between common stock and preferred stock?

6. What is the distinction between par value and no-par value capital stock?

7. What are the usual characteristics of preferred stock?

8. What items are included in Accumulated Other Comprehensive Income (Loss)?

9. What is treasury stock? Why do corporations acquire their own stock to hold in treasury?

10. How is treasury stock reported on the balance sheet? How is the "gain or loss" on reissued treasury stock reported on the financial statements?

11. What are the two financial requirements to support the declaration of a cash dividend? What are the effects of a cash dividend on assets and stockholders' equity?

12. What is the difference between cumulative and noncumulative preferred stock?

13. What is a stock dividend? How does a stock dividend differ from a cash dividend?

14. What are the primary reasons for issuing a stock dividend?

15. Your company has been very profitable and expects continued financial success. Its stock price has reached a point where the company needs to make it more affordable. Would you recommend a stock dividend or a stock split? Why? ●

16. Identify and explain four important dates with respect to dividends.

17. Why is the EPS number so popular? What are its limitations?

18. How do stock repurchases affect the EPS and ROE ratios?

19. What is one interpretation of a high P/E ratio?

20. You work for a public company that has relied heavily on debt financing in the past and is now considering a preferred stock issuance to reduce its debt-to-assets ratio. Debt-to-assets is one of the key ratios in your company's loan covenants. Should the preferred stock have a fixed annual dividend rate or a dividend that is determined yearly? In what way might this decision be affected by IFRS? ●

MULTIPLE CHOICE

1. Which feature is not applicable to common stock ownership?

   a. Right to receive dividends before preferred stock shareholders.

   b. Right to vote on appointment of external auditor.

   c. Right to receive residual assets of the company should it cease operations.

   d. All of the above are applicable to common stock ownership.

2. Which statement regarding treasury stock is false?

   a. Treasury stock is considered to be issued but not outstanding.

   b. Treasury stock has no voting, dividend, or liquidation rights.

   c. Treasury stock reduces total stockholders' equity on the balance sheet.

   d. None of the above are false.

3. Which of the following statements about stock dividends is true?

   a. Stock dividends are reported on the income statement.

   b. Stock dividends increase total stockholders' equity.

   c. Stock dividends decrease total stockholders' equity.

   d. None of the above.

4. Which of the following is ordered from the largest number of shares to the smallest number of shares?

   a. Shares authorized, shares issued, shares outstanding.

   b. Shares issued, shares outstanding, shares authorized.

   c. Shares outstanding, shares issued, shares authorized.

   d. Shares in treasury, shares outstanding, shares issued.

5. Which of the following statements about the relative advantages of equity and debt financing is false?

   a. An advantage of equity financing is that it does not have to be repaid.

   b. An advantage of equity financing is that dividends are optional.

   c. An advantage of debt financing is debtholders get to vote on company decisions.

   d. An advantage of debt financing is that interest is tax deductible.

6. A journal entry is not recorded on what date?

   a. Date of declaration.

   b. Date of record.

   c. Date of payment.

   d. A journal entry is recorded on all of the above dates.

7. Which of the following transactions will increase the return on equity?

    a. Declare and issue a stock dividend.
    b. Split the stock 2-for-1.
    c. Repurchase the company's stock.
    d. None of the above.

8. Which statement regarding dividends is false?

    a. Dividends represent a sharing of corporate profits with owners.
    b. Both stock and cash dividends reduce retained earnings.
    c. Cash dividends paid to stockholders reduce net income.
    d. None of the above statements are false.

9. When stock is purchased with cash and held in treasury, what is the impact on the balance sheet equation?

    a. No change—the reduction of the asset Cash is offset with the addition of the asset Treasury Stock.

    b. Assets decrease and stockholders' equity increases.
    c. Assets increase and stockholders' equity decreases.
    d. Assets decrease and stockholders' equity decreases.

10. In what situation does total stockholders' equity decrease?

    a. When a cash dividend is declared.
    b. When a stock dividend is declared.
    c. When a stock split is announced.
    d. When a previously declared cash dividend is paid.

> For answers to the Multiple-Choice Questions **see page Q1** located in the last section of the book.

MINI-EXERCISES

M11-1 Equity versus Debt Financing

LO 11-1

Indicate whether each of the following relates to equity (E) or debt (D) financing and whether it makes that form of financing more, or less, favorable.

_____ 1. Interest is tax deductible.
_____ 2. Dividends are optional.
_____ 3. It must be repaid.
_____ 4. Additional stock issuances dilute existing stockholders' control.

M11-2 Computing the Number of Issued Shares

LO 11-1

Face 2 Face Corporation reports 100 outstanding shares, 500 authorized shares, and 50 shares of treasury stock. How many shares are issued?

M11-3 Computing the Number of Unissued Shares

LO 11-1

The balance sheet for Crutcher Corporation reported 200,000 shares outstanding, 300,000 shares authorized, and 20,000 shares in treasury stock. Compute the maximum number of new shares that Crutcher could issue.

M11-4 Analyzing and Recording the Issuance of Common Stock

LO 11-2

To expand operations, Aragon Consulting issued 1,000 shares of previously unissued common stock with a par value of $1. The price for the stock was $50 per share. Analyze the accounting equation effects and record the journal entry for the stock issuance. Would your answer be different if the par value were $2 per share? If so, analyze the accounting equation effects and record the journal entry for the stock issuance with a par value of $2.

M11-5 Analyzing and Recording the Issuance of No-Par Value Common Stock

LO 11-2

Refer to M11-4. Assume the issued stock has no par value. Analyze the accounting equation effects and record the journal entry for the issuance of the no-par value stock at $50. Do the effects on total assets, total liabilities, and total stockholders' equity differ from those in M11-4?

M11-6 Determining the Effects of Stock Issuance and Treasury Stock Transactions

LO 11-2

Trans Union Corporation issued 5,000 shares for $50 per share in the current year, and it issued 10,000 shares for $37 per share in the following year. The year after that, the company reacquired 20,000 shares of its own stock for $45 per share. Determine the impact (increase, decrease, or no change) of each of these transactions on the following classifications:

1. Total assets.
2. Total liabilities.
3. Total stockholders' equity.
4. Net income.

LO 11-3   **M11-7 Determining the Amount of a Dividend**

Netpass Company has 300,000 shares of common stock authorized, 270,000 shares issued, and 100,000 shares of treasury stock. The company's board of directors declares a dividend of $1 per share of common stock. What is the total amount of the dividend that will be paid?

LO 11-3   **M11-8 Recording Dividends**

On May 20, the board of directors for Auction.com declared a cash dividend of 50 cents per share payable to stockholders of record on June 14. The dividends are paid on July 14. The company has 500,000 shares of stock outstanding. Closing entries are recorded on July 31. Prepare any necessary journal entries for each date.

LO 11-3   **M11-9 Determining the Impact of a Stock Dividend**

Sturdy Stone Tools, Inc., announced a 100 percent stock dividend. Determine the impact (increase, decrease, no change) of this dividend on the following:

1. Total assets.
2. Total liabilities.
3. Common stock.

4. Total stockholders' equity.
5. Market value per share of common stock.

LO 11-3   **M11-10 Determining the Impact of a Stock Split**

Complete the requirements of M11-9 assuming that the company announced a 2-for-1 stock split.

LO 11-4   **M11-11 Determining the Amount of a Preferred Dividend**

Colliers, Inc., has 100,000 shares of cumulative preferred stock outstanding. The preferred stock pays dividends in the amount of $2 per share, but because of cash flow problems, the company did not pay any dividends last year. The board of directors plans to pay dividends in the amount of $600,000 this year. What amount will go to preferred stockholders? How much will be available for common stock dividends?

LO 11-4   **M11-12 Determining the Amount of a Preferred Dividend**

Refer to M11-11. Assume the preferred stock is noncumulative. What amount will go to preferred stockholders? How much of the cash dividends will be available for common stockholders?

LO 11-5   **M11-13 Calculating and Interpreting Earnings per Share (EPS) and Return on Equity (ROE)**

Academy Driving School reported the following amounts in its financial statements:

	Year 1	Year 2
Number of common shares	11,500	11,500
Net income	$ 18,000	$ 23,000
Cash dividends paid on common stock	$ 3,000	$ 3,000
Total stockholders' equity	$220,000	$240,000

Calculate EPS and ROE for Year 2. Another driving school in the same city reported a higher net income ($45,000), yet its EPS and ROE ratios were lower than those for the Academy Driving School. Explain how this apparent inconsistency could occur.

LO 11-5   **M11-14 Inferring Financial Information Using the P/E Ratio**

Last year, Rec Room Sports reported earnings per share of $8.50 when its stock price was $212.50. This year, its earnings increased by 20 percent. If the P/E ratio remains constant, what is likely to be the price of the stock? Explain.

LO 11-S1   **M11-15 (Supplement 11A) Comparing Owner's Equity to Stockholders' Equity**

On January 2, Daniel Harrison contributed $20,000 to start his business. At the end of the year, the business had generated $30,000 in sales revenues, incurred $18,000 in operating expenses, and distributed $5,000 for Daniel to use to pay some personal expenses. Prepare (a) a statement of owner's equity, assuming this is a sole proprietorship; (b) the owner's equity section of the balance sheet, assuming this is a sole proprietorship; and (c) the stockholder's equity section of the balance sheet, assuming this is a corporation with no-par value stock.

M11-16 (Supplement 11B) Recording a Stock Dividend

To reduce its stock price, Shriver Food Systems, Inc., declared and issued a 100 percent stock dividend. The company has 800,000 shares authorized and 200,000 shares outstanding. The par value of the stock is $1 per share and the market value is $100 per share. Prepare the journal entry to record this large stock dividend.

EXERCISES

E11-1 Computing Shares Outstanding

The annual report for General Mills disclosed that 1 billion shares of common stock have been authorized. At the beginning of 2017, 755 million shares had been issued and the number of shares in treasury stock was 178 million. During 2017, the only common share transactions were that 11 million common shares were reissued from treasury and 27 million common shares were purchased and held as treasury stock.

Required:

Determine the number of common shares (*a*) issued, (*b*) in treasury, and (*c*) outstanding at the end of 2017.

E11-2 Reporting Stockholders' Equity and Determining Dividend Policy

Incentive Corporation was authorized to issue 12,000 shares of common stock, each with a $1 par value. During its first year, the following selected transactions were completed:

a. Issued 6,000 shares of common stock for cash at $20 per share.
b. Issued 2,000 shares of common stock for cash at $23 per share.

Required:

1. Show the effects of each transaction on the accounting equation.
2. Give the journal entry required for each of these transactions.
3. Prepare the stockholders' equity section as it should be reported on the year-end balance sheet. At year-end, the accounts reflected a profit of $100.
4. Incentive Corporation has $30,000 in the company's bank account. What is the maximum amount of cash dividends the company can declare and distribute?

E11-3 Preparing the Stockholders' Equity Section of the Balance Sheet

North Wind Aviation received its charter during January authorizing the following capital stock:

> Preferred stock: 8 percent, par $10, authorized 20,000 shares.
> Common stock: par $1, authorized 50,000 shares.

The following transactions occurred during the first year of operations in the order given:

a. Issued a total of 40,000 shares of the common stock for $15 per share.
b. Issued 10,000 shares of the preferred stock at $16 per share.
c. Issued 3,000 shares of the common stock at $20 per share and 1,000 shares of the preferred stock at $16.
d. Net income for the first year was $48,000, but no dividends were declared.

Required:

Prepare the stockholders' equity section of the balance sheet at December 31.

E11-4 Reporting the Stockholders' Equity Section of the Balance Sheet

Shelby Corporation was organized in January to operate an air-conditioning sales and service business. The charter issued by the state authorized the following capital stock:

> Common stock, $1 par value, 200,000 shares.
> Preferred stock, $10 par value, 6 percent, 50,000 shares.

During January and February, the following stock transactions were completed:

a.   Collected $400,000 cash and issued 20,000 shares of common stock.
b.   Issued 15,000 shares of preferred stock at $30 per share; collected in cash.

Net income for the year was $50,000; cash dividends declared and paid at year-end were $10,000.

Required:

Prepare the stockholders' equity section of the balance sheet at December 31.

LO 11-2, 11-4   **E11-5   Determining the Effects of the Issuance of Common and Preferred Stock**

Inside Incorporated was issued a charter on January 15 authorizing the following capital stock:

> Common stock, $6 par, 100,000 shares, one vote per share.
> Preferred stock, 7 percent, par value $10 per share, 5,000 shares, nonvoting.

The following selected transactions were completed during the first year of operations in the order given:

a.   Issued 20,000 shares of the $6 par common stock at $18 cash per share.
b.   Issued 3,000 shares of preferred stock at $22 cash per share.
c.   At the end of the year, the accounts showed net income of $38,000. No dividends were declared.

Required:

1.   Prepare the stockholders' equity section of the balance sheet at December 31.
2.   Assume that you are a common stockholder of Inside Incorporated. If the company needed additional capital, would you prefer to have it issue additional common stock or additional preferred stock? Explain.

LO 11-2, 11-4   **E11-6   Recording and Reporting Stockholders' Equity Transactions**

Ava School of Learning obtained a charter at the start of the year that authorized 50,000 shares of no-par common stock and 20,000 shares of preferred stock, par value $10. During the year, the following selected transactions occurred:

a.   Collected $40 cash per share from four individuals and issued 5,000 shares of common stock to each.
b.   Issued 6,000 shares of common stock to an outside investor at $40 cash per share.
c.   Issued 8,000 shares of preferred stock at $20 cash per share.

Required:

1.   Give the journal entries indicated for each of these transactions.
2.   Prepare the stockholders' equity section of the balance sheet at December 31. At the end of the year, the accounts reflected net income of $36,000. No dividends were declared.

LO 11-2, 11-4   **E11-7   Finding Amounts Missing from the Stockholders' Equity Section**

The stockholders' equity section on the December 31 balance sheet of Chemfast Corporation reported the following amounts:

Contributed Capital	
Preferred Stock (par $20; authorized 10,000 shares, ? issued,	
of which 1,000 shares are held as treasury stock)	$104,000
Additional Paid-In Capital, Preferred	14,300
Common Stock (no-par; authorized 20,000 shares, issued and	
outstanding 6,000 shares)	600,000
Retained Earnings	30,000
Treasury Stock, 1,000 Preferred shares at cost	(9,500)

Assume that no shares of treasury stock have been sold in the past.

Required:

Complete the following statements and show your computations.

1. The number of shares of preferred stock issued was _____.
2. The number of shares of preferred stock outstanding was _____.
3. The average issue price of the preferred stock was $_____ per share.
4. The average issue price of the common stock was $_____.
5. The treasury stock transaction increased (decreased) stockholders' equity by _____.
6. The treasury stock cost $_____ per share.
7. Total stockholders' equity is $_____.

E11-8 Recording Treasury Stock Transactions and Analyzing Their Impact LO 11-2, 11-3

The following selected transactions occurred for Corner Corporation:

Feb. 1   Purchased 400 shares of the company's own common stock at $20 cash per share;
             the stock is now held in treasury.
July 15   Issued 100 of the shares purchased on February 1 for $30 cash per share.
Sept. 1   Issued 60 more of the shares purchased on February 1 for $15 cash per share.

Required:

1. Show the effects of each transaction on the accounting equation.
2. Give the indicated journal entries for each of the transactions.
3. What impact does the purchase of treasury stock have on dividends paid?
4. What impact does the reissuance of treasury stock for an amount higher than the purchase price have on net income?

E11-9 Recording and Reporting Stockholders' Equity Transactions, Including Closing Entry LO 11-2, 11-3

The annual report for Malibu Beachwear reported the following transactions affecting stockholders' equity:

a. Purchased $350,000 of common stock now held in treasury.
b. Declared cash dividends in the amount of $260,000.
c. Paid the dividends in (b).
d. Issued 100,000 new shares of $0.10 par value common shares for $2 per share.
e. Closed the Dividends account.

Required:

1. Indicate the effect (increase, decrease, or no effect) of each of these transactions on total assets, liabilities, and stockholders' equity.
2. Prepare journal entries to record each of these events.
3. Prepare a statement of stockholders' equity, assuming the following opening balances: Common Stock, $12,500; Additional Paid-In Capital, $190,000; Retained Earnings, $150,000; and Treasury Stock, $0. Net income for the current year was $270,000.

E11-10 Computing Dividends on Preferred Stock and Analyzing Differences LO 11-3, 11-4

The records of Hoffman Company reflected the following balances in the stockholders' equity accounts at December 31, 2021:

> Common stock, par $12 per share, 40,000 shares outstanding.
> Preferred stock, 8 percent, par $10 per share, 6,000 shares outstanding.
> Retained earnings, $220,000.

On January 1, 2022, the board of directors was considering the distribution of a $62,000 cash dividend. No dividends were paid during 2020 and 2021.

Required:

1. Determine the total and per-share amounts that would be paid to the common stockholders and to the preferred stockholders under two independent assumptions:
   a. The preferred stock is noncumulative.
   b. The preferred stock is cumulative.

2. Briefly explain why the dividends per share of common stock in requirements 1a and 1b could be different.

3. What factors would cause a more favorable dividend for the common stockholders?

LO 11-2, 11-3   **E11-11 Recording Dividends and Preparing a Statement of Retained Earnings**

The annual report for Sneer Corporation disclosed that the company declared and paid preferred dividends in the amount of $100,000 in the current year. It also declared and paid dividends on common stock in the amount of $2 per share. During the current year, Sneer had 1 million common shares authorized; 300,000 shares had been issued; and 100,000 shares were in treasury stock. The opening balance in Retained Earnings was $800,000 and Net Income for the current year was $300,000.

Required:

1. Prepare journal entries to record the declaration, and payment, of dividends on (*a*) preferred and (*b*) common stock.

2. Using the information given above, prepare a statement of retained earnings for the year ended December 31.

3. Prepare a journal entry to close the Dividends account.

LO 11-3   **E11-12 Analyzing Stock Dividends**

On December 31, the stockholders' equity section of the balance sheet of R & B Corporation reflected the following:

Common stock (par $10; 60,000 shares authorized; 25,000 issued and outstanding)	$250,000
Additional paid-in capital	12,000
Retained earnings	75,000

On February 1 of the following year, a 12 percent stock dividend was issued. The market value of the stock on February 1 was $18 per share.

Required:

1. For comparative purposes, prepare the stockholders' equity section of the balance sheet (*a*) immediately before the stock dividend and (*b*) immediately after the stock dividend.
   TIP: Use two columns for the amounts in this requirement.

2. How would your answer to requirement 1 change if the stock dividend were 100%?

LO 11-3   **E11-13 Accounting for Dividends**

Stanley Black & Decker

Stanley Black & Decker is a leading global manufacturer and marketer of power tools, hardware, and home improvement products. A press release contained the following announcement:

> NEW BRITAIN, Conn.—(BUSINESS WIRE)—Oct. 15, 2019—Stanley Black & Decker (NYSE: SWK) announced today that its Board of Directors approved a regular fourth-quarter cash dividend of $0.69 per common share. This extends the company's record for the longest consecutive annual and quarterly dividend payments among industrial companies listed on the New York Stock Exchange. The dividend is payable on Tuesday, December 17, 2019, to shareholders of record as of the close of business on Friday, November 29, 2019.

At the time of the press release, the company had 300 million shares authorized and 148 million outstanding. The par value for the company's stock is $2.50 per share.

Required:

1. Prepare journal entries as appropriate for each of the three dates mentioned above.
2. Assuming no other dividends were declared during the year, prepare the closing entry.

E11-14 Comparing 100 Percent Stock Dividend and 2-for-1 Split

LO 11-3

On July 1, Jones Corporation had the following capital structure:

Common Stock, par $1; 8,000,000 authorized shares, 100,000 issued and outstanding	$100,000
Additional Paid-In Capital	90,000
Retained Earnings	170,000
Treasury Stock	None

Required:

Complete the following table based on two independent cases involving stock transactions:

> **Case 1:** The board of directors declared and issued a 100 percent stock dividend when the stock price was $8 per share.
>
> **Case 2:** The board of directors voted a 2-for-1 stock split. The stock price prior to the split was $8 per share.

Items	Before Stock Transactions	Case 1 After 100% Stock Dividend	Case 2 After Stock Split
Number of shares outstanding			
Par per share	$ 1	$	$
Common stock account	$	$	$
Additional paid-in capital	90,000		
Retained earnings	170,000		
Total stockholders' equity	$	$	$

E11-15 Journalizing Cash Dividends

LO 11-3

Bogscraft Company has outstanding 60,000 shares of $10 par value common stock and 25,000 shares of $20 par value preferred stock (8 percent). On February 1, the board of directors voted in favor of an 8 percent cash dividend on the preferred stock. The cash dividends were paid on March 15. The company closed its books at its fiscal year-end, June 30.

Required:

Prepare journal entries to record the events on (*a*) February 1, (*b*) March 15, and (*c*) June 30.

E11-16 Preparing a Statement of Retained Earnings and Partial Balance Sheet and Evaluating Dividend Policy

LO 11-3, 11-5

The following account balances were selected from the records of beverage maker Blake Corporation at December 31 after all adjusting entries were completed:

Common stock (par $15; authorized 100,000 shares, issued 35,000 shares, of which 1,000 shares are held as treasury stock)	$525,000
Additional paid-in capital—common stock	180,000
Dividends	28,000
Retained earnings, beginning of year	76,000
Treasury stock at cost (1,000 shares)	20,000

Net income for the year was $48,000.

Required:

1. Prepare the statement of retained earnings for the year ended December 31 and the stockholders' equity section of the balance sheet at December 31.
2. Determine the number of shares of stock that received dividends.
3. Compute the ROE ratio for the current year, assuming total stockholders' equity was $629,000 on December 31 of the previous year.

LO 11-2, 11-5 **E11-17 Determining the Effect of a Stock Repurchase on EPS and ROE**

Swimtech Pools Inc. (SPI) reported the following in its financial statements for the quarter ended March 31, 2021.

	December 31, 2020	March 31, 2021
Common Stock, $1 par, 50,000 shares issued and outstanding	$ 50,000	$ 50,000
Additional Paid-In Capital	30,000	30,000
Retained Earnings	20,000	20,000
Total Stockholders' Equity	$100,000	$100,000

During the quarter ended March 31, SPI reported Net Income of $5,000 and declared and paid cash dividends totaling $5,000.

Required:

1. Calculate earnings per share (EPS) and return on equity (ROE) for the quarter ended March 31.
2. Assume SPI repurchases 10,000 of its common stock at a price of $2 per share on April 1, 2021. Also assume that during the quarter ended June 30, 2021, SPI reported Net Income of $5,000 and declared and paid cash dividends totaling $5,000. Calculate earnings per share (EPS) and return on equity (ROE) for the quarter ended June 30, 2021.
3. Based on your calculations in requirements 1 and 2, what can you conclude about the impact of a stock repurchase on EPS and ROE?

LO 11-S1 **E11-18 (Supplement 11A) Comparing Stockholders' Equity Sections for Alternative Forms of Organization**

Assume for each of the following independent cases that the annual accounting period ends on December 31 and that the total of all revenue accounts was $150,000 and the total of all expense accounts was $130,000.

Case A: Assume that the business is a *sole proprietorship* owned by Proprietor A. Prior to the closing entries, the Capital account reflected a credit balance of $50,000 and the Drawings account showed a balance of $8,000.

Case B: Assume that the business is a *partnership* owned by Partner A and Partner B. Prior to the closing entries, the owners' equity accounts reflected the following balances: A, Capital, $40,000; B, Capital, $38,000; A, Drawings, $5,000; and B, Drawings, $9,000. Profits and losses are divided equally.

Case C: Assume that the business is a *corporation*. Prior to the closing entries, the stockholders' equity accounts showed the following: Capital Stock, par $10, authorized 30,000 shares, issued and outstanding 15,000 shares; Additional Paid-In Capital, $5,000; Retained Earnings, $65,000. No dividends were declared.

Required:

1. Give all the closing entries required at December 31 for each of the separate cases.
2. Show how the equity section of the balance sheet would appear at December 31 for each case. Show computations.

LO 11-S2 **E11-19 (Supplement 11B) Journalizing Small and Large Stock Dividends**

Refer to E11-12. Prepare the journal entry to record (*a*) the small 12 percent stock dividend and, alternatively, (*b*) the large 100 percent stock dividend mentioned in requirement 2 of E11-12.

COACHED PROBLEMS

 connect

CP11-1 Analyzing Accounting Equation Effects, Recording Journal Entries, and Preparing a Partial Balance Sheet Involving Stock Issuance, Purchase, and Reissuance Transactions

LO 11-2

Worldwide Company obtained a charter from the state in January that authorized 200,000 shares of common stock, $10 par value. During the first year, the company earned $38,200 and declared no dividends; the following selected transactions occurred in the order given:

a. Issued 60,000 shares of the common stock at $12 cash per share.

b. Reacquired 2,000 shares at $15 cash per share from stockholders; the shares are now held in treasury.

c. Reissued 1,000 of the shares in transaction (*b*) two months later at $18 cash per share.

Required:

1. Indicate the effects of each transaction on the accounting equation.
2. Prepare journal entries to record each transaction.
3. Prepare the stockholders' equity section of the balance sheet at December 31.
   TIP: Because this is the first year of operations, Retained Earnings has a zero balance at the beginning of the year.

CP11-2 Recording Stock Dividends

LO 11-3

Activision Blizzard, Inc., reported the following in the notes to its financial statements.

Activision Blizzard, Inc.

> *Stock Split*—In July, the Board of Directors approved a two-for-one split of our outstanding common shares effected in the form of a stock dividend ("the split"). The split was paid September 5 to share-holders of record as of August 25. The par value of our common stock was maintained at the pre-split amount of $.000001 per share.

Required:

1. Describe the effects that this transaction would have had on the company's financial statements. Assume that 600 million shares were outstanding at the time of the transaction, trading at a stock price of $33.
   TIP: Although the financial statements refer to a stock split, the transaction actually involved a 100% stock dividend. Large stock dividends, such as a 100% dividend, are recorded at par value.
2. Why might the board of directors have decided to declare a stock dividend rather than a stock split?

CP11-3 Finding Missing Amounts

LO 11-2, 11-3, 11-5

At December 31, the records of Nortech Corporation provided the following selected and incomplete data:

LEVEL UP

> Common stock (par $1; no changes during the current year).
> Shares authorized, 500,000.
> Shares issued, __?__ ; issue price $22 per share.
> Common Stock account, $200,000.
> Shares held as treasury stock, 3,000 shares, cost $20 per share.
> Net income for the current year, $147,750.
> Dividends declared and paid during the current year, $49,250.
> Retained Earnings balance, beginning of year, $155,000.

Required:

1. Complete the following:
   Shares authorized _____.
   Shares issued _____.
   Shares outstanding _____.
   TIP: To determine the number of shares issued, divide the balance in the Common Stock account by the par value per share.

2. The balance in Additional Paid-In Capital would be $_____.

3. Earnings per share is $_____.

4. Dividends paid per share of common stock is $_____.

5. Treasury stock should be reported in the stockholders' equity section of the balance sheet in the amount of $_____.

6. Assume that the board of directors approved a 2-for-1 stock split. After the stock split, the par value per share will be $_____.

LO 11-2, 11-3, 11-4

CP11-4 Calculating Common and Preferred Cash Dividends

Tower Corp. had the following stock outstanding and Retained Earnings at December 31, 2021:

Common Stock (par $8; issued and outstanding, 30,000 shares)	$240,000
Preferred Stock, 8% (par $10; issued and outstanding, 6,000 shares)	60,000
Retained Earnings	280,000

On December 31, 2021, the board of directors is considering the distribution of a cash dividend to the common and preferred stockholders. No dividends were declared during 2019 or 2020, and none have been declared yet in 2021. Three independent cases are assumed:

Case A: The preferred stock is noncumulative; the total amount of 2021 dividends would be $12,600.

Case B: The preferred stock is cumulative; the total amount of 2021 dividends would be $14,400. Dividends were not in arrears prior to 2019.

Case C: Same as Case B, except the total dividends are $66,000.

Required:

Compute the amount of 2021 dividends, in total and per share, that would be payable to each class of stockholders if dividends were declared as described in each case. Show computations.

TIP: Preferred stockholders with cumulative dividends are to be paid dividends for any prior years (in arrears) and for the current year before common stockholders are paid.

LO 11-5

Delta Air Lines, Inc.
Southwest Airlines Co.

CP11-5 Computing and Interpreting Return on Equity (ROE) and Price/Earnings (P/E) Ratios

Delta Air Lines, Inc., and Southwest Airlines Co. are two publicly traded airline companies. They reported the following in their financial statements (in millions of dollars, except per-share amounts and stock prices):

	Delta		Southwest	
	2018	2017	2018	2017
Net income	$ 3,935	$ 3,577	$2,465	$ 3,488
Total stockholders' equity	13,687	13,910	9,853	10,430
Earnings per share	5.69	4.53	4.30	5.80
Stock price when annual results reported	51.08	53.46	57.88	55.50

Required:

1. Compute the 2018 ROE for each company. Express ROE as a percentage rounded to one decimal place. Which company appears to generate greater returns on stockholders' equity in 2018?

   TIP: Remember the bottom of the ROE ratio uses the average stockholders' equity.

2. Compute the 2018 P/E ratio for each company (rounded to one decimal place). Do investors appear to value one company's earnings more than the other's? Explain.

GROUP A PROBLEMS

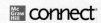

LO 11-2

PA11-1 Analyzing Accounting Equation Effects, Recording Journal Entries, and Preparing a Partial Balance Sheet Involving Stock Issuance and Purchase Transactions

Global Marine obtained a charter from the state in January that authorized 1,000,000 shares of common stock, $5 par value. During the first year, the company earned $400,000 of net income and declared no dividends; the following selected transactions occurred in the order given:

a. Issued 100,000 shares of the common stock at $55 cash per share.
b. Reacquired 25,000 shares at $50 cash per share.
c. Reissued 10,000 shares from treasury for $51 per share.
d. Reissued 10,000 shares from treasury for $49 per share.

Required:

1. Indicate the effects of each transaction on the accounting equation.
2. Prepare journal entries to record each transaction.
3. Prepare the stockholders' equity section of the balance sheet at December 31.

PA11-2 Recording Cash Dividends

LO 11-3

National Chocolate Corp. produces chocolate bars and snacks under the brand names Blast and Soothe. A press release contained the following information:

> March 5—National Chocolate Corp. today announced that its Board of Directors has declared a special "one-time" cash dividend of $1 per share on its 100,000 outstanding common shares. The dividend will be paid on April 29 to shareholders of record at the close of business on March 26. The Company's fiscal year will end April 30.

Required:

1. Prepare any journal entries that National Chocolate Corp. should make on the four dates mentioned in the press release.
2. What two requirements would the board of directors have considered before making the dividend decisions?

PA11-3 Finding Missing Amounts

LO 11-2, 11-3, 11-5

LEVEL
UP

At December 31, the records of Kozmetsky Corporation provided the following selected and incomplete data:

> Common stock (par $2; no changes during the current year).
> Shares authorized, 5,000,000.
> Shares issued, __?__ ; issue price $8 per share.
> Shares held as treasury stock, 10,000 shares, cost $6 per share.
> Net income for the current year, $481,000.
> Common Stock account, $150,000.
> Dividends declared and paid during the current year, $2 per share.
> Retained Earnings balance, beginning of year, $800,000.

Required:

1. Complete the following:
   Shares issued _____.
   Shares outstanding _____.
2. The balance in Additional Paid-In Capital would be $_____.
3. Earnings per share is $_____. Round your answer to two decimal places.
4. Total dividends paid on common stock during the current year is $_____.
5. Treasury stock should be reported in the stockholders' equity section of the balance sheet in the amount of $_____.
6. Assume that the board of directors voted a 2-for-1 stock split. After the stock split, the par value per share will be $_____.

PA11-4 Calculating Common and Preferred Cash Dividends

LO 11-2, 11-3, 11-4

Ritz Company had the following stock outstanding and Retained Earnings at December 31, 2021:

> | | |
> |---|---:|
> | Common stock (par $1; issued and outstanding, 500,000 shares) | $500,000 |
> | Preferred stock, 8% (par $10; issued and outstanding, 21,000 shares) | 210,000 |
> | Retained earnings | 900,000 |

On December 31, 2021, the board of directors is considering the distribution of a cash dividend to the common and preferred stockholders. No dividends were declared during 2019 or 2020. Three independent cases are assumed:

Case A: The preferred stock is noncumulative; the total amount of 2021 dividends would be $30,000.

Case B: The preferred stock is cumulative; the total amount of 2021 dividends would be $30,000. Dividends were not in arrears prior to 2019.

Case C: Same as Case B, except the amount is $75,000.

Required:

Compute the amount of dividends, in total and per share, payable to each class of stockholders if dividends were declared as described in each case. Show computations. Round per-share amounts to two decimal places.

LO 11-5

PA11-5 Computing and Interpreting Return on Equity (ROE) and Price/Earnings (P/E) Ratios

Two online magazine companies reported the following in their financial statements:

	BusinessWorld		Fun and Games	
	2021	2020	2021	2020
Net income	$110,000	$108,604	$ 91,420	$172,173
Total stockholders' equity	587,186	512,814	447,151	467,049
Earnings per share	3.20	3.19	2.10	3.98
Stock price when annual results reported	54.40	51.04	32.55	59.70

Required:

1. Compute the 2021 ROE for each company (express ROE as a percentage rounded to one decimal place). Which company appears to generate greater returns on stockholders' equity in 2021?

2. Compute the 2021 P/E ratio for each company. Do investors appear to value one company's earnings more than the other's? Explain.

GROUP B PROBLEMS

LO 11-2

PB11-1 Analyzing Accounting Equation Effects, Recording Journal Entries, and Preparing a Partial Balance Sheet Involving Stock Issuance and Purchase Transactions

Whyville Corporation obtained its charter from the state in January that authorized 500,000 shares of common stock, $1 par value. During the first year, the company earned $58,000 and declared no dividends; the following selected transactions occurred in the order given:

a. Issued 200,000 shares of the common stock at $23 cash per share.
b. Reacquired 5,000 shares at $24 cash per share to use as stock incentives for senior management.

Required:

1. Indicate the effects of each transaction on the accounting equation.
2. Prepare journal entries to record each transaction.
3. Prepare the stockholders' equity section of the balance sheet at December 31.

LO 11-3

PB11-2 Recording Cash Dividends

Yougi Corp. is an animation studio that issued the following recent press release:

April 1—Yougi Corp. today announced that its Board of Directors has declared a cash dividend of $0.50 per share on 605,000 outstanding preferred shares. The dividend will be paid on or before May 31, to preferred shareholders of record at the close of business on May 26. The Company's fiscal year will end on June 30.

Required:

1. Prepare any journal entries that Yougi Corp. should make on the four dates mentioned in the press release.
2. What two requirements would the board of directors have considered before making the dividend decision?

PB11-3 Finding Missing Amounts

LO 11-2, 11-3, 11-5

At December 31, the records of Seacrest Enterprises provided the following selected and incomplete data:

Common stock (par $1; no changes during the current year).
Shares authorized, 10,000,000.
Shares issued, __?__; issue price $10 per share.
Shares held as treasury stock, 50,000 shares, cost $11 per share.
Net income for the current year, $1,400,000
Common Stock account, $750,000.
Dividends declared and paid during the current year, $1 per share.
Retained Earnings balance, beginning of year, $36,400,000.

Required:

1. Complete the following:
   Shares issued _____.
   Shares outstanding _____.
2. The balance in Additional Paid-In Capital would be $_____.
3. Earnings per share is $_____. Round your answer to two decimal places.
4. Total dividends paid on common stock during the current year is $_____.
5. Treasury stock should be reported in the stockholders' equity section of the balance sheet in the amount of $_____.
6. Assume that the board of directors voted a 2-for-1 stock split. After the stock split, the par value per share will be $_____.

PB11-4 Comparing Stock and Cash Dividends

LO 11-2, 11-3, 11-4

Carlos Company had the following stock outstanding and Retained Earnings at December 31, 2021:

Common Stock (par $1; issued and outstanding, 490,000 shares)	$490,000
Preferred Stock, 8% (par $10; issued and outstanding, 19,000 shares)	190,000
Retained Earnings	966,000

On December 31, 2021, the board of directors is considering the distribution of a cash dividend to the common and preferred stockholders. No dividends were declared during 2019 or 2020. Three independent cases are assumed:

Case A: The preferred stock is noncumulative; the total amount of 2021 dividends would be $24,000.

Case B: The preferred stock is cumulative; the total amount of 2021 dividends would be $24,000. Dividends were not in arrears prior to 2019.

Case C: Same as Case B, except the amount is $67,000.

Required:

Compute the amount of 2021 dividends, in total and per share, payable to each class of stockholders for each case. Show computations. Round per-share amounts to two decimal places.

LO 11-5 **PB11-5 Computing and Interpreting Return on Equity (ROE)**

Two music companies reported the following in their financial statements:

	Urban Youth		Sound Jonx	
	2021	**2020**	**2021**	**2020**
Net income	$ 27,500	$ 24,302	$ 41,500	$ 36,739
Total stockholders' equity	387,101	300,399	516,302	521,198
Earnings per share	1.10	1.00	0.95	0.85
Stock price when annual results reported	20.35	18.50	16.15	14.45

Required:

1. Compute the 2021 ROE for each company (express ROE as a percentage rounded to one decimal place). Which company appears to generate greater returns on stockholders' equity in 2021?
2. Compute the 2021 P/E ratio for each company. Do investors appear to value one company's earnings more than the other's? Explain.

COMPREHENSIVE PROBLEMS

LO 4-2, 4-5, 8-2, 9-3, 10-3, **C11-1 Financial Reporting of Depreciation, Write-off, Bond Issuance and Common Stock**
11-2, 11-3 **Issuance, Purchase, Reissuance, and Cash Dividends (Chapters 4, 8, 9, 10, and 11)**

American Laser, Inc., reported the following account balances on January 1.

	Debit	Credit
Accounts Receivable	$ 5,000	
Accumulated Depreciation		$ 30,000
Additional Paid-In Capital		90,000
Allowance for Doubtful Accounts		2,000
Bonds Payable		0
Buildings	247,000	
Cash	10,000	
Common Stock, 10,000 shares of $1 par		10,000
Notes Payable (long-term)		10,000
Retained Earnings		120,000
Treasury Stock	0	
TOTALS	$262,000	$262,000

The company entered into the following transactions during the year.

Jan. 15	Issued 5,000 shares of $1 par common stock for $50,000 cash.
Jan. 31	Collected $3,000 from customers on account.
Feb. 15	Reacquired 3,000 shares of $1 par common stock into treasury for $33,000 cash.
Mar. 15	Reissued 2,000 shares of treasury stock for $24,000 cash.
Aug. 15	Reissued 600 shares of treasury stock for $4,600 cash.
Sept. 15	Declared (but did not yet pay) a $1 cash dividend on each outstanding share of common stock.
Oct. 1	Issued 100, 10-year, $1,000 bonds, at a quoted bond price of 101.
Oct. 3	Wrote off a $1,500 balance due from a customer who went bankrupt.
Dec. 29	Recorded $230,000 of service revenue, all of which was collected in cash.
Dec. 30	Paid $200,000 cash for this year's wages through December 31. (Ignore payroll taxes and payroll deductions.)
Dec. 31	Calculated $10,000 of depreciation for the year to be recorded. (Ignore accrual adjustments for interest and income taxes.)

Required:

1. Analyze the effects of each transaction on total assets, liabilities, and stockholders' equity.
2. Prepare journal entries to record each transaction.
3. Enter the January 1 balances into T-accounts, post the journal entries from requirement 2, and determine ending balances.
4. Prepare a closing journal entry for the income statement accounts, assuming the events on December 29–31 were the only transactions to affect income statement accounts.
5. Prepare the closing entry for Dividends.
6. Prepare a classified balance sheet at December 31.
7. Calculate the debt-to-assets ratio at January 1 and December 31. Round the ratio to three decimal places and also express it as a percentage rounded to one decimal place. Does the company rely more (or less) on debt financing at the end of the year than at the beginning of the year?

C11-2 Recording Daily and Adjusting Entries, and Preparing and Evaluating Financial Statements (Part A: Chapters 3, 4, 6, 7, 8, 9, 10, and 11; Part B: Chapter 11, Supplement 11B; Part C: Appendix C)

LO 3-3, 4-2, 4-3, 4-4, 6-3, 6-4, 7-3, 8-2, 9-2, 9-3, 9-5, 10-2, 10-3, 11-2, 11-3, 11-S2

One Product Corp. (OPC) incorporated at the beginning of last year. The balances on its post-closing trial balance prepared on December 31, at the end of its first year of operations, were

Cash	$19,500	Withheld Income Taxes Payable	$ 500
Accounts Receivable	8,250	Salaries and Wages Payable	1,600
Allowance for Doubtful Accounts	885	Unemployment Tax Payable	300
Inventory	12,060	Deferred Revenue	4,500
Prepaid Rent	1,600	Interest Payable	495
Equipment	25,000	Notes Payable (long-term)	22,000
Accumulated Depreciation	2,400	Common Stock	13,300
Accounts Payable	0	Additional Paid-In Capital, Common	19,210
Sales Tax Payable	500	Retained Earnings	4,120
FICA Payable	600	Treasury Stock	4,000

The following information is relevant to the first month of operations in the following year:

- OPC sells its inventory at $150 per unit, plus sales tax of 6 percent. OPC's January 1 inventory balance consists of 180 units at a total cost of $12,060. OPC's policy is to use the FIFO method, recorded using a perpetual inventory system.

- The $1,600 in Prepaid Rent relates to a payment made in December for January rent this year.

- The equipment was purchased on July 1 of last year. It has a residual value of $1,000 and an expected life of five years. It is being depreciated using the straight-line method.

- Employee wages are $4,000 per month. Employees are paid on the 16th for the first half of the month and on the first day of the following month for the second half of each month. Withholdings each pay period include $250 of income taxes and $150 of FICA taxes. These withholdings and the employer's matching contribution are paid monthly on the second day of the following month. In addition, unemployment taxes of $50 are accrued each pay period, and will be paid on March 31.

- Deferred Revenue is for 30 units ordered and paid for in advance by two customers in late December. One order of 25 units is to be filled in January, and the other will be filled in February.

- Notes Payable arises from a three-year, 9 percent bank loan received on October 1 last year.

- The par value on the common stock is $2 per share.

- Treasury Stock arises from the reacquisition of 500 shares at a cost of $8 per share.

January Transactions

a. On 1/01, OPC paid employees' salaries and wages that were previously accrued on December 31.
b. A truck is purchased on 1/02 for $10,000 cash. It is estimated this vehicle will be used for 50,000 miles, after which it will have no residual value.
c. Payroll withholdings and employer contributions for December are remitted on 1/03.
d. OPC declares a $0.50 cash dividend on each share of common stock on 1/04, to be paid on 1/10.
e. A $950 customer account is written off as uncollectible on 1/05.

 f. On 1/06, recorded sales of 175 units of inventory on account. Sales tax is charged but not yet collected or remitted to the state.

 g. Sales taxes of $500 that had been collected and recorded in December are paid to the state on 1/07.

 h. On 1/08, OPC issued 300 shares of treasury stock for $2,400.

 i. Collections from customers on account, totaling $8,500, are recorded on 1/09.

 j. On 1/10, OPC distributes the $0.50 cash dividend declared on January 4. The company's stock price is currently $5 per share.

 k. OPC purchases on account and receives 70 units of inventory on 1/11 for $4,410.

 l. The equipment purchased last year for $25,000 is sold on 1/15 for $23,000 cash. Record depreciation for the first half of January prior to recording the equipment disposal.

 m. Payroll for January 1–15 is recorded and paid on 1/16. Be sure to accrue unemployment taxes and the employer's matching share of FICA taxes.

 n. Having sold the equipment, OPC pays off the note payable in full on 1/17. The amount paid is $22,585, which includes interest accrued in December and an additional $90 interest through January 17.

 o. On 1/27, OPC records sales of 30 units of inventory on account. Sales tax is charged but not yet collected or remitted.

 p. A portion of the advance order from December (25 units) is delivered on 1/29. No sales tax is collected on this transaction because the customer is a U.S. governmental organization that is exempt from sales tax.

 q. To obtain funds for purchasing new equipment, OPC issued bonds on 1/30 with a total face value of $90,000, stated interest rate of 5 percent, annual compounding, and six-year maturity date. OPC received $81,420 from the bond issuance, which implies a market interest rate of 7 percent.

 r. On 1/31, OPC records units-of-production depreciation on the vehicle (truck), which was driven 1,900 miles this month.

 s. OPC estimates that 2 percent of the ending accounts receivable balance will be uncollectible. Adjust the applicable accounts on 1/31, using the allowance method.

 t. On 1/31, adjust for January rent expired.

 u. Accrue January 31 payroll on 1/31, which will be payable on February 1. Be sure to accrue unemployment taxes and the employer's matching share of FICA taxes.

 v. Accrue OPC's corporate income taxes on 1/31, estimated to be $3,750.

Required:

Part A

 1. Prepare all January journal entries and adjusting entries for items (*a*)–(*v*).

 2. If you are completing this problem manually, set up T-accounts using the December 31 balances as the beginning balances, post the journal entries from requirement 1, and prepare an unadjusted trial balance at January 31. If you are completing this problem in Connect using the general ledger tool, this requirement will be completed using your previous answers.

 3. Prepare an income statement, statement of stockholders' equity, and classified balance sheet at the end of January.

 4. What was OPC's total payroll cost for January?

 5. Will the carrying value of the bond increase or decrease after recording interest in February?

 6. What is the interest payment OPC will need to pay annually on the bond?

 7. What was the gain or loss recognized on the issuance of Treasury Stock on Jan. 8?

Part B (Supplement 11B)

 8. Rather than distribute a cash dividend in January (see item *j*), OPC considered issuing a 30 percent stock dividend on common stock. What journal entry would OPC record had a 30 percent stock dividend been issued?

 9. What journal entry would OPC record had a 10 percent stock dividend been issued?

Part C (Appendix C)

 10. Show how the total bond issuance proceeds of $81,420 were determined in item (*q*) by calculating the present value of (*a*) the $90,000 face value and (*b*) the annual interest payments.

 11. Rather than issue bonds to obtain cash for purchasing new equipment, OPC could have saved up and invested cash over several years. If OPC can earn 7 percent interest compounded annually, what single lump sum would it have to invest now to reach $98,000 in three years?

 12. Instead of investing one large amount of cash, OPC could invest equal amounts over the next three years. If OPC can earn 7 percent interest compounded annually, how much cash would OPC need to invest equally at the end of each of the next three years to have saved $98,000?

SKILLS DEVELOPMENT CASES

Mc Graw Hill **connect**

S11-1 Finding Financial Information

LO 11-2, 11-3, 11-5

The Home Depot

Refer to the financial statements of The Home Depot in Appendix A at the end of this book. (Note: Fiscal 2019 for The Home Depot runs from February 4, 2019, to February 2, 2020. See S1-1 for further explanation.)

1. As of February 2, 2020, how many shares of common stock were authorized? How many shares were issued? How many shares were held in treasury?
   a. $0.05 authorized; 10,000 issued; 1,786 in treasury
   b. $0.05 authorized; 10,000 issued; 709 in treasury
   c. 10 billion authorized; 1.786 billion issued; 709 million in treasury
   d. 10 billion authorized; 1.786 billion issued; 1.077 billion in treasury

2. According to the Retained Earnings section in the Statement of Stockholders' Equity, what was the total dollar amount of cash dividends declared during the year ended February 2, 2020?
   a. $11,242 million   c. $11,121 million
   b. $5,958 million   d. $4,704 million

3. According to the income statement, how has The Home Depot's net earnings and basic earnings per share changed over the past three years?
   a. Both net earnings and EPS increased.
   b. Net earnings increased and EPS decreased.
   c. Net earnings decreased and EPS increased.
   d. Both net earnings and EPS decreased.

S11-2 Comparing Financial Information

LO 11-2, 11-3, 11-5

Lowe's

Refer to the financial statements of Lowe's Companies, Inc. in Appendix B. (Note: Fiscal 2019 for Lowe's runs from February 2, 2019, to January 31, 2020. See S1-1 for further explanation.)

1. As of January 31, 2020, how many shares of common stock were issued? How many shares were outstanding? How many were shares were held in treasury?
   a. 763 million; 801 million; 381 million   c. 801 million; 801 million; 381 million
   b. 763 million; 763 million; 0   d. 381 million; 1,727 million; 136 million

2. According to the Retained Earnings column in the Statement of Stockholders' Equity, what was the total dollar amount of cash dividends declared during the year ended January 31, 2020?
   a. $1,324 million   c. $1,653 million
   b. $1,500 million   d. $4,090 million

3. According to the income statement, how has Lowe's net earnings and basic earnings per share changed over the past two years?
   a. Both net earnings and EPS increased.
   b. Net earnings increased and EPS decreased.
   c. Net earnings decreased and EPS increased.
   d. Both net earnings and EPS decreased.

S11-3 Internet-Based Team Research: Examining an Annual Report

LO 11-3, 11-5

As a team, select an industry to analyze. Using your web browser, each team member should access the annual report or 10-K for one publicly traded company in the industry, with each member selecting a different company. (See S1-3 in Chapter 1 for a description of possible resources for these tasks.)

Required:

1. On an individual basis, each team member should write a short report that incorporates the following:
   a. Has the company declared cash or stock dividends during the past three years?
   b. What is the trend in the company's EPS over the past three years?
   c. Compute and analyze the return on equity ratio over the past two years.

2. Then, as a team, write a short report comparing and contrasting your companies using these attributes. Discuss any patterns across the companies that you as a team observe. Provide potential explanations for any differences discovered.

LO 11-1, 11-2

Activision

S11-4 Ethical Decision Making: A Real-Life Example

Activision became a public company with an initial public offering of stock on June 9, 1983, at $12 per share. In June 2002, Activision issued 7.5 million additional shares to the public at approximately $33 per share in a seasoned new issue. In October 2002, when its stock was trading at about $22 per share, Activision executives announced that the company would spend up to $150 million to reacquire stock from investors. On January 8, 2003, *The Wall Street Journal* reported several analysts were criticizing Activision's executives because the company had issued the shares to the public at a high price ($33) and then were offering to reacquire them at the going stock market price, which was considerably lower than the issue price in 2002.

Required:

1. Do you think it was inappropriate for Activision to offer to reacquire the stock at a lower stock price in October 2002?
2. Would your answer to requirement 1 be different if Activision had not issued additional stock in June 2002?
3. The above *Wall Street Journal* article also reported that, in December 2002, Activision executives had purchased, for their own personal investment portfolios, 530,000 shares of stock in the company at the then-current price of $13.32 per share. If you were an investor, how would you feel about executives buying stock in their own company?
4. Would your answer to requirement 3 be different if you also learned that the executives had disposed of nearly 2.5 million shares of Activision stock earlier in the year, when the price was at least $26.08 per share?

LO 11-3

S11-5 Ethical Decision Making: A Mini-Case

You are the president of a very successful Internet company that has had a remarkably profitable year. You have determined that the company has more than $10 million in cash generated by operating activities not needed in the business. You are thinking about paying it out to stockholders as a special dividend. You discuss the idea with your vice president, who reacts angrily to your suggestion:

> Our stock price has gone up by 200 percent in the last year alone. What more do we have to do for the owners? The people who really earned that money are the employees who have been working 12 hours a day, six or seven days a week to make the company successful. Most of them didn't even take vacations last year. I say we have to pay out bonuses and nothing extra for the stockholders.

As president, you are hired by the board of directors, which is elected by the stockholders.

Required:

What is your responsibility to both groups? To which group would you give the $10 million? Why?

LO 11-3

S11-6 Critical Thinking: Making a Decision as an Investor

You have retired after a long and successful career as a business executive and now spend a good portion of your time managing your retirement portfolio. You are considering three basic investment alternatives. You can invest in (1) corporate bonds paying 7 percent interest, (2) conservative stocks that pay substantial dividends (typically 5 percent of the stock price every year), and (3) growth-oriented technology stocks that pay no dividends.

Required:

Analyze each of these alternatives and select one. Justify your selection.

S11-7 Charting Stock Price Movement around Important Announcement Dates

LO 11-1, 11-3

Using a web search engine such as Google, find either an earnings or dividend announcement for two different companies. Using a source such as bigcharts.com, determine the closing stock price for each company for each day during the five business days before and after the announcement. Using a separate worksheet for each company, prepare a line chart of its stock price movement.

Required:

Examine the charts for each company. Does the stock price appear to change as a consequence of their announcements? Explain why or why not.

CONTINUING CASE

CC11-1 Accounting for Equity Financing

LO 11-1, 11-2, 11-3, 11-4, 11-5

Nicole has been financing Nicole's Getaway Spa (NGS) using equity financing. Currently NGS has authorized 100,000 no-par preferred shares and 200,000 $2 par common shares. Outstanding shares include 50,000 preferred shares and 40,000 common shares.

Recently the following transactions have taken place.

a. NGS issues 1,000 preferred shares for $12 a share.
b. NGS repurchases 1,000 common shares for $11 a share.
c. On November 12, the board of directors declares a $0.10 cash dividend on each outstanding preferred share.
d. The dividend is paid December 20.

Required:

1. Prepare the journal entries needed for each of the transactions.
2. If you were a common shareholder concerned about your voting rights, would you prefer Nicole to issue additional common shares or additional preferred shares? Why?
3. Describe the overall effect of each transaction on the assets, liabilities, and shareholders' equity of the company. (Use + for increase, − for decrease, and NE for no effect.)
4. How would each transaction affect the ROE ratio?

DATA ANALYTICS EXERCISES

Data Analytics Exercises are auto-graded exercises offering detailed data visualization, interpretation, and analysis, and are available for assignment in *Connect*.

12

CHAPTER TWELVE

Statement of Cash Flows

YOUR LEARNING OBJECTIVES

LO 12-1 Identify cash flows arising from operating, investing, and financing activities.

LO 12-2 Report cash flows from operating activities, using the indirect method.

LO 12-3 Report cash flows from investing activities.

LO 12-4 Report cash flows from financing activities.

LO 12-5 Interpret cash flows from operating, investing, and financing activities.

LO 12-6 Report and interpret cash flows from operating activities, using the direct method.

LO 12-S1 Report cash flows from PPE disposals using the indirect method.

LO 12-S2 Use the T-account approach for preparing an indirect method statement of cash flows.

THAT WAS THEN

In the previous chapters, you learned about the income statement, statement of retained earnings, and balance sheet.

andresr/Getty Images

FOCUS COMPANY: DAVE & BUSTER'S ENTERTAINMENT, INC.

This chapter is all about cash. Cash McCool. That was the company name Dave Corriveau gave to a games parlor he started as a 24-year-old entrepreneur. But Dave's dreams were bigger than pool tables and video games. He had noticed his customers regularly going next door to eat and drink at Buster's restaurant and bar. Dave didn't see this as competition, but rather, to him, it was opportunity. He approached his neighbor with the idea of combining Dave's games and entertainment business with Buster's restaurant and bar to create the first-ever Dave & Buster's. That was about 40 years ago, but, even today, the company continues to focus on the same core concept: "offer customers the opportunity to Eat Drink Play and Watch all in one location."*

Dave & Buster's is now a public company with its stock traded on the NASDAQ under the ticker symbol PLAY. It has more than 120 locations across the United States. One of the key goals for managers at Dave & Buster's is to ensure the company generates enough cash from day-to-day operations to upgrade its existing locations and expand into new locations. Management is particularly excited to introduce 50-foot LED screens and new VR games for its customers to watch and play. But they also are aware that investors and creditors will be closely monitoring the company's cash inflows and outflows. Investors want to know whether Dave & Buster's is likely to pay dividends, and creditors want to know whether Dave & Buster's is likely to pay them the amounts they are owed. They find information for making such predictions in the statement of cash flows, as we will discuss in the following sections.

*Source: Dave & Buster's 2019 Form 10-K.

Understand the business	Study the accounting methods	Evaluate the results	Supplement 12A	Supplement 12B	Review the chapter
• Business activities and cash flows • Classifying cash flows	• Relationship to other financial statements • Preparing the statement of cash flows	• Evaluating cash flows • Operating cash flows revisited (direct method)	• Reporting disposals of property, plant, and equipment (indirect method)	• T-account approach (indirect method)	• Demonstration cases • Chapter summary • Key terms • Homework helper • Practice material

Understand the Business

BUSINESS ACTIVITIES AND CASH FLOWS

To this point in the course, we've analyzed business activities to identify their financial effects on assets, liabilities, stockholders' equity, revenues, and expenses. We've emphasized that business activities have financial effects even when they don't involve cash. That's why accrual accounting exists. When accurately reported, accrual-based net income is the best measure of a company's profitability during the period.

Despite its importance, net income is not what companies use when they pay wages, dividends, or loans. These activities require cash, so financial statement users need information about changes in a company's cash. Neither the balance sheet nor the income statement provides this information. The balance sheet shows a company's cash balance at a point in time, but it doesn't explain the activities that caused changes in its cash. Cash may have been generated by the company's day-to-day operations, by the sale of the company's buildings, or by advances on loans. The income statement doesn't explain changes in cash because it focuses on just the operating results of the business, excluding cash that is received or paid when taking out or paying down loans, issuing or acquiring the company's own stock, and selling or investing in long-lived assets. Also, the timing of cash receipts and payments may differ from the accrual-based income statement, which reports revenues when goods or services are provided and expenses when they are incurred. Such differences between net income and cash flows are the reason GAAP requires every company to report a statement of cash flows.

The statement of cash flows shows the major types of business activity that caused a company's cash to increase or decrease during the accounting period. For purposes of this statement, cash is defined to include cash, cash equivalents, and restricted cash. Cash equivalents are short-term, highly liquid investments purchased within three months of maturity. They are considered equivalent to cash because they are both (1) readily convertible to known amounts of cash and (2) so near to maturity their value is unlikely to change. Restricted cash is money that is legally or contractually required to be set aside such that it is not available for use in day-to-day operations.

SPOTLIGHT ON | Ethics

Cash Isn't Estimated

Critics of accrual-based net income claim it can be manipulated because it relies on many estimates (of bad debts, inventory market values, assets' useful lives), but cash flows do not involve estimates so they are not easily manipulated. A cash balance changes only when cash has been received or paid. One particularly dramatic illustration of the subjectivity of net income, but not cash, involved the bankruptcy of a department store chain operated by the W. T. Grant Company. Through biased estimates, the company reported net income for nine consecutive years but then shocked everyone when it declared bankruptcy and shut down after the following year. At the time, a statement of cash flows wasn't required. Had it been required, the company would have reported negative operating cash flows in seven of the ten years.

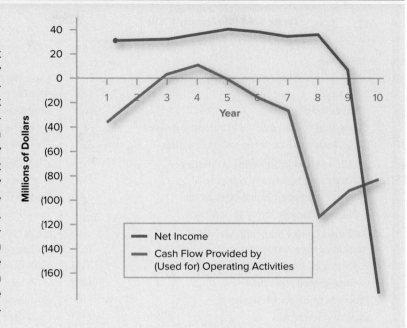

Source: James A. Largay III and Clyde P. Stickney, "Cash Flows, Ratio Analysis and the W. T. Grant Company Bankruptcy," *Financial Analysts Journal* 36, no. 4 (July/August 1980), pp. 51–54.

CLASSIFYING CASH FLOWS

The statement of cash flows requires all cash inflows and outflows to be classified as relating to the company's operating, investing, or financing activities. This classification of cash flows is useful because most companies experience different cash flow patterns as they develop and mature. Think back to Chapter 2 when Noodlecake Studios had just started. The first thing Jordan and Ty needed to get their idea off the ground was **financing,** which the company could then use to **invest** in assets that later would be needed to **operate** the business. At this early stage, financing and investing cash flows were crucial for Noodlecake. For an established business, like Walmart in Chapter 6, operating activities often are the focus. Financial statement users are interested in a company's ability to generate operating cash flows that will allow it to continue investing in additional assets and repay the financing it originally obtained. Creditors and investors will tolerate poor operating cash flows for only so long before they stop lending to or investing in the company. For any company to survive in the long run, the amount of cash generated through daily operating activities has to exceed the amount spent on them.

A condensed (and somewhat simplified) version of Dave & Buster's statement of cash flows is presented in Exhibit 12.1. Don't worry about the details in the three cash flow categories yet. For now, focus on the categories' totals. Notice that each category can result in net cash inflows (represented by a positive number) or net cash outflows (represented by a negative number by using parentheses). The sum of these three categories ($305 − $187 − $116 = $2) represents the overall change in cash on the balance sheet between the beginning and end of the period ($2 + $20 = $22).

Dave & Buster's cash flows in Exhibit 12.1 suggest the company is financially healthy. The company generated enough cash from its day-to-day operations ($305 million) to pay for investments in store upgrades ($185 million) and to return some cash to stockholders through stock repurchases ($149 million) and dividends ($11 million). To learn more about these cash flows, you would consider the details of each category, as we will do now.

EXHIBIT 12.1	Dave & Buster's Condensed Statement of Cash Flows

DAVE & BUSTER'S ENTERTAINMENT, INC. Statement of Cash Flows For the Year Ended February 3, 2019		Explanation
(in millions)		
Cash Flows from Operating Activities		**Cash flows related to day-to-day activities**
Net income	$ 117	Assume net income (NI) generates cash inflow
Depreciation	105	Depreciation decreased NI but didn't decrease cash
Changes in current assets and current liabilities	83	Differences in the timing of net income and cash flows
Net cash provided by operating activities	305	Indicates overall cash impact of operating activities
Cash Flows Used in Investing Activities		**Cash flows related to long-term assets**
Purchase of property and equipment	(185)	Cash was used to upgrade stores and purchase equipment
Purchase of intangible and other assets	(2)	Cash was used to purchase intangibles
Net cash used in investing activities	(187)	Indicates overall cash impact of investing activities
Cash Flows from Financing Activities		**Cash flows from transactions with lenders, investors**
Additional long-term notes	265	Cash received from borrowing
Payments on long-term notes	(231)	Cash used to repay amounts previously borrowed
Common stock repurchase	(149)	Cash used to buy previously issued stock
Proceeds from stock issuance	10	Cash received from issuing stock
Cash dividends paid	(11)	Cash used to pay dividends
Net cash provided by financing activities	(116)	Indicates overall cash impact of financing activities
Net Change in Cash and Cash Equivalents	2	$305 + $(187) + ($116) = $2
Cash and cash equivalents, beginning of year	20	Cash balance at beginning of the period
Cash and cash equivalents, end of year	$ 22	Cash balance at end of the period (**on balance sheet**)

Operating Activities

Cash flows from operating activities (or **cash flows from operations**) are the cash inflows and outflows related directly to the revenues and expenses reported on the income statement. Operating activities involve day-to-day business activities with customers, suppliers, employees, landlords, and others. Typical cash flows from operating activities include:

Inflows	Outflows
Cash provided by	*Cash used for*
Collecting from customers	Purchasing services (electricity, etc.) and goods for resale
Receiving dividends	Paying salaries and wages
Receiving interest	Paying income taxes
	Paying interest

The difference between these cash inflows and outflows is reported on the statement of cash flows as a subtotal, Net Cash Provided by (Used for) Operating Activities.

Investing Activities

Cash flows from investing activities are the cash inflows and outflows related to the purchase and disposal of investments and long-lived assets. Typical cash flows from investing activities include:

Inflows	Outflows
Cash provided by	*Cash used for*
Sale or disposal of equipment	Purchase of equipment or intangibles
Sale or maturity of investments in securities	Purchase of investments in securities

The difference between these cash inflows and outflows is reported on the statement of cash flows as a subtotal, Net Cash Provided by (Used in) Investing Activities.

Financing Activities

YOU SHOULD KNOW

Cash Flows from Financing Activities: Cash inflows and outflows related to financing sources external to the company (owners and lenders).

Cash flows from financing activities include exchanges of cash with stockholders and cash exchanges with lenders (for principal on loans). Common cash flows from financing activities include:

Inflows	Outflows
Cash provided by	**Cash used for**
Borrowing from lenders through formal debt contracts	Repaying principal to lenders
Issuing stock to owners	Repurchasing stock from owners
	Paying cash dividends to owners

The difference between these cash inflows and outflows is reported on the statement of cash flows as a subtotal, Net Cash Provided by (Used in) Financing Activities.

One way to classify cash flows into operating, investing, and financing categories is to think about the balance sheet accounts to which the cash flows relate. **Although exceptions exist, a general rule is that operating cash flows cause changes in current assets and current liabilities, investing cash flows affect noncurrent assets, and financing cash flows affect noncurrent liabilities or stockholders' equity accounts.**[1] Exhibit 12.2 shows how this general rule relates the three sections of the statement of cash flows (SCF) to each of the main sections of a classified balance sheet.

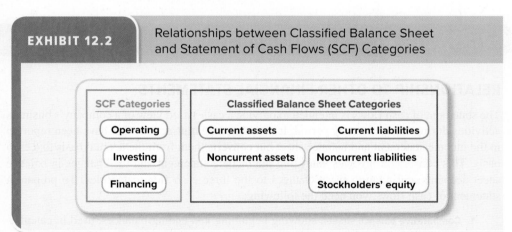

EXHIBIT 12.2 Relationships between Classified Balance Sheet and Statement of Cash Flows (SCF) Categories

SCF Categories	Classified Balance Sheet Categories	
Operating	Current assets	Current liabilities
Investing	Noncurrent assets	Noncurrent liabilities
Financing		Stockholders' equity

How's it going? Self-Study Practice

Brunswick Corporation produces the Life Fitness line of gym equipment. A listing of some of its cash flows follows. Indicate whether each item is disclosed in the operating activities (O), investing activities (I), or financing activities (F) section of the statement of cash flows.

☐ *a.* Stock issued to stockholders. ☐ *d.* Purchase of equipment.
☐ *b.* Collections from customers. ☐ *e.* Purchase of investment securities.
☐ *c.* Interest paid on debt. ☐ *f.* Cash dividends paid.

After you have finished, check your answers with the solution.

Solution to Self-Study Practice
a. F, *b.* O, *c.* O, *d.* I, *e.* I, *f.* F

---

[1]Intermediate accounting courses discuss in detail exceptions to this general rule. Exceptions include investing activities that affect current assets (for example, short-term investments) and financing activities that affect current liabilities (for example, dividends payable and short-term notes payable).

SPOTLIGHT ON

The World

Classification Choices under IFRS

To create consistency across companies, GAAP restricts interest and dividend classifications to a single category. IFRS, on the other hand, allows managers to choose between categories, as follows:

	COMPANY PAYS		COMPANY RECEIVES	
	Dividends	Interest	Dividends	Interest
GAAP	F	O	O	O
IFRS	O, F	O, F	O, I	O, I

GAAP classifies dividends paid as financing (F) because they are transactions with stockholders. IFRS allows dividends paid to also be classified as operating (O) to assist users in determining the company's ability to pay dividends out of operating cash flows. GAAP requires the other three items to be classified as operating because they enter into the determination of net income. IFRS allows interest paid to also be classified as financing because it is a cost of obtaining financial resources. IFRS allows interest and dividends received to also be classified as investing (I) because they are returns on investments.

Study the Accounting Methods

RELATIONSHIP TO OTHER FINANCIAL STATEMENTS

The statement of cash flows is intended to provide a cash-based view of a company's business activities during the accounting period. It uses the same transactions that have been reported in the income statement and balance sheet but converts them from the accrual basis to a cash basis. This conversion involves analyzing the income statement and the changes in balance sheet accounts and relating these changes to the three cash flow categories. To prepare a statement of cash flows, you need the following:

1. **Comparative balance sheets,** showing beginning and ending balances, used in calculating the cash flows from all activities (operating, investing, and financing).

2. **A complete income statement,** used primarily in calculating cash flows from operating activities.

3. **Additional data** concerning selected accounts that increase and decrease as a result of investing and/or financing activities.

The approach to preparing the cash flow statement focuses on changes in the balance sheet accounts. It relies on a simple rearrangement of the balance sheet equation:

$$\text{Assets} = \text{Liabilities} + \text{Stockholders' Equity}$$

First, assets can be split into cash and all other assets, which we'll call **noncash assets:**

$$\text{Cash} + \text{Noncash Assets} = \text{Liabilities} + \text{Stockholders' Equity}$$

If we move the noncash assets to the right side of the equation, we get

$$\text{Cash} = \text{Liabilities} + \text{Stockholders' Equity} - \text{Noncash Assets}$$

Given this relationship, the **change** in cash between the beginning and end of the period must equal the **change** in the amounts on the right side of the equation between the beginning and end of the period:

$$\text{Change in Cash} = \text{Change in (Liabilities} + \text{Stockholders' Equity} - \text{Noncash Assets)}$$

This equation says **changes in cash must be accompanied by and can be accounted for by the changes in liabilities, stockholders' equity, and noncash assets.**

PREPARING THE STATEMENT OF CASH FLOWS

Based on the idea that the change in cash equals the sum of the changes in all other balance sheet accounts, we use the following steps to prepare the statement of cash flows:

1. **Determine the change in each balance sheet account.** From this year's ending balance, subtract this year's beginning balance (i.e., last year's ending balance).

2. **Identify the cash flow category or categories to which each account relates.** Use Exhibit 12.2 as a guide, but be aware that some accounts may include two categories of cash flows. Retained Earnings, for example, can include both financing cash flows (paying dividends) and operating cash flows (generating net income). Similarly, Accumulated Depreciation can be affected by operating activities (depreciation for using equipment in daily operations) as well as investing activities (disposing of equipment).

3. **Create schedules that summarize operating, investing, and financing cash flows.** Let's start with operating cash flows.

Direct and Indirect Reporting of Operating Cash Flows

Two alternative methods may be used when presenting the operating activities section of the statement of cash flows:

1. The **direct method** reports the total cash inflow or outflow from each main type of transaction (that is, transactions with customers, suppliers, employees, etc.). The difference between these cash inflows and outflows equals the Net Cash Provided by (Used in) Operating Activities.

2. The **indirect method** starts with net income from the income statement and adjusts it by eliminating the effects of items that do not involve cash (for example, depreciation) and including items that do have cash effects. Adjusting net income for these items yields the Net Cash Provided by (Used in) Operating Activities.

YOU SHOULD KNOW

Direct Method: Reports the components of cash flows from operating activities as gross receipts and gross payments.
Indirect Method: Presents the operating activities section of the cash flow statement by adjusting net income to compute cash flows from operating activities.

Direct Method		Indirect Method	
Cash collected from customers	$1,274	Net income	$117
Cash paid to suppliers of inventory	(204)	Depreciation	105
Cash paid to employees and suppliers of services	(721)		
Cash paid for interest	(13)	Changes in current assets and current liabilities	83
Cash paid for income tax	(31)		
Net cash provided by (used in) operating activities	$ 305	Net cash provided by (used in) operating activities	$305

The point to remember about the direct and indirect methods is that they are simply different ways to arrive at the same number. **Net cash flows provided by (used in) operating activities is always the same under the direct and indirect methods.** Also, the choice between the two methods affects only the operating activities section of the statement of cash flows, not the investing and financing sections.

We focus on the indirect method in the following section because it is currently used by about 99 percent of large companies in the United States. The direct method is presented in the last section of this chapter.

Determining Operating Cash Flows Using the Indirect Method

Learning Objective 12-2
Report cash flows from operating activities, using the indirect method.

When using the indirect method, operating cash flows are calculated as follows. We explain each of these items below and then we demonstrate how to use Dave & Buster's financial information to create such a schedule.

> **Net income**
> Items included in net income that do not involve cash
>   **+ Depreciation**
> Changes in current assets and current liabilities
>   **+ Decreases in current assets**
>   **− Increases in current assets**
>   **− Decreases in current liabilities**
>   **+ Increases in current liabilities**
> **Net cash flow provided by (used in) operating activities**

Net income. When determining operating cash flows using the indirect method, start with net income as reported on the last line of the company's income statement. By starting with net income, it's as if we are assuming all revenues resulted in cash inflows and all expenses resulted in cash outflows. But we know this is not true, so we add and subtract various amounts to convert that net income number into cash flows from operating activities. The additions and subtractions are explained below.

+ Depreciation. When initially recording depreciation in the accounting system, we increase Depreciation Expense (with a debit) and increase Accumulated Depreciation (with a credit). Notice that this entry for depreciation does not involve cash. To **eliminate** the effect of having deducted Depreciation Expense from Net Income in the income statement, we add it back in the statement of cash flows.

+ Decreases in current assets. Adding decreases in current assets serves two purposes. First, it **eliminates** the effects of some transactions that decreased net income but did not affect cash in the current period. For example, when Supplies are used, net income decreases, but cash is not affected. To eliminate these noncash effects from our cash flow computations, we must add back decreases in Supplies and other current assets. Second, adding decreases in current assets allows us to **include** the cash effects of other transactions that did not affect net income in the current period but did increase cash. For example, Cash increases when Accounts Receivable are collected. These cash inflows are captured by adding the amount by which this current asset had decreased.

− Increases in current assets. Subtracting increases in current assets similarly serves two purposes. First, it **eliminates** the effects of transactions that increased net income but did not affect cash in the current period. For example, net income increases when a company provides services on account to its customers, but cash is not affected. We eliminate these noncash effects by subtracting increases in current assets. Second, subtracting increases in current assets allows us to **include** the cash effects of other transactions that did not affect net income in the current period but did decrease cash. For example, Cash decreases when a company prepays its insurance or rent, but net income isn't affected until these assets are used up. The cash outflows can be captured by subtracting the increase in these current assets.

COACH'S TIP

Use this table to remember how to adjust for changes in current assets and liabilities. The + and − indicate whether balance sheet changes are added (+) or subtracted (−) in the statement of cash flows.

	Current Assets	Current Liabilities
Increase	−	+
Decrease	+	−

− Decreases in current liabilities. Subtracting decreases in current liabilities serves two purposes. First, it **eliminates** the effects of transactions that increased net income but did not affect cash. For example, a company decreases Deferred Revenue and increases net income in the current period when it fulfills prior obligations to provide services, but cash is not affected. To eliminate these noncash effects, we subtract decreases in current liabilities. Second, subtracting decreases in current liabilities allows us to **include** the cash effects of other transactions that did not affect net income in the current period but did decrease cash. For example, Cash decreases when a company pays wages that were incurred and expensed in a previous period. These cash outflows are captured by subtracting decreases in current liabilities.

+ Increases in current liabilities. Adding increases in current liabilities serves two purposes. First, it **eliminates** the effects of transactions that decreased net income but did not affect cash. For example, when interest is accrued on a bank loan, a company decreases net income, but its cash is not affected. To eliminate these noncash effects, we add back increases in current liabilities. Second, adding increases in current liabilities allows us to **include** the cash effects of other transactions that did not affect net income in the current period but did increase cash. For example, Cash and Deferred Revenue increase when the company receives cash in advance of providing services. Adding the increase in current liabilities captures these cash inflows.

Reporting Operating Cash Flows—Indirect Method

The preceding approach to preparing an operating cash flow schedule can be applied to Dave & Buster's information in Exhibit 12.3. We start by calculating the changes in all balance sheet accounts (Step ❶, as shown to the right of the balances). Then, using the additional data provided below, classify whether the changes involve operating (**O**), investing (**I**), and/or financing (**F**) activities (in Step ❷). Cash is not classified as O, I, or F because the change in Cash is reported at the bottom of the statement of cash flows rather than within its three sections.

Next, we use the amount of the change in each account marked by an O in Exhibit 12.3 to complete Step ❸, which involves preparing the operating cash flow schedule in Exhibit 12.4. Have a quick look at Exhibit 12.4 right now and then take your time reading the following explanations and make sure you understand the reasons for each item.

Net Income + Depreciation   Net income and depreciation are the first two lines to appear in a statement of cash flows prepared using the indirect method. They begin the process of converting net income to operating cash flows. They also begin the process of explaining the change in Cash by accounting for changes in the other balance sheet accounts. In the case of Dave & Buster's, the $117 million of net income accounts for the increase in Retained Earnings (the decrease caused by dividends are reported later, in the financing cash flows section). The $105 million of depreciation accounts for the change in Accumulated Depreciation (assuming the company had no disposals).[2]

Decrease in Accounts Receivable   Accounts Receivable increases when sales are made on account and it decreases when cash is collected from customers. An overall decrease in this account, then, implies sales on account were less than cash collections. To convert from the lower sales number that is included in net income to the higher cash collected from customers, we add the difference ($9 million).

Another way to remember whether to add or subtract the difference is to think about whether the overall change in the account balance is explained by a debit or credit. If the change in the account is explained by a credit, the adjustment in the cash flow schedule is reported like a corresponding debit to cash (added). In Dave & Buster's case, the decrease in

>  **COACH'S TIP**
>
> The depreciation addback is not intended to suggest depreciation creates an increase in cash. Rather, it's just showing that depreciation does not cause a decrease in cash. This is a subtle, but very important, difference in interpretation.

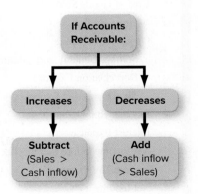

---

[2]Amortization and impairment losses (discussed in Chapter 9) would be handled in the same way as depreciation. Gains and losses on fixed asset disposals also would be dealt with in a similar manner, as discussed in Chapter Supplement 12A.

EXHIBIT 12.3	Information for Preparing a Statement of Cash Flows

DAVE & BUSTER'S ENTERTAINMENT, INC.
Balance Sheet*

(in millions)	February 3, 2019	February 4, 2018		Change	Related Cash Flow Section
Assets					
Current Assets:					
Cash and Cash Equivalents	$ 22	$ 20		+2	Cash
Accounts Receivable	21	30		–9	O
Inventory	27	28		–1	O
Prepaid Expenses	21	19		+2	O
Total Current Assets	91	97			
Property and Equipment	1,385	1,200		+185	I (see notes 1 and 3 below)
Accumulated Depreciation	(580)	(475)		–105	O (see notes 2 and 3 below)
Intangible and Other Assets	377	375		+2	I (see notes 1 and 3 below)
Total Assets	$1,273	$1,197			
Liabilities and Stockholders' Equity					
Current Liabilities:					
Accounts Payable	$ 88	$ 73		+15	O
Accrued Liabilities	380	320		+60	O
Total Current Liabilities	468	393			
Notes Payable (long-term)	417	383		+34	F (see note 4 below)
Total Liabilities	885	776			
Stockholders' Equity:					
Common Stock	331	321		+10	F (see note 5 below)
Retained Earnings	354	248		+106	O, F (see note 6 below)
Treasury Stock	(297)	(148)		–149	F (see note 7 below)
Total Stockholders' Equity	388	421			
Total Liabilities and Stockholders' Equity	$1,273	$1,197			

Step **1**   Step **2**

DAVE & BUSTER'S ENTERTAINMENT, INC.
Income Statement*
For the Year Ended February 3, 2019

(in millions)	
Net Sales	$1,265
Cost of Goods Sold	220
Gross Profit	1,045
Operating Expenses:	
Selling, General, and Administrative Expense	779
Depreciation Expense	105
Total Operating Expenses	884
Income from Operations	161
Interest Expense	13
Net Income before Income Tax Expense	148
Income Tax Expense	31
Net Income	$ 117

Additional data

1. Equipment costing $185 million and Intangibles and Other Assets costing $2 million were purchased with cash.

2. Accumulated Depreciation increased by $105 million for depreciation.

3. No disposals or impairments of property and equipment, or intangibles occurred.

4. Notes payable of $231 million were paid and $265 million in new notes were borrowed.

5. Shares of common stock were issued for $10 million.

6. Retained Earnings increased by $117 million of net income and decreased by $11 million of cash dividends paid.

7. Shares of common stock were repurchased into treasury for $149 million.

*Certain items have been revised to simplify presentation.

Source: Dave & Buster's 2019 Form 10-K.

EXHIBIT 12.4   Dave & Buster's Schedule of Operating Cash Flows

Step 3 Items	Amount (in millions)	Explanations
Net income	**$ 117**	Starting point, from the income statement
Items included in net income that do not involve cash		
+ **Depreciation**	105	Depreciation is a noncash expense
Changes in current assets and current liabilities		
+ **Decrease in Accounts Receivable**	9	Cash collections more than sales on account
+ **Decrease in Inventory**	1	Purchases less than cost of goods sold
− **Increase in Prepaid Expenses**	(2)	Prepayments greater than related expenses
+ **Increase in Accounts Payable**	15	Purchases greater than payments to suppliers
+ **Increase in Accrued Liabilities**	60	Accrued expenses more than cash payments
Net cash flow provided by (used in) operating activities	**$ 305**	Overall increase in cash from operations

Accounts Receivable is explained by a credit, so the adjustment in the cash flow schedule is reported like a debit to cash (added), as follows:

Accounts Receivable (A)			
Beg. bal.	30		
		Decrease	9
End. bal.	21		

> **CASH FLOWS FROM OPERATING ACTIVITIES**
>
> | Net income | 117 |
> |---|---|
> | + Accounts receivable decrease | +9 |
> | . . . | . . . |
> | Net cash inflow | — |

Decrease in Inventory   The income statement reports the cost of goods sold during the period, but cash flow from operating activities must report cash purchases of inventory. As shown in the T-account on the left, purchases of goods increase the balance in inventory, and recording the cost of goods sold decreases the balance in inventory.

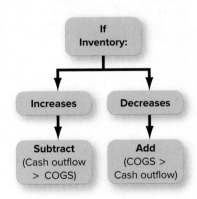

Inventory (A)			
Beg. bal.			
Purchases		Cost of goods sold	
End. bal.			

Inventory (A)			
Beg. bal.	28		
		Decrease	1
End. bal.	27		

The above T-account on the right shows a $1 million inventory decrease, which means that the cost of goods sold deducted on the income statement was more than the cash outflow for inventory purchases. This difference must be added back to net income to convert it to cash flow from operating activities in Exhibit 12.4. (An increase would be subtracted.)

Increase in Prepaid Expenses   The income statement reports expenses of the period, but cash flow from operating activities must reflect the cash payments. Cash prepayments increase the balance in prepaid expenses, and recording of expenses decreases the balance in prepaid expenses.

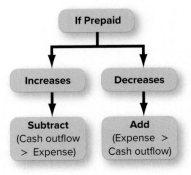

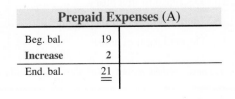

Prepaid Expenses (A)			
Beg. bal.			
Cash prepayments		Used-up / expensed	
End. bal.			

Prepaid Expenses (A)			
Beg. bal.	19		
Increase	2		
End. bal.	21		

Dave & Buster's $2 million increase in Prepaid Expenses means cash prepayments this period were more than expenses. These extra cash prepayments must be subtracted in Exhibit 12.4. (A decrease would be added.)

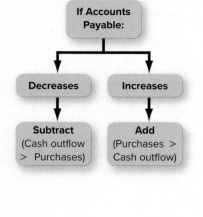

Increase in Accounts Payable Cash flow from operations must reflect cash purchases, but not all purchases are for cash. Purchases on account increase Accounts Payable and cash paid to suppliers decreases Accounts Payable.

Accounts Payable (L)		Accounts Payable (L)	
	Beg. bal.	Beg. bal.	73
Cash payments	Purchases on account	Increase	15
	End. bal.	End. bal.	88

Accounts Payable increased by $15 million, which means that purchases on account were greater than cash payments to suppliers. Thus, to show the lower cash outflow, the increase in Accounts Payable must be added back in Exhibit 12.4. (A decrease would be subtracted.)

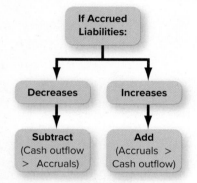

Increase in Accrued Liabilities The income statement reports all accrued expenses, but the cash flow statement must reflect only the actual cash payments for expenses. Recording accrued expenses increases the balance in Accrued Liabilities and cash payments for the expenses decreases Accrued Liabilities.

Accrued Liabilities (L)		Accrued Liabilities (L)	
	Beg. bal.	Beg. bal.	320
Cash payments	Accrued expenses	Increase	60
	End. bal.	End. bal.	380

Dave & Buster's Accrued Liabilities increased by $60 million, which indicates that more expenses were accrued than paid. To convert to the smaller cash outflow, this difference must be added in Exhibit 12.4. (A decrease would be subtracted.)

By scanning Exhibit 12.3 you can see that you have now considered the changes in all balance sheet accounts that relate to operating activities (marked by the letter O). The last step in determining the net cash flow provided by (used in) operating activities is to calculate a total. As shown in Exhibit 12.4, the combined effects of all operating cash flows is a net inflow of $305 million.

Now that you have seen how to compute operating cash flows using the indirect method, take a moment to complete the following Self-Study Practice.

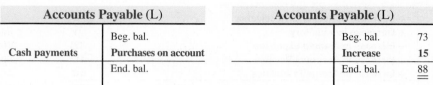

How's it going?   Self-Study Practice

Indicate whether the following items taken from **Brunswick Corporation**'s cash flow statement would be added (+), subtracted (−), or not included (0) in the reconciliation of net income to cash flow from operations.

- ☐ *a.* Decrease in inventory.
- ☐ *b.* Increase in accounts payable.
- ☐ *c.* Depreciation expense.
- ☐ *d.* Increase in accounts receivable.
- ☐ *e.* Increase in accrued liabilities.
- ☐ *f.* Increase in prepaid expenses.

After you have finished, check your answers with the solution.

Reporting Investing Cash Flow Calculations

To prepare the investing section of the statement of cash flows, you must analyze accounts related to long-lived tangible and intangible assets.[3] Unlike the analysis of operating activities, where you were concerned only with the *net* change in selected balance sheet accounts, an analysis of investing (and financing) activities requires that you identify and separately report the causes of *both* increases and decreases in account balances. The following relationships are the ones you will encounter most:

Related Balance Sheet Accounts	Investing Activity	Cash Flow Effect
Property and Equipment	Purchase of property and equipment for cash	Outflow
	Sale of property and equipment for cash	Inflow
Intangible Assets	Purchase of intangible assets	Outflow
	Sale of intangible assets	Inflow

Dave & Buster's balance sheet (Exhibit 12.3) shows two investing assets (noted with an I) that changed during the year: Property and Equipment, and Intangible and Other Assets.

Property and Equipment To determine the cause of the change in the Property and Equipment account, accountants would examine the detailed accounting records for purchases (increases) and disposals (decreases). The additional data in Exhibit 12.3 indicate Dave & Buster's purchased equipment for $185 million cash. This purchase is a cash outflow, which we subtract in the schedule of investing activities in Exhibit 12.5. In our example, this purchase fully accounts for the change in the Property and Equipment balance, as shown in the following T-account. Note 3 of the additional data in Exhibit 12.3 confirms there were no disposals or impairments during the year. Chapter Supplement 12A explains how disposals affect the statement of cash flows.

Property and Equipment (A)

Beg. bal.	1,200		
Purchases	185	Disposals	0
End. bal.	1,385		

EXHIBIT 12.5 Dave & Buster's Schedule of Investing Cash Flows

Items	Amount (in millions)	Explanations
Purchase of property and equipment	$(185)	Paid cash for property and equipment
Purchase of intangible and other assets	(2)	Paid cash for intangibles
Net cash provided by (used in) investing activities	(187)	Subtotal for the statement of cash flows

---

[3]Investing activities also affect other assets described in Appendix D (investments in other companies). Although not shown here, the cash flows for investments are similar to those shown in this section for equipment and intangible assets.

Intangible and Other Assets A similar approach is used to determine cash flows associated with intangible assets. For our example, analysis of Dave & Buster's additional data indicates the company did not have any reductions in its intangible assets as a result of disposals, impairments, or amortization during the year. However, Dave & Buster's did purchase intangible assets for $2 million cash, as noted in the additional data in Exhibit 12.3. This cash outflow is subtracted in the schedule of investing activities in Exhibit 12.5.

Reporting Financing Cash Flow Calculations

Learning Objective 12-4
Report cash flows from financing activities.

This section of the cash flow statement includes changes in liabilities owed to owners (Dividends Payable) and financial institutions (Notes Payable and other types of debt), as well as changes in stockholders' equity accounts. Interest is considered an operating activity so it is excluded from financing cash flows. The following relationships are the ones you will encounter most often:

COACH'S TIP

Dividends paid are financing cash flows. Dividends received, however, are operating cash flows.

Related Balance Sheet Accounts	Financing Activity	Cash Flow Effect
Notes Payable	Borrowing cash from banks or other financial institutions	Inflow
	Repayment of loan principal	Outflow
Bonds Payable	Issuance of bonds for cash	Inflow
	Repayment of bond face value	Outflow
Common Stock	Issuance of stock for cash	Inflow
Treasury Stock	Repurchase of stock with cash	Outflow
Retained Earnings	Payment of cash dividends	Outflow

To compute cash flows from financing activities, you should review changes in all debt and stockholders' equity accounts. Increases and decreases must be identified and reported separately. Dave & Buster's balance sheet in Exhibit 12.3 indicates that Notes Payable, Common Stock, Retained Earnings, and Treasury Stock changed during the period as a result of financing cash flows (noted with an F).

Notes Payable The additional data in Exhibit 12.3 indicate Notes Payable (long-term) was affected by both cash inflows and outflows, as shown in the T-account below. These cash flows are reported separately in the schedule of financing activities shown in Exhibit 12.6.

Notes Payable (long-term) (L)			
		Beg. bal.	383
Repayments	231	Borrowings	265
		End. bal.	417

Common Stock and Treasury Stock The additional data in Exhibit 12.3 indicate Dave & Buster's issued $10 million of common stock and repurchased treasury stock for $149 million cash.[4] These stock transactions fully account for the change in Common Stock and Treasury Stock, as shown in the following T-accounts. These cash flows are listed in the schedule of financing activities in Exhibit 12.6.

Common Stock (SE)		
	Beg. bal.	321
	Stock issued	10
	End. bal.	331

Treasury Stock (SE)		
Beg. bal.	148	
Stock repurchased	149	
End. bal.	297	

---

[4] This description was simplified by eliminating stock options and by illustrating no-par, rather than par value, common stock.

EXHIBIT 12.6   Dave & Buster's Schedule of Financing Cash Flows

Items	Amount (in millions)	Explanations
Additional long-term notes	$ 265	Cash received when new notes signed
Payments on long-term notes	(231)	Cash paid on principal of notes
Proceeds from stock issuance	10	Cash received from stockholders for new stock
Repurchase of stock into treasury	(149)	Cash paid to repurchase stock into treasury
Cash dividends paid	(11)	Cash paid to stockholders
Net cash from (used in) financing activities	(116)	Subtotal for the statement of cash flows

Retained Earnings   Net income increases Retained Earnings and any declared dividends decrease Retained Earnings. Net income has already been accounted for as an operating cash flow. The declared dividends were $11 million (see the additional data in Exhibit 12.3), which decreased Retained Earnings as shown in the following T-account. Because the balance sheet does not report Dividends Payable, we assume all of these declared dividends were paid in cash. This cash outflow is reported in the financing section of the statement of cash flows, as summarized in Exhibit 12.6.

	Retained Earnings (SE)	
	Beg. bal.	248
Dividends 11	**Net income**	**117**
	End. bal.	354

Reporting the Statement of Cash Flows

Now that you have determined the cash flows for the three main types of business activities in Exhibits 12.4, 12.5, and 12.6, you can prepare the statement of cash flows in a proper format. Exhibit 12.7 shows the statement of cash flows for Dave & Buster's using the indirect method. Notice that the $2 million subtotal for "Net increase (decrease) in cash and cash equivalents" combines cash flows from operating, investing, and financing activities to produce an overall net change in cash. This net change is added to the beginning cash balance to arrive at the ending cash balance, which is the same cash balance as reported on the balance sheet.

Noncash Transactions and Other Supplemental Disclosures   In addition to cash flows, all companies are required to report material investing and financing transactions that did not have cash flow effects (called **noncash investing and financing activities**). For example, the purchase or lease of a $10,000 piece of equipment with a $10,000 note payable to the equipment supplier does not cause either an inflow or an outflow of cash. As a result, these activities are not listed in the three main sections of the statement of cash flows. This important information is normally presented for users in a supplementary schedule to the statement of cash flows or in the financial statement notes. Companies using the indirect method also must disclose the amount of cash paid for interest and for income taxes. Examples of these supplemental disclosures are shown at the bottom of Exhibit 12.7.

 **COACH'S TIP**

When doing homework problems, assume all changes in noncurrent account balances are caused by cash transactions (unless the problem also describes changes caused by noncash investing and financing activities).

EXHIBIT 12.7 Dave & Buster's Statement of Cash Flows (Indirect Method)

DAVE & BUSTER'S ENTERTAINMENT, INC.
Statement of Cash Flows*
For the Year Ended February 3, 2019

(in millions)

Cash Flows from Operating Activities	
Net income	$117
Adjustments to reconcile net income to net cash provided by operating activities:	
Depreciation	105
Changes in current assets and current liabilities:	
Accounts Receivable	9
Inventory	1
Prepaid Expenses	(2)
Accounts Payable	15
Accrued Liabilities	60
Net cash provided by (used in) operating activities	305
Cash Flows from Investing Activities	
Purchase of property and equipment	(185)
Purchase of intangible and other assets	(2)
Net cash provided by (used in) investing activities	(187)
Cash Flows from Financing Activities	
Additional long-term notes	265
Payments on long-term notes	(231)
Proceeds from stock issuance	10
Repurchase of stock into treasury	(149)
Cash dividends paid	(11)
Net cash provided by (used in) financing activities	(116)
Net increase (decrease) in cash and cash equivalents	2
Cash and cash equivalents, beginning of year	20
Cash and cash equivalents, end of year	$ 22
Supplemental Disclosures	
Cash paid for interest	$ 13
Cash paid for income tax	31

Note: These supplemental disclosures also could include significant noncash transactions (e.g., issued a promissory note to purchase $x of equipment).

*Certain amounts have been adjusted to simplify the presentation.

Evaluate the Results

Unlike the income statement, which summarizes its detailed information in one number (net income), the statement of cash flows does not provide a summary measure of cash flow performance. Instead, it must be evaluated in terms of the cash flow pattern suggested by the subtotals of each of the three main sections. As we discussed at the beginning of this chapter, expect different patterns of cash flows from operating, investing, and financing activities depending on how well established a company is. Exhibit 12.8 illustrates typical cash flow

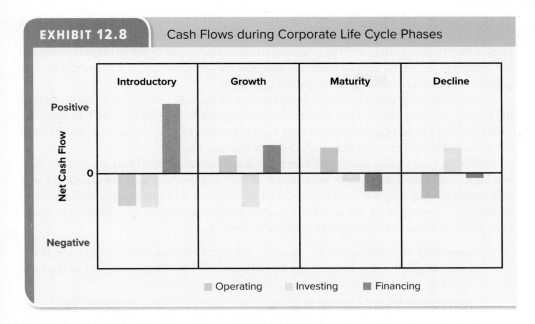

EXHIBIT 12.8 Cash Flows during Corporate Life Cycle Phases

patterns for a company as it evolves from an **introductory phase** when the company is being established to a **growth phase** when the company's presence expands to a **maturity phase** when the company stabilizes and finally to a **decline phase**. Although exceptions can exist, knowing the patterns in Exhibit 12.8 can help you to better understand and evaluate a company's cash flows.

Most companies in the introductory (start-up) phase experience negative net operating cash flows, as suggested by the blue bar in Exhibit 12.8. Negative cash flows arise during this phase because companies pay cash out to employees and suppliers but haven't established a large enough customer base to generate sizable cash inflows from customers. Also during the introductory phase, these companies are spending significant amounts of cash on long-term assets (e.g., property and equipment), resulting in negative investing cash flows, as suggested by the yellow bar in Exhibit 12.8. To fund these negative investing and operating cash flows, companies in the introductory phase rely heavily on cash obtained through financing activities (e.g., borrowing from lenders and obtaining contributions from shareholders), as suggested by the grey bar in Exhibit 12.8.

If a company survives the introductory phase, it will enter a growth phase, which is similar to the introductory phase except that operating cash flows turn positive because the company has improved its cash inflows from customers. Having positive operating cash flows, a growth company relies less on financing cash flows than a company in the introductory phase. In the maturity phase, the company continues to enjoy positive operating cash flows but no longer has opportunities for expanding the business, so it reduces its spending on investing activities and instead uses its cash for financing activities such as repaying lenders and returning excess cash to shareholders. Finally, during the decline phase, a company's operating cash flows again become negative, prompting lenders to demand repayment of loans (i.e., negative financing cash flows). To fund these repayments, the company sells off its long-term assets, resulting in significantly positive investing cash flows.

EVALUATING CASH FLOWS

After considering a company's overall pattern of cash flows, you should then look at the details within each of the three sections of the SCF.

Evaluating Cash Flows from Operating Activities

The operating activities section indicates how well a company is able to generate cash internally through its operations and management of current assets and current liabilities.

Most analysts believe this is the most important section of the statement because, in the long run, operations are the only continuing source of cash. Investors will not invest in a company if they believe cash generated from operations is inadequate to pay dividends or expand the company. Similarly, creditors will not lend money or extend credit if they believe cash generated from operations is insufficient to repay them.

When evaluating the operating activities section of the statement of cash flows, consider the absolute amount of cash flow (is it positive or negative?), keeping in mind that operating cash flows have to be positive over the long run for a company to be successful. Also, look at the relationship between operating cash flows and net income.

All other things being equal, when net income and operating cash flows are similar, there is a high likelihood that revenues are realized in cash and that expenses are associated with cash outflows. Any major deviations should be investigated. In some cases, a deviation may be nothing to worry about, but in others, it could be the first sign of big problems to come. Four potential causes of deviations to consider include:

1. **Seasonality.** In some industries, seasonal variations in sales and inventory levels can cause the relationship between net income and cash flow from operations to fluctuate from one quarter to the next. Usually, this isn't cause for alarm.

2. **The corporate life cycle (growth in sales).** New companies often experience rapid sales growth. When sales are increasing, accounts receivable and inventory normally increase faster than the cash flows being collected from sales. This often causes operating cash flows to be lower than the related net income. This isn't a big deal, provided the company can obtain cash from financing activities until operating activities begin to generate more positive cash flows.

3. **Changes in revenue and expense recognition.** Most cases of fraudulent financial reporting involve aggressive revenue recognition (recording revenues before performance obligations are fulfilled) or delayed expense recognition (failing to report expenses when they are incurred). Both of these tactics cause net income to increase in the current period, making it seem as though the company has improved its performance. Neither of these tactics, though, affects cash flows from operating activities. As a result, if revenue and expense recognition policies are changed to boost net income, cash flow from operations will be significantly lower than net income, providing one of the first clues the financial statements might contain errors or fraud.

4. **Changes in working capital management.** Working capital is a measure of the amount by which current assets exceed current liabilities. If a company's current assets (such as accounts receivable and inventory) are allowed to grow out of control, its operating cash flows will decrease. More efficient management will have the opposite effect. To investigate this potential cause more closely, use the inventory and accounts receivable turnover ratios covered in Chapters 7 and 8.

Evaluating Cash Flows from Investing Activities

Although it might seem counterintuitive at first, healthy companies tend to show negative cash flows in the investing section of the statement of cash flows. A negative total for this section means the company is spending more to acquire new long-term assets than it is taking in from selling its existing long-term assets. That's normal for any healthy, growing company. In fact, if you see a positive total cash flow in the investing activities section, you should be concerned because it could mean the company is selling off its long-term assets just to generate cash inflows. If a company sells off too many long-term assets, it may not have a sufficient base to continue running its business effectively, which would likely lead to further decline in the future.

Evaluating Cash Flows from Financing Activities

Unlike the operating and investing activities sections, where a healthy company typically shows positive and negative cash flows, respectively, the financing activities section does not have an obvious expected direction for cash flows. For example, a healthy company that is growing rapidly could need financing cash inflows to fund its expansion. In this case, the company could take out new loans or issue new shares, both of which would result in positive net cash flows from financing activities. Alternatively, a healthy company could use its cash resources to repay existing loans, pay dividends, or repurchase shares, all of which would result in negative net cash flows from financing activities. Thus, it's not possible to evaluate the company's financing cash flows by simply determining whether they are positive or negative on an overall basis. Rather, you will need to consider detailed line items within this section to assess the company's overall financing strategy (is the company moving toward greater reliance on risky debt financing?).

SPOTLIGHT ON | Financial Reporting

Free Cash Flow

At a recent investor conference, **Dave & Buster's** presented a performance measure called **free cash flow.**[*] This measure combines selected operating, investing, and financing cash flows. Free cash flow is not defined in accounting standards, so companies differ in how they calculate it. The most common calculation is:

Free Cash Flow = Operating Cash Flow − Capital Expenditures − Cash Dividends

Capital expenditures are cash purchases of fixed assets (e.g., property and equipment). Using the data in Exhibit 12.7, Dave & Buster's free cash flow for 2019 was $109 million ($109 = $305 − $185 − $11). This implies the company had more than enough cash flow for property and equipment purchases as well as dividend payments. Seeing $109 million of "free" cash available, the company's board of directors authorized an increase in its share repurchase program.

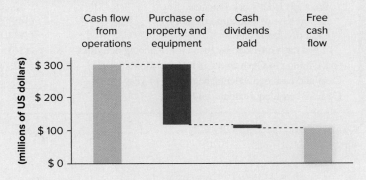

[*]Dave & Buster's *Fall 2019 Investor Presentation,* PowerPoint slideshow downloaded from http://ir.daveandbusters.com/events-and-presentations on November 7, 2019.

OPERATING CASH FLOWS REVISITED (DIRECT METHOD)

Learning Objective 12-6
Report and interpret cash flows from operating activities, using the direct method.

In this section, we demonstrate how to determine operating cash flows using the direct method of presentation. You might ask whether it's worth learning how to use this approach when fewer than 1 percent of public companies report with it. That's a fair question. But you also should ask why *aren't* more companies using it when the FASB recommends it over the indirect method. Some argue companies do not use the direct method of presentation because it reveals too much about their operations. As we show below, useful insights can be gained about a company by analyzing its operating cash flows using the direct method of presentation.

Exhibit 12.9 presents **Dave & Buster's** statement of cash flows using the direct method. Because this method lists each operating cash flow component, it allows more detailed analyses of operating cash flows. For example, the direct method would allow Dave & Buster's managers to determine that a 10 percent increase in product costs would have required an additional cash outflow to inventory suppliers of $20 million (= 10% × $204 million). To cover these additional cash outflows, Dave & Buster's could raise prices by 1.5 percent, which could increase cash inflow from customer collections by $19 million (= 1.5% × $1,274 million).

The direct method also provides financial statement users with more information to identify potential relationships between cash inflows and outflows. An increase in some activities, such as sales, generally leads to an increase in cash inflows from customers and cash outflows

EXHIBIT 12.9	Dave & Buster's Statement of Cash Flows (Direct Method)

DAVE & BUSTER'S ENTERTAINMENT, INC.
Statement of Cash Flows
For the Year Ended February 3, 2019

(in millions)		**Explanations**
Cash Flows from Operating Activities		**Cash flows related to day-to-day activities**
Cash collected from customers	$1,274	Cash collected on account and from any cash sales
Cash paid to suppliers of inventory	(204)	Cash paid in the current period to acquire inventory
Cash paid to employees and suppliers of services	(721)	Cash paid for salaries, wages, utilities, rent, etc.
Cash paid for interest	(13)	Separate reporting of these items fulfills the role of
Cash paid for income tax	(31)	the supplemental disclosures in Exhibit 12.7
Net cash provided by (used in) operating activities	305	**Indicates overall cash impact of operating activities**
Cash Flows from Investing Activities		**Cash flows related to long-term assets**
Purchase of property and equipment	(185)	Cash was used to purchase property and equipment
Purchase of intangible and other assets	(2)	Cash was used to purchase intangibles
Net cash provided by (used in) investing activities	(187)	**Indicates overall cash impact of investing activities**
Cash Flows from Financing Activities		**Cash flows from transactions with lenders, investors**
Additional long-term notes	265	Cash received from borrowing
Payments on long-term notes	(231)	Cash used to repay amounts previously borrowed
Proceeds from stock issuance	10	Cash received from issuing stock
Repurchase of stock into treasury	(149)	Cash paid to repurchase stock into treasury
Cash dividends paid	(11)	Cash used to pay dividends
Net cash provided by (used in) financing activities	(116)	**Indicates overall cash impact of financing activities**
Net Change in Cash and Cash Equivalents	2	$305 + $(187) + $(116) = $2
Cash and cash equivalents, beginning of year	20	Cash balance at beginning of the period
Cash and cash equivalents, end of year	$ 22	Cash balance at end of the period (**on balance sheet**)

to inventory suppliers. However, an increase in sales activity only loosely affects other cash outflows, such as interest paid on loans. Knowing the detailed components of operating cash flows allows analysts to more reliably predict a company's future cash flows.

In the remainder of this section, we describe how to prepare the statement of cash flows using the direct method. We focus on preparing just the operating activities section. Instructions on preparing the investing and financing activities sections, which are identical under both the direct and indirect methods, were presented earlier in this chapter.

Reporting Operating Cash Flows with the Direct Method

The direct method presents a summary of all operating transactions that result in either a debit or a credit to cash. It is prepared by adjusting each revenue and expense on the income statement from the accrual basis to the cash basis. We will complete this process for all of the revenues and expenses reported in the Dave & Buster's income statement in Exhibit 12.3 to show the calculations underlying the operating cash flows in Exhibit 12.9. Notice that, with the direct method, we work directly with each revenue and expense listed on the income statement and ignore any totals or subtotals (such as net income).

Converting Sales Revenues to Cash Inflows When sales are recorded, Accounts Receivable increases, and when cash is collected, Accounts Receivable decreases. This means that if Accounts Receivable decreases by $9 million, then cash collections were $9 million more than sales on account. To convert sales revenue to the cash collected, we need to add $9 million to Sales Revenue. The following flowchart shows this visually:

Using information from Dave & Buster's income statement and balance sheet presented in Exhibit 12.3, we compute cash collected from customers as follows:

Net Sales	$1,265
+ Decrease in Accounts Receivable	9
Cash collected from customers	$1,274

Accounts Receivable (A)

Beg. bal.	30		
		Decrease	9
End. bal.	21		

Converting Cost of Goods Sold to Cash Paid to Suppliers Cost of Goods Sold represents the cost of merchandise sold during the accounting period, which may be more or less than the amount of cash paid to suppliers during the period. In Dave & Buster's case, Inventory decreased during the year, implying the company bought less merchandise than it sold. If the company paid cash to suppliers of inventory, it would have paid less cash to suppliers than the amount of Cost of Goods Sold. So, the decrease in Inventory must be subtracted from Cost of Goods Sold to compute cash paid to suppliers.

Typically, companies buy inventory on account from suppliers (as indicated by an Accounts Payable balance on the balance sheet). Consequently, we need to consider more than just the change in Inventory to convert Cost of Goods Sold to cash paid to suppliers. The credit purchases and payments that are recorded in Accounts Payable also must be considered. Credit purchases increase Accounts Payable and cash payments decrease it. The overall increase in Accounts Payable reported by Dave & Buster's in Exhibit 12.3 indicates that cash payments were less than credit purchases, so the difference must be subtracted in the computation of total cash payments to suppliers.

In summary, to fully convert Cost of Goods Sold to a cash basis, you must consider changes in both Inventory and Accounts Payable as follows:

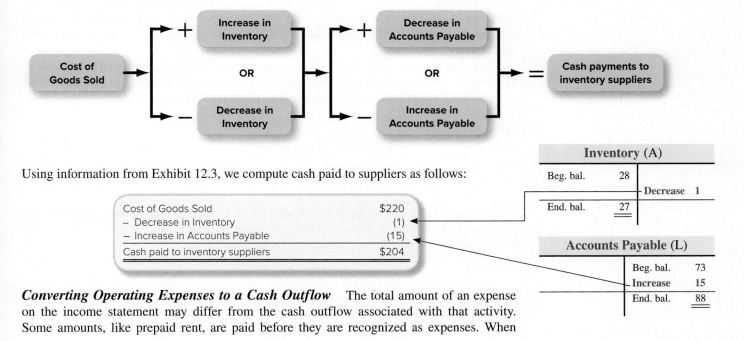

Using information from Exhibit 12.3, we compute cash paid to suppliers as follows:

Cost of Goods Sold	$220
− Decrease in Inventory	(1)
− Increase in Accounts Payable	(15)
Cash paid to inventory suppliers	$204

Inventory (A)

Beg. bal.	28		
		Decrease	1
End. bal.	27		

Accounts Payable (L)

	Beg. bal.	73
	Increase	15
	End. bal.	88

Converting Operating Expenses to a Cash Outflow The total amount of an expense on the income statement may differ from the cash outflow associated with that activity. Some amounts, like prepaid rent, are paid before they are recognized as expenses. When prepayments are made, the balance in the asset Prepaid Expenses increases. When expenses are recorded, Prepaid Expenses decreases. When we see Dave & Buster's prepaids increase by $2 million during the year, it means the company paid more cash than it recorded as operating expenses. This amount must be added in computing cash paid to service suppliers for operating expenses.

Some other expenses, like wages, are paid for after they are incurred. In this case, when expenses are recorded, the balance in Accrued Liabilities increases. When payments are made, Accrued Liabilities decreases. When Dave & Buster's Accrued Liabilities increase by $60 million, it means the company paid that much less cash than it recorded as operating expenses. This amount must be subtracted when computing cash paid to employees and service suppliers for operating expenses.

Generally, operating expenses such as Selling, General, and Administrative Expense can be converted from the accrual basis to the cash basis in the following manner:

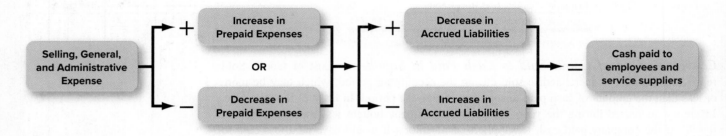

Prepaid Expenses (A)

Beg. bal.	19
Increase	2
End. bal.	21

Accrued Liabilities (L)

Beg. bal.	320
Increase	60
End. bal.	380

Using information from Exhibit 12.3, we can compute the total cash paid as follows:

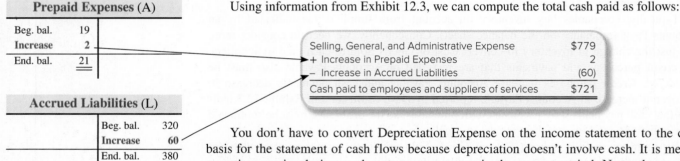

Selling, General, and Administrative Expense	$779
+ Increase in Prepaid Expenses	2
− Increase in Accrued Liabilities	(60)
Cash paid to employees and suppliers of services	$721

You don't have to convert Depreciation Expense on the income statement to the cash basis for the statement of cash flows because depreciation doesn't involve cash. It is merely reporting previously incurred costs as an expense in the current period. Noncash expenses like depreciation (or, similarly, revenues that don't affect cash) are omitted when the statement of cash flows is prepared using the direct method. Because of this, be sure to exclude any Depreciation Expense that might have been included in Selling, General, and Administrative Expense.

The next account listed on the income statement in Exhibit 12.3 is Interest Expense of $13 million. Because the balance sheet does not report Interest Payable, we will assume all of the interest was paid in cash. Thus, interest expense equals interest paid.

Interest Expense	$13
No change in Interest Payable	0
Cash paid for interest	$13

The same logic can be applied to income taxes. Dave & Buster's presents Income Tax Expense of $31 million. Exhibit 12.3 does not report an Income Tax Payable balance, so we assume income tax paid is equal to income tax expense.

Income Tax Expense	$31
No change in Income Tax Payable	0
Cash paid for income tax	$31

You have now seen, in this section, how to determine each amount reported in the operating activities section of the statement of cash flows in Exhibit 12.9 prepared using the direct method. For a quick check on your understanding of this material, complete the following Self-Study Practice.

💡 How's it going? — Self-Study Practice

Indicate whether the following items taken from a cash flow statement would be added (+), subtracted (−), or not included (0) when calculating cash flow from operations using the direct method.

- ☐ *a.* Cash paid to suppliers.
- ☐ *b.* Payment of dividends to stockholders.
- ☐ *c.* Cash collections from customers.
- ☐ *d.* Purchase of equipment for cash.
- ☐ *e.* Payments of interest to lenders.
- ☐ *f.* Payment of taxes to the government.

After you have finished, check your answers with the solution.

Solution to Self-Study Practice
a. −, b. 0, c. +, d. 0, e. −, f. −

SUPPLEMENT 12A | REPORTING DISPOSALS OF PROPERTY, PLANT, AND EQUIPMENT (INDIRECT METHOD)

Learning Objective 12-S1
Report cash flows from PPE disposals using the indirect method.

Whenever a company sells property, plant, and equipment (PPE), it records three things: (1) decreases in the PPE accounts for the assets sold, (2) an increase in the Cash account for the cash received on disposal, and (3) a gain if the cash received is more than the book value of the assets sold (or a loss if the cash received is less than the book value of the assets sold). The only part of this transaction that qualifies for the statement of cash flows is the cash received on disposal. This cash inflow is classified as an investing activity, just like the original equipment purchase.

Okay, that seems straightforward, so why do we have a separate chapter supplement for this kind of transaction? Well, there is one complicating factor. Gains and losses on disposal are included in the computation of net income, which is the starting point for the operating activities section when prepared using the indirect method. So, just as we had to add back the depreciation subtracted on the income statement, we also have to add back losses reported on disposals of PPE. As the following example shows, the flip side is true for gains on disposal (they are subtracted).

To illustrate, assume **Dave & Buster's** sold equipment for $7 million. The equipment originally cost $15 million and had $10 million of accumulated depreciation at the time of disposal. The disposal would have been analyzed and recorded as follows (in millions):

COACH'S TIP

If you're a little rusty on accounting for disposals, it would be worth your time to review that part of Chapter 9.

① Analyze

Assets		= Liabilities +	Stockholders' Equity	
Cash	+7		Gain on Disposal (+R)	+2
Accumulated Depreciation (−xA)	+10			
Equipment	−15			

2 Record

	Debit	Credit
Cash	7	
Accumulated Depreciation—Equipment (−xA)	10	
Equipment		15
Gain on Disposal		2

The $7 million inflow of cash would be reported as an investing activity. The $10 million and $15 million are taken into account when considering changes in the Accumulated Depreciation and Equipment account balances. Lastly, the $2 million Gain on Disposal was included in net income, so we must remove (subtract) it in the operating activities section of the statement. Thus, the disposal would affect two parts of the statement of cash flows:

Cash flows provided by (used in) operating activities

Net income	$117
Adjustments to reconcile net income to net cash from operations:	
. . .	. . .
Gain on disposal of equipment	(2)
. . .	. . .
Net cash provided by (used in) operating activities	. . .

Cash provided by (used in) investing activities

Additions to equipment	. . .
Cash received from disposal of equipment	7
. . .	. . .
Net cash provided by (used in) investing activities	. . .

Learning Objective 12-S2
Use the T-account approach for preparing an indirect method statement of cash flows.

SUPPLEMENT 12B T-ACCOUNT APPROACH (INDIRECT METHOD)

When we began our discussion of preparing the statement of cash flows, we noted that changes in cash must equal the sum of the changes in all other balance sheet accounts. Based on this idea, we used the following three steps to prepare the statement of cash flows:

1. Determine the change in each balance sheet account. From this year's ending balance, subtract this year's beginning balance (i.e., last year's ending balance).

2. Identify the cash flow category or categories to which each account relates. Use Exhibit 12.2 as a guide, but be aware that some accounts may include two categories of cash flows. Retained Earnings, for example, can include both financing cash flows (paying dividends) and operating cash flows (generating net income). Similarly, Accumulated Depreciation can be affected by operating activities (depreciation for using equipment in daily operations) as well as investing activities (disposing of equipment).

3. Create schedules that summarize operating, investing, and financing cash flows.

Instead of creating separate schedules for each section of the statement, many accountants prefer to prepare a single large T-account to represent the changes that have taken place in cash subdivided into the three sections of the cash flow statement. Such an account is presented in Panel A of Exhibit 12B.1. The cash account in Panel A shows increases in cash as debits and decreases in cash as credits. Note how each section matches the three schedules we prepared for Dave & Buster's cash flows presented in Exhibits 12.4, 12.5,

EXHIBIT 12B.1	T-Account Approach to Preparing the Statement of Cash Flows (Indirect Method)

Panel A: Changes in Cash Account

Cash (A)			
Operating			
(1) Net Income	117		
(2) Depreciation Expense	105		
(3) Accounts Receivable	9		
(4) Inventory	1	2	(5) Prepaid Expenses
(6) Accounts Payable	15		
(7) Accrued Liabilities	60		
Net cash flow provided by operating activities	305		
Investing			
		185	(8) Purchased Property and Equipment
		2	(9) Purchased Intangibles
		187	Net cash used in investing activities
Financing			
(10) Additional long-term notes	265	231	(11) Payment of long-term notes
(12) Proceeds from stock issuance	10	149	(13) Stock repurchased
		11	(14) Payment of cash dividends
		116	Net cash used in financing activities
Net increase in cash	2		
Beg. bal.	20		
End. bal.	22		

Panel B: Changes in Noncash Accounts

Accounts Receivable (A)			
Beg. bal.	30		
		(3) Decrease	9
End. bal.	21		

Inventory (A)			
Beg. bal.	28		
		(4) Decrease	1
End. bal.	27		

Prepaid Expenses (A)			
Beg. bal.	19		
(5) Increase	2		
End. bal.	21		

Property and Equipment (A)			
Beg. bal.	1,200		
(8) Purchases	185	Disposals	0
End. bal.	1,385		

Accumulated Depreciation (xA)			
		Beg. bal.	475
Disposals	0	(2) Depreciation	105
		End. bal.	580

Intangible and Other Assets (A)			
Beg. bal.	375		
(9) Purchases	2	Disposals	0
End. bal.	377		

Accounts Payable (L)			
		Beg. bal.	73
		(6) Increase	15
		End. bal.	88

Accrued Liabilities (L)			
		Beg. bal.	320
		(7) Increase	60
		End. bal.	380

Notes Payable (long-term) (L)			
		Beg. bal.	383
(11) Payments	231	(10) Borrowings	265
		End. bal.	417

Common Stock (SE)			
		Beg. bal.	321
		(12) Stock issued	10
		End. bal.	331

Treasury Stock (SE)			
Beg. bal.	148		
(13) Stock repurchased	149		
End. bal.	297		

Retained Earnings (SE)			
		Beg. bal.	248
(14) Dividends	11	(1) Net income	117
		End. bal.	354

and 12.6. Panel B includes the same T-accounts for the noncash balance sheet accounts we used in our discussion of each cash flow statement section in the body of the chapter. Note how each change in the noncash balance sheet accounts has a number referencing its accompanying change in the cash account. You can use the information in the cash flow T-account in Exhibit 12B.1 to prepare the statement of cash flows in proper format, as shown in Exhibit 12.7.

REVIEW THE CHAPTER

DEMONSTRATION CASE A: INDIRECT METHOD

During a recent year (ended April 30), Best Beverage Corp. reported net income of $25,000. The company also reported the following activities:

a.   Purchased equipment for $6,000 in cash.
b.   Issued common stock for $1,000 in cash.
c.   Depreciation of equipment was $9,000 for the year.

Its comparative balance sheet is presented below.

BEST BEVERAGE CORP.
Balance Sheet
Year Ended April 30

	Current Year	Prior Year
Assets		
Current assets:		
Cash and cash equivalents	$ 84,000	$ 48,700
Accounts receivable	53,600	50,000
Inventory	39,600	39,000
Prepaid expenses	5,500	15,000
Equipment	206,000	200,000
Accumulated depreciation	(126,700)	(117,700)
Total assets	$ 262,000	$ 235,000
Liabilities and Stockholders' Equity		
Current liabilities:		
Accounts payable	$ 48,000	$ 49,000
Accrued liabilities	44,000	42,000
Total current liabilities	92,000	91,000
Stockholders' equity:		
Common Stock	10,000	9,000
Retained earnings	160,000	135,000
Total stockholders' equity	170,000	144,000
Total liabilities and stockholders' equity	$ 262,000	$ 235,000

Required:

Based on this information, prepare the cash flow statement using the indirect method. Evaluate cash flows reported in the statement.

Suggested Solution

BEST BEVERAGE CORP. Balance Sheet At April 30			STEP ① CHANGE	STEP ② SCF SECTION
	Current Year	**Prior Year**		
Assets				
Cash and Cash Equivalents	$ 84,000	$ 48,700	+35,300	Cash
Accounts Receivable	53,600	50,000	+3,600	O
Inventory	39,600	39,000	+600	O
Prepaid Expenses	5,500	15,000	−9,500	O
Equipment	206,000	200,000	+6,000	I
Accum. Depreciation	(126,700)	(117,700)	−9,000	O
Total Assets	$ 262,000	$ 235,000		
Liabilities and Stockholders' Equity				
Accounts Payable	$ 48,000	$ 49,000	−1,000	O
Accrued Liabilities	44,000	42,000	+2,000	O
Common Stock	10,000	9,000	+1,000	F
Retained Earnings	160,000	135,000	+25,000	O
Total Liabilities and Stockholders' Equity	$ 262,000	$ 235,000		

BEST BEVERAGE CORP. Statement of Cash Flows For the Year Ended April 30	
Cash Flows from Operating Activities	
Net income	$25,000
Adjustments to reconcile net income to net cash provided by operating activities:	
Depreciation	9,000
Changes in current assets and current liabilities:	
Accounts Receivable	(3,600)
Inventory	(600)
Prepaid Expenses	9,500
Accounts Payable	(1,000)
Accrued Liabilities	2,000
Net cash provided by operating activities	40,300
Cash Flows from Investing Activities	
Purchase of equipment	(6,000)
Net cash used in investing activities	(6,000)
Cash Flows from Financing Activities	
Proceeds from issuance of common stock	1,000
Net cash provided by financing activities	1,000
Net Increase in Cash and Cash Equivalents	35,300
Cash and cash equivalents, beginning of year	48,700
Cash and cash equivalents, end of year	$84,000

Best Beverage reported positive profits but even higher cash flows from operations for the year. The difference between the two is caused primarily by depreciation and decreases in prepaid expenses. That operating cash flows are higher than net income suggests Best Beverage is carefully managing its current assets and current liabilities so that it has sufficient cash to cover the costs of purchases of additional equipment without the need to borrow additional funds. This increase in cash can be used for future expansion or to pay future dividends to stockholders.

DEMONSTRATION CASE B: DIRECT METHOD

The managers at Best Beverage Corp. would like to know the impact on cash flows of a 10 percent increase in product costs.

Required:

Based on the information given in Demonstration Case A and the following income statement, prepare a statement of cash flows using the direct method. By what amount would cash outflows have increased if product costs were 10 percent higher? By what percentage would Best Beverage have to increase its prices to cover a 10 percent increase in cash outflows for product costs? (Assume a price increase will not adversely affect sales volume.)

Given Information

BEST BEVERAGE CORP.
Income Statement
For the Year Ended April 30

Sales Revenue	$636,000
Cost of Goods Sold	240,000
Gross Profit	396,000
Office Expense	242,000
Depreciation Expense	9,000
Income from Operations	145,000
Interest Expense	0
Income before Income Taxes	145,000
Income Tax Expense	120,000
Net Income	$ 25,000

Suggested Solution

BEST BEVERAGE CORP.
Statement of Cash Flows
For the Year Ended April 30

Cash Flows from Operating Activities	
Cash collected from customers	$632,400
Cash paid to suppliers of inventory	(241,600)
Cash paid to employees and suppliers of services	(230,500)
Cash paid for income taxes	(120,000)
Net cash provided by operating activities	40,300
Cash Flows from Investing Activities	
Purchase of equipment	(6,000)
Net cash used in investing activities	(6,000)
Cash Flows from Financing Activities	
Proceeds from issuance of common stock	1,000
Net cash provided by financing activities	1,000
Net Increase in Cash and Cash Equivalents	35,300
Cash and cash equivalents, beginning of year	48,700
Cash and cash equivalents, end of year	$ 84,000

Cash collected from customers = Sales Revenue − Increase in Accounts Receivable
= $636,000 − 3,600 = $632,400
Cash paid for inventory = Cost of Goods Sold + Increase in Inventory
+ Decrease in Accounts Payable
= $240,000 + 600 + 1,000 = $241,600
Cash paid to employees, etc. = Office Expense − Decrease in Prepaids −
Increase in Accrued Liabilities
= $242,000 − 9,500 − 2,000 = $230,500

If product costs were 10 percent higher, total cash paid to inventory suppliers would have increased by $24,160 ($241,600 × 10%). To cover these additional cash outflows, Best Beverage could increase prices by $24,160, which compared to current collections from customers is 3.8 percent ($24,160 ÷ $632,400).

CHAPTER SUMMARY

LO 12-1   **Identify cash flows arising from operating, investing, and financing activities.**

- The statement has three main sections: Cash flows from operating activities, which are related to earning income from normal operations; Cash flows from investing activities, which are related to the acquisition and sale of productive assets; and Cash flows from financing activities, which are related to external financing of the enterprise.

- The net cash inflow or outflow for the period is the same amount as the increase or decrease in cash and cash equivalents for the period on the balance sheet. Cash equivalents are highly liquid investments purchased within three months of maturity.

Report cash flows from operating activities, using the indirect method.

- The indirect method for reporting cash flows from operating activities reports a conversion of net income to net cash flow from operating activities.

- The conversion involves additions and subtractions for (1) noncash expenses (such as depreciation expense) and revenues that do not affect current assets or current liabilities and (2) changes in each of the individual current assets (other than cash) and current liabilities (other than debt to financial institutions, which relates to financing).

Report cash flows from investing activities. LO 12-3

- Investing activities reported on the cash flow statement include cash payments to acquire fixed assets and investments and cash proceeds from the sale of fixed assets and investments.

Report cash flows from financing activities. LO 12-4

- Cash inflows from financing activities include cash proceeds from issuance of debt and common stock. Cash outflows include principal payments on debt, cash paid for the repurchase of the company's stock, and cash dividend payments. Cash payments associated with interest are a cash flow from operating activities.

Interpret cash flows from operating, investing, and financing activities. LO 12-5

- A healthy company will generate positive cash flows from operations, some of which will be used to pay for equipment purchases and dividends. Any additional cash (called free cash flow) can be used to further expand the business, pay down some of the company's debt, or simply build up the cash balance. A company is in trouble if it is unable to generate positive cash flows from operations in the long run because eventually creditors will stop lending to the company and stockholders will stop investing in it.

Report and interpret cash flows from operating activities, using the direct method. LO 12-6

- The direct method for reporting cash flows from operating activities accumulates all of the operating transactions that result in either a debit or a credit to cash into categories. The most common inflows are cash received from customers and dividends and interest on investments. The most common outflows are cash paid for purchase of services and goods for resale, salaries and wages, income taxes, and interest on liabilities. It is prepared by adjusting each item on the income statement from an accrual basis to a cash basis.

KEY TERMS

Cash Flows from Financing Activities p. 559

Cash Flows from Investing Activities p. 558

Cash Flows from Operating Activities (Cash Flows from Operations) p. 558

Direct Method p. 561

Indirect Method p. 561

See complete definitions in the glossary in the back of this text.

HOMEWORK HELPER

Helpful reminders

- Although some exceptions exist, operating activities typically affect current assets and current liabilities; investing activities typically affect noncurrent assets; and financing activities typically affect noncurrent liabilities and stockholders' equity accounts.

- The typical additions and subtractions to reconcile net income with cash flows from operating activities when using the indirect method are as follows:

COACH'S TIP

Notice in this table that, to reconcile net income to cash flows from operations, you
- add the change when the current asset decreases or current liability increases.
- subtract the change when the current asset increases or current liability decreases.

Item	Additions and Subtractions to Reconcile Net Income to Cash Flows from Operating Activities*	
	When Item Increases	When Item Decreases
Depreciation	+	n/a
Accounts Receivable	–	+
Inventory	–	+
Prepaid Expenses	–	+
Accounts Payable	+	–
Accrued Liabilities	+	–

*Certain items have been eliminated from this statement to simplify presentation; these items (gains/losses on asset disposals) are discussed in Supplement 12A.

- The following adjustments are commonly made to convert income statement items to the related operating cash flow amounts for the direct method:

Income Statement Account	+/– Change in Balance Sheet Account(s)	= Operating Cash Flow
Sales Revenue	+ Decrease in Accounts Receivable (A) – Increase in Accounts Receivable (A)	= Cash collected from customers
Cost of Goods Sold	+ Increase in Inventory (A) – Decrease in Inventory (A) – Increase in Accounts Payable (L) + Decrease in Accounts Payable (L)	= Cash paid to suppliers of inventory
Other Expenses	+ Increase in Prepaid Expenses (A) – Decrease in Prepaid Expenses (A) – Increase in Accrued Expenses (L) + Decrease in Accrued Expenses (L)	= Cash paid to employees and suppliers of services (e.g., wages, rent, utilities)
Interest Expense	– Increase in Interest Payable (L) + Decrease in Interest Payable (L)	= Cash paid for interest
Income Tax Expense	– Increase in Income Taxes Payable (Deferred Taxes) (L) + Decrease in Income Taxes Payable (Deferred Taxes) (L)	= Cash paid for income tax

Frequent mistakes

- Do not merely report the net change in all balance sheet accounts. Some accounts (typically those affected by investing and financing activities) include both inflows and outflows of cash, which must be reported separately.

PRACTICE MATERIAL

QUESTIONS (⊖Symbol indicates questions that require analysis from more than one perspective.)

1. Compare the purposes of the income statement, the balance sheet, and the statement of cash flows.

2. What information does the statement of cash flows report that is not reported on the other required financial statements?

3. What are cash equivalents? How are they reported on the statement of cash flows?

4. What are the major categories of business activities reported on the statement of cash flows? Define each of these activities.

5. What are the typical cash inflows from operating activities? What are the typical cash outflows from operating activities?

6. Describe the types of items used to compute cash flows from operating activities under the two alternative methods of reporting.

7. Under the indirect method, depreciation expense is added to net income to report cash flows from operating activities. Does depreciation cause an inflow of cash?

8. Explain why cash outflows during the period for purchases and salaries are not specifically reported on a statement of cash flows prepared using the indirect method.

9. Explain why a $50,000 increase in inventory during the year must be included in computing cash flows from operating activities under both the direct and indirect methods.

10. Loan covenants require that E-Gadget Corporation (EGC) generate $200,000 cash from operating activities each year. Without intervening during the last month of the current year, EGC will generate only $180,000 cash from operations. What are the pros and cons of each of the following possible interventions: (*a*) pressuring customers to pay overdue accounts, (*b*) delaying payment of amounts owing to suppliers, and (*c*) purchasing additional equipment to increase depreciation? ⊖

11. As a junior analyst, you are evaluating the financial performance of Digilog Corporation. Impressed by this year's growth in sales (20 percent increase), receivables (40 percent increase), and inventories (50 percent increase), you plan to report a favorable evaluation of the company. Your supervisor cautions you that those increases may signal difficulties rather than successes. When you ask what she means, she just says you should look at the company's statement of cash flows. What do you think you will find there? What are the cash flow effects when the balances in a company's receivables and inventory increase faster than its sales? ⊖

12. What are the typical cash inflows from investing activities? What are the typical cash outflows from investing activities?

13. What are the typical cash inflows from financing activities? What are the typical cash outflows from financing activities?

14. What are noncash investing and financing activities? Give one example. How are noncash investing and financing activities reported on the statement of cash flows?

15. (Supplement 12A) How is the sale of equipment reported on the statement of cash flows using the indirect method?

MULTIPLE CHOICE

1. Where is the overall change in cash shown in the statement of cash flows?

   a. In the top part, before the operating activities section.
   b. In one of the operating, investing, or financing activities sections.
   c. In the bottom part, following the financing activities section.
   d. None of the above.

2. In what order do the three sections of the statement of cash flows appear when reading from top to bottom?

   a. Financing, investing, operating.
   b. Investing, operating, financing.
   c. Operating, financing, investing.
   d. Operating, investing, financing.

3. Total cash inflow in the operating section of the statement of cash flows should include which of the following?

   a. Cash received from customers at the point of sale.
   b. Cash collections from customer accounts receivable.
   c. Cash received in advance of revenue recognition (deferred revenue).
   d. All of the above.

4. If the balance in Prepaid Expenses increased during the year, what action should be taken on the statement of cash flows when following the indirect method, *and why*?

   a. The change in the account balance should be subtracted from net income because the net increase in Prepaid Expenses did not impact net income but did reduce the cash balance.
   b. The change in the account balance should be added to net income because the net increase in Prepaid Expenses did not impact net income but did increase the cash balance.

   c. The net change in Prepaid Expenses should be subtracted from net income to eliminate the effect of adding it in the income statement.
   d. The net change in Prepaid Expenses should be added to net income to eliminate the effect of subtracting it in the income statement.

5. Which of the following would not appear in the investing section of the statement of cash flows?

   a. Purchase of inventory.
   b. Sale of investments.
   c. Purchase of land.
   d. All of the above would appear in the investing section of the statement of cash flows.

6. Which of the following items would not appear in the financing section of the statement of cash flows?

   a. The issuance of the company's own stock.
   b. The repayment of debt.
   c. The payment of dividends.
   d. All of the above would appear in the financing section of the statement of cash flows.

7. Which of the following is not added when computing cash flows from operations using the indirect method?

   a. The net increase in accounts payable.
   b. The net decrease in accounts receivable.
   c. The net decrease in inventory.
   d. All of the above should be added.

8. If a company engages in a material noncash transaction, which of the following is required?

   a. The company must include an explanatory narrative or schedule accompanying the statement of cash flows.
   b. No disclosure is necessary.

c. The company must include an explanatory narrative or schedule accompanying the balance sheet.

d. It must be reported in the investing and financing sections of the statement of cash flows.

9. The *total* change in cash shown on the statement of cash flows for the year should agree with which of the following?

   a. The difference in Retained Earnings when reviewing the comparative balance sheet.

   b. Net income or net loss as found on the income statement.

   c. The difference in cash when reviewing the comparative balance sheet.

   d. None of the above.

10. If a company's current assets (such as accounts receivable and inventories) are allowed to grow out of control, which of the following would occur?

   a. Cash flows from investing activities would be reduced.

   b. Cash flows from operating activities would be reduced.

   c. Cash flows from financing activities would increase.

   d. None of the above.

For answers to the Multiple-Choice Questions **see page Q1** located in the last section of the book.

MINI-EXERCISES

LO 12-1, 12-5

M12-1 Identifying Companies from Cash Flow Patterns

Based on the cash flows shown, classify each of the following cases as a growing start-up company (S), a healthy established company (E), or an established company facing financial difficulties (F).

	Case 1	Case 2	Case 3
Cash provided by (used for) operating activities	$ 3,000	$(120,000)	$ 80,000
Cash provided by (used for) investing activities	(70,000)	10,000	(40,000)
Cash provided by (used for) financing activities	75,000	75,000	(30,000)
Net change in cash	8,000	(35,000)	10,000
Cash position at beginning of year	2,000	40,000	30,000
Cash position at end of year	$ 10,000	$ 5,000	$ 40,000

LO 12-1, 12-2

The Buckle, Inc.

M12-2 Matching Items Reported to Cash Flow Statement Categories (Indirect Method)

The Buckle, Inc., included the following in its statement of cash flows presented using the indirect method. Indicate whether each item is disclosed in the operating activities (O), investing activities (I), or financing activities (F) section of the statement or use (NA) if the item does not appear on the statement.

____ 1. Purchase of investments.

____ 2. Proceeds from issuance of stock.

____ 3. Purchase of equipment.

____ 4. Depreciation.

____ 5. Accounts payable (decrease).

____ 6. Inventory (increase).

LO 12-2

M12-3 Determining the Effects of Account Changes on Cash Flows from Operating Activities (Indirect Method)

Indicate whether each item would be added (+) or subtracted (−) in the computation of cash flows from operating activities using the indirect method.

____ 1. Depreciation.

____ 2. Inventory decrease.

____ 3. Accounts payable decrease.

____ 4. Accounts receivable increase.

____ 5. Accrued liabilities increase.

LO 12-2

M12-4 Computing Cash Flows from Operating Activities (Indirect Method)

For each of the following independent cases, compute cash flows from operating activities. Assume the list below includes all balance sheet accounts related to operating activities.

	Case A	Case B	Case C
Net income	$310,000	$ 15,000	$420,000
Depreciation expense	40,000	150,000	80,000
Accounts receivable increase (decrease)	100,000	(200,000)	(20,000)
Inventory increase (decrease)	(50,000)	35,000	50,000
Accounts payable increase (decrease)	(50,000)	120,000	70,000
Accrued liabilities increase (decrease)	60,000	(220,000)	(40,000)

M12-5 Computing Cash Flows from Operating Activities (Indirect Method)

LO 12-2

For the following two independent cases, show the cash flows from operating activities section of the statement of cash flows for year 2 using the indirect method.

	Case A		Case B	
	Year 2	Year 1	Year 2	Year 1
Sales Revenue	$11,000	$9,000	$21,000	$18,000
Cost of Goods Sold	6,000	5,500	12,000	11,000
Gross Profit	5,000	3,500	9,000	7,000
Depreciation Expense	1,000	1,000	1,500	1,500
Salaries and Wages Expense	2,500	2,000	5,000	5,000
Net Income	$ 1,500	$ 500	$ 2,500	$ 500
Accounts Receivable	$ 300	$ 400	$ 750	$ 600
Inventory	750	500	730	800
Accounts Payable	800	700	800	850
Salaries and Wages Payable	1,000	1,200	200	250

M12-6 Computing Cash Flows from Investing Activities

LO 12-3

Based on the following information, compute cash flows from investing activities under GAAP.

Cash collections from customers	$800
Purchase of used equipment	200
Depreciation expense	200
Sale of investments	450
Dividends received	100
Interest received	200

M12-7 Computing Cash Flows from Financing Activities

LO 12-4

Based on the following information, compute cash flows from financing activities under GAAP.

Purchase of investments	$ 250
Dividends paid	1,200
Interest paid	400
Additional borrowing from bank	2,800

M12-8 Computing Cash Flows under IFRS

LO 12-1

Using the data from M12-6, calculate the maximum investing cash inflows that could be reported under IFRS. Using data from M12-7, calculate the maximum financing cash flows that could be reported under IFRS.

M12-9 Reporting Noncash Investing and Financing Activities

LO 12-3, 12-4

Which of the following transactions would be considered noncash investing and financing activities?

_____ 1. Additional borrowing from bank.

_____ 2. Purchase of equipment with investments.

_____ 3. Dividends paid in cash.

_____ 4. Purchase of a building with a promissory note.

LO 12-5 **M12-10 Interpreting Cash Flows from Operating, Investing, and Financing Activities**

Quantum Dots, Inc., is a nanotechnology company that manufactures "quantum dots," which are tiny pieces of silicon consisting of 100 or more molecules. Quantum dots can be used to illuminate very small objects, enabling scientists to see the blood vessels beneath a mouse's skin ripple with each heartbeat, at the rate of 100 times per second. Evaluate this research-intensive company's cash flows, assuming the following was reported in its statement of cash flows.

	Current Year	Previous Year
Cash Flows from Operating Activities		
Net cash provided by (used for) operating activities	$ (50,790)	$ (46,730)
Cash Flows from Investing Activities		
Purchases of research equipment	(250,770)	(480,145)
Proceeds from selling all short-term investments	35,000	—
Net cash provided by (used for) investing activities	(215,770)	(480,145)
Cash Flows from Financing Activities		
Additional long-term debt borrowed	100,000	200,000
Proceeds from stock issuance	140,000	200,000
Cash dividends paid	—	(10,000)
Net cash provided by (used for) financing activities	240,000	390,000
Net increase (decrease) in cash	(26,560)	(136,875)
Cash at beginning of period	29,025	165,900
Cash at end of period	$ 2,465	$ 29,025

LO 12-5 **M12-11 Evaluating Cash Flows**

Based on the following cash flow graphs, determine whether each of the companies shown would be considered in the Introductory, Growth, Mature, or Decline phase for the year indicated.

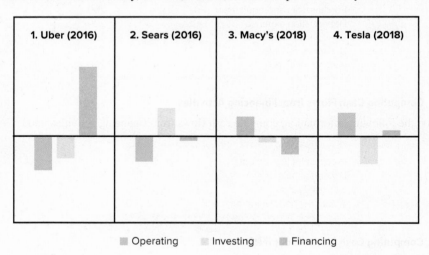

1. Uber (2016)	2. Sears (2016)	3. Macy's (2018)	4. Tesla (2018)

■ Operating   ■ Investing   ■ Financing

LO 12-5 **M12-12 Calculating Cash Flows**

Assume Weartronics Clothing reported net cash provided by operating activities of $200,000, cash paid for dividends of $20,000, cash received from stock issuance of $50,000, cash paid for equipment purchases of $120,000, cash received from bank loan advances of $10,000, and cash paid for intangible assets of $10,000. Calculate the following:

1. Net cash provided by (used in) investing activities.
2. Net cash provided by (used in) financing activities.

3. Net increase (decrease) in cash.
4. Free cash flow.

M12-13 Calculating Cash Flows

LO 12-5

Tech Gear Corp. started the year with $100,000 cash and reported net cash provided by operating activities of $200,000, cash paid for dividends of $40,000, cash received from stock issuance of $30,000, cash paid for equipment purchases of $150,000, cash paid for intangible assets of $100,000, and cash paid on bank loan of $35,000. Calculate the following:

1. Net cash provided by (used in) investing activities.
2. Net cash provided by (used in) financing activities.
3. Ending cash.
4. Free cash flow.

M12-14 Matching Items Reported to Cash Flow Statement Categories (Direct Method)

LO 12-1, 12-6

Prestige Manufacturing Corporation reports the following items in its statement of cash flows presented using the direct method. Indicate whether each item is disclosed in the operating activities (O), investing activities (I), or financing activities (F) section of the statement under GAAP or use (NA) if the item does not appear on the statement.

____ 1. Payment for equipment purchase.

____ 2. Repayments of bank loan.

____ 3. Dividends paid.

____ 4. Proceeds from issuance of stock.

____ 5. Interest paid.

____ 6. Receipts from customers.

M12-15 Computing Cash Flows from Operating Activities (Direct Method)

LO 12-6

For each of the following independent cases, compute cash flows from operating activities using the direct method. Assume the list below includes all items relevant to operating activities.

	Case A	Case B	Case C
Sales revenue	$65,000	$55,000	$96,000
Cost of goods sold	35,000	26,000	65,000
Depreciation expense	10,000	2,000	26,000
Salaries and wages expense	5,000	13,000	8,000
Net income (loss)	$15,000	$14,000	$ (3,000)
Accounts receivable increase (decrease)	$ (1,000)	$ 4,000	$ 3,000
Inventory increase (decrease)	2,000	0	(3,000)
Accounts payable increase (decrease)	0	2,500	(1,000)
Salaries and wages payable increase (decrease)	1,500	(2,000)	1,100

M12-16 Computing Cash Flows from Operating Activities (Direct Method)

LO 12-6

Refer to the two cases presented in M12-5, and for each case show the cash flow from operating activities section of the Year 2 statement of cash flows using the direct method.

EXERCISES

🅜 **connect**

E12-1 Matching Items Reported to Cash Flow Statement Categories (Indirect Method)

LO 12-1, 12-2

NIKE, Inc.

NIKE, Inc., is the best-known sports shoe, apparel, and equipment company in the world because of its association with athletes such as LeBron James, Brooks Koepka, and Bianca Andreescu. Some of the items included in its recent statement of cash flows presented using the indirect method are listed here.

Indicate whether each item is disclosed in the operating activities (O), investing activities (I), or financing activities (F) section of the statement or use (NA) if the item does not appear on the statement.

____ 1. Additions to long-term debt.

____ 2. Depreciation.

____ 3. Additions to equipment.

____ 4. Increase (decrease) in notes payable. (The amount is owed to financial institutions.)

____ 5. (Increase) decrease in other current assets.

____ 6. Cash received from disposal of equipment.

____ 7. Reductions in long-term debt.

____ 8. Issuance of stock.

____ 9. (Increase) decrease in inventory.

____ 10. Net income.

LO 12-2

E12-2 Understanding the Computation of Cash Flows from Operating Activities (Indirect Method)

Suppose your company sells services of $180 in exchange for $110 cash and $70 on account.

Required:

1. Show the journal entry to record this transaction.
2. Identify the amount that should be reported as net cash flow from operating activities.
3. Identify the amount that would be included in net income.
4. Show how the indirect method would convert net income (requirement 3) to net cash flow from operating activities (requirement 2).
5. What general rule about converting net income to operating cash flows is revealed by your answer to requirement 4?

LO 12-2

E12-3 Understanding the Computation of Cash Flows from Operating Activities (Indirect Method)

Suppose your company sells services for $325 cash this month. Your company also pays $100 in salaries and wages, which includes $15 that was payable at the end of the previous month and $85 for salaries and wages of this month.

Required:

1. Show the journal entries to record these transactions.
2. Calculate the amount that should be reported as net cash flow from operating activities.
3. Calculate the amount that should be reported as net income.
4. Show how the indirect method would convert net income (requirement 3) to net cash flow from operating activities (requirement 2).
5. What general rule about converting net income to operating cash flows is revealed by your answer to requirement 4?

LO 12-2

E12-4 Understanding the Computation of Cash Flows from Operating Activities (Indirect Method)

Suppose your company sells services of $150 in exchange for $120 cash and $30 on account. Depreciation of $50 relating to equipment also is recorded.

Required:

1. Show the journal entries to record these transactions.
2. Calculate the amount that should be reported as net cash flow from operating activities.
3. Calculate the amount that should be reported as net income.
4. Show how the indirect method would convert net income (requirement 3) to net cash flow from operating activities (requirement 2).
5. What general rule about converting net income to operating cash flows is revealed by your answer to requirement 4?

E12-5 Understanding the Computation of Cash Flows from Operating Activities (Indirect Method)

Suppose your company sells goods for $300, of which $200 is received in cash and $100 is on account. The goods cost your company $125 and were paid for in a previous period. Your company also recorded salaries and wages of $70, of which only $30 has been paid in cash.

Required:

1. Show the journal entries to record these transactions.
2. Calculate the amount that should be reported as net cash flow from operating activities.
3. Calculate the amount that should be reported as net income.
4. Show how the indirect method would convert net income (requirement 3) to net cash flow from operating activities (requirement 2).
5. What general rule about converting net income to operating cash flows is revealed by your answer to requirement 4?

E12-6 Preparing and Evaluating a Simple Statement of Cash Flows (Indirect Method)

Suppose your company reports $160 of net income and $40 of cash dividends paid, and its comparative balance sheet indicates the following.

	Beginning	Ending
Cash	$ 35	$205
Accounts Receivable	75	175
Inventory	245	135
Total	$355	$515
Salaries and Wages Payable	$ 10	$ 50
Common Stock	100	100
Retained Earnings	245	365
Total	$355	$515

Required:

1. Prepare the operating activities section of the statement of cash flows, using the indirect method.
2. Identify the most important cause of the difference between the company's net income and net cash flow from operating activities.

E12-7 Preparing and Evaluating a Simple Statement of Cash Flows (Indirect Method)

Suppose the income statement for Goggle Company reports $95 of net income, after deducting depreciation of $35. The company bought equipment costing $60 and obtained a long-term bank loan for $70. The company's comparative balance sheet, at December 31, is presented here.

	Previous Year	Current Year	Change
Cash	$ 35	$ 240	
Accounts Receivable	75	175	
Inventory	260	135	
Equipment	500	560	
Accumulated Depreciation—Equipment	(45)	(80)	
Total	$825	$1,030	
Salaries and Wages Payable	$ 10	$ 50	
Notes Payable (long-term)	445	515	
Common Stock	10	10	
Retained Earnings	360	455	
Total	$825	$1,030	

Required:

1. Calculate the change in each balance sheet account and indicate whether each account relates to operating, investing, and/or financing activities.
2. Prepare a statement of cash flows using the indirect method.
3. In one sentence, explain why an increase in accounts receivable is subtracted.
4. In one sentence, explain why a decrease in inventory is added.
5. In one sentence, explain why an increase in salaries and wages payable is added.
6. Are the cash flows typical of a start-up, healthy, or troubled company? Explain.

LO 12-2   **E12-8 Reporting Cash Flows from Operating Activities (Indirect Method)**

The following information pertains to Guy's Gear Company:

Sales		$80,000
Expenses:		
Cost of Goods Sold	$50,000	
Depreciation Expense	6,000	
Salaries and Wages Expense	12,000	68,000
Net Income		$12,000
Accounts Receivable decrease	$ 4,000	
Inventory increase	8,000	
Salaries and Wages Payable increase	750	

Required:

Present the operating activities section of the statement of cash flows for Guy's Gear Company using the indirect method.

LO 12-2, 12-5   **E12-9 Reporting and Interpreting Cash Flows from Operating Activities from an Analyst's Perspective (Indirect Method)**

New Vision Company completed its income statement and balance sheet and provided the following information:

Service Revenue		$66,000
Expenses:		
Salaries and Wages	$42,000	
Depreciation	7,300	
Utilities	6,000	
Office	1,700	57,000
Net Income		$ 9,000
Decrease in Accounts Receivable	$12,000	
Paid cash for equipment	5,000	
Increase in Salaries and Wages Payable	9,000	
Decrease in Accounts Payable	4,250	

Required:

1. Present the operating activities section of the statement of cash flows for New Vision Company using the indirect method.
2. Of the potential causes of differences between cash flow from operations and net income, which are the most important to financial analysts?

E12-10 Computing and Interpreting Cash Flows from Operating Activities from an Analyst's Perspective (Indirect Method)

LO 12-2, 12-5

Pizza International, Inc., reported the following information (in thousands):

Operating Activities			
Net Income	$ 100	Decrease in accounts payable	$ 8,720
Depreciation	33,305	Increase in accrued liabilities	719
Increase in receivables	170	Decrease in income taxes payable	2,721
Decrease in inventory	643	Payments on notes payable	12,691
Increase in prepaid expenses	664	Cash paid for equipment	29,073

Required:

1. Based on this information, compute cash flow from operating activities using the indirect method.
2. What was the primary reason that Pizza International was able to report large positive cash flow from operations despite nearly having a net loss?

E12-11 Inferring Balance Sheet Changes from the Cash Flow Statement (Indirect Method)

LO 12-2

Colgate-Palmolive

Colgate-Palmolive was founded in 1806. Its statement of cash flows reported the following information (in millions) for the six months ended June 30, 2019:

Operating Activities	
Net Income	$1,218
Depreciation	256
Cash effect of changes in	
Accounts Receivable	(178)
Inventory	(63)
Accounts Payable	(14)
Other	30
Net Cash Provided by Operations	$1,249

Required:

Based on the information reported in the operating activities section of the statement of cash flows for Colgate-Palmolive, indicate whether the following accounts increased (I) or decreased (D) during the period: (a) Accounts Receivable, (b) Inventory, and (c) Accounts Payable.

E12-12 Inferring Balance Sheet Changes from the Cash Flow Statement (Indirect Method)

LO 12-2

A statement of cash flows contained the following information:

Operating Activities	
Net Income	$14,013
Depreciation	1,027
Changes in current assets and current liabilities:	
Accounts Receivable	(2,142)
Inventory	596
Accounts Payable	6,307
Accrued Liabilities	(1,217)
Net Cash Provided by Operations	$18,584

Required:

Determine whether the following account balances increased (I) or decreased (D) during the period: (*a*) Accounts Receivable, (*b*) Inventory, (*c*) Accounts Payable, and (*d*) Accrued Liabilities.

LO 12-1, 12-2, 12-3, 12-4, 12-5

E12-13 Preparing and Evaluating a Statement of Cash Flows (Indirect Method) from Comparative Balance Sheets and Income Statements

Consultex, Inc., was founded in 2018 as a small financial consulting business. The company had done reasonably well in 2018–2020 but started noticing its cash dwindle early in 2021. In January 2021, Consultex had paid $16,000 to purchase land and repaid $2,000 principal on an existing promissory note. In March, the company paid $2,000 cash for dividends and $1,000 to repurchase and eliminate Consultex stock that had previously been issued for $1,000. To improve its cash position, Consultex borrowed $5,000 by signing a new promissory note in May and also issued stock to a new private investor for $12,000 cash. Year-end comparative balance sheets and income statements are presented below.

CONSULTEX, INC.
Balance Sheet
October 31

	2021	2020
Assets		
Cash	$11,000	$14,000
Accounts Receivable	14,000	12,000
Prepaid Rent	2,000	3,000
Land	26,000	10,000
Total Assets	$53,000	$39,000
Liabilities and Stockholders' Equity		
Salaries and Wages Payable	$ 2,000	$ 3,000
Income Taxes Payable	1,000	1,000
Notes Payable (long-term)	15,000	12,000
Common Stock	20,000	9,000
Retained Earnings	15,000	14,000
Total Liabilities and Stockholders' Equity	$53,000	$39,000

CONSULTEX, INC.
Income Statement
For the Year Ended October 31

	2021	2020
Sales Revenue	$158,000	$161,000
Salaries and Wages Expense	98,000	97,000
Rent Expense	36,000	30,000
Utilities Expenses	19,700	20,000
Income before Income Tax Expense	4,300	14,000
Income Tax Expense	1,300	4,200
Net Income	$ 3,000	$ 9,800

Requirements:

1. Prepare a properly formatted Statement of Cash Flows for Consultex, Inc., for the year ended October 31, 2021 (using the indirect method).
2. What one thing can Consultex reasonably change in 2022 to avoid depleting its cash?

E12-14 Calculating and Understanding Operating Cash Flows Relating to Inventory Purchases   **LO 12-2**
       (Indirect Method)

The following information was reported by three companies. When completing the requirements, assume that any and all purchases on account are for inventory.

	Aztec Corporation	Bikes Unlimited	Campus Cycles
Cost of goods sold	$175,000	$175,000	$350,000
Inventory purchases from suppliers made using cash	200,000	0	200,000
Inventory purchases from suppliers made on account	0	200,000	200,000
Cash payments to suppliers on account	0	160,000	160,000
Beginning inventory	100,000	100,000	200,000
Ending inventory	125,000	125,000	250,000
Beginning accounts payable	0	80,000	80,000
Ending accounts payable	0	120,000	120,000

Required:

1. What amount did each company deduct on the income statement related to inventory?
2. What total amount did each company pay out in cash during the period related to inventory purchased with cash and on account?
3. By what amount do your answers in requirements 1 and 2 differ for each company?
4. By what amount did each company's inventory increase (decrease)? By what amount did each company's accounts payable increase (decrease)?
5. Using the indirect method of presentation, what amount(s) must each company add (deduct) from net income to convert from accrual to cash basis?
6. Describe any similarities between your answers to requirements 3 and 5. Are these answers the same? Why or why not?

E12-15 Reporting Cash Flows from Investing and Financing Activities   **LO 12-3, 12-4**

Zumiez Inc. is a Washington-based clothing and ski/skate accessories retailer. In a recent quarter,   Zumiez Inc.
it reported the following activities:

Net income	$1,770	Payments to reduce notes payable (long-term)	$24,233
Purchase of equipment	9,061	Proceeds from sale of marketable securities	41,200
Borrowings under line of credit (bank)	29,227	Purchase of marketable securities	35,046
Proceeds from issuance of common stock	426	Income taxes paid	7,362
Cash received from customers	421,158	Other fixed assets purchased with promissory notes	3,496

Required:

Based on this information, present the cash flows from investing and financing activities sections of the cash flow statement.

E12-16 Reporting and Interpreting Cash Flows from Investing and Financing Activities with   **LO 12-3, 12-4**
       Discussion of Management Strategy

Gibraltar Industries, Inc., is a manufacturer of steel products for customers such as Home   Gibraltar Industries, Inc.
Depot, Lowe's, Chrysler, Ford, and General Motors. In the year ended December 31, 2018, it reported the following activities (amounts in thousands):

Net income	$63,800	Depreciation	$20,370
Purchase of equipment	17,700	Proceeds from sale of equipment	3,150
Payments on notes payable to bank	400	Decrease in accounts receivable	9,700
Net proceeds from stock issuance	1,400	Payments to acquire treasury stock	7,200

Required:

Based on this information, present the cash flows from the investing and financing activities sections of the cash flow statement.

LO 12-2, 12-5

E12-17 Interpreting the Cash Flow Statement

Walt Disney Company

The Walt Disney Company reported the following in its 2018 annual report (in millions):

	2016	2017	2018
Net income	$ 9,790	$ 9,366	$13,066
Net cash provided by operating activities	13,136	12,343	14,295
Purchase of parks, resorts, and equipment	(5,758)	(4,111)	(5,336)

Required:

1. Note that in all three years, net cash provided by operating activities is greater than net income. Given the above information and what you know about the Walt Disney Company from your own personal observations, provide one reason that could explain the sizable difference between net income and net cash provided by operating activities.

2. Based solely on the results reported above for the three years, did Walt Disney Company need external financing to purchase parks, resorts, and equipment during these years?

LO 12-2, 12-6

E12-18 Comparing the Direct and Indirect Methods

To compare statement of cash flows reporting under the direct and indirect methods, enter check marks to indicate which line items are reported on the statement of cash flows with each method.

	Statement of Cash Flows Method	
Cash Flows (and Related Changes)	Direct	Indirect
1. Net income		
2. Receipts from customers		
3. Accounts receivable increase or decrease		
4. Payments to suppliers		
5. Inventory increase or decrease		
6. Accounts payable increase or decrease		
7. Payments to employees		
8. Salaries and wages payable, increase or decrease		
9. Depreciation expense		
10. Cash flows from operating activities		
11. Cash flows from investing activities		
12. Cash flows from financing activities		
13. Net increase or decrease in cash during the period		

LO 12-5, 12-6

E12-19 Reporting and Interpreting Cash Flows from Operating Activities from an Analyst's Perspective (Direct Method)

Refer to the information for New Vision Company in E12-9.

Required:

1. Present the operating activities section of the statement of cash flows for New Vision Company using the direct method. Assume that Accounts Payable relate to Utilities and Office Expenses on the income statement.

2. If payments for salaries and wages were to increase by 10 percent throughout the year, by what dollar amount and in what direction would operating cash flows change?

E12-20 Reporting and Interpreting Cash Flows from Operating Activities from an Analyst's   LO 12-5, 12-6
Perspective (Direct Method)

Refer back to the information given for E12-10, plus the following summarized income statement for Pizza International, Inc. (in thousands):

Revenues	$143,551
Cost of Sales	45,500
Gross Profit	98,051
Salary and Wages Expense	56,835
Depreciation	33,305
Office Expense	7,781
Net Income before Income Tax Expense	130
Income Tax Expense	30
Net Income	$ 100

Required:

1. Based on this information, compute cash flow from operating activities using the direct method. Assume Prepaid Expenses and Accrued Liabilities relate to office expenses.

2. What was the primary reason that Pizza International was able to report large positive cash flow from operations despite nearly having a net loss?

E12-21 (Supplement 12A) Determining Cash Flows from the Sale of Equipment   LO 12-S1

Cedar Fair operates amusement parks in the United States and Canada. During 2018, it reported   Cedar Fair
the following (in millions):

From the income statement	
Loss on sale of equipment	$ 10
Depreciation expense	155
From the balance sheet	
Equipment, beginning	1,740
Equipment, ending	1,810
Accumulated depreciation, beginning	1,610
Accumulated depreciation, ending	1,730

Equipment costing $190 was purchased during the year.

Required:

For the equipment that was disposed of during the year, compute the following: (*a*) its original cost, (*b*) its accumulated depreciation, and (*c*) cash received from the disposal.

E12-22 (Supplement 12A) Determining Cash Flows from the Sale of Equipment   LO 12-S1

During the period, Teen's Trends sold some excess equipment at a loss. The following information was collected from the company's accounting records:

From the income statement	
Depreciation expense	$ 500
Loss on sale of equipment	4,000
From the balance sheet	
Beginning equipment	12,500
Ending equipment	6,500
Beginning accumulated depreciation	2,000
Ending accumulated depreciation	2,200

No new equipment was bought during the period.

Required:

For the equipment that was sold, determine (*a*) its original cost, (*b*) its accumulated depreciation, and (*c*) the cash received from the sale.

LO 12-S2 **E12-23 (Supplement 12B) Preparing a Statement of Cash Flows, Indirect Method: T-Account Approach**

Golf Goods Inc. is a regional and online golf equipment retailer. The company reported the following for the current year:

- Purchased a long-term investment for cash, $15,000.
- Paid cash dividend, $12,000.
- Sold equipment for $6,000 cash (cost, $21,000; accumulated depreciation, $15,000).
- Issued shares of no-par stock, 500 shares at $12 cash per share.
- Net income was $20,200.
- Depreciation expense was $3,000.

Its comparative balance sheet is presented below.

	Ending Balances	Beginning Balances
Cash	$ 19,200	$ 20,500
Accounts Receivable	22,000	22,000
Inventory	75,000	68,000
Investments	15,000	0
Equipment	93,500	114,500
Accumulated Depreciation—Equipment	(20,000)	(32,000)
Total	$204,700	$193,000
Accounts Payable	$ 14,000	$ 17,000
Salaries and Wages Payable	1,500	2,500
Income Taxes Payable	4,500	3,000
Notes Payable (long-term)	54,000	54,000
Common Stock	106,000	100,000
Retained Earnings	24,700	16,500
Total	$204,700	$193,000

Required:

1. Following Supplement 12B, complete a T-account worksheet to be used to prepare the statement of cash flows for the current year.
2. Based on the T-account worksheet, prepare the statement of cash flows for the current year in proper format.

COACHED PROBLEMS

LO 12-1 **CP12-1 Determining Cash Flow Statement Effects of Transactions**

For each of the following transactions, indicate whether operating (O), investing (I), or financing (F) activities are affected and whether the effect is a cash inflow (+) or outflow (−). Use (NE) if the transaction has no effect on cash.

TIP: Think about the journal entry recorded for the transaction. The transaction affects net cash flows if and only if the account Cash is affected.

_____ 1. Purchased new equipment with cash.
_____ 2. Recorded and paid income taxes to the federal government.
_____ 3. Issued shares of stock for cash.
_____ 4. Prepaid rent for the following period.

_____ 5. Paid cash to repurchase stock into treasury.

_____ 6. Issued long-term promissory notes for cash.

_____ 7. Collected payments on account from customers.

_____ 8. Recorded and paid salaries and wages to employees.

CP12-2 Computing Cash Flows from Operating Activities (Indirect Method)

LO 12-2

Hamburger Heaven's income statement for the current year and selected balance sheet data for the current and prior years ended December 31 are presented below.

Income Statement	
Sales Revenue	$2,060
Expenses:	
Cost of Goods Sold	900
Depreciation Expense	200
Salaries and Wages Expense	500
Rent Expense	250
Insurance Expense	80
Interest Expense	60
Utilities Expense	50
Net Income	$ 20

Selected Balance Sheet Accounts	Current Year	Prior Year
Inventory	$ 82	$ 60
Accounts Receivable	380	450
Accounts Payable	200	210
Salaries/Wages Payable	29	20
Utilities Payable	20	60
Prepaid Rent	2	10
Prepaid Insurance	14	5

TIP: Prepaid Rent decreased because the amount taken out of Prepaid Rent (and subtracted from net income as Rent Expense) was more than the amount paid for rent in cash during the current year.

Required:

Prepare the cash flows from operating activities section of the statement of cash flows using the indirect method.

CP12-3 Preparing a Statement of Cash Flows (Indirect Method)

LO 12-2, 12-3, 12-4, 12-5

Hunter Company is developing its annual financial statements at December 31. The statements are complete except for the statement of cash flows. The completed comparative balance sheets and income statement are summarized:

	Current Year	Prior Year
Balance Sheet at December 31		
Cash	$ 44,000	$ 18,000
Accounts Receivable	27,000	29,000
Inventory	30,000	36,000
Equipment	111,000	102,000
Accumulated Depreciation—Equipment	(36,000)	(30,000)
Total Assets	$176,000	$155,000
Accounts Payable	$ 25,000	$ 22,000
Salaries and Wages Payable	800	1,000
Notes Payable (long-term)	38,000	48,000
Common Stock	80,000	60,000
Retained Earnings	32,200	24,000
Total Liabilities and Stockholders' Equity	$176,000	$155,000
Income Statement (current year)		
Sales Revenue	$100,000	
Cost of Goods Sold	61,000	
Other Expenses	27,000	
Net Income	$ 12,000	

Additional Data:

a. Bought equipment for cash, $9,000.
b. Paid $10,000 on the long-term notes payable.
c. Issued new shares of stock for $20,000 cash.
d. Declared and paid a $3,800 cash dividend.
e. Other expenses included depreciation, $6,000; salaries and wages, $10,000; taxes, $3,000; utilities, $8,000.
f. Accounts Payable includes only inventory purchases made on credit. Because there are no liability accounts relating to taxes or other expenses, assume that these expenses were fully paid in cash.

Required:

1. Prepare the statement of cash flows for the year ended December 31 using the indirect method.
2. Use the statement of cash flows to evaluate Hunter's cash flows.
   TIP: Demonstration Case A provides a good example of information to consider when evaluating cash flows.

LO 12-2, 12-3, 12-4, 12-5   **CP12-4 Preparing and Interpreting a Statement of Cash Flows (Indirect Method)**

Soft Touch Company was started several years ago by two golf instructors. The company's comparative balance sheets and income statement are presented below, along with additional information.

	Current Year	Previous Year
Balance Sheet at December 31		
Cash	$13,500	$ 8,000
Accounts Receivable	2,500	3,500
Equipment	11,000	10,000
Accumulated Depreciation—Equipment	(3,000)	(2,500)
Total Assets	$24,000	$19,000
Accounts Payable	$ 1,000	$ 2,000
Salaries and Wages Payable	1,000	1,500
Notes Payable (long-term)	3,000	1,000
Common Stock	10,000	10,000
Retained Earnings	9,000	4,500
Total Liabilities and Stockholders' Equity	$24,000	$19,000
Income Statement		
Service Revenue	$75,000	
Salaries and Wages Expense	68,000	
Depreciation Expense	500	
Income Tax Expense	2,000	
Net Income	$ 4,500	

Additional Data:

a. Bought new golf clubs using cash, $1,000.
b. Borrowed $2,000 cash from the bank during the year.
c. Accounts Payable includes only purchases of services made on credit for operating purposes. Because there are no liability accounts relating to income tax, assume that Income Tax Expense was fully paid in cash.

Required:

1. Prepare the statement of cash flows for the current year ended December 31 using the indirect method.

2. Use the statement of cash flows to evaluate the company's cash flows.
   TIP: Demonstration Case A provides an example of information to consider when evaluating cash flows.

CP12-5 Computing Cash Flows from Operating Activities (Direct Method)   LO 12-6

Refer to the information in CP12-2.

Required:

Prepare the cash flows from operating activities section of the statement of cash flows using the direct method.
TIP: Convert the cost of goods sold to cash paid to suppliers by adding the increase in inventory and adding the decrease in accounts payable.

CP12-6 Preparing and Interpreting a Statement of Cash Flows (Direct Method)   LO 12-3, 12-4, 12-5, 12-6

Refer to CP12-4.

Required:

Complete requirements 1 and 2 using the direct method.
TIP: Remember to exclude depreciation expense when converting to the cash basis.

CP12-7 (Supplement 12A) Preparing and Interpreting a Statement of Cash Flows with Loss on Disposal (Indirect Method)   LO 12-S1

Assume the same facts as CP12-4, except for additional data item (*a*) and the income statement. Instead of item (*a*) from CP12-4, assume that the company bought new golf clubs for $3,000 cash and sold existing clubs for $1,000 cash. The clubs that were sold had cost $2,000 and had Accumulated Depreciation of $500 at the time of sale. The corrected income statement follows.

Income Statement	
Service Revenue	$75,000
Salaries and Wages Expense	68,000
Depreciation Expense	1,000
Loss on Disposal of Equipment	500
Income Tax Expense	1,000
Net Income	$ 4,500

Required:

1. Prepare the statement of cash flows for the year ended December 31 using the indirect method.
2. Use the statement of cash flows to evaluate the company's cash flows.

GROUP A PROBLEMS

Mc Graw Hill **connect**

PA12-1 Determining Cash Flow Statement Effects of Transactions   LO 12-1

For each of the following first-quarter transactions, indicate whether operating (O), investing (I), or financing (F) activities are affected and whether the effect is a cash inflow (+) or outflow (−). Use (NE) if the transaction has no effect on cash.

_____ 1. Bought used equipment for cash.

_____ 2. Paid cash to purchase new equipment.

_____ 3. Declared and paid cash dividends to stockholders.

_____ 4. Collected payments on account from customers.

_____ 5. Recorded and paid interest on debt to creditors.

_____ 6. Repaid principal on loan from bank.

_____ 7. Prepaid rent for the following period.

_____ 8. Made payment to suppliers on account.

LO 12-2

PA12-2 Computing Cash Flows from Operating Activities (Indirect Method)

The income statement and selected balance sheet information for Direct Products Company for the year ended December 31 are presented below.

Income Statement	
Sales Revenue	$48,600
Expenses:	
Cost of Goods Sold	21,000
Depreciation Expense	2,000
Salaries and Wages Expense	9,000
Rent Expense	4,500
Insurance Expense	1,900
Interest Expense	1,800
Utilities Expense	1,400
Net Income	$ 7,000

Selected Balance Sheet Accounts	Ending Balances	Beginning Balances
Accounts Receivable	$560	$580
Inventory	990	770
Accounts Payable	420	460
Prepaid Rent	25	20
Prepaid Insurance	25	28
Salaries and Wages Payable	100	60
Utilities Payable	20	15

Required:

Prepare the cash flows from operating activities section of the statement of cash flows using the indirect method.

LO 12-2, 12-3, 12-4, 12-5

PA12-3 Preparing a Statement of Cash Flows (Indirect Method)

XS Supply Company is developing its annual financial statements at December 31. The statements are complete except for the statement of cash flows. The completed comparative balance sheets and income statement are summarized:

	Current Year	Previous Year
Balance Sheet at December 31		
Cash	$ 34,000	$ 29,000
Accounts Receivable	35,000	28,000
Inventory	41,000	38,000
Equipment	121,000	100,000
Accumulated Depreciation—Equipment	(30,000)	(25,000)
Total Assets	$201,000	$170,000
Accounts Payable	$ 36,000	$27,000
Salaries and Wages Payable	1,200	1,400
Notes Payable (long-term)	38,000	44,000
Common Stock	88,600	72,600
Retained Earnings	37,200	25,000
Total Liabilities and Stockholders' Equity	$201,000	$170,000
Income Statement		
Sales Revenue	$120,000	
Cost of Goods Sold	70,000	
Other Expenses	37,800	
Net Income	$ 12,200	

Additional Data:

a. Bought equipment for cash, $21,000.

b. Paid $6,000 on the long-term notes payable.

c. Issued new shares of stock for $16,000 cash.

d. No dividends were declared or paid.

e. Other expenses included depreciation, $5,000; salaries and wages, $20,000; taxes, $6,000; utilities, $6,800.

f. Accounts Payable includes only inventory purchases made on credit. Because there are no liability accounts relating to taxes or other expenses, assume that these expenses were fully paid in cash.

Required:

1. Prepare the statement of cash flows for the current year ended December 31 using the indirect method.

2. Evaluate the statement of cash flows.

PA12-4 Preparing and Interpreting a Statement of Cash Flows (Indirect Method)   LO 12-2, 12-3, 12-4, 12-5

Heads Up Company was started several years ago by two hockey instructors. The company's comparative balance sheets and income statement follow, along with additional information.

	Current Year	Previous Year
Balance Sheet at December 31		
Cash	$ 6,300	$4,000
Accounts Receivable	900	1,750
Equipment	5,500	5,000
Accumulated Depreciation—Equipment	(1,500)	(1,250)
Total Assets	$11,200	$9,500
Accounts Payable	$ 500	$1,000
Salaries and Wages Payable	500	750
Notes Payable (long-term)	1,700	500
Common Stock	5,000	5,000
Retained Earnings	3,500	2,250
Total Liabilities and Stockholders' Equity	$11,200	$9,500
Income Statement		
Service Revenue	$37,500	
Salaries and Wages Expense	35,000	
Depreciation Expense	250	
Income Tax Expense	1,000	
Net Income	$ 1,250	

Additional Data:

a. Bought new hockey equipment for cash, $500.

b. Borrowed $1,200 cash from the bank during the year.

c. Accounts Payable includes only purchases of services made on credit for operating purposes. Because there are no liability accounts relating to income tax, assume that this expense was fully paid in cash.

Required:

1. Prepare the statement of cash flows for the current year ended December 31 using the indirect method.

2. Use the statement of cash flows to evaluate the company's cash flows.

LO 12-6 **PA12-5 Computing Cash Flows from Operating Activities (Direct Method)**

Refer to the information in PA12-2.

Required:

Prepare the cash flows from operating activities section of the statement of cash flows using the direct method.

LO 12-3, 12-4, 12-5, 12-6 **PA12-6 Preparing and Interpreting a Statement of Cash Flows (Direct Method)**

Refer to PA12-4.

Required:

Complete requirements 1 and 2 using the direct method.

LO 12-S1 **PA12-7 (Supplement 12A) Preparing and Interpreting a Statement of Cash Flows with Loss on Disposal (Indirect Method)**

Assume the same facts as PA12-4, except for the income statement and additional data item (*a*). The new income statement is shown below. Instead of item (*a*) from PA12-4, assume that the company bought new equipment for $1,800 cash and sold existing equipment for $500 cash. The equipment that was sold had cost $1,300 and had Accumulated Depreciation of $250 at the time of sale.

Income Statement	
Service Revenue	$37,500
Salaries and Wages Expense	35,000
Depreciation Expense	500
Loss on Disposal of Equipment	550
Income Tax Expense	200
Net Income	$ 1,250

Required:

1. Prepare the statement of cash flows for the year ended December 31 using the indirect method.
2. Use the statement of cash flows to evaluate the company's cash flows.

GROUP B PROBLEMS

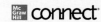

LO 12-1 **PB12-1 Determining Cash Flow Statement Effects of Transactions**

For each of the following transactions, indicate whether operating (O), investing (I), or financing (F) activities are affected and whether the effect is a cash inflow (+) or outflow (−). Use (NE) if the transaction has no effect on cash.

_____ 1. Received deposits from customers for products to be delivered the following period.

_____ 2. Principal repayments on loan.

_____ 3. Paid cash to purchase new equipment.

_____ 4. Received proceeds from loan.

_____ 5. Collected payments on account from customers.

_____ 6. Recorded and paid salaries and wages to employees.

_____ 7. Paid cash for building construction.

_____ 8. Recorded and paid interest to debt holders.

PB12-2 Computing Cash Flows from Operating Activities (Indirect Method)   **LO 12-2**

The income statement and selected balance sheet information for Calendars Incorporated for the year ended December 31 are presented below.

Income Statement	
Sales Revenue	$78,000
Expenses:	
Cost of Goods Sold	36,000
Depreciation Expense	16,000
Salaries and Wages Expense	10,000
Rent Expense	2,500
Insurance Expense	1,300
Interest Expense	1,200
Utilities Expense	1,000
Net Income	$10,000

Selected Balance Sheet Accounts	Ending Balances	Beginning Balances
Inventory	$ 430	$ 490
Accounts Receivable	1,800	1,500
Accounts Payable	1,200	1,300
Salaries and Wages Payable	450	250
Utilities Payable	100	0
Prepaid Rent	80	100
Prepaid Insurance	70	90

Required:

Prepare the cash flows from operating activities section of the statement of cash flows using the indirect method.

PB12-3 Preparing a Statement of Cash Flows (Indirect Method)   **LO 12-2, 12-3, 12-4, 12-5**

Audio City, Inc., is developing its annual financial statements at December 31. The statements are complete except for the statement of cash flows. The completed comparative balance sheets and income statement are summarized below:

	Current Year	Previous Year
Balance Sheet at December 31		
Cash	$ 60,000	$ 65,000
Accounts Receivable	15,000	20,000
Inventory	22,000	20,000
Equipment	223,000	150,000
Accumulated Depreciation—Equipment	(60,000)	(45,000)
Total Assets	$260,000	$210,000
Accounts Payable	$ 8,000	$ 19,000
Salaries and Wages Payable	2,000	1,000
Notes Payable (long-term)	60,000	75,000
Common Stock	100,000	70,000
Retained Earnings	90,000	45,000
Total Liabilities and Stockholders' Equity	$260,000	$210,000
Income Statement		
Sales Revenue	$200,000	
Cost of Goods Sold	90,000	
Other Expenses	60,000	
Net Income	$ 50,000	

Additional Data:

a. Bought equipment for cash, $73,000.
b. Paid $15,000 on the long-term notes payable.
c. Issued new shares of stock for $30,000 cash.
d. Dividends of $5,000 were paid in cash.

    e.   Other expenses included depreciation, $15,000; salaries and wages, $20,000; taxes, $25,000.

    f.   Accounts Payable includes only inventory purchases made on credit. Because a liability relating to taxes does not exist, assume that they were fully paid in cash.

Required:

1. Prepare the statement of cash flows for the current year ended December 31 using the indirect method.
2. Evaluate the statement of cash flows.

LO 12-2, 12-3, 12-4, 12-5   **PB12-4   Preparing and Interpreting a Statement of Cash Flows (Indirect Method)**

Dive In Company was started several years ago by two diving instructors. The company's comparative balance sheets and income statement, as well as additional information, are presented below.

	Current Year	Previous Year
Balance Sheet at December 31		
Cash	$ 3,200	$4,000
Accounts Receivable	1,000	500
Prepaid Rent	100	50
Total Assets	$ 4,300	$4,550
Salaries and Wages Payable	$ 350	$1,100
Common Stock	1,200	1,000
Retained Earnings	2,750	2,450
Total Liabilities and Stockholders' Equity	$ 4,300	$4,550
Income Statement		
Service Revenue	$33,950	
Salaries and Wages Expense	30,000	
Rent and Office Expenses	3,650	
Net Income	$ 300	

Additional Data:

    a.   Rent is paid in advance each month, and Office Expenses are paid in cash as incurred.

    b.   An owner contributed capital by paying $200 cash in exchange for the company's stock.

Required:

1. Prepare the statement of cash flows for the current year ended December 31 using the indirect method.
2. Use the statement of cash flows to evaluate the company's cash flows.

LO 12-6   **PB12-5   Computing Cash Flows from Operating Activities (Direct Method)**

Refer to the information in PB12-2.

Required:

Prepare the cash flows from operating activities section of the statement of cash flows using the direct method.

LO 12-3, 12-4, 12-5, 12-6   **PB12-6   Preparing and Interpreting a Statement of Cash Flows (Direct Method)**

Refer to PB12-4.

Required:

Complete requirements 1 and 2 using the direct method.

SKILLS DEVELOPMENT CASES

Mc Graw Hill **connect**

S12-1 Finding Financial Information

LO 12-1, 12-5

Refer to the financial statements of **The Home Depot** in Appendix A at the end of this book. (Note: Fiscal 2019 for The Home Depot runs from February 4, 2019, to February 2, 2020. See S1-1 for further explanation.)

The Home Depot

1. Which of the two basic reporting approaches for the cash flows from operating activities did The Home Depot use?
   a. Direct
   b. Indirect

2. What amount of income tax payments did The Home Depot make during the year ended February 2, 2020?
   a. $44 million
   b. $55 million
   c. $3,220 million
   d. $3,473 million

3. In the fiscal year ended February 2, 2020, The Home Depot generated $13,723 million from operating activities. Indicate where this cash was spent by listing the two largest cash outflows.
   a. Share Repurchase ($6,965 million) and Cash Dividends ($5,958 million)
   b. Share Repurchase ($6,965 million) and Capital Expenditures ($2,678 million)
   c. Long-Term Debt Repayments ($1,070 million) and Share Repurchase ($6,965 million)
   d. Cash Dividends ($5,958 million) and Share Repurchase ($6,965 million)

S12-2 Comparing Financial Information

LO 12-1, 12-5

Refer to the financial statements of **Lowe's Companies, Inc.** in Appendix B. (Note: Fiscal 2019 for Lowe's runs from February 2, 2019, to January 31, 2020. See S1-1 for further explanation.)

Lowe's

1. Which of the two basic reporting approaches for the cash flows from operating activities did Lowe's use?
   a. Indirect
   b. Direct

2. What was the main source of cash inflow during the year ended January 31, 2020?
   a. Cash provided by operating activities
   b. Proceeds from sale/maturity of investments
   c. Proceeds from issuance of debt
   d. Repurchase of common stock

3. What was the main source of cash outflow during the year ended January 31, 2020?
   a. Capital expenditures
   b. Purchases of investments
   c. Repayment of long-term debt
   d. Repurchase of common stock

S12-3 Internet-Based Team Research: Examining an Annual Report

LO 12-5

As a team, select an industry to analyze. Using your web browser, each team member should access the annual report or 10-K for one publicly traded company in the industry, with each member selecting a different company. (See S1-3 in Chapter 1 for a description of possible resources for these tasks.)

Required:

1. On an individual basis, each team member should write a short report that incorporates the following:
   a. Has the company generated positive or negative operating cash flows during the past three years?
   b. Has the company been expanding over the period? If so, what appears to have been the source of financing for this expansion (operating cash flows, additional borrowing, issuance of stock)?
   c. Compare and analyze the difference between net income and operating cash flows over the past three years.

2. Then, as a team, write a short report comparing and contrasting your companies using these attributes. Discuss any patterns across the companies that you as a team observe. Provide potential explanations for any differences discovered.

LO 12-1, 12-5

Enron

S12-4 Ethical Decision Making: A Real-Life Example

This case is based on a cash flow reporting fraud at Enron. The case is available online in the Connect eBook. To complete this case, you will evaluate the statement of cash flow effects of misclassifying a loan as a sale.

LO 12-1, 12-5

S12-5 Ethical Decision Making: A Mini-Case

This case is available online in the Connect eBook. To complete this case, you will evaluate two alternatives for increasing a sports club's reported operating cash flows.

LO 12-2

S12-6 Critical Thinking: Interpreting Adjustments Reported on the Statement of Cash Flows from a Management Perspective (Indirect Method)

QuickServe, a chain of convenience stores, was experiencing some serious cash flow difficulties because of rapid growth. The company did not generate sufficient cash from operating activities to finance its new stores, and creditors were not willing to lend money because the company had not produced any income for the previous three years. The new controller for QuickServe proposed a reduction in the estimated life of store equipment to increase depreciation expense; thus, "we can improve cash flows from operating activities because depreciation expense is added back on the statement of cash flows." Other executives were not sure that this was a good idea because the increase in depreciation would make it more difficult to report positive earnings: "Without income, the bank will never lend us money."

Required:

What action would you recommend for QuickServe? Why?

LO 12-2

S12-7 Using a Spreadsheet That Calculates Cash Flows from Operating Activities (Indirect Method)

You've recently been hired by B2B Consultants to provide financial advisory services to small business managers. B2B's clients often need advice on how to improve their operating cash flows and, given your accounting background, you're frequently called upon to show them how operating cash flows would change if they were to speed up their sales of inventory and their collections of accounts receivable or delay their payment of accounts payable. Each time you're asked to show the effects of these business decisions on the cash flows from operating activities, you get the uneasy feeling that you might inadvertently miscalculate their effects. To deal with this once and for all, you e-mail your friend Owen and ask him to prepare a template that automatically calculates the net operating cash flows from a simple comparative balance sheet. You received his reply today.

From: Owentheaccountant@yahoo.com
To: Helpme@hotmail.com
Cc:
Subject: Excel Help

Hey pal. I like your idea of working smarter, not harder. Too bad it involved me doing the thinking. Anyhow, I've created a spreadsheet file that contains four worksheets. The first two tabs (labeled BS and IS) are the input sheets where you would enter the numbers from each client's comparative balance sheets and income statement. Your clients are small, so this template allows for only the usual accounts. Also, I've assumed that depreciation is the only reason for a change in accumulated depreciation. If your clients' business activities differ from these, you'll need to contact me for more complex templates. The third worksheet calculates the operating cash flows using the indirect method and the fourth does this calculation using the direct method. I'll attach the screenshots of each of the worksheets so you can create your own. To answer "what if" questions, all you'll need to do is change selected amounts in the balance sheet and income statement.

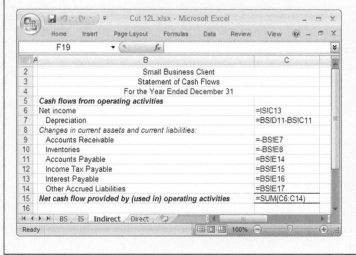

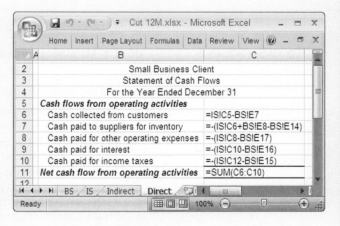

Source: Microsoft Excel

Required:

Copy the account balances from the worksheets for the balance sheet and income statement into a spreadsheet file. Enter formulas into the balance sheet worksheet to compute the change in each account balance, and then enter the formulas for the statement of cash flows (indirect method only) into a third worksheet. From this third worksheet, report the net cash flow provided by (used in) operating activities.

LO 12-6 **S12-8 Using a Spreadsheet that Calculates Cash Flows from Operating Activities (Direct Method)**

Refer to the information presented in S12-7.

Required:

Complete the same requirements, except use the direct method only.

LO 12-5 **S12-9 Using a Spreadsheet to Answer "What If" Management Decisions (Indirect or Direct Method)**

Change the amounts for selected balance sheet accounts in the spreadsheets created for either S12-7 or S12-8 to calculate the net cash flows from operating activities if, just before the current year-end, the company's management took the actions listed in the following requirements. Consider each question independently, unless indicated otherwise.

Required:

1. What if the company collected $10,000 of the accounts receivable?
2. What if the company had paid down its interest payable by an extra $2,000?
3. What if the company waited an additional month before paying $6,000 of its accounts payable?
4. What if the company had reported $5,000 more depreciation expense?
5. What if all four of the above events had taken place at the same time?

CONTINUING CASE

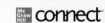

LO 12-2, 12-3, 12-4, 12-5 **CC12-1 Accounting for Cash Flows**

During a recent year, Nicole's Getaway Spa (NGS) reported net income of $2,300. The company reported the following activities:

a. Increase in inventory of $400.
b. Depreciation of $3,000.
c. Increase of $2,170 in prepaid expenses.
d. Payments of $4,600 on long-term debt.
e. Purchased new spa equipment for $7,582.
f. Payments on accounts payable exceeded purchases by $320.
g. Collections on accounts receivable exceeded credit sales by $859.
h. Issued $10,000 of common stock.

Required:

Based on this information, prepare a statement of cash flows for the year ended December 31 using the indirect method. Assume the cash balance at the beginning of the year was $7,000.

DATA ANALYTICS EXERCISES

Data Analytics Exercises are auto-graded exercises offering detailed data visualization, interpretation, and analysis, and are available for assignment in *Connect*.

13

Measuring and Evaluating Financial Performance

CHAPTER THIRTEEN

YOUR LEARNING OBJECTIVES

LO 13-1 Describe the purposes and uses of horizontal, vertical, and ratio analyses.

LO 13-2 Use horizontal (trend) analyses to recognize financial changes that unfold over time.

LO 13-3 Use vertical (common size) analyses to understand important relationships within financial statements.

LO 13-4 Calculate financial ratios to assess profitability, liquidity, and solvency.

LO 13-5 Interpret the results of financial analyses.

LO 13-6 Describe how analyses depend on key accounting decisions and concepts.

LO 13-S1 Describe how discontinued operations and comprehensive income are reported.

LO 13-S2 Describe significant differences between GAAP and IFRS.

THAT WAS THEN

In the previous chapters, you learned how to report and interpret the financial effects of various business activities.

Ariel Skelley/Getty Images

Measuring and evaluating financial performance is like judging gymnastics or figure skating at the Olympics. You have to know three things: (1) the general categories to evaluate for each event, (2) the particular elements to consider within each category, and (3) how to measure performance for each element. When assessing financial performance, managers and analysts follow the same process. They evaluate general categories such as profitability, liquidity, and solvency, which are separated into particular elements such as gross profit margin and net profit margin. For each of these elements, managers and analysts measure performance by computing various percentages and ratios, which themselves are based on information reported in the financial statements.

In this chapter, we focus on Lowe's, the second largest home improvement retailer in the world. Lowe's is a giant with more than 1,900 stores and 320,000 employees. The company's success depends on increasing sales in existing markets and successfully entering new markets. At the same time, Lowe's must control costs while maintaining a high level of customer service in its stores. Finally, Lowe's management must anticipate the actions of its larger rival, The Home Depot, and address changes in overall demand for building products over which it has little control.

How do managers, analysts, investors, and creditors assess Lowe's success in meeting these challenges? This is the purpose of financial statement analysis. Our discussion begins with an explanation of how to analyze financial statements to understand the financial results of a company's business activities. We conclude the chapter with a review of the key accounting decisions analysts consider when evaluating financial statements.

THIS IS NOW

This chapter synthesizes previous chapters by evaluating the financial statements and accounting decisions of a publicly traded company.

Understand the business	Study the accounting methods	Evaluate the results	Supplement 13A	Supplement 13B	Review the chapter
• Horizontal, vertical, and ratio analyses	• Horizontal (trend) computations • Vertical (common size) computations • Ratio computations	• Interpreting horizontal and vertical analyses • Interpreting ratio analyses • Underlying accounting decisions and concepts	• Discontinued operations and comprehensive income	• Reviewing and contrasting IFRS and GAAP	• Demonstration case • Chapter summary • Key terms • Homework helper • Practice material

Understand the Business

Learning Objective 13-1
Describe the purposes and uses of horizontal, vertical, and ratio analyses.

As you first learned in Chapter 1, the goal of accounting is to provide information that allows decision makers to understand and evaluate the results of business activities. Throughout the course, you have learned how financial statements are used in a variety of decisions. Managers analyze financial statements to evaluate past financial performance and make future decisions. Creditors use financial statements to assess compliance with loan covenants. And, of course, analysts use financial statements to generate advice for investors and others. You have learned that no single number fully captures the results of all business activities nor predicts a company's success or failure. Instead, to understand and evaluate the results of business activities, you need to look at a business from many different angles. An understanding of whether a business is successful will emerge only after you have learned to combine all of your evaluations into a complete picture or story that depicts the company's performance. Our goal for this chapter is to demonstrate how you can do this, relying on horizontal, vertical, and ratio analyses to develop the "story" of how well a company has performed.

HORIZONTAL, VERTICAL, AND RATIO ANALYSES

Most good stories have a plot, which the reader comes to understand as it unfolds over time or as one event relates to another. This is the same way financial analyses work. **Horizontal (trend) analyses are conducted to help financial statement users recognize important financial changes that unfold over time.** Horizontal analyses compare individual financial statement line items horizontally (from one period to the next), with the general goal of identifying significant sustained changes (trends). These changes are typically described in terms of dollar amounts and year-over-year percentages. For example, trend analyses could be used to determine the dollar amount and percentage by which Cost of Goods

Sold increased this year, relative to prior years. **Vertical analyses focus on important relationships between items on the same financial statement.** These items are compared vertically (one account balance versus another) and are typically expressed as percentages to reveal the relative contributions made by each financial statement item. For example, vertical analyses could show that operating expenses consume one quarter of a company's net sales revenue. **Ratio analyses are conducted to understand relationships among various items reported in one or more of the financial statements.** Ratio analyses allow you to evaluate how well a company has performed given the level of other company resources. For example, while vertical analyses can show that Cost of Goods Sold consumes 65 percent of Net Sales and horizontal analyses can show that this percentage has increased over time, ratio analyses can relate these amounts to inventory levels to evaluate inventory management decisions.

Before we show you how to calculate horizontal, vertical, and ratio analyses (in the next section), we must emphasize that **no analysis is complete unless it leads to an interpretation that helps financial statement users understand and evaluate a company's financial results.** Without interpretation, these computations can appear as nothing more than a list of disconnected numbers.

Study the Accounting Methods

HORIZONTAL (TREND) COMPUTATIONS

Horizontal (trend) analyses help financial statement users recognize financial changes that unfold over time. This approach compares individual financial statement items from year to year with the general goal of identifying significant changes. Because this type of analysis compares results over a series of periods, it is sometimes called **time-series analysis.**

Regardless of the name, trend analyses are usually calculated in terms of year-to-year dollar and percentage changes. A year-to-year percentage change expresses the current year's dollar change as a percentage of the prior year's total by using the following calculation:

$$\frac{\text{Year-to-Year}}{\text{Change (\%)}} = \frac{\text{Change This Year}}{\text{Prior Year's Total}} = \frac{(\text{Current Year's Total} - \text{Prior Year's Total})}{\text{Prior Year's Total}}$$

To demonstrate how to calculate a trend, we analyze Lowe's financial statements. Summaries of Lowe's balance sheets and income statements from two recent years appear in Exhibits 13.1 and 13.2. Dollar and percentage changes from fiscal year 2018 to 2019[1] are shown to the right of the balance sheet and income statement. The dollar changes were calculated by subtracting the fiscal 2018 balances from the fiscal 2019 balances. The percentage changes were calculated by dividing those differences by the fiscal 2018 balances. For example, according to Exhibit 13.1, Cash increased by $205 (= $716 − $511) in fiscal 2019 relative to fiscal 2018 (all numbers in millions). That dollar amount represented an increase of 0.401, or 40.1 percent (= $205 ÷ $511).

---

[1]Like many retail companies, Lowe's 2019 fiscal year ends in early 2020 (on January 31).

EXHIBIT 13.1

EXHIBIT 13.1 Horizontal (Trend) Analysis of Lowe's Summarized Balance Sheets

LOWE'S
Balance Sheets
(in millions)

	January 31, 2020 ("Fiscal 2019")	February 1, 2019 ("Fiscal 2018")	Increase (Decrease) Amount	Percent*
Assets				
Current Assets				
Cash	$ 716	$ 511	$ 205	40.1
Short-Term Investments	160	218	(58)	(26.6)
Accounts Receivable	—	—	—	—
Inventory	13,179	12,561	618	4.9
Other Current Assets	1,263	938	325	34.6
Total Current Assets	15,318	14,228	1,090	7.7
Property and Equipment, Net	18,669	18,432	237	1.3
Other Assets	5,484	1,848	3,636	196.8
Total Assets	$39,471	$34,508	$ 4,963	14.4
Liabilities and Stockholders' Equity				
Current Liabilities	$15,182	$14,497	$ 685	4.7
Long-Term Liabilities	22,317	16,367	5,950	36.4
Total Liabilities	37,499	30,864	6,635	21.5
Stockholders' Equity	1,972	3,644	(1,672)	(45.9)
Total Liabilities and Stockholders' Equity	$39,471	$34,508	$ 4,963	14.4

*Amount of Increase (Decrease) ÷ Fiscal 2018

EXHIBIT 13.2 Horizontal (Trend) Analysis of Lowe's Summarized Income Statements

LOWE'S
Income Statements
(in millions)

Year Ended:	January 31, 2020 ("Fiscal 2019")	February 1, 2019 ("Fiscal 2018")	Increase (Decrease) Amount	Percent*
Net Sales Revenue	$72,148	$71,309	$ 839	1.2
Cost of Sales	49,205	48,401	804	1.7
Gross Profit	22,943	22,908	35	0.2
Operating and Other Expenses	16,629	18,890	(2,261)	(12.0)
Interest Expense	691	624	67	10.7
Income Tax Expense	1,342	1,080	262	24.3
Net Income	$ 4,281	$ 2,314	$1,967	85.0
Earnings per Share	$ 5.49	$ 2.84	$ 2.65	93.3

*Amount of Increase (Decrease) ÷ Fiscal 2018

In a later section, we will explain and evaluate the underlying causes of significant changes in account balances. But before we leave this topic, we must note that not all large percentage changes will be significant. For example, the 40.1 percent increase in Cash is the third-largest percentage change on the balance sheet (Exhibit 13.1), but the $205 increase is relatively small when compared to other changes, such as the $618 increase in Inventory. To avoid focusing on unimportant changes, use the percentage changes to identify potentially significant changes, but then check the dollar change to make sure that it too is significant.

VERTICAL (COMMON SIZE) COMPUTATIONS

A second type of analysis, **vertical (common size) analysis**, focuses on important relationships within a financial statement. When a company is growing or shrinking overall, it is difficult to tell from the dollar amounts whether the proportions within each statement category are changing. Common size financial statements provide this information by expressing each financial statement amount as a percentage of another amount on that statement. The usefulness of common size statements is illustrated by the fact that Lowe's actually presents its balance sheet and income statements in the common size format, illustrated in Exhibits 13.3 and 13.4.

In a common size balance sheet, each asset appears as a percent of total assets, and each liability or stockholders' equity item appears as a percent of total liabilities and stockholders' equity. For example, in Exhibit 13.3, which presents Lowe's common size balance sheets, Cash was 1.8 percent of total assets ($716 ÷ $39,471 = 0.018) at the end of fiscal 2019.

> **Learning Objective 13-3**
> Use vertical (common size) analyses to understand important relationships within financial statements.

> **YOU SHOULD KNOW**
> **Vertical (Common Size) Analysis:** Expressing each financial statement amount as a percentage of another amount on the same financial statement.

EXHIBIT 13.3 Vertical (Common Size) Analysis of Lowe's Summarized Balance Sheets

LOWE'S
Balance Sheets
(in millions)

	Fiscal 2019		Fiscal 2018	
	Amount	Percent	Amount	Percent
Assets				
Current Assets				
Cash	$ 716	1.8%	$ 511	1.5%
Short-Term Investments	160	0.4	218	0.6
Inventory	13,179	33.4	12,561	36.4
Other Current Assets	1,263	3.2	938	2.7
Property and Equipment, Net	18,669	47.3	18,432	53.4
Other Assets	5,484	13.9	1,848	5.4
Total Assets	$39,471	100.0%	$34,508	100.0%
Liabilities and Stockholders' Equity				
Current Liabilities	$15,182	38.5%	$14,497	42.0%
Long-Term Liabilities	22,317	56.5	16,367	47.4
Total Liabilities	37,499	95.0	30,864	89.4
Stockholders' Equity	1,972	5.0	3,644	10.6
Total Liabilities and Stockholders' Equity	$39,471	100.0%	$34,508	100.0%

EXHIBIT 13.4   Vertical (Common Size) Analysis of Lowe's Summarized Income Statements

LOWE'S
Income Statements
(in millions)

	Fiscal 2019		Fiscal 2018	
	Amount	Percent	Amount	Percent
Net Sales Revenue	$ 72,148	100.0%	$ 71,309	100.0%
Cost of Sales	49,205	68.2	48,401	67.9
Gross Profit	22,943	31.8	22,908	32.1
Operating and Other Expenses	16,629	23.0	18,890	26.5
Interest Expense	691	1.0	624	0.9
Income Tax Expense	1,342	1.9	1,080	1.5
Net Income	$ 4,281	5.9%	$ 2,314	3.2%

The common size income statement reports each income statement item as a percentage of sales. For example, in Exhibit 13.4, Cost of Sales was equal to 68.2 percent of Net Sales Revenue in fiscal 2019 ($49,205 ÷ $72,148 = 0.682).

RATIO COMPUTATIONS

Ratio analyses help financial statement users understand relationships among various items reported in the financial statements. These analyses compare the amounts for one or more line items to the amounts for other line items in the same year. Ratio analyses are useful because they consider differences in the size of the amounts being compared, similar to common size statements. In fact, some of the most popular ratios, such as net profit margin and the debt-to-assets ratio, are taken directly from the common size statements. Ratios allow users to evaluate how well a company has performed given the level of its other resources.

Most analysts classify ratios into three categories:

1. **Profitability** ratios, which relate to the company's performance in the current period—in particular, the company's ability to generate income.

2. **Liquidity** ratios, which relate to the company's short-term survival—in particular, the company's ability to use current assets to repay liabilities as they become due.

3. **Solvency** ratios, which relate to the company's long-run survival—in particular, the company's ability to repay lenders when debt matures and to make required interest payments prior to the date of maturity.

Exhibit 13.5 organizes the ratios introduced in previous chapters according to these three categories and demonstrates their calculations for Lowe's in fiscal 2019 using data from Exhibits 13.1 and 13.2.

EXHIBIT 13.5	Common Ratios Used in Financial Statement Analysis

Profitability Ratios	**Fiscal 2019 Calculations**
(1) Net Profit Margin $= \dfrac{\text{Net Income}}{\text{Revenues}}$ (Ch. 3, p. 117)	$\dfrac{\$4{,}281}{\$72{,}148} = 5.9\%$
(2) Gross Profit Percentage $= \dfrac{\text{Net Sales} - \text{Cost of Goods Sold}}{\text{Net Sales}}$ (Ch. 6, p. 275)	$\dfrac{\$72{,}148 - \$49{,}205}{\$72{,}148} = 31.8\%$
(3) Fixed Asset Turnover $= \dfrac{\text{Net Revenue}}{\text{Average Net Fixed Assets}}$ (Ch. 9, p. 414)	$\dfrac{\$72{,}148}{(\$18{,}669 + \$18{,}432)/2} = 3.89$
(4) Return on Equity (ROE) $= \dfrac{\text{Net Income} - \text{Preferred Dividends*}}{\text{Average Common Stockholders' Equity}}$ (Ch. 11, p. 523)	$\dfrac{\$4{,}281 - \$13^*}{(\$1{,}972 + \$3{,}644)/2} = 152.0\%$
(5) Earnings per Share (EPS) $= \dfrac{\text{Net Income} - \text{Preferred Dividends*}}{\text{Average Number of Common Shares Outstanding}}$ (Ch. 11, p. 523)	$\dfrac{\$4{,}281 - \$13^*}{777^\ddagger} = \$5.49$
(6) Price/Earnings Ratio $= \dfrac{\text{Stock Price (per share)}^\dagger}{\text{Earnings per Share (annual)}}$ (Ch. 11, p. 523)	$\dfrac{\$113.30}{\$5.49} = 20.6$
Liquidity Ratios	
(7) Receivables Turnover $= \dfrac{\text{Net Sales Revenue}}{\text{Average Net Receivables}}$ (Ch. 8, p. 364)	n/a
Days to Collect $= \dfrac{365}{\text{Receivables Turnover Ratio}}$ (Ch. 8, p. 364)	n/a
(8) Inventory Turnover $= \dfrac{\text{Cost of Goods Sold}}{\text{Average Inventory}}$ (Ch. 7, p. 318)	$\dfrac{\$49{,}205}{(\$13{,}179 + \$12{,}561)/2} = 3.8$
Days to Sell $= \dfrac{365}{\text{Inventory Turnover Ratio}}$ (Ch. 7, p. 318)	$\dfrac{365}{3.8} = 96.1$
(9) Current Ratio $= \dfrac{\text{Current Assets}}{\text{Current Liabilities}}$ (Ch. 2, p. 68)	$\dfrac{\$15{,}318}{\$15{,}182} = 1.01$
Solvency Ratios	
(10) Debt-to-Assets $= \dfrac{\text{Total Liabilities}}{\text{Total Assets}}$ (Ch. 10, p. 462)	$\dfrac{\$37{,}499}{\$39{,}471} = 0.95$
(11) Times Interest Earned $= \dfrac{\text{Net Income} + \text{Interest Expense} + \text{Income Tax Expense}}{\text{Interest Expense}}$ (Ch. 10, p. 462)	$\dfrac{\$4{,}281 + \$691 + \$1{,}342}{\$691} = 9.1$

* Note 13 of Lowe's financial statements indicated the company committed to paying a $13 million dividend to its "participating" and other securities, similar to a preferred dividend.

‡ Note 15 of Lowe's financial statements reports the average number of common shares outstanding.

† Stock price is the closing price on the day the company first reports its annual earnings in a press release.

How's it going?   Self-Study Practice

For the year ended February 3, 2019, **The Home Depot** reported net income of $11.1 billion on sales of $108.2 billion. If the company's cost of goods sold that year was $71.0 billion, what were the company's gross profit percentage and net profit margin? If sales were $100.1 billion in the prior year, what was the year-over-year percentage increase in the most recent year?

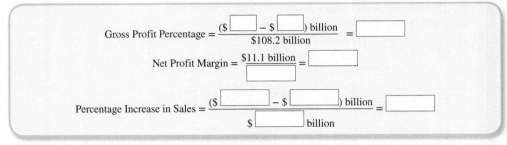

After you have finished, check your answers with the solution.

Solution to Self-Study Practice

Gross Profit Percentage = [($108.2 − $71.0)/$108.2]
  = 34.4%
Net Profit Margin = ($11.1/$108.2) = 10.3%
Percentage Increase in Sales = [($108.2 − $100.1)/$100.1]
  = 8.1%

Evaluate the Results

Learning Objective 13-5
Interpret the results of financial analyses.

INTERPRETING HORIZONTAL AND VERTICAL ANALYSES

As noted in the previous section, financial statement analyses are not complete unless they lead to interpretations that help users understand and evaluate a company's financial results. When interpreting analyses, your goals should be to understand what each analysis is telling you and then combine your findings into a coherent "story" that explains the results of the company's business activities. We demonstrate how to do this, beginning with interpretations of each set of analyses shown in Exhibits 13.1–13.5 and later concluding with an overall summary of **Lowe's** results.

Trends Revealed in Horizontal Analyses

Horizontal (trend) analysis of Lowe's balance sheet in Exhibit 13.1 shows the company grew in fiscal 2019. Overall, total assets increased 14.4 percent. The financing for this growth came from debt. In fact, during fiscal 2019, Lowe's total liabilities increased by 21.5 percent (whereas stockholders' equity *decreased* by 45.9 percent). The notes to Lowe's financial statements explain that Lowe's liabilities increased because it issued about $3.0 billion of new bonds; its stockholders' equity decreased because it paid $1.6 billion in dividends and repurchased about $4.3 billion of its common shares that were immediately retired and returned to authorized and unissued status.

Horizontal analysis of Lowe's income statement in Exhibit 13.2 shows a 1.2 percent increase in Net Sales Revenue, a 1.7 percent increase in Cost of Sales, and a 12.0 percent decrease in Operating and Other Expenses in fiscal 2019. The company explains in the Management's Discussion and Analysis (MD&A) section of its annual report that Lowe's decided to close underperforming stores in the United States, Canada, and Mexico in 2018 and 2019. The reduction in number of Lowe's stores caused a slight decrease in Net Sales Revenue and Cost of Sales, but in fiscal 2019 that was more than offset at its remaining stores by a greater number of customer transactions at a higher average ticket price. When Lowe's decided to close its stores in fiscal 2018, it recorded significant impairment losses that year; of course, similar losses were not recorded in fiscal 2019, leading to a 12.0 percent decrease in Operating and Other Expenses. The final changes in Lowe's fiscal 2019 expenses related to interest and income tax expenses, which increased as a direct result of carrying more debt and earning more income.

Relationships Noted in Vertical Analyses

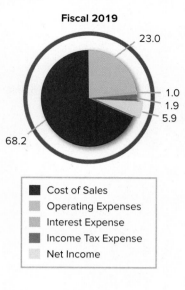

Fiscal 2019

- ■ Cost of Sales
- Operating Expenses
- Interest Expense
- ■ Income Tax Expense
- Net Income

Vertical (common size) analysis of Lowe's balance sheet in Exhibit 13.3 highlights key elements of the company. Its most significant assets have always been Inventory and Property and Equipment, but their prominence declined somewhat when the company recently closed underperforming stores. This decline can be seen in Exhibit 13.3, where these two assets now account for just 33.4 and 47.3 percent of total assets at the end of fiscal 2019, as compared to 36.4 and 53.4 percent in the previous year. Financing for assets comes from debt and equity. As a result of the bond issuance and stock repurchases in 2019, debt became a significantly greater source of financing (95.0 percent) than equity (5.0 percent) at the end of fiscal 2019.

Vertical analysis of Lowe's income statement in Exhibit 13.4 indicates that Cost of Sales and Operating Expenses are the most important determinants of the company's profitability. Cost of Sales consumed 68.2 percent of Sales in fiscal 2019 and Operating Expenses consumed an additional 23.0 percent. Much of the increase in the company's Net Income (from 3.2 percent of Sales in fiscal 2018 to 5.9 percent in fiscal 2019) is explained by a reduction in Operating Expenses, as was noted earlier in the horizontal analyses.

These findings from the vertical analyses serve to underscore findings from the horizontal analyses. The emerging story is that Lowe's success depends on its ability to focus its investments in Inventory and Property and Equipment on stores that meet performance goals for generating sales while also controlling expenses.

INTERPRETING RATIO ANALYSES

As shown throughout other chapters in this book, benchmarks help when interpreting a company's ratios. These benchmarks can include the company's prior-year results, as well as the results of close competitors or the average for the industry. In a competitive economy, companies strive to outperform one another, so comparisons against industry competitors can provide clues about who is likely to survive and thrive in the long run.

In the following analyses, we compare Lowe's financial ratios to the prior year and in some cases to those for The Home Depot and the home improvement industry as a whole. (Excerpts from both Lowe's and The Home Depot's annual reports for fiscal 2019 are presented in Appendices A and B at the end of this book.)

Profitability Ratios

The analyses in this section focus on the level of profits the company generated during the period. We will analyze ratios (1) through (6) from Exhibit 13.5. The first two profitability ratios come right from the common size income statement in Exhibit 13.4.

(1) Net Profit Margin   Net profit margin represents the percentage of revenue that ultimately makes it into net income, after deducting expenses. Using the equation in Exhibit 13.5, the calculation of Lowe's net profit margin for each of the last two years yields

Fiscal Year	2019	2018
Net profit margin = $\dfrac{\text{Net Income}}{\text{Revenues}}$	5.9%	3.2%

As discussed in the previous sections, Lowe's decided in fiscal 2018 to dispose of underperforming stores in Mexico, Canada, and the United States. This decision led to higher-than-normal expenses in fiscal 2018, followed by greater sales and profits in fiscal 2019 from its more successful stores. Overall, Lowe's net profit margin increased from 3.2 percent in 2018 to 5.9 percent in 2019. The Home Depot's net profit margin was steady over these two years, at 10.3 and 10.2 percent.

(2) Gross Profit Percentage   The horizontal analysis indicated that Lowe's earned more total dollars of gross profit in 2019 than in 2018, as a result of a greater number of sales transactions. However, it did not indicate whether that increase was caused solely by greater total sales volume or also by more profit per sale. The gross profit percentage addresses these

COACH'S TIP

Industry averages are reported in the Annual Statement Studies, which are published by the Risk Management Association. You can obtain industry averages also from csimarket.com or finance.yahoo.com, both of which were available free of charge at the time this book was written.

possibilities by indicating how much profit was made, on average, on each dollar of sales after deducting the cost of goods sold. Lowe's gross profit percentage for the last two years was

Fiscal Year		2019	2018
Gross Profit Percentage =	$\dfrac{\text{Net Sales} - \text{Cost of Goods Sold}}{\text{Net Sales}}$	31.8%	32.1%

This analysis shows that in 2019, after deducting the cost of merchandise sold, 31.8 cents of each sales dollar were left to cover other costs, such as employee wages, advertising, and utilities, and to provide profits to the stockholders. The decrease in the gross profit percentage from 2018 to 2019 (32.1% − 31.8%) means that Lowe's made 0.3¢ less gross profit on each dollar of sales in 2019 than in 2018. Thus, the increase in dollars of gross profit is explained only by an increase in total sales volume. Financial statement users also would want to know which of two potential explanations accounts for the decrease in gross profit percentage: (1) Lowe's reduced its selling prices and (2) Lowe's had to pay higher unit costs to initially acquire merchandise. The MD&A section of Lowe's annual report suggests the decrease in gross profit percentage largely resulted from the second of these two reasons (i.e., higher unit costs). Specifically, an escalating trade war between the United States and China in 2019 resulted in 25 percent tariffs on the cost of building materials imported into the United States, which Lowe's sold without corresponding increases in selling prices.

(3) Fixed Asset Turnover   The fixed asset turnover ratio indicates how much revenue the company generates for each dollar invested in fixed assets, such as store buildings and the property they sit on. Lowe's fixed asset turnover ratios for the two years were

Fiscal Year		2019	2018
Fixed Asset Turnover =	$\dfrac{\text{Net Revenue}}{\text{Average Net Fixed Assets}}$	3.89	3.73

This analysis shows Lowe's had $3.89 of sales in 2019 for each dollar invested in fixed assets. Looking at the components of this ratio, we see the decrease in net fixed assets that resulted from closing stores in the United States, Canada, and Mexico was the main factor contributing to the ratio's increase in 2019.

Although Lowe's fixed asset turnover ratio improved in 2019, it is low compared to that of its main competitor, The Home Depot, whose fixed asset turnover ratio was 4.88 in 2019. In terms of using fixed assets to generate sales revenue, The Home Depot has a competitive advantage over Lowe's.

(4) Return on Equity (ROE)   The return on equity ratio compares the amount of net income earned for common stockholders to the average amount of common stockholders' equity. (The amount of net income earned for common stockholders is net income minus any dividends on preferred or "participating" stock.) Like the interest rate on your bank account, ROE reports the net amount earned during the period as a percentage of each dollar contributed by common stockholders and retained in the business. Lowe's ROE ratios for the past two years were

Fiscal Year		2019	2018
Return on Equity (ROE) =	$\dfrac{\text{Net Income} - \text{Preferred Dividends}}{\text{Average Common Stockholders' Equity}}$	152.0%	48.5%

Lowe's ROE increase from 48.5 to 152.0 percent is consistent with our previous analyses. Specifically, horizontal analysis indicated dividends and stock repurchases decreased common stockholders' equity and lower operating expenses increased 2019 net income. Taken together, these results imply net income as a percentage of average common stockholders' equity was sure to rise in 2019. The Home Depot's ROE was even more extreme because that company reported negative stockholders' equity as a result of significant stock repurchases. To address issues of low (or negative) stockholders' equity balances, companies such as

Lowe's and The Home Depot are increasingly analyzing a different measure of return on investment called **Return on Invested Capital** (ROIC). This measue is similar to ROE, except it compares earnings to both equity and debt, reflecting the view that executives use both forms of capital to finance the business. Methods for calculating ROIC are discussed in advanced courses in financial statement analysis.

(5) Earnings per Share (EPS)   Earnings per share (EPS) indicates the amount of earnings generated for each share of outstanding common stock. Consistent with the increase in ROE, the EPS ratio increased from $2.84 in 2018 to $5.49 in 2019, as shown below. This represents an increase of $2.65 per share ($5.49 − $2.84).

Fiscal Year	2019	2018
Earnings per Share (EPS) = $\dfrac{\text{Net Income} - \text{Preferred Dividends}}{\text{Average Number of Common Shares Outstanding}}$	$5.49	$2.84

(6) Price/Earnings (P/E) Ratio   The P/E ratio relates the company's stock price to its EPS, as follows:

Fiscal Year	2019	2018
Price/Earnings Ratio = $\dfrac{\text{Stock Price (per share)}}{\text{Earnings per Share (annual)}}$	20.6	37.9

Using the stock price immediately after Lowe's announced its fiscal 2019 and 2018 earnings (on February 26, 2020, and February 27, 2019), the P/E ratio was 20.6 and 37.9, respectively. This means investors were willing to pay 20.6 times earnings to buy a share of Lowe's stock in early 2020 (versus 37.9 times earnings a year earlier). The decrease from the prior year suggests investors were less optimistic about the company's future than they were the year before. The effects of increased tariffs and uncertainty about the economic consequences of the COVID-19 pandemic dampened investors' outlook for 2020 and beyond.

Let's pause to summarize what we've learned so far. Lowe's had a mixed year in fiscal 2019. On the positive side, the company saw a slight increase in 2019 sales revenue despite having closed more than 150 stores over the previous two years. More revenue combined with fewer stores led to an increase in Lowe's fixed asset turnover in 2019. Lowe's also enjoyed an increase in net income in 2019, causing EPS and ROE to increase significantly over the previous year. However, the increase in net income wasn't all good news because it was partly attributable to higher-than-normal impairment losses in 2018 rather than across-the-board improvements in 2019. Gross profit percentage, for example, declined in 2019 because Lowe's was unable to pass on to consumers increased tariff costs on imported building materials. This news, combined with the COVID-19 pandemic and resulting global recession, was concerning to investors, as indicated by Lowe's decreased P/E ratio.

Liquidity Ratios

The analyses in this section focus on the company's ability to survive in the short term, by converting assets to cash that can be used to pay current liabilities as they come due. We interpret ratios (7) through (9) from Exhibit 13.5.

(7) Receivables Turnover   Most home improvement retailers have low levels of accounts receivable relative to sales revenue because they either collect the majority of their sales immediately in cash or sell credit card receivables to finance companies (as Lowe's does, as explained in the "Sale of Business Accounts Receivable and Credit Programs" section of its financial statement Note 1). Consequently, the receivables turnover ratio is not terribly meaningful for Lowe's or The Home Depot. The formula is presented in Exhibit 13.5 simply to remind you of how it is calculated.

(8) Inventory Turnover   The inventory turnover ratio indicates how frequently inventory is bought and sold during the year. The measure "days to sell" converts the inventory turnover ratio into the average number of days needed to sell inventory.

Fiscal Year	2019	2018
Inventory Turnover = $\dfrac{\text{Cost of Goods Sold}}{\text{Average Inventory}}$	3.8	4.0
Days to Sell = $\dfrac{365}{\text{Inventory Turnover Ratio}}$	96.1	91.3

Lowe's inventory turned over slightly slower in 2019 than in 2018. On average, its inventory took 4.8 more days to sell (96.1 − 91.3). Lowe's executives explained this decline was the result of a strategic decision they made in 2019 to increase inventory levels so that in-stock quantities would better meet the needs of professional contractors. But their decision hasn't yet increased sales to pro contractors, leading the inventory turnover ratio to decrease in 2019. Lowe's expects this will change in the future and help it catch up to The Home Depot, where inventory turns over much faster (71.6 days to sell in 2019).

Turnover ratios vary significantly from one industry to the next. Companies in the food industry (restaurants and grocery stores) have high inventory turnover ratios because their inventory is subject to spoilage. Companies that sell expensive merchandise (automobiles and high-fashion clothes) have much slower turnover because sales of those items are infrequent, but these companies tend to carry lots of inventory so that customers have a wide selection to choose from when shopping.

(9) Current Ratio   The current ratio compares current assets to current liabilities, as follows:

Fiscal Year	2019	2018
Current Ratio = $\dfrac{\text{Current Assets}}{\text{Current Liabilities}}$	1.01	0.98

The current ratio measures the company's ability to pay its current liabilities. Lowe's ratio was virtually unchanged between 2018 and 2019, ending fiscal 2019 with a ratio of 1.01. In some instances, a current ratio near 1.0 is a cause for concern. But in this industry, a current ratio near 1.0 is deemed acceptable because it arises from entering into financing arrangements that benefit the company and its suppliers, as explained in the following Spotlight.

SPOTLIGHT ON | **Business Decisions**

Lowe's Helps Suppliers Collect on Account

Lowe's has a low current ratio because it carries a large balance in Accounts Payable. The large Accounts Payable balance arises because suppliers give Lowe's favorable payment terms, including a longer period to pay its Accounts Payable. Why would suppliers be willing to allow this? The reason is that Lowe's participates in supply chain financing, or what some call "reverse factoring." The way this works is Lowe's tells a finance company what it owes to particular suppliers. The finance company then contacts the suppliers and offers to take over the collection of Lowe's account balance. Just like a normal factoring arrangement (discussed in Chapter 8), the finance company pays the supplier right away. The finance company charges the supplier a smaller-than-normal factoring fee because it knows Lowe's balance will be easily collected because Lowe's has openly told the finance company how much it owes. The supplier appreciates collecting right away and being charged a smaller factoring fee, so it gives Lowe's more favorable payment terms. Lowe's fiscal 2019 annual report indicates it has made this supply chain financing possible for 17 percent of its suppliers.

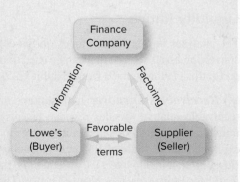

Solvency Ratios

The analyses in this section focus on Lowe's ability to survive over the long term—that is, its ability to repay debt at maturity and pay interest prior to that time. We interpret ratios (10) and (11) from Exhibit 13.5.

(10) Debt-to-Assets   The debt-to-assets ratio indicates the proportion of total assets that creditors finance. Remember that creditors must be paid regardless of how difficult a year the company may have had. The higher this ratio, the riskier is the company's financing strategy. Lowe's ratios at the end of fiscal 2019 and 2018 follow.

Fiscal Year	2019	2018
Debt-to-Assets = $\dfrac{\text{Total Liabilities}}{\text{Total Assets}}$	0.95	0.89

Lowe's ratio of 0.95 in 2019 indicates that creditors contributed 95 percent of the company's financing, implying that it was the company's main source of financing. The debt-to-assets ratio increased from 2018 to 2019 as a result of issuing new bonds (and reducing equity financing by declaring dividends and repurchasing its common stock). Although this increase suggests greater financing risk, it is not out of line with others in the home improvement industry. The Home Depot, for example, had an even higher debt-to-assets ratio at the end of fiscal 2019 (106 percent). The Home Depot's ratio was greater than 100 percent because the company repurchased its stock in 2019 at a price greater than its original issue price, resulting in negative stockholders' equity.

(11) Times Interest Earned   The times interest earned ratio indicates how many times the company's interest expense was covered by its operating results. This ratio is calculated using accrual-based interest expense and net income before interest and income taxes, as follows:

Fiscal Year	2019	2018
Times Interest Earned = $\dfrac{\text{Net Income} + \text{Interest Expense} + \text{Income Tax Expense}}{\text{Interest Expense}}$	9.1	6.4

A times interest earned ratio above 1.0 indicates that net income (before the costs of financing and taxes) is sufficient to cover the company's interest expense. Lowe's ratio of 9.1 indicates that, despite its heavy reliance on debt, the company is generating more than enough profit to cover its interest expense.

COACH'S TIP

Instead of the debt-to-assets ratio, analysts might use a debt-to-equity ratio, which gives the same basic information as debt-to-assets. Debt-to-equity typically is calculated as total liabilities ÷ total stockholders' equity. As with debt-to-assets, the higher the debt-to-equity ratio, the more the company relies on debt (rather than equity) financing.

COACH'S TIP

If a company reports a net loss, rather than net income, include the loss as a negative number in the times interest earned formula. A negative ratio indicates operating results (before the costs of financing and taxes) are insufficient to cover interest costs.

How's it going?   Self-Study Practice

Show the computations for the following two ratios for Lowe's for the prior year (fiscal 2018). Use the information in Exhibits 13.1 and 13.2.

a.   Times interest earned ratio

b.   Current ratio

After you have finished, check your answers with the solution.

Solution to Self-Study Practice
a. ($2,314 + $624 + $1,080)/$624 = 6.4
b. $14,228 ÷ $14,497 = 0.98

UNDERLYING ACCOUNTING DECISIONS AND CONCEPTS

Accounting Decisions

In the analyses just presented, we compared Lowe's results with those of The Home Depot. When appropriate, we discussed how differences in the two companies' strategies (for example, relying on debt versus equity financing) and business operations (for example, carrying more

Learning Objective 13-6
Describe how analyses depend on key accounting decisions and concepts.

inventory) affected their financial ratios. We should also consider whether differences between the two companies' financial ratios might be caused by differences in their accounting decisions.

The first item to note is both companies' financial statements have been audited by an independent public accounting firm. Their auditors' reports immediately precede the financial statements in Appendixes A and B. These reports indicate **unqualified opinions** that the companies' financial statements can be relied upon because they are fairly presented. With this overall assurance, we then consider the specific accounting decisions that are summarized in the first note to the financial statements. Exhibit 13.6 shows the policies that three home improvement retailers follow in accounting for inventory and depreciation.

EXHIBIT 13.6	Comparison of Accounting Methods		
	Lowe's	**The Home Depot**	**Builders FirstSource**
Inventory	FIFO	FIFO	Weighted Average Cost
Depreciation	Straight line Buildings: 5–40 yrs Equipment: 2–15 yrs	Straight line Buildings: 5–45 yrs Equipment: 2–20 yrs	Straight line Buildings: 10–40 yrs Equipment: 3–10 yrs

As you can see, the three companies follow similar but not identical policies. Lowe's and The Home Depot use the FIFO method of accounting for inventory and cost of goods sold, so direct comparison between these two companies is straightforward and appropriate. On the other hand, Builders FirstSource uses the weighted average method, which yields higher Cost of Goods Sold, lower Inventory, and higher inventory turnover measures than FIFO in times of rising costs. The impact of its weighted average cost method (versus FIFO) is likely to be relatively minor in the current period because inventory costs have not been rising rapidly over this time. But analysts will exercise caution when comparing this company to the other two should costs change significantly in the future.

All three companies calculate depreciation using the straight-line method with a similar range of estimated useful lives for buildings and equipment. Because buildings and equipment make up such a large portion of each company's assets, these similarities go a long way toward making their financial results comparable. In conclusion, although the companies' accounting policies differ somewhat, they are unlikely to materially affect our comparisons.

Accounting Concepts

Before wrapping up this chapter, it's worth revisiting the accounting concepts that were introduced in previous chapters. Exhibit 13.7 summarizes the conceptual framework for financial accounting and reporting that was first introduced in Chapter 1. The concepts that you have already learned about in prior chapters are highlighted in red in Exhibit 13.7.

EXHIBIT 13.7	Conceptual Framework for Financial Accounting and Reporting

Objective of External Financial Reporting
To provide useful financial information to external users for decision making (Ch. 1)
- It must be relevant and a faithful representation of the business
- It is more useful if it is comparable, verifiable, timely, and understandable

Elements to Be Measured and Reported
- Assets, Liabilities, Stockholders' Equity, Revenues, Expenses, Dividends (Ch. 1)

Concepts for Measuring and Reporting Information
- Assumptions: Unit of Measure (Ch.1), Separate Entity (Ch.1), Going Concern, Time Period (Ch. 3)
- Principles: Cost (Ch. 2), Revenue and Expense Recognition (Ch. 3), Full Disclosure

As shown in Exhibit 13.7, the primary objective of financial accounting and reporting is to provide useful financial information for people external to a company to use in making decisions about the company. To be useful, this information must be relevant and faithfully represent the underlying business.

As Exhibit 13.7 indicates, only two accounting concepts have not been introduced in previous chapters, so we will explain them here. The **full disclosure principle** states that financial reports should present all information that is needed to properly interpret the results of the company's business activities. This doesn't mean every single transaction needs to be explained in detail, but rather adequate information needs to be presented to allow financial statement users to fairly interpret reports about the company's income, financial position, and cash flows.

The **going-concern** (also called *continuity*) **assumption** quietly underlies all accounting rules. It is the belief that any business will be capable of continuing its operations long enough to realize the economic benefits of its assets and meet its obligations in the normal course of business. If a company judges it probable that it will be unable to meet its obligations for at least one year after the financial statements are issued, it must disclose this in the financial statement notes. An example of this disclosure is presented in the Spotlight box that follows. In severe cases, the company may need to adjust the amount and classification of items in its financial statements. Some of the factors that commonly contribute to going-concern uncertainties are listed in Exhibit 13.8. Notice that some of the analyses presented earlier in this chapter are key considerations.

> **YOU SHOULD KNOW**
>
> **Full Disclosure Principle:** The financial statements should present information needed to understand the financial results of the company's business activities.
> **Going-Concern (Continuity) Assumption:** A business is assumed to be capable of continuing its operations long enough to meet its obligations.

EXHIBIT 13.8	Factors Contributing to Going-Concern Uncertainties

Revealed by Financial Analyses	Revealed by Other Analyses
• Declining sales	• Loss of a key supplier or customer
• Declining gross profit	• Insufficient product innovation/quality
• Significant one-time expenses	• Significant barriers to expansion
• Fluctuating net income	• Loss of key personnel without replacement
• Insufficient current assets	• Unfavorable long-term commitments
• Excessive reliance on debt financing	• Inadequate maintenance of long-lived assets
• Negative operating cash flows	• Loss of a key franchise, license, or patent

SPOTLIGHT ON Financial Reporting

COVID-19 Impacts Companies' Going Concern Status

The unprecedented COVID-19 pandemic that struck the world in 2020 had a major adverse impact on many businesses, after governments urged people to isolate by issuing stay-at-home orders and adopting physical-distancing measures. Particularly hard hit were airlines, automakers, dine-in restaurants, hotels, movie theatres, retailers, sports and fitness companies, and theme parks. In addition, layoffs and unemployment reached historic levels, leading to a massive decrease in consumer spending. The financial impact on the economy was unparalleled, leading many companies to report doubts about their ability to remain in business. An excerpt from Dave & Buster's financial disclosures is presented below as an example:

> During the period from March 14, 2020 to March 20, 2020, the Company closed 100% of its 137 operating stores . . . to combat the spread of the COVID-19 pandemic. These developments have caused a material adverse impact on the Company's revenues, results of operations and cash flows, including the Company's ability to meet its obligations when due. These conditions raise substantial doubt about the Company's ability to continue as a going concern.

Source: Dave & Buster's Entertainment, Inc., Form 10-Q filed on June 11, 2020.

Before closing the book on these key accounting concepts (and possibly this course), take a moment to complete the following Self-Study Practice. It'll give you a good idea of whether you need a detailed review of the concepts introduced in earlier chapters or whether you're ready to move on to review and practice the new topics introduced in this chapter.

 How's it going?   Self-Study Practice

Match each statement below to the concept to which it most closely relates.

1. Everything comes down to dollars and cents.	*(a)* Separate entity
2. That's not our issue. It's for somebody else to report.	*(b)* Revenue and expense recognition
3. If it relates to this period's earnings, you'd better report it.	*(c)* Going concern
4. I've told you everything you need to know.	*(d)* Unit of measure
5. At that rate, you may not survive past the end of the year.	*(e)* Time period
6. I know it's a long time, but let's break it down into stages.	*(f)* Full disclosure

After you have finished, check your answers with the solution.

You have now seen enough to interpret most basic financial statements. When analyzing real-world financial statements, you may encounter two other items: discontinued operations and comprehensive income. These items are discussed in Chapter Supplement 13A.

Learning Objective 13-S1
Describe how discontinued operations and comprehensive income are reported.

SUPPLEMENT 13A   DISCONTINUED OPERATIONS AND COMPREHENSIVE INCOME

Discontinued Operations

YOU SHOULD KNOW

Discontinued Operations: Result from the disposal of a major component of the business and are reported net of income tax effects.
Comprehensive Income: Comprehensive Income = Net Income + Other Comprehensive Income (OCI). OCI includes gains and losses arising from changes in the values of certain assets and liabilities (see Appendix D).

Discontinued operations result from a strategic shift, such as abandoning or selling a major business component. Because an abandoned or sold business unit will not affect financial results in future years, its results for the current year are reported on a separate line of the income statement following Income Tax Expense. This discontinued operations line includes any gain or loss on disposal of the discontinued operation as well as any operating income generated before its disposal, net of related tax effects.

Lowe's did not consider its Mexico operations a separate business unit, so its exit from Mexico in 2019 was not reported as a discontinued operation. So, to provide an example, we turn to a smaller competitor (Builders FirstSource) that reported discontinued operations in 2013. The highlighted line in Exhibit 13A.1 shows how the income statement distinguishes net income (loss) from continuing and discontinued operations.

Comprehensive Income

Companies with pensions, foreign currencies, and certain debt securities are required to report not only net income but also a second type of income called **comprehensive income**. Comprehensive income includes net income, as reported on the income statement, as well as unrealized gains and losses on pensions, foreign currencies, and certain debt securities. Comprehensive income is reported either immediately after net income at the bottom of the income statement or in a separate Statement of Comprehensive Income (see page B5 at the end of this book for an example involving Lowe's). These unrealized gains and losses are excluded from net income because they may disappear before they are ever realized. For this reason, most analysts will consider the size of these special items in relation to net income. If the amount is not large, they will exclude the items when calculating profitability ratios.

EXHIBIT 13A.1	Discontinued Operations Reported Net of Tax on the Income Statement

BUILDERS FIRSTSOURCE, INC.
Condensed Income Statements
For the Year Ended December 31, 2013
(in thousands)

Sales	$1,489,900
Cost of Sales	1,170,000
Gross Profit	319,900
Selling, General, and Administrative Expenses	271,900
Income from Operations	48,000
Interest Expense, Net	89,600
Income (Loss) from Continuing Operations before Income Tax Expense	(41,600)
Income Tax Expense	800
Net Income (Loss) from Continuing Operations	(42,400)
Income (Loss) from Discontinued Operations, Net of Tax	(300)
Net Income (Loss)	$ (42,700)

SUPPLEMENT 13B REVIEWING AND CONTRASTING IFRS AND GAAP

Learning Objective 13-S2
Describe significant differences between GAAP and IFRS.

In this supplement, we review and contrast IFRS and GAAP as they relate to topics raised in earlier chapters of the text. We begin with a theoretical discussion of similarities and differences between IFRS and GAAP that potentially affect the accounting rules for specific topics. We then follow with a summary of specific topic discussions.

Overview

Generally speaking, IFRS and GAAP are similar. Both aim to guide businesses in reporting financial information that is relevant and that faithfully represents the underlying activities of businesses. At a basic level, these accounting rules describe (1) when an item should be recognized in the accounting system, (2) how that item should be classified (e.g., asset or expense, revenue or liability), and (3) the amount at which each item should be measured.

Many differences between IFRS and GAAP that we have noted in this book relate to cases where IFRS requires or allows companies to report items using values that differ from those required or allowed by GAAP. For example, in Chapter 9, we noted that IFRS allows companies to report fixed assets at fair values. Researchers studying a sample of European and Canadian companies found that financial ratios changed significantly when the companies switched from GAAP to IFRS.[2] Thus, it is useful for you to consider the effects of possible accounting differences when doing your own analyses. A summary of the differences introduced in this text is presented in the next section.

[2]See Anna-Maija Lantto and Petri Sahlström, "Impact of International Financial Reporting Standard Adoption on Key Financial Ratios," *Accounting and Finance* 49 (2009), pp. 341–361; and Michel Blanchette, François-Eric Raciot, and Jean-Yves Girard, *The Effects of IFRS on Financial Ratios: Early Evidence in Canada* (CGA-Canada, 2011).

Specific IFRS Topics Integrated in Earlier Chapters

Chapter 1

- **Page 18.** Spotlight discusses the joint work of the Financial Accounting Standards Board and the International Accounting Standards Board to establish accounting rules and a unified conceptual framework.

Chapter 7

- **Page 315.** Spotlight explains that IFRS prohibits LIFO and discusses the potential financial impact of switching from LIFO to FIFO.

Chapter 9

- **Page 399.** Spotlight discusses IFRS's accounting for component costs.
- **Page 412.** Spotlight discusses IFRS's accounting for R&D and revaluation at fair value.

Chapter 10

- **Page 462.** Spotlight discusses IFRS's threshold for accruing contingent liabilities.
- **Page 463.** Spotlight discusses IFRS's current classification of long-term debt involving violated loan covenants.

Chapter 11

- **Page 520.** Spotlight discusses classification of some preferred stock as a liability.

Chapter 12

- **Page 560.** Spotlight illustrates differences in classification of dividends and interest received and paid, under IFRS and GAAP.

REVIEW THE CHAPTER

DEMONSTRATION CASE

The following information was reported in The Home Depot's annual report.

(in millions of dollars)	February 2, 2020 (Fiscal 2019)	
Net Sales Revenue	$110,225	
Cost of Goods Sold	72,653	
Other Expenses	26,330	
Net Income	11,242	
	February 2, 2020 (Fiscal 2019)	February 3, 2019 (Fiscal 2018)
Inventory	$14,531	$13,925
Current Assets	19,810	18,529
Property and Equipment, Net	22,770	22,375
Total Assets	51,236	44,003
Current Liabilities	18,375	16,716
Total Liabilities	54,352	45,881

Required:

1. Conduct a horizontal analysis of Inventory and a vertical analysis of the income statement.
2. Compute the following ratios for The Home Depot for the year ended February 2, 2020.

   Fixed Asset Turnover   Inventory Turnover   Current Ratio

   Gross Profit Percentage   Days to Sell   Debt-to-Assets

3. Interpret the meaning of the ratios you calculated in requirement 2.

Suggested Solution

1.

Horizontal Analysis	February 2, 2020	February 3, 2019	Increase
Inventory	$14,531	$13,925	$606 4.4%

Vertical Analysis		
Net Sales Revenue	$110,225	100.0%
Cost of Goods Sold	72,653	65.9
Other Expenses	26,330	23.9
Net Income	$ 11,242	10.2%

2. Calculating ratios:

Fixed Asset Turnover = Net Sales Revenue/Average Net Fixed Assets
= $110,225 ÷ [($22,770 + $22,375) ÷ 2]
= 4.88

Gross Profit Percentage = (Net Sales − Cost of Goods Sold)/Net Sales
= ($110,225 − $72,653) ÷ $110,225
= 0.341 or 34.1%

Inventory Turnover = Cost of Goods Sold/Average Inventory
= $72,653 ÷ [($14,531 + $13,925) ÷ 2]
= 5.11

Days to Sell = 365 ÷ Inventory Turnover Ratio
= 365 ÷ 5.11
= 71.4 days

Current Ratio = Current Assets/Current Liabilities
= $19,810 ÷ $18,375
= 1.08

Debt-to-Assets = Total Liabilities/Total Assets
= $54,352 ÷ $51,236
= 1.06

3. Interpreting ratios

- The fixed asset turnover ratio of 4.88 means that, on average, The Home Depot generated $4.88 of sales for each dollar of fixed assets.
- The gross profit percentage of 34.1 means each dollar of sales generated 34.1 cents of profit, before considering other expenses related to administration, interest, and income taxes.
- The inventory turnover ratio of 5.11 means that The Home Depot turned over (bought and sold) the equivalent of its entire inventory an average of 5.11 times during the year.
- The days to sell ratio of 71.4 means that, on average, 71.4 days elapsed between the time The Home Depot acquired the inventory and the time the company sold it.
- The current ratio of 1.08 means that at year-end, The Home Depot had $1.08 of current assets for each dollar of current liabilities.
- The debt-to-assets ratio of 1.06 means that The Home Depot had more total liabilities than total assets. The Home Depot was able to carry so much debt because, according to its annual report, it had arranged more than $6 billion in additional financing to draw on should further cash flow be needed to pay current liabilities as they come due.

CHAPTER SUMMARY

Describe the purposes and uses of horizontal, vertical, and ratio analyses.   **LO 13-1**

- Horizontal analyses (also called trend analyses) compare financial statement items to comparable amounts in prior periods with the goal of identifying sustained changes, or trends.
- Vertical analyses create common size financial statements that express each line of the income statement (or balance sheet) as a percentage of total sales (or total assets).
- Ratio analyses compare one or more financial statement items to an amount for other items for the same year. Ratios take into account differences in the size of amounts to allow for evaluations of performance given existing levels of other company resources.

Use horizontal (trend) analyses to recognize financial changes that unfold over time.   **LO 13-2**

- Trend analyses involve computing the dollar amount by which each account changes from one period to the next and expressing that change as a percentage of the balance for the prior period.

LO 13-3 **Use vertical (common size) analyses to understand important relationships within financial statements.**

- Vertical (common size) analyses indicate the proportions within each financial statement category.

LO 13-4 **Calculate financial ratios to assess profitability, liquidity, and solvency.**

- Financial ratios are commonly classified with relation to profitability, liquidity, or solvency. Exhibit 13.5 lists common ratios in these three categories and shows how to compute them.
- Profitability ratios focus on measuring the adequacy of a company's income by comparing it to other items reported on the financial statements.
- Liquidity ratios measure a company's ability to meet its current debt obligations.
- Solvency ratios measure a company's ability to meet its long-term debt obligations.

LO 13-5 **Interpret the results of financial analyses.**

- Financial analyses are not complete unless they lead to an interpretation that helps financial statement users understand and evaluate a company's financial results.
- An understanding of whether a business is successful emerges only after you have learned to combine analyses into a complete picture or story that depicts the company's performance.
- To assist in developing this picture or story, most analysts compare to benchmarks such as the company's performance in prior years or to competitors' performance in the current year.

LO 13-6 **Describe how analyses depend on key accounting decisions and concepts.**

- Before comparing across companies or time periods, users should determine the extent to which differences in accounting decisions (e.g., methods used to account for inventory, depreciation, contingent liabilities, etc.) might reduce the comparability or consistency of the financial information being compared.
- Many accounting concepts were presented throughout earlier chapters, all of which aim to make accounting information more useful for creditors and investors. Two new concepts were explained in this chapter:
  - Full disclosure principle—a company's financial statements should provide all information that is important to users' decisions.
  - Going-concern (continuity) assumption—a business is assumed to continue to operate into the foreseeable future.

Accounting Decision Tools
See Exhibit 13.5 for a summary

KEY TERMS

Comprehensive Income p. 628

Discontinued Operations p. 628

Full Disclosure Principle p. 627

Going-Concern (Continuity)
   Assumption p. 627

Horizontal (Trend) Analyses p. 615

Liquidity p. 618

Profitability p. 618

Solvency p. 618

Vertical (Common Size) Analysis p. 617

See complete definitions in the glossary in the back of this text.

HOMEWORK HELPER

Helpful reminders

- Ratios that include both income statement and balance sheet accounts require you to calculate an average for the balance sheet accounts rather than just use the end-of-period balance. An average ensures the balance sheet data cover the same period as the income statement data.

- To calculate averages for the current and prior years, you will need three years of balance sheet data. (The statement of stockholders' equity reports three years of stockholders' equity data. To calculate averages for other balance sheet accounts, you will need comparative balance sheets from at least two annual reports.)
- The pronoun for referring to a specific company is "its," not "their."

Frequent mistakes

- In calculating year-over-year percentages, divide the change in the account balance by its balance from the prior year, not the current year.

PRACTICE MATERIAL

QUESTIONS (⊖ Symbol indicates questions that require analysis from more than one perspective.)

1. What is the general goal of trend analysis?

2. How is a year-over-year percentage calculated?

3. What is ratio analysis? Why is it useful?

4. What benchmarks are commonly used for interpreting ratios?

5. Into what three categories of performance are most financial ratios reported? To what in particular does each of these categories relate?

6. Why are some analyses called *horizontal* and others called *vertical*?

7. Slow Cellar's current ratio increased from 1.2 to 1.5. What is one favorable interpretation of this change? What is one unfavorable interpretation of this change? ⊖

8. From last year to this year, Colossal Company's current ratio increased and its inventory turnover decreased. Does this imply a higher, or lower, risk of obsolete inventory? ⊖

9. From last year to this year, Berry Barn reported that its Net Sales increased from $300,000 to $400,000 and its Gross Profit increased from $90,000 to $130,000. Was the Gross Profit increase caused by (a) an increase in sales volume only, (b) an increase in gross profit per sale only, or (c) a combination of both? Explain your answer. ⊖

10. Explain whether the following situations, taken independently, would be favorable or unfavorable: (a) increase in gross profit percentage, (b) decrease in inventory turnover ratio, (c) increase in earnings per share, (d) decrease in days to collect, and (e) increase in net profit margin.

11. What are the two essential characteristics of useful financial information? What other characteristics enhance the usefulness of financial information?

12. What is the primary objective of financial reporting?

13. What is the full disclosure principle?

14. What is the going-concern assumption? What is a going-concern problem? What factors can contribute to such a problem?

15. (Supplement 13A) Explain where and how discontinued operations are reported on the income statement.

16. (Supplement 13B) Techgear is an electronics company in the United States. It uses the LIFO inventory method. You plan to compare its ratios to those of Eurotext, but you are concerned because Eurotext uses IFRS. What accounting policy difference is certain to exist between the two companies? Of the ratios in Exhibit 13.5, name five that will be affected by this difference. ⊖

MULTIPLE CHOICE

1. Which of the following ratios is *not* used to analyze profitability?

   a. Net profit margin ratio.
   b. Gross profit percentage.
   c. Current ratio.
   d. Return on equity.

2. Which of the following would *not* directly change the receivables turnover ratio for a company?

   a. Selling your inventory on credit at higher prices.
   b. A change in your credit policy.
   c. Increases in the cost you incur to purchase inventory.
   d. All of the above would directly change the receivables turnover ratio.

3. Which of the following ratios is used to analyze liquidity?

   a. Earnings per share.
   b. Debt-to-assets.
   c. Current ratio.
   d. Both *b* and *c*.

4. Analysts use ratios to

   a. Compare different companies in the same industry.
   b. Track a company's performance over time.
   c. Compare a company's performance to industry averages.
   d. All of the above describe ways that analysts use ratios.

5. Which of the following ratios incorporates stock market data?

   a. Inventory turnover.
   b. Earnings per share.
   c. Price/earnings ratio.
   d. All of the above.

6. Given the following ratios for four companies, which company is least likely to experience problems paying its current liabilities promptly?

	Current Ratio	Receivables Turnover Ratio
a.	1.2	7.0
b.	1.2	6.0
c.	1.0	6.0
d.	0.5	7.0

7. A decrease in Selling and Administrative Expenses would directly impact what ratio?

   a. Fixed asset turnover ratio.
   b. Times interest earned.
   c. Current ratio.
   d. Gross profit percentage.

8. A bank is least likely to use which of the following ratios when analyzing the likelihood that a borrower will pay interest and principal on its loans?

   a. Current ratio.   c. Times interest earned ratio.
   b. Debt-to-assets ratio.   d. Price/earnings ratio.

9. Which of the following accounting concepts do accountants and auditors assess by using financial analyses?

   a. Time period.
   b. Separate entity.
   c. Full disclosure.
   d. Going-concern assumption.

10. (Supplement 13A) Which of the following items is reported net of related income taxes?

   a. Gain or loss from discontinued operations.
   b. Gain or loss from disposal of property, plant, and equipment.
   c. Interest on long-term debt.
   d. Gain or loss from early extinguishment of debt.

> For answers to the Multiple-Choice Questions **see page Q1** located in the last section of the book.

MINI-EXERCISES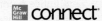

LO 13-2   **M13-1 Calculations for Horizontal Analyses**

Using the following income statements, perform the calculations needed for horizontal analyses. Round percentages to one decimal place.

		LOCKEY FENCING CORPORATION Income Statements For the Years Ended December 31	
		Current	**Previous**
Net Sales		$100,000	$75,000
Cost of Goods Sold		58,000	45,000
Gross Profit		42,000	30,000
Selling, General, and Administrative Expenses		9,000	4,500
Income from Operations		33,000	25,500
Interest Expense		3,000	3,750
Income before Income Tax		30,000	21,750
Income Tax Expense		9,000	6,525
Net Income		$ 21,000	$15,225

LO 13-3   **M13-2 Calculations for Vertical Analyses**

Refer to M13-1. Perform the calculations needed for vertical analyses. Round percentages to one decimal place.

LO 13-5   **M13-3 Interpreting Horizontal Analyses**

Refer to the calculations from M13-1. What are the two most significant year-over-year changes in terms of dollars and in terms of percentages? Give one potential cause of each of these changes.

LO 13-5   **M13-4 Interpreting Vertical Analyses**

Refer to the calculations from M13-2. Which of the ratios from Exhibit 13.5 have been included in these calculations? Have these two ratios improved or deteriorated in the current year compared to the previous year?

M13-5 Inferring Financial Information Using Gross Profit Percentage   LO 13-4

Your campus computer store reported Sales Revenue of $168,000. The company's gross profit percentage was 60.0 percent. What amount of Cost of Goods Sold did the company report?

M13-6 Inferring Financial Information Using Gross Profit Percentage   LO 13-2, 13-4
and Year-over-Year Comparisons

A consumer products company reported a 25 percent increase in sales from last year to this year. Sales last year were $200,000. This year, the company reported Cost of Goods Sold in the amount of $150,000. What was the gross profit percentage this year? Round to one decimal place.

M13-7 Computing the Return on Equity Ratio   LO 13-4

Given the following data, compute the return on equity ratio for the current year (expressed as a percentage with one decimal place).

	Current	Previous
Net income	$ 1,850	$ 1,600
Stockholders' equity	10,000	13,125
Total assets	24,000	26,000
Interest expense	400	300

M13-8 Analyzing the Inventory Turnover Ratio   LO 13-4, 13-5

A manufacturer reported an inventory turnover ratio of 8.6 last year. During the current year, management introduced a new inventory control system that was expected to reduce average inventory levels by 25 percent without affecting sales volume. Given these circumstances, would you expect the inventory turnover ratio to increase or decrease during the current year? Explain.

M13-9 Inferring Financial Information Using the Current Ratio   LO 13-4

Mystic Laboratories reported total assets of $11,200,000 and noncurrent assets of $1,480,000. The company also reported a current ratio of 1.5. What amount of current liabilities did the company report?

M13-10 Inferring Financial Information Using the P/E Ratio   LO 13-4

Last year, Big W Company reported earnings per share of $2.50 when its stock was selling for $50.00. If its earnings this year increase by 10 percent and the P/E ratio remains constant, what will be the price of its stock? Explain.

M13-11 Identifying Relevant Ratios   LO 13-4, 13-5

Identify the ratio that is relevant to answering each of the following questions.

a. How much net income does the company earn from each dollar of sales?
b. Is the company financed primarily by debt or equity?
c. How many dollars of sales were generated for each dollar invested in fixed assets?
d. How many days, on average, does it take the company to collect on credit sales made to customers?
e. How much net income does the company earn for each dollar owners have invested in it?
f. Does the company have sufficient assets to convert into cash for paying liabilities as they come due in the upcoming year?

M13-12 Interpreting Ratios   LO 13-4, 13-5

Generally speaking, do the following indicate good news or bad news?

a. Increase in times interest earned ratio.
b. Decrease in days to sell.
c. Increase in gross profit percentage.
d. Decrease in EPS.
e. Increase in fixed asset turnover ratio.

M13-13 Analyzing the Impact of Accounting Alternatives   LO 13-6

Nevis Corporation operates in an industry where costs are falling. The company is considering changing its inventory method from FIFO to LIFO and wants to determine the impact that the change would have on selected accounting ratios in future years. In general, what impact would you expect on the following ratios: net profit margin, fixed asset turnover, and current ratio?

LO 13-6   **M13-14 Describing the Effect of Accounting Decisions on Ratios**

For each of the following three accounting choices, indicate the decision that will yield (*a*) a higher net profit margin and (*b*) a lower current ratio. If the decision does not affect the ratio, indicate "no effect."

1. Straight-line versus accelerated depreciation (in the first year of the asset's life).
2. FIFO versus LIFO (in periods of constantly rising costs and rising inventory levels).
3. Straight-line depreciation with a four-year useful life versus a seven-year useful life (no residual value).

EXERCISES

LO 13-2, 13-3, 13-5   **E13-1 Preparing and Interpreting a Schedule for Horizontal and Vertical Analyses**

Chevron Corporation

The average price of a gallon of gas in 2018 increased $0.30 (12.4 percent) from $2.42 in 2017 (to $2.72 in 2018). Let's see whether these changes are reflected in the income statement of Chevron Corporation for the year ended December 31, 2018 (amounts in billions).

	2018	2017
Revenues	$166	$142
Costs of Purchased Crude Oil and Products	95	76
Other Operating Costs	50	57
Income before Income Tax Expense	21	9
Income Tax Expense	6	—
Net Income	$ 15	$ 9

Required:

1. Conduct a horizontal analysis by calculating the year-over-year changes in each line item, expressed in dollars and in percentages (rounded to one decimal place). How did the change in gas prices compare to the changes in Chevron's total revenues and costs of crude oil and products?
2. Conduct a vertical analysis by expressing each line as a percentage of total revenues (round to one decimal place). Excluding income tax and other operating costs, did Chevron earn more gross profit per dollar of revenue in 2018 compared to 2017?

LO 13-4, 13-5   **E13-2 Computing and Interpreting Profitability Ratios**

Chevron Corporation

Use the information for Chevron Corporation in E13-1 to complete the following requirements.

Required:

1. Compute the gross profit percentage for each year (rounded to one decimal place). Assuming that the change from 2017 to 2018 is the beginning of a sustained trend, is Chevron likely to earn more or less gross profit from each dollar of sales in 2019?
2. Compute the net profit margin for each year (expressed as a percentage with one decimal place). Given your calculations here and in requirement 1, explain whether Chevron did a better or worse job of controlling expenses other than the costs of crude oil and products in 2018 relative to 2017.
3. Chevron reported average net fixed assets of $342 billion in 2018 and $340 billion in 2017. Compute the fixed asset turnover ratios for both years (round to two decimal places). Did the company better utilize its investment in fixed assets to generate revenues in 2018 or 2017?
4. Chevron reported average stockholders' equity of $152 billion in 2018 and $148 billion in 2017. The company has not issued preferred stock. Compute the return on equity ratios for both years (expressed as a percentage with one decimal place). Did the company generate greater returns for stockholders in 2018 or 2017?

E13-3 Preparing and Interpreting a Schedule for Horizontal and Vertical Analyses

LO 13-2, 13-3, 13-5

According to the producer price index database maintained by the Bureau of Labor Statistics, the average cost of computer equipment fell 3.6 percent between January and December 2018. Let's see whether these changes are reflected in the income statement of Computer Tycoon Inc. for the year ended December 31, 2018.

	2018	2017
Sales Revenue	$100,000	$120,000
Cost of Goods Sold	60,000	71,500
Gross Profit	40,000	48,500
Selling, General, and Administrative Expenses	36,000	37,000
Interest Expense	500	475
Income before Income Tax Expense	3,500	11,025
Income Tax Expense	1,000	5,000
Net Income	$ 2,500	$ 6,025

Required:

1. Conduct a horizontal analysis by calculating the year-over-year changes in each line item, expressed in dollars and in percentages (rounded to one decimal place). How did the change in computer prices compare to the changes in Computer Tycoon's sales revenues?

2. Conduct a vertical analysis by expressing each line as a percentage of total revenues (round to one decimal place). Excluding income tax, interest, and operating expenses, did Computer Tycoon earn more profit per dollar of sales in 2018 compared to 2017?

E13-4 Computing Profitability Ratios

LO 13-4, 13-5

Use the information in E13-3 to complete the following requirements.

Required:

1. Compute the gross profit percentage for each year (rounded to one decimal place). Assuming that the change from 2017 to 2018 is the beginning of a sustained trend, is Computer Tycoon likely to earn more or less gross profit from each dollar of sales in 2019?

2. Compute the net profit margin for each year (expressed as a percentage with one decimal place). Given your calculations here and in requirement 1, explain whether Computer Tycoon did a better or worse job of controlling operating expenses in 2018 relative to 2017.

3. Computer Tycoon reported average net fixed assets of $54,200 in 2018 and $45,100 in 2017. Compute the fixed asset turnover ratios for both years (round to two decimal places). Did the company better utilize its investment in fixed assets to generate revenues in 2018 or 2017?

4. Computer Tycoon reported average stockholders' equity of $54,000 in 2018 and $40,800 in 2017. The company has not issued preferred stock. Compute the return on equity ratios for both years (expressed as a percentage with one decimal place). Did the company generate greater returns for stockholders in 2018 than in 2017?

E13-5 Computing a Commonly Used Solvency Ratio

LO 13-4, 13-5

Use the information in E13-3 to complete the following requirement.

Required:

Compute the times interest earned ratios for 2018 and 2017. In your opinion, does Computer Tycoon generate sufficient net income (before taxes and interest) to cover the cost of debt financing?

E13-6 Matching Each Ratio with Its Computational Formula

LO 13-4

Match each ratio or percentage with its formula by entering the appropriate letter for each numbered item.

Ratios or Percentages	Formula
____ 1. Current ratio	A. Net income ÷ Total revenue
____ 2. Net profit margin	B. (Net sales revenue − Cost of goods sold) ÷ Net sales revenue
____ 3. Inventory turnover ratio	C. Current assets ÷ Current liabilities
____ 4. Gross profit percentage	D. Cost of goods sold ÷ Average inventory
____ 5. Fixed asset turnover	E. Net credit sales revenue ÷ Average net receivables
____ 6. Return on equity	F. (Net income − Preferred dividends) ÷ Average number of common shares outstanding
____ 7. Times interest earned	G. Total liabilities ÷ Total assets
____ 8. Debt-to-assets ratio	H. (Net income + Interest expense + Income tax expense) ÷ Interest expense
____ 9. Price/earnings ratio	I. Current market price per share ÷ Earnings per share
____ 10. Receivables turnover ratio	J. (Net income − Preferred dividends) ÷ Average common stockholders' equity
____ 11. Earnings per share	K. Total revenue ÷ Average net fixed assets

LO 13-4, 13-5

E13-7 Computing and Interpreting Selected Liquidity Ratios

Double West Suppliers (DWS) reported sales for the year of $300,000, all on credit. The average gross profit percentage was 40 percent on sales. Account balances follow:

	Beginning	Ending
Accounts receivable (net)	$45,000	$55,000
Inventory	60,000	40,000

Required:

1. Compute the turnover ratios for accounts receivable and inventory (round to one decimal place).
2. By dividing 365 by your ratios from requirement 1, calculate the average days to collect receivables and the average days to sell inventory (round to one decimal place).
3. Explain what each of these ratios and measures means for DWS.

LO 13-4, 13-5

Cintas Corporation

E13-8 Computing and Interpreting Liquidity Ratios

Cintas Corporation is the largest uniform supplier in North America. Selected information from its annual report follows. For the 2019 fiscal year, the company reported sales revenue of $5.6 billion and Cost of Goods Sold of $3.0 billion.

Fiscal Year	2019	2018
Balance Sheet (amounts in millions)		
Cash and Cash Equivalents	$ 97	$139
Accounts Receivable, Net	910	805
Inventory	335	280
Prepaid Rent and Other Current Assets	894	754
Accounts Payable	226	215
Salaries and Wages Payable	156	141
Notes Payable (short-term)	312	0
Other Current Liabilities	434	420

Required:

Assuming that all sales are on credit, compute the current ratio (two decimal places), inventory turnover ratio (one decimal place), and accounts receivable turnover ratio (one decimal place) for 2019. Explain what each ratio means for Cintas.

LO 13-4, 13-5

Procter & Gamble

E13-9 Computing the Accounts Receivable and Inventory Turnover Ratios

Procter & Gamble (P&G) manufactures and markets many products you use every day. In 2019, sales for the company were $67,684 (all amounts in millions). The annual report did not report the amount of credit sales, so we will assume that all sales were on credit. The average gross profit percentage was 48.6 percent. Account balances for the year follow:

	Beginning	Ending
Accounts receivable (net)	$4,686	$4,951
Inventory	4,738	5,017

Required:

1. Rounded to one decimal place, compute the turnover ratios for accounts receivable and inventory.
2. By dividing 365 by your ratios from requirement 1, calculate the average days to collect receivables and the average days to sell inventory.
3. Interpret what these ratios and measures mean for P&G.

E13-10 Inferring Financial Information from Profitability and Liquidity Ratios

LO 13-4, 13-5

Dollar General Corporation

Dollar General Corporation operates general merchandise stores that feature quality merchandise at low prices to meet the needs of middle-, low-, and fixed-income families in southern, eastern, and midwestern states. For the year ended February 1, 2019, the company reported average inventory of $3,850 (in millions) and an inventory turnover of 4.63. Average total fixed assets were $2,836 (million) and the fixed asset turnover ratio was 9.04.

Required:

1. Calculate Dollar General's gross profit percentage (expressed as a percentage with one decimal place). What does this imply about the amount of gross profit made from each dollar of sales?
   TIP: Work backward from the fixed asset turnover and inventory turnover ratios to compute the amounts needed for the gross profit percentage.
2. Is this an improvement from the gross profit percentage of 30.8 percent earned during the previous year?

E13-11 Analyzing the Impact of Selected Transactions on the Current Ratio

LO 13-4, 13-5

In its most recent annual report, Appalachian Beverages reported current assets of $54,000 and a current ratio of 1.80. Assume that the following transactions were completed: (1) purchased merchandise for $6,000 on account and (2) purchased a delivery truck for $10,000, paying $1,000 cash and signing a two-year promissory note for the balance.

Required:

Compute the updated current ratio, rounded to two decimal places, after each transaction.

E13-12 Analyzing the Impact of Selected Transactions on the Current Ratio

LO 13-4, 13-5

In its most recent annual report, Sunrise Enterprises reported current assets of $1,090,000 and current liabilities of $602,000. Sunrise Enterprises uses a perpetual inventory system.

Required:

Determine for each of the following transactions whether the current ratio, and each of its two components, for Sunrise will increase, decrease, or have no change: (1) sold long-term assets for cash, (2) accrued severance pay for terminated employees, (3) wrote down the carrying value of certain inventory items that were deemed to be obsolete, and (4) acquired new inventory by signing an 18-month promissory note (the supplier was not willing to provide normal credit terms).

E13-13 Analyzing the Impact of Selected Transactions on the Current Ratio

LO 13-4, 13-5

Good Sports, Inc., is a private full-line sporting goods retailer. Assume one of the Good Sports stores reported current assets of $88,000 and its current ratio was 1.75, and then completed the following transactions: (1) paid $6,000 on accounts payable, (2) purchased a delivery truck for $10,000 cash, (3) wrote off a bad account receivable for $2,000, and (4) paid previously declared dividends in the amount of $25,000.

Required:

Compute the updated current ratio, rounded to two decimal places, after each transaction.

E13-14 Analyzing the Impact of Selected Transactions on the Current Ratio

LO 13-4, 13-5

A company has current assets that total $500,000, has a current ratio of 2.00, and uses the perpetual inventory method. Assume that the following transactions are then completed: (1) sold $12,000 in merchandise on short-term credit for $15,000, (2) declared but did not pay dividends of $50,000, (3) paid prepaid rent in the amount of $12,000, (4) paid previously declared dividends in the amount of $50,000, (5) collected an account receivable in the amount of $12,000, and (6) reclassified $40,000 of long-term debt as a current liability.

Required:

Compute the updated current ratio, rounded to two decimal places, after each transaction.

LO 13-6   **E13-15 Analyzing the Impact of Alternative Inventory Methods on Selected Ratios**

Company A uses the FIFO method to cost inventory and Company B uses the LIFO method. The two companies are exactly alike except for the difference in inventory costing methods. Costs of inventory items for both companies have been falling steadily in recent years and each company has increased its inventory each year. Ignore income tax effects.

Required:

Identify which company will report the higher amount for each of the following ratios. If it is not possible to identify which will report the higher amount, explain why.

1. Current ratio.
2. Debt-to-assets ratio.
3. Earnings per share.

COACHED PROBLEMS

LO 13-2, 13-5   **CP13-1 Analyzing Comparative Financial Statements Using Horizontal Analyses**

Golden Corporation declared and paid $3,000 of cash dividends during the current year ended December 31. Its financial statements also reported the following summarized data:

	Current	Previous	Increase (Decrease) in Current (versus Previous)	
			Amount	Percentage
Income Statement				
Sales revenue	$180,000	$165,000		
Cost of goods sold	110,000	100,000		
Gross profit	70,000	65,000		
Operating expenses	53,300	50,400		
Interest expense	2,700	2,600		
Income before income taxes	14,000	12,000		
Income tax expense	4,000	3,000		
Net income	$ 10,000	$ 9,000		
Balance Sheet				
Cash	$ 4,000	$ 8,000		
Accounts receivable (net)	19,000	23,000		
Inventory	40,000	35,000		
Property and equipment (net)	45,000	38,000		
Total assets	$108,000	$104,000		
Current liabilities	$ 16,000	$ 19,000		
Notes payable (long-term)	45,000	45,000		
Common stock (par $5)	30,000	30,000		
Additional paid-in capital	5,000	5,000		
Retained earnings	12,000	5,000		
Total liabilities and stockholders' equity	$108,000	$104,000		

Required:

1. Complete the two final columns shown beside each item in Golden Corporation's comparative financial statements. Round the percentages to one decimal place.

   TIP: Calculate the increase (decrease) by subtracting the previous year from the current year. Calculate the percentage by dividing the amount of increase (decrease) by the previous-year balance.

2. Use the horizontal (trend) analyses to identify (*a*) a large percentage change in one account that is accompanied by a small dollar change and (*b*) a directional change in one account balance that is inconsistent with the direction of change in a related account balance.

CP13-2 Analyzing Comparative Financial Statements Using Selected Ratios

LO 13-4, 13-5

Use the data given in CP13-1 for Golden Corporation.

Required:

1. Compute the gross profit percentage for the current and previous years. Round the percentages to one decimal place. Are the current-year results better, or worse, than those for the previous year?

2. Compute the net profit margin for the current and previous years. Round the percentages to one decimal place. Are the current-year results better, or worse, than those for the previous year?

3. Compute the earnings per share for the current and previous years. Are the current-year results better, or worse, than those for the previous year?

   TIP: To calculate EPS, use the balance in Common Stock to determine the number of shares outstanding. Common Stock equals the par value per share times the number of shares.

4. Stockholders' equity totaled $30,000 at the beginning of the previous year. Compute the return on equity (ROE) ratios for the current and previous years. Express the ROE as percentages rounded to one decimal place. Are the current-year results better, or worse, than those for the previous year?

5. Net property and equipment totaled $35,000 at the beginning of the previous year. Compute the fixed asset turnover ratios for the current and previous years. Round the ratios to two decimal places. Are the current-year results better, or worse, than those for the previous year?

6. Compute the debt-to-assets ratios for the current and previous years. Round the ratios to two decimal places. Is debt providing financing for a larger or smaller proportion of the company's asset growth? Explain.

7. Compute the times interest earned ratios for the current and previous years. Round the ratios to one decimal place. Are the current-year results better, or worse, than those for the previous year? Explain.

8. After Golden released its current year's financial statements, the company's stock was trading at $30. After the release of its previous year's financial statements, the company's stock price was $21 per share. Compute the P/E ratios for both years, rounded to one decimal place. Does it appear that investors have become more (or less) optimistic about Golden's future success?

CP13-3 Vertical Analysis of a Balance Sheet

LO 13-3, 13-5

A condensed balance sheet for Jerma Games, Inc., and a partially completed vertical analysis are presented below.

JERMA GAMES, INC.
Balance Sheet (summarized)
March 31, 2019
(in millions of U.S. dollars)

Cash and Cash Equivalents	$3,834	54%	Accounts Payable	$ 960	14%
Accounts Receivable, Net	233	3	Deferred Revenue	1,458	*d*
Inventory	33	1	Notes Payable (long-term)	1,236	17
Other Current Assets	254	*a*	Total Liabilities	3,654	52
Intangibles	1,767	*b*	Common Stock	1,352	*e*
Property and Equipment, Net	439	*c*	Retained Earnings	2,044	29
Other Assets	490	7	Total Stockholders' Equity	3,396	48
Total Assets	$7,050	100%	Total Liabilities & Stockholders' Equity	$7,050	100%

Required:

1. Complete the vertical analysis by computing each line item (*a*)–(*e*) as a percentage of total assets. Round to the nearest whole percentage.

   TIP: Accounts Receivable was 3 percent, computed as ($233 ÷ $7,050).

2. What percentages of Jerma Games's assets relate to intangibles versus property and equipment? Which of these two asset groups is more significant to Jerma Games's business?

LO 13-3, 13-5 **CP13-4 Vertical Analysis of an Income Statement**

A condensed income statement for Jerma Games, Inc., and a partially completed vertical analysis follow.

JERMA GAMES, INC.				
Income Statement (summarized)				
For the Year Ended March 31				
(in millions of U.S. dollars)				
	2019		**2018**	
Net Revenues	$4,396	100%	$4,515	100%
Cost of Goods Sold	1,354	*a*	1,429	32
Research and Development Expense	1,109	*b*	1,094	24
Sales and Marketing Expense	622	*c*	647	14
General and Administrative Expense	413	10	397	9
Income from Operations	898	20	948	21
Other Expenses	21	0	23	1
Income before Income Tax	877	20	925	20
Income Tax Recovery (Expense)	279	6	(50)	(1)
Net Income	$1,156	*d*%	$ 875	19

Required:

1. Complete the vertical analysis by computing each line item (*a*)–(*d*) as a percentage of net revenues. Round to the nearest whole percentage.

   TIP: In the prior year, Cost of Goods Sold was 32 percent of Net Revenues, computed as ($1,429 ÷ $4,515).

2. Does Cost of Goods Sold, as a percentage of Net Revenues, represent better or worse performance in 2019 as compared to 2018?

LO 13-4, 13-5 **CP13-5 Interpreting Profitability, Liquidity, Solvency, and P/E Ratios**

Kohl's Corporation

Macy's

Kohl's Corporation is a national retail department store. The company's total revenues for the twelve months ended August 2, 2019, were $20.0 billion. Macy's is a larger department store company with $24.9 billion of revenues for the same period. The following ratios for the two companies were obtained for this period from csimarket.com:

Ratio	Kohl's	Macy's
a. Gross profit percentage	39.6%	38.5%
b. Net profit margin	3.7%	4.1%
c. Return on equity	13.5%	16.6%
d. EPS	$4.54	$3.35
e. Inventory turnover ratio	3.08	2.67
f. Current ratio	1.83	1.47
g. Debt-to-assets	0.62	0.70
h. P/E ratio	10.7	4.8

Required:

1. For each ratio listed, indicate whether it would be used to compare profitability (P), liquidity (L), or solvency (S). If any measure is not applicable to comparing companies, indicate NA.

2. Which company appears more profitable? Describe the ratio(s) that you used to reach this decision.

3. Which company appears more liquid? Describe the ratio(s) that you used to reach this decision.

4. Which company appears more solvent? Describe the ratio(s) that you used to reach this decision.

5. Are the conclusions from your analyses in requirements 2–4 consistent with the value of the two companies, as suggested by their P/E ratios? If not, offer one explanation for any apparent inconsistency.

   TIP: The stock price in the top of the P/E ratio represents investors' expectations about future financial performance whereas the bottom number reports past financial performance.

CP13-6 Using Ratios to Compare Alternative Investment Opportunities

LO 13-4, 13-5, 13-6

The financial statements for Armstrong and Blair companies are summarized here:

	Armstrong Company	Blair Company
Balance Sheet		
Cash	$ 35,000	$ 22,000
Accounts Receivable, Net	40,000	30,000
Inventory	100,000	40,000
Equipment, Net	180,000	300,000
Other Assets	45,000	408,000
Total Assets	$400,000	$800,000
Current Liabilities	$100,000	$ 50,000
Notes Payable (long-term)	60,000	370,000
Total Liabilities	160,000	420,000
Common Stock (par $10)	150,000	200,000
Additional Paid-In Capital	30,000	110,000
Retained Earnings	60,000	70,000
Total Liabilities and Stockholders' Equity	$400,000	$800,000
Income Statement		
Sales Revenue	$450,000	$810,000
Cost of Goods Sold	245,000	405,000
Other Expenses	160,000	315,000
Net Income	$ 45,000	$ 90,000
Other Data		
Estimated value of each share at end of year	$ 18	$ 27
Selected Data from Previous Year		
Accounts Receivable, Net	$ 20,000	$ 38,000
Inventory	92,000	45,000
Equipment, Net	180,000	300,000
Note Payable (long-term)	60,000	70,000
Total Stockholders' Equity	231,000	440,000

The companies are in the same line of business and are direct competitors in a large metropolitan area. Both have been in business approximately 10 years and each has had steady growth. Despite these similarities, the management of each has a different viewpoint in many respects. Blair is more conservative, and as its president said, "We avoid what we consider to be undue risk." Both companies use straight-line depreciation, but Blair estimates slightly shorter useful lives than Armstrong. No shares were issued in the current year and neither company is publicly held. Blair Company has an annual audit by a CPA, but Armstrong Company does not. Assume the end-of-year total assets and net equipment balances approximate the year's average and all sales are on account.

Required:

1. Calculate the ratios in Exhibit 13.5 for which sufficient information is available. Round all calculations to two decimal places.

   TIP: To calculate EPS, use the balance in Common Stock to determine the number of shares outstanding. Common Stock equals the par value per share times the number of shares.

2. A venture capitalist is considering buying shares in one of the two companies. Based on the data given, prepare a comparative written evaluation of the ratio analyses (and any other available information) and conclude with your recommended choice.

> **TIP:** Comment on how accounting differences affect your evaluations, if at all.

LO 13-5   **CP13-7 Analyzing an Investment by Comparing Selected Ratios**

You have the opportunity to invest $10,000 in one of two companies from a single industry. The only information you have follows. The word *high* refers to the top third of the industry; *average* is the middle third; *low* is the bottom third.

Ratio	Company A	Company B
Current	High	Average
Inventory turnover	Low	Average
Debt-to-assets	High	Average
Times interest earned	Low	Average
Price/earnings	Low	Average

Required:

Which company should you select? Write a brief explanation for your recommendation.

> **TIP:** When interpreting ratios, think about how they are related to one another. For example, the current ratio and the inventory turnover ratio both include the Inventory balance. This means that the low inventory turnover ratio can help you to interpret the high current ratio.

GROUP A PROBLEMS

LO 13-2, 13-5   **PA13-1 Analyzing Financial Statements Using Horizontal Analyses**

Pinnacle Plus declared and paid a cash dividend of $6,600 in the current year. Its comparative financial statements, prepared at December 31, reported the following summarized information:

	Current	Previous	Increase (Decrease) in Current (versus Previous) Amount	Percentage
Income Statement				
Sales Revenue	$110,000	$ 99,000		
Cost of Goods Sold	52,000	48,000		
Gross Profit	58,000	51,000		
Operating Expenses	36,000	33,000		
Interest Expense	4,000	4,000		
Income before Income Tax Expense	18,000	14,000		
Income Tax Expense (30%)	5,400	4,200		
Net Income	$ 12,600	$ 9,800		
Balance Sheet				
Cash	$ 69,500	$ 38,000		
Accounts Receivable, Net	17,000	12,000		
Inventory	25,000	38,000		
Property and Equipment, Net	95,000	105,000		
Total Assets	$206,500	$193,000		
Accounts Payable	$ 42,000	$ 35,000		
Income Tax Payable	1,000	500		
Notes Payable (long-term)	40,000	40,000		
Total Liabilities	83,000	75,500		
Common Stock (par $10)	90,000	90,000		
Retained Earnings	33,500	27,500		
Total Liabilities and Stockholders' Equity	$206,500	$193,000		

Required:

1. Complete the two final columns shown beside each item in Pinnacle Plus's comparative financial statements. Round the percentages to one decimal place.
2. Which account increased by the largest dollar amount? Which account increased by the largest percentage?

PA13-2 Analyzing Comparative Financial Statements Using Selected Ratios   LO 13-4, 13-5

Use the data given in PA13-1 for Pinnacle Plus.

Required:

1. Compute the gross profit percentage in the current and previous years. Round the percentages to one decimal place. Are the current-year results better, or worse, than those for the previous year?
2. Compute the net profit margin for the current and previous years. Round the percentages to one decimal place. Are the current-year results better, or worse, than those for the previous year?
3. Compute the earnings per share for the current and previous years. Are the current-year results better, or worse, than those for the previous year?
4. Stockholders' equity totaled $100,000 at the beginning of the previous year. Compute the return on equity (ROE) ratios for the current and previous years. Express the ROE as percentages rounded to one decimal place. Are the current-year results better, or worse, than those for the previous year?
5. Net property and equipment totaled $110,000 at the beginning of the previous year. Compute the fixed asset turnover ratios for the current and previous years. Round the ratios to two decimal places. Are the current-year results better, or worse, than those for the previous year?
6. Compute the debt-to-assets ratios for the current and previous years. Round the ratios to two decimal places. Is debt providing financing for a larger or smaller proportion of the company's asset growth?
7. Compute the times interest earned ratios for the current and previous years. Round the ratios to one decimal place. Are the current-year results better, or worse, than those for the previous year?
8. After Pinnacle Plus released its current year's financial statements, the company's stock was trading at $18. After the release of its previous year's financial statements, the company's stock price was $15 per share. Compute the P/E ratios for both years, rounded to one decimal place. Does it appear that investors have become more (or less) optimistic about Pinnacle's future success?

PA13-3 Vertical Analysis of a Balance Sheet   LO 13-3, 13-5

A condensed balance sheet for Simultech Corporation and a partially completed vertical analysis are presented below.

SIMULTECH CORPORATION Balance Sheet (summarized) January 31 (in millions of U.S. dollars)					
Cash	$ 433	29%	Current Liabilities	$ 409	27%
Accounts Receivable	294	19	Long-Term Liabilities	495	33
Inventory	206	14	Total Liabilities	904	b
Other Current Assets	109	a	Common Stock	118	c
Property and Equipment	27	2	Retained Earnings	492	32
Other Assets	445	29	Total Stockholders' Equity	610	d
Total Assets	$1,514	100%	Total Liabilities & Stockholders' Equity	$1,514	100%

Required:

1. Complete the vertical analysis by computing each line item (a)–(d) as a percentage of total assets. Round to the nearest whole percentage.

2. What percentages of Simultech's assets relate to inventory versus property and equipment? Which of these two asset groups is more significant to Simultech's business?

3. What percentage of Simultech's assets is financed by total stockholders' equity? By total liabilities?

LO 13-3, 13-5   **PA13-4   Vertical Analysis of an Income Statement**

A condensed income statement for Simultech Corporation and a partially completed vertical analysis are presented below.

SIMULTECH CORPORATION Income Statement (summarized) (in millions of U.S. dollars)				
	Current Year		**Previous Year**	
Sales Revenues	$2,062	100%	$2,200	100%
Cost of Goods Sold	1,637	79	1,721	d
Selling, General, and Administrative Expenses	333	a	346	16
Other Operating Expenses	53	3	12	1
Interest Expense	22	b	26	1
Income before Income Tax Expense	17	1	95	e
Income Tax Expense	6	0	33	1
Net Income	$ 11	c%	$ 62	f%

Required:

1. Complete the vertical analysis by computing each line item (a)–(f) as a percentage of sales revenues. Round to the nearest whole percentage.

2. Does Simultech's Cost of Goods Sold for the current year, as a percentage of revenues, represent better or worse performance as compared to that for the previous year?

3. Has Simultech's net profit margin increased, or decreased, over the two years?

LO 13-4, 13-5   **PA13-5   Interpreting Profitability, Liquidity, Solvency, and P/E Ratios**

Coca-Cola Co.
PepsiCo

Coke and Pepsi are well-known international brands. Coca-Cola Co. sells more than $34.5 billion each year while annual sales of PepsiCo products exceed $66 billion. Compare the two companies as a potential investment based on the following ratios as reported by csimarket.com for the twelve months ended September 27, 2019:

Ratio	Coca-Cola	PepsiCo
a. Gross profit percentage	61.3%	55.0%
b. Net profit margin	22.7%	18.8%
c. EPS	$1.66	$8.82
d. Inventory turnover ratio	4.2	8.3
e. Current ratio	0.62	0.95
f. Debt-to-assets	0.76	0.82
g. P/E ratio	32.5	15.5

Required:

1. For each ratio listed, indicate whether it would be used to compare profitability (P), liquidity (L), or solvency (S), or whether it is not applicable (NA) to comparing companies.

2. Which company appears more profitable? Describe the ratio(s) that you used to reach this decision.

3. Which company appears more liquid? Describe the ratio(s) that you used to reach this decision.

4. Which company appears more solvent? Describe the ratio(s) that you used to reach this decision.

5. Are the conclusions from your analyses in requirements 2–4 consistent with the value of the two companies, as suggested by their P/E ratios? If not, offer one explanation for any apparent inconsistency.

PA13-6 Using Ratios to Compare Loan Requests from Two Companies

LO 13-4, 13-5, 13-6

The financial statements for Royale and Cavalier companies are summarized here:

	Royale Company	Cavalier Company
Balance Sheet		
Cash	$ 25,000	$ 45,000
Accounts Receivable, Net	55,000	16,000
Inventory	110,000	25,000
Equipment, Net	550,000	160,000
Other Assets	140,000	46,000
Total Assets	$880,000	$292,000
Current Liabilities	$120,000	$ 15,000
Notes Payable (long-term)	190,000	55,000
Common Stock (par $20)	480,000	210,000
Additional Paid-In Capital	50,000	4,000
Retained Earnings	40,000	8,000
Total Liabilities and Stockholders' Equity	$880,000	$292,000
Income Statement		
Sales Revenue	$800,000	$280,000
Cost of Goods Sold	480,000	150,000
Other Expenses	240,000	95,000
Net Income	$ 80,000	$ 35,000
Other Data		
Per share price at end of year	$ 14.00	$ 11.00
Selected Data from Previous Year		
Accounts Receivable, Net	$ 47,000	$ 14,000
Notes Payable (long-term)	190,000	55,000
Equipment, Net	550,000	160,000
Inventory	95,000	38,000
Total Stockholders' Equity	570,000	202,000

These two companies are in the same business and state but different cities. Each company has been in operation for about 10 years. Both companies received an unqualified audit opinion on the financial statements. Royale Company wants to borrow $75,000 cash and Cavalier Company is asking for $30,000. The loans will be for a two-year period. Both companies estimate bad debts based on an aging analysis, but Cavalier has estimated slightly higher uncollectible rates than Royale. Neither company issued stock in the current year. Assume the end-of-year total assets and net equipment balances approximate the year's average and all sales are on account.

Required:

1. Calculate the ratios in Exhibit 13.5 for which sufficient information is available. Round all calculations to two decimal places.

2. Assume that you work in the loan department of a local bank. You have been asked to analyze the situation and recommend which loan is preferable. Based on the data given, your analysis prepared in requirement 1, and any other information (e.g., accounting policies and decisions), give your choice and the supporting explanation.

PA13-7 Analyzing an Investment by Comparing Selected Ratios

LO 13-5

You have the opportunity to invest $10,000 in one of two companies from a single industry. The only information you have is shown here. The word *high* refers to the top third of the industry; *average* is the middle third; *low* is the bottom third.

Ratio	Company A	Company B
Current	Low	High
Inventory turnover	High	Low
Debt-to-assets	Low	Average
Times interest earned	High	Average
Price/earnings	High	Average

Required:

Which company should you select? Write a brief explanation for your recommendation.

GROUP B PROBLEMS

LO 13-2, 13-4, 13-5   **PB13-1 Analyzing Financial Statements Using Horizontal and Ratio Analyses**

Tiger Audio declared and paid a cash dividend of $5,525 in the current year. Its comparative financial statements, prepared at December 31, reported the following summarized information:

	Current	Previous	Increase (Decrease) in Current (versus Previous) Amount	Percentage
Income Statement				
Sales Revenue	$222,000	$185,000		
Cost of Goods Sold	127,650	111,000		
Gross Profit	94,350	74,000		
Operating Expenses	39,600	33,730		
Interest Expense	4,000	3,270		
Income before Income Tax Expense	50,750	37,000		
Income Tax Expense (30%)	15,225	11,100		
Net Income	$ 35,525	$ 25,900		
Balance Sheet				
Cash	$ 40,000	$ 38,000		
Accounts Receivable, Net	18,500	16,000		
Inventory	25,000	22,000		
Property and Equipment, Net	127,000	119,000		
Total Assets	$210,500	$195,000		
Accounts Payable	$ 27,000	$ 25,000		
Income Tax Payable	3,000	2,800		
Notes Payable (long-term)	75,500	92,200		
Total Liabilities	105,500	120,000		
Common Stock (par $1)	25,000	25,000		
Retained Earnings	80,000	50,000		
Total Liabilities and Stockholders' Equity	$210,500	$195,000		

Required:

1. Complete the two final columns shown beside each item in Tiger Audio's comparative financial statements. Round the percentages to one decimal place.
2. Which account increased by the largest dollar amount? Which account increased by the largest percentage?

LO 13-4, 13-5   **PB13-2 Analyzing Comparative Financial Statements Using Selected Ratios**

Use the data given in PB13-1 for Tiger Audio.

Required:

1. Compute the gross profit percentage in the current and previous years. Are the current-year results better, or worse, than those for the previous year?

2. Compute the net profit margin for the current and previous years. Are the current-year results better, or worse, than those for the previous year?

3. Compute the earnings per share for the current and previous years. Are the current-year results better, or worse, than those for the previous year?

4. Stockholders' equity totaled $65,000 at the beginning of the previous year. Compute the return on equity ratios for the current and previous years. Are the current-year results better, or worse, than those for the previous year?

5. Net property and equipment totaled $115,000 at the beginning of the previous year. Compute the fixed asset turnover ratios for the current and previous years. Are the current-year results better, or worse, than those for the previous year?

6. Compute the debt-to-assets ratios for the current and previous years. Is debt providing financing for a larger or smaller proportion of the company's asset growth?

7. Compute the times interest earned ratios for the current and previous years. Are the current-year results better, or worse, than those for the previous year?

8. After Tiger released its current-year financial statements, the company's stock was trading at $17. After the release of its previous-year financial statements, the company's stock price was $12 per share. Compute the P/E ratios for both years. Round to one decimal place. Does it appear that investors have become more (or less) optimistic about Tiger's future success?

PB13-3 Vertical Analysis of a Balance Sheet

LO 13-3, 13-5
Southwest Airlines

A condensed balance sheet for Southwest Airlines and a partially completed vertical analysis are presented below.

SOUTHWEST AIRLINES Balance Sheet (summarized) December 31, 2018 (in millions of U.S. dollars)					
Cash	$ 1,854	*a*%	Current Liabilities	$ 7,905	30%
Short-Term Investments	1,835	7	Long-Term Liabilities	8,485	32
Accounts Receivable	568	*b*	Total Liabilities	16,390	62
Inventory of Parts and Supplies	461	2	Common Stock	2,338	9
Other Current Assets	310	1	Retained Earnings	15,967	61
Property and Equipment, Net	19,525	*c*	Treasury Stock	(8,452)	(32)
Other Assets	1,690	6	Total Stockholders' Equity	9,853	38
Total Assets	$26,243	100%	Total Liabilities & Stockholders' Equity	$26,243	100%

Required:

1. Complete the vertical analysis by computing each line item (*a*)–(*c*) as a percentage of total assets. Round to the nearest whole percentage. Total of percentages may not sum to 100% due to rounding.

2. What percentages of Southwest's assets relate to inventory of parts and supplies versus property and equipment? Round to the nearest whole percentage. Which of these two asset groups is more significant to Southwest's business?

3. What percentage of Southwest's assets is financed by total stockholders' equity? By total liabilities? Round to the nearest whole percentage.

PB13-4 Vertical Analysis of an Income Statement

LO 13-3, 13-5
Southwest Airlines

A condensed income statement for Southwest Airlines and a partially completed vertical analysis follow.

	SOUTHWEST AIRLINES Income Statement (summarized) For the Year Ended December 31 (in millions of U.S. dollars)				
		2018		**2017**	
Sales Revenues		$21,965	100%	$21,146	100%
Salaries and Wages Expense		7,649	*a*	7,305	35
Fuel, Oil, Repairs, and					
Maintenance		5,723	*b*	5,077	*d*
Other Operating Expenses		5,387	25	5,357	*e*
Other Expenses (Revenues)		42	0	142	1
Income before Income Tax Expense		3,164	14	3,265	15
Income Tax Expense (Recovery)		699	3	(92)	(1)
Net Income		$ 2,465	*c*%	$ 3,357	*f*%

Required:

1. Complete the vertical analysis by computing each line item (*a*)–(*f*) as a percentage of sales revenues. Round to the nearest whole percentage.

2. Does the percentage that you calculated in 1(*b*) and (*d*) suggest that fuel costs, as a percentage of sales, decreased, increased, or stayed the same in 2018 compared to 2017?

3. Refer to the percentages that you calculated in 1(*c*) and (*f*). Is Southwest's net profit margin improving, declining, or staying the same?

LO 13-4, 13-5

Mattel
Hasbro

PB13-5 Interpreting Profitability, Liquidity, Solvency, and P/E Ratios

Mattel and Hasbro are the two biggest makers of games and toys in the world. Mattel sells over $4.5 billion of products each year while annual sales of Hasbro products exceed $4.6 billion. Compare the two companies as a potential investment based on the following ratios reported by csimarket.com for twelve months ending in September 2019:

Ratio	Mattel	Hasbro
a. Gross profit percentage	43.5%	60.9%
b. Net profit margin	(5.0)%	13.5%
c. Return on equity	(45.9)%	15.0
d. EPS	$(0.60)	$2.07
e. Receivables turnover ratio	5.0	4.6
f. Inventory turnover ratio	4.0	3.5
g. Current ratio	1.6	2.33
h. Debt-to-assets	0.92	0.67

Required:

1. For each ratio listed, indicate whether it would be used to compare profitability (P), liquidity (L), or solvency (S), or whether it is not applicable (NA) to comparing companies.

2. Which company appears more profitable? Describe the ratio(s) that you used to reach this decision.

3. Which company appears more liquid? Describe the ratio(s) that you used to reach this decision.

4. Which company appears more solvent? Describe the ratio(s) that you used to reach this decision.

LO 13-4, 13-5, 13-6

PB13-6 Using Ratios to Compare Loan Requests from Two Companies

The financial statements for Thor and Gunnar companies are summarized here:

	Thor Company	Gunnar Company
Balance Sheet		
Cash	$ 35,000	$ 32,000
Accounts Receivable, Net	77,000	28,000
Inventory	154,000	30,000
Equipment, Net	770,000	192,000
Other Assets	196,000	68,400
Total Assets	$1,232,000	$350,400
Current Liabilities	$ 168,000	$ 18,000
Notes Payable (long-term) (12% interest rate)	266,000	66,000
Common Stock (par $20)	672,000	252,000
Additional Paid-In Capital	70,000	4,800
Retained Earnings	56,000	9,600
Total Liabilities and Stockholders' Equity	$1,232,000	$350,400
Income Statement		
Sales Revenue	$1,120,000	$336,000
Cost of Goods Sold	672,000	180,000
Other Expenses	336,000	114,000
Net Income	$ 112,000	$ 42,000
Other Data		
Per share price at end of year	$ 13.20	$ 19.60
Selected Data from Previous Year		
Accounts Receivable, Net	$ 65,800	$ 27,200
Inventory	133,000	45,600
Equipment, Net	770,000	192,000
Notes Payable (long-term) (12% interest rate)	266,000	66,000
Total Stockholders' Equity	798,000	266,400

These two companies are in the same business and state but different cities. Each company has been in operation for about 10 years. Both companies received an unqualified audit opinion on the financial statements. Thor Company wants to borrow $105,000 and Gunnar Company is asking for $36,000. The loans will be for a two-year period. Neither company issued stock in the current year. Assume the end-of-year total assets and net equipment balances approximate the year's average and all sales are on account.

Required:

1. Calculate the ratios in Exhibit 13.5 for which sufficient information is available. Round all calculations to two decimal places.

2. Assume that you work in the loan department of a local bank. You have been asked to analyze the situation and recommend which loan is preferable. Based on the data given, your analysis prepared in requirement 1, and any other information, give your choice and the supporting explanation.

PB13-7 Analyzing an Investment by Comparing Selected Ratios   LO 13-5

You have the opportunity to invest $10,000 in one of two companies from a single industry. The only information you have is shown here. The word *high* refers to the top third of the industry; *average* is the middle third; *low* is the bottom third.

Ratio	Company A	Company B
EPS	High	High
Return on equity	High	Average
Debt-to-assets	High	Low
Current	Low	Average
Price/earnings	Low	High

Required:

Which company should you select? Write a brief explanation for your recommendation.

SKILLS DEVELOPMENT CASES

LO 13-4

The Home Depot

S13-1 Computing Ratios

Compute the following three ratios for The Home Depot's year ended February 2, 2020: (i) fixed asset turnover, (ii) days to sell, and (iii) debt-to-assets. To calculate the ratios, use the Fiscal 2019 financial statements of The Home Depot in Appendix A at the end of this book. (Note: Fiscal 2019 for The Home Depot runs from February 4, 2019, to February 2, 2020. See S1-1 for further explanation.)

a.   4.88; 71.4; 0.94
b.   4.84; 71.4; 1.06
c.   2.15; 71.4; 1.06
d.   4.88; 71.4; 1.06

LO 13-5

Lumber Liquidators, Inc.
Lowe's

S13-2 Evaluating Financial Information

Lumber Liquidators, Inc., competes with Lowe's in product lines such as hardwood flooring, moldings, and noise-reducing underlay. The two companies reported the following financial results in fiscal 2019:

	Lumber Liquidators	Lowe's
Gross profit percentage	38.6%	31.8%
Net profit margin	0.9%	5.9%
Current ratio	1.51	1.01
Earnings per share (EPS)	$ 0.34	$ 5.49

Which of the following is an appropriate statement for the reported data?

a.   Compared to Lumber Liquidators, Lowe's earns less profit on each dollar of sales but is better at controlling other expenses related to operations, interest, and taxes.

b.   Earnings per share (EPS) indicates Lumber Liquidators is worse off than Lowe's.

c.   Lowe's has a faster inventory turnover than Lumber Liquidators.

d.   Lumber Liquidators buys more inventory on credit than Lowe's.

LO 13-1, 13-2, 13-3, 13-4, 13-5, 13-6

S13-3 Internet-Based Team Research: Examining an Annual Report

As a team, select an industry to analyze. Using your web browser, each team member should access the annual report or 10-K for one publicly traded company in the industry, with each member selecting a different company. (See S1-3 in Chapter 1 for a description of possible resources for these tasks.)

Required:

1.   On an individual basis, each team member should write a short report that incorporates horizontal and vertical analyses and as many of the ratios from the chapter as are applicable given the nature of the selected company.

2.   Then, as a team, write a short report comparing and contrasting your companies using these attributes. Discuss any patterns across the companies that you as a team observe. Provide potential explanations for any differences discovered. Consider the impact of differences in accounting policies.

LO 13-6

S13-4 Ethical Decision Making: A Real-Life Example

This case is available online in the Connect eBook. To complete this case, you will consider the negative effects of auditors (a) failing to identify going-concern problems that exist and (b) reporting going-concern problems that do not exist.

LO 13-4, 13-5

S13-5 Ethical Decision Making: A Mini-Case

Capital Investments Corporation (CIC) requested a sizable loan from First Federal Bank to acquire a large piece of land for future expansion. CIC reported current assets of $1,900,000 (including $430,000 in cash) and current liabilities of $1,075,000. First Federal denied the loan request for a number of reasons, including the fact that the current ratio was below 2:1. When CIC was informed of the loan denial, the controller of the company immediately paid $420,000 that was owed to several trade creditors. The controller then asked First Federal to reconsider the loan application. Based on these abbreviated facts, would you recommend that First Federal approve the loan request? Why? Are the controller's actions ethical?

S13-6 Critical Thinking: Analyzing the Impact of Alternative Depreciation Methods on Ratio Analysis

LO 13-4, 13-5, 13-6

Speedy Company uses the double-declining-balance method to depreciate its property, plant, and equipment and Turtle Company uses the straight-line method. The two companies are exactly alike except for the difference in depreciation methods.

Required:

1. Identify the financial ratios discussed in this chapter that are likely to be affected by the difference in depreciation methods.
2. Which company will report the higher amount for each ratio that you have identified in response to requirement 1? If you cannot be certain, explain why.

S13-7 Using a Spreadsheet to Calculate Financial Statement Ratios

LO 13-2, 13-3

Enter the account names and dollar amounts from the comparative balance sheets in Exhibit 13.1 into a worksheet in a spreadsheet file. Create a second copy of the worksheet in the same spreadsheet file.

Required:

1. To the right of the comparative numbers in the first worksheet, enter the necessary formulas to compute the amount and percent change as shown in Exhibit 13.1.
2. To the right of each column in the second worksheet, enter the necessary formulas to create common size statements similar to those shown in Exhibit 13.3.

CONTINUING CASE

Mc Graw Hill **connect**

CC13-1 Evaluating Profitability, Liquidity, and Solvency

LO 13-4, 13-5

Looking back over the last few years, it is clear that Nicole Mackisey has accomplished a lot running her business, Nicole's Getaway Spa (NGS). Nicole is curious about her company's performance as she compares its financial statements.

	2021	2020	2019
Balance Sheet			
Cash	$ 6,700	$ 4,200	$ 3,800
Accounts Receivable, Net	2,000	2,500	1,800
Inventory	1,200	3,000	1,600
Prepaid Expenses	750	1,050	200
Other Current Assets	300	350	200
Total Current Assets	10,950	11,100	7,600
Property and Equipment, Net	64,000	79,000	27,000
Total Assets	$74,950	$ 90,100	$34,600
Current Liabilities	$ 8,000	$ 8,000	$ 9,000
Long-Term Liabilities	35,000	50,000	14,000
Total Liabilities	43,000	58,000	23,000
Common Stock	25,000	30,000	10,900
Retained Earnings	6,950	2,100	700
Total Stockholders' Equity	31,950	32,100	11,600
Total Liabilities and Stockholders' Equity	$74,950	$ 90,100	$34,600
Income Statement			
Sales Revenue	$80,000	$56,000	$44,000
Cost of Goods Sold	65,000	48,000	35,000
Gross Profit	15,000	8,000	9,000
Operating Expenses	4,000	2,000	7,000
Income from Operations	11,000	6,000	2,000
Interest Expense	1,000	3,100	800
Income before Income Tax Expense	10,000	2,900	1,200
Income Tax Expense	3,050	800	500
Net Income	$ 6,950	$ 2,100	$ 700

Required:

1. Was NGS more profitable in 2021 or 2020? Use the net profit margin, gross profit percentage, return on equity, and fixed asset turnover ratios to help in making a decision (where possible, express each measure as a percentage, rounded to two decimal places).

2. Was NGS more liquid in 2021 or 2020? Use the current ratio to help in making a decision (where possible, express each measure as a percentage, rounded to two decimal places).

3. Was NGS more solvent in 2021 or 2020? Use the debt-to-assets ratio and times interest earned ratio to help in making a decision (where possible, express each measure as a percentage, rounded to two decimal places).

DATA ANALYTICS EXERCISES

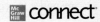

Data Analytics Exercises are auto-graded exercises offering detailed data visualization, interpretation, and analysis, and are available for assignment in *Connect*.

Excerpts from the Fiscal 2019 10-K Annual Report of The Home Depot, Inc.

Note: The materials in Appendix A are selected from the 10-K Annual Report of The Home Depot, Inc., for fiscal year 2019, which ended February 2, 2020. The complete Form 10-K filing is available online at https://ir.homedepot.com/financial-reports/sec-filings.

MANAGEMENT'S REPORT ON INTERNAL CONTROL OVER FINANCIAL REPORTING

Our management is responsible for establishing and maintaining adequate internal control over financial reporting, as such term is defined in Rule 13a-15(f) promulgated under the Exchange Act. Under the supervision and with the participation of our management, including our Chief Executive Officer and Chief Financial Officer, we conducted an evaluation of the effectiveness of our internal control over financial reporting as of February 2, 2020 based on the framework in *Internal Control—Integrated Framework (2013)* issued by the Committee of Sponsoring Organizations of the Treadway Commission. Based on our evaluation, our management concluded that our internal control over financial reporting was effective as of February 2, 2020 in providing reasonable assurance regarding the reliability of financial reporting and the preparation of financial statements for external purposes in accordance with GAAP. The effectiveness of our internal control over financial reporting as of February 2, 2020 has been audited by KPMG LLP, an independent registered public accounting firm, as stated in their report which is included herein.

/S/ CRAIG A. MENEAR

Craig A. Menear

Chairman, Chief Executive Officer and President

/S/ RICHARD V. MCPHAIL

Richard V. McPhail

Executive Vice President and Chief Financial Officer

REPORT OF INDEPENDENT REGISTERED PUBLIC ACCOUNTING FIRM

To the Stockholders and Board of Directors
The Home Depot, Inc.:

Opinion on Internal Control Over Financial Reporting

We have audited The Home Depot, Inc. and Subsidiaries' (the Company) internal control over financial reporting as of February 2, 2020, based on criteria established in *Internal Control—Integrated Framework (2013)* issued by the Committee of Sponsoring Organizations of the Treadway Commission. In our opinion, the Company maintained, in all material respects, effective internal control over financial reporting as of February 2, 2020, based on criteria established in *Internal Control—Integrated Framework (2013)* issued by the Committee of Sponsoring Organizations of the Treadway Commission.

We also have audited, in accordance with the standards of the Public Company Accounting Oversight Board (United States) (PCAOB), the Consolidated Balance Sheets of the Company as of February 2, 2020 and February 3, 2019, the related Consolidated Statements of Earnings, Comprehensive Income, Stockholders' Equity, and Cash Flows for each of the fiscal years in the three-year period ended February 2, 2020, and the related notes (collectively, the Consolidated Financial Statements), and our report dated March 25, 2020 expressed an unqualified opinion on those Consolidated Financial Statements.

Basis for Opinion

The Company's management is responsible for maintaining effective internal control over financial reporting and for its assessment of the effectiveness of internal control over financial reporting, included in the accompanying Management's Report on Internal Control Over Financial Reporting. Our responsibility is to express an opinion on the Company's internal control over financial reporting based on our audit. We are a public accounting firm registered with the PCAOB and are required to be independent with respect to the Company in accordance with the U.S. federal securities laws and the applicable rules and regulations of the Securities and Exchange Commission and the PCAOB.

We conducted our audit in accordance with the standards of the PCAOB. Those standards require that we plan and perform the audit to obtain reasonable assurance about whether effective internal control over financial reporting was maintained in all material respects. Our audit of internal control over financial reporting included obtaining an understanding of internal control over financial reporting, assessing the risk that a material weakness exists, and testing and evaluating the design and operating effectiveness of internal control based on the assessed risk. Our audit also included performing such other procedures as we considered necessary in the circumstances. We believe that our audit provides a reasonable basis for our opinion.

Definition and Limitations of Internal Control Over Financial Reporting

A company's internal control over financial reporting is a process designed to provide reasonable assurance regarding the reliability of financial reporting and the preparation of financial statements for external purposes in accordance with generally accepted accounting principles. A company's internal control over financial reporting includes those policies and procedures that (1) pertain to the maintenance of records that, in reasonable detail, accurately and fairly reflect the transactions and dispositions of the assets of the company; (2) provide reasonable assurance that transactions are recorded as necessary to permit preparation of financial statements in accordance with U.S. generally accepted accounting principles, and that receipts and expenditures of the company are being made only in accordance with authorizations of management and directors of the company; and (3) provide reasonable assurance regarding prevention or timely detection of unauthorized acquisition, use, or disposition of the company's assets that could have a material effect on the financial statements.

Because of its inherent limitations, internal control over financial reporting may not prevent or detect misstatements. Also, projections of any evaluation of effectiveness to future periods are subject to the risk that controls may become inadequate because of changes in conditions, or that the degree of compliance with the policies or procedures may deteriorate.

/s/ KPMG LLP

Atlanta, Georgia
March 25, 2020

REPORT OF INDEPENDENT REGISTERED PUBLIC ACCOUNTING FIRM

To the Stockholders and Board of Directors
The Home Depot, Inc.:

Opinion on the Consolidated Financial Statements

We have audited the accompanying Consolidated Balance Sheets of The Home Depot, Inc. and Subsidiaries (the Company) as of February 2, 2020 and February 3, 2019, the related Consolidated Statements of Earnings, Comprehensive Income, Stockholders' Equity, and Cash Flows for each of the fiscal years in the three-year period ended February 2, 2020, and the related notes (collectively, the Consolidated Financial Statements). In our opinion, the Consolidated Financial Statements present fairly, in all material respects, the financial position of the Company as of February 2, 2020 and February 3, 2019, and the results of its operations and its cash flows for each of the fiscal years in the three-year period ended February 2, 2020, in conformity with U.S. generally accepted accounting principles.

We also have audited, in accordance with the standards of the Public Company Accounting Oversight Board (United States) (PCAOB), the Company's internal control over financial reporting as of February 2, 2020, based on criteria established in *Internal Control—Integrated Framework (2013)* issued by the Committee of Sponsoring Organizations of the Treadway Commission, and our report dated March 25, 2020 expressed an unqualified opinion on the effectiveness of the Company's internal control over financial reporting.

Change in Accounting Principle

As discussed in Note 1 to the Consolidated Financial Statements, the Company has changed its method of accounting for leases as of February 4, 2019 due to the adoption of Accounting Standards Update No. 2016-02, *Leases (Topic 842),* and related amendments.

Basis for Opinion These Consolidated Financial Statements are the responsibility of the Company's management. Our responsibility is to express an opinion on these Consolidated Financial Statements based on our audits. We are a public accounting firm registered with the PCAOB and are required to be independent with respect to the Company in accordance with the U.S. federal securities laws and the applicable rules and regulations of the Securities and Exchange Commission and the PCAOB.

We conducted our audits in accordance with the standards of the PCAOB. Those standards require that we plan and perform the audit to obtain reasonable assurance about whether the Consolidated Financial Statements are free of material misstatement, whether due to error or fraud. Our audits included performing procedures to assess the risks of material misstatement of the Consolidated Financial Statements, whether due to error or fraud, and performing procedures that respond to those risks. Such procedures included examining, on a test basis, evidence regarding the amounts and disclosures in the Consolidated Financial Statements. Our audits also included evaluating the accounting principles used and significant estimates made by management, as well as evaluating the overall presentation of the Consolidated Financial Statements. We believe that our audits provide a reasonable basis for our opinion.

Critical Audit Matters

The critical audit matters communicated below are matters arising from the current period audit of the Consolidated Financial Statements that were communicated or required to be communicated to the audit committee and that: (1) relate to accounts or disclosures that are material to the Consolidated Financial Statements and (2) involved our especially challenging, subjective, or complex judgments. The communication of critical audit matters does not alter in any way our opinion on the Consolidated Financial Statements, taken as a whole, and we are not, by communicating the critical audit matters below, providing separate opinions on the critical audit matters or on the accounts or disclosures to which they relate.

Evaluation of the Self-Insurance Liability

As discussed in Note 1 to the Consolidated Financial Statements, the Company is self-insured for certain losses related to general liability (including product liability), workers' compensation, employee group medical, and automobile claims. The Company recognizes the expected ultimate cost for claims incurred at the balance sheet date as a liability. The expected ultimate cost for claims incurred is estimated based upon an analysis of historical data and actuarial estimates determined by the Company's third-party actuary.

We identified the evaluation of certain self-insurance liabilities as a critical audit matter, specifically those liabilities related to general liability (including product liability) and workers' compensation. Specialized skills were required to evaluate the actuarial methods and assumptions used in determining certain self-insurance liabilities. There was a high degree of judgment required to evaluate the Company's key assumptions such as loss development factors and the selection of ultimate losses among estimates derived using the various actuarial methods.

The primary procedures we performed to address this critical audit matter included the following. We tested certain internal controls over the Company's self-insurance liabilities process including controls over the review of the third-party actuarial report and the actuarial methods and key assumptions used by the actuary in determining certain self-insurance liabilities. We analyzed the key assumptions underlying the actuarial estimates by evaluating the reported claims and claims payments. We involved actuarial professionals with specialized skills and knowledge, who assisted in:

- Assessing the actuarial methods used by the Company's third-party actuary, for consistency with generally accepted actuarial standards and practices;
- Evaluating the key assumptions by comparing to historical data; and
- Developing an independent actuarial range of certain self-insurance liabilities, based on the Company's underlying historical paid and incurred loss data, and comparing the range to the Company's estimated liabilities.

Evaluation of Gross Unrecognized Income Tax Benefits

As discussed in Notes 1 and 5 to the Consolidated Financial Statements, the Company recognizes the effect of income tax positions if those positions are more likely than not of being sustained at the largest amount that is greater than 50% likely of being realized. The Company's tax positions are subject to examination by domestic and foreign taxing authorities and the resolution of such examinations may span multiple years. Since tax law is complex and often subject to interpretations, there is uncertainty that some of the Company's tax positions will be sustained upon examination.

We identified the evaluation of the Company's gross unrecognized tax benefits as a critical audit matter. Complex auditor judgment was required to evaluate the Company's interpretation of tax law and its identification and determination of the ultimate resolution of its tax positions.

The primary procedures we performed to address this critical audit matter included the following. We tested certain internal controls over the Company's tax process to evaluate gross unrecognized tax benefits, including controls related to (1) interpreting tax law, (2) evaluating which of the Company's tax positions may not be sustained upon examination, and (3) determination of the more-likely-than-not amount of the positions to be upheld. We involved tax professionals with specialized skills and knowledge, who assisted in:

- Assessing the transfer pricing studies for compliance with applicable laws and regulations;
- Evaluating the Company's interpretation of tax laws by developing an independent assessment based on our understanding and interpretation of the tax laws;
- Inspecting settlements with applicable taxing authorities, and evaluating the expiration of statutes of limitations; and
- Analyzing the Company's assumptions and data used to determine the amount of tax benefits to recognize as well as testing the Company's calculations and comparing the results to the Company's assessment.

/s/ KPMG LLP
We have served as the Company's auditor since 1979.

Atlanta, Georgia
March 25, 2020

THE HOME DEPOT, INC.
Consolidated Balance Sheets

in millions, except per share data	February 2, 2020 "Fiscal 2019"	February 3, 2019 "Fiscal 2018"
ASSETS		
Current assets:		
Cash and cash equivalents	$ 2,133	$ 1,778
Receivables, net	2,106	1,936
Merchandise inventories	14,531	13,925
Other current assets	1,040	890
Total current assets	19,810	18,529
Net property and equipment	22,770	22,375
Operating lease right-of-use assets	5,595	—
Goodwill	2,254	2,252
Other assets	807	847
Total assets	$ 51,236	$ 44,003
LIABILITIES AND STOCKHOLDERS' EQUITY		
Current liabilities:		
Short-term debt	$ 974	$ 1,339
Accounts payable	7,787	7,755
Accrued salaries and related expenses	1,494	1,506
Sales taxes payable	605	656
Deferred revenue	2,116	1,782
Income taxes payable	55	11
Current installments of long-term debt	1,839	1,056
Current operating lease liabilities	828	—
Other accrued expenses	2,677	2,611
Total current liabilities	18,375	16,716
Long-term debt, excluding current installments	28,670	26,807
Long-term operating lease liabilities	5,066	—
Deferred income taxes	706	491
Other long-term liabilities	1,535	1,867
Total liabilities	54,352	45,881
Common stock, par value $0.05; authorized: 10,000 shares; issued: 1,786 shares at February 2, 2020 and 1,782 shares at February 3, 2019; outstanding: 1,077 shares at February 2, 2020 and 1,105 shares at February 3, 2019	89	89
Paid-in capital	11,001	10,578
Retained earnings	51,729	46,423
Accumulated other comprehensive loss	(739)	(772)
Treasury stock, at cost, 709 shares at February 2, 2020 and 677 shares at February 3, 2019	(65,196)	(58,196)
Total stockholders' (deficit) equity	(3,116)	(1,878)
Total liabilities and stockholders' equity	$ 51,236	$ 44,003

See accompanying notes to consolidated financial statements.

THE HOME DEPOT, INC.
Consolidated Statements Of Earnings

in millions, except per share data	Fiscal 2019	Fiscal 2018	Fiscal 2017
NET SALES	$110,225	$108,203	$100,904
Cost of sales	72,653	71,043	66,548
GROSS PROFIT	37,572	37,160	34,356
Operating expenses:			
Selling, general and administrative	19,740	19,513	17,864
Depreciation and amortization	1,989	1,870	1,811
Impairment loss	—	247	—
Total operating expenses	21,729	21,630	19,675
OPERATING INCOME	15,843	15,530	14,681
Interest and other (income) expense:			
Interest and investment income	(73)	(93)	(74)
Interest expense	1,201	1,051	1,057
Other	—	16	—
Interest and other, net	1,128	974	983
EARNINGS BEFORE PROVISION FOR INCOME TAXES	14,715	14,556	13,698
Provision for income taxes	3,473	3,435	5,068
NET EARNINGS	$ 11,242	$ 11,121	$ 8,630
Basic weighted average common shares	1,093	1,137	1,178
BASIC EARNINGS PER SHARE	$ 10.29	$ 9.78	$ 7.33
Diluted weighted average common shares	1,097	1,143	1,184
DILUTED EARNINGS PER SHARE	$ 10.25	$ 9.73	$ 7.29

Fiscal 2019 and fiscal 2017 include 52 weeks. Fiscal 2018 includes 53 weeks.
See accompanying notes to consolidated financial statements.

THE HOME DEPOT, INC.
Consolidated Statements Of Comprehensive Income

in millions	Fiscal 2019	Fiscal 2018	Fiscal 2017
Net earnings	$11,242	$11,121	$8,630
Other comprehensive income (loss):			
Foreign currency translation adjustments	53	(267)	311
Cash flow hedges, net of tax	8	53	(1)
Other	3	8	(9)
Total other comprehensive income (loss)	64	(206)	301
COMPREHENSIVE INCOME	$11,306	$10,915	$8,931

Fiscal 2019 and fiscal 2017 include 52 weeks. Fiscal 2018 includes 53 weeks.
See accompanying notes to consolidated financial statements.

THE HOME DEPOT, INC.
Consolidated Statements Of Stockholders' Equity

in millions	Fiscal 2019	Fiscal 2018	Fiscal 2017
Common Stock:			
Balance at beginning of year	$ 89	$ 89	$ 88
Shares issued under employee stock plans	—	—	1
Balance at end of year	89	89	89
Paid-in Capital:			
Balance at beginning of year	10,578	10,192	9,787
Shares issued under employee stock plans	172	104	132
Stock-based compensation expense	251	282	273
Balance at end of year	11,001	10,578	10,192
Retained Earnings:			
Balance at beginning of year	46,423	39,935	35,519
Cumulative effect of accounting changes	26	75	—
Net earnings	11,242	11,121	8,630
Cash dividends	(5,958)	(4,704)	(4,212)
Other	(4)	(4)	(2)
Balance at end of year	51,729	46,423	39,935
Accumulated Other Comprehensive Income (Loss):			
Balance at beginning of year	(772)	(566)	(867)
Cumulative effect of accounting changes	(31)	—	—
Foreign currency translation adjustments	53	(267)	311
Cash flow hedges, net of tax	8	53	(1)
Other	3	8	(9)
Balance at end of year	(739)	(772)	(566)
Treasury Stock:			
Balance at beginning of year	(58,196)	(48,196)	(40,194)
Repurchases of common stock	(7,000)	(10,000)	(8,002)
Balance at end of year	(65,196)	(58,196)	(48,196)
Total stockholders' (deficit) equity	$ (3,116)	$ (1,878)	$ 1,454

Fiscal 2019 and fiscal 2017 include 52 weeks. Fiscal 2018 includes 53 weeks.
See accompanying notes to consolidated financial statements.

THE HOME DEPOT, INC.
Consolidated Statements Of Cash Flows

in millions	Fiscal 2019	Fiscal 2018	Fiscal 2017
CASH FLOWS FROM OPERATING ACTIVITIES:			
Net earnings	$ 11,242	$ 11,121	$ 8,630
Reconciliation of net earnings to net cash provided by operating activities:			
Depreciation and amortization	2,296	2,152	2,062
Stock-based compensation expense	251	282	273
Impairment loss	—	247	—
Changes in receivables, net	(170)	33	139
Changes in merchandise inventories	(593)	(1,244)	(84)
Changes in other current assets	(135)	(257)	(10)
Changes in accounts payable and accrued expenses	68	743	352
Changes in deferred revenue	334	80	128
Changes in income taxes payable	44	(42)	29
Changes in deferred income taxes	202	26	92
Other operating activities	184	(103)	420
Net cash provided by operating activities	13,723	13,038	12,031
CASH FLOWS FROM INVESTING ACTIVITIES:			
Capital expenditures	(2,678)	(2,442)	(1,897)
Payments for businesses acquired, net	—	(21)	(374)
Proceeds from sales of property and equipment	37	33	47
Other investing activities	(12)	14	(4)
Net cash used in investing activities	(2,653)	(2,416)	(2,228)
CASH FLOWS FROM FINANCING ACTIVITIES:			
(Repayments of) proceeds from short-term debt, net	(365)	(220)	850
Proceeds from long-term debt, net of discounts and premiums	3,420	3,466	2,991
Repayments of long-term debt	(1,070)	(1,209)	(543)
Repurchases of common stock	(6,965)	(9,963)	(8,000)
Proceeds from sales of common stock	280	236	255
Cash dividends	(5,958)	(4,704)	(4,212)
Other financing activities	(176)	(26)	(211)
Net cash used in financing activities	(10,834)	(12,420)	(8,870)
Change in cash and cash equivalents	236	(1,798)	933
Effect of exchange rate changes on cash and cash equivalents	119	(19)	124
Cash and cash equivalents at beginning of year	1,778	3,595	2,538
Cash and cash equivalents at end of year	$ 2,133	$ 1,778	$ 3,595
SUPPLEMENTAL DISCLOSURES:			
Cash paid for income taxes	$ 3,220	$ 3,774	$ 4,732
Cash paid for interest, net of interest capitalized	1,112	1,035	991
Non-cash capital expenditures	136	248	150

Fiscal 2019 and fiscal 2017 include 52 weeks. Fiscal 2018 includes 53 weeks.
See accompanying notes to consolidated financial statements.

THE HOME DEPOT, INC. NOTES TO CONSOLIDATED FINANCIAL STATEMENTS

1. Summary of significant accounting policies

Business   The Home Depot, Inc., together with its subsidiaries (the "Company," "Home Depot," "we," "our" or "us"), is a home improvement retailer that sells a wide assortment of building materials, home improvement products, lawn and garden products, and décor items and provides a number of services, in stores and online. We operate in the U.S. (including the Commonwealth of Puerto Rico and the territories of the U.S. Virgin Islands and Guam), Canada, and Mexico.

Consolidation and Presentation   Our consolidated financial statements include our accounts and those of our wholly-owned subsidiaries. All significant intercompany transactions have been eliminated in consolidation. Certain amounts in prior fiscal years have been reclassified to conform with the presentation adopted in the current fiscal year. Our fiscal year is a 52- or 53-week period ending on the Sunday nearest to January 31st. Fiscal 2019 and fiscal 2017 include 52 weeks while fiscal 2018 includes 53 weeks.

Use of Estimates   We have made a number of estimates and assumptions relating to the reporting of assets and liabilities, the disclosure of contingent assets and liabilities, and reported amounts of revenues and expenses in preparing these financial statements in conformity with GAAP. Actual results could differ from these estimates.

Cash Equivalents   We consider all highly liquid investments purchased with original maturities of three months or less to be cash equivalents. Our cash equivalents are carried at fair market value and consist primarily of money market funds.

Receivables   The components of receivables, net, follow:

in millions	February 2, 2020	February 3, 2019
Card receivables	$ 778	$ 696
Rebate receivables	668	660
Customer receivables	292	284
Other receivables	368	296
Receivables, net	$2,106	$1,936

Card receivables consist of payments due from financial institutions for the settlement of credit card and debit card transactions. Rebate receivables represent amounts due from vendors for volume and co-op advertising rebates. Customer receivables relate to credit extended directly to certain customers in the ordinary course of business. The valuation allowance related these receivables was not material to our consolidated financial statements at the end of fiscal 2019 or fiscal 2018.

Merchandise Inventories   The substantial majority of our merchandise inventories are stated at the lower of cost (first-in, first-out) or market, as determined by the retail inventory method, which is based on a number of factors such as markups, markdowns, and inventory losses (or shrink). As the inventory retail value is adjusted regularly to reflect market conditions, inventory valued using the retail method approximates the lower of cost or market. Certain subsidiaries, including retail operations in Canada and Mexico, and distribution centers, record merchandise inventories at the lower of cost or net realizable value, as determined by a cost method. These merchandise inventories represent approximately 29% of the total merchandise inventories balance. We evaluate the inventory valued using a cost method at the end of each quarter to ensure that it is carried at the lower of cost or net realizable value. The valuation allowance for merchandise inventories valued under a cost method was not material to our consolidated financial statements at the end of fiscal 2019 or fiscal 2018.

Source: The Home Depot Form 10-K

Independent physical inventory counts or cycle counts are taken on a regular basis in each store and distribution center to ensure that amounts reflected in merchandise inventories are properly stated. Shrink (or in the case of excess inventory, swell) is the difference between the recorded amount of inventory and the physical inventory. We calculate shrink based on actual inventory losses occurring as a result of physical inventory counts during each fiscal period and estimated inventory losses occurring between physical inventory counts. The estimate for shrink occurring in the interim period between physical inventory counts is calculated on a store-specific basis based on recent shrink results and current trends in the business.

Property and Equipment   Buildings, furniture, fixtures, and equipment are recorded at cost and depreciated using the straight-line method over their estimated useful lives. Leasehold improvements are amortized using the straight-line method over the original term of the lease or the useful life of the improvement, whichever is shorter.

The estimated useful lives of our property and equipment follow:

	Life
Buildings	5–45 years
Furniture, fixtures and equipment	2–20 years
Leasehold improvements	5–45 years

We capitalize certain costs, including interest, related to construction in progress and the acquisition and development of software. Costs associated with the acquisition and development of software are amortized using the straight-line method over the estimated useful life of the software, which is three to six years. Certain development costs not meeting the criteria for capitalization are expensed as incurred.

We evaluate our long-lived assets each quarter for indicators of potential impairment. Indicators of impairment include current period losses combined with a history of losses, our decision to relocate or close a store or other location before the end of its previously estimated useful life, or when changes in other circumstances indicate the carrying amount of an asset may not be recoverable. The evaluation for long-lived assets is performed at the lowest level of identifiable cash flows, which is generally the individual store level. The assets of a store with indicators of impairment are evaluated for recoverability by comparing its undiscounted future cash flows with its carrying value. If the carrying value is greater than the undiscounted future cash flows, we then measure the asset's fair value to determine whether an impairment loss should be recognized. If the resulting fair value is less than the carrying value, an impairment loss is recognized for the difference between the carrying value and the estimated fair value. Impairment losses on property and equipment are recorded as a component of SG&A. When a leased location closes, we also recognize, in SG&A, the net present value of future lease obligations less estimated sublease income. Impairments and lease obligation costs on closings and relocations were not material to our consolidated financial statements in fiscal 2019, fiscal 2018, or fiscal 2017.

Leases   On February 4, 2019, we adopted the new leases standard using the modified retrospective transition method. See "Recently Adopted Accounting Pronouncements—ASU No. 2016-02" in the complete Form 10-K for more information.

Goodwill   Goodwill represents the excess of purchase price over the fair value of net assets acquired. We do not amortize goodwill, but assess the recoverability of goodwill in the third quarter of each fiscal year, or more often if indicators warrant, by determining whether the fair value of each reporting unit supports its carrying value.

Other Intangible Assets   We amortize the cost of other finite-lived intangible assets over their estimated useful lives, which range up to 12 years. Intangible assets with indefinite lives are tested in the third quarter of each fiscal year for impairment, or more often if indicators warrant. Intangible assets other than goodwill are included in other assets.

Debt   We record any premiums or discounts associated with an issuance of long-term debt as a direct addition or deduction to the carrying value of the related senior notes. We also record debt issuance costs associated with an issuance of long-term debt as a direct deduction to the carrying value of the related senior notes. Premium, discount, and debt issuance costs are amortized over the term of the respective notes using the effective interest rate method.

Insurance   We are self-insured for certain losses related to general liability (including product liability), workers' compensation, employee group medical, and automobile claims. We recognize the expected ultimate cost for claims incurred (undiscounted) at the balance sheet date as a liability. The expected ultimate cost for claims incurred is estimated based upon analysis of historical data and actuarial estimates.

Our self-insurance liabilities, which are included in accrued salaries and related expenses, other accrued expenses and other long-term liabilities in the consolidated balance sheets, were $1.3 billion at February 2, 2020 and February 3, 2019.

We also maintain network security and privacy liability insurance coverage to limit our exposure to losses such as those that may be caused by a significant compromise or breach of our data security. Insurance-related expenses are included in SG&A.

Treasury Stock   Treasury stock is reflected as a reduction of stockholders' equity at cost. We use the weighted-average purchase cost to determine the cost of treasury stock that is reissued, if any.

Net Sales   On January 29, 2018, we adopted the new revenue recognition guidance per ASU No. 2014-09 using the modified retrospective transition method, which requires that we recognize revenue differently pre- and post-adoption.

Fiscal 2018 and Subsequent Periods. We recognize revenue, net of expected returns and sales tax, at the time the customer takes possession of merchandise or when a service is performed. The liability for sales returns, including the impact to gross profit, is estimated based on historical return levels and recognized at the transaction price. We also recognize a return asset, and corresponding adjustment to cost of sales, for our right to recover the goods returned by the customer, measured at the former carrying amount of the goods, less any expected recovery cost. At each financial reporting date, we assess our estimates of expected returns, refund liabilities, and return assets.

Net sales include services revenue generated through a variety of installation, home maintenance, and professional service programs. In these programs, the customer selects and purchases material for a project, and we provide or arrange for professional installation. These programs are offered through our stores, online, and in-home sales programs. Under certain programs, when we provide or arrange for the installation of a project and the subcontractor provides material as part of the installation, both the material and labor are included in services revenue. We recognize this revenue when the service for the customer is complete, which is not materially different from recognizing the revenue over the service period as the substantial majority of our services are completed within one week.

For product sold in stores or online, payment is typically due at the point of sale. For services, payment in full is due upon completion of the job. When we receive payment from customers before the customer has taken possession of the merchandise or the service has been performed, the amount received is recorded as deferred revenue until the sale or service is complete. Such performance obligations are part of contracts with expected original durations of three months or less. We further record deferred revenue for the sale of gift cards and recognize the associated revenue upon the redemption of those gift cards in net sales. Gift card breakage income, which is our estimate of the non-redeemed gift card balance and recognized in net sales, was immaterial in fiscal 2019 and fiscal 2018.

We also have agreements with third-party service providers who directly extend credit to customers, manage our PLCC program, and own the related receivables. We have evaluated the third-party entities holding the receivables under the program and concluded that they should not be consolidated. The agreement with the primary third-party service provider for our PLCC program expires in 2028, with us having the option, but no obligation, to purchase the existing receivables at the end of the agreement. Deferred interest charges incurred for our deferred financing programs offered to these customers, interchange fees charged to us for their use of the cards, and any profit sharing with the third-party service providers are included in net sales.

Cost of Sales Cost of sales includes the actual cost of merchandise sold and services performed; the cost of transportation of merchandise from vendors to our distribution network, stores, or customers; shipping and handling costs from our stores or distribution network to customers; and the operating cost and depreciation of our sourcing and distribution network and online fulfillment centers. In fiscal 2017, cost of sales also included cost of deferred interest programs offered through our PLCC programs.

Vendor Allowances Vendor allowances primarily consist of volume rebates that are earned as a result of attaining certain purchase levels and co-op advertising allowances for the promotion of vendors' products that are typically based on guaranteed minimum amounts with additional amounts being earned for attaining certain purchase levels. These vendor allowances are accrued as earned, with those allowances received as a result of attaining certain purchase levels accrued over the incentive period based on estimates of purchases. Volume rebates and certain co-op advertising allowances reduce the carrying cost of inventory and are recognized in cost of sales when the related inventory is sold.

Advertising Expense Television and radio advertising production costs, along with media placement costs, are expensed when the advertisement first appears. Certain co-op advertising allowances are recorded as an offset against advertising expense.

Income Taxes Income taxes are accounted for under the asset and liability method. We provide for federal, state, and foreign income taxes currently payable, as well as for those deferred due to timing differences between reporting income and expenses for financial statement purposes versus tax purposes. Deferred tax assets and liabilities are recognized for the future tax consequences attributable to temporary differences between the financial statement carrying amounts of existing assets and liabilities and their respective tax bases. Deferred tax assets and liabilities are measured using enacted income tax rates expected to apply to taxable income in the years in which those temporary differences are expected to be recovered or settled. The effect of a change in income tax rates is recognized as income or expense in the period that includes the enactment date.

We recognize the effect of income tax positions only if those positions are more likely than not of being sustained. Recognized income tax positions are measured at the largest amount that is greater than 50% likely of being realized. Changes in recognition or measurement are reflected in the period in which the change in judgment occurs.

We file a consolidated U.S. federal income tax return which includes certain eligible subsidiaries. Non-U.S. subsidiaries and certain U.S. subsidiaries, which are consolidated for financial reporting purposes, are not eligible to be included in our consolidated U.S. federal income tax return. Separate provisions for income taxes have been determined for these entities. For unremitted earnings of our non-U.S. subsidiaries, we are required to make an assertion regarding reinvestment or repatriation for tax purposes. For any earnings that we do not make a permanent reinvestment assertion, we recognize a provision for deferred income taxes. For earnings where we have made a permanent reinvestment assertion, no provision is recognized. See Note 5 for further discussion.

Comprehensive Income Comprehensive income includes net earnings adjusted for certain gains and losses that are excluded from net earnings under GAAP, which consists primarily of foreign currency translation adjustments.

Foreign Currency Translation Assets and liabilities denominated in a foreign currency are translated into U.S. dollars at the current rate of exchange on the last day of the reporting period. Revenues and expenses are translated using average exchange rates for the period and equity transactions are translated using the actual rate on the day of the transaction.

Other notes to the financial statements can be downloaded from sec.gov or the investor relations section of the company's website.

Excerpts from the Fiscal 2019 10-K Annual Report of Lowe's Companies, Inc.

Note: The materials in Appendix B are selected from the 10-K Annual Report of Lowe's Companies, Inc., for fiscal year 2019, which ended January 31, 2020. The complete Form 10-K filing is available online at https://lowes.gcs-web.com/financial-information/sec-filings.

MANAGEMENT'S REPORT ON INTERNAL CONTROL OVER FINANCIAL REPORTING

Management of Lowe's Companies, Inc. and its subsdiaries is responsible for establishing and maintaining adequate internal control over financial reporting (Internal Control) as defined in Rule 13a-15(f) under the Securities Exchange Act of 1934, as amended. Our Internal Control was designed to provide reasonable assurance to our management and the Board of Directors regarding the reliability of financial reporting and the preparation and fair presentation of published financial statements.

All internal control systems, no matter how well designed, have inherent limitations, including the possibility of human error and the circumvention or overriding of controls. Therefore, even those systems determined to be effective can provide only reasonable assurance with respect to the reliability of financial reporting and financial statement preparation and presentation. Further, because of changes in conditions, the effectiveness may vary over time.

Our management, with the participation of the Chief Executive Officer and Chief Financial Officer, evaluated the effectiveness of our Internal Control as of January 31, 2020. In evaluating our Internal Control, we used the criteria set forth by the Committee of Sponsoring Organizations of the Treadway Commission (COSO) in *Internal Control— Integrated Framework (2013)*. Based on our management's assessment, we have concluded that, as of January 31, 2020, our Internal Control is effective.

Deloitte & Touche LLP, the independent registered public accounting firm that audited the financial statements contained in this Annual Report, was engaged to audit our Internal Control.

REPORT OF INDEPENDENT REGISTERED PUBLIC ACCOUNTING FIRM

To the Board of Directors and Shareholders of Lowe's Companies, Inc.

Opinion on the Financial Statements

We have audited the accompanying consolidated balance sheets of Lowe's Companies, Inc. and subsidiaries (the "Company") as of January 31, 2020 and February 1, 2019, the related consolidated statements of earnings, comprehensive income, shareholders' equity, and cash flows, for each of the three fiscal years in the period ended January 31, 2020, and the related notes and the schedule listed in the Index at Item 15 (collectively referred to as the "financial statements"). In our opinion, the financial statements present fairly, in all material respects, the financial position of the Company as of January 31, 2020 and February 1, 2019, and the results of its operations and its cash flows for each of the three fiscal years in the period ended January 31, 2020, in conformity with accounting principles generally accepted in the United States of America.

We have also audited, in accordance with the standards of the Public Company Accounting Oversight Board (United States) (PCAOB), the Company's internal control over financial reporting as of January 31, 2020, based on criteria established in *Internal Control— Integrated Framework (2013)* issued by the Committee of Sponsoring Organizations of the Treadway Commission and our report dated March 23, 2020, expressed an unqualified opinion on the Company's internal control over financial reporting.

Accounting Pronouncement Recently Adopted

As discussed in Note 1 to the financial statements, the Company has changed its method of accounting for leases in the fiscal year ended January 31, 2020 due to the adoption of Financial Accounting Standards Board Accounting Standards Update 2016-02, *Leases (Topic 842)*.

Basis for Opinion

These financial statements are the responsibility of the Company's management. Our responsibility is to express an opinion on the Company's financial statements based on our audits. We are a public accounting firm registered with the PCAOB and are required to be independent with respect to the Company in accordance with the U.S. federal securities laws and the applicable rules and regulations of the Securities and Exchange Commission and the PCAOB.

We conducted our audits in accordance with the standards of the PCAOB. Those standards require that we plan and perform the audit to obtain reasonable assurance about whether the financial statements are free of material misstatement, whether due to error or fraud. Our audits included performing procedures to assess the risks of material misstatement of the financial statements, whether due to error or fraud, and performing procedures that respond to those risks. Such procedures included examining, on a test basis, evidence regarding the amounts and disclosures in the financial statements. Our audits also included evaluating the accounting principles used and significant estimates made by management, as well as evaluating the overall presentation of the financial statements. We believe that our audits provide a reasonable basis for our opinion.

Critical Audit Matter

The critical audit matter communicated below is a matter arising from the current-period audit of the financial statements that was communicated or required to be communicated to the audit committee and that (1) relates to accounts or disclosures that are material to the financial statements and (2) involved our especially challenging, subjective, or complex judgments. The communication of critical audit matters does not alter in any way our opinion on the financial statements, taken as a whole, and we are not, by communicating the critical audit matter below, providing a separate opinion on the critical audit matter or on the accounts or disclosures to which it relates.

Merchandise Inventory - Vendor Funds - Refer to Note 1 to the Financial Statements

Critical Audit Matter Description The Company receives funds from its vendors in the normal course of business, principally as a result of purchase volumes, sales, early payments or promotions of vendors' products. In the fiscal year ended January 31, 2020, the Company purchased inventory from a significant number of vendors. Many of the vendor funds associated with these purchases are earned under agreements that are negotiated on an annual basis or shorter. The funds are recorded as a reduction to the cost of inventory as they are earned. As the related inventory is sold, the amounts are recorded as a reduction to cost of sales.

We identified vendor funds as a critical audit matter because of the number, complexity, and diversity of the individual vendor agreements. This required an increased extent of effort when performing audit procedures to evaluate whether the vendor funds were recorded in accordance with the terms of the vendor agreements.

How the Critical Audit Matter Was Addressed in the Audit Our audit procedures related to whether the vendor funds were recorded in accordance with the terms of the vendor agreements included the following, among others:

- We tested the effectiveness of controls over vendor funds, including management's controls over the accrual and recording of vendor funds as a reduction to the cost of inventory or cost of sales in accordance with the terms of the vendor agreements.

- We selected a sample of vendor funds and recalculated the amount earned using the terms of the vendor agreement, including the amount recorded as a reduction to the cost of inventory and/or the amount recorded as a reduction to cost of sales.

- We selected a sample of vendor funds and confirmed the amount earned and terms of the agreement directiy with the vendor.

/S/ DELOITTE & TOUCHE LLP
We have served as the Company's auditor since 1962.

Charlotte, North Carolina
March 23, 2020

REPORT OF INDEPENDENT REGISTERED PUBLIC ACCOUNTING FIRM

To the Board of Directors and Shareholders of Lowe's Companies, Inc.

Opinion on Internal Control over Financial Reporting

We have audited the internal control over financial reporting of Lowe's Companies, Inc. and subsidiaries (the "Company") as of January 31, 2020, based on criteria established in *Internal Control—Integrated Framework (2013)* issued by the Committee of Sponsoring Organizations of the Treadway Commission (COSO). In our opinion, the Company maintained, in all material respects, effective internal control over financial reporting as of January 31, 2020, based on criteria established in *Internal Control—Integrated Framework (2013)* issued by COSO.

We have also audited, in accordance with the standards of the Public Company Accounting Oversight Board (United States) (PCAOB), the consolidated financial statements and financial statement schedule as of and for the fiscal year ended January 31, 2020 of the Company and our report dated March 23, 2020, expressed an unqualified opinion on those financial statements and included an explanatory paragraph regarding the Company's adoption of Financial Accounting Standards Board Accounting Standards Update 2016-02, *Leases (Topic 842)*.

Basis for Opinion

The Company's management is responsible for maintaining effective internal control over financial reporting and for its assessment of the effectiveness of internal control over financial reporting, included in the accompanying Management's Report on Internal Control over Financial Reporting. Our responsibility is to express an opinion on the Company's internal control over financial reporting based on our audit. We are a public accounting firm registered with the PCAOB and are required to be independent with respect to the Company in accordance with the U.S. federal securities laws and the applicable rules and regulations of the Securities and Exchange Commission and the PCAOB.

We conducted our audit in accordance with the standards of the PCAOB. Those standards require that we plan and perform the audit to obtain reasonable assurance about whether effective internal control over financial reporting was maintained in all material respects. Our audit included obtaining an understanding of internal control over financial reporting, assessing the risk that a material weakness exists, testing and evaluating the design and operating effectiveness of internal control based on the assessed risk, and performing such other procedures as we considered necessary in the circumstances. We believe that our audit provides a reasonable basis for our opinion.

Definition and Limitations of Internal Control over Financial Reporting

A company's internal control over financial reporting is a process designed to provide reasonable assurance regarding the reliability of financial reporting and the preparation of financial statements for external purposes in accordance with generally accepted accounting principles. A company's internal control over financial reporting includes those policies and procedures that (1) pertain to the maintenance of records that, in reasonable detail, accurately and fairly reflect the transactions and dispositions of the assets of the company; (2) provide reasonable assurance that transactions are recorded as necessary to permit preparation of financial statements in accordance with generally accepted accounting principles, and that receipts and expenditures of the company are being made only in accordance with authorizations of management and directors of the company; and (3) provide reasonable assurance regarding prevention or timely detection of unauthorized acquisition, use, or disposition of the company's assets that could have a material effect on the financial statements.

Because of its inherent limitations, internal control over financial reporting may not prevent or detect misstatements. Also, projections of any evaluation of effectiveness to future periods are subject to the risk that controls may become inadequate because of changes in conditions, or that the degree of compliance with the policies or procedures may deteriorate.

/S/ DELOITTE & TOUCHE LLP

Charlotte, North Carolina
March 23, 2020

LOWE'S COMPANIES, INC.
CONSOLIDATED STATEMENTS OF EARNINGS

(In millions, except per share and percentage data)

Fiscal Years Ended	January 31, 2020		February 1, 2019		February 2, 2018	
	"Fiscal 2019"	% Sales	"Fiscal 2018"	% Sales	"Fiscal 2017"	% Sales
Net sales	$72,148	100.00%	$71,309	100.00%	$68,619	100.00%
Cost of sales	49,205	68.20	48,401	67.88	46,185	67.31
Gross margin	22,943	31.80	22,908	32.12	22,434	32.69
Expenses:						
Selling, general and administrative	15,367	21.30	17,413	24.41	14,444	21.04
Depreciation and amortization	1,262	1.75	1,477	2.07	1,404	2.05
Operating income	6,314	8.75	4,018	5.64	6,586	9.60
Interest—net	691	0.96	624	0.88	633	0.92
Loss on extinguishment of debt	—	—	—	—	464	0.68
Pre-tax earnings	5,623	7.79	3,394	4.76	5,489	8.00
Income tax provision	1,342	1.86	1,080	1.52	2,042	2.98
Net earnings	$ 4,281	5.93%	$ 2,314	3.24%	$ 3,447	5.02%
Basic earnings per common share	$ 5.49		$ 2.84		$ 4.09	
Diluted earnings per common share	$ 5.49		$ 2.84		$ 4.09	
Cash dividends per share	$ 2.13		$ 1.85		$ 1.58	

LOWE'S COMPANIES, INC.
CONSOLIDATED STATEMENTS OF COMPREHENSIVE INCOME

(In millions, except percentage data)

Fiscal Years Ended	January 31, 2020		February 1, 2019		February 2, 2018	
	"Fiscal 2019"	% Sales	"Fiscal 2018"	% Sales	"Fiscal 2017"	% Sales
Net earnings	$4,281	5.93%	$2,314	3.24%	$3,447	5.02%
Foreign currency translation adjustments—net of tax	94	0.13	(221)	(0.30)	251	0.37
Other	(21)	(0.03)	1	—	—	—
Other comprehensive income/(loss)	73	0.10	(220)	(0.30)	251	0.37
Comprehensive income	$4,354	6.03%	$2,094	2.94%	$3,698	5.39%

See accompanying notes to consolidated financial statements.

LOWE'S COMPANIES, INC.
CONSOLIDATED BALANCE SHEETS

(In millions, except par value)

		January 31, 2020	February 1, 2019
Assets			
Current assets:			
Cash and cash equivalents		$ 716	$ 511
Short-term investments		160	218
Merchandise inventory—net		13,179	12,561
Other current assets		1,263	938
Total current assets		15,318	14,228
Property, less accumulated depreciation		18,669	18,432
Operating lease right-of-use assets		3,891	—
Long-term investments		372	256
Deferred income taxes—net		216	294
Goodwill		303	303
Other assets		702	995
Total assets		$39,471	$34,508
Liabilities and shareholders' equity			
Current liabilities:			
Short-term borrowings		$ 1,941	$ 722
Current maturities of long-term debt		597	1,110
Current operating lease liabilities		501	—
Accounts payable		7,659	8,279
Accrued compensation and employee benefits		684	662
Deferred revenue		1,219	1,299
Other current liabilities		2,581	2,425
Total current liabilities		15,182	14,497
Long-term debt, excluding current maturities		16,768	14,391
Noncurrent operating lease liabilities		3,943	—
Deferred revenue—extended protection plans		894	827
Other liabilities		712	1,149
Total liabilities		37,499	30,864
Commitments and contingencies			
Shareholders' equity:			
Preferred stock—$5 par value, none issued		—	—
Common stock—$0.50 par value;			
Shares issued and outstanding			
January 31, 2020	763		
February 1, 2019	801	381	401
Capital in excess of par value		—	—
Retained earnings		1,727	3,452
Accumulated other comprehensive loss		(136)	(209)
Total shareholders' equity		1,972	3,644
Total liabilities and shareholders' equity		$39,471	$34,508

See accompanying notes to consolidated financial statements.

LOWE'S COMPANIES, INC.
CONSOLIDATED STATEMENTS OF SHAREHOLDERS' EQUITY

(In millions, except per share data)

	Common Stock		Capital in Excess of Par Value	Retained Earnings	Accumulated Other Comprehensive Income/(Loss)	Total Shareholders' Equity
	Shares	Amount				
Balance February 3, 2017	866	$433	$ —	$6,241	$(240)	$ 6,434
Net earnings				3,447		3,447
Other comprehensive income					251	251
Cash dividends declared, $1.58 per share				(1,324)		(1,324)
Share-based payment expense			99			99
Repurchase of common stock	(40)	(20)	(215)	(2,939)		(3,174)
Issuance of common stock under share-based payment plans	4	2	138			140
Balance February 2, 2018	830	$415	$ 22	$5,425	$ 11	$ 5,873
Cumulative effect of accounting change				33		33
Net earnings				2,314		2,314
Other comprehensive loss					(220)	(220)
Cash dividends declared, $1.85 per share				(1,500)		(1,500)
Share-based payment expense			74			74
Repurchase of common stock	(32)	(16)	(209)	(2,820)		(3,045)
Issuance of common stock under share-based payment plans	3	2	113			115
Balance February 1, 2019	801	$401	$ —	$3,452	$(209)	$ 3,644
Cumulative effect of accounting change				(263)		(263)
Net earnings				4,281		4,281
Other comprehensive income					73	73
Cash dividends declared, $2.13 per share				(1,653)		(1,653)
Share-based payment expense			98			98
Repurchase of common stock	(41)	(21)	(214)	(4,090)		(4,325)
Issuance of common stock under share-based payment plans	3	1	116			117
Balance January 31, 2020	763	$381	$ —	$1,727	$(136)	$ 1,972

See accompanying notes to consolidated financial statements.

Source: Lowe's Form 10-K

LOWE'S COMPANIES, INC.
CONSOLIDATED STATEMENTS OF CASH FLOWS

(In millions)

	Fiscal Year Ended		
	January 31, 2020 "Fiscal 2019"	February 1, 2019 "Fiscal 2018"	February 2, 2018 "Fiscal 2017"
Cash flows from operating activities:			
Net earnings	$ 4,281	$ 2,314	$ 3,447
Adjustments to reconcile net earnings to net cash provided by operating activities:			
Depreciation and amortization	1,410	1,607	1,540
Noncash lease expense	468	—	—
Deferred income taxes	177	(151)	53
Loss on property and other assets—net	117	630	40
Impairment of goodwill	—	952	—
Loss on extinguishment of debt	—	—	464
Loss/(gain) on cost method and equity method investments	12	9	(82)
Share-based payment expense	98	74	99
Changes in operating assets and liabilities:			
Merchandise inventory—net	(600)	(1,289)	(791)
Other operating assets	(376)	(110)	250
Accounts payable	(637)	1,720	(92)
Other operating liabilities	(654)	437	137
Net cash provided by operating activities	**4,296**	**6,193**	**5,065**
Cash flows from investing activities:			
Purchases of investments	(743)	(1,373)	(981)
Proceeds from sale/maturity of investments	695	1,393	1,114
Capital expenditures	(1,484)	(1,174)	(1,123)
Proceeds from sale of property and other long-term assets	163	76	45
Acquisition of business—net	—	—	(509)
Other—net	—	(2)	13
Net cash used in investing activities	**(1,369)**	**(1,080)**	**(1,441)**
Cash flows from financing activities:			
Net change in commercial paper	220	(415)	625
Net proceeds from issuance of debt	3,972	—	2,968
Repayment of long-term debt	(1,113)	(326)	(2,849)
Proceeds from issuance of common stock under share-based payment plans	118	114	139
Cash dividend payments	(1,618)	(1,455)	(1,288)
Repurchase of common stock	(4,313)	(3,037)	(3,192)
Other—net	(1)	(5)	(10)
Net cash used in financing activities	**(2,735)**	**(5,124)**	**(3,607)**
Effect of exchange rate changes on cash	**1**	**(12)**	**13**
Net increase/(decrease) in cash and cash equivalents, including cash classified within current assets held for sale	193	(23)	30
Less: Net increase/(decrease) in cash classified within current assets held for sale	12	(54)	—
Net increase/(decrease) in cash and cash equivalents	**205**	**(77)**	**30**
Cash and cash equivalents, beginning of year	511	588	558
Cash and cash equivalents, end of year	**$ 716**	**$ 511**	**$ 588**

See accompanying notes to consolidated financial statements.

Source: Lowe's Form 10-K

NOTES TO CONSOLIDATED FINANCIAL STATEMENTS

YEARS ENDED JANUARY 31, 2020, FEBRUARY 1, 2019 AND FEBRUARY 2, 2018

NOTE 1: Summary of Significant Accounting Policies

Lowe's Companies, Inc. and subsidiaries (the Company) is the world's second-largest home improvement retailer and operated 1,977 stores in the United States and Canada at January 31, 2020. Below are those accounting policies considered by the Company to be significant.

Fiscal Year   The Company's fiscal year ends on the Friday nearest the end of January. Each of the fiscal years presented contained 52 weeks. All references herein for the years 2019, 2018, and 2017 represent the fiscal years ended January 31, 2020, February 1, 2019, and February 2, 2018, respectively.

Principles of Consolidation   The consolidated financial statements include the accounts of the Company and its wholly-owned or controlled operating subsidiaries. All intercompany accounts and transactions have been eliminated.

Foreign Currency   The functional currencies of the Company's international subsidiaries are generally the local currencies of the countries in which the subsidiaries are located. Foreign currency denominated assets and liabilities are translated into U.S. dollars using the exchange rates in effect at the balance sheet date. Results of operations and cash flows are translated using the average exchange rates throughout the period. The effect of exchange rate fluctuations on translation of assets and liabilities is included as a component of shareholders' equity in accumulated other comprehensive loss. Gains and losses from foreign currency transactions are included in selling, general and administrative (SG&A) expense.

Use of Estimates   The preparation of the Company's financial statements in accordance with accounting principles generally accepted in the United States of America requires management to make estimates that affect the reported amounts of assets, liabilities, sales and expenses, and related disclosures of contingent assets and liabilities. The Company bases these estimates on historical results and various other assumptions believed to be reasonable, all of which form the basis for making estimates concerning the carrying values of assets and liabilities that are not readily available from other sources. Actual results may differ from these estimates.

Cash and Cash Equivalents   Cash and cash equivalents include cash on hand, demand deposits, and short-term investments with original maturities of three months or less when purchased. Cash and cash equivalents are carried at amortized cost on the consolidated balance sheets. The majority of payments due from financial institutions for the settlement of credit card and debit card transactions process within two business days and are, therefore, classified as cash and cash equivalents.

Investments   Investments generally consist of money market funds, corporate debt securities, agency securities, and governmental securities, all of which are classified as available-for-sale. Available-for-sale debt securities are recorded at fair value, and unrealized gains and losses are recorded, net of tax, as a component of accumulated other comprehensive loss. Gross unrealized gains and losses were not significant for any of the periods presented.

The proceeds from sales of available-for-sale debt securities were $121 million, $506 million, and $523 million for 2019, 2018, and 2017, respectively. Gross realized gains and losses on the sale of available-for-sale debt securities were not significant for any of the periods presented.

Investments with a stated maturity date of one year or less from the balance sheet date or that are expected to be used in current operations are classified as short-term investments. All other investments are classified as long-term. Investments classified as long-term at January 31, 2020, will mature in one to three years, based on stated maturity dates.

The Company classifies as investments restricted balances primarily pledged as collateral for the Company's extended protection plan program. Restricted balances included in short-term investments were $160 million at January 31, 2020, and $218 million at February 1, 2019. Restricted balances included in long-term investments were $372 million at January 31, 2020, and $256 million at February 1, 2019.

Merchandise Inventory   The majority of the Company's inventory is stated at the lower of cost and net realizable value using the first-in, first-out method of inventory accounting. Inventory for certain subsidiaries representing approximately 6% and 7% of the consolidated inventory balances as of January 31, 2020 and February 1, 2019, respectively, are stated at lower of cost and net realizable value using the weighted average cost method. The cost of inventory includes certain costs associated with the preparation of inventory for resale, including distribution center costs, and is net of vendor funds.

The Company records an inventory reserve for the anticipated loss associated with selling inventories below cost. This reserve is based on management's current knowledge with respect to inventory levels, sales trends, and historical experience. Management does not believe the Company's merchandise inventories are subject to significant risk of obsolescence in the near term, and management has the ability to adjust purchasing practices based on anticipated sales trends and general economic conditions. However, changes in consumer purchasing patterns could result in the need for additional reserves. The Company also records an inventory reserve for the estimated shrinkage between physical inventories. This reserve is based primarily on actual shrink results from previous physical inventories. Changes in the estimated shrink reserve are made based on the timing and results of physical inventories.

The Company receives funds from vendors in the normal course of business, principally as a result of purchase volumes, sales, early payments, or promotions of vendors' products. Generally, these vendor funds do not represent the reimbursement of specific, incremental, and identifiable costs incurred by the Company to sell the vendor's product. Therefore, the Company treats these funds as a reduction in the cost of inventory and are recognized as a reduction of cost of sales when the inventory is sold. Funds that are determined to be reimbursements of specific, incremental, and identifiable costs incurred to sell vendors' products are recorded as an offset to the related expense. The Company develops accrual rates for vendor funds based on the provisions of the agreements in place. Due to the complexity and diversity of the individual vendor agreements, the Company performs analyses and reviews historical trends throughout the year and confirms actual amounts with select vendors to ensure the amounts earned are appropriately recorded. Amounts accrued throughout the year could be impacted if actual purchase volumes differ from projected annual purchase volumes, especially in the case of programs that provide for increased funding when graduated purchase volumes are met.

Sale of Business Accounts Receivable and Credit Programs   The Company has branded and private label proprietary credit cards which generate sales that are not reflected in receivables. Under an agreement with Synchrony Bank (Synchrony), credit is extended directly to customers by Synchrony. All credit program-related services are performed and controlled directly by Synchrony. The Company has the option, but no obligation, to purchase the receivables at the end of the agreement.

The Company also has an agreement with Synchrony under which Synchrony purchases at face value commercial business accounts receivable originated by the Company and services these accounts. The Company primarily accounts for these transfers as sales of the accounts receivable. When the Company transfers its commercial business accounts receivable, it retains certain interests in those receivables, including the funding of a loss reserve and its obligation related to Synchrony's ongoing servicing of the receivables sold. Any gain or loss on the sale is determined based on the previous carrying amounts of the transferred assets allocated at fair value between the receivables sold and the interests retained. Fair value is based on the present value of expected future cash flows, taking into account the key assumptions of anticipated credit losses, payment rates, late fee rates, Synchrony's servicing costs, and the discount rate commensurate with the uncertainty involved. Due to the short-term nature of the receivables sold, changes to the key assumptions would not materially impact the recorded gain or loss on the sales of receivables or the fair value of the retained interests in the receivables.

Total commercial business accounts receivable sold to Synchrony were $3.2 billion in 2019, $3.1 billion in 2018, and $3.1 billion in 2017. The Company recognized losses of $41 million in 2019, $41 million in 2018, and $39 million in 2017 on these receivable sales, which primarily relates to the fair value of obligations related to servicing costs that are remitted to Synchrony monthly.

Property and Depreciation   Property is recorded at cost. Costs associated with major additions are capitalized and depreciated. Capital assets are expected to yield future benefits and have original useful lives which exceed one year. The total cost of a capital asset generally includes all applicable sales taxes, delivery costs, installation costs, and other appropriate costs incurred by the Company, including interest in the case of self-constructed assets. Upon disposal, the cost of properties and related accumulated depreciation is removed from the accounts, with gains and losses reflected in SG&A expense in the consolidated statements of earnings.

Property consists of land, buildings and building improvements, equipment, finance lease assets, and construction in progress. Buildings and building improvements includes owned buildings, as well as buildings under finance lease and leasehold improvements. Equipment primarily includes store racking and displays, computer hardware and software, forklifts, vehicles, finance lease equipment, and other store equipment.

Depreciation is recognized over the estimated useful lives of the depreciable assets. Assets are depreciated using the straight-line method. Leasehold improvements and finance lease assets are depreciated and amortized, respectively, over the shorter of their estimated useful lives or the term of the related lease. The amortization of these assets is included in depreciation and amortization expense in the consolidated statements of earnings.

Long-Lived Asset Impairment   The carrying amounts of long-lived assets are reviewed whenever certain events or changes in circumstances indicate that the carrying amounts may not be recoverable. A potential impairment has occurred for long-lived assets held-for-use if projected future undiscounted cash flows expected to result from the use and eventual disposition of the assets are less than the carrying amounts of the assets. The carrying value of a location's asset group includes inventory, property, operating and finance lease right-of-use assets, and operating liabilities, including inventory payables, salaries payable and operating lease liabilities. Financial and non-operating liabilities are excluded from the carrying value of the asset group. An impairment loss is recorded for long-lived assets held-for-use when the carrying amount of the asset is not recoverable and exceeds its fair value.

Excess properties that are expected to be sold within the next 12 months and meet the other relevant held-for-sale criteria are classified as long-lived assets held-for-sale. Excess properties consist primarily of retail outparcels and property associated with relocated or closed locations. An impairment loss is recorded for long-lived assets held-for-sale when the carrying amount of the asset exceeds its fair value less cost to sell. A long-lived asset is not depreciated while it is classified as held-for-sale.

For long-lived assets to be abandoned, the Company considers the asset to be disposed of when it ceases to be used. Until it ceases to be used, the Company continues to classify the asset as held-for-use and tests for potential impairment accordingly. If the Company commits to a plan to abandon a long-lived asset before the end of its previously estimated useful life, its depreciable life is re-evaluated.

Impairment losses are included in SG&A expense in the consolidated statements of earnings. Fair value measurements associated with long-lived asset impairments are further described in Note 6 to the consolidated financial statements.

Goodwill   Goodwill is the excess of the purchase price over the fair value of identifiable assets acquired, less liabilities assumed, in a business combination. The Company reviews goodwill for impairment at the reporting unit level, which is the operating segment level or one level below the operating segment level. Goodwill is not amortized but is evaluated for impairment at least annually on the first day of the fourth quarter or whenever events or changes in circumstances indicate that it is more likely than not that the carrying amount may not be recoverable.

Leases   Effective February 2, 2019, the Company adopted ASU 2016-02, *Leases (Topic 842),* which requires leases to be recognized on the balance sheet. Leases with an original term of 12 months or less are not recognized on the Company's balance sheet, and the lease expense related to those short-term leases is recognized over the lease term. The Company does not account for lease and non-lease (e.g. common area maintenance) components of contracts separately for any underlying asset class.

The Company leases certain retail stores, warehouses, distribution centers, office space, land and equipment under finance and operating leases. Lease commencement occurs on the date the Company takes possession or control of the property or equipment. Original terms for facility-related leases are generally between five and twenty years. These leases generally contain provisions for four to six renewal options of five years each. Original terms for equipment-related leases, primarily material handling equipment and vehicles, are generally between one and seven years. Some of the Company's leases also include rental escalation clauses and/or termination provisions. Renewal options and termination options are included in the determination of lease payments when management determines the options are reasonably certain of exercise, considering financial performance, strategic importance and/or invested capital.

Accounts Payable   The Company has agreements with third parties to provide accounts payable tracking systems which facilitate participating suppliers' ability to finance payment obligations from the Company with designated third-party financial institutions. Participating suppliers may, at their sole discretion, make offers to finance one or more payment obligations of the Company prior to their scheduled due dates at a discounted price to participating financial institutions. The Company's goal in entering into these arrangements is to capture overall supply chain savings in the form of pricing, payment terms, or vendor funding, created by facilitating suppliers' ability to finance payment obligations at more favorable discount rates, while providing them with greater working capital flexibility.

The Company's obligations to its suppliers, including amounts due and scheduled payment dates, are not impacted by suppliers' decisions to finance amounts under these arrangements. However, the Company's right to offset balances due from suppliers against payment obligations is restricted by these arrangements for those payment obligations that have been financed by suppliers. The Company's outstanding payment obligations placed on the accounts payable tracking systems were $1.9 billion as of January 31, 2020 and $2.1 billion as of February 1, 2019, and are included in accounts payable on the consolidated balance sheets, and participating suppliers financed $1.3 billion and $1.5 billion, respectively, of those payment obligations to participating financial institutions. Total payment obligations that were placed and settled on the accounts payable tracking system were $8.7 billion and $8.4 billion for each of the years ended January 31, 2020 and February 1, 2019, respectively.

Other Current Liabilities   Other current liabilities on the consolidated balance sheets consist of:

(In millions)	January 31, 2020	February 1, 2019
Self-insurance liabilities	$ 501	$ 378
Accrued dividends	420	385
Accrued interest	221	184
Sales return reserve	194	194
Sales tax liabilities	153	179
Accrued property taxes	104	108
Other	988	997
Total	**$2,581**	**$2,425**

Self-Insurance   The Company is self-insured for certain losses relating to workers' compensation, automobile, property, and general and product liability claims. The Company has insurance coverage to limit the exposure arising from these claims. The Company is also self-insured for certain losses relating to extended protection plan and medical and dental claims. Self-insurance claims filed and claims incurred but not reported are accrued based upon management's estimates of the discounted ultimate cost for self-insured claims incurred using actuarial assumptions followed in the insurance industry and historical experience. Although management believes it has the ability to reasonably estimate losses related to claims, it is possible that actual results could differ from recorded self-insurance liabilities. The total self-insurance liability, including the current and non-current portions, was $1.1 billion and $953 million at January 31, 2020, and February 1, 2019, respectively.

The Company provides surety bonds issued by insurance companies to secure payment of workers' compensation liabilities as required in certain states where the Company is self-insured. Outstanding surety bonds relating to self-insurance were $262 million and $246 million at January 31, 2020, and February 1, 2019, respectively.

Income Taxes   The Company establishes deferred income tax assets and liabilities for temporary differences between the tax and financial accounting bases of assets and liabilities. The tax effects of such differences are reflected in the consolidated balance sheets at the enacted tax rates expected to be in effect when the differences reverse. A valuation allowance is recorded to reduce the carrying amount of deferred tax assets if it is more likely than not that all or a portion of the asset will not be realized. The tax balances and income tax expense recognized by the Company are based on management's interpretation of the tax statutes of multiple jurisdictions.

The Company establishes a liability for tax positions for which there is uncertainty as to whether or not the position will be ultimately sustained. The Company includes interest related to tax issues as part of net interest on the consolidated financial statements. The Company records any applicable penalties related to tax issues within the income tax provision.

Shareholders' Equity   The Company has a share repurchase program that is executed through purchases made from time to time either in the open market or through private market transactions. Shares purchased under the repurchase program are retired and returned to authorized and unissued status. Any excess of cost over par value is charged to additional paid-in capital to the extent that a balance is present. Once additional paid-in capital is fully depleted, remaining excess of cost over par value is charged to retained earnings.

Revenue Recognition   The Company recognizes revenue to depict the transfer of goods or services to customers in an amount that reflects the consideration to which the Company expects to be entitled in exchange for those goods and services. A description of the Company's principle revenue generating activities is as follows:

- *Products*—Revenue from products primarily relates to in-store and online merchandise purchases, which are recognized at the point in time when the customer obtains control of the merchandise. This occurs at the time of in-store purchase or delivery of the product to the customer. A provision for anticipated merchandise returns is provided through a reduction of sales and cost of sales in the period that the related sales are recorded. The merchandise return reserve is presented on a gross basis, with a separate asset and liability included in the consolidated balance sheets.

- *Services*—Revenues from services primarily relate to professional installation services the Company provides through subcontractors related to merchandise purchased by a customer. In certain instances, installation services include materials provided by the subcontractor, and both product and installation are included in service revenue. The Company recognizes revenue associated with services as they are rendered, and the majority of services are completed within one week from initiation.

Deferred revenue is presented for merchandise that has not yet transferred control to the customer and for services that have not yet been provided, but for which tender has been accepted. Deferred revenue is recognized in sales either at a point in time when the customer obtains control of merchandise through pickup or delivery, or over time as services are provided to the customer. In addition, the Company defers revenues from stored-value cards, which include gift cards and returned merchandise credits, and recognizes revenue into sales when the cards are redeemed.

The Company also defers revenues for its separately-priced extended protection plan contracts, which is a Lowe's-branded program for which the Company is ultimately self-insured. The Company recognizes revenue from extended protection plan sales on a straight-line basis over the respective contract term. Extended protection plan contract terms primarily range from one to five years from the date of purchase or the end of the manufacturer's warranty, as applicable.

Cost of Sales and Selling, General and Administrative Expenses   The following lists the primary costs classified in each major expense category:

Cost of Sales	*Selling, General and Administrative*
• Total cost of products sold, including: — Purchase costs, net of vendor funds; — Freight expenses associated with moving merchandise inventories from vendors to selling locations; — Costs associated with operating the Company's distribution network, including payroll and benefit costs and occupancy costs; — Depreciation of assets associated with the Company's distribution network; • Costs of installation services provided; • Costs associated with shipping and handling to customers, as well as directly from vendors to customers by third parties; • Depreciation of assets used in delivering product to customers; • Costs associated with inventory shrinkage and obsolescence; • Costs of services performed under the extended protection plan.	• Payroll and benefit costs for retail and corporate employees; • Occupancy costs of retail and corporate facilities; • Advertising; • Third-party, in-store service costs; • Tender costs, including bank charges, costs associated with credit card interchange fees; • Costs associated with self-insured plans, and premium costs for stop-loss coverage and fully insured plans; • Long-lived asset impairment losses, gains/losses on disposal of assets, and exit costs; • Other administrative costs, such as supplies, and travel and entertainment.

Advertising   Costs associated with advertising are charged to expense as incurred. Advertising expenses were $871 million, $963 million, and $968 million in 2019, 2018, and 2017, respectively.

Store Opening Costs   Costs of opening new or relocated retail stores, which include payroll and supply costs incurred prior to store opening and grand opening advertising costs, are charged to expense as incurred.

Comprehensive Income   The Company reports comprehensive income in its consolidated statements of comprehensive income and consolidated statements of shareholders' equity. Comprehensive income represents changes in shareholders' equity from non-owner sources and is comprised of net earnings adjusted primarily for foreign currency translation adjustments. Net foreign currency translation losses, net of tax, classified in accumulated other comprehensive loss were $115 million and $209 million at January 31, 2020 and February 1, 2019, respectively. Net foreign currency translation gains, net of tax, classified in accumulated other comprehensive income were $11 million at February 2, 2018.

Segment Information The Company's home improvement retail operations represent a single reportable segment. Key operating decisions are made at the Company level in order to maintain a consistent retail store presentation. The Company's home improvement retail and hardware stores sell similar products and services, use similar processes to sell those products and services, and sell their products and services to similar classes of customers. In addition, the Company's operations exhibit similar long-term economic characteristics. The amounts of long-lived assets and net sales outside of the U.S. were approximately 7.7% and 6.9%, respectively, at January 31, 2020. The amounts of long-lived assets and net sales outside of the U.S. were approximately 9.1% and 7.6%, respectively, at February 1, 2019. The amounts of long-lived assets and net sales outside of the U.S. were approximately 9.8% and 7.8%, respectively, at February 2, 2018.

Other notes to the financial statements can be downloaded from sec.gov or the investor relations section of the company's website.

Present and Future Value Concepts

The concepts of present value (PV) and future value (FV) are based on the time value of money. The **time value of money** is the idea that, quite simply, money received today is worth more than money to be received one year from today (or at any other future date) because it can be used to earn interest. If you invest $1,000 today at 10 percent, you will have $1,100 in one year. So $1,000 in one year is worth $100 less than $1,000 today because you lose the opportunity to earn the $100 in interest.

In some business situations, you will know the dollar amount of a cash flow that occurs in the future and will need to determine its value now. This type of situation is known as a **present value** problem. The opposite situation occurs when you know the dollar amount of a cash flow that occurs today and need to determine its value at some point in the future. These situations are called **future value** problems. The value of money changes over time because money can earn interest. The following table illustrates the basic difference between present value and future value problems:

	Now	Future
Present value	?	$1,000
Future value	$1,000	?

Present and future value problems may involve two types of cash flow: a single payment or an annuity (which is the fancy word for a series of equal cash payments). Combining two types of time value of money problems with two types of cash flows yields four different situations:

1. Future value of a single payment
2. Present value of a single payment
3. Future value of an annuity
4. Present value of an annuity

The detailed arithmetic computations required to solve future value and present value problems can be performed using a spreadsheet program such as Excel, an online app such as EZ Calculator, or Tables C.1 through C.4 at the end of this appendix. We demonstrate all three approaches.

> ### YOU SHOULD KNOW
>
> **Time Value of Money:** The idea that money received today is worth more than the same amount received in the future because money received today can be invested to earn interest over time.
> **Present Value:** The current value of an amount to be received in the future. It is calculated by discounting a future amount for compound interest.
> **Future Value:** The sum to which an amount will increase as the result of compound interest.

Future Value of a Single Amount

In future value of a single amount problems, you will be asked to calculate how much money you will have in the future as the result of investing a certain amount in the present. If you were to receive a gift of $10,000, for instance, you might decide to put it in a savings account and use the money as a down payment on a house after you graduate. The future value computation would tell you how much money will be available when you graduate.

To solve a future value problem, you need to know three items:

1. Amount to be invested.
2. Interest rate (i) the amount will earn.
3. Number of periods (n) in which the amount will earn interest.

The future value concept is based on compound interest, which simply means that interest is calculated on top of interest. Thus, the amount of interest for each period is calculated using the principal plus any interest not paid out in prior periods. Graphically, the calculation of the future value of $1 for three periods at an interest rate of 10 percent may be represented as follows:

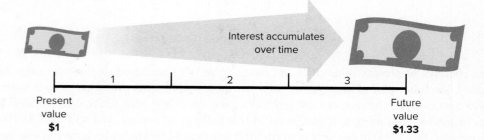

ARITHMETIC CALCULATIONS

Assume that on January 1 you deposit $1,000 in a savings account at 10 percent annual interest, compounded annually. At the end of three years, the $1,000 will have increased to $1,331 as follows:

Year	Amount at Start of Year	+	Interest During the Year	=	Amount at End of Year
1	$1,000	+	$1,000 × 10% = $100	=	$1,100
2	1,100	+	1,100 × 10% = 110	=	1,210
3	1,210	+	1,210 × 10% = 121	=	1,331

USING TABLES

The detailed arithmetic calculations can be avoided by referring to Table C.1, Future Value of $1. This table shows a Future Value Factor for various combinations of interest rates (i) and interest periods (n). To determine the future value of an amount invested today, find the Future Value Factor at the intersection of the applicable interest rate and number of periods and then multiply that factor by the amount invested today.

For example, $1,000 invested today to earn 10 percent interest compounded annually for three years ($i = 10$, $n = 3$) requires a Future Value Factor of 1.33100, as shown in the nearby excerpt from Table C.1. Thus, the future value of $1,000 invested today at 10 percent for three years is calculated as **$1,000 × 1.33100 = $1,331.**

Periods	9%	10%
0	1.00000	1.00000
1	1.09000	1.10000
2	1.18810	1.21000
3	1.29503	1.33100
4	1.41158	1.46410

USING EXCEL

Excel provides another way to calculate the future value of a single sum of money. As the help function in Excel shows, all you need to do is enter the required information in the proper order in any cell in Excel. Excel's labels differ slightly from ours; using our abbreviations for consistency, the proper order is shown below. Be sure to include the equals sign first.

=FV(i, n, FV pmt, PV)

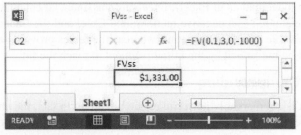

Source: Microsoft Excel

Replace the *i* with the interest rate (**expressed as a decimal**), *n* with the number of interest periods, FV pmt with the number 0, and PV with the amount invested today (**expressed as a negative number with no commas**).

For example, the future value of $1,000 invested today to earn 10 percent interest compounded annually for three years would be entered in a cell in Excel as

$$=FV(0.10,3,0,-1000)$$

After entering the above function and pressing Enter, the Excel cell will show a value of **$1,331.00.** Notice that, unlike the Table method, Excel produces the future value amount (you do not have to multiply it by the amount invested).

USING A FINANCIAL CALCULATOR APP

A search for "financial calculator app" on the Internet will return about 5 million matches. To help narrow it down, we recommend you try the TVM (time value of money) app made by Bishinew Incorporated. This free app can be used with a web browser at fncalculator.com or downloaded for a tablet or smartphone from the App Store or Google Play.

The inputs for this app are similar to those used in Excel, as indicated by the nearby accompanying screen capture. When using this app to calculate the future value of a single sum of money, leave the "Mode" selection at its default (End), enter the present value invested today as a negative number, enter the number 0 in the payment field, leave the Future Value field blank, enter the annual interest rate as a whole number (not its decimal equivalent), enter the number of interest periods, and select the applicable compounding frequency (annually for all examples in this book). To obtain the future value, click the FV button to the right of that empty field and then wait. Soon, the future value (1,331.00) will appear in the Future Value field.

The following table presents a summary of the steps to follow when using these three methods to compute the **future value of a single amount,** assuming an initial investment of **$1,000** that earns **10 percent** interest compounded annually for **three years.**

TVM Calculator

Mode	● End ○ Beginning	
Present Value	-1,000	PV
Payment	0	PMT
Future Value		FV
Annual Rate (%)	10	Rate
Periods	3	Periods
Compounding	Annually ▼	

Source: Financial Calculators

Problem Type	Using Tables	Using Excel	Using EZ Calculator App
FV—single amount	Go to Table C.1	Enter in any cell: =FV(*i*, *n*, FV pmt, PV)	Go to fncalculator.com Select TVM Calculator
Inputs	Find value for *i* = 10%, *n* = 3 ↓ **1.33100** ×1,000	Where . . . *i* = 0.10, *n* = 3, FV pmt = 0, PV = −1000	Present Value = −1000 Payment = 0 Future Value = [blank] Annual Rate = 10 Periods = 3 Compounding = Annually Click on FV button
Outputs	$1,331.00	$1,331.00	Future Value = $1,331.00

When using these different methods to calculate future values, watch out for the following subtle differences. The tables and financial calculator app specify the interest rate as a whole number (not a decimal as in Excel); Excel and the financial calculator app require the initial amount to be entered as a negative number; and Excel and the financial calculator app compute the future value as a dollar amount (whereas the tables provide only a Future Value Factor, which must be multiplied by the initial payment to reach the future value).

The Power of Compounding

Compound interest is a remarkably powerful economic force. In fact, the ability to earn interest on interest is the key to building economic wealth. If you save $1,000 per year for the first 10 years of your career, you will have more money when you retire than you would if you had saved $15,000 per year for the last 10 years of your career. This surprising outcome occurs because the money you save early in your career will earn more interest than the money you save at the end of your career. If you start saving money now, the majority of your wealth will not be the money you saved but the interest your money was able to earn.

The period/value table shows how a single investment of $1,000 today grows over time, at the investment community's historic average growth rate of 10 percent. Two important lessons are revealed in the table: **(1) you can earn a lot of interest through the effects of compounding** (in just 10 years, you will earn $1,600 interest on a $1,000 investment) and **(2) start early** (notice the balance more than doubles every 10 years, so letting your investment sit an extra decade could make you twice as rich).

Period	Value
Now	$ 1,000
10 years	$ 2,600
20 years	$ 6,700
30 years	$ 17,400
40 years	$ 45,300
50 years	$117,400
60 years	$304,500
70 years	$789,700

Present Value of a Single Amount

The present value of a single amount is the worth to you today of receiving that amount sometime in the future. For instance, you might be offered an opportunity to invest in a financial instrument that would pay you $1,000 in three years. Before you decided whether to invest, you would want to determine the present value of the instrument.

To compute the present value of an amount to be received in the future, we must discount (a procedure that is the opposite of compounding) at i interest rate for n periods. In discounting, the interest is subtracted rather than added, as it is in compounding. Graphically, the present value of $1 due at the end of the third period with an interest rate of 10 percent can be represented as follows:

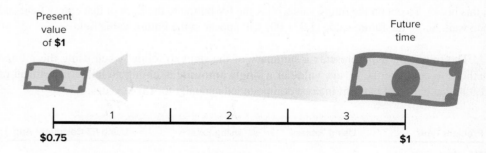

Assume that today is January 1 and you have the opportunity to receive $1,000 cash three years from now on December 31. At an interest rate of 10 percent per year, how much is the $1,000 payment worth to you today? You could discount the amount year by year,[1] but it is easier to use a table, Excel, or a financial calculator app.

---

[1]The detailed discounting is as follows:

Periods	Interest for the Year	Present Value*
1	$1,000 − ($1,000 × 1/1.10) = $90.91	$1,000 − $90.91 = $909.09
2	$909.09 − ($909.09 × 1/1.10) = $82.65	$909.09 − $82.65 = $826.44
3	$826.44 − ($826.44 × 1/1.10) = $75.13	$826.44 − $75.13 = $751.31

*Verifiable in Table C.2.

USING TABLES

For a present value of a single amount, refer to Table C.2, Present Value of $1. As shown nearby, for $i = 10\%$, $n = 3$, the Present Value Factor is 0.75131. Thus, the present value of $1,000 to be received at the end of three years can be calculated as **$1,000 × 0.75131 = $751.31.**

Periods	9%	10%
1	0.91743	0.90909
2	0.84168	0.82645
3	0.77218	0.75131
4	0.70843	0.68301

USING EXCEL

To compute the present value of a single amount in Excel, enter amounts in any cell in the order of our abbreviations shown below. Be sure to include the equals sign first.

=PV(_i_, _n_, PV pmt, FV)

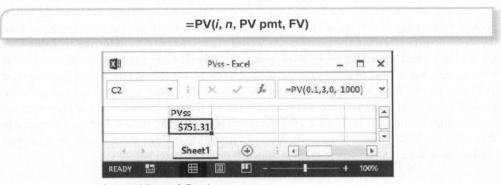
Source: Microsoft Excel

Replace the i with the interest rate (**expressed as a decimal**), n with the number of interest periods, PV pmt with the number 0, and FV with the amount to be received in the future (**shown as a negative number with no commas**). Thus, the present value of $1,000 to be received after three years, discounted to today at 10% annual interest, is calculated in Excel as

=PV(0.10,3,0,−1000)

After entering the above function and pressing Enter, the Excel cell will show **$751.31.**

USING A FINANCIAL CALCULATOR APP

The present value inputs are similar to the future value inputs (shown earlier) with one exception: Rather than entering the amount invested as the present value and leaving the Future Value field blank, **leave the Present Value field blank and enter the future value amount** (as a negative number). The nearby screen capture shows the inputs for our example: Leave the Mode selection at its default (End), leave the Present Value field blank, enter the number 0 in the Payment field, enter the Future Value as a negative number (−1,000), enter the annual interest rate as a whole number (10), enter the number of interest periods (3), and select the compounding frequency (annually). To obtain the present value, click the PV button to the right of that empty field. Soon, the present value (751.31) will appear in the Present Value field.

TVM Calculator

Mode	● End ○ Beginning	
Present Value		PV
Payment	0	PMT
Future Value	-1,000	FV
Annual Rate (%)	10	Rate
Periods	3	Periods
Compounding	Annually ▾	

Source: Financial Calculators

The following table presents a summary of the steps to follow when using these methods to compute the **present value of a single amount,** assuming **$1,000** will be received after **three years** discounted using a **10 percent** interest rate.

Problem Type	Using Tables	Using Excel	Using EZ Calculator App
PV—single amount	Go to Table C.2	Enter in any cell: =PV(_i_, _n_, PV pmt, FV)	Go to fncalculator.com Select TVM Calculator
Inputs	Find value for $i = 10\%$, $n = 3$	Where . . . $i = 0.10$, $n = 3$, PV pmt = 0, FV = −1000	Present Value = [blank] Payment = 0 Future Value = −1000 Annual Rate = 10 Periods = 3 Compounding = Annually Click PV
	0.75131 × 1,000		
Outputs	$751.31	$751.31	Present Value = $751.31

It's important to learn not only how to compute a present value but also to understand what it means. The $751.31 is the amount you would pay now to have the right to receive $1,000 at the end of three years, assuming an interest rate of 10 percent. Conceptually, you should be indifferent between having $751.31 today and receiving $1,000 in three years. If you had $751.31 today but wanted $1,000 in three years, you would deposit the money in a savings account that pays 10 percent interest and it would grow to $1,000 in three years. Alternatively, if you had a contract that promised you $1,000 in three years, you could sell it to an investor for $751.31 in cash today because it would permit the investor to earn the difference in interest.

What if you could only earn 6 percent during the three-year period? What would be the present value today of receiving $1,000 three years from now? To answer this, we would take the same approach, except the interest rate would change to $i = 6\%$. Referring to Table C.2, we see the present value factor for $i = 6\%$, $n = 3$, is 0.83962. Thus, the present value of $1,000 to be received at the end of three years, assuming a 6 percent interest rate, would be computed as $1,000 × 0.83962 = $839.62. (Excel and the financial calculator app similarly calculate the present value as $839.62.) Notice when we assume a 6 percent interest rate, the present value is greater than when we assumed a 10 percent interest rate. The reason for this difference is that, to reach $1,000 three years from now, you'd need to deposit more money in a savings account now if it earns 6 percent interest than if it earns 10 percent interest.

 How's it going?   Self-Study Practice

1. If the interest rate in a present value problem increases from 8 percent to 10 percent, will the present value increase or decrease?

2. What is the present value of $10,000 to be received 10 years from now if the interest rate is 5 percent, compounded annually?

3. If $10,000 is deposited now in a savings account that earns 5 percent interest compounded annually, how much will it be worth 10 years from now?

After you have finished, check your answers with the solution.

Solution to Self-Study Practice
1. The present value will decrease.
2. $10,000 × 0.61391 = $6,139.10
3. $10,000 × 1.62889 = $16,288.90

Future Value of an Annuity

Instead of a single payment, many business problems involve multiple cash payments over a number of periods. An **annuity** is a series of consecutive payments characterized by

1. An equal dollar amount each interest period.
2. Interest periods of equal length (year, half a year, quarter, or month).
3. An equal interest rate each interest period.

YOU SHOULD KNOW

Annuity: A series of periodic cash receipts or payments that are equal in amount each interest period.

If you are saving money for some purpose, such as a new car or a trip to Europe, you might decide to deposit a fixed amount of money in a savings account each month. The future value of an annuity computation will tell you how much money will be in your savings account at some point in the future. Other examples of annuities include monthly payments on a car or house, yearly contributions to a savings account, and monthly pension benefits.

The future value of an annuity includes compound interest on each payment from the date of payment to the end of the term of the annuity. Each new payment accumulates less interest than prior payments, only because the number of periods remaining in which to accumulate interest decreases. The future value of an annuity of $1 for three periods at 10 percent may be represented graphically as

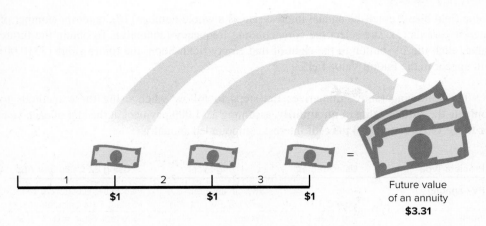

Future value
of an annuity
$3.31

Assume that each year for three years you deposit $1,000 cash in a savings account at 10 percent interest per year. You make the first $1,000 deposit on December 31, 2020, the second one on December 31, 2021, and the third and last one on December 31, 2022. The first $1,000 deposit earns compound interest for two years (for a total principal and interest of $1,210); the second deposit earns interest for one year (for a total principal and interest of $1,100). The third deposit earns no interest because it was made on the day that the balance is computed. Thus, the total amount in the savings account at the end of three years is $3,310 ($1,210 + $1,100 + $1,000).

USING TABLES

To calculate the future value of this annuity, we could compute the interest on each deposit, similar to what's described above. However, a faster way is to refer to Table C.3, Future Value of Annuity of $1. For $i = 10\%$, $n = 3$, we find the value 3.31000. The future value of the three deposits of $1,000 each can be computed as follows: **$1,000 × 3.31000 = $3,310.**

Periods*	9%	10%
1	1.00000	1.00000
2	2.09000	2.10000
3	3.27810	3.31000
4	4.57313	4.64100

USING EXCEL

To compute the future value of an annuity in Excel, enter amounts in any cell in the order of our abbreviations shown below:

=FV(*i*, *n*, PV pmt, PV)

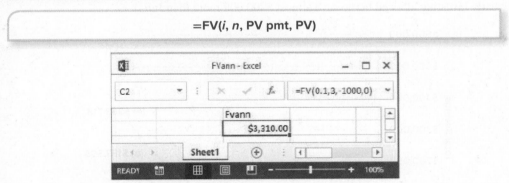

Source: Microsoft Excel

Replace the *i* with the interest rate (**expressed as a decimal**), *n* with the number of interest periods, PV pmt with the amount of the annuity payment (**shown as a negative number with no commas**), and PV as the number 0. Thus, the future value of an annuity of $1,000 paid each year for three years, earning 10 percent interest compounded annually, is calculated in Excel as

=FV(0.10,3,−1000,0)

After entering the above function, the Excel cell will show a value of **$3,310.00.**

USING A FINANCIAL CALCULATOR APP

The nearby screen capture shows the inputs for our future value of an annuity example: Leave the Mode selection at its default (End), enter the number 0 in the Present Value field, enter the annuity amount (−1,000) in the Payment field (as a negative number), leave the Future

Source: Financial Calculators

Value field blank, enter the annual interest rate as a whole number (10), enter the number of interest periods (3), and select the compounding frequency (annually). To obtain the future value, click the FV button to the right of that empty field. Soon, the future value (3310.00) will appear in the Future Value field.

The following table summarizes the steps to follow when using these methods to compute the **future value of an annuity,** assuming a **$1,000** payment at the end of each year for **three years** earning **10 percent** interest compounded annually.

Problem Type	Using Tables	Using Excel	Using EZ Calculator App
FV—annuity	Go to Table C.3	Enter in any cell: =FV(*i, n*, PV pmt, PV)	Go to fncalculator.com Select TVM Calculator
Inputs	Find value for *i* = 10%, *n* = 3 ↓ **3.31000** × 1,000	Where . . . *i* = 0.10, *n* = 3, PV pmt = −1000, PV = 0	Present Value = 0 Payment = −1000 Future Value = [blank] Annual Rate = 10 Periods = 3 Compounding = Annually Click FV
Outputs	$3,310.00	$3,310.00	Future Value = $3,310.00

THE POWER OF COMPOUNDING AND REGULAR SAVING

You've already seen the powerful effects of compound interest. Now, combine that with regular saving (an annuity), and you have the secret to becoming wealthy. The following graph shows three profiles: **(a) Start early then stop:** Julia invests $1,200 per year for the first 10 years of her career but then stops, leaving her investment to grow over the last 30 years until she retires; **(b) Start later and never stop:** Kevin invests $1,200 per year for each of the last 30 years of his career; and **(c) Start early and never stop:** Brooklyn invests $1,200 per year for her entire career. The big lessons here are that it really pays to (1) **start early** (Julia invested only $12,000 total whereas Kevin invested $36,000 total, yet at age 65 Julia has $136,325 more money to spend in retirement) and (2) **never stop** (Brooklyn's continued yearly investing allowed her to save almost $200,000 more than Julia).

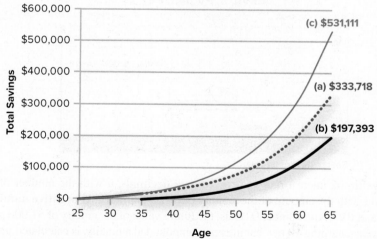

(Assumes 10 percent interest, compounded annually.)

Present Value of an Annuity

The present value of an annuity is the value now of a series of equal amounts to be received (or paid out) for some specified number of periods in the future. It is computed by discounting each of the equal periodic amounts. A good example of this type of problem is a retirement program that offers employees a monthly income after retirement. The present value of an annuity of $1 for three periods at 10 percent may be represented graphically as

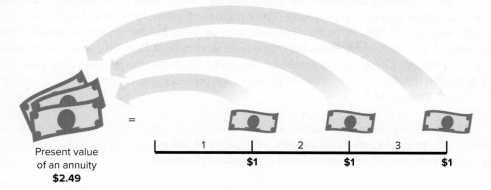

Present value
of an annuity
$2.49

Assume you are to receive $1,000 cash on each December 31, 2020, 2021, and 2022. How much would the sum of these three $1,000 future amounts be worth on January 1, 2020, assuming an interest rate of 10 percent per year?

USING TABLES

One way to determine the present value of an annuity is to use Table C.2 to calculate the present value of each single amount as follows:

Year	Amount		FACTOR FROM TABLE C.2 i = 10%		Present Value
1	$1,000	×	0.90909 (n = 1)	=	$ 909.09
2	$1,000	×	0.82645 (n = 2)	=	826.45
3	$1,000	×	0.75131 (n = 3)	=	751.31
			Total present value	=	$2,486.85

Alternatively, we can compute the present value of this annuity more easily by using Table C.4, Present Value of Annuity of $1, as follows: **$1,000 × 2.48685 = $2,486.85.**

Periods*	9%	10%
1	0.91743	0.90909
2	1.75911	1.73554
3	2.53129	2.48685
4	3.23972	3.16987

USING EXCEL

To compute the present value of an annuity in Excel, enter amounts in any cell in the order of our abbreviations shown below:

=PV(i, n, FV pmt)

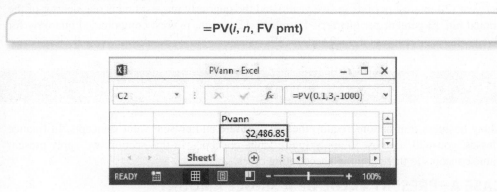

Source: Microsoft Excel

Replace the *i* with the interest rate (**expressed as a decimal**), *n* with the number of interest periods, and FV pmt with the amount of the annuity payment (**shown as a negative number with no commas**). Thus, the present value of an annuity of $1,000 paid each year for three years, earning 10 percent interest compounded annually, is calculated in Excel as

=PV(0.10,3,−1000)

After entering the preceding function, the Excel cell will show a value of **$2,486.85.**

USING A FINANCIAL CALCULATOR APP

TVM Calculator

Mode	● End ○ Beginning
Present Value	[blank] PV
Payment	-1,000 PMT
Future Value	0 FV
Annual Rate (%)	10 Rate
Periods	3 Periods
Compounding	Annually ▾

Source: Financial Calculators

The nearby screen capture shows the inputs for our future value of an annuity example: Leave the Mode selection at its default (End), leave the Present Value field blank, enter the annuity amount (−1,000) in the Payment field (as a negative number), enter the number 0 in the Future Value field, enter the annual interest rate as a whole number (10), enter the number of interest periods (3), and select annual compounding. To obtain the present value, click the PV button to the right of that empty field. Soon, the present value (2,486.85) will appear in the Present Value field.

The following table summarizes the steps to follow when using these methods to compute the **present value of an annuity,** assuming a **$1,000** payment at the end of each year for **three years** earning **10 percent** interest compounded annually.

Problem Type	Using Tables	Using Excel	Using EZ Calculator App
PV—annuity	Go to Table C.4	Enter in any cell: =PV(i, n, PV pmt)	Go to fncalculator.com Select TVM Calculator
Inputs	Find value for $i = 10\%, n = 3$ ↓ **2.48685** × 1,000	Where . . . $i = 0.10$, $n = 3$, PV pmt = −1000	Present Value = [blank] Payment = −1000 Future Value = 0 Annual Rate = 10 Periods = 3 Compounding = Annually Click PV
Outputs	$2,486.85	$2,486.85	Present Value = $2,486.85

INTEREST RATES AND INTEREST PERIODS

The preceding illustrations assumed annual periods for compounding and discounting. Although interest rates are quoted on an annual basis, many compounding periods encountered in business are less than one year. When interest periods are less than a year, the values of n and i must be restated to be consistent with the length of the interest compounding period.

To illustrate, 12 percent interest compounded annually for five years requires the use of $n = 5$ and $i = 12\%$. If compounding is quarterly, however, there will be four interest periods per year (20 interest periods in five years) and the quarterly interest rate is one quarter of the annual rate (3 percent per quarter). Therefore, 12 percent interest compounded quarterly for five years requires use of $n = 20$ and $i = 3\%$.

Accounting Applications of Present Values

Many business transactions require the use of future and present value concepts. In finance classes, you will see how to apply future value concepts. In this section, we apply present value concepts to three common accounting cases.

CASE A—PRESENT VALUE OF A SINGLE AMOUNT

On January 1, 2021, General Mills bought equipment. The company signed a note and agreed to pay $200,000 on December 31, 2022, an amount representing the cash equivalent price of the equipment plus interest for two years. The market interest rate for this note was 9 percent.

1. How should the accountant record the purchase?

Answer   This case requires the computation of the present value of a single amount. In conformity with the cost principle, the cost of the equipment is its current cash equivalent price excluding interest, which is the present value of the future payment. The problem can be shown graphically as follows:

| January 1, 2021 | December 31, 2021 | December 31, 2022 |

?

$200,000

The present value of the $200,000 is computed using any of the three methods:

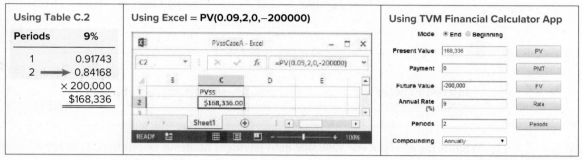

Using Table C.2

Periods	9%
1	0.91743
2 →	0.84168
	× 200,000
	$168,336

Using Excel = PV(0.09,2,0,−200000)

Using TVM Financial Calculator App

Mode	● End ○ Beginning	
Present Value	168,336	PV
Payment	0	PMT
Future Value	-200,000	FV
Annual Rate (%)	9	Rate
Periods	2	Periods
Compounding	Annually	

Source: Microsoft Excel

Source: Financial Calculators

For all examples, we record the transaction in dollars without cents ($168,336). The transaction has the following financial effects and would be recorded with the journal entry shown below.

1 Analyze

Assets	=	Liabilities	+	Stockholders' Equity
Equipment +168,336		Note Payable +168,336		

2 Record

	Debit	Credit
Equipment	168,336	
Note Payable		168,336

2. How should the effects of interest be reported at the end of 2021 and 2022?

Answer Interest expense would be calculated, reported, and recorded as follows:

December 31, 2021

Interest = Principal × Rate × Time
= $168,336 × 9% × 12/12 = $15,150 (rounded)

1 Analyze

Assets	=	Liabilities	+	Stockholders' Equity
		Note Payable +15,150		Interest Expense (+E) −15,150

2 Record

	Debit	Credit
Interest Expense	15,150	
Note Payable		15,150

COACH'S TIP

The interest is recorded in the Note Payable account because it would be paid as part of the note at maturity.

December 31, 2022

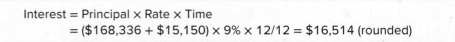

Interest = Principal × Rate × Time
= ($168,336 + $15,150) × 9% × 12/12 = $16,514 (rounded)

1 Analyze

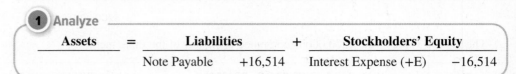

Assets	=	Liabilities	+	Stockholders' Equity	
		Note Payable +16,514		Interest Expense (+E)	−16,514

2 Record

	Debit	Credit
Interest Expense	16,514	
Note Payable		16,514

Note Payable (L)	
	168,336 Jan. 1, 2021
	15,150 Interest 2021
	16,514 Interest 2022
200,000 Dec. 31, 2022	

3. What is the effect of the $200,000 debt payment made on December 31, 2022?

Answer At this date, the amount to be paid is the balance in Note Payable, after it has been updated for interest pertaining to 2022, as shown in the nearby T-account. Notice that, just prior to its repayment, the balance for the note on December 31, 2022, is the same as the maturity amount on the due date.

The debt payment has the following financial effects and would be recorded with the journal entry shown below.

1 Analyze

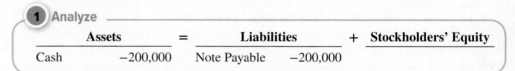

Assets	=	Liabilities	+	Stockholders' Equity
Cash −200,000		Note Payable −200,000		

2 Record

	Debit	Credit
Note Payable	200,000	
Cash..		200,000

CASE B—PRESENT VALUE OF AN ANNUITY

On January 1, General Mills bought new milling equipment. The company elected to finance the purchase with a note payable to the equipment supplier to be paid off in three years in annual installments of $163,685. Each installment includes principal plus interest on the unpaid balance at 11 percent per year. The annual installments are due on December 31, 2021, 2022, and 2023. This problem can be shown graphically as follows:

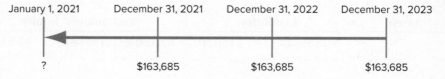

January 1, 2021	December 31, 2021	December 31, 2022	December 31, 2023
?	$163,685	$163,685	$163,685

1. What is the amount of the note?

Answer The note is the present value of each installment payment, $i = 11\%$ and $n = 3$. This is an annuity because the note repayment is made in three equal installments. The amount of the note is computed as follows:

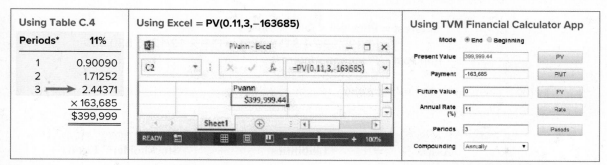

Using Table C.4		Using Excel = PV(0.11,3,−163685)	Using TVM Financial Calculator App

Source: Microsoft Excel   Source: Financial Calculators

Using the present value of $399,999, the purchase on January 1, 2021, would be accounted for as follows:

1 Analyze

Assets		=	Liabilities		+	Stockholders' Equity
Equipment	+399,999		Note Payable	+399,999		

2 Record

	Debit	Credit
Equipment	399,999	
Note Payable		399,999

2. How should the payments made at the end of each year be accounted for?

Answer:

December 31, 2021

Each payment includes both interest and principal. The interest part of the first payment is calculated as

$$\text{Interest} = \text{Principal} \times \text{Rate} \times \text{Time}$$
$$= \$399,999 \times 11\% \times 12/12 = \$44,000$$

Now that we know the interest component, the principal portion of the first payment of $163,685 can be calculated ($163,685 − $44,000 = $119,685). Thus, the first payment on December 31, 2021, would be accounted for as

1 Analyze

Assets		=	Liabilities		+	Stockholders' Equity	
Cash	−163,685		Note Payable	−119,685		Interest Expense (+E)	−44,000

2 Record

	Debit	Credit
Interest Expense	44,000	
Note Payable ($163,685 − $44,000)	119,685	
Cash		163,685

December 31, 2022

The interest portion of the second and third payments would be calculated in the same way, although notice the principal balance in the Note Payable account changes after each payment.

$$Interest = Principal \times Rate \times Time$$
$$= [(\$399,999 - \$119,685) \times 11\% \times 12/12] = \$30,835$$
$$Principal = Payment - Interest$$
$$= \$163,685 - \$30,835 = \$132,850$$

1 Analyze

Assets	=	Liabilities	+	Stockholders' Equity	
Cash −163,685		Note Payable −132,850		Interest Expense (+E)	−30,835

2 Record

	Debit	Credit
Interest Expense	30,835	
Note Payable	132,850	
Cash		163,685

December 31, 2023

$$Interest = Principal \times Rate \times Time$$
$$= [(\$399,999 - \$119,685 - \$132,850) \times 11\% \times 12/12]$$
$$= \$16,221$$
$$Principal = Payment - Interest$$
$$= \$163,685 - \$16,221 = \$147,464$$

Note Payable (L)

	$399,999	Jan. 1, 2021
Dec. 31, 2021	119,685	
Dec. 31, 2022	132,850	
Dec. 31, 2023	147,464	
	0	Dec. 31, 2023

1 Analyze

Assets	=	Liabilities	+	Stockholders' Equity	
Cash −163,685		Note Payable −147,464		Interest Expense (+E)	−16,221

2 Record

	Debit	Credit
Interest Expense	16,221	
Note Payable	147,464	
Cash		163,685

CASE C—PRESENT VALUE OF A SINGLE AMOUNT AND AN ANNUITY (BOND PRICING)

On January 1, 2021, General Mills issued 100 four-year, $1,000 bonds. The bonds pay interest annually at a stated rate of 6 percent of face value. What total amount would investors be willing to pay for the bonds if the investors require an annual return (i.e., market interest rate) of (*a*) 4 percent, (*b*) 6 percent, or (*c*) 8 percent?

Answer This case requires the computation of the present value of a single amount (the $100,000 face value paid at maturity) plus the present value of an annuity (the annual interest payments of $6,000). The problem can be shown graphically as follows:

(a) 4 Percent Market Interest Rate

The present value of the single payment of $100,000 face value and the annuity of $6,000 per year for interest can be separately calculated and summed, as follows, using either the tables or Excel:

Using Tables

Present Value of $100,000 Face Value: **$100,000 × 0.85480** (Table C.2) = $ 85,480.00
Present Value of $6,000 Annuity: **$6,000 × 3.62990** (Table C.4) =   21,779.40
Total Present Value of Bond Payments = $107,259.40

Using Excel

Present Value of $100,000 Face Value: **=PV(0.04,4,0,−100000)** = $ 85,480.42   (see below left)
Present Value of $6,000 annuity: **=PV(0.04,4,−6000)** =   21,779.37   (see below right)
Total Present Value of Bond Payments = $107,259.79

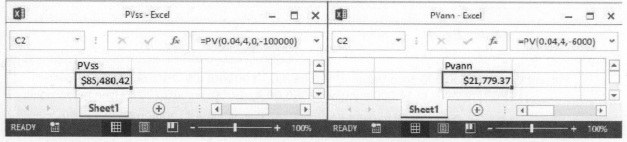

Source: Microsoft Excel   Source: Microsoft Excel

Using a Financial Calculator App These bond calculations can be simplified even further using the smartphone/tablet app or by going to fncalculator.com. Rather than select the TVM Calculator, choose the Bond Calculator. Use this calculator to solve for any missing value by inputting the other values. For example, **to use the app to determine the market interest rate, enter all the bond details except for the Annual Yield and then click the Yield button to determine the market interest rate.**

In the current case, we want to calculate the bond issue price. As shown in the accompanying screen capture, to calculate the bond issue price, leave the Bond Price field blank, enter the amount to be paid at maturity as a negative amount in the Face Value field (−100,000), enter the **dollar amount** paid for interest each year as a negative value in the Annual Coupon Payment field (−6,000), enter the market interest rate in the Annual Yield field (as a whole number, such as 4.0, not the decimal equivalent), enter the number of years for the bond (4), and select the compounding frequency (annually for all examples in this textbook). Next, click on the Price button to the right of the Bond Price field. For the General Mills bond, the inputs return a bond price of $107,259.79.

Bond Calculator

Bond Price	107,259.79	Price
Face Value	-100,000	Face Value
Annual Coupon Payment	-6,000	Coupon
Annual Yield (%)	4.000	Yield
Years to Maturity	4	Years
Compounding	Annually ▼	

Source: Financial Calculators

(b) 6 Percent Market Interest Rate

Using Tables

Present Value of $100,000 Face Value: **$100,000** × **0.79209** (Table C.2) = $79,209.00
Present Value of $6,000 Annuity: **$6,000** × **3.46511** (Table C.4) =   20,790.66
Total Present Value of Bond Payments = $99,999.66

This calculation is 34 cents short of $100,000 because the tables are rounded to five decimal places.

Using Excel

Present Value of $100,000 Face Value: **=PV(0.06,4,0,−100000)** = $ 79,209.37 (see below left)
Present Value of $6,000 annuity: **=PV(0.06,4,−6000)** =   20,790.63 (see below right)
Total Present Value of Bond Payments = $100,000.00

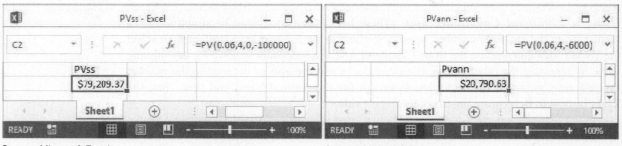

Source: Microsoft Excel   Source: Microsoft Excel

Using a Financial Calculator App

As shown in the accompanying screen capture, to calculate the bond issue price, leave the Bond Price field blank, enter the amount to be paid at maturity as a negative amount in the Face Value field (−100,000), enter the **dollar amount** paid for interest each year as a negative value in the Annual Coupon Payment field (−6,000), enter the market interest rate in the Annual Yield field (as a whole number, such as 6.0, not the decimal equivalent), enter the number of years for the bond (4), and select the compounding frequency (annually for all examples in this textbook). Next, click on the Price button to the right of the Bond Price field. For the General Mills bond, the inputs return a bond price of exactly $100,000.

Bond Calculator

Bond Price	100,000	Price
Face Value	-100,000	Face Value
Annual Coupon Payment	-6,000	Coupon
Annual Yield (%)	6.000	Yield
Years to Maturity	4	Years
Compounding	Annually ▾	

Source: Financial Calculators

(c) 8 Percent Market Interest Rate

Using Tables

Present Value of $100,000 Face Value: **$100,000 × 0.73503** (Table C.2) = $73,503.00
Present Value of $6,000 Annuity: **$6,000 × 3.31213** (Table C.4) = 19,872.78
Total Present Value of Bond Payments = $93,375.78

Using Excel

Present Value of $100,000 Face Value: **=PV(0.08,4,0,−100000)** = $73,502.99 (see below left)
Present Value of $6,000 Annuity: **=PV(0.08,4,−6000)** = 19,872.76 (see below right)
Total Present Value of Bond Payments = $93,375.75

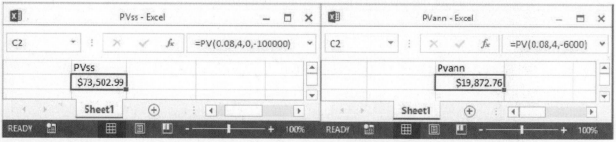

Source: Microsoft Excel   Source: Microsoft Excel

Using a Financial Calculator App   As shown in the accompanying screen capture, to calculate the bond issue price, leave the Bond Price field blank, enter the amount to be paid at maturity as a negative amount in the Face Value field (−100,000), enter the **dollar amount** paid for interest each year as a negative value in the Annual Coupon Payment field (−6,000), enter the market interest rate in the Annual Yield field (as a whole number, such as 8.0, not the decimal equivalent), enter the number of years for the bond (4), and select the compounding frequency (annually for all examples in this textbook). Next, click on the Price button to the right of the Bond Price field. For the General Mills bond, the inputs return a bond price of $93,375.75.

Bond Calculator

Bond Price	93,375.75	Price
Face Value	-100,000	Face Value
Annual Coupon Payment	-6,000	Coupon
Annual Yield (%)	8.000	Yield
Years to Maturity	4	Years
Compounding	Annually ▾	

Source: Financial Calculators

Summary

The following table summarizes the preceding (rounded) calculations for the $100,000, four-year, 6 percent bonds, assuming market interest rates of 4, 6, and 8 percent.

	MARKET INTEREST RATES		
	4%	6%	8%
Present value of $100,000 face value (principal) paid four years from now	$ 85,480	$ 79,210	$ 73,503
Present value of $6,000 (interest) paid once a year for four years	21,780	20,790	19,873
Bond price	**$107,260**	**$100,000**	**$93,376**

Of course, these calculations are just the starting point for understanding how bond liabilities are determined and reported. You'll need to read Chapter 10 for information about how to account for these values when reporting bond liabilities.

| TABLE C.1 | | Future Value of $1 |

Periods	2%	3%	3.75%	4%	4.25%	5%	6%	7%	8%
0	1.00000	1.00000	1.00000	1.00000	1.00000	1.00000	1.00000	1.00000	1.00000
1	1.02000	1.03000	1.03750	1.04000	1.04250	1.05000	1.06000	1.07000	1.08000
2	1.04040	1.06090	1.07641	1.08160	1.08681	1.10250	1.12360	1.14490	1.16640
3	1.06121	1.09273	1.11677	1.12486	1.13300	1.15763	1.19102	1.22504	1.25971
4	1.08243	1.12551	1.15865	1.16986	1.18115	1.21551	1.26248	1.31080	1.36049
5	1.10408	1.15927	1.20210	1.21665	1.23135	1.27628	1.33823	1.40255	1.46933
6	1.12616	1.19405	1.24718	1.26532	1.28368	1.34010	1.41852	1.50073	1.58687
7	1.14869	1.22987	1.29395	1.31593	1.33824	1.40710	1.50363	1.60578	1.71382
8	1.17166	1.26677	1.34247	1.36857	1.39511	1.47746	1.59385	1.71819	1.85093
9	1.19509	1.30477	1.39281	1.42331	1.45440	1.55133	1.68948	1.83846	1.99900
10	1.21899	1.34392	1.44504	1.48024	1.51621	1.62889	1.79085	1.96715	2.15892
20	1.48595	1.80611	2.08815	2.19112	2.29891	2.65330	3.20714	3.86968	4.66096

Periods	9%	10%	11%	12%	13%	14%	15%	20%	25%
0	1.00000	1.00000	1.00000	1.00000	1.00000	1.00000	1.00000	1.00000	1.00000
1	1.09000	1.10000	1.11000	1.12000	1.13000	1.14000	1.15000	1.20000	1.25000
2	1.18810	1.21000	1.23210	1.25440	1.27690	1.29960	1.32250	1.44000	1.56250
3	1.29503	1.33100	1.36763	1.40493	1.44290	1.48154	1.52088	1.72800	1.95313
4	1.41158	1.46410	1.51807	1.57352	1.63047	1.68896	1.74901	2.07360	2.44141
5	1.53862	1.61051	1.68506	1.76234	1.84244	1.92541	2.01136	2.48832	3.05176
6	1.67710	1.77156	1.87041	1.97382	2.08195	2.19497	2.31306	2.98598	3.81470
7	1.82804	1.94872	2.07616	2.21068	2.35261	2.50227	2.66002	3.58318	4.76837
8	1.99256	2.14359	2.30454	2.47596	2.65844	2.85259	3.05902	4.29982	5.96046
9	2.17189	2.35795	2.55804	2.77308	3.00404	3.25195	3.51788	5.15978	7.45058
10	2.36736	2.59374	2.83942	3.10585	3.39457	3.70722	4.04556	6.19174	9.31323
20	5.60441	6.72750	8.06231	9.64629	11.52309	13.74349	16.36654	38.33760	86.73617

| TABLE C.2 | | Present Value of $1 |

Periods	2%	3%	3.75%	4%	4.25%	5%	6%	7%	8%
1	0.98039	0.97087	0.96386	0.96154	0.95923	0.95238	0.94340	0.93458	0.92593
2	0.96117	0.94260	0.92902	0.92456	0.92013	0.90703	0.89000	0.87344	0.85734
3	0.94232	0.91514	0.89544	0.88900	0.88262	0.86384	0.83962	0.81630	0.79383
4	0.92385	0.88849	0.86307	0.85480	0.84663	0.82270	0.79209	0.76290	0.73503
5	0.90573	0.86261	0.83188	0.82193	0.81212	0.78353	0.74726	0.71299	0.68058
6	0.88797	0.83748	0.80181	0.79031	0.77901	0.74622	0.70496	0.66634	0.63017
7	0.87056	0.81309	0.77283	0.75992	0.74725	0.71068	0.66506	0.62275	0.58349
8	0.85349	0.78941	0.74490	0.73069	0.71679	0.67684	0.62741	0.58201	0.54027
9	0.83676	0.76642	0.71797	0.70259	0.68757	0.64461	0.59190	0.54393	0.50025
10	0.82035	0.74409	0.69202	0.67556	0.65954	0.61391	0.55839	0.50835	0.46319
20	0.67297	0.55368	0.47889	0.45639	0.43499	0.37689	0.31180	0.25842	0.21455

Periods	9%	10%	11%	12%	13%	14%	15%	20%	25%
1	0.91743	0.90909	0.90090	0.89286	0.88496	0.87719	0.86957	0.83333	0.80000
2	0.84168	0.82645	0.81162	0.79719	0.78315	0.76947	0.75614	0.69444	0.64000
3	0.77218	0.75131	0.73119	0.71178	0.69305	0.67497	0.65752	0.57870	0.51200
4	0.70843	0.68301	0.65873	0.63552	0.61332	0.59208	0.57175	0.48225	0.40960
5	0.64993	0.62092	0.59345	0.56743	0.54276	0.51937	0.49718	0.40188	0.32768
6	0.59627	0.56447	0.53464	0.50663	0.48032	0.45559	0.43233	0.33490	0.26214
7	0.54703	0.51316	0.48166	0.45235	0.42506	0.39964	0.37594	0.27908	0.20972
8	0.50187	0.46651	0.43393	0.40388	0.37616	0.35056	0.32690	0.23257	0.16777
9	0.46043	0.42410	0.39092	0.36061	0.33288	0.30751	0.28426	0.19381	0.13422
10	0.42241	0.38554	0.35218	0.32197	0.29459	0.26974	0.24718	0.16151	0.10737
20	0.17843	0.14864	0.12403	0.10367	0.08678	0.07276	0.06110	0.02608	0.01153

TABLE C.3   Future Value of Annuity of $1

Periods*	2%	3%	3.75%	4%	4.25%	5%	6%	7%	8%
1	1.00000	1.00000	1.00000	1.00000	1.00000	1.00000	1.00000	1.00000	1.00000
2	2.02000	2.03000	2.03750	2.04000	2.04250	2.05000	2.06000	2.07000	2.08000
3	3.06040	3.09090	3.11391	3.12160	3.12931	3.15250	3.18360	3.21490	3.24640
4	4.12161	4.18363	4.23068	4.24646	4.26230	4.31013	4.37462	4.43994	4.50611
5	5.20404	5.30914	5.38933	5.41632	5.44345	5.52563	5.63709	5.75074	5.86660
6	6.30812	6.46841	6.59143	6.63298	6.67480	6.80191	6.97532	7.15329	7.33593
7	7.43428	7.66246	7.83861	7.89829	7.95848	8.14201	8.39384	8.65402	8.92280
8	8.58297	8.89234	9.13255	9.21423	9.29671	9.54911	9.89747	10.25980	10.63663
9	9.75463	10.15911	10.47503	10.58280	10.69182	11.02656	11.49132	11.97799	12.48756
10	10.94972	11.46388	11.86784	12.00611	12.14622	12.57789	13.18079	13.81645	14.48656
20	24.29737	26.87037	29.01739	29.77808	30.56250	33.06595	36.78559	40.99549	45.76196

Periods*	9%	10%	11%	12%	13%	14%	15%	20%	25%
1	1.00000	1.00000	1.00000	1.00000	1.00000	1.00000	1.00000	1.00000	1.00000
2	2.09000	2.10000	2.11000	2.12000	2.13000	2.14000	2.15000	2.20000	2.25000
3	3.27810	3.31000	3.34210	3.37440	3.40690	3.43960	3.47250	3.64000	3.81250
4	4.57313	4.64100	4.70973	4.77933	4.84980	4.92114	4.99338	5.36800	5.76563
5	5.98471	6.10510	6.22780	6.35285	6.48027	6.61010	6.74238	7.44160	8.20703
6	7.52333	7.71561	7.91286	8.11519	8.32271	8.53552	8.75374	9.92992	11.25879
7	9.20043	9.48717	9.78327	10.08901	10.40466	10.73049	11.06680	12.91590	15.07349
8	11.02847	11.43589	11.85943	12.29969	12.75726	13.23276	13.72682	16.49908	19.84186
9	13.02104	13.57948	14.16397	14.77566	15.41571	16.08535	16.78584	20.79890	25.80232
10	15.19293	15.93742	16.72201	17.54874	18.41975	19.33730	20.30372	25.95868	33.25290
20	51.16012	57.27500	64.20283	72.05244	80.94683	91.02493	102.44358	186.68800	342.94470

*There is one payment each period.

TABLE C.4   Present Value of Annuity of $1

Periods*	2%	3%	3.75%	4%	4.25%	5%	6%	7%	8%
1	0.98039	0.97087	0.96386	0.96154	0.95923	0.95238	0.94340	0.93458	0.92593
2	1.94156	1.91347	1.89287	1.88609	1.87936	1.85941	1.83339	1.80802	1.78326
3	2.88388	2.82861	2.78831	2.77509	2.76198	2.72325	2.67301	2.62432	2.57710
4	3.80773	3.71710	3.65138	3.62990	3.60861	3.54595	3.46511	3.38721	3.31213
5	4.71346	4.57971	4.48326	4.45182	4.42073	4.32948	4.21236	4.10020	3.99271
6	5.60143	5.41719	5.28507	5.24214	5.19974	5.07569	4.91732	4.76654	4.62288
7	6.47199	6.23028	6.05790	6.00205	5.94699	5.78637	5.58238	5.38929	5.20637
8	7.32548	7.01969	6.80280	6.73274	6.66378	6.46321	6.20979	5.97130	5.74664
9	8.16224	7.78611	7.52077	7.43533	7.35135	7.10782	6.80169	6.51523	6.24689
10	8.98259	8.53020	8.21279	8.11090	8.01089	7.72173	7.36009	7.02358	6.71008
20	16.35143	14.87747	13.89620	13.59033	13.29437	12.46221	11.46992	10.59401	9.81815

Periods*	9%	10%	11%	12%	13%	14%	15%	20%	25%
1	0.91743	0.90909	0.90090	0.89286	0.88496	0.87719	0.86957	0.83333	0.80000
2	1.75911	1.73554	1.71252	1.69005	1.66810	1.64666	1.62571	1.52778	1.44000
3	2.53129	2.48685	2.44371	2.40183	2.36115	2.32163	2.28323	2.10648	1.95200
4	3.23972	3.16987	3.10245	3.03735	2.97447	2.91371	2.85498	2.58873	2.36160
5	3.88965	3.79079	3.69590	3.60478	3.51723	3.43308	3.35216	2.99061	2.68928
6	4.48592	4.35526	4.23054	4.11141	3.99755	3.88867	3.78448	3.32551	2.95142
7	5.03295	4.86842	4.71220	4.56376	4.42261	4.28830	4.16042	3.60459	3.16114
8	5.53482	5.33493	5.14612	4.96764	4.79877	4.63886	4.48732	3.83716	3.32891
9	5.99525	5.75902	5.53705	5.32825	5.13166	4.94637	4.77158	4.03097	3.46313
10	6.41766	6.14457	5.88923	5.65022	5.42624	5.21612	5.01877	4.19247	3.57050
20	9.12855	8.51356	7.96333	7.46944	7.02475	6.62313	6.25933	4.86958	3.95388

*There is one payment each period.

KEY TERMS

Annuity p. C6 **Present Value** p. C1 **Time Value of Money** p. C1
Future Value p. C1

See complete definitions in the glossary in the back of this text.

PRACTICE MATERIAL

QUESTIONS

1. Explain the concept of the time value of money.

2. Explain the basic difference between future value and present value.

3. If you deposited $10,000 in a savings account that earns 10 percent, how much would you have at the end of 10 years? Use a convenient format to display your computations and round to the nearest dollar.

4. If you hold a valid contract that will pay you $8,000 cash 10 years from now and the going rate of interest is 10 percent, what is its present value? Use a convenient format to display your computations and round to the nearest dollar.

5. What is an annuity?

6. Use Tables C.1 to C.4 to complete the following schedule:

	Table Values		
	i = 5%, *n* = 4	*i* = 10%, *n* = 7	*i* = 14%, *n* = 10
FV of $1			
PV of $1			
FV of annuity of $1			
PV of annuity of $1			

7. If you deposit $1,000 at the end of each period for 10 interest periods and you earn 8 percent interest, how much would you have at the end of period 10? Use a convenient format to display your computations and round to the nearest dollar.

MULTIPLE CHOICE

1. You are saving up for a Mercedes-Benz SLR McLaren, which currently sells for nearly half a million dollars. Your plan is to deposit $15,000 at the end of each year for the next 10 years. You expect to earn 5 percent each year. How much will you have saved after 10 years, rounded to the nearest 10 dollars?

   a. $150,000.
   b. $188,670.
   c. $495,990.
   d. None of the above.

2. Which of the following is a characteristic of an annuity?

   a. An equal dollar amount each interest period.
   b. Interest periods of equal length.
   c. An equal interest rate each interest period.
   d. All of the above are characteristics of an annuity.

3. Which of the following is most likely to be an annuity?

   a. Monthly payments on a credit card bill.
   b. Monthly interest earned on a checking account.
   c. Monthly payments on a home mortgage.
   d. Monthly utility bill payments.

4. Assume you bought a state-of-the-art entertainment system, with no payments to be made until two years from now, when you must pay $6,000. If the going rate of interest on most loans is 5 percent, which table in this appendix would you use to calculate the system's equivalent cost if you were to pay for it today?

   a. Table C.1 (Future Value of $1)
   b. Table C.2 (Present Value of $1)
   c. Table C.3 (Future Value of Annuity of $1)
   d. Table C.4 (Present Value of Annuity of $1)

5. Assuming the facts in question 4, what is the system's equivalent cost if you were to pay for it today?

   a. $5,442
   b. $11,100
   c. $6,615
   d. $12,300

6. Assume you bought a car using a loan that requires payments of $3,000 to be made at the end of every year for the next three years. The loan agreement indicates the annual interest rate is 6 percent. Which table in this appendix would you use to calculate the car's equivalent cost if you were to pay for it in full today?

   a. Table C.1 (Future Value of $1)
   b. Table C.2 (Present Value of $1)
   c. Table C.3 (Future Value of Annuity of $1)
   d. Table C.4 (Present Value of Annuity of $1)

7. Assuming the facts in question 6, what is the car's equivalent cost if you were to pay for it today? Round to the nearest hundred dollars.

   a. $2,600
   b. $3,600
   c. $8,000
   d. $9,600

8. Which of the following statements is true?

   a. When the interest rate increases, the present value of a single amount decreases.

   b. When the number of interest periods increases, the present value of a single amount increases.

   c. When the interest rate increases, the present value of an annuity increases.

   d. None of the above are true.

9. Which of the following describes how to calculate a bond's issue price?

Face Value	Interest Payments
a. Present value of single amount	Future value of annuity
b. Future value of single amount	Present value of annuity
c. Present value of single amount	Present value of annuity
d. Future value of single amount	Future value of annuity

10. If interest is compounded quarterly, rather than yearly, how do you adjust the number of years and annual interest rate when using the present value tables?

Number of years	Annual interest rate
a. Divide by 4	Divide by 4
b. Divide by 4	Multiply by 4
c. Multiply by 4	Divide by 4
d. Multiply by 4	Multiply by 4

Solutions to Multiple-Choice Questions can be found on **page Q1.**

MINI-EXERCISES

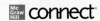

MC-1 Computing the Present Value of a Single Payment with Tables

Use present value tables to compute the present value of $500,000 to be paid in 10 years, with an interest rate of 8 percent. Round to the nearest dollar.

MC-2 Computing the Present Value of an Annuity with Tables

Use present value tables to compute the present value of 10 equal payments of $15,000, with an interest rate of 10 percent. Round to the nearest dollar.

MC-3 Computing the Present Value of a Complex Contract with Tables

As a result of a slowdown in operations, Mercantile Stores is offering to employees who have been terminated a severance package of $100,000 cash, another $100,000 to be paid in one year, and an annuity of $30,000 to be paid each year for 20 years. Use present value tables to compute the present value of the complete package, assuming an interest rate of 8 percent. Round to the nearest dollar.

MC-4 Computing the Future Value of an Annuity with Tables

You plan to retire in 20 years. Use the time value of money tables to calculate whether it is better for you to save $25,000 a year for the last 10 years before retirement or $15,000 for each of the 20 years. Assume you are able to earn 10 percent interest on your investments. Round to the nearest dollar.

MC-5 Computing the Present Value of a Single Payment in Excel

Use Excel to answer MC-1. Round to the nearest dollar.

MC-6 Computing the Present Value of an Annuity in Excel

Use Excel to answer MC-2. Round to the nearest dollar.

MC-7 Computing the Present Value of a Complex Contract in Excel

Use Excel to answer MC-3. Round to the nearest dollar.

MC-8 Computing the Future Value of an Annuity in Excel

Use Excel to answer MC-4. Round to the nearest dollar.

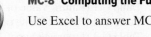

MC-9 Computing the Present Value of an Annuity Using a Financial Calculator App

Use the financial calculator app shown in the appendix to answer MC-1. Round to the nearest dollar.

MC-10 Computing the Present Value of an Annuity Using a Financial Calculator App

Use the financial calculator app shown in the appendix to answer MC-2. Round to the nearest dollar.

MC-11 Computing the Present Value of a Complex Contract Using a Financial Calculator App

Use the financial calculator app shown in the appendix to answer MC-3. Round to the nearest dollar.

MC-12 Computing the Future Value of an Annuity Using a Financial Calculator App

Use the financial calculator app shown in the appendix to answer MC-4. Round to the nearest dollar.

EXERCISES

EC-1 Computing Growth from a Single Amount (All Methods)

On January 1, you deposited $6,000 in an investment account. The account will earn 10 percent annual compound interest, which will be added to the fund balance at the end of each year.

Required (round to the nearest dollar):

1. What will be the balance in the account at the end of 10 years?
2. What is the interest for the 10 years?
3. How much interest revenue did the fund earn in the first year? the second year?

EC-2 Computing Deposit Required for a Single Sum (All Methods)

On January 1, Alan King decided to transfer an amount from his checking account into an investment account that later will provide $80,000 to send his son to college (four years from now). The investment account will earn 8 percent, which will be added to the fund each year-end.

Required (show computations and round to the nearest dollar):

1. How much must Alan deposit on January 1?
2. What is the interest for the four years?

EC-3 Growth in an Investment Account with Equal Periodic Payments (All Methods)

On each December 31, you plan to transfer $2,000 from your checking account into an investment account. The investment account will earn 4 percent annual interest, which will be added to the account balance at each year-end. The first deposit will be made December 31, 2021 (at the end of the period).

Required (show computations and round to the nearest dollar):

1. What will be the balance in the account at the end of the 10th year (i.e., 10 deposits)?
2. What is the total amount of interest earned on the 10 deposits?
3. How much interest revenue did the fund earn in 2022? 2023?

EC-4 Computing Growth for a Savings Fund with Periodic Deposits (All Methods)

On January 1, you plan to take a trip around the world upon graduation four years from now. Your grandmother wants to deposit sufficient funds for this trip in an investment account for you. On the basis of a budget, you estimate that the trip currently would cost $15,000. Being the generous and sweet lady she is, your grandmother decided to deposit $3,500 in the fund at the end of each of the next four years, starting on December 31, 2021. The account will earn 6 percent annual interest, which will be added to the account at each year-end.

Required (show computations and round to the nearest dollar):

1. How much money will you have for the trip at the end of year 4 (i.e., after four deposits)?
2. What is the total amount of interest earned over the four years?
3. How much interest revenue did the fund earn in each of the four years, starting in 2021?

EC-5 Computing Value of an Asset Based on Present Value (All Methods)

You have the chance to purchase an oil well. Your best estimate is that the oil well's net royalty income will average $25,000 per year for five years. There will be no residual value at that time. Assume that the cash inflow occurs at each year-end and that considering the uncertainty in your estimates, you expect to earn 5 percent per year on the investment. What should you be willing to pay for this investment right now (round to the nearest dollar)?

EC-6 Computing Bond Issue Proceeds and Issue Price (All Methods)

Your company plans to issue bonds later in the upcoming year. But with the economic uncertainty and varied interest rates, it is not clear how much money the company will receive when the bonds are issued. The company is committed to issuing 2,000 bonds, each of which will have a face value of $1,000, a stated interest rate of 8 percent paid annually, and a period to maturity of 10 years.

Required:

1. Compute the bond issue proceeds assuming a market interest rate of 8 percent. (Do not round until totaling the bond proceeds, at which point you should **round the total bond proceeds to the nearest thousand dollars.**) Also, express the bond issue price as a percentage by comparing the (rounded) total proceeds to the total face value.

2. Compute the bond issue proceeds assuming a market interest rate of 7 percent. (Do not round until totaling the bond proceeds, at which point you should **round the total bond proceeds to the nearest thousand dollars.**) Also, express the bond issue price as a percentage by comparing the (rounded) total proceeds to the total face value.

3. Compute the bond issue proceeds assuming a market interest rate of 9 percent. (Do not round until totaling the bond proceeds, at which point you should **round the total bond proceeds to the nearest thousand dollars.**) Also, express the bond issue price as a percentage by comparing the (rounded) total proceeds to the total face value.

EC-7 Computing Missing Present or Future Values Involving Single Amounts or Annuities (All Methods)

Each of the following situations is independent.

Case	Present Value	Annuity	Future Value	Annual Interest Rate	Number of Years
A	$100,000	—	(i)	4%	5
B	(ii)	—	$100,000	5%	4
C	(iii)	$2,000	—	3%	10
D	—	$3,000	(iv)	4%	20

Required:

Compute the missing amounts for (i) through (iv), rounded to the nearest dollar.

COACHED PROBLEMS

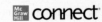

CPC-1 Comparing Options Using Present Value Concepts (Using Tables)

Assume you won the big prize of "$20 million" on a game show. This prize will be paid out in one of three ways: (1) you can receive $1 million per year for the next 20 years, (2) you can have $8 million today, or (3) you can have $2 million today and receive $700,000 for each of the next 20 years. Your financial adviser tells you that it is reasonable to expect to earn 10 percent on investments. Which option do you prefer? What factors influence your decision?

> **TIP:** All three scenarios require you to determine today's value of the various payment options. These are present value problems.

CPC-2 Comparing Options Using Present Value Concepts (Using Excel or a Financial Calculator)

Use Excel or a financial calculator to answer CPC-1.

CPC-3 Recording Equipment Purchase with Two-Year Note

Stellar Corporation purchased equipment and in exchange signed a two-year promissory note. The note requires Stellar to make a single payment of $100,000 in two years. Stellar has other promissory notes that charge interest at the annual rate of 5 percent.

Required:

1. Compute the present value of the note, rounded to the nearest dollar, using Stellar's typical interest rate of 5 percent.

2. Show the journal entry to record the equipment purchase (round to the nearest dollar).
3. Show the adjusting journal entry at the end of the first year to record interest on the note.
4. Show the adjusting journal entry at the end of the second year to record interest on the note (but do not record the payment of $100,000 yet).
5. Show the journal entry at the end of the second year to record the payment of $100,000.
   TIP: Notes Payable should show a zero balance after the final payment is recorded.

CPC-4 Recording Equipment Purchase with Installment Note (All Methods)

Legendary Corporation purchased equipment and in exchange signed a three-year promissory note. The note requires Legendary to make equal annual payments of $10,000 at the end of each of the next three years. Legendary has other promissory notes that charge interest at the annual rate of 6 percent.

Required:

1. Compute the present value of the note, rounded to the nearest dollar, using Legendary's typical interest rate of 6 percent.
2. Show the journal entry to record the equipment purchase (round to the nearest dollar).
   TIP: Record the liability as Notes Payable.
3. Show the journal entry at the end of the first year to record the first payment of $10,000.
4. Show the journal entry at the end of the second year to record the second payment of $10,000.
5. Show the journal entry at the end of the third year to record the third payment of $10,000.

CPC-5 Using the Financial Calculator App to Compute Bond Issue Details

The following table shows three cases, each with one missing element.

	Case a	Case b	Case c
Total face value	$500,000	$400,000	$300,000
Total bond proceeds	463,200	b	320,033
Stated interest rate	5%	6%	c
Market interest rate (yield)	a	5%	4%
Bond term (years)	10	15	5

Required:

Use the bond calculator at fncalculator.com to determine the missing element for each case. Assume simple annual compounding and round dollar amounts to the nearest dollar or interest rate percentages to one decimal place.

GROUP A PROBLEMS

PAC-1 Comparing Options Using Present Value Concepts (Using Tables)

After completing a long and successful career as senior partner at Pearson Hardman, you are preparing for retirement. After visiting the human resources office, you have found that you have several retirement options: (1) you can receive an immediate cash payment of $1 million, (2) you can receive $60,000 per year for life (your remaining life expectancy is 20 years), or (3) you can receive $50,000 per year for 10 years and then $70,000 per year for life (this option is intended to give you some protection against inflation). You have determined that you can earn 8 percent on your investments. Which option do you prefer and why?

PAC-2 Comparing Options Using Present Value Concepts (Using Excel or a Financial Calculator)

Use Excel or a financial calculator to answer PAC-1.

PAC-3 Recording Equipment Purchase with Two-Year Note

Peabody Corporation purchased equipment and in exchange signed a three-year promissory note. The note requires Peabody to make a single payment of $20,000 in three years. Peabody has other promissory notes that charge interest at the annual rate of 6 percent.

Required:

1. Compute the present value of the note, rounded to the nearest dollar, using Peabody's typical interest rate of 6 percent.
2. Show the journal entry to record the equipment purchase (round to the nearest dollar).
3. Show the adjusting journal entry at the end of the first year to record interest on the note.
4. Show the adjusting journal entry at the end of the second year to record interest on the note.
5. Show the adjusting journal entry at the end of the third year to record interest on the note (but do not record the payment of $20,000 yet).
6. Show the journal entry at the end of the third year to record the payment of $20,000.

PAC-4 Recording Equipment Purchase with Installment Note (All Methods)

Moseby Corporation purchased equipment and in exchange signed a two-year promissory note. The note requires Moseby to make equal annual payments of $30,000 at the end of each of the next two years. Moseby has other promissory notes that charge interest at the annual rate of 5 percent.

Required:

1. Compute the present value of the note, rounded to the nearest dollar, using Moseby's typical interest rate of 5 percent.
2. Show the journal entry to record the equipment purchase (round to the nearest dollar).
3. Show the journal entry at the end of the first year to record the first payment of $30,000.
4. Show the journal entry at the end of the second year to record the second payment of $30,000.

PAC-5 Using the Financial Calculator App to Compute Bond Issue Details

The following table shows three cases, each with one missing element.

	Case a	Case b	Case c
Total face value	$200,000	$400,000	$600,000
Total bond proceeds	183,884	b	653,442
Stated interest rate	5%	5%	c
Market interest rate (yield)	a	6%	4%
Bond term (years)	10	15	5

Required:

Use the bond calculator at fncalculator.com to determine the missing element for each case. Assume simple annual compounding and round dollar amounts to the nearest dollar or interest rate percentages to one decimal place.

GROUP B PROBLEMS

PBC-1 Comparing Options Using Present Value Concepts (Using Tables)

After incurring a serious injury caused by a manufacturing defect, your friend has sued the manufacturer for damages. Your friend received three offers from the manufacturer to settle the lawsuit: (1) receive an immediate cash payment of $100,000, (2) receive $6,000 per year for life (your friend's remaining life expectancy is 20 years), or (3) receive $5,000 per year for 10 years and then $7,000 per year for life (this option is intended to compensate your friend for increased aggravation of the injury over time). Your friend can earn 8 percent interest and has asked you for advice. Which option would you recommend and why?

PBC-2 Comparing Options Using Present Value Concepts (Using Excel or a Financial Calculator)

Use Excel or a financial calculator to answer PBC-1.

PBC-3 Recording Equipment Purchase with Two-Year Note

Southtown Corporation purchased equipment and in exchange signed a two-year promissory note. The note requires Southtown to make a single payment of $100,000 in two years. Southtown has other promissory notes that charge interest at the annual rate of 6 percent.

Required:

1. Compute the present value of the note, rounded to the nearest dollar, using Southtown's typical interest rate of 6 percent.
2. Show the journal entry to record the equipment purchase (round to the nearest dollar).
3. Show the adjusting journal entry at the end of the first year to record interest on the note.
4. Show the adjusting journal entry at the end of the second year to record interest on the note (but do not record the payment of $100,000 yet).
5. Show the journal entry at the end of the second year to record payment of the $100,000.

PBC-4   Recording Equipment Purchase with Installment Note (All Methods)

Marshall Corporation purchased equipment and in exchange signed a three-year promissory note. The note requires Marshall to make equal annual payments of $20,000 at the end of each of the next three years. Marshall has other promissory notes that charge interest at the annual rate of 6 percent.

Required:

1. Compute the present value of the note, rounded to the nearest dollar, using Marshall's typical interest rate of 6 percent.
2. Show the journal entry to record the equipment purchase (round to the nearest dollar).
3. Show the journal entry at the end of the first year to record the first payment of $20,000.
4. Show the journal entry at the end of the second year to record the second payment of $20,000.
5. Show the journal entry at the end of the third year to record the third payment of $20,000.

PBC-5   Using Financial Calculator App to Compute Bond Issue Details

The following table shows three cases, each with one missing element.

	Case a	Case b	Case c
Total face value	$100,000	$200,000	$100,000
Total bond proceeds	105,786	b	109,295
Stated interest rate	6%	6%	c
Market interest rate (yield)	a	5%	6%
Bond term (years)	7	11	14

Required:

Use the bond calculator at fncalculator.com to determine the missing element for each case. Assume simple annual compounding and round dollar amounts to the nearest dollar or interest rate percentages to one decimal place.

Investments in Other Corporations

Available in *Connect*.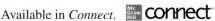

Appendix Introduction

At the website abc.xyz, the founders of Google describe how they created a new company called Alphabet. As they say, Alphabet owns a collection of companies that includes Google as well as many other different types of companies. In fact, Alphabet has quickly become a major corporate investor. As of March 31, 2019, Alphabet had invested as much money in corporate securities as the 40th largest bank in the United States. Alphabet's investment of more than $90 billion in marketable securities was greater than even the amount invested by E*TRADE Financial Corporation ($68 billion).[1] Appendix D explains why Alphabet invests in other companies and how it accounts for its various types of investments.

To access a copy of Appendix D, go to the eBook in Connect. The following topics are discussed in the appendix.

An Overview	**Accounting for Passive Investments**	**Accounting for Influential Investments**
• Reasons companies invest • Identifying investment types and accounting methods	• Debt investments held to maturity: Amortized cost method • Passive investments in equity securities: Fair value method • Passive investments in equity securities without readily determinable fair values	• Investments for significant influence: Equity method • Investments with controlling interests: Consolidated statements

---

[1] Federal Financial Institutions Examination Council, National Information Center. Retrieved November 18, 2019, from https://www.ffiec.gov/npw/Institution/TopHoldings.

Solutions to Multiple-Choice Questions

Chapter 1

1. b 2. a 3. c 4. c 5. a 6. c 7. c 8. d 9. b 10. d

Chapter 2

1. d 2. a 3. d 4. a 5. d 6. c 7. a 8. d 9. d 10. b

Chapter 3

1. b 2. b 3. d 4. d 5. a 6. c 7. c 8. a 9. b 10. c

Chapter 4

1. b 2. a 3. d 4. c 5. d 6. d 7. a 8. c 9. c 10. a

Chapter 5

1. b 2. a 3. a 4. d 5. d 6. c 7. c 8. c 9. c 10. b

Chapter 6

1. b 2. b 3. b 4. a 5. a 6. b 7. c 8. c 9. a 10. b

Chapter 7

1. b 2. d 3. d 4. b 5. d 6. d 7. c 8. c 9. c 10. b

Chapter 8

1. d 2. b 3. b 4. d 5. c 6. d 7. c 8. b 9. d 10. d

Chapter 9

1. d 2. d 3. c 4. c 5. d 6. a 7. d 8. b 9. d 10. b

Chapter 10

1. c 2. b 3. c 4. a 5. c 6. b 7. c 8. c 9. d 10. c

Chapter 11

1. a 2. d 3. d 4. a 5. c 6. b 7. c 8. c 9. d 10. a

Chapter 12

1. c 2. d 3. d 4. a 5. a 6. d 7. d 8. a 9. c 10. b

Chapter 13

1. c 2. c 3. c 4. d 5. c 6. a 7. b 8. d 9. d 10. a

Appendix C

1. b 2. d 3. c 4. b 5. a 6. d 7. c 8. a 9. c 10. c

Appendix D

Included in the ebook.

1. c 2. d 3. c 4. d 5. c 6. c 7. a 8. b 9. c 10. c

Name of Account	Acct #	Financial Statement	Type	Normal Balance
Cash	100	Balance Sheet	Asset, Current	Debit
Cash Equivalents	101	Balance Sheet	Asset, Current	Debit
Petty Cash	102	Balance Sheet	Asset, Current	Debit
Restricted Cash (short-term)	103	Balance Sheet	Asset, Current	Debit
Accounts Receivable	110	Balance Sheet	Asset, Current	Debit
Allowance for Doubtful Accounts	111	Balance Sheet	Asset, Current, Contra	Credit
Notes Receivable (short-term)	120	Balance Sheet	Asset, Current	Debit
Interest Receivable	121	Balance Sheet	Asset, Current	Debit
Short-Term Investments	122	Balance Sheet	Asset, Current	Debit
Investment in Marketable Equity Securities	123	Balance Sheet	Asset, Current	Debit
Inventory	130	Balance Sheet	Asset, Current	Debit
Inventory—Estimated Returns	131	Balance Sheet	Asset, Current	Debit
Supplies	140	Balance Sheet	Asset, Current	Debit
Prepaid Insurance	150	Balance Sheet	Asset, Current	Debit
Prepaid Rent	151	Balance Sheet	Asset, Current	Debit
Prepaid Advertising	152	Balance Sheet	Asset, Current	Debit
Other Current Assets	160	Balance Sheet	Asset, Current	Debit
Land	170	Balance Sheet	Asset, Noncurrent	Debit
Buildings	171	Balance Sheet	Asset, Noncurrent	Debit
Accumulated Depreciation—Buildings	172	Balance Sheet	Asset, Noncurrent, Contra	Credit
Equipment	173	Balance Sheet	Asset, Noncurrent	Debit
Accumulated Depreciation—Equipment	174	Balance Sheet	Asset, Noncurrent, Contra	Credit
Vehicles	175	Balance Sheet	Asset, Noncurrent	Debit
Accumulated Depreciation—Vehicles	176	Balance Sheet	Asset, Noncurrent, Contra	Credit
Goodwill	180	Balance Sheet	Asset, Noncurrent	Debit
Logo and Trademarks	181	Balance Sheet	Asset, Noncurrent	Debit
Patents	182	Balance Sheet	Asset, Noncurrent	Debit
Copyrights	183	Balance Sheet	Asset, Noncurrent	Debit
Licensing Rights	184	Balance Sheet	Asset, Noncurrent	Debit
Franchise Rights	185	Balance Sheet	Asset, Noncurrent	Debit
Software	186	Balance Sheet	Asset, Noncurrent	Debit
Accumulated Amortization	187	Balance Sheet	Asset, Noncurrent, Contra	Credit
Investment in Affiliates	188	Balance Sheet	Asset, Noncurrent	Debit
Restricted Cash (long-term)	190	Balance Sheet	Asset, Noncurrent	Debit
Notes Receivable (long-term)	191	Balance Sheet	Asset, Noncurrent	Debit
Natural Resource Assets	192	Balance Sheet	Asset, Noncurrent	Debit
Other Noncurrent Assets	193	Balance Sheet	Asset, Noncurrent	Debit
Accounts Payable	201	Balance Sheet	Liability, Current	Credit
Interest Payable	202	Balance Sheet	Liability, Current	Credit
Salaries and Wages Payable	203	Balance Sheet	Liability, Current	Credit
Withheld Income Taxes Payable	204	Balance Sheet	Liability, Current	Credit
FICA Payable	205	Balance Sheet	Liability, Current	Credit
Unemployment Tax Payable	206	Balance Sheet	Liability, Current	Credit
Charitable Contributions Payable	207	Balance Sheet	Liability, Current	Credit
Sales Tax Payable	208	Balance Sheet	Liability, Current	Credit
Income Tax Payable	209	Balance Sheet	Liability, Current	Credit
Dividends Payable	210	Balance Sheet	Liability, Current	Credit
Deferred Revenue	211	Balance Sheet	Liability, Current	Credit
Notes Payable (short-term)	212	Balance Sheet	Liability, Current	Credit

Name of Account	Acct #	Financial Statement	Type	Normal Balance
Refund Liability	213	Balance Sheet	Liability, Current	Credit
Notes Payable (long-term)	220	Balance Sheet	Liability, Noncurrent	Credit
Bonds Payable	221	Balance Sheet	Liability, Noncurrent	Credit
Discount on Bonds Payable	222	Balance Sheet	Liability, Noncurrent, Contra	Debit
Premium on Bonds Payable	223	Balance Sheet	Liability, Noncurrent	Credit
Other Noncurrent Liabilities	230	Balance Sheet	Liability, Noncurrent	Credit
Common Stock	301	Balance Sheet	Stockholders' Equity	Credit
Additional Paid-In Capital, Common Stock	302	Balance Sheet	Stockholders' Equity	Credit
Preferred Stock	303	Balance Sheet	Stockholders' Equity	Credit
Additional Paid-In Capital, Preferred Stock	304	Balance Sheet	Stockholders' Equity	Credit
Retained Earnings	305	Balance Sheet	Stockholders' Equity	Credit
Accumulated Other Comprehensive Income	306	Balance Sheet	Stockholders' Equity	Credit
Treasury Stock	307	Balance Sheet	Stockholders' Equity, Contra	Debit
Additional Paid-In Capital, Treasury Stock	308	Balance Sheet	Stockholders' Equity	Credit
Service Revenue	401	Income Statement	Revenue	Credit
Donation Revenue	402	Income Statement	Revenue	Credit
Interest Revenue	410	Income Statement	Revenue	Credit
Dividend Revenue	411	Income Statement	Revenue	Credit
Equity in Affiliate Earnings	412	Income Statement	Revenue	Credit
Gain on Equity Securities	413	Income Statement	Revenue	Credit
Rent Revenue	420	Income Statement	Revenue	Credit
Gain on Disposal of PPE	430	Income Statement	Revenue	Credit
Gain on Bond Retirement	431	Income Statement	Revenue	Credit
Other Revenue	432	Income Statement	Revenue	Credit
Sales Revenue	440	Income Statement	Revenue	Credit
Sales Returns and Allowances	441	Income Statement	Revenue, Contra	Debit
Cost of Goods Sold	501	Income Statement	Expense	Debit
Advertising Expense	502	Income Statement	Expense	Debit
Amortization Expense	503	Income Statement	Expense	Debit
Bad Debt Expense	504	Income Statement	Expense	Debit
Delivery Expense	505	Income Statement	Expense	Debit
Depreciation Expense	506	Income Statement	Expense	Debit
Impairment Loss	507	Income Statement	Expense	Debit
Insurance Expense	508	Income Statement	Expense	Debit
Interest Expense	509	Income Statement	Expense	Debit
Legal Expense	510	Income Statement	Expense	Debit
Office Expense	511	Income Statement	Expense	Debit
Payroll Tax Expense	512	Income Statement	Expense	Debit
Rent Expense	513	Income Statement	Expense	Debit
Repairs and Maintenance Expense	514	Income Statement	Expense	Debit
Salaries and Wages Expense	515	Income Statement	Expense	Debit
Supplies Expense	516	Income Statement	Expense	Debit
Travel Expense	517	Income Statement	Expense	Debit
Utilities Expense	518	Income Statement	Expense	Debit
Other Operating Expenses	519	Income Statement	Expense	Debit
Loss on Disposal of PPE	520	Income Statement	Expense	Debit
Loss on Bond Retirement	521	Income Statement	Expense	Debit
Cash Shortage	522	Income Statement	Expense	Debit
Income Tax Expense	523	Income Statement	Expense	Debit
Cash Overage	524	Income Statement	Revenue	Credit
Loss on Equity Securities	525	Income Statement	Expense	Debit
Bank Charges Expense	526	Income Statement	Expense	Debit
Dividends	600	Statement of Retained Earnings	Dividends	Debit

A

Accounting A system of analyzing, recording, and summarizing the results of a business's operating, investing, and financing activities and then reporting them to decision makers.

Accounts A standardized format that organizations use to accumulate the dollar effects of transactions on each financial statement item.

Accounts Receivable Amounts owed to a business by its customers.

Accrual Basis Accounting Recording revenues when generated and expenses when incurred, regardless of the timing of cash receipts or payments.

Accrued Liabilities Liabilities for expenses that have been incurred but not paid at the end of the accounting period.

Adjusted Trial Balance A list of all accounts and their adjusted balances to check on the equality of recorded debits and credits.

Adjusting Journal Entries Entries necessary at the end of each accounting period to report revenues and expenses in the proper period and assets and liabilities at appropriate amounts. Also called *Adjustments.*

Adjustments Entries necessary at the end of each accounting period to report revenues and expenses in the proper period and assets and liabilities at appropriate amounts. Also called *Adjusting Journal Entries.*

Aging of Accounts Receivable Method Estimates uncollectible accounts based on the age of each account receivable. Also called the *balance sheet approach.*

Allowance Method A method of accounting that reduces accounts receivable (as well as net income) for an estimate of uncollectible accounts (bad debts).

Amortization For intangible assets, this is the systematic and rational allocation of the cost of an intangible asset over its useful life.

Amortization Schedule A table showing the gradual reduction in a balance over its life; in the context of loans and notes, an amortization schedule shows the payment of interest and repayment of principal on balances owed.

Annuity A series of periodic cash receipts or payments that are equal in amount each interest period.

Assets Probable future economic benefits owned by the business as a result of past transactions.

Authorized Shares The maximum number of shares of capital stock of a corporation that can be issued, as specified in the charter.

B

Bad Debt Expense Reports the estimated amount of this period's credit sales that customers will fail to pay.

Balance Sheet Reports the amount of assets, liabilities, and stockholders' equity of an accounting entity at a point in time.

Bank Reconciliation Process of using both the bank statement and the cash accounts of a business to determine the appropriate amount of cash in a bank account, after taking into consideration delays or errors in processing cash transactions.

Basic Accounting Equation Assets = Liabilities + Stockholders' Equity.

Book Value The acquisition cost of an asset less accumulated depreciation. Also called *Carrying Value, Net Book Value.*

C

Capitalize To record a cost as an asset, rather than an expense.

Carrying Value The amount at which an asset or liability is reported after deducting any contra-accounts. Also called *Book Value, Net Book Value.*

Cash Money or any instrument that banks will accept for deposit and immediately credit to the company's account, such as a check, money order, or bank draft.

Cash Basis Accounting Recording revenues when cash is received and expenses when cash is paid.

Cash Equivalents Short-term, highly liquid investments purchased within three months of maturity.

Cash Flows from Financing Activities Cash inflows and outflows related to financing sources external to the company (owners and lenders).

Cash Flows from Investing Activities Cash inflows and outflows related to the sale or purchase of investments and long-lived assets.

Cash Flows from Operating Activities (Cash Flows from Operations) Cash inflows and outflows related to components of net income.

Chart of Accounts A summary of all account names and corresponding account numbers used to record financial results in the accounting system.

Classified Balance Sheet A balance sheet that classifies assets and liabilities into current and other (long-term) categories.

Common Stock The basic voting stock issued by a corporation to stockholders.

Comprehensive Income Comprehensive Income = Net Income + Other Comprehensive Income (OCI). OCI includes gains and losses arising from changes in the values of certain assets and liabilities (see Appendix D).

Consolidated Financial Statements Combine the financial statements of parent and subsidiary companies into a single set of financial statements.

Contingent Liabilities Potential liabilities that have arisen as a result of a past transaction or event; their ultimate outcome will not be known until a future event occurs or fails to occur.

Contra-Account An account that is an offset to, or reduction of, another account.

Copyright A form of protection provided to the original authors of literary, musical, artistic, dramatic, and other works of authorship.

Cost of Goods Sold Equation Expresses the relationship between inventory on hand, purchased, and sold; BI + P − EI = CGS or BI + P − CGS = EI.

Cost Principle Requires assets to be initially recorded at the historical cash-equivalent cost, which is the amount paid or payable on the date of the transaction.

Credit When used as a noun, credit is the right side of an account; when used as a verb, credit is the act of recording the credit portion of a journal entry to a particular account.

Cumulative Dividend Preference The preferred stock feature that requires current dividends not paid in full to accumulate for every year in which they are not paid. These cumulative unpaid amounts (called **dividends in arrears**) must be paid before any common dividends can be paid.

Current Assets Assets that will be used up or turned into cash within 12 months or the next operating cycle, whichever is longer.

Current Dividend Preference The feature of preferred stock that grants priority on preferred dividends over common dividends.

Current Liabilities Short-term obligations that will be paid in cash (or fulfilled with other current assets) within 12 months or the next operating cycle, whichever is longer.

D

Data Visualization Presenting large quantities of data in maps, charts, and graphs, to reveal important relationships and trends within the data.

Days to Collect A measure of the average number of days from the time a sale is made on account to the time it is collected.

Days to Sell Measure of the average number of days from the time inventory is bought to the time it is sold.

Debit When used as a noun, debit is the left side of an account; when used as a verb, debit is the act of recording the debit portion of a journal entry to a particular account.

Debt-to-Assets Ratio Indicates financing risk by computing the proportion of total assets financed by debt, computed as total liabilities divided by total assets.

Declaration Date The date on which the board of directors officially approves a dividend.

Declining-Balance Depreciation Method Allocates the cost of an asset over its useful life based on a multiple of (often two times) the straight-line rate.

Deferred Revenue A liability representing a company's obligation to provide goods or services to customers in the future.

Depletion Process of allocating a natural resource's cost over the period of its extraction or harvesting.

Depreciable Cost The portion of the asset's cost that will be used up during its life. It is calculated as asset cost minus residual value and allocated to depreciation expense throughout the asset's life.

Depreciation Process of allocating the cost of buildings, equipment, and other similar long-lived "productive" assets over their productive lives using a systematic and rational method of allocation.

Direct Method A method of presenting the operating activities section of the statement of cash flows; reports the components of cash flows from operating activities as gross receipts and gross payments.

Direct Write-Off Method Records bad debt expense only when accounts are written off; not allowed under GAAP.

Discontinued Operations Result from the disposal of a major component of the business and are reported net of income tax effects.

Discount The amount by which a bond's issue price is less than its face value.

Dividends in Arrears Dividends on cumulative preferred stock that have not been declared in prior years.

E

EBITDA Abbreviation for "earnings before interest, taxes, depreciation, and amortization," which is a measure of operating performance that some managers and analysts use in place of net income.

Effective-Interest Method of Amortization Allocates the amount of bond premium or discount over each period of a bond's life in amounts corresponding to the bond's carrying value and market interest rate.

Expense Recognition Principle Expenses are recorded when incurred in earning revenue; also called "matching."

Expenses Decreases in assets or increases in liabilities arising from providing goods or services during the current period.

Extraordinary Repairs Infrequent expenditures that increase an asset's economic usefulness in the future and that are capitalized.

F

Face Value The payment made when the bond matures; used to compute interest payments.

Factoring An arrangement where receivables are sold to another company (called a *factor*) for immediate cash (minus a factoring fee).

Financial Statements Reports that summarize the financial results of business activities.

First-In, First-Out (FIFO) Method Assumes that the first goods purchased (the first in) are the first goods sold.

FOB Destination Term of sale indicating that goods are owned by the seller until delivered to the buyer.

FOB Shipping Point Term of sale indicating that goods are owned by the buyer the moment they leave the seller's premises.

Franchise A contractual right to sell certain products or services, use certain trademarks, or perform activities in a certain geographical region.

Fraud An attempt to deceive others for personal gain.

Full Disclosure Principle The financial statements should present information needed to understand the financial results of the company's business activities.

Future Value The sum to which an amount will increase as the result of compound interest.

G

Generally Accepted Accounting Principles (GAAP) The rules used in the United States to calculate and report information in the financial statements.

Going-Concern (Continuity) Assumption A business is assumed to be capable of continuing its operations long enough to meet its obligations.

Goods Available for Sale The sum of beginning inventory and purchases for the period.

Goodwill (Cost in Excess of Net Assets Acquired) For accounting purposes, the excess of the purchase price of a business over the market value of the business's assets and liabilities.

Gross Profit (Gross Margin, Margin) Net sales less cost of goods sold.

Gross Profit Percentage Indicates how much above cost a company sells its products; calculated as Gross Profit divided by Net Sales.

H

Horizontal (Trend) Analyses Comparing results across time, often expressing changes in account balances as a percentage of prior-year balances.

I

Impairment Occurs when the cash to be generated by an asset is estimated to be less than the carrying value of that asset and requires that the carrying value of the asset be written down.

Imprest System A process that controls the amount paid to others by limiting the total amount of money available for making payments to others.

Income Statement (Statement of Income, Statement of Profit and Loss, Statement of Operations) Reports the revenues less the expenses of the accounting period.

Indirect Method Presents the operating activities section of the cash flow statement by adjusting net income to compute cash flows from operating activities.

Interest Formula $I = P \times R \times T$, where I = interest calculated, P = principal, R = annual interest rate, and T = time period covered in the interest calculation (number of months out of 12).

Internal Control Actions taken to promote efficient and effective operations, protect assets, enhance accounting information, and adhere to laws and regulations.

International Financial Reporting Standards (IFRS) The rules used internationally to calculate and report information in the financial statements.

Inventory Goods held for sale in the normal course of business or used in producing other goods for sale.

Inventory Turnover The process of buying and selling inventory.

Issue Price The amount of money that a lender pays (and the company receives) when a bond is issued.

Issued Shares Shares of stock that have been distributed by the corporation.

J

Journal A record of each day's transactions.

Journal Entry An accounting method for expressing the effects of a transaction on accounts in a debits-equal-credits format.

L

Last-In, First-Out (LIFO) Method Assumes that the most recently purchased units (the last in) are sold first.

Ledger A collection of records that summarizes, for each account, the effects of transactions entered in the journal.

Liabilities Probable debts or obligations of the entity that result from past transactions, which will be fulfilled by providing assets or services.

Licensing Right The limited permission to use property according to specific terms and conditions set out in a contract.

Liquidity The extent to which a company is able to pay its currently maturing obligations.

Loan Covenants Terms of a loan agreement that, if broken, entitle the lender to renegotiate loan terms or force repayment.

Long-Lived Assets Tangible and intangible resources owned by a business and used in its operations over several years.

Lower of Cost or Market/Net Realizable Value (LCM/NRV) Valuation method departing from the cost principle; recognizes a loss when inventory value drops below cost.

M

Market Interest Rate The rate of interest that investors demand from a bond. Also called *yield, discount rate*, or *effective interest rate*.

Maturity Date The date on which the bonds are due to be paid in full.

Merchandising Company A company that sells goods that have been obtained from a supplier.

Multistep Income Statement Reports alternative measures of income by calculating subtotals for core and peripheral business activities.

N

Net Assets Shorthand term used to refer to assets minus liabilities.

Net Income Equal to revenues minus expenses.

Net Profit Margin Profit earned from each dollar of revenue.

No-Par Value Stock Capital stock that has no par value specified in the corporate charter.

Noncurrent Long-term; assets and liabilities that do not meet the definition of current.

Notes Receivable Promises that require other parties to pay the business according to written agreements.

NSF (Non-Sufficient Funds) Checks Checks written for an amount greater than the funds available to cover them.

O

Ordinary Repairs and Maintenance Expenditures for the normal operating upkeep of long-lived assets, recorded as expenses.

Outstanding Shares Shares that are currently held by stockholders (not the corporation itself).

P

Par Value An insignificant value per share of capital stock specified in the charter.

Parent Company The entity that controls another company.

Patent A right to exclude others from making, using, selling, or importing an invention.

Payment Date The date on which a cash dividend is paid to the stockholders of record.

Percentage of Credit Sales Method Estimates bad debts based on the percentage of sales expected to lead to bad debt losses. Also called the *income statement approach*.

Periodic Inventory System A system in which ending inventory and cost of goods sold are determined only at the end of the accounting period based on a physical inventory count.

Permanent Accounts The balance sheet accounts that carry their ending balances into the next accounting period.

Perpetual Inventory System A system in which a detailed inventory record is maintained by recording each purchase and sale of inventory during the accounting period.

Post-Closing Trial Balance Prepared to check that debits equal credits and that all temporary accounts have been closed.

Preferred Stock Stock that has specified rights over common stock.

Premium The amount by which a bond's issue price exceeds its face value.

Present Value The current value of an amount to be received in the future. It is calculated by discounting a future amount for compound interest.

Profitability The extent to which a company generates income.

Purchase Discount Cash discount received for prompt payment of an account.

Purchase Returns and Allowances A reduction in the cost of purchases associated with unsatisfactory goods.

R

Receivable Write-Off The act of removing an uncollectible account receivable and its corresponding allowance from the accounting records.

Receivables Turnover The process of selling and collecting on account. The receivables turnover ratio determines the average number of times this process occurs during the period.

Record Date The date on which the corporation prepares the list of current stockholders as shown on its records; dividends can be paid only to the stockholders who own stock on that date.

Research and Development Expenses Expenditures that may someday lead to patents, copyrights, or other intangible assets, but the uncertainty about their future benefits requires they be expensed.

Residual (or Salvage) Value Estimated amount to be recovered, less disposal costs, at the end of the company's estimated useful life of an asset.

Restricted Cash Not available for general use but rather restricted for a specific purpose.

Revenue Recognition Principle Revenues are recorded when (or as) the seller provides goods or services to customers, in the amount the seller expects to be entitled to receive.

Revenues Increases in assets or settlements of liabilities arising from providing goods or services.

Robotic process automation (RPA) Using automation and artificial intelligence to create software bots that capture data, execute sequences, and make simple decisions.

S

Sales (or Cash) Discount Cash discount offered to customers to encourage prompt payment of an account receivable.

Sales Returns and Allowances Reduction of sales revenues for return of or allowances for unsatisfactory goods.

Sarbanes-Oxley Act (SOX) A set of laws established to strengthen corporate reporting in the United States.

Segregation of Duties An internal control designed into the accounting system to prevent an employee from making a mistake or committing a dishonest act as part of one assigned duty and then also covering it up through another assigned duty.

Separate Entity Assumption States that business transactions are separate from and should exclude the personal transactions of the owners.

Service Company A company that sells services rather than physical goods.

Shrinkage The cost of inventory lost to theft, fraud, and error.

Solvency The ability to survive long enough to repay lenders when debt matures.

Specific Identification Method A method of assigning costs to inventory that identifies the cost of each specific item purchased and sold.

Stated Interest Rate The rate stated on the face of the bond that is used to compute interest payments. Also called the *coupon rate* or *contract rate*.

Statement of Cash Flows Reports inflows and outflows of cash during the accounting period in the categories of operating, investing, and financing.

Statement of Retained Earnings Reports the way that net income and the distribution of dividends affected the financial position of the company during the accounting period.

Stock Dividend A dividend that distributes additional shares of a corporation's own stock.

Stock Split An increase in the total number of authorized shares by a specified ratio; does not affect retained earnings.

Stockholders' Equity (Owners' Equity or Shareholders' Equity) The financing provided by the owners and the operations of the business.

Straight-Line Depreciation Method Allocates the depreciable cost of an asset in equal periodic amounts over its useful life.

Straight-Line Method of Amortization Evenly allocates the amount of bond premium or discount over each period of a bond's life to adjust interest expense for differences between its stated interest rate and market interest rate.

Subsidiary Company The entity that is controlled by the parent.

T

T-Account A simplified version of a ledger account used for summarizing transaction effects and determining balances for each account.

Technology Assets Capitalized computer software and web development costs; an intangible asset.

Temporary Accounts Income statement accounts that are closed to *Retained Earnings* at the end of the accounting period.

Time Period Assumption The assumption that allows the long life of a company to be reported in shorter time periods.

Time Value of Money The idea that money received today is worth more than the same amount received in the future because money received today can be invested to earn interest over time.

Times Interest Earned Ratio Divides net income before interest and taxes by interest expense to determine the extent to which earnings before taxes and financing costs are sufficient to cover interest incurred on debt.

Trademark An exclusive legal right to use a special name, image, or slogan.

Transaction An exchange or an event that has a direct economic effect on the assets, liabilities, or stockholders' equity of a business.

Treasury Stock Issued shares that have been reacquired by the company.

Trial Balance A list of all accounts with their balances to provide a check on the equality of the debits and credits.

U

Unadjusted Trial Balance An internal report, prepared before end-of-period adjustments, listing the unadjusted balances of each account to check the equality of total debits and credits.

Unit of Measure Assumption The financial results of a company's worldwide business activities should be measured and reported using a single monetary unit, such as the U.S. dollar.

Units-of-Production Depreciation Method Allocates the depreciable cost of an asset over its useful life based on its output during the period in relation to its total estimated output.

Useful Life The expected service life of an asset to the present owner.

V

Vertical (Common Size) Analysis Expressing each financial statement amount as a percentage of another amount on the same financial statement.

Voucher System A process for approving and documenting all purchases and payments on account.

W

Weighted Average Cost Method Uses the weighted average unit cost of goods available for sale for calculations of both the cost of goods sold and ending inventory.